2001 8TH EDITION

TOYS & PRICES

Edited by
Sharon Korbeck
&
Elizabeth Stephan

Published by

**krause
publications**

700 E. State Street • Iola, WI 54990-0001
Telephone: 715/445-2214

www.krause.com

Please call or write for our free catalog of publications.
Our toll-free number to place an order or obtain a free catalog is 800-258-0929 or please use
our regular business telephone 715-445-2214 for editorial comment and further information.

Library of Congress Catalog Number: 93-77554
ISBN: 0-87341-938-3

Printed in the United States of America

Contents

Hey? What's on the Cover? IV
Acknowledgments V
Introduction VI
Using the Grading Guides in *Toys &
Prices* IX

Action Figures 1
Advertising Toys 43
Banks 53
    Mechanical 56
    Still 71
Barbie 91
    Dolls 95
    Fashions 131
    Accessories 135
Battery-Operated Toys 137
Beanbag Toys 145
Character Toys 160
Coloring Books 277
Erector Sets 287
Fisher-Price 293
    Plastic 300
    Wooden 295
Games 311
    Prewar Games 316
    Postwar Games 342
    Tabletop 378
G.I. Joe 380
Guns 408
Lunch Boxes 429
Marx Play Sets 447
Model Kits 467
PEZ Candy Dispensers 482
Restaurant Premiums 493
Robots 536
Rock and Roll 545
Space/Science Fiction 550
Star Wars 589
    Action Figures 592
    Non-Action Figures 604

Tin Toys 610
TV Toys 630
Vehicle Toys 654
    Arcade 659
    Auburn 668
    Bandai 668
    Barclay 671
    Brooklin 671
    Buddy L 672
    Corgi 700
    Dinky 735
    Doepke 744
    Hess 744
    Hot Wheels 746
    Hubley 810
    Japanese 814
    Johnny Lightning/Playing
       Mantis 816
    Johnny Lightning/Topper . 833
    Keystone 837
    Majorette 838
    Marx 846
    Matchbox 860
    Nylint 882
    Schuco 882
    Smith-Miller 883
    Structo 887
    Tonka 888
    Tootsietoy 897
    Williams, A.C. 906
    Winross 907
    Wyandotte 914
View-Master Reels 915
Weebles 924
Western Toys 931

Toy Manufacturer Directory . . . 943
Directory of Auction Houses . . . 945

Hey! What's on the Cover?

MINT

Front Cover

The Dating Game board game, Hasbro $40
Steve Canyon Jet Helmet, Ideal 130
Space Gun, Remco. 30
Strawberry Shortcake lunch box, 1980s 10
Monopoly board game, 1940s. 25
Mini Bus, Fisher-Price, plastic, 1970s. 10
Magnetic Pick-Up Stix, Novel Novelties, 1952 15
Rock 'Em Sock 'Em Robots, Marx, 1960s. 130
Black Edventurer G.I. Joe, 1970s 300

Back Cover

Birthday Bear, Ty. $15
Have Gun Will Travel thermos 150
Silken Flame Barbie, modern reproduction, 1998. 30
Howdy Doody hand puppet. 50
Winnie the Pooh pull toy 15

Toys supplied by Sharon Korbeck, Mark Rich, Ken Boyer, Lisa Jacobsen, Tom Michael and Michael Jacquart.

Acknowledgments

Welcome to *Toys & Prices 2001:* A toy odyssey!

Every year, as we prepare a new edition of *Toys & Prices,* we face the same challenge. How can we make this book as comprehensive as possible and still keep it manageable?

As we close in on 1,000 pages in this our eighth edition, we think we've done a pretty good job. While it may be impossible to list every toy ever made and collected, this book hits what we feel are the highlights. We're sure you'll find not only your favorite toys, but other toys you may have forgotten from your childhood. Remembering them is half the fun — finding them again and buying them complete the experience.

In this edition, a special thanks goes out to the readers for their interest and our many contributors for their expertise.

Numerous experts contribute their time and knowledge each year to make this book bigger and better. Active collectors may be familiar with their names from ads in *Toy Shop.* And we welcome back some of last year's contributors as well.

Veteran collectors will recognize these people as widely-respected authorities in their various fields, from restaurant premiums and model kits to G.I. Joes and Barbie dolls. They took time from their busy schedules to sift through almost 30,000 toys worth — correcting errors, verifying values, adding toy listings, and weeding out duplications. It took the labors and long hours of many people to produce this book, and all of them deserve much thanks.

Special thanks goes to the staff of Krause Publications — *Toy Cars & Vehicles* Associate Editor Merry Dudley; Shelly Johnson, Cheryl Hayburn, Bonnie Tetzlaff and lauren Borth of the book production staff; Chris Pritchard and Ross Hubbard for cover design/photography; and the production staff for turning copy and photos into a cohesive, coherent package.

Outside contributors/reviewers (we hope we haven't forgotten anyone) include Chris Fawcett, Gus Lopez, Jon Brecka, Corey LeChat, Patricia Long, Bob Pierce, John K. Snyder Jr., Danny Fuchs, Paul Fink, Jeffrey Lowe, Steve Giannangelo, Sean and Debbie Craig, John Devlin, Richard Belyski, Edwin Price Jr., Andrew Dudek, Jim Wilson, Steve and Anna Cinnamon, Ray C. Falcoa, Fred Berecz and Mary Ann and Wolfgang Sell.

The main reason we publish this book is for you — the thousands of toy collectors nationwide and around the world — and we continue to thank you for your support of the book and the hobby.

Here's hoping your year is filled with plenty of toys, good deals and the time to enjoy them both.

Elizabeth A. Stephan and Sharon Korbeck
Editors

Introduction

This book, *Toys & Prices*, is now in its eighth edition, we've has added hundreds of pages and dozens of categories since the first edition in 1994.

Toy collecting has changed quite a bit over the years, especially in terms of the type of toys collected. No longer are the oldest "antique" toys generating the most attention. Now new toys, fresh off store shelves, are eagerly anticipated and quickly scarfed up by anxious collectors. Baby Boomer toys have hit their heyday, but not yet their peak.

This book is for you, the avid toy enthusiast. But even if you're a casual admirer of the quality and charm of old toys, you may be amazed at what some of those banks, cars, tin toys and other remnants of childhood can sell for today.

This book is designed to not only reacquaint you with lost favorites, but also to introduce you to newer, collectible toys. And you may be surprised to learn what collectors are grabbing up and selling for top dollar.

It's never too late for you to get started or add to your collection. *Toys & Prices* is designed to help you get the most value for the toys you own now and for the toys you may purchase tomorrow.

From the day we shoot the cover photo to the time the final values are entered into the computer, *Toys & Prices* is a year-long, cooperative process. And like any price guide on the market, it takes the time and talents of dealers, collectors, editors, photographers, designers and marketing specialists to put together a quality product.

When the long task is finally finished, we have a true picture of what we set out to produce — a concise, compact, and current price guide for over twenty toy collecting areas representing almost 30,000 toys. No price guide of its nature can be all-inclusive, but we've tried to offer a variety of the main collecting areas.

So whether your interest is Star Wars or space robots, Barbie or board games, *Toys & Prices* offers both casual and veteran collectors a better handle on buying and selling both vintage, and newer, collectible toys.

What's New?

A current trend in toy collecting is the rising popularity of "new" toys as instant collectibles. Often, toys purchased directly from a store shelf become coveted by collectors — who are often willing to pay top dollar for these sometimes rare, sometimes regional, often elusive treasures.

To address this trend, we've included more "new" toy lines, like action figures and Hot Wheels.

Other new sections this year include Weebles (another emerging Gen-X collectible), Robots and TV Toys.

Once again, we feature Top Ten lists, offering a quick glance at the most valuable toys in each section.

Generating price lists for *Toys & Prices* is a year-long process. As we feature articles and price guides in our bi-weekly magazine *Toy Shop*, we keep in mind what toys collectors are most interested in. To do that, we attend toy shows nationwide, study the advertisements in *Toy Shop*, conduct readership surveys and listen to calls and letters from those of you in the collecting trenches.

Keeping Pace in a Hot Hobby

As most of you already know, toy collectors are a fun, albeit sometimes obsessive, bunch. They'll travel miles out of their way to hit a garage sale, destined to uncover a true treasure on the dollar table — and it does happen.

Thousands of people from all walks of life are becoming toy collectors each month, from kids spending their allowances to investment advisors seeking high returns. Toy collectors come in all sizes, ages and nationalities and live all over the globe, but we all share a love of collecting and an appreciation of the artistry, charm, history and just plain fun toys have always offered, and still do.

Toy collecting has been called the hottest collecting field of the 1990s. Television shows now exist devoted to collecting, museum and library displays spotlight large toy collections, and even some of today's hottest celebrities have admitted their voracious appetites for toys. A quick search of the Internet will show dozens upon dozens of web sites devoted to toys. Toy manufacturers are quickly keeping pace preparing for the secondary market, issuing limited-edition items destined (hopefully) to increase in value.

This hobby has everything going for it — a colorful universe of plentiful and affordable items, the thrill of the hunt, intellectual and emotional gratification, camaraderie and investment potential.

As evidenced in this book, toy collecting is a vast field, discriminating against no one. Novice collectors with little to spend can edge in on the action figure field by purchasing today's "new" collectibles or relatively inexpensive toys such as restaurant premiums and PEZ dispensers. Character toy aficionados are continually bombarded with new characters from Disney, Warner Bros. and the like. More seasoned and affluent collectors can concentrate on some of the older and revered favorites like cast-iron banks or 1930s classic tin.

Where Do Those Prices Come From?

So just where do the prices in this book originate? Our primary sources are print retail ads in *Toy Shop*, dealer price lists, observed prices at toy shows, prices realized from auction houses across the country and Internet auctions. Information is compiled by category and entered into databases. These databases are then reviewed for accuracy by the editors of *Toys & Prices*.

Each database is then sent out for final review by recognized authorities in the subject fields. These contributing experts are some of the leading collectors and dealers in America, and we are proud to list them on our acknowledgments page.

The final results listed in this book are what we believe to be accurate, current retail prices, listed across a range of grades for each item.

While we've proofed and reproofed this book for accuracy, some typos may have slipped in. If you spot a price that seems way off base, don't take it as gospel. It may be a typo, or based on incomplete information. If you do notice what looks like a glaring error, we'd like to know about it so we can be sure to double check it for the next edition.

Likewise, if you own an item not listed here, we would appreciate the chance to add it to our database, especially if you can give us a clean photo of it along with information on its size, maker, year, and any other descriptions that might apply. Photos are welcome, but send only duplicates, as we regret we cannot return them.

A Cautionary Note

Veteran collectors know that a toy listed for $500 Mint in a price guide may or may not bring such a value — especially since dealers will pay less than book value for items that they will, in turn, mark up. But guides do serve as a starting point for those unfamiliar with the popularity or potential collectibility of particular toys.

Remember, values listed in this book are not offers to buy or sell, but are guidelines as to what you could expect to pay for an item at a show or by mail.

Price guides can be helpful, but they can also be frustrating — both for the editor and the user — if used improperly. Prices for the same item can vary widely from source to source, depending on factors such as geographical differences, personal economics and target market.

Because of this, price guides are meant to be just that — a guide — and not a bible. Feel free to use the values as gauges to aid your purchasing and negotiation, but remember that a dealer's agenda is to get the best price and make a profit too.

"I Had That Doll"

The next time you find yourself at a flea market saying longingly, "I had that doll," or "My brother and I played with that very same truck in our sandbox," you'll know the toy collecting bug is nearby. When you start to negotiate on the price, that bug is moving in . . . fast. When you decide you've got to have that toy at any cost, it's all over — the toy collecting bug has bitten. But it may only sting for a minute . . . then the real fun sets in.

Having fun, after all, should be the ultimate goal of toy collecting. If you aren't having fun, what's the point?

It may take years before you find "the perfect toy" to add to your collection. But that quest and the excitement that fuels it are what keep the hobby going.

Want to Know More?

Whether you use *Toys & Prices* to guide you as you begin your collection or consult it on weekly shopping trips, we're glad you picked us. And we'd love to see you further your hobby with other books on toy collecting from Krause Publications.

A Final Note

For those of you new to toy collecting, WELCOME! Enjoy the ride as you retrieve your past.

To veteran collectors, you already know the emotional and financial benefits this hobby can bring. Share this joy of toys with your children and grandchildren . . . and it just may make you feel like a kid again.

Using The Grading Guides in *Toys & Prices*

Prices listed in *Toys & Prices* are intended only as guidelines of what you might expect to pay for an item in today's market, either at a show or through the mail. The values listed are not offers to buy or sell toys; the publisher does not engage in buying or selling toys, but in compiling information and prices.

Values listed represent our best assessment of current market values at press time and are derived from various printed sources, toy show observations, auction results and the input of expert contributors.

Prices are generally listed for more than one grade of condition. Toy collectors and dealers know grading can be difficult and subjective. It's usually easy to reach agreement on a toy that's Mint In Box, but beyond that, grading becomes a somewhat imprecise science.

In order to provide general guidelines, the editors of *Toys & Prices* have adopted the following grade descriptions. Bear in mind that since various types of toys are looked at in different ways, no single grading system will apply to all of them. Some descriptions may not apply to certain toys, depending on how they are categorized, when they were produced, how they were originally packaged and how they are collected today.

Good, Excellent . . . C10?

Toys & Prices uses a Good, Excellent and Mint grading scale. Many of you, however, may be familiar with the 'C6' or 'C10' numbers used in *O'Brien's Collecting Toys* book.

Don't sweat it; our Good, Excellent and Mint prices roughly figure out to C6, C8 and C10 respectively. Items in less than Good condition may often be considered poor; prices should be lowered accordingly depending on condition.

MIB or MIP (Mint In Box, Mint In Package, C10) — Just like new, in the original package, preferably still sealed. Boxes may have been opened, but any packages inside remain unopened. Blister cards should be intact and unopened. Factory-sealed boxes often command higher prices.

MNP or MNB (Mint No Package, Mint No Box, C10) — This describes a toy typically produced in the 1960s or later in Mint condition, but not in its original package. A toy outside its original package is often referred to as 'loose.'

NM (Near Mint, C9) — A toy that appears like new in overall appearance but exhibits very minor wear and does not have the original box. An exception would be a toy that comes in kit form. A kit toy in Near Mint condition would be expected to have the original box, but the box would display some wear.

EX (Excellent, C8) — A toy that is complete and has been played with. Signs of minor wear may be evident, but the toy is very clean and well cared for.

VG (Very Good, C7) — A toy that obviously has been played with and shows general wear overall. Paint chipping is readily apparent. In metal toys, some minor rust may be evident. In sets, some minor pieces may be missing.

GD (Good, C6) — A toy with evidence of heavy play, dents, chips, and possibly moderate rust. The toy may be missing a major replaceable component, such as a battery compartment door, or may be in need of repair. In sets, several pieces may be missing.

Ultimately, the market is driven by the checkbook, and the bottom line final value of a toy is often the last price at which it was sold. In this sense the toy hobby, like many others, operates in a vacuum, with individual toys setting their own values. Repeated sales of specific items create precedents and establish standards for asking prices across the market. It is by comparison of such multiple transactions that price guides such as this one are created. In the end, the value of a toy is decided by one person, the buyer.

Action Figures

Adventure heroes and superheroes are everywhere, on comic pages, television and movie screens, and, of course, in toy store aisles. The action figure likenesses produced by numerous toy companies are among today's hottest collectibles.

Action figure collecting is one of the fastest growing and potentially largest collectible areas since the baseball card boom of the 1980s. A stroll through the toy section of any store is proof enough. Plus, it is a given that a percentage of today's teen and preteen action figure buyers will become collectors, and their potential numbers are huge. Action figures could bring more collectors into the hobby than G.I. Joe, Hot Wheels and model kits combined.

Hundreds of figures are for sale currently, and they are commonplace in toy stores. In some places, action figures are literally climbing the walls. Why collect them if they can be bought directly from current store shelves? For many collectors, that's exactly how the collecting frenzy begins.

For many action figure collectors, time began in the 1960s. While boys had played with toy soldiers for hundreds of years, these were typically iron or lead figures with no movable parts. The same held true for the hard plastic Marx figures of the 1950s. By definition, however, the term "action figure" was born in the 1960s.

That decade also saw American culture and technologies come of age in ways that changed countless aspects of everyday life, including how toys would be made and sold.

Heroes from the TV Screen

By the late 1950s, television had replaced the dinner table and parlor radio as the family hearth. The sturdy cabinet in the living room captivated with a power only hinted at by radio and which has never been challenged since. It was a working window not only into a wide world of people and places, but also, increasingly, of neat things to buy. Youngsters clustered on the floor, soaking up the names and lore of their new friends and heroes — Wonder Woman, Superman, Batman.

From 1961 to 1963, toy makers watched with envy and despair as Mattel's Barbie, aided by TV, took the world of girls' toys by storm. Of course, no one would dream of selling dolls to boys, so this barrier seemed insurmountable. But the wheels of industry would not be easily stopped, and the simple solution to this dilemma ranks as one of the greatest marketing spins of all time. If boys won't play with dolls, why not rename them "action figures?"

Hasbro's first test of G.I. Joe, the male answer to Barbie, debuted at New York's International Toy Fair in early 1964. Toy Fair is where buyers, retailers and manufacturers meet to view upcoming lines — and in the process, make or break a toy's success.

G.I. Joe was the first true fully-articulated action figure for boys, but he wouldn't be alone for long. A.C.

Comic Heroine Posin' Dolls
Batgirl, 1967, Ideal

Gilbert introduced James Bond figures in 1965, but for the first time in his career, Ian Fleming's super spy failed in his mission. Marx also entered the ring with the Best of the West series, but G.I. Joe had a seemingly limitless arsenal of battle-geared appeal.

The first reasonably successful challenge to G.I. Joe came from Ideal's Captain Action. While Joe's identity was well established, Captain Action was a man of many faces. Ideal designed Captain Action to establish not only his own identity, but also to capitalize on those of many popular superheroes. Joe was just Joe, but Captain Action could become Spider-Man, Batman, the Phantom, Green Hornet and others. Today, Captain Action figures and sets command the second highest prices in the action figure market, second only to classic G.I. Joes.

Ideal's brief foray into the world of superhero action figures paved the way for many to come. By 1969, Ideal tired of Captain Action's complex licensing agreements and discontinued the series, but another company was waiting in the wings. It was Mego.

Mighty Mego

In 1972, Mego released its first superhero series, the six-figure set of Official World's Greatest Super Heroes. These eight-inch tall cloth and plastic figures were joined by 28 others by the time the series ended 10 years later. Mego supplemented this superhero line with licensed film and TV characters from, most notably, *Planet of the Apes, Star Trek* and *The Dukes of Hazzard*, as well as historic figures representing the Old West and the World's Greatest Super Knights.

Another milestone in action figure history took place in 1977. Out of nowhere, George Lucas's Star Wars had become a worldwide smash, but nobody except Kenner had bothered to secure rights to merchandise toys. When Kenner realized the magnitude of Star Wars' potential, it rushed toys through production, but it didn't have time to get action figures on the shelves by Christmas. Instead, Kenner essentially pre-sold the figures as the mail-order Early Bird set.

By Christmas 1978, the line had grown to 17 figures and the first wave of a deluge of accessories and related toys. The Star Wars figures also established a third standard size for action figures. G.I. Joe and Captain Action were 12-inch figures, Mego figures measured eight inches, and Kenner's Star Wars figures were just 3-3/4 inches tall. Their tremendous popularity cemented that size as a new standard that holds to this day.

Next came the six-inch figure, set by Mattel's highly successful and lucrative 1981 Masters of the Universe series. This series was the first to be reverse licensed; in other words, Mattel made the toys first, and then sold the licensing to television and film, not the other way around. Mattel also upped the manufacturing ante by endowing the figures with action features such as punching and grabbing movements, thus enhancing their play value and setting another standard in the process.

Hasbro then scored again with the 1985 introduction of the next level in the evolution of action figures, the transforming figure. The aptly-named Transformers did just that, changing from innocuous-looking vehicles into menacing robots with a few deft twists, and then back again. Hasbro's mutating robots also transformed the toy industry, spawning numerous competitors and introducing the element of interchangeability into toy design. Hasbro, however, did not invent the transforming robot. That credit, as far as research shows, goes to a Japanese line called GoDaiKins. But Hasbro perfected the mass merchandising of the concept.

Today's generation of microchip-powered voice simulation and sound effect-laden toys are now the industry standard, but this will undoubtedly be made obsolete by future evolutions of controllability and interaction.

Action figures are big business, and hot series like Star Trek and Spawn are now regularly ranked in the top 20 best selling lines by industry trade magazines. An enduring character identity is a key to continued demand and future appreciation. Star Trek

KISS: Psycho Circus Peter Criss with Animal Wrangler, 1998, McFarlane

has proven itself a worthy long term franchise and is joining the ranks of Star Wars as the blue chip stocks of the action figure market.

The action figure aisles are now attracting more adults, and they are not always buying for their kids. More adults today are buying action figures as collectibles and investments. And those investments will in years hence feed the needs of tomorrow's collectors — the ones who are now sitting on the floor playing with Captain Picard, Batman and Spawn.

The Top 10 Action Figures
(excluding Captain Actionand G.I. Joe)
(in Mint in Box condition)

1. Batgirl, Comic Heroine Posin' Dolls, Ideal, 1967 .... $4,500
2. Wonder Woman, Comic Heroine Posin' Dolls, Ideal, 1967 3,000
3. Supergirl, Comic Heroine Posin' Dolls, Ideal, 1967 3,000
4. Mera, Comic Heroine Posin' Dolls, Ideal, 1967 3,000
5. Scorpio, Major Matt Mason, Mattel, 1967-70 2,250
6. Batman's Wayne Foundation Penthouse, 1977, fiberboard, World's
    Greatest Super Heroes, Mego, 1972-78 1,200
7. Mission Team Four-Pack, Major Matt Mason, Mattel, 1967-70, ... 625
8. Romulan, Star Trek, Mego, 1976 600
9. Callisto, Major Matt Mason, Mattel, 1967-70 600
10. Mad Monster Castle, vinyl, Mad Monster Series, Mego 600

Contributors to this section: Anthony Balasco, Figures, P.O. Box 19482, Johnston, RI 02919

ACTION FIGURES

ACTION JACKSON (MEGO, 1974)

	MNP	MIP
8" FIGURES		
Action Jackson, Black version	25	60
Action Jackson, blond, brown, or black beard	15	30
Action Jackson, blond, brown, or black hair	15	30
ACCESSORIES		
Parachute Plunge	5	15
Strap-On Helicopter	5	15
Water Scooter	5	15
OUTFITS		
Air Force Pilot	7	15
Army Outfit	7	15
Aussie Marine	7	15
Baseball	7	15
Fisherman	7	15
Football	7	15
Frog Man	7	15
Hockey	7	15
Jungle Safari	7	15
Karate	7	15
Navy Sailor	7	15
Rescue Squad	7	15
Scramble Cyclist	7	15
Secret Agent	7	15
Ski Patrol	7	15
Snowmobile Outfit	7	15
Surf and Scuba Outfit	7	15
Western Cowboy	7	15
PLAY SETS		
Jungle House	40	85
Lost Continent Play Set	40	85
VEHICLES		
Adventure Set	40	85
Campmobile	40	85
Dune Buggy	30	60
Formula Racer	30	60
Mustang	30	60
Rescue Helicopter	40	85
Safari Jeep	40	85
Scramble Cycle	20	40
Snowmobile	15	30

ALIENS (KENNER, 1979)

	MNP	MIP
18" FIGURE		
Alien	200	500

ALIENS (KENNER, 1992-94)

	MNP	MIP
1993, SERIES 2		
Alien vs. Predator	15	30
Flying Queen Alien	5	15
Queen Face Hugger	5	15
Snake Alien	5	15
1994		
Arachnid Alien	6	25
Atax	5	20
Clan Leader Predator	5	25
Cracked Tusk Predator	5	15
Invisible Predator (mail-in)	20	40
Kill Krab Alien	5	15
King Alien	10	25
Lasershot Predator (electronic)	15	30
Lava Predator	5	15
Mantis Alien	5	15

ALIENS (KENNER, 1992-94)

	MNP	MIP
Night Cougar Alien	5	15
Night Storm Predator	6	15
Panther Alien	5	15
Rhino Alien	7	15
Spiked Tail Predator	4	15
Stalker Predator	4	15
Swarm Alien (electronic)	15	25
Wild Boar Alien	4	15
5" FIGURES, 1992, SERIES 1		
Apone	5	15
Bull Alien	7	15
Drake	5	15
Gorilla Alien	8	15
Hicks	5	15
Queen Alien	10	25
Ripley	5	15
Scorpion Alien	7	15
ACCESSORIES		
Evac Fighter	7	20
Hovertread	5	20
Power Loader	5	20
Stinger XT-37	5	20

AMERICAN WEST (MEGO, 1973)

	MNP	MIP
8" FIGURES		
Buffalo Bill Cody, boxed	40	75
Buffalo Bill Cody, carded	40	100
Cochise, boxed	40	75
Cochise, carded	40	100
Davy Crockett, boxed	70	110
Davy Crockett, carded	70	140
Shadow (horse), carded	70	140
Sitting Bull, boxed	45	90
Sitting Bull, carded	45	125
Wild Bill Hickok, boxed	40	75
Wild Bill Hickok, carded	40	125
Wyatt Earp, boxed	40	75
Wyatt Earp, carded	40	125
PLAY SETS		
Dodge City Play Set, vinyl	100	200

ARCHIES (MARX, 1975)

	MNP	MIP
Archie	15	75
Betty	15	75
Jughead	15	75
Veronica	15	75

ASTRONAUTS (MARX, 1969)

	MNP	MIP
Jane Apollo Astronaut	35	75
Johnny Apollo Astronaut	35	75
Kennedy Space Center Astronaut	35	75

A-TEAM (GALOOB, 1984)

	MNP	MIP
3-3/4" FIGURES AND ACCESSORIES		
Armored Attack Adventure with B.A. Figure	8	20
A-Team Four Figure Set	12	30
Bad Guys Figure Set: Viper, Rattle, Cobra, Python	10	25
Combat Attack Gyrocopter	10	25
Command Center Play Set	14	35
Corvette with Face Figure	8	20

4

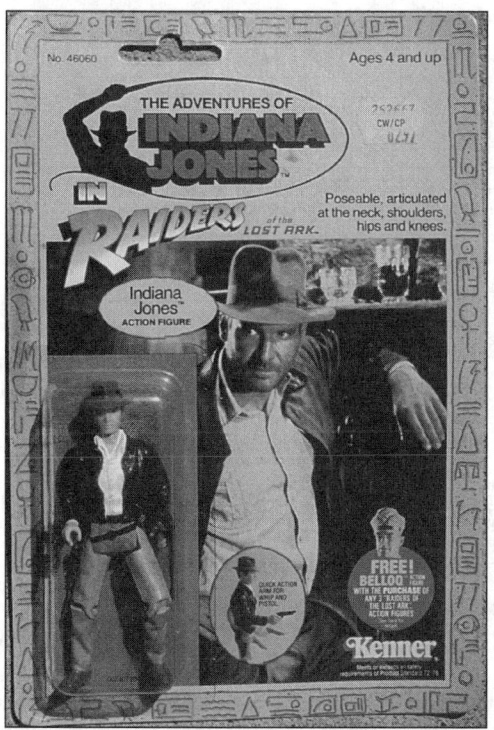

Adventures of Indiana Jones Indiana Jones, 1982-83, Kenner

Adventures of Indiana Jones Toht, 1982-83, Kenner

A-TEAM (GALOOB, 1984)

	MNP	MIP
Interceptor Jet Bomber with Murdock	10	25
Tactical Van Play Set	6	15

6-1/2" FIGURES AND ACCESSORIES

	MNP	MIP
Amy Allen	10	30
B.A. Baracus	8	25
Cobra	6	15
Face	6	25
Hannibal	6	25
Murdock	8	25
Off Road Attack Cycle	8	20
Python	6	15
Rattler	6	15
Viper	6	15

AUSTIN POWERS (MCFARLANE, 1999)

	MNP	MIP
FIGURES		
Austin in Union Jack underwear	4	8
Austin in velvet suit	4	8
Dr. Evil with Mr. Biggleworth	4	8
Felicity Shagwell	4	8

AVENGERS (TOY BIZ, 1998)

	MNP	MIP
FIGURES		
Iron Man	5	10
Loki	5	10
Scarlett Witch	5	10
The Mighty Thor	5	10

BANANA SPLITS (SUTTON, 1970)

	MNP	MIP
Bingo the Bear	45	125
Drooper the Lion	45	125
Fleagle Beagle	45	125
Snorky the Elephant	45	125

BATMAN CRIME SQUAD (KENNER, 1995)

	MNP	MIP
ACCESSORIES		
Attack Jet	7	15
FIGURES		
Air Assault Batman	5	15
Land Strike Batman	5	15
Pirahna Blade Batman	5	15
Sea Claw Batman	5	15
Ski Blast Robin	5	15
Stealthwing Batman	5	15
Torpedo Batman	5	15

BATMAN DARK KNIGHT (KENNER, 1990-91)

	MNP	MIP
FIGURES		
Blast Shield Batman	12	25
Bruce Wayne	7	20
Claw Climber Batman	12	25
Crime Attack Batman	7	15
Iron Winch Batman	7	15
Knockout Joker	25	75
Night Glider Batman	20	35
Power Wing Batman	12	25
Shadow Wing Batman	7	15

BATMAN DARK KNIGHT (KENNER, 1990-91)

	MNP	MIP
Sky Escape Joker	10	30
Thunder Whip Batman	12	25
Wall Scaler Batman	7	15

BATMAN FOREVER (KENNER, 1995)

	MNP	MIP
FIGURES		
Blast Cape Batman	5	15
Fireguard Batman	5	15
Hydro Claw Robin	5	15
Manta Ray Batman	5	15
Night Hunter Batman	5	15
Riddler	10	20
Sonar Sensor Batman	4	10
Street Biker Robin	4	10
Transforming Bruce Wayne	4	10
Transforming Dick Grayson	4	10
Two Face	10	20

BATMAN RETURNS (KENNER, 1992-94)

	MNP	MIP
FIGURES		
Aerostrike Batman	5	15
Air Attack Batman	4	15
Arctic Batman	4	15
Bola Strike Batman	4	15
Bruce Wayne	10	20
Catwoman	10	25
Claw Climber Batman	4	15
Crime Attack Batman	4	15
Deep Dive Batman	5	15
Glider Batman	4	15
High Wire Batman	4	15
Hydrocharge Batman	4	15
Jungle Tracker Batman	4	15
Laser Batman	4	15
Night Climber Batman	4	15
Penguin	15	40
Penguin Commandos	10	25
Polar Blast Batman	4	15
Power Wing Batman	6	15
Robin	10	25
Shadow Wing Batman	4	15
Sky Winch Batman	4	15
Thunder Strike Batman	4	15
Thunder Whip Batman	5	15
VEHICLES		
B.A.T.V. Vehicle	5	15
Bat Cycle	5	25
Batmobile	20	75
Bat-Signal Jet	3	15
Bruce Wayne Custom Coupe	12	50
Camo Attack Batmobile	30	75

BATMAN: THE ANIMATED SERIES (KENNER 1993-95)

	MNP	MIP
ACCESSORIES		
Batmobile	10	45
Bat-Signal Jet	3	6
Hoverbat Vehicle	5	15
Joker Mobile	6	20
Robin Dragster	75	250

BATMAN: THE ANIMATED SERIES (KENNER 1993-95)

	MNP	MIP
Street Jet	15	25
Turbo Batplane	6	20
FIGURES		
Anti-Freeze Batman	4	15
Bane	10	25
Bruce Wayne	10	20
Catwoman	7	25
Clay Face	7	25
Combat Belt Batman	7	40
Dick Grayson	5	15
Ground Assault Batman	5	10
Infrared Batman	5	10
Jet Pack Joker (green face)	10	25
Jet Pack Joker (white face)	10	25
Joker	7	20
Killer Croc	8	30
Knight Star Batman	4	10
Lightning Strike Batman	4	10
Manbat	7	25
Mechwing Batman	4	10
Mr. Freeze	8	20
Ninja Power Pack Batman and Robin	10	25
Ninja Robin	8	15
Parawing Robin	8	15
Penguin	12	85
Phantasm	15	40
Poison Ivy	20	30
Power Vision Batman	8	15
Riddler	10	50
Scarecrow	7	30
Skydive Batman	5	10
Total Armor Batman	4	10
Turbojet Batman	7	15
Two Face	7	20
Ultimate Batman (15")	25	50

BATTLESTAR GALACTICA (MATTEL, 1978-79)

	MNP	MIP
12" FIGURES		
Colonial Warrior	20	55
Cylon Centurian	20	55
3-3/4" FIGURES, 1978, SERIES 1		
Commander Adama	15	40
Cylon Centurian	15	40
Daggit (brown)	15	30
Daggit (tan)	15	30
Imperious Leader	15	30
Ovion	12	35
Starbuck	15	40
3-3/4" FIGURES, 1979, SERIES 2		
Baltar	30	75
Boray	30	75
Cylon Commander	55	110
Lucifer	55	110

BEATLES YELLOW SUBMARINE (MCFARLANE, 1999)

	MNP	MIP
FIGURES		
George with Yellow Submarine	4	10
John with Nowhere Man	4	10
Paul with Glove	4	10
Ringo with Blue Meanie	4	10

BEETLEJUICE (KENNER, 1989-90)

	MNP	MIP
ACCESSORIES		
Creepy Cruiser	5	25
Phantom Flyer	7	15
Snake Mask	7	15
Vanishing Vault	10	20
FIGURES		
Adam Maitland	8	20
Exploding Beetlejuice	5	10
Harry the Haunted Hunter	8	20
Old Buzzard	8	20
Ortho the Obnoxious	8	20
Shipwreck Beetlejuice	5	15
Shish Kabab Beetlejuice	5	15
Showtime Beetlejuice	5	15
Spinhead Beetlejuice	5	15
Street Rat	8	20
Talking Beetlejuice, 12" tall	20	50
Teacher Creature	10	20

BEST OF THE WEST (MARX, 1960S)

	MNP	MIP
FIGURES		
Bill Buck, 1967	100	200
Brave Eagle, 1967	45	90
Buckboard with Horse and Harness	35	75
Chief Cherokee, 1965	45	90
Daniel Boone, 1965	100	200
Davy Crockett	100	200
Fighting Eagle, 1967	45	90
General Custer, 1965	40	80
Geronimo and Pinto	40	80
Geronimo, 1967	45	90
Jamie West, 1967	32	65
Jane West, 1966	40	80
Janice West, 1967	32	65
Jay West, 1967	32	65
Johnny West Covered Wagon, with horse and harness	35	75
Johnny West with Comanche	80	125
Johnny West, 1965	40	80
Josie West, 1967	32	65
Pancho Horse, for 9" figures, 1968	20	40
Princess Wildflower, 1974	50	100
Sam Cobra, 1972	45	90
Sheriff Garrett, 1973	40	80
Thunderbolt Horse	35	75
Zeb Zachary, 1967	40	80

BLACK HOLE (MEGO, 1979-80)

	MNP	MIP
12" FIGURES		
Captain Holland	25	50
Dr. Alan Durant	25	50
Dr. Hans Reinhardt	25	50
Harry Booth	30	60
Kate McCrae	35	80
Pizer	25	50
3-3/4" FIGURES		
Captain Holland, 1979	10	20
Dr. Alan Durant, 1979	10	20
Dr. Hans Reinhardt, 1979	10	25
Harry Booth, 1979	10	25
Humanoid, 1980	70	135
Kate McCrae, 1979	10	25
Maximillian, 1979	17	40

7

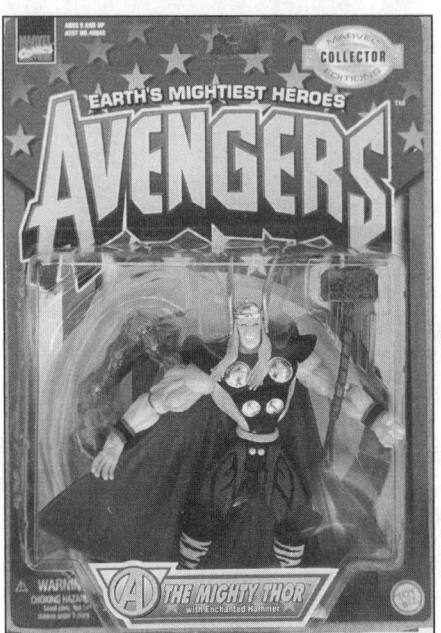

Avengers The Mighty Thor, 1998, Toy Biz

Battlestar Galactica Colonial Warrior, 1979, Mattel

Beatles Yellow Submarine John with Nowhere Man, 1999, McFarlane

BLACK HOLE (MEGO, 1979-80)

	MNP	MIP
Old B.O.B., 1980	60	120
Pizer, 1979	15	25
S.T.A.R., 1980	60	120
Sentry Robot, 1980	25	60
V.I.N.cent., 1979	30	60

BUCK ROGERS (MEGO, 1979)

	MNP	MIP
12" FIGURES		
Buck Rogers	30	80
Doctor Huer	30	60
Draco	30	60
Draconian Guard	30	60
Killer Kane	30	60
Tiger Man	30	80
Walking Twiki	30	60
3-3/4" FIGURES		
Ardella	6	15
Buck Rogers	20	40
Doctor Huer	6	20
Draco	6	20
Draconian Guard	10	20
Killer Kane	6	15
Tiger Man	6	15
Twiki	20	30
Wilma Deering	12	25
3-3/4" PLAY SETS		
Star Fighter Command Center	35	100
3-3/4" VEHICLES		
Draconian Marauder	25	50
Land Rover	20	40
Laserscope Fighter	20	40
Star Fighter	25	50
Starseeker	30	60

BUFFY THE VAMPIRE SLAYER (MOORE, 1999)

	MNP	MIP
FIGURES		
Angel	3	11
Buffy	3	11
Master, The	3	11
Willow	3	11

CAPTAIN ACTION (IDEAL, 1966-68)

	MNP	MIP
12" FIGURES		
Captain Action, box photo, 1966	200	900
Captain Action, parachute offer on box, 1967	275	1150
Captain Action, photo box, 1967	200	1250
Captain Action, with blue-shirted Lone Ranger on box, 1966	200	900
Captain Action, with red-shirted Lone Ranger on box, 1966	200	900
Dr. Evil, 1967	300	1200
9" FIGURES		
Action Boy, 1967	275	650
Action Boy, with space suit, 1968	350	825
ACCESSORIES		
Action Cave Carrying Case, vinyl, 1967	400	700
Directional Communicator Set, 1966	110	300
Dr. Evil Sanctuary, 1967	600	750

CAPTAIN ACTION (IDEAL, 1966-68)

	MNP	MIP
Jet Mortar, 1966	110	300
Parachute Pack, 1966	100	225
Power Pack, 1966	125	250
Quick Change Chamber, Cardboard, Sears Exclusive, 1967	750	900
Silver Streak Amphibian, 1967	500	1000
Silver Streak Garage (with Silver Streak Vehicle, Sears Exclusive)	400	500
Survival Kit, 20 pieces, 1967	125	275
Vinyl Headquarters Carrying Case, Sears Exclusive, 1967	200	500
Weapons Arsenal, 10 pieces, 1966	110	225
ACTION BOY COSTUMES		
Aqualad, 1967	300	900
Robin, 1967	300	1200
Superboy, 1967	300	1000
CAPTAIN ACTION COSTUMES		
Aquaman, 1966	160	600
Aquaman, with flasher ring, 1967	180	750
Batman, 1966	225	1000
Batman, with flasher ring, 1967	250	1100
Buck Rogers, with flasher ring, 1967	450	2700
Captain America, 1966	220	900
Captain America, with flasher ring, 1967	225	900
Flash Gordon, 1966	200	1250
Flash Gordon, with flasher ring, 1967	225	1000
Green Hornet, with flasher ring, 1967	1500	5500
Lone Ranger, blue shirt, with flasher ring, 1967	300	1500
Lone Ranger, red shirt, 1966	170	1350
Phantom, 1966	150	875
Phantom, with flasher ring, 1967	175	900
Sergeant Fury, 1966	200	1000
Spider-Man, with flasher ring, 1967	550	6000
Steve Canyon, 1966	150	1000
Steve Canyon, with flasher ring, 1967	175	1200
Superman, 1966	200	1200
Superman, with flasher ring, 1967	225	1300
Tonto, with flasher ring, 1967	375	1100

CAPTAIN ACTION (PLAYING MANTIS, 1998-99)

	MNP	MIP
FIGURES AND COSTUMES		
Captain Action	15	35
Dr. Evil	15	35
Flash Gordon	15	35
Green Hornet	15	45
Green Hornet	15	45
Kato	15	40
Lone Ranger	15	35
Ming the Merciless	15	35
Tonto	15	35

CHiPS (Mego, 1979)

	MNP	MIP
3-3/4" CARDED FIGURES & ACCESSORIES		
Jimmy Squeaks	5	15
Jon	10	20
Launcher with Motorcycle	25	50
Motorcycle (boxed)	5	30
Ponch	8	20
Sarge	10	30
Wheels Willie	5	15

CHiPS (Mego, 1979)

	MNP	MIP
8" CARDED FIGURES & ACCESSORIES		
Jon	20	50
Motorcycle	30	75
Ponch	15	40
Sarge	25	50

COMIC ACTION HEROES (MEGO, 1975)

	MNP	MIP
3-3/4" FIGURES		
Aquaman	30	60
Batman	20	50
Captain America	20	50
Green Goblin	22	55
Hulk	20	50
Joker	20	50
Penguin	20	50
Robin	20	50
Shazam	20	50
Spider-Man	20	50
Superman	20	45
Wonder Woman	20	40
ACCESSORIES		
Collapsing Tower (w/Invisible Plane & Wonder Woman)	50	125
Exploding Bridge with Batmobile	75	150
Fortress of Solitude with Superman	100	200
Mangler	55	110

COMIC HEROINE POSIN' DOLLS (IDEAL, 1967)

	MNP	MIP
12" BOXED FIGURES		
Batgirl	1000	4500
Mera	600	3000
Supergirl	600	3000
Wonder Woman	600	3000

COMMANDER POWER (MEGO, 1975)

	MNP	MIP
FIGURE WITH VEHICLE		
Commander Power with Lightning Cycle	20	40

DC COMICS SUPER HEROES (TOY BIZ, 1989)

	MNP	MIP
Aquaman	10	30
Batman	5	15
Bob The Goon	10	20
Flash	7	15
Flash II	10	25
Green Lantern	15	40
Hawkman	15	30
Joker, no Facial Hair	5	15
Joker, w/Facial Hair	10	25
Lex Luthor	5	15
Penguin, long missile	15	25
Penguin, short missile	15	30
Penguin, umbrella-firing	5	15
Riddler	7	15
Superman	20	50
Two Face	15	30
Wonder Woman	8	15

DIE-CAST SUPER HEROES (MEGO, 1979)

	MNP	MIP
6" FIGURES		
Batman	30	75
Hulk	25	65
Spider-Man	30	75
Superman	30	75

DUKES OF HAZZARD (MEGO, 1981-82)

	MNP	MIP
3-3/4" CARDED FIGURES		
Bo Duke	8	15
Boss Hogg	8	20
Cletus	15	30
Cooter	15	30
Coy Duke	15	30
Daisy Duke	12	25
Luke Duke	8	20
Rosco Coltrane	15	30
Uncle Jesse	15	30
Vance Duke	15	30
3-3/4" FIGURES WITH VEHICLES		
Daisy Jeep with Daisy, 1981, boxed	25	50
General Lee Car with Bo and Luke, 1981, boxed	25	50
8" CARDED FIGURES		
Bo Duke	15	30
Boss Hogg	20	40
Coy Duke (card says Bo)	25	50
Daisy Duke	25	50
Luke Duke	15	30
Vance Duke (card says Luke)	25	50

EARTHWORM JIM (PLAYMATES, 1995)

	MNP	MIP
Bob	5	12
Earthworm Jim w/Battle Damage	5	8
Earthworm Jim w/Snott	5	8
Hench Rat w/Evil Cat	5	10
Monstrous Peter Puppy	5	8
Peter Puppy	5	8
Pocket Rocket	5	8
Princess What's Her Name	7	12
Psycrow w/Major Mucus	4	8

FANTASTIC FOUR (TOY BIZ, 1995)

	MNP	MIP
10" BOXED FIGURES		
Dr. Doom	6	12
Human Torch	6	12
Silver Surfer	10	15
5" FIGURES		
Annihilus	3	10
Attuma	3	10
Black Bolt	3	10
Blastaar	3	10
Dr. Doom	3	10
Dragon Man	3	10
Firelord	3	10
Gorgon	3	10
Human Torch	3	10
Invisible Woman	10	20
Mole Man	5	10
Mr. Fantastic	3	10

*Best of the West Fighting Eagle,
1967, Marx*

*Best of the West Jane West, 1966,
Marx*

*Best of the West Johnny West Covered Wagon,
1960s, Marx*

*Best of the West Johnny West,
1965, Marx*

FANTASTIC FOUR (TOY BIZ, 1995)

	MNP	MIP
Namor the Sub-Mariner	3	10
Silver Surfer	6	10
Super Skrull	3	10
Terrax	3	10
Thanos	3	10
Thing	5	10
Thing II	5	10
Triton	3	10

ELECTRONIC 14" FIGURES

	MNP	MIP
Galactus	10	40
Talking Thing	10	20

VEHICLES

	MNP	MIP
Fantasticar	7	15
Mr. Fantastic Sky Shuttle	7	15
The Thing's Sky Cycle	7	15

FLASH GORDON (MEGO, 1976)

9" FIGURES

	MNP	MIP
Dale Arden	35	70
Dr. Zarkow	55	110
Flash Gordon	55	110
Ming	30	60

PLAY SETS

	MNP	MIP
Flash Gordon Play Set	55	125

FORT APACHE FIGHTERS (MARX, 1960S)

	MNP	MIP
Captain Maddox, 1967	35	70
Fighting Eagle and Comanche	50	100
Fighting Eagle, 1967	35	70
General Custer, 1967	35	70
Geronimo, 1967	35	70

GARGOYLES (KENNER, 1995)

ACCESSORIES

	MNP	MIP
Gargoyle Castle	20	40
Night Striker	10	20
Rippin' Rider Cycle	7	12

FIGURES

	MNP	MIP
Battle Goliath	3	15
Broadway	3	15
Bronx	3	15
Brooklyn	4	15
Claw Climber Goliath	3	15
Demona	4	15
Lexington	3	15
Mighty Roar Goliath	5	15
Power Wing Goliath	5	15
Quick Strike Goliath	3	15
Steel Clan Robot	3	15
Stone Armor Goliath	5	15
Strike Hammer Macbeth	3	15
Xanatos	3	15

GHOSTBUSTERS (KENNER, 1986-91)

1986

	MNP	MIP
Bad to the Bone Ghost	5	15
Banshee Bomber Gooper Ghost with Ecto-Plazm	5	15
Bug-Eye Ghost	5	15

GHOSTBUSTERS (KENNER, 1986-91)

	MNP	MIP
Ecto-1	20	40
Egon Spengler & Gulper Ghost	6	15
Firehouse Headquarters	25	50
Ghost Pooper	5	10
Ghost Zapper	5	15
Gooper Ghost Sludge Bucket	5	15
Gooper Ghost Squisher with Ecto-Plazm	5	15
H2 Ghost	5	15
Peter Venkman & Grabber Ghost	6	15
Proton Pack	20	40
Ray Stantz & Wrapper Ghost	6	15
Slimer Plush Figure, 13"	20	35
Slimer with Pizza	20	40
Stay-Puft Marshmallow Man Plush, 13"	15	30
Winston Zeddmore & Chomper Ghost	7	18

1988

	MNP	MIP
Brain Blaster Ghost Haunted Human	5	15
Ecto-2 Helicopter	5	15
Fright Feature Egon	5	15
Fright Feature Janine Melnitz	5	15
Fright Feature Peter	5	15
Fright Feature Ray	5	15
Fright Feature Winston	5	15
Gooper Ghost Slimer	12	25
Granny Gross Haunted Human	5	15
Hard Hat Horror Haunted Human	5	15
Highway Haunter	10	20
Mail Fraud Haunted Human	5	15
Mini Ghost Mini-Gooper	5	10
Mini Ghost Mini-Shooter	5	10
Mini Ghost Mini-Trap	5	10
Pull Speed Ahead Ghost	5	15
Terror Trash Haunted Human	5	15
Tombstone Tackle Haunted Human	5	15
X-Cop Haunted Human	5	15

1989

	MNP	MIP
Dracula	5	15
Ecto-3	5	15
Fearsome Flush	5	10
Frankenstein	3	15
Hunchback	3	15
Mummy	3	15
Screaming Hero Egon	5	15
Screaming Hero Janine Melnitz	5	15
Screaming Hero Peter	5	15
Screaming Hero Ray	5	15
Screaming Hero Winston	5	15
Slimer with Proton Pack, red or blue	15	35
Super Fright Egon with Slimy Spider	5	15
Super Fright Janine with Boo Fish Ghost	5	15
Super Fright Peter Venkman & Snake Head	5	15
Super Fright Ray	5	15
Super Fright Winston Zeddmore & Meanie Wienie	5	15
Wolfman	5	15
Zombie	5	15

1990

	MNP	MIP
Ecto Bomber with Bomber Ghost	5	15
Ecto-1A with Ambulance Ghost	20	40
Ghost Sweeper	5	15
Gobblin' Goblin Nasty Neck	6	15
Gobblin' Goblin Terrible Teeth	6	15
Gobblin' Goblin Terror Tongue	6	15

GHOSTBUSTERS (KENNER, 1986-91)

	MNP	MIP
Slimed Hero Egon	5	15
Slimed Hero Louis Tully & Four Eyed Ghost	5	15
Slimed Hero Peter Venkman & Tooth Ghost	5	15
Slimed Hero Ray Stantz & Vapor Ghost	5	15
Slimed Hero Winston	5	15
1991		
Ecto-Glow Egon	10	30
Ecto-Glow Louis Tully	10	30
Ecto-Glow Peter	10	30
Ecto-Glow Ray	10	30
Ecto-Glow Winston Zeddmore	10	30

GHOSTBUSTERS, FILMATION (SCHAPER, 1986)

	MNP	MIP
Belfry and Brat-A-Rat	10	15
Bone Troller	10	15
Eddie	10	15
Fangster	10	15
Fib Face	10	15
Futura	10	15
Ghost Popper Ghost Buggy	20	40
Haunter	10	15
Jake	10	15
Jessica	10	15
Mysteria	10	15
Prime Evil	10	15
Scare Scooter Vehicle	10	20
Scared Stiff	6	15
Time Hopper Vehicle	10	15
Tracy	10	15

HAPPY DAYS (MEGO, 1978)

	MNP	MIP
Fonzie, boxed	30	75
Fonzie, carded	30	75
Potsie, carded	30	75
Ralph, carded	30	75
Richie, carded	30	75
PLAY SETS		
Fonzie, boxed	30	75
Fonzie, carded	30	75
Fonzie's Garage Play Set, 1978	60	150
Potsie, carded	30	75
Ralph, carded	30	75
Richie, carded	30	75
VEHICLES		
Fonzie, boxed	30	75
Fonzie, carded	30	75
Fonzie's Jalopy, 1978	40	80
Fonzie's Motorcycle, 1978	40	80
Potsie, carded	30	75
Ralph, carded	30	75
Richie, carded	30	75

INDEPENDENCE DAY (TRENDMASTERS, 1996)

	MNP	MIP
FIGURES		
Alien Attacker Pilot	5	10
Alien in Bio Chamber	8	12
Alien Science Officer	5	10
Alien Shock Trooper	5	10

INDEPENDENCE DAY (TRENDMASTERS, 1996)

	MNP	MIP
Alien Supreme Commander	15	25
David Levinson	5	10
President Thomas Whitmore	5	10
Steve Hiller	5	10
Ultimate Alien Commander	20	35
Weapons Expert	10	20
Zero Gravity	8	15

INDIANA JONES, ADVENTURES OF (KENNER, 1982-83)

	MNP	MIP
Belloq	12	35
Belloq in Ceremonial Robe, in mailer box	8	20
Belloq in Ceremonial Robe, on card	200	500
Cairo Swordsman	8	20
Convoy Truck	15	35
German Mechanic	15	35
Indiana Jones	50	100
Indiana Jones in German Uniform	20	45
Indiana Jones, 12"	125	250
Map Room Set	20	50
Marion Ravenwood	70	175
Sallah	20	45
Streets of Cairo Set	18	45
Toht	5	15
Well of Souls	30	75

JAMES BOND: MOONRAKER (MEGO, 1979)

	MNP	MIP
12" FIGURES		
Drax	150	200
Holly	150	200
James Bond	125	150
James Bond, deluxe version	350	500
Jaws	400	500

JOHNNY WEST (MARX, 1975)

	MNP	MIP
Jeb Gibson	125	275
Johnny West with Quick Draw	35	70
Sam Cobra with Quick Draw	40	80
Sheriff Garrett	35	70
Thunderbolt, Western Ranch Horse	25	50

JONNY QUEST (GALOOB, 1996)

	MNP	MIP
ACCESSORIES		
Cyber Copter	5	15
Quest Porpoise w/Deep Sea Jonny	5	15
Quest Rover	5	15
QUEST WORLD FIGURES		
Cyber Cycle Jonny Quest	5	10
Cyber Jet Race	5	10
Cyber Suit Hadji	5	10
Cyber Trax Surd	5	10
REAL WORLD FIGURES		
Deep Sea Race Bannon & Hadji	4	8
Jungle Commando Dr. Quest & Ezekiel Rage	4	8
Night Stryker Jonny Quest & Jessie	5	10
Shuttle Pilot Jonny Quest & Race Bannon	4	8
X-Treme Action Jonny Quest & Hadji	4	8

Captain Action Dr. Evil, 1967, Ideal

CHiPs Motorcycle, 1979, Mego

KISS (McFARLANE, 1997)

	MNP	MIP
6" CARDED FIGURES		
Ace Frehley w/album	5	10
Ace Frehley w/letter stand	7	15
Gene Simmons w/album	5	10
Gene Simmons w/letter base	7	15
Paul Stanley w/album	4	10
Paul Stanley w/letter stand	7	15
Peter Criss w/album	5	10
Peter Criss w/letter stand	7	15

KISS (MEGO, 1978)

	MNP	MIP
12" BOXED FIGURES		
Ace Frehley	100	260
Gene Simmons	110	260
Paul Stanley	100	260
Peter Criss	100	260

KISS: PSYCHO CIRCUS (McFARLANE, 1998)

	MNP	MIP
FIGURES		
Ace Frehley with Stiltman	5	10
Gene Simmons with Ring Master	5	10
Paul Stanley with The Jester	5	10
Peter Criss with Animal Wrangler	5	10

KISS: PSYCHO CIRCUS TOUR (McFARLANE, 1999)

	MNP	MIP
FIGURES		
Ace Frehley	4	8
Gene Simmons	4	8
Paul Stanley	4	8
Peter Criss	4	8

LARA CROFT (PLAYMATES, 1999)

	MNP	MIP
FIGURES		
Lara in Area 51 outfit	10	20
Lara in jungle outfit	10	20
Lara in wet suit	10	20
Talking Lara	15	30

LAVERNE AND SHIRLEY (MEGO, 1978)

	MNP	MIP
12" BOXED FIGURES		
Laverne and Shirley	60	125
Lenny and Squiggy	90	175

LEGENDS OF BATMAN (KENNER, 1994)

	MNP	MIP
FIGURES		
Catwoman	8	25
Crusader Batman	4	10
Crusader Robin	4	10
Cyborg Batman	4	10
Dark Rider Batman	10	15
Dark Warrior Batman	4	10
Desert Knight Batman	5	10
Flightpak Batman	5	10

LEGENDS OF BATMAN (KENNER, 1994)

	MNP	MIP
Future Batman	5	10
Joker	10	25
Knightquest Batman	5	10
Knightsend Batman	4	10
Long Bow Batman	4	10
Nightwing Robin	5	10
Power Guardian Batman	5	10
Riddler	10	25
Samurai Batman	4	10
Silver Knight Batman	5	10
Viking Batman	4	10
VEHICLES		
Batcycle	10	20

LEGENDS OF BATMAN (KENNER, 1994)

	MNP	MIP
VEHICLES		
Batmobile	20	75

LONE RANGER RIDES AGAIN (GABRIEL, 1979)

	MNP	MIP
FIGURES		
Dan Reid	25	50
Little Bear w/Hawk	25	50
Lone Ranger	20	40
Red Sleeves	25	50
Tonto	20	40

LONE RANGER, LEGEND OF (GABRIEL, 1982)

	MNP	MIP
FIGURES		
Buffalo Bill Cody	10	25
Butch Cavendish	10	20
General Custer	10	20
Lone Ranger	15	40
Lone Ranger w/Silver	25	90
Scout	10	20
Silver	15	30
Smoke	10	25
Tonto	7	15
Tonto w/Scout	25	50

LORD OF THE RINGS (TOY VAULT, 1998-99)

	MNP	MIP
FIGURES		
Balrog	7	13
Frodo in Lorien	7	13
Frodo in the Barrow	8	18
Gandalf	7	13
Gimli in Battle	7	13
Gimli in Lorien	7	13
Gimli of the Fellowship	8	18
Gollum	7	13
Gollum the Fisherman	7	13
Ugluk at War	7	13
Ugluk on the Hunt	7	13

LOST IN SPACE
(TRENDMASTERS, 1998)

	MNP	MIP
FIGURES		
Battle Armor Don West	4	8
Cryo Chamber Judy Robinson	4	8
Cryo Chamber Judy Robinson	4	8
Cryo Chamber Will Robinson	4	8
Cyclops	7	15
Dr. Smith	7	15
Judy Robinson	7	15
Proteus Armor Dr. Smith	4	8
Proteus Armor John Robinson	4	8
Tybo the Carrot Man	7	15
Will Robinson	7	15
PLAY SETS		
Jupiter 2 play set	10	25

LOVE BOAT (MEGO, 1981)

	MNP	MIP
4" CARDED FIGURES		
Captain Stubing	10	20
Doc	10	20
Gopher	10	20
Isaac	10	20
Julie	10	25
Vicki	10	25

M*A*S*H (TRISTAR, 1982)

	MNP	MIP
3-3/4" FIGURES AND VEHICLES		
B.J.	5	15
Colonel Potter	5	15
Father Mulcahy	5	15
Hawkeye	5	15
Hawkeye with Ambulance	15	35
Hawkeye with Helicopter	8	20
Hawkeye with Jeep	10	25
Hot Lips	10	20
Klinger	5	15
Klinger in Drag	15	35
M*A*S*H Figures Collectors Set	26	65
Winchester	5	15
8" CARDED FIGURES		
B.J.	15	35
Hawkeye	15	35
Hot Lips	12	30

MAD MONSTER SERIES
(MEGO, 1974)

	MNP	MIP
8" FIGURES		
The Dreadful Dracula	80	160
The Horrible Mummy	50	100
The Human Wolfman	75	150
The Monster Frankenstein	45	90
ACCESSORIES		
Mad Monster Castle, vinyl	300	600

MAJOR MATT MASON
(MATTEL, 1967-70)

	MNP	MIP
FIGURES		
Callisto, 6"	100	600
Captain Lazer, 12"	125	520
Doug Davis, 6"	100	300

MAJOR MATT MASON
(MATTEL, 1967-70)

	MNP	MIP
Jeff Long, 6"	100	500
Major Matt Mason, 6"	75	225
Mission Team Four-Pack	175	625
Scorpio, 7"	500	2250
Sergeant Storm, 6"	100	400
VEHICLES AND ACCESSORIES		
Astro-Trak	35	75
Firebolt Space Cannon	35	80
Gamma Ray Guard	30	125
Moon Suit Pak	25	70
Reconojet Pak	25	75
Rocket Launch	25	75
Satellite Launch Pak	25	75
Satellite Locker	30	80
Space Power Suit	30	110
Space Probe Pak	25	75
Space Shelter Pak	25	75
Space Station Set	150	350
Star Seeker	85	180
Supernaut Power Limbs	30	110
Uni-Tred & Space Bubble	50	125
XRG-1 Reentry Glider	75	200

MARS ATTACKS!
(TRENDMASTERS, 1997)

	MNP	MIP
FIGURES		
Martian Ambassador	6	12
Martian Leader	6	12
Martian Spy Girl	45	65
Martian Trooper	8	15

MARVEL FAMOUS COVERS
(TOY BIZ, 1997)

	MNP	MIP
FIGURES		
Aunt May	10	15
Green Goblin	10	15
Spider-Man	10	15
Storm	12	18
Wolverine	10	15

MARVEL GOLD (TOY BIZ, 1998)

	MNP	MIP
FIGURES		
Black Panther	8	16
Marvel Girl	8	16
Moon Knight	8	16
Power Man	8	16
Vision	8	16

MARVEL SECRET WARS
(MATTEL, 1984-85)

	MNP	MIP
4" FIGURES		
Baron Zemo	15	35
Captain America	10	25
Constrictor (foreign release)	30	75
Daredevil	15	35
Doctor Doom	10	20
Doctor Octopus	10	20
Electro (foreign release)	30	75
Falcon	20	40
Hobgoblin	30	60

Dukes of Hazzard Luke Duke, 1981-82, Mego

Happy Days Ralph, 1978, Mego

KISS: Psycho Circus Tour Gene Simmons, 1999, McFarlane

Major Matt Mason Space Probe Pak, 1967-70, Mattel

17

MARVEL SECRET WARS
(MATTEL, 1984-85)

	MNP	MIP
Ice Man (foreign release)	30	75
Iron Man	20	35
Kang	10	20
Magneto	10	20
Spider-Man, black outfit	25	50
Spider-Man, red and blue outfit	20	40
Three-Figure Set	40	90
Two-Figure Set	25	50
Wolverine, black claws	25	60
Wolverine, silver claws	25	50

ACCESSORIES

Secret Messages Pack	1	5
Tower of Doom	10	25

VEHICLES

Doom Copter	10	35
Doom Copter with Doctor Doom	15	55
Doom Cycle	6	20
Doom Cycle with Doctor Doom	10	40
Doom Roller	10	20
Doom Star Glider with Kang	15	30
Freedom Fighter	10	30
Star Dart with Spider-Man (black outfit)	25	50
Turbo Copter	10	40
Turbo Cycle	5	20

MARVEL SUPER HEROES
(TOY BIZ, 1990-92)

	MNP	MIP
SERIES 1, 1990		
Captain America	10	25
Daredevil	15	50
Doctor Doom	10	25
Doctor Octopus	10	25
Hulk	5	15
Punisher (cap firing)	5	15
Silver Surfer	10	30
Spider-Man (suction cups)	5	20
SERIES 2, 1991		
Green Goblin (back lever)	15	40
Green Goblin (no lever)	10	25
Iron Man	10	25
Punisher (machine gun sound)	5	15
Spider-Man (web climbing)	15	35
Spider-Man (web shooting)	10	30
Thor (back lever)	15	40
Thor (no lever)	10	25
Venom	10	20
SERIES 3, 1992		
Annihilus	5	15
Deathlok	5	15
Human Torch	5	15
Invisible Woman	75	150
Mister Fantastic	5	15
Silver Surfer (chrome)	5	15
Spider-Man (ball joints)	5	15
Spider-Man (web tracer)	5	15
Thing	5	15
Venom (tongue flicking)	15	20
TALKING HEROES		
Cyclops	10	20
Hulk	10	20
Magneto	10	20
Punisher	10	20
Spider-Man	10	20

MARVEL SUPER HEROES
(TOY BIZ, 1990-92)

	MNP	MIP
Venom	10	25
Wolverine	10	20

MASTERS OF THE UNIVERSE
(MATTEL, 1981-90)

	MNP	MIP
5-3/4" FIGURES		
Battle Armor He-Man	10	20
Battle Armor Skeletor	5	20
Beast Man	10	20
Blade	10	25
Blast-Attak	5	15
Buzz-Off	5	15
Buzz-Saw Hordak	5	15
Clamp Champ	5	15
Clawful	10	20
Dragstor	5	15
Evil-Lyn	15	30
Extendar	5	15
Faker	15	40
Faker (reissue)	5	15
Fisto	5	15
Grizzlor	5	15
Gwildor	5	15
He-Man, original version	15	30
Hordak	5	15
Horde Trooper	5	15
Jitsu	10	20
King Hiss	5	15
King Randor	10	25
Kobra Khan	5	20
Leech	5	15
Man-At-Arms	10	20
Man-E-Faces	10	20
Mantenna	5	15
Mekaneck	5	15
Mer-Man	5	25
Modulok	5	20
Mosquitor	5	15
Moss Man	5	15
Multi-Bot	5	20
Ninjor	5	20
Orko	5	20
Prince Adam	10	25
Ram Man	15	35
Rattlor	5	15
Rio Blast	5	15
Roboto	5	15
Rokkon	5	15
Rotar	5	15
Saurod	5	20
Scare Glow	15	35
Skeletor, original version	10	25
Snake Face	5	20
Snout Spout	6	20
Sorceress	10	25
Spikor	10	20
SSSqueeze	10	20
Stinkor	5	15
Stonedar	5	15
Stratos, blue wings	10	20
Stratos, red wings	10	20
Sy-Klone	10	20
Teela	10	25
Trap Jaw	10	25
Tri-Klops	30	100
Tung Lashor	5	15

18

MASTERS OF THE UNIVERSE (MATTEL, 1981-90)

	MNP	MIP
Twistoid	5	15
Two-Bad	5	15
Webstor	5	15
Whiplash	5	15
Zodac	10	20

ACCESSORIES

	MNP	MIP
Battle Bones Carrying Case	5	10
Battle Cat	10	25
Battle Cat with He-Man (original version)	20	40
Beam-Blaster and Artilleray	15	30
Jet Sled	10	25
Mantisaur	8	15
Megalaser	10	20
Monstroid Creature	15	30
Night Stalker	5	15
Night Stalker with Jitsu	10	25
Panthor (evil cat)	10	25
Panthor with Skeletor (original version)	15	40
Screech	5	15
Screech with Skeletor (original version)	10	25
Stilt Stalkers	5	15
Stridor Armored Horse	5	15
Stridor with Fisto	10	25
Weapons Pak	2	5
Zoar	5	15
Zoar with Teela	15	30

FIFTH ANNIVERSARY FIGURES

	MNP	MIP
Dragon Blaster Skeletor	10	25
Flying Fists He-Man	10	25
Hurricane Hordak	10	25
Terror Claws Skeletor	10	25
Thunder Punch He-Man	15	30

GRAYSKULL DINOSAUR SERIES

	MNP	MIP
Bionatops	10	25
Turbodaltyl	10	25
Tyrantisaurus Rex	10	25

METEORBS

	MNP	MIP
Astro Lion	15	30
Comet Cat	15	30
Cometroid	15	30
Crocobite	15	30
Dinosorb	15	30
Gore-illa	15	30
Orbear	15	30
Rhinorb	15	30
Tuskor	15	30
Ty-Gyr	15	30

PLAY SETS

	MNP	MIP
Castle GraySkull	25	100
Eternia	100	200
Fright Zone	25	50
Slime Pit	10	20
Snake Mountain	25	50

VEHICLES

	MNP	MIP
Attak Trak	15	40
Bashasaurus	10	40
Battle Ram	10	40
Blasterhawk	15	40
Dragon Walker	10	25
Fright Fighter	10	40
Land Shark	10	25
Laser Bolt	15	30
Point Dread	10	50

MASTERS OF THE UNIVERSE (MATTEL, 1981-90)

	MNP	MIP
Road Ripper	10	25
Roton	10	30
Spydor	15	40
Wind Raider	10	40

METAL GEAR SOLID (MCFARLANE, 1998)

FIGURES

	MNP	MIP
Liquid Snake	4	8
Meryl Silverburgh	4	8
Ninja	4	8
Psycho Mantis	4	8
Revolver Ocelot	4	8
Sniper Wolf	4	8
Solid Snake	4	8
Vulcan Raven	4	8

MICRONAUTS (MEGO, 1976-80)

ALIEN INVADERS CARDED

	MNP	MIP
Antron, 1979	15	30
Centaurus, 1980	35	70
Karrio, 1979	10	20
Kronos, 1980	35	70
Lobros, 1980	35	70
Membros, 1979	15	30
Repto, 1979	13	25

ALIEN INVADERS PLAY SETS

	MNP	MIP
Rocket Tubes, 1978	23	50

ALIEN INVADERS VEHICLES

	MNP	MIP
Alphatron	5	10
Aquatron, 1977	10	20
Betatron	5	10
Gammatron	5	10
Hornetroid, 1979	20	40
Hydra, 1976	7	15
Mobile Exploration Lab, 1976	17	35
Solarion, 1978	15	30
Star Searcher, 1978	15	40
Taurion, 1978	11	22
Terraphant, 1979	20	40

BOXED FIGURES

	MNP	MIP
Andromeda, 1977	10	25
Baron Karza, 1977	15	30
Biotron, 1976	10	25
Force Commander, 1977	10	25
Giant Acroyear, 1977	10	25
Megas, 1981	10	25
Microtron, 1976	5	20
Nemesis Robot, 1978	7	15
Oberon, 1977	10	25
Phobos Robot, 1978	12	25

CARDED FIGURES

	MNP	MIP
Acroyear II, 1977, red, blue, orange	7	15
Acroyear, 1976, red, blue, orange	10	20
Galactic Defender, 1978, white, yellow	7	15
Galactic Warriors, 1976, red, blue, orange	4	10
Pharoid with Time Chamber, 1977, blue, red, gray	10	20
Space Glider, 1976, blue, green, orange	5	10
Time Traveler, 1976, clear plastic, yellow, orange	3	10

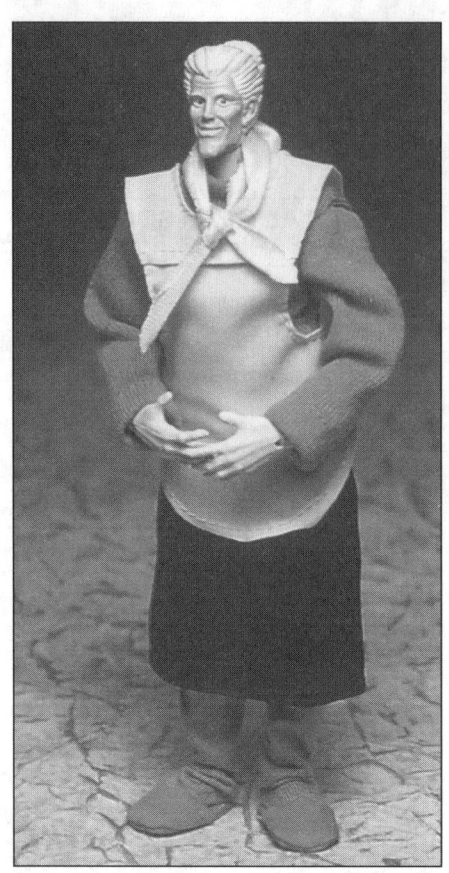

Marvel Famous Covers Aunt May, 1997, Toy Biz

Masters of the Universe Blast-Attak, 1981-90, Mattel

Masters of the Universe Dragon Walker, 1981-90, Mattel

MICRONAUTS (MEGO, 1976-80)

	MNP	MIP
Time Traveler, 1976, solid plastic, yellow, orange	5	15

MICROPOLIS PLAY SETS

	MNP	MIP
Galactic Command Center, 1978	20	40
Interplanetary Headquarters, 1978	20	40
Mega City, 1978	20	30
Microrail City, 1978	20	40

PLAY SETS

	MNP	MIP
Astro Station, 1976	10	20
Stratstation, 1976	15	30

VEHICLES

	MNP	MIP
Battle Cruiser, 1977	30	60
Crater Cruncher with figure, 1976	5	15
Galactic Cruiser, 1976	7	17
Hydro Copter, 1976	10	25
Neon Orbiter, 1977	6	20
Photon Sled with figure, 1976	5	15
Rhodium Orbiter, 1977	6	20
Thorium Orbiter, 1977	6	20
Ultronic Scooter with figure, 1976	5	15
Warp Racer with figure, 1976	5	15

MIGHTY MORPHIN POWER RANGERS (BANDAI, 1993-95)

	MNP	MIP

3" FIGURES

	MNP	MIP
Black Ranger	5	15
Blue Ranger	5	15
Pink Ranger	5	15
Red Ranger	5	15
Yellow Ranger	5	15

5" FIGURES W/THUNDER BIKES

	MNP	MIP
Black Ranger	6	15
Blue Ranger	6	15
Pink Ranger	6	15
Red Ranger	6	15
Yellow Ranger	6	15

5-1/2" CARDED FIGURES

	MNP	MIP
Black Ranger	3	15
Blue Ranger	3	15
Green Ranger	3	15
Pink Ranger	3	15
Red Ranger	2	15
Yellow Ranger	3	15

8" FIGURES, 1993

	MNP	MIP
Black Ranger	7	20
Blue Ranger	7	20
Pink Ranger	10	20
Red Ranger	5	20
Yellow Ranger	10	20

8" MOVIE FIGURES, 1995

	MNP	MIP
Black Ranger	6	15
Blue Ranger	6	15
Pink Ranger	6	15
Red Ranger	6	15
White Ranger	6	15
Yellow Ranger	6	15

ALIENS, 1993

	MNP	MIP
Baboo	10	20
Bones	10	20
Finster	10	20
Goldar	10	20
King Sphinx	10	20
Putty Patrol	10	20
Squatt	10	20

MIGHTY MORPHIN POWER RANGERS (BANDAI, 1993-95)

	MNP	MIP

ALIENS, 1994

	MNP	MIP
Evil Eye	7	15
Goo Fish	7	15
Guitardo	7	15
Lord Zed	8	18
Pirantus Head	7	15
Pudgy Pig	7	15
Rhino Blaster	7	15
Socaddillo	7	15
Super Puttys	7	15

KARATE ACTION FIGURES, 1994

	MNP	MIP
Black Ranger	6	12
Blue Ranger	6	12
Pink Ranger	8	16
Red Ranger	5	10
Yellow Ranger	8	16

POWER RANGERS FOR GIRLS

	MNP	MIP
Kimberly	10	20
Kimberly/Trini Set	20	40
Trini	10	20

ZORDS, 1993

	MNP	MIP
Dragon Dagger	20	50
Dragon Zord w/Green Ranger	25	55
MegaZord	15	30
MegaZord Deluxe	20	40
Titanus the Carrier Zord	35	75

ZORDS, 1994

	MNP	MIP
MegaZord, black/gold, limit. ed.	50	100
Power Cannon	15	35
Power Dome Morphin Set	25	55
Red Dragon Thunder Zord	25	45
Saba (White Sword)	15	30
Thunder Zord Assault Team	25	45
TOR the Shuttle Zord	30	60
Ultra Thunder Zord	35	70
White Tiger Zord w/White Ranger	25	50

MONSTERS-SERIES 2 (McFARLANE, 1998)

	MNP	MIP

PLAY SETS

	MNP	MIP
Dr. Frankenstein	6	12
The Mummy	6	12
The Phantom of the Opera	6	12
The Sea Creature	6	12

MOVIE MANIACS (McFARLANE, 1998)

	MNP	MIP

FIGURES

	MNP	MIP
Eve	4	8
Freddy Krueger	4	15
Jason	4	8
Leatherface	4	15
Patrick	4	8

MOVIE MANIACS II (McFARLANE, 1999)

	MNP	MIP

FIGURES

	MNP	MIP
Eric Dravin from The Crow	4	15
Ghostface from Scream	4	15
Michael myers from Halloween	4	15

MOVIE MANIACS II
(McFARLANE, 1999)

	MNP	MIP
Norman Bates from Psycho	4	15
Pumpkinhead	4	15

NOBLE KNIGHTS (MARX, 1968)

	MNP	MIP
Black Knight	75	190
Bravo Armor Horse	100	130
Gold Knight	60	120
Silver Knight	60	120
Valiant Armor Horse	100	130
Valor Armor Horse	100	130
Victor Armor Horse	100	130

ONE MILLION YEARS, B.C.
(MEGO, 1976)

	MNP	MIP
Dimetrodon, 1976, boxed	75	150
Grok, 1976, carded	25	50
Hairy Rino, 1976, boxed	75	150
Mada, 1976, carded	25	50
Orm, 1976, carded	25	50
Trag, 1976, carded	25	50
Tribal Lair Gift Set (Five figures), 1976	70	180
Tribal Lair, 1976	60	120
Tyrannosaur, 1976, boxed	75	150
Zon, 1976, carded	25	50

OUTER SPACE MEN
(COLORFORMS, 1968)

	MNP	MIP
CARDED FIGURES		
Alpha 7 / Man from Mars	90	250
Astro-Nautilus / Man from Neptune	90	250
Colossus Rex / Man from Jupiter	100	300
Commander Comet / Man from Venus	90	250
Electron / Man from Pluto	90	250
Orbitron / Man from Uranus	90	250
Xodiac / Man from Saturn	90	250

PLANET OF THE APES
(MEGO, 1973-75)

	MNP	MIP
8" FIGURES		
Astronaut Burke, 1975, boxed	50	130
Astronaut Burke, 1975, carded	50	100
Astronaut Verdon, 1975, boxed	50	140
Astronaut Verdon, 1975, carded	50	125
Astronaut, 1973, boxed	50	150
Astronaut, 1975, carded	50	100
Cornelius, 1973, boxed	40	140
Cornelius, 1975, carded	40	100
Dr. Zaius, 1973, boxed	40	150
Dr. Zaius, 1975, carded	40	100
Galen, 1975, boxed	40	140
Galen, 1975, carded	40	100
General Urko, 1975, boxed	50	130
General Urko, 1975, carded	50	100
General Ursus, 1975, boxed	50	120
General Ursus, 1975, carded	50	100
Soldier Ape, 1973, boxed	50	140
Soldier Ape, 1975, carded	50	100
Zira, 1973, boxed	30	150
Zira, 1975, carded	30	100

PLANET OF THE APES
(MEGO, 1973-75)

	MNP	MIP
ACCESSORIES		
Action Stallion, brown motorized, 1975, boxed	50	100
Battering Ram, 1975, boxed	20	40
Dr. Zaius' Throne, 1975, boxed	20	40
Jail, 1975, boxed	20	40
PLAY SETS		
Forbidden Zone Trap, 1975	65	150
Fortress, 1975	60	120
Treehouse, 1975	50	100
Village, 1975	60	130
VEHICLES		
Catapult and Wagon, 1975, boxed	25	50

PLANET OF THE APES
(HASBRO, 1998)

	MNP	MIP
FIGURES		
Cornelius	8	20
Dr. Zaius	8	20
General Ursus	8	20

POCKET SUPER HEROES
(MEGO, 1976-79)

	MNP	MIP
3-3/4" FIGURES		
Aquaman, 1976, white card	50	100
Batman, 1976, red card	20	40
Batman, 1976, white card	20	40
Captain America, 1976, white card	50	100
Captain Marvel, 1979, red card	20	40
General Zod, 1979, red card	5	15
Green Goblin, 1976, white card	50	100
Hulk, 1976, white card	15	40
Hulk, 1979, red card	15	30
Joker, 1979, red card	20	40
Jor-El (Superman), 1979, red card	10	20
Lex Luthor (Superman), 1979, red card	10	20
Penguin, 1979, red card	20	40
Robin, 1976, white card	20	40
Robin, 1979, red card	20	40
Spider-Man, 1976, white card	15	40
Spider-Man, 1979, red card	15	30
Superman, 1976, white card	15	30
Superman, 1979, red card	15	30
Wonder Woman, 1979, white card	20	45
ACCESSORIES		
Batcave, 1981	120	300
VEHICLES		
Batmachine, 1979	40	100
Batmobile, 1979, with Batman	80	200
Invisible Jet, 1979	50	125
Spider-Car, 1979, with Spider-Man	30	75
Spider-Machine, 1979	40	100

PUPPET MASTER
(FULL MOON TOYS, 1997-98)

	MNP	MIP
FIGURES		
Blade	15	45
Cyclops	7	13
Jester	7	13

*Masters of the Universe King Randor,
1981-90, Mattel*

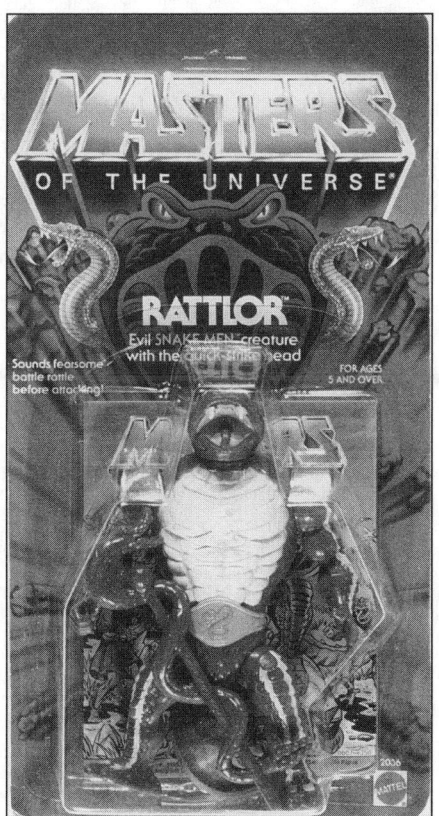

*Masters of the Universe Rattlor,
1981-90, Mattel*

23

PUPPET MASTER (FULL MOON TOYS, 1997-98)

	MNP	MIP
Leech Woman	10	25
Pinhead	7	13
Radu	7	13
Retro Blade	7	13
Shrieker	7	13
Six Shooter	10	40
Totem	7	13
Tunneler	10	25

RAMBO (COLECO, 1985)

	MNP	MIP
FIGURES		
Black Dragon	8	20
Chief	8	20
Colonel Troutman	7	15
Dr. Hyde	10	25
General Warhawk	8	20
Gripper	8	20
K.A.T.	10	20
Mad Dog	8	20
Nomad	10	20
Rambo	10	25
Rambo w/Fire Power	10	25
Sargeant Havoc	8	20
Turbo	8	20
White Dragon	8	20

ROBIN HOOD AND HIS MERRY MEN (MEGO, 1974)

	MNP	MIP
8" FIGURES		
Friar Tuck	25	75
Little John	45	100
Robin Hood	75	150
Will Scarlett	75	150

ROBIN HOOD PRINCE OF THIEVES (KENNER, 1991)

	MNP	MIP
ACCESSORIES		
Battle Wagon	15	30
Bola Bomber	5	10
Net Launcher	5	10
Sherwood Forest Play Set	30	60
FIGURES		
Azeem	7	15
Friar Tuck	15	30
Little John	7	15
Robin Hood, Crossbow	5	18
Robin Hood, Crossbow, Costner Head	7	20
Robin Hood, Long Bow	8	17
Robin Hood, Long Bow, Costner Head	10	20
Sheriff of Nottingham	5	15
The Dark Warrior	8	20
Will Scarlett	8	20

ROBOCOP AND THE ULTRA POLICE (KENNER, 1989-90)

	MNP	MIP
ACCESSORIES		
Robo-Glove	25	45
Robo-Helmet	15	40
FIGURES		
Ace Jackson	5	15
Anne Lewis	5	15

ROBOCOP AND THE ULTRA POLICE (KENNER, 1989-90)

	MNP	MIP
Birdman Barnes	8	15
Chainsaw	5	15
Claw Callahan	7	15
Dr. McNamara	5	15
Ed-260	10	25
Headhunter	5	15
Nitro	5	15
RoboCop	9	20
RoboCop Night Fighter	6	20
RoboCop, Gatlin' Gun	15	30
Scorcher	6	15
Sgt. Reed	6	15
Toxic Waster	10	20
Wheels Wilson	6	15
VEHICLES		
Robo-1	10	25
Robo-Command	10	30
Robo-Copter	15	35
Robo-Cycle	5	10
Robo-Hawk	10	35
Robo-Jailer	15	40
Robo-Tank	10	35
Skull-Hog	5	10
Vandal-1	5	20

SHOGUN WARRIORS (MATTEL, 1979)

	MNP	MIP
FIGURES		
Daimos	75	150
Dragun	75	175
Dragun (2nd figure)	75	150
Gaiking	75	150
Godzilla	100	200
Godzilla (2nd figure)	100	250
Mazinga	85	175
Mazinga (2nd figure)	75	150
Raydeen	75	150

SIMPSONS (MATTEL, 1990)

	MNP	MIP
Bart	10	20
Bartman	10	20
Homer	10	20
Lisa	15	30
Maggie	15	30
Marge	10	20
Nelson	10	20
Sofa Set	10	30

SIMPSONS (PLAYMATES, 2000)

	MNP	MIP
ACCESSORIES		
Interactive Living Room with Marge and maggie	5	25
Interactive Nuclear Power Plant with Homer	5	25
FIGURES		
Bart Simpson	3	10
Grandpa Simpson	3	12
Homer Simpson	4	15
Krusty the Clown	4	17
Lisa Simpson	3	10
Mr. Burns	4	17

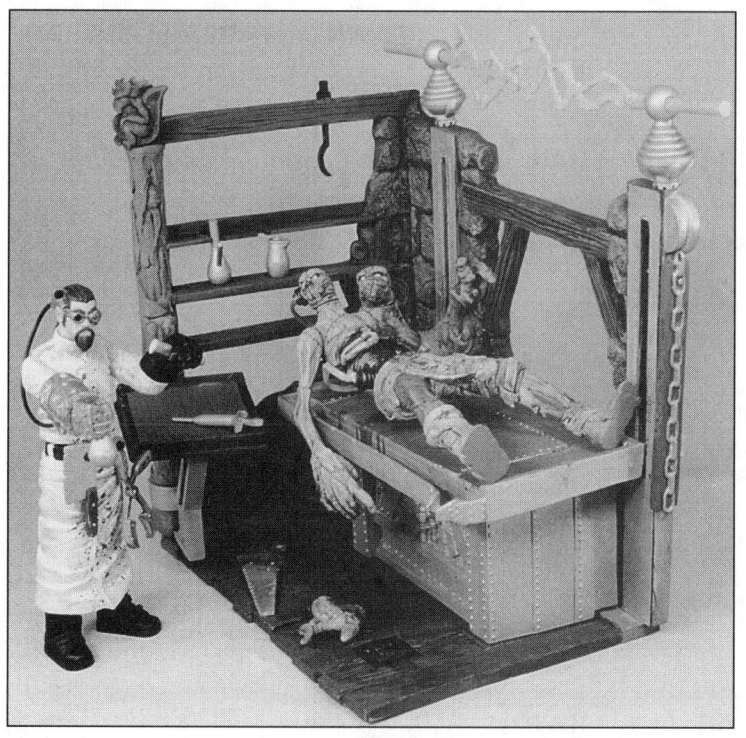

Monsters-Series 2 Dr. Frankenstein, 1998, McFarlane

Movie Maniacs II Norman Bates from Psycho, 1999, McFarlane

SIN CITY (McFARLANE, 1999)

	MNP	MIP
FIGURES		
MARV	5	15

SIX MILLION DOLLAR MAN (KENNER, 1975-78)

	MNP	MIP
ACCESSORIES		
Backpack Radio	10	20
Bionic Cycle	10	20
Bionic Mission Vehicle	25	55
Bionic Transport	10	30
Bionic Video Center	25	65
Critical Assignment Arms	15	30
Critical Assignment Legs	15	30
Dual Launch Drag Set	45	80
Flight Suit	15	30
Mission Control Center	25	50
Mission to Mars Space Suit	15	30
OSI Headquarters	30	70
OSI Undercover Blue Denims	15	30
Porta-Communicator	20	50
Tower & Cycle Set	25	50
Venus Space Probe	50	80
FIGURES		
Bionic Bigfoot	75	120
Maskatron	40	100
Oscar Goldman	50	100
Steve Austin	50	100

SPAWN (McFARLANE, 1994-97)

	MNP	MIP
ACCESSORIES		
Spawn Alley Play Set	15	50
Spawnmobile	12	40
Violator Monster Rig	12	45
FIGURES		
Alien Spawn	5	15
Angela	5	25
Badrock	8	15
Battleclad Spawn	5	20
Chapel	6	20
Clown	6	20
Clown w/Violator Head	6	20
Commando Spawn	7	20
Cosmic Angela	5	15
Crutch	5	15
Curse, The	5	15
Freak, The	5	15
Future Spawn	10	15
Malebolgia	40	80
Mangler, The	5	15
Medieval Spawn	5	20
Ninja Spawn	7	15
No-Body	5	15
Nuclear Spawn	4	15
Overtkill	7	20
Overtkill II	5	15
Pilot Spawn	10	20
Redeemer	5	15
Sam and Twitch	5	15
Sansker	5	15
Scourge	5	15
Spawn	5	30
Spawn (unmasked, 1st card)	15	30
Spawn II	10	15
Spawn III	7	25

SPAWN (McFARLANE, 1994-97)

	MNP	MIP
Superpatriot	5	10
Tiffany	5	15
Tremor	8	15
Tremor II	5	10
Vandalizer	5	10
Vertebreaker	10	25
Viking Spawn	5	25
Violator	5	20
Violator II	10	20
Violator w/Chrome Card	10	40
Widow Maker	5	15
Zombie Spawn	5	10

SPAWN SERIES 12 (McFARLANE, 1998)

	MNP	MIP
FIGURES		
Bottom Line	5	15
Cy-Gor	5	25
Reanimated Spawn	5	15
Spawn IV	5	15
The Creech	5	20
The Heap	5	15
Top Gun	5	15

SPAWN STORE EXCLUSIVES (McFARLANE, 1998)

	MNP	MIP
FIGURES		
Manga Spawn	15	30
Poacher with Gun	15	30
Spawn III	15	30
Spiked Spawn	15	30

SPAWN, DARK AGES (McFARLANE, 1998)

	MNP	MIP
FIGURES		
Spawn-The Black Knight	4	8
The Horrid	4	8
The Ogre	4	15
The Raider	4	8
The Skull Queen	4	15

SPAWN, MANGA (McFARLANE, 1997)

	MNP	MIP
FIGURES		
Clown	6	10
Curse	6	10
Goddess	10	15
Manga Ninja Spawn	6	10
Manga Spawn	7	12
Violator	6	12

SPAWN, MANGA II (McFARLANE, 1998)

	MNP	MIP
FIGURES		
Beast	4	15
Cyber Violator	4	8
Dead Spawn	4	8
Freak	4	8
Overtkill	4	8
Samurai Spawn	4	8

Planet of the Apes General Ursus, 1975, Mego

Spawn Cosmic Angela, 1994-96, McFarlane

SPAWN: THE MOVIE (McFARLANE, 1997)

	MNP	MIP
FIGURES		
Al Simmons	4	10
Burnt Spawn	4	10
Clown	4	10
Jason Wynn	4	10
Jessica Priest	4	10
Malebolgia (boxed)	10	30
Spawn (boxed)	10	30
Violator (boxed)	10	30
PLAY SETS		
Final Battle	10	20
Graveyard	10	20
Spawn Alley	10	20

SPIDER-MAN: THE ANIMATED SERIES (TOY BIZ, 1994)

	MNP	MIP
10" DELUXE FIGURES		
Dr. Octopus	7	15
Hobgoblin	7	15
Kraven	7	15
Lizard	7	15
Spider-Man (hanging)	7	15
Spider-Man w/Suction Cups	7	15
Venom	7	15
Vulture	10	20
15" TALKING FIGURES		
Spider-Man	12	25
Venom	12	25
2-1/2" DIE-CAST FIGURES		
Spider-Man vs. Carnage	2	4
Spider-Man vs. Dr. Octopus	2	4
Spider-Man vs. Hobgoblin	2	4
Spider-Man vs. Venom	2	4
4-1/2" FIGURES		
Alien Spider Slayer	4	8
Carnage	5	15
Dr. Octopus	5	12
Green Goblin	4	15
Hobgoblin	5	12
Kingpin	5	15
Kraven	5	12
Lizard	5	15
Peter Parker	6	15
Rhino	6	25
Scorpion	5	15
Shocker	4	15
Smythe	5	12
Spider-Man (multi-jointed)	3	15
Spider-Man w/Spider Armor	3	15
Spider-Man w/Web Parachute	8	15
Spider-Man w/Web Racer	5	15
Spider-Man w/Web Shooter	5	15
Venom	4	15
Vulture	5	15
ACCESSORIES		
Daily Bugle Play Set	10	15
PROJECTORS		
Hobgoblin	5	15
Spider-Man	5	15
Venom	5	15
VEHICLES		
Hobgoblin Pumpkin Bomber	7	15
Hobgoblin Wing Bomber	10	25

SPIDER-MAN: THE ANIMATED SERIES (TOY BIZ, 1994)

	MNP	MIP
Smythe Battle Chair Attack Vehicle	15	40
Spider-Man Wheelie Cycle	7	15
Spider-Man's Cycle (radio-controlled)	15	30
Tri-Spider Slayer	10	25
Venom Assault Racer	7	15

STAR TREK (MEGO, 1974-80)

	MNP	MIP
12" BOXED FIGURES		
Arcturian, 1979	30	60
Captain Kirk, 1979	25	55
Decker, 1979	45	115
Ilia, 1979	25	50
Klingon, 1979	40	85
Mr. Spock, 1979	35	75
3-3/4" CARDED FIGURES		
Acturian, 1980	75	150
Betelgeusian, 1980	75	150
Captain Kirk, 1979	12	35
Decker, 1979	12	35
Dr. McCoy, 1979	12	35
Ilia, 1979	10	20
Klingon, 1980	75	150
Megarite, 1980	75	150
Mr. Spock, 1979	12	35
Rigellian, 1980	75	150
Scotty, 1979	12	35
Zatanite, 1980	75	150
8" CARDED FIGURES		
Andorian, 1976	200	400
Captain Kirk, 1974	25	50
Cheron, 1975	85	175
Dr. McCoy, 1974	35	75
Gorn, 1975	80	180
Klingon, 1974	25	50
Lt. Uhura, 1974	50	135
Mr. Spock, 1974	25	50
Mugato, 1976	150	300
Neptunian, 1975	100	225
Romulan, 1976	300	600
Scotty, 1974	35	80
Talos, 1976	165	300
The Keeper, 1975	75	175
PLAY SETS		
Command Bridge (for 3-3/4" figures), 1980	45	105
Enterprise Bridge (for 8" figures), 1976	60	150
Enterprise Bridge with Figures, 1976	95	250
Mission to Gamma VI (for 8" figures), 1976	200	500

STAR TREK ALIEN COMBAT (PLAYMATES, 1999)

	MNP	MIP
FIGURES		
Borg Drone	15	40
Klingon Warrior	15	40

STAR TREK COLLECTOR ASSORTMENT (PLAYMATES, 1999)

	MNP	MIP
FIGURES		
Andorian Ambassador	14	28
Captain Janeway	14	28

Star Trek Dr. McCoy, 1979, Mego

*Star Trek Klingon, 1980, Mego
(Italian Package)*

29

STAR TREK COLLECTOR ASSORTMENT (PLAYMATES, 1999)

	MNP	MIP
Counselor Troi	14	28
Dr. McCoy	14	28
Ensign Chekov	14	28
Geordi LaForge	14	28
Gorn Captain	14	28
Khan	14	28
Lieutenant Sulu	14	28
Lieutenant Uhura	14	28
Locutus of Borg	14	28
Mr. Spock	14	28
Mugatu	14	28
Q	14	28
Scotty	14	28
Seven of Nine	14	28

STAR TREK COLLECTOR SERIES (PLAYMATES, 1994-95)

	MNP	MIP
9-1/2" BOXED FIGURES		
Borg	10	25
Captain Benjamin Sisko (Command Edition)	10	25
Captain Jean-Luc Picard (Command Edition)	10	25
Captain Jean-Luc Picard (Movie Edition)	10	25
Captain Kirk (Command Edition)	10	25
Captain Kirk (Movie Edition)	10	25
Commander Riker	10	25
Data (Movie Edition)	10	25
Dr. Beverly Crusher	10	25
Geordi La Forge (Movie Edition)	10	25

STAR TREK ELECTRONIC DISPLAY ASSORTMENT (PLAYMATES, 1999)

	MNP	MIP
FIGURES		
Captain Kirk	20	40
Captain Picard	20	40
Commander Riker	20	40
Lieutenant Commander Data	20	40
Lieutenant Worf	20	40
Mr. Spock	20	40

STAR TREK MILLENNIUM COLLECTOR'S SET (PLAYMATES, 1999)

	MNP	MIP
FIGURES		
Captain Janeway/Commander Chakotay	15	40
Captain Kirk/Mr. Spock	15	40
Captain Picard/Commander Riker	15	40
Captain Sisko/Commander Riker	15	40

STAR TREK V (GALOOB, 1989)

	MNP	MIP
BOXED FIGURES		
Captain Kirk	15	75
Dr. McCoy	15	75
Klaa	15	75
Mr. Spock	15	75
Sybok	15	75

STAR TREK: FIRST CONTACT (PLAYMATES, 1996)

	MNP	MIP
FIGURES		
Borg	8	15
Data	12	18
Data	5	10
Deanna Troi	5	10
Dr. Beverly Crusher	6	12
Geordi LaForge	5	10
Jean-Luc Picard	5	10
Jean-Luc Picard in 21st century outfit	15	23
Jean-Luc Picard in space suit	6	12
Lily	8	15
William Riker	5	10
Worf	5	10
Zefram Cochrane	5	10

STAR TREK: INSURRECTION (PLAYMATES, 1998)

	MNP	MIP
FIGURES		
Counselor Troi	10	20
Data	10	20
Geordi LaForge	10	20
Jean-Luc Picard	10	20
Ru' Afo	10	20
Worf	10	20

STAR TREK: SPACE TALK SERIES (PLAYMATES, 1995)

	MNP	MIP
SPACE TALK SERIES		
Borg	5	20
Picard	5	10
Q	5	20
Riker	5	10

STAR TREK: STARFLEET ACADEMY (PLAYMATES, 1996)

	MNP	MIP
FIGURES		
Cadet Geordi LaForge	8	15
Cadet Jean-Luc Picard	8	15
Cadet William Riker	8	15
Cadet Worf	8	15

STAR TREK: THE NEXT GENERATION (GALOOB, 1988-89)

	MNP	MIP
3-3/4" FIGURES, SERIES 1		
Data, blue face	70	160
Data, brown face	30	60
Data, flesh face	15	30
Data, spotted face	15	30
Geordi La Forge	5	15
Jean-Luc Picard	5	15
Lt. Worf	5	15
Tasha Yar	10	25
William Riker	5	15
3-3/4" FIGURES, SERIES 2		
Antican	35	100
Ferengi	35	100
Q	35	100
Selay	35	100

Starsky and Hutch Chopper, 1976, Mego

Super Powers Braniac, 1984, Kenner

STAR TREK: THE NEXT GENERATION (GALOOB, 1988-89)

	MNP	MIP
ACCESSORIES		
Enterprise	10	35
Ferengi Fighter	15	50
Galileo Shuttle	15	50
Phaser	20	40

STAR TREK: THE NEXT GENERATION (PLAYMATES, 1992-1996)

	MNP	MIP
SERIES 1, 1992		
Borg	10	20
Commander Riker	10	18
Data	10	20
Deanna Troi	15	30
Ferengi	10	25
Geordi LaForge	10	25
Gowron the Klingon	12	25
Jean-Luc Picard	10	20
Romulan	15	30
Worf	10	20
SERIES 2, 1993		
Admiral McCoy	5	12
Benzite	7	15
Borg	5	10
Captain Scott (Scotty)	5	10
Commander Riker	6	12
Commander Sela	6	12
Data	6	12
Dathon	7	15
Deanna Troi	6	12
Dr. Beverly Crusher	6	12
Geordi LaForge	7	15
Guinan	7	15
Jean-Luc Picard	6	12
K'Ehleyr	6	12
Locutus	6	12
Lore	7	15
Q	6	12
Spock	6	12
Vorgon	10	20
Wesley Crusher	6	12
Worf	6	12
SERIES 3, 1994		
Barclay	5	15
Beverly Crusher	5	15
Data as Romulan	5	15
Data, dress uniform	5	15
Data, Redemption outfit	75	300
Deanna Troi	3	15
Dr. Noonian Soong	5	15
Ensign Ro Laren	10	20
Esoqq	20	75
Geordi La Forge	5	15
Gowron	10	40
Guinan	5	15
Hugh Borg	5	15
Lore	3	15
Lwaxana Troi	3	15
Nausicaan	5	15
Picard as Dixon Hill	5	15
Picard as Romulan	3	15
Picard, red uniform	3	15
Q, judge's robes	5	15
Riker, Malcorian	3	15
Riker, red uniform	65	200

STAR TREK: THE NEXT GENERATION (PLAYMATES, 1992-1996)

	MNP	MIP
Sarek	5	15
Sela	5	15
Spock	5	15
Tasha Yar	5	15
Wesley Crusher	5	15
Worf	8	15

STAR TREK: VOYAGER (PLAYMATES, 1995-1996)

	MNP	MIP
5" FIGURES		
B'Elanna Torres	15	25
Chakotay	5	10
Chakotay as a Maquis	8	15
Doctor	8	15
Harry Kim	8	15
Kathryn Janeway	15	25
Kazon	5	10
Kes the Ocampa	12	18
Neelix	5	10
Seska	5	10
Tom Paris	5	10
Tuvok	5	10

STARSKY AND HUTCH (MEGO, 1976)

	MNP	MIP
8" FIGURES & ACCESSORIES		
Captain Dobey	25	50
Car	65	125
Chopper	25	45
Huggy Bear	25	50
Hutch	20	45
Starsky	20	45

SUPER HERO BENDABLES (MEGO, 1972)

	MNP	MIP
5" FIGURES		
Aquaman	50	120
Batgirl	50	120
Batman	35	90
Captain America	35	90
Catwoman	70	175
Joker	60	150
Mr. Mxyzptlk	50	125
Penguin	60	150
Riddler	60	150
Robin	30	75
Shazam	50	125
Supergirl	70	175
Superman	30	75
Tarzan	25	60
Wonder Woman	40	100

SUPER POWERS (KENNER, 1984-86)

	MNP	MIP
5" FIGURES		
Aquaman, 1984	15	35
Batman, 1984	25	55
Braniac, 1984	15	30
Clark Kent, mail-in figure, 1986	100	

32

*Super Powers Darkseid,
1985, Kenner*

*Super Powers Flash,
1984, Kenner*

SUPER POWERS
(KENNER, 1984-86)

	MNP	MIP
Cyborg, 1986	75	200
Cyclotron, 1986	35	75
Darkseid, 1985	5	15
Desaad, 1985	10	30
Doctor Fate, 1985	25	50
Firestorm, 1985	15	35
Flash, 1984	10	25
Golden Pharoah, 1986	30	65
Green Arrow, 1985	25	55
Green Lantern, 1984	30	60
Hawkman, 1984	25	50
Joker, 1984	15	30
Kalibak, 1985	5	15
Lex Luthor, 1984	5	15
Mantis, 1985	10	30
Martian Manhunter, 1985	10	30
Mr. Freeze, 1986	15	35
Mr. Miracle, 1986	75	200
Orion, 1986	20	40
Parademon, 1985	15	35
Penguin, 1984	20	40
Plastic Man, 1986	40	80
Red Tornado, 1985	25	55
Robin, 1984	25	50
Samurai, 1986	25	50
Shazam (Captain Marvel), 1986	20	40
Steppenwolf, in mail-in bag, 1985	15	
Steppenwolf, on card, 1985	15	75
Superman, 1984	20	35
Tyr, 1986	25	50
Wonder Woman, 1984	10	20
ACCESSORIES		
Collector's Case, 1984	20	40
PLAY SETS		
Hall of Justice, 1984	75	175
VEHICLES		
Batcopter, 1986	40	75
Batmobile, 1984	50	100
Darkseid Destroyer, 1985	25	50
Delta Probe One, 1985	15	30
Justice Jogger Wind-Up, 1986	20	40
Kalibak Boulder Bomber, 1985	10	25
Lex-Soar 7, 1984	10	25
Supermobile, 1984	15	30

TEEN TITANS (MEGO, 1976)

	MNP	MIP
6-1/2" CARDED FIGURES		
Aqualad	175	350
Kid Flash	175	300
Speedy	300	500
Wondergirl	200	450

TEENAGE MUTANT NINJA
TURTLES (PLAYMATES, 1988-92)

	MNP	MIP
1988, SERIES 1		
April O'Neil (no stripe)	60	150
Bebop	3	8
Donatello	8	20
Donatello (w/fan club form)	12	50
Foot Soldier	8	20
Leonardo	8	20
Leonardo (w/fan club form)	12	50
Michaelangelo	8	20

TEENAGE MUTANT NINJA
TURTLES (PLAYMATES, 1988-92)

	MNP	MIP
Michaelangelo (w/fan club form)	12	50
Raphael	8	20
Raphael (w/fan club form)	12	50
Rocksteady	8	20
Shredder	8	20
Splinter	8	20
1989, SERIES 2		
Ace Duck (hat off)	5	40
Ace Duck (hat on)	5	15
April O'Neil (blue stripe)	12	30
Baxter Stockman	10	25
Genghis Frog (black belt)	5	15
Genghis Frog (black belt, bagged weapons)	5	30
Genghis Frog (yellow belt)	30	75
Krang	5	15
1989, SERIES 3		
Casey Jones	5	15
General Traag	5	15
Leatherhead	25	50
Metalhead	5	15
Rat King	5	15
Usagi Yojimbo	5	15
1990, SERIES 4		
Mondo Gecko	5	15
Muckman and Joe Eyeball	5	15
Scumbag	5	15
Wingnut & Screwloose	5	15
1990, SERIES 5		
Fugitoid	5	15
Slash (black belt)	3	25
Slash (purple belt, red "S")	25	75
Triceraton	5	15
1990, SERIES 6		
Mutagen Man	5	15
Napoleon Bonafrog	5	15
Panda Khan	5	15
1991, GIANT TURTLES, 13"		
Donatello	20	40
Leonardo	20	40
Michaelangelo	20	40
Raphael	20	40
1991, SERIES 10		
Grand Slam Raph	5	15
Hose'em Down Don	5	15
Lieutenant Leo	5	15
Make My Day Leo	5	15
Midshipman Mike	5	15
Pro Pilot Don	5	15
Raph the Green Teen Beret	5	15
Slam Dunkin' Don	5	15
Slapshot Leo	5	15
T.D. Tossin' Leonardo	5	15
1991, SERIES 7		
April O'Neil	25	125
April O'Neil ("Press")	10	20
Pizza Face	5	15
Ray Fillet (purple body, red "V")	10	25
Ray Fillet (red body, maroon "V")	10	30
Ray Fillet (yellow body, blue "V")	10	15
1991, SERIES 8		
Don The Undercover Turtle	5	15
Leo the Sewer Samurai	5	15
Mike the Sewer Surfer	5	15
Raph The Space Cadet	5	15

Total Justice Aquaman, 1996, Kenner

Total Justice Robin, 1996, Kenner

Total Justice The Flash, 1996, Kenner

TEENAGE MUTANT NINJA TURTLES (PLAYMATES, 1988-92)

	MNP	MIP
1991, SERIES 9		
Chrome Dome	5	15
Dirt Bag	5	15
Ground Chuck	5	15
Storage Shell Don	5	15
Storage Shell Leo	5	15
Storage Shell Michaelangelo	5	15
Storage Shell Raphael	5	15
1991, WACKY ACTION		
Breakfightin' Raphael	5	15
Creepy Crawlin' Splinter	5	15
Headspinnin' Bebop	5	15
Machine Gunnin' Rocksteady	5	15
Rock & Roll Michaelangelo	5	15
Sewer Swimmin' Don	5	15
Slice 'n Dice Shredder	10	25
Sword Slicin' Leonardo	8	15
Wacky Walkin' Mouser	10	20
1992, GIANT TURTLES, 13"		
Bebop	20	40
Movie Don	20	40
Movie Leo	20	40
Movie Mike	20	40
Movie Raph	20	40
Rocksteady	20	40
1992, SERIES 11		
Rahzer (black nose)	5	15
Rahzer (red nose)	7	25
Skateboard'n Mike	5	15
Super Shredder	5	15
Tokka (brown trim)	9	25
Tokka (gray trim)	5	15
1992, SERIES 12		
Movie Don	5	15
Movie Leo	5	15
Movie Mike	5	15
Movie Raph	5	15
Movie Splinter, no tooth	5	15
Movie Splinter, w/tooth	25	75
VEHICLES/ACCESSORIES		
Flushomatic	4	10
Foot Cruiser	14	35
Foot Ski	4	10
Mega Mutant Killer Bee	3	8
Mega Mutant Needlenose	8	20
Mike's Pizza Chopper Backpack	4	10
Mutant Sewer Cycle with Sidecar	4	10
Ninja Newscycle	5	12
Oozey	4	10
Pizza Powered Sewer Dragster	5	15
Pizza Thrower	14	35
Psycho Cycle	10	25
Raph's Sewer Dragster	6	16
Raph's Sewer Speedboat	5	12
Retrocatapult	4	10
Retromutagen Ooze	2	4
Sewer Seltzer Cannon	4	10
Sludgemobile	7	18
Technodrome, 22"	24	60
Toilet Taxi	5	12
Turtle Blimp, 30" green vinyl	12	30
Turtle Party Wagon	16	40
Turtle Trooper Parachute, 22"	4	10
Turtlecopter	16	40

TOTAL CHAOS (MCFARLANE, 1996)

	MNP	MIP
FIGURES		
Al Simmons	5	15
Dragon Blade	5	15
Gore	5	15
Hoof	5	15
Thorax	5	15
Thresher	5	30

TOTAL JUSTICE (KENNER, 1996)

	MNP	MIP
5" FIGURES		
Aquaman, black armor	5	15
Aquaman, gold armor	7	20
Batman	5	15
Black Lightning	7	20
Darkseid	5	15
Despero	5	15
Flash, The	5	15
Green Arrow	5	20
Green Lantern	5	15
Hawkman	5	15
Huntress	5	20
Parallax	5	20
Robin	5	15
Superman	5	15

TOY STORY (THINKWAY, 1996)

	MNP	MIP
5" FIGURES		
Alien	5	15
Boxer Buzz	4	8
Crawling Baby Face	3	9
Fighting Woody	3	9
Flying Buzz (Rocket)	4	8
Hamm	4	8
Karate Buzz	4	8
Kicking Woody	4	8
Quick-Draw Woody	4	8
Rex	4	8
Super Sonic Buzz	3	9
LARGE FIGURES		
Talking Buzz Lightyear	15	50
Talking Woody	15	60

TUFF TALKIN' WRESTLERS (TOY BIZ, 1999)

	MNP	MIP
FIGURES		
Goldberg/Kevin Nash	20	40
Sting/Diamond Dallas Page	20	40

UNIVERSAL MONSTERS (HASBRO, 1998)

	MNP	MIP
FIGURES		
Frankenstein	10	25
The Bride of Frankenstein	10	25
The Mummy	10	25
The Wolf Man	10	25

VIKINGS (MARX, 1960S)

	MNP	MIP
Eric the Viking	35	65
Mighty Viking Horse	30	60
Odin the Viking Chieftan	35	65

WALTONS (MEGO, 1975)

	MNP	MIP
8" FIGURES		
Grandma and Grandpa	25	50
John Boy and Ellen	25	50
Mom and Pop	25	50
ACCESSORIES		
Barn	50	100
Country Store	50	100
Truck	40	80
PLAY SETS		
Farm House	50	100
Farm House with Six Figures	50	200

WETWORKS (McFARLANE, 1995-96)

	MNP	MIP
FIGURES		
Assassin One	5	15
Blood Queen	8	30
Dane	4	15
Delta Commander	5	15
Dozer	4	15
Frankenstein	5	15
Grail	4	15
Mendoza	5	15
Mother One	7	15
Pilgrim	10	30
Vampire	10	15
Werewolf	10	30

WIZARD OF OZ (MEGO, 1974)

	MNP	MIP
4" BOXED FIGURES		
Munchkin Dancer	75	150
Munchkin Flower Girl	75	150
Munchkin General	75	150
Munchkin Lollipop Kid	75	150
Munchkin Mayor	75	150
8" BOXED FIGURES		
Cowardly Lion	25	50
Dorothy with Toto	25	50
Glinda the Good Witch	25	50
Scarecrow	25	50
Tin Woodsman	25	25
Wicked Witch	50	100
Witch's Monkey	75	150
Wizard of Oz	35	100
PLAY SETS		
Emerald City with eight 8" figures	125	350
Emerald City with Wizard of Oz	45	100
Munchkin Land	150	300
Witch's Castle, Sears Exclusive	250	450

WORLD WRESTLING FEDERATION (HASBRO, 1990-94)

	MNP	MIP
FIGURES		
1-2-3 Kid	30	75
Adam Bomb	20	35

WORLD WRESTLING FEDERATION (HASBRO, 1990-94)

	MNP	MIP
Akeem	30	75
Andre the Giant	50	150
Ax	10	30
Bam Bam Bigelow	12	30
Bart Gunn	20	35
Berzerker	6	15
Big Bossman (1990)	8	16
Big Bossman (1992)	7	15
Billy Gunn	20	35
Bret Hart (1992)	10	25
Bret Hart (1993 mail-in)	75	
Bret Hart (1994)	7	15
British Bulldog	7	15
Brutus the Barber (1990)	12	25
Brutus the Barber (1992)	12	25
Bushwackers (two-pack)	10	20
Butch Miller	5	15
Crush (1993)	12	25
Crush (1994)	6	15
Demolition (two-pack)	20	45
Doink the Clown	7	15
Dusty Rhodes	125	300
Earthquake	15	30
El Matador	6	15
Fatu	5	15
Giant Gonzales	5	15
Greg the Hammer	9	30
Hacksaw Jim Duggan (1991)	5	15
Hacksaw Jim Duggan (1994)	5	15
Honky Tonk Man	25	50
Hulk Hogan (1990)	12	25
Hulk Hogan (1991)	10	20
Hulk Hogan (1992)	10	20
Hulk Hogan (1993, mail-in)	75	100
Hulk Hogan (1993, no shirt)	10	20
I.R.S.	7	15
Jake the Snake Roberts	9	20
Jim Neidhart	6	15
Jimmy Superfly Snuka	12	25
Kamala	10	25
Koko B. Ware	20	60
Legion of Doom (two-pack)	20	40
Lex Luger	15	30
Ludwig Borga	20	35
Luke Williams	5	15
Macho Man (1990)	12	25
Macho Man (1991)	15	35
Macho Man (1992)	15	35
Macho Man (1993)	7	15
Marty Jannetty	5	15
Mountie	6	15
Mr. Perfect (1992)	15	35
Mr. Perfect (1994)	12	25
Nailz	12	25
Nasty Boys (two-pack)	15	80
Owen Hart	20	35
Papa Shango	7	15
Razor Ramon (1993)	15	30
Razor Ramon (1994)	9	18
Repo Man	7	15
Ric Flair	7	15
Rick Martel	5	15
Rick Rude	15	30
Rick Steiner	9	18
Ricky "The Dragon" Steamboat	7	15
Rockers (two-pack)	10	20
Rowdy Roddy Piper	15	30
Samu	5	15

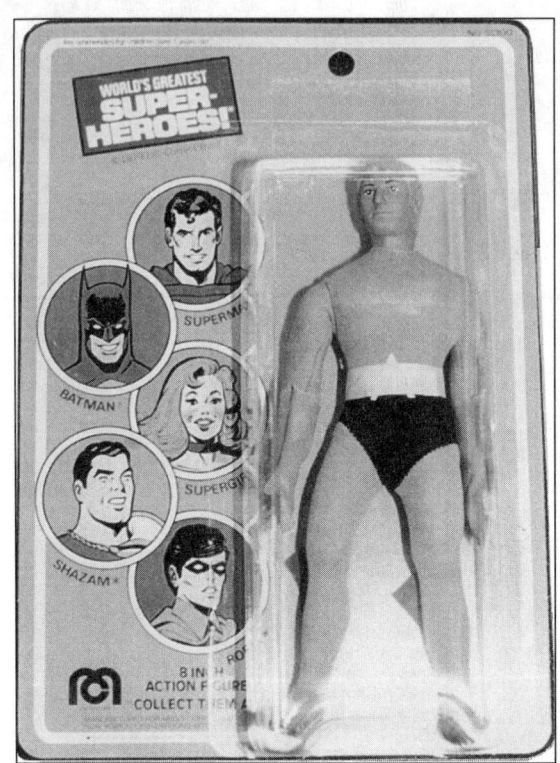

World's Greatest Super Heroes
Aquaman, 1972, Mego

World's Greatest Super
Heroes Isis, 1976, Mego

WORLD WRESTLING FEDERATION (HASBRO, 1990-94)

	MNP	MIP
Scott Steiner	8	18
Sgt. Slaughter	15	30
Shawn Michaels (1993)	10	25
Shawn Michaels (1994)	6	15
Sid Justice	6	15
Skinner	6	15
Smash	12	25
Tatanka (1993)	7	15
Tatanka (1994)	7	15
Ted Diabiase (1990)	10	20
Ted Diabiase (1991)	7	15
Ted Diabiase (1994)	7	15
Texas Tornado	10	50
Typhoon	15	30
Ultimate Warrior (1990)	12	25
Ultimate Warrior (1991)	10	20
Ultimate Warrior (1992)	20	40
Undertaker (1992)	9	18
Undertaker (1993, mail-in)	25	50
Undertaker (1994)	15	25
Virgil	7	15
Warlord	6	15
Yokozuna	15	30

WORLD'S GREATEST SUPER HEROES (MEGO, 1972-78)

	MNP	MIP
12-1/2" BOXED FIGURES		
Amazing Spider-Man, 1978	40	100
Batman, 1978	60	125
Captain America, 1978	75	150
Hulk, 1978	30	60
8" FIGURES		
Aquaman, 1972, boxed	50	150
Aquaman, 1972, carded	50	150
Batgirl, 1973, boxed	125	300
Batgirl, 1973, carded	125	250
Batman, fist fighting, 1975, boxed	150	350
Batman, painted mask, 1972, boxed	60	150
Batman, painted mask, 1972, carded	60	100
Batman, removable mask, 1972, boxed	200	350
Batman, removable mask, 1972, Kresge card only	200	450
Bruce Wayne, 1974, boxed, Montgomery Ward exclusive	400	500
Captain America, 1972, boxed	60	200
Captain America, 1972, carded	60	150
Catwoman, 1973, boxed	100	225
Catwoman, 1973, carded	100	225
Clark Kent, 1974, boxed, Montgomery Ward exclusive	400	500
Conan, 1975, boxed	120	300
Conan, 1975, carded	120	300
Dick Grayson, 1974, boxed, Montgomery Ward exclusive	400	500
Falcon, 1974, boxed	60	150
Falcon, 1974, carded	60	200
Green Arrow, 1973, boxed	100	250
Green Arrow, 1973, carded	100	400
Green Goblin, 1974, boxed	90	225
Green Goblin, 1974, carded	90	300
Human Torch, Fantastic Four, 1975, boxed	25	90
Human Torch, Fantastic Four, 1975, card	25	50
Incredible Hulk, 1974, boxed	20	100

WORLD'S GREATEST SUPER HEROES (MEGO, 1972-78)

	MNP	MIP
Incredible Hulk, 1974, carded	20	50
Invisible Girl, Fantastic Four, 1975, boxed	30	150
Invisible Girl, Fantastic Four, 1975, card	30	60
Iron Man, 1974, boxed	75	125
Iron Man, 1974, carded	75	250
Isis, 1976, boxed	75	250
Isis, 1976, carded	75	125
Joker, 1973, boxed	60	150
Joker, 1973, carded	60	150
Joker, fist fighting, 1975, boxed	150	400
Lizard, 1974, boxed	75	200
Lizard, 1974, carded	75	250
Mr. Fantastic, Fantastic Four, 1975, boxed	30	140
Mr. Fantastic, Fantastic Four, 1975, carded	30	60
Mr. Mxyzptlk, open mouth, 1973, boxed	50	75
Mr. Mxyzptlk, open mouth, 1973, carded	50	150
Mr. Mxyzptlk, smirk, 1973, boxed	60	150
Penguin, 1973, boxed	60	150
Penguin, 1973, carded	60	125
Peter Parker, 1974, boxed, Montgomery Ward exclusive	400	500
Riddler, 1973, boxed	100	250
Riddler, 1973, carded	100	400
Riddler, fist fighting, 1975, boxed	150	400
Robin, fist fighting, 1975, boxed	125	350
Robin, painted mask, 1972, boxed	60	150
Robin, painted mask, 1972, carded	60	90
Robin, removable mask, 1972, boxed	250	400
Shazam, 1972, boxed	75	200
Shazam, 1972, carded	75	150
Spider-Man, 1972, boxed	20	100
Spider-Man, 1972, carded	20	50
Supergirl, 1973, boxed	300	450
Supergirl, 1973, carded	300	450
Superman, 1972, boxed	50	125
Superman, 1972, carded	50	100
Tarzan, 1972, boxed	50	150
Tarzan, 1976, Kresge card only	60	225
Thing, Fantastic Four, 1975, boxed	40	150
Thing, Fantastic Four, 1975, carded	40	60
Thor, 1975, boxed	150	300
Thor, 1975, carded	150	300
Wonder Woman, boxed	100	250
Wonder Woman, Kresge card only	100	350
Wondergirl	100	240
ACCESSORIES		
Super Hero Carry Case, 1973	40	100
Supervator, 1974	60	120
PLAY SETS		
Aquaman vs. the Great White Shark, 1978	200	500
Batcave Play Set, 1974, vinyl	125	250
Batman's Wayne Foundation Penthouse, 1977, fiberboard	600	1200
Hall of Justice, 1976, vinyl	125	250
SUPERMAN SERIES		
General Zod, 1978	50	100
Jor-El, 1978	50	100
Lex Luthor, 1978	50	100
Superman Play Set, 1978	75	150
Superman, 1978	50	125

WORLD'S GREATEST SUPER HEROES (MEGO, 1972-78)

	MNP	MIP
VEHICLES		
Batcopter, 1974, boxed	75	150
Batcopter, 1974, carded	55	110
Batcycle, black, 1975, boxed	75	185
Batcycle, black, 1975, carded	60	150
Batcycle, blue, 1974, boxed	75	170
Batcycle, blue, 1974, carded	75	135
Batmobile and Batman	40	100
Batmobile, 1974, boxed	50	125
Batmobile, 1974, carded	50	120
Captain Americar, 1976	100	200
Green Arrowcar, 1976	175	350
Jokermobile, 1976	150	300
Mobile Bat Lab, 1975	125	250
Spidercar, 1976	50	125
WONDER WOMAN SERIES		
Major Steve Trevor, 1978	26	65
Queen Hippolyte, 1978	40	100
Queen Nubia, 1978	40	100
Wonder Woman Play Set, 1978	50	100
Wonder Woman with Diana Prince outfit, 1978	55	80

WORLD'S GREATEST SUPER KNIGHTS (MEGO, 1975)

	MNP	MIP
8" BOXED FIGURES		
Black Knight	80	160
Ivanhoe	60	120
King Arthur	60	120
Sir Galahad	75	150
Sir Lancelot	75	150
ACCESSORIES		
Castle Play Set	80	160
Jousting Horse, battery operated	40	70

WORLD'S GREATEST SUPER PIRATES (MEGO, 1974)

	MNP	MIP
8" BOXED FIGURES		
Blackbeard	70	150
Captain Patch	70	150
Jean LaFitte	80	160
Long John Silver	80	160

X-FILES (MCFARLANE, 1998)

	MNP	MIP
FIGURES		
Fireman with Cryolitter	4	8
Mulder in Arctic wear	4	8
Mulder with docile alien	4	8
Mulder with Human Host and Cryopod Chamber	4	8
Mulder with victim	4	8
Primitive Man with Attack Alien	4	8
Scully in Arctic wear	4	8
Scully with docile alien	4	8
Scully with Human Host and Cryopod Chamber	4	8
Scully with victim	4	8

X-MEN/X-FORCE (TOY BIZ, 1991-1995)

	MNP	MIP
FIGURES		
Ahab	5	15
Apocalypse #1, 1991	7	15
Apocalypse #1, 1993	4	15
Apocalypse #2	4	15
Archangel	7	15
Archangel #2	4	15
Banshee, 1992	7	15
Banshee, 1993	3	15
Beast	10	20
Bishop	7	15
Black Tom	5	15
Blob	5	15
Bonebreaker	3	15
Bridge	5	15
Bridge	4	15
Brood	4	15
Cable	5	15
Cable #1, 1992	6	15
Cable #1, 1993	4	15
Cable #2	4	15
Cable #3	4	15
Cable #4	3	15
Cable Cyborg	4	15
Caliban	4	15
Cameron Hodge	4	15
Cannonball, Pink	15	35
Cannonball, Purple	10	20
Colossus, 1991	10	20
Colossus, 1993	6	15
Corsair	3	15
Cyclops #1, blue	10	20
Cyclops #1, stripes	5	15
Cyclops #2	5	15
Deadpool	15	35
Deadpool, 1992	15	35
Deadpool, 1995	6	15
Domino	5	15
Forearm	10	20
Forearm	10	20
Forge	10	25
Gambit, 1992	10	20
Gambit, 1993	7	15
Gideon	4	15
Gideon	5	15
Gladiator	3	15
Grizzly	4	15
Havok	4	15
Ice Man #2	4	15
Ice Man, 1992	20	45
Ice Man, 1993	10	25
Juggernaut, 1991	10	25
Juggernaut, 1993	4	15
Kane	5	15
Kane #1	7	15
Kane #2	4	15
Killspree	7	15
Krule	3	15
Kylun	3	15
Longshot	7	15
Magneto #1	6	15
Magneto #2	5	15
Maverick	3	15
Morph	10	20
Mr. Sinister	7	15
Nightcrawler	10	25
Nimrod	4	15
Omega Red	6	15

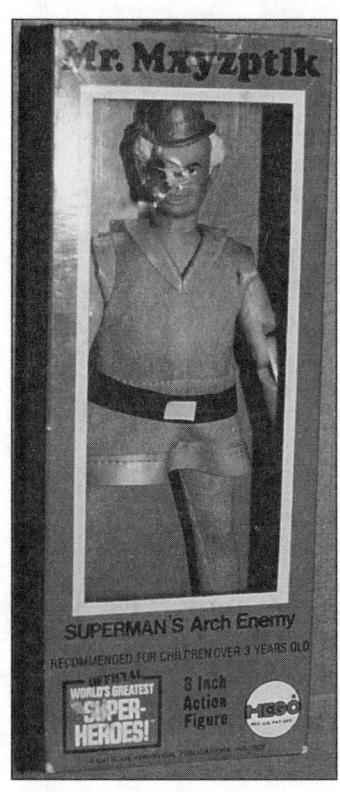

World's Greatest Super Heroes
Mr. Mxyzptlk, 1973, Mego

X-Files Mulder with Human Host and
Cryopod Chamber, 1998, McFarlane

ACTION FIGURES

X-MEN/X-FORCE
(TOY BIZ, 1991-1995)

	MNP	MIP
Phoenix	10	25
Professor X	6	15
Pyro	5	15
Quark	3	15
Random	3	15
Raza	3	15
Rictor	3	15
Rogue	10	25
Sabretooth #1	7	15
Sabretooth #2	6	15
Sabretooth #3	4	15
Sauron	3	15
Shatterstar	5	15
Shatterstar #1	5	15
Shatterstar #2	3	15
Silver Samurai	3	15
Slayback	3	15
Spiral	4	15
Storm, 1991	20	40
Storm, 1993	10	20
Strong Guy	3	15
Stryfe	8	15
Stryfe	10	25
Sunfire	4	15
Sunspot	3	15
Trevor Fitzroy	3	15
Tusk	5	15
Warpath	10	25
Warpath #1	7	15
Warpath #2	5	15
Warstar	6	15
Wolverine #1, 1991	10	20
Wolverine #1, 1993	7	15

X-MEN/X-FORCE
(TOY BIZ, 1991-1995)

	MNP	MIP
Wolverine #2, 1992	7	15
Wolverine #2, 1993	5	15
Wolverine #3	12	25
Wolverine #4	7	15
Wolverine #5	7	15
Wolverine #6	4	15
Wolverine Fang	4	15
Wolverine, space armor	6	15
Wolverine, street clothes	4	15
X-Cutioner	4	15
X-Treme	4	15

YOUNGBLOOD
(MCFARLANE, 1995)

FIGURES	MNP	MIP
Crypt	5	10
Die Hard	4	8
Dutch	4	8
Sentinel	4	8
Shaft	4	8
Troll	10	20

ZORRO (GABRIEL, 1982)

FIGURES	MNP	MIP
Amigo	10	25
Captain Ramon	10	25
Picaro	15	35
Sergeant Gonzales	10	25
Tempest	10	25

Advertising Toys

Almost everyone is familiar with advertising characters — how many can you name? Snap, Crackle and Pop; the Pillsbury Doughboy; Speedy Alka Seltzer; the Jolly Green Giant.

What is the purpose of the advertising character? Its primary purpose is to attract the consumer's attention so he or she will buy a product.

Let's face it, many times the store brand item tastes the same or even better than a name brand, so why buy a product that is twice the price? Advertisers hope it's because the character is so familiar and beloved.

Advertising characters are a colorful part of everyday life and can take many forms. The favorite of many collectors are PVC vinyl figures. Such figures are brightly colored, almost unbreakable and make great display pieces. Advertising figures are also found as bendy figures, wind-up toys, radios, telephones and beanbag toys.

Some of the ad characters of today have been around for over 100 years. Aunt Jemima, known for touting maple syrup, is one such example. Aunt Jemima was first used for advertising pancake flour at the World's Fair in the late 1800s. She was a great success; soon after, a paper doll set was used as a promotional item.

Kellogg's has long delighted collectors with their many premiums depicting characters. A 1920s Kellogg's premium was a set of Goldilocks and the three bears dolls. The consumer received a piece of fabric with the image of the doll printed on it. Consumers were supposed to cut, stuff and sew the doll themselves.

Popular cereal pixies Snap, Crackle and Pop were first offered as make-your-own dolls in the 1940s.

Advertising characters have been used to promote everything from tires (remember the Michelin Man?) and shoes (Buster Brown) to fast food (McDonald's Speedee) and dairy products (Elsie the Cow). But cereal characters seem to be among the most popular with collectors.

Oscar Mayer Foods Wienermobile Beanbag, 1998

Quisp is extremely popular, but collectibles are hard to find today. Rare collectibles, like a Quisp bank, can run up to $1,000. Other popular cereal characters include the General Mills monsters (Frankenberry, Boo Berry, Count Chocula and Fruit Brute); Tony the Tiger; and Snap, Crackle and Pop.

Also popular are vintage advertising characters that presented stereotypical (often negative) ethnic characters — think Aunt Jemima and Uncle Mose (pancake mix), Mohawk Carpet Indian and Rastus, the black character used to advertise Cream of Wheat cereal. Because such stereotypes are considered politically incorrect today, such items are extremely collectible.

The Top 10 Advertising Toys
(in Mint condition)

1. Quisp Bank, Quaker Oats, 1960s..$850
2. Reddy Kilowatt Bobbin' Head, Reddy Communications, 1960s........................ 450
3. Mr. Peanut Figure, Planters Peanuts, 1930s.. 375
4. Esky Store Display, Esquire Magazine, 1940s.. 375
5. Elsie the Cow Cookie Jar, Borden's, 1950s 350
6. Speedy Figure, Alka-Seltzer, 1963... 350
7. Vegetable Man Display, Kraft, 1980 275
8. Barnum's Animal Crackers Cookie Jar, Nabisco, 1972................................... 275
9. Vegetable Man Bank, Kraft, 1970s... 275
10. Clark Bar Figure, Beatrice Foods, 1960s 275

Contributor to this section: Carren Kopleton, Queen's Collection, P.O. Box 235, Clifton, NJ 07011, toyqueenie@aol.com.

NAME	YEAR	DESCRIPTION	GOOD	EX	MINT
7-ELEVEN					
Big Bite Figures	1987	3-1/2" hot dog men holding snacks	7	10	12
7-UP					
Spot Wind-Up	1990	3" red circular figure w/sunglasses	8	12	15
AIR INDIA					
Air India Man Figure	1973	4-1/2" statue of man wearing turban standing on flying carpet	10	20	25
ALKA-SELTZER					
Speedy Figure	1963	5-1/2" vinyl boy holding Alka-Seltzer figure	275	300	350
ALPO					
Dan the Dog Cookie Jar	1980s	7" ceramic gray and white sheep dog	35	50	70
Dan the Dog Wind-Up	1979	3" wind-up figure of shaggy gray dog walking on his front paws	10	15	25
AMERICAN HOME FOOD PRODUCTS					
Marky Maypo Figure	1960	9" vinyl figure	35	45	55
AUNT JEMIMA SYRUP					
Aunt Jemima Doll	1950s	13" cloth doll wearing red checkered dress	60	70	90
BASKIN ROBBINS					
Pinky the Spoon Figure	1993	5" bendable figure	4	5	10
BAZOOKA					
Bazooka Joe Doll	1973	19" plush boy pirate	20	25	30
BEATRICE FOODS					
Clark Bar Figure	1960s	8-1/2" vinyl boy holding a Clark bar wearing a striped shirt	200	225	275
BEECH-NUT					
Fruit Stripe Gum Figure	1967	7-1/2" bendable man shaped like a pack of gum riding a motorcycle	150	200	225
BOB'S BIG BOY					
Big Boy Doll	1973	8" plastic jointed doll holding a hamburger, made by Dakin	75	125	150
Big Boy Doll	1978	14" cloth boy doll wearing checkerboard outfit	15	25	30
Big Boy Lamp	1960	6-1/2" vinyl figural lamp	40	60	75
Dolly Doll	1978	14" cloth girl doll w/Dolly nametag	15	25	30
Nugget Doll	1978	10" cloth dog doll w/"Nugget" on collar	15	25	30
BORDEN'S					
Elsie the Cow Cookie Jar	1950s	12" Elsie w/her head popping out of barrel	275	300	350
Elsie the Cow Doll	1950s	12" plush cow that moos when shaken	50	75	85
Elsie the Cow Lamp	1947	electric lamp, ceramic	150	175	225
BRADFORD HOUSE RESTAURANTS					
Bucky Bradford Figure	1960s	9-1/2" blond pilgrim boy holding dish that reads "It's Yum Yum Time"	25	30	35
CAMPBELL					
Campbell's Kid Doll	1950s	9-1/2" vinyl jointed cheerleader wearing a white shirt w/"C" in middle	45	65	80
Campbell's Kid Doll	1973	16" blonde girl w/red hair	25	35	40
Campbell's Kid Figure	1950s	7" boy chef doll w/"C"on hat and spoon in his hand	40	50	65
Campbell's Kid Figure	1970s	7" vinyl Campbell boy w/blue overalls	30	40	50
Christmas Ornament	1989	ball ornament w/picture of Campbell Kid dressed as Santa	5	10	15
Wizard of O's Figure	1978	7-1/2" vinyl wizard w/Spaghetti O's on his hat and bow tie	15	25	30
CHAMPION AUTO STORES					
Champ Man Figure	1991	6" bendable man; head is a flag	7	10	15
CHICKEN DELIGHT INTERNATIONAL					
Chicken Delight Bank	1960s	6" yellow and red chicken holding a tray of biscuits	85	125	150
CHIQUITA					
Chiquita Banana Doll	1974	16" plush dancing banana w/fruit on its head	18	20	25

ADVERTISING TOYS

NAME	YEAR	DESCRIPTION	GOOD	EX	MINT
CRACKER JACK					
Cracker Jack Doll	1974	15" plush sailor holding small box of Cracker Jacks snacks	15	20	25
CREST TOOTHPASTE					
Sparkle Telephone	1980s	11" blue and silver snowman-type character	25	35	40
CURAD					
Taped Crusader Figure	1977	7-1/2" male cartoon superhero	65	75	85
CURITY					
Miss Curity Display	1950s	18" plastic store display of a nurse on a base	125	150	185
DEL MONTE					
Clown Bank		colorful, smiling clown	5	10	20
DOUGLAS OIL COMPANY					
Freddy Fast Figure	1976	7" freckled face boy; hat says "Freddy Fast"	90	110	125
DOW BRANDS					
Scrubbing Bubble Brush	1980s	3-1/2" light blue scrub brush	8	10	12
ESQUIRE MAGAZINE					
Esky Store Display	1940s	11" old man dressed in a tuxedo standing on an Esquire magazine	300	350	375
ESSO					
Esso Tiger Figure	1960s	8-1/2" plastic tiger	20	25	30
Esso Tiger Garbage Can	1970s	10" metal garbage can w/picture of the Esso tiger	15	20	30
EVEREADY BATTERIES					
Energizer Bunny Plush		22" plush	15	40	65
Eveready Cat Bank	1981	black cat w/Eveready battery on side	10	15	20
FACIT ADDING MACHINES					
Facit Man Figure	1964	4" man wearing yellow outfit w/black wizard hat	20	25	30
FLORIDA CITRUS DEPARTMENT					
Florida Orange Bird Hat	1970s	child's-size hat w/visor, pictures Orange Bird on front and back	10	15	20
Florida Orange Bird Nodder	1970s	7" plastic	50	60	75
Florida Orange Bird Stick Pin	1980s	metal, depicts the Florida Orange Bird	5	10	15
FUNNY FACE DRINK					
Choo Choo Cherry Ramp Walker	1971	3" round, red figure w/conductor's hat	70	90	110
Funny Face Mugs	1969	3" mugs of Funny Face characters, each	7	10	15
Goofy Grape Pitcher	1973	10" pitcher of smiling, purple character wearing lime green captain's hat	75	95	125
Lefty Lemon Frisbee	1980s	plastic w/picture of Lefty Lemon	5	10	12
GENERAL MILLS					
Boo Berry Figure	1975	7-1/2" white and light blue ghost w/hat and bow tie	75	95	120
Cereal Card Game	1981	card game w/different cereal characters	10	15	20
Count Chocula Figure	1975	7-1/2" vinyl vampire	70	85	110
Frankenberry Figure	1975	8" vinyl pink Frankenstein	70	95	135
Fruit Brute Figure	1975	8" vinyl werewolf w/striped shirt	75	90	120
Lucky Charms Leprechaun Doll	1978	17" plush	20	25	30
Monster Cereal Pencil Case	1980s	8" x 5", vinyl case featuring Count Chocula, Frankenberry and Boo Berry	10	15	20
Trix Rabbit Figure	1977	9" vinyl white rabbit	30	40	50
GERBER PRODUCTS					
Gerber Boy figure	1985	8" vinyl boy w/baseball cap turned sideways that reads "I'm a Gerber Kid"	25	27	30
GOOD HUMOR					
Good Humor Bar	1975	8" vinyl ice cream bar w/a bite out of it	175	200	275
GRANDMA'S COOKIES					
Grandma Bank	1988	7-1/2" hard plastic Grandma wearing a blue dress	25	30	35

Funny Face Drink Goofy Grape Pitcher, 1973

General Mills Boo Berry Figure, 1975

ADVERTISING TOYS

NAME	YEAR	DESCRIPTION	GOOD	EX	MINT
H.P. HOOD					
Harry Hood Figure	1981	7-1/2" delivery man w/"Hood" inscription on chest	55	70	80
HEINZ					
Aristocrat Tomato	1939	6" Aristocrat Tomato bust wearing top hat	150	200	225
HERSHEY'S					
Hershey's Chocolate Figure	1987	4-1/2" bendable candy bar shaped like a man	5	8	10
HUSH PUPPIES					
Hush Puppies Figure	1970s	8" tan and brown basset hound	20	25	35
ICEE					
ICEE Bear Figure	1970s	8" vinyl polar bear drinking an ICEE	25	30	35
INSTY-PRINTS					
Insty-Prints Wizard Figure	1980s	9" vinyl figure of wizard dressed in red outfit w/ moons and stars	75	100	135
IRON FIREMAN FURNACE					
Iron Fireman Figure	1943	5" metal man shoveling coal	65	75	85
KAHN'S WIENERS					
Beefy Frank Figure	1980	5-1/2" vinyl figural hot dog mustard dispenser	15	18	22
KEEBLER COMPANY					
Ernie the Keebler Elf Figure	1974	7" figure of Ernie wearing oange and yellow hat and green jacket	15	25	30
Ernie the Keebler Elf Mug	1972	3" plastic figural mug	8	12	15
KELLOGG'S					
Coppertone	1998	Coppertone Beach Set: Coppertone girl, black dog, drawstring tote, suntan lotion, towel, radio and umbrella; Madame Alexander, the set	25	50	100
Dig 'Em Bendy Figure	1970	3-1/2" bendable frog figure w/"Dig 'Em" on shirt	10	15	25
Dig 'Em Doll	1973	16" smiling frog w/baseball hat wearing shirt that reads "Dig Em"	15	20	30
Dig 'Em Slide Puzzle	1979	4" plastic squares that make a scene when put together	8	10	15
Milton The Toaster Figure	1980	5" white, smiling toaster	50	70	90
Newton the Owl License Plate	1973	5" x 7" plastic license plate w/Newton the Owl; made in several colors	5	8	10
Rice Krispies Dolls	1998	Snap, Crackle and Pop, the set	100	150	200
Rice Krispies Dolls	1998	8" Snap, Crackle, Pop; Madame Alexander, each	20	40	65
Rice Krispies Towel	1972	20 x 38" towel featuring Snap, Crackle and Pop!	10	20	25
Snap, Crackle and Pop Figures	1975	7-1/2" vinyl, arms at side, each	20	25	30
Snap, Crackle and Pop Figures	1975	7-1/2" vinyl, arms extended, each	25	30	35
Snap, Crackle and Pop Hand Puppets	1950s	cloth body and vinyl head, each	25	35	40
Tony the Tiger Cookie Jar	1968	7" plastic	70	95	125
Tony the Tiger Figure	1974	7-1/2" vinyl tiger	45	60	75
Toucan Sam Backpack	1983	12" blue backpack that pictures Toucan Sam sitting on a schoolhouse	15	20	25
Toucan Sam Figure	1984	3" plastic jointed figure w/blue body and multi-colored beak	12	15	20
Toucan Sam Wallet	1984	plastic w/picture of Toucan Sam	10	15	20
KEN-L-RATION					
Ken-L-Ration Wall Pockets	1960s	3" pair of plastic wall pockets; cat's head and a dog's head	40	50	65
KENDALL COMPANY					
Curad Taped Crusader Figure	1977	7-1/2" vinyl figure	65	75	85
KENTUCKY FRIED CHICKEN					
Colonel Sanders Nodder	1960s	7" plastic nodder of Colonel holding bucket of chicken	70	85	100

NAME	YEAR	DESCRIPTION	GOOD	EX	MINT
KIDDIE CITY TOY STORE					
Kaycee Kangaroo Figure	1980s	vinyl kangaroo w/baby in pouch	40	55	65
KRAFT					
Cheesasaurus Rex Figure	1990s	5-1/2" orange dinosaur figures wearing different outfits	3	5	7
Mr. Wiggle Hand Puppet	1966	6" red rubber	150	185	225
Vegetable Man Bank	1970s	8" vegetable man w/tomato for a head and a celery body	200	250	275
Vegetable Man Display	1980	3' plastic vacuuform store display of Vegetable Man	150	225	275
LABATT'S BREWERY					
Labatt's Beer Man Figure	1972	6" man standing next to wood barrel	20	25	30
MAGIC CHEF					
Magic Chef Figure	1980s	7" chef dressed in tuxedo and chef's hat	10	12	15
MICHELIN TIRES					
Mr. Bib Figure	1980s	12" plastic figure w/Michelin sash across chest	30	40	50
MOHAWK CARPET COMPANY					
Mohawk Tommy Doll	1970	16" stuffed doll of a little boy marked "Mohawk Tommy" across front	10	15	20
NABISCO					
Barnum's Animal Crackers Cookie Jar	1972	ceramic, shaped like a box of animal crackers	175	225	275
Chips Ahoy Girl Figure	1983	4-1/2" vinyl figure of girl w/Chips Ahoy cookie on her head and in her hand	15	18	20
Fig Newton Girl Figure	1983	4-1/2" girl w/Fig Newton on her head	15	18	20
Nabisco Thing	1996	5" multi-colored bendable figure w/Nabisco logo for its head	5	10	15
Oreo Cookie Girl Figure	1983	4-1/2" vinyl figure of girl w/Oreo Cookie on head and in her hand	15	18	20
NESTLE'S					
Quik Bunny Doll	1976	24" plush rabbit w/letter "Q" on his chest	25	35	40
Quik Bunny Figure	1991	6" bendable brown and tan rabbit w/the letter "Q" hanging from his neck	3	7	10
NOVOTEL HOTEL					
Dolphi Figure	1990s	4-1/2" bendable dolphin figures; set of four produced each year	5	8	10
OSCAR MAYER FOODS					
Hot Wheels Wienermobile		die-cast Wienermobile	2	4	6
Little Oscar Puppet		thin plastic, theme song on back	1	3	6
Wienermobile	1950s	11" car; Little Oscar pops up when car is rolled	75	95	135
Wienermobile Bank		plastic	3	7	15
Wienermobile Beanbag	1998	7" plush beanbag	3	5	8
PEPPERIDGE FARM					
Goldfish Plush	1970s	16" plush figure	15	20	25
PILLSBURY					
Biscuit the Cat Puppet	1974	2-1/2" vinyl cat finger puppet	18	25	30
Grandpopper & Grandmommer Figures	1974	5" vinyl pair of figures	80	120	150
Jolly Green Giant Figure	1970s	9-1/2" vinyl green man wearing loincloth of leaves	85	100	125
Little Sprout Figure	1970s	6-1/2" vinyl green figure w/leaves on head and body	7	10	15
Little Sprout Inflatable Figure	1976	24" vinyl	25	30	35
Little Sprout Salt and Pepper Shakers	1988	3" ceramic figural shakers	25	30	35
Poppin' Fresh Doll	1972	white velour doll w/hat and scarf	20	25	30
Poppin' Fresh Figure	1971	6-1/2" vinyl white baker w/blue eyes and blue dot on hat	5	7	10
PIZZA HUT					
Pizza Hut Pete Bank	1969	7-1/2" plastic	20	35	50
PIZZA TIME THEATRE					
Chuck E. Cheese Bank	1980s	6-1/2" plastic	8	12	15

Kellogg's Tony the Tiger Figure, 1974

Starkist Charlie the Tuna Figure, 1973

NAME	YEAR	DESCRIPTION	GOOD	EX	MINT
PLANTERS PEANUTS					
Mr. Peanut Doll	1967	21" pillow doll	15	20	25
Mr. Peanut Figure	1930s	8-1/2" painted wood figure w/hat and cane	275	300	375
Mr. Peanut Figure	1992	8-1/2" yellow and black plastic	12	15	20
Mr. Peanut Wind-Up	1984	3" yellow peanut man w/traditional hat and cane	20	25	30
POST CEREAL					
California Raisins PVC Figure	1987	2" male raisin playing drums	3	5	8
California Raisins Wind-Up	1987	4" female raisin w/tambourine	5	7	10
Sugar Bear Doll	1970s	12" plush brown bear w/blue "Sugar Bear" shirt	20	25	30
Sugar Bear Doll	1988	12" plush bear w/blue "Sugar Bear" shirt	15	20	25
PROCTOR & GAMBLE					
24 Hour Bug	1970s	7" spotted green bug	50	65	80
Hawaiian Punch Doll	1983	15" plush Punchy w/red hair and blue and white striped shirt	20	22	25
Hawaiian Punch Radio	1970s	6" figural radio of Punchy	25	35	45
Mr. Clean Figure	1961	8" bald man wearing white clothes w/earring; arms are folded	85	100	135
PURINA CHUCK WAGON					
Chuck Wagon	1975	8" vinyl team of horses and checker board covered wagon	25	30	35
QUAKER OATS					
Cap'n Crunch Bank	1969	8" captain wearing blue outfit and sword	45	65	85
Jean LaFoote Bank	1975	8" vinyl pirate wearing green suit and purple hat	60	85	125
Quake Cereal Doll	1965	9" man w/raised arms and letter "Q" across chest	85	95	125
Quisp Bank	1960s	6-1/2" papier-mâché	500	750	850
Quisp Cereal Doll	1965	10" doll w/pink body, green clothes and letter "Q" across stomach	70	85	125
QUISP CEREAL/QUAKER					
Quisp Powered Sugar Space Gun		7" long, red, mail away premium	150	250	400
R.J. REYNOLDS					
Joe Camel Can Cooler	1991	4" vinyl	5	10	12
RAID					
Raid Bug	1989	plush green bug	20	25	30
Raid Bug Radio	1980s	Raid bug in standing position w/clock on one side and radio on the other	70	200	135
Raid Bug Wind-Up	1983	4" yellow and green angry bug	40	50	70
RALSTON PURINA					
Meow Mix Cat	1976	4-1/2" vinyl yellow cat w/black stripes	20	25	30
RECKITT & COLMAN					
Mr. Bubble Figure	1990	8" pink vinyl	20	30	35
REDDY COMMUNICATIONS					
Reddy Kilowatt Bobbin' Head	1960s	6-1/2" Reddy wearing cowboy outfit	225	275	450
Reddy Kilowatt Figure	1961	6" plastic figure w/lightbulb for head and lightning bolts for body	150	185	225
RITALIN					
Ritalin Man Statue	1970s	7" smiling plastic statue w/hat	55	65	75
SEA HOST					
Clem the Clam Push Puppets	1969	4" fish push puppets; four different fish were issued	15	30	40
SHOP RITE					
Scrunchy Bear Doll	1970s	16" plush bear w/Shop-Rite shirt	20	25	30
SMILE ORANGE DRINK					
Drink Smile Statue	1930s	8" plaster statue of character w/orange for head; "Drink Smile" written across base	150	200	250
SMITH KLINE & FRENCH LAB					
Tagamet Figure	1989	2-1/2" bendable pink figure standing on base	15	20	25

ADVERTISING TOYS

NAME	YEAR	DESCRIPTION	GOOD	EX	MINT
SONY					
Sony Boy Figure	1960s	4" vinyl boy wearing yellow "Sony" shirt	150	200	225
SQUIRT BEVERAGE					
Squirt Doll	1961	17" vinyl boy w/blond hair and removable clothing; "Squirt" written across shirt	100	150	175
STARKIST					
Charlie the Tuna Doll	1970	15" pull string talking doll	40	50	75
Charlie the Tuna Figure	1973	7-1/2" vinyl Charlie; arms pointed down	50	70	85
Charlie the Tuna Radio	1970	6" radio	50	60	90
Charlie the Tuna Scale	1972	oval shaped bathroom scale w/Charlie the Tuna	50	65	80
STERLING DRUG					
Diaparene Baby Doll	1980	5" baby w/movable arms and legs; baby wears diaper	35	40	50
TASTYKAKE					
Tastykake Baker Doll	1974	13" pillow doll wearing chef outfit	15	20	25
TONY'S PIZZA					
Mr. Tony Figure	1972	8" vinyl Italian pizza chef	30	35	40
TOYS R US					
Geoffrey Doll	1967	2-1/2" plush Geoffrey wearing red and white striped shirt	20	25	35
Geoffrey Flashlight	1989	8-1/2" plastic figural flashlight of Geoffrey the Giraffe	8	10	12
TRAVELODGE					
Sleepy Bear Squeeze Toy	1970s	5-1/2" bear wearing pajamas	25	30	35
TROPICANA					
Tropic-Ana Doll	1977	17" pillow doll of Hawaiian girl	15	20	25
U.S. FORESTRY DEPARTMENT					
Woodsy Owl Bank	1970s	8-1/2" ceramic figural bank	100	125	150
U.S. POSTAL SERVICE					
Mr. ZIP Statue	1960s	6-1/2" wood statue w/mailbag and pop-up hat	150	180	225
WONDER BREAD					
Fresh Guy Figure	1975	4" smiling loaf of bread w/polka dots, smiling face and "Wonder" on side	100	150	175

Banks

Mechanical Banks

Mechanical banks are often considered the royalty of American toys, mainly because they developed at an eventful time in American history, when industrialization was changing every aspect of life, including the change in toys from wood and tin to the newly-discovered cast iron.

The age of mechanical banks began with the end of the Civil War and the dawning of the industrial age and for collecting purposes ended with the beginning of World War II.

The rise of factories during the Civil War laid the groundwork for the coming industrial revolution, and iron was the main metal utilized. Prior to the Civil War, most toys were made of wood, tin or sheet metal. The new process of "casting" iron, with its durability and lower cost, made iron the metal of choice for toy makers. The new process allowed design innovations not previously possible, and toy makers were quick to exploit its potential.

Toys of the day reflected the attitudes, activities, personalities and morals of the day. Americans believed in frugality both as a morally-dictated behavior and as a means toward a secure future, and parents of the day strove to instill the virtue in their children. Many of the nursery rhymes and songs of the time espoused the value of thrift, and children were encouraged to save their pennies at every turn. Toy makers saw to it that those parents had clever and colorful allies in the banks themselves.

In 1869, the first patent was issued for a cast-iron mechanical bank, Hall's Excelsior Bank. It was also the first of many banks designed as buildings, a concept which by imitation and variation grew into the largest category in the related field of non-mechanical or still banks.

What's a Mechanical Bank?

Mechanical banks have parts which are set in motion when a coin is deposited. Still banks are receptacles only; depositing coins in them causes no action. In short, if you drop in the coin and something happens, the bank is most likely mechanical. If nothing happens, the bank is classified as still.

The degree of action varies from the simple closing of a mouth or nod of a head to complex multiple figure actions involving music, acrobatics, pratfalls and sports. Along with rarity and subject matter, this complexity of design and action is a primary factor in determining the value of a mechanical bank. From a manufacturing standpoint, intricacy of design and action increased production costs, resulting in higher retail prices and lower overall unit sales. Many years later, that results in rarity.

Some banks never made it into commercial production at all. Bank designers were required to submit working pattern samples with their patent applications, and sometimes these patterns are all that remains of a failed patent bid. Other banks were never intended for commercial

Girl Skipping Rope, 1890, J.& E. Stevens

Panorama Bank, 1876, J.& E. Stevens

production, but were made instead for personal reasons. As one-of-a-kind examples, surviving banks of this type are obviously very rare and command prices in accordance with their rarity.

Think You've Got an Original?

Both mechanical and still cast-iron banks are prime targets for reproduction. Whether intended as forgeries or as honest replicas and marked as such, these items can and do find their way into dealer stock, priced as genuine antique articles. Reproduction labels and imprints can be filed away, metals can be artificially aged, and other telltale areas can be altered in hopes of turning an honest $50 profit into $5,000 or $15,000.

Collectors entering this field are well advised to confine their initial dealings to reputable dealers and auction houses with qualified and impartial expert staffs.

Still Banks

The same companies that made mechanical banks often made still banks as less expensive alternatives. Several banks can be found in both still and mechanical versions. Companies such as Arcade, Ives, Kenton and Stevens are familiar to still and mechanical bank collectors alike.

Again, building-shaped banks are perhaps the single largest type of still banks, with others fashioned as animals, people and busts, and appliances like safes, clocks, mail boxes and globes.

Building-shaped banks span a range from Lincoln's Cabin in pottery to cottages, Victorian houses, mansions and skyscrapers in cast iron. Commemorative banks were particularly popular, such as banks resembling the Washington Monument, National Bank of Los Angeles, Century of Progress building and Eiffel Tower. Other building banks offered variations on general themes such as Home Savings Banks, State Banks and churches.

One notable class of still bank is the registering bank. Often in the shape of a safe or cash register, these banks typically accept only certain coins, such as dimes or nickels. They keep a running tally of deposits and pop open once the bank is filled, typically at $5 or $10. While their delayed reaction mechanism has earned them places in some mechanical collections, they are generally classified as still banks.

A note on restoration: As in many other areas of collecting, restoration of banks is strongly discouraged in the marketplace. Unless undertaken by an experienced professional, the restoration of a bank can result in irreparable damage to its collector value.

While most still banks were made of cast iron, other materials frequently used included glass, pottery and other ceramics, brass, lead, tin, wood, composition and even plastic. This book concentrates on cast-iron banks. Modern ceramic and plastic banks may also be found under their respective character headings in the Character Toys and Advertising Toys sections of this book.

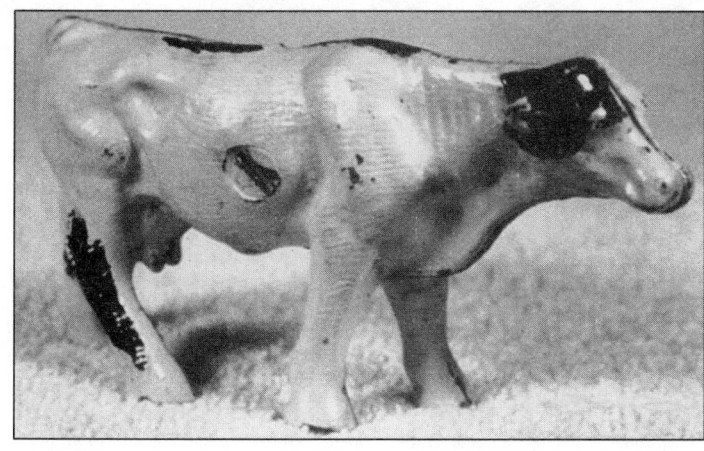

*Cow, 1920,
A.C. Williams*

Trends

Bank collecting, like other hobbies, is ultimately a matter of discretionary income. The prices of many cast-iron mechanical banks have put them in the realm of the wealthy and major investors only. Still banks are also frequently priced beyond the means of casual collectors, but their values are in general a fraction of mechanicals, making them more attractive investment vehicles for collectors of moderate means. Both types offer the collector a piece of history and beauty, and each field has its unique attractions and benefits.

The Top 10 Mechanical Banks
(in Excellent condition)

1. Mikado, Kyser & Rex, 1886 .... $55,000
2. Jonah and the Whale, Jonah Emerges, Stevens, J.& E., 1880s 55,000
3. Rollerskating Bank, Kyser & Rex, 1880s 45,000
4. Girl Skipping Rope, Stevens, J.& E., 1890 45,000
5. Circus Bank, Shepard Hardware, 1888 45,000
6. Calamity, Stevens, J.& E., 1905 35,000
7. Harlequin, Stevens, J.& E., 1907 22,000
8. Turtle Bank, Kilgore, 1920s 20,000
9. Picture Gallery Bank, Shepard Hardware, 1885 20,000
10. Motor Bank, Kyser & Rex, 1889 20,000

The Top 10 Still Banks
(in Excellent condition)

1. Indiana Paddle Wheeler, Unknown, 1896 .... $8,000
2. Tug Boat, Unknown 7,500
3. San Gabriel Mission, Unknown 7,500
4. Chanticleer (Rooster), Unknown, 1911 7,500
5. Eagle with Ball, Building, Unknown 6,500
6. Coin Registering Bank, Kyser & Rex, 1890 6,500
7. Hippo, Unknown 6,000
8. Dormer Bank, Unknown 6,000
10. Battleship Maine, Stevens, J. & E., 1901 6,000

Contributor to this section: Bob Pierce, Henry/Pierce Auctions, 1525 S. Arcadian Dr., New Berlin, WI 53151.

BANKS

NAME	COMPANY	YEAR	DESCRIPTION	GOOD	VG	EX
Acrobat	Stevens, J.& E.	1883	deposit coin in opening, press lever which causes the gymnast to kick the clown causing the clown to stand on his head while coin is deposited in bank; cast iron	2000	3000	10000
Artillery Bank	Stevens, J.& E.	1900s	#24668, 8" long, 6" tall; put coin in barrel, press lever, making soldier drop arm to signal firing, hammer snaps and fires coin through building window; cast iron	550	1200	3200
Artillery Bank	Shepard Hardware	1892	nickel plate version, coin is placed in the cannon, the hammer is pushed back; pressing the thumb piece fires the coin into the fort; cast iron	500	1100	2600
Atlas Bank	Unknown		iron base w/white metal figure holding wooden globe w/paper litho map; put coin in slot, pulling lever makes coin fall into bank, making globe spin; Iron and wood	1000	1500	3500
Bad Accident Mule	Stevens, J.& E.	1890s	10" long, painted; deposit coin under the feet of the driver, press lever, boy jumps into the road, frightening the mule; he rears, the cart and driver are thrown backwards and coin falls in cart; cast iron	850	1500	4200
Bear and Tree Stump	Judd	1880s	5" tall; put coin on bear's tongue; pressing lever makes tongue lift coin and drop it into bank; cast iron	500	700	1200
Bear, Slot in Chest	Kenton	1870s	deposit coin in the bear's chest and his mouth opens and closes; cast iron	750	1000	1500
Bill E. Grin Bank	Judd	1887	4-1/2" tall; dropping coin on top of head makes tongue jut and eyes blink; cast iron	500	900	2200
Billy Goat Bank	Stevens, J.& E.	1910	deposit coin in slot and pull wire loop forward, goat jumps forward and coin falls in bank; cast iron	600	1000	1850
Bird on Roof	Stevens, J.& E.	1878	deposit coin in slot on bird's head, pull the wire lever on left side of house, the bird tilts forward, coin rolls into the chimney; cast iron	650	1000	2200
Bismark Pig	Stevens, J.& E.	1883	lock mechanism, put coin in slot over tail, press the pig's tail, Bismark figure pops up and coin drops; lead	1800	3500	6000
Boy and Bulldog	Judd	1870s	deposit coin between the boy and the dog; pulling lever makes boy lean forward and 'push' coin into bank, the dog moves backwards at the same time and coin falls; cast iron	600	900	1850
Boy on Trapeze	J. Barton & Smith Co.	1891	9-1/2" tall, painted; place a coin in the slot on the boy's head and he revolves; cast iron	600	1500	6500
Boy Robbing Bird's Nest	Stevens, J.& E.	1906	8" tall; deposit coin in slot and press the lever on the tree; as the boy falls, the coin disappears in the tree; cast iron	1000	3000	10500
Boy Scout Camp	Stevens, J.& E.	1912	9-1/2" long; drop coin into tent; pressing lever makes Scout raise flag as coin drops; cast iron	1500	3500	12000
Boys Stealing Watermelon	Kyser & Rex	1880s	6 1/2" long; put coin in slot on top of dog house; pressing lever makes boy move toward watermelon, dog comes out of house, and coin drops; cast iron	600	1200	3000
Breadwinners	Stevens, J.& E.	1886	put coin in end of club, cock hammer; pressing button makes 'Labor' hit 'Monopoly', "sending the rascals up" and dropping coin into loaf of bread; cast iron	3500	7000	18000
Bucking Mule, Miniature	Judd	1870s	put coin in slot; releasing donkey makes him throw man, knocking coin into bank; cast iron	600	900	1800
Bull and Bear, Single Pendulum	Stevens, J.& E.	1930s	put coin in pendulum on tree stump; pressing lever releases pendulum to swing, dropping coin into either bull or bear; Iron and lead	800	1200	1800
Bull Tosses Boy In Well	Unknown		7" long; put coin in boy's hands; pressing lever makes bull spring and boy jumps back, dropping coin in well; brass	750	1200	1700
Bulldog Bank	Stevens, J.& E.	1880s	put coin on dog's nose, pull his tail, the dog opens his mouth and swallows the coin; cast iron	400	1200	3500

NAME	COMPANY	YEAR	DESCRIPTION	GOOD	VG	EX
Bulldog Savings Bank	Ives	1878	8-1/2" long; put coin in man's hand, press lever, making dog jump, bite coin, and fall back, dropping coin into bank; cast iron	1000	2000	3000
Bulldog Standing	Judd	1870s	coin is placed on dog's tongue and tail is lifted; when tail is released the coin is deposited; cast iron	350	600	1200
Bureau, Five Knob	James A. Serrill	1869	place coin in open drawer; closing drawer makes coin drop; wood	200	350	500
Bureau, Three Knob	James A. Serrill	1869	place coin in open drawer; closing drawer makes coin drop; wood	300	400	550
Butting Buffalo	Kyser & Rex	1888	place coin into tree trunk; pressing lever makes buffalo 'butt' boy up trunk while raccoon flees into tree; cast iron	1200	2000	4500
Butting Goat	Judd	1870s	deposit coin on holder on tree trunk; lifting the tail causes the goat to spring forward depositing coin in bank; base length 4-3/4"; cast iron	600	1000	2000
Butting Ram	Ole Storle	1895	put coin on tree limb; pressing lever makes ram butt coin into bank while boy thumbs his nose; cast iron	2000	6000	12000
Cabin Bank	Stevens, J.& E.	1885	3-1/2" tall, shows darkie in front of cabin; put coin on roof, flip lever to make figure flip and push coin into bank w/his feet; cast iron	300	850	2000
Calamity	Stevens, J.& E.	1905	cock tackles into position, put coin in slot in front of fullback; pressing lever activates tackles and coin drops in the collision; cast iron	3000	8000	35000
Called Out Bank	Stevens, J.& E.	1900	9" tall; push soldier into bank, drop coin into slot, making soldier pop up and drop coin into bank; cast iron	4000	10000	20000
Calumet, Large	Calumet Baking Powder	1924	put coin in slot, making box sway back and forth in 'thanks'; cardboard	150	250	350
Cat and Mouse: Cat Balancing	Stevens, J.& E.	1891	8-1/2" tall; put coin in slot and lock mouse into position; pressing lever makes mouse disappear and kitten appears holding mouse on a ball; cast iron	1000	2200	4200
Chandlers Bank	National Brass Works	1900s	open the drawer, put in coin, closing drawer drops coin into bank; cast iron	400	600	1250
Chief Big Moon	Stevens, J.& E.	1899	10" long; put coin in slot in fish tail, push lever, making frog spring up from pond, dropping coin; cast iron	1200	2200	6000
Chimpanzee Bank	Kyser & Rex	1880	green version; push coin slide toward monkey w/log book, making monkey lower head and arm to 'log in' deposit, ringing a bell; cast iron	1200	2000	3200
Chimpanzee Bank	Kyser & Rex	1880	red variant; push coin slide toward monkey w/ log book, making monkey lower head and arm to 'log in' deposit, ringing a bell; cast iron	1400	2200	3200
Circus Bank	Shepard Hardware	1888	place coin on money receptacle, turn the crank and pony goes around the ring and the clown deposits coin; cast iron	5000	8000	45000
Circus Ticket Collector	Judd	1830	deposit coin on top of barrel and the man's head nods his thanks; cast iron	550	850	1500
Clown Bust	Chamberlain & Hill	1880s	English bank; put coin in hand; pressing lever makes arm lift coin and clown swallows it; cast iron	1700	2500	4000
Clown on Globe	Stevens, J.& E.	1890	clown straddles globe on footed base; pressing lever makes globe and clown move and change positions, leaving clown standing on head; 9" tall; cast iron	900	1500	4500
Coin Registering Bank	Kyser & Rex	1890s	when the last nickel or dime is deposited totaling $5 the door will pop off and the money can be taken out; cast iron	1200	2500	6500
Columbian Magic	Introduction	1892	swing open the shelf and place a coin on it, close the shelf and the coin is deposited in bank; cast iron	150	300	550

BANKS

Artillery Bank, 1900s, J.& E. Stevens

Bad Accident Mule, 1890s, J.& E. Stevens

MECHANICAL BANKS

NAME	COMPANY	YEAR	DESCRIPTION	GOOD	VG	EX
Confectionery Bank	Kyser & Rex	1881	8-1/2" tall; depicts lady at candy counter; coin dropped into slot, button pushed, making figure slide to receive candy; bell rings as coin drops; cast iron	2000	4000	8500
Creedmore Bank	Stevens, J.& E.	1877	9-3/4" long, painted; pull back lever on gun, put coin in slot; pressing man's foot shoots coin into tree; cast iron	600	900	1500
Cupola Circular Building	Stevens, J.& E.	1874	push the doorbell lever and the top pops up exposing the cashier, who pivots back and returns to his forward position; cast iron	4000	8000	12000
Darkie in the Chimney	Unknown		pull the drawer out and the darkie emerges; front door knob when turned counterclockwise allows the trap door in base of bank to be removed; wood	550	1000	1400
Darktown Battery Bank	Stevens, J.& E.		#24670, 10" long, 7-1/4" tall, painted; three lads play ball, red, blue and yellow pitcher's uniform; put coin in pitcher's hand; pressing lever to pitch coin, batter swings and misses, catcher drops; cast iron	1200	2800	8000
Dentist	Stevens, J.& E.	1880s	9-1/2" long; coin drops into dentist's pocket; press lever at figure's feet, making dentist pull patient's tooth, patient falls backward, dropping coin into gas bag; cast iron	2000	5500	9500
Dinah	J. Harper & Co.	1911	deposit coin in Dinah's hand and press the lever; she raises her hand, her eyes roll back and her tongue flips in as she swallows the coin; cast iron	600	900	1450
Dog on Turntable	Judd	1870s	5-1/4" long, 5" tall; turn the handle and dog goes in and deposits penny, coming out of the other door for more; cast iron	400	800	1200
Dog Tray Bank	Kyser & Rex	1880	place coin on plate; the dog faithfully deposits it in the vault; cast iron	2000	3500	6500
Eagle and Eaglets	Stevens, J.& E.	1883	#24671, 7-3/4" long, 6" tall, painted; put coin in eagle's beak; pressing lever makes eaglets rise, eagle tilts forward and drops coin into nest; cast iron	600	1200	1800
Electric Safe	Louis	1904	twist the center knob in a clockwise direction until it stops, coin slot becomes operational, rotate dial counterclockwise and the coin falls into the bank; sheet metal	200	450	650
Elephant and Three Clowns	Stevens, J.& E.	1883	6" tall, painted; place coin between the rings held by acrobat, move the ball on the feet of the other acrobat and the elephant hits coin w/his trunk and coin falls into bank; cast iron	600	1200	2800
Elephant Howdah Bank, Pull Tail	Hubley	1934	put coin in elephant's trunk; pulling tail makes animal lift coin over head, dropping coin in howdah; cast iron	300	500	1250
Elephant Moves Trunk, Large	Williams, A.C.	1905	the trunk of the elephant moves when coin is inserted, trunk automatically closes the slot as soon as coin is deposited, 6-3/4" long; cast iron	150	250	400
Elephant Three Stars	Unknown	1884	place coin in the elephant's trunk, touch his tail and the coin will be thrown into his head; cast iron	300	650	1250
Elephant, Man Pops Out	Enterprise	1884	push man into howdah or lift trunk to cock mechanism, close howdah lid, put coin in elephant's mouth; pressing lever drops trunk into mouth, dropping coin and man pops up from howdah; 5-3/8" tall; cast iron and wood	400	800	1250
Feed the Goose	Banker's Thrift	1927	press the tail feathers lever and the goose opens his mouth; toss in a coin and release, the mouth closes, coin is swallowed and his wings rotate; white metal	250	400	600
Football	J. Harper & Co.	1895	place a coin on the platform in front of the player's foot, press the lever and he kicks the coin into the goal net; cast iron	1200	2200	3500

BANKS

59

BANKS

NAME	COMPANY	YEAR	DESCRIPTION	GOOD	VG	EX
Fortune Teller Savings Bank	Nickel, Baumgarter & Co.	1901	drop a nickel in the slot of the lever give a sharp jerk backwards, the wheel will spin; when it stops pull lever forward and your fortune will appear in window; cast iron	500	800	1400
Frog on Rock	Kilgore	1920s	press small lever under frog's mouth and he opens to deposit coin; cast iron	200	400	1100
Frog on Round Base	Stevens, J.& E.	1872	press frog's right foot and put coin in his mouth; release lever and he swallows coin and winks; cast iron	350	550	1000
Gem Bank	Judd	1878	pull dog back from bank, put coin on tray, lift dog's tail making dog move and drop coin into building; cast iron	200	550	850
Gem Registering Bank	Stevens, J.& E.	1893	floral embossed rectangular bank w/dials at one end; turn thumb piece to top, insert coin, turn thumb piece to bottom, dropping coin into bank; cast iron	600	1200	3000
Germania Exchange	Stevens, J.& E.	1880s	goat on a keg; put coin on goat's tail; turning faucet makes goat drop coin and lifts up a glass of beer; cast iron and lead	3500	7000	12000
Giant in Tower	J. Harper & Co.	1892	put coin in slot and giant leans forward; cast iron	6000	10000	15000
Girl in Victorian Chair	W.S. Reed	1880	girl in blue dress sits w/dog in her lap in a highback wicker chair; put coin in chair top and press lever, making coin drop and dog lean forward; cast iron	2000	3000	4500
Girl Skipping Rope	Stevens, J.& E.	1890	blonde girl in light blue dress jumps rope by means of an ornately housed mechanism; cast iron	10000	15000	45000
Give Me a Penny	F. W. Smith	1870	bureau w/drawer; open drawer and picture rises at back, saying "Give Me A Penny"; putting coin in drawer and closing it makes coin drop and picture fall back into cabinet; wood	1100	2000	3000
Grenadier Bank	J. Harper & Co.	1890s	soldier shoots coin into tree stump; cast iron	350	650	1100
Guessing Bank, Man's Figure	McLoughlin Brothers	1877	man sits atop a clock w/numbers from 1 to 6 repeated around dial; dropping coin makes dial spin and land on a number; bank reads, "Pays Five For One If You Call the Number"; cast iron	1200	2000	3500
Haley's Elephant	Unknown		8" long, painted gray w/red and gold blanket; cast iron	350	500	650
Hall's Excelsior Bank	Stevens, J.& E.	1869	value varies according to color of bank; 5" tall, yellow version, monkey sits atop building; put coin on tray in monkey's lap, pull string and monkey disappears inside; cast iron and wood	300	600	850
Hall's Liliput	Stevens, J.& E.	1877	coin laid on plate is carried around by the cashier and placed in the bank; cashier returns to its place and cycle can begin again; cast iron	350	700	1600
Hall's Liliput, No Tray	Stevens, J.& E.	1877	coin laid on plate is carried around by the cashier and placed in the bank, cashier returns to its place and cycle can begin again; cast iron and brass Figure	400	750	1600
Harlequin	Stevens, J.& E.	1907	bring figure's hand halfway around to position and place coin in slot and press lever; cast iron	5000	10000	22000
Hen and Chick	Stevens, J.& E.	1901	place coin in front of hen in slot, raise the lever and as the hen calls, the chicken springs from under her for the coin and disappears; cast iron	1100	1700	5500
Hindu	Kyser & Rex	1882	deposit coin in mouth and press the lever on the back of the head, his eyes roll down and his tongue swings down, causing the coin to fall into the bank; cast iron	800	1300	1850
Hold the Fort, Seven Hole	Unknown	1877	pull back the ring until rod is in position, tip the bank, place the coin on target and drop the shot in the cannon; shot follows the coin into the bank and escapes out of the bottom; cast iron	3000	5000	9500

Cat and Mouse: Cat Balancing, 1891, J.& E. Stevens

BANKS

NAME	COMPANY	YEAR	DESCRIPTION	GOOD	VG	EX
Home Bank with Dormers	Stevens, J.& E.	1872	pull knob, place penny on its edge in front of the cashier, push the knob to the right, and the coin is deposited in the rear of the bank in vault; cast iron	800	1200	3500
Hoop-La Bank	J. Harper & Co.	1895	place coin in dog's mouth and press the lever, the dog jumps through the hoop and deposits the coin in the barrel; cast iron	800	1200	5500
Horse Race, Straight Base	Stevens, J.& E.	1870	pull cord to start spring, place the horses' heads opposite the star, deposit the coin in the opening and the race will begin; cast iron	3500	5500	8000
Humpty Dumpty Bank	Shepard Hardware	1882	8-1/2" tall; put coin in Humpty's hand, press lever, making him drop coin into bank; cast iron	800	2200	4000
I Always Did 'Spise a Mule-Bench	Stevens, J.& E.	1897	put the mule and boy into position; when the knob is touched, the base causes the mule to kick the boy over, throwing the coin from the bench into the receptacle below; cast iron	800	1200	3500
I Always Did 'Spise a Mule-Jockey	Stevens, J.& E.	1879	#24672, 10-1/2" long, 8" tall; put coin in jockey's mouth; pressing lever makes mule kick, throwing jockey which drops coin into bank; cast iron	800	1200	3500
Independence Hall	Enterprise	1875	semi-mechanical bronze finish bank; drop coin in tower and pull lever to make bell ring; cast iron	350	550	1050
Indian Shooting Bear	Stevens, J.& E.	1883	10-3/8" long; put coin on rifle barrel; pressing level makes Indian shoot coin into bear; cast iron	900	2500	5500
Initiating Bank, First Degree	Mechanical Novelty Works	1880	10-1/2" long, Eddy's patent on base; place coin on boy's tray, push lever, the goat butts boy forward and the frog moves upward as the coin slides from the tray into the frog's mouth; cast iron	5000	7000	9000
Initiating Bank, Second Degree	Mechanical Novelty Works	1880	goat is pressed down to lock mechanism; put coin on man's tray; pressing lever makes goat butt man, dropping coin into frog's mouth; cast iron	3000	5000	8000
Jolly Nigger in High Hat	Starkie (England)	1920	put coin in hand; pressing lever makes figure swallow coin while eyes roll and ears wiggle; aluminum	250	400	650
Jolly Nigger in High Hat	J. Harper & Co.	1880s	put coin in hand; pressing lever makes arm raise, dropping coin into mouth, eyes roll and tongue moves back into mouth as coin drops; cast iron	250	400	650
Jolly Nigger, String Tie	Unknown (England)	1890s	put coin in his hand; pressing lever makes him lift coin and swallow it, tongue pulling back and eyes rolling; aluminum	175	300	500
Jonah and the Whale	Shepard Hardware	1890s	put coin on Jonah's back; pressing lever makes Jonah turn toward whale's mouth, dropping coin into mouth.; cast iron	1200	2500	5500
Jonah and the Whale, Jonah Emerges	Stevens, J.& E.	1880s	deposit coin in side of whale; pull Jonah into position by pulling tail backwards; press the lever, the coin is deposited and Jonah will appear; cast iron	12000	20000	55000
Kick Inn	Melvisto Novelty	1921	place coin on the ledge and push the lever on edge of base, the donkey kicks the ledge w/his hind feet; ledge moves upward and tosses the coin into the side of the inn; wood	200	500	900
Kiltie	J. Harper & Co.	1931	deposit coin in Scotchman's hand and press the lever; he raises his arm, lowers his eyes and deposits coin in his shirt pocket; cast iron	750	1200	3000
Leap Frog Bank	Shepard Hardware	1891	7-1/2" long; put standing boy behind stooping one, put coin in slot; pressing lever makes standing boy leap over other one, who pushes lever on tree, dropping coin into bank; cast iron	750	1500	5500
Lighthouse	Unknown	1891	two slots, one is a still bank, other on top of tower takes nickels; the button on top of tower will permit the bank to open only after 100 nickels are deposited; cast iron	1200	1800	5500

NAME	COMPANY	YEAR	DESCRIPTION	GOOD	VG	EX
Lion and Two Monkeys	Kyser & Rex	1883	9" long; put coin in monkey's hand; pressing lever makes monkey lower hand and drop coin into lion's mouth; cast iron	650	1400	4200
Lion Hunter	Stevens, J.& E.	1911	hunter figure shoots coin into lion's mouth; cast iron	2000	5000	10000
Little Jocko	Ferdinand Strauss	1912	drop penny into cup, turn the crank, the monkeys dance and music plays; steel/white metal	500	1200	2200
Little Joe (Darkie Bank)	J. Harper & Co.	1910	put coin in Joe's hand; pressing lever makes him lift and swallow coin; cast iron	150	350	575
Little Moe	Chamberlin & Hill	1931	place coin in Moe's hand, press the lever on his left shoulder, he raises his right arm, his tongue flips in and he swallows the coin as he lowers his arm, tipping his hat; cast iron	250	400	600
Magic Bank	Stevens, J.& E.	1873	6" tall; open door to find cashier, put coin on his tray; pressing lever makes cashier disappear and drop coin in building; cast iron	800	1400	2800
Magician Bank	Stevens, J.& E.	1901	8" tall; put coin on table; pressing lever makes magician lower hat over coin, dropping coin into bank while magician nods head; cast iron	2500	3500	6500
Mama Katzenjammer	Kenton	1908	deposit coin in Mama's back in slot; her eyes roll up and return to their original position; cast iron	3000	5000	7500
Mammy and Child	Kyser & Rex	1884	put coin on apron; pressing lever makes Mammy lower spoon to baby, Mammy's head lowers and baby's leg lifts as coin drops; cast iron	3000	4500	6500
Mason Bank	Shepard Hardware	1887	7-1/4" long; drop coin onto hod, press lever, making hod move and drop coin into brick wall; cast iron	2000	4000	7500
Memorial Money Bank	Enterprise	1876	slide the lever forwards to expose the coin slot, deposit coin, release the lever and it snaps back to ring the Liberty Bell; cast iron	600	1200	1850
Merry-Go-Round	Kyser & Rex	1888	put coin in slot, turn the handle and chimes will ring, the figures will revolve and the attendant turns, raises stick, and coin drops; cast iron	7500	11000	15000
Mikado	Kyser & Rex	1886	put coin under right hat and turn crank, making coin mysteriously move to left hat, which is lifted to display coin; cast iron	15000	25000	55000
Milking Cow	Stevens, J.& E.	1885	deposit coin in cow's back, the lever under the cow's throat is pressed, the cow will kick up its hind leg, upset the boy and the milk pail and deposit coin; cast iron	3000	5000	7000
Monkey and Coconut	Stevens, J.& E.	1886	8-1/2" tall; put coin in monkey's hand; pressing lever makes monkey drop coin into coconut; cast iron	350	900	2500
Monkey Bank	Hubley	1920s	9" long, painted dark green base, put coin in monkey's mouth; pressing lever makes monkey spring forward, dropping coin into organ; cast iron	600	1000	1600
Mosque Bank	Judd	1880s	9" tall, electroplated; put coin on tray on gorilla's head, turning lever makes gorilla turn, dropping coin into bank; cast iron	600	1400	2600
Motor Bank	Kyser & Rex	1889	wind the rod w/key, drop a coin in slot and the trolley car is set in motion; cast iron	10000	15000	20000
Mule Entering Barn	Kyser & Rex	1880	8-1/2" long, gray barn version; put coin between mule's hind legs; pushing lever makes mule kick coin into barn and dog appears; cast iron	600	1200	3500
Musical Savings Bank, Regina	Regina Music Box	1894	bank is styled like a mantle clock; wind up mechanism, drop in coin, music plays; wood and metal	2500	4000	6000
National Bank	Stevens, J.& E.	1873	place coin on door ledge and push doorbell; the door revolves, slinging the coin into the bank, the man behind the window of the door quickly moves to the right to get out of the way; cast iron	2000	3500	6000

63

Chief Big Moon, 1899, J.& E. Stevens

Columbian Magic, 1892

MECHANICAL BANKS

NAME	COMPANY	YEAR	DESCRIPTION	GOOD	VG	EX
National, Your Savings	Unknown	1900s	replica cash register, w/one slot and key each for pennies, nickels, dimes and quarters; dropping coin and pressing key rings a bell; cast iron	275	550	850
New Creedmore Bank	Stevens, J.& E.	1891	place coin on barrel of rifle, press right foot and coin is shot into the bull's eye of the target; as coin enters it strikes gong bell; cast iron	550	950	1850
Novelty Bank	Stevens, J.& E.	1873	open door and put coin on tray, release door which closes by a spring and teller turns and drops coin into vault; cast iron	550	1000	2250
Octagonal Fort Bank	Unknown	1890	also called Fort Sumter, cock mechanism, put coin in barrel end; pressing lever makes coin fire into tower; 10-3/4" long; cast iron	1200	2200	3500
Organ Bank	Kyser & Rex	1881	6" tall, brown organ, monkey in blue pants and coat, yellow hat; turn handle and a chime of bells will ring while monkey deposits coins placed in tambourine, tipping his hat in thanks; cast iron	350	500	850
Organ Bank with Boy and Girl	Kyser & Rex	1882	7-1/2" tall; put coin on tray; turning crank makes monkey lower tray, dropping coin into bank while boy and girl turn; cast iron	500	850	1650
Organ Bank with Cat and Dog	Kyser & Rex	1882	#24663, 8-1/2" tall; put coin on tray; turning crank makes monkey lower tray dropping coin into bank while cat and dog rotate; cast iron	500	850	1650
Organ Bank, Miniature	Kyser & Rex	1890s	put coin in slot; turning crank makes bells ring, monkey turn, and coin drop; cast iron	500	850	1800
Owl, Slot in Book	Kilgore	1926	5-3/4"; deposit a coin in the slot and Blinkey's eyes will roll down and back; cast iron	350	650	1200
Owl, Slot in Head	Kilgore	1926	5-5/8", deposit coin in slot, eyes roll forward; cast iron	350	650	1200
Owl, Turns Head	Stevens, J.& E.	1880	7-1/2" tall, brown bird w/yellow highlights, glass eyes; insert coin in branch; pressing lever makes owl turn head as coin drops; cast iron	250	500	900
Paddy and the Pig	Stevens, J.& E.	1882	8-1/2" tall; put coin in pig's nose; pressing lever makes pig kick coin into Paddy's mouth; cast iron	900	2500	6500
Panorama Bank	Stevens, J.& E.	1876	place coin in slot on roof and next picture appears in the window; cast iron	2500	4500	6500
Patronize the Blind Man	Stevens, J.& E.	1878	place coin in the blind man's hand, the dog takes the coin and deposits it in the bank and returns to his position; cast iron	2000	3000	4500
Peg-Leg Beggar	Judd	1875s	insert coin in slot on hat and the beggar nods his thanks; cast iron	750	1200	1700
Pelican Bank, Baseball Player	Stevens, J.& E.	1878	8" tall; close bird's beak, put coin into top of head which makes beak open revealing a baseball player's head; cast iron	2000	3500	5000
Picture Gallery Bank	Shepard Hardware	1885	place coin in hand of center figure and he deposits coin; all the letters of the alphabet and numbers 1 to 26 are shown in rotation; also 26 animals or objects w/short word for each letter; cast iron	4500	7500	20000
Pig in a High Chair	Stevens, J.& E.	1897	5-1/4" tall; put coin on tray; pressing lever makes tray bring coin to pig's mouth; cast iron	350	550	1400
Pistol Bank	Richard Elliot	1909	5-1/2" long; pull trigger halfway back, a hook appears from end of the barrel, place a dime on hook and pull trigger; coin is snatched and pistol fires when deposited; cast iron	450	750	1650
Presto Bank	Kyser & Rex	1894	pull drawer open and deposit coin, release drawer and coin is deposited in bank; cast iron	250	525	950
Professor Pug Frog's Great Bicycle Feat	Stevens, J.& E.	1886	place coin on rear wheel; turning crank makes frog spin, dropping coin into bank; cast iron	1500	3500	8500
Punch and Judy	Banks & Sons	1929	pressing lever makes figures rise, put coin in slot; releasing lever makes figures fall back into bank as coin drops; Iron and Tin	2700	5000	7000

BANKS

NAME	COMPANY	YEAR	DESCRIPTION	GOOD	VG	EX
Punch and Judy, Large Letters	Shepard Hardware	1884	7-1/2" tall; put coin on Judy's tray, press lever and Judy deposits coin while Punch tries to hit her w/stick; cast iron	600	2500	5500
Punch and Judy, Small Letters	Shepard Hardware	1884	7-1/2" tall; put coin on Judy's tray, press lever and Judy deposits coin while Punch tries to hit her w/stick; cast iron	600	1500	5500
Queen Victoria Bust	J. Harper & Co.	1887	drop coin into slot in crown, making eyes roll; also made in brass; cast iron	3000	5000	7500
Rabbit in Cabbage	Kilgore	1925	4-1/2" long, white w/a green base; press coin into the slot and ears will rise and then flop back down; cast iron	200	650	1400
Rabbit Standing, Small	Lockwood Mfg.		put coin in rabbit's paws; pressing tail moves ears and drops coin; cast iron	450	850	1250
Reclining Chinaman	Stevens, J.& E.	1882	8-1/4" long; put coin in slot on log, press lever to make figure raise hand, showing hand of cards and saluting the depositor; as coin falls, rat runs out of the end of the log; cast iron	1500	2500	8500
Red Riding Hood	W.S. Reed	1880s	put coin in slot in pillow; moving lever makes Grandma's mask shift, revealing the wolf; Red turns her head in 'fear' and coin drops; cast iron	8500	14000	18000
Registering Dime Savings Bank	Ives	1890	deposit dime in chute and pull lever to right, then left and the dime will be deposited and door locked, amount registered on dial; when $10 is deposited door will unlock and pop out; cast iron	800	1600	2500
Rollerskating Bank	Kyser & Rex	1880s	place coin in roof slot, press lever, the skaters glide to the rear of the rink as the coin is deposited in bank, the man turns to give a little girl a wreath; cast iron	12000	18000	45000
Rooster Bank	Kyser & Rex	1900s	6-1/4", put coin on rooster's tail; pressing lever causes the rooster to move his head in a crowing position, money is deposited; cast iron	600	900	1800
Safety Locomotive	Edward J. Colby	1887	weight of money dropped on cab loosens the smokestack, then it can be lifted out and the money poured from the opening; cast iron	650	1400	2200
Santa at the Chimney	Shepard Hardware	1889	6" tall, painted; put coin in his hand; pressing lever makes him drop coin into chimney; cast iron	800	1800	5500
Schley Bottling Up Cervera	Unknown	1899	bottle neck shows two portraits, Schley and Cervera; coins can only be dropped when Cervera is visible; shake bank to pull up Cervera picture, dropping coin will make Schley's picture return; cast iron	4500	8000	18000
Smyth X-Ray Bank	Henry C. Hart	1898	set coin in the path of the scope slot and look into the eyepiece; you will see through the coin and out the other end of the bank; press lever and the coin is deposited in the bank; cast iron	900	1800	3200
Speaking Dog	Shepard Hardware	1885	deposit coin on girl's plate; when thumb piece is pressed the girl's arm moves, depositing coin through trap door on bench and dog wags his tail and moves his mouth.; cast iron	850	1500	4500
Sportsman, Fowler	Stevens, J.& E.	1892	place a coin in slot, set the trap, place the bird on the trap and push the lever; bird rises in the air and the sportsman fires, downing bird; bank can use paper caps; cast iron	7500	12000	18000
Springing Cat	Charles Bailey	1882	lock cat in place, put coin in slot; pulling lever makes cat move toward coin as a mouse appears, knocks coin into bank, and escapes back into bank, leaving cat w/open jaws; lead and wood	3500	6000	8000
Squirrel and Tree Stump	Mechanical Novelty Works	1881	pressing lever makes squirrel move and drop coin into stump; cast iron	850	1250	2250
Starkie's Aeroplane	Starkie (England)	1919	move plane up pole and lock in place, put coin in slot on plane; pressing lever makes plane coast down pole, dropping coin in bank base; aluminum	1200	1800	3500

Eagle and Eaglets, 1883, J.& E. Stevens

Elephant and Three Clowns, 1883, J.& E. Stevens

Hall's Liliput, 1877, J.& E. Stevens

BANKS

NAME	COMPANY	YEAR	DESCRIPTION	GOOD	VG	EX
Stump Speaker Bank	Shepard Hardware	1886	9-3/4" tall, painted; place coin in hand, press the small knob on top of the box, which lowers the arm and opens the satchel to deposit the coin; release lever and mouth moves up and down; cast iron	850	2200	4500
Tabby Bank	Unknown	1887	cat sits atop large egg, waiting for chick to hatch; drop coin in slot in cat's back and the chick moves its head; cast iron	250	650	1050
Tammany Bank	Stevens, J.& E.	1873	6" tall; fat politician sits in chair, yellow vest, brown jacket, blue pants; put coin in his hand and he drops it into his pocket; cast iron	400	800	3000
Tank and Cannon	Starkie (England)	1919	cannon fires coin into tank bank; cast iron or aluminum	650	900	1500
Teddy and the Bear	Stevens, J.& E.	1907	10" long, painted; cock gun and put coin in it, push bear into tree and close cover; pressing lever makes Teddy lower head in aim, gun fires coin into tree and bear pops up; cast iron	1000	2200	4500
Toad on Stump	Stevens, J.& E.	1886	press lever to open toad's mouth, put coin on mouth and release lever, dropping coin into bank; cast iron	550	875	1650
Tommy Bank	J. Harper & Co.	1914	cock the rifle, lay a coin in front of the launcher and press the lever on top of soldier's left side; the coin is shot into the tree as his head rises; cast iron	2500	3500	6500
Treasure Chest Musical Bank	Faith Mfg.	1930	bronze or silver finish domed chest; wind mechanism, dropping coin in slot makes music play; white metal	300	500	700
Trick Dog Bank (Six-Part Base)	Hubley	1888	deposit coin in dog's mouth; pressing lever makes dog jump through clown's hoop and coin is deposited in his barrel; cast iron	500	800	1800
Trick Dog Bank, Solid Base	Hubley	1920s	deposit coin in dog's mouth; pressing lever makes dog jump through clown's hoop and coin is deposited in his barrel; cast iron	200	450	1000
Trick Pony	Shepard Hardware	1885	7" long, 8" tall; put coin in horse's mouth, pulling lever makes pony drop coin in trough; cast iron	900	1250	3500
Trick Savings Bank	Unknown		5-1/2", deposit coin, coin disappears w/drawer closed; wood	55	125	200
Turtle Bank	Kilgore	1920s	press a coin in the slot and Pokey's neck extends and then returns; cast iron	7500	12000	20000
Uncle Remus	Kyser & Rex	1891	5-3/4" long, painted; deposit coin on roof and press the chicken's head, the policeman moves toward Uncle Remus who slams the door to prevent getting caught; cast iron	1700	2300	3500
Uncle Sam with Carpet Bag	Shepard Hardware	1886	11-1/2" tall; put coin in Sam's hand; pressing lever lowers coin into his carpet bag; cast iron	1000	2800	9500
Uncle Tom, No Star, Lapels	Kyser & Rex	1882	put coin on tongue; pressing lever makes Tom swallow coin and move eyes; cast iron	250	650	1250
Uncle Tom, With Lapels and Star	Kyser & Rex	1882	put coin on tongue; pressing lever makes Tom swallow coin and move eyes; cast iron	250	650	1250
United States and Spain	Stevens, J.& E.	1898	U.S. cannon faces Spanish ship; cock cannon and insert paper cap; pressing lever fires cap and shot which strikes ship's mast while coin drops; cast iron	2000	4500	7500
United States Safe Bank	Stevens, J.& E.	1880	drop coin in slot, making top flip up showing a small bank book in which to write entry of deposit; cast iron	800	2200	4000
Victorian Money Box	Unknown (England)		dropping coin into box makes girl in doorway curtsy; wood	800	1300	1800
Volunteer Bank	J. Harper & Co.	1885	length 10"; cock rifle and put coin in slot; pressing lever makes man fire rifle, shooting coin into tree stump; cast iron	750	1250	1850
Watch Dog Safe	Stevens, J.& E.	1890s	drop coin in top of bank, lift lever, coin falls into the bank as the dog opens his mouth and barks; release and mouth closes; cast iron	350	675	1250

MECHANICAL BANKS

NAME	COMPANY	YEAR	DESCRIPTION	GOOD	VG	EX
William Tell	Stevens, J.& E.	1896	10-1/2" long; lock lever on gun, lower head to aim; lowering boy's arm reveals apple, put coin on gun, press shooter's foot to fire coin into castle, knocking down apple, ringing a gong; cast iron	600	1250	2800
Wimbledon Bank	J. Harper & Co.	1885	cock rifle in reclining redcoat's hands, put coin on barrel; pressing lever shoots coin into tree as soldier's head rises; cast iron	3500	5500	8000
Wireless Bank	Hugo Mfg.	1926	battery operated; putting coin on roof of bank and clapping hands makes cover swing over, dropping coin into bank; Iron, Tin, wood	350	650	850
World's Fair Bank, with Lettering	Stevens, J.& E.	1893	deposit coin on Columbus' feet; pressing lever makes the Indian Chief pop up from log, offering peace pipe as Columbus salutes him; cast iron	850	1250	1850
Zoo Bank	Kyser & Rex	1890s	building bank; put coin in slot; pressing monkey's face makes coin drop and shutters open on lower windows, and faces of lion and tiger appear through windows; cast iron	850	1650	2250

BANKS

Leap Frog Bank, 1891, Shepard Hardware

Magic Bank, 1873, J.& E. Stevens

Memorial Money Bank, 1876, Enterprise

NAME	COMPANY	YEAR	DESCRIPTION	GOOD	EX
$100,000 Money Bag	Unknown		3-5/8" tall, silver gray finish	300	650
1 Pounder Shell Bank	Grey Iron Casting	1918	8" artillery shell, "1 Pounder Bank"	25	95
1876 Bank, Large	Judd, H.L.	1895	3-3/8" tall, building bank w/bronze/copper finish	75	250
1926 Sesquicentennial Bell	Grey Iron Casting	1926	3-3/4" x 3-7/8" diam.	75	200
A.A.O.S.M.S. Shriner's Fez	Allen Mfg.	1920s	2-3/8" red fez w/tassel and gold lettering	250	650
Administration Building	Magic Introduction	1893	5", unpainted	250	650
Air Mail Bank on Base	Dent	1920	6-3/8" tall, red	375	1400
Alamo	Alamo Iron Works	1930s	1-7/8" tall, 3-3/8" wide, unpainted bronze finish	200	450
Alphabet Bank	Unknown		3-1/2", octagonal	1200	3500
Amherst Buffalo	Unknown	1930s	5-1/4" tall, 8" long	150	350
Amish Boy	Wright, John	1970	5" tall, painted	10	65
Amish Boy in White Shirt	Wright, John	1971	5" tall, blue coveralls, black hat	10	65
Amish Girl	Wright, John	1970	5" tall, painted	10	65
Andy Gump	Arcade	1928	4-3/8" tall, Andy sits reading a paper, painted	500	1200
Apollo 8	Wright, John	1968	4-1/4", red, white and blue	20	75
Apollo, Plain	Wright, John	1968	4-1/4", unpainted	20	65
Apple	Kyser & Rex	1882	5-1/4" tall, painted apple on twig w/leaves	600	2400
Arabian Safe	Kyser & Rex	1882	4-9/16" x 4-1/4"	100	300
Armoured Car	Williams, A.C.	1900s	3-3/4" tall, 6-3/4" long, red car on gold wheels	650	3500
Art Deco Elephant	Unknown		4-3/8" tall, red	100	350
Aunt Jemima	Williams, A.C.	1900s	5-7/8", also called Mammy w/Spoon	125	325
Auto	Williams, A.C.	1910?	5-3/4" long, black, red wheels, four passengers	500	1200
Baby in Cradle	Unknown	1890s	3-1/4" tall, rocking cradle	500	1500
Bank of Columbia	Arcade	1800s	4-7/8", unpainted, "Bank of Columbia"	150	375
Bank of England Safe	Kyser & Rex	1882	identical to Egyptian Safe except front is embossed Bank of England	350	750
Barrel	Judd, H.L.	1873	2-3/4" tall	100	225
Baseball on Three Bats	Hubley	1914	5-1/4"	350	1850
Baseball Player	Williams, A.C.	1910s	5-3/4" tall, several colors	200	750
Baseball Player	Williams, A.C.	1909	5-3/4 inches, gold	100	550
Basket Puzzle Bank	Nicol	1894	2-3/4" tall, 3-1/2" wide, unpainted	300	650
Basket Registering Bank, Woven	Braun, Chas. A.	1902	2-7/8" x 3-3/4"	50	125
Basset Hound	Unknown		3-1/8", bronze finish	650	1500
Battleship Maine	Stevens, J. & E.	1901	6" tall, 10-1/4" long, white	500	6000
Battleship Maine	Grey Iron Casting	1800s	5-1/4" tall, 6-5/8" long, "Maine"	650	4500
Battleship Oregon	Stevens, J. & E.	1890s	4-7/8" long, silver finish	200	450
Be Wise Owl	Williams, A.C.	1900s	4-7/8" x 2-1/2"	150	375
Bean Pot	Unknown		3", red cooking pot, nickel registering	150	450
Bear Seated on Log	Unknown		7"	400	950
Bear Stealing Pig	Ober	1913	5-1/2" tall, painted	400	1000
Bear with Honey Pot	Hubley		6-1/2" tall, painted	75	175
Bear, Begging	Williams, A.C.	1900s	5-3/8", bronze finish	75	150
Beehive Bank	Kyser & Rex	1882	2-3/8"	250	500
Beehive Registering Savings Bank	Unknown	1891	5-3/8" x 6-1/2"	200	425
Beehive with Brass Top	Gobeille, W.M.		5-1/2" tall on base, unpainted	350	750

STILL BANKS

NAME	COMPANY	YEAR	DESCRIPTION	GOOD	EX
Bethel College Administration Building	Service Foundry	1935	2-7/8" x 5-1/4"	175	350
Bicentennial Bell	Unknown	1976	4" x 4"	25	45
Billiken	Williams, A.C.	1909	4-1/4" tall, on square base, bronze finish, red cap	55	125
Billiken on Throne	Williams, A.C.	1909	6-1/2" tall	65	175
Billy Bounce	Hubley	1900s	4-11/16" tall, silver painted body	375	1200
Billy Possum ("Possum & Taters")	Harper, J.M.	1909	3" x 4-3/4", on base "Billy Possum"	1200	5500
Bird Bank Building	Unknown		5-7/8" unpainted cupola building w/bird on top, "Bank New York"	650	3500
Bird Cage Bank	Arcade	1900s	3-7/8" tall, similar to Crystal Bank #926, but glass is replaced by open mesh	50	125
Bismark Bank, (Pig)	Unknown	1883	3-3/8", "Bismark Bank"	100	300
Bismark Pig with Rider	Unknown	1880s	7-1/4" tall 6-1/2" long, bronze finish	1000	3500
Boss Tweed	Unknown	1870s	3-7/8" tall	1500	3500
Boston State House	Smith & Egge	1800s	6-3/4" tall, painted	3000	6000
Boxer Bulldog	Hubley	1900s	4-1/2", seated, bronze finish	125	225
Boy Scout	Williams, A.C.	1910s	5-7/8" tall, brown finish	50	150
Boy with Large Football	Hubley	1914	5-1/8" tall, brown	2000	3200
Buckeye (SBCCA)	Filler, Lou	1973	3-1/2", painted "Ohio The Buckeye State", "SBCC 1973"	25	100
Buffalo Bank	Williams, A.C.	1900s	3-1/8" x 4-3/8", gold	50	175
Buffalo Nickel	Knerr, George	1970s	3-7/8"	35	100
Building with Belfry	Kenton		8" tall, in browns	650	4500
Bull on Base	Unknown		4" tall, unpainted	200	450
Bull with Long Horns	Unknown		3-11/16" tall, painted	50	125
Bulldog, Large	Wright, John	1960s	6", painted	25	65
Bulldog, Seated	Hubley	1928	3-7/8"	200	400
Bulldog, Standing	Arcade	1900s	2-1/4", painted	250	450
Bungalow Bank	Grey Iron Casting	1900s	3-3/4" x 3", white cottage w/green roof	225	650
Bust of Man	Unknown		5"	100	350
Buster Brown & Tige	Williams, A.C.	1900s	5-1/2"	100	375
Cadet	Hubley	1905	5-3/4" tall, blue uniform w/gold trim	300	750
Camel, Kneeling	Kyser & Rex	1889	2-1/2" tall, 4-3/4" long	350	1050
Camel, Large	Williams, A.C.	1900s	7-1/4" x 6-1/4"	200	650
Camel, Small	Hubley	1920s	4-3/4" x 3-7/8"	100	225
Camera	Wrightsville Hardware	1888		1000	5000
Camera Bank	Wrightsville Hdw.	1800s	4-5/16" tall, bronze finish bellows camera on tripod	2500	5000
Campbell Kids	Williams, A.C.	1900s	3-5/16" x 4-1/8"	150	350
Cannon	Hubley	1914	3" tall, 6-7/8" long, black cannon on red wheels	2500	5000
Capitalist, The (Everett True)	Ober	1913	5" tall, painted	1200	2000
Capitol Bank	Riverside Foundry	1981	5-1/8"	25	50
Captain Kidd	Unknown	1900s	5-5/8" tall, Kidd stands by tree trunk w/ shovel, base reads "Captain Kidd"	275	850
Carpenter Safe	Harper, J.M.	1907	4-3/8"	2500	5000
Cash Register Savings Bank	Hubley	1906	4-3/4", unpainted, "Cash Register Savings Bank"	500	750
Cash Register Savings Bank	Unknown	1880s	5-5/8" tall, round face on three claw foot feet, "Cash Register Savings Bank"	350	850
Cash Register with Mesh	Arcade	1900s	3-3/4" tall, red finish w/gold-bronze mesh	50	125
Castle Bank, Small	Kyser & Rex	1882	3" x 2-13/16"	200	650
Cat on Tub	Williams, A.C.	1920s	4-1/8" tall, bronze finish	100	200

Mikado, 1886, Kyser & Rex

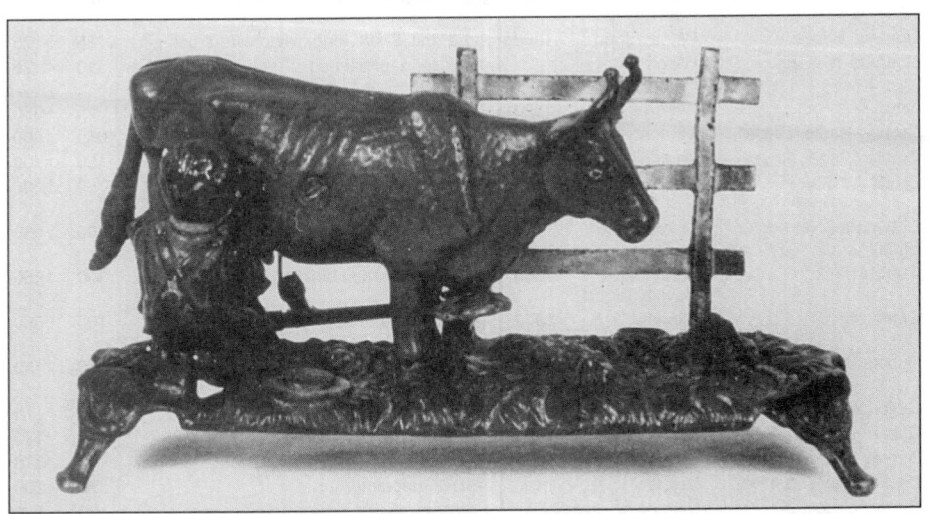

Milking Cow, 1885, J.& E. Stevens

STILL BANKS

NAME	COMPANY	YEAR	DESCRIPTION	GOOD	EX
Cat with Ball	Williams, A.C.	1900s	2-1/2" tall	200	375
Cat with Bow	Hubley	1930s	4-1/8"	275	575
Cat with Bow, Seated	Grey Iron Casting	1922	4-3/8" tall, brown finish	225	475
Cat with Bow, Seated	Wright, John		4-3/8" x 2 7/8", painted, white body, red bow	25	50
Cat with Long Tail	Grey Iron Casting	1910s	4-3/8" tall, 6-3/4" long	375	1250
Cat with Soft Hair, Seated	Arcade	1900s	4-1/4" x 2 7/8"	85	225
Century of Progress Building	Arcade	1933	4-1/2" x 7", white, "A Century Of Progress" building from Chicago World's Fair	800	3000
Champion Safe	Unknown		4-1/8" green and black, "Champion"	125	500
Chanticleer (Rooster)	Unknown	1911	4-5/8", bronze finish, painted face and comb	850	7500
Chicken Feed Bag	Knerr, George	1973	4-5/8", "Chicken Feed"	35	350
Chipmunk with Nut	Unknown		4-1/16", black	300	950
Church Towers	Unknown		6-3/4"	850	1900
Church Window Safe	Shimer Toy	1890s	3 1/16"	50	165
City Bank with Chimney	Unknown	1870s	6-3/4" tall, painted	650	3500
City Bank with Crown	Unknown	1870s	5-1/2" tall	600	4500
City Bank with Teller	Judd, H.L.		5-1/2", bronze finish	400	750
Clown	Williams, A.C.	1908	6-1/4", gold and red w/tall curved hat	125	250
Clown Bust	Knerr, George	1973	4-7/8", painted	100	350
Coca-Cola Bank	Unknown		3-3/8" tall, red and green w/logo	600	2200
Coin Registering Bank	Kyser & Rex	1890	6-3/4" w/red doors and dome	2500	6500
Colonial House with Porch, Large	Williams, A.C.	1900s	4" tall, white	100	375
Colonial House with Porch, Small	Williams, A.C.	1910s	3 " tall, brown finish w/red, green or gold roof	75	250
Columbia	Kenton		4-1/2" tall, silver finish building bank	600	900
Columbia Bank	Kenton	1890s	5-3/4" tall, unpainted silver finish	300	700
Columbia Bank	Kenton	1890s	8-3/4" tall, bronze finish	600	1000
Columbia Magic Savings Bank	Magic Introduction	1892	5", unpainted, "Columbia Magic Savings Bank"	300	700
Columbia Tower	Grey Iron Casting	1897	6-7/8", unpainted three-story tower	450	950
Covered Bridge	Wright, John	1960s	2-1/2" tall, 6-1/8" long, white w/red roof	35	75
Covered Wagon	Wilton Products		6-5/8" long, unpainted	10	25
Cow	Williams, A.C.	1920	3-3/8" x 5-1/4", brown or red finish	75	550
Crosley Radio, Large	Kenton	1930s	5-1/8" tall, green w/gold highlights	650	1800
Crosley Radio, Small	Kenton	1930s	4-5/16" tall, green	150	700
Cross	Unknown		9-1/4" tall, dark finish, "God Is Love" on base	750	2200
Crown Bank on Legs, Small	Unknown		4-5/8", painted	600	950
Cupola Bank	Vermont Novelty Works	1869	5-1/2" tall, painted building w/center roof cupola	300	1250
Cupola Bank	Stevens, J. & E.	1872	4-1/4" x 3-3/8", red and gray	100	850
Cupola Bank	Stevens, J. & E.	1870s	3-1/4" tall, black	75	450
Cutie Dog	Hubley	1914	3-7/8", painted	65	175
Daisy	Shimer Toy	1899	2-1/8" tall, red safe bank	50	175
Darkey Sharecropper	Williams, A.C.	1900s	5-1/2" tall, toes visible on one foot	75	375
Decker's Iowana, (Pig)	Unknown		2-5/16", unpainted	75	200
Derby	Unknown		1-5/8" tall, 3-1/8" long, "Pass Around the Hat"	100	325

STILL BANKS

NAME	COMPANY	YEAR	DESCRIPTION	GOOD	EX
Dime Registering Coin Barrel	Kyser & Rex	1889	4" x 2-1/2", unpainted	125	225
Dime Savings	Shimer Toy	1899	2-1/2" safe, "Dime Savings"	200	425
Dog on Tub	Williams, A.C.	1920s	4-1/16" x 2" diam., bronze finish	125	200
Dog Smoking Cigar	Hubley		4-1/4", painted, white body, red bow tie	450	850
Dolphin Boat Bank	Grey Iron Casting	1900s	4-1/2" tall, sailor boy in boat holds anchor	500	850
Domed Bank	Williams, A.C.	1899	3" tall	20	95
Domed Mosque Bank	Grey Iron Casting	1900s	4-1/4" tall, gold/bronze finish	85	175
Domed Mosque Bank	Grey Iron Casting	1900s	3-1/8" tall, bronze finish	65	145
Donkey	Unknown		3-1/4" tall, black w/red yoke	100	200
Donkey "I Made St. Louis Famous"	Arcade	1903	4-11/16" tall, gray finish	800	1800
Donkey on Base	Unknown		6-9/16" tall	250	650
Donkey with Blanket	Kenton	1930s	3-7/8" tall, painted, gray w/red blanket	450	950
Donkey, Large	Williams, A.C.	1920s	6-13/16" tall, painted	150	450
Donkey, Small	Arcade	1910s	4-1/2" tall, blue, gold or gray finish	85	200
Dormer Bank	Unknown		4-3/4" tall, painted building bank w/red roof	3500	6000
Double Door	Williams, A.C.	1900s	5-7/16" building w/two doors, painted white w/gold highlights	200	425
Doughboy	Grey Iron Casting	1919	7" tall, painted World War I soldier	350	850
Dry Sink	Wright, John	1970	3" x 2-3/4", dark finish	25	45
Duck	Hubley	1930s	4-3/4", white painted body	150	275
Duck Bank	Williams, A.C.	1900s	4-7/8", unpainted	150	275
Duck on Tub "Save for a Rainy Day"	Hubley	1930s	5-3/8"	95	450
Duck, Round	Kenton	1930s	4" tall, painted, yellow body, red beak and top of head	225	650
Dutch Boy	Grey Iron Casting		6-3/4" tall	600	850
Dutch Boy	Unknown		8-1/4" tall, doorstop conversion	150	275
Dutch Boy on Barrel	Hubley	1930s	5-5/8"	75	275
Dutch Girl	Grey Iron Casting		6-1/2" tall, bronze finish	600	850
Dutch Girl Holding Flowers	Hubley	1930s	5-1/2" tall, painted, iron trap in base	100	275
Eagle Bank Building	Unknown		9-3/4" tall, painted building w/gold eagle on roof	450	1250
Eagle with Ball, Building	Unknown		10-3/4" tall, building w/eagle and ball on roof	850	6500
Edison Bust	Blevins, Charlotte	1972	5-5/16"	35	65
Eggman (Wm. Howard Taft)	Arcade	1910	4-1/8" tall	850	3500
Egyptian Tomb	Kyser & Rex	1882	6-1/4 " square safe on base, decorated w/Sphinx and obelisk on front, sides show, pyramid, walled ruins and urn w/ flowers, gold	450	750
Electric Railroad	Shimer Toy	1893	8-1/4" long	2500	6000
Elephant on Bench on Tub	Williams, A.C.	1920s	3-7/8"	125	225
Elephant on Tub	Williams, A.C.	1920s	5-3/8", in bronze finish	100	185
Elephant on Tub, Decorated	Williams, A.C.	1920s	5-3/8", painted version of #483	125	200
Elephant on Wheels	Williams, A.C.	1920s	4" tall, unpainted	150	300
Elephant Trumpeting	Wright, John	1971	7-1/4" tall, black finish	15	35
Elephant with Bent Knee	Kenton	1904	3-1/2", tan finish	200	375

Punch and Judy, Large Letters, 1884, Shepard Hardware

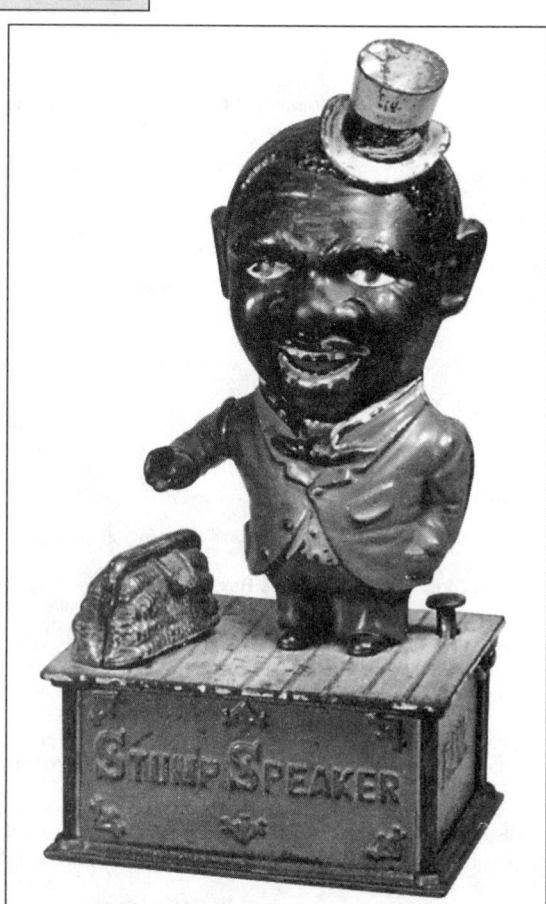

Stump Speaker Bank, 1886, Shepard Hardware

NAME	COMPANY	YEAR	DESCRIPTION	GOOD	EX
Elephant with Chariot, Large	Hubley	1900s	4-3/4" tall, also made without chariot	2000	3000
Elephant with Chariot, Small	Hubley	1906	7" long, gray elephant, red chariot, yellow wheels	1400	2200
Elephant with Howdah, Large	Williams, A.C.	1900s	4-7/8" x 6-3/8"	65	125
Elephant with Howdah, Large	Williams, A.C.	1900s	6-3/4", gold	85	150
Elephant with Howdah, Short Trunk	Hubley	1910	3-3/4" tall, painted gray w/red belt	125	275
Elephant with Howdah, Small	Williams, A.C.	1900s	3-1/2" x 5"	65	125
Elephant with Raised Slot	Unknown		4-1/2" tall, gray body, gold blanket	150	350
Elephant with Swivel Trunk	Unknown		2-1/2", black finish w/gold swivel trunk	125	250
Elephant with Tin Chariot	Wing	1900s	8" long, red chariot	1000	1600
Elephant with Tucked Trunk	Arcade	1900s	2-3/4" x 4-5/8", red or green	65	125
Elephant with Turned Trunk, Seated	Unknown		4-1/4", unpainted	450	950
Elephant, "GOP 1936"	Hubley	1936	3-1/2" tall, "GOP 1936"	750	1200
Elephant, Circus	Hubley	1930s	3-7/8", painted, w/lavender pants and red dotted white shirt	150	350
Elf	Unknown		10" tall, painted, converted doorstop	150	450
English Setter	Wright, John	1970	8-1/2" tall, black	125	275
Fidelity Safe, Large	Kyser & Rex	1880	3-5/8" tall, green w/gold trim, "Fidelity Safe"	150	300
Fidelity Trust Vault, Lord Fauntleroy	Barton Smith Co.	1890	6-1/2" x 5-7/8"	300	650
Fido	Hubley	1914	5", painted, white body, black eyes and ears, red collar	60	225
Fido on Pillow	Hubley	1920s	7-3/8" long, painted	100	550
Finial Bank	Kyser & Rex	1887	5-3/4" tall, 4-3/8" wide, building bank w/ single finial on roof	275	1400
Flags Bank (SBCCA)	Littlestown Harware	1976	3-1/4" tall, 6" square white pyramid w/ color US flags	75	125
Flat Iron Building Bank	Kenton	1900s	5-1/2" tall, silver	135	450
Floral Safe (National Safe)	Stevens, J. & E.	1898	4-5/8" x 4-1/8"	125	350
Football Player	Williams, A.C.	1910s	5-7/8" tall, bronze finish	250	550
Foreman	Grey Iron Casting	1951	4-1/2", painted	175	350
Fort	Unknown	1910s	4-1/8", unpainted bronze finish	125	275
Fort Mt. Hope	Unknown		2-7/8" tall	125	425
Four Tower	Stevens, J. & E.		5-3/4", unpainted w/gold highlights	125	450
Four Tower	Ohio Foundry	1949	5-3/8", painted white building w/red roof	35	85
Foxy Grandpa	Hubley	1920s	5-1/2" tall, painted	150	375
Frog	Iron Art	1973	4-1/8", deep green finish	75	125
Frowning Face	Unknown		5-5/8" tall, hanging bank, chin drops below surface level	850	1750
G.E. Radio Bank	Arcade	1930s	3-3/4" tall, brown cabinet radio on four legs	125	325
G.E. Refrigerator, Small	Hubley	1930s	3-3/4", blue	75	225
Gas Pump	Unknown		5-3/4" tall, red	275	650
Gem Stove	Abendroth Bros.		4-3/4", brown finish	75	175
General Butler	Stevens, J. & E.	1884	6-1/2" tall, painted head on frog body	1500	3500

BANKS

BANKS

NAME	COMPANY	YEAR	DESCRIPTION	GOOD	EX
General Pershing Bust	Grey Iron Casting	1918	7-3/4" tall, bronze finish	75	175
General Sheridan on Base	Arcade	1910s	6" tall, General seated on rearing horse	250	650
George Washington Bust on Safe	Harper, J.M.	1903	5-7/8" tall	1000	2500
Gettysburg Bank	Wilton Products	1960	4-3/4" x 7-1/4" gray monument w/ reclining soldier	75	200
Give Me A Penny	Hubley	1900s	5-1/2" tall Black figure in hat, painted	200	450
Globe Bank With Eagle	Enterprise Mfg.	1875	5-3/4", red w/eagle on globe	125	450
Globe on Arc	Grey Iron Casting	1900s	5-1/4" tall, red	100	300
Globe on Claw Feet	Kenton		6"	175	375
Globe on Hand	Unknown	1893	4", bronze finish	375	1275
Globe on Wire Arc	Arcade	1900s	4-5/8" tall, painted spinning globe, red continents	125	450
Globe Safe with Hinged Door	Kenton	1900s	5"	100	250
Globe Savings Fund Bank	Kyser & Rex	1889	7-1/8", painted "Globe Savings Fund 1888"	1800	4000
Gold Eagle	Wright, John	1970	5-3/4"	5	20
Good Luck Horseshoe	Arcade	1908	4-1/4" tall, Buster Brown & Tige w/ horse inside horseshoe	150	550
Goose Bank	Arcade	1920s	3-3/4", unpainted	85	175
Graf Zeppelin	Williams, A.C.	1920s	6-5/8" long, silver gray finish	85	375
Graf Zeppelin on Wheels	Williams, A.C.	1934	7-3/4" long silver pull toy bank	150	475
Grandpa's Hat	Unknown		2-1/4" tall, 3-7/8" wide, top hat	225	450
Grenade with Pin	Bartlett Mayward		4-1/4"	85	175
Gunboat	Kenton		8-1/2" long, blue hull, white top, twin masts	650	1800
Hall Clock	Arcade	1923	5-5/8" tall, dark finish w/gold highlights	300	700
Hall Clock	Hubley	1900s	5-1/4" tall, brown finish, paper face	275	475
Hall Clock with Cast Face	Hubley	1920s	5-3/26" tall	275	425
Hanging Mailbox	Williams, A.C.	1920s	5-1/8" tall, green, wall mount mailbox replica, gold lettering	65	175
Hanging Mailbox on Platform	Unknown	1800s	7-1/4" tall, red box hangs on post in platform base	650	1500
Hard Hat	Knerr, George	1970s	1-15/16" tall, white w/red lettering	100	250
Harleysville Bank	Unicast Foundry	1959	2-5/8" tall, 5-1/4" long, white w/gray roof	75	225
Hen on Nest	Unknown	1900s	3", bronze finish w/red highlights	100	1750
High Rise Building	Kenton		7" tall	200	550
High Rise, Tiered	Kenton		5-3/4"	125	350
Hippo	Unknown		2" tall, 5-3/16" long, bronze w/red highlights	3500	6000
Holstein Cow	Arcade	1910s	2-1/2" tall, 4-5/8" long, black finish	125	650
Home Bank	Judd, H.L.	1890s	4" x 3-1/2", dark finish	175	500
Home Bank with Crown	Stevens, J. & E.	1872	5-1/4", painted, "Home Bank"	475	1400
Home Savings Bank	Unknown		10-1/2" painted, "Property of Peoples Savings Bank, Grand Rapids, Mich."	175	650
Home Savings Bank	Shimer Toy	1899	5-7/8", painted	150	525
Home Savings Bank	Unknown		9-5/8" tall, painted	175	650
Home Savings Bank with Dog Finial	Stevens, J. & E.	1891	5-3/4" tall	125	550
Home Savings Bank with Finial	Stevens, J. & E.	1891	3-1/2" tall, mustard finish	125	375
Honey Bear	Unknown		2-1/2", silver finish unpainted bear sits eating honey	675	1200

Dutch Girl, Grey Iron Casting

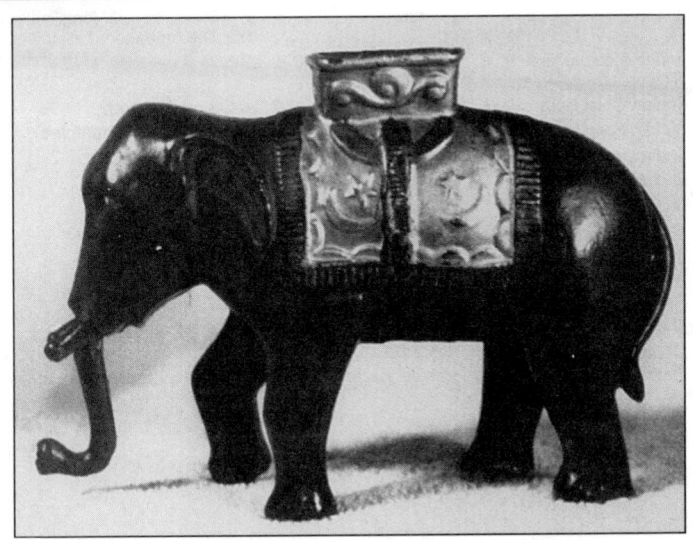

*Elephant with
Swivel Trunk*

STILL BANKS

NAME	COMPANY	YEAR	DESCRIPTION	GOOD	EX
Hoover/Curtis Elephant "GOP"	Hubley	1928	3-3/8", ivory finish	675	1600
Horse on Tub, Decorated	Williams, A.C.	1920s	5-5/6"	135	300
Horse on Wheels	Williams, A.C.	1920	4-1/4", deep red finish	150	450
Horse, "Beauty"	Arcade	1900s	4-1/8" x 4-3/4", black w/raised "Beauty" on side	85	175
Horse, Prancing	Arcade	1910s	4-1/4" tall, black w/gray hooves	55	150
Horse, Prancing with Belly Band	Unknown		4-1/2", light bronze finish	175	375
Horse, Prancing, Large	Williams, A.C.	1910s	7-3/16" tall, bronze finish	75	165
Horse, Rearing on Oval Base	Williams, A.C.	1920s	5-1/8" x 4-7/8"	95	250
Horse, Rearing on Pebbled Base	Unknown		7-1/4" x 6-1/2", gold finish	85	165
Horseshoe with Mesh	Williams, A.C.		Horse head inside horseshoe that forms end of mesh coin cage, bronze finish	65	145
Hot Point Electric Stove	Arcade	1925	6", white, on legs	350	1250
House with Basement	Ohio Foundry Co.	1893	4-5/8" square, painted	850	1800
House with Bay Window	Unknown	1874	5-5/8" tall, painted	900	2200
House with Chimney Slot	Unknown		2-7/8" x 2-13/16", painted	275	850
House with Knight	Unknown		7-1/4" unpainted "Savings Bank" w/ knight figure on roof peak	375	950
Hub	Magic Introduction	1892	5" x 5-1/4" x 1-5/8"	300	850
Humphrey-Muskie Donkey	Unknown	1968	4-1/2" tall, pale silver finish, "Humphrey Muskie 68"	10	35
Humpty Dumpty	Unknown	1930s	5-1/2" tall, painted, white egg, red brick wall	375	850
Humpty Dumpty, Seated	Russell, Edward K.	1974	5-3/8" tall, painted	75	125
Husky	Grey Iron Casting	1910s	5"	200	550
I Made Chicago Famous, Large Pig	Harper, J.M.	1902	2-5/8" x 5-5/16"	250	550
I Made Chicago Famous, Small Pig	Harper, J.M.	1902	2-1/8" x 4-1/8"	200	400
Ice Box	Arcade		4-1/4" tall, white, "Save For Ice"	175	650
Independence Hall	Enterprise Mfg.	1875	10" tall, deep red/brown finish	450	1150
Independence Hall	Unknown	1875	8-1/8" tall, 15-1/2" long, mustard building on base w/bell tower	1800	3500
Independence Hall Tower	Enterprise Mfg.	1876	9-1/2"	225	525
Indian Chief Bust	Unknown	1978	4-7/8", unpainted	35	85
Indian Family	Harper, J.M.	1905	3-5/8" x 5-1/8", unpainted	850	2800
Indian Head Penny	Knerr, George	1972	3-1/4" diam.	35	75
Indian Seated on Log	Ouve, A.	1970s	3-5/8" tall, unpainted	85	150
Indian with Tomahawk	Hubley	1900s	5-7/8"	175	550
Indiana Paddle Wheeler	Unknown	1896	7-1/8" long, black w/red trim	4000	8000
International Eagle on Globe	Unknown		8" x 8", unpainted	1200	2500
Ironmaster's House	Kyser & Rex	1884	4-1/2", unpainted	600	2200
Japanese Safe	Kyser & Rex	1883	5-1/2" tall, painted	125	375
Japanese Safe	Kyser & Rex	1882	5-3/8" tall	100	300
Jarmulowsky Building	Stevens, J. & E.		7-3/4" tall, bronze finish building bank	1200	2800
Jewel Safe	Stevens, J. & E.	1907	5-3/8", unpainted	125	350
John Brown Fort	Unknown		3" tall, red w/white cupola	85	135

NAME	COMPANY	YEAR	DESCRIPTION	GOOD	EX
Junior Cash Register, Small	Stevens, J. & E.	1920s	5-1/4" x 4-5/8" elaborate cast w/slot at top	175	375
Kelvinator Bank	Arcade	1930s	#832, 4-1/2" tall, white w/gray trim replica refrigerator	150	375
Key	Somerville, W.J.	1905	5-1/2" long, silver finish skeleton key	250	650
Key, St. Louis World's Fair	Unknown	1904	5-3/4" long, dark finish	275	700
King Midas	Hubley	1930s	4-1/2" tall, painted	1250	2500
Kitty Bank	Hubley	1930s	4-3/4" tall, painted, white body w/blue bow	65	150
Klondyke	Unknown		3-1/4" cube	650	1400
Kodak Bank	Stevens, J. & E.	1905	4-1/4" tall, 5" wide, "Kodak Bank"	200	450
L'il Tot	Watkins, Bob	1982	5-7/8"	125	175
Labrador Retriever	Unknown		4-1/2" black finish w/gold collar	125	375
Lamb	Wright, John	1970	3-1/4" tall, painted white w/black highlights	35	75
Lamb, Small	Unknown		3-3/16", painted white	200	375
Laughing Pig	Hubley		2-1/2", painted	125	275
Liberty Bell	Harper, J.M.	1905	3-3/4"	275	550
Liberty Bell with Yoke	Arcade	1920s	3-1/2"	25	65
Liberty Bell, Miniature	Penncraft		3-1/2" x 1-3/4"	20	35
Lighthouse	Lane Art	1950s	9-1/2" tall, "Light of the World"	125	250
Lighthouse	Unknown	1891	10-1/4" tall, red tower rises from unpainted base	1200	5500
Limousine	Arcade	1921	same as #1478, but w/steel wheels	1200	2800
Limousine	Arcade	1920s	8-1/16" long, black w/white rubber tires	750	2500
Limousine Yellow Cab	Arcade	1921	repaint of #1478	1400	2800
Lincoln High Hat	Unknown	1880s	2-3/8" tall, black finish, "Pass Around the Hat"	125	225
Lion on Tub, Decorated	Williams, A.C.	1920s	5-1/2" tall	125	225
Lion on Tub, Plain	Williams, A.C.	1920s	7-1/2" tall, bronze finish	100	200
Lion on Tub, Small	Williams, A.C.	1920s	4-1/8" tall, brown or green finish	85	175
Lion on Wheels	Williams, A.C.	1920s	4-1/2" x 5-1/2", gold	145	225
Lion, Ears Up	Williams, A.C.	1930s	3-5/8" x 4-1/2"	75	125
Lion, Small	Williams, A.C.	1934	2-1/2" x 3-5/8"	85	150
Lion, Tail Between Legs	Unknown		3" x 5-1/4"	85	145
Lion, Tail Left	Hubley	1910s	3-3/4" tall, bronze finish	100	175
Lion, Tail Right	Arcade	1900s	4" tall	55	100
Lion, Tail Right	Williams, A.C.	1900s	5-1/4" tall, bronze finish	55	150
Lion, Tail Right	Williams, A.C.	1920s	3-1/2" x 4-15/16"	55	100
Little Red Riding Hood Safe	Harper, J.M.	1907	5-1/16" tall, painted	2000	4000
Log Cabin	Kyser & Rex	1882	2-1/2" x 3-1/4", painted	175	550
Lost Dog	Judd H.L.	1890s	5-3/8", unpainted	275	850
Lucky Cabin	Wright, John	1970	4-1/8" tall, painted w/horseshoe over door	35	65
Mailbox on Legs, Large	Hubley	1920s	5-1/2" tall, green street corner box replica	85	225
Mailbox on Legs, Small	Hubley	1928	3-3/4" tall, green replica street corner mailbox	35	100
Main Street Trolley with People	Williams, A.C.	1920s	3" x 6-3/4" bronze finish	175	475
Main Street Trolley without People	Williams, A.C.	1920s	6-3/4" long	175	400
Majestic Radio Bank	Arcade	1930s	4-1/2" tall, mahogany finish replica of a floor standing radio on four legs, coin slot in back, w/key	125	200

BANKS

Indian with Tomahawk, 1900s, Hubley

*Mammy with Hands on Hips,
1900s, Hubley*

STILL BANKS

NAME	COMPANY	YEAR	DESCRIPTION	GOOD	EX
Majestic Refrigerator Bank	Arcade	1930s	4-1/2" tall, in red, green or blue w/gold trim, replica of single door fridge on four legs, coin slot in back, w/key lock	375	600
Mammy	Unknown	1970s	8-1/4" tall, doorstop conversion, red dress, white apron	10	25
Mammy with Hands on Hips	Hubley	1900s	5-1/4" tall, red dress, white apron	85	400
Man in Barrel	Stevens, J. & E.	1890s	3-3/4" tall, painted	175	550
Man on Cotton Bale	US Hardware	1898	4-7/8" tall, painted darkie sits on hay bale, red scarf, yellow pants	1500	3500
Marietta Silo	Unknown		5-1/2" gray finish	275	850
Marshall Stove	Unknown		3-7/8", red	125	225
Mary & Little Lamb	Unknown	1901	4-3/8" tall, painted white w/red trim	350	1500
Mascot	Hubley	1914	5-3/4" tall, boy stands on baseball	850	2400
McKinley/Teddy Elephant	Unknown	1900	2-1/2" tall, bronze finish	650	2200
Mean Standing Bear	Hubley		5-1/2"	100	225
Mellow Furnace	Liberty Toy		3-9/16" x 3-1/8", brown finish	125	225
Mermaid Boat	Grey Iron Casting	1900s	4-1/2" tall, companion piece to Dolphin, girl in boat holds fish	350	850
Merry-Go-Round	Grey Iron Casting	1920s	4-5/8" tall, unpainted	175	550
Metropolitan Bank	Stevens, J. & E.	1872	5-7/8", "Metropolitan Bank"	125	275
Mickey Mouse	Wright, John	1970s	5" x 3-3/4" bookend bank, painted	85	150
Mickey Mouse, Hands on Hips	Unknown		9" tall, painted	125	450
Middy with Clapper	Unknown	1887	5-1/4" brown finish	150	350
Minuteman	Hubley	1905	6" tall, painted	200	650
Model T Ford	Arcade	1920s	4" tall, black	650	1250
Moody & Sankey	Smith & Egge	1870	5" painted, two oval portraits on front	800	3500
Mosque, Large, Three-Story	Williams, A.C.	1920s	3-1/2" tall	45	125
Mosque, Small, Two-Story	Unknown		2-7/8" tall	35	115
Mother Hubbard Safe	Harper, J.M.	1907	4-1/2" tall	1500	5000
Mulligan Policeman (Keystone Cop)	Williams, A.C.	1900s	5-3/4", painted	175	400
Multiplying Bank	Stevens, J. & E.	1883	6-1/2" painted building	700	3500
Mutt & Jeff	Williams, A.C.	1900s	4-1/4" x 3-1/2", gold	75	275
National Safe	Stevens, J. & E.	1800s	3-3/8" tall, unpainted	65	125
Nest Egg	Smith & Egge	1873	3-3/8" tall on base, bronze finish egg on side, "Horace"	450	850
Nesting Doves Safe	Harper, J.M.	1907	5-1/4", bronze finish	1500	3500
New Heatrola Bank	Kenton	1920s	4-1/2" tall, green finish w/red trim	85	375
Newfoundland Dog	Arcade	1930s	3-5/8" x 5-3/8", blue or green finish	100	225
Newfoundland Dog with Pack	Unknown		4-11/16" tall	85	175
Nixe	Unknown		4-1/2" tall, silver boy in boat, "Nixe"	350	1450
Nixon Bust	Blevins, Charlotte	1972	5-5/16"	45	85
Nixon/Agnew Elephant	Unknown	1968	2-5/8"	15	35
North Pole Bank	Grey Iron Casting	1920s	4-1/4", unpainted, "Save Your Money And Freeze It"	375	775
Oak Stove	Shimer Toy	1899	2-3/8" tall, unpainted	125	475
Old Abe with Shield, Eagle	Unknown	1880	3-7/8", unpainted	450	1300
Old South Church	Unknown		10" tall, bronze finish	2000	5000

STILL BANKS

NAME	COMPANY	YEAR	DESCRIPTION	GOOD	EX
One Car Garage	Williams, A.C.	1920s	2-1/2", painted	125	350
One Story House	Grey Iron Casting	1900s	3" tall	65	175
Oregon Gunboat	Kenton		11" long, blue hull, gray guns, black and red stacks, "Oregon"	850	1800
Organ Grinder	Hubley		6-3/16" x 2-1/8", painted	125	350
Oriental Boy on Pillow	Hubley	1920s	5-1/2" tall, painted	85	200
Oriental Camel	Unknown		3-3/4" tall, on rockers	300	875
Ornate Hall Clock	Hubley	1900s	5-7/8" tall, tan finish, paper face	200	425
Osborn Pig	Unknown		2" x 4", "You can bank on the Osborn..."	100	350
Oscar the Goat	Unknown		7-3/4" tall, black w/silver hooves and horns	75	175
Owl	Vindex Toys	1930	4-1/4", painted	75	325
Owl on Stump	Unknown		3-5/8", red	65	125
Ox	Kenton		4-3/8", painted	85	150
Palace	Ives	1885	7-1/2" tall, 8" wide	850	3500
Park Bank Building	Unknown		4-3/8" painted	450	2200
Parlor Stove	Unknown		6-7/8", gray and black	275	425
Parrot on Stump	Unknown		6-1/4", painted	125	450
Pavillion	Kyser & Rex	1880	3-1/8" x 3"	225	550
Pay Phone Bank	Stevens, J. & E.	1926	7-3/16", unpainted	450	1800
Pearl Street Bank	Unknown		4-1/4", unpainted, silver finish	350	1400
Peg Legged Pirate	Unknown		5-1/4", unpainted	25	85
Pelican	Hubley	1930s	4-3/4", painted white	350	1500
Penny Register Pail	Kyser & Rex	1889	2-3/4", unpainted	125	250
Penthouse Building	Williams, A.C.		5-7/8" tall, silver finish	350	850
Peters Weatherbird	Arcade		4-1/4" tall	750	2500
Phoenix Dime Register Trunk	Piaget	1890	3-3/4" x 5" steamer trunk	125	250
Pig, A Christmas Roast	Unknown		3-1/4" x 7-1/8"	85	250
Pig, Seated	Williams, A.C.	1900s	3" x 4-9/16"	35	125
Plymouth Rock 1620	Unknown		3-7/8" long, "1620"	650	1850
Polar Bear, Begging	Arcade	1900s	5-1/4", white	275	450
Policeman Bank	Arcade	1930s	5-5/8" tall, blue w/aluminum finish on gloves and star, gold buttons, black shoes, flesh face and hands	250	1000
Policeman Safe	Harper, J.M.	1907	5-1/4"	1250	4500
Polish Rooster	Unknown		5-1/2" tall, painted	850	2200
Pooh Bank	Unknown		5" x 4-7/8"	5	15
Possum	Arcade	1910s	2-3/8" tall, 4-3/8" long, silver finish	125	575
Postal Savings Mailbox	Nicol	1920s	6-3/4"	85	275
Pot Bellied Stove	Knerr, George	1968	5-3/4" tall, flat black finish	25	65
Potato	Martin, Mary A.	1897	5-1/4" long, "Bank"	850	1850
Presto Bank	Williams, A.C.	1900s	3-5/8" tall, silver finish w/gold dome	85	175
Presto Bank	Unknown		4-1/4" tall building, silver w/gold dome	85	175
Presto Bank	Unknown		3-1/4" tall, silver finish, "Bank"	65	150
Presto Trick Bank	Kyser & Rex	1894	4-1/2" tall, red doors and roof	250	950
Professor Pug Frog Bank	Williams, A.C.	1900s	3-1/4"	275	550
Pugdog, Seated	Kyser & Rex	1889	3-1/2", painted	250	475
Puppo	Hubley	1920s	4-7/8" tall, painted bee on body	125	250
Puppo on Pillow	Hubley	1920s	5-5/8" x 6", painted brown, cream, black, pink	150	275
Put Money in Thy Purse	Unknown	1886	2-3/4" tall change purse, black	625	950
Puzzle Try Me	Unknown	1868	2-11/16" tall, safe, "Puzzle Try Me"	475	975
Quadrafoil House	Several Makers	1900s	3-1/8" tall	125	225
Queen Stove	Wright, John	1975	3-3/4" to cook top, "Queen" on oven door	25	65

Pavillion, 1880, Kyser & Rex

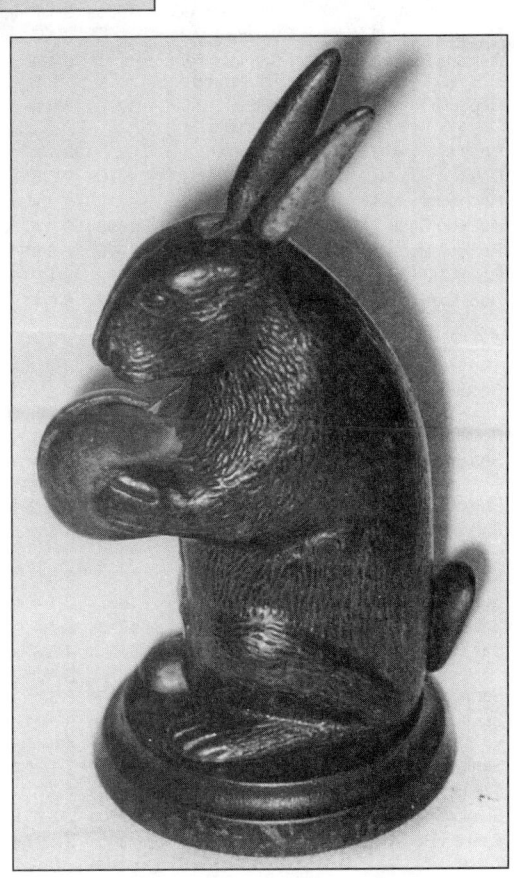

Rabbit Standing, large, 1908, A.C. Williams

STILL BANKS

NAME	COMPANY	YEAR	DESCRIPTION	GOOD	EX
Quilted Lion	Unknown		3-3/4" tall, 4-3/4" long, bronze finish	185	450
Rabbit Lying Down	Unknown		2-1/8" x 5-1/8", unpainted	175	575
Rabbit Standing, Large	Williams, A.C.	1908	6-1/4" tall, brown metal finish	125	325
Rabbit with Carrot	Knerr, George	1972	3-3/8", painted white, orange and green carrot	85	200
Rabbit, Begging	Williams, A.C.	1900s	5-1/8"	85	275
Rabbit, Large, Seated	Hubley	1900s	4-5/8" tall, painted white w/pink highlights	125	375
Rabbit, Small, Seated	Arcade	1910s	3-5/8" tall	125	325
Radio Bank	Hubley	1928	3-5/16" tall, metallic blue	100	375
Radio Bank with Three Dials	Kenton	1920s	3" tall, 4-5/8" long, red	100	350
Radio with Combination Door	Kenton	1930s	4-1/2" red, metal sides and back	125	375
Reclining Cow	Unknown		2-1/8" tall, 4" long, black	100	400
Recording Bank	Unknown		6-5/8" x 4-1/4"	200	575
Red Ball Safe	Unknown		3", red ball on base	175	425
Red Goose Shoes on Base	Arcade	1920s	5-1/2", on pedestal w/base	300	750
Red Goose Shoes on Pedestal	Unknown		4-7/16" red goose on bronze base	175	350
Red Goose Shoes, Squatty	Arcade	1920s	4" tall, red body, yellow feet	275	500
Reindeer on Base	Wright, John	1973	10" x 8"	75	125
Reindeer, Large	Williams, A.C.	1900s	9-1/2" tall, bronze finish	125	250
Reindeer, Small	Williams, A.C.		6-1/4" tall, bronze finish	75	150
Reliable Parlor Stove	Schneider & Trenkramp		6-1/4"	425	850
Republic Pig	Wilton Products	1970s	7" tall, painted pig in business suit	35	85
Rhesus Monkey	Unknown		8-1/2" converted doorstop, painted	35	125
Rhino	Arcade	1910s	2-5/8" tall, 5" long, gold	225	650
Rochester Clock	Unknown		5" tall w/working clock	225	750
Rocking Chair	Manning, C.J.	1898	6-3/4" tall, brown finish	1500	2750
Rocking Horse	Knerr, George	1975	5-5/8", white w/red saddle, "SBCC"	350	550
Roller Safe	Kyser & Rex	1882	3-11/16" x 2-7/8"	125	245
Roof Bank	Stevens, J. & E.	1887	5-1/4" x 3-3/4"	125	450
Roof Bank	Grey Iron Casting	1900s	5-1/4"	125	300
Rooster	Hubley/ Williams	1910s	4-3/4", brown finish w/red comb and wattle	125	350
Rooster	Arcade	1910s	4-5/8", black w/red comb	125	400
Rooster, Large	Unknown	1913	6-3/4", unpainted except for red comb and wattle	550	1250
Rumplestiltskin	Unknown	1910s	6" x 2-1/4"	200	500
Saddle Horse	Grey Iron Casting	1928	4-3/8" tall	375	650
Safe Deposit	Shimer Toy	1899	3-5/8", "Safe Deposit"	85	150
Safety Locomotive	Unknown	1887	3-1/4" tall, gray	650	2200
Sailor, Medium	Hubley	1910s	5-1/4" tall	225	475
San Gabriel Mission	Unknown		4-5/8" x 3-3/4", painted, musical building	2000	7500
Santa Claus	Hubley	1900s	5-3/4", painted w/arms folded in front	450	950
Santa Claus with Tree	Hubley	1910s	5-3/4" tall, arms folded in front, tree at back, painted	450	950
Santa with Wire Tree	Ives	1890s	7-1/4" tall, w/removable ornate tree	875	1500
Scottie, Seated	Hubley	1930s	4-7/8" x 6", black finish, red collar	125	300
Scrollwork Safe	Unknown	1900s	2-3/4" tall	85	225
Seal on Rock	Arcade	1900s	3-1/2", black	175	500

STILL BANKS

NAME	COMPANY	YEAR	DESCRIPTION	GOOD	EX
Security Safe	Unknown	1894	4-1/2" tall, red door	125	275
Security Safe Deposit	Unknown	1881	3-7/8" tall	95	150
Shell Out	Stevens, J. & E.	1882	4-3/4" long, conch shell on base, off white	225	850
Show Horse	Lane Chair	1973	5-7/8" tall	75	150
Six Sided Building, Two Story	Unknown		3-3/8" tall	100	275
Six-Sided Building	Unknown		2-3/8" tall, unpainted	225	650
Skyscraper Bank	Williams, A.C.	1900s	5-1/2" tall, silver building, four gold posts	85	150
Skyscraper Bank	Williams, A.C.	1900s	4-3/8" tall, silver building, four gold posts	85	125
Skyscraper with Six Posts	Williams, A.C.	1900s	6-1/2" tall, silver building, gold posts	125	450
Songbird on Stump	Williams, A.C.	1900s	4-3/4", bronze finish	300	950
Space Heater with Bird	Chamberlain & Hill	1890s	English, 6-1/2" tall	175	375
Space Heater with Flowers	Unknown	1890s	English, 6-1/2" tall, Far East motif, red finish	175	375
Spaniel, Large	Wright, John	1960s	10-1/2" long, painted	65	125
Spitz	Grey Iron Casting	1928	4-1/4", bronze finish	225	575
Squirrel with Nut	Unknown		4-1/8"	425	1250
St. Bernard with Pack, Large	Williams, A.C.	1900s	5-1/2" x 7-3/4"	125	225
St. Bernard with Pack, Small	Williams, A.C.	1900s	3-3/4" x 5-1/2"	85	175
Star Safe	Kyser & Rex	1882	2-5/8" tall	150	450
State Bank	Kenton	1900	8" x 7"	550	1200
State Bank	Kenton	1890s	3" tall, unpainted building bank	95	200
State Bank	Arcade	1910s	4-1/8" tall, bronze finish	85	175
State Bank	Kyser & Rex	1890s	5-1/2" tall, bronze building bank	125	325
Statue of Liberty	Williams, A.C.		6-3/8" tall	85	125
Statue of Liberty	Kenton	1900s	6-3/8" tall, silver finish w/gold highlights	100	175
Statue of Liberty	Kenton	1900s	6-1/16" tall	85	125
Statue of Liberty, Large	Kenton	1900s	9-1/2" tall, silver gray finish, gold highlights	350	1200
Steamboat	Williams, A.C.	190s	7-5/8" long, brown finish	125	375
Steamboat with Small Wheels	Kenton		7-7/16" long, silver finish	175	425
Stop Sign	Dent	1920	5-5/8" tall, green w/red and gold highlights	325	1450
Stork Safe	Harper, J.M.	1907	5-1/2"	850	1750
Street Car	Grey Iron Casting	1891	4-1/2" long, painted	250	650
Sun Dial	Arcade	1900s	4-5/16" tall	650	2000
Sunbonnet Sue	Unknown	1970	7-1/2", painted	65	165
Tabernacle Savings	Keyless Lock Co.		2-1/4" x 5", unpainted	850	1250
Taft-Sherman Bust	Harper, J.M.	1908	4" tall, one side Smiling Jim, other side Peaceful Bill	1000	2200
Tank Bank 1918, Large	Williams, A.C.	1920s	3" tall x 3-11/16" long, gold finish	100	200
Tank Bank 1918, Small	Williams, A.C.	1920s	2-3/8"long, gold finish	65	150
Tank Bank 1919	Unknown		3" x 5-1/2", silver finish, "1919"	125	350
Tank Savings Bank	Ferrosteel	1919	9-1/2" long, "Tank Savings Bank"	175	525
Teddy Bear	Arcade	1900	2-1/2" x 3-7/8"	125	350
Teddy Roosevelt Bust	Williams, A.C.	1919	5" tall	175	450
Templetone Radio	Arcade	1930s	4-1/2", red	275	650
Thoroughbred	Hubley	1946	5-1/4", bronze finish	75	150
Three Wise Monkeys	Williams, A.C.	1900s	3-1/4" tall, 3-1/2" wide	225	550

Sailor, medium, 1910s, Hubley

*Santa Claus with Tree,
1910s, Hubley*

STILL BANKS

NAME	COMPANY	YEAR	DESCRIPTION	GOOD	EX
Time Is Money Clock Bank	Williams, A.C.	1910s	3-1/2" tall, alarm clock shaped, gold finish, "Time Is Money"	125	200
Time Safe	Roche, E.M. Co.		7" tall, 3-3/4" wide, unpainted	375	750
Tower	Kenton	1915	4-1/8", unpainted	175	375
Tower Bank	Kyser & Rex	1890	6-7/8" building w/tower rising from roof, "Tower Bank 1890"	1200	2200
Tower Bank	Harper, J.M.	1900s	9-1/4" tall, unpainted, brown finish	175	375
Town Hall Bank	Kyser & Rex	1882	4-5/8", red, "Town Hall Bank"	375	950
Toy Soldier	Worley, Laverne A.	1982	7-1/2" tall, painted, "SBCCA"	15	65
Treasure Chest	Wright, John	1970	2-3/4" x 4", smaller version is #928	60	35
Triangular Building	Hubley	1914	6" tall, "Bank"	325	675
Trick Buffalo	Unknown		5-1/2" tall, black	750	1500
Trolley Car	Kenton	1900s	5-1/4" long, painted silver	225	650
Trunk on Dolly	Piaget	1890	2-5/8" x 3-9/16"	175	350
Trust Bank	Stevens, J. & E.	1800s	7-1/4"	1800	3500
Tug Boat	Unknown		5-1/2" long, red, pull toy	4500	7500
Turkey, Large	Williams, A.C.	1900s	4-1/4" x 4", painted wattle	250	600
Turkey, Small	Williams, A.C.	1900s	3-3/8" tall, red head and wattle	150	275
Turtle Bank	Unknown		1" tall, 3-7/16" long	2000	3500
Two Car Garage	Williams, A.C.	1920s	2-1/2", painted	125	350
Two Goats Butting	Harper, J.M.		4-1/2", two goats on tree stump, "Two Kids" on base	950	2000
Two Story House	Williams, A.C.	1930s	3-1/16" tall, brown finish w/red roof	75	150
Two-Faced Black Boy, Large	Williams, A.C.	1900s	4-1/8" tall	125	350
Two-Faced Black Boy, Small	Williams, A.C.	1900s	3-1/8" x 2-3/4"	85	300
Two-Faced Devil	Williams, A.C.	1004	4-1/4" tall, deep red	550	1250
Two-Faced Indian	Williams, A.C.	1900s	4-5/16" tall, bronze finish w/painted highlights	1500	2750
U.S. Bank, Eagle Finial	Unknown	1890s	9-1/4" tall, green w/gold trim	850	1500
U.S. Mail	Kenton	1900s	4-3/4" tall, silver gray w/red lettering	100	375
U.S. Mail Bank with Combination Lock	Fish, O.B.	1903	6-7/8" tall, silver gray w/red lettering	225	775
U.S. Mail with Eagle	Hubley	1906	4" x 4"	175	325
U.S. Mail with Eagle	Kenton	1930s	4-1/8" x 3-1/2"	85	175
U.S. Mail, Small	Kenton	1900s	3-5/8" x 2-3/4", silver or green mail box w/red lettering	75	150
U.S. Navy Akron Zeppelin	Williams, A.C.	1930	6-5/8" long, silver finish, "US Navy Akron"	175	500
U.S. Treasury Bank	Grey Iron Casting	1920s	3-1/4", painted	250	475
Ulysses S. Grant Bust	Unknown	1976	5-1/2" tall	125	250
Ulysses S. Grant Bust on Safe	Harper, J.M.	1903	5-5/8" tall	1750	3000
Uncle Sam Hat	Knerr, George		2" x 3", red, white and blue	125	350
United Banking and Trust, Building Bank	Williams, A.C.		3" tall, bronze finish	225	550
Victorian House	Stevens, J. & E.	1892	4-1/2", unpainted deep gray finish	175	375
Victorian House	Unknown		3-1/4" tall, gray metallic finish	150	275
Villa	Kyser & Rex	1894	5-9/16" unpainted except for red finial	375	850
Villa Bank	Kyser & Rex	1882	3-7/8" x 3-3/8", "1882"	375	700
Vindex Bulldog	Vindex Toys	1931	5-1/4" tall, painted, "Vindex Toys"	125	275
Washington Bell with Yoke	Grey Iron Casting	1932	2-3/4", red	125	325
Washington Monument	Williams, A.C.	1900s	6" tall	150	325

BANKS

STILL BANKS

NAME	COMPANY	YEAR	DESCRIPTION	GOOD	EX
Washington, George, Bust	Grey Iron Casting	1920s	8" tall, bronze finish	850	1450
Watch Dog Safe	Unknown		5-1/8", w/brass handle, dog stands guard on front	1850	4000
Water Spaniel with Pack (I Hear A Call)	Harper, J.M.	1900	5-3/8" x 7-7/8"	225	450
Weaver Hen	Unknown	1970s	6", white w/red comb and wattle, "Weaver"	20	50
Westside Presbyterian Church	Unknown	1916	3-3/4" x 3-5/8", silver finish	350	950
Whale of a Bank	Knerr, George	1975	2-3/4" x 5-3/16", "A Whale of a Bank"	85	200
Whippet on Base	Unknown		3-1/2" tall, gold finish	75	125
White City Barrel #1 on Cart	Nicol	1894	5" long, unpainted, "White City Puzzle Savings Bank, A Barrel of Money"	275	475
White City Barrel, Large	Nicol	1893	5-1/8" tall, silver finish barrel	175	275
White City Pail	Nicol	1893	2-5/8" tall, silver finish pail w/handle	125	225
White City Puzzle Safe #10	Nicol	1893	4-5/8", unpainted	125	225
White City Puzzle Safe #12	Nicol	1893	4-7/8", unpainted	150	325
White Horse on Base	Knerr, George	1973	9-1/2" tall	125	225
Wirehaired Terrier	Hubley	1920s	4-5/8", painted	125	275
Wisconsin Beggar Boy	Unknown		6-7/8" tall, "Help the Crippled Children of Wisconsin"	525	900
Wisconsin War Eagle	Unknown	1880	2-7/8"	675	1500
Wise Pig, The	Hubley	1930s	6-5/8" tall, painted off white pig holding plaque	85	275
Woolworth Building	Kenton	1915	5-3/4" x 1-1/4"	85	175
Woolworth Building	Kenton	1915	7-7/8" tall, bronze finish	100	275
Work Horse on Base	Unknown		9" tall, painted white	75	125
Work Horse with Flynet	Arcade	1910s	4" tall	300	800
World's Fair Administration Building	Unknown	1893	6" x 6", painted	1400	2250
Yellow Cab	Arcade	1921	7-7/8" long, orange and black, rubber tires	1500	2400
York Stove	Abendroth Bros.		4" tall, unpainted, "York Stove"	225	525
Young America	Kyser & Rex	1882	4-3/8" x 3-1/8" safe	125	275

Barbie Dolls, Fashions and Accessories

Mattel's fashion doll icon still captures the essence of little girls' imaginations and dreams. Since her inception, Barbie has seen cosmetic changes (like hairstyle, facial expression and a slight change in body style) and more major changes (literally dozens of careers, computer technological advances, etc.). But through it all, Barbie has come out ahead of her competitors. Today, Mattel sells close to two billion in Barbie dolls per year.

How It All Began

Barbie's beginnings were modest really. Mattel co-founder Ruth Handler watched her young daughter, Barbara, playing "make-believe" with paper dolls. Handler immediately recognized that playing make-believe and pretending about the future was an important part of growing up. In researching the marketplace, she discovered a void and was determined to fill the niche with a three-dimensional fashion doll. Her all-male design staff, however, harbored doubts. Barbie, after all, would be much different than other dolls of the time. Several designs later, Mattel introduced Barbie, the Teen-Age Fashion Model to skeptical toy buyers at New York's annual Toy Fair in 1959. Never before had they seen a doll so completely unlike the baby and toddler dolls popular at the time. A major point of controversy? Barbie's ample bosom. Undaunted, Mattel used innovative television advertising to reach its audience and instantly had a hit!

A Collector's Dream

Barbie's charm as a children's toy may have been immediate, but it wasn't until decades later than collectors started paying more attention. Collectors who had grown up with Barbie wanted to reclaim her. There was, after all, plenty to recapture—the memories of playing dolls with friends, Barbie's fabulous fancy outfits, dream dates with Ken and—who could forget?—Barbie's dream house!

But since Barbie dolls were well-loved and played-with by girls, many of the 1959 and early 1960s dolls were in less-than-perfect shape. That's why examples of the earliest Barbie dolls regularly command hundreds, and sometimes even thousands, of dollars each. Having original boxes and clothing only increases a doll's value.

Collectors today are interested in both vintage and newer, collector-edition Barbie dolls. And collecting Barbie dolls is no small hobby. Full-time dealers make their livings off Barbie, and several publications exist solely to cover what's new in Barbie's world.

Nostalgia and investment potential are perhaps the two biggest motivators for Barbie collectors. And investment potential has proven itself over the last decades.

Barbie and Ken Cut-Outs, 1962

BARBIE

91

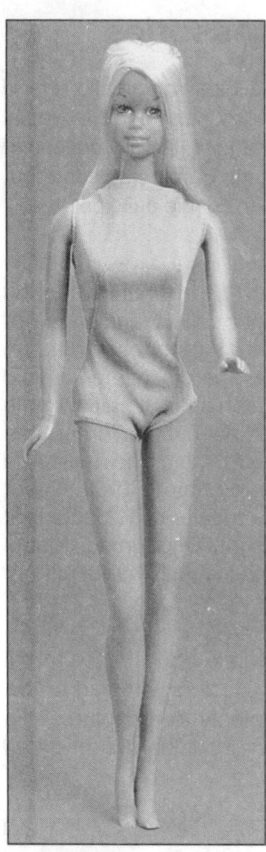

Malibu Barbie, 1975

BARBIE

Collecting Trends

Vintage dolls, particularly early 1960s issues, have consistently held their values. And auction prices have soared. An early Ponytail Barbie (so called by collectors because of the early dolls' hairstyle) sold at a 1999 auction for more than $13,000. The condition of the doll, and the fact that it was wearing an extremely rare outfit, led to that record price.

The very first Barbie, known to collectors as Ponytail #1, has hovered around the $5,000-$9,000 range for one in Mint in Box condition. Lesser condition #1s will bring only a fraction of that spectacular price.

Other hot prospects for collectors have been newer (1970s-1980s) dolls. Here are some worthy of mention:

• **Happy Holidays Barbie.** This series began in 1988 and ended in 1998. The decade-long series has been immensely popular with collectors. Each doll, introduced mid-year for the Christmas season, has worn an elaborate gown. The first issue from 1988 remains a collector favorite and can command up to $900 in Mint in Box condition. Later Happy Holidays dolls do not hold their values as well since so many were made. Happy Holidays dolls from the late 1990s, especially, fell victim to less demand and early clearance sales.

• **Teen Talk Barbie.** Issued in 1992, this doll featured a voice chip. About one percent of the dolls had a voice chip that said, among other things, "Math is tough." This phrases was met with disdain by many, and use of the chip was halted. Mattel even offered a refund for any doll voicing the offending phrase. Its current value on the secondary market is around $275. Other Teen Talk versions are valued between $15-$45.

• **Series Dolls.** Certain collectors like to buy all the dolls in a particular series. Current popular series, for example, are the Children's Collector Series, Harley-Davidson exclusives and designer lines (including dolls wearing Bob Mackie fashions). Not every doll in a series is a winner, in collectors' eyes, however.

Tips for Collecting

Although many Barbie dolls do increase in value, others do not. Here are some tips for smart collecting:

• **Avoid regular issue (also known as pink box) dolls.** These are the ones that generally retail for under $15. These have limited investment potential. Buy them because you like them, not because you expect them to increase in value.

• **Look for limited-edition exclusives.** Certain dolls are called "exclusives" because they are made only for one retail outlet—like Target or FAO Schwarz—to sell. Many of these dolls have gone on to increase in value; others, however, showed less success. Harley-Davidson Barbie, exclusive to Toys R Us, for example, was next to impossible to find in stores. Its secondary market price immediately soared to $250 or more.

- **Look for dolls in the best possible condition.** Dolls in top condition command higher prices than dolls in poor condition. And watch for accessories, apparel and original boxes. They can all add value to a doll.
- **Don't be fooled by dates!** Barbie dolls have distinct markings on their buttocks, but be aware that the date on a doll may be the date the doll's body style was copyrighted—not necessarily the date the doll was made. Therefore, dolls with a 1960s date may actually be made in the 1990s. Plenty of books exist with photos of dolls and markings, making identifying your doll much more accurate.
- **Don't overlook licensed Barbie products.** Mattel licenses the Barbie name to companies who make paper dolls, clothing, watches, cases and other collectibles. Anything with the Barbie name is collectible, but not necessarily valuable.

The Top Ten Barbie Accessories
(in Mint in Box condition)

1. Barbie's Airplane, 1964 .... $3,500
2. Barbie's Sport Plane, 1964 3,500
3. Skipper's Speedboat, 1965 1,850
4. Barbie's Speedboat, 1964 1,800
5. Vanity Fair Transistor Radio, 1963 1,350
6. Barbie's Austin Healy, lavender, 1964 1,000
7. Ken's Hot Rod, 1963 950
8. Barbie Starbright Boudoir Clock, 1964 775
9. Barbie Personal Photo Clock, 1964 675
10. Skipper's Schoolroom, 1965 600

The Top 10 Barbie Dolls
(in Mint in Box condition)

1. Ponytail Barbie #1, brunette, 1959 .... $8,000
2. Ponytail Barbie #1, blond, 1959 7,500
3. Ponytail Barbie #2, brunette, 1959 6,650
4. Ponytail Barbie #2, blond, 1959 6,350
5. American Girl Side-Part Barbie, brunette, blond, titian, 1965 3,875
6. Color Magic Barbie, midnight hair, 1966 3,200
7. Midge's Ensemble Gift Set, 1964 3,150
8. Barbie's Round the Clock Gift Set, Bubblecut, 1964 3,000
9. Barbie Beautiful Blues Gift Set, 1967 3,000
10. Fashion Queen Barbie & Ken Trousseau Gift Set, 1964 2,800

The Top 10 Barbie Fashions
(in Never-Removed-From-Box condition)

1. Roman Holiday, #968 .... $4,800
2. Pan American Stewardess, #1678 4,000
3. Easter Parade, #947 4,000
4. Gay Parisienne, #964 4,000
5. Beautiful Bride, #1698 2,100
6. Campus Sweetheart, #1616 1,600
7. Gold n' Glamour, #1647 1,600
8. Shimmering Magic, #1664 1,600
9. Commuter Set, #916 1,500
10. Here Comes The Groom, #1426 1,400

Contributor to this section: Patricia Long, 5608 S. Kingshighway, St. Louis, MO 63109.

BARBIE

Looking Out for #1

To the non-collector, the first Ponytail Barbies all look some-what similar. There are, however, subtle and important differ-ences. the first Barbie (1959), known to collectors as Ponytail Barbie #1, featured:

- *holes in the bottom of the feet with copper tubes*
- *zebra-stripe one-piece swimsuit*
- *blonde or brunette hair with soft curly bangs*
- *red fingernails, toenails and lips*
- *gold hoop earrings*
- *white irises and severely pointed black eyebrows*
- *heavy, black facial paint*
- *pale, almost white, ivory skin tone*
- *body markings: Barbie T.M./ Pats. Pend. / ©MCMLVIII/ by/Mattel/Inc.*

Ponytail Barbie #1, blond, 1959

BARBIE & FRIENDS

NO.	NAME	YEAR	MNB	MIB
9423	All American Barbie	1991	4	20
9425	All American Christie	1991	4	25
9424	All American Ken	1991	4	15
9427	All American Kira	1991	4	20
9426	All American Teresa	1991	4	30
3553	All Star Ken	1981	7	25
9099	All Stars Barbie	1989	5	25
9352	All Stars Christie	1989	5	20
9361	All Stars Ken	1989	5	20
9360	All Stars Midge	1989	5	30
9353	All Stars Teresa	1989	5	30
1010	Allan, bendable leg	1965	150	400
1000	Allan, straight leg	1964	55	125
4930	American Beauties Mardi Gras Barbie	1988	40	100
3137	American Beauty Queen	1991	5	45
3245	American Beauty Queen, black doll	1991	5	35
1070	American Girl Barbie "Color Magic Face"	1966	1200	2700
1070	American Girl Barbie, all blonds	1965	800	1800
1070	American Girl Barbie, brunette, titian	1966	1200	2700
1070	American Girl Side-Part Barbie, brunette, blond, titian	1965	2225	3875
5640	Angel Face Barbie	1982	8	40
4828	Animal Lovin' Barbie, black doll	1989	5	75
1350	Animal Lovin' Barbie, white doll	1989	5	40
1395	Animal Lovin' Ginger Giraffe	1989	7	20
1351	Animal Lovin' Ken	1989	5	20
1352	Animal Lovin' Nikki	1989	7	20
1393	Animal Lovin' Zizi Zebra	1989	7	20
1207	Astronaut Barbie, black doll	1985	30	40
2449	Astronaut Barbie, white doll	1985	25	75
	Baby Krissy Layette Set, Play Line	2000	5	10
9434	Babysitter Courtney	1991	4	15
9433	Babysitter Skipper	1991	4	15
1599	Babysitter Skipper, black doll	1991	4	10
9000	Baggy Casey, blond (Baggie)	1975	25	100
9613	Ballerina Barbie on Tour, gold, 1st version	1976	45	125
9093	Ballerina Barbie, 1st version	1976	20	65
9528	Ballerina Cara	1976	25	65
9805	Barbie & Her Fashion Fireworks	1976	20	60
3751	Barbie & the Beat	1990	5	30
2752	Barbie & the Beat Christie	1990	5	15
2754	Barbie & the Beat Midge	1990	6	20
1144	Barbie with Growin' Pretty Hair	1971	100	300
9601	Bathtime Fun Barbie	1991	3	20
9603	Bathtime Fun Barbie, black doll	1991	3	15
3237	Beach Blast Barbie	1989	3	20
3253	Beach Blast Christie	1989	4	15
3238	Beach Blast Ken	1989	4	15
3244	Beach Blast Miko	1989	4	15
3242	Beach Blast Skipper	1989	4	15
3251	Beach Blast Steven	1989	4	15
3249	Beach Blast Teresa	1989	5	15
9907	Beautiful Bride Barbie	1978	60	125
1290	Beauty Secrets Barbie, 1st issue	1980	12	65
1295	Beauty Secrets Christie	1980	12	65
1018	Beauty, Barbie's Dog	1979	12	30
9404	Benetton Barbie	1991	6	45
9407	Benetton Christie	1991	6	35
9409	Benetton Marina	1991	6	35
1293	Black Barbie, 1st issue, black doll	1980	20	80

BARBIE

BARBIE & FRIENDS

NO.	NAME	YEAR	MNB	MIB
1142	Brad, bendable leg	1970	75	150
850	Bubblecut Barbie	1962	300	500
850	Bubblecut Barbie Brownette	1961	900	1400
850	Bubblecut Barbie Sidepart, all hair colors	1961	350	800
850	Bubblecut Barbie, all blonds	1961	150	385
850	Bubblecut Barbie, black haired	1961	200	425
850	Bubblecut Barbie, brunette	1961	200	425
850	Bubblecut Barbie, titian	1961	200	425
850	Bubblecut Barbie, white ginger	1962	450	1000
3311	Busy Barbie	1972	145	280
3313	Busy Francie	1972	250	425
13675	Busy Gal Barbie, Nostalgic Collection	1995	25	55
3314	Busy Ken	1972	70	165
3312	Busy Steffie	1972	170	350
4547	Calgary Olympic Skating Barbie	1987	25	60
4439	California Dream Barbie	1988	5	20
4443	California Dream Christie	1988	6	15
4441	California Dream Ken	1988	8	15
4442	California Dream Midge	1988	3	15
4440	California Dream Skipper	1988	13	20
4403	California Dream Teresa	1988	15	20
7377	Carla, European exclusive	1976	65	140
1180	Casey, brunette, blond, Twist and Turn	1967	85	300
1180	Casey, titian, Twist and Turn	1967	150	400
3570	Chris, titian, blond, brunette (Tutti's friend)	1967	100	250
	Coach Ken & Tommy, white or black dolls	2000	7	15
1150	Color Magic Barbie, blond, plastic box	1966	800	2400
1150	Color Magic Barbie, midnight hair	1966	1200	3200
4893	Cool City Blues: Barbie, Ken, Skipper	1989	20	45
15469	Cool Shavin' Ken	1996	10	15
3022	Cool Times Barbie	1989	5	25
3217	Cool Times Christie	1989	5	20
3219	Cool Times Ken	1989	5	20
3216	Cool Times Midge	1989	7	20
3218	Cool Times Teresa	1989	9	20
7079	Cool Tops Courtney	1989	7	20
9351	Cool Tops Kevin	1989	5	20
4989	Cool Tops Skipper	1989	7	15
5441	Cool Tops Skipper, black doll	1989	5	15
	Corduroy Cool Barbie	2000	5	10
	Corduroy Cool Teresa	2000	5	10
7123	Costume Ball Barbie	1991	6	25
7134	Costume Ball Barbie, black doll	1991	6	15
7154	Costume Ball Ken	1991	6	30
7160	Costume Ball Ken, black doll	1991	6	20
4859	Crystal Barbie, black doll	1984	10	25
4598	Crystal Barbie, white doll	1984	10	35
9036	Crystal Ken, black doll	1983	15	25
4898	Crystal Ken, white doll	1983	8	30
3509	Dance Club Barbie	1989	5	45
3513	Dance Club Devon	1989	5	40
3512	Dance Club Kayla	1989	5	85
3511	Dance Club Ken	1989	5	40
4836	Dance Magic Barbie	1990	7	25
7080	Dance Magic Barbie, black doll	1990	7	25
7081	Dance Magic Ken	1990	6	20
7082	Dance Magic Ken, black doll	1990	6	20
7945	Day-to-Night Barbie, black doll	1985	10	35
7944	Day-to-Night Barbie, Hispanic doll	1985	17	40

Skipper Jeweled Bed, 1965

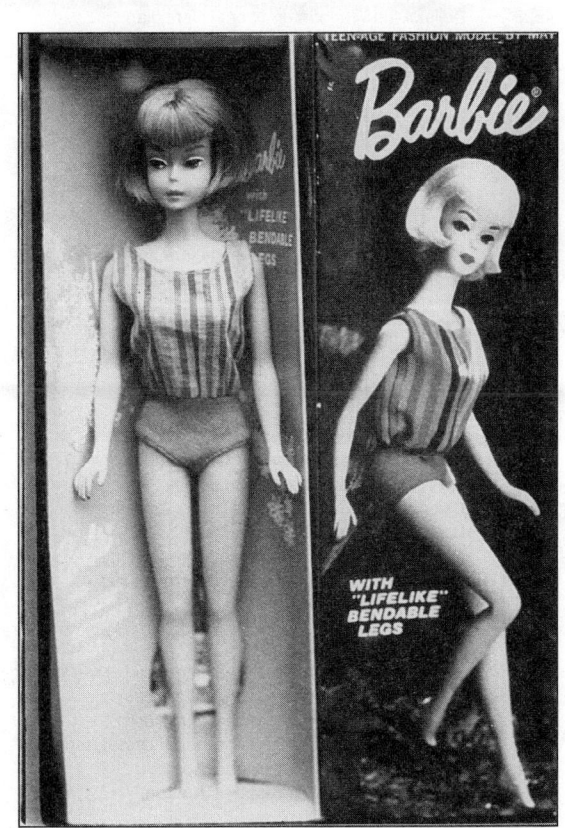

American Girl Barbie, 1966

BARBIE & FRIENDS

NO.	NAME	YEAR	MNB	MIB
7929	Day-to-Night Barbie, white doll	1985	10	40
9018	Day-to-Night Ken, black doll	1984	8	20
9019	Day-to-Night Ken, white doll	1984	8	25
9217	Deluxe Quick Curl Barbie	1976	20	95
9219	Deluxe Quick Curl Cara	1976	20	80
9218	Deluxe Quick Curl P.J.	1976	20	50
9428	Deluxe Quick Curl Skipper	1976	20	50
	Deluxe Tropical Barbie	1986	18	40
	Dentist Barbie	1997	15	30
	Disney Fun Barbie	1998	12	30
	Disney Fun Barbie	1994	20	45
	Disney Fun Barbie	1993	20	48
	Disney Fun Barbie	1995	12	35
	Disney Fun Barbie	1997	12	30
	Disney's Animal Kingdom Barbie	1998	15	30
	Disney's Animal Kingdom Barbie, black doll	1998	15	35
	Disneyland Resort Vacation, Barbie Tommy Kelly Ken Gift Set, Disneyland exc	1998	35	80
	Disneyland Resort Vacation, Barbie Tommy Kelly Ken Gift Set, Walt Disney Wo	1998	35	80
3850	Doctor Barbie	1988	8	45
4118	Doctor Ken	1988	5	40
	Dolls of the World/International Arctic	1997	20	30
3626	Dolls of the World/International Australian, two box variations	1993	10	35
21553	Dolls of the World/International Austrian	1999	15	25
9094	Dolls of the World/International Brazillian	1990	15	60
4928	Dolls of the World/International Canadian	1988	15	75
	Dolls of the World/International Chilean	1998	10	20
11180	Dolls of the World/International Chinese	1994	10	30
7330	Dolls of the World/International Czechoslovakian	1991	30	110
11104	Dolls of the World/International Dutch	1994	10	35
4973	Dolls of the World/International English	1992	12	80
3898	Dolls of the World/International Eskimo	1982	30	100
9844	Dolls of the World/International Eskimo, reissue	1991	8	60
	Dolls of the World/International French	1997	10	25
3188	Dolls of the World/International German	1987	45	100
12598	Dolls of the World/International German, reissue	1995	10	25
	Dolls of the World/International Ghanian	1996	15	25
12043	Dolls of the World/International Gift Set (Chinese, Dutch, Kenyan)	1994	30	70
	Dolls of the World/International Gift Set (Irish, German, Polynesian)	1995	30	65
	Dolls of the World/International Gift Set (Japanese, Indian, Norwegian)	1996	30	60
2997	Dolls of the World/International Greek	1986	30	80
3189	Dolls of the World/International Iceland	1987	30	100
3897	Dolls of the World/International India	1982	50	120
14451	Dolls of the World/International India, reissue	1995	12	25
	Dolls of the World/International Indian	1996	10	20
7517	Dolls of the World/International Irish	1984	45	115
12998	Dolls of the World/International Irish, reissue	1995	10	40
1601	Dolls of the World/International Italian	1980	65	175
2256	Dolls of the World/International Italian, reissue, two box versions	1993	10	50
4647	Dolls of the World/International Jamaican, silver earrings	1992	12	55
9481	Dolls of the World/International Japanese	1985	55	125
	Dolls of the World/International Japanese	1996	10	20
14163	Dolls of the World/International Japanese, reissue	1986-87	12	150
11181	Dolls of the World/International Kenyan	1994	10	35
4929	Dolls of the World/International Korean	1988	15	75

BARBIE

NO.	NAME	YEAR	MNB	MIB
7329	Dolls of the World/International Malaysian	1991	10	50
1917	Dolls of the World/International Mexican	1989	15	50
	Dolls of the World/International Mexican	1996	10	20
	Dolls of the World/International Mexican, reissue	1995	12	25
21507	Dolls of the World/International Moroccan	1999	15	25
1753	Dolls of the World/International Native American #1, two box versions	1993	12	45
11609	Dolls of the World/International Native American #2	1994	10	35
12699	Dolls of the World/International Native American #3	1995	10	30
7376	Dolls of the World/International Nigerian	1990	15	60
14450	Dolls of the World/International Norwegian, pink flowers	1996	12	65
24671	Dolls of the World/International NW Coast Native American Barbie	2000	12	25
3262	Dolls of the World/International Oriental	1981	55	130
1600	Dolls of the World/International Parisian	1980	65	150
9843	Dolls of the World/International Parisian, reissue	1991	8	60
2995	Dolls of the World/International Peruvian	1986	30	80
21506	Dolls of the World/International Peruvian, reissue	1999	15	25
	Dolls of the World/International Polish	1998	15	25
12700	Dolls of the World/International Polynesian	1995	10	30
	Dolls of the World/International Puerto Rican	1997	15	25
1602	Dolls of the World/International Royal	1980	65	175
1916	Dolls of the World/International Russian	1989	20	25
	Dolls of the World/International Russian	1997	20	75
3263	Dolls of the World/International Scottish	1981	50	130
9845	Dolls of the World/International Scottish, reissue	1991	8	60
4031	Dolls of the World/International Spanish	1983	40	110
24670	Dolls of the World/International Spanish	2000	12	25
4963	Dolls of the World/International Spanish, reissue	1992	12	45
24672	Dolls of the World/International Swedish	2000	12	25
4032	Dolls of the World/International Swedish	1983	35	100
7451	Dolls of the World/International Swiss	1984	35	100
	Dolls of the World/International Thai	1998	10	20
1116	Dramatic New Living Barbie, all hair colors	1970	65	275
1117	Dramatic New Living Skipper	1970	50	175
1623	Dream Bride	1992	10	40
2242	Dream Glow Barbie, black doll	1986	12	25
1647	Dream Glow Barbie, Hispanic doll	1986	25	70
2248	Dream Glow Barbie, white doll	1986	12	45
2421	Dream Glow Ken, black doll	1986	13	20
2250	Dream Glow Ken, white doll	1986	13	15
9180	Dream Time Barbie, pink	1985	10	25
	Earring Magic Barbie	1993	15	25
2290	Earring Magic Ken	1993	15	40
7093	Fabulous Fur Barbie	1983	20	65
5313	Fashion Jeans Barbie	1981	15	65
5316	Fashion Jeans Ken	1982	12	25
2210	Fashion Photo Barbie, two versions	1978	20	75
2324	Fashion Photo Christie	1978	20	75
2323	Fashion Photo P.J.	1978	35	85
7193	Fashion Play Barbie	1983	10	30
4835	Fashion Play Barbie	1987	10	25
9429	Fashion Play Barbie	1990	2	30
9629	Fashion Play Barbie	1991	2	20
5953	Fashion Play Barbie, black doll	1991	2	15
5954	Fashion Play Barbie, Hispanic doll	1990	2	15
870	Fashion Queen Barbie	1963	145	500
1189	Feelin' Fun Barbie, two versions, white, 1st issue	1988	5	20
9916	Flight Time Barbie, black doll	1990	5	20
9584	Flight Time Barbie, white doll	1990	5	30

Corduroy Cool Barbie, 2000

Francie Twist and Turn with bendable legs, 1967

NO.	NAME	YEAR	MNB	MIB
9600	Flight Time Ken	1990	5	20
1143	Fluff	1971	100	210
1122	Francie Hair Happenin's	1970	150	400
1170	Francie Twist and Turn, bendable leg, all hair colors, long hair	1967	150	400
	Francie Twist and Turn, flip hair	1969	200	400
1129	Francie with Growin' Pretty Hair	1971	75	225
1170	Francie, bendable leg, black doll	1968	900	1600
1130	Francie, bendable leg, white doll, blond, brunette	1966	150	350
1140	Francie, straight leg, brunette, blond	1966	200	450
7270	Free Moving Barbie	1974	50	100
7283	Free Moving Cara	1974	40	80
7280	Free Moving Ken	1974	30	70
7281	Free Moving P.J.	1974	30	80
4939	Fun to Dress Barbie, black doll	1989	2	15
1373	Fun to Dress Barbie, black doll	1988	3	15
7668	Fun to Dress Barbie, black doll	1987	3	15
7373	Fun to Dress Barbie, Hispanic doll	1989	3	15
4808	Fun to Dress Barbie, white doll	1989	3	15
4372	Fun to Dress Barbie, white doll	1988	3	15
4558	Fun to Dress Barbie, white doll	1987	3	20
1739	Funtime Barbie, black doll	1987	5	25
1738	Funtime Barbie, white doll	1987	5	25
7194	Funtime Ken	1987	7	20
1953	Garden Party Barbie	1989	8	18
1922	Gift Giving Barbie	1986	5	30
1205	Gift Giving Barbie	1989	5	30
7262	Gold Medal Olympic Barbie Skater	1975	20	100
7264	Gold Medal Olympic Barbie Skier	1975	20	100
7263	Gold Medal Olympic P.J. Gymnast	1975	20	85
7261	Gold Medal Olympic Skier Ken	1975	20	85
7274	Gold Medal Olympic Skipper	1975	20	85
3533	Golden Dreams Barbie Glamorous Night	1981	18	65
1974	Golden Dreams Barbie, two versions	1981	15	60
3249	Golden Dreams Christie	1981	15	65
15121	Got Milk? Barbie	1996	15	30
15122	Got Milk? Barbie, black	1996	15	30
7834	Great Shapes Barbie, black	1984	5	25
7025	Great Shapes Barbie, w/Walkman	1984	12	40
7025	Great Shapes Barbie, white doll	1984	5	35
7310	Great Shapes Ken	1984	5	25
7417	Great Shapes Skipper	1984	5	25
4253	Groom Todd	1982	15	45
	Growing Pretty Hair Barbie	1970	135	295
9222	Growing Up Ginger	1977	30	140
	Hair Clip Barbie, Christie, Teresa, white or black doll	2000	7	15
1922	Happy Birthday Barbie	1981	8	45
1922	Happy Birthday Barbie	1984	8	35
9561	Happy Birthday Barbie	1991	8	20
9561	Happy Birthday Barbie, black doll	1991	8	30
7470	Hawaiian Barbie	1977	30	80
7470	Hawaiian Barbie	1975	25	68
5040	Hawaiian Fun Barbie	1991	3	20
5044	Hawaiian Fun Christie	1991	3	20
9294	Hawaiian Fun Jazzie	1991	3	20
5041	Hawaiian Fun Ken	1991	3	15
5043	Hawaiian Fun Kira	1991	3	15
5042	Hawaiian Fun Skipper	1991	3	15
5045	Hawaiian Fun Steven	1991	3	15
7495	Hawaiian Ken	1984	7	30

BARBIE

BARBIE & FRIENDS

NO.	NAME	YEAR	MNB	MIB
2960	Hawaiian Ken	1979	13	50
3698	High School Chelsie	1989	5	20
3600	High School Dude, Jazzie's boyfriend	1989	5	20
3635	High School Jazzie	1989	5	20
3636	High School Stacie	1989	5	20
1292	Hispanic Barbie	1980	15	75
	Hollywood Nails Barbie, white or black doll	1999	7	15
	Hollywood Nails Teresa, white or black doll	1999	7	15
2249	Home Pretty Barbie	1990	8	18
2390	Homecoming Queen Skipper, black doll	1988	8	20
1952	Homecoming Queen Skipper, white doll	1988	12	25
1757	Horse Lovin' Barbie	1983	10	40
3600	Horse Lovin' Ken	1983	8	25
5029	Horse Lovin' Skipper	1983	8	25
7927	Hot Stuff Skipper	1984	5	18
7365	Ice Capades Barbie, 50th Anniversary	1990	5	35
7348	Ice Capades Barbie, black doll, 50th Anniversary	1990	5	25
7375	Ice Capades Ken	1990	5	25
15473	Inline Skating Barbie	1996	5	25
15474	Inline Skating Ken	1996	5	25
15475	Inline Skating Midge	1996	5	25
4061	Island Fun Barbie	1988	3	20
4092	Island Fun Christie	1988	3	20
4060	Island Fun Ken	1988	3	15
4064	Island Fun Skipper	1988	3	15
4093	Island Fun Steven	1988	3	15
4117	Island Fun Teresa	1988	3	15
3633	Jazzie Workout	1989	5	12
	Jewel Girl Barbie (new body style, belly button)	2000	15	30
1756	Jewel Secrets Barbie, black doll, two box versions	1987	6	55
1737	Jewel Secrets Barbie, white doll, two box versions	1987	6	35
3232	Jewel Secrets Ken, black doll	1987	6	25
1719	Jewel Secrets Ken, rooted hair	1987	6	25
3133	Jewel Secrets Skipper	1987	6	25
3179	Jewel Secrets Whitney	1987	8	25
750	Ken, bendable leg, brunette	1965	155	275
1124	Ken, bendable leg, talking Ken	1970	60	125
750	Ken, flocked hair, brunette, blond	1961	100	350
750	Ken, painted hair, brunette, blond	1962	50	145
9325	Kevin	1991	5	10
2597	Kissing Barbie, two versions	1979	8	65
2955	Kissing Christie	1979	10	65
9725	Lights & Lace Barbie	1991	4	30
9728	Lights & Lace Christie	1991	4	30
9727	Lights & Lace Teresa	1991	4	25
1155	Live Action Barbie	1971	60	150
1152	Live Action Barbie Onstage	1971	75	250
1175	Live Action Christie	1971	60	250
1159	Live Action Ken	1971	55	150
1172	Live Action Ken on Stage	1971	40	150
1156	Live Action P.J.	1971	65	250
1153	Live Action P.J. on Stage	1971	75	175
1116	Living Barbie	1970	65	250
7072	Lovin' You Barbie	1983	20	100
3989	Magic Curl Barbie, black doll	1982	8	25
3856	Magic Curl Barbie, white doll	1982	10	35
3137	Magic Moves Barbie, black doll	1985	15	35
2126	Magic Moves Barbie, white doll	1985	15	35
	Major League Baseball	1999	20	45

Live Action Barbie, 1971

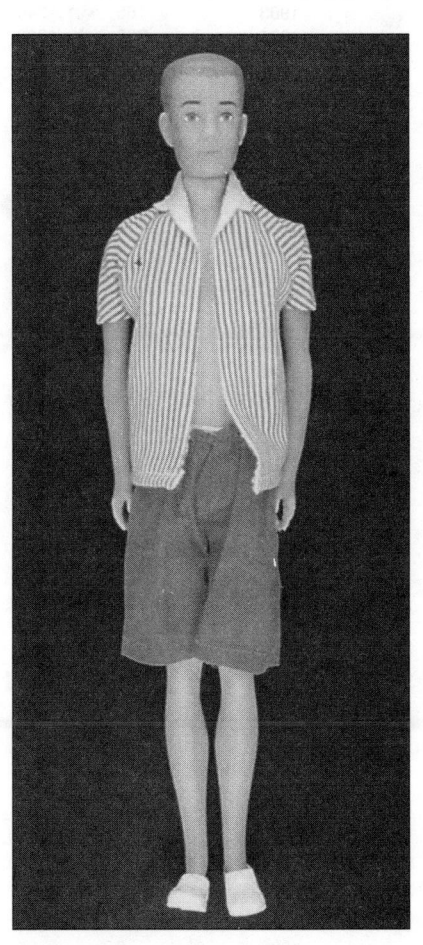

Ken with painted hair, 1962

BARBIE & FRIENDS

NO.	NAME	YEAR	MNB	MIB
1067	Malibu Barbie	1975	15	40
1067	Malibu Barbie	1971	15	60
7745	Malibu Christie	1975	10	40
7745	Malibu Christie	1977	15	40
1068	Malibu Francie	1971	15	45
1088	Malibu Ken	1976	8	25
1087	Malibu P.J.	1975	5	45
1069	Malibu Skipper	1977	8	45
	Mickey's Toontown Stacie	1994	12	30
1080	Midge, bendable leg, blond, titian, brunette	1965	325	600
860	Midge, straight leg, blond	1963	75	200
860	Midge, straight leg, brunette, titian	1963	100	225
860	Midge, w/teeth, all hair colors	1963	165	340
1060	Miss Barbie (Sleep-eye)	1964	700	1300
4224	Mod Hair Ken	1973	45	65
9988	Music Lovin' Barbie	1985	15	45
2388	Music Lovin' Ken	1985	15	45
2854	Music Lovin' Skipper	1985	20	75
9942	My First Barbie	1991	3	25
1875	My First Barbie, aqua and yellow dress	1981	10	30
9944	My First Barbie, black doll	1990	4	20
9943	My First Barbie, black doll	1991	3	20
9943	My First Barbie, Hispanic doll	1990	5	25
9944	My First Barbie, Hispanic doll	1991	3	20
1875	My First Barbie, pink checkered dress	1983	5	35
1801	My First Barbie, pink tutu, black doll	1987	5	20
1788	My First Barbie, pink tutu, white doll	1987	5	20
9942	My First Barbie, white doll	1990	4	20
9858	My First Barbie, white dress, black doll	1984	7	25
1875	My First Barbie, white dress, white doll	1984	5	30
1281	My First Barbie, white tutu, black doll	1988	6	15
1282	My First Barbie, white tutu, Hispanic doll	1988	6	20
1280	My First Barbie, white tutu, white doll	1988	5	20
9940	My First Ken	1991	3	15
9940	My First Ken	1990	4	15
1389	My First Ken, 1st issue	1989	4	15
1124	New Good Lookin' Ken	1970	75	150
9342	New Look Ken	1976	23	65
7807	Newport Barbie, two versions	1974	25	140
1170	No Bangs Francie	1970	900	1600
1127	Nurse Julia, 1-piece outfit	1970	100	300
1127	Nurse Julia, two-piece outfit, twist and turn	1969	100	285
4405	Nurse Whitney	1987	20	45
15430	Ocean Friends Barbie, Ocean Magic	1996	5	17
15430	Ocean Friends Ken, Ocean Magic	1996	5	17
15431	Ocean Friends Kira, Ocean Magic	1996	5	17
15123	Olympic Gymnast, blond	1996	10	25
4885	Party Treats Barbie	1989	8	25
9516	Peaches n' Cream Barbie, black doll	1984	8	40
7926	Peaches n' Cream Barbie, white doll	1984	8	45
4555	Perfume Giving Ken, black doll	1989	6	25
4554	Perfume Giving Ken, white doll	1989	6	25
4552	Perfume Pretty Barbie, black doll	1989	8	25
4551	Perfume Pretty Barbie, white doll	1989	8	25
4557	Perfume Pretty Whitney	1987	8	35
3551	Pink n' Pretty Barbie	1982	12	45
3554	Pink n' Pretty Christie	1982	10	40
5336	Playtime Barbie	1984	15	20
850	Ponytail Barbie #1, blond	1959	4000	7500

NO.	NAME	YEAR	MNB	MIB
850	Ponytail Barbie #1, brunette	1959	4500	8000
850	Ponytail Barbie #2, blond	1959	3500	6350
850	Ponytail Barbie #2, brunette	1959	4000	6650
850	Ponytail Barbie #3, blond	1960	600	1400
850	Ponytail Barbie #3, brunette	1960	800	1550
850	Ponytail Barbie #4, blond	1960	300	675
850	Ponytail Barbie #4, brunette	1960	350	675
850	Ponytail Barbie #5, blond	1961	175	600
850	Ponytail Barbie #5, brunette	1961	250	600
850	Ponytail Barbie #5, titian	1961	250	700
850	Ponytail Barbie #6, blond	1962	200	545
850	Ponytail Barbie #6, brunette	1962	200	545
850	Ponytail Barbie #6, titian	1962	250	545
850	Ponytail Swirl Style Barbie, blond	1964	350	625
850	Ponytail Swirl Style Barbie, brunette	1964	350	625
850	Ponytail Swirl Style Barbie, platinum	1964	500	1200
850	Ponytail Swirl Style Barbie, titian	1964	350	625
1117	Pose n' Play Skipper (baggie)	1973	20	55
2598	Pretty Changes Barbie	1978	8	45
7194	Pretty Party Barbie	1983	12	30
4220	Quick Curl Barbie	1973	20	80
7291	Quick Curl Cara	1975	20	60
4222	Quick Curl Francie	1973	20	55
4221	Quick Curl Kelley	1973	20	75
8697	Quick Curl Miss America, blond	1974	35	75
8697	Quick Curl Miss America, brunette	1973	45	175
4223	Quick Curl Skipper	1973	20	50
1090	Ricky	1965	55	160
1140	Rocker Barbie, 1st issue	1986	7	40
3055	Rocker Barbie, 2nd issue	1987	7	25
1196	Rocker Dana, 1st issue	1986	7	40
3158	Rocker Dana, 2nd issue	1987	7	20
1141	Rocker Dee-Dee, 1st issue	1986	7	30
3160	Rocker Dee-Dee, 2nd issue	1987	7	20
2428	Rocker Derek, 1st issue	1986	7	30
3173	Rocker Derek, 2nd issue	1987	7	20
2427	Rocker Diva, 1st issue	1986	7	30
3159	Rocker Diva, 2nd issue	1987	7	20
3131	Rocker Ken, 1st issue	1986	7	30
1880	Rollerskating Barbie	1980	8	60
1881	Rollerskating Ken	1980	8	40
4973	Safari Barbie	1983	8	30
1019	Scott	1979	15	60
9109	Sea Lovin' Barbie	1984	8	35
9110	Sea Lovin' Ken	1984	8	30
	Secret Messages Barbie, white or black doll	2000	7	15
4931	Sensations Barbie	1987	5	12
4977	Sensations Becky	1987	5	12
4976	Sensations Belinda	1987	5	12
4967	Sensations Bopsy	1987	5	12
4960	Sensations Bopsy Bibops	1987	15	95
	Sit 'n Style Barbie, Teresa or Christie, white or black doll	2000	7	15
7511	Ski Fun Barbie	1991	6	15
7512	Ski Fun Ken	1991	6	15
7513	Ski Fun Midge	1991	6	25
1030	Skipper, bendable leg, brunette, blond, titian	1965	100	300
950	Skipper, straight leg, brunette, blond, titian	1964	50	195
950	Skipper, straight leg, reissues, brunette, blond, titian	1971	125	400
1120	Skooter, bendable leg, brunette, blond, titian	1966	100	350

BARBIE

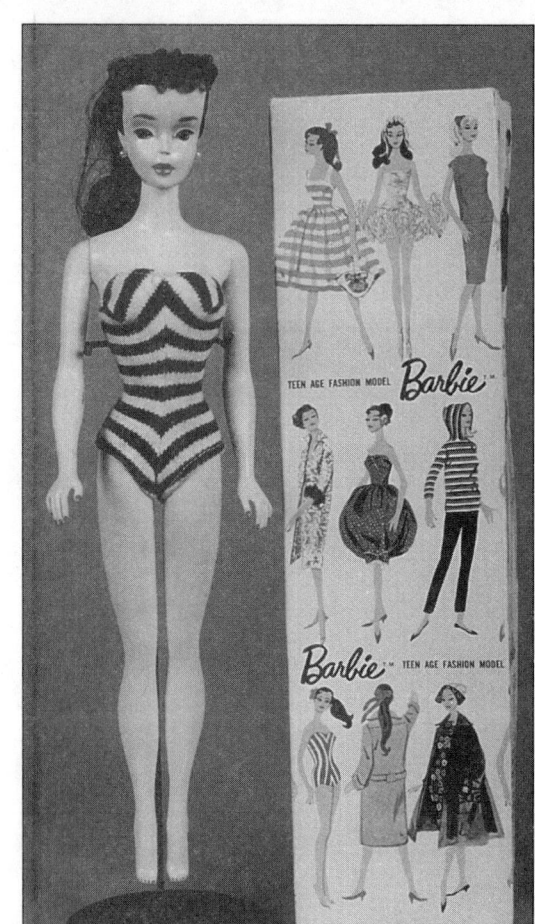

Ponytail Barbie #3, brunette, 1960

Ponytail Barbie #5, blond, 1961

NO.	NAME	YEAR	MNB	MIB
1040	Skooter, straight leg, brunette, blond, titian	1965	55	180
15408	Snowboard Barbie	1996	10	20
13534	Solo in the Spotlight, blond	1995	12	25
13820	Solo in the Spotlight, brunette	1995	12	25
15419	Sparkle Barbie	1996	10	20
	Spiegel Winner's Circle Barbie	1997	18	40
1294	Sport n' Shave Ken	1980	8	40
1190	Standard Barbie, blond, brunette	1970	300	600
1190	Standard Barbie, blond, brunette	1967	300	550
1190	Standard Barbie, titian	1970	500	1000
1190	Standard Barbie, titian	1967	500	1000
1281	Starr Kelley	1979	8	35
1283	Starr Shaun	1979	8	40
1280	Starr Starr	1979	8	35
1282	Starr Tracy	1979	8	35
3360	Stars & Stripes Air Force Barbie	1990	15	50
3966	Stars & Stripes Army Barbie	1989	10	40
9693	Stars & Stripes Navy Barbie	1991	10	35
9694	Stars & Stripes Navy Barbie, black doll	1991	10	35
	Stars 'n Stripes Air Force Barbie, black or white doll	1994	15	25
	Stars 'n Stripes Air Force Ken, black or white doll	1994	15	25
	Stars 'n Stripes Army Barbie	1993	15	30
	Stars 'n Stripes Army Ken	1993	15	30
	Stars 'n Stripes Marine Corps Barbie, black or white doll	1992	15	35
	Stars 'n Stripes Marine Corps Ken, black or white doll	1992	20	40
1283	Style Magic Barbie	1989	5	20
1288	Style Magic Christie	1989	5	20
1915	Style Magic Skipper	1989	10	20
1290	Style Magic Whitney	1989	5	20
7027	Summit Barbie	1990	8	25
7029	Summit Barbie, Asian version	1990	10	25
	Summit Barbie, Asian, black or white doll	1990	12	25
7028	Summit Barbie, black doll	1990	8	25
	Summit Barbie, Hispanic	1990	15	30
7030	Summit Barbie, Hispanic doll	1990	10	28
7745	Sun Gold Malibu Barbie, black doll	1983	5	15
4970	Sun Gold Malibu Barbie, Hispanic doll	1985	3	20
1067	Sun Gold Malibu Barbie, white doll	1983	5	15
3849	Sun Gold Malibu Ken, black doll	1983	3	15
	Sun Gold Malibu Ken, Hispanic doll	1985	3	20
1088	Sun Gold Malibu Ken, white doll	1983	3	15
1187	Sun Gold Malibu P.J.	1983	5	15
1069	Sun Gold Malibu Skipper	1983	5	15
1067	Sun Lovin' Malibu Barbie	1978	5	20
1088	Sun Lovin' Malibu Ken	1978	5	20
1187	Sun Lovin' Malibu P.J.	1978	5	20
1069	Sun Lovin' Malibu Skipper	1978	5	20
7806	Sun Valley Barbie	1974	20	130
7809	Sun Valley Ken	1974	20	100
4970	Sunsational Hispanic Barbie	1984	20	35
1067	Sunsational Malibu Barbie	1982	6	25
4970	Sunsational Malibu Barbie, Hispanic doll	1982	8	25
7745	Sunsational Malibu Christie	1982	6	20
3849	Sunsational Malibu Ken, black doll	1982	15	35
1187	Sunsational Malibu P.J.	1982	6	30
1069	Sunsational Malibu Skipper	1982	5	35
7745	Sunset Malibu Christie	1973	20	65
1068	Sunset Malibu Francie	1971	25	65
1088	Sunset Malibu Ken	1972	15	50

BARBIE

BARBIE

NO.	NAME	YEAR	MNB	MIB
1187	Sunset Malibu P.J.	1971	10	50
1069	Sunset Malibu Skipper	1971	20	50
3296	Super Hair Barbie, black doll	1987	8	20
3101	Super Hair Barbie, white doll	1987	8	25
	Super Size Bridal Barbie	1977	150	295
5839	Super Sport Ken	1982	8	20
	Super Talk Barbie	1995	10	20
2756	Super Teen Skipper	1978	7	20
9828	Supersize Barbie	1977	75	200
9839	Supersize Christie	1977	75	275
2844	Supersize Super Hair Barbie	1979	85	175
4983	Superstar Ballerina Barbie, 1st version	1976	20	60
	Superstar Barbie #2	1978	45	95
1605	Superstar Barbie 30th Anniversary, black doll	1989	6	35
1604	Superstar Barbie 30th Anniversary, white doll	1989	8	25
9720	Superstar Barbie, first version	1977	15	70
9950	Superstar Christie	1977	20	75
2211	Superstar Ken	1978	17	75
1550	Superstar Ken 30th Anniversary, black doll	1989	5	30
1535	Superstar Ken 30th Anniversary, white doll	1989	7	50
1067	Superstar Malibu Barbie	1977	10	35
	Superstar Promotional	1976	50	110
7796	Sweet 16 Barbie	1974	25	125
7455	Sweet Roses P.J.	1983	15	25
	Swimming Champion Barbie	2000	7	15
2064	Tahiti, Barbie's Pet Parrot	1985	3	15
	Talk With Me Barbie	1997	25	50
1115	Talking Barbie	1970	175	350
1115	Talking Barbie, all hair colors (nape curls)	1968	200	385
1114	Talking Brad	1970	65	150
1195	Talking Busy Barbie	1972	150	300
1196	Talking Busy Ken	1972	80	160
1186	Talking Busy Steffie	1972	175	350
1126	Talking Christie	1970	65	200
1115	Talking Christie	1970	120	200
1128	Talking Julia	1969	65	250
1111	Talking Ken	1969	40	175
1111	Talking Ken	1970	75	175
1113	Talking P.J.	1970	65	250
1125	Talking Stacey	1970	235	475
1125	Talking Stacey	1968	175	355
1125	Talking Stacey, blond, titian	1970	200	475
1107	Talking Truly Scrumptious	1969	300	650
13915	Teacher Barbie, black doll, painted on panties	1996	15	20
13914	Teacher Barbie, painted on panties	1996	15	25
3634	Teen Dance Jazzie	1989	7	35
5893	Teen Fun Skipper Cheerleader	1987	5	15
5899	Teen Fun Skipper Party Teen	1987	5	15
5889	Teen Fun Skipper Workout	1987	5	15
3634	Teen Jazzie (Teen Dance)	1989	4	35
3631	Teen Looks Jazzie Cheerleader	1989	4	20
3633	Teen Looks Jazzie Workout	1989	4	20
5507	Teen Scene Jazzie, two box versions	1991	5	35
4855	Teen Sweetheart Skipper	1988	5	25
5745	Teen Talk Barbie, must say "Math is Tough"	1992	50	275
5745	Teen Talk Barbie, two box versions	1992	15	45
1950	Teen Time Courtney	1988	5	10
1951	Teen Time Skipper	1988	5	10
1760	Tennis Barbie	1986	5	25

Quick Curl Barbie, 1973

Skipper with bendable legs, 1965

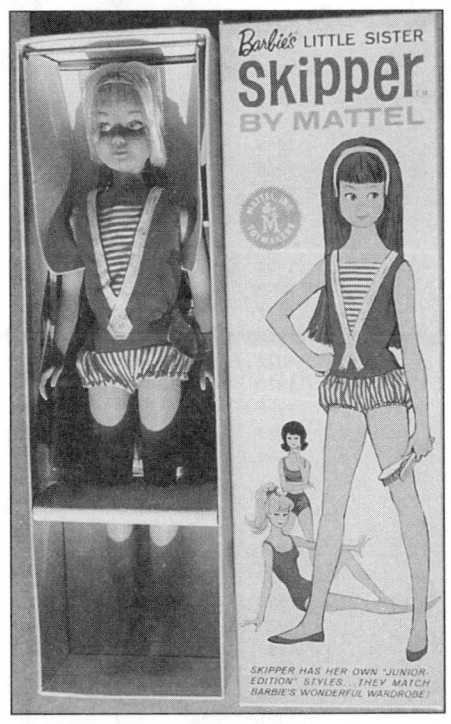

Skipper with straight legs, 1964

Solo in the Spotlight, 1995

BARBIE & FRIENDS

NO.	NAME	YEAR	MNB	MIB
1761	Tennis Ken	1986	5	25
3590	Todd	1967	95	200
4103	Tracey Bride	1983	8	45
1022	Tropical Barbie, black doll	1986	3	15
1017	Tropical Barbie, white doll	1986	3	20
1023	Tropical Ken, black doll	1986	3	15
4060	Tropical Ken, white doll	1986	3	20
2056	Tropical Miko	1986	3	20
4064	Tropical Skipper	1986	3	20
1108	Truly Scrumptious, non-talking	1969	250	650
3580	Tutti, all hair colors, floral dress w/yellow ribbon	1967	45	150
3550	Tutti, all hair colors, pink, white gingham suit, hat	1966	50	170
8128	Tutti, Germany	1978	40	125
1185	Twiggy	1967	150	350
5723	Twirley Curls Barbie, black doll	1983	10	35
5724	Twirley Curls Barbie, Hispanic doll	1982	10	40
5579	Twirley Curls Barbie, white doll	1982	10	40
1160	Twist and Turn Barbie	1968	225	500
1160	Twist and Turn Barbie Flip Hair	1970	250	475
1160	Twist and Turn Barbie, blonds and brunettes	1967	150	525
1160	Twist and Turn Barbie, titian	1967	200	600
1119	Twist and Turn Christie	1969	100	300
1160	Twist and Turn Flip Barbie, all hair colors	1969	150	400
1170	Twist and Turn Francie	1967	200	450
1170	Twist and Turn Francie	1969	300	650
1127	Twist and Turn Julia	1970	165	300
1118	Twist and Turn P.J., blond	1970	75	200
1118	Twist and Turn PJ		140	275
1105	Twist and Turn Skipper	1970	165	350
1107	Twist and Turn Skipper	1970	157	275
1105	Twist and Turn Skipper, all hair colors	1968	50	350
1165	Twist and Turn Stacey	1970	325	750
1165	Twist and Turn Stacey	1969	240	475
1165	Twist and Turn Stacey, blond, titian	1968	200	475
4774	UNICEF Barbie, Asian version	1989	17	30
4770	UNICEF Barbie, black doll	1989	7	25
4782	UNICEF Barbie, Hispanic doll	1989	7	30
1920	UNICEF Barbie, white doll	1989	7	25
	University Barbie	1997	12	18
1182	Walk Lively Barbie	1972	100	225
1184	Walk Lively Ken	1972	40	150
3200	Walk Lively Miss America Barbie, brunette	1972	95	200
1183	Walk Lively Steffie	1972	150	300
1132	Walking Jamie	1970	200	400
	Walt Disney World Barbie	1996	12	30
7011	Wedding Fantasy Barbie, black doll	1989	7	25
2125	Wedding Fantasy Barbie, white doll	1989	7	40
9607	Wedding Party Alan	1991	7	20
9608	Wedding Party Barbie	1991	7	20
9852	Wedding Party Kelly & Todd	1991	15	35
9609	Wedding Party Ken	1991	7	20
9606	Wedding Party Midge	1991	7	15
3469	Western Barbie, three hair styles	1981	8	40
2930	Western Fun Barbie, black doll	1989	5	15
9932	Western Fun Barbie, white doll	1989	5	15
9934	Western Fun Ken	1989	5	15
9933	Western Fun Nia	1989	5	15
3600	Western Ken	1981	7	40
5029	Western Skipper	1982	8	30

BARBIE & FRIENDS

NO.	NAME	YEAR	MNB	MIB
4103	Wet n' Wild Barbie	1990	8	35
4121	Wet n' Wild Christie	1989	3	15
4104	Wet n' Wild Ken	1989	3	15
4120	Wet n' Wild Kira	1989	3	15
4138	Wet n' Wild Skipper	1989	3	15
4137	Wet n' Wild Steven	1989	3	15
4136	Wet n' Wild Teresa	1989	3	15
1009	Wig Wardrobe Midge	1965	200	500
	Working Woman	1999	15	30
7808	Yellowstone Kelley	1974	100	275

COLLECTORS' EDITIONS, STORE EXCLUSIVES, GIFT SETS

NO.	NAME	YEAR	MNB	MIB
21384/ 22336	40th Anniversary Barbie, white or black doll	1999	25	50
	40th Anniversary Gala	1999	30	90
	Addams Family Barbie & Ken as Morticia & Gomez	2000	40	80
17341	After the Walk, Coca-Cola, Fashion Classic Series	1997	100	200
3712	All American Barbie & Starstepper	1991	12	35
17313	American Stories American Indian	1997	10	20
	American Stories American Indian Barbie #2		15	28
14612	American Stories Civil War Nurse Barbie	1996	10	25
12578	American Stories Colonial Barbie	1995	10	25
14715	American Stories Indian and Papoose	1996	10	25
17312	American Stories Patriot Barbie	1997	10	25
12577	American Stories Pilgrim Barbie	1995	10	25
12680	American Stories Pioneer Barbie	1995	10	25
	American Stories Pioneer Barbie #2	1996	15	25
14756	American Stories Shopkeeper Barbie	1996	10	25
5854	Ames Country Looks Barbie	1993	12	25
2452	Ames Denim 'N Lace Barbie	1992	10	30
5756	Ames Hot Looks Barbie	1992	10	25
	Ames Ice Cream Barbie	1998	8	15
	Ames Lady Bug Barbie	1997	5	20
	Ames Magna Doodle Barbie	1999	8	15
2909	Ames Party in Pink	1991	10	30
	Ames Strawberry Party Barbie	1999	8	15
	Angel Lights Barbie	1993	45	100
	Angels of Music Harpist Angel Barbie, black or white	1998	35	75
	Angels of Music Heartstring Angel Barbie, black or white	1999	40	85
17603	Anne Klein Barbie	1997	35	70
3406	Applause Barbie Holiday	1991	20	40
5313	Applause Style Barbie	1990	10	35
23884	Artist Series, Reflections of Light Barbie, Renoir	1999	40	80
19366	Artist Series, Sunflower Barbie, Van Gogh	1998	40	80
	Artist Series, Water Lily Barbie	1997	50	110
15204	Autumn Glory, Enchanted Seasons Collection	1996	40	90
	Avon Fruit Fantasy Barbie, blonde	1999	10	25
	Avon Fruit Fantasy Barbie, brunette	1999	15	30
	Avon Lemon-Lime Barbie	1999	10	25
17690	Avon Mrs. P.F.E. Albee	1997	22	65
	Avon Mrs. P.F.E. Albee #2	1998	30	75
	Avon Representative Barbie, black, white, Hispanic	1999	20	50
	Avon Snow Sensation, black or white doll	1999	15	40
15202	Avon Spring Blossom, black doll	1996	10	20
15201	Avon Spring Blossom, white	1996	10	25
	Avon Spring Petals Barbie, black doll	1997	15	30
	Avon Spring Petals Barbie, blond or brunette	1997	15	30
	Avon Spring Tea Party Barbie, black doll		15	30

COLLECTORS' EDITIONS, STORE EXCLUSIVES, GIFT SETS

NO.	NAME	YEAR	MNB	MIB
	Avon Spring Tea Party Barbie, blond or brunette		15	30
	Avon Strawberry Sorbet Barbie	1999	10	25
	Avon Winter Rhapsody Barbie, black doll		15	30
	Avon Winter Rhapsody Barbie, blond or brunette		15	30
	Avon Winter Splendor Barbie, black	1998	20	40
	Avon Winter Splendor Barbie, white	1998	15	35
15587	Avon Winter Velvet, black doll	1996	10	85
15571	Avon Winter Velvet, white	1996	17	75
11182	B Mine Barbie	1993	7	25
3208	Back To School	1993	15	35
9613	Ballerina on Tour Gift Set	1976	25	125
17763	Ballroom Beauties Moonlight Waltz Barbie, 3rd	1997	40	80
14070	Ballroom Beauties Starlight Waltz Barbie	1995	35	85
27409/ 27410	Barbie 2000, white or black doll	2000	30	59
4431	Barbie and Friends: Ken, Barbie, P.J.	1983	25	75
	Barbie and Ken Camping Out	1983	25	65
892	Barbie and Ken Tennis Gift Set	1962	450	1000
	Barbie at Bloomingdale's	1996	15	35
3303	Barbie Beautiful Blues Gift Set	1967	1600	3000
17450	Barbie Loves Elvis Gift Set	1997	30	55
	Barbie Loves Frankie Sinatra Gift Set	1999	40	70
	Barbie Millicent Roberts Final Touches & Lime Time		8	15
	Barbie Millicent Roberts Final Touches Red Hot	1997	8	15
16079	Barbie Millicent Roberts Gift Set, Matinee Today	1996	22	60
19433	Barbie Millicent Roberts Green Thumb Fashion	1998	10	20
16076	Barbie Millicent Roberts Homecoming Fan, Goin' to the Game	1996	10	20
	Barbie Millicent Roberts Jet Set Luggage	1997	8	18
17567	Barbie Millicent Roberts Perfectly Suited	1997	30	45
16077	Barbie Millicent Roberts Picnic in the Park	1996	10	20
19791	Barbie Millicent Roberts Pinstripe Power Gift Set	1998	30	50
19772	Barbie Millicent Roberts Snow Chic, So Chic Fashion	1998	10	20
1013	Barbie's Round the Clock Gift Set, Bubblecut	1964	1200	3000
1011	Barbie's Sparkling Pink Gift Set, Bubblecut	1964	1000	2400
1017	Barbie's Wedding Party Gift Set	1964	1000	2400
	Beautiful Bride Barbie	1976	75	200
1702	Beauty Secrets Barbie Pretty Reflections Gift Set	1979	40	100
17040	Bill Blass Barbie	1997	35	75
17641	Billions of Dreams Barbie	1997	150	350
3421	Billy Boy Feelin' Groovy Barbie	1987	100	175
	Billy Boy Le Nouveau Theatre de la Mode Barbie	1985	100	200
19365	Birds of Beauty #1 Peacock Barbie	1998	32	70
22957	Birds of Beauty #2 Flamingo Barbie	1999	50	100
27682	Birds of Beauty #3 Swan Barbie	2000	40	80
11589	Birthday Fun at McDonald's Gift Set	1994	15	35
21128	Birthday Wishes #1, black or white doll	1999	15	35
	Birthday Wishes #2, black or white doll	2000	20	40
9385	BJ's Children's Palace, black doll	1990	15	45
4385	BJ's Children's Palace, white	1990	20	45
15987	BJ's Rose Bride Barbie	1996	15	45
	Bloomingdale's Calvin Klein Barbie	1996	20	55
14595	Bloomingdale's Donna Karan, blond	1994	35	90
14452	Bloomingdale's Donna Karan, blond	1995	45	100
14452	Bloomingdale's Donna Karan, brunette	1996	35	145
20376	Bloomingdale's Oscar de la Renta	1998	45	100
15950	Bloomingdale's Ralph Lauren Barbie	1997	40	80
12152	Bloomingdale's Savvy Shopper	1994	50	100
5405	Bob Mackie Designer Gold	1990	350	700
4247	Bob Mackie Empress Bride Barbie	1992	500	900

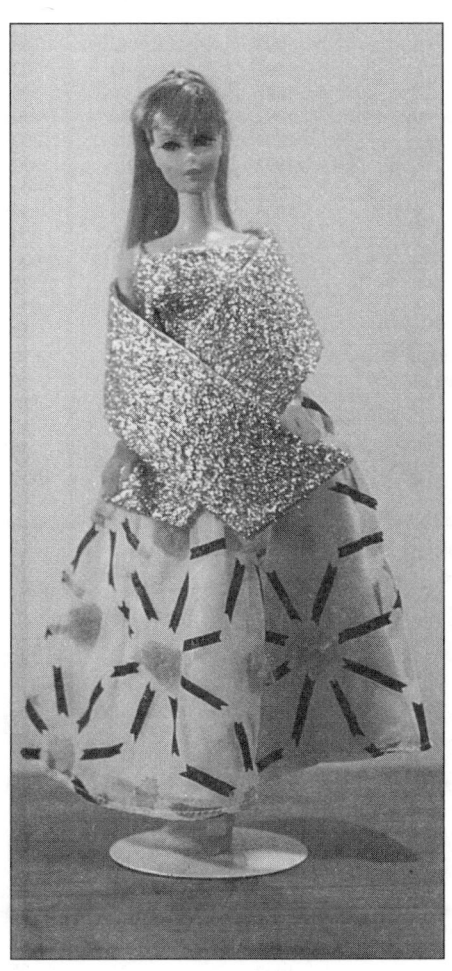

Twist and Turn Barbie, titian, 1967

Twist and Turn Christie, 1969

COLLECTORS' EDITIONS, STORE EXCLUSIVES, GIFT SETS

NO.	NAME	YEAR	MNB	MIB
22044	Bob Mackie Fantasy Goddess of Africa	1999	120	225
SA415	Bob Mackie Fantasy Goddess of Asia	1998	120	225
25859	Bob Mackie Fantasy Goddess of the Americas	2000	125	240
14056	Bob Mackie Goddess of the Sun	1995	75	225
15522	Bob Mackie Jewel Essence Amethyst Aura	1997	40	120
15519	Bob Mackie Jewel Essence Diamond Dazzle	1997	40	140
15521	Bob Mackie Jewel Essence Emerald Embers	1997	40	120
15520	Bob Mackie Jewel Essence Ruby Radiance	1997	40	120
15523	Bob Mackie Jewel Essence Sapphire Splendor	1997	40	120
	Bob Mackie Le Papillon	1999	70	200
17934	Bob Mackie Madame du Barbie	1997	100	250
10803	Bob Mackie Masquerade Ball Barbie	1993	250	400
14105	Bob Mackie Moon Goddess	1996	75	180
4248	Bob Mackie Neptune Fantasy Barbie	1992	500	900
2703	Bob Mackie Platinum	1991	300	600
12046	Bob Mackie Queen of Hearts Barbie	1994	125	275
2704	Bob Mackie Starlight Splendor	1991	300	600
25871	Bowling Champ Barbie	2000	15	35
27674	Bridal Collection Millenium Wedding, white, black or Hispanic	2000	25	50
19848	Byron Lars Cinnabar Sensation, black or white doll	1999	35	95
17031	Byron Lars In the Limelight	1997	40	175
23478	Byron Lars Plum Royale	1998	40	95
13966	Caroling Fun Barbie	1995	8	20
3304	Casey Goes Casual Gift Set	1967	800	1650
27690	Celestial Collection #1 Evening Star	2000	25	49
27688	Celestial Collection #2 Morning Sun	2000	25	49
27689	Celestial Collection #3 Midnight Moon Princess	2000	25	49
4385	Child's World Disney Barbie	1990	15	35
9835	Child's World Disney Barbie, black doll	1990	15	35
16900	Children's Collector Series Cinderella	1997	25	40
14960	Children's Collector Series Little Bo Peep	1995	80	175
13016	Children's Collector Series Rapunzel	1995	25	50
	Children's Collector Series Sleeping Beauty	1998	20	45
21130	Children's Collector Series Snow White	1999	20	40
24673	Children's Collector Series, Barbie as Belle (Beauty and the Beast)	2000	20	40
16013	Christian Dior 50th Anniversary Barbie	1997	35	75
13168	Christian Dior Barbie	1995	60	100
14615	Chuck E. Cheese	1996	15	30
22257	City Seasons Autumn in London	1999	20	50
19367	City Seasons Autumn in Paris	1998	18	50
	City Seasons Spring in Tokyo	1999	25	50
	City Seasons Spring in Tokyo, nostalgic face mold, Internet exclusive	1999	30	65
19431	City Seasons Summer in Rome	1999	25	50
22258	City Seasons Winter in Montreal	1999	20	50
19429	City Seasons Winter in New York	1998	18	50
20581	Classic Ballet Marzipan	1999	15	30
25642	Classic Ballet Snowflake	2000	15	30
17056	Classic Ballet Sugar Plum Fairy	1997	15	35
18509	Classic Ballet Swan Lake, black or white doll	1998	15	30
1521	Classique Benefit Ball Barbie	1992	50	125
10149	Classique City Style Barbie	1993	30	100
11622	Classique Evening Extravaganza	1994	25	65
11638	Classique Evening Extravaganza, black doll	1994	25	75
19361	Classique Evening Sophisticate	1998	18	50
12999	Classique Midnight Gala	1995	25	70
10148	Classique Opening Night Barbie	1993	30	95
17136	Classique Romantic Interlude Barbie	1997	15	45
17137	Classique Romantic Interlude Barbie, black doll	1997	15	45

COLLECTORS' EDITIONS, STORE EXCLUSIVES, GIFT SETS

NO.	NAME	YEAR	MNB	MIB
15461	Classique Starlight Dance	1996	20	45
15819	Classique Starlight Dance, black doll	1996	20	45
11623	Classique Uptown Chic Barbie	1994	25	70
2366	Club-Doll-Jewel Jubilee	1991	10	25
24637	Coca-Cola Barbie as 1950s Teenager	2000	25	59
22831	Coca-Cola Barbie, carhop	1999	20	65
	Coca-Cola Fashion Classic #1, After the Walk	1997	75	160
19739	Coca-Cola Fashion Classic #2, Summer Daydreams	1998	50	100
	Coca-Cola Ken	2000	25	59
	Coca-Cola Soda Fountain Sweetheart	1996	90	180
	Coca-Cola, Disney Teddy & Doll Convention, brunette, limited to 1,500		45	95
21510	Collectors' Request Commuter Set Barbie	1999	25	50
24930	Collectors' Request Sophisticated Lady	1999	25	59
18941	Collectors' Request Twist and Turn Smasheroo, brunette	1998	25	40
	Collectors' Request Twist N' Turn Smasheroo, red hair	1998	25	50
25525	Cool Collecting Barbie (w/mini toys)	2000	25	59
15528	Couture Collection Portrait in Taffeta Barbie	1996	65	150
17572	Couture Collection Serenade in Satin Barbie	1997	65	150
4917	Dance Club Barbie Gift Set	1989	25	60
5409	Dance Magic Gift Set Barbie & Ken	1990	15	35
9058	Dance Sensation Barbie Gift Set	1984	15	40
2996	Deluxe Tropical Barbie	1986	10	30
11276	Easter Fun Barbie	1994	10	20
12793	Easter Party	1995	20	45
15846	Empress Sissy, Barbie as	1996	35	80
14992	Enchanted Evening Barbie, blond	1996	25	30
15407	Enchanted Evening Barbie, brunette	1996	25	30
25639	Enchanted World of Fairies, Fairy of the Forest Barbie	2000	25	49
15948	Escada Barbie	1996	40	70
	Essence of Nature #1 Water Rhapsody	1998	40	90
22834	Essence of Nature #2 Whispering Wind	1999	40	80
26327	Essence of Nature #3 Dancing Fire	2000	35	79
	Evergreen Princess Barbie, Winter Princess Collection	1994	35	100
3196	Fantastica Barbie	1992	20	40
	FAO Schwarz Barbie as George Washington (American Beauty Series)	1996	35	75
	FAO Schwarz Bob Mackie Le Papillion Barbie,	1999	80	155
13257	FAO Schwarz Circus Star Barbie	1995	35	110
	FAO Schwarz City Seasons Summer in San Francisco	1998	40	95
	FAO Schwarz City Seasons Summer in San Francisco, red hair		200	750
	FAO Schwarz Floral Signature #1 Antique Rose Barbie	1996	50	150
	FAO Schwarz Floral Signature #2 Lily Barbie	1997	50	145
7734	FAO Schwarz Golden Greetings Barbie	1989	65	225
	FAO Schwarz Golden Hollywood Barbie, white or black doll	1999	55	100
14061	FAO Schwarz Jeweled Splendor (125th Anniversary)	1995	100	225
1539	FAO Schwarz Madison Ave. Barbie	1992	100	200
24636/ 24998	FAO Schwarz Mann's Chinese Theatre Barbie, white or black doll	2000	35	75
2921	FAO Schwarz Night Sensation	1991	75	165
2017	FAO Schwarz Rockettes Barbie	1993	75	200
11652	FAO Schwarz Silver Screen Barbie	1994	65	200
14684	FAO Schwarz Statue of Liberty Barbie (American Beauty Series)	1996	40	100
	FAO Schwarz Summer in San Francisco	1998	30	95
5946	FAO Schwarz Winter Fantasy	1990	100	235
	FAO Schwarz, Barbie at FAO	1997	12	25
17382	Fashion Luncheon	1997	25	55
26929	Fashion Model Collection, Delphine Barbie	2000	35	80

BARBIE

COLLECTORS' EDITIONS, STORE EXCLUSIVES, GIFT SETS

NO.	NAME	YEAR	MNB	MIB
26930/ 26931	Fashion Model Collection, Lingerie Barbie, blonde or brunette	2000	20	40
863	Fashion Queen Barbie & Her Friends	1964	1000	2400
864	Fashion Queen Barbie & Ken Trousseau Gift Set	1964	1200	2800
17860	Fashion Savvy #1 Tangerine Twist	1997	14	45
19632	Fashion Savvy #2 Uptown Chic	1998	20	45
1194	Francie Rise n' Shine Gift Set	1971	600	1200
1042	Francie Swingin' Separates Gift Set	1966	700	1500
17601	Francie Wild Bunch	1997	20	55
14808	Francie, 30th Anniversary	1996	20	45
3826	Fun to Dress Barbie Gift Set	1993	8	15
18547	Gap Barbie and Kelly Gift Set	1997	15	45
	Gap Barbie and Kelly Gift Set, black doll	1997	15	45
16450	Gap Barbie, black doll	1996	20	60
16449	Gap Barbie, white	1996	30	60
22237	Garden of Flowers Rose Barbie	1999	25	50
	General Mills Winter Dazzle, black doll	1997	5	20
18456	General Mills Winter Dazzle, white	1997	5	20
	Givenchy Barbie	2000	35	80
24635	Givenchy Barbie	2000	40	80
12009	Gold Jubilee Barbie, Jubilee Series	1994	500	750
	Graduation, Class of 1996	1996	5	15
	Graduation, Class of 1997	1997	5	10
17782	Grand Ole Opry #1 Country Rose Barbie	1997	40	80
17864	Grand Ole Opry #2 Rising Star Barbie	1998	50	100
23498	Grand Ole Opry Barbie and Kenny Duet	1999	55	99
16708	Great Eras Chinese Empress	1997	35	50
11397	Great Eras Egyptian Queen	1994	20	120
12792	Great Eras Elizabethan Queen	1995	25	60
4063	Great Eras Flapper	1993	25	175
16707	Great Eras French Lady	1997	35	50
3702	Great Eras Gibson Girl	1993	25	125
15005	Great Eras Grecian Goddess	1996	35	50
12791	Great Eras Medieval Lady	1995	25	60
11478	Great Eras Southern Belle	1994	20	100
14900	Great Eras Victorian Lady	1996	35	50
18630	Great Fashions of the 20th Century #1, Promenade in the Park	1998	20	65
19631	Great Fashions of the 20th Century #2, Dance 'til Dawn	1998	30	65
21531	Great Fashions of the 20th Century #3, Steppin Out Barbie	1999	30	60
22162	Great Fashions of the 20th Century #4, Fabulous Forties	2000	25	59
27675	Great Fashions of the 20th Century #5, Nifty Fifties	2000	25	59
27676	Great Fashions of the 20th Century #6, Groovy Sixties	2000	25	59
	Hallmark Fair Valentine Barbie	1998	20	45
14108	Hallmark Holiday Memories Barbie	1995	20	50
17094	Hallmark Holiday Traditions Barbie	1997	25	50
	Hallmark Holiday Voyage Barbie	1998	25	60
	Hallmark Sentimental Valentine Barbie	1997	23	50
14880	Hallmark Valentine Barbie (Sweet Valentine Barbie)	1996	20	60
12579	Hallmark Victorian Skater Barbie (Victorian Elegance Barbie)	1994	75	80
15621	Hallmark Yuletide Romance Barbie	1996	20	50
	Hanae Mori Barbie		50	99
	Happy Birthday Barbie Gift Set	1985	20	40
9519	Happy Birthday Barbie Gift Set	1984	35	85
1703	Happy Holidays 1988	1988	100	750
3253	Happy Holidays 1989	1989	50	250
4098	Happy Holidays 1990	1990	25	150
4543	Happy Holidays 1990, black doll	1990	20	100
1871	Happy Holidays 1991	1991	40	175
2696	Happy Holidays 1991 black doll	1991	40	100

BARBIE

Avon Mrs. P.F.E. Albee, 1997

*Barbie Millicent
Roberts Gift Set,
Matinee Today, 1996*

COLLECTORS' EDITIONS, STORE EXCLUSIVES, GIFT SETS

NO.	NAME	YEAR	MNB	MIB
1429	Happy Holidays 1992	1992	30	145
2396	Happy Holidays 1992, black doll	1992	30	80
10824	Happy Holidays 1993	1993	30	130
10911	Happy Holidays 1993, black doll	1993	30	60
12155	Happy Holidays 1994	1994	30	155
12156	Happy Holidays 1994, black doll	1994	30	80
14123	Happy Holidays 1995	1995	20	65
14124	Happy Holidays 1995, black doll	1995	20	55
15646	Happy Holidays 1996, white or black doll	1996	30	55
17832	Happy Holidays 1997	1997	5	25
17833	Happy Holidays 1997, black doll	1997	5	25
	Happy Holidays 1998, white or black doll	1998	10	25
	Harrods Easy Chic Barbie, limited to 250	1996	250	800
0175	Harvey Nichols Special Edition (250 made)	1995	500	900
7470	Hawaiian Barbie	1982	25	100
1879	Hills Blue Elegance Barbie	1992	12	40
3274	Hills Evening Sparkle	1990	10	35
3549	Hills Moonlight Rose	1991	7	30
4843	Hills Party Lace Barbie	1989	15	35
12412	Hills Polly Pocket Barbie	1994	12	25
13940	Hills Sea Pearl Mermaid Barbie	1995	8	35
28081	Holiday Angel #1, black doll	2000	20	50
26914	Holiday Angel #1, white doll	2000	20	50
12192	Holiday Dreams Barbie	1994	10	20
10280	Holiday Hostess Barbie	1993	25	50
15581	Holiday Season	1996	5	15
10928	Hollywood Hair Deluxe Gift Set	1993	15	35
12701	Hollywood Legends Dorothy (Wizard of Oz)	1995	20	180
15498	Hollywood Legends Eliza Doolittle (My Fair Lady), green coat	1996	30	65
15500	Hollywood Legends Eliza Doolittle (My Fair Lady), lace ball gown	1996	30	95
15501	Hollywood Legends Eliza Doolittle (My Fair Lady), pink	1996	30	75
15497	Hollywood Legends Eliza Doolittle (My Fair Lady), white lace gown w/parasol	1996	30	75
14901	Hollywood Legends Glinda (Wizard of Oz)	1996	35	75
16573	Hollywood Legends Ken as Cowardly Lion (Wizard of Oz)	1996	35	75
15499	Hollywood Legends Ken as Henry Higgins (My Fair Lady)	1996	25	65
	Hollywood Legends Ken as Rhett Butler	1994	25	65
	Hollywood Legends Ken as Scarecrow (Wizard of Oz)	1996	35	65
14902	Hollywood Legends Ken as Tin Man (Wizard of Oz)	1996	35	65
13676	Hollywood Legends Maria (Sound of Music)	1995	20	50
17451	Hollywood Legends Marilyn Monroe, pink	1997	20	45
17452	Hollywood Legends Marilyn Monroe, red	1997	20	45
17155	Hollywood Legends Marilyn Monroe, white	1997	20	45
13254	Hollywood Legends Scarlett O'Hara, black/white dress	1993	25	70
12045	Hollywood Legends Scarlett O'Hara, green velvet curtain	1994	25	70
12997	Hollywood Legends Scarlett O'Hara, green/white silk dress	1995	25	65
12815	Hollywood Legends Scarlett O'Hara, red velvet dress	1994	25	70
26914	Hollywood Movie Star #1, Hollywood Premiere	2000	25	50
27684	Hollywood Movie Star #2, Between Takes	2000	25	50
1865	Home Shopping Club Evening Flame	1991	70	125
	Home Shopping Club Golden Allure Barbie	1999	5	30
	Japanese Living Eli	1970	700	1400
1596	JC Penney Barbie Pink Premier Gift Set		600	1500
2702	JCPenney Enchanted Evening (Evening Elegance Series)	1991	40	70
7057	JCPenney Evening Elegance (Evening Elegance Series)	1990	40	60
	JCPenney Evening Enchantment Barbie	1998	20	48
1278	JCPenney Evening Sensation (Evening Elegance Series)	1992	12	55
10684	JCPenney Golden Winter (Evening Elegance Series)	1993	12	55
	JCPenney My Wardrobe Barbie		15	30

COLLECTORS' EDITIONS, STORE EXCLUSIVES, GIFT SETS

NO.	NAME	YEAR	MNB	MIB
12191	JCPenney Night Dazzle (Evening Elegance Series)	1994	15	55
	JCPenney Original Arizona Jean Co. Barbie	1998	12	25
	JCPenney Original Arizona Jean Co. Barbie	1996	12	28
	JCPenney Original Arizona Jean Co. Barbie	1997	12	25
	JCPenney Royal Enchantment Barbie	1995	20	40
14010	JCPenney Royal Enchantment Barbie	1995	25	40
	JCPenney Winter Renaissance Barbie	1996	15	30
21923	Jubilee Series, Crystal Jubilee, limited to 20,000	1999	150	325
	Jubilee Series, Gold Jubilee	1994	300	750
3756	Jubilee Series, Pink Jubilee, limited to 1,200	1989	800	2200
	Julia Simply Wow Gift Set	1969	400	1500
	K-B Fantasy Ball Barbie	1997	10	20
	K-B Fashion Avenue Barbie	1998	8	15
	K-B Starlight Carousel Barbie	1998	10	20
	K-B Toys Glamour Barbie	1997	10	20
	K-B Toys Glamour Barbie, black doll	1997	10	20
	Kmart March of Dimes Walk America Barbie & Kelly Gift Set	1999	15	25
	Kmart March of Dimes Walk America Barbie, black or white doll	1998	10	24
4870	Kmart Peach Pretty Barbie	1989	10	30
3117	Kmart Pretty in Purple	1992	12	25
3121	Kmart Pretty in Purple, black doll	1992	12	25
	Keepsake Treasures Barbie and the Tale of Peter Rabbit	1998	15	40
2977	Kissing Barbie Gift Set	1978	25	65
	Kool-Aid Barbie	1996	15	40
10309	Kool-Aid Wacky Warehouse Barbie I	1993	25	60
11763	Kool-Aid Wacky Warehouse Barbie II	1994	25	50
	Kraft Treasures Barbie	1992	30	55
	L.E. Festival Holiday Barbie (540 made)	1994	700	1200
	Life Ball Barbie #1	1998	200	500
	Life Ball Barbie #2	1999	200	500
	Little Debbie #2, bent arms	1996	15	30
	Little Debbie #2, straight arms	1996	15	25
	Little Debbie #3	1998	15	25
10123	Little Debbie Barbie	1993	25	60
1585	Living Barbie Action Accents Gift Set	1970	500	1500
1117	Living Skipper	1970	40	175
7583	Loving You Barbie Gift Set	1983	45	100
	Macy's Anne Klein Barbie	1997	30	70
	Macy's City Shopper Barbie	1996	25	70
27287	Magic & Mystery Morgan LeFay and Merlin	2000	50	100
23882	Major League Baseball #1 Los Angeles Dodgers	1999	20	40
23881	Major League Baseball #1 New York Yankees	1999	20	40
23883	Major League Baseball #3 Chicago Cubs	1999	20	40
23883	Major League Baseball Chicago Cubs	1999	20	45
23882	Major League Baseball Los Angeles Dodgers	1999	20	45
23881	Major League Baseball New York Yankees	1999	20	45
1703	Malibu Barbie "The Beach Party", w/case	1979	17	35
1248	Malibu Ken Surf's Up Gift Set	1971	75	200
18667	Masquerade #1 Illusion	1997	50	120
20647	Masquerade #2 Rendezvous	1998	50	85
24501	Masquerade #3 Venetian Opulence	2000	50	100
	Mattel Festival 35th Anniversary (3,500 made)	1994	250	200
11591	Mattel Festival 35th Anniversary Gift Set (975 made)	1994	400	550
	Mattel Festival Banquet, blond	1994	175	225
	Mattel Festival Banquet, brunette	1994	125	250
	Mattel Festival Banquet, redhead	1994	225	225
11160	Mattel Festival Doctor, brunette (1,500 made)	1994	75	100
11921	Mattel Festival Gymnast (1,500 made)	1994	75	80

BARBIE

COLLECTORS' EDITIONS, STORE EXCLUSIVES, GIFT SETS

NO.	NAME	YEAR	MNB	MIB
12155	Mattel Festival Happy Holiday	1994	270	1200
	Mattel Festival Haute Couture, rainbow (500 made)	1994	200	300
	Mattel Festival Haute Couture, red velvet (480 made)	1994	200	375
12191	Mattel Festival Night Dazzle, brunette (420 made)	1994	150	400
12905	Mattel Festival Snow Princess, brunette (285 made)	1994	600	1250
10051	Meijers Shopping Fun	1993	10	20
863	Meijers Something Extra	1992	10	20
4983	Mervyns Ballerina Barbie	1983	30	75
7093	Mervyns Fabulous Fur	1986	25	65
1012	Midge's Ensemble Gift Set	1964	1200	3150
17780	Midnight Princess	1997	30	60
24505	Millennium Bride, limited to 10,000	1999	150	300
	Millennium Princess Barbie, black or white doll		20	40
	Millennium Princess Teresa		20	40
857	Mix n' Match Gift Set	1962	800	1850
3210	Montgomery Wards (mail order box)	1972	30	700
3210	Montgomery Wards Barbie (pink box)	1972	350	800
2483	My First Barbie Gift Set	1991	8	20
1979	My First Barbie Gift Set, pink tutu	1986	15	35
5386	My First Barbie Gift Set, pink tutu	1987	18	40
1875	My First Barbie, pink tutu, Zayre's Hispanic	1987	8	45
20442	NASCAR Barbie #1, Kyle Petty #44	1998	20	25
22954	NASCAR Barbie #2, Bill Elliott #94	1999	20	45
	National Convention, Barbie and the Bandstand	1996	225	450
	National Convention, Barbie Around the World Festival	1985	125	300
	National Convention, Barbie Convention 1980	1980	125	350
	National Convention, Barbie Forever Young	1989	125	300
	National Convention, Barbie Loves a Fairytale	1991	150	250
	National Convention, Barbie Loves New York	1984	125	275
	National Convention, Barbie Ole	1995	225	400
	National Convention, Barbie Wedding Dreams	1992	50	200
	National Convention, Barbie's Pow Wow	1983	125	350
	National Convention, Barbie's Reunion	1986	125	275
	National Convention, Beach Blanket Barbie	1997	225	375
	National Convention, Christmas With Barbie	1987	125	300
	National Convention, Come Rain or Shine	1988	125	250
	National Convention, Deep in the Heart of Texas	1990	125	250
	National Convention, Michigan Entertains Barbie	1982	125	275
	National Convention, The Magic of Barbie	1994	175	375
	National Convention, You've Come a Long Way	1993	225	450
23205	New Lifestyles of the West Western Plains	1999	40	80
16289	Nicole Miller	1996	30	65
	Nolan Miller #1	1998	70	150
23495	Nolan Miller #2 Evening Illusion	1999	70	110
11591	Nostalgic 35th Anniversary Gift Set	1994	75	150
11590	Nostalgic 35th Anniversary, blond	1994	25	50
11782	Nostalgic 35th Anniversary, brunette	1994	50	80
	Nostalgic Wedding Day, blond	1997	10	25
21740	Nursery Rhymes Barbie Had a Little Lamb	1999	20	40
5472	Nutcracker Barbie	1992	85	250
16442	Ocean Friends Gift Set	1996	20	45
16443	Olympic Barbie Gift Set	1996	15	30
1014	On Parade Gift Set, Barbie, Ken, Midge	1964	800	2300
3803	Osco Picnic Pretty	1993	20	40
14024	Oshagatsu Barbie	1995	40	80
1588	P.J.'s Swinging Silver Gift Set	1970	700	1500
10926	Paint 'N Dazzle Deluxe Gift Set	1993	17	35
2001	Party Premier	1992	15	30
9025	Party Sensation	1990	30	70

Birthday Wishes #2, 2000

*Bob Mackie Queen of Hearts
Barbie, 1994*

COLLECTORS' EDITIONS, STORE EXCLUSIVES, GIFT SETS

NO.	NAME	YEAR	MNB	MIB
7009	Peach Blossom Barbie	1992	15	30
13598	Peppermint Princess Barbie, Winter Princess Collection	1995	35	85
20377	Phantom of the Opera gift set, FAO Schwarz	1998	60	145
5239	Pink & Pretty Barbie Gift Set	1982	35	90
16091	Pink Splendor	1996	200	550
15280	Poodle Parade	1996	25	55
2598	Pretty Changes Barbie Gift Set	1978	35	75
2901	Pretty Hearts Barbie	1992	7	15
1135	Pretty Pairs Angie N' Tangie	1970	125	250
1133	Pretty Pairs Lori N' Rori	1970	125	250
1134	Pretty Pairs Nan N' Fran	1970	125	250
25192	Radio Shack Earring Magic	1991	20	40
3161	Red Romance Barbie	1993	7	15
25680	Royal Jewels Empress of Emeralds, QVC exclusive	2000	50	100
	Royal Jewels Queen of Sapphires	2000	50	100
1858	Royal Romance	1992	20	45
	Runway Collection, Indigo Obsession	2000	40	99
	Russell Stover Candie Barbie	1997	5	15
14617	Russell Stover Easter (w/Easter basket)	1996	10	25
14956	Russell Stover Easter (w/software package)	1996	10	25
	Sam's Club 70s Disco Barbie, blond	1998	12	25
	Sam's Club 70s Disco Barbie, brunette	1998	15	30
	Sam's Club Dinner Date Barbie, blond	1998	8	15
	Sam's Club Dinner Date Barbie, red hair	1998	9	20
10339	Sam's Club Festiva Barbie	1993	15	35
	Sam's Club Fifties Fun Barbie	1996	20	40
2366	Sam's Club Jewel Jubilee	1991	25	65
	Sam's Club Jewel Jubilee Barbie	1991	25	60
	Sam's Club Party Sensation Barbie	1990	20	50
	Sam's Club Peach Blossom Barbie	1992	20	40
	Sam's Club Season's Greetings Barbie	1994	25	60
	Sam's Club Sixties Fun Barbie, blond	1997	15	25
17693	Sam's Club Sixties Fun Barbie, red hair	1997	10	28
	Sam's Club Sixties Fun Barbie, red hair	1997	15	30
17252	Sam's Club Sixties Fun, blond	1997	10	25
	Sam's Club Sweet Moments Barbie	1997	10	20
	Sam's Club Sweet Moments Barbie	1997	12	20
	Sam's Club Wedding Fantasy Barbie Gift Set	1993	30	70
	Sam's Club Winter Fantasy Barbie	1996	10	25
	Sam's Club Winter Fantasy Barbie, black doll	1997	20	50
	Sam's Club Winter Fantasy Barbie, blond or brunette	1997	10	20
	Sam's Club Winter's Eve Barbie	1995	12	28
13741	Schooltime Fun	1995	15	30
25636	Scuderia Ferrari Barbie	2000	20	39
2998	Sears 100th Celebration Barbie	1986	20	75
1866	Sears Barbie Twinkle Town Set	1969	800	1600
3817	Sears Blossom Beautiful Barbie	1992	100	275
	Sears Blue Starlight	1997	15	30
2306	Sears Dream Princess	1992	25	50
10292	Sears Enchanted Princess	1993	35	60
3596	Sears Evening Enchantment Barbie	1989	10	40
	Sears Evening Flame	1996	15	30
5588	Sears Lavender Surprise	1990	8	35
9049	Sears Lavender Surprise, black doll	1990	8	30
7669	Sears Lilac and Lovely Barbie	1988	10	45
1193	Sears Perfectly Plaid Gift Set	1971	800	1500
	Sears Pink Reflections	1998	10	25
13011	Sears Ribbons and Roses Barbie	1995	10	50
12410	Sears Silver Sweetheart Barbie	1994	17	50

NO.	NAME	YEAR	MNB	MIB
1036	Sears Skooter Cut n' Button Gift Set	1967	150	650
2586	Sears Southern Belle	1991	10	40
4550	Sears Star Dream Barbie	1987	10	60
9042	Sears Winter Sports	1975	65	115
12384	Season's Greetings Barbie	1994	50	85
10929	Secret Hearts Gift Set	1993	17	35
1364	Service Merchandise Blue Rhapsody	1991	125	175
12005	Service Merchandise City Sophisticate	1994	20	85
	Service Merchandise Definitely Diamonds	1998	45	110
	Service Merchandise Dream Bride, black or white		10	25
	Service Merchandise Evening Symphony	1998	10	25
13612	Service Merchandise Ruby Romance Barbie	1995	25	50
1886	Service Merchandise Satin Nights, two earring versions	1992	20	80
	Service Merchandise Sea Princess	1996	15	30
10994	Service Merchandise Sparkling Splendor	1993	17	50
5716	Sharin Sisters Gift Set	1992	12	25
10143	Sharin Sisters Gift Set	1993	12	25
3142	Shopko/Venture Blossom Beauty	1991	10	40
1876	Shopko/Venture Party Perfect	1992	12	35
	Shopko/Venture Party Perfect Barbie	1992	15	30
	Silken Flame, blond or brunette	1998	15	30
15951	Silver Royale	1996	25	65
1021	Skipper Party Time Gift Set	1964	100	550
1172	Skipper Swing 'a' Rounder Gym Gift Set	1972	100	400
2262	Snap 'N Play Gift Set (Snap 'N Play Deluxe)	1992	12	35
	Snow Princess Barbie	1994	75	150
	Spiegel Golden Qi-Pao Barbie	1998	30	65
4116	Spiegel Regal Reflections Barbie	1992	75	275
10969	Spiegel Royal Invitation Barbie	1993	35	100
14009	Spiegel Shopping Chic Barbie	1995	35	75
3347	Spiegel Sterling Wishes	1991	45	130
	Spiegel Summer Sophisticate	1996	20	45
12077	Spiegel Theatre Elegance	1994	150	180
	Spiegel Theatre Elegance Barbie	1994	55	165
17441	Spiegel Winners Circle	1997	35	50
	Splash 'N Color Barbie Gift Set	1997	10	20
3477	Spring Bouquet Barbie	1993	10	20
7008	Spring Parade Barbie	1992	15	25
2257	Spring Parade Barbie, black doll	1992	15	25
15006	Star Trek Barbie and Ken	1996	15	30
24639	Storybook Favorites, Kelly and Tommy as Raggedy Ann and Andy,	2000	10	18
1648	Swan Lake Barbie	1991	65	200
3208	Sweet Spring Barbie	1992	10	20
25644/ 26302	Sydney 2000 Olympic Pin Collector, black or white doll	2000	20	40
	Target 35th Anniversary Barbie, black doll	1997	10	24
	Target 35th Anniversary Barbie, white doll	1997	10	20
4583	Target Baseball Date Barbie	1993	10	30
	Target City Style Barbie	1998	8	15
	Target City Style Barbie	1996	10	20
	Target Club Wedd Barbie, black doll	1999	10	20
	Target Club Wedd Barbie, blond or brunette,	1999	10	20
	Target Club Wedd Barbie, brunette or Hispanic	1998	10	24
	Target Club Wedd Barbie, white doll	1998	10	20
2954	Target Cute'n Cool	1991	8	30
3203	Target Dazzlin' Date Barbie	1992	10	25
	Target Easter Bunny Fun Barbie & Kelly	1999	15	30
	Target Easter Egg Hunt Barbie & Kelly	1998	15	40
7476	Target Gold and Lace Barbie	1989	10	30

BARBIE

COLLECTORS' EDITIONS, STORE EXCLUSIVES, GIFT SETS

NO.	NAME	YEAR	MNB	MIB
2587	Target Golden Evening	1991	6	45
10202	Target Golf Date Barbie	1993	10	25
	Target Halloween Fun Barbie & Kelly, white or black dolls	1999	15	25
	Target Halloween Fun Li'l Friends of Kelly	1999	15	25
	Target Halloween Party Barbie & Ken (pirate suits)	1998	20	40
	Target Happy Halloween Barbie & Kelly	1997	30	60
5955	Target Party Pretty Barbie	1990	6	25
5413	Target Pretty in Plaid Barbie	1992	15	30
14110	Target Steppin' Out Barbie	1995	8	20
	Target Valentine Style Barbie, black doll	1999	8	18
	Target Valentine Style Barbie, white doll	1999	8	15
	Target Wild Style Barbie	1992	10	24
	Target With Love Barbie	2000	8	15
7801	Tennis Star Barbie & Ken	1988	18	40
1199	Tiff Pose N' Play	1972	175	400
22955	Timeless Sentiments Angel of Hope	1999	25	50
19633	Timeless Sentiments Angel of Joy	1998	25	50
24240	Timeless Sentiments Angel of Peace	1999	25	50
24241	Timeless Sentiments Angel of Peace, black doll	1999	25	50
	Todd Oldham (Designer)	1999	35	70
19364	Together Forever Collection Romeo & Juliet	1998	50	100
23880	Together Forever King Arthur and Queen Guinevere	1999	50	100
	Toys R Us 101 Dalmatians Barbie	1997	15	28
	Toys R Us 101 Dalmatians Barbie, black	1999	12	20
	Toys R Us 101 Dalmatians Barbie, brunette or strawberry blond	1999	12	20
	Toys R Us 35th Anniversary Midge	1998	25	50
	Toys R Us 35th Anniversary Midge	1998	25	40
12149	Toys R Us Astronaut Barbie (Career Collection)	1994	15	45
12150	Toys R Us Astronaut Barbie, black doll	1994	15	45
10217	Toys R Us Back to School Barbie	1993	10	20
3722	Toys R Us Barbie for President	1992	17	65
3940	Toys R Us Barbie for President, black doll	1992	17	40
	Toys R Us Barbie For President, black doll	1992	15	40
	Toys R Us Barbie For President, white doll	1992	20	60
7970	Toys R Us Bath Time Skipper	1992	12	25
9342	Toys R Us Beauty Pagent Skipper	1991	10	25
	Toys R Us Bicyclin' Barbie, black or white doll	1995	15	25
	Toys R Us Birthday Fun Kelly Gift Set	1996	15	28
1490	Toys R Us Cool 'N Sassy	1992	10	20
4110	Toys R Us Cool 'N Sassy, black doll	1992	10	20
	Toys R Us Crystal Splendor	1996	12	25
	Toys R Us Crystal Splendor Barbie, white or black doll	1996	10	25
9180	Toys R Us Dream Date Barbie	1982	7	30
4077	Toys R Us Dream Date Ken	1982	5	30
5869	Toys R Us Dream Date P.J.	1982	8	40
	Toys R Us Dream Date Skipper	1990	10	25
4817	Toys R Us Dream Date Skipper	1990	6	20
9180	Toys R Us Dream Time Barbie	1988	10	30
10712	Toys R Us Dream Wedding Gift Set	1993	20	45
10713	Toys R Us Dream Wedding Gift Set, black doll	1993	22	45
12322	Toys R Us Emerald Elegance (Society Style Collection)	1994	15	40
	Toys R Us Emerald Elegance Barbie, white or black doll	1994	15	30
12323	Toys R Us Emerald Elegance, ethnic doll	1994	15	40
17443	Toys R Us Emerald Enchantment Barbie	1997	25	50
	Toys R Us Fashion Brights Barbie, white or black doll	1992	10	20
	Toys R Us Fashion Fun Barbie Gift Set	1999	15	25
	Toys R Us Fire Fighter Barbie, white or black doll	1995	25	5
2721	Toys R Us Fun School	1991	6	40
	Toys R Us Gardening Fun Barbie & Kelly Gift Set	1997	12	23
	Toys R Us Golden Anniversary Barbie	1998	40	95
	Toys R Us Got Milk? Barbie, white or black doll		8	20
	Toys R Us Gran Gala Teresa	1997	8	15

Escada Barbie, 1996

Gold Jubilee Barbie, Jubilee
Series, 1994

COLLECTORS' EDITIONS, STORE EXCLUSIVES, GIFT SETS

NO.	NAME	YEAR	MNB	MIB
	Toys R Us Harley-Davidson Barbie #3	1999	50	100
17692	Toys R Us Harley-Davidson Barbie #1	1997	200	400
	Toys R Us Harley-Davidson Barbie #2	1998	100	200
	Toys R Us Harley-Davidson Ken #1	1999	50	100
	Toys R Us I'm A Toys R Us Kid Barbie, white or black doll	1998	15	30
	Toys R Us International Pen Friend Barbie	1995	7	16
10507	Toys R Us Love to Read Barbie	1993	12	40
4581	Toys R Us Malt Shop Barbie	1993	10	25
10608	Toys R Us Moonlight Magic Barbie	1993	15	65
10609	Toys R Us Moonlight Magic Barbie, black doll	1993	15	55
	Toys R Us My Size Bride Barbie, brunette	1995	60	135
	Toys R Us My Size Bride Barbie, red hair	1995	60	135
	Toys R Us Olympic Gymnast Barbie, red hair, box w/o special edition marking	1996	15	30
	Toys R Us Olympic Gymnast Barbie, red hair, Special Edition box	1996	15	35
	Toys R Us Oreo Fun Barbie	1997	8	18
	Toys R Us Paleontologist Barbie, black or white doll	1997	12	24
	Toys R Us Party Time Barbie, black or white doll	1994	10	20
	Toys R Us Party Time Theresa	1994	12	24
4869	Toys R Us Pepsi Spirit Barbie	1989	18	70
4867	Toys R Us Pepsi Spirit Skipper	1989	15	65
	Toys R Us Pink Inspiration Barbie, black doll	1999	15	25
	Toys R Us Pink Inspiration Barbie, blond or brunette	1999	15	25
13233	Toys R Us POG Barbie	1995	7	15
10688	Toys R Us Police Officer Barbie	1993	15	70
10689	Toys R Us Police Officer Barbie, black doll	1993	15	65
13555	Toys R Us Purple Passion	1995	10	30
13554	Toys R Us Purple Passion, ethnic doll	1995	10	30
1276	Toys R Us Radiant in Red Barbie	1992	12	55
4113	Toys R Us Radiant in Red Barbie, black doll	1992	12	55
13256	Toys R Us Sapphire Dream Barbie (Society Style Collection)	1995	50	70
	Toys R Us Sapphire Sophisticate	1997	12	25
2721	Toys R Us School Fun Barbie	1992	10	20
4411	Toys R Us School Fun Barbie, black doll	1992	10	20
10682	Toys R Us School Spirit Barbie	1993	10	25
10683	Toys R Us School Spirit Barbie, black doll	1993	10	30
	Toys R Us Share A Smile Barbie	1997	7	15
	Toys R Us Share A Smile Becky	1997	15	28
	Toys R Us Share A Smile Christie	1997	7	15
7799	Toys R Us Show and Ride Barbie	1988	10	35
7799	Toys R Us Show n' Ride Barbie	1988	10	35
	Toys R Us Space Camp Barbie, white or black doll	1999	12	28
10491	Toys R Us Spots 'N Dots Barbie	1993	12	35
10885	Toys R Us Spots 'N Dots Teresa	1993	12	40
	Toys R Us Spring Parade Barbie, white or black doll	1992	15	30
	Toys R Us Sunflower Barbie	1995	9	20
	Toys R Us Sunflower Teresa	1995	9	20
	Toys R Us Super Talk Barbie, black or white doll	1995	12	28
2917	Toys R Us Sweet Romance	1991	8	30
	Toys R Us Sweet Romance Barbie	1991	15	30
	Toys R Us Sweet Roses Barbie	1989	12	28
7635	Toys R Us Sweet Roses Barbie	1989	7	25
1433	Toys R Us Totally Hair Courtney	1992	10	25
1430	Toys R Us Totally Hair Skipper	1992	10	25
7735	Toys R Us Totally Hair Whitney	1992	20	40
	Toys R Us Travelin' Sisters Gift Set	1995	30	65
1675	Toys R Us Vacation Sensations Barbie, blue	1986	10	40
1675	Toys R Us Vacation Sensations Barbie, pink	1988	12	48
	Toys R Us Wedding Fantasy Barbie & Ken Gift Set	1997	20	45

BARBIE

NO.	NAME	YEAR	MNB	MIB
5949	Toys R Us Winter Fun Barbie	1990	10	40
	Toys R Us Winter Fun Barbie	1990	15	35
	Toys R Us Winter Sports Midge	1995	15	35
	Toys R Us/FAO Schwarz Sea Holiday Barbie #1, with lip gloss	1993	15	30
	Toys R Us/FAO Schwarz Sea Holiday Barbie #2, with lip gloss	1993	15	24
	Toys R Us/FAO/JC Penney, Winter Sports Barbie	1995	15	30
	Toys R Us/FAO/JC Penney, Winter Sports Ken	1995	15	30
2783	Trail Blazin'	1991	10	25
22833	Trend Forecaster Barbie	1999	20	45
2996	Tropical Barbie Deluxe Gift Set	1985	20	45
3556	Tutti and Todd Sundae Treat Set	1966	150	350
3554	Tutti Me n' My Dog	1966	150	350
3553	Tutti Nighty Night Sleep Tight	1965	100	300
4097	Twirley Curls Barbie Gift Set	1982	30	85
21911	Twist and Turn Far Out Barbie	1999	20	40
12675	Valentine Barbie	1994	7	20
774505	Valerie	1978	125	225
19788	Vera Wang #1, bride	1998	75	150
23027	Vera Wang #2, lavender dress	1999	55	140
1859	Very Violet Barbie	1992	10	20
	Victorian Barbie with Cedric Bear	2000	25	59
25507	Victorian Tea Orange Pekoe Barbie	2000	110	220
4589	Wal-Mart 25th Year Pink Jubilee Barbie	1987	20	50
	Wal-Mart 35th Anniversary Barbie, black or white doll		10	24
	Wal-Mart 35th Anniversary Teresa	1997	12	25
	Wal-Mart Anniversary Star Barbie	1992	15	30
2282	Wal-Mart Anniversary Star Barbie (30th Anniversary)	1992	15	30
3678	Wal-Mart Ballroom Beauty	1991	8	30
9601	Wal-Mart Bathtime Fun Barbie	1991	5	25
13014	Wal-Mart Country Bride	1995	8	15
13015	Wal-Mart Country Bride, black doll	1995	8	15
13016	Wal-Mart Country Bride, Hispanic	1995	8	15
	Wal-Mart Country Star Barbie, white, Hispanic, or black	1994	7	20
	Wal-Mart Country Western Star Barbie, black or Hispanic	1994	12	30
	Wal-Mart Country Western Star Barbie, white doll	1994	10	25
7335	Wal-Mart Dream Fantasy	1990	8	35
1374	Wal-Mart Frills and Fantasy Barbie	1988	7	45
	Wal-Mart Jewel Skating Barbie, black or white doll	1999	6	12
3963	Wal-Mart Lavender Look Barbie	1989	7	30
	Wal-Mart Portrait in Blue Barbie, black doll	1998	10	20
	Wal-Mart Portrait in Blue Barbie, white doll	1998	8	18
	Wal-Mart Pretty Choices Barbie, black doll	1997	8	18
	Wal-Mart Pretty Choices Barbie, blond or brunette	1997	8	18
	Wal-Mart Puzzle Craze Barbie, white or black doll	1998	6	14
	Wal-Mart Puzzle Craze Teresa	1998	6	14
	Wal-Mart Shopping Time Barbie, black or white doll	1997	7	15
	Wal-Mart Shopping Time Teresa	1997	7	15
	Wal-Mart Skating Dream	1997	5	15
15510	Wal-Mart Skating Star Barbie	1996	10	15
10592	Wal-Mart Superstar Barbie	1993	15	30
	Wal-Mart Superstar Barbie, black doll	1993	15	40
	Wal-Mart Superstar Barbie, white doll	1993	12	28
	Wal-Mart Sweet Magnolia Barbie, black, white or Hispanic	1996	9	15
11645	Wal-Mart Tooth Fairy #1	1994	7	20
	Wal-Mart Tooth Fairy #2	1995	5	20
	Wal-Mart Tooth Fairy Barbie	1998	6	14
1247	Walking Jamie Strollin' in Style Gift Set	1972	300	600
17783	Water Lily (Artist Series, Monet)	1997	40	75

BARBIE

COLLECTORS' EDITIONS, STORE EXCLUSIVES, GIFT SETS

NO.	NAME	YEAR	MNB	MIB
17119	Wedding Day Barbie, blond	1997	15	35
17120	Wedding Day Barbie, redhead	1997	15	35
10924	Wedding Fantasy Gift Set	1993	50	125
	Wedding Flower Blushing Orchid Bride	1997	100	200
	Wedding Flower Romantic Rose Bride	1996	100	220
9852	Wedding Party Gift Set, Six Dolls	1991	45	125
25641	Wedgwood Barbie	2000	40	80
15186	Wessco Carnival Cruise Barbie	1997	25	40
13912	Wessco International Traveler #1	1995	35	60
16158	Wessco International Traveler #2	1996	25	50
5408	Western Fun Gift Set Barbie & Ken	1989	12	30
5408	Western Fun Gift Set Barbie & Ken	1990	12	30
	Western Plains Barbie	2000	40	95
7637	Winn Dixie Party Pink Barbie	1989	7	25
5410	Winn Dixie Pink Sensation	1990	6	20
3284	Winn Dixie Southern Beauty	1991	10	25
	Winter Fantasy Assortment	1997	10	20
	Winter Fantasy, black doll	1997	10	20
15334	Winter Fantasy, blond	1996	20	45
15530	Winter Fantasy, brunette	1996	30	65
10655	Winter Princess Barbie	1993	100	350
10658	Winter Royale	1993	20	40
13513	Winter's Eve Barbie	1995	15	35
24638	Wonder Woman, Barbie as	2000	25	49
2583	Woolworth's Special Expressions, black doll, blue dress	1991	4	10
3200	Woolworth's Special Expressions, black doll, peach dress	1992	5	30
5505	Woolworth's Special Expressions, black doll, pink dress	1990	4	10
7326	Woolworth's Special Expressions, black doll, white dress	1989	5	20
10048	Woolworth's Special Expressions, blue dress, pastel print	1993	5	15
5504	Woolworth's Special Expressions, pink dress	1990	3	20
4842	Woolworth's Special Expressions, white doll	1989	5	20
2582	Woolworth's Special Expressions, white doll, blue dress	1991	4	15
3197	Woolworth's Special Expressions, white doll, peach dress	1992	5	20
	Woolworth's Sweet Lavender Barbie, black or white doll	1992	12	28
	Workin' Out Barbie Gift Set	1997	10	25
	X-Files Barbie and Ken as Scully and Mulder	1998	15	45

MATTEL DOLLS, NON-BARBIE

NO.	NAME	YEAR	MNB	MIB
3577	Buffy and Mrs. Beasley	1968	125	275
	Celebrity Series, Audrey Hepburn Pink Princess	1998	40	90
	Celebrity Series, Audrey Hepburn, Breakfast At Tiffany's, black dress	1998	40	90
23782	Chatty Cathy, 1999 reissue	1999	50	100
23288	Coca-Cola Holiday Series, Santa Claus	1999	25	60
	Daytime Drama, Erica Kane #1	1998	20	50
	Daytime Drama, Erica Kane #2	1999	20	45
	Daytime Drama, Marlena Evans	1999	20	45
	Disney Series, Jolly Holiday Mary Poppins	2000	20	40
	Elizabeth Taylor as Cleopatra	1999	35	60
26836	Elizabeth Taylor in Father of the Bride	2000	30	70
20544	Elvis Presley #1	1998	20	50
21912	Elvis Presley #2 The Army Years	1999	20	50
	Great Villains, Captain Hook (Peter Pan)	1999	30	75
16295	Great Villains, Cruella DeVil, Power in Pinstripes	1996	35	75
	Great Villains, Cruella DeVil, Ruthless in Red	1997	35	75
18626	Great Villains, Evil Queen (Snow White)	1998	30	75
	Great Villains, Maleficent (Sleeping Beauty)	1999	25	75
17575	Great Villains, Ursula (Little Mermaid)	1997	30	75

Barbie in Switzerland

Black Magic

Roman Holiday

MATTEL DOLLS, NON-BARBIE

NO.	NAME	YEAR	MNB	MIB
23783	Holiday Chatty Cathy	1999	50	125
	Lucille Ball as Lucy Ricardo, Vitameatavegemin	1998	25	45
21268	Lucy Ricardo "Job Switching"	1999	20	35
25527	Lucy's Italian Movie	2000	20	40
	Rosie O'Donnell	1999	10	25

PORCELAIN BARBIES

NO.	NAME	YEAR	MNB	MIB
1110	30th Anniversary Ken	1991	75	175
7957	30th Anniversary Midge	1993	65	150
11396	30th Anniversary Skipper	1994	50	150
5475	Benefit Performance Barbie	1988	200	425
1708	Blue Rhapsody Barbie, first porcelain Barbie	1986	300	600
16962	Blushing Orchid Bride Barbie	1997	75	175
23451	Bob Mackie Tango	1999	150	200
1553	Crystal Rhapsody, blond, Presidential Porcelain Barbie collection	1992	100	300
10201	Crystal Rhapsody, brunette, Presidential Porcelain Barbie collection	1993	100	600
3415	Enchanted Evening Barbie	1987	175	400
19816	Faberge Imperial Elegance Barbie, limited to 15,000	1999	150	350
9973	Gay Parisienne, brunette, Disney Porcelain Treasures collection	1991	150	225
9973	Gay Parisienne, redhead, Disney Porcelain Treasures collection	1991	225	625
9973	Gay Parisiennte, blond, Disney Porcelain Treasures collection	1991	225	625
10246	Gold Sensation, Gold and Silver Porcelain Barbie Set	1993	175	350
18326	Holiday Ball, Holiday Porcelain #3	1997	75	200
15760	Holiday Caroler, Holiday Porcelain #2	1996	60	200
20128	Holiday Gift, Holiday Porcelain #4	1998	100	200
14311	Holiday Jewel, Holiday Porcelain #1	1995	55	225
14479	Mattel's 50th Anniversary Barbie	1995	300	350
	Mint Memories, Victorian Tea Porcelain Collection	1999	100	215
7526	Plantation Belle, blond, Porcelain Treasures Collection	1992	100	575
5351	Plantation Belle, red, Porcelain Treasures Collection	1992	100	200
	Presidential Porcelain Evening Pearl Barbie	1996	95	225
14541	Romantic Rose Bride	1995	75	175
10950	Royal Splendor, Presidential Porcelain Collection	1993	100	250
1249	Silken Flame Barbie, brunette, Porcelain Treasures Collection	1993	100	200
11099	Silken Flame, blond	1993	250	500
11875	Silver Starlight, Gold and Silver Porcelain Barbie Set	1994	175	350
7613	Solo in the Spotlight	1990	100	200
5313	Sophisticated Lady	1990	125	200
12953	Star Lily Bride Barbie, Wedding Flower Collection	1995	125	250
2641	Wedding Day Barbie	1989	300	400
26834	Wizard of Oz Dorothy	2000	70	150
26835	Wizard of Oz Wicked Witch	2000	70	150

NO.	OUTFIT	MNP	MIP
1631	Aboard Ship	245	475
934	After Five	68	135
984	American Airlines Stewardess	110	225
917	Apple Print Sheath	68	135
989	Ballerina	50	200
0874	Barbie Arabian Nights	275	410
953	Barbie Baby-Sits (1963)	200	325
1605	Barbie in Hawaii	140	275
0823	Barbie in Holland	85	200
0821	Barbie in Japan	350	475
0820	Barbie in Mexico	205	275
0822	Barbie in Switzerland	130	250
1634	Barbie Learns to Cook	195	500
1608	Barbie Skin Diver	45	110
962	Barbie-Q Outfit	72	155
1651	Beau Time	235	500
1698	Beautiful Bride	650	2100
1667	Benefit Performance	550	1375
1609	Black Magic	150	300
947	Bride's Dream	160	300
1628	Brunch Time	140	350
981	Busy Gal	225	400
956	Busy Morning	175	275
1616	Campus Sweetheart	615	1600
0889	Candy Striper Volunteer	200	365
954	Career Girl	120	275
1687	Caribbean Cruise	80	200
0876	Cheerleader	115	195
0872	Cinderella	265	460
1672	Club Meeting	145	375
1670	Coffee's On	70	150
916	Commuter Set	700	1500
1627	Country Club Dance	265	450
1603	Country Fair	55	165
1604	Crisp'n Cool	85	175
918	Cruise Stripes	85	165
1626	Dancing Doll	220	450
1666	Debutante Ball	600	1200
946	Dinner At Eight	90	225
1633	Disc Date	155	295
1613	Dog n' Duds	155	325
1669	Dreamland	120	200
0875	Drum Majorette	120	200
971	Easter Parade	1500	4000
983	Enchanted Evening	207	385
1695	Evening Enchantment	300	500
1660	Evening Gala	130	350
961	Evening Splendor	177	355
1676	Fabulous Fashion	280	525
943	Fancy Free	30	75
1635	Fashion Editor	290	650
1656	Fashion Luncheon	600	1200
1691	Fashion Shiner	90	220
1696	Floating Gardens	220	500
921	Floral Petticoat	27	55
1697	Formal Occasion	190	500
1638	Fraternity Dance	240	610

NO.	OUTFIT	MNP	MIP
979	Friday Night Date	130	245
1624	Fun At The Fair	140	285
1619	Fun n' Games	135	300
931	Garden Party	47	150
1606	Garden Tea Party	70	175
1658	Garden Wedding	240	500
964	Gay Parisienne	1100	4000
1647	Gold n' Glamour	775	1600
992	Golden Elegance	225	350
1610	Golden Evening	115	250
911	Golden Girl	87	175
1645	Golden Glory	230	425
945	Graduation	48	95
0873	Guinevere	190	300
1665	Here Comes The Bride	440	995
1639	Holiday Dance	325	595
942	Icebreaker	60	120
1653	International Fair	365	500
1632	Invitation To Tea	285	525
0819	It's Cold Outside, brown	45	110
0819	It's Cold Outside, red	65	165
1620	Junior Designer	200	350
1614	Junior Prom	375	600
1621	Knit Hit	165	225
1602	Knit Separates	70	160
957	Knitting Pretty, blue	80	190
957	Knitting Pretty, pink	200	475
978	Let's Dance	115	230
0880	Little Red Riding Hood & The Wolf	385	585
1661	London Tour	170	400
1600	Lunch Date	45	125
1649	Lunch On The Terrace	210	325
1673	Lunchtime	150	285
1646	Magnificence	350	595
944	Masquerade	75	175
1640	Matinee Fashion	320	525
1617	Midnight Blue	415	800
1641	Miss Astronaut	395	650
1625	Modern Art	360	550
940	Mood For Music	107	190
933	Movie Date	30	50
1633	Music Center Matinee	380	600
965	Nighty Negligee	46	92
1644	On The Avenue	245	525
985	Open Road	225	350
987	Orange Blossom (1961)	55	165
1650	Outdoor Art Show	235	500
1637	Outdoor Life	115	275
1601	Pajama Party	20	50
1678	Pan American Stewardess	1500	4000
958	Party Date	85	175
1692	Patio Party	140	325
915	Peachy Fleecy	75	150
1648	Photo Fashion	150	375
967	Picnic Set	205	410
1694	Pink Moonbeams	110	300

BARBIE

BARBIE VINTAGE FASHIONS
1959-1966

NO.	OUTFIT	MNP	MIP
966	Plantation Belle	240	475
1643	Poodle Parade	620	950
1652	Pretty As A Picture	225	450
1686	Print Aplenty	140	275
949	Rain Coat	50	95
1654	Reception Line	350	500
939	Red Flare	80	165
991	Registered Nurse	98	245
963	Resort Set	103	205
1668	Riding In The Park	300	595
968	Roman Holiday	1500	4800
1611	Satin n' Rose	190	375
1615	Saturday Matinee	525	900
951	Senior Prom	115	225
986	Sheath Sensation	80	150
1664	Shimmering Magic	800	1600
977	Silken Flame	60	145
988	Singing In The Shower	65	130
1629	Skater's Waltz	180	395
948	Ski Queen	75	165
1636	Sleeping Pretty	100	350
1674	Sleepytime Gal	125	220
1642	Slumber Party	135	260
982	Solo In The Spotlight	235	470
993	Sophisticated Lady	240	425
937	Sorority Meeting	120	240
1671	Sporting Casuals	60	165
0949	Stormy Weather	50	95
1622	Student Teacher	235	400
1690	Studio Tour	110	250
969	Suburban Shopper	180	360
1675	Sunday Visit	210	450
1683	Sunflower	140	245
976	Sweater Girl	75	175
973	Sweet Dreams, pink	240	425
973	Sweet Dreams, yellow	80	145
955	Swingin' Easy	125	245
941	Tennis Anyone	74	150
1612	Theatre Date (1963)	100	175
959	Theatre Date (1964)	75	200
1688	Travel Togethers	110	240
1655	Under Fashions	265	500
919	Undergarments	31	65
1685	Underprints	55	225
1623	Vacation Time	110	240
972	Wedding Day Set	195	385
1607	White Magic	125	275
975	Winter Holiday	82	165

FRANCIE FASHIONS 1966

NO.	OUTFIT	MNP	MIP
1259	Checkmates	85	140
1258	Clam Diggers	130	250
1256	Concert In The Park	135	260
1257	Dance Party	180	250
1260	First Formal	100	175
1252	First Things First	55	100
1254	Fresh As A Daisy	85	140
1250	Gad-About	120	220

FRANCIE FASHIONS 1966

NO.	OUTFIT	MNP	MIP
1251	It's A Date	70	125
1255	Polka Dots N' Raindrops	55	100
1261	Shoppin' Spree	100	140
1253	Tuckered Out	55	125

KEN VINTAGE FASHIONS
1961-1966

NO.	OUTFIT	MNP	MIP
0779	American Airlines Captain #1	205	300
797	Army and Air Force	135	245
1425	Best Man	700	1100
1424	Business Appointment	800	1150
1410	Campus Corduroys	20	65
770	Campus Hero	35	95
0782	Casuals, striped shirt	70	100
782	Casuals, yellow shirt	40	65
1416	College Student	190	400
1400	Country Clubbin'	40	85
793	Dr. Ken	55	130
785	Dreamboat	40	95
0775	Drum Major	75	175
1407	Fountain Boy	230	325
1408	Fraternity Meeting	25	55
791	Fun On Ice	55	105
1403	Going Bowling	20	35
1409	Going Huntin'	50	100
795	Graduation	35	65
1426	Here Comes The Groom	1000	1400
1412	Hiking Holiday	100	210
1414	Holiday	48	100
780	In Training	30	50
1420	Jazz Concert	135	250
1423	Ken A Go Go	500	700
0774	Ken Arabian Nights	100	200
1404	Ken In Hawaii	100	195
0777	Ken In Holland	155	250
0778	Ken In Mexico	150	250
0776	Ken In Switzerland	150	200
1406	Ken Skin Diver	30	50
0773	King Arthur	225	375
794	Masquerade (Ken)	60	145
1427	Mountain Hike	150	300
1415	Mr. Astronaut	395	650
1413	Off To Bed	82	150
792	Play Ball	55	110
788	Rally Day	66	130
1405	Roller Skate Date, w/ hat	40	125
1405	Roller Skate Date, w/ slacks	40	150
1417	Rovin' Reporter	175	295
796	Sailor	65	120
786	Saturday Date	40	105
1421	Seein' The Sights	195	455
798	Ski Champion	85	155
0781	Sleeper Set, blue	60	120
781	Sleeper Set, brown	38	70
1401	Special Date	70	145

Sweet Dreams

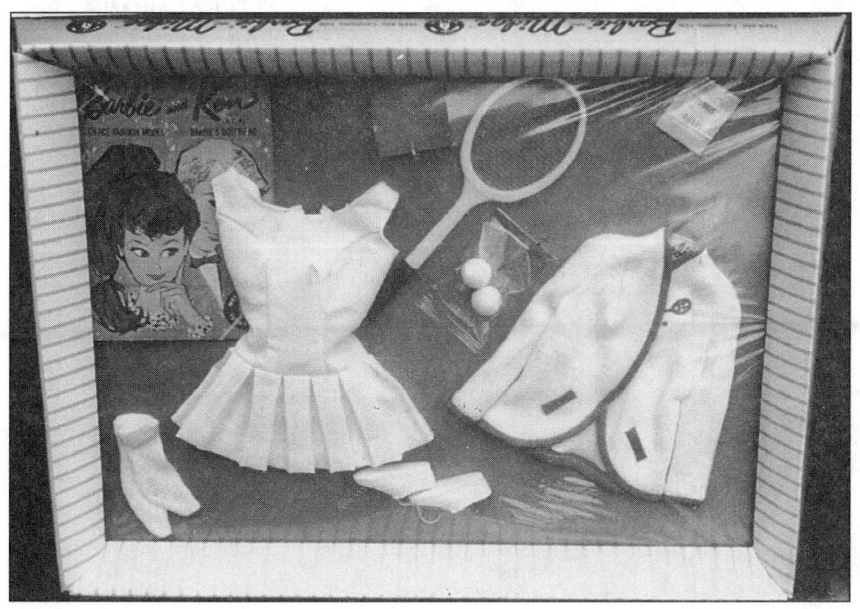

Tennis Anyone

KEN VINTAGE FASHIONS
1961-1966

NO.	OUTFIT	MNP	MIP
783	Sport Shorts	20	55
1422	Summer Job	290	475
784	Terry Togs	60	90
0772	The Prince	285	375
789	The Yachtsman, no hat	45	90
0789	The Yachtsman, w/hat	235	475
790	Time For Tennis	70	140
1418	Time To Turn In	80	175
799	Touchdown	55	125
787	Tuxedo	125	245
1419	TV's Good Tonight	110	250
1411	Victory Dance	60	135

RICKY FASHIONS 1965-1966

NO.	OUTFIT	MNP	MIP
1506	Let's Explore	35	85
1501	Lights Out	55	100
1504	Little Leaguer	65	95
1502	Saturday Show	45	70
1505	Skateboard Set	55	100
1503	Sunday Suit	45	65

SKIPPER VINTAGE FASHIONS
1964-1966

NO.	OUTFIT	MNP	MIP
1905	Ballet Class	60	135
1923	Can You Play?	60	125
1926	Chill Chasers	55	100
1912	Cookie Time	85	150
1933	Country Picnic	300	450
1911	Day At The Fair	120	200
1929	Dog Show	190	300
1909	Dreamtime	60	125
1906	Dress Coat	60	80

SKIPPER VINTAGE FASHIONS
1964-1966

NO.	OUTFIT	MNP	MIP
1904	Flower Girl	80	150
1920	Fun Time	100	200
1919	Happy Birthday	355	500
1934	Junior Bridesmaid	285	475
1917	Land & Sea	90	155
1935	Learning To Ride	185	275
1932	Let's Play House	125	250
1930	Loungin' Lovelies	55	125
1903	Masquerade (Skipper)	80	155
1913	Me N' My Doll	150	260
1915	Outdoor Casuals	85	135
1914	Platter Party	75	125
1916	Rain Or Shine	50	90
1928	Rainy Day Checkers	155	300
1901	Red Sensation	65	125
1907	School Days	60	130
1921	School Girl	200	295
1918	Ship Ahoy	155	275
1902	Silk N' Fancy	60	125
1908	Skating Fun	48	110
1936	Sledding Fun	155	275
1910	Sunny Pastels	60	125
1924	Tea Party	185	300
1922	Town Togs	95	170
1900	Under-Pretties	25	50
1925	What's New At The Zoo?	50	120

TUTTI FASHIONS 1966

NO.	OUTFIT	MNP	MIP
3601	Puddle Jumpers	20	45
3603	Sand Castles	55	98
3602	Ship Shape	55	90
3604	Skippin' Rope	55	95

BARBIE & FRIENDS ACCESSORIES

NAME	COMPANY	YEAR	EX	MINT
Colorforms Sets				
Barbie Sport Fashion	Colorforms	1975	4	8
Barbie's 3-D Fashion Theatre	Colorforms	1970	9	20
Dress-Up Kit New Living Barbie	Colorforms	1970	10	38
Malibu Barbie	Colorforms	1972	7	20
Francie Fashions 1966				
Fur Out		1966	235	400
Go Granny Go		1966	110	200
Hip Knits		1966	125	200
Leather Limelight		1966	110	255
Orange Cozy		1966	170	235
Quick Shift		1966	90	180
Style Setters		1966	140	260
Swingin' Skimmy		1966	140	245
Miscellaneous				
Barbie & Ken Wipe Away Cloths		1964	100	280
Barbie and Ken Hangers	SPP	1960s	20	35
Barbie Beauty Kit	Roclar	1961	100	200
Barbie Bubble Bath	Roclar	1961	45	100
Barbie Carry-All Wallet	SPP	1963	145	255
Barbie Disco Record Player		1976	85	160
Barbie Dresser Accessories		1962	175	300
Barbie Ge-Tar	Mattel	1963	200	400
Barbie Hair Fair	Mattel	1966	75	145
Barbie Mattel-A-Phone		1968	75	140
Barbie Nurse Kit	Pressman	1962	100	275
Barbie Powder Mitt		1961	75	140
Barbie Pretty Up Time		1960s	50	125
Barbie Record	Columbia Records	1965	70	120
Barbie Store Display	Mattel	1980	10	30
Barbie Wig Wardrobe	Mattel	1960s	75	150
Barbie's Dog Snowball	Arco/Mattel	1990s	20	35
Barbie, Ken, Midge Pencil Case	SPP	1964	100	260
Francie Electric Drawing Table		1966	65	130
Jack and Jill magazine advertisements		1960s	15	35
Jigsaw Puzzle	Whitman	1963-65	30	60
Jumbo Trading Cards	Dynamic	1962	225	365
Record Player	Emenee	1961	700	950
Record Tote	Ponytail	1961	75	180
Vanity Fair Transistor Radio	Vanity Fair	1962	700	1350
Wine Set		1986	40	75
Paper Dolls				
Barbie and Ken Cut-Outs	Whitman	1962	50	135
Barbie and Ken Paper Dolls	Whitman	1970	35	60
Barbie and Skipper Stand-Up Dolls	Whitman	1964	50	125
Barbie Costume Dolls	Whitman	1964	60	125
Barbie Cut-Outs		1962	55	125
Barbie Doll Cut-Outs	Whitman	1963	45	95
Barbie Dolls and Clothes		1969	35	70
Barbie Has a New Look Paper Dolls	Whitman	1967	40	100
Barbie Paper Dolls	Whitman	1967	20	60
Barbie's Travel Wardrobe		1964	50	125
Barbie, Christie and Stacey	Whitman	1968	35	80
Barbie, Ken and Midge Paper Dolls	Whitman	1963	50	90
Barbie, Ken and Midge Paper Dolls	Whitman	1963	40	90
Barbie, Two Magic Dolls w/stay-on clothes		1969	30	70
Francie and Casey Paper Dolls	Whitman	1967	30	60
Francie Paper Dolls	Whitman	1966	40	80
Malibu Barbie Paper Dolls	Whitman	1972	20	45
Meet Francie Paper Dolls	Whitman	1966	35	80
Midge Cut-Outs	Whitman	1963	45	90
P.J. Cover Girl Paper Dolls	Whitman	1971	20	40
Skipper Paper Dolls	Whitman	1965	25	50
Skipper Paper Dolls	Whitman	1965	25	50
Skooter Paper Dolls	Whitman	1965	35	95

BARBIE

135

BARBIE

NAME	COMPANY	YEAR	EX	MINT
Paper Dolls				
Tutti, Barbie and Skipper's Tiny Sister Paper Dolls		1967	30	60
Twiggy Paper Dolls	Whitman	1967	25	48
Structures				
Barbie Café Today		1971	200	400
Barbie Fashion Stage	Mattel	1971	60	100
Barbie Goes to College	Mattel	1964	250	600
Barbie's 2nd Dream House	Mattel	1964	100	250
Barbie's Dream House	Mattel	1962	125	300
Barbie's Dream Kitchen	Mattel	1965	300	500
Fashion Shop	Mattel	1962	200	550
Francie and Casey Studio		1967	75	150
Francie House		1965	90	140
Jamie's Penthouse (Sears)		1971	220	475
Little Theatre	Mattel	1964	200	400
Quick Curl Boutique		1973	40	80
Skipper Jeweled Bed		1965	125	250
Skipper's Dream Room	Mattel	1965	300	575
Skipper's Schoolroom	Mattel	1965	375	600
Tutti Ice Cream Stand		1967	130	225
Tutti's Playhouse		1966	75	125
Timepieces				
Barbie Personal Photo Clock	Bradley/Elgin	1964	520	675
Barbie Starbright Boudoir Clock	Bradley/Elgin	1964	640	775
Brokn' Heart Pendant	Bradley/Elgin	1965	425	575
Brokn' Heart Wristwatch	Bradley/Elgin	1964	325	425
Curly Bangs Pendant	Bradley/Elgin	1963-64	200	450
Curly Bangs Wristwatch	Bradley/Elgin	1963-64	150	375
Midge Wristwatch	Bradley/Elgin	1964	350	500
Skipper Wristwatch	Bradley/Elgin	1964	350	500
Swirl Ponytail Wristwatch	Bradley/Elgin	1964	175	350
Vehicles				
Allan's Mercedes Roadster	Irwin	1964	150	575
Barbie and Ken and Midge Convertible	Irwin	1964	125	200
Barbie's Airplane	Irwin	1964	1000	3500
Barbie's Austin Healey Convertible	Irwin	1962	125	450
Barbie's Austin Healey, lavender	Irwin	1964	800	1000
Barbie's Speedboat	Irwin	1964	100	1800
Barbie's Sport Plane	Irwin	1964	1800	3500
Ken's Hot Rod	Irwin	1963	175	350
Skipper's Speedboat	Irwin	1965	1450	1850
Skipper's Sports Car	Irwin	1965	175	400
Vinyl Cases				
Barbie & Francie Case	SPP	1967	35	50
Barbie & Stacey Sleep & Keep Case		1969	75	100
Barbie Double Case	SPP	1963	12	25
Barbie Double Case	Ponytail	1961	15	30
Barbie Goes Travelin' Case	SPP	1965	100	325
Barbie Single Case	SPP	1963	7	15
Barbie Single Case	Ponytail	1961	10	20
Barbie Train Case	SPP	1961	45	70
Fashion Queen Case	SPP	1963	75	150
Hatbox-Style Cases	Mattel	1961	20	50
Ken Cases (U.S. versions)	Ponytail	1961	12	25
Midge Cases (U.S. versions)		1963	20	45
Miss Barbie Case	SPP	1964	75	150
Skipper Cases (U.S. versions)		1964	12	25

Battery-Operated Toys

Armies of colorful, playful tin toys are frequently found at toy shows and flea markets. Among the most popular are battery-operated toys.

The heyday of battery-operated toys began in the 1940s, with Japanese companies leading the charge. Popular wind-up and friction toys were soon replaced with longer-lasting battery-operated versions.

Thousands of designs were made with toys featuring a variety of creative characters — from bubble-blowing monkeys to robots to cigar-smoking clowns. Disney creations and other cartoon characters like Popeye were also popular. The ingenuity of the Japanese created some truly unique novelty toys, valued today for their motion, design and humorous appeal.

Toys were often complex and could replicate several motions, such as walking, lifting or drumming. Tin lithography was usually quite interesting and detailed.

It is often difficult to identify the manufacturer of a battery-operated toy. Many companies used only initials to mark toys; some didn't mark them at all. Major manufacturers of battery-operated toys from the 1940s-1960s include Marx, Linemar (Marx's Japanese subsidiary), Alps, Marusan, Yonezawa, Bandai, Asahi Toy and Modern Toy (MT).

Manufacture of tin toys dropped off in the 1960s in favor of cheaper methods and materials.

Determining Value

As in other collecting areas, toys with character ties generally command more money. Space-related battery-operated toys are also popular.

It's difficult to find most battery-operated toys in Mint condition in original boxes. Battery-operated toys are highly susceptible to rust, corrosion and yellowing of fabric or plush.

Having the original box greatly increases the toy's desirability. Instructions were often printed on the box, and the name of the toy on the box often didn't match the toy exactly.

The complexity of the toy also determines value. A toy with three or more actions will generally be worth more than a toy that performs only one action. Even though they may be nice display pieces, toys that don't work command much less.

This book lists toys in Good, Excellent and Mint in Box conditions.

To be graded in Mint condition, a toy should be operational, clean, free of rust or corrosion, and have the original box. Note that those in Good condition will exhibit wear, but will still be operational. Lesser condition toys and those that are not operational are not graded here. Some collectors acquire them for parts.

Barber Bear, 1950s, Linemar. Photo Courtesy Don Hultzman

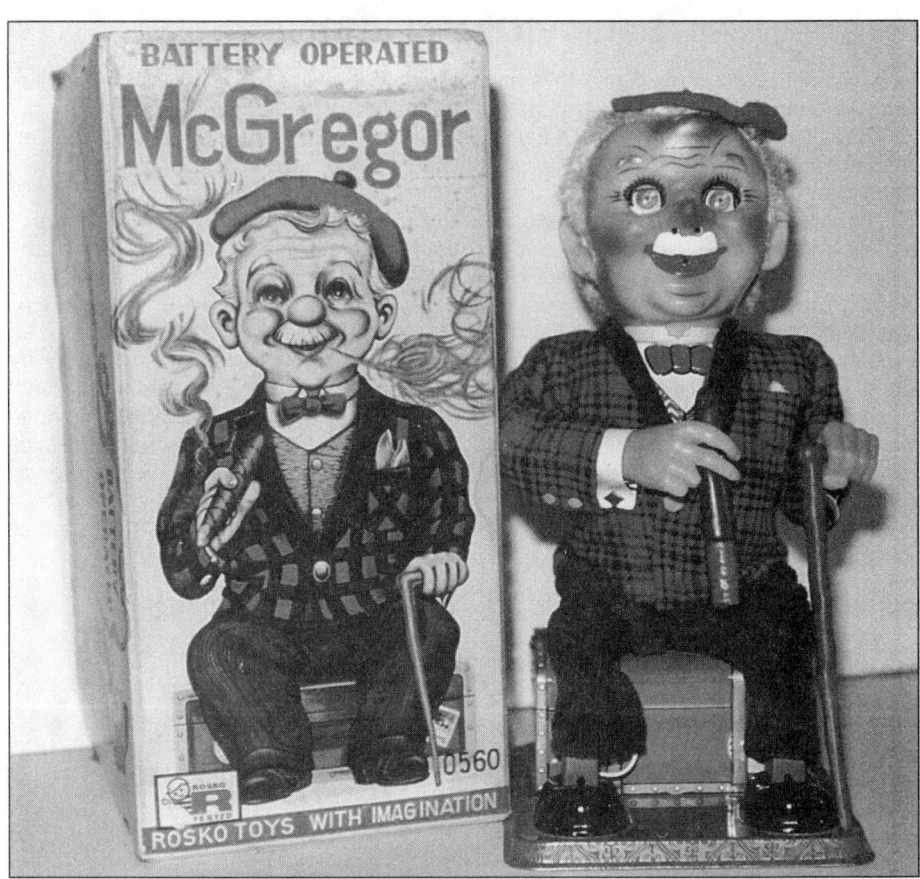

McGregor, 1960s, Rosko

The Top 10 Battery-Operated Toys
(in Mint condition)

1. Mickey the Magician, Linemar, 1960s $2,500
2. Bubble Blowing Popeye, Linemar, 1950s 2,500
3. Gypsy Fortune Teller, Ichida, 1950s 2,200
4. Smoking Spaceman, Linemar, 1950s 1,600
5. Kooky-Spooky Whistling Tree, Marx, 1950s 1,600
6. Drumming Mickey Mouse, Linemar, 1950s 1,600
7. Nutty Nibs, Linemar, 1950s 1,400
8. Main Street, Linemar, 1950s 1,200
9. Tarzan, Marusan, 1960s 1,000
10. Super Susie, Linemar, 1950s 1,000

BATTERY-OPERATED TOYS

NAME	COMPANY	YEAR	DESCRIPTION	GOOD	EX	MIB
ABC Fairy Train	MT	1950s	14-1/2" long	80	95	160
Accordion Player Bunny	Alps	1950s	12" tall	200	325	400
Air Cargo Prop-Jet Airplane	Marx	1960s	Seaboard World Airlines, 12" long	150	300	425
Air Control Tower	Bandai	1960s	11" tall, 37" span	210	315	450
Air Defense Pom-Pom Gun	Linemar	1950s	14" long	115	175	200
Aircraft Carrier	Marx	1950s	20" long	275	450	625
Alley, the Exciting New Roaring Stalking Alligator	Marx	1960s	17-1/2" long	145	225	310
American Airlines DC-7	Linemar	1960s	17-1/2" long, 19" wingspan	200	325	450
American Airlines Electra	Linemar	1950s	18" long, 19-1/2" wingspan	175	300	450
American Airlines Flagship Caroline	Linemar	1950s	18" long, 19-1/2" wingspan	175	300	400
Anti-Aircraft Unit No. 1	Linemar	1950s	12-1/2" long	140	225	310
Army Radio Jeep—J1490	Linemar	1950s	7-1/4" long	75	125	165
Arthur A-Go-Go	Alps	1960s	10" tall	135	200	295
Atomic Rocket X-1800	MT	1960s	9" long	145	225	325
B-58 Hustler Jet	Marx	1950s	21" long, 12" wingspan	425	650	925
Ball Playing Dog	Linemar	1950s	9"	125	200	250
Barber Bear	Linemar	1950s	9-1/2" tall	175	300	400
Barking Boxer Dog	Marx	1950s	7" long	45	65	85
Barney Bear Drummer	Alps	1950s	11" tall	110	185	250
Barnyard Rooster	Marx	1950s	10" tall	100	150	200
Bartender	TN	1960s	11-1/2" tall	50	75	100
Bear the Cashier	MT	1950s	7-1/2" tall	200	300	400
Bengali—The Exciting New Growling, Prowling Tiger	Linemar	1961	18-1/2" tall	100	150	200
Big John	Alps	1960s	12" tall	55	75	125
Big John the Indian Chief	TN	1960s	12-1/2" tall	100	150	200
Big Max Robot	Remco	1958	7" tall	80	125	175
Big Parade	Marx	1963	15" long	300	450	600
Bimbo the Clown	Alps	1950s	9-1/4" tall	190	325	400
Blushing Gunfighter	Y Co.	1960s	11" tall	120	200	235
Blushing Willie	Y Co.	1960s	10" tall	65	85	110
Bobby the Drumming Bear	Alps	1950s	10" tall	175	275	380
Bongo Player	Alps	1960s	10" tall	75	110	160
Bongo the Drumming Monkey	Alps	1960s	9-1/2" tall	75	115	165
Brave Eagle	TN	1950s	11" tall	100	150	200
Brewster the Rooster	Marx	1950s	9-1/2" tall	150	200	250
Bubble Blowing Bear	MT	1950s	9-1/2" tall	150	225	300
Bubble Blowing Monkey	Alps	1950s	10" tall	125	150	225
Bubble Blowing Popeye	Linemar	1950s	11-3/4" tall	750	1200	2500
Bubbling Bull	Linemar	1950s	8" tall	100	150	200
Bunny the Magician	Alps	1950s	14-1/2" tall	300	400	500
Burger Chef	Y Co.	1950s	9" tall	150	225	300
Busy Housekeeper	Alps	1950s	8-1/2" tall	175	300	375
Busy Secretary	Linemar	1950s	7-1/2" tall	125	200	300
Busy Shoe Shining Bear	Alps	1950s	10" tall	125	200	250
Cabin Cruiser with Outboard Motor	Linemar	1950s	12" long	100	135	200
Calypso Joe	Linemar	1950s	11" tall	190	310	400
Camera Shooting Bear	Linemar	1950s	11" tall	350	475	700
Cappy the Baggage Porter Dog	Alps	1960s	12" tall	100	150	200
Caterpillar	Alps	1950s	16" long	80	125	175
Central Choo Choo	MT	1960s	15" long	30	40	60
Charlie the Drumming Clown	Alps	1950s	9-1/2" tall	135	200	275
Charlie Weaver	TN	1962	12"	75	100	125
Charm the Cobra	Alps	1960s	6" tall	90	130	175
Chee Chee Chihuahua	Mego	1960s	8" tall	50	75	100
Chef Cook	Y Co.	1960s	11-1/2" tall	100	200	300
Chippy the Chipmunk	Alps	1950s	12" long	75	120	155
Circus Fire Engine	MT	1960s	11" long	110	175	235
Clancy the Great	Ideal	1960s	19-1/2" tall	85	135	200
Climbing Donald Duck on Friction Fire Engine	Linemar	1950s	12" long	300	525	700
Clown Circus Car	MT	1960s	8-1/2" long	100	175	235
Clown on Unicycle	MT	1960s	10-1/2" tall	180	280	375
Colonel Hap Hazard Robot	Marx	1968	11-1/4" tall	300	440	600

139

*Bongo the Drumming Monkey,
1960s, Alps*

*Cragstan Crapshooter,
1950s, Y Co.*

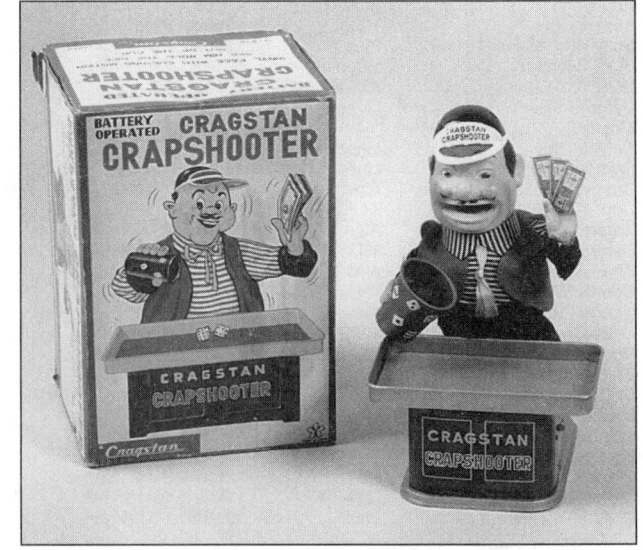

BATTERY-OPERATED TOYS

NAME	COMPANY	YEAR	DESCRIPTION	GOOD	EX	MIB
Coney Island Penny Machine	Remco	1950s	13" tall	90	130	300
Coney Island Rocket Ride	Alps	1950s	13-1/2" tall	300	450	600
Cragstan Beep Beep Greyhound Bus	Cragstan	1950s	20" long	100	150	220
Cragstan Crapshooter	Y Co.	1950s	9-1/2" tall	100	150	200
Cragstan Crapshooting Monkey	Alps	1950s	9" tall	100	150	200
Cragstan Mother Goose	Y Co.	1960s	8-1/4" tall	100	150	200
Cragstan Playboy	Cragstan	1960s	13" tall	100	150	200
Cragstan Roulette, A Gambling Man	Y Co.	1960s	9" tall	150	225	300
Crawling Baby	Linemar	1940s	11" long	45	75	100
Daisy, the Jolly Drumming Duck	Alps	1950s	9" tall	120	180	240
Dancing Merry Chimp	Kuramochi	1960s		100	150	200
Dandy, the Happy Drumming Pup	Alps	1950s	8-1/2" tall	100	150	200
Dennis the Menace	Rosko	1950s	9" tall, with xylophone	120	180	240
Disney Acrobats	Linemar	1950s	9" tall; Mickey, Donald, and Pluto	300	625	800
Disney Fire Engine	Linemar	1950s	11" long	425	650	870
Disneyland Fire Engine	Linemar	1950s	18" long	350	550	750
Donald Duck	Linemar	1960s	8" tall	200	300	400
Doxie the Dog	Linemar	1950s	9" long	20	25	45
Drinking Captain	S & E	1960s		100	150	200
Drummer Bear	Alps	1950s	10" tall	130	200	275
Drumming Mickey Mouse	Linemar	1950s	10" tall	800	1000	1600
Drumming Polar Bear	Alps	1960s	12"	75	120	165
Ducky Duckling	Alps	1960s	8"	35	55	85
El Toro, Cragstan Bullfighter	TN	1950s	9-1/2" long	90	145	200
Feeding Bird Watcher	Linemar	1950s	9" tall	300	350	600
Fido the Xylophone Player	Alps	1950s	8-3/4" tall	115	170	240
Flintstone Yacht	Remco	1961	17" long	90	145	200
Frankenstein Monster	TN	1960s	14" tall	130	200	275
Frankie the Rollerskating Monkey	Alps	1950s	12"	90	150	200
Fred Flintstone Bedrock Band	Alps	1962	9-1/2" tall	400	500	900
Fred Flintstone Flivver	Marx	1960s	7" long	400	600	900
Friendly Jocko, My Favorite Pet	Alps	1950s	8" tall	110	175	245
Gino, Neapolitan Balloon Blower	Tomiyama	1960s	10" tall	80	130	180
Girl with Baby Carriage	TN	1960s	8" tall	100	150	200
Godzilla Monster	Marusan	1970s	11-1/2" tall	125	160	250
Good Time Charlie	MT	1960s	12" tall	90	130	175
Grandpa Panda Bear	MT	1950s	9" tall	100	175	245
Great Garloo	Marx	1960s	23" tall green monster	300	450	600
Green Caterpillar	Daiya	1950s	19-1/2" long	150	250	350
Gypsy Fortune Teller	Ichida	1950s	12" tall, 20 cards	1100	1700	2200
Happy & Sad Face Cymbal Clown	Y Co.	1960s	10" tall	120	180	200
Happy Fiddler Clown	Alps	1950s	9-1/2" tall	200	300	425
Happy Naughty Chimp	Daishin	1960s	9-1/2" tall	75	100	150
Happy Santa One-Man Band	Alps	1950s	9" tall	100	185	245
Hippo Chef	Y Co.	1960s	10" tall	100	160	600
Hobo Clown with Accordion	Alps	1950s	10-1/2" tall	275	425	525
Hoop Zing Girl	Linemar	1950s	11-1/2" tall	115	185	245
Hoopy the Fishing Duck	Alps	1950s	10" tall	275	375	525
Hooty the Happy Owl	Alps	1960s	9" tall	65	100	145
Hungry Cat	Linemar	1960s	9" tall	250	450	700
Hungry Hound Dog	Y Co.	1950s	9-1/2" tall	150	275	300
Ice Cream Baby Bear	MT	1950s		200	300	400
Indian Joe	Alps	1960s	12" tall	75	110	150
Jo-Jo the Flipping Monkey	TN	1970s	10" tall	35	55	80
Jocko the Drinking Monkey	Linemar	1950s	11" tall	100	150	200
Jolly Bambino	Alps	1950s	9" tall	200	300	400
Jolly Bear Peanut Vendor	TN	1950s	8" tall	250	285	500
Jolly Daddy	Marusan	1950s	8-3/4" tall	165	250	350
Jolly Drummer Chimpy	Alps	1950s	9" tall	100	125	150

141

BATTERY-OPERATED TOYS

NAME	COMPANY	YEAR	DESCRIPTION	GOOD	EX	MIB
Jolly Pianist	Marusan	1950s	8" tall	90	145	200
Jolly Santa on Snow	Alps	1950s	12-1/2" tall	100	200	300
Josie the Walking Cow	Daiya	1950s	14" long	125	175	225
Jumbo the Bubble Blowing Elephant	Y Co.	1950s	7-1/4" tall	75	100	125
Jungle Trio	Linemar	1950s	8" tall	400	600	800
King Zor	Ideal	1962	blue plastic dinosaur, 30" long	100	250	550
Kissing Couple	Ichida	1950s	10-3/4" long	145	200	300
Knitting Grandma	T-N	1950s	8-1/2" tall	175	250	350
Kooky-Spooky Whistling Tree	Marx	1950s	14-1/4" tall	450	760	1600
Lambo Elephant	Alps	1950s	16" long with trailer	260	385	525
Linemar Music Hall	Linemar	1950s	8" tall	100	120	200
Lion	Linemar	1950s	9" long	100	150	200
Loop the Loop Clown	T-N	1960s	10" tall	60	120	175
Mac the Turtle	Y Co.	1960s	8" tall	85	135	185
Magic Man Clown	Marusan	1950s	11" tall	250	385	525
Magic Snowman	MT	1950s	11-1/4" tall	125	190	265
Main Street	Linemar	1950s	19-1/2" long	600	1000	1200
Major Tooty	Alps	1960s	14" tall	85	130	175
Mambo the Jolly Drumming Elephant	Alps	1950s	9-1/2" tall	90	150	200
Marching Bear	Alps	1960s	10" tall	150	225	300
Marshal Wild Bill	Y Co.	1950s	10-1/2" tall	180	280	375
Marvelous Mike	Saunders	1950s	17" long	100	175	245
Maxwell Coffee-Loving Bear	TN	1960s	10" tall	100	150	200
McGregor	Rosko	1960s	12" tall	125	175	225
Mickey the Magician	Linemar	1960s	10" tall	785	1200	2500
Mighty Kong	Marx	1950s	11" tall	250	325	500
Mischievous Monkey	MT	1950s	18" tall	200	300	400
Miss Friday the Typist	TN	1950s	8" tall	150	225	300
Mr. MacPooch	SAN	1950s	8" tall	150	200	300
Mr. Traffic Policeman	A-I	1950s	14" tall	175	270	365
Mumbo Jumbo	Alps	1960s	9-3/4" tall	85	120	160
Musical Bear	Linemar	1950s	10" tall	200	300	400
Musical Jackal	Linemar	1950s	10" tall	150	225	600
Musical Marching Bear	Alps	1950s	11" tall	115	170	600
Nutty Mad Indian	Marx	1960s	12" tall	100	150	200
Nutty Nibs	Linemar	1950s	11-1/2" tall	700	850	1400
Odd Ogg	Ideal	1962	large plastic turtle-frog creature	75	200	450
Ol' Sleepy Head RIP	Y Co.	1950s	9" tall	150	250	320
Panda Bear	MT	1970s	10" long	30	45	65
Pat the Roaring Elephant	Y Co.	1950s	9" long	100	160	225
Peppermint Twist Doll	Haji	1950s	12" tall	150	225	300
Peppy Puppy	Y Co.	1950s	8" long	45	70	100
Pet Turtle	Alps	1960s	7" long	65	100	145
Pete the Space Man	Bandai	1960s	5" tall	60	90	130
Peter the Drumming Rabbit	Alps	1950s	13" tall	145	200	275
Phantom Raider	Ideal	1963	33", freighter turned warship	35	100	225
Picnic Bear	Alps	1950s	10" tall	100	150	200
Picnic Bunny	Alps	1950s	10" tall	100	150	200
Picnic Monkey	Alps	1950s	10" tall	100	150	200
Picnic Poodle	STS	1950s	7" long	40	60	80
Pierrot Monkey Cycle	M-T	1950s	8" tall	325	460	650
Pinkee the Farmer	MT	1950s	9-1/2" long	100	155	200
Pipie the Whale	Alps	1950s	12" long	90	100	180
Pistol Pete	Marusan	1950s	10-1/4" tall	250	270	500
Playful Puppy	MT	1950s	5" tall	100	150	200
Polar Bear	Alps	1970s	8" long	50	75	100
Popcorn Eating Bear	MT	1950s	9" tall	100	150	200
Rambling Ladybug	M-T	1960s	8" long	60	90	125
Reading Bear	Alps	1950s	9" tall	100	175	225
Rembrandt the Monkey Artist	Alps	1950s	8" tall	170	240	365
Ricki the Begging Poodle	Rock Valley	1950s	9" long	35	45	65
Roarin' Jungle Lion	Marx	1950s	16" long	175	250	325
Rock 'N Roll Monkey	Rosko	1950s	13" tall	150	225	300
Rocking Chair Bear	MT	1950s	10" tall	125	175	200
Roller Skater	Alps	1950s	12" tall	100	125	200
Root Beer Counter	K Co.	1960s	8" tall	100	160	230

*Saxophone Playing Monkey,
1950s, Alps*

*Suzette the Eating
Monkey, 1950s, Linemar*

*Walking Bear with
Xylophone, 1950s,
Linemar. Photo
Courtesy Don
Hultzman*

BATTERY-OPERATED TOYS

NAME	COMPANY	YEAR	DESCRIPTION	GOOD	EX	MIB
Sam the Shaving Man	Plaything Toy	1960s	11-1/2" tall	125	180	245
Sammy Wong the Tea Totaler	TN	1950s	10" tall	140	200	285
Santa Claus on Handcar	MT	1960s	10" tall	100	140	200
Santa Claus on Reindeer Sleigh	M-T	1950s	17" long	400	600	825
Santa Claus on Scooter	MT	1960s	10" tall	100	140	180
Santa Copter	MT	1960s	8-1/2" high	100	150	200
Saxophone Playing Monkey	Alps	1950s	9-1/2" tall	200	300	400
Serpent Charmer	Linemar	1950s	7" tall	175	300	425
Shaggy the Friendly Pup	Alps	1960s	8" long	35	45	65
Shoe Maker Bear	TN	1960s	8-1/2" tall	125	200	250
Shoe Shine Bear	T-N	1950s	9" tall	150	225	300
Shoe Shine Joe	Alps	1950s	11" tall	150	225	300
Shoe Shine Monkey	TN	1950s	9" tall	150	225	300
Shooting Gorilla	MT	1950s	12" tall	155	235	325
Shutterbug Photographer	T-N	1950s		420	620	820
Skating Circus Clown	TPS	1950s	6" tall	450	595	800
Skiing Santa	MT	1960s	12" tall	160	230	300
Skipping Monkey	TN	1960s	9-1/2" tall	45	60	80
Slalom Game	T-N	1960s	15-1/4" long	100	160	225
Sleeping Baby Bear	Linemar	1950s	9" long	195	285	400
Sleeping Pup	Alps	1960s	9" long	45	75	100
Slurpy Pup	TN	1960s	6-1/2" long	45	60	100
Smokey Bear	SAN	1950s	9" tall	250	300	500
Smoking Bunny	SAN	1950s	10-1/2" tall	125	150	200
Smoking Elephant	Marusan	1950s	8-3/4" tall	115	165	225
Smoking Spaceman	Linemar	1950s	12" tall	750	1200	1600
Sneezing Bear	Linemar	1950s	9" tall	200	300	400
Snoopy Sniffer	MT	1960s	8" long	40	60	80
Spanking Bear	Linemar	1950s	9" tall	160	200	320
Strutting Sam	Haji	1950s	10-1/2" tall	250	350	450
Sunday Driver	MT	1950s	10" long	55	90	125
Super Susie	Linemar	1950s	9" tall	500	750	1000
Suzette the Eating Monkey	Linemar	1950s	8-3/4" tall	300	450	625
Switchboard Operator	Linemar	1950s	7-1/2" tall	250	380	800
Tarzan	Marusan	1960s	13" tall	480	765	1000
Teddy Bear Swing	T-N	1950s	17" tall	300	380	600
Teddy the Boxing Bear	Y Co.	1950s	9" tall	115	190	240
Teddy the Rhythmical Drummer	Alps	1960s	11" tall	100	150	200
Teddy-Go-Kart	Alps	1960s	10-1/2" long	75	125	160
Telephone Bear	Linemar	1950s	7-1/2" tall	200	300	400
Television Spaceman	Alps	1960s	14-1/2" tall	400	600	825
Tinkling Trolley	M-T	1950s	10-1/2" long	150	200	250
Tom and Jerry Choo Choo	M-T	1960s	10-1/4" long	125	185	255
Tom and Jerry Handcar	M-T	1960s	7-3/4" long	150	225	300
Tom-Tom Indian	Y Co.	1960s	10-1/2" tall	80	120	160
Topo Gigio Playing the Xylophone	TN	1960s		265	440	525
Traveler Bear	Linemar	1950s	8" tall	100	150	200
Trumpet Playing Bunny	Alps	1950s	10" tall	145	200	280
Trumpet Playing Monkey	Alps	1950s	9" tall	150	225	300
Tubby the Turtle	Y Co.	1950s	7" long	50	75	100
Tumbles the Bear	Yanoman	1960s	8-1/2" tall	100	150	200
Twirly Whirly	Alps	1950s	13-1/2" tall	290	450	600
Walking Bear with Xylophone	Linemar	1950s	10" tall	175	270	365
Walking Elephant	Linemar	1950s	8-1/2" tall	80	120	155
Walking Esso Tiger	Marx	1950s	11-1/2" tall	250	350	450
Walking Itchy Dog	Alps	1950s	9" long	45	75	100
Western Locomotive	MT	1950s	10-1/2" long	45	65	80
Windy the Elephant	TN	1950s	9-3/4" tall	150	200	250
Yeti the Abominable Snowman	Marx	1960s	12" tall	250	335	500
Yo-Yo Clown	Alps	1960s	9" tall	150	190	300
Yo-Yo Monkey	YM	1960s	12" tall	85	135	180
Yo-Yo Monkey	Alps	1960s	9" tall	100	185	245
Yummy Yum Kitty	Alps	1950s	9-1/2" tall	170	270	325
Zero Fighter Plane	Bandai	1950s	15" wingspan	150	230	300

Beanbag Toys

What recent toy craze has caused lines to form at stores, incited adults to push and shove and resulted in an immediate boom in secondary market prices?

Plush beanbag toys, led by Ty, Inc.'s Beanie Babies, have surged forward in the last five years — creating a thriving market for the cute and tiny toys.

According to the Toy Manufacturers of America, sales of plush toys increased nineteen percent in 1998 over the previous year — amounting to more than $1.6 billion in sales, led by Beanie Babies.

The beanbag craze escalated around 1987 when Ty announced it would "retire" or cease production of some of its popular $5 plush animals. Collectors and speculators alike, worried that they could no longer purchase the Beanie they wanted, began paying more than retail — sometimes ten times the retail price or more.

Prices skyrocketed and continued to do so as retirements and speculation about the market continued. But escalating prices aren't the only phenomenon to grow out of the Beanie Babies craze.

Sensing a hungry public and a lucrative opportunity, dozens of manufacturers have vied for attention in the plush market. Copycat toys abounded.

Russ and Applause — two leaders in plush toy manufacturing — turned their attention to beanbag toys. Smaller companies, like Idea Factory and others, entered the

Garcia the Bear, Ty

game as well. Even toy giant Kenner opted to turn its prize license, *Star Wars*, into a beanbag product with Star Wars Buddies.

Disney and Warner Bros. made beanbags of their most popular characters, and even advertising characters morphed into beanbag form.

Everything and every license seemed targeted at the beanbag market — sports, advertising, cartoon characters, ecology, music, entertainment, wrestling and more.

Ty created a stir when they announced they would retire all Beanie Babies. While some thought they would cease production of Beanies altogether, many Beanie experts believed this was a way to energize a slumping market. While it worked initially, there has been little demand for the new line of Beanie Babies or the Beanie Kids.

Market Trends

The market is seemingly glutted — especially with non-Ty beanbags. It doesn't appear likely that prices will skyrocket into the astronomical ranges any longer, except possibly for special editions or rare variations. The laws of supply and demand have taken over, leaving collectors with lots of choices for their dollars. Disney and Warner Bros. beanbags remain popular among collectors, but don't expect them to hold on to any significant secondary market value.

The very rare and earliest Beanie Babies will continue to hold their values since they were not initially purchased or saved as collectibles. Few exist in pristine condition with original tags. Uncommon variations of Beanies and other beanbag toys may still hold interest and value for collectors and completists.

Beanbag toys in the most demand are those with variations, and those that contain mistakes (such as misspelled names). Beanie Babies with "old" tags tend to be more popular than those with newer ones.

Beanie Babies bears have seen incredible increases in popularity, especially those with embroidered logos on their chests, like Peace (with a peace sign), Signature Bear (bearing Ty Warner's signature) and Millenium (a year 2000 commemorative edition). Collectors beware, just because one pays top dollar for a beanbag bear does not mean it will bring that kind of price on the secondary market.

The Top 10 Beanbag Toys
(Prices are for items in Mint condition)

1. #1 Bear, Ty, employee-only bear, limited edition $7,000
2. Billionaire 2 the Bear, Ty, employee-only bear, purple, limited edition 3,200
3. Nana the Monkey, Ty, retired 1995 3,200
4. Peanut the Elephant, Ty, royal blue, retired 10/2/95 3,200
5. Punchers the Lobster, Ty, retired 1993 2,500
6. Brownie the Bear, Ty, retired 1993 2,400
7. Billionaire the Bear, Ty, employee-only bear, brown, limited edition 2,200
8. 1997 Employee Bear, Ty, purple with red or green ribbon, limited edition 1,800
9. Derby the Horse, Ty, fine mane, retired 1995 1,700
10. Humphrey the Camel, Ty, retired 6/15/95 1,600

Contributor to this section: Shawn Brecka, P.O. Box 441, Plover, WI 54467

BAMMERS
(Salvinos)

NAME	DESCRIPTION	MINT
Cal Ripken Jr.	commemorative gold set	45
Dante Bichette	commemorative gold set	25
Derek Jeter	commemorative gold set	45
Frank Thomas	commemorative gold set	30
Gary Sheffield	commemorative gold set	25
Greg Maddux	commemorative gold set	40
John Elway	Promo	75
Juan Gonzalez	commemorative gold set	30
Ken Griffey Jr.	commemorative gold set	60
Kerry Wood	commemorative gold set	30
Mark McGwire	commemorative gold set	90
Mark McGwire	Promo	150
Mike Piazza	commemorative gold set	40
Muhammad Ali, bear	Promo	30
Roberto Clemente Bamm Beano	Puerto Rico Exclusive	40
Sammy Sosa	Promo	45
Tony Gwynn	commemorative gold set	30
Wayne Gretzky, baby size	Promo	25
Wayne Gretzky, full size	Promo	100

BEANIE BABIES
(Ty)

NAME	DESCRIPTION	MINT
#1 Bear	Employee-only Bear	7000
1997 Employee Bear	purple with red or green ribbon	1800
1997 Holiday Teddy	brown, red Santa hat	55
1998 Holiday Teddy	white with holly print	50
1999 Holiday Teddy	blue with snowflake print	1500
1999 Signature Bear	brown	8
2000 Signature Bear	white	22
Ally the Alligator		45
Almond the Beige Bear		5
Amber the Gold Tabby		5
Ants the Anteater		10
Aurora the Polar Bear		20
B.B. Bear		15
Baldy the Eagle		9
Batty the Bat		8
Beak the Kiwi		5
Bernie the St. Bernard		6
Bessie the Cow		45
Billionaire 2 the Bear	Employee-only Bear, Purple	3200
Billionaire the Bear	Employee-only Bear, Brown	2200
Blackie the Bear		8
Blizzard the Snow Tiger		9
Bones the Dog		8

BEANIE BABIES
(Ty)

NAME	DESCRIPTION	MINT
Bongo the Monkey	brown tail	40
Bongo the Monkey	tan tail	8
Britannia the Bear	European Exclusive	90
Bronty the Brontosaurus		600
Brownie the Bear		2400
Bruno the Terrier		5
Bubbles the Fish		90
Bucky the Beaver		18
Bumble the Bee		375
Bushy the Lion		13
Butch the Bull Terrier		5
Canyon the Mountain Lion		6
Caw the Crow		450
Cheeks the Baboon		6
Chilly the Polar Bear		1450
Chip the Calico Cat		6
Chipper the Chipmunk		6
Chocolate the Moose		7
Chops the Lamb		100
Claude the Crab	tie-dyed	6
Clubby II the Bear	Official Collectors' Club Bear	15
Clubby the Bear	Official Collectors' Club Bear	25
Congo the Gorilla		5
Coral the Fish		100
Crunch the Shark		5
Cubbie the Bear		18
Curly the Bear		10
Daisy the Cow		7
Derby the Horse	coarse mane, star	8
Derby the Horse	furry mane, star	7
Derby the Horse	fine mane	1700
Derby the Horse	coarse mane, no star	15
Digger the Crab	orange	450
Digger the Crab	red	75
Doby the Doberman		8
Doodle the Rooster		22
Dotty the Dalmatian		8
Early the Robin		5
Ears the Bunny		8
Echo the Dolphin		8
Echo the Dolphin	w/"Waves" tags	10
Eggbert the Baby Chick		9
Erin the Bear	green w/shamrock on chest	12
Eucalyptus the Koala		10
Ewey the Lamb		7
Fetch the Golden Retriever		12
Flash the Dolphin		85

BEANIE BABIES
(Ty)

NAME	DESCRIPTION	MINT
Fleece the Lamb		7
Fleecie the Lamb		12
Flip the Cat		22
Flitter the Butterfly		14
Floppity the Bunny	lavender	12
Flutter the Butterfly		600
Fortune the Panda		7
Freckles the Leopard		7
Frigid the Penguin		10
Fuzz the Bear		9
Garcia the Bear	tie-dyed, old tag	140
Germania the Bear	European exclusive w/German flag	100
Gigi the Black Poodle		6
Glory the Bear		25
Glow the Lightning Bug		11
Goatee the Mountain Goat		6
Gobbles the Turkey		5
Goldie the Goldfish		24
Goochy the Jellyfish		6
Grace the Bunny		12
Gracie the Swan		6
Groovy the Ty-Dye Bear		14
Grunt the Razorback		90
Halo II the Angel Bear		20
Halo the Angel Bear		12
Happy the Hippo	lavender, old tag	12
Happy the Hippo	gray	400
Hippie the Tie-Dyed Bunny		12
Hippity the Bunny	mint green	12
Hissy the Snake		6
Honks the Goose		6
Hoot the Owl		28
Hope the Prayer Bear		8
Hoppity the Bunny	pink	10
Humphrey the Camel		1600
Iggy the Iguana	dark blue, spine	8
Iggy the Iguana	tie-dyed, spine	10
Iggy the Iguana	tie-dyed, spine, tongue	8
Inch the Worm	yarn antenna	14
Inch the Worm	felt antenna	100
Inky the Octopus	tan, no mouth	550
Inky the Octopus	tan, with mouth	450
Inky the Octopus	pink	15
Jabber the Parrot		5
Jake the Mallard Duck		5

BEANIE BABIES
(Ty)

NAME	DESCRIPTION	MINT
Jolly the Walrus		8
Kicks the Soccer Bear		8
Kiwi the Toucan		100
Knuckles the Pig		5
Kuku the Cockatoo		5
Lefty the Donkey		175
Legs the Frog		14
Libearty the Bear	w/flag	300
Lips the Fish		9
Lizzy the Lizard	blue w/black spots, new tag	16
Lizzy the Lizard	tie-dye	650
Loosy the Goose		5
Lucky the Ladybug	w/seven felt dots	150
Lucky the Ladybug	w/eleven spots	12
Lucky the Ladybug	w/twenty-one spots	250
Luke the Black Labrador		8
Mac the Cardinal		5
Magic the Dragon		35
Manny the Manatee		90
Maple the Bear	Canadian exclusive	100
Maple the Bear	w/"Pride" tag	400
Mel the Koala		5
Millenium the Bear		14
Mooch the Spider Monkey		6
Morrie the Eel		12
Mystic the Unicorn	coarse mane, iridescent horn	8
Mystic the Unicorn	fine mane, tan horn	250
Mystic the Unicorn	coarse mane, tan horn	15
Mystic the Unicorn	rainbow mane, iridescent horn	10
Nana the Monkey		3200
Nanook the Husky		6
Neon the Seahorse		6
Nibbler the Rabbit	white	7
Nibbly the Rabbit	brown/gray	7
Niles the Camel		12
Nip the Cat	gold face, white paws	12
Nip the Cat	white face and belly	400
Nip the Cat	all gold	700
Nuts the Squirrel		6
Osito the Mexican Bear	US Exclusive	12
Patti the Platypus	dark magenta	350
Patti the Platypus	light magenta	10
Paul the Walrus		6
Peace the Tie-Dyed Bear		11
Peanut the Elephant	royal blue	3200

Tigger, Disney Mini Bean Bags, Disney

Winnie-the-Pooh, Disney Mini Bean Bags, Disney

Early the Robin, Ty

Kuku the Cockatoo, Ty

BEANBAG TOYS

NAME	DESCRIPTION	MINT
Peanut the Elephant	light blue	12
Pecan the Gold Bear		6
Peking the Panda		1000
Pinchers the Lobster		12
Pinky the Flamingo		5
Pouch the Kangaroo		5
Pounce the Cat		5
Prance the Cat		5
Prickles the Hedgehog		5
Princess the Bear	PVC pellets	50
Princess the Bear	PE pellets	14
Puffer the Puffin		5
Pugsly the Pug Dog		6
Pumkin the Pumpkin		15
Punchers the Lobster		2500
Quackers the Duck	without wings	1100
Quackers the Duck	with wings	10
Radar the Bat		85
Rainbow the Chameleon	tie-dyed	9
Rainbow the Chameleon	blue	9
Rex the Tyrannosaurus		600
Righty the Elephant		185
Ringo the Raccoon		7
Roam the Buffalo		7
Roary the Lion		8
Rocket the Blue Jay		5
Rover the Dog		15
Rufus the Dog		14
Sakura the Bear	Japanese Exclusive	175
Sammy the Bear Cub		6
Santa		20
Sarge the German Shepherd		12
Scaly the Lizard		6
Scat the Cat		5
Schweetheart the Orangutan		6
Scoop the Pelican		5
Scorch the Dragon		8
Scottie the Terrier		12
Scurry the Beetle		10

NAME	DESCRIPTION	MINT
Seamore the Seal		75
Seaweed the Otter		12
Sheets the Ghost		8
Silver the Grey Tabby		5
Slippery the Seal		6
Slither the Snake		1100
Slowpoke the Sloth		6
Sly the Fox	brown belly	90
Sly the Fox	white belly	8
Smoochy the Frog		6
Sneaky the Leopard		12
Snip the Cat	Siamese	6
Snort the Bull		6
Snowball the Snowman		22
Spangle the American Bear	blue face	40
Spangle the American Bear	white face	15
Spangle the American Bear	pink face	22
Sparky the Dalmatian		80
Speedy the Turtle		20
Spike the Rhinoceros		6
Spinner the Spider		6
Spinner the Spider	w/"Creepy" tush tag	45
Splash the Orca Whale		75
Spooky the Ghost		20
Spot the Dog	without spot	1200
Spot the Dog	with spot	34
Springy the Lavender Bunny		12
Spunky the Cocker Spaniel		7
Squealer the Pig		15
Steg the Stegosaurus		600
Stilts the Stork		4
Sting the Stingray		100
Stinger the Scorpion		6
Stinky the Skunk		7
Stretch the Ostrich		6
Stripes the Tiger	dark gold	230
Stripes the Tiger	light tan	10
Strut the Rooster		5
Swampy the Alligator		12
Swirly the Snail		6
Swoop the Pterodactyl		15

BEANIE BABIES
(Ty)

NAME	DESCRIPTION	MINT
Tabasco the Bull		90
Tabasco the Bull		140
Tank the Armadillo	nine lines, no shell	225
Tank the Armadillo	shell	45
Tank the Armadillo	seven lines, no shell	125
Teddy the Bear	brown, new face	75
Teddy the Bear	teal, new face	1150
Teddy the Bear	magenta, new face	1150
Teddy the Bear	violet, new face	1150
Teddy the Bear	cranberry, new face	1150
Teddy the Bear	teal, old face	1350
Teddy the Bear	magenta, old face	1300
Teddy the Bear	jade, old face	1300
Teddy the Bear	cranberry, old face	1300
Teddy the Bear	brown, old face	1500
Teddy the Bear	jade, new face	1150
Teddy the Bear	violet, old face	1350
The Beginning the Bear		22
The End the Bear		24
Tiny the Chihuahua		6
Tiptoe the Mouse		7
Tracker the Basset Hound		6
Trap the Mouse		1000
Trumpet the Elephant		12
Tuffy the Terrier		7
Tusk the Walrus		80
Tusk the Walrus	w/"Tuck" tag	90
Twigs the Giraffe		12
Ty 2K the Bear		14
Valentina the Bear		8
Valentino the Bear		14
Velvet the Panther		20
Waddle the Penguin		15
Wallace the Scottish Bear		16
Waves the Whale		8
Waves the Whale	w/"Echo" tags	10
Web the Spider		900
Weenie the Dog		15
Whisper the Deer		6
Wiggly the Octopus		12
Wise the Owl		8
Wiser the Owl		8
Wrinkles the Dog		7
Zero the Christmas Penguin		12
Ziggy the Zebra		9
Zip the Cat	white paws	15
Zip the Cat	white face and belly	400
Zip the Cat	all black	800

CVS
(CVS/Stuffins)

NAME	DESCRIPTION	MINT

CHRISTMAS 1999

Boss Elf		6
Coach Reindeer		6
Frosty the Snowman		6
Herbie		6
Karen		6
Misfit Cowboy		6
Misfit Jelly Gun		6
Misfit Plane		6
Mystery Millennium Character		
Professor Hinkle		6
Sam the Snowman		6
Santa		6
Tall Elf		6
Traffic Cop		6
Yukon Cornelius		6

EASTER 1999

Hickory Dickory Dock		6
Humpty Dumpty		6
Mother Goose		6
Mrs. Cottontail		6
Peter Cottontail		6
The Cow Jumped Over the Moon		6
This Little Piggy		6
Three Little Kittens	Gray	12
Three Little Kittens	Tan	12
Three Little Kittens	Red	12

ISLAND OF MISFIT TOYS

Abominable Snowman	15
Charlie-in-the-Box	10
Clarice	12
Herbie	12
King Moonracer	12
Misfit Doll	8
Misfit Train	8
Rudolph	15
Sam the Snowman	12
Santa Claus	10
Spotted Elephant	12
Yukon Cornelius	15

ROCKY AND BULLWINKLE AND FRIENDS

Boris	7
Bullwinkle	7
Horse	7
Mr. Peabody	7
Natasha	7
Rocky	7
Sherman	7
Snidely	7

Abominable Snowman, CVS

Santa Claus, CVS

Clarice, CVS

DISNEY MINI BEAN BAGS
(Disney)

NAME	DESCRIPTION	MINT
101 Dalmatians Pup	test – no "V" on forehead, no spots on belly	40
2000 Bean Bag Set – Mickey, Goofy, Donald		25
Abominable Snowman	Disneyland Exclusive	12
Alien		7
Baby Pegasus		16
Bashful		12
Buzz Lightyear	Version 2 - no "V," no kneepads	7
Buzz Lightyear	Version 1 - "V" on chest, kneepads	10
Christopher Robin		8
Cuppy Bunny		10
Daisy	Version 2 - Plastic Eyes	9
Daisy	Version 1 - Sewn Eyes	9
Doc		12
Donald	Test - sewn tuck on hat, flag on front of hat	15
Donald	Version 2 - untucked hat, flag on back	7
Donald	Version 3 - plastic eyes	8
Donald – Soccer	UK Exclusive	70
Dopey	Version 2 - "Bean Bag" two words on tag	10
Dopey	Test - "Beanbag" all one word on tag	25
Eeyore	Test - smaller, shorter nose, more plush	15
Eeyore	Version 2 - longer, longer nose	7
Eeyore	Version 3 - much darker	8
Eeyore	Version 4 - gray	14
Eeyore – As Pooh	Catalog Exclusive	25
Eeyore – Classic		7
Eeyore – Cupid		15
Eeyore – Dinosaur		12
Eeyore – Graduation		10
Eeyore – Reindeer	Version 1 - lighter blue, smaller bow	14
Eeyore – Reindeer	Version 2 - darker blue, bigger bow	14
Eeyore – Sugar Plum Fairy		70
Figment	Epcot Center Exclusive	10
Flubber		15
Goofy	Version 3, plastic eyes	8
Goofy	Test - Beans in arms and legs	15
Goofy	Version 2, beans not in legs	8
Gopher		9
Gopher – Bunny		10
Grumpy	Test- "Beanbag" all one word on tag	20
Grumpy	Version 2 - "Bean Bag" two words on tag	9
Hag		7
Hamm	Japan Tag	12
Hamm		7
Happy		12

DISNEY MINI BEAN BAGS
(Disney)

NAME	DESCRIPTION	MINT
Heffalump #4	blue/pink/yellow	9
Herbie		9
Huey/Dewey/ Louie	Version 2 - corrected colors (red/blue/green)	24
Huey/Dewey/ Louie	Version 1 - Mistake colors (blue/green/red)	36
Hunny Bee	Club Disney Exclusive	15
Kanga	Version 1 - 8"	8
Kanga	Version 2 - 7"	7
Merlin	signed (stamped tag), Club Disney Exclusive	24
Merlin	Club Disney Exclusive	9
Mickey	Version 3 - smaller, completely beans	8
Mickey	Version 4 - plastic eyes, more plush	9
Mickey	Version 2 - 8", less stuffing, more beans	12
Mickey	Test-9", no black stitching around eyes and mouth	45
Mickey – 1930s-style	Japan Exclusive	25
Mickey – 70th Anniversary Set	in hat pants	30
Mickey – Cast Member		350
Mickey – Chinese New Year	Version 2 - black lines on gloves, Japan Exclusive	20
Mickey – Chinese New Year	Version 1 - all white gloves, Japan Exclusive	75
Mickey – Gradnite, Disneyland	red shorts	22
Mickey – Gradnite, WDW	floral shorts	25
Mickey – Jester		35
Mickey – Jester	Christmas version	46
Mickey – Kimono		30
Mickey – Monochrome	Japan Exclusive	25
Mickey – Oklahoma		75
Mickey – Santa		9
Mickey – Scarecrow		11
Mickey – Soccer	UK Exclusive	100
Mickey – Spirit of Mickey		14
Mickey – Valentine		17
Minnie	Version 4 - plastic eyes, more plush	9
Minnie	Version 2 - 8", less dots on dress	10
Minnie	Version 3 - 7", more dots on dress	9
Minnie	Test - 9", no black around eyes and mouth	45
Minnie – 1930s-style	Japan Exclusive	25
Minnie – Chinese New Year	Version 1 - all white gloves, Japan Exclusive	75

BEANBAG TOYS

DISNEY MINI BEAN BAGS
(Disney)

NAME	DESCRIPTION	MINT
Minnie – Chinese New Year	Version 2 - black lines on gloves, Japan Exclusive	20
Minnie – Jester		35
Minnie – Jester	Christmas version	46
Minnie – Kimono		30
Minnie – Monochrome	Japan Exclusive	25
Minnie – Santa		9
Minnie – Spirit of Mickey		14
Minnie – Sugar Plum Fairy		12
Minnie – Valentine		17
Owl	Version 1 - plain chin	7
Owl	Version 2 - fuzzy chin	9
Pain		8
Panic		8
Piglet	Version 2 - no footpads	7
Piglet	Test - footpads	35
Piglet – As Tigger	Catalog Exclusive	25
Piglet – Classic		8
Piglet – Easter Egg		15
Piglet – Pumpkin	UK Exclusive	25
Piglet – Valentine	UK Exclusive	35
Pluto	Test - tag says 9", longer ears, footpads on hind feet	24
Pluto	Version 3 - plastic eyes, more plush	8
Pluto	Version 2 - tag has no measurement, no footpads	7
Pluto – Reindeer		21
Prince from Snow White		8
Rabbit	Version 2 - white tail	8
Rabbit	Version 1 - yellow tail	7
Rex		7
Rocket	Disney Quest Exclusive	14
Roo		25
Sleepy		12
Sneezy		10
Snow White		9
Sound Flubber		9
Tigger	Version 5 - footpads, curly tail, bigger eyebrows	7
Tigger	Version 4 - no footpads, straight tail, more stripes	10
Tigger	Grandite	10
Tigger	Version 3 - no footpads, curly tail, more stripes	8
Tigger	Version 2 - no footpads, curly tail, fewer stripes	20
Tigger	Test - footpads, straight tail, fewer stripes	32
Tigger – As Piglet	Catalog Exclusive	9
Tigger – As Pooh		9
Tigger – Classic	Version 2 - brownish/orange	7
Tigger – Classic	Version 1 - orange	7
Tigger – Gradnite		n/a
Tigger – Mad Scientist		15

DISNEY MINI BEAN BAGS
(Disney)

NAME	DESCRIPTION	MINT
Tigger – St. Patrick's Day		24
Tigger – Xmas	Version 1 - small eyebrows, no footpads	25
Tigger – Xmas	Version 2 - bigger eyebrows, footpads, UK Exclusive	32
Timothy	sitting, WDCC tag	36
Winnie the Pooh Picnic		8
Winnie-the-Pooh	Version 3 - no footpads, stitched nose	7
Winnie-the-Pooh	Test - footpads, hard nose	32
Winnie-the-Pooh	Version 2 - no footpads, hard nose	12
Winnie-the-Pooh – As Eeyore	Catalog Exclusive	9
Winnie-the-Pooh – As Tigger		9
Winnie-the-Pooh – Baseball		8
Winnie-the-Pooh – Bumblebee		8
Winnie-the-Pooh – Choo-Choo		9
Winnie-the-Pooh – Classic		7
Winnie-the-Pooh – Easter Bunny	white, Japan Exclusive	25
Winnie-the-Pooh – Easter Bunny, blue		14
Winnie-the-Pooh – Easter, lavender bunny suit	Disney Store Exclusive	7
Winnie-the-Pooh – Easter, red shirt, bunny ears		35
Winnie-the-Pooh – Fishing		7
Winnie-the-Pooh – Friendship Set		40
Winnie-the-Pooh – Gradnite	Disneyland Exclusive	24
Winnie-the-Pooh – Gradnite	WDW - floral shorts	28
Winnie-the-Pooh – Hanukkah		12
Winnie-the-Pooh – Jumping Bean		12
Winnie-the-Pooh – Nautical		8
Winnie-the-Pooh – Picnic		n/a
Winnie-the-Pooh – Pilot		8
Winnie-the-Pooh – Pumpkin		12
Winnie-the-Pooh – Reindeer		8
Winnie-the-Pooh – Santa	Version 1 - hard nose	24

DISNEY MINI BEAN BAGS
(Disney)

NAME	DESCRIPTION	MINT
Winnie-the-Pooh – Santa	Version 2 - stitched nose	18
Winnie-the-Pooh – Snowflake		52
Winnie-the-Pooh – Snowman		13
Winnie-the-Pooh – Valentine		82
Winnie-the-Pooh – w/red sweater		12
Winnie-the-Pooh – Xmas	green scarf	30
Woody	Version 2 - no buttons on shirt, no cuffs, no lines on hat	7
Woody	Version 1 - buttons on shirt, cuffs, lines on hat	9
Woozle #2	pink/fuscia	9
Woozle #3	yellow/green	9

GRATEFUL DEAD BEARS
(Liquid Blue)

NAME	DESCRIPTION	MINT
Aiko	purple turtle	10
All Access		35
Alligator		10
Althea		22
Ashbury		10
August West		10
Bertha		15
Bird Song		10
Black Peter		50
Blues Man		10
C.C. Rider		10
Candy Man		10
Casey Jones		42
Cassidy		15
China Cat		10
Cosmic Charlie		25
Crazy Fingers		17
Daisy		10
Dark Hollow		10
Dark Star		10
Daydream		15
Deal		10
Delilah		25
Delilah	w/o black paws	60
Doodah Man		10
Dupree		12
Esau		10
Eyes of the World		10
Fall Tour		10
Father Time		10
Fire		10
Foolish Heart		10
Franklin		15
Haight		10
Irie		15
Jack A Roe		10
Jack Straw		30
Jerry		20
Lost Sailor		10
Masterpiece		10

GRATEFUL DEAD BEARS
(Liquid Blue)

NAME	DESCRIPTION	MINT
Pearly Baker		10
Peggy-O		15
Picasso Moon		10
Poppa Bear		35
Reuben		10
Ripple		15
Samson		20
Scarlet		10
Snowflake		10
St. Stephen		15
Stagger Lee		15
Sugaree		35
Sunshine		15
Tennessee Jed		25
Terrapin	green turtle	10
Touch of Grey		42
Uncle John		10
Uncle Sam		10
Wharf Rat		35

MEANIES
(Idea Factory)

NAME	DESCRIPTION	MINT
Alien Iverson		250
Armydillo Dan		15
Bare Bear		10
Bart the Elephart		15
Bessie Got Milked		10
Boris the Mucousaurus		15
Buddy the Dog	Infamous Meanies, first series	20
Bull Clinton	Infamous Meanies, first series	15
Burny the Bear		10
Chicken Pox		10
Cod Father		12
Cold Turkey		5
Dennis Rodmantis	Infamous Meanies, second series	10
Digger the Snottish Terrier		10
Donkyng	Infamous Meanies, first series	12
Donnie Didn't Duck		10
Fi & Do the Dalmutation		10
Floaty the Fish		10
Got Lucky		5
Heartless Bear	red	18
Heartless Bear	white	5
Hurley Pukin' Toucan		12
Jerry Stinger	Infamous Meanies, second series	15
Lucky the Rabbit		10
Mallard Stern	Infamous Meanies, second series	15
Matt the Fat Bat		20
Mick Jaguar	Infamous Meanies, second series	15

Franklin, Liquid Blue

Tin Man, Warner Bros.

Dorothy, Warner Bros.

MEANIES
(Idea Factory)

NAME	DESCRIPTION	MINT
Mike Bison	Infamous Meanies, first series	12
Moodonna	Infamous Meanies, second series	15
Navy Seal		15
Otis the Octo-punk		12
Peeping Tom Cat		10
Peter Gotta Peegull		10
Phlemingo		10
Pirate Jack		200
Quack Nicholson	Infamous Meanies, second series	10
Sledge the Hammered-head Shark		18
Slushy the Snowman		5
Snake Eyes Jake		15
Splat in the Hat		5
Splat the Road Kill Kat		15
Stupid Cupid		5
Sunny the Preemie Chicken		10
Velocirapper		15

PLUSH BEAN BAG TOYS
(Applause)

NAME	DESCRIPTION	MINT

HUSH PUPPIES

Beet		12
Berry Frappe		8
Blue Bayou		12
Bunting Blue		8
Chantilly		8
Jet Black		8
Logo Basset		18
Miami Coral		12
Royal Purple		20
Salad Green		20

PEANUTS

Charlie Brown		7
Snoopy		7
Woodstock		7

RUGRATS

Angelica		6
Chuckie		6
Reptar		6
Spike		6
Tommy		6

STAR BEANS
(Mattel)

NAME	DESCRIPTION	MINT

101 DALMATIANS

Freckles	1999 Mail-in Offer	10
Patch	1999 Mail-in Offer	10
Penny	1999 Mail-in Offer	10
Pepper	1999 Mail-in Offer	10

BEAR IN THE BIG BLUE HOUSE

Bear	6
Luna	6
Ojo	6
Pip	6
Pop	6
Treelo	6
Tutter	6

DISNEY CLASSICS SERIES

Baloo		5
Bambi		7
Dumbo		5
Gus		5
Jaq		5
Jiminy Cricket		5
King Louie		7
Lady	Wal-Mart Exclusive	6
Pinocchio		5
Thumper		7
Timothy		7
Tramp		5

MICKEY MOUSE SERIES

Chip	7
Daisy Duck	5
Dale	7
Dewey	5
Donald Duck	5
Double Dribble Goofy	5
Goofy	5
Half-Time Minnie	5
Home-Run Mickey	5
Huey	5
Louie	5
Mickey Mouse	5
Minnie Mouse	5
Pluto	5
Touchdown Donald	5
Uncle Scrooge	5

SPOT A STAR

Hamm	10
Sheriff Tigger	10
Soccer Mickey	10
Tinker Bell	10

TOY STORY

Buzz Lightyear	5
Rex	5
Woody	5

TOY STORY II

Angelic Rex	Target Exclusive	6
Bullseye		5
Buzz Lightyear		5

BEANBAG TOYS

STAR BEANS
(Mattel)

NAME	DESCRIPTION	MINT
Gift Bearing Woody	Target Exclusive	6
Jessie		5
Jolly St. Buzz	Target Exclusive	6
Prospector		5
Reindeer Bullseye	Target Exclusive	6
Rex		5
Woody		5

WINNIE THE POOH SERIES

Kanga & Roo		5
Cool Pal Rabbit		5
Cowboy Pooh		5
Eeyore		5
Frosty Friend Tigger		5
Giddy-Up Pooh		5
Gopher		5
High Country Gopher		5
Lasso Roping Piglet		5
Nap Time Owl		5
Nightie Nightie Rabbit		5
Owl		8
Pajama Party Pooh		5
Piglet		5
Pillow Time Piglet		5
Rabbit		5
Sheriff Tigger		5
Sleepwalking Gopher		5
Snow Buddy Piglet		5
Sweet Dreams Eeyore		5
Sweet Lullabye Kanga	KMart Exclusive	5
Tigger		5
Wake-Up Tigger		5
Winnie-The-Pooh		5
Winter Winnie-the-Pooh		5
Yippee-Yay Rabbit		5

TEENIE BEANIE BABIES/ MCDONALD'S

See Restaurant Premiums

WARNER BROS. BEAN BAGS
(Warner Bros.)

NAME	DESCRIPTION	MINT
Aquaman		7
Astro		12
Augie Doggie		12
Bamm Bamm		7

WARNER BROS. BEAN BAGS
(Warner Bros.)

NAME	DESCRIPTION	MINT
Barney		7
Batgirl		7
Batman		7
Betty		7
Bladebeak		8
Blossom		8
Boo Boo		11
Brain		8
Bubbles		8
Bugs Bunny	Santa	10
Bugs Bunny	Trick 'r Treat	12
Bugs Bunny	talking	15
Bugs Bunny	Stars & Stripes	12
Bugs Bunny	snowman	15
Bugs Bunny	Rabbit Season	10
Bugs Bunny	Millooneyum	12
Bugs Bunny	Easter '98	50
Bugs Bunny	Carrot Easter '99	14
Bugs Bunny	Birthday	8
Buttercup		8
Catwoman		7
Cowardly Lion		12
Daffy Duck		10
Daphne		7
Devon and Cornwall		18
Dino		12
Dot		8
Droopy		15
Elroy		7
Flash		7
Flintmobile	QVC/Catalog Exclusive	12
Foghorn Leghorn		10
Fred (Scooby-Doo)		7
Fred Flintstone		7
George		7
Gizmo		12
Gossamer		10
Great Gazoo	QVC/Catalog Exclusive	10
Green Lantern		10
Harley Quinn		7
Hong Kong Phooey		10
Huckleberry Hound		10
Jack Frost		20
Jane		7
Jerry		10
Judy		7
K-9		10
K-9	Reindeer	12
Lola Bunny		9
Lollipop Boy		12
Lollipop Girl		12
Marc Antony		18
Martian Manhunter		7
Marvin the Martian		25
Marvin the Martian	Millooneyum	12
Michigan J. Frog		10
Morocco Mole		9
Pebbles		7
Penelope		10

WARNER BROS. BEAN BAGS
(Warner Bros.)

NAME	DESCRIPTION	MINT
Pepe Le Pew		15
Petunia Pig		10
Poison Ivy		7
Porky Pig		10
Pussyfoot		10
Riddler		7
Road Runner		10
Robin		7
Rosie the Robot		7
Scooby Doo	Witch	16
Scooby Doo	letters SD on collar	15
Scooby Doo	Xmas '99	10
Scooby Doo	Vampire	16
Scooby Doo	Year 2000	12
Scooby Doo	Easter '98	40
Scooby Doo	Reindeer '97	125
Scooby Doo	Antlers '98	14
Scooby Doo	letter S on collar	30
Scrappy Doo		7
Shaggy		7
Shazam		7
Snagglepuss		10
Space Ghost		10
Speed Buggy		10
Speedy Gonzalez		10
Squiddly-Diddly		10
Supergirl		7
Superman		10

WARNER BROS. BEAN BAGS
(Warner Bros.)

NAME	DESCRIPTION	MINT
Sylvester		10
Sylvester	Millooneyum	12
Tasmanian Devil		20
Tasmanian Devil	Millooneyum	12
The Joker		7
Tom		10
Touche Turtle		10
Tweety		20
Tweety	Millooneyum	12
Velma		7
Wakko		8
Wicked Witch		12
Wile E. Coyote		10
Wilma		7
Wonder Woman		7
Yakko		8
Yakky Doodle		10
Yosemite Sam		10

WIZARD OF OZ SERIES

Dorothy		12
Flying Monkey		12
Glinda the Good Witch		12
Scarecrow		12
Tin Man		12
Toto		15
Wizard		10

Character Toys

Everybody loves a character — right? In the field of toy collecting, characters are those familiar faces created by comic books, television cartoons, movies and more.

Character toy collecting remains the broadest field in the hobby. If time and space would permit, we could easily fill this book with character toys and still only skim its colorful surface.

From Atom Ant to Mickey Mouse, from Popeye to Zorro and everywhere in between, the choices are mind boggling. Collectors are restricted only by their budgets, as the variety even within single categories like Mickey Mouse or Popeye is wide enough to comprise entire collections. Tin wind-ups, bisques, dolls, books, puppets, play sets, puzzles, models, coloring books, games — it never ends.

Beginning collectors are soon faced with either narrowing their collecting into specialties or being overwhelmed by choices, and the options are so tempting that many collectors never specialize at all. Flash Gordon and Mickey Mouse not only look just fine together, they belong together. Dick Tracy, Li'l Abner and Donald Duck look great side by side on a shelf, and whatever configuration a developing toy collection takes, it will tell a fascinating story of its time and its relationship to other toys around it. For this reason, those diverse and eclectic collections can be the most satisfying of all.

For those who are already engaged in or are considering specialization, a few words of introduction to some of the major classes in this section are in order.

Disney Mania!

Walt Disney has often been called the single greatest contributor to American culture. Disneyana is one of the largest and most vigorous areas of toy collecting, and it shows no signs of slowing.

No comic creations have ever been as honored (or as frequently pirated) as Disney characters. From the rat-snouted mouse of 1928 to the virtually human version of the 1990s, the various stages of Mickey Mouse have adorned more toys and trinkets than any other image in modern history. And he is hardly alone.

Mickey Mouse Alarm Clock, 1975, Bradley

The wide world of Walt has grown full, is richly populated, and the theory of cosmic expansion holds true — each new Disney film brings new planets of characters into being. And across our planet, millions of budding little collectors line up to be first for their movie tickets, popcorn, and every piece of merchandise their allowances will buy.

The implication is clear. The market demand for the classic toys of Mickey, Donald, Pinocchio, and other early Disney characters is secure and will likely stay that way. We can only guess what those first 1930s Disney toys will be worth when they finally turn 100 years old, or what *Toy Story 2* or *Tarzan* toys will be worth in 2099.

Just How Popular?

Not all toys endlessly escalate in value. Enduring popularity is a key element in predicting future demand for pop culture collectibles. How popular was it when it was new? How long did it stay at the top? These and other factors all impact on future collectibility.

As collectibles mature and their active collecting public increases, their prices can be expected to rise. But once the collector base begins to erode, once it gets old or loses interest or gets interrupted by a war or replaced by the next big thing, then values can begin to slide. When collectors go away, sometimes an entire hobby goes with them. The best insurance against this is the continued popularity of some aspect of their identity, particularly if it is character based.

Another prime example of this longevity is Popeye, who made his first appearance in 1929 in a comic strip

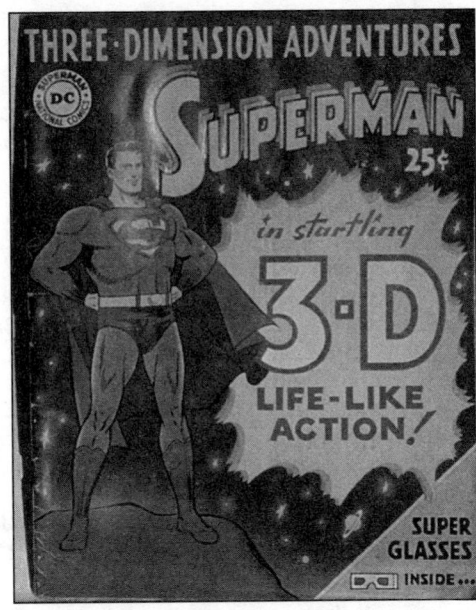

3-D Adventures of Superman Comic Book, 1950s, DC Comics

called Thimble Theatre, created by E.C. Segar. The spinach-eating sailor rapidly became one of the most popular characters of his day, bringing fame to his cartoon companions as well.

That fame manifested itself in some of the most beautiful and well-designed toys of the 1930s. Classic Marx toys like Popeye the Champ and Popeye and Olive Oyl Jiggers have continually topped price lists not only because they are superb examples of the toy makers' art, but also because their characters continue to charm to this day.

Durability translates into collectibility, and the power to draw new collectors from each maturing generation. The universal and continuing appeal of Mickey and Minnie Mouse, Superman, Snoopy, Popeye, Batman and others are assurances that future generations of collectors will seek out their toys and place them proudly on their shelves, someday perhaps right next to their 50-year-old Buzz Lightyear action figures.

Trends

Character toys see little chance of waning popularity, with new characters cropping up with every movie, TV show and book. Especially hot in 2000 were toys related to movies, like *X-Men*, the ever-popular rock group KISS. With interest in pop culture shifting from the 1960s to the 1970s and the popularity of such TV shows as That '70s Show has generated lots of interest in vintage games, lunch boxes, dolls and other toys from that era — particularly those that remembered TV shows like *H.R. PufnStuf*, *The Dukes of Hazzard* and *The Partridge Family* (see TV Toys for values).

Among newer toys, Batman and Superman toys failed to generate as much interest as vintage toys bearing those superheroes. And while new Superman toys don't excited collectors much today, Superman premiums from the 1940s continue to lead lists of the top-selling character collectibles.

Demand for a particular character may ebb and flow according to times and market whims, but overall this is one of the strongest and most reliable areas of toy collecting.

Some Good prices were lowered, accounting for the increasing desire for toys in Excellent or better condition.

The Top 10 Character Collectibles
(in Mint condition)

1. Superman Member Ring, 1940 .... $185,000
2. Action Comics #1, DC Comics, 1938, first appearance of
   Superman 70,000
3. Superman Gum Ring, Gum, Inc., 1940 30,000
4. Little Orphan Annie Altascope Ring, Quaker, 1942 25,000
5. Superman Candy Ring, Leader Novelty Candy, 1940 20,000
6. Donald Duck Bicycle, Shelby, 1949 10,000
7. Superman-Tim Club Ring, 1940s 10,000
8. Superman Trading Cards, Gum Inc., 1940 10,000
9. Batman Play Set, Ideal, 1966 10,000
10. Superman Patch, 1939 9,000

Contributor to this section: John Snyder, Jr., Diamond International Galleries, 1966 Greenspring Dr., Suite 401, Timonium, MD 21093.

101 DALMATIANS

TOY	COMPANY	YEAR	DESCRIPTION	GOOD	EX	MIB
101 Dalmatians Snow Dome	Marx	1961	3" x 5" x 3-1/2" tall	35	65	100
101 Dalmatians Wind-Up	Linemar	1959		70	125	400
Dalmatian Pups Figures	Enesco	1960s	4-1/2" tall, set of three	25	50	160
Lucky Figure	Enesco	1960s	4" tall	35	65	100
Lucky Squeeze Toy	Dell		7" tall, squeakers in the bottom	10	15	45

ALICE IN WONDERLAND

TOY	COMPANY	YEAR	DESCRIPTION	GOOD	EX	MIB
Adventures in Costumeland Game	Walt Disney World	1980s	created for Disney costume division members, game board and pieces in a small vinyl garment bag	75	125	200
Alice and White Rabbit Mug	TDL/Daiichi Seimei	1991	promo piece	25	40	65
Alice Bank	Leeds	1950s	figural	55	90	175
Alice Cookie Jar	Regal		13-1/2" tall	375	1000	1500
Alice Cookie Jar	Leeds	1950s	printed in relief	75	125	275
Alice Costume	Ben Cooper	1950s	costume made until 1970s	25	50	125
Alice Disneykin	Marx	1950s	hard plastic	10	20	40
Alice Disneykin	Marx	1950s	unpainted, soft plastic	10	16	30
Alice Doll	Horsman	1970s	Alice has a castle on her apron	15	30	65
Alice Doll	Pedigree	1970s	Great Britain	15	30	65
Alice Doll	Gund	1950s	flat vinyl, stuffed	15	50	100
Alice Doll	Duchess	1951	12-1/2" tall	45	85	250
Alice Doll	Duchess	1951	#739, 7-1/2" tall	35	70	175
Alice Doll	Horsman	1970s	#1071, Walt Disney Classics	15	30	65
Alice Figure	Shaw	1951		110	210	375
Alice Figure	Marx	1950s	painted w/"Holland" stamped on the bottom	15	30	65
Alice Figure	Aldon Industries	1950s	plastic, cut-out standup	30	75	125
Alice Figure	Sears	1980s	Magic Kingdom Collection, bone china	10	15	35
Alice Figure	Hagen-Renaker	1956		125	275	475
Alice Figure	Bully	1984	Germany, PVC, wearing a blue or red dress, each	10	15	20
Alice in Wonderland and Cinderella Book	Collins	1950s	Great Britain version	20	50	85
Alice in Wonderland Big Coloring Book	Whitman	1951	#301 Big Golden	25	65	135
Alice in Wonderland Book	Whitman	1951	#426, Big Golden Book	20	50	125
Alice in Wonderland Book	Whitman	1951	Sandpiper Book w/dust jacket	15	30	90
Alice in Wonderland Book	Dell Publishing	1951	#331	25	50	125
Alice in Wonderland Book	Whitman	1950s	#10426, Big Golden Book, gold foil backing	25	60	125
Alice in Wonderland Book	Whitman	1950s	#10426, without gold backing	15	30	75
Alice in Wonderland Book	Whitman	1950s	#2074 Cozy Corner Book, green endpapers	10	20	50
Alice in Wonderland Card Game	Thos. De LaRue	1980s		4	8	15
Alice in Wonderland Classic Series with Disney Book	Whitman	1950s	#2140 Lewis Carroll text w/Disney dust jacket	15	40	75
Alice in Wonderland Coloring Book	Whitman	1974	#1049	5	15	35
Alice in Wonderland Paint Book	Whitman	1951	#2167	25	60	120
Alice in Wonderland Punch-Out Book	Whitman	1951	#2164	30	100	210
Alice in Wonderland Sticker Fun	Whitman	1950s	#2193 stencil and coloring book	15	30	75

CHARACTER

CHARACTER

TOY	COMPANY	YEAR	DESCRIPTION	GOOD	EX	MIB
Alice Marionette	Peter Puppet	1950s	comes in two different boxes, one "Alice in Wonderland" the other Peter Puppet Disney	40	100	300
Alice Meets the White Rabbit Book	Whitman	1951	#D-19, Little Golden Book	15	25	65
Alice Mug	Disney	1970s		12	20	40
Alice Paper Dolls	Whitman	1976	#1948	8	20	40
Alice Paper Dolls	Whitman	1972	#4712	10	20	50
Alice Snow Dome	Marx	1961	3" tall featuring Alice and the White Rabbit in front of tree	15	30	75
Alice Stationery and Notepad	Pak-Well	1970s	#77065 w/a fan card cover	8	15	30
Alice Wristwatch	U.S. Time	1950s	came w/ceramic statue	80	200	400
Alice Wristwatch	Alba	1990s	Japan, gold tone face	15	30	45
Alice Wristwatch	U.S. Time	1950s	Alice peeking through pink flowers and a plastic statue	80	200	400
Balloons	Eagle Rubber	1951		12	18	35
Balloons	Oak Rubber	1951	four different designs	12	18	35
Blocks	Chad Valley	1950s	five cylindrical tin blocks w/color graphics	60	125	250
Bread Labels	NBC	1950s	twelve different styles, each	10	25	50
Bread Seal Poster	NBC	1950s		10	25	50
Bread Stickers	Continental Baking/Wonder	1974	five styles, each	3	7	12
Bridge Card Game	Whitman	1950s	two decks of cards	35	75	150
Canasta Card Game	Whitman	1950s	two Canasta decks of White Rabbit cards	30	65	125
Candy Tin	Edward Sharp and Sons	1950s	Great Britain English Toffee Tin	55	100	225
Cards	Royal Desserts	1951	sixteen different cards on the back of dessert packages, each	10	25	40
Caterpillar Figure	Hagen-Renaker	1956		125	275	450
Cereal Box with Record	General Mills	1956	Wheaties	70	200	375
Cheshire Cat Costume Pattern	McCall's	1951		25	40	75
Cheshire Cat Doll	Disneyland	1970s	plush	10	25	50
Child's Vanity	Neevel	1950s	illustrated w/film scenes	40	80	160
Clock Radio	General Electric	1970s	features characters on face	20	40	75
Disneykin Play Set	Marx	1950s		175	350	650
Disneyland Figures Set	United China	1960s	large set, each piece	10	25	50
Disneyland Figures Set	United China	1970s	small figures, each piece	10	15	30
Dormouse Doll	Lars/Italy	1950s	stuffed	160	330	525
Dormouse Figure	Shaw	1951		130	225	375
Fan Card	Walt Disney	1951	original release w/1973 invitation to studio screening	30	60	80
Fan Card	Walt Disney	1951	premium sent to fans who wrote letters to studio	15	30	60
Film Viewer	Tru-Vue	1950s	viewer and filmstrip	30	55	85
Glass	Pepsi Cola	1970s	featuring Alice, part of Wonderful World of Disney set	10	16	30
Glasses	Libbey	1951	eight styles released for film opening, each	40	60	120
Handbag	Salient	1950s	child's pink vinyl shoulder bag, Alice w/rocking fly	20	50	85
Handbag	ACME Briefcase	1950s	child's red leather shoulder bag	20	50	85
Hatbox	Neevel	1950s	Caterpillar or Tea Party graphics	55	85	150
Jingle Ball	Vanguard	1951		12	25	50
Looking Glass Cookie Jar	Fred Roberts		raised characters on the body of the jar w/a mirror lid	130	275	600
Mad Hatter Costume	Ben Cooper	1950s	costume made until 1970s	25	35	85
Mad Hatter Costume Pattern	McCall's	1951		20	35	55
Mad Hatter Disneykin	Marx	1950s		25	45	85

TOY	COMPANY	YEAR	DESCRIPTION	GOOD	EX	MIB
Mad Hatter Disneykin	Marx	1950s	unpainted, soft plastic	10	16	30
Mad Hatter Doll	Gund	1950s	flat vinyl, stuffed	20	40	75
Mad Hatter Doll	Gund	1950s	plush	125	250	375
Mad Hatter Figure	Hagen-Renaker	1956		125	250	375
Mad Hatter Figure	Shaw	1951		65	175	325
Mad Hatter Figure	Marx	1950s	painted w/"Holland" stamped on the bottom	15	20	35
Mad Hatter Figure	Sydney Pottery	1950s	large size, sold only in Australia	200	350	525
Mad Hatter Figure	Schmid	1980s	playing xylophone	20	40	75
Mad Hatter Hand Puppet		1960s	hand puppet w/cloth body	20	40	75
Mad Hatter Marionette	Peter Puppet	1950s		45	85	175
Mad Hatter Nodder	Marx	1950s		30	100	200
Mad Hatter Snap Eeze	Marx	1950s		15	25	35
Mad Hatter Snow Dome	New England Collectors Society	1980s	crystal, Mad Hatter, St. Patrick's Day	15	25	45
Mad Hatter Teapot	Regal	1950s		500	1000	1550
Mad Hatter/March Hare Figure	TDL	1980s	Mad Hatter, March Hare w/saxophone	20	40	60
Mad Hatter's Tea Party Book	Whitman	1951	#D-23 Little Golden Book	15	25	35
Mad Tea Party/Cheshire Cat Mug	Applause	1988	Cheshire Cat handle w/Tea Party on the mug	12	18	30
Magic Picture Kit Set	Jiffy Pop	1974	set of four	12	20	40
Make-Up Kit	Hasbro	1951		25	55	85
March Hare Costume	Ben Cooper	1950s	costume made until 1970s	20	35	85
March Hare Costume Pattern	McCall's	1951	pattern	15	30	60
March Hare Disneykin	Marx	1950s	unpainted and soft plastic	12	18	35
March Hare Doll	Gund	1950s	flat vinyl, stuffed	25	45	75
March Hare Doll	Gund	1950s	plush	175	350	550
March Hare Figure	Hagen-Renaker	1956		110	250	410
March Hare Figure	Sydney Pottery	1950s	large size, sold only in Australia	155	330	525
March Hare Figure	Shaw	1951		170	320	475
March Hare Figure	Marx	1950s	painted w/"Holland" stamped on the bottom	15	20	35
March Hare Marionette	Peter Puppet	1950s		35	100	175
March Hare Snap Eeze	Marx	1950s		15	20	40
March Hare Twistoy	Marx	1950s		15	20	40
Molding Set	Model Craft	1951		45	75	150
Molding Set	Great Britain	1952	similar to Model Craft set	50	95	175
Music Box	TDL	1980s	ceramic teacup	45	70	150
Music Box	TDL	1980s	plastic, tea cup rotates	45	70	150
Music Box	Disneyland	1980s	Wooden box features Alice and White Rabbit "I'm Late"	25	50	100
Picture Frame	Dexter-Mahnke	1970s	cloth picture frame, featuring Mad Tea Party	20	35	55
Pitcher	Regal	1950s	King of Hearts	175	350	550
Plaque	Disneyland	1970s	wooden, w/Alice and live flowers	15	25	50
Poster	Disneyland	1958	Alice attraction	175	525	850
Poster	Walt Disney World	1980s	costume division poster featuring Cheshire Cat	15	30	65
Poster	Kraft	1980	Disneyland 25th Anniversary Family Reunion	15	30	65
Puppet Theatre	Peter Puppet	1950s		85	150	250
Puzzle	TDL	1980s	#18, Mad Tea Party and Cast	5	10	20
Puzzle	Jaymar	1951	Tea Party scene	20	65	100
Puzzle	Stafford/England	1979	wooden, Great Britain Tea Party	10	25	40
Puzzle	Jaymar	1951	Croquet cast scene	20	65	100
Puzzle	Jaymar	1951	Alice under a tree	20	65	100
Puzzle	Jaymar	1951	Alice and Rabbit	20	65	100
Queen of Hearts Card Game	Edu-Cards	1975		20	30	45

CHARACTER

ALICE IN WONDERLAND

TOY	COMPANY	YEAR	DESCRIPTION	GOOD	EX	MIB
Queen of Hearts Disneykin	Marx	1950s		30	55	85
Queen of Hearts Disneykin	Marx	1950s	unpainted, soft plastic	15	20	35
Queen of Hearts Doll	Gund	1950s	flat vinyl, stuffed	25	60	100
Queen of Hearts Figure	Sears	1980s	Magic Kingdom Collection, bone china	15	25	35
Queen of Hearts Figure	Marx	1950s	painted w/"Holland" stamped on the bottom	10	18	35
Ramp Walker	Marx	1950s	Mad Hatter and White Rabbit	20	35	65
Record Player	RCA Victor	1951	45 rpm	75	125	200
Record/Little Nipper Giant Storybook	RCA Victor	1951	LY-437, 33, 45, or 78 rpm, each	50	100	150
Rubber Stamp Set	Multiprint	1970s	Italy, #177	20	30	55
Rubber Stamp Set	All Night Media	1989		10	15	25
Salt and Pepper Shakers	Regal	1950s	featuring TweedleDee and TweedleDum	150	300	500
Salt and Pepper Shakers	Regal	1950s	blue or white featuring Alice	150	300	500
School Bag	ACME Briefcase	1950s	fabric and leather	30	70	120
Sewing Cards	Whitman	1951		25	50	100
Sewing Kit	Hasbro	1951	7" sewing machine and 5" doll, all plastic	35	75	125
Soap Set		1951		30	75	150
Tea Cake Box	TDL	1980s	w/a Mad Tea Party lid	10	15	30
Tea Cup and Saucer	TDL	1986	ceramic, Mad Tea Party	60	120	200
Tea Cup Wristwatch	U.S. Time	1950s	picture of Mad Hatter w/an overlay	175	350	600
The Unbirthday Party Book	Whitman	1974	#22, Walt Disney Showcase	8	15	25
Thimble	New England Collectors Society	1980s	Mad Hatter and Alice	5	15	25
Ticket	Disneyland	1970s	employee screening ticket featuring Cheshire Cat	5	10	20
TV Scene, White Rabbit and March Hare	Marx	1950s		30	65	100
TweedleDee and TweedleDum Dolls	Gund	1950s	flat vinyl, stuffed, each	25	50	100
TweedleDee and TweedleDum Dolls	TDL	1980s	plush, each	15	30	55
TweedleDee Figure	Shaw	1951		70	150	225
TweedleDee Figure	Sydney Pottery	1950s	large size, sold only in Australia	175	330	525
TweedleDum Figure	Shaw	1951		70	150	225
TweedleDum Figure	Sydney Pottery	1950s	large size, sold only in Australia	160	350	525
Vase	Enesco	1960s	featuring Alice's head	50	100	200
View-Master Set	GAF	1970s	three reels, Disney	10	15	30
Wall Decor	Dolly Toy	1951	#260 contains Alice, Mad Hatter, March Hare and a lamp	50	100	200
Wall Plaque	Leisuramics	1974	bisque, oval shape, featuring Mad Hatter	20	40	75
Wall Plaque	Leisuramics	1974	bisque, oval shape, featuring TweedleDee and TweedleDum	20	40	60
Wallet	Salient	1950s	vinyl, featuring White Rabbit	20	40	60
Wallet	Salient	1950s	vinyl, featuring Mad Tea Party	20	40	75
Walrus Doll	Lars/Italy	1950s	stuffed	150	325	500
Walrus Figure	Shaw	1951		110	230	360
Walrus Figure	Sydney Pottery	1950s	large size, sold only in Australia	160	350	525
White Rabbit Creamer	Regal	1950s		110	260	425
White Rabbit Disneykin	Marx	1950s		30	60	85
White Rabbit Disneykin	Marx	1950s	unpainted and soft plastic	10	20	35
White Rabbit Doll	Gund	1950s		110	250	375
White Rabbit Doll	TDL	1980s	plush	10	25	50
White Rabbit Doll	Buena Vista/Disney	1974	plush	50	100	150

ALICE IN WONDERLAND

TOY	COMPANY	YEAR	DESCRIPTION	GOOD	EX	MIB
White Rabbit Doll	Disneyland	1970s	small w/black spectacles	10	20	40
White Rabbit Doll	Sears	1970s	plush w/waistcoat and umbrella	12	20	40
White Rabbit Doll	Gund	1950s	flat vinyl, stuffed	20	50	100
White Rabbit Doll	Disneyland	1970s	large, plush w/yellow spectacles	12	20	40
White Rabbit Ears	TDL	1980s		8	15	30
White Rabbit Figure	Sears	1980s	Magic Kingdom Collection, bone china	10	18	35
White Rabbit Figure	Shaw	1951		65	135	225
White Rabbit Figure	Marx	1950s	painted w/"Holland" stamped on the bottom	10	16	35
White Rabbit Figure	Italy		5-1/2" tall, ceramic	15	35	55
White Rabbit Rolykin	Marx	1950s		20	40	60
White Rabbit Sugar Bowl	Regal	1950s		160	340	525

AMOS AND ANDY

TOY	COMPANY	YEAR	DESCRIPTION	GOOD	EX	MIB
Amos and Andy Card Party	A.M. Davis	1930	6" x 8", score pads and tallies	30	80	175
Amos and Andy Fresh Air Taxi	Marx	1930s	5" x 8" long, tin wind-up	550	1200	1800
Amos Wind-Up	Marx	1930	12" tall, tin	550	1200	1800
Contest Winner Check	Pepsodent	1936	$2.00 winner's check for contest	500	800	1200
Puzzle	Pepsodent	1932	8-1/2" x 10", pictured Amos, Andy and other characters	40	125	275
Stock Certificate	Bogus Taxi Company	1930s	premium	125	175	300

ANDY GUMP

TOY	COMPANY	YEAR	DESCRIPTION	GOOD	EX	MIB
Andy Gump Automobile	Arcade		7" x 6", cast iron w/a large figure	375	800	1350
Brush and Mirror			4" diameter, red on ivory colored surface of brush	20	75	150
Chester Gump Playstone Funnies Mold Set		1940s		55	120	175
Chester Gump/Herby Nodders		1930s	ceramic 2-1/4" string nodders, each	55	200	300

ARCHIES

TOY	COMPANY	YEAR	DESCRIPTION	GOOD	EX	MIB
Archie Halloween Costume	Ben Cooper	1969		20	55	85
Archies Paper Dolls	Whitman	1969		20	40	75
Jalopy	Marx	1975	12", plastic	30	55	150
Puzzle	Jaymar	1960s	"Swinging Malt Shop"	10	30	75

ATOM ANT AND FRIENDS

TOY	COMPANY	YEAR	DESCRIPTION	GOOD	EX	MIB
Atom Ant Kite	Roalex	1960s		25	80	150
Atom Ant Punch-Out Set	Whitman	1966		40	100	200
Atom Ant Push Puppet	Kohner	1960s		20	50	75
Atom Ant Puzzle	Whitman	1966		15	50	100
Atom Ant Soaky	Purex	1966		20	65	85
Morocco Mole Bubble Club Soaky	Purex	1960s	7" hard plastic	20	60	100
Squiddly Diddly Bubble Club Soaky	Purex	1960s	10-1/2" hard plastic	20	60	100
Winsome Witch Bubble Club Soaky	Purex	1960s	10-1/2" hard plastic	20	60	100

BABES IN TOYLAND

TOY	COMPANY	YEAR	DESCRIPTION	GOOD	EX	MIB
Babes in Toyland Go Mobile Friction Car	Linemar	1961	4" x 5"x 6"	65	120	385
Babes in Toyland Hand Puppets	Gund		Silly Dilly Clown, Soldier, or Gorgonzo, each	35	65	125
Babes in Toyland Twist 'N Bend Toy	Marx	1963	4" tall flexible toy w/Private Valiant holding a baton	10	25	50
Babes in Toyland Wind-Up Toy	Linemar	1950s	tin	80	180	400
Cadet Doll	Gund		15-1/2" tall, fabric	20	50	100
Puzzle	Jaymar	1961		15	30	50

BAMBI

TOY	COMPANY	YEAR	DESCRIPTION	GOOD	EX	MIB
Bambi Book	Grosset and Dunlap	1942	black and white illustrations	15	35	75
Bambi Prints	New York Graphic Society	1947	11" x 14" framed	25	50	100
Bambi Soaky	Colgate-Palmolive			15	40	65
Flower Bank		1940s	5" x 5"x 7" tall, plaster	50	100	200
Lamp			Bambi and Thumper	40	120	250
Throw Rug		1960s	21" x 39", Bambi and Thumper	25	50	75
Thumper Ashtray	Goebel	1950s	4" tall	30	75	150
Thumper Bank	Leeds	1950s	ceramic, figural	45	85	165
Thumper Book	Grosset and Dunlap	1942	color and black/white illustrations	15	35	75
Thumper Doll			16" tall, plush	15	30	50
Thumper Pull Toy	Fisher-Price	1942	#533, 7-1/2" x 12", wood and metal, Thumper's tail rings the bell	30	100	200
Thumper Soaky	Colgate-Palmolive	1960s		25	60	85

BARNEY GOOGLE

TOY	COMPANY	YEAR	DESCRIPTION	GOOD	EX	MIB
Barney Google and Spark Plug	Nifty	1920s	7-1/2" tall, wind-up	400	800	1650
Barney Google and Spark Plug Figurines			3" x 3", bisque, on white bisque pedestal	75	175	300
Barney Google Doll	Schoenhut	1922	8-1/2" tall, wood and wood composition	180	475	900
Spark Plug Doll	Schoenhut	1922	9" long x 6-1/2" tall, jointed wood construction w/fabric	180	475	900
Spark Plug in Bathtub		1930	5" long die-cast, white	100	225	375
Spark Plug Pull Toy			10" x 8" tall, wood	80	160	275
Spark Plug Squeaker Toy		1923	5" long, rubber w/squeaker in mouth	25	90	150
Spark Plug Toy		1920s	5" tall, wood, on wheels	45	150	225

BATMAN

TOY	COMPANY	YEAR	DESCRIPTION	GOOD	EX	MIB
Bat Bomb	Mattel	1966		50	75	150
Bat Cycle	Toy Biz	1989		5	12	25
Bat Machine	Mego	1979		30	55	110
Bat Ring		1966	yellow plastic, originally for a gumball machine	15	40	65
Batboat	Duncan	1987		10	20	40
Batboat Pullstring Toy	Eidai		made in Japan	60	120	185
Batcave Play Set	Mego	1974	vinyl	150	250	500
Batcoin Lot	Space Magic Limited	1966	Four 1-1/2" diameter metal coins, each depicting a scene featuring Batman and Robin battling villains	30	75	100
Batman "Punch-O" Drink Mix		1966	small paper packet	25	35	70
Batman 3-D Comic Book	DC Comics	1966	9" x 11" comic w/3-D pages and glasses	50	150	375
Batman and Robin Hand Puppets	Ideal	1966	12" soft vinyl head, plastic body, each	40	150	250

TOY	COMPANY	YEAR	DESCRIPTION	GOOD	EX	MIB
Batman and Robin Society Membership Button	Button World	1966	full color litho metal button featuring Batman and Robin and the words "Charter Member-Batman and Robin Society"	15	25	35
Batman and Robin Valentine		1966		10	20	50
Batman and Superman Record Album	Wonderland	1969-71	45 rpm record Batman theme song from the 1966 television show and "The Superman Song"	20	75	100
Batman Annual		1965-66	8" x 10" hardback annual contains reprinted stories from 1950s Batman and Detective Comics	20	30	60
Batman Arcade Game	Bluebox	1989	electronic	75	120	165
Batman Bank		1989	figural bank given away w/Batman Cereal	4	7	15
Batman Bank		1966	7" tall glazed china figural bank depicts Batman w/hands on hip	45	90	125
Batman Batarang Toss	Pressman	1966		125	250	400
Batman Bendy Figure	Diener	1960s	on card	35	65	85
Batman Candy Box	Phoenix Candy	1966	2-1/2" x 3-1/2" x 1", several color scenes	30	100	200
Batman Cartoon Kit	Colorforms	1966		25	55	85
Batman Cast and Paint Set		1960s	plaster casting mold and paint set	35	75	150
Batman Cereal Box	Kellogg's	1966	w/Yogi Bear on front	250	800	1800
Batman Cereal Box	Ralston	1989		20	55	80
Batman Comic Book and Record Set	Golden Records	1966	33-1/3 rpm record, full size Batman comic book, official Batman membership card w/secret Batman code on back	30	60	120
Batman Crazy Foam		1974		20	40	80
Batman Crusader Sundae Fudgesicle	Popsicle	1966	7" white and brown paper wrapper	8	15	25
Batman Dinner Set		1966	ceramic; three pieces	40	70	150
Batman Drinking Glass	Pepsi	1976	7" tall glass tumbler, all Batman characters, each	10	20	30
Batman Figure	Applause	1988	15" tall w/stand	15	25	45
Batman Figure	Takara/Japan	1989		40	80	150
Batman Figure	Presents	1989	15-1/2" tall vinyl and cloth figure on base, 1970s logo, metal stand	20	40	75
Batman Figure	Bully	1989	7" bendy	8	15	25
Batman Figure	Billiken	1989	8" on card	8	15	25
Batman Figure	Ideal	1966	3" yellow plastic, detachable gray plastic cape	12	25	50
Batman Figure and Parachute	CDC	1966	11" x 9" card, metallic blue figure of Batman and working parachute	25	45	85
Batman Figure with Flyaway Action	Mego	1976	12-1/2" tall	55	120	225
Batman Flying Copter	Remco	1966	12" plastic w/guide-wire control	40	85	175
Batman Flying Figure on String	Ben Cooper	1973	6" rubber figure of Batman w/rubber cape	10	20	40
Batman Fork	Imperial	1966	6" stainless steel w/embossed figure of Batman, w/"Batman" engraved towards the bottom	8	25	50
Batman Halloween Costume	Ben Cooper	1965	plastic Halloween mask and purple and yellow cape, several versions, some feature logo on chest	20	40	85
Batman Helmet and Cape Set	Ideal	1966	blue hard plastic cowl shaped helmet and soft blue vinyl cape w/drawstring	100	250	500

CHARACTER

TOY	COMPANY	YEAR	DESCRIPTION	GOOD	EX	MIB
Batman Inflated Gliding Figure	Ideal	1966	16" soft plastic inflatable Batman w/free flowing cape and hard plastic cable rail	30	60	125
Batman Kite	Hiflyer	1982		8	15	25
Batman Lamp	Vanity Fair		Made in Taiwan	45	75	150
Batman Lobby Display	Warner Bros.	1989	Michael Keaton cardboard stand up	50	100	175
Batman Lucky Charm Display Card		1966	4" x 4" paper display card used in bubble gum machines, card shows Bat logo and red "Be protected—Get your Batman lucky charm now"	12	25	50
Batman Meets Blockbuster Coloring Book	Whitman	1966	40 pages	20	40	75
Batman on a String Figure	Fun Things	1966	4" rubber, flexible arms, legs and removable cape	15	30	60
Batman Paint by Number Set	Hasbro	1965	five pre-numbered sketches, ten oil paint vials and brush	40	85	175
Batman Pencil Box	Empire Pencil	1966	gun-shaped pencil box w/set of Batman pencils	25	55	125
Batman Pillow		1966	10" x 12" w/1940s logo	20	40	75
Batman Pinball Game	Marx	1960s	tin litho w/plastic casing	35	80	175
Batman Play Set	Ideal	1966	eleven pieces including characters and vehicles	1000	4000	10000
Batman Postcards	Dexter Press	1966	three full color postcards, each taken from a comic panel from Batman comics, each	8	15	30
Batman Postcards	Dexter Press	1966	set of eight postcards w/Carmine Infantino artwork	30	100	150
Batman Push Puppet	Kohner	1966	3" plastic w/push button on bottom	20	45	85
Batman Radio Belt and Buckle		1966		25	75	150
Batman Record	SPC	1966	45 rpm, sleeve shaped like Batman's head; also available in Robin, Joker, Penguin, Riddler and Batmobile versions	15	50	100
Batman Returns Display	Warner Bros.	1992		10	50	75
Batman Returns Lobby Display	Warner Bros.	1992	Michael Keaton life-size cardboard stand up	30	100	175
Batman Returns Watch	Consort	1989	gray or yellow Bat logo	10	20	50
Batman Road Race Set		1960s	slot car racing set	100	250	400
Batman Slot Car	Magicar (England)	1966	5" long Batmobile being driven by Batman and Robin in illustrated display window box	100	250	450
Batman Soundtrack Record	20th Century Fox	1966	mono and stereo versions, each	50	140	250
Batman String Puppet	Madison	1977		35	75	150
Batman Super Powers Stain and Paint Set		1984		10	25	50
Batman Superfriends Lite Brite Refill Pack		1980		5	15	25
Batman Superhero Stamp Set		1970s		10	20	40
Batman Switch and Go Play Set	Mattel	1966	9" plastic Batmobile, 40 feet of track, figures, etc.	125	250	500
Batman Target Game	Hasbro	1966	tin litho target w/plastic revolver and rubber-tipped darts	40	80	175
Batman Trace-a-Graph	Emenee	1966		30	75	150
Batman Utility Belt	Ideal	1960s		1000	3000	5000
Batman vs. the Joker Book	Signet	1966	160-page paperback	5	10	15

BATMAN

TOY	COMPANY	YEAR	DESCRIPTION	GOOD	EX	MIB
Batman Wastepaper Basket		1966	10" tall, color tin litho	30	60	125
Batman Wind-Up	Billiken	1989	Tin litho	25	50	100
Batman Wristwatch	Quintel	1991	digital	8	15	25
Batman Yo-Yo	SpectraStar	1989		4	10	25
Batman/Robin Flicker-Flasher Ring	Vari-Vue	1966	silver plastic base	10	20	25
Batmobile	Azrak-Hamway	1974	battery operated	40	80	175
Batmobile	Rich Man's Toys	1989	remote control	85	160	350
Batmobile	Aoshinu (Japan)	1980s	motorized	30	60	150
Batmobile	Toy Biz	1989	remote control	12	30	65
Batmobile	Apollo (Japan)		radio-controlled	60	125	250
Batmobile	Matsushiro		radio-controlled	60	125	250
Batmobile	Bandai	1980s	pullback vehicle w/machine guns	25	60	125
Batmobile	AHI	1972	11" long tin litho battery-operated mystery action car w/blinking light and jet engine noise	75	150	275
Batmobile	Duncan	1977	12" x 8" on card	25	50	100
Batmobile	Simms	1960s	plastic car on card	20	45	75
Batmobile AM Radio	Bandai	1970s		45	90	175
Batmobile Display Sign	Burry's	1969	34" x 48" die-cut 3-D plastic story display, raised images of Batman, Robin, and Batmobile, bright orange w/yellow lettering	300	800	1200
Batmobile Motorized Kit	Aoshinu (Japan)	1980s	smaller snap kit	20	35	75
Batphone	Marx	1966		70	125	250
Batscope Dart Launcher	Tarco	1966		25	45	85
Bat-Troll Doll	Wish-Nik	1966	vinyl, dressed in a blue felt Batman outfit w/cowl and cape	75	150	300
Batwing	Toy Biz	1980s		15	25	50
Beach Towel		1966	34" x 58" white, Batman hitting a crook	40	95	180
Bread Wrapper	New Century Bread	1966	plastic	20	45	75
Button Display Card		1966	full color display card used in bubble gum machines which offered Batman buttons	15	40	75
Cake Decoration		1960s	2" hard plastic figure of Robin or Batman, each	8	15	25
Cake Decorations	Space Magic Limited	1966	4" plastic one dimensional figures of Batman, Robin and old 1940s Batman logo	15	33	65
Candy Cigarettes		1960s	made in England	15	35	75
Catwoman Iron-On Patch		1966	Catwoman w/the words "Batkids Fan Club"	10	50	75
Catwoman Returns	Horizon	1990s	vinyl model kit	10	20	40
Catwoman Watch	Consort	1991	Batman Returns	7	20	40
Catwoman Watch	Quintel	1991	digital	5	15	30
Catwoman's Revenge Record	Power Records	1975	33-1/3 rpm story record	5	20	40
Cave Tun-L	New York Toy	1966	26" x 26" x 2" tunnel	500	1100	2100
Charm Bracelet		1966	on card	30	60	125
Child's Belt		1960s	elastic w/bronze logo buckle	22	40	75
Child's Dinner Plate	Boontonware	1966	7" plastic w/image of Batman and Robin	15	30	50
Child's Mittens		1973	children's blue plastic vinyl, raised illustration of Batman and logo	12	25	50
Child's Pajamas	Wormser	1966	light blue, two piece pajamas, full color Batman logo on chest	200	450	900

BATMAN

TOY	COMPANY	YEAR	DESCRIPTION	GOOD	EX	MIB
Chocolate Milk Carton	Reiter and Hart	1966	one-quart carton in yellow, red and brown, features front and back panels of Batman in action poses	100	200	400
Christmas Ornament	Presents	1989		5	10	20
Coffee Mug	Anchor-Hocking	1966	milk glass, action pose of Batman on one side and the Bat logo on the opposite side	15	30	50
Coins	Transogram	1966	plastic, set	25	50	100
Costume Patterns	McCalls	1960s	patterns for making Batman, Robin, and Superman costumes, paper envelope, each	15	35	75
Costume Store Poster	Ben Cooper	1966	12" x 24", yellow	30	125	175
Dot-To-Dot and Coloring Book	Vasquez Brothers	1967	Batman w/Robin the Boy Wonder, printed in the Phillipines, 20 pages	20	40	85
Drinking Glass		1989	5", made in France	10	20	35
Escape Gun	Lincoln	1966	red plastic spring-loaded pistol w/Batman decal, two separate firing barrels	30	100	175
Flicker Pictures Display Card		1966	bubble gum machine display card	10	25	45
Frame Tray Puzzle	Whitman	1966	11" x 14", Batman and Robin thwarting the Joker	15	30	60
From Alfred to Zowie! Book	Golden Press	1966		10	20	35
Give-A-Show Projector Cards	Kenner	1960s	four slide cards in box	10	25	50
Glow-in-the Dark Poster	Ciro Art	1966	18" x 14" poster of Batman and Robin swinging across Gotham City	20	75	100
Gotham City Stunt Set	Tonka	1989		15	55	85
Inflatable TV Chair		1982		10	20	35
Jelly Jar	W.H. Marvin	1966	5"-6" glass jar w/color label, "Bat" Pure Apple Jelly	200	400	600
Joker Bank	Mego	1974	plastic	30	60	125
Joker Cereal Bowl	Sun Valley	1966	5" hard plastic	12	25	50
Joker Figure	Presents		15" vinyl figure	10	20	40
Joker Figure	Ideal	1966	3" blue plastic	10	20	45
Joker Figure	Applause	1988	vinyl w/stand	10	20	40
Joker Record	SPC	1966	45 rpm, sleeve shaped like Joker's head	20	40	85
Joker Van	Ertl	1989	die-cast vehicle on card	5	10	20
Joker Wind-up	Billiken	1989		40	80	150
Joker Wristwatch	Quintell	1989	digital	10	20	40
Joker Wristwatch	Fossil	1980s		25	60	100
Joker Yo-Yo	SpectraStar	1989		5	15	30
Lapel Pin	Mamsell	1966	2" bat-shaped metal, black w/yellow eyes	20	35	50
Life Magazine		1966	March 11, 1966 issue, Adam West as Batman on cover	15	50	100
Magic Magnetic Gotham City Play Set	Remco	1966	cardboard city, character figures	200	450	850
Mug		1966	5" clear plastic; color wrap around sheet	30	60	100
Official Bat-Signal Stickers	Alan-Whitney	1966		10	20	35
Paint-By-Number Book	Whitman	1966		20	40	75
Paper Mask		1943	newspaper premium, announced first newspaper comic	500	1500	2500
Party Hat	Amscan/Canadian	1972	7" child's cardboard hat depicts Batman and Robin	8	15	25
Penguin Returns Model Kit	Horizon			10	20	40

172

BATMAN

TOY	COMPANY	YEAR	DESCRIPTION	GOOD	EX	MIB
Pennant		1966	11 x 29" white felt, illustration of the Dynamic Duo swinging on ropes w/the Bat-signal in the background	20	100	175
Projector Gun	Toy Biz	1989		10	20	50
Puppet Theater Stage	Ideal	1966	marketed by Sears, 19" x 11" x 20" cardboard stage w/hand puppets	80	225	450
Ray Gun		1960s	7" long blue and black futuristic space gun w/bat sights and bats on handgrip	80	250	400
Riddler/Batman Punching Riddler Flicker-Flasher Ring	Vari-Vue	1966	silver plastic base	10	25	45
Robin Character Sponge	Epic	1966	5"	10	30	75
Robin Figure	Palitoy	1970s	8" figure on card	15	40	80
Robin Figure	Presents		cloth and vinyl, on base	10	20	35
Robin Figure	Ideal	1966	3" plastic, detachable yellow plastic cape	10	20	40
Robin Figure	Applause	1988	vinyl w/stand	10	20	35
Robin Iron-on Patch		1966	2-1/2" diameter patch, Batkids Fan Club	8	35	50
Robin on a String Figure	Ben Cooper		4" tall, rubber	10	20	35
Robin Ornament	Presents	1989		5	13	20
Robin Placemat		1966	13" x 18" vinyl	15	45	75
Robin Push Puppet	Kohner	1966	3", plastic, push button on bottom	25	60	100
Robin Shuttle	Mego	1979	sized for British-made Mego figures, in box	20	40	85
Robin/Dick Grayson Flicker-Flasher Ring	Vari-Vue	1966	silver plastic base	10	25	45
Rubber Stamp Set	Kellogg's	1966	2" x 5" hard black plastic case, set of six plastic stamps plus ink pad: Batman, Robin, Batmobile, Joker, Riddler and Penguin	60	150	300
Shooting Arcade	AHI	1970s	graphics of Joker, Catwoman and Penguin	25	75	150
Sip-A-Drink Cup		1966	British, 6" tall, white plastic	50	100	200
Slam Bang Ice Cream Carton	Cabarrus Creamery	1966	features Batman and Robin on side panels	15	40	55
Sparkle Paint Set	Kenner	1966	paint and six pre-numbered sketches of Batman	30	75	150
Sticker Fun with Batman Book	Watkins-Strathmore	1966	8" x 11" softbound w/stickers	15	40	90
Super Accelerator Batmobile	AHI	1970s	on card	15	40	85
Talking Alarm Clock	Janex	1975	plastic clock w/Bat logo on face	40	85	175
Three Villains of Doom Book	Signet	1966	160 pages	10	30	60
Turbine-Sound Batmobile	Toy Biz	1989		10	15	25
TV Guide	TV Guide	1966	March 26-April 1 issue, photo cover of Adam West as Batman	50	175	300
Video Game Watch	Tiger	1989	w/alarm	8	15	30

BETTY BOOP

TOY	COMPANY	YEAR	DESCRIPTION	GOOD	EX	MIB
Betty Boop Delivery Truck	Schylling	1990	tin litho	15	30	50
Betty Boop Doll		1930s	wood w/composition head	125	400	700
Betty Boop Doll	M-Toy	1986	12" vinyl jointed	10	20	50

BETTY BOOP

TOY	COMPANY	YEAR	DESCRIPTION	GOOD	EX	MIB
Betty Boop Doll Clothing	M-Toy	1986	outfits for 12" dolls high fashion boutique, each	5	10	25
Betty Boop Figure		1980s	3" PVC figure, eight different poses and outfits, each	2	4	10
Betty Boop Figure	NJ Croce	1988	9" bendy	5	10	25

BLONDIE AND DAGWOOD

TOY	COMPANY	YEAR	DESCRIPTION	GOOD	EX	MIB
Blondie Figure		1940s	2-1/2" tall, lead	12	50	100
Blondie Paint Book	Whitman	1947		25	100	200
Blondie Paint Set	American Crayon	1946		25	100	200
Blondie Paper Dolls	Whitman	1955		30	90	150
Blondie Paper Dolls	Whitman	1944		75	125	300
Blondie's Peg Board Set	King Features	1934	9" x 15-1/2", multi-colored pegs, hammer, cut-outs of Dagwood, Blondie, etc.	45	150	300
Blondie's Presto Slate	Presto	1944	10" x 13" illustration of Blondie and Dagwood and other characters	20	60	85
Dagwood and Kids Figures	King Features	1944	Dagwood, Alexander, and Cookie, each	30	85	150
Dagwood Marionette		1945	14"	75	125	275
Dagwood's Solo Flight Airplane	Marx	1935	12" wingspan, plane 9" in length	275	750	1250
Lucky Safety Card		1953	2" x 4" cards, Dagwood offers safety tips	10	55	60
Puzzle		1930s	Featured Funnies	25	85	125

BUGS BUNNY

TOY	COMPANY	YEAR	DESCRIPTION	GOOD	EX	MIB
Bugs Bunny Bank		1940s	5-3/4" x 5-1/2", pot metal, figure on base	45	120	225
Bugs Bunny Bank	Dakin	1971	on a basket of carrots	15	30	60
Bugs Bunny Bendy	Applause	1980s	4" tall	5	10	25
Bugs Bunny Charm Bracelet		1950s	brass charms of Bugs Bunny, Tweety, Sniffles, Fudd, etc.	20	50	100
Bugs Bunny Chatter Chum	Mattel	1982		10	25	45
Bugs Bunny Clock	Litech	1972	12" x 14"	35	85	175
Bugs Bunny Colorforms Set	Colorforms	1958		15	40	75
Bugs Bunny Costume	Collegeville	1960s	mask and costume	9	20	40
Bugs Bunny Figure	Dakin	1976	yellow globes in "Cartoon Theater" box	12	25	50
Bugs Bunny Figure	Dakin	1971	10" tall	10	35	60
Bugs Bunny Figure	Warner Bros.	1975	5-1/2" tall, ceramic, holding carrot	20	50	100
Bugs Bunny Figure	Warner Bros.	1975	2-3/4" tall, ceramic	10	25	50
Bugs Bunny in Uncle Sam Outfit	Dakin	1976	distributed through Great America Theme Park, Illinois	20	60	100
Bugs Bunny Mini Snow Dome	Applause	1980s		5	12	30
Bugs Bunny Musical Ge-Tar	Mattel	1977		10	35	75
Bugs Bunny Night Light	Applause	1980s		5	10	15
Bugs Bunny Soaky			soft rubber	9	20	40
Bugs Bunny Talking Alarm Clock	Janex	1974	battery-operated	40	80	175
Bugs Bunny Talking Doll	Mattel	1971		30	75	150
Bugs Bunny Wristwatch	Lafayette	1978		25	60	125

Alice in Wonderland March Hare Marionette, 1950s, Peter Puppet

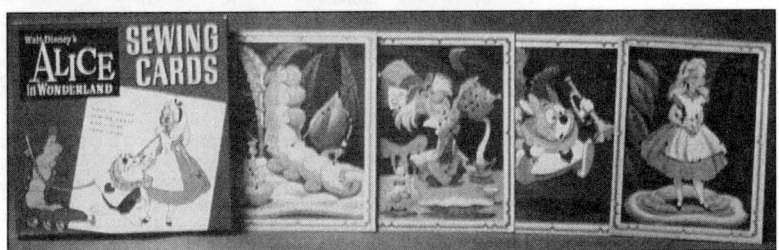

Alice in Wonderland Sewing Cards, 1951, Whitman

Batcave Play Set, 1974, Mego

CALIFORNIA RAISINS

TOY	COMPANY	YEAR	DESCRIPTION	GOOD	EX	MIB
California Raisins Chalkboard	Rose Art	1988		5	10	20
California Raisins Clay Factory	Rose Art	1988		10	30	50
California Raisins Colorforms Play Set	Colorforms	1987		8	20	40
California Raisins Crayon By Number	Rose Art	1988		10	30	45
California Raisins Wind-Up Walkers	Rasta	1987		4	12	20

CAPTAIN AMERICA

TOY	COMPANY	YEAR	DESCRIPTION	GOOD	EX	MIB
Captain America Club Kit		1941	includes two badges (copper and bronze), card, envelope	600	1250	2600
Captain America Figure	Lakeside	1970s	bendy	30	75	125
Captain America Rocket Racer	Buddy L	1984	Secret Wars remote controlled battery operated car	30	100	150

CAPTAIN MARVEL

TOY	COMPANY	YEAR	DESCRIPTION	GOOD	EX	MIB
Adventures of Captain Marvel Ink Blotter/Ruler	Republic/Fawcett	1940s	6" blotter w/ruler advertises the 12-part serial, theatre premium	250	750	1000
Boy Who Never Heard of Captain Marvel Mini Comic	Bond Bread	1940s		40	80	175
Captain Marvel and Billy's Big Game Mini Comic		1940s		90	180	375
Captain Marvel Beanbags		1940s	Captain Marvel, Mary Marvel or Hoppy, each	50	150	250
Captain Marvel Beanie		1940s	cap shows image of Captain Marvel flying toward word "Shazam," blue	85	250	425
Captain Marvel Beanie		1940s	girls' cap shows image of Captain Marvel flying toward word "Shazam," pink, rare	300	1000	1500
Captain Marvel Booklet	Fawcett	1940s		35	55	350
Captain Marvel Brunch Bag		1940s	red rectangular vinyl w/strap handle	60	200	400
Captain Marvel Button		1940s	celluloid, pinback	30	70	110
Captain Marvel Buzz Bomb	Fawcett	1950s	paper airplane in envelope	25	60	100
Captain Marvel Club Button		1941	tin litho, showing Captain Marvel in bust 3/4 view, w/"Shazam" in lightning bolts at bottom	30	70	110
Captain Marvel Club Felt Shoulder Patches	Fawcett	1940s	Captain Marvel diving towards Earth, blue	30	80	175
Captain Marvel Club Felt Shoulder Patches	Fawcett	1940s	Captain Marvel diving towards Earth, yellow	75	300	525
Captain Marvel Club Membership Card	Fawcett	1940s		15	50	85
Captain Marvel Code Finder		1943		150	400	600
Captain Marvel Comic Hero Punch-Outs	Lowe	1942	cardboard figures	75	150	300
Captain Marvel Felt Pennant	Fawcett	1940s	blue, shows Captain Marvel flying	40	90	175
Captain Marvel Felt Pennant	Fawcett	1940s	yellow, shows Captain Marvel flying	60	150	275

TOY	COMPANY	YEAR	DESCRIPTION	GOOD	EX	MIB
Captain Marvel Film Viewer Gun		1940s	gun-shaped movie viewer w/film strips from Paramount series	100	200	375
Captain Marvel Flannel Patch	Fawcett	1940s		25	65	150
Captain Marvel Glow Pictures	Fawcett	1940s	set of four	250	650	1000
Captain Marvel Iron-Ons	Fawcett	1950s	sheet	15	35	65
Captain Marvel Jr. Ski Jump	Reed and Associates	1947	paper, in envelope	10	20	50
Captain Marvel Jr. Statuette	Fawcett	1940s	hand-painted plastic	550	1800	3000
Captain Marvel Jr. Wristwatch		1940s	blue band, round dial w/blue costumed Jr.	325	650	1000
Captain Marvel Key Chain	Fawcett	1940s		40	125	175
Captain Marvel Lightning Wind-Up Race Car	Fawcett	1947	4" long tin wind-up in green, yellow, orange or blue, four cars and box	500	1200	1600
Captain Marvel Magic Dime Register Bank	Fawcett	1948	available in three colors	55	175	300
Captain Marvel Magic Flute		1940s	on die-cut card, shows Captain Marvel on side	40	100	150
Captain Marvel Magic Lightning Box	Fawcett	1940s		50	100	165
Captain Marvel Magic Membership Card	Fawcett	1940s		20	55	85
Captain Marvel Magic Picture	Reed and Associates	1940s	paper, shows Billy Batson "transforming" into Captain Marvel	20	55	100
Captain Marvel Magic Whistle	Fawcett	1948	seed company premium, picture of Captain Marvel on both sides, on card	45	120	175
Captain Marvel Meets the Weatherman Mini Comic	Bond Bread	1940s	Bond Bread premium	45	90	150
Captain Marvel Neck Tie	Fawcett	1940s		30	120	200
Captain Marvel Overseas Cap		1940s	rare	80	400	600
Captain Marvel Paint Set		1940s	paint set w/five chalk figurines	175	500	1000
Captain Marvel Paper Horn	Fawcett	1940s		20	40	75
Captain Marvel Patch	Fawcett	1940s		30	75	150
Captain Marvel Pinback Pattern	Fawcett	1940s	pattern for original pinback	15	30	100
Captain Marvel Portrait	Whiz Comics/Fawcett	1940s		50	125	250
Captain Marvel Portrait	Republic	1940s	different version than Whiz Comics portrait	50	125	250
Captain Marvel Power Siren	Fawcett	1940s		45	125	175
Captain Marvel Puzzle	Reed and Associates	1940s	in envelope	40	200	375
Captain Marvel Puzzle	Fawcett	1941	in box	30	175	300
Captain Marvel Secret Code Sheet	Fawcett	1940s		15	30	75
Captain Marvel Sirocco Figurine	Fawcett	1940s		1500	4000	6000
Captain Marvel Skull Cap		1940s		70	220	425
Captain Marvel Soap	Fawcett	1947	three illustrated bars in box	70	175	350
Captain Marvel Stationary	Fawcett	1940s	paper and envelopes in box	100	200	325
Captain Marvel Statuette	Fawcett	1940s	hand-painted plastic, shows Captain Marvel standing w/arms crossed, on base w/name engraved	1100	2800	4000

CAPTAIN MARVEL

TOY	COMPANY	YEAR	DESCRIPTION	GOOD	EX	MIB
Captain Marvel Suspenders	Fawcett	1940s		50	125	175
Captain Marvel Sweater		1940s	white or off-white, red Captain Marvel logo	60	225	300
Captain Marvel Tattoo Transfers	Fawcett	1940s		30	100	150
Captain Marvel Tie Bar		1940s	on card	35	65	150
Captain Marvel Wristwatch		1948	in box, shows Captain Marvel holding an airplane	200	650	1200
Captain Marvel, Jr. Booklet	Fawcett	1940s		25	50	100
Fawcett's Comic Stars Christmas Tree Ornaments	Fawcett	1940s	metal star-shaped ornaments w/art of Captain Marvel and Hoppy	25	40	75
Giveaway Comics #1, Captain Marvel and the Lt. of Safety		1950	Danger Flies a Kite	125	600	1250
Giveaway Comics #2, Captain Marvel and the Lt. of Safety		1950	Danger Takes to Climbing	100	500	1000
Giveaway Comics #3, Captain Marvel and the Lt. of Safety		1951	Danger Smashes Street Lights	100	500	1000
Mary Marvel Figurine			5"	525	1650	2650
Mary Marvel Illustrated Soap	Fawcett	1947	three soap bars in box	100	250	350
Mary Marvel Patch	Fawcett	1940s		100	250	400
Mary Marvel Pin	Fawcett	1940s	fiberboard	100	200	400
Mary Marvel Stationery	Fawcett	1940s	boxed	75	175	300
Mary Marvel Statuette	Fawcett	1940s	hand-painted plastic	750	2200	3550
Mary Marvel Wristwatch		1940s	in box	200	500	1000
Membership Secret Code Card	Fawcett	1940s		20	100	200
Rocket Raider	Fawcett	1940s	paper airplane in envelope	12	20	40

CAPTAIN MIDNIGHT

TOY	COMPANY	YEAR	DESCRIPTION	GOOD	EX	MIB
Air Heroes Stamp Album		1930s	twelve stamps	30	80	175
Captain Midnight Badge Brass		1930s	gold, wings and words "Flight Commander," fying cross	85	200	375
Captain Midnight Cup			plastic, 4" tall, "Ovaltine-The Heart of a Hearty Breakfast"	30	70	150
Captain Midnight Map	Skelly Oil	1940	11" x 17"	150	600	1100
Captain Midnight Membership Manual		1930s	Secret Squadron official code and manual guide	55	125	250
Captain Midnight Secret Society Decoder		1949	w/key	75	150	300

CARTOON/COMIC CHARACTERS

TOY	COMPANY	YEAR	DESCRIPTION	GOOD	EX	MIB
Alfred E. Neuman Figurine		1960s	base says "What Me Worry?"	45	90	175
Andy Panda Bank	Walter Lantz	1977	7" tall, hard plastic	12	35	65
Beetle Bailey Comic Strip Stamper Set	Ja-Ru	1981	7 stampers, book, crayon	8	20	40
Beetle Bailey Gun Set	Ja-Ru	1981	cord gun and target	10	35	65
Bloom County Opus Doll		1986	10" tall, plush, penguin Opus wearing a Santa Claus cap	10	30	50
Breezley Soaky	Purex	1967	9" tall, plastic	25	60	110
Cadbury the Butler Figure	DFC	1981	3-1/2" figure from Richie Rich	7	15	25
Chilly Willy Doll	Walter Lantz	1982	plush	7	20	35
Daffy Dog Poster			10" x 13", The Morning After	10	17	30

CARTOON/COMIC CHARACTERS

TOY	COMPANY	YEAR	DESCRIPTION	GOOD	EX	MIB
Dan Dunn Pinback Button		1930s	1-1/4"	30	125	275
Doggie Daddy Metal Trivet		1960s	says "You have to work like a dog to live like one"	15	35	50
Dudley Do-Right Doll	Wham-O	1972	bendy	15	35	65
Dudley Do-Right Jigsaw Puzzle	Whitman	1975	Dudley and Snidley	15	35	65
Easy Show Movie Projector Films	Kenner	1965	numerous cartoon characters, each film	8	15	30
Favorite Funnies Printing Set		1930s	#4004, Orphan Annie, Herby, and Dick Tracy, six stamps, pad, paper and instructions	50	130	225
Geoffrey Jack-in-the-Box	Toys R Us	1970s	jack-in-the-box	20	40	75
Hagar the Horrible Doll		1983	12" tall	12	22	50
Hair Bear Bunch Mug		1978	Square Bear figural mug	5	13	20
Hair Bear Bunch Wristwatch		1972	medium gold tone case, base metal back, articulated hands, red leather snap down band	30	70	125
Harold Teen Playstone Funnies Mold Set		1940s		30	80	175
Henry on Trapeze Toy	G. Borgfeldt		6" x 9", celluloid, wind-up, jointed Henry suspended from trapeze	175	500	875
Herman and Katnip Punch Out Kite	Saalfield	1960s	folds into a kite	12	22	40
Josie and the Pussycats Paper Doll Book	Whitman	1971		22	45	85
Katzenjammer Kids Jigsaw Puzzle		1930s	9-1/2" x 14", Featured Funnies	30	120	250
King Leonardo Doll	Holiday Fair	1960s	cloth plush dressed in royal robe	35	75	160
Little Audrey Dress Designer Kit	Saalfield	1962	die cut doll and accessories in illustrated box	20	50	100
Little Audrey Shoulder Bag Leathercraft Kit	Jewel	1961		25	600	100
Little Lulu Bank			8" tall hard plastic w/black fire hydrant	25	60	100
Little Lulu Dish		1940s	5-1/2" hand painted ceramic, pictures of Lulu, Tubby and her friends	50	125	200
Little Lulu Paint Book	Whitman	1944		25	100	175
Little Lulu Puzzles	Whitman	1973	four frame tray puzzles	25	55	100
Mush Mouse Pull Toy	Ideal	1960s	pull toy w/vinyl figure	40	100	180
Nancy Music Box	United Feature	1968	ceramic	30	85	125
Peter Potamus Soaky			11" tall	20	40	75
Rosie's Beau Puzzle		1930s	9-1/2" x 14", Featured Funnies	25	75	100
Scrappy Bank			3" x 3-1/2" metal, embossed illustration of Scrappy and his dog	40	175	300
Smilin' Jack Puzzle		1930s	9-1/2" x 14", Featured Funnies	20	100	150
Supercar Molding Color Kit	Sculptorcraft	1960s	set of rubber plaster casting models of vehicle and show characters, including Mike Mercury, Beaker and Popkiss, Jimmy and Mitch, Masterspy	35	150	200
Touche Turtle Soaky		1960s	standing	25	60	110
Touche Turtle Soaky		1960s	lying down	15	40	65
Winnie Winkle Playstone Funnies Mold Set		1940s		30	55	110
Wonder Woman Figure	Presents		14" tall cloth and vinyl figure on base	9	25	50
Yipee Pull Toy	Ideal	1960s	w/vinyl figures of Yipee, Yapee and Yahoee	40	80	150

CASPER THE FRIENDLY GHOST

TOY	COMPANY	YEAR	DESCRIPTION	GOOD	EX	MIB
Casper Costume	Collegeville		"Ghostland" costume, #216	25	40	75
Casper Doll			7-3/4" tall squeeze doll holds black spotted puppy	25	50	100
Casper Doll		1960s	15" cloth	20	50	100
Casper Doll	Sutton and Sons	1972	rubber squeeze doll w/logo	10	20	40
Casper Figure Lamp	Archlamp	1950	17" tall	30	100	175
Casper Halloween Costume	Collegeville	1960s	mask and costume	12	30	60
Casper Hand Puppet		1960s	8" tall, cloth and plastic head	15	40	75
Casper Jigsaw Puzzle	Ja-Ru	1988		4	10	15
Casper Light Shade		1960s		20	50	100
Casper Night Light	Duncan	1975	6-1/2" tall	15	40	75
Casper Soaky	Colgate-Palmolive			20	55	85
Casper Spinning Top		1960s	blue top w/figure of Casper inside	20	50	75
Casper the Friendly Ghost Talking Doll	Mattel	1961	15" tall, terry cloth, plastic head w/a pull string voice box	35	100	150
Casper Wind-Up Toy	Linemar	1950s	tin	125	325	600
Wendy the Good Witch Soaky				20	55	85

CHARLIE CHAPLIN

TOY	COMPANY	YEAR	DESCRIPTION	GOOD	EX	MIB
Charlie Chaplin Cloth Doll			patterned fabric	100	200	400
Charlie Chaplin Doll			11-1/2" tall, wind-up	225	500	1000
Charlie Chaplin Figure			2-1/2" tall, lead	40	175	325
Charlie Chaplin Figure			8-1/2" tall, tin w/cast iron feet, wind-up	325	625	1350
Charlie Chaplin Pencil Case			8" long	25	75	150
Charlie Chaplin Toy			4" tall, spring mechanism tips his hat when string is pulled	35	110	250
Charlie Chaplin Wristwatch	Bubbles/Cadeaux	1972	Swiss, large chrome case, black and white dial, articulated sweep cane second hand, black leather band	45	100	225
Charlie Chaplin Wristwatch	Bradley	1985	oldies series, quartz, large black plastic case and band, sweep seconds, shows Chaplin as Little Tramp	20	50	100

CHARLIE'S ANGELS

TOY	COMPANY	YEAR	DESCRIPTION	GOOD	EX	MIB
Charlie's Angels Paper Dolls	Toy Factory	1977	Farrah, Kate or Jaclyn sets, each	15	40	75
Charlie's Angels Pendant	Fleetwood Toys	1977	4" plastic figure of Farrah hangs from pendant	10	25	40
Cheryl Ladd Doll	Mattel	1978	12" tall	15	30	60
Farrah Fawcett Doll	Mattel	1977	12"	25	75	150
Kate Jackson Doll	Mattel	1978	12"	20	40	75
Kelly Doll	Hasbro	1977	8"	10	25	50
Kris Doll	Hasbro	1977	8"	10	25	45
River Race Outfits	Palitoy	1977		15	35	60
Sabrina Doll	Hasbro	1977	8"	15	65	100
Sabrina, Kelly, and Kris Gift Set	Hasbro	1977		20	65	100
Slalom Caper Outfits	Palitoy			10	20	40
Underwater Intrigue Outfits	Palitoy			10	20	40

CHIPMUNKS

TOY	COMPANY	YEAR	DESCRIPTION	GOOD	EX	MIB
Alvin Doll	Knickerbocker	1963	14" tall plush w/vinyl head	15	40	75
Chipmunks Bean Bags		1998	three in set, talking	18	36	50

CHIPMUNKS

TOY	COMPANY	YEAR	DESCRIPTION	GOOD	EX	MIB
Chipmunks Soaky		1960s	10" tall, Alvin, Simon, or Theodore, each	10	40	75
Chipmunks Toothbrush		1984	battery-operated	10	25	45
Chipmunks Wallet		1959	vinyl	10	25	50

CINDERELLA

TOY	COMPANY	YEAR	DESCRIPTION	GOOD	EX	MIB
Cinderella Alarm Clock	Westclox		2-1/2" x 4-1/2" x 4" tall	35	75	165
Cinderella Bank		1950s	ceramic, Cinderella holding magic wand	20	55	100
Cinderella Charm Bracelet		1950	golden brass link w/five charms, Cinderella, Fairy Godmother, slipper, pumpkin coach and Prince	25	50	85
Cinderella Doll	Horsman		8" tall in illustrated box	20	65	120
Cinderella Doll			11" tall, blue stain ballgown w/white bridal gown, glass slippers, holding Little Little Golden Book	20	40	85
Cinderella Figurine			5" tall, ceramic	12	40	90
Cinderella Figurine			5" tall, plastic	10	20	35
Cinderella Molding Set	Model Craft	1950s	set of character molds in illustrated box	40	75	150
Cinderella Musical Jewelry Box			mahogany music box plays "So This Is Love"	15	35	75
Cinderella Paper Dolls	Whitman	1965		20	50	100
Cinderella Puzzle	Jaymar	1960s		10	20	35
Cinderella Soaky		1960s	11" tall, blue	15	30	50
Cinderella Wind-Up Toy	Irwin	1950	5" tall, Cinderella and Prince dancing	40	125	275
Cinderella Wristwatch	US Time	1950		50	130	350
Cinderella Wristwatch	Timex	1958	Cinderella and castle, pink leather band	40	100	175
Fairy Godmother Pitcher			7" tall figural pitcher	22	50	85
Gus Doll	Gund	1950s	13" tall, gray doll w/dark red shirt and green felt hat	55	150	200
Gus/Jaq Serving Set	Westman	1960s	creamer, pitcher and sugar bowl	40	75	150
Prince Charming Hand Puppet	Gund	1959	10" tall	20	45	85

CRUSADER RABBIT

TOY	COMPANY	YEAR	DESCRIPTION	GOOD	EX	MIB
Crusader Rabbit Book	Wonder Book	1958		12	40	75
Crusader Rabbit in Bubble Trouble Book	Whitman	1960		10	35	65
Crusader Rabbit Paint Set		1960s	13" x 19"	25	75	150
Crusader Rabbit Soaky	Purex	1960s		30	80	150
Crusader Rabbit Trace and Color Book	Whitman	1959		25	75	125

DANGER MOUSE

TOY	COMPANY	YEAR	DESCRIPTION	GOOD	EX	MIB
Danger Mouse Doll	Russ	1988	15" tall	15	40	75
Danger Mouse ID Set	Gordy	1985		7	15	25
Danger Mouse Pendant Necklace	Gordy	1986		7	15	25

DENNIS THE MENACE

TOY	COMPANY	YEAR	DESCRIPTION	GOOD	EX	MIB
Dennis the Menace and Ruff Book	Whitman	1959	Little Golden Book	10	18	35
Dennis the Menace and Ruff Book Ends		1974	ceramic	30	65	125
Dennis the Menace Colorforms Set	Colorforms	1961		15	45	80
Dennis the Menace Giant Mischief Kit	Hasbro	1950s		40	100	200
Dennis the Menace Paint Set	Pressman	1954	paints, crayons, brush and trays	22	75	125
Dennis the Menace Tiddley Winks	Whitman	1961		20	35	65
Dennis the Menace TV Show Puzzle	Whitman	1960		15	30	60

DEPUTY DAWG

TOY	COMPANY	YEAR	DESCRIPTION	GOOD	EX	MIB
Deputy Dawg Doll	Ideal	1960s	14" tall, cloth w/plush arms and vinyl head	25	90	135
Deputy Dawg Figure	Dakin	1977	6 " tall, plastic body w/vinyl head	30	45	80
Deputy Dawg Soaky		1966	9-1/2" tall, plastic	15	45	75

DICK TRACY

TOY	COMPANY	YEAR	DESCRIPTION	GOOD	EX	MIB
45 Special Water Handgun	Tops Plastics	1950s	plastic	30	75	100
Ace Detective Book	Whitman	1943		10	40	65
Adventures of Dick Tracy and Dick Tracy Jr. Book	Whitman	1933	320 pages, hardcover Big Little Book	85	325	650
Adventures of Dick Tracy the Detective Book	Whitman	1933	first of Big Little Book series, hardcover	175	525	1000
Air Detective Bracelet		1938		250	500	750
Air Detective Cap	Quaker	1938		50	275	450
Air Detective Member Badge	Quaker	1938	brass, wing shape	30	100	150
Auto Magic Picture Gun		1950s	6-1/2" x 9" metal picture gun and filmstrip	30	75	150
Automatic Police Station	Marx	1950s	tin litho police station and car	150	600	1250
Automatic Target Range Gun	Marx	1967	BB gun mounted in an enclosed plastic shooting gallery	55	110	225
B.O. Plenty Figure	Marx	1950s	Famous Comic Figures series, waxy cream, pink, 60mm tall	20	40	65
B.O. Plenty Wind-Up	Marx	1940s	8-1/2" tall holding baby Sparkle, litho tin, walks, hat tips up and down when key is wound	115	230	475
Baby Sparkle Plenty Coloring Book	Saalfield	1948	#1015, cover has Baby Sparkle sitting in a chair	22	55	100
Baby Sparkle Plenty Paper Dolls	Saalfield	1948	#1510, on cover, Baby Sparkle is standing by a clothes line	22	65	125
Baking Set	Pillsbury	1937	cookie cutter, six press-out sheets w/pictures of Dick Tracy and his pals	50	100	200
Big Boy Figure	Playmates	1990		6	12	25
Black Light Magic Kit	Stroward	1952	ultra-violet bulb, cloth, invisible pen, brushes and fluorescent dyes	50	100	200
Bonny Braids Coloring Book	Saalfield		#1174, Dick Tracy's New Daughter	25	45	85
Bonny Braids Doll		1950s	6" tall, plastic, walking wobble doll	25	60	125
Bonny Braids Doll	Ideal	1952	8" tall, crawls when wound	80	170	325
Bonny Braids Doll	Ideal	1951	14" tall w/toothbrush	90	180	375

DICK TRACY

TOY	COMPANY	YEAR	DESCRIPTION	GOOD	EX	MIB
Bonny Braids Paper Dolls	Saalfield	1951	#1559, Dick Tracy's new daughter and Tess	25	80	135
Bonny Braids Pin	Charmore	1951	1-1/4" figure plastic pin on full color card	20	60	100
Bonny Braids Store Contest Card		1951	5-1/2" x 5-1/2"	25	65	125
Bonny Braids Stroll Toy	Charmore	1951	tin litho, Bonny doll in carriage	35	80	160
Booklet	Big Thrill Chewing Gum	1934	five different premium books, eight pages, each	25	60	120
Breathless Mahoney Figure	Applause	1990	14" tall	5	10	20
Camera Dart Gun	Larami	1971	8mm camera-shaped toy w/dart-shooting viewer	25	55	100
Candy Box	Novel Package	1940s	box w/cartoons and story on back; comic strips on bottom	35	200	300
Christmas Tree Light Bulb		1930s	early painted figure of Dick Tracy	30	70	125
Coloring Set	Hasbro	1967	six pre-sketched, numbered pictures to color, w/pencils	30	65	110
Convertible Squad Car	Marx	1948	20", friction power w/flashing lights	110	325	750
Copmobile	Ideal	1963	24" long, white and blue plastic, battery-operated w/a microphone w/amplified speaker on top	55	120	200
Crimestopper Club Kit	Chicago Tribune	1961	premium kit containing badge, whistle, decoder, magnifying glass, fingerprinting kit, ID card, crimestopper textbook	25	45	85
Crimestopper Play Set	Hubley	1970s	Dick Tracy cap gun, holster, handcuffs, wallet, flashlight, badge and magnifying glass	35	70	50
Crimestoppers Set	Larami	1973	handcuffs, nightstick and badge	12	25	50
Decoder Card	Post Cereal		cereal premium, red or green	15	45	85
Detective Button		1930s	celluloid pinback w/portrait, newspaper premium	25	50	90
Detective Club Belt		1937	leather w/secret pouch	75	225	400
Detective Club Crime Stoppers Badge	Guild	1940s		25	50	90
Detective Club Pin		1942	yellow, tab back	25	50	90
Detective Dick Tracy and the Spider Gang Book	Whitman	1937	240 pages, Big Little Book	25	60	120
Detective Kit		1944	Dick Tracy Junior Detective Manual, Secret Decoder, ruler, Certificate of Membership and badge	175	425	750
Dick Tracy and His G-Men Book	Whitman	1941	432 pages, Big Little Book, hardcover w/flip pictures	25	60	120
Dick Tracy and Little Orphan Annie Button	Genung Promo			250	750	1000
Dick Tracy and the Bicycle Gang Book	Whitman	1948	288 pages, Big Little Book, hardcover	25	50	100
Dick Tracy and the Boris Arson Gang Book	Whitman	1935	432 pages, Big Little Book, hardcover	25	60	120
Dick Tracy and the Hotel Murders Book	Whitman	1937	432 pages, hardcover Big Little Book	25	60	120
Dick Tracy and the Invisible Man Book	Whitman	1939	Quaker premium, 132 pages, softcover Big Little Book	50	150	250
Dick Tracy and the Mad Killer Book	Whitman	1947	288 pages, hardcover Big Little Book	25	55	95
Dick Tracy and the Mystery of the Purple Cross Book	Whitman	1938	320 pages, Big Big Book, hardcover	85	225	500
Dick Tracy and the Phantom Ship Book	Whitman	1940	432 pages, hardcover Big Little Book	25	50	110

TOY	COMPANY	YEAR	DESCRIPTION	GOOD	EX	MIB
Dick Tracy and the Racketeer Gang Book	Whitman	1936	432 pages, hardcover Big Little Book	25	60	120
Dick Tracy and the Stolen Bonds Book	Whitman	1934	320 pages, hardcover, Big Little Book	25	60	120
Dick Tracy and the Tiger Lilly Gang Book	Whitman	1949	288 pages, hardcover Big Little Book	20	45	90
Dick Tracy and the Wreath Kidnapping Case Book	Whitman	1945	432 pages, hardcover Big Little Book	25	50	100
Dick Tracy and Yogee Yamma Book	Whitman	1946	352 pages, hardcover Big Little Book	20	45	90
Dick Tracy Bingo, Lock Them Up in Jail and Harmonize with Tracy Game		1940s	object of each is to roll BBs into different holes on the face of a glass framed game card for points	45	90	160
Dick Tracy Braces	Deluxe	1940s	Chicago Tribune premium, suspenders on colorful card	25	80	175
Dick Tracy Braces for Smart Boys and Girls	Deluxe	1950s	Police badge, metal handcuffs, whistle, suspenders w/a Dick Tracy badge as a holder and magnifying glass	35	80	175
Dick Tracy Candid Camera	Seymour Sales	1950s	w/50mm lens, plastic carrying case and 127 film	45	85	175
Dick Tracy Car	Marx	1950s	6-1/2" long, light blue w/machine gun pointing out of the front window	80	225	400
Dick Tracy Cartoon Kit	Colorforms	1962		20	45	85
Dick Tracy Comic Book	Popped Wheat Cereal	1947	premium	6	10	20
Dick Tracy Crime Lab	Ja-Ru	1980s	click pistol, fingerprint pad, badge and magnifying glass, available in orange and bright yellow	8	15	30
Dick Tracy Crime Stopper Badge		1960s	star shape giveaway badge from WGN "9 Official Dick Tracy Crimestopper" TV Badge	30	65	125
Dick Tracy Crime Stopper Game	Ideal	1963	workstation contains crime indicator dial, decoder knobs, criminal buttons, clue cards and holders and clue windows	40	90	180
Dick Tracy Crime Stoppers Laboratory	Porter Chemical	1955	60 power microscope, fingerprint pack, glass slides and magnifying glass and textbook	85	175	350
Dick Tracy Detective Club Belt Badge with belt			premium	35	100	350
Dick Tracy Detective Club Wrist Radios	Gaylord	1945		85	170	350
Dick Tracy Detective Set	Pressman	1930s	color graphics of Junior and Dick Tracy, ink roller, glass plate, and Dick Tracy fingerprint record paper	85	170	350
Dick Tracy Doll		1930s	13" tall, composition, grey trench coat w/moveable head and mouth that operates w/back pull string, gray or yellow coat	150	300	600
Dick Tracy Encounters Facey Book	Whitman	1967	260 pages, hardcover Big Little Book, cover price 39 cents	10	15	30
Dick Tracy Figure	Lakeside		bendy	15	30	50
Dick Tracy Figure	Professional Art	1940s	7" unpainted, detailed white chalk figure or painted	80	175	375
Dick Tracy Figures	Marx	1950s	Famous Comic Figures series, several characters, each	40	75	150
Dick Tracy From Colorado to Nova Scotia Book	Whitman	1933	320 pages, hardcover Big Little Book	25	60	120

DICK TRACY

TOY	COMPANY	YEAR	DESCRIPTION	GOOD	EX	MIB
Dick Tracy Hand Puppet	Ideal	1961	10-1/2", fabric and vinyl, w/record	35	80	150
Dick Tracy in 3-D Comic Book	Blackthorne	1986	Ocean Death Trap	2	5	10
Dick Tracy in Action Model Kit	Aurora	1968	plastic	85	175	375
Dick Tracy in Chains of Crime Book	Whitman	1936	432 pages, hardcover, Big Little Book	25	60	120
Dick Tracy Jr. Bombsight	Miller Bros. Hat	1940s	cardboard	40	70	175
Dick Tracy Jr. Click Pistol #78	Marx	1930s	aluminum	35	100	250
Dick Tracy Jr. Detective Agency Tie Clasp		1930s	silver or brass, each	25	50	100
Dick Tracy Junior Detective Kit Book	Golden Press	1962	punchout book of Tracy tools, including badges, revolver, wrist radio	25	50	100
Dick Tracy Lamp		1950s	painted ceramic bust of Tracy in black coat, yellow hat and red tie	700	1500	3000
Dick Tracy Little Golden Book	Golden Press	1962	features characters from the TV show	17	25	50
Dick Tracy Mask	Philadelphia Inquirer	1933	paper	70	225	375
Dick Tracy Meets a New Gang Book	Whitman	1939	Quaker premium, 132 pages, softcover Big Little Book	60	180	275
Dick Tracy Monogram Ring	Quaker	1938	ring shows initials only, no Tracy name or picture	230	650	1000
Dick Tracy Nodder		1960s	6-1/2" tall, ceramic nodding head bust	230	650	1200
Dick Tracy on the High Seas Book	Whitman	1939	432 pages, hardcover Big Little Book	25	60	120
Dick Tracy on the Trail of Larceny Lu Book	Whitman	1935	432 pages, hardcover Big Little Book	30	65	125
Dick Tracy on Voodoo Island Book	Whitman	1944	352 pages, hardcover Big Little Book	22	45	90
Dick Tracy Original Radio Broadcast Album	Coca-Cola	1972	presents the cast from "The Case of the Firebug Murders" radio show	20	60	100
Dick Tracy Out West Book	Whitman	1933	300 pages, hardcover, Big Little Book	30	60	120
Dick Tracy Paint Book	Saalfield	1930s	96 pages	60	150	300
Dick Tracy Picture	Pillsbury	1940s	part of set of eight, each 7" x 10" in mat, shows Tracy and Junior	60	130	250
Dick Tracy Pinball Game	Marx	1967	14 x 24", shows characters from TV show pilot	40	90	175
Dick Tracy Play Set	Ideal	1973	contains 18 cardboard figures that measure 3-1/2" to 5" tall, w/carrying case	50	120	225
Dick Tracy Play Set	Placo	1982	plastic dart gun, targets of different villians and a set of handcuffs	10	30	50
Dick Tracy Pop-Pop Game	Ja-Ru	1980s	Diet Smith and Flattop are targets	10	15	25
Dick Tracy Puzzle		1952	11" x 14" frame tray	25	75	125
Dick Tracy Returns Book	Whitman	1939	432 pages, hardcover Big Little Book, Republic movie serial tie-in	25	60	120
Dick Tracy Ring	Miller Bros. Hat	1940s	enameled portrait	50	140	250
Dick Tracy Service Patrol Ring		1966	premium	20	40	60
Dick Tracy Soaky	Colgate-Palmolive	1965	10" tall	25	60	100
Dick Tracy Solves the Penfield Mystery Book	Whitman	1934	320 pages, hardcover, Big Little Book	25	60	120
Dick Tracy Sparkle Paints	Kenner	1963	paints, brushes and six pictures to paint	25	50	100

TOY	COMPANY	YEAR	DESCRIPTION	GOOD	EX	MIB
Dick Tracy Special FBI Operative Book	Whitman	1943	432 pages, hardcover, Big Little Book	25	45	90
Dick Tracy Special Ray Gun	Larami	1964	Remington .41 derringer w/a metal Dick Tracy New York Police Detective Badge	25	65	120
Dick Tracy Super Detective Book	Whitman	1941		25	45	90
Dick Tracy Target	Marx	1941	10" square tin litho w/"Recovery" and "Rescuing" points on front and bullseye target on back	45	115	250
Dick Tracy Target Game	Marx	1940s	17" circular cardboard target, w/dart gun and box	75	200	450
Dick Tracy Target Set	Larami	1969	red, green or blue; shoots rubber bands	15	35	75
Dick Tracy the Man with No Face Book	Whitman	1938	432 pages, hardcover, Big Little Book	25	60	120
Dick Tracy the Super Detective Book	Whitman	1939	432 pages, hardcover Big Little Book	25	60	120
Dick Tracy Two-Way Wristwatch	Playmates	1990	watch w/no radio function	4	7	15
Dick Tracy vs. Crooks in Disguise Book	Whitman	1939	352 pages, hardcover, Big Little Book w/flip pictures	25	60	120
Dick Tracy Wristwatch	New Haven	1937	oblong, round, or square face, in box	100	375	850
Dick Tracy Wristwatch	Omni	1981	digital; police car box	15	40	80
Dick Tracy Wristwatch	Bradley	1959		50	100	200
Dick Tracy Wristwatch with Animated Gun	New Haven	1951		65	190	400
Dick Tracy's Ghost Ship Book	Whitman	1939	Quaker premium, 132 pages, softcover Big Little Book	40	150	250
Dick Tracy's Two-in-One Mystery Puzzle	Jaymar	1958	one puzzle shows the crime and the other the solution	30	60	110
Dinnerware Set	Zak Designs	1980s	plate, cup, bowl	10	15	30
Dinnerware Set	Homer Laughlin	1950s	bowl, dinner plate, and mug	70	150	290
Famous Funnies Deluxe Printing Set		1930s	14 stamps, paper and stamp pad, in illustrated box	45	90	190
Favorite Funnies Printing Set	Stampercraft	1935	features Tracy and other cartoon characters	35	70	135
Film Strip Viewer	Acme	1948	viewer and two films in colorful illustrated box	45	90	185
Film Strip Viewer	Acme	1964	viewer w/two boxes of film, on card, jumbo movie style	20	45	85
Film Viewer	Larami	1973	mini color televiewer w/two paper filmstrips	10	20	45
Fingerprint Set	Pressman	1933	microscope, fingerprint pad, magnifying glass and badge	100	225	425
Flashlight	Bantam Lite	1961	metal wrist light	25	55	150
Flashlight	Quaker	1939	3" pen light, black	45	75	175
Flashlight	Quaker	1939	red, green, and black; bullet shaped w/shield tag, pocket size	45	100	250
Flattop Story Double Record Set	Mercury Records	1947	record, book, comics	55	125	225
Get Away Car	Playmates	1990		15	25	45
Gravel Gertie Figure	Marx	1950s	Famous Comic Figures series	10	15	30
Handcuffs	John Henry	1946	metal toy handcuffs on display header card	25	55	110
Hat	Miller Bros. Hat	1940s	wool fedora, blue/gray	40	100	175
Hemlock Holmes Hand Puppet	Ideal	1961	includes record	40	90	175
Hingees "Dick Tracy and his Friends to Life" Punch-outs	Reed and Associates	1944	6-1/2" tall figures, Tess Trueheart, Chief Brandon, Junior, Pat Patton and Tracy	25	50	100
Joe Jitsu Hand Puppet	Ideal	1961	10-1/2", fabric and vinyl, includes record	45	125	200
Junior Detective Kit	Sweets Company	1944	certificate, secret code dial, wall chart, file cards and tape measure	60	150	375

CHARACTER

DICK TRACY

TOY	COMPANY	YEAR	DESCRIPTION	GOOD	EX	MIB
Junior Dick Tracy Crime Detection Folio		1942	radio premium, contained detective's notebook, decoder w/three mystery sheets, and puzzle	60	150	375
Little Honey Moon Doll	Ideal	1965	16" space baby, bubble helmet and outfit w/white pigtails, doll sitting on half a moon w/stars in the background	75	170	350
Luger Water Gun	Larami	1971		15	35	75
Mobile Commander	Larami	1973	toy telephone w/plastic connecting tube, plastic gun and badge	20	40	85
Motorola Presents Dick Tracy Comic Book	Motorola	1953	premium comic book w/paper mask and vest	40	80	150
Offical Holster Outfit	Classy Products	1940s	leather holster w/painted Tracy profile	60	225	375
Pep B.O. Plenty Pin	Kellogg's	1945	tin litho button	20	30	50
Pep Chief Brandon Pin	Kellogg's	1945	tin litho button	10	15	30
Pep Dick Tracy Pin	Kellogg's	1945	tin litho button	25	40	75
Pep Flattop Pin	Kellogg's	1945	tin litho button	20	35	60
Pep Flintheart Pin	Kellogg's	1945	tin litho button	10	20	40
Pep Gravel Gertie Pin	Kellogg's	1945	tin litho button	20	35	50
Pep Junior Tracy Pin	Kellogg's	1945	tin litho button	10	20	40
Pep Pat Patten Pin	Kellogg's	1945	tin litho button	10	20	35
Pep Tess Trueheart Pin	Kellogg's	1945	tin litho button	12	20	35
Playstone Funnies Kasting Kit	Allied	1930s	molds for casting figures of Tracy and other characters	40	80	35
Police Car	Marx		9" long, green litho tin, friction drive when wond up siren on the side of station turns rapidly	80	180	325
Police Car	Linemar	1949	tin, battery-operated remote control	180	385	775
Police Whistle No. 64	Marx		tin	20	40	80
Pop Gun	Tip Top Bread	1944	7-1/2" x 4-1/2" paper pop gun, premium	35	100	175
Power Jet Squad Gun	Mattel	1962	29" long cap and water rifle	45	100	200
Puzzle, "Dick Tracy's New Daughter"	Saalfield	1951	tray puzzle of Bonny Braids	22	65	125
Puzzle, "The Bank Holdup"	Jaymar	1960s	triple-thick interlocking pieces featuring the TV cartoon	20	65	110
Puzzles, Dick Tracy Big Little Book Picture Puzzles	Whitman	1938	8" x 10" x 2" contains two puzzles of BLB scenes	55	185	350
Rapid Fire Tommy Gun	Parker Johns	1940s	20" long tommy gun w/Tracy on stock	75	250	375
Repeater Cap Gun	Larami	1972		15	35	75
Riot Car	Marx	1950s	friction, sparkling, 7-1/2" long, 1946	80	200	425
Secret Code Book	Quaker	1938	premium	35	75	150
Secret Code Writer and Pencil		1939		45	100	250
Secret Compartment Ring	Quaker	1938	removable cover picturing Tracy and good luck symbols	90	200	300
Secret Detective Methods and Magic Tricks Book	Quaker	1939	cereal premium	25	80	175
Secret Detector Kit	Quaker	1938	Secret Formula Q-11 and negatives	75	250	525
Secret Service Patrol Badge	Quaker	1938	Inspector General, brass, 2-1/2"	250	500	850
Secret Service Patrol Badge	Quaker	1938	Sergeant	40	90	175
Secret Service Patrol Badge	Quaker	1938	Lieutenant	50	175	300
Secret Service Patrol Badge	Quaker	1938	brass girl's division badge	20	50	90

Batman Helmet and Cape Set, 1966, Ideal

Batman Talking Alarm Clock, 1975, Janex

DICK TRACY

TOY	COMPANY	YEAR	DESCRIPTION	GOOD	EX	MIB
Secret Service Patrol Badge	Quaker	1938	brass Captain badge	75	175	325
Secret Service Patrol Badge	Quaker	1938	2nd year chevron	10	25	50
Secret Service Patrol Bracelet	Quaker	1938	chain bracelet w/small head of Dick Tracy and Junior and four leaf clover	70	150	250
Secret Service Patrol Leader Pin	Quaker	1938	litho bar pin, Patrol Leader, rare	425	1100	1600
Secret Service Patrol Member Button	Quaker	1938	1-1/4" blue and silver, pinback	20	45	80
Secret Service Phones	Quaker	1938	cardboard phones, walkie talkie type	75	190	300
Shoulder Holster Set	J. Hapern	1950s	leather holster w/Dick Tracy's profile	45	90	185
Siren Pistol	Marx	1930s	pressed steel, 8-1/2" long	90	250	450
Space Coupe	Aurora	1968	assembly required, all plastic	100	250	525
Sparkle Plenty Bank	Jayess	1940s	12" tall, base features a medallion of Dick Tracy as Godfather	120	250	500
Sparkle Plenty Christmas Tree Lights	Mutual Equipment	1940s	seven-light set	30	65	125
Sparkle Plenty Christmas Tree Lights	Mutual Equipment	1940s	15-light set	40	90	175
Sparkle Plenty Doll	Ideal	1947	12" tall	125	250	450
Sparkle Plenty Figure	Marx	1950s	Famous Comic Figures series	10	15	40
Sparkle Plenty Islander Ukette	Styron	1950	musical instrument, junior size, w/instruction book	60	130	275
Sparkle Plenty Washing Machine	Kalon Radio	1940s	12" tall tin litho, pictured outside on tub is Gravel Gertie doing the wash as B.O. Plenty holds baby Sparkle	70	150	325
Squad Car	Marx	1950s	20" long, green litho tin, convertible w/friction drive w/a battery operated flashing light to the driver's side	125	275	575
Squad Car No. 1	Marx	1950s	11" long, w/characters painted on windows, Dick Tracy badge on door, equipped w/red light and machine gun	100	225	475
Squad Car No. 1 Pedal Car	Murray	1950s	deep green w/yellow markings and white plastic light on hood	600	1300	2500
Steve the Tramp Figure	Playmates	1990	discontinued	8	20	40
Sub-Machine Gun	Tops Plastics	1950s	12" long, red, green or blue, water gun "holds over 500 shots on one filling," Dick Tracy decal on magazine	75	130	275
Sunday Funnies Board Game	Ideal	1972		25	50	100
Super 8 Color Film	Republic	1965	b/w cartton "Trick or Treat"	10	25	50
Talking Phone	Marx	1967	green w/ivory handle, battery-operated w/10 different phrases	35	75	125
The Blank Figure	Playmates	1990	figure w/gun and hat w/featureless face attached	60	100	150
The Capture of Boris Arson Book	Pleasure Books	1935	pop-up book	90	300	500
Transistor Radio Receivers	American Doll and Toy	1961	shoulder holster and secret ear plug w/two transistor radio receivers	40	80	160
Two-Way Electronic Wrist Radios	Remco	1950s	2-1/2" x 9 1/2" x 13-1/2", plastic battery-operated wrist radios	60	125	225
Two-Way Wrist Radios	American Doll and Toy	1960s	plastic w/power pack, battery-operated	50	100	185
Two-Way Wrist Radios	Ertl	1990	battery-operated	15	20	30

DICK TRACY

TOY	COMPANY	YEAR	DESCRIPTION	GOOD	EX	MIB
Wall Clock		1990s	16" x 20" battery power quartz, face shows Disney movie Tracy talking into wrist radio	15	20	35
Wallpaper Section		1950s	shows comic strip scenes of Tracy and seven other characters	15	40	75
Wrist Band AM Radio	Creative Creations	1976	w/earphone and two mercury batteries; box shows Tracy and Flattop	30	65	125
Wrist Radio	Da-Myco Products	1947	crystal set w/receiver on a leather band, 30" wires and connectors for aerial and ground, no batteries, no tubes and no electric	150	290	550
Wrist TV	Ja-Ru	1980s	paper roll of cartoon strips are threaded through the TV viewer	10	20	35

DISNEY

TOY	COMPANY	YEAR	DESCRIPTION	GOOD	EX	MIB
Aristocats Thomas O'Malley Figure	Enesco	1967	8" tall ceramic	30	65	125
Black Hole Puzzle	Whitman	1979	jigsaw puzzle, V.I.N.C.E.N.T. or Cygnus	6	20	40
Carousel	Linemar		7" tall w/3" figures, wind-up	150	300	500
Casey Jr. Disneyland Express Train	Marx	1950s	12" long, tin, wind-up	70	250	450
Character Molding and Coloring Set		1950s	red rubber molds of Bambi, Thumper, Dumbo, Goofy, Flower and Jose Carioca to make plaster figures	35	75	150
Color Television Bank	Linemar	1950s	4" x 4-1/2", tin, Mickey or Donald on side panels, litho screen rotates	200	350	500
Disney "Sea Scouts" Puzzle	Williams Ellis	1930s		20	75	150
Disney Figure Golf Balls			set of twelve	12	23	35
Disney Filmstrips	Craftman's Guild	1940s	13 color filmstrips	95	180	275
Disney Rattle	Noma	1930s	4" tall w/Mickey and Minnie, Donald and Pluto carrying a Christmas tree	60	115	275
Disney Shooting Gallery	Welso Toys	1950s	8" x 12" x 1-1/2" tin target w/molded figures of Mickey, Donald, Goofy and Pluto	60	115	225
Disney Tin Tray	Ohio Art		8" x 10", pictures Mickey and Minnie Mouse, Goofy, Horace, Pluto, Donald Duck and Clarabelle	25	50	75
Disney Treasure Chest Set	Craftman's Guild	1940s	red plastic film viewer and filmstrips in blue box designed like a chest	65	125	190
Disney World Globe	Rand McNally	1950s	6-1/2" metal base, 8" diameter w/Disney characters	30	75	185
Disneyland Ashtray		1950s	5" diameter, china, w/Tinker Bell and castle	15	50	125
Disneyland Auto Magic Picture Gun and Theater		1950s	battery-operated metal gun w/oval filmstrip	50	90	150
Disneyland Bagatelle	Wolverine	1970s	large game w/Disneyland graphics	15	25	100
Disneyland Electric Light	Econlite	1950s	picture of Disney characters leaving a bus on a drum base	45	80	225
Disneyland F.D. Fire Truck	Linemar		18" long, battery-operated, moveable, Donald Duck fireman climbs the ladder	70	150	275
Disneyland Felt Banner	Disney	1960s	"The Magic Kingdom," 24-1/2" red/white/blue coat of arms	25	50	75

DISNEY

TOY	COMPANY	YEAR	DESCRIPTION	GOOD	EX	MIB
Disneyland Give-A-Show Projector Color Slides		1960s	112 color slides	60	115	200
Disneyland Haunted House Bank	Japanese	1960s		35	65	225
Disneyland Metal Craft Tapping Set	Pressman	1950s		25	40	100
Disneyland Miniature License Plates	Marx	1966	2" x 4" plates w/Mickey, Minnie and Pluto, or Snow White, Donald and Goofy, each	12	23	35
Disneyland Pen		1960s	6" long w/a picture of a floating riverboat	15	25	40
Disneyland Puzzle	Whitman	1956	frame tray	15	50	85
Duck Tales Travel Tote		1980s	travel agency premium	5	10	20
Early Settlers Log Set	Halsam	1960s	log building set based on Disneyland's Tom Sawyer's Island	25	50	150
Fantasia Bowl	Vernon Kilns	1940	12" diameter and 2-1/2" tall, pink bowl w/a winged nymph from Fantasia	120	220	400
Fantasia Cup and Saucer Set	Vernon Kilns	1940	6-1/4" diameter saucer and 2" tall cup	65	120	200
Fantasia Figure	Vernon Kilns		half-woman, half-zebra centaur	85	150	350
Fantasia Musical Jewelry Box	Schmid Bros.	1990	box features Mickey and plays "The Sorcerer's Apprentice"	30	55	85
Fantasia Unicorn Figure	Vernon Kilns	1940s	ceramic black-winged unicorn	50	90	200
Figural Light Switch Plates	Monogram		hand-painted switch plates: Goofy, Donald, Mickey, on card, each	6	12	25
Happy Birthday/Pepsi Placemats	Pepsi	1978	set of four mats	10	25	50
Horace Horsecollar Hand Puppet	Gund	1950s		25	50	125
Johnny Tremain Figure and Horse	Marx	1957	plastic, 9-1/2" tall horse and 5-1/2" tall Johnny	60	120	200
Jose Carioca Figure	Marx	1960s	5-1/2" tall plastic, wire arms and legs	50	85	160
Jose Carioca Figure	Marx	1960s	2" tall, plastic	30	55	50
Jose Carioca Wind-Up Toy	France	1940s	3-1/2" x 5" x 7-1/2" tall	100	225	375
Lap Trays	Hasko	1960s	set of four: Donald, Goofy and Pluto, Peter Pan, and the Seven Dwarfs	35	65	150
Nautilus Expanding Periscope	Pressman	1954	inspired by 20,000 Leagues Under the Sea, 19" long	40	125	220
Nautilus Wind-Up Submarine	Sutcliffe/England	1950s		85	150	325
Official Santa Fe and Disneyland R.R. Scale Model Train	Tyco	1966	HO scale, electric	160	300	500
Pecos Bill Wind-Up Toy	Marx	1950s	10" tall, riding his horse Widowmaker and holding a metal lasso	40	120	275
Robin Hood of the Range Better Little Book	Whitman	1942		7	20	50
Sand Pail and Shovel	Ohio Art	1930s	features pie-eyed Mickey selling cold drinks to Pluto, Minnie and Clarabelle	35	100	250
Second National Duck Bank	Chein		3-1/2" tall x 7" long	90	150	300
Silly Symphony Lights	Noma		set of eight	55	100	350
Toby Tyler Circus Playbook	Whitman	1959	punch-out character activity book	25	50	75
Walt Disney Movie Viewer and Cartridge	Action Films	1972	#9312 w/the cartridge "Lonesome Ghosts"	9	16	25

DISNEY

TOY	COMPANY	YEAR	DESCRIPTION	GOOD	EX	MIB
Walt Disney's Character Scramble	Plane Facts	1940s	10 cardboard figures, 6" tall	25	50	150
Walt Disney's Clock Cleaners Book	Whitman	1938	linen-like illustrated book	45	125	200
Walt Disney's Game/Parade/Acade my Award Winners	American Toy Works		15 games for all ages	60	115	175
Walt Disney's Realistic Noah's Ark	W.H. Greene	1940s	6" x 7" x 18" Ark, 101 2" animals, and 4" human figures on cardboard	130	350	650
Walt Disney's Silly Symphony Bells	Noma		Christmas tree bells	40	100	250
Walt Disney's Snap-Eeze Set	Marx	1963	12-1/2" x 15" x 1" box w/12 flat plastic figures	60	115	275
Walt Disney's Television Car	Marx		8" long, friction toy lights up a picture on the roof when motor turns	140	450	850

DOC SAVAGE

TOY	COMPANY	YEAR	DESCRIPTION	GOOD	EX	MIB
Club Kit		1975	comics premium; includes card, button and mailer	10	35	75
Club Pin		1930s	Pulp premium, brass	100	200	350
Medal of Honor Award		1930s	brass	1000	3500	5200

DONALD DUCK

TOY	COMPANY	YEAR	DESCRIPTION	GOOD	EX	MIB
Carpet Sweeper	Ohio Art	1930s	3" w/wooden handle, Donald Duck and Minnie Mouse	50	125	250
Crayon Box	Transogram	1946	tin, pictures Donald and Mickey	30	55	150
Daisy Duck Wristwatch	US Time	1948		110	300	650
Donald Duck Alarm Clock	Glen Clock/Scotland	1950s	5-1/2" x 5-1/2" x 2", Donald pictured w/blue bird on his hand	100	250	600
Donald Duck Alarm Clock	Bayard	1960s	2" x 4-1/2" x 5"	90	250	550
Donald Duck and Pluto Car	Sun Rubber		6-1/2" long, hard rubber	30	75	250
Donald Duck Bank	Crown Toy	1938	6" tall, composition, movable head	65	200	500
Donald Duck Bank		1940s	4-1/2" x 4-1/2" x 6-1/2" tall, ceramic, Donald holding a rope w/a large brown fish by his side	50	75	250
Donald Duck Bank		1940s	5-1/2" x 6" x 7-1/2" tall, china, Donald seated holding a coin in one hand	75	175	300
Donald Duck Bicycle	Shelby	1949		2000	5000	10000
Donald Duck Camera	Herbert-George	1950s	3" x 4" x 3"	40	100	250
Donald Duck Car	Sun Rubber	1950s	2-1/2" x 3-1/2" x 6-1/2", rubber	40	100	300
Donald Duck Doll	Knickerbocker	1938	17" tall, red jacket, black plush hat, Donald as drum major	100	600	1200
Donald Duck Doll	Mattel	1976	talking doll	30	150	300
Donald Duck Driving Pluto Toy			9" long, wind-up, celluloid	300	750	1500
Donald Duck Dump Truck	Linemar	1950s		80	150	500
Donald Duck Figure	Japanese	1930s	celluloid, long-billed Donald	60	175	555
Donald Duck Figure	Seiberling		6" tall, hollow rubber w/squeaker in the base	80	200	300
Donald Duck Figure	Seiberling		6" tall, solid rubber w/movable head	80	200	300
Donald Duck Figure	Dell	1950s	7" tall, rubber	50	100	200
Donald Duck Figure	Seiberling		5" tall, rubber	80	200	300
Donald Duck Fun-E-Flex Figure	Fun-E-Flex	1930s	wooden Donald on red sled w/rope	50	100	350

DONALD DUCK

TOY	COMPANY	YEAR	DESCRIPTION	GOOD	EX	MIB
Donald Duck Funnee Movie Set	Transogram	1940	box features Donald, Mickey, and the nephews	50	175	275
Donald Duck Funnee Movie Set	Irwin	1949	hand-crank viewer and four films in box	85	150	250
Donald Duck Lamp	Dolly Toy	1970s	Donald on a tug boat	30	75	175
Donald Duck Lamp		1940s	9" tall, china, Donald holding an axe standing next to a tree trunk	60	130	250
Donald Duck Light Switch Cover	Dolly Toy	1976	plastic, Donald on a boat	5	10	15
Donald Duck Marionette	Peter Puppet	1950s	6-1/2" tall	30	100	200
Donald Duck Music Box	Anri	1971	Donald w/guitar, plays "My Way"	40	70	150
Donald Duck Nodder		1960s	5-1/2" tall on green base	25	90	160
Donald Duck Paint Box	Transogram	1938		25	90	250
Donald Duck Pinback		1935	Jackets premium, cello	250	800	950
Donald Duck Pinback		1930s	Wanna Fight movie premium	250	800	950
Donald Duck Projector	Stephens	1950s	projector w/four films	55	125	250
Donald Duck Puppet	Pelham Puppets	1960s	10" tall, hollow composition	40	75	200
Donald Duck Push Puppet	Kohner	1950s	sailor Donald	30	100	160
Donald Duck Push Toy	Gong Bell	1950s		35	60	100
Donald Duck Puzzle	Jaymar	1940s	frame tray	12	60	100
Donald Duck Ramp Walker	Marx	1950s	1-1/4" x 3-1/2" x 3" tall, Donald is pulling red wagon w/his nephews	110	150	300
Donald Duck Sand Pail	Ohio Art	1939	4-1/2" tall, tin, Donald at beach playing tug-of-war w/his two nephews	40	110	200
Donald Duck Sand Pail	Ohio Art	1950s	3-1/2" tall, tin, Donald in life preserver fighting off seagulls	35	60	100
Donald Duck Scooter	Marx	1960s	tin wind-up, 4" x 4" x 2"	85	150	250
Donald Duck Skating Rink Toy	Mettoy	1950s	4" diameter, Donald is skating while other Disney characters circle the rink	40	70	150
Donald Duck Sled	S.L. Allen	1935	36" long wooden slat and metal runner sled w/character decals, Donald and nephews	100	350	700
Donald Duck Snow Shovel	Ohio Art		wood, tin, litho	60	130	185
Donald Duck Soaky		1950s	7" tall	15	50	95
Donald Duck Soap	Disney		figural castile soap	40	70	110
Donald Duck Squeeze Toy	Dell	1960s	8" tall, rubber	15	30	65
Donald Duck Tea Set	Ohio Art		7-1/2" tray, 2-1/4" diameter cups, saucers	45	85	200
Donald Duck Telephone Bank	N.N. Hill Brass	1938	5" tall w/cardboard figure	75	175	300
Donald Duck the Drummer	Marx	1940s	5" x" 7 x 10" tall, Donald beats on a metal drum	175	310	485
Donald Duck Toothbrush Holder		1930s	bisque, figural	200	400	600
Donald Duck Toy	Schuco		5-1/2" tall, wind-up w/a bellows, quacking sound	325	600	900
Donald Duck Toy Raft	Ideal	1950s	2" tall, blue plastic raft w/yellow sail w/Donald looking through a telescope	400	75	110
Donald Duck Trapeze Toy	Linemar		5" tall, celluloid, wind-up	60	120	500
Donald Duck Umbrella Handle		1930s	3-1/4" tall	40	65	150
Donald Duck Watering Can	Ohio Art	1938	6" tall, tin litho	25	40	150
Donald Duck Wind-Up	Durham Plastic	1972	6-1/2" tall, hard plastic	15	30	75
Donald Duck Wristwatch	US Time	1940s		150	400	700

193

DONALD DUCK

TOY	COMPANY	YEAR	DESCRIPTION	GOOD	EX	MIB
Donald Duck WWI Pencil Box	Dixon		5" x 8-1/2" x 1-1/4" deep, Donald flying a plane, holding a tomahawk	40	65	150
Donald Tricycle Toy	Linemar	1950s	tin	240	450	750
Huey, Dewey and Louie Dolls	Gund	1950s	set of three 8" tall dolls	65	125	350
Louie Doll	Gund	1940s	8" tall, white/light green plush	40	70	115
Ludwig Von Drake Figure	Marx	1961	3" tall, from the "Snap-Eeze" collection	10	20	40
Ludwig Von Drake in Go Cart	Linemar	1960s	tin and plastic	115	250	500
Ludwig Von Drake Mug		1961	3-1/2" white china	15	20	50
Ludwig Von Drake Squeeze Toy	Dell	1961	8" tall, rubber	10	20	50
Ludwig Von Drake Tiddly Winks	Whitman	1961		10	20	50
Ludwig Von Drake Wonderful World of Color Pencil Box	Hasbro	1961	box shows Ludwig and the nephews	25	55	85
Uncle Scrooge Wallet		1970s	3" x 4", Uncle Scrooge tossing coins	12	35	75

DR. DOOLITTLE

TOY	COMPANY	YEAR	DESCRIPTION	GOOD	EX	MIB
Dr. Doolittle Figure	Mattel	1967	5" tall w/parrot	15	30	50
Dr. Doolittle Figure	Mattel	1967	7" tall	15	35	75
Dr. Doolittle Giraffe-in-the-Box			jack-in-the-box	40	80	175

DR. SEUSS

TOY	COMPANY	YEAR	DESCRIPTION	GOOD	EX	MIB
Cat in the Hat Doll	Coleco	1983	plush	10	35	70
Cat in the Hat Ge-Tar	Mattel	1970		55	85	175
Cat in the Hat Jack-in-the-Box	Mattel	1969		50	125	250
Cat in the Hat Riding Toy	Coleco	1983		25	50	125
Cat in the Hat Rocking Toy	Coleco	1983		25	50	125
Cat in the Hat Talking Puppet	Mattel	1970	vinyl head	40	100	250
Grinch Doll	Coleco	1983		35	60	250
Horton the Elephant Doll	Coleco	1983		25	50	120
Lorax Doll	Coleco	1983		25	50	120
Mattel-O-Phone	Mattel	1970		40	55	200
Star-Bellied Sneetch Doll	Coleco	1983		40	55	125
Talking Cat in the Hat Doll	Mattel	1970		50	125	275
Talking Hedwig Doll	Mattel	1970		50	100	225
Talking Horton Doll	Mattel	1970		60	150	325
Thidwick the Moose Doll	Coleco	1983		10	30	75
Yertle the Turtle Doll	Coleco	1983	12" plush	10	35	75

DUMBO

TOY	COMPANY	YEAR	DESCRIPTION	GOOD	EX	MIB
Dumbo Christmas Ornament			2" porcelain bisque, 50th anniversary	8	12	20
Dumbo Doll			12" plush	10	18	30
Dumbo Figure	Dakin			12	22	45
Dumbo Milk Pitcher		1940s	6" tall	30	65	175
Dumbo Roll Over Wind-Up Toy	Marx	1941	4" tall, tin w/tumbling action	150	250	500
Dumbo Squeeze Toy	Dell	1950s	5" tall	12	22	50

194

ELMER FUDD

TOY	COMPANY	YEAR	DESCRIPTION	GOOD	EX	MIB
Elmer Fudd Figure	Dakin	1977	Fun Farm	18	33	65
Elmer Fudd Figure		1950s	metal 5", on green base w/his name embossed, Elmer in hunting outfit	55	120	235
Elmer Fudd Figure	Dakin	1971	in a red hunting outfit	30	65	125
Elmer Fudd Figure	Dakin	1968	8" tall	20	50	85
Elmer Fudd Mini Snow Dome	Applause	1980s		10	20	35
Elmer Fudd Mug	Applause	1980s	figural	5	10	20
Elmer Fudd Pull Toy	Brice Toys	1940s	9", wooden, Elmer in fire chief's car	65	150	300

FELIX THE CAT

TOY	COMPANY	YEAR	DESCRIPTION	GOOD	EX	MIB
Felix Cartoon Lamp Shade			6" tall	30	85	175
Felix Doll		1920s	13" tall, jointed arms	115	275	550
Felix Doll		1920s	8" tall, wood, fully jointed	100	285	575
Felix Figure	Schoenhut	1920s	4" tall, wood, leather ears, stands on a white wood base	50	250	500
Felix Flashlight		1960s	contains whistle	20	175	300
Felix Manual Dexterity Game	German	1920s	2", round, metal	60	150	235
Felix on a Scooter	Nifty	1924	tin wind-up	200	400	725
Felix Pencil Case		1950s		25	75	120
Felix Punching Bag		1960s	11" tall inflatable bobber	25	60	110
Felix Sip-a-Drink Cup			5" tall	15	25	50
Felix Soaky		1960s	10" tall, black plastic	15	50	90
Felix Soaky		1960s	10" tall, red plastic	20	60	100
Felix Soaky		1960s	10" tall, blue plastic	20	60	100
Felix Squeak Toy		1930s	6" tall, soft rubber	35	90	150
Felix the Cat Pull Toy	Nifty	1920s	5-1/2" tall, 8" long, tin, cat is chasing two red mice on the front of the cart, litho pictures of Felix on side	150	325	675
Felix Wristwatch		1960s		65	150	275

FERDINAND THE BULL

TOY	COMPANY	YEAR	DESCRIPTION	GOOD	EX	MIB
Ferdinand Doll	Knickerbocker	1938	5" x 9" x 8-1/2" tall, joint composition w/cloth tail and flower stapled in his mouth	100	190	300
Ferdinand Figure			9" tall, plastic	20	35	150
Ferdinand Figure	Disney	1940s	composition	75	150	300
Ferdinand Figure			3-1/2" bisque	15	25	100
Ferdinand Figure	Seiberling	1930s	3" x 5-1/2" x 4" tall, rubber	30	80	175
Ferdinand Figure	Delco	1938	4-1/2" tall, ceramic, bull seated w/a purple garland around his neck	40	80	175
Ferdinand Hand Puppet	Crown Toy	1938	9-1/2" tall	50	85	210
Ferdinand Savings Bank	Crown Toy		5" tall, wood composition w/silk flower w/metal trap door	25	45	200
Ferdinand the Bull Book	Whitman	1938	linen picture book	30	75	150
Ferdinand the Bull/ The Matador Wind-Up Toy	Marx	1938	5-1/2" high by 8" long, wind-up action between the matador and Ferdinand "bull fight"	250	450	800
Ferdinand Toy	Knickerbocker	1940	wood composition w/jointed head and legs w/flower in his mouth	45	100	275
Ferdinand Wind-Up Toy	Marx	1938	6" long, tin, wind-up, when wound the wire tail spins and causes him to jump around	175	375	475

FLIPPER

TOY	COMPANY	YEAR	DESCRIPTION	GOOD	EX	MIB
Flipper Halloween Costume	Collegeville	1964		20	40	80
Flipper Magic Slate	Lowe	1960s		9	18	35
Flipper Model Kit	Revell	1965		15	33	65
Flipper Puzzle	Whitman	1960s	several variations, each	10	20	30
Flipper Ukelele	Mattel	1968		12	22	35

FOGHORN LEGHORN

TOY	COMPANY	YEAR	DESCRIPTION	GOOD	EX	MIB
Foghorn Leghorn Figure	Applause	1980s	PVC	3	50	75
Foghorn Leghorn Figure	Dakin	1970	6-1/4" tall	22	45	85
Foghorn Leghorn Hand Puppet		1960s	9", fabric w/vinyl head	15	65	125

FONTAINE FOX

TOY	COMPANY	YEAR	DESCRIPTION	GOOD	EX	MIB
Powerful Katrinka Toy		1923	5-1/2" tall, wind-up, pushing Jimmy in a wheelbarrow	250	600	1000
Toonerville Trolley		1922	7-1/2" tall, wind-up	300	600	1100
Toonerville Trolley	Nifty		miniature, 2" tall	95	200	400
Toonerville Trolley			3" tall	100	200	400
Toonerville Trolley			4" tall, red pot metal	175	610	1200

GARFIELD

TOY	COMPANY	YEAR	DESCRIPTION	GOOD	EX	MIB
Garfield Chair Bank	Enesco	1981		10	20	50
Garfield Easter Figure	Enesco	1978		6	12	25
Garfield Figure	Enesco	1978	Garfield as graduate	5	10	20
Garfield Figure Bank	Enesco	1981	4-3/4"	10	22	40
Garfield Music Box	Enesco	1981	Garfield dancing	15	40	75

GASOLINE ALLEY

TOY	COMPANY	YEAR	DESCRIPTION	GOOD	EX	MIB
Skeezix Comic Figure		1930s	6" chalk statue	10	30	75
Skeezix Stationery		1926	6" x 8-1/2"	10	25	50
Uncle Walt and Skeezix Figure Set			bisque, Uncle Walt, Skeezix, Herby and Smitty	60	175	320
Uncle Walt and Skeezix Pencil Holder	F.A.S.		5" tall, bisque	50	200	300

GOOFY

TOY	COMPANY	YEAR	DESCRIPTION	GOOD	EX	MIB
Backwards Goofy Wristwatch	Pedre		silver case 2nd edition	35	65	150
Backwards Goofy Wristwatch	Helbros	1972		275	500	800
Goofy Car	Spain		vinyl head Goofy drives tin litho car	25	40	75
Goofy Doll		1970s	5" x 6" x 13" tall, fabric and vinyl, laughing doll	30	60	125
Goofy Figure	Marx		Snap-Eeze figure	12	35	50
Goofy Figure	Arco		bendy	10	15	25
Goofy Lil' Headbobber	Marx			20	35	100
Goofy Night Light	Horsman	1973	green, figural	16	30	45
Goofy Rolykin	Marx			25	50	75
Goofy Safety Scissors	Monogram	1973	on card	5	10	20
Goofy Toothbrush	Pepsodent	1970s		5	10	20
Goofy Twist'N Bend Figure	Marx	1963	4" tall	11	20	30
Goofy with Bump 'N Go Action Lawn Mower	Illfelder	1980s	3-1/2" x 10" x 11", plastic figure pushing lawn mower w/silver handle	40	70	125

GUMBY

TOY	COMPANY	YEAR	DESCRIPTION	GOOD	EX	MIB
Adventures of Gumby Electric Drawing Set	Lakeside	1966		22	45	75
Gumby Adventure Costume	Lakeside	1960s	fireman, cowboy, knight and astronaut, each	25	50	85
Gumby Colorforms Set	Colorforms	1988		8	12	30
Gumby Figure		1980s	large, foam rubber	20	30	50
Gumby Figure	Applause	1980s	12" tall, poseable	10	20	30
Gumby Figure	Applause	1980s	5-1/2 " bendy, three styles	4	8	20
Gumby Hand Puppet	Lakeside	1965	9" tall w/vinyl head	15	35	75
Gumby Modeling Dough	Chemtoy	1960s		25	50	85
Gumby's Jeep	Lakeside	1960s	yellow tin litho, Gumby and Pokey's names are printed on seat	85	190	300
Pokey Figure	Lakeside	1960s		20	40	85
Pokey Modeling Dough	Chemtoy	1960s		25	50	90

HAPPY HOOLIGAN

TOY	COMPANY	YEAR	DESCRIPTION	GOOD	EX	MIB
Happy Hooligan Nesting Toys	Anri		4" tall, wooden set of four nesting pieces	60	100	225
Happy Hooligan Songsheet		1905	newspaper premium	60	150	250
Happy Hooligan Toy	Chein	1932	6" tall, wind-up, walking figure	150	350	650

HECKLE AND JECKLE

TOY	COMPANY	YEAR	DESCRIPTION	GOOD	EX	MIB
Heckle and Jeckle Figures			7" soft foam figures	15	35	75
Heckle and Jeckle Skooz-It Game	Ideal	1963	cylindrical container	25	45	80
Heckle and Jeckle Story Book	Wonder Book	1957		10	30	50
Little Roquefort Figure		1959	8-1/2" tall, wood	20	40	70

HONEY WEST

TOY	COMPANY	YEAR	DESCRIPTION	GOOD	EX	MIB
Formal Outfit	Gilbert	1965		30	55	110
Honey West Accessory Set	Gilbert	1965	telephone purse, lipstick, handcuffs and telescope lens necklace	25	45	90
Honey West Accessory Set	Gilbert	1965	cap-firing pistol, binoculars, shoes and glasses	25	45	90
Honey West Doll	Gilbert	1965	12" tall w/black leotards, belt, shoes, binoculars and gun	100	200	350
Karate Outfit	Gilbert	1965		25	50	110
Pet Set with Ocelot	Gilbert	1965		30	60	110
Secret Agent Outfit	Gilbert	1965		25	50	100

HUCKLEBERRY HOUND

TOY	COMPANY	YEAR	DESCRIPTION	GOOD	EX	MIB
Hokey Wolf Figure	Marx	1961	TV-Tinykin	15	40	75
Hokey Wolf Figure	Dakin	1970		30	75	140
Huckleberry Hound Bank	Dakin	1980	5" tall figural bank of Huck sitting	15	25	60
Huckleberry Hound Bank	Knickerbocker	1960	10" tall, hard plastic figural	10	25	60
Huckleberry Hound Doll	Knickerbocker	1959	18" plush, vinyl hands and face	20	60	100
Huckleberry Hound Figure	Marx	1961	TV-Tinykins	15	25	50
Huckleberry Hound Figure		1960s	6" tall, glazed china	15	30	65

HUCKLEBERRY HOUND

TOY	COMPANY	YEAR	DESCRIPTION	GOOD	EX	MIB
Huckleberry Hound Figure	Dakin		8" tall	20	40	85
Huckleberry Hound Figure Set	Marx	1961	TV-Tinykins	30	70	100
Huckleberry Hound Go-Cart	Linemar	1960s	6-1/2" tall, friction	80	160	325
Huckleberry Hound Wind-Up Toy	Linemar	1962	4" tall, tin	75	160	325
Huckleberry Hound Wristwatch	Bradley	1965	chrome case, wind-up mechanism, gray leather band, face shows Huck in full view	35	90	175
Mr. Jinks Doll	Knickerbocker	1959	13" tall, plush, vinyl face	25	100	200
Mr. Jinks Soaky	Purex	1960s	10" tall, Pixie and Dixie, hard plastic	15	30	60
Pixie and Dixie Dolls	Knickerbocker	1960	12" tall, each	25	45	75
Pixie and Dixie Magic Slate		1959		15	25	50

HUMPTY DUMPTY

TOY	COMPANY	YEAR	DESCRIPTION	GOOD	EX	MIB
Humpty Dumpty Bubble Bath	Avon	1960s	figural plastic container	7	30	75
Humpty Dumpty Crib Toy	Mattel	1980s	plastic, sits on crib rail	4	8	15
Humpty Dumpty Figural Soap	Avon	1990s		3	6	12
Humpty Dumpty Figure	Marx	1950s	Fairy Tale series, plastic	3	8	20
Humpty Dumpty Game	Orchard Toys	1981	British matching game	8	15	30
Humpty Dumpty Magazine		1960s		2	5	10
Humpty Dumpty Musical Toy	Alladin Plastics	1960s	plastic, record inside toy	12	25	50
Humpty Dumpty Potato Chip Tin		1990s	large blue and gold tin	7	15	35
Humpty Dumpty Pull Toy	Fisher-Price	1970s	plastic, several color variations	2	5	10
Humpty Dumpty Puzzle			wood frame tray puzzles, several varieties	4	12	25

INDIANA JONES

TOY	COMPANY	YEAR	DESCRIPTION	GOOD	EX	MIB
Indiana Jones 3-D View-Master Gift Set	View-Master			15	30	65
Indiana Jones Backpack	Pepsi			20	45	90
Indiana Jones The Legend Mug				5	10	15
Last Crusade Button	Pepsi		retailer button	5	10	25
Patch		1990		10	15	25
Temple of Doom Calendar				5	10	30
Temple of Doom Storybook			hardbound	7	15	25

JAMES BOND

TOY	COMPANY	YEAR	DESCRIPTION	GOOD	EX	MIB
007 Bullet Hole Stickers		1987	simulated bullet holes, magnetic license holder	6	15	25
007 Dart Gun	Imperial	1984	photo of Roger Moore	10	25	50
007 Exploding Cigarette Lighter	Coibel			6	15	30
007 Exploding Coin	Coibel		on blister pack	6	15	30
007 Exploding Pen	Coibel		on blister pack	6	15	30
007 Exploding Spoon	Coibel		on blister pack	6	15	30

JAMES BOND

TOY	COMPANY	YEAR	DESCRIPTION	GOOD	EX	MIB
007 Flicker Rings		1967	set of 11	50	90	200
007 Radio Trap	Multiple Toys	1966	radio w/secret business cards	40	85	175
007 Submachine Gun	Imperial	1984	photo of Roger Moore	10	25	50
007 Toy Pistol	Edgemark			5	15	30
007 Video Disc Promo Kit	RCA	1980s	disc, poster, pamphlet	15	30	60
Bond Golf Tees		1987	British, six tees and pencil in leather pouch	8	15	30
Bond Pocket Diary		1988	British leather bound	5	15	30
Electric Drawing Set	Lakeside	1965	plastic tracing board, pencils, sharpener, adventure sheets	50	100	200
Goldfinger II Role Playing Game				6	10	25
Goldfinger Puzzle	Milton Bradley	1965	Bond's Bullets Blaze	20	40	85
Goldfinger Puzzle	Milton Bradley	1965	Bond and Golden Girl	25	50	100
James Bond .380 Pistol	Imperial	1984	w/photo of Roger Moore	10	25	50
James Bond Action Figure	Gilbert	1965	12"	80	165	350
James Bond Action Figure Accessory Set	Gilbert	1965	trench coat, mask, shoes, binoculars, glasses, grenade, pants and hat	50	150	400
James Bond Action Figure Action Apparel Set	Gilbert	1965	scuba tanks, spear gun, knife	25	75	250
James Bond Alarm Clock			painting of Roger Moore in center	20	40	85
James Bond Aston Martin	Gilbert	1965	12", battery operated	130	275	525
James Bond Aston Martin Slot Car	Gilbert	1965		60	110	250
James Bond B.A.R.K. Attache Case	Multiple Toys	1965	007 luger, missles, hideaway pistol and rocket launching device, case and gun bears 007 logo	90	175	375
James Bond Computer Game "The Stealth Affair"		1990	based on Licence to Kill	15	30	60
James Bond Disguise Kit	Gilbert	1965		40	80	160
James Bond Disguise Kit #2	Gilbert	1965		40	80	160
James Bond Hand Puppet	Gilbert	1965		40	85	125
James Bond Harpoon Gun (Thunderball)	Lone Star	1960s	box illustrated w/undersea fight scene graphics	40	100	200
James Bond Hideaway Pistol	Coibel	1985		12	35	75
James Bond Jr. Action Ninja Figure	Hasbro			8	15	60
James Bond Jr. Bath Towel				10	20	20
James Bond Jr. Buddy Mitchell Figure	Hasbro			5	10	20
James Bond Jr. Capt. Walker D. Plank figure	Hasbro			3	6	15
James Bond Jr. CD Player/Weapons Kit	Hasbro			10	20	30
James Bond Jr. Corvette				10	25	50
James Bond Jr. Crime Fighter Set			includes handcuffs, watch and walkie-talkie	5	10	20
James Bond Jr. Dr. Derange figure	Hasbro			3	6	15
James Bond Jr. Dr. No. figure	Hasbro			3	6	20
James Bond Jr. Figure	Hasbro		w/scuba gear	3	6	20
James Bond Jr. Figure	Hasbro		w/pistol	3	6	20

JAMES BOND

TOY	COMPANY	YEAR	DESCRIPTION	GOOD	EX	MIB
James Bond Jr. Gordo Leiter figure	Hasbro			3	6	20
James Bond Jr. I.Q. figure	Hasbro		w/weapon device	3	6	15
James Bond Jr. Jaws Figure	Hasbro			5	10	25
James Bond Jr. Karate Punch Target Game			gun w/boxing glove and targets of villain	8	15	25
James Bond Jr. Ninja Play Set			throw stars, nunchukas and badge	8	15	35
James Bond Jr. Ninja Wrist Weapon Set				5	10	30
James Bond Jr. Odd Job figure	Hasbro			5	10	25
James Bond Jr. Scum Shark Mobile				10	15	30
James Bond Jr. Sticker Book				3	6	15
James Bond Jr. Sub Cycle				5	12	30
James Bond Jr. Vehicles	Ertl		S.C.U.M. Helicopter, Bond's car and van; set of three	18	50	100
James Bond Parachute Set	Imperial	1984	orange and green parachutist figures	10	25	50
James Bond Pocket Watch		1981	Roger Moore on face	25	60	125
James Bond Ring		1964	glass oval w/photo of Sean Connery	10	25	40
James Bond Roadrace Set	Gilbert	1965	scenery tracks, Aston Martin and other cars	175	325	650
James Bond Secret Attache Case	MPC	1965		130	275	675
James Bond Secret Service Game	Spears	1965		40	150	600
James Bond Sting Pistol	Coibel		8-shot cap pistol and booklet from On Her Majesty's Secret Service	18	35	75
James Bond Tarot Game		1973		15	30	60
James Bond Video Game	Coleco	1983		15	25	50
James Bond Wall Clock		1981	large clock w/painting of Roger Moore in action	25	45	90
Jaws Figure	Mego	1979		135	275	550
Licence to Kill Car Set	Matchbox		jeep, seaplane, oil tanker, and copter	25	50	100
Living Daylights German Pistol	Wicke	1980s	25-shot cap gun	10	25	50
Living Daylights Record Mobile		1980s		5	15	30
May Day Pistol		1985		10	20	40
Moonraker Drax Copter	Corgi			15	30	60
Moonraker Halloween Costume		1979	mask of Roger Moore and space suit costume	20	50	125
Moonraker Jr. Set	Corgi		Aston Martin and Lotus	20	40	150
Moonraker Jr. Shuttle	Corgi			10	20	50
Moonraker Shuttle and Drax Copter Jr.'s	Corgi		set of two	15	30	60
Moonraker Space Shuttle	Corgi			25	50	125
Moonraker Spanish Card Game			33 cards w/different color stills	15	30	60
Multi-Action Aston Martin		1960s	friction operated car for Agent 711	70	130	275
Octopussy Gift Set	Corgi		plane, truck and horse trailer	35	75	150
Odd Job Action Figure	Gilbert	1965	12" doll in karate outfit, w/derby	130	260	525
Odd Job Puppet	Gilbert		plastic hand puppet	60	310	560
Scuba Outfit #2	Gilbert	1965		20	35	70

Laurel and Hardy Banks, 1974, Play Pal

Mickey Mouse Steamboat, 1988, Masudaya

Mickey Mouse Wristwatch, 1958, Timex

JAMES BOND

TOY	COMPANY	YEAR	DESCRIPTION	GOOD	EX	MIB
Scuba Outfit #3	Gilbert	1965		20	35	80
Scuba Outfit #4	Gilbert	1965		20	35	70
Scuba Outfit Deluxe	Gilbert	1965		30	65	80
Ski Outfit	Gilbert	1965		50	100	200
Spy Who Loved Me Helicopter Jr.	Corgi			10	20	40
Spy Who Loved Me Jr. Set	Corgi		Lotus and Copter	15	35	75
Spy Who Loved Me Puzzle	Milton Bradley		several scenes, each	20	40	80
Stromberg Helicopter	Corgi			25	55	85
The James Bond Box		1965	rare game played w/dice	40	75	150
Thunderball Balloon Target Game		1965		40	80	160
Thunderball Puzzle	Milton Bradley	1965	several pictures, each	20	40	85
Thunderball Set	Gilbert	1965		40	90	200
Tuxedo Outfit	Gilbert	1965		50	100	210
View to a Kill Michelin Button			Bond on large size pinback w/Midas man	5	10	20

JETSONS

TOY	COMPANY	YEAR	DESCRIPTION	GOOD	EX	MIB
Elroy Toy	Transogram	1963		10	20	35
Jetson Figures	Applause	1990	10" tall; Judy, George, Elroy, Rosie, each	50	100	185
Jetsons Birthday Surprise Book	Whitman	1963	Tell-A-Tale Book	12	25	65
Jetsons Colorforms Kit	Colorforms	1963		40	75	150
Puzzle	Whitman	1962	70 pieces	25	95	175

JUNGLE BOOK

TOY	COMPANY	YEAR	DESCRIPTION	GOOD	EX	MIB
Baloo Doll			12" tall, plush	10	50	100
Jungle Book Carrying Case	Ideal	1966	5" x 14" x 8"	25	50	100
Jungle Book Dinner Set			vinyl placemat, bowl, plate and cup	10	18	40
Jungle Book Fun-L Tun-L	New York Toy	1966	108" x 24"	40	70	125
Jungle Book Magic Slate	Watkins-Strathmore	1967		10	22	40
Jungle Book Sand Pail and Shovel	Chein	1966	tin litho, illustrated w/Jungle Book characters	25	50	85
Jungle Book Tea Set	Chein	1966	tin litho, plates, saucers, tea cups and serving tray	25	50	95
Jungle Book Utensils			fork and spoon w/melamine handles	5	10	25
Mowgli Figure	Holland Hill	1967	8", vinyl	20	40	70
Mowgli/Baloo Wristwatch			digital, clear plastic band	5	10	25
Mowgli's Hut Mobile and Figures	Multiple Toymakers	1968	2" x 3" x 3" mobile w/Baloo and King Louis figures	35	65	120
Shere Kahn Figure	Enesco	1965	5" tall, ceramic	15	20	35

LADY AND THE TRAMP

TOY	COMPANY	YEAR	DESCRIPTION	GOOD	EX	MIB
Lady and Tramp Figures	Marx	1955	Lady is 1-1/2" tall and white, Tramp is 2" tall and tan	25	50	100
Lady Doll	Woolikin	1955	5" x 8" x 8-1/2", light tank w/burnt orange accents on face, ears, stomach and tail, plastic eyes, nose and a white silk ribbon around neck	45	60	150
Modeling Clay	Pressman	1955		30	120	185
Perri Doll	Steiff	1950s	6" tall, plush	40	70	150
Puzzle	Whitman	1954	11" x 15", frame tray	20	35	75

LADY AND THE TRAMP

TOY	COMPANY	YEAR	DESCRIPTION	GOOD	EX	MIB
Toy Bus	Modern Toys/Japan	1966	3-1/2" x 4" x 14" long	20	40	75
Tramp Doll	Schuco	1955	8" tall, brown w/a white underside and face, hard plastic eyes and nose	55	120	250

LAUREL AND HARDY

TOY	COMPANY	YEAR	DESCRIPTION	GOOD	EX	MIB
Laurel and Hardy Die-Cut Puppets	Dell	1982	soft vinyl, each	20	75	150
Laurel and Hardy Die-Cut Puppets	Larry Harmon	1970s	moveable, each	25	125	250
Laurel and Hardy TV Set		1976	w/paper filmstrips	20	35	70
Oliver Hardy Bank	Play Pal	1974	13-1/2" tall, plastic	15	30	50
Oliver Hardy Doll	Dakin	1974	5" tall wind-up dancing/shaking vinyl doll	35	40	75
Oliver Hardy Figure	Dakin	1974	7-1/2" tall	25	90	175
Stan Laurel Bank		1972	15" tall, vinyl figural bank	20	40	75
Stan Laurel Bank	Play Pal	1974	13-1/2" tall, plastic	10	30	50
Stan Laurel Figure	Dakin	1974	8" tall	30	60	125

LITTLE MERMAID

TOY	COMPANY	YEAR	DESCRIPTION	GOOD	EX	MIB
Ariel Jewelry Box			5-3/4" x 4-1/2", musical	9	16	30
Ariel Toothbrush			battery operated w/holder	9	16	25
Eric Doll			9-1/2" tall in full dress uniform	9	16	30
Flounder and Ariel Faucet Cover			plastic	5	10	20
Flounder Doll			15" plush fish	9	16	30
Flounder Pillow			14" x 24" shaped like Flounder	7	13	25
Little Mermaid Figures	Applause		several PVC characters, each	2	5	10
Little Mermaid Purse			6" diameter, vinyl, canteen style purse	5	12	20
Little Mermaid Snow Globe			4" water globe	9	16	30
Scuttle Doll			15" seagull, plush	12	20	35
Sebastian Doll			16" crab, plush	10	16	30
Under the Sea Jewelry Box			4" mahogany, musical	18	35	60

LITTLE ORPHAN ANNIE

TOY	COMPANY	YEAR	DESCRIPTION	GOOD	EX	MIB
Annie Doll	Knickerbocker	1982	10" doll without locket	2	5	10
Annie Doll	Knickerbocker	1982	10" tall, w/two dresses and removable heart locket	5	10	20
Annie Figures	Knickerbocker	1982	six figures, 2" tall, each	2	5	10
Beetleware Mug	Ovaltine	1933		25	65	100
Beetleware Mug	Ovaltine	1935		35	55	110
Daddy Warbucks Doll	Knickerbocker	1982		10	50	90
ID Bracelet	Ovaltine	1934		25	50	100
Little Orphan Annie Altascope Ring	Quaker	1942	premium, only eight known to exist	2500	7500	25000
Little Orphan Annie and Chizzler Book		1930s	Big Little Book	25	65	120
Little Orphan Annie and Sandy Ashtray		1930s	3" tall, ceramic	50	100	200
Little Orphan Annie and Sandy Dolls	Famous Artists Syndicate	1930	9-3/4" tall, each	45	100	200
Little Orphan Annie and Sandy Toothbrush Holder		1930s	bisque	50	100	175
Little Orphan Annie and the Gooneyville Mystery Book	Whitman	1947		20	100	160

LITTLE ORPHAN ANNIE

TOY	COMPANY	YEAR	DESCRIPTION	GOOD	EX	MIB
Little Orphan Annie and the Haunted House Comic Book	Cupples and Leon	1928		50	125	250
Little Orphan Annie Bucking the World Comic Book	Cupples and Leon	1929	hardcover	40	125	300
Little Orphan Annie Clothespins	Gold Medal	1938	clothesline and pulley	20	40	80
Little Orphan Annie Colorforms Set	Colorforms	1970s		10	20	40
Little Orphan Annie Costume		1930s	mask and slip-over paper dress w/belt	75	200	350
Little Orphan Annie Cut-Outs	Miller Toys	1960s	Sandy, Grunts the Pig, Pee Wee the Elephant	20	100	200
Little Orphan Annie Doll	Well Toy	1973	7" tall	15	20	50
Little Orphan Annie Figure		1940s	1-1/2" tall, lead	15	25	50
Little Orphan Annie Glassips		1936	drinking straws	200	450	650
Little Orphan Annie in the Circus Comic Book	Cupples and Leon	1927	9" x 7", 86 pages	50	115	300
Little Orphan Annie Light Up the Candles Game	Ovaltine		3-1/2" x 5", premium	30	150	300
Little Orphan Annie Mug	Ovaltine	1930	Uncle Wiggily	30	75	150
Little Orphan Annie Music Box	N.Y. News	1970	figural	25	60	100
Little Orphan Annie Periscope	Quaker	1942	offered in handbook	100	275	525
Little Orphan Annie Punch-Outs	King, Larson, McMahon	1944	3-D punch-outs of Annie, Sandy, Punjab and Daddy Warbucks	30	60	125
Little Orphan Annie Rummy Cards	Whitman	1937	5" x 6", colored silhouettes of Annie on the back	20	80	160
Little Orphan Annie Shipwrecked Comic Book	Cupples and Leon	1931	9" x 7", 86 pages	40	100	300
Little Orphan Annie Stamper	Quaker	1941	premium, w/wood handle; secret guard	250	500	750
Little Orphan Annie Stove		1930s	non-electric model, gold-brass lithographed labels of Annie and Sandy, oven doors functional	60	120	250
Little Orphan Annie Stove		1930s	electric version, 8" x 9", gold metal, litho plates, functional oven doors and back burner	70	150	275
Little Orphan Annie Wind-Up Toy	Marx	1930s	5" tall, tin	190	400	750
Miss Hannigan Doll	Knickerbocker	1982		5	10	20
Molly Doll	Knickerbocker	1982		5	10	20
Punjab Doll	Knickerbocker	1982		5	15	25
Puzzle	Novelty Dist.		Famous Comics	20	60	125
Radio Annie's Secret Society Booklet		1936	6" x 9"	30	65	150
Radio Annie's Secret Society Manual		1938	6" x 9", 12 pages	50	90	175
Round Decoder Pin	Ovaltine	1936		30	120	200
Sandy Figure		1940s	3/4" tall, lead	20	55	100
Sandy Wind-Up Toy	Marx	1930s	4" tall, tin	15	40	75
Secret Compartment Decoder Pin	Ovaltine	1936		20	150	300
Shake-Up Mug	Ovaltine	1931		30	65	110
Sunburst Decoder Pin	Ovaltine	1937		30	65	150

204

LOONEY TUNES

TOY	COMPANY	YEAR	DESCRIPTION	GOOD	EX	MIB
Bugs Bunny Hand Puppet	Zany	1940s	rubber head	35	75	150
Daffy Duck Bank	Applause	1980s	figural	10	20	30
Daffy Duck Figure	Applause	1980s	4" bendy	10	20	30
Daffy Duck Figure	Dakin	1968	8-1/2" tall	15	25	50
Daffy Duck Figure	Dakin	1970s		15	30	58
Elmer Fudd Hand Puppet	Zany	1940s	rubber head	30	70	150
Foghorn Leghorn Hand Puppet	Zany	1940s	rubber head	30	60	150
Pepe Le Pew Figure	Dakin	1971	8" tall	25	50	100
Pepe Le Pew Goofy Gram	Dakin	1971		25	50	100
Speedy Gonzales Figure	Dakin	1970	7-1/2" tall, vinyl	15	25	50
Speedy Gonzales Figure	Dakin		5", vinyl	10	20	40
Sylvester and Tweety Bank		1972	vinyl	15	25	50
Sylvester and Tweety Figures	Warner Bros.	1975	6" tall	10	16	30
Sylvester Figure	Oak Rubber	1950	6", rubber	20	45	100
Sylvester Figure	Dakin	1971	Sylvester on a fish crate	15	25	45
Sylvester Figure	Dakin	1969		12	22	45
Sylvester Figure	Dakin	1976	Cartoon Theater	10	16	30
Sylvester Hand Puppet	Zany	1940s	rubber head	32	70	150
Sylvester Soaky	Colgate			10	25	50
Tasmanian Devil Bank	Applause	1980s		5	20	35
Tasmanian Devil Doll	Mighty Star	1971	13" tall, plush	9	30	60
Tasmanian Devil Figure	Superior	1989	7", plastic, on base	3	8	20
Tweety Doll	Dakin	1969	6", moveable head and feet	9	16	35
Tweety Figure	Dakin	1971	Goofy Gram, holding red heart	15	25	50
Tweety Figure	Dakin	1971	on bird cage	14	25	50
Tweety Figure	Dakin	1976	Cartoon Theater	9	16	35
Tweety Hand Puppet	Zany	1940s	rubber head	30	70	150
Tweety Soaky	Colgate	1960s	8-1/2", plastic	10	25	50

MAGILLA GORILLA

TOY	COMPANY	YEAR	DESCRIPTION	GOOD	EX	MIB
Droop-A-Long Coyote Soaky	Purex	1960s	12", plastic	20	45	85
Droop-A-Long Hand Puppet	Ideal		vinyl head	25	50	100
Magilla Gorilla Book	Golden	1964	Big Golden Book	12	25	50
Magilla Gorilla Cannon	Ideal	1964		30	70	150
Magilla Gorilla Cereal Bowl	MB Inc.			10	35	75
Magilla Gorilla Doll	Ideal	1966	18-1/2" plush w/vinyl head	50	100	300
Magilla Gorilla Doll		1960s	11" tall, cloth body, hard arms and legs, hard plastic head	25	50	175
Magilla Gorilla Plate		1960s	8" diameter, plastic	7	16	30
Magilla Gorilla Pull Toy	Ideal	1960s	w/vinyl figure	40	80	200
Magilla Gorilla Puppet	Ideal			40	100	200
Magilla Gorilla Push Puppet	Kohner	1960s	brown plastic figure in pink shorts and shoes, yellow base	25	50	100
Punkin' Puss Soaky	Purex	1960s	11-1/2" tall, plastic	20	40	75
Ricochet Rabbit Hand Puppet	Ideal	1960s	11", vinyl head	30	42	85
Ricochet Rabbit Soaky	Purex	1960s	10-1/2" tall, plastic	30	65	130

MARY POPPINS

TOY	COMPANY	YEAR	DESCRIPTION	GOOD	EX	MIB
Mary Poppins Doll	Gund	1964	11-1/2" tall, bendable	40	100	200
Mary Poppins Figure			8" tall, ceramic	20	40	75

MARY POPPINS

TOY	COMPANY	YEAR	DESCRIPTION	GOOD	EX	MIB
Mary Poppins Manicure Set	Tre-Jur	1964		20	40	85
Mary Poppins Paper Dolls	Whitman	1973	w/magic tote bag	20	40	85
Mary Poppins Pencil Case		1964	vinyl w/zipper top	10	20	40
Mary Poppins Puzzle	Jaymar	1964	frame tray	8	15	30
Mary Poppins Tea Set	Chein	1964	tin, creamer, plates, place settings, cups, serving tray	30	75	150

MICKEY AND MINNIE MOUSE

TOY	COMPANY	YEAR	DESCRIPTION	GOOD	EX	MIB
50 Years with Mickey Wristwatch	Bradley	1983	small round chrome case, inscription and serial number on back	45	85	175
Adventures of Mickey Mouse Book	David McKay	1931	full color illustrations, softcover	60	200	400
Crayons	Transogram	1946		20	40	75
Mickey and Donald Alarm Clock	Jerger/Germany	1960s	2-1/2" x 5" x 7"; metal case, dark brass finish, 3-D plastic figures of Mickey and Donald on either side	55	100	160
Mickey and Donald Jack-in-the-Box	Lakeside	1966	Donald pops out	30	75	175
Mickey and Minnie and Donald Throw Rug			26" x 41", Mickey and Minnie in an airplane w/Donald parachuting	60	120	200
Mickey and Minnie Carpet			27" x 41", Peg Leg Pete is lassoed by Mickey; all characters in western outfits	115	225	350
Mickey and Minnie Dolls	Gund	1940s	13" tall, each	100	250	650
Mickey and Minnie Flashlight	Usalite Co.	1930s	6" long, Mickey leading Minnie through the darkness guided by flashlight and Pluto	40	70	125
Mickey and Minnie Sand Pail	Ohio Art		5" x 5", tin, Mickey, Minnie, Pluto and Donald in boat looking across water at castle, w/swivel handle	45	110	300
Mickey and Minnie Sled	S.L. Allen	1935	32" long, wooden slat sled, metal runners, "Mickey Mouse" decal on steering bar	120	275	475
Mickey and Minnie Snow Dome	Monogram	1970s	3" x 4" x 3" tall, Mickey and Minnie w/a pot of gold at the end of the rainbow	12	25	50
Mickey and Minnie Tea Set	Ohio Art	1930s	5" x 8", pitcher pictures Mickey at piano and cups picture Mickey, Pluto and Minnie	50	100	250
Mickey and Minnie Toothbrush Holder			4-1/2" tall, bisque, toothbrush holes are located behind their heads	55	150	300
Mickey and Minnie Toothbrush Holder			2-1/2" x 4" x 3-1/2", Mickey and Minnie on sofa w/Pluto at their feet	70	160	350
Mickey and Minnie Trash Can	Chein	1970s	13" tall tin litho, Mickey and Minnie fixing a flat tire on one side, other side shows Mickey feeding Minnie soup	25	75	150
Mickey and Minnie Tray	Ohio Art	1930s	5-1/2" x 7-1/4", tin, Mickey and Minnie in rowboat	25	50	150
Mickey and Pluto Ashtray			3" x 4" x 3" tall, ceramic, Mickey and Pluto playing banjos while sitting on the edge of the ashtray	120	240	450
Mickey and Pluto Wristwatch	Bradley	1980	LCD quartz, black vinyl band	20	45	100
Mickey and Three Pigs Spinning Top	Lackawanna		9" diameter, tin	35	85	175

MICKEY AND MINNIE MOUSE

TOY	COMPANY	YEAR	DESCRIPTION	GOOD	EX	MIB
Mickey Mouse Activity Book	Whitman	1936	40 pages	25	75	150
Mickey Mouse Alarm Clock	House Martin	1988	5" x 7" x 2"	11	20	40
Mickey Mouse Alarm Clock	Bayard	1960s	2" x 4-1/2" x 4-1/2" tall, 1930s style Mickey w/movable head that ticks off the seconds	100	190	300
Mickey Mouse Alarm Clock	Bradley	1975	travel alarm, large red cube case, shut off button on top, separate alarm wind, in sleeve box	30	55	90
Mickey Mouse Ashtray			3-1/2" tall, wood composition figure of Mickey	40	100	200
Mickey Mouse Baby Gift Set		1930s	silver-plated cup, fork, spoon, cup and napkin holder	100	170	275
Mickey Mouse Band Drum		1936	7" x 14" diameter, cloth mesh and paper drum heads	50	100	275
Mickey Mouse Band Leader Bank	Knickerbocker		7-1/2" tall, plastic	10	25	50
Mickey Mouse Band Sand Pail	Ohio Art	1938	6" tall, tin, pictures of Mickey Mouse, Minnie, Horace, Pluto, and Clarabelle the cow parading down street	30	90	250
Mickey Mouse Band Spinning Top			9" diameter	25	50	125
Mickey Mouse Bank		1930s	2-1/2" x 6", shaped like a mailbox w/Mickey holding an envelope	60	150	350
Mickey Mouse Bank	Fricke and Nacke	1978	3" x 5" x 7" tall, embossed image of Mickey in front, side panels have Minnie, Goofy, Donald and Pluto	15	25	175
Mickey Mouse Bank	Crown Toy	1938	6" tall, composition, key locked trap door on base, w/figure standing next to treasure chest and head is movable	60	125	400
Mickey Mouse Bank		1950s	5" x 5-1/2" x 6", china, shaped like Mickey's head w/slot between his ears	30	60	150
Mickey Mouse Bank	German	1934	2-1/2" x 3", tin, bright yellow bank shaped like a beehive, Mickey approaching door holding a honey jar in one arm and key to open the door in the other	180	350	650
Mickey Mouse Bank	Transogram	1970s	5" x 7-1/2" x 19" tall, plastic w/Mickey standing on a white chest	15	25	40
Mickey Mouse Bank	Wolverine	1960s	1-1/2" x 5-1/2" x 1" tall, plastic	50	60	125
Mickey Mouse Bank		1930s	2" x 3" x 2-1/4", tin, shaped like a treasure chest w/Mickey and Minnie on the "Isle of the Thrift"	175	300	500
Mickey Mouse Bean Bag Game	Marks Bros.	1930s		100	130	210
Mickey Mouse Beanie		1950s	blue/yellow felt hat w/Mickey on front	45	150	350
Mickey Mouse Boxed Lantern Slides	Ensign	1930s	5" x 6" x 2", cartoons: Traffic Troubles, Gorilla Mystery, Cactus Kid, Castaway, Delivery Boy, Fishin' Around, Firefighters, Moose Hunt and Mickey Steps Out	160	300	450
Mickey Mouse Bubble Buster Gun	Kilgore	1936	8" long, cork gun	55	120	200
Mickey Mouse Bump-N-Go Spaceship	Matsudaya	1980s	battery operated tin litho w/clear dome, has six flashing lights, rotating antenna	35	65	125
Mickey Mouse Camera	Ettelson	1960s	3" x 3" x 5"	18	35	50
Mickey Mouse Camera	Child Guidance	1970s	4" x 7" x 7"	10	20	40

MICKEY AND MINNIE MOUSE

TOY	COMPANY	YEAR	DESCRIPTION	GOOD	EX	MIB
Mickey Mouse Camera	Helm Toy	1970s	2" x 5" x 4-1/2", Mickey in engineer's uniform riding on top of the train	13	25	50
Mickey Mouse Car	Polistil	1970s	2" x 4" x 1-1/2" tall plastic car w/rubber figure, Mickey in driver's seat	30	55	85
Mickey Mouse Cardboard House	O.B. Andrews	1930s	14" x 12" x 13" tall	120	225	375
Mickey Mouse Chatty Chums	Mattel	1979		8	15	35
Mickey Mouse Christmas Lights	Noma	1930s	eight lamps w/holiday decals of characters	125	225	350
Mickey Mouse Clock	Elgin	1970s	10" x 15" x 3", electric wall clock	12	25	35
Mickey Mouse Club Bank	Play Pal Plastics	1970s	4-1/2" x 6" x 11-1/2" tall, vinyl	16	30	50
Mickey Mouse Club Coffee Tin		1950s	illustrated lid promotes the club, tin included MM badge	30	55	120
Mickey Mouse Club Fun Box	Whitman	1957	box includes stamp book, club scrapbook, six coloring books and four small gameboards	45	75	150
Mickey Mouse Club Magic Divider	Jacmar	1950s	arithmetic game	30	55	85
Mickey Mouse Club Magic Kit	Mars Candy	1950s	two 8" x 20" punch-out sheets	30	55	125
Mickey Mouse Club Magic Subtractor	Jacmar	1950s	arithmetic game	11	20	40
Mickey Mouse Club Marionette		1950s	3" x 6-1/2" x 13-1/2" tall, composition figure of a girl w/black felt hat and mouse ears	100	250	400
Mickey Mouse Club Mouseketeer Doll	Horsman	1960s	8" tall, denim outfit	25	65	100
Mickey Mouse Club Mousketeer Ears	Kohner		7" x 12-1/2"	11	20	40
Mickey Mouse Club Mousketeer Handbag	Connecticut Leather		leather/vinyl crafting set	45	60	85
Mickey Mouse Club Newsreel with Sound	Mattel	1950s	4" x 4-1/2" x 9" tall, orange box, plastic projector w/two short filmstrips, record, cardboard screen, cartoons "Touchdown Mickey" and "No Sail"	75	170	285
Mickey Mouse Club Plastic Plate	Arrowhead	1960s	9" diameter, clubhouse w/Goofy, Pluto and Donald wearing mouse ears and sweaters w/club emblems	16	30	45
MIckey Mouse Club Rhythm Makers Set	Emenee			65	100	325
Mickey Mouse Club Toothbrush	Pepsodent	1970s		4	7	15
Mickey Mouse Colorforms Set	Colorforms	1976	8" x 12-1/2" x 1", Spirit of '76	10	30	75
Mickey Mouse Cup	Cavalier	1950s	3" tall, silver-plated cup w/a 2-1/2" opening	25	50	100
Mickey Mouse Dart Gun Target	Marks Brothers	1930s	10" target, dart gun and suction darts	35	65	250
Mickey Mouse Dinner Set	Empresa Electro	1930s	china, 2" creamer, 3-4-1/2" plates and 3-5" plates, 7" long dish, two oval platters	140	250	400
Mickey Mouse Doll		1930s	4" x 7" x 10-1/2" tall, movable arms and legs, swivel head, black velveteen body and red felt pants	325	600	950
Mickey Mouse Doll	Schuco	1950s	10" tall	110	215	360
Mickey Mouse Doll	Knickerbocker		5" x 7" x 12" tall, fabric, Mickey in checkered shorts and green jacket w/white felt flower stapled to it	190	350	575
Mickey Mouse Doll	Gund	1960s	12", Mickey as fireman	30	55	85

MICKEY AND MINNIE MOUSE

TOY	COMPANY	YEAR	DESCRIPTION	GOOD	EX	MIB
Mickey Mouse Doll	Knickerbocker	1935	11" tall, stuffed w/removable shoes and jointed head, red shorts	115	210	325
Mickey Mouse Doll	Hasbro	1970s	4" x 5-1/2" x 7-1/2" tall, talks	20	40	60
Mickey Mouse Doll	Horsman	1972	3" x 10" x 12" tall, talking doll, says five different phrases	20	35	60
Mickey Mouse Dominoes	Halsam		Mickey and Pluto on dominoes	80	100	160
Mickey Mouse Drum	Ohio Art	1930s	6" diameter	35	60	190
Mickey Mouse Electric Casting Set	Home Foundary	1930s	9-1/2" x 16" x 2"	65	120	185
Mickey Mouse Electric Table Radio	General Electric	1960s	4-1/2" x 10-1/2" x 6" tall	30	55	135
Mickey Mouse Figure	Marx	1970	6" tall, vinyl	10	20	40
Mickey Mouse Figure	Seiberling	1930s	3-1/2" tall, latex	60	110	160
Mickey Mouse Figure		1930s	3" tall, bisque, plays saxophone	35	80	175
Mickey Mouse Figure		1930s	3" tall, bisque, holding a parade flag and sword	35	80	175
Mickey Mouse Figure	Seiberling	1930s	3-1/2" tall, black hard rubber	25	80	175
Mickey Mouse Figure			composition, part of the Lionel Circus Train Set	60	110	160
Mickey Mouse Figure	Goebel	1930s	3-1/2" tall, in a hunting outfit reading a book	35	65	120
Mickey Mouse Figure			4" tall, bisque, dressed in a green nightshirt	35	65	110
Mickey Mouse Figure	Seiberling	1930s	6-1/2" tall, rubber	70	135	200
Mickey Mouse Fire Engine	Sun Rubber		7" long, rubber, push toy	45	85	150
Mickey Mouse Fire Truck with Figure	Sun Rubber		2-1/2" x 6-1/2" x 4", Mickey driving and mold-in image of Donald standing on the back holding onto his helmet	45	85	150
Mickey Mouse Fun-E-Flex Figure	Fun-E-Flex	1930s	7", bendy	245	455	725
Mickey Mouse Gumball Bank	Hasbro	1968		15	30	50
Mickey Mouse Has a Busy Day Book	Whitman	1937	16 pages	25	40	75
Mickey Mouse in Giantland Book	David McKay	1934	45 pages, hardcover	50	85	175
Mickey Mouse Jack-In-the-Box		1970s	5-1/2" square tin litho box shows Mickey, Pluto, Donald and Goofy, Mickey pops out	25	50	75
Mickey Mouse Lamp	Soreng-Manegold	1935	10-1/2" tall	75	150	375
Mickey Mouse Lionel Circus Train	Lionel	1935	five cars w/Mickey, 30" train, 84 inches of track, circus tent, Sunoco station, truck, tickets, Mickey composition statue	550	1200	2500
Mickey Mouse Lionel Circus Train Handcar	Lionel		metal, 9" long w/6" tall composition/rubber figures of Mickey and Minnie	240	450	750
Mickey Mouse Magic Slate	Watkins-Strathmore	1950s	8-1/2" x 14" tall	20	30	50
Mickey Mouse Map of the United States	Dixon	1930s	9-1/4" x 14"	40	100	300
Mickey Mouse Marbles	Monarch		marbles and Mickey bag, on card	5	10	25
Mickey Mouse Mechanical Pencil		1930s	head of Mickey on one end and decal of Mickey walking on other side of pencil	40	70	150
Mickey Mouse Mechanical Robot	Gabriel			70	125	150
Mickey Mouse Mousegetar		1960s	10" x 30" x 2-1/2" black plastic	40	80	150
Mickey Mouse Movie Projector	Keystone	1934	5-1/2" x 11-1/2" x 11" tall for 8mm movies	150	275	550
Mickey Mouse Movie-Fun Shows	Mastercraft	1940s	7-1/2" square by 4" deep, animated action movies	100	200	300

TOY	COMPANY	YEAR	DESCRIPTION	GOOD	EX	MIB
Mickey Mouse Music Box	Schmid		3" x 6" x 7-1/2" tall, bisque, Spirit of '76, plays "Yankee Doodle;" Mickey, Goofy and Donald are dressed as Revolutionary War Minutemen	60	120	185
Mickey Mouse Music Box	Japan	1970s	4" x 6" tall, china, plays "Side by Side," Mickey is brushing a kitten in a washtub	15	25	60
Mickey Mouse Music Box			4-1/2" x 5" x 7", plays "It's a Small World," Mickey in conductor's uniform standing on cake	20	35	60
Mickey Mouse Music Box	Anri	1971	5" x 3-1/2", plays "If I Were Rich Man"	50	85	135
Mickey Mouse Music Box	Schmid	1970s	3-1/2" x 5-1/2", plays "Mickey Mouse Club March," ceramic, Mickey in western clothes standing next to a cactus	35	60	90
Mickey Mouse Musical Money Box		1970s	3" x 6", tin box w/Mickey, Pluto, Donald and Goofy	30	55	90
Mickey Mouse Night Light	Disney	1938	4" tall, tin	100	175	275
Mickey Mouse Old Timers Fire Engine	Matsudaya	1980s	red, tin and plastic fire truck w/Mickey at the wheel	40	70	125
Mickey Mouse Pencil Box	Dixon	1930s	5-1/2" x 10-1/2" x 1-1/4", Mickey in a gymnasium	35	100	185
Mickey Mouse Pencil Box	Dixon	1937	5" x 8-1/2" x 1-1/4", Mickey is a circus ringmaster and Donald riding a seal	35	100	175
Mickey Mouse Pencil Box	Dixon	1930s	Mickey ready to hitch Horace to a carriage in which Minnie is sitting	35	100	175
Mickey Mouse Pencil Box	Dixon	1937	5-1/2" x 9" x 3/4", Mickey, Goofy and Pluto riding a rocket	35	100	175
Mickey Mouse Pencil Holder	Dixon	1930s	4-1/2" tall	60	100	175
Mickey Mouse Pencil Sharpener	Hasbro	1960s	shape of Mickey's head, pencil goes into mouth	12	25	50
Mickey Mouse Pencil Sharpener			3" tall, celluloid, sharpener located on base	65	125	250
Mickey Mouse Picture Gun	Stephens	1950s	6-1/2" x 9-1/2" x 3", metal, lights to show filmstrips	55	100	250
Mickey Mouse Pitcher	Germany	1930s	2" x 3" diameter, china, white w/green shading around the base, Mickey on each side	65	125	250
Mickey Mouse Play Tiles	Halsam	1964	336 tiles	15	25	50
Mickey Mouse Pocket Watch	Bradley	1976	3-1/2" x 4-1/2" x 3/4", Mickey in his Bicentennial outfit	35	50	120
Mickey Mouse Pocket Watch	Ingersoll	1930s	2" diameter	200	600	1350
Mickey Mouse Pocket Watch	Bradley	1970s		35	70	150
Mickey Mouse Pocket Watch	Lorus	1988	#2202, quartz, small gold bezel, gold chain and clip fob, articulated hands	25	50	100
Mickey Mouse Presents a Silly Symphony Book	Whitman	1934	Big Little Book	25	60	120
Mickey Mouse Print Shop Set	Fulton Specialty	1930s	6-1/2" x 6-1/2", ink pad, stamper, metal tweezers, wooden tray	75	150	275
Mickey Mouse Pull Toy	Toy Kraft		7" x 22" x 8" tall, horse cart drawn by wooden horses	300	575	875
Mickey Mouse Pull Toy	N.N. Hill Brass	1935	14" tall, wood and metal	135	250	400
Mickey Mouse Puppet Forms	Colorforms	1960s		10	25	60
Mickey Mouse Radio	Philgee	1970s		20	35	65

TOY	COMPANY	YEAR	DESCRIPTION	GOOD	EX	MIB
Mickey Mouse Radio	Emerson	1934	wood composition cabinet w/designs of Mickey playing musical instruments	350	1000	4000
Mickey Mouse Record Player	General Electric	1970s	playing arm is the design of Mickey's arm	60	125	175
Mickey Mouse Riding Toy	Mengel	1930s	6" x 17" x 16" tall	390	725	1200
Mickey Mouse Rodeo Rider	Matsudaya	1980s	plastic wind-up, cowboy Mickey rides a bucking bronco	25	45	75
Mickey Mouse Rolykin	Marx		1-1/2" tall, ball bearing action	12	20	60
Mickey Mouse Rub 'N Play Magic Transfer Set	Colorforms	1978		15	30	70
Mickey Mouse Safety Blocks	Halsam	1930s	nine blocks	90	150	250
Mickey Mouse Sand Pail	Ohio Art	1938	6" tall, tin, Mickey, Donald and Goofy playing golf	25	85	250
Mickey Mouse Sand Pail	Ohio Art	1938	3" tall, tin	25	75	150
Mickey Mouse Sand Shovel	Ohio Art		10" long, tin	20	55	125
Mickey Mouse Saxophone		1930s	16" tall	120	225	350
Mickey Mouse Scissors	Disney		3" long, child's scissors w/Mickey figure	20	35	65
Mickey Mouse Serving Tray		1960s	11" diameter, tin	11	20	60
Mickey Mouse Sewing Cards	Colorforms	1978	7-1/2" x 12" cut-out card designs of Mickey, Minnie, Pluto, Clarabelle, Donald Duck and Horace	10	20	75
Mickey Mouse Sled	Flexible Flyer	1930s	18" x 30" x 6" tall, wood	120	350	850
Mickey Mouse Squeeze Toy	Dell	1950s	rubber, Mickey as hitchhiking hobo	35	65	150
Mickey Mouse Squeeze Toy	Dell	1960s	8" tall	15	30	50
Mickey Mouse Squeeze Toy	Sun Rubber	1950s	10" tall, rubber	20	45	75
Mickey Mouse Stamp Pad		1930s	3" long	25	75	150
Mickey Mouse Steamboat	Matsudaya	1988	wind-up plastic steamboat w/Mickey as Steamboat Willie, runs on floor as smokestacks go up and down, box says "60 Years w/You"	30	60	135
Mickey Mouse Tea Set		1930s	3" saucer, 2" pitcher, 2-1/2" sugar bowl each piece shows Mickey and Minnie in a rowboat	30	100	250
Mickey Mouse Tea Set	Wolverine		plastic	50	175	175
Mickey Mouse Telephone Bank	N.N. Hill Brass	1938	5" tall w/cardboard figure of Mickey	75	150	300
Mickey Mouse Throw Rug	Alex. Smith Carpet	1935	26" x 42"	130	250	375
Mickey Mouse Tractor	Sun Rubber		5" long, rubber	30	60	150
Mickey Mouse Transistor Radio	Gabriel	1950s	6-1/2" x 7" x 1-1/2"	40	70	150
Mickey Mouse Tricycle Toy	Steiff	1932	8-1/2" x 7", wood and metal frame, action movement	330	790	3500
Mickey Mouse Twirling Tail Toy	Marx	1950s	3" x 5-1/2" x 5-1/2" tall, w/a built-in key, metal tail spins around as the toy vibrates	120	225	375
Mickey Mouse Utensils	Wm. Rogers and Son	1947	6" fork and 5-1/2" spoon	50	90	150
Mickey Mouse Viewer	Craftsmen's Guild	1940s	film viewer w/12 films	70	125	200
Mickey Mouse Wall Clock	Elgin	1978	9" diameter dial, 15" long, shaped like oversize watchband, "50 Happy Years" logo on dial	30	55	85

TOY	COMPANY	YEAR	DESCRIPTION	GOOD	EX	MIB
Mickey Mouse Wash Machine	Ohio Art		8" tin litho w/Mickey and Minnie Mouse pictured doing their wash	45	85	275
Mickey Mouse Water Globes		1970s	3" x 4-1/2" x 5" tall, three dimensional plastic figures of Mickey seated w/a plastic water globe between his legs	25	50	100
Mickey Mouse Watering Can	Ohio Art	1938	6" tin litho	40	125	250
Mickey Mouse Wind-Up Musical Toy	Illco	1970s	6" tall, plays "Lullaby and Goodnight," 3-D figure of Mickey in red pants and yellow shirt	25	35	65
Mickey Mouse Wind-Up Toy	Gabriel	1978	plastic transparent figure of Mickey w/visible metal gears	10	20	50
Mickey Mouse Wind-Up Trike	Korean	1960s	tin litho trike w/plastic Mickey w/flag and balloon on handle, bell on back	85	150	250
Mickey Mouse Wristwatch	Timex	1960s	large round case, stainless back, articulated hands, red vinyl band	50	80	100
Mickey Mouse Wristwatch			two-gun Mickey, saddle tan western style band	25	45	75
Mickey Mouse Wristwatch	Bradley	1970s	2-1/2" x 6" x 2-1/2", plastic case, white dial w/Mickey playing tennis, the second hand has a tennis ball on the end of it	35	65	125
Mickey Mouse Wristwatch	Ingersoll	1939	rectangular w/standard second hand between Mickey's legs	225	380	750
Mickey Mouse Wristwatch	Bradley	1983	medium black octagonal case, articulated hands, no numbers on face, in plastic window box	25	260	385
Mickey Mouse Wristwatch	Bradley	1978	commemorative edition	65	125	200
Mickey Mouse Wristwatch	Bradley	1970s	white plastic case, watch on pendant, bubble crystal, articulated hands, gold chain	25	55	85
Mickey Mouse Wristwatch	Timex	1958	electric	120	225	350
Mickey Mouse Wristwatch	Bradley	1984	medium white case, articulated hands, black face, sweep seconds, white vinyl band, in plastic window box	20	35	65
Mickey Mouse Yarn Sewing Kit	Marks Bros.	1930s	seven cards, yarn, needle	40	160	275
Mickey's Air Mail Plane	Sun Rubber	1940s	3-1/2" x 6" long, 5" wingspan, rubber	45	75	250
Minnie Mouse Alarm Clock	Bradley	1970s	pink metal electric two-bell clock w/articulated hands	25	50	75
Minnie Mouse Car	Matchbox	1979		5	10	30
Minnie Mouse Choo-Choo Train Pull Toy	Linemar	1940s	3" x 8-1/2" x 7" tall, green metal base and green wooden wheels	70	150	300
Minnie Mouse Clock	Phinney-Walker	1970s	8" diameter by 1-1/2" deep, plastic, "Behind Every Great Man, There is a Woman!"	40	70	125
Minnie Mouse Doll	Petz	1940s	10" tall	125	225	400
Minnie Mouse Doll	Knickerbocker	1935	14" tall, stuffed, cloth, polka-dot skirt and lace pantaloons	115	200	550
Minnie Mouse Figure	Ingersoll	1958	5-1/2" tall, plastic	35	60	100
Minnie Mouse Fun-E-Flex Figure	Fun-E-Flex	1930s	5", bendy	130	250	375
Minnie Mouse Hand Puppet		1940s	11" tall, white on red polka-dot, fabric hard cover and a pair of black and white felt hands	55	125	200
Minnie Mouse Music Box	Schmid	1970s	3-1/2" diameter, plays "Love Story"	12	25	60

MICKEY AND MINNIE MOUSE

TOY	COMPANY	YEAR	DESCRIPTION	GOOD	EX	MIB
Minnie Mouse Rocker	Marx	1950s	tin wind-up, rocker moves back and forth w/gravity motion of her head and ears	250	460	700
Minnie Mouse Wristwatch	Timex	1958	small round chrome case, stainless back, articulated hands, yellow vinyl band	60	120	200
Minnie Mouse Wristwatch	Bradley	1978	gold case, sweep seconds, red vinyl band, articulated hands	16	30	50
Minnie with Bump-n-Go Action Shopping Cart	Illfelder	1980s	4" x 9-1/2" x 11-1/2" tall, plastic, battery operated Minnie pushing cart	30	55	80
Mouseketeer Cut-Outs	Whitman	1957	figures and accessories	25	50	100
Mouseketeer Fan Club Typewriter		1950s	lithographed tin	50	90	175
Puzzle	Whitman	1957	Adventureland, 11" x 15" frame tray; Mickey, Minnie, Donald and his nephew in boat surrounded by jungle beasts	15	30	60
Puzzle	Jaymar	1960s	Pluto's Wash and Scrub Service	15	25	65
Puzzle	Marks Brothers	1930s	10" x 12", Mickey polishing the boiler on his "Mickey Mouse R.R." train engine and Minnie waving from the cab	45	85	150
Spinning Top	Chein	1950s	tin litho, features Mickey in cowboy outfit and other characters	40	120	250
Spinning Top	Fritz Bueschel	1930s	7" diameter, 7" tall, Mickey, Minnie, a nephew, Donald and Horace playing a musical instrument	55	120	275

MIGHTY MOUSE

TOY	COMPANY	YEAR	DESCRIPTION	GOOD	EX	MIB
Charm Bracelet		1950s	brass charms of Gandy Goose, Terry Bear, Mighty Mouse and other Terrytoon characters	25	50	100
Mighty Mouse Ball Game	Ja-Ru	1981		5	10	20
Mighty Mouse Cinema Viewer	Fleetwood	1979	w/four strips	7	15	35
Mighty Mouse Doll		1942	ruber head, wering red suit	300	750	1000
Mighty Mouse Doll	Ideal	1950s	14" tall, stuffed, cloth	30	80	150
Mighty Mouse Doll		1942	large, rubber head, yellow sui w/cape	250	600	850
Mighty Mouse Dynamite Dasher	Takara	1981		50	110	225
Mighty Mouse Figure	Dakin	1977	hard and soft vinyl figure	20	50	85
Mighty Mouse Figure	Dakin	1978	Fun Farm	20	55	90
Mighty Mouse Figure		1950s	9-1/2" rubber, squeaks	20	50	100
Mighty Mouse Flashlight	Dyno	1979	3-1/2" figural light	20	65	100
Mighty Mouse Hit the Claw Target Set	Parks			55	110	225
Mighty Mouse Make-a-Face Sheet	Towne	1958	w/dials to change face parts	15	35	90
Mighty Mouse Mighty Money	Fleetwood	1979		2	55	85
Mighty Mouse Money Press	Ja-Ru	1981	stampers, pads and money	8	15	30
Mighty Mouse Movie Viewer	Chemtoy	1980		8	15	30
Mighty Mouse Picture Play Lite	Janex	1983		8	15	30
Mighty Mouse Sneakers	Randy Co.	1960s	children's, graphics on box, picture on sneakers	25	45	110
Mighty Mouse Wallet	Larami	1978		10	20	50

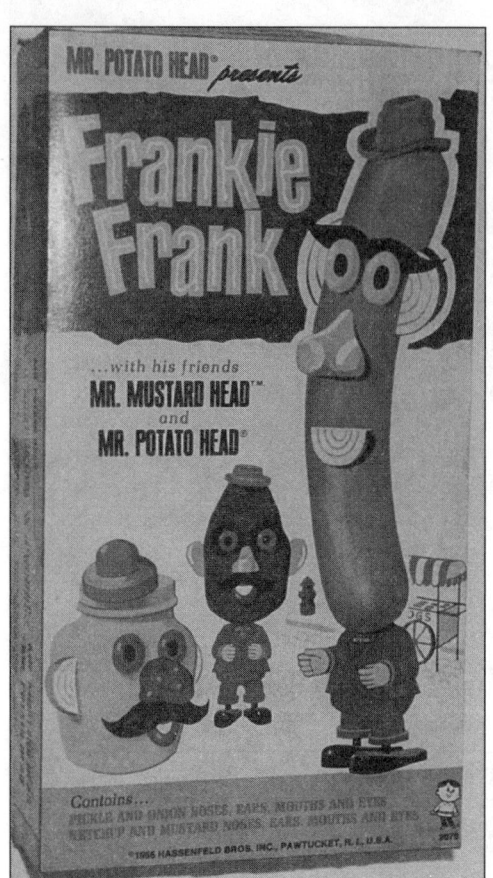

*Mr. Potato Head Frankie Frank,
1966, Hasbro*

*Snoopy in the Music Box,
1969, Mattel*

MIGHTY MOUSE

TOY	COMPANY	YEAR	DESCRIPTION	GOOD	EX	MIB
Mighty Mouse Wristwatch	Bradley	1979	chrome case	15	20	50
Puzzle	Fleetwood	1979	Mighty Mouse/Heckle and Jeckle	10	75	125
Puzzle			tray puzzle; Mighty Mouse and his TV Pals	6	12	35

MISCELLANEOUS CHARACTERS

TOY	COMPANY	YEAR	DESCRIPTION	GOOD	EX	MIB
Amy Carter Paper Dolls	Toy Factory	1970s	14" cardboard doll w/accessories	15	25	50
Bonzo Scooter Toy			7" scooter w/6" Bonzo, wind-up	125	250	500
Bruce Lee Figure	Largo	1986	8" w/weapon	20	40	70
Daktari Puzzle	Whitman	1967	100 pieces	10	30	100
Diamond Jim Figure		1930s	5-1/2" tall	30	70	150
Evel Knievel Stunt Stadium	Ideal	1974	large vinyl case w/accessories	35	80	160
George Bush Figure			7" tall	8	15	35
Hardy Boys Dolls	Kenner	1979	12" tall Joe Hardy (Shaun Cassidy) or Frank Hardy (Parker Stevenson)	20	40	80
Holly Hobbie Wristwatch	Bradley	1982	small gold tone case, base metal back, yellow plastic band	5	10	35
Jimmy Carter Radio			peanut-shaped transistor radio	20	42	85
Jimmy Carter Wind-Up Walking Peanut			5" tall	10	20	40
Joan Palooka Stringless Marionette	Nat'l Mask and Puppet	1952	12-1/2" tall "daughter of Joe Palooka" doll comes w/pink blanket and birth certificate	50	100	225
Kennedy Kards		1960s	red, white, and blue playing cards w/cartoon artwork	10	15	30
Komic Kamera Film Viewer Set		1950s	5" long, Dick Tracy, Little Orphan Annie, Terry and the Pirates and The Lone Ranger	40	80	125
Little King Lucky Safety Card	New York Journal	1953	2" x 4" cards, Little King warns of safety	10	20	50
Lyndon Johnson Figure	Remco	1960s		17	35	50
Mr. and Mrs. Potato Head Set	Hasbro	1960s	cars, boats, shopping trailer, etc.	25	50	100
Mr. Potato Head Frankie Frank	Hasbro	1966	companion to Mr. Potato Head, w/accessories	20	40	90
Mr. Potato Head Frenchy Fry	Hasbro	1966	companion to Mr. Potato Head, w/accessories	20	40	90
Mr. Potato Head Ice Pops	Hasbro	1950s	plastic molds for freezing treats, in box	16	35	70
Patton Figure	Excel Toy		poseable doll w/clothing and accessories	20	40	80
Prince Charles of Wales Figure	Goldberger	1982	13" tall, dressed in palace guard uniform	18	35	70
Red Ranger Ride 'Em Cowboy	Wyandotte	1930s	tin wind-up rocker	115	230	575
Ringling Bros. and Barnum and Bailey Circus Play Set		1970s	vinyl, w/animals, trapeze personnel, clowns and assorted circus equipment	25	45	90
Rin-Tin-Tin Magic Erasable Pictures	Transogram	1955		50	130	250
Sandra Dee Paper Dolls	Saalfield	1959	two cardboard dolls w/outfits	25	45	85
Sir Reginald Play-N-Save Bank		1960s	7" tall plastic lion and hunter, on a 15" green plastic base, the hunter fires the coin into the lion's mouth	45	115	160
Space Ghost Puzzle	Whitman	1967		20	50	100
Sylvester Stallone Rambo Figure		1986	18" tall, poseable figure	10	15	30

215

MISCELLANEOUS CHARACTERS

TOY	COMPANY	YEAR	DESCRIPTION	GOOD	EX	MIB
Tuesday Weld Paper Dolls	Saalfield	1960	two cardboard dolls w/outfits	25	50	85
Uncle Don's "Puzzy and Sizzy" Membership Card		1950s		10	25	50
Willie Whopper Pencil Case		1930s	green w/illustrations of Willie, Pirate and his gal	45	75	125

MOON MULLINS

TOY	COMPANY	YEAR	DESCRIPTION	GOOD	EX	MIB
Moon Mullins and Kayo Railroad Handcar Toy	Marx	1930s	6" long, wind-up, both figures bendable arms and legs	250	500	950
Moon Mullins and Kayo Toothbrush Holder			4" tall, bisque	40	80	175
Moon Mullins Figure Set			bisque, Uncle Willie, Kayo, Moon Mullins and Emmy, 2-1/4" to 3-1/2"	85	260	475
Moon Mullins Playstone Funnies Mold Set		1940s		40	75	160
Puzzle		1930s	9-1/2" x 14", Featured Funnies	20	50	100

MR. MAGOO

TOY	COMPANY	YEAR	DESCRIPTION	GOOD	EX	MIB
Mr. Magoo Car	Hubley	1961	7-1/2" x 9" long, metal, battery-operated	120	350	475
Mr. Magoo Doll	Ideal	1970	12" tall	20	45	90
Mr. Magoo Doll	Ideal	1962	5" tall, vinyl head w/cloth body	454	95	185
Mr. Magoo Drinking Glass		1962	5-1/2" tall	10	25	45
Mr. Magoo Figure	Dakin		7" tall	30	80	160
Mr. Magoo Hand Puppet		1960s	vinyl head, cloth body	30	60	125
Mr. Magoo Puzzle	Warren	1978	frame tray	10	20	45
Mr. Magoo Soaky	Palmolive	1960s	10" tall, vinyl and plastic	20	50	85

MUTT AND JEFF

TOY	COMPANY	YEAR	DESCRIPTION	GOOD	EX	MIB
Mutt and Jeff Bank			5" tall, cast iron, two piece construction held together by screw in the back	50	100	200
Mutt and Jeff Caroon Book	Ball Publications	1910	68 pages	250	850	1500
Mutt and Jeff Dolls		1920s	8" x 6-1/2" tall, composition hands and heads w/heavy cast iron feet, movable arms and legs, fabric clothing; pair	130	300	600
Mutt and Jeff Figures	A. Steinhardt and Bros	1911	ceramic, w/a coin inserted into base; pair	80	200	325

NIGHTMARE BEFORE CHRISTMAS

TOY	COMPANY	YEAR	DESCRIPTION	GOOD	EX	MIB
Bandanna	Fashion Victim		two styles: Jack or Lock, Shock and Barrel	5	10	25
Baseball Caps	Fashion Victim		three styles: Fishbone w/metal keychain; Lock, Shock and Barrel; or Jack "Bone Daddy"	8	10	15
Beach Towel	Fashion Victim			22	29	35
Bionic Airwalker Balloon	Anagram		featuring Jack Skellington; over 7" tall	15	20	40
Bookmarks	OSP Publishing		set of eight styles including wallet cards	10	15	25
Boxer Shorts	Stanley DeSantis		Lock, Shock and Barrel or Jack styles; cotton	6	8	10

NIGHTMARE BEFORE CHRISTMAS

TOY	COMPANY	YEAR	DESCRIPTION	GOOD	EX	MIB
Brass Keychain	Disney		Jack Skellington's Tombstone	3	7	15
Buttons			set of 12 featuring logo, characters, etc.	15	20	40
Cardboard Store Display	Applause		over 6" wide	50	90	150
Comforter	Wamsutta		twin size featuring Lock, Shock and Barrel	45	55	85
Cookie Jar	Treasure Craft		ceramic; Jack on Tombstone	45	85	175
Drawstring Bag			Jack Skellington on front	10	15	25
Gift Bags	Cleo		five styles available	6	10	20
Glow Oogie Boogie Figure	Applause		PVC figure	7	20	40
Greeting Cards			set of six featuring various characters	15	25	50
Handheld Video Game	Tiger			25	30	65
Jack Figure	Hasbro		bendy on card	6	15	35
Jack in Coffin Figure	Applause		12"	30	100	275
Jack Soaky			glow head	7	15	50
Kaleidoscope	C. Bennett Scopes			16	20	50
Lock, Shock and Barrel Dolls	Applause		set of three; 6" cloth and vinyl dolls	25	50	100
Lock, Shock and Barrel Figures	Applause		set of three, 3" PVC figures	10	20	50
Magic Action Figures	Applause		set of three; 4" figures has its own action when rolled	20	30	50
Mayor Figure	Hasbro		bendy on card	10	25	50
Mayor Wind-Up Music Box	Schmid		head spins while music plays "What's This?"	40	75	125
Mug	Selandia		10 oz. acrylic mug w/floating snowflakes and glitter	5	10	25
Mug	Selandia		16 oz. acrylic mug w/floating snowflakes and glitter	5	10	25
Mylar Balloons	Anagram		five variations, each	10	15	30
Notepad	Beach		75-sheet pad featuring Lock, Shock and Barrel	3	5	10
Oogie Boogie Doll	Applause		16"; makes farting noise when squeezed	15	35	75
Partyware	Beach		65 pieces	14	16	30
Pencil			Whirly Sally or Whirly Jack	4	10	20
Pin	Oopsa Daisy		several character styles, pewter	10	18	25
Pop-Up Book				15	35	75
Postcard Book			30 full-color postcards	5	12	25
Purse			multi-compartment w/mirror	5	15	40
PVC Figure on Drinking Straws			Jack or Sally	3	7	10
Rhinestone Pin			white stones featuring Jack Skellington	30	55	75
Rhinestone Pin	Oopsa Daisy		red stones featuring Jack Skellington	40	65	85
Sally Doll	Hasbro		removable limbs	50	150	400
Sally Figure	Hasbro		bendy on card	15	30	75
Sally in Coffin Figure	Applause		12"	60	175	450
Santa Claus Doll	Applause		10" plush	10	25	50
Santa Jack Figure	Hasbro		bendy on card	6	10	20
Santa Puppet Doll	Hasbro			25	45	75
Silk Necktie			many styles/patterns	15	20	40
Sky Floater Kite	Spectra Star			5	10	25
Stickers	Gibson		featuring movie characters	2	5	10
Sunglasses	Jet Vision Limited			12	15	25
Talking Jack Doll	Hasbro			50	120	350
Temporary Tattoos	US Kids			2	4	10
Tumbler	Selandia		7 oz., acrylic	10	13	20
Vest	Fashion Victim		Lock, Shock and Barrel or Jack styles	12	15	35
Video Release Poster	Touchstone		24" x 36"	15	40	65
Wooden Ornaments	Kurt S. Adler		set of 10; 4" to 6" tall; individually packaged	20	60	75
Wristwatch	Timex		six styles available, each	10	30	50
Yo-Yo	Spectra Star			5	20	40

PEANUTS

TOY	COMPANY	YEAR	DESCRIPTION	GOOD	EX	MIB
Batter-Up Snoopy Colorforms	Colorforms	1979		10	30	45
Big Quart-O-Snoopy Bubbles	Chemtoy	1970s		9	13	15
Camp Kamp Play Set	Child Guidance	1970s	rubber camp building w/characters	20	50	80
Can You Catch It, Charlie Brown? Game	Ideal	1976		50	120	175
Charlie Brown Costume	Collegeville		w/mask	12	20	35
Charlie Brown Deluxe View-Master Gift Pak	GAF/View-Master	1970s	cylindrical container holds seven reels and viewer	20	50	65
Charlie Brown Doll	Determined	1970s	plastic; wearing baseball gear	30	65	100
Charlie Brown Doll	Ideal	1976	removable clothing	25	40	60
Charlie Brown Doll	Hungerford Plastics	1958	8-1/2" plastic	35	75	150
Charlie Brown Nodder	Japanese	1960s	5-1/2" tall, bobbing head	25	100	200
Charlie Brown Pocket Doll	Boucher	1968	7"	20	32	60
Charlie Brown Punching Bag	Determined	1970s		15	30	50
Charlie Brown Push Puppet	Ideal	1977		20	40	60
Charlie Brown Wristwatch	Determined	1970s	Charlie Brown in baseball gear, yellow face, black band	55	160	225
Charlie Brown's All-Star Dugout Play Set	Child Guidance	1970s		20	40	50
Charlie Brown's Backyard Play Set	Child Guidance	1970s		10	30	40
Chirping Woodstock	Aviva	1977	plastic w/electronic sound	18	25	35
Dolls	Simon Simple	1960s	7-1/2", Charlie Brown, Lucy, or Linus	20	40	65
Dress Me Belle Doll	Knickerbocker	1983	Belle wearing pink dress w/blue dots	15	35	45
Dress Me Snoopy Doll	Knickerbocker	1983	Snoopy wearing blue jeans and red/yellow shirt	15	35	45
Electronic Snoopy Playmate	Romper Room/Hasbro	1980		60	125	175
Express Station Set	Aviva	1977	Snoopy riding locomotive	20	50	70
Formula-1 Racing Car	Aviva	1978	11-1/2" plastic w/Woodstock or Snoopy	75	110	150
Joe Cool Punching Bag	Ideal	1976		20	35	50
Joe Cool Push Puppet	Ideal	1977		20	35	75
Kaleidorama	Determined	1979		12	17	25
Linus Doll	Hungerford Plastics	1958	8-1/2" plastic	50	75	150
Linus Doll	Ideal	1976	removable clothing	55	80	175
Linus Music Box	Anri		wood, Linus in pumpkin patch on cover, plays "Who Can I Turn To?"	85	120	150
Linus Pocket Doll	Boucher	1968	7"	15	25	40
Lucy and Charlie Brown Music Box	Anri	1971	4", each character beside large mushroom, plays "Rose Garden"	75	150	185
Lucy Candlestick Holder	Hallmark		7-1/4" figural composition	15	21	25
Lucy Doll	Ideal	1976	removable clothing	25	50	75
Lucy Doll	Hungerford Plastics	1958	8-1/2" plastic	50	75	100
Lucy Music Box	Anri	1971	5", Lucy w/mushrooms on ground, plays "Love Story"	80	195	250
Lucy Music Box	Anri	1969	6-1/2", Lucy behind psychiatrist booth, plays "Try to Remember"	80	195	250
Lucy Nurse Push Puppet	Ideal	1977		20	35	50
Lucy Pocket Doll	Boucher	1968	7" smiling	15	30	50
Lucy Pocket Doll	Boucher	1968	7" open mouth	15	25	45
Lucy Tea Party Game	Milton Bradley	1972		25	35	50

PEANUTS

TOY	COMPANY	YEAR	DESCRIPTION	GOOD	EX	MIB
Lucy Wristwatch	Timex	1970s	small chrome case, articulated arms, sweep seconds, white vinyl band	25	55	100
Lucy's Watch Wardrobe	Determined	1970s	white face, comes w/blue, white, and pink bands	60	100	175
Lucy's Winter Carnival Colorforms	Colorforms	1973		20	40	50
Official Peanuts Baseball	Wilson	1969	illustrated w/characters	25	95	130
Parade Drum	Chein	1969	large tin drum features characters in director's chairs	90	160	195
Peanuts Banks	United Features	1970	set of five	45	80	150
Peanuts Coloring Books	Saalfield	1960s	boxed set of five, cover features baseball scene	30	75	100
Peanuts Deluxe Play Set	Determined	1975	includes Lucy's psychiatrist booth and three action figures	90	200	250
Peanuts Drum	Chein	1974	tin, features characters w/instruments	75	110	180
Peanuts Kindergarten Rhythm Set	Chein	1972	four percussion instruments	90	160	210
Peanuts Magic Catch Puppets	Synergistics	1978	four characters w/Velcro balls	10	20	40
Peanuts Music Box	Schmid	1972	8" wooden ferris wheel box/bank, plays "Spinning Wheel"	100	235	300
Peanuts Music Box	Schmid	1985	ceramic, characters piled on car, "Clown Capers", plays "Be a Clown"	75	110	140
Peanuts Music Box	Schmid	1984	8", ceramic, characters revolve around Christmas tree, plays "Joy to the World"	75	175	225
Peanuts Pelham Puppets	Pelham/Tiderider	1979	7"-8" Charlie Brown, Snoopy or Woodstock	45	75	150
Peanuts Projects	Determined	1963	activity book	30	45	60
Peanuts Puppets Display	Pelham/Tiderider	1979	display theater	110	340	550
Peanuts Show Time Finger Puppets	Ideal	1977	several rubber character puppets	25	35	50
Peanuts Skediddler Clubhouse Set	Mattel	1970	three rubber skediddlers, Snoopy, Lucy, Charlie Brown	125	185	220
Peanuts Stackables	Determined	1979	four hard rubber figures	18	25	35
Peanuts Tea Set		1961	one tray, two plates, two cups, four small plates	25	50	100
Peanuts Trace and Color	Saalfield	1960s	five book set	35	50	75
Peanuts: A Book to Color	Saalfield		cover features Snoopy and Charlie Brown on skateboard	33	47	75
Peppermint Patty Doll			14" tall, cloth	10	13	25
Peppermint Patty Doll	Ideal	1976	removable clothing	30	40	50
Piano	Ely	1960s	wood w/characters on top	165	250	375
Picture Maker	Mattel	1971	plastic character stencils	45	65	80
Pigpen Doll	Hungerford Plastics	1958	8-1/2" plastic	65	90	125
Playmate Snoopy Doll	Determined	1971	6" plush	10	20	35
Push and Play with the Peanuts Gang	Child Guidance	1970s	plastic w/rubber characters	30	50	75
Push 'N' Fly Snoopy	Romper Room/Hasbro	1980	pull toy featuring Snoopy the Flying Ace	12	20	30
Puzzle	Determined	1971	four "Love Is" scenes, 1,000 pieces	25	40	50
Puzzle	Milton Bradley	1973	Schroeder, Charlie Brown, Snoopy, and Lucy on baseball mound	10	20	35
Puzzle	Determined	1971	eight-panel cartoon strip, 1,000 pieces	15	25	35
Puzzle	Playskool	1979	six pieces, Snoopy leaning on bat	5	8	10
Rowing Snoopy	Mattel	1981		20	40	50
Sally Doll	Hungerford Plastics	1958	6-1/2" plastic	65	95	140

TOY	COMPANY	YEAR	DESCRIPTION	GOOD	EX	MIB
Schroeder and Piano Doll	Hungerford Plastics	1958	7" plastic	110	240	350
Schroeder Music Box	Anri	1971	5", Schroeder at the piano, plays "Beethoven's Emperor's Waltz"	90	125	200
Schroeder's Piano	Child Guidance	1970s		50	95	150
Schroeder's Piano	Aviva			25	45	65
See 'N' Say Snoopy Says	Mattel	1969		40	80	95
Snoopy Action Toys	Aviva	1977	wind-up Snoopy as drummer or boxer	25	45	50
Snoopy and Charlie Brown Copter	Aviva/Hasbro	1979	plastic	15	25	35
Snoopy and his Bugatti Race Car Model Kit	Monogram/Mattel	1971		55	110	125
Snoopy and his Flyin' Doghouse	Mattel	1974		60	95	120
Snoopy and his Motorcycle Model Kit	Monogram/Mattel	1971		65	90	110
Snoopy and his Sopwith Camel Model Kit	Monogram/Mattel	1971		65	110	130
Snoopy and Woodstock in Wagon	Aviva		green die-cast w/white wheels	10	15	20
Snoopy and Woodstock on Skateboard	Aviva			10	15	20
Snoopy and Woodstock Radio	Determined	1970s	plastic, two-dimensional doghouse	20	35	65
Snoopy as Astronaut Doll	Determined	1969	9", rubber head, plastic body	30	60	125
Snoopy as Astronaut Doll	Knickerbocker		5" vinyl	30	60	125
Snoopy as Astronaut Doll	Ideal	1977	14" plush w/helmet and space suit	90	155	200
Snoopy as Astronaut Music Box	Schmid	1970s		25	40	65
Snoopy as Beagle Scout in Bus	Hasbro	1983	die-cast	4	8	15
Snoopy as Flying Ace Costume	Collegeville		w/mask	15	20	35
Snoopy as Flying Ace in Wagon	Aviva		yellow die-cast w/red wheels	10	15	25
Snoopy as Joe Cool in Wagon	Aviva		purple die-cast w/orange wheels	10	15	20
Snoopy as Magician Doll	Ideal	1977	14" plush w/cape, hat, and mustache	95	155	185
Snoopy as Rock Star Doll	Ideal	1977	14" plush w/wig, shoes and microphone	90	155	185
Snoopy Autograph Doll	Determined	1971	10-1/2"	20	25	35
Snoopy Bank	United Feature	1968	7" figural bank	15	25	50
Snoopy Bank Radio	Concept 2000	1978	plastic, Snoopy dancing	45	70	90
Snoopy Biplane	Aviva	1977	die-cast, Snoopy as Flying Ace	15	25	40
Snoopy Color 'N' Recolor	Avalon	1980		30	50	60
Snoopy Copter Pull Toy	Romper Room	1980	sound and action toy	6	10	15
Snoopy Costume	Collegeville		w/mask	12	17	25
Snoopy Deep Diver Submarine	Knickerbocker	1980s	plastic	35	55	70
Snoopy Doghouse Radio	Determined	1970s	plastic	35	55	85
Snoopy Doll	Determined	1970s	plastic jointed	25	40	50
Snoopy Doll	Hungerford Plastics	1958	7" plastic	45	75	120
Snoopy Doll	Determined	1971	15" plush, felt eyes, eyebrows, and nose; red tag around neck	20	35	60
Snoopy Doll	Ideal		7" rag doll	8	15	30

PEANUTS

TOY	COMPANY	YEAR	DESCRIPTION	GOOD	EX	MIB
Snoopy Drive-In Movie Theater	Kenner	1975		95	150	200
Snoopy Emergency Set	Hasbro		Snoopy in three vehicles	20	50	60
Snoopy Express	Aviva	1977	mechanical wind-up train, wood, includes track, tunnel, and signs	20	55	75
Snoopy Express	Aviva	1982	mechanical wind-up train, plastic	20	30	40
Snoopy Family Car	Aviva	1978		40	70	80
Snoopy Family Car	Aviva	1977	die-cast convertible, 2-1/4"	35	55	70
Snoopy Gravity Raceway	Aviva	1977		40	60	85
Snoopy Gyro Cycle	Aviva/Hasbro	1982	plastic friction toy	20	45	60
Snoopy Handfuls	Hasbro		twin pack; characters in die-cast racers	15	35	60
Snoopy Hero Time Watch	Determined	1970s	Snoopy in dancing pose, red band	55	110	185
Snoopy Hi-Fi Radio	Determined	1977	three-dimensional Snoopy wearing headphones, plastic	35	65	125
Snoopy High Wire Act	Monogram/Mattel	1973		25	45	60
Snoopy in the Music Box	Mattel	1969	metal jack-in-the-box	15	30	75
Snoopy in Tow Truck	Hasbro	1983	die-cast	5	8	15
Snoopy is Joe Cool Model Kit	Monogram/Mattel	1971	Snoopy rides surfboard	40	75	100
Snoopy Jack-in-the-Box	Romper Room/Hasbro	1980	plastic doghouse jack-in-the-box	8	15	25
Snoopy Magician Push Puppet	Ideal	1977		15	30	45
Snoopy Marionette	Pelham/Tiderider	1979	27", Pelham Puppets	210	450	550
Snoopy Movie Viewer	Kenner	1975		15	25	40
Snoopy Music Box	Schmid	1984	7" ceramic, Snoopy and Woodstock on seesaw, plays "Playmates"	75	110	130
Snoopy Music Box	Aviva	1974	6", Snoopy w/hobo pack w/Woodstock, plays "Born Free"	30	45	60
Snoopy Music Box	Aviva	1982	ceramic heart-shaped base w/Snoopy and Woodstock hugging on top, plays "Love Makes the World Go Round"	30	60	75
Snoopy Music Box	Aviva	1979	8", Snoopy on doghouse shaped box, roof is removable lid, plays "Candy Man"	35	75	100
Snoopy Music Box	Quantasia	1984	ceramic Snoopy and musical note on base, plays "Fur Elise"	35	45	65
Snoopy Music Box	Quantasia	1985	plastic, Snoopy in boat inside waterglobe, plays "Blue Hawaii"	20	40	60
Snoopy Music Box	Schmid	1986	6" ceramic, Snoopy as Lion Tamer, plays "Pussycat, Pussycat"	45	65	100
Snoopy Music Box	Schmid	1986	7-1/2" ceramic, Snoopy next to Christmas tree, plays "O, Tannenbaum"	95	150	200
Snoopy Musical Ge-tar	Mattel	1969	crank handle	25	45	75
Snoopy Musical Guitar	Aviva	1980	plastic, crank handle	15	35	50
Snoopy Nodder	Japanese	1960s	5-1/2" tall, bobbing head	20	45	90
Snoopy Paint-by-Number Set	Craft House	1980s	12" x 16"	10	20	35
Snoopy Paper Dolls	Determined	1976	w/10 outfits	20	40	50
Snoopy Phonograph	Vanity Fair	1979	features picture of dancing Snoopy	75	110	150
Snoopy Playhouse	Determined	1977	plastic doghouse w/furniture, Snoopy, and Woodstock	40	70	100
Snoopy Playland	Aviva	1978	Snoopy in bus and six other characters	45	65	90
Snoopy Pocket Doll	Boucher	1968	7" w/Flying Ace outfit	20	35	65

PEANUTS

TOY	COMPANY	YEAR	DESCRIPTION	GOOD	EX	MIB
Snoopy Racing Car Stickshifter	Aviva	1978		90	150	200
Snoopy Radio	Determined	1977	plastic square radio w/Snoopy pointing to dial	30	65	80
Snoopy Radio	Determined	1975	plastic two-dimensional	30	65	80
Snoopy Radio	Determined	1970s	figural radio, Snoopy on green grass, plastic	20	30	40
Snoopy Radio-Controlled Doghouse	Aviva	1980		35	60	75
Snoopy Radio-Controlled Fire Engine	Aviva	1980	w/Woodstock transmitter	50	75	90
Snoopy Sheriff Push Puppet	Ideal	1977		20	30	50
Snoopy Sign Mobile	Avalon	1970s		50	80	90
Snoopy Skediddler and His Sopwith Camel	Mattel	1969	w/carrying case	110	250	325
Snoopy Slot Car Racing Set	Aviva	1977		50	90	150
Snoopy Slugger	Playskool	1979	ball, bat and cap	15	22	40
Snoopy Snack Attack Game	Gabriel	1980		25	40	50
Snoopy Snippers Scissors	Mattel	1975	plastic	30	45	60
Snoopy Soaper	Kenner	1975	gold soap dispenser w/Snoopy on top	20	45	60
Snoopy Tea Set	Chein	1970	metal, features tray, plate, cups, and saucers	50	150	200
Snoopy the Critic	Aviva	1977	Snoopy and Woodstock on doghouse w/microphone	90	200	250
Snoopy the Flying Ace Push Puppet	Ideal	1977		20	30	50
Snoopy Toothbrush	Kenner	1972	Snoopy on doghouse holder	15	30	40
Snoopy Wristwatch	Lafayette Watch	1970s	Snoopy dancing, Woodstock is the second hand, silver case w/red face and black band	65	120	150
Snoopy Wristwatch	Timex	1970s	gold bezel, tennis ball circles Snoopy on clear disk, articulated hands holding racket, denim background and band	30	55	80
Snoopy Wristwatch	Determined	1969	Snoopy in dancing pose, silver or gold case, various colors	70	100	150
Snoopy, Woodstock, and Charlie Brown Radio	Concept 2000	1970s	two-dimensional plastic	20	35	45
Snoopy-Matic Instant Load Camera	Helm Toy	1970s	uses 110 film	95	150	182
Snoopy's Beagle Bugle	Child Guidance	1970s	plastic	55	80	100
Snoopy's Bubble Blowing Bubble Tub	Chemtoy	1970s		20	45	50
Snoopy's Dog House	Romper Room/Hasbro	1978	Snoopy walks on roof	20	45	50
Snoopy's Dream Machine	DCS	1980	small version, no blinking lights, laminated cardboard	55	80	100
Snoopy's Dream Machine	DCS	1979	w/blinking lights	95	155	185
Snoopy's Fantastic Automatic Bubble Pipe	Chemtoy	1970s		5	10	14
Snoopy's Good Grief Glider	Child Guidance	1970s	spring load launcher	35	65	80
Snoopy's 'Lectric Comb and Brush	Kenner	1975		35	50	60
Snoopy's Pencil Sharpener	Kenner	1974		15	40	80

CHARACTER

PEANUTS

TOY	COMPANY	YEAR	DESCRIPTION	GOOD	EX	MIB
Snoopy's Pound-A-Ball Game	Gabriel/Child Guidance	1980		35	65	80
Snoopy's Shape Register	Gabriel/Child Guidance	1980	plastic cash register	28	50	65
Snoopy's Soft House	Knickerbocker	1980	soft cloth house	25	40	50
Snoopy's Spaceship AM Radio	Concept 2000	1978	plastic	50	95	150
Snoopy's Stunt Spectacular	Child Guidance	1978	Snoopy on motorcycle	35	50	64
Snoopy's Swim and Sail Club	Child Guidance	1970s	characters and water vehicles	45	75	92
Snoopy's Take-a-Part Doghouse	Gabriel/Child Guidance	1980		15	25	45
Speak Up, Charlie Brown Talking Storybook	Mattel	1971	cardboard w/vinyl pages	80	120	150
Spinning Top	Ohio Art		5", Snoopy and the Gang	10	20	40
Spinning Top	Chein	1960s	faces of Snoopy, Charlie Brown, Lucy, and Linus	32	55	100
Stack-Up Snoopy	Romper Room/Hasbro	1980		10	13	18
Super Cartoon Maker	Mattel	1970	molds to make character figures	65	120	140
Swimming Snoopy	Concept 2000	1970s		20	40	48
Table Top Snoopy Game	Nintendo	1980s		65	125	150
Tabletop Hockey	Munro Games	1972		65	115	150
Talking Peanuts Bus	Chein	1967	metal, chracters seen in windows	100	325	575
Tell Time Clock	Concept 2000	1980s	three styles: Snoopy, Woodstock or Charlie Brown	18	25	35
Tell Us a Riddle, Snoopy Game	Colorforms	1974		20	55	85
Tub Time Snoopy Doll	Knickerbocker	1980s	rubber	20	35	40
Vaporizer/Humidifier	Milton Bradley		plastic, 13" x 16", Snoopy on doghouse	45	75	100
Woodstock Climbing String Action	Aviva/Hasbro	1977	plastic	15	28	40
Woodstock Costume	Collegeville		w/mask	15	20	30
Woodstock in Ice Cream Truck	Aviva		friction vehicle	6	9	15
Yankee Doodle Snoopy	Colorforms	1975		20	35	45

PETER PAN

TOY	COMPANY	YEAR	DESCRIPTION	GOOD	EX	MIB
Captain Hook Figure			8" tall, plastic	10	20	35
Captain Hook Hand Puppet	Gund	1950s	9" tall	33	65	135
Peter Pan Baby Figure	Sun Rubber	1950s		35	75	150
Peter Pan Charm Bracelet		1974		20	30	75
Peter Pan Doll	Duchess Doll	1953	11-1/2" tall, brown trim fabric shoes, green mesh stockings w/flocked outfit, hat w/a large red feather, shiny silver white metal dagger in belt, eyes, arms and head move	140	300	520
Peter Pan Doll	Ideal	1953	18" tall	100	200	325
Peter Pan Hand Puppet	Oak Rubber	1953	rubber	30	55	110
Peter Pan Map of Neverland		1953	18" x 24", collectors issue for users of Peter Pan Beauty Bar	40	150	225
Peter Pan Nodder		1950s	6" tall	70	140	300
Peter Pan Paper Dolls	Whitman	1952	11 die-cut cardboard figures	30	90	175
Peter Pan Push Puppet	Kohner	1950s	6" tall, green and flesh colored beads, plastic head, light green plastic hat	20	45	90

223

PETER PAN

TOY	COMPANY	YEAR	DESCRIPTION	GOOD	EX	MIB
Peter Pan Sewing Cards	Whitman	1952		15	25	50
Puzzle	Jaymar	1950s	frame tray puzzle shows Peter, Wendy, John and Michael flying over Neverland	15	35	75
Tinker Bell Doll	Duchess Doll	1953	8" tall, flocked green outfit w/a pair of large white fabric wings w/gold trim, eyes open and close, jointed arms and head moves	90	200	400
Tinker Bell Figure	Sutton	1960s	7" tall, plastic and rubber figure	25	50	85
Tinker Bell Pincushion		1960s	w/1-1/2" tall Tinker Bell figure, in clear plastic display can	25	40	90
Wendy Doll	Duchess Doll	1953	8" tall, full purple length skirt w/purple bow in back of dress, eyes open and close, jointed arms and head moves	90	200	400

PHANTOM

TOY	COMPANY	YEAR	DESCRIPTION	GOOD	EX	MIB
Oil Paint by Numbers Set	Hasbro	1967		225	320	550
Phantom 2040 Carded Toys	Ja-Ru	1995	sword, crossbow, gun or whistle light	8	12	20
Phantom 2040 Rubber Ball	Unice	1995		12	17	30
Phantom Archery Set	Larami	1976	bow, arrows, animals	75	125	175
Phantom Binoculars	Larami	1976		120	155	225
Phantom Candy Jar	KFS	1996	plastic w/figural lid	12	22	40
Phantom Club Rubber Stamper Skull Ring		1950s		850	1200	1600
Phantom Costume	Ben Cooper	1950s		175	225	325
Phantom Costume	CHaracter Costumes	1989		40	55	75
Phantom Costume	Collegeville	1970s		70	90	150
Phantom Dagger Set	Larami	1976	knife and sheath	100	120	200
Phantom Desert Survival Kit	Larami	1976	canteen and Thermos bottle	80	120	175
Phantom Figure		1980s	6" dark blue PVC figure	25	35	50
Phantom Figure	Street Players	1996	4" action figure w/skull throne or horse	10	15	30
Phantom Figure		1990s	6" purple PVC figure	12	25	50
Phantom Figures	Spain	1990	3-1/2", two pieces, purple PVC	10	15	30
Phantom Giant Games Book	World Distributors	1968		80	125	175
Phantom Jungle Play Set	Larami	1976	figure, palm trees, animals	110	160	225
Phantom Pathfinder Set	Larami	1976	compass, canteen, binoculars, case	80	120	175
Phantom Pinback		1940s	club member cello, Australia	250	700	1000
Phantom Puffy Magnet	Hanna-Barbera	1975		40	50	70
Phantom Safari Set	Larami	1976	figure, truck, trailer, animals	130	180	275
Phantom Squirt Camera	Larami	1976		80	120	175
Phantom Water Pistol	Nasta	1974		80	120	175
Phantom Water Pistol	Nasta	1974	w/holster	70	80	150
Playing Cards	Bulls Dist.	1990	Swedish	16	22	35
Playing Cards	John Sands	1990		16	22	35
Rub-On Transfer Set	Hasbro	1967		100	120	200
Syrocco Figure	Pillsbury Mills	1944	brown	1100	1300	1850
Syrocco Figure	Pillsbury Mills	1944	purple	520	850	1300

PINK PANTHER

TOY	COMPANY	YEAR	DESCRIPTION	GOOD	EX	MIB
Pink Panther and The Fancy Party Book	Golden			5	10	15
Pink Panther and The Haunted House Book	Golden			5	10	15

CHARACTER

PINK PANTHER

TOY	COMPANY	YEAR	DESCRIPTION	GOOD	EX	MIB
Pink Panther at Castle Kreep Book	Whitman			5	10	15
Pink Panther at The Circus Sticker Book	Golden	1963		8	15	35
Pink Panther Coloring Book	Whitman	1976	cover shows Pink Panther roasting hot dogs	8	15	35
Pink Panther Figure	Dakin	1971	8" tall, w/legs closed	15	30	75
Pink Panther Figure	Dakin	1971	8" tall, w/legs open	15	30	75
Pink Panther Memo Board			write on/wipe off memo board	5	10	15
Pink Panther Motorcycle			2-1/2" plastic	5	10	20
Pink Panther Music Box	Royal Orleans	1983	Christmas limited edition	25	60	100
Pink Panther Music Box	Royal Orleans	1984	Christmas limited edition	25	60	100
Pink Panther Music Box	Royal Orleans	1982	Christmas limited edition	25	60	100
Pink Panther One-Man Band	Illco	1980	10" tall, battery-operated, plush body w/vinyl head	25	55	85
Pink Panther Pool Game	Ja-Ru	1980s		4	10	20
Pink Panther Putty	Ja-Ru	1970s		4	7	10
Pink Panther Wind-Up			3" tall, plastic, walking wind-up w/trench coat and glasses	10	15	35
Puzzle	Whitman	1960s	100 pieces, several pictures available, each	10	20	45

PINOCCHIO AND JIMINY CRICKET

TOY	COMPANY	YEAR	DESCRIPTION	GOOD	EX	MIB
Figaro Figure	Knickerbocker	1940s	composition, movable limbs and head	95	160	275
Figaro Figure	Multi-Wood Products	1940	3" tall, wood composition	32	80	200
Figaro Friction Toy	Linemar	1960s	1-1/2" x 3" x 1-1/2", tin	55	125	250
Figaro Roll Over Wind-Up Toy	Marx	1940	5" long w/ears and tail, tin	130	230	450
Gepetto Figure	Multi-Wood Products	1940	5-1/2" tall, wood composition	55	100	160
Gideon Figure	Multi-Wood Products		5" tall	40	70	185
Honest John Figure	Multi-Wood Products		2-1/2" x 3" base w/a 7" tall figure	50	90	250
Jiminy Cricket Doll	Ideal	1940	wooden jointed	130	260	500
Jiminy Cricket Figure	Marx		3-1/2" x 4-3/4" tall, Snap-Eeze, white plastic base w/movable arms and legs	30	55	85
Jiminy Cricket Figure	Ideal	1940s	wood jointed, hand painted	160	220	375
Jiminy Cricket Hand Puppet	Gund	1950s	11" tall	20	45	110
Jiminy Cricket Marionette	Pelham Puppets	1950s	3" x 6" x 10" tall, dark green head with, large eyes, gray felt hat	75	150	300
Jiminy Cricket Ramp Walker	Marx	1960s	1" x 3" x 3" tall, pushing a bass fiddle	80	130	260
Jiminy Cricket Soaky			7" tall bottle	12	45	70
Jiminy Cricket Toothbrush Set	Dupont	1950s	plastic wall hanging Jiminy holds a toothbrush	30	55	85
Jiminy Cricket Wristwatch	US Time	1948	Birthday Series	55	155	350
Lampwick Figure	Multi-Wood Products	1940	5-1/2" tall, wood composition	40	100	200
Pin the Nose on Pinocchio Game	Parker Brothers	1939	15-1/2" x 20"	35	90	175
Pinocchio and Jiminy Cricket Dolls	Knickerbocker	1962	6" tall, vinyl, titled "Knixies", each	25	50	100
Pinocchio and Jiminy Push Puppet	Marx	1960s	2-1/2" x 5" x 4" tall, double puppet	30	45	100
Pinocchio Bank	Play Pal Plastics	1970s	7" x 7" x 10" tall, vinyl, 3-D molded head of Pinocchio	10	20	35
Pinocchio Bank	Crown Toy	1939	5" tall, wood composition w/metal trap door on back	65	125	300

PINOCCHIO AND JIMINY CRICKET

TOY	COMPANY	YEAR	DESCRIPTION	GOOD	EX	MIB
Pinocchio Bank	Play Pal Plastics	1960s	11-1/2" tall, plastic	15	25	40
Pinocchio Book		1940	Big Little Book	25	60	120
Pinocchio Book	Grosset and Dunlap	1939	9-1/2" x 13", laminated cover	25	50	110
Pinocchio Book	Whitman	1939	96 pages	18	32	75
Pinocchio Book Set	Whitman	1940	8-1/2" x 11-1/2", set of six books, 24 pages each	80	180	360
Pinocchio Color Box	Transogram		also known as paint box	18	35	75
Pinocchio Crayon Box	Transogram	1940s	4-1/2" x 5-1/2" x 1/2" deep, tin	18	35	70
Pinocchio Cut-Out Book	Whitman	1940		35	75	160
Pinocchio Doll	Knickerbocker	1940	3-1/2" x 4" x 9 1/2" tall, jointed composition doll w/movable arms and head	200	430	800
Pinocchio Doll	Ideal	1939	12" tall w/wire mesh arms and legs	85	190	425
Pinocchio Doll	Ideal	1940	19-1/2" tall, composition	230	450	785
Pinocchio Doll	Ideal	1940	10" tall, wood composition head, jointed arms and legs attached to body	60	135	350
Pinocchio Doll	Ideal	1940	8" tall, wood composition head, others are jointed wood	65	110	275
Pinocchio Figure	Crown Toy		9-1/2" tall, jointed arms	45	95	200
Pinocchio Figure	Multi-Wood Products	1940	5" tall, wood composition	45	85	210
Pinocchio Hand Puppet	Gund	1950s	10" tall, w/squeaker	25	50	125
Pinocchio Hand Puppet	Knickerbocker	1962		25	50	85
Pinocchio Hand Puppet	Crown Toy		9" tall, composition	25	45	50
Pinocchio Music Box			plays "Puppet on a String"	15	30	60
Pinocchio Paint Book	Disney	1939	11" x 15", heavy paper cover	30	65	150
Pinocchio Paperweight and Thermometer	Plastic Novelties	1940		25	50	85
Pinocchio Plastic Cup	Safetyware	1939	2-3/4" tall, plastic	25	50	100
Pinocchio Push Puppet	Kohner	1960s	5" tall	15	25	65
Pinocchio Snow Dome	Disney	1970s	3" x 4-1/2" x 5" tall, Pinocchio holds plastic dome between hands and feet	15	40	75
Pinocchio Soaky				12	35	70
Pinocchio Tea Set	Ohio Art	1939	tin tray, plates, saucers, serving platter, cups, bowls and smaller plates	55	100	250
Pinocchio the Acrobat Wind-Up Toy	Marx	1939	2-1/2" x 11" x 17" tall, turning on a trapeze-like frame	300	560	925
Pinocchio Walker	Marx	1939	9" tall, tin, animated eyes, rocking action	210	420	775
Pinocchio Wind-Up Toy	Linemar		6" tall, tin wind-up, arms and legs move	100	180	375
Puzzle	Jaymar	1960s	5" x 7", "Pinocchio's Expedition"	12	22	35
Walt Disney Tells the Story of Pinocchio Book	Whitman	1939	4-1/4" x 6-1/2" paperback, 144 pages	30	55	80
Walt Disney's Pinocchio Book	Random House	1939	8-1/2" x 11-1/2", hardcover	20	45	70

PLUTO

TOY	COMPANY	YEAR	DESCRIPTION	GOOD	EX	MIB
Pluto Alarm Clock	Allied	1955	4" x 5-1/2" x 10" tall, eyes and hands shaped like dog bones, glow in the dark	60	125	250
Pluto Bank	Animal Toys Plus	1970s	9" tall vinyl, Pluto standing in front of a doghouse	20	35	60
Pluto Bank	Disney	1940s	4" x 4-1/2" x 6-1/2", ceramic	35	65	120
Pluto Figure	Seiberling	1930s	3-1/2" long, rubber	35	80	150
Pluto Figure	Seiberling	1930s	7" tall, rubber	35	80	150

CHARACTER

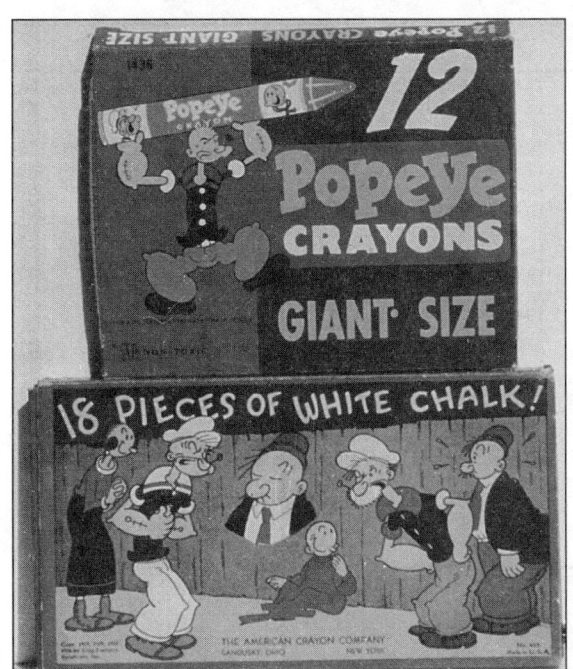

*Popeye Crayons, 1933,
American Crayon*

Popeye Soaky, 1987, KFS

PLUTO

TOY	COMPANY	YEAR	DESCRIPTION	GOOD	EX	MIB
Pluto Fun-E-Flex Figure	Fun-E-Flex	1930s	wood	30	55	135
Pluto Hand Puppet	Gund	1950s	9" tall	15	35	75
Pluto Lantern Toy	Linemar	1950s		130	280	475
Pluto Pop-A-Part Toy	Multiple Toymakers	1965	9" long, plastic	20	35	50
Pluto Pop-Up Critter Figure	Fisher-Price	1936	wooden, Pluto standing on base 10-1/2" long	80	150	200
Pluto Purse	Gund	1940s	9" x 14" x 2"	25	55	100
Pluto Push Toy	Fisher-Price	1936	8" long, wood	70	150	300
Pluto Rolykin	Marx		1" x 1" x 1-1/2" tall, ball bearing action	15	35	70
Pluto Sports Car	Empire		2" long	10	18	30
Pluto the Acrobat Trapeze Toy	Linemar		10" tall, metal, celluloid, wind-up	65	210	275
Pluto the Drum Major	Marx/Linemar	1950s	tin, mechanical	180	350	750
Pluto Toy	Linemar		4" long, friction motor makes tongue wag	35	80	275
Pluto Toy	Linemar		9" friction toy, Pluto pulling red wagon	65	130	300
Pluto Tricycle Toy	Linemar	1950s	tin	155	330	675
Pluto Watch Me Roll Over	Marx	1939	8" long, tin, Pluto turns over as his tail passes beneath him	155	300	500

POPEYE

TOY	COMPANY	YEAR	DESCRIPTION	GOOD	EX	MIB
60th Anniversary Bank	Presents	1988	metal, P5988	5	15	30
60th Anniversary Candle Box	Presents	1989	metal, heart shaped, #P5979	5	10	20
60th Anniversary Collection Book	Hawk Books	1990		20	35	50
Adventures of Popeye Book	Saalfield	1934		25	100	275
Adventures of Popeye Game	Transogram	1957		35	75	150
Apprentice Printer	MSS	1970s		6	15	30
Ball and Jacks Set	MSS			6	10	20
Ball and Paddle	BC			6	10	20
Balloon Pump		1957	inflato-pump	25	50	100
Barber Shop	Larami	1970s		5	15	25
Baseball	Ja-Ru	1983		5	10	35
Beach Boat	H.G. Industries	1980	red or yellow	5	10	35
Bell	Vandor	1980	Popeye on top, ceramic	8	15	25
Belt Buckle	U.S. Spinach Growers		Strength thru Spinach	8	15	25
Belt Buckle	Pyramid Belt	1973	Popeye w/sailor hat	10	20	40
Belt Buckle	Lee	1980	Popeye w/spinach	8	15	25
Biffbat-Fly Back Paddle		1935		15	30	75
Big Surprise Book	Wonder Books	1976		5	10	25
Billion Bubbles	Larami	1984		4	8	15
Blackboard	Bar Zim	1962		15	33	75
Blinky Cup	Beacon Plastics			8	15	25
Bluto Button	Lisa Frank	1979	2", Bluto getting socked	2	3	10
Bluto Dippy Dumper	Marx	1935	wind-up	210	450	850
Bluto Figure	Cristallerie Antonio		Italian crystal	10	25	60
Bluto Wind-Up Toy	Marx	1938	celluloid, w/Brutus, horse, and cart	350	530	800
Bookends	Vandor	1980	ceramic, Popeye and Brutus	20	45	75
Bop Bag	Miner Industries	1981		6	12	25
Bowl	National Home Products	1979	plastic	5	10	20
Bowl	Deka	1971	oval, plastic	10	20	30
Bowl	Vandor	1980	ceramic, 1 of 3	8	18	30
Boxing Game	Harmony	1981		5	10	20
Boxing Gloves	Everlast	1960s		25	55	110
Brutus Button	Strand	1985	3", "Gonna Eat You for Breakfast"	2	3	6

POPEYE

TOY	COMPANY	YEAR	DESCRIPTION	GOOD	EX	MIB
Brutus Button	Strand	1985	3", "Ya Little Runt"	2	3	6
Brutus Button	Mini Media	1983	1", "I'm Mean"	2	3	6
Brutus Button	Factors	1980	3", movie	2	3	6
Brutus Dog Toy	Petex	1986		5	10	20
Brutus Doll	Presents	1985	large with tag	9	30	75
Brutus Doll	Presents	1985	small	5	15	40
Brutus Figure	Presents	1990	PVC	2	3	6
Brutus Figure	Comic-Spain	1984	Brutus w/club	4	7	12
Brutus Figure	Bully	1981	pink shirt	5	13	25
Brutus Figure	Japan Olympics	1962	wood, Brutus in barrel	75	175	325
Brutus Figure	KFS-Hearst	1991	wood	4	7	12
Brutus Figure Painting Kit	Avalon	1980		6	10	30
Brutus Hand Puppet	Gund	1960s		18	30	85
Brutus Hi-Pop Ball	Ja-Ru	1981		6	10	18
Brutus Hookies	Tiger	1977		5	18	50
Brutus in Jeep		1950s	tiny plastic car	15	30	55
Brutus in Steamroller	Lesney/Matchbox	1980	Matchbox	8	18	40
Brutus Jump-Up	Imperial	1970s		8	18	35
Brutus Mini Bank	KFS	1979		10	20	35
Brutus Music Box	Presents	1989	#P5984	8	15	30
Brutus Music Box	KFS	1980	Brutus dancing	10	15	30
Brutus Painting Kit	Avalon	1980		8	15	25
Brutus Soaky	Colgate-Palmolive	1960s		15	35	70
Brutus Sports Car		1950s	tiny plastic car	10	25	55
Brutus Wind-Up Toy	Durham	1980		5	10	25
Bubble Blower	Transogram	1958		15	35	60
Bubble Blower Boat	Larami	1984		6	10	20
Bubble Blowing Popeye	Linemar	1950s		275	550	1200
Bubble Blowing Train	Hong Kong	1970s	pink	8	18	30
Bubble 'N Clean	Woolfoam	1960s		20	45	75
Bubble Pipe	KFS	1960s	yellow w/red end	10	25	50
Bubble Pipe	Ja-Ru	1985		5	10	20
Bubble Set	Transogram	1936	two wooden pipes, tray, soap in 5" x 7-1/2" box	25	80	175
Bubble Shooter	Ja-Ru	1980s	orange or yellow body	5	10	20
Bubbleblaster	Carlin Playthings	1980		10	15	25
Bubbles Blaster	Larami	1984		5	10	18
Bubbles with Dip Pow Bubbles	MSS	1986		5	10	18
Button	Offset Gravure	1930s	1", New York Evening Journal	15	35	85
Button	Mini Media	1983	1", "No Wimps"	2	4	8
Cabinet			mirrored	30	55	125
Candy	Alberts	1980	bonbons	6	10	15
Candy Box	Phoenix Candy	1960	Popeye and his pals	15	25	65
Candy Cigarettes	Primrose Confectionery - England	1959		10	20	40
Candy Rings	Alberts	1989		6	15	20
Candy Sticks	World Candies	1990	48 count	6	15	20
Candy Sticks	Hearst	1989	red box	6	15	20
Cap Gun	Ja-Ru	1981		6	15	30
Captain George Presents Popeye Book	Memory Lane	1970		5	10	35
Cereal Bowl	National Home Products	1979		5	10	25
Cereal Box	Cocoa-Puffs	1987	w/gum	3	10	25
Chain Bubbles Maker	Larami	1984	red Popeye	6	10	20
Chalk	American Crayon	1936	white, 18 pieces	10	35	85
Change Purse	Sanrio	1990		5	10	20
Character Figures	Popeye's Chicken	1991	blue plastic, several characters available	1	3	8

POPEYE

TOY	COMPANY	YEAR	DESCRIPTION	GOOD	EX	MIB
Character Figures	Spoontiques	1980	2" figures: Popeye w/barbell, Popeye w/parrot, Olive walking, Popeye flexing muscles, Popeye w/spinach, each	10	20	35
Character Figures	Spoontiques	1981	pewter, three 1" figures: Olive w/hands clasped, Popeye w/muscles, Jeep standing, each	10	20	30
Character Figures	Spoontiques	1980	two 1" figures: Jeep lifting tail, Swee'Pea w/feet showing, each	10	20	30
Charm Bracelet	Peter Brams	1990	silver or gold	10	18	25
Checker Board	Ideal	1959		15	30	65
Chimes Doll	J. Swedlin	1950s	gray plush body, chimes	15	45	75
Chinese Jump Rope	MSS			4	10	20
Chocolate Mold		1940s	metal, Popeye	35	80	150
Chocolate Mold	Turmic Plastics	1991	plastic, Popeye	3	6	10
Christmas Lamp Shades	General Electric	1930s	set of ten	60	160	350
Christmas Light Covers	General Electric Textolite	1929	"Cheers"	30	85	350
Christmas Ornament	Bully	1981	Dufus	8	15	25
Christmas Ornament	Bully	1981	Bluto	8	15	25
Christmas Ornament	Presents	1987	Alice the Goon, Swee'Pea, Wimpy, Popeye, Olive Oyl or Brutus, each	4	8	20
Christmas Ornament	Presents	1989	Season's Greetings	4	8	20
Christmas Tree Lamp Set	General Electric	1935		70	160	300
Circus Man Film	Brumberger	1950s	8mm	10	25	50
Clothes Brush	KFS	1929	wooden, black or brown	20	60	175
Color Markers	Sanrio	1990	six	2	5	8
Colorforms Birthday Party Set	Colorforms	1961		20	60	110
Colorforms Movie Version	Colorforms	1980		7	15	30
Color-Me Stickers	Diamond Toymakers	1983		5	10	20
Color-Vue Pencil-by-Numbers	Hasbro	1979		10	18	30
Comb and Brush	KFS	1979		7	15	40
Construction Trucks	Larami	1981		6	12	25
Cookie Jar	McCoy	1965	ceramic white-suited Popeye	50	175	300
Cook's Catch-All	KFS	1980	ceramic, Wimpy	10	20	35
Crayons	Dixon	1958	12 giant crayons	10	20	50
Crayons	American Crayon	1950s		10	20	50
Crayons	American Crayon	1933	12 giant crayons	10	25	75
Cup	New Zealand	1940s	Popeye on skis, ceramic	18	40	70
Daily Dime Bank	KFS	1956		20	75	150
Daily Quarter Bank	Kalon	1950s	4-1/2" tall, metal	60	125	225
Danger Ahoy! Book	Whitman	1969	Big Little Book	5	10	20
Deep Sea Danger Book	Whitman	1980	Big Little Book	2	4	10
Dice		1990	w/Popeye head	1	3	5
Dime Register Bank	KFS	1929	square, window shows total deposits	40	175	300
Dish	New Zealand	1940s	ceramic, Popeye and Olive	20	45	90
Dish Set	Boontonware	1964	three piece plastic	20	45	80
Dockside Presto Magix	APC	1980		3	6	12
Double Action Water Gun Set	MSS			4	10	20
Drawing Board	KFS	1978	slate w/rope attached	8	16	30
Drawing Desk	Carlin Playthings	1980		10	20	40
Duck Shoot	Ja-Ru	1980s		5	10	25
Dufus Figure	Bully	1981	w/hand on stomach	8	15	28
Egg Cup	Japan	1940s	Popeye sitting at table w/spinach	30	65	125
Egg Cup and Mug	Magna	1989	Great Britain	15	40	75

POPEYE

TOY	COMPANY	YEAR	DESCRIPTION	GOOD	EX	MIB
Erase-O-Board and Magic Screen Set	Hassenfeld Bros.	1957		25	60	100
Film Card	Tru-Vue	1959	T-28	8	20	50
Film Projector	Cinexin-Spain		8mm w/13 movies	65	140	210
Finger Puppet Family	Denmark Plastics	1960s		20	45	85
Flashlight	Bantam-Lite	1960s	three color, wrist light	8	15	25
Flashlight	Larami	1983	blue, yellow, or red	5	10	20
Fleas A Crowd Record	Peter Pan	1962	78 rpm	8	15	25
Foto-Fun Printing Kit	Fun Bilt	1958		20	45	100
Freezicles	Imperial	1980		5	15	20
Fun Booklets	Spot-O-Gold	1980	set of 10	10	25	60
Funny Color Foam	Creative Aerosol	1983		5	15	60
Funny Face Maker	Jaymar	1962		15	30	65
Funny Films Viewer	Acme	1940s		20	40	85
Funny Fire Fighters	Marx	1930s	celluloid figures, Popeye on ladder and Bluto drives fire truck--both figures wear boxing gloves	250	1100	2000
Ghost Ship to Treasure Island Book	Whitman	1967	Big Little Book	8	15	25
Giant 24 Big Picture Coloring Book	Merrigold Press	1981		4	8	20
Giant Paint Book	Whitman	1937	blue or red	25	65	150
Give-A-Show Projector	Kenner		projector w/slides	35	75	150
Great Big Popeye Paint and Crayon Book	McLoughlin Bros.	1937		25	65	150
Gumball Dispenser	Superior Toys	1983	pocket pack	5	10	20
Gumball Machine	Hasbro	1968	6", shape of Popeye's head	10	20	65
Gumball Machine	Superior Toys	1983	Popeye eating spinach	7	15	35
Gumball Machine	Superior Toys	1983	Popeye gives Olive flowers	7	15	35
Hag of the Seven Seas Pop-Up Book	Blue Ribbon Books	1935		45	150	300
Halloween Bucket	Renz	1979	shaped like Popeye's head, red, yellow or blue	10	15	35
Harmonica	Larami	1973		10	25	60
Hat and Pipe	Empire Plastics	1950s		18	35	75
Holster Set	Halco	1960s		25	75	175
Horseshoe Magnets	Larami	1984		5	10	20
House that Popeye Built Book	Wonder Books	1960		5	12	35
Hunting Knife	Larami	1973		10	25	60
ID Set	Gordy	1982		5	13	20
In a Sock for Susan's Sake Book	Whitman	1940	Big Little Book	20	60	120
In Quest of Poopdeck Pappy Book	Whitman	1937	Big Little Book	20	60	120
Indian Fighter Film	Atlas Films		8mm	5	10	20
Jack-in-the-Box	Mattel	1961		40	80	150
Jack-in-the-Box	Nasta	1979		15	35	65
Jack-in-the-Box	Nasta	1983		10	20	40
Jackknife	Imperial	1940s	green Popeye on pearl handle	30	85	160
Jeep Doll	Presents	1985	two sizes	8	13	35
Jeep Figure	KFS-Hearst	1991	wood	4	10	20
Jeep Lucky Spinner	KFS	1936		30	85	200
Jeep Wall Plaque			ceramic	5	10	25
Jiffy Pop Fun 'N Games Booklet	Spot-O-Gold	1980		5	10	20
Jumbo Card Game	House of Games	1978		8	15	25
Jumbo Trading Card Game	Dynamic Toy	1960s		8	20	50
Kaleidoscope	Larami	1979		6	15	35
Kazoo and Harmonica	Larami	1979		6	15	25
Kazoo Pipe	Northwestern Products	1934		20	35	85
Kazoo Pipe	Peerless Playthings	1960s	yellow	10	20	50
King of the Jungle Film	Atlas Films	1960s	8mm	5	10	25

TOY	COMPANY	YEAR	DESCRIPTION	GOOD	EX	MIB
Kite	Sky-Way	1980	inflatable	6	12	20
Kite	Sky-Way	1980	regular	4	8	18
Knapsack	Fabil	1979		10	15	30
Knockout Bank	Straits	1935		190	450	875
Kooky Straw	Imperial	1980		4	10	20
Lamp		1940s	boat w/Popeye light bulb	210	500	900
Lantern	Linemar	1950s	7-1/2" tall, battery operated, light in belly	130	230	450
Life Raft	KFS	1979	large, blue	10	20	30
Little Pops the Ghost Book	Random House	1981		5	10	20
Little Pops the Magic Flute Book	Random House	1981		5	10	20
Little Pops the Spinach Burgers Book	Random House	1981		5	10	20
Little Pops the Treasure Hunt Book	Random House	1981		5	10	20
Magic Eyes Film Card	Tru-Vue	1962	set of three	15	25	60
Magic Glow Putty	FC Famous Toys			6	10	15
Magic Play Around Game	Amsco	1960s		20	45	85
Magic Slate	Lowe	1959		10	20	60
Magic Slate Paper Saver	Whitman	1981		4	8	15
Make-A-Picture Premium	Quaker	1934		10	50	100
Marble		1940s	1" blue/white w/black/white or red Popeye	8	20	25
Marble Set	Imperial	1980		5	10	25
Marble Set	Akro Agate	1935	#116	100	350	800
Marble Shooter		1940s	milk glass container	15	30	45
Metal Tapping Set	Carlton Dank	1950s		25	50	100
Metal Target Set	Ja-Ru	1983		8	15	30
Metal Whistle	Ja-Ru	1981		5	10	20
Micro-Movie	Fascinations	1990	Popeye-Ali Baba	4	8	15
Mini Hurricane Lamp	Presents	1989	P5981-1993, 60th year	4	8	15
Mini Lunch Box	Sanrio	1990	plastic	4	8	15
Mini Memo Board	Freelance	1980		5	10	15
Miniature Train Set	Larami	1980		6	11	20
Mirror	Freelance	1979	Olive w/mirror	7	13	20
Mirror	Freelance	1978	Popeye lifting weights	8	13	18
Mirror Rattle	Cribmates	1979		8	13	20
Mix or Match Storybook	Random House	1981		5	10	20
Model Kit	Carto	1970s	Popeye and Olive Oyl	25	50	110
Modeling Clay	American Crayon	1936		25	65	175
Motor Friend	Nasta	1976		10	20	50
Mug	Schmid	1950s	ceramic	10	20	40
Muscle Builder Bluto	Carlin Playthings	1980		6	12	20
Muscle Builder Popeye	Carlin Playthings	1980		6	12	20
Music Box	Vandor	1980	revolving Olive w/Popeye dancing, ceramic	18	35	75
Music Box	Vandor	1980	Wimpy on top of hamburger, ceramic	18	35	75
Music Box	Vandor	1980	revolving Popeye spanks Swee'Pea, ceramic	18	35	75
Music Lovers Film	Atlas Films	1960s	8mm	8	15	20
Musical Mug	KFS	1982	ceramic	10	20	35
Musical Rattle	Cribmates	1979		8	13	20
My Popeye Coloring Kit	American Crayon	1957		20	60	120
Official Popeye Pipe		1958	5" stem w/2" bowl, battery operated, "It lites, it toots"	20	75	150
Old Time Wild West Train	Larami	1984		5	10	25
Olive Oyl and Swee'Pea Hot Water Bottle	Duarry	1970		30	85	150

POPEYE

TOY	COMPANY	YEAR	DESCRIPTION	GOOD	EX	MIB
Olive Oyl and Swee'Pea Snow Globe	Presents	1989	several styles	4	10	20
Olive Oyl and Swee'Pea Telephone Shoulder Rest	Comvu	1982		5	10	25
Olive Oyl and Swee'Pea Thermometer	KFS	1981		8	13	18
Olive Oyl and Swee'Pea Wash Up Book	Tuffy Books	1980		3	8	15
Olive Oyl Bank		1940s	cast iron	65	175	300
Olive Oyl Bike Bobbers	KFS	1960s		15	25	50
Olive Oyl Button	Factors	1980	3"	1	2	5
Olive Oyl Button	Pep	1946		8	22	38
Olive Oyl Button	Mini Media	1983	1", "More than just a pretty face"	1	2	5
Olive Oyl Costume	Collegeville	1950s		15	35	85
Olive Oyl Costume	Ben Cooper	1976		8	20	50
Olive Oyl Cup	Coke	1977	Coke Kollect-A-Set	4	8	20
Olive Oyl Doll	Presents	1991	Christmas, small	8	13	20
Olive Oyl Doll	Dakin	1970s	Cartoon Theatre, in box	15	40	85
Olive Oyl Doll	Rempel	1950s	small	15	40	85
Olive Oyl Doll	Presents	1990	small molded plastic, musical # P5948	8	13	20
Olive Oyl Doll	Presents	1991	small molded plastic, # P5966	4	8	15
Olive Oyl Doll	Presents	1985	Christmas, large	14	25	35
Olive Oyl Doll	Toy Toons	1990		4	7	12
Olive Oyl Doll			9" vinyl sqeeze doll, Olive w/Swee'Pea	12	25	60
Olive Oyl Doll	Dakin	1960s	8" tall	18	35	75
Olive Oyl Doll	Uneeda	1979	removable clothing	10	25	50
Olive Oyl Doll	Dakin	1970s	hard plastic w/removable clothes	15	35	75
Olive Oyl Doll	Presents	1985	small	8	15	20
Olive Oyl Figure	Chester	1990	10", Olive w/rolling pin	5	12	25
Olive Oyl Figure	Presents	1990	3" tall, plastic	1	3	6
Olive Oyl Figure		1940s	lead	10	25	50
Olive Oyl Figure	KFS	1980	arms clamped together, hanging figure	5	10	25
Olive Oyl Figure	Bully	1981	w/hands clasp	8	15	25
Olive Oyl Figure	Bully	1981	holding flower	8	15	25
Olive Oyl Figure	Multiple Toymakers	1950s	2" tall	7	15	35
Olive Oyl Figure	Comics Spain	1984	PVC, Olive w/flower	3	7	15
Olive Oyl Figure	Presents	1990	PVC	1	3	6
Olive Oyl Figure		1940s	5" wooden jointed	30	100	250
Olive Oyl Figure	KFS-Hearst	1991	wood	4	7	12
Olive Oyl Figure	Mexico	1990	ceramic	5	12	25
Olive Oyl Figure	Amscan	1980	large bendy	6	12	20
Olive Oyl Figure	Jesco	1988	small bendy	2	4	10
Olive Oyl Figure	Jesco	1988	large bendy	3	6	15
Olive Oyl Figure	Comics Spain	1986	6" bendy	4	8	15
Olive Oyl Figure	Ben Cooper	1974	rubber	10	25	50
Olive Oyl Figure	KFS	1940	8" tall	30	90	200
Olive Oyl Figure	Cristallerie Antonio		Italian crystal	10	15	35
Olive Oyl Figure Painting Kit	Avalon	1980		6	12	20
Olive Oyl Foam Toy	Cribmates	1979		8	15	35
Olive Oyl Hairbrush	Cribmates	1979	musical	8	15	35
Olive Oyl Hand Puppet	Gund	1960s	comic strip body	20	45	100
Olive Oyl Hi-Pop Ball	Ja-Ru	1981		5	10	30
Olive Oyl Hookies	Tiger	1977		4	10	30
Olive Oyl in a Sports Car	Lesney/Matchbox	1980		8	15	40
Olive Oyl in Airplane	Corgi	1970s		8	15	40
Olive Oyl Jump-Up	Imperial			5	10	20
Olive Oyl Marionette	Gund	1950s	11-1/2" tall	30	75	175
Olive Oyl Mini Bank	KFS	1979		10	20	40

TOY	COMPANY	YEAR	DESCRIPTION	GOOD	EX	MIB
Olive Oyl Mug	Schmid	1950s	musical ceramic	15	40	75
Olive Oyl Mug	Vandor	1980	ceramic	8	15	25
Olive Oyl Music Box	Presents	1989	#P5983	8	15	30
Olive Oyl Music Box	KFS	1980	Olive dancing	8	15	30
Olive Oyl on Troubled Waters Record	Peter Pan	1976	45 rpm	5	10	30
Olive Oyl Painting Kit	Avalon	1980		5	10	20
Olive Oyl Push Puppet	Kohner	1960s	4" tall, plastic	15	30	60
Olive Oyl Sports Car		1950s	tiny plastic car	10	15	50
Olive Oyl Squeak Toy	Cribmates	1979	on a stick	5	13	20
Olive Oyl Squeeze Toy	Rempel	1950s	vinyl	15	35	85
Olive Oyl Swim Ring	Wet Set-Zee Toys	1979		5	10	15
Olive Oyl Tiles	Italy	1970s	3" x 5" w/stand	12	25	40
Olive Oyl Toboggan	KFS	1979		6	15	25
Olive Oyl Wall Plaque			ceramic	3	7	10
Original Radio Broadcasts Record	Golden Age	1977	33 rpm	5	20	40
Paint 'N Puff Set	Art Award	1979	two versions	6	12	20
Paint with Water Book	Whitman	1981		3	6	15
Painting and Crayon Book	England	1960		15	25	60
Paper Party Blowouts	Gala/James River	1988		2	4	8
Paperweight		1937	"Popeye Eats Del Monte Spinach"	35	85	150
Pencil Case	Hassenfeld Bros.	1950s	red	20	45	80
Pencil Case	Sanrio	1990		4	8	15
Pencil Case	Eagle	1936	beige, #9027	25	75	150
Pencil Sharpener	KFS	1929	orange celluloid	15	30	85
Pick-Up Sticks	Lido	1957		12	30	65
Picture Disc Record	Peter Pan	1982	33 rpm	6	10	25
Picture Disc Record	Record of America	1948	78 rpm	15	30	80
Pig for a Friend Mug	Vandor	1980	ceramic	6	12	50
Pin	JCPenney	1935	Back to School Days w/Popeye	12	30	65
Pirate Island Presto Magix	American Pub.	1980		4	8	15
Plane and Parachute	Fleetwood	1980		6	12	18
Play Money	The Toy House	1970		5	10	30
Play Money		1930s	color bucks-framed	10	25	60
Playing Cards	Presents	1988	metal box, #P5998, two decks, 60th year	4	9	18
Pocket Pin Ball	Nintendo/Ja-Ru	1983	cups	5	10	15
Pocket Pin Ball	Nintendo/Ja-Ru	1983	holes	5	10	15
Pollution Solution Record	Peter Pan	1970s	45 rpm	4	8	25
Pool Table	Larami	1984		4	8	15
Poopdeck Pappy Doll	Presents	1985	with tag	15	40	100
Pop Maker and Son	Ja-Ru	1987		2	4	10
Pop Pistol	Larami	1984		4	8	25
Popeye Activity Coloring Book	Grosset and Dunlap	1978		5	10	20
Popeye Activity Pad	Merrigold Press	1982		3	7	13
Popeye Air Mattress	Zee Toys	1979		8	20	25
Popeye Alarm Clock	Smiths	1967	British	75	150	300
Popeye All Picture Comic Book	Whitman	1942	Big Little Book	18	45	90
Popeye and Betty Boop Film	Exclusive Films	1935	8mm film	11	25	45
Popeye and Brutus Punch Me Bop Bag	Dartmore	1960s		15	30	50
Popeye and Cast Cigar Box				10	15	35
Popeye and Friends Record	Merry Records	1981	33 rpm	3	8	15
Popeye and his Jungle Pet Book	Whitman	1937		20	45	100
Popeye and Olive Oyl Button	Lisa Frank	1980	1", cowboy Popeye and Indian Olive	2	4	8

TOY	COMPANY	YEAR	DESCRIPTION	GOOD	EX	MIB
Popeye and Olive Oyl Button		1970s	1-1/2", "I Love You"	2	4	8
Popeye and Olive Oyl Music Box	Schmid		8-1/4" figural box	40	80	150
Popeye and Olive Oyl Sand Set	Peer Products	1950s	bucket, shovel	15	40	85
Popeye and Olive Oyl Suspenders	KFS	1979	blue	6	12	20
Popeye and Olive Oyl Toy Watch	Unknown	1970s	flicker	5	10	20
Popeye and Oscar Flicker Ring			blue	8	15	25
Popeye and Shark Swim Ring	Laurel Star-Japan	1960s		10	25	35
Popeye and Swee'Pea Coloring Book	Whitman	1970	1056-31	6	13	25
Popeye and Swee'Pea Flicker Badge	Varivue	1960s		8	15	35
Popeye and Swee'Pea Flicker Ring			blue	8	15	30
Popeye and Swee'Pea Snow Globe	Presents	1989	several varieties	3	7	12
Popeye and the Deep Sea Mystery Big Little Book	Whitman	1939		20	60	120
Popeye and the Jeep Book	Whitman	1937	Big Little Book	20	60	120
Popeye and the Pet Book	Peter Haddock	1987	book three of four	3	5	10
Popeye and the Time Machine Book	Quaker	1990	mini comic	1	3	6
Popeye and Wimpy Flicker Badge	Varivue	1960s		8	15	35
Popeye and Wimpy Flicker Ring			blue	8	15	30
Popeye and Wimpy Walk-A-Way Toy	Marx	1964		25	50	95
Popeye Apron	Chester	1990		4	8	15
Popeye Arcade	Fleetwood	1980		6	12	25
Popeye Arcade Game	Parker Bros.	1980	card game	5	10	15
Popeye at the Wheel	Woolnough	1950s	musical	125	250	500
Popeye Ball			rubber kick ball	7	13	20
Popeye Ball Toss Game	KFS	1950s		30	55	100
Popeye Bank	Play Pal	1972	shape of Popeye's head, plastic	15	30	50
Popeye Bank	Vandor	1980	ceramic	130	260	525
Popeye Bank	Leonard	1980	silver, Popeye sitting	15	25	50
Popeye Bank	Mexico	1990	ceramic bust	10	25	45
Popeye Bank			ceramic, Popeye in light blue cap	5	10	25
Popeye Bank	Vandor	1980	ceramic, Popeye sitting on rope	10	20	40
Popeye Bank	Renz	1979	beige bust	10	20	40
Popeye Bank	Play Pal	1970s	plastic, Popeye sitting on rope	10	30	40
Popeye Bank		1940s	Popeye w/life preserver	30	80	175
Popeye Bank	Sanrio	1990	w/padlock	4	8	15
Popeye Bank	Presents	1991	vinyl, Popeye w/removable pipe	6	12	19
Popeye Bank		1940s	9" cast iron	65	130	275
Popeye Bathtub Toy	Stahlwood	1960s	floating boat	15	30	65
Popeye Beach Set	Peer Products/KFS	1950s	plastic rowboat, accessories	15	35	60
Popeye Bend-I-Face	Lakeside	1967		15	35	65
Popeye Bingo	Nasta	1980		6	10	20
Popeye Bingo	Bar Zim	1929		15	50	100
Popeye Blow Me Down Airport	Marx	1935		250	650	1350
Popeye Book	Random House	1980	hardcover, based on movie	3	5	10
Popeye Break-A-Plate Game	Combex	1963		30	70	150

TOY	COMPANY	YEAR	DESCRIPTION	GOOD	EX	MIB
Popeye Bubble Liquid	M. Shimmel Sons	1970s	shaped like Popeye w/necktie similar to a sailor's knot	8	15	25
Popeye Button	Lowe	1959	sew-on card	12	20	40
Popeye Button	KFS	1950s	1", Famous Studios	15	25	50
Popeye Button	KMOX TV	1960s	1", S.S. Popeye	5	10	20
Popeye Button	S. Cruz	1990	2", Santa Cruz boardwalk	2	3	5
Popeye Button	Factors	1980	3", movie	2	3	5
Popeye Button	KFS	1989	3", marine conservation	2	3	5
Popeye Button	Pep	1946		15	35	60
Popeye Button	Strand	1985	3", several styles	2	3	10
Popeye Calls on Olive Oyl Book	Whitman	1937	8-1/2" x 9-1/2"	25	60	125
Popeye Car	Vandor	1980	Popeye and Olive in blue or pink car	20	45	85
Popeye Carnival	Toymaster	1965		50	100	200
Popeye Charm			solid gold	100	150	200
Popeye Charm		1930s	celluloid	12	25	65
Popeye Charm			silver w/dangly parts	10	20	40
Popeye Climbs a Mountain Book	Wonder Books	1983		2	4	8
Popeye Color and Recolor Book	Jack Built	1957	color, wipe and color again	15	25	60
Popeye Coloring Set	Hasbro	1960s	numbered, w/pencils	12	25	45
Popeye Costume	Collegeville	1980s		6	10	20
Popeye Costume	Ben Cooper	1984		4	8	20
Popeye Costume	Collegeville	1950s		15	40	85
Popeye Cup	Deca Plastics	1979	plastic	4	7	20
Popeye Cup	Popeye Picnic	1989	plastic	1	2	5
Popeye Cup and Saucer	Japan	1930s		40	75	150
Popeye Dog Toy	Petex	1986		3	6	10
Popeye Doll	Uneeda	1979		20	40	80
Popeye Doll	Presents	1985	small	8	13	25
Popeye Doll	Etone	1983	8" plush	5	10	25
Popeye Doll	Woolikin	1950s	white plush	20	45	100
Popeye Doll	Chad Valley	1950s	7" tall, squeaks	20	45	95
Popeye Doll	Dakin	1974	squeaks	15	30	70
Popeye Doll	Dakin	1970s	Cartoon Theatre, in box	25	50	100
Popeye Doll	Rempel	1950s	small	20	45	75
Popeye Doll	Presents	1990	small molded plastic, musical #P5949	10	15	25
Popeye Doll	Sears/Cameo	1957	13" in box	150	310	650
Popeye Doll			23" china	90	175	350
Popeye Doll	Presents	1985	small doll w/pipe molded into hand	10	15	35
Popeye Doll	Toy Toons	1990		5	10	25
Popeye Doll	Lakeside	1968	12" tall, sponge rubber	10	25	60
Popeye Doll		1960s	9" vinyl squeeze doll, Popeye w/Swee'Pea	12	30	60
Popeye Doll	Chicago Herald American	1950s		20	65	125
Popeye Doll	Uneeda	1979	16" tall	15	35	70
Popeye Doll	Cameo	1935		100	250	525
Popeye Doll	Quaker	1960s	12" cloth	10	25	60
Popeye Doll	Dakin	1970s	hard plastic w/removable clothes	15	40	95
Popeye Doll	Gund	1958	20" tall	30	75	175
Popeye Doll	Stack	1936	12" tall, wood jointed, w/pipe	80	200	450
Popeye Figure	KFS-Hearst	1991	wood	8	12	20
Popeye Figure	Presents	1990	PVC	1	2	4
Popeye Figure	Cristallerie Antionio Imperatore		Italian crystal	10	18	35
Popeye Figure	England	1950s	7", bendy, yellow pants	25	50	150
Popeye Figure		1940s	celluloid w/wooden feet	25	50	150
Popeye Figure		1950s	plastic, Popeye on four wheels w/telescope	20	40	85
Popeye Figure	Japan	1950s	celluloid	15	30	85
Popeye Figure	Comics Spain	1984	PVC, Popeye w/spinach	4	7	12

236

TOY	COMPANY	YEAR	DESCRIPTION	GOOD	EX	MIB
Popeye Figure	Bully	1981	several variations	9	18	30
Popeye Figure		1940s	lead	15	25	50
Popeye Figure	Presents	1990	3" tall, plastic	2	3	5
Popeye Figure	Sirocco-KFS	1944	5", wood	40	80	175
Popeye Figure	Chester	1990	10", ceramic, Popeye w/spinach	6	10	20
Popeye Figure	Mexico	1990	ceramic	7	15	25
Popeye Figure	Japan Olympics	1962	wood, Popeye at bat	125	250	500
Popeye Figure	Duncan	1970	8" tall	15	30	60
Popeye Figure	Imperial	1979		6	10	15
Popeye Figure	Bronco	1978	bendy	6	10	20
Popeye Figure		1970s	ceramic, removeable head Popeye	20	45	75
Popeye Figure	Dakin		8" tall w/spinach can	15	30	60
Popeye Figure		1930s	5" tall, wood jointed, held together w/string	50	100	275
Popeye Figure	Ben Cooper	1974	rubber	8	15	35
Popeye Figure	Combex	1960s	rubber, Popey w/a can of spinach	15	25	60
Popeye Figure	Amscan	1980	large bendy	6	12	16
Popeye Figure	Lakeside	1968	miniflex	10	25	50
Popeye Figure	Lakeside	1969	superflex	10	25	50
Popeye Figure	Jesco	1988	bendy	6	10	15
Popeye Figure	Comics Spain	1986	6" bendy, white pants	3	6	15
Popeye Figure	Jesco	1988	small bendy	2	5	10
Popeye Figure	Amscan	1980	small bendy	4	7	12
Popeye Figure		1930s	12" tall, chalk, w/pipe and hat, ashtray base	40	90	200
Popeye Figure Painting Kit	Avalon	1980		4	8	15
Popeye Finger Rings	Post Toasties	1949		18	40	90
Popeye Fishing Game	Fleetwood	1980		5	10	20
Popeye Fishing Game	Transogram	1962	magnetic	15	30	60
Popeye Flicker Badge	Varivue	1960s	Popeye eating spinach	8	15	30
Popeye Flickers	Sonwell	1960s		8	15	30
Popeye French Record	Polygram	1981	45 rpm	6	10	25
Popeye Galley Steward Figure	KFS	1980	ceramic	9	20	35
Popeye Games	Ed-U-Card	1960s	set of four games	10	25	50
Popeye Ge-tar	Mattel	1960s	14" long, shaped like Popeye's face, plays "I'm Popeye the Sailor Man"	20	45	100
Popeye Glass	Coke	1977	Coke Kollect-A-Set	4	7	20
Popeye Glow Putty	Larami	1984		3	6	10
Popeye Goes Swimming Colorforms	Colorforms	1963		15	35	65
Popeye Goes to School Television	Zaboly	1950s		15	40	85
Popeye Hammer Game	Holgate	1960s		60	130	250
Popeye Hand Puppet	Gund	1960s	Popeye's head on cloth body	20	45	85
Popeye Hand Puppet	Gund	1950s	plush	15	30	75
Popeye Hi-Pop Ball	Ja-Ru	1981		4	8	15
Popeye Hot Water Bottle	Duarry	1970		40	90	175
Popeye How to Draw Cartoons Book	Joe Musial/D. McKay	1939		25	80	175
Popeye in a Spinach Truck	Lesney/Matchbox	1980		8	15	30
Popeye in Boat	Corgi	1970s		8	20	40
Popeye in Puddleburg Book	Saalfield	1934	Big Little Book	25	60	120
Popeye in the Movies Record	Peter Pan		33 rpm w/book	6	10	20
Popeye Jump-Up	Imperial	1970s		8	20	35

TOY	COMPANY	YEAR	DESCRIPTION	GOOD	EX	MIB
Popeye Lamp	Alan Jay	1959	Popeye w/legs folded holding spinach	35	75	175
Popeye Lamp		1940s	telescope w/Popeye at base	40	90	225
Popeye Launches His New Song Hits Record	Peter Pan	1958	45 rpm	10	20	50
Popeye Learn and Play Activity Book	Allen Canning	1985		2	5	10
Popeye Magic Play Around	Amsco	1950s	characters w/magnetic bases that slide across play set	30	65	135
Popeye Marionette	Gund	1950s	11-1/2" tall	50	100	275
Popeye Marionette	Create-Japan		wood	90	190	375
Popeye Mechanical Pencil	Eagle	1929	10-1/2" long illustrated pencil w/box	25	60	150
Popeye Meets his Rival Book	Whitman	1937	8-1/2" x 11-1/2"	25	50	120
Popeye Menu Pinball Game	Durable Toy and Novelty	1935		50	95	195
Popeye Mini Bank	KFS	1979		4	8	20
Popeye Mini Tennis Game	Nordic	1970s		10	15	25
Popeye Mini Winder	Durham	1980		4	10	20
Popeye Model Kit	Tokyo Plamo	1964	#808	35	80	180
Popeye Nail-On Game	Colorforms	1963		20	45	100
Popeye Night Light	Arrow Plastic			8	13	20
Popeye on Parade/Strike Me Pink Record	Cricket	1950s	45 rpm	10	20	40
Popeye on Rocket Coloring Book	Whitman - France	1980		8	15	25
Popeye on Safari Book	Quaker	1990	mini comic	2	3	5
Popeye on Tricycle	Linemar		4-1/2", tin wind-up w/celluloid arms and legs, bell rings behind Popeye	100	250	600
Popeye One Man Band	Larami	1980s		6	10	20
Popeye Paddle Ball	Larami	1984	w/color photo of Popeye	6	10	20
Popeye Paint and Crayon Set	Milton Bradley	1934		30	60	160
Popeye Paint Book	McLoughlin Bros.	1932	blue	25	75	150
Popeye Paint By Numbers	Hasbro	1960s		12	25	50
Popeye Paint Coloring Book	Whitman	1951		15	30	70
Popeye Paint Set	American Crayon	1933	6", tin	25	60	150
Popeye Paint-By-Numbers	Hasbro	1981		8	13	20
Popeye Painting Kit	Avalon	1980		6	10	15
Popeye Party Game	Whitman	1937	posters, paper pipes, game box	30	60	125
Popeye Pencil-By-Numbers	Hasbro	1979		10	25	40
Popeye Peppy Puppet	Kohner	1970		10	25	35
Popeye Picture	KFS-Sears		silver foil	10	15	30
Popeye Pin			Popeye at steering wheel, stick pin	4	8	15
Popeye Pinball Game	Ja-Ru	1983		6	10	20
Popeye Pipe	KFS	1970s	plastic kazoo, red and blue	6	20	35
Popeye Pipe		1940s	red wooden	15	25	40
Popeye Pipe	MSS	1970s	plastic, white	8	20	35
Popeye Pipe	Edmonton Pipe	1970	figural head	15	25	45
Popeye Pipe	Harmony	1980		6	10	15
Popeye Pipe	Micro-Lite-KFS	1958		10	25	60
Popeye Pipe Toss Game	Rosebud Art	1935	small version w/wooden pipe	20	50	150
Popeye Pistol	Marx	1935		60	500	1000
Popeye Pistol	Delcast		Super mini cap w/24 caps No. 807-BB	6	20	50

TOY	COMPANY	YEAR	DESCRIPTION	GOOD	EX	MIB
Popeye Play Set	Cribmates	1979	Popeye, Olive Oyl, and Swee'Pea squeak toys, mirror, rattle and pillow	15	30	45
Popeye Playing Card Game	Parker Bros.	1983		6	10	15
Popeye Playing Card Game	Whitman	1934	5" x 7", green box	15	50	100
Popeye Playing Card Game	Whitman	1938	blue box	15	50	100
Popeye Popcorn	Purity Mills	1949	in can	20	35	75
Popeye Pop-Up Book	Random House	1981		6	12	20
Popeye Presto Paints	Kenner	1961		15	50	65
Popeye Pull Toy	Metal Masters	1950s	10-1/2" x 11-1/2", xylophone, wood w/paper litho labels, metal wheels	100	225	450
Popeye Punch-Out Play Book	Whitman	1961		12	22	35
Popeye Puppet	Kohner		pull string, Popeye jumps	10	15	25
Popeye Puppet Show Book	Pleasure Books	1936		25	40	100
Popeye Push Puppet	Kohner	1960	4" tall	20	40	80
Popeye Record	Peter Pan	1977	33 rpm, four stories, #1114	6	10	25
Popeye Ring Toss Game	Fleetwood	1980		6	10	25
Popeye Ring Toss Game	Transogram	1957		30	50	100
Popeye Sailboat	KFS	1976		9	15	35
Popeye Sees the Sea Book	Whitman	1936	Big Little Book	15	50	110
Popeye Service Station	Larami	1979		6	15	40
Popeye Shipwreck Game	Einson-Freeman	1933		40	65	150
Popeye Snow Globe	KFS	1960s	Popeye holds globe between legs	25	40	75
Popeye Soaky	Colgate-Palmolive	1960s		15	35	65
Popeye Soaky	KFS	1987	British	12	20	40
Popeye Song Folio Book	Famous Music	1936		20	65	150
Popeye Sparkler	Chein	1959		90	125	175
Popeye Speed Boat	Harmony	1981		10	16	30
Popeye Speedboard Pull Toy		1960s		175	350	675
Popeye Spinach Eater Pull Toy	Fisher-Price	1939	#488, standing Popeye drums on spinach can drum	200	375	550
Popeye Spinach Target Game	Gardner	1960s		40	65	100
Popeye Sports Car	Linemar	1950s		225	375	650
Popeye Squeeze Toy	Rempel	1950s	8" tall, vinyl	15	35	70
Popeye Squeeze Toy	Cribmates	1979	Popeye on a stick	8	13	20
Popeye Stay in Shape Book	Tuffy Books	1980		6	10	15
Popeye Supergyro	Larami	1980s		6	10	15
Popeye Surprise Present Book	Peter Haddock	1987		4	7	10
Popeye the Juggler Bead Game	Bar-Zim	1929	3-1/2" x 5", covered w/glass	20	35	85
Popeye the Ladies Man Record			33 rpm	8	13	30
Popeye the Movie Book	Avon Printing	1980		6	10	20
Popeye the Movie Soundtrack Record	Paramount	1980		6	10	20
Popeye the Pilot	Chein	1940s	tin wind-up airplane, 8" long, 8" wingspan	320	600	1000
Popeye the Sailor Man and His Friends Record	Golden	1960s	33 rpm	6	10	25

Bullwinkle and Rocky Movie Viewer, 1960s

Bullwinkle's Double Boomerangs, 1969, Larami

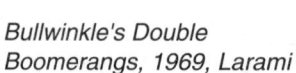

POPEYE

TOY	COMPANY	YEAR	DESCRIPTION	GOOD	EX	MIB
Popeye the Sailor Man Book	Whitman	1942	Big Little Book	25	55	110
Popeye the Sailor Man Record	Diplomat Records	1960	33 rpm	6	10	30
Popeye the Sailor Man Record	Peter Pan	1976	33 rpm	6	10	30
Popeye the Sailor Man Record	Golden	1959	45 rpm	6	10	25
Popeye the Weatherman Colorforms	Colorforms	1959		20	50	110
Popeye Thimble		1990		4	7	10
Popeye Tiles	Italy	1970s	3" x 5" w/stand	15	35	65
Popeye Toboggan	KFS	1979		6	10	15
Popeye Toothbrush Holder	Vandor		5" tall, figural	10	15	25
Popeye Toothbrush Set	Nasta	1980s	holds two toothbrushes	6	15	20
Popeye Train Pull Toy	Larami			135	225	375
Popeye Train Set	Larami	1973		6	15	25
Popeye Transit Company Moving Van	Linemar	1950	tin	300	650	1200
Popeye Tricky Trapeze	Kohner	1970		15	35	65
Popeye Tricky Walker	Jaymar	1960s	plastic	10	25	55
Popeye Tricycling	Linemar	1950s		250	500	900
Popeye Tug and Dingy Pull Toy	Fisher-Price	1950s	wood	135	225	350
Popeye Tugboat	Ideal	1961	inflatable	15	35	55
Popeye TV Cartoon Kit	Colorforms	1966		20	40	75
Popeye TV Magic Putty	MSS	1970s		6	10	15
Popeye Utensils	Arrow Plastic	1970s	spoon and fork	8	13	20
Popeye Video Game	Nintendo	1983		12	20	30
Popeye vs. Bluto the Bad Book	Quaker	1990	mini comic	2	3	5
Popeye Wall Hanging	Amscan	1979	42", jointed	8	13	20
Popeye Water Colors	American Crayon	1933		20	40	85
Popeye Water Sprinkler	KFS	1960s	w/rubbber head	15	25	40
Popeye with his Friends Book	Whitman	1937		15	50	110
Popeye Wristwatch	Armitron	1991		20	35	50
Popeye Wristwatch	Bradley	1964	#308, green case	115	195	300
Popeye Wristwatch	KFS-Japan	1990	Popeye in ship's wheel	40	65	100
Popeye Wristwatch	Unique	1987	Popeye's head pops open, digital	12	22	35
Popeye Wristwatch	New Haven	1938		125	400	850
Popeye Wristwatch	Bradley	1979		60	100	150
Popeye Writing Tablet	KFS	1929	Popeye w/spinach hypo	22	40	100
Popeye/Olive Oyl/Swee'Pea Lamp Shade		1950s		40	65	125
Popeye/Olive Oyl/Wimpy Decals	IGS Stores	1935		8	15	40
Popeye/Olive Oyl/Wimpy Skill Games	Lido	1965		10	16	25
Popeye's Adventure Book	Purnell	1958	England	12	20	40
Popeye's Ark Book	Saalfield	1936	Big Little Book	20	40	100
Popeye's Favorite Sea Shanties Record	RCA Camden	1960		10	20	40
Popeye's Favorite Sea Songs Record	Peter Pan	1959	45 rpm	10	20	40
Popeye's Favorite Stories Record	RCA Camden	1960	33 rpm	10	20	35

TOY	COMPANY	YEAR	DESCRIPTION	GOOD	EX	MIB
Popeye's Gang Pinball Game	MSS	1970s		13	25	45
Popeye's Lucky Jeep Game	Northwestern Products	1936		40	65	175
Popeye's Official Wallet	KFS	1959		10	25	60
Popeye's Peg Board Game	Bar Zim	1934		45	110	250
Popeye's Sliding Boards and Ladders	Warren Built-Rite	1958		12	25	75
Popeye's Songs About...... Record	Golden	1961	33 rpm	8	18	35
Popeye's Spinach Hunt Game	Whitman	1976		10	20	40
Popeye's Submarine	Larami	1973		10	25	45
Popeye's Three Game Set	Built-Rite	1956		20	35	75
Popeye's Tiddly Winks	Parker Bros.	1948		20	35	75
Popeye's Treasure Map Game	Whitman	1977		12	20	40
Popeye's Where's Me Pipe Game				30	45	75
Popsicle Harmonica	Czech	1929		60	150	250
Punch Ball	National Latex	1970s		10	20	35
Punch'Em Talking Rattle Toy	Sanitoy	1950s		15	35	70
Punching Bag	Dartmore	1960s		15	30	50
Punching Bag Film	Brumberger	1950s	8mm	8	15	25
Puppetforms	Colorforms	1950s		25	40	65
Puzzle	Illco	1987	11 pieces, Popeye 3-D	4	7	15
Puzzle	Jaymar	1991	63 pieces, jumbo, Popeye's boat	6	10	20
Puzzle	Saalfield	1932	Popeye in Four	35	60	150
Puzzle	Tower Press	1962	wood, Popeye	10	16	30
Puzzle	Roalex	1960s	tile	20	35	50
Puzzle	Ja-Ru	1987	Popeye and Son TV show	6	10	20
Puzzle	Opera Mundi	1977	tile, "Popeye's Riddle"	11	18	25
Puzzle	Illco	1987	11 pieces, Olive 3-D	6	10	20
Puzzle	Jaymar	1991	63 pieces, jumbo, Popeye rescues Olive	6	10	20
Puzzle	Ja-Ru	1989	boating and dancing	6	10	20
Puzzle	Jaymar	1991	63 pieces, jumbo, Popeye and Olive surfing	4	8	15
Puzzle	American Pub. Corp.	1976	5-1/2" round can	10	16	30
Puzzle	Jaymar	1991	Christmas scene, inlaid, 12 pieces	4	8	15
Puzzle	Jaymar	1991	12 pieces, Popeye holding turkey	4	8	15
Puzzle	Jaymar	1945	22" x 13-1/2", Popeye	25	50	75
Puzzle	Jaymar	1991	12 pieces, Popeye gang swimming	4	8	15
Puzzle	England	1959	120 pieces, "What a Catch"	25	50	75
Puzzle	Larami	1973	magnetic	6	12	25
Puzzle	Waddington's House of Games	1978	27" x 18" floor puzzle	8	15	25
Puzzle	Ja-Ru	1981	comic	6	10	20
Puzzle	Jaymar	1991	63 pieces, Popeye blowing candles	6	10	20
Puzzle	Ja-Ru	1989	"Birthday Cake and Ice Cream"	6	10	20
Puzzle Game	Waddington's House of Games	1978		10	18	35
Puzzle Party Book	Cinnamon House	1979		6	10	20
Quest for the Rainbird Book	Whitman	1943	Big Little Book	15	50	100
Race Set	Ja-Ru	1989		6	10	20
Race to Pearl Peak Book	Golden	1982		6	10	15
Rain Boots	KFS	1950s	spinach power	13	30	60

TOY	COMPANY	YEAR	DESCRIPTION	GOOD	EX	MIB
Record Player	Emerson	1960s	Dynamite Music Machine	35	70	150
Ring the Bell with Hammer Game	Harett-Gilmar	1960s		25	42	65
Ring Toss Stand-Up Game	Transogram	1958		15	30	55
Road Building Set	Larami	1979		6	10	15
Roller Skating Popeye	Linemar	1950s		250	525	100
Roly Poly and Cork Gun Game	Knickbocker	1958		50	90	150
Roly Poly Popeye		1940s	w/beaded arms and celluloid	75	150	225
Rub 'N Win Party Game	Spot-O-Gold	1980		5	10	15
S.S. Funboat Coloring Book	Merrigold Press	1981		4	7	20
Sailboats	Larami	1981		6	10	15
Sailor and the Spinach Stalk Coloring Book	Whitman	1982	1150-1	4	7	20
Sailor's Knife	Ja-Ru	1981		6	10	20
Scott Fun 'N Games Booklet	Spot-O-Gold	1980	set of five	10	15	30
Screen-A Show Projector	Denys Fisher	1973		35	85	150
Sea Hag Doll	Presents	1985		20	45	85
Sea Hag Hand Puppet	Presents	1987		8	15	40
Secret Message Pen	Gordy	1981		6	10	20
Shaving Kit	Larami	1979		6	10	20
Six Popeye Songs Record	Wonderland Records	1950s	45 rpm	8	15	50
Skeet Shoot Game	Irwin	1950		40	80	150
Sketchbook	Japan	1960		12	25	45
Skoozit Pick-A-Puzzle Game	Ideal	1966	8-1/4" round can	15	35	70
Sleeping Bag	KFS	1979		15	35	65
Sling Darts	KFS			20	35	50
Soap Dispenser	Woolfoam	1970s		15	25	35
Soap on a Rope	KFS		white, shaped like Popeye's head	15	25	40
Soap Set	Kerk Guild	1930s	Olive Oyl, Swee'Pea, and Popeye soap figures	40	100	200
Soapy Popeye Boat	Kerk Guild	1950s		20	40	85
Song and Story Skin Diver Record	KFS	1964		8	15	35
Songs of Health Record	Golden	1960s	45 rpm	6	10	20
Songs of Safety Record	Golden	1960s	45 rpm	6	10	20
Spinach Can Bank	KFS	1975	blue can w/raised characters	15	25	50
Squirt Face	Ja-Ru	1981		6	10	15
Stationery	Presents	1989	metal box, heart-shaped note paper, #P5976	6	10	15
Stitch-A-Story	KFS			12	20	30
Storage Box	Sanrio	1990	smoke colored	6	10	15
Sunday Funnies Soda Can	Flavor Valley	1970s		8	13	20
Sun-Eze Pictures	Tillman Toy	1962		10	20	40
Sunglasses	Larami	1980s	red, yellow, or blue	6	10	15
Super Race with Launcher	Fleetwood	1980		6	10	15
Surf Rider	Wet Set-Zee Toys	1979		10	20	40
Suspenders		1970s	red, white and blue w/plastic emblems	8	18	30
Swee'Pea Bank	Vandor	1980	6-1/2" figural	15	50	100
Swee'Pea Bean Bag	Dakin	1974		10	20	35
Swee'Pea Button	Lisa Frank	1980	1", Swee'Pea w/Jeep	2	4	8
Swee'Pea Cup	Coke	1977	Coke Kollect-A-Cup	4	7	10
Swee'Pea Doll	Presents	1991	small molded plastic, # P5968	8	13	20
Swee'Pea Doll	Presents	1985	small	8	13	35
Swee'Pea Doll	Presents	1985	large	10	16	30

POPEYE

TOY	COMPANY	YEAR	DESCRIPTION	GOOD	EX	MIB
Swee'Pea Doll	Uneeda	1979		8	13	35
Swee'Pea Doll	Presents	1991	Christmas, small	8	13	35
Swee'Pea Egg Cup	Vandor	1980	ceramic	10	16	30
Swee'Pea Figure	Comics Spain	1984	PVC, Swee'Pea w/cake	4	8	15
Swee'Pea Figure	Presents	1990	3" tall, plastic	4	8	15
Swee'Pea Figure	Presents	1984	PVC	2	4	8
Swee'Pea Figure			ceramic, one of five	5	10	25
Swee'Pea Figure	Cristallerie Antonio Imperatore		Italian crystal	12	20	35
Swee'Pea Hand Puppet	Gund	1960s	bonnet on head, cloth body decorated w/baby lambs	15	30	65
Swee'Pea Hand Puppet	Presents	1987		8	15	35
Swee'Pea Hi-Pop Ball	Ja-Ru	1981		6	12	20
Swee'Pea Mini Bank	KFS	1979		10	20	45
Swee'Pea Music Box	Presents	1989	#P5986	8	13	25
Swee'Pea Music Box	KFS	1980	Swee'Pea dancing	8	13	25
Swee'Pea Night Light	Presents	1978	bone china	10	25	50
Swee'Pea Snow Globe	Presents	1989	several styles	5	10	20
Swee'Pea Squeak Toy		1970s	frowning or smiling	12	22	40
Swee'Pea Wall Plaque		1950s	ceramic	12	30	50
Swee'Pea's Lemonade Stand Television Film	Zaboly	1950s		10	20	40
Swirler Flying Barrel Toy	Imperial	1980		8	15	30
Talking View-Master Set	GAF	1962	old type	12	25	50
Tambourine	Larami	1980s		6	10	20
Tambourine	Santa Cruz	1990		6	10	15
Target Ball	Ja-Ru	1981		6	10	20
Telephone	Comvu	1982		15	25	45
Telescope	Larami	1973		8	15	35
The Outer Space Zoo Book	Golden	1980		6	12	30
Thimble Theatre Book	Whitman	1935	Big Big Book	45	150	350
Thimble Theatre Cut-Outs	Aldon	1950s		25	50	85
Toy Watch	Sekonda-Japan	1987	comic strip band	30	50	85
Trace and Color	Fleetwood	1980		6	10	15
Training Cup	Deka	1971		8	13	25
Transistor Radio	Philgee	1960s		22	45	75
Trash Can	KFS			10	15	25
Trinket Box	Vandor	1980	Popeye laying on top, ceramic	10	16	25
Trinket Box	Vandor	1980	Popeye's head in preserver, ceramic	10	16	25
Trumpet Bubble Blower	Larami	1984	pink or yellow pan	6	12	20
Tube-A-Loonies	Larami	1973	five small tubes on card	6	12	20
Turn-A-Scope	Larami	1979		6	12	30
TV Set with Three Film Scrolls		1957		12	20	45
TV Tray	KFS	1979		8	13	20
Umbrella	KFS	1979	blue and white	12	20	40
View-Master Set	Sawyers	1959	three reels	15	25	50
View-Master Set	GAF	1962	three pack	8	15	30
View-Master Set	GAF	1959	"The Fish Story"	8	15	35
View-Master Set	GAF	1959	"The Hunting Bird"	8	15	30
Wagon Works Film	Atlas Films	1960s	8mm	6	10	20
Wallet	Larami	1978		8	15	35
Wallet	Sanrio	1990		6	10	18
Wallet	Presents	1991	P-5432, tri-fold	6	10	18
Water Ball Game	Nintendo	1983	one basket	6	10	15
Whale of a Tale Record	Peter Pan	1981	45 rpm	6	10	15
What! No Spinach? Book	Golden	1981		6	10	25
Whistle Candy	Alberts	1989		6	10	15

POPEYE

TOY	COMPANY	YEAR	DESCRIPTION	GOOD	EX	MIB
Whistling Flashlights	Bantam-Lite	1960s	six w/display	140	230	375
Whistling Wing Ding	Mego	1950s		20	35	60
Wimpy Button	Strand	1985	3", "Must Go Home and Water the Ducks"	2	3	8
Wimpy Button	Lisa Frank	1979	2"	2	3	6
Wimpy Button	Pep	1946		10	16	30
Wimpy Cup	Coke	1977	Coke Kollect-A-Set	4	7	10
Wimpy Dog Toy	Petex	1986		8	13	20
Wimpy Doll	Presents	1985	holding a hamburger	15	30	75
Wimpy Doll	KFS	1950s	rubber	22	40	75
Wimpy Figure		1940s	lead	12	20	50
Wimpy Figure	Sirocco-KFS	1944	5", wood	30	60	150
Wimpy Figure	Cristallerie Antionio Imperatore		Italian crystal	10	15	40
Wimpy Figure	Buitoni	1950s	premium	30	60	120
Wimpy Figure	Presents	1990	PVC	2	4	8
Wimpy Figure	Bully	1981	yellow hat	6	12	25
Wimpy Figure	Comics Spain	1984	Wimpy w/hamburger	4	8	15
Wimpy Hand Puppet	Gund	1950s	fabric hand cover, vinyl squeaker head and voice	15	35	85
Wimpy Hand Puppet	Gund	1960s	cloth body	15	30	65
Wimpy Hand Puppet	Presents	1987		8	13	30
Wimpy in Back to his First Love Book			eight pages	6	10	15
Wimpy Magnet				6	10	15
Wimpy Music Box	Presents	1989	#P5985	8	15	25
Wimpy Ring	Post Toasties	1949		12	30	75
Wimpy Squeeze Toy	Rempel	1950s	vinyl	20	40	60
Wimpy Squeeze Toy	Cribmates	1979		12	20	35
Wimpy the Hamburger Eater Book	Whitman	1938	Big Little Book	15	50	110
Wimpy Thermometer	KFS	1981		8	13	20
Wimpy Tricks Popeye and Roughhouse Book	Whitman	1937		35	65	125
Wimpy Tricks Popeye Book	Whitman	1937		45	65	110
Wimpy Tugboat	Ideal	1961	inflatable	20	35	55
Wimpy What's Good to Eat? Book	Tuffy Books	1980		6	10	20
Wood Slate	Ja-Ru	1983		6	10	20
Write on/Wipe Off Board	Freelance	1979		6	10	20

PORKY PIG

TOY	COMPANY	YEAR	DESCRIPTION	GOOD	EX	MIB
Porky and Petunia Figures	Warner Bros.	1975	4-1/2" tall	9	16	25
Porky Pig Bank		1930s	bisque, orange, blue, and yellow	60	120	200
Porky Pig Doll	Dakin	1968	7-3/4" tall in black velvet jacket	11	22	50
Porky Pig Doll	Gund	1950	14" tall	50	90	150
Porky Pig Doll	Mattel	1960s	17", cloth, vinyl head	15	30	50
Porky Pig Soaky				15	35	65
Porky Pig Umbrella		1940s	hard plastic 3" figure on end, Porky and Bugs printed in red cloth	40	75	125

QUICK DRAW MCGRAW

TOY	COMPANY	YEAR	DESCRIPTION	GOOD	EX	MIB
Auggie Doggie Doll	Knickerbocker	1959	10" tall, plush w/vinyl face	16	30	75
Auggie Doggie Soaky	Purex	1960s	10" tall, plastic	15	45	75
Baba Looey Bank	Knickerbocker	1960s	9" tall, vinyl, plastic head	16	30	50
Baba Looey Doll	Knickerbocker	1959	20" tall, plush w/vinyl donkey ears and sombrero	35	80	150
Blabber Doll	Knickerbocker	1959	15" tall, plush w/vinyl face	25	60	120

QUICK DRAW MCGRAW

TOY	COMPANY	YEAR	DESCRIPTION	GOOD	EX	MIB
Blabber Soaky	Purex	1960s	10-1/2" tall, plastic	18	40	75
Quick Draw McGraw Bank		1960	9-1/2", plastic, orange, white, and blue	20	40	85
Quick Draw McGraw Book	Whitman	1960		15	25	60
Quick Draw McGraw Doll	Knickerbocker	1959	16", plush w/vinyl face, cowboy hat	45	100	200
Quick Draw McGraw Moving Target Game	Knickerbocker	1960s		95	125	225
Quick Draw Mold and Model Cast Set		1960		30	60	85
Scooper Doll	Knickerbocker	1959	20", plush w/vinyl face	30	60	110

RAGGEDY ANN AND ANDY

TOY	COMPANY	YEAR	DESCRIPTION	GOOD	EX	MIB
Camel with the Wrinkled Knees Book		1924		75	120	200
Raggedy Andy Bank	Play Pal		11"	15	20	30
Raggedy Andy Figure		1970s	rubber/wire, 4" tall	5	10	15
Raggedy Andy Puppet	Dakin	1975	cloth	15	25	35
Raggedy Ann Bank	Play Pal	1974	11"	15	20	30
Raggedy Ann Coloring Book		1968		6	12	30
Raggedy Ann Puppet	Dakin	1975	cloth	15	25	35
Raggedy Ann/Andy Paper Doll Book	Whitman	1974	#1962	15	25	45
Raggedy Ann/Andy Record Player		1950s	plastic, heart shaped	80	95	150
Raggedy Ann/Andy Record Player			square, cardboard	45	60	95
Raggedy Ann/Andy Wastebasket		1972	tin	8	15	40

ROAD RUNNER AND WILE E. COYOTE

TOY	COMPANY	YEAR	DESCRIPTION	GOOD	EX	MIB
Road Runner and Coyote Lamp		1977	12-1/2", figures standing on base	30	60	175
Road Runner Bank			standing on base	8	15	25
Road Runner Costume	Collegeville	1960s		20	30	65
Road Runner Doll	Mighty Star	1971	13" tall	9	20	50
Road Runner Figure	Dakin	1968	8-3/4" tall	15	25	60
Road Runner Figure	Dakin		plastic, Cartoon Theater	9	25	75
Road Runner Figure	Dakin	1971	Goofy Gram	15	25	50
Road Runner Hand Puppet	Japanese	1970s	10", vinyl head	5	10	35
Wile E. Coyote and Road Runner Figures	Royal Crown	1979	7" tall, each	11	20	50
Wile E. Coyote Doll	Mighty Star	1971	18" tall, plush	9	25	60
Wile E. Coyote Doll	Dakin	1970	on explosive box	15	35	70
Wile E. Coyote Figure	Dakin	1976	Cartoon Theater	10	20	40
Wile E. Coyote Figure	Dakin	1971	Goofy Gram, fused bomb in right hand	14	25	60
Wile E. Coyote Figure	Dakin	1968	10" tall	14	35	75
Wile E. Coyote Hand Puppet	Japanese	1970s	10" vinyl head	5	10	30
Wile E. Coyote Night Light	Applause	1980s		13	25	50

ROCKY

TOY	COMPANY	YEAR	DESCRIPTION	GOOD	EX	MIB
Apollo Creed Doll	Phoenix Toys	1983	8" tall	5	10	25
Clubber Lang Doll	Phoenix Toys	1983	8" tall	6	12	30
Rocky Balboa Doll	Phoenix Toys	1983	8" tall	6	12	30

TOY	COMPANY	YEAR	DESCRIPTION	GOOD	EX	MIB
Bullwinkle and Rocky Clock Bank	Larami	1969	4-1/2" tall, plastic	30	55	110
Bullwinkle and Rocky Movie Viewer		1960s	#225, red and white plastic viewer w/three movies	25	50	75
Bullwinkle and Rocky Wastebasket		1961	11" tall, metal w/Jay Ward cast pictured	35	65	135
Bullwinkle Bank		1960s	6" tall, glazed china	75	125	400
Bullwinkle Bank	Play Pal	1972	11-1/2", plastic	35	50	100
Bullwinkle Cartoon Kit	Colorforms	1962		35	50	160
Bullwinkle Dinner Set	Boonton Molding	1960s	plate and cup pictures Bullwinkle and the Cheerios Kid	25	50	85
Bullwinkle Figure	Dakin	1976	Cartoon Theater, 7-1/2" tall, plastic	25	50	90
Bullwinkle Flexy Figure	Larami	1970		10	20	60
Bullwinkle for President Bumper Sticker		1972		10	16	40
Bullwinkle Jewelry Hanger		1960s	5" tall, suction cup on back	15	25	50
Bullwinkle Magic Slate		1963		15	35	75
Bullwinkle Make Your Own Badge Set	Larami	1960s		20	35	75
Bullwinkle Paintless Paint Book	Whitman	1960		15	30	70
Bullwinkle Spell and Count Board		1969		10	20	40
Bullwinkle Stamp Set	Larami	1970		11	20	35
Bullwinkle Stickers		1984	Bullwinkle, Sherman and Peabody, Snidely Whiplash	5	10	20
Bullwinkle Talking Doll	Mattel	1970		25	60	125
Bullwinkle Travel Adventure Board Game	Transogram	1960s		30	70	125
Bullwinkle Travel Game	Larami	1971	magnetic	15	30	60
Bullwinkle's Circus Time Toy		1969	Rocky on a circus horse	20	35	85
Bullwinkle's Circus Time Toy		1969	Bullwinkle on a elephant	20	35	85
Bullwinkle's Double Boomerangs	Larami	1969	set of two on illustrated card	15	25	50
Dudley Do-Right Figure	Wham-O	1972	5" tall, flexible	10	30	75
Dudley Do-Right Figure	Dakin	1976	Cartoon Theater	15	30	75
Dudley Do-Right Puzzle	Whitman	1975		12	25	50
Mr. Peabody Bank		1960s	6" tall, glazed china	90	180	375
Mr. Peabody Figure	Wham-O	1972	4" tall, flexible	10	20	60
Natasha Figure	Wham-O	1972		10	20	60
Rocky and Bullwinkle Bank		1960	5" tall, glazed china	85	180	375
Rocky and Bullwinkle Coloring Book	Watkins-Strathmore	1962		15	30	75
Rocky and Bullwinkle Presto Sparkle Painting Set	Kenner	1962	six cartoon pictures and two comic strip panels	30	65	125
Rocky and Bullwinkle Puzzle	Whitman	1972	boxed	15	30	70
Rocky and Bullwinkle Toothpaste Holder		1960s	glazed china	80	190	375
Rocky and His Friends Book	Whitman	1960s	Little Golden Book	10	25	50
Rocky Bank		1950s	5" tall, slot in large tail, glazed china	75	200	400
Rocky Figure	Dakin	1976	Cartoon Theater, 6-1/2" tall, plastic	30	60	125

ROCKY AND BULLWINKLE

TOY	COMPANY	YEAR	DESCRIPTION	GOOD	EX	MIB
Rocky Flexy Figure	Larami	1970		10	25	50
Rocky Soaky			10-1/2" tall, plastic	15	45	75
Rocky the Flying Squirrel Coloring Book	Whitman	1960		18	35	75
Sherman Figure	Wham-O	1972	4" tall, flexible	15	30	60
Snidely Whiplash Figure	Wham-O	1972	5" tall, flexible	10	30	75

ROGER RABBIT

TOY	COMPANY	YEAR	DESCRIPTION	GOOD	EX	MIB
Animates		1988	Doom, Roger, Eddie and Smart Guy, each	5	8	15
Baby Herman and Roger Rabbit Mug	Applause			5	8	15
Baby Herman Figure	LJN	1988	ceramic	9	15	30
Baby Herman Figure	LJN	1987	6" figure on card	9	15	30
Benny the Cab	LJN			20	40	75
Benny the Cab Doll	Applause	1988	6" long	6	12	25
Boss Weasel Figure	LJN	1988	4" bendable	4	8	15
Deluxe Color Activity Book	Golden		#5523	5	10	20
Dip Flip Game	LJN			8	15	30
Eddie Valiant Animate	LJN	1988	6" tall, bendable	4	8	15
Eddie Valiant Figure	LJN	1988	4", flexible	4	8	15
Jessica License Plate				6	12	20
Jessica Zipper Pull				5	10	15
Judge Doom Animate	LJN	1988	6" tall poseable	5	10	20
Judge Doom Figure	LJN	1988	4" bendable	3	6	20
Paint with Water Book	Golden		#1702	6	12	25
Paint-A-Cel Set			Benny the Cab and Roger pictures	8	15	30
Roger Rabbit Animate	LJN	1988	6" poseable	4	8	15
Roger Rabbit Blow-Up Buddy			36" tall	5	10	20
Roger Rabbit Bullet Hole Wristwatch	Shiraka	1987	white case and leather band, in plastic display box	20	40	100
Roger Rabbit Doll	Applause		17" tall	8	20	50
Roger Rabbit Doll	Applause		8-1/2" tall	5	10	25
Roger Rabbit Figure	LJN	1988	4" bendable	4	8	15
Roger Rabbit Silhouette Wristwatch	Shiraka	1987	large gold case, black band	20	40	100
Roger Wacky Head Puppets	Applause		hand puppets	5	10	20
Roger Wind-Up	Matsudaya	1988		18	35	60
Smart Guy Figure	LJN	1988	flexible	4	8	15
Talking Roger in Benny the Cab			17" tall	12	25	50
Trace and Color Book	Golden		#2355	5	10	20
View-Master Gift Set	View-Master			8	15	40

ROOTIE KAZOOTIE

TOY	COMPANY	YEAR	DESCRIPTION	GOOD	EX	MIB
Rootie Kazootie Club Button		1950s	1" tin litho	18	42	65
Rootie Kazootie Drum		1950s	8" diameter drum, Rootie on the drum head	25	50	85
Rootie Kazootie Fishing Tackle Box	RK Inc.	1950s	tin litho, bright graphics	15	25	50

RUFF AND REDDY

TOY	COMPANY	YEAR	DESCRIPTION	GOOD	EX	MIB
Ruff and Reddy Draw Cartoon Set Color	Wonder Art			50	85	150

248

RUFF AND REDDY

TOY	COMPANY	YEAR	DESCRIPTION	GOOD	EX	MIB
Ruff and Reddy Go To A Party Tell-A-Tale Book	Whitman	1958		15	30	60
Ruff and Reddy Magic Rub-Off Picture Set	Transogram	1958		45	80	150

SECRET SQUIRREL

TOY	COMPANY	YEAR	DESCRIPTION	GOOD	EX	MIB
Secret Squirrel Bubble Club Soaky	Purex	1960s		20	30	75
Secret Squirrel Push Puppet	Kohner	1960s	plastic figure in white coat, blue hat holding binoculars	20	35	70
Secret Squirrel Puzzle		1967	frame tray	14	25	50
Secret Squirrel Ray Gun				14	25	60

SHIRLEY TEMPLE

TOY	COMPANY	YEAR	DESCRIPTION	GOOD	EX	MIB
Baby Take A Bow Dress		1934	red cotton, red polka dots on collar and reverse on the bottom w/silk ribbons, fits 16" doll	85	95	120
Ballerina Outfit		1957-58	blue/green nylon and tulle, flower hair piece; fits 12" vinyl doll	80	85	100
Blue Bird Doll		1939	18", felt skirt and vest, organdy blouse and apron w/blue bird appliques	910	975	1200
Blue Bird Doll		1939	20" composition	800	925	1200
Bridge Cards	U.S. Playing Card	1934		35	45	55
Bright Eyes Doll		1936	13" composition, plaid dress, leather shoes	610	650	750
Bright Eyes Dress		1934	fits 16" dolls, several colors variations	85	90	120
Bright Eyes Outfit			white corduroy coat and hat w/original pin, fits 16" doll	100	150	200
Captain January Doll	Ideal		22", dark blue sailor suit w/white trim	800	860	1000
Captain January Doll	Ideal	1957	12", vinyl head, dark blonde hair, plastic body, arms and legs	175	200	300
Captain January Doll	Ideal	1936	20", blue floral print, cotton school dress w/ruffled collar	725	775	950
Captain January Doll		1936	18", cotton sailor suit w/anchor applique and red silk tie	650	725	900
Captain January Doll		1936	16", green pique w/silk ribbons	650	725	800
Captain January Doll		1936	13", white sailor suit, red bow tie, white hat, original pin	600	675	850
Captain January Outfit		1936	red or green pleated pique, silk ribbons; fits a 16" doll	85	95	120
Coat and Hat			velveteen coat and hat w/red buttons; fits 16" doll	80	90	100
Coat and Hat	Ideal	1958	red corduroy coat and hat, fits 12" doll	60	70	75
Composition Book	Western	1935		25	30	60
Curly Top Doll		1935	11", dotted swiss dress, blue silk ribbons	600	660	800
Curly Top Doll		1935	16" composition; different versions available	675	725	800
Curly Top Doll		1935	18" composition, mohair hair, hazel eyes	600	675	800
Curly Top Doll		1935	18", pleated dotted swiss w/blue silk ribbons, red or lavender	600	675	800
Curly Top Doll	Ideal	1935	11", pink organdy dress	875	1000	1250
Curly Top Dress		1935	striped cotton dress, fits 20" doll	85	95	120

TOY	COMPANY	YEAR	DESCRIPTION	GOOD	EX	MIB
Dimples Outfit		1936	heavy felt jacket w/red trim; fits 16" doll	85	95	120
Doll Buggy	F.A. Whitney Carriage	1935	wicker, hubcaps are labeled Shirley Temple	300	375	450
Doll Trunk			18" tall w/"Our Little Girl" decal on the side, photo of Shirley	100	175	250
Doll Wardrobe Trunk			20" heavy cardboard/wood steamer trunk for 18" doll, leather strap, metal latch w/lock and key, two drawers, and four cardboard hangers	120	175	250
Dress	Ideal	1958	nylon w/loop details; fits 12" doll	65	75	80
Dress			light blue organdy; fits 16" doll	85	95	120
Dress, Jacket, and Purse		1959	nylon	65	70	75
Hair Ribbon and Band	Ribbon Mills	1934	Several colors/styles	15	25	50
Hanger			cardboard; picture of Shirley Temple, came w/all outfits	15	25	40
Heidi Doll	Ideal	1957	12", vinyl head, dark blonde hair and plastic body, arms and legs	200	275	325
Heidi Doll		1960-61	17"	250	325	400
Heidi Doll		1937	18", striped cotton skirt, black velveteen top w/red braid, apron, mohair pigtails w/red ribbons	950	1050	1350
Jumper and Blouse	Ideal	1959	blue velveteen jumper w/floral applique, cotton blouse	60	70	80
Jumpsuit			red/white checkered	35	40	50
Jumpsuit			red w/white flowers	80	85	100
Little Colonel Doll			13", variations in pantaloons, bonnets and shoes	775	825	1050
Little Colonel Doll		1934	13", light blue dress w/bonnet, pantaloons and shoes w/buckles	775	825	1050
Little Colonel Doll			13", taffeta outfit, variations in the collar, ruffles and pantaloons	775	825	1050
Little Colonel Doll	Ideal	1934	13", smiling, pink hat w/feather and dress and bloomers	775	825	1050
Little Colonel Doll	Alexander		13", pink hat w/ruffle, pink dress and bloomers	475	550	800
Little Colonel Doll		1934	18", pink organdy dress, bonnet, white pantaloons	775	825	1050
Little Colonel Doll			20", blue organdy, bonnet w/pink feather	925	975	1350
Littlest Rebel Doll		1935	13", yellow/brown dress, white ruffled collar, yellow shoes	775	825	1050
Littlest Rebel Doll		1935	16", polka dot outfit, pantaloons, gray felt hat	625	675	850
Littlest Rebel Doll		1935	18", cotton and organdy outfit	675	725	875
Littlest Rebel Doll		1935	22", red/white cotton dress w/organdy collar	775	825	1050
Littlest Rebel Dress		1935	yellow/brown, fits an 18" doll	150	175	275
Littlest Rebel Outfit			checkered dress, rick rack ribbon on sleeves, lace collar and apron	85	100	175
My Life and Times by Shirley Temple Book	Saalfield	1936	Big Little Book #116	25	75	110
Nightcoat and Cap	Ideal	1958-59	flannel; fits 12" doll	60	70	80
Our Little Girl Outfit		1935	blue or white pique, white dog appliques, fits 16" doll	85	100	175
Our Little Girl Outfit		1935	red or blue dress w/music appliques, matching hat, fits 16" doll	85	100	175
Paper Doll Book	Whitman	1976	#1986	8	15	30
Paper Dolls	Saalfield	1934	four 8" dolls and 30 outfits; first licensed set, #2112	60	200	350
Paper Dolls	Saalfield	1958	#4435	35	50	125

TOY	COMPANY	YEAR	DESCRIPTION	GOOD	EX	MIB
Paper Dolls	Saalfield	1959	18" folding doll w/easel, costumes, and accessories, #5110	10	40	80
Pen and Pencil Set	David Kahn	1930s		90	125	200
Pin	Reliable		"The World's Darling/Genuine Shirley Temple, A Reliable Doll"	65	75	85
Polka Dot Dancing Dress		1935	blue organdy w/matching hat and sunsuit	85	90	110
Poor Little Rich Girl Doll		1936	18", pique sunsuit w/matching tam	325	700	900
Poor Little Rich Girl Doll		1936	13", sailor dress w/white trim and matching tam	275	350	725
Poor Little Rich Girl Doll		1936	13", blue silk pajamas	325	700	900
Poor Little Rich Girl Outfit		1935	pique and organdy dress, fits 16" doll	90	100	125
Poor Little Rich Girl Outfit		1936	pleated red plaid w/white collar, fits 16" doll	90	100	125
Poor Little Rich Girl Outfit		1935	blue sailor dress, fits 16" doll	90	100	125
Promo Photo			8" x 10" photo of Shirley w/facsimile autograph, came w/all composition dolls and outfits	30	40	55
Purse		1950s	red, white, and black w/Shirley Temple lettering	30	40	60
Rain Cape and Umbrella			plaid red or blue rain cape w/hood and matching umbrella; fits 18" doll	80	100	150
Rebecca of Sunnybrook Farm Doll		1957	12" vinyl, blue bib overalls, blue polka dot blouse, straw hat	125	220	310
Rebecca of Sunnybrook Farm Doll		1957	12" vinyl, red felt jumper and plastic purse	175	220	310
Rebecca of Sunnybrook Farm Doll		1957	12" vinyl, blue bib overalls w/plaid blouse, black low shoes	125	175	210
Rebecca of Sunnybrook Farm Doll	Ideal	1957	12", vinyl head, dark blonde hair, plastic body, arms and legs	175	220	310
Scrap Book	Saalfield	1935	#1714	60	75	100
Shirley Standing Doll	Saalfield	1935	cardboard doll on platform and different outfits, #1719	35	70	250
Shirley Temple A Great Big Book to Color	Saalfield	1936	#1717	35	45	75
Shirley Temple at Play Book	Saalfield	1935	#1712	40	50	85
Shirley Temple Baby			16", mohair wig, flirty eyes	525	725	1200
Shirley Temple Baby			20", composition head, arms and legs, cloth body	700	900	1350
Shirley Temple Baby	Ideal		18", painted hair, chubby toddler body w/dimpled cheeks, flirty eyes, dressed in pink organdy w/silk ribbons	600	850	1250
Shirley Temple Doll			16" composition	375	625	800
Shirley Temple Doll	Ideal		22" jointed, composition body, blonde mohair, hazel glass eyes, open mouth, red/white polka dot dress	225	450	950
Shirley Temple Doll	Ideal/Hong Kong	1972	15" vinyl manufactured for Montgomery Ward's	190	210	235
Shirley Temple Doll	Ideal/Hong Kong	1972	16", vinyl, red polka dot dress, Stand Up and Cheer	155	185	210
Shirley Temple Doll	Reliable (Ideal/Canada)		13", yellow organdy dress, silk ribbon	460	760	1000

TOY	COMPANY	YEAR	DESCRIPTION	GOOD	EX	MIB
Shirley Temple Doll			13", pleated pique w/white applique	275	525	750
Shirley Temple Doll			16", light blue organdy w/pink hemstitching and silk ribbons	275	525	800
Shirley Temple Doll			18" composition w/facial molding	525	675	850
Shirley Temple Doll			22" composition w/facial molding	600	800	950
Shirley Temple Doll	Ideal		19" vinyl, twinkle eyes, dressed in pink nylon, black purse	180	325	450
Shirley Temple Doll	Made in Japan		8" composition w/pink silk undies	175	200	275
Shirley Temple Doll			16", black velveteen coat and hat	180	325	800
Shirley Temple Doll			27" composition w/pink taffeta, bonnet and pantaloons	850	1200	1750
Shirley Temple Doll		1957	12", vinyl, molded hands and feet, synthetic rooted wig, pink slip trimmed w/lace	125	225	400
Shirley Temple Doll		1935	18" facial molding doll w/mohair wig (parted in the center), light complexion, outfit from "Curly Top"	260	475	1000
Shirley Temple Doll	Ideal	1960s	17", yellow nylon dress and Twinkle Eyes wrist tag	210	320	450
Shirley Temple Doll		1957	12" vinyl, molded hands and feet, synthetic rooted wig, two piece slip/undies	110	225	350
Shirley Temple Doll		1958	15" vinyl, red nylon dress w/floral detailing at collar, hair ribbon, purse	110	210	310
Shirley Temple Doll			20" composition w/facial molding	500	725	900
Shirley Temple Doll		1960	15" vinyl, blue jumper w/red/white gingham blouse and pocket facing	100	200	310
Shirley Temple Doll		1960s	17", yellow party dress, white purse w/Shirley Temple lettering	225	325	450
Shirley Temple Doll	Blossom		18" cloth w/Little Colonel dress	210	310	450
Shirley Temple Doll	Ideal	1934	18", light pink organdy	475	625	900
Shirley Temple Doll	Ideal	1934	18", pleated pale green, pink, or blue dress, embroidered collar and pink silk ribbon	520	625	900
Shirley Temple Doll	Ideal	1958	15" vinyl, yellow nylon dress trimmed w/lace and ribbon around skirt	175	320	425
Shirley Temple Doll	Ideal	1958-59	17" vinyl, brown twinkle eyes, pink/blue dress	210	320	425
Shirley Temple Doll		1957	12" vinyl, pink/blue nylon dress w/daisy appliques, hat, purse	125	250	375
Shirley Temple Dolls and Dresses	Saalfield	1960	Two dolls w/different outfits, #1789	12	18	35
Shirley Temple Five Books About Me	Saalfield	1936	Just a Little Girl, Twinkletoes, On the Movie Lot, In Starring Roles, and Little Playmate, #1730	90	120	150
Shirley Temple in The Littlest Rebel	Saalfield	1935	Big Little Book, #1595	18	25	65
Shirley Temple My Book to Color	Saalfield	1937	#1768	35	40	65
Shirley Temple Pastime Box	Saalfield	1937	Four activity books: Favorite Puzzles, Favorite Games, Favorite Sewing Cards, and Favorite Coloring Book, #1732	55	125	165
Shirley Temple Scrap Book	Saalfield	1936	#1722	65	70	110

Superman Scrap Book, 1940, Saalfield

Cindy Bear Doll, 1959, Knickerbocker

Yogi Bear Doll, 1959, Knickerbocker

SHIRLEY TEMPLE

TOY	COMPANY	YEAR	DESCRIPTION	GOOD	EX	MIB
Shirley Temple Scrap Book	Saalfield	1937	#1763	70	75	110
Shirley Temple Story Book	Saalfield	1935	#1726	25	30	65
Shirley Temple Treasury Book	Random House	1959		20	30	40
Shirley Temple with Lionel Barrymore in The Little Colonel	Saalfield	1935	Big Little Book, #1095	15	25	60
Shirley Temple's Blue Bird Coloring Book	Saalfield	1939		35	55	85
Shirley Temple's Busy Book	Saalfield	1958	Activity book, #5326	40	50	60
Shirley Temple's Favorite Poems	Saalfield	1936	#1720	20	30	60
Stand Up and Cheer Doll		1934	11", dotted red, blue, or green organdy dress w/silk ribbon	450	650	900
Stand Up and Cheer Doll		1934	13" composition, dotted organdy green dress	150	200	375
Stand Up and Cheer Doll			11" composition, short rayon dress w/blue polka dots	675	875	1000
Stand Up and Cheer Doll Trunk		1934		125	200	275
Stowaway Doll		1936	25", pink taffeta, mohair hair	700	900	1250
Stowaway Doll		1936	20", two-piece linen w/brass buttons	650	800	1200
Stowaway Outfit		1936	red or blue pique, fits 16" doll	90	125	210
Texas Ranger Doll			20", plaid shirt, leather vest w/trim, chaps, holster, and metal gun	700	900	1300
Texas Ranger Doll			17", plaid shirt, leather vest w/trim	550	650	1000
Texas Ranger/Cowgirl Doll			11", plaid cotton shirt, leather vest, chaps, holster, metal gun, felt 10 gallon hat w/"Ride 'Em Cowboy" printed band	450	700	1250
Texas Ranger/Cowgirl Gun			Came w/Texas Ranger outfit	35	50	125
The Story of Shirley Temple Book	Saalfield	1934	Big Little Book, #1089	18	25	60
This Is My Crayon Book	Saalfield	1936	#1711	35	55	85
Wee Willie Winkie Doll		1937	18", long sleeve cotton jacket, two pockets and six brass buttons, plaid wool skirt, tan belt w/brass buckle	700	1000	1350
Wee Willie Winkie Doll	Ideal	1957	12", vinyl head, dark blonde hair, plastic body, arms and legs	190	225	350
Wee Willie Winkie Outfit		1937	pique outfit and tam, slip/undies; fits 16" doll	125	150	225
Wool Coat			fits 18" dolls, from Little Miss Marker	60	80	135

SLEEPING BEAUTY

TOY	COMPANY	YEAR	DESCRIPTION	GOOD	EX	MIB
Fairy Godmother Hand Puppets		1958	set of three: 10-1/2" tall, Flora, Merryweather, and Fauna, each	60	75	210
King Huber/King Stefan Hand Puppets	Gund	1956	10" tall, molded rubber heads w/fabric hand cover	30	75	150
Puzzle	Whitman	1958	11-1/2" x 14-1/2", Three Good Fairies circling around a baby in a crib	15	35	55
Puzzle	Whitman	1958	11-1/2" x 14-1/2", Sleeping Beauty w/Prince Phillip and Three Good Fairies circling	15	35	55

SLEEPING BEAUTY

TOY	COMPANY	YEAR	DESCRIPTION	GOOD	EX	MIB
Puzzle	Whitman	1958	11-1/2" x 14-1/2", Sleeping Beauty w/forest animals	15	35	55
Sleeping Beauty Alarm Clock	Phinney-Walker	1950s	2-1/2" x 4" x 4-1/2" tall, Sleeping Beauty surrounded by three birds and petting a rabbit	50	75	150
Sleeping Beauty Doll Crib Mattress		1960s	9" x 17", Sleeping Beauty and the fairies	15	25	50
Sleeping Beauty Jack-In-The-Box	Enesco	1980s	Princess Aurora, wooden box, plays "Once Upon A Dream"	40	75	160
Sleeping Beauty Magic Paint Set	Whitman			25	50	75
Sleeping Beauty Squeeze Toy	Dell	1959	4" x 4" x 5" tall, rubber, Sleeping Beauty w/rabbit	25	50	75
Sleeping Beauty Sticker Fun Book	Whitman	1959		15	30	50

SMOKEY BEAR

TOY	COMPANY	YEAR	DESCRIPTION	GOOD	EX	MIB
Smokey Bank			6" tall, china	20	40	100
Smokey Bear and the Campers Book	Golden	1961		10	20	40
Smokey Bear Coloring Book	Whitman	1958		10	20	50
Smokey Bear Record	Peter Pan		45 rpm	5	10	30
Smokey Bobbing Head Figure		1960s	6-1/4" tall	40	125	300
Smokey Doll	Ideal	1950s	15" plush, vinyl face	50	125	250
Smokey Figure	Dakin	1971	figure on a tree stump	30	75	150
Smokey Soaky		1960s	9" tall, plastic	10	25	50
Smokey Wristwatch	Hawthorne	1960s		45	100	225

SNOW WHITE AND THE SEVEN DWARFS

TOY	COMPANY	YEAR	DESCRIPTION	GOOD	EX	MIB
Baby Rattle	Krueger	1938	Snow White at piano, Dwarfs playing instruments	150	250	400
Bashful Doll	Ideal	1930s		65	150	350
Dime Register Bank	Disney	1938	holds up to five dollars	65	150	350
Doc Doll	Ideal	1930s		65	150	350
Doc Lamp	LaMode Studios	1938	8" tall, plaster	60	150	275
Dopey Bank	Crown Toy	1938	7-1/2" tall, wood composition	60	125	275
Dopey Dime Register Bank	Disney	1938	holds up to $5	50	125	350
Dopey Doll	Ideal	1930s		65	125	300
Dopey Doll	Chad Valley	1938	cloth body	55	100	250
Dopey Doll	Krueger		14" tall	100	175	325
Dopey Doll	Knickerbocker	1938	11" tall composition	100	200	450
Dopey Figure		1960s	ceramic figure and barrel	15	30	75
Dopey Lamp		1940s	9" tall, ceramic base w/Dopey	50	100	250
Dopey Rolykin	Marx		2"	35	75	125
Dopey Soaky		1960s	10" tall	11	30	60
Dopey Ventriloquist Doll	Ideal	1938	18" tall	120	250	600
Dopey Walker	Marx	1938	9" tall, tin, rocking walker	300	550	850
Grumpy Doll	Knickerbocker	1938	11" tall, composition	100	250	550
Happy Doll		1930s	5-1/2" tall, composition, holding a silver pick w/a black handle	50	100	250
Happy Toy	YS Toys (Taiwan)		battery operated, Happy fries eggs	50	100	250
Ironing Board	Wolverine		tin board and cover	15	25	50
Pencil Box	Venus Pencil		3" x 8" x 1"	75	125	185
Puzzle	Jaymar	1960s	11" x 14"	20	35	60
Puzzles	Whitman	1938	set of two	60	120	200
Radio	Emerson	1938	8" x 8" w/characters on cabinet	450	1000	3200
Refrigerator	Wolverine	1970s	15", tin, single door, white and yellow depicting Snow White	25	50	100
Safety Blocks	Halsam	1938	7-1/2" x 14-1/2"	50	125	225

255

SNOW WHITE AND THE SEVEN DWARFS

TOY	COMPANY	YEAR	DESCRIPTION	GOOD	EX	MIB
Sand Pail	Ohio Art	1938	8", tin, Snow White plays hide-n-seek w/the dwarfs	50	125	300
Seven Dwarfs Figures	Seiberling	1938	5-1/2", rubber	130	300	650
Seven Dwarfs Target Game	Chad Valley	1930s	6-1/2" x 11-1/2" target, spring locked gun	125	250	400
Sled	S. L. Allen	1938	40" long wood slat and metal runner sled w/character decals	150	275	500
Sneezy Doll	Krueger		14" tall	125	225	400
Snow White and the Seven Dwarfs Book	Whitman	1938	Big Little Book	25	60	125
Snow White and the Seven Dwarfs Dolls	Deluxe	1940s	22" Snow White and 7" dwarfs	350	700	1600
Snow White Doll	Knickerbocker	1939	3" x 7" x 3-1/2", composition w/movable arms and legs	60	250	600
Snow White Doll	Ideal	1938	3-1/2" x 6-1/2" x 16" tall, fabric face and arms, red/white dress w/dwarf and forest animal design	250	600	900
Snow White Doll	Horsman		8", in illustrated box	25	50	100
Snow White Doll	Knickerbocker	1940	12" tall, composition	80	250	600
Snow White Lamp	LaMode Studios	1938	8-1/2" tall	40	90	300
Snow White Marionette	Tony Sarg/Alexander	1930s	12-1/2" tall	65	125	375
Snow White Mirror		1940s	9-1/2", plastic handle	25	50	125
Snow White Model Making Set	Sculptorcraft	1930s		65	125	375
Snow White Paper Dolls	Whitman	1938	10" x 15" x 1-1/2"	85	250	500
Snow White Sewing Set	Ontex	1940s		30	55	100
Snow White Sink	Wolverine	1960s	tin	15	25	50
Snow White Soaky				15	40	75
Snow White Table Quoits	Chad Valley	1930s	9-1/2" x 21" x 1-1/4" deep	125	225	350
Tea Set	Marx	1960s	teapot, five saucers, large plates and tea cups	40	70	150
Tea Set	Ohio Art	1937	plates, cups, tray, saucers	50	150	325
Tea Set	Wadeheath	1930s	white china, teapot, cups, saucers, and creamer	125	250	400

SPORTS

TOY	COMPANY	YEAR	DESCRIPTION	GOOD	EX	MIB
Dorothy Hamill Doll	Ideal	1975	11-1/4" tall	30	55	85
Evel Knievel Doll	Ideal		6" tall	20	35	75
Julius Erving (Dr. J) Doll		1974		20	40	75
Muhammed Ali Wristwatch	Bradley	1980	chrome case, sweep seconds, brown leather band, face shows Ali in trunks and gloves, w/signature beneath	35	65	150
O.J. Simpson Doll		1974		30	75	250
Wayne Gretzky Doll	Mattel		12" tall	25	50	75

STEVE CANYON

TOY	COMPANY	YEAR	DESCRIPTION	GOOD	EX	MIB
Steve Canyon Costume	Halco	1959		25	50	175
Steve Canyon's Interceptor Station Punch Out	Golden	1950s		40	80	160
Steve Canyon's Membership Card and Badge			1/2" x 4" Milton Caniff membership card for the Airagers, Morse code on back, 3" tin litho color badge w/gold feathers w/Steve's face centered	70	130	200

SUPERHEROES

TOY	COMPANY	YEAR	DESCRIPTION	GOOD	EX	MIB
Amazing Spider-Car	Mego	1976	10" long, red plastic	25	35	85
Aquaman Halloween Costume	Ben Cooper	1967		20	55	80
Aquaman Jigsaw Puzzle	Whitman	1968	100 pieces; Aquaman and Mera	20	40	60
Aquaman Scourge of the Sea Book	Whitman	1968	Big Little Book	15	25	50
Captain America Bendy Figure	Lakeside	1966	6", rubber	50	85	150
Captain America Halloween Costume	Ben Cooper	1967		55	125	250
Captain America Rocket Racer	Buddy L	1984	Secret Wars, remote control battery-operated car	20	35	125
Captain America Scooter	Marx	1967	4", yellow plastic friction toy w/figure	100	225	350
Comic Book Tattoos	Topps	1967	Aquaman, Wonder Woman, Superman, or Batman	20	30	50
Flash Glass	Pepsi	1978		20	40	65
Green Lantern Halloween Costume	Ben Cooper	1967		80	175	260
Hawkman Button	Button World	1966	3", "Hawkman Superhero Club"	20	30	40
Justice League of America Display Card	Fleer	1970	cardboard display from inside gumball machine	30	45	75
Marvel Superheroes Card Game	Milton Bradley	1978		20	25	50
Marvel Superheroes Colorforms Set	Colorforms	1983		10	20	40
Marvel Superheroes Easy Show Projector	Kenner	1967	projector and three cartridges	55	150	250
Marvel Superheroes Puzzle	Milton Bradley	1967	100 pieces	40	80	175
Marvel Superheroes Sparkle Paint Set	Kenner	1967		40	80	175
Marvel World Adventure Play Set	Amsco	1975	w/stand-up scenes and figures	60	150	250
Mr. Bubble Superfriends Box		1984	bubble bath box features Superman, Wonder Woman, Batman, and Robin	20	30	75
Spider-Man Button	Button World	1966	3", "Superhero Club"	15	35	60
Spider-Man Coloring Book	Marvel Books	1983	oversized, "The Arms of Doctor Octopus"	10	20	40
Spider-Man Crazy Foam	American Aerosol	1974		10	30	45
Spider-Man Friction Vehicle	Marx	1968	tin litho w/Spider-Man figure at wheel	80	175	400
Spider-Man Hand Puppet	Imperial	1976	9", vinyl head, plastic body	15	30	50
Wonder Woman Glass	Pepsi	1978	6"	10	25	40
Wonder Woman Record	Peter Pan Records	1977	33-1/3" rpm record w/comic book	10	25	35

SUPERMAN

TOY	COMPANY	YEAR	DESCRIPTION	GOOD	EX	MIB
3-D Adventures of Superman Comic Book	DC Comics	1950s	w/3-D goggles	50	100	250
Action Comics #1	DC Comics	1938	first appearance of Superman	70000	100000	185000
Adventures of Superman Book	Random House	1942	6-1/2" x 9" hardcover, 220 pages, author George Lowther, full color dust jacket	500	750	1200
Adventures of Superman Book	Random House	1942	6-1/2" x 9" hardcover by George Lowther, no dust jacket	150	200	250
Adventures of Superman Book	Random House	1942	4" x 5-1/2" armed services edition	100	200	400
Bicycle Siren	Empire	1970s		10	20	30
Book and Record Set	Musette Records	1947	The Flying Train	40	100	125

TOY	COMPANY	YEAR	DESCRIPTION	GOOD	EX	MIB
Book and Record Set	Musette Records	1947	The Magic Ring	40	100	125
Book, With Superman at the Gilbert Hall of Science	Gilbert	1948	32-page promo catalog for Gilbert's Erector Sets and other toys, illustrated w/Superman	75	100	150
Bubble Gum Badge	Fo-Lee Gum Corp.	1948	shield-shaped brass finish badge shows a variant of the chain breaking pose inside a sun burst pattern ringed w/stars	1000	3500	5000
Children's Dish Set	Boontonware	1966	7" plate, 5-1/2" bowl, 3-1/2" cup, all white plastic w/Superman image	50	100	150
Cinematic Picture Pistol	Daisy	1940	non-electric, film is viewed through view in back of gun, metal gun w/one pre-loaded 28 scene Superman film	300	750	1500
Crayon-by-Numbers Set	Transogram	1954	16 crayons and 44 action scenes	100	200	300
Daily Planet Jetcopter	Corgi	1979		20	40	60
Dangle Dandies Mobile	Kellogg's	1955	set of eight cut outs on boxes of Rice Krispies and Corn Flakes	75	100	150
Energized Superman Figure	Remco	1979	12" tall battery operated hard body figure, in box	35	65	150
Fan Card	National Comics	1950s	5" x 7" promo b/w post card w/signature "Best Wishes, George Reeves"	75	150	200
Fan Card		1942	7" x 10", shows full color Superman in hands on hips pose, reads, "Best wishes from your friend Superman"	250	700	1000
Film Viewer		1965	plastic hand viewer w/two boxes of film, on illustrated card	25	40	65
Film Viewer		1947	1-1/2" x 4" x 6-1/2" wide boxed set of hand-held viewer and six films	250	500	700
Film Viewer	Acme	1947	1-1/2" x 6-1/2" wide boxed set of hand-held viewer and two films	100	400	600
Flying Noise Balloon	Van Dam	1966	oversized balloon makes noise in flight, Superman illustration on balloon and card	12	23	35
Flying Superman	Transogram	1955	12-1/2" tall molded plastic figure propelled by "super flight launcher", a rubber band attached to a pistol grip holder, on illustrated card	55	100	150
Flying Superman	Kellogg's	1950s	premium, 5" x 6 1/2", rubber band propelled, w/instruction sheet and mailer	100	200	300
Flying Superman	Kellogg's	1950s	plastic premium, 5" x 6-1/2", toy only	50	100	150
Hair Brush	Monarch	1940	wood, full length decal of Superman, brush came in handle and no-handle styles w/box	50	150	300
Hair Brush	Avon	1976	Superman handle, illustrated box	15	25	50
Jumbo Movie Viewer	Acme	1950s	blue/yellow plastic viewer w/35 mm "theatre size" film, on illustrated card, w/one filmstrip	90	165	250
Junior Defense League of America Membership Certificate	Superman, Inc.	1940s	Superman Bread premium, red/blue print and Superman bust and logo on paper, "signed" by Clark Kent	250	500	1000
Kryptonite Rock		1970s	glow-in-the-dark rocks sold as kryptonite chunks, in illustrated box	10	15	25

TOY	COMPANY	YEAR	DESCRIPTION	GOOD	EX	MIB
Krypto-Raygun Film Viewer	Daisy	1940	battery-operated metal projector gun, seven Superman filmstrips, illustrated box	500	1000	2500
Membership Certificate		1965	last year of club	50	75	150
Mini Comic Book	Kellogg's	1955	cereal premium, #1-B, Supershow of Metropolis	90	175	300
Mini Comic Book	Kellogg's	1955	cereal premium, #1-A, Duel in Space	90	175	300
Mini Comic Book	Kellogg's	1955	cereal premium, #1, The Superman Time Capsule	125	230	350
Movie Viewer	Acme	1950s	black/red plastic viewer w/two individually boxed Superman films	70	130	200
Movie Viewer	Acme Plastics	1940	tortoise shell plastic, and three individually boxed Superman films, in large full color die-cut box	200	500	800
Movie Viewer	Acme Plastics	1947	black plastic viewer, white knob and two individually boxed Superman films, in red/blue die-cut box	100	300	500
Movie Viewer	Acme Plastics	1948	red plastic viewer and three individually boxed Superman films, in small full color die-cut box	100	300	500
Official Magic Kit	Bar-Zim	1956	magic balls, disappearing cards, multiplying corks, vanishing trick, shell game, balancing belt and directions, in illustrated box	350	750	1200
Official Superman Costume	Ben Cooper	1954	blue/red suit w/red/yellow monogram and belt, in box	140	260	400
Official Superman Krypto-Raygun Film Viewer	Daisy	1940	includes raygun, battery, bulb, lens and one film strip, in illustrated box	500	1000	1500
Official Superman Playsuit	Ben Cooper	1970	cloth suit in illustrated box	20	40	60
Official Superman Playsuit	Funtime Playwear	1954	rayon outfit, red cap w/screened Superman image, navy and red suit w/5" gold monogram and belt	200	400	600
Official Superman Two-Piece Kiddie Swim Set		1950s	set of rubber swim fins and goggles w/Superman's image or "S" symbol, in box	50	150	225
Original Radio Broadcasts Record	Nostalgia Lane	1977	old Superman radio teleplays, in illustrated sleeve showing chain breaking pose in color and b/w strip panels	10	25	50
Paint-by-Numbers Watercolor Set	Transogram	1954	16 watercolors and 44 action scenes	75	200	250
Patch		1970s	cloth diamond-shaped patch of "S" logo in gold/red, several sizes, each	5	10	15
Patch		1970s	rectangular white patch w/green border shows full color Superboy running toward viewer	20	40	65
Patch		1970s	rectangular white cloth patch w/green border shows full color Supergirl flying	5	10	15
Patch		1940s	3-1/2" round patch shows chain breaking pose	750	2000	5700
Patch	Superman Bread	1942	cardboard shield	200	500	1300

TOY	COMPANY	YEAR	DESCRIPTION	GOOD	EX	MIB
Patch		1973	diamond-shaped cloth patch shows Superman standing against vertical red/white stripes, wide yellow border has stars and reads "Superman Junior Olympics"	5	10	15
Patch		1970s	triangular orange cloth patch w/red border shows Superman flying over desert scene	5	10	15
Patch		1939	5-1/2" diameter fabric premium patch, shows 3/4 profile of Superman breaking chains off chest, Supermen of America - - Action Comics	1500	7000	9000
Pen	Jaffe	1947	red/blue pen on illustrated card	200	400	625
Pencil Box	Mattel	1966		25	50	75
Pencil Holder	Superman, Inc.	1940s	hollow holder in shape of large pencil, illustrated on shaft w/red and blue on white images and Superman-Tim Club logos	400	800	1200
Pennant		1973	35th anniversary item, felt pennant has Amazing World of Superman logo and reads "Metropolis, Illinois, Home of Superman", came in two sizes, each	12	25	50
Pennant		1940s	yellow pennant w/Superman image and raised logo	300	800	1200
Pillow		1960s	12" square felt pillow w/color art of flying Superman	35	65	100
Pin	Kellogg's	1940s	7/8" round pin w/black/red/blue bust of Superman, most common pin in Pep Cereal series of late 1940s	12	25	35
Puzzle	APC	1973		10	15	20
Puzzle	Whitman	1966	150 pieces, 14" X 18", Superman	12	25	35
Puzzle	Whitman	1966	two frame tray puzzles: one shows Superman fighting space robot, other shows him flying past manned rocket ship in outer space, each	25	50	75
Puzzle	Saalfield	1940	300 pieces, 12 x 16", Superman w/Muscles Like Steel	150	350	500
Puzzle	Saalfield	1940	500 pieces, 16 x 20", Superman Stands Alone	200	500	750
Puzzle	Saalfield	1940	500 pieces, 16 x 20", Superman Saves a Life	200	500	750
Puzzle	Saalfield	1940	300 pieces, 12 x 16", Superman Shows his Super Strength	150	350	500
Puzzle	Saalfield	1940	300 pieces, 12 x 16", Superman Saves the Streamliner	150	350	500
Puzzle	Saalfield	1940	300 pieces, 12 x 16", Superman the Man of Tomorrow	150	350	500
Puzzle		1940	set of two Superman puzzles	300	600	1200
Puzzles	Saalfield	1940	set of six small puzzles w/42 pieces each	500	1000	1500
Record and Club Membership Kit		1966	33-1/3 rpm record of the original comic, Superman Club card, shoulder patch and 1" tin litho club button, in 12" square illustrated box	100	150	200
Super Babe Doll	Imperial Crown Toy	1947	15" tall, rubber skin, movable arms and legs, sleep eyes, composition head	500	1000	2500
Super Candy and Toy	Phoenix Candy	1967	boxed candy w/a small toy inside each box	50	75	125

TOY	COMPANY	YEAR	DESCRIPTION	GOOD	EX	MIB
Super Heroes String Puppets	Madison	1978	string controlled cloth and vinyl marionette	25	40	65
Superman 3-D Cut-Out Picture	Kellogg's	1950s	4-1/2 x 6-1/2" premium framed cut-out of Superman from the back of cereal box, reads "Best Wishes From Your Friend Superman"	60	80	100
Superman Action Game	American Toy Works	1940s	wood and cardboard wartime game, Superman holds tottering bridge and kids shoot darts at tanks on bridge	750	1500	2000
Superman and Supergirl Push Puppets	Kohner	1968	set of two: 5-1/4" on bases, in window box	200	600	1000
Superman Back-a-Wack	Dell	1966	blue plastic paddle w/gold imprinted "S" logo and name, elastic string and red ball, on illustrated card	50	100	150
Superman Balloon		1966	small balloon w/centered image	5	15	25
Superman Bank		1949	9-1/2" painted ceramic shows youthful looking Superman standing on a cloud, possibly an unlicensed import or carnival prize	300	500	800
Superman Bank		1974	bust of Superman	50	75	100
Superman Beanie		1940s	hat w/two-color Superman embossed images on brim	500	700	1400
Superman Belt	Pioneer	1940s	brown leather w/Superman images and rectangular buckle, in box	300	500	750
Superman Belt	Pioneer	1940s	clear plastic w/color images and round brass buckle in box	300	500	700
Superman Belt	Kellogg's	1950s	28" long red plastic, aluminum "S" symbol buckle in red/yellow	100	250	325
Superman Belt Buckle		1940s	square metal buckle shows red/blue chain breaking pose	100	150	400
Superman Book and Record Set	Peter Pan	1970s	two stories w/record	5	10	15
Superman Button	WABC Radio	1966	radio premium button for "It's a Bird, It's a Plane..." production, shows faceless Superman w/"WABC 77" across chest	100	150	300
Superman Candy	Leader Novelty Candy	1940	boxed candy w/punch-out trading cards on box back and coupons redeemable for Superman items, red box, front shows chain-breaking pose	500	750	1500
Superman Candy Ring	Leader Novelty Candy	1940	gold finish hidden compartment ring, face is embossed w/"M", lightning bolt and eyeball symbol, compartment shows Superman decal image	1300	6000	20000
Superman Christmas Card		1940s	4" x 5", Superman Brings You Christmas Greetings, shows him flying w/small tree in hands	50	150	300
Superman Cigarette Lighter	Dunhill	1940s	battery-operated table-top lighter has chrome finish figure standing on black base	500	1000	1500
Superman City Game	Remco	1966	board game w/magnetic figures and buildings	150	300	500
Superman Club Button		1966	3-1/2" celluloid button, shows 3/4 profile thigh-up view of Superman in hands on hips pose, reads, "Official Member Superman Club"	10	20	30

TOY	COMPANY	YEAR	DESCRIPTION	GOOD	EX	MIB
Superman Costume		1950s	red pants and tie-on cape, blue shirt w/red, blue and yellow "S" emblem on chest, yellow belt	100	260	400
Superman Crazy Foam	American Aerosol	1970s	spray bath soap in full color illustrated can	25	50	75
Superman Crusader Ring		1940s	brass or silver finish ring shows forward facing bust of Superman	50	120	250
Superman Cup	Burger King	1984	one of four in set w/figural handles, others are Batman, Wonder Woman and Darkseid	5	7	10
Superman Cut-Outs	Saalfield	1940	perforated figures, heavy stock paper, blue cover	500	1700	3000
Superman Cut-Outs	Saalfield	1940	red cover, lighter paper than blue book, non-perforated cut-outs	500	1700	3000
Superman Dime Register Bank		1940s	1/2" x 2-1/2" x 2 1/2" yellow tin, front shows full color Superman breaking chains off chest, held $5 in dimes	100	250	400
Superman Doll	Ideal	1940	13-1/2" tall, wood jointed body w/composition head, movable head, arms and legs, ball knob hands	500	1000	2500
Superman Doll	Toy Works	1977	25-1/2" tall, cloth, w/cape	12	25	35
Superman Doll	Knickerbocker		20" tall plush in box	12	25	35
Superman Electronic Question and Answer Quiz Machine	Lisbeth Whiting Co.	1966	battery operated quiz game in full color illustrated box	50	100	200
Superman Figure	Fun Things		6" rubber figure on card	9	16	25
Superman Figure	Chemtoy		rubber, three different poses, on card, each	25	40	50
Superman Figure	Presents		15" vinyl/cloth figure on base	25	40	50
Superman Figure	Japan	1979	plastic body w/soft vinyl head, movable arms and head, in illustrated window box	40	60	75
Superman Figure	Palitoy		8" figure on card	35	65	100
Superman Figurine	Ideal	1966	3" tall hard plastic painted or unpainted figure on base, removable cape, part of Justice League series	35	65	85
Superman Figurine	Craft Master	1984	solid figurine and paint set, on illustrated card	25	50	75
Superman Golden Muscle Building Set	Peter Puppets Playthings	1954	handles, springs, hand grippers, jump rope, wall hooks, measuring tape, progress chart, membership certificate and button, illustrated box	700	1000	1500
Superman Gum Ring	Gum, Inc.	1940	gold finish hidden compartment ring, face is embossed w/"S", lightning bolt and Superman bust, compartment shows Superman image	2500	10000	30000
Superman Hand Puppet	Ideal	1966	11", cloth body, vinyl head	25	40	65
Superman Hood Ornament	Lee	1940s	chrome finish, shows Superman in stylized running pose w/box	500	2000	3500
Superman II Trading Cards	Topps	1981	set of 88 cards, complete set	20	30	40
Superman II Trading Cards	Costa Rican	1981	set of 88 cards, complete set	18	35	50
Superman II View-Master Set			three reels, based on film	5	10	20
Superman III Trading Cards	Topps	1983	set of 99 cards, complete set	5	10	15

TOY	COMPANY	YEAR	DESCRIPTION	GOOD	EX	MIB
Superman III View-Master Set			three reels, based on film	5	10	15
Superman Junior Defense League Pin		1940s	die cut pin in shape of flying Superman holding banner aloft, gold finish pin w/red/white/blue detailing	75	150	250
Superman Junior Horseshoe Set	Super Swim	1950s	four rubber horseshoes, two rubber bases and two wood pegs and Official Sports Club card and rules for sportsmanship	50	100	200
Superman Junior Swim Goggles	Super Swim	1950s	plastic lenses, rubber goggles w/red strap, "S" logo and membership card for Superman Safety Swim Club	35	80	175
Superman Kite	Hiflyer	1982		5	10	15
Superman Kite	Pressman	1966		50	75	125
Superman Krypton Rocket	Park Plastics	1956	2" x 9" x 9-1/2" water powered rocket w/Krypton generating pump, reserve fuel tank and Krypton Rocket, in illustrated box, same as Kellogg's rocket but in mass market packaging w/added fuel tank	150	300	400
Superman Krypton Rocket	Kellogg's	1954	2" x 9" x 9-1/2" water powered rocket w/"Krypton generating pump," in mailer box	150	300	400
Superman Krypto-Raygun Filmstrips	Daisy	1940s	extra boxed films for Krypto-Raygun, each	15	30	45
Superman Member Ring		1940		5000	20000	70000
Superman Moccasins	Penobscot Shoe	1940s	leather moccasins w/Superman chain breaking pose on toe upper	300	1000	2000
Superman Mug		1966	white glass, red and blue logo w/Superman image, reverse picture is Superman breaking chain	20	40	65
Superman Mug		1950s	left handed mug, shows Superman on front and name across cape in back, handle has arrow and star	75	150	250
Superman Muscle Building Club Button	Peter Puppets Playthings	1954	part of Golden Muscle Building set, full color bust in sunburst circle in white button, reads "Superman Muscle Building Club"	50	250	500
Superman Necktie		1940s		100	200	300
Superman Necktie Set		1940s	boxed set of two ties, small tie shows Superman standing w/arms crosses, larger tie shows Superman landing	500	1000	1500
Superman of Metropolis Award Certificate		1973	premium given out during Metropolis, Illinois' 1973 35th anniversary of Superman celebration	20	40	65
Superman Official Eight-Piece Junior Quoit Set		1940s	game in illustrated box includes wood and rubber game pieces, instruction booklet and membership card for "Superman Official Sports Club"	75	100	150
Superman Paint Set	American Toy Works	1940s	larger version, shows Superman in front of pallet background	250	750	1200
Superman Paint Set	American Toy Works	1940	three brushes, small palette, water cup, 14 different paints and four b/w cartoon panels, in 11" x 14-1/2" color illustrated box	250	750	1200

TOY	COMPANY	YEAR	DESCRIPTION	GOOD	EX	MIB
Superman Paint Set	American Toy Works	1940s	box shows Superman flying up toward upper right corner of box, w/pallet and brushes at lower right, "Paint Set" inside pallet	250	750	1200
Superman Paint-by-Number Book	Whitman	1966	11" x 13-1/2", 40 pictures plus coloring guide on back cover	15	25	50
Superman Phone Booth Radio	Vanity Fair	1978	battery operated AM radio of green British-style booth has color bas-relief Superman exiting	35	75	150
Superman Pinball Game	Bally	1978	full-sized arcade game	200	500	1000
Superman Planter		1970s	3" diameter painted ceramic	5	10	15
Superman Play Set	Ideal	1973	self-contained vinyl covered full color snap-close case opens to three backdrops, Fortress of Solitude, Daily Planet and villain's hideout, for staging action scenes w/supplied color punch-outs	50	75	150
Superman Playsuit	Fishback	1940	red and blue imprinted blue smock shirt and pants w/tie-on red cape	150	500	1200
Superman Pogo Stick		1977	48" w/a vinyl bust on top	25	50	100
Superman Pop-Up Book	Random House	1979	hardcover, full color	15	25	50
Superman Press-Out Book	Whitman	1966	punch out, assemble and hang scenes and characters	20	35	65
Superman Push Puppet	Kohner	1966	5-1/4" on base, in window box	50	75	100
Superman Radio		1973	transistor radio made in punch-out shape of Superman from waist up	50	75	150
Superman Record Player		1978	latching box briefcase type record player illustrated on all sides in full color, also features b/w origin strip on back	55	100	150
Superman Ring	Nestle's	1978	premium ring, gold finish w/white circle center and yellow/red diamond "S" logo in middle	5	15	25
Superman Roller Skates	Larami	1975	plastic w/color bust of Superman shaped around front of each skate, in illustrated window box	20	50	75
Superman Rub-Ons	Hasbro	1966	magic picture transfers in box illustrated w/picture of Superman flying	50	100	150
Superman School Bag	Acme	1950s	red/blue fold-over clasp vinyl bag, screened full color Superman figure, black plastic handle and shoulder strap	75	150	300
Superman Scrap Book	Saalfield	1940	cover shows Superman flying over mountains toward stylized S.O.S. transmission	1000	1500	3000
Superman Senior Rubber Horseshoe Set		1950s	in box	55	100	150
Superman Senior Swim Goggles	Super Swim	1950s	plastic lenses, rubber goggles w/red strap, "S" logo on bridge, membership card for Superman Safety Swim Club	40	80	150
Superman Sky Hero	Marx	1977	rubber band glider w/color Superman image, on card	25	40	75
Superman Soaky	Avon	1978	9-1/2" bubble bath bottle, Superman stands atop building	30	40	50

SUPERMAN

TOY	COMPANY	YEAR	DESCRIPTION	GOOD	EX	MIB
Superman Soaky	Colgate Palmolive	1965	10" soap bottle, shows him standing w/hands at sides	20	40	75
Superman Song Record	A.A. Records	1950s	6" two-song, 45 rpm record in sleeve, other song is "Tarzan Song"	25	50	100
Superman Space Satellite Launcher Set	Kellogg's	1950s	premium set of generic plastic gun w/firing "satellite wheel" and illustrated instruction sheet, in mailer box	150	450	1000
Superman Stamp Set		1965	set of six wood-backed character stamps	25	50	100
Superman Statue		1940s	15" tall, crude painted plaster carnival prize	75	250	400
Superman Statue	Syracuse Ornament	1942	5-1/2" tall composition statue of Superman in hands on hips pose, finished in brown patina w/red/black highlights	750	2000	4000
Superman Super Watch	Toy House	1967	plastic toy watch w/moveable hands, watch "case" is large "S" chest symbol, on illustrated card	15	30	75
Superman Supertime Wristwatch	National Comics	1950s	gray band, stamped red "S" logo, silver western style buckle, full color hands on hips pose inside chrome finish case, second hand, even-hour numbers around face, in full color box	250	750	1500
Superman Suspenders	Pioneer	1948	elastic, illustrated box	350	500	900
Superman Tank	Linemar	1958	large battery operated tin, 3-D Superman w/a cloth cape, in illustrated box	350	1750	3000
Superman Telephone	ATE	1979	plastic phone w/large figure of Superman in hands on hips pose standing over key pad, receiver hangs up into back of his cape, illustrated box	150	750	1200
Superman the Movie Trading Cards	Topps	1979	set of 88 cards, second issue	12	25	35
Superman the Movie Trading Cards	Topps	1978	set of 77 cards, first issue	7	13	20
Superman the Movie Trading Cards	OPC	1979	set of 132 cards	12	25	35
Superman the Movie Trading Cards	French	1979	set of 180 cards	18	35	50
Superman the Movie View-Master Set		1979	three reels, based on film	5	10	15
Superman Tilt Track	Kohner	1966	marble skill game, in illustrated window box	65	95	175
Superman To The Rescue Coloring Book	Whitman	1964	cover shows Superman rescuing woman	25	50	85
Superman Toothbrush	Janex	1970s	figural, battery operated	20	35	65
Superman Towels	G.H. Wood	1970s	children's sponge towels, illustrated	12	25	50
Superman Trading Cards	Gum Inc.	1940	2-1/2" x 3-1/4" cards, each	25	50	100
Superman Trading Cards	Topps	1966	set of 66 cards, shows George Reeves TV series scenes, each card	5	7	10
Superman Trading Cards	Gum Inc.	1940	2-1/2" x 3-1/4" cards, set of 72	2500	8000	10000
Superman Trading Cards	Topps	1966	set of 66 cards, George Reeves TV series scenes	90	165	300
Superman Trading Cards Display Box	Topps	1966	2" x 4" x 8" display box of 24 unopened packs, box shows George Reeves bust	500	750	1300

Yogi Bear Friction Toy, 1960s

Yogi Bear Bubble Pipe, 1963, Transogram

TOY	COMPANY	YEAR	DESCRIPTION	GOOD	EX	MIB
Superman Trading Cards Wrapper	Gum Inc.	1940	4-1/2" x 6" waxed paper	300	500	750
Superman Turnover Tank	Linemar	1950s	tin wind-up, flat tin Superman wears yellow suit and red cape, olive drab tank is marked M-25, rare in box	500	1200	2500
Superman Turnover Tank	Marx	1940	2-1/2 x 3" x 4" long tin wind-up	500	1200	2500
Superman Utility Belt	Remco	1979	illustrated window box, decoder glasses, kryptonite detector, nonworking watch, handcuffs, ring, decoder map, press card and secret message	50	150	250
Superman View-Master Set	GAF		three reels, based on cartoon series	5	10	15
Superman Wall Clock	New Haven	1978	plastic and cardboard battery operated framed wall clock showing Superman fighting alien shaceship	30	60	100
Superman Wallet	Croyden	1950s	brown, color embossed flying Superman and logo	50	150	200
Superman Wallet		1960s	brown leather	25	40	65
Superman Water Gun	Multiple Toymakers	1967	6" plastic	30	100	175
Superman Workbook	DC Comics	1940s	English grammar workbook	100	450	750
Superman Wristwatch	Bradley	1959	dial shows Superman flying over city, second hand, chrome finish case	600	800	1400
Superman Wristwatch	New Haven Clock	1939	flattened oval face, shows color image of standing Superman from knees up, leather band	600	1400	2000
Superman Wristwatch		1977	gold bezel, stainless back, blue leather band, face shows Superman flying upward from below	35	65	150
Superman Wristwatch	Una-Donna	1986	plastic case and band, several color and face illustrations, each	10	20	50
Superman Wristwatch	New Haven Clock	1940s	squared-oval faced watch, leather band, dial shows Superman standing, hands on hips, in illustrated box	600	1400	2200
Superman's Christmas Adventure Comic Book	Macy's	1940	1940 Macy's holiday premium	700	1500	2500
Superman's Christmas Adventure Record	Decca	1940s	set of three 78 rpm records in illustrated sleeves	150	400	800
Superman's Christmas Play Book		1944	department store premium	200	500	1000
Superman-Tim Club Button	Superman, Inc.	1940s	two different, both say Superman-Tim Club and have red/blue lettering and images on white background	50	75	100
Superman-Tim Club Membership Card	Superman, Inc.	1940s	blue/red or red/black card	750	125	300
Superman-Tim Club Press Card		1940s	blue/red card for identifying self as an Official Reporter for club	100	150	325
Superman-Tim Club Redbacks	Superman, Inc.	1940s	red on white imprinted coupons styled to look like money, denominations of $1, $5 and $10 "redbacks", each	10	20	30
Superman-Tim Club Ring		1940s	bronze finish metal ring w/embossed image of Superman in flight, w/initials S and T near his feet	800	4000	8000
Superman-Tim Magazine		1940s	5" x 7" monthly store premium, each	50	75	150
Supermen of America Membership Certificate		1948	8-1/2" x 11", signed by "Clark Kent"	75	150	350

SUPERMAN

TOY	COMPANY	YEAR	DESCRIPTION	GOOD	EX	MIB
Toy Wristwatch	Germany	1950s	non-working toy watch, blue plastic band, rectangular case w/full color full standing pose on white dial	35	65	150
Trick Picture Sun Camera	Made in Japan	1950s	when left in the sun for two minutes, the camera "develops" a picture of Superman fighting a space monster	75	150	225
Utensil Set	Imperial Knife	1966	stainless steel spoon and fork set w/Superman on the handles, on 4-1/2 x 10" illustrated card	50	75	175
Wall Banner		1966	16" x 25" w/hanging rod at top, shows large central picture of Superman in front of city skyline and two lower panels of him smashing rocks and flying through space	40	70	150

TARZAN

TOY	COMPANY	YEAR	DESCRIPTION	GOOD	EX	MIB
Bracelet		1965	drink more milk radio premium	1000	2000	3000
Figure		1930s	2-1/2" tall, celluloid, French	300	750	1200
Jungle Map		1933	radio premium	150	400	650
Kala Ape Figure	Dakin	1984	3" tall	5	10	20
Poster	Paper Mills	1933	three masks; premium	350	600	1250
Tarzan Flasher Ring	Vari-Vue	1960s		10	20	40
Tarzan Party Set	Amscan	1977		10	20	30
Young Tarzan Figure	Dakin	1984	4", bendable	10	15	20

THREE LITTLE PIGS

TOY	COMPANY	YEAR	DESCRIPTION	GOOD	EX	MIB
Big Bad Wolf Pocket Watch	Ingersoll	1934		200	750	1500
Puzzle	Jaymar	1940s	7" x 10" x 2"	45	75	150
Three Little Pigs Bracelet		1930s	1/2" x 2-1/4", wolf blowing down a house w/pig running away	75	200	325
Three Little Pigs Sand Pail	Ohio Art	1930s	4-1/2", tin	50	90	250
Three Little Pigs Soaky Set	Drew Chemical	1960s	8" tall each: Three Little Pigs and the Big Bad Wolf	70	125	250
Three Little Pigs Wind-Up Toy	Schuco	1930s	4-1/2" pigs playing fiddle, fife and drum	250	475	750
Who's Afraid of the Big Bad Wolf Game	Parker Brothers	1930s		65	300	500

TOM AND JERRY

TOY	COMPANY	YEAR	DESCRIPTION	GOOD	EX	MIB
Jerry Figure	Marx	1973	4" tall	15	25	50
Puzzles	Whitman		four frame tray puzzles	20	30	65
Tom and Jerry Bank	Gorham	1980	6" tall	20	35	65
Tom and Jerry Figure Set		1975	walking, Tom, Jerry, and Droopy	20	40	85
Tom and Jerry Go Kart	Marx	1973	plastic, friction drive	30	60	95
Tom and Jerry on Scooter	Marx	1971	plastic friction drive	15	25	40
Tom and Jerry Wristwatch	Bradley	1985	quartz, oldies series, small white plastic case and band, sweep seconds, face shows Tom squirting Jerry w/hose	15	20	50
Tom Figure	Marx	1973	6" tall	15	25	55

TONY THE TIGER

TOY	COMPANY	YEAR	DESCRIPTION	GOOD	EX	MIB
Cookie Jar	Kellogg's	1960s	plastic, figural	25	60	100
Figural Bank	Kellogg's	1967		30	45	60
Inflatable Tiger	Kellogg's	1950s		7	20	35
Plush Tiger	Kellogg's	1970s		10	20	40
Radio		1980s	plastic, figural	20	40	65

TOP CAT

TOY	COMPANY	YEAR	DESCRIPTION	GOOD	EX	MIB
Top Cat Figure	Marx	1961	TV-Tinykins, plastic	20	35	50
Top Cat Soaky		1960s	10" tall, vinyl	25	45	75
Viewmarx Micro-Viewer	Marx	1963	plastic	20	35	65

WINNIE THE POOH

TOY	COMPANY	YEAR	DESCRIPTION	GOOD	EX	MIB
Jack-In-The-Box	Carnival Toys	1960s		20	35	65
Kanga and Roo Squeak Toy	Holland Hill	1966	vinyl	15	30	50
Lamp	Dolly Toy	1964	7" tall	30	60	100
Magic Slate	Western Publishing	1965	8-1/2" x 13-1/2"	20	35	50
Puzzle	Whitman	1964	frame tray	10	15	40
Radio	Thilgee	1970s	5" x 6" x 1-1/2" tall	30	55	100
Winnie the Pooh and Christopher Robin Dolls	Horsman	1964	Winnie the Pooh 3-1/2" tall and Christopher 11" tall, set	65	125	225
Winnie the Pooh Button		1960s	3-1/2" celluloid	10	15	25
Winnie the Pooh Doll		1960s	12" tall	15	25	50
Winnie the Pooh Snow Globe			5-1/2", musical	15	30	45

WIZARD OF OZ

TOY	COMPANY	YEAR	DESCRIPTION	GOOD	EX	MIB
Carpet Sweeper	Bissell	1939	child-sized	125	175	275
Cast 'N Paint Set		1975	makes six 6" figures	15	25	35
Chalk Board	Roth American	1975	wood frame, steel stand w/chalk, chalk holder and eraser	16	27	40
Christmas Ornaments	Presents	1989	cloth and vinyl: Dorothy, Scarecrow, Tin Man, Cowardly Lion, Glinda and Wicked Witch, each	8	10	15
Christmas Ornaments	Bradford Novelty	1977	4-1/2" tall, Dorothy, Scarecrow, Tin Man, Cowardly Lion, each	5	8	20
Cookie Jar	Clay Art	1990	white w/relief figures of characters	25	40	85
Cowardly Lion Bank		1960s	ceramic, red nose	30	50	100
Cowardly Lion Costume	Ben Cooper	1975	costume and mask	15	25	50
Cowardly Lion Costume	Collegeville	1989	plastic mask and vinyl bodysuit	10	15	20
Cowardly Lion Costume	Collegeville	1989	deluxe	20	40	50
Cowardly Lion Doll	Presents	1988	vinyl	20	35	50
Cowardly Lion Doll	Largo Toys	1989	rag doll	8	15	25
Cowardly Lion Doll	M-D Tissue	1971	cloth, light brown body w/white snout	8	15	25
Cowardly Lion Doll	Ideal	1984	9", Character Dolls series	20	35	60
Cowardly Lion Mask	Newark Mask Company	1939	linen, hand painted	55	90	150
Cowardly Lion Mask	Don Post Studios	1983	rubber	35	55	85
Cowardly Lion Music Box	Schmid	1983		20	35	50
Cowardly Lion Wind-Up	Durham Industries	1975	on illustrated card	15	20	30
Crayon Box	Cheinco	1975	rectangular, metal	5	8	12

TOY	COMPANY	YEAR	DESCRIPTION	GOOD	EX	MIB
Cut and Make Masks	Dover	1982	eight cut-out color masks	5	10	15
Dandy Lion Doll	Artistic	1962	14" tall, cloth and vinyl	35	55	90
Decoupage Kit		1975	two wooden plaques, scenes based on film	15	25	35
Doodle Dolls	Whiting	1979	three dolls: cardboard parts, yarn, Styrofoam balls, fabric	6	10	25
Dorothy and Friends Visit Oz Book	Curtis Candy	1967	candy premium	5	10	20
Dorothy and Toto Doll	Ideal	1984	9", Character Dolls series	20	35	50
Dorothy Bank		1960s	ceramic, blue dress w/brown wicker basket	30	45	80
Dorothy Costume	Ben Cooper	1975	costume and mask	15	25	40
Dorothy Costume	Collegeville	1989	plastic mask and vinyl bodysuit	8	15	20
Dorothy Costume	Collegeville	1989	deluxe, includes red metallic glitter chips for shoes	20	35	50
Dorothy Doll	Effanbee	1984	14-1/2" tall, vinyl, Judy Garland, blue dress and hair ribbons, ruby slippers, Legend Series	40	70	100
Dorothy Doll	Largo Toys	1989	Judy Garland	8	15	25
Dorothy Doll	Presents	1988	vinyl, blue checkered jumper, white blouse, red slippers, yellow brick road base	20	35	50
Dorothy Doll	M-D Tissue	1971	cloth, stuffed, yellow hair, orange jumper	6	12	30
Dorothy Doll	Ideal	1939	18", Judy Garland, blue checked jumper, open and close brown eyes	475	800	1500
Dorothy Doll	Ideal	1939	15-1/2", Judy Garland, blue checked jumper, open and close brown eyes	350	625	1200
Dorothy Doll	Ideal	1939	13", Judy Garland, blue checked jumper, open and close brown eyes	300	450	850
Dorothy Doll	Madame Alexander	1991	8", blue checked jumper w/white blouse, basket w/Toto and red shoes, Storyland Dolls series	20	35	50
Dorothy Doll	Sears	1939	15-1/2", Judy Garland, red or blue checked jumper w/black pin curls	400	650	1300
Dorothy Meets the Wizard Book	Curtis Candy	1967	candy premium	8	15	35
Dorothy Music Box	Schmid	1983	plays "Over the Rainbow"	25	40	60
Dorothy Squeak Toy	Burnstein	1939	7", hollow rubber	75	120	275
Erasers	Applause	1989	set of six: figural, Scarecrow, Cowardly Lion, Dorothy, Wicked Witch, Tin Man, Glinda, set	15	20	30
Fun Shades	Multi Toys	1989	children's sunglasses w/character images	3	6	10
Game of The Wizard of Oz	Whitman	1939		100	155	300
Give-A-Show Projector Slides	Kenner	1968	35 color slides, five different shows	20	30	60
Glinda Doll	Presents	1989	vinyl, pink dress w/pink crown and wand, yellow brick road base	20	35	60
Glinda Squeak Toy	Burnstein	1939	7", hollow rubber	80	150	300
Glinda's Magic Wand	Multi Toys	1989	battery operated wand w/red glitter star on end, lights up, on illustrated card	5	8	15
Jack Pumpkinhead and the Sawhorse of Oz Book	Rand McNally	1939	hardcover, also contains "Tik Tok and the Gnome King of Oz"	35	55	125
Jack Pumpkinhead Doll	Oz Doll and Toy	1924	13"	400	700	1350
Jack Pumpkinhead Figure	Heart and Heart	1985	Return to Oz, 3"-4" tall, plastic jointed	35	55	85

270

TOY	COMPANY	YEAR	DESCRIPTION	GOOD	EX	MIB
Little Dorothy and Toto of Oz Book	Rand McNally	1939	hardcover, also contains "The Cowardly Lion and the Hungry Tiger"	35	55	175
Little Golden Book Series		1951	The Road to Oz, The Emerald City of Oz, and The Tin Woodman of Oz, each	8	15	25
Lollipop Guild Boy Doll	Presents	1989	vinyl, plaid shirt, green shorts and striped socks, on a yellow brick road base	20	35	50
Lullabye League Girl Doll	Presents	1989	vinyl, pink ballerina dress and slippers w/hat on a yellow brick road base	20	35	50
Magic Picture Kit	Jiffy Pop Popcorn	1968		5	10	20
Magic Slate	Lowe	1961	art based on animated TV show	12	20	35
Magic Slate	Whitman	1976		6	9	15
Magic Slate	Western	1985	Return to Oz	4	8	12
Magic Slate	Western	1989		3	6	9
Magic Story Cloth	Raco	1978	38" x 44" plastic sheet, eight crayons and sponge	6	12	20
Magnets	Grynnen Barrett	1987	six character magnets in box	6	10	15
Magnets	Vanderbilt Products	1989	several characters available, each	2	3	5
Mask Book	Watermill Press	1990	four paper masks	3	5	10
Mayor of Munchkinland Doll	Presents	1989	vinyl, black suit and shoes on a yellow brick road base	20	35	50
Munchkins Figures	Presents	1988	PVC, 1-3/4" to 2-3/4": Mayor, Lollipop Guild Boy, Sleepyhead Girl, Lady, Soldier and Ballerina, each	4	6	10
Off to See the Wizard Colorforms	Colorforms	1967		25	40	60
Off to See the Wizard Dancing Toys	Marx	1967	mechanical, dancing Tin Man, the Cowardly Lion and the Scarecrow, Montgomery Ward's exclusive, each	50	80	150
Off to See the Wizard Flasher Rings	Vari-Vue	1967	gumball machine prizes, silver painted resin, gold painted, dark or light blue plastic, each	6	12	25
Off to See the Wizard Hand Puppet	Mattel	1968	talking, four vinyl heads on finger tips, Toto and Cowardly Lion on thumb pad, ten phrases	30	45	75
Oz Time Wristwatch	Macy's	1989	50th anniversary premium, round face w/Emerald City, black plastic band	30	40	85
Oz-Kins Figures	Aurora	1967	plastic Burry Biscuit premium: set of 10	40	70	125
Pails	Swift and Company	1950s	Oz Peanut Butter, red and yellow and red, yellow and white tin	25	40	75
Paint by Number 'N Frame Set	Hasbro	1969	16" x 18", two plastic frames, 18 watercolors, brush and eight pictures to paint	20	30	50
Paint by Number Set	Craft Master	1968	six paints, brush, picture of Tin Man, Cowardly Lion, or the Scarecrow	20	30	50
Paint by Number Set	Art Award	1989	three different versions	4	6	10
Paint by Number Set	Craft House	1979	two 10" x 14" panels, 15 colors, brush and instructions	10	15	25
Paint by Number Set	Hasbro	1973	six oil paint vials and brush	6	12	20
Paint with Crayons Set	Art Award	1989	four pictures based on MGM film characters, in illustrated box	3	5	10
Paper Dolls	The Toy Factory	1975	Dorothy, Tin Man, Scarecrow, Cowardly Lion and Toto, clothes and accessories	10	20	40
Patchwork Girl Doll	Oz Doll and Toy	1924	13"	75	125	275
Playing Cards	Presents	1988	tin holds two decks	5	8	20

TOY	COMPANY	YEAR	DESCRIPTION	GOOD	EX	MIB
Puppet Theatre	Proctor and Gamble	1965	cardboard theater designed for P and G puppets	35	55	120
Puzzle	American Puzzle Company	1976	200 piece puzzle in canister	4	8	15
Puzzle	Western	1989	frame tray, 100 pieces, Glinda and Dorothy in Munchkinland	5	8	15
Puzzle	Milton Bradley	1990	1000 piece jigsaw featuring the 1989 Norman James Company poster	6	10	15
Puzzle	Effanbee	1984	in canister	8	15	25
Puzzle	Whitman	1976	frame tray	4	6	10
Puzzle	Haret-Gilmar	1960s	10" x 14" puzzle in canister	7	13	20
Puzzle	Reilly and Lee	1932	#1, two softcover editions of the Scarecrow and the Tin Man, Ozma and the Little Wizard, plus two puzzles, in box	175	295	450
Puzzle	Crisco Oil	1985	Return to Oz, mail away premium, 200 piece puzzle	8	15	30
Puzzles	Reilly and Lee	1932	set #2, two softcover editions of Tik-Tok and Jack Pumpkinhead and the Sawhorse, plus 25 piece puzzles	200	300	500
Puzzles	Whitman	1967	set of three: Peter Pan, Alice in Wonderland and The Wizard of Oz, in box	12	18	30
Puzzles	Jaymar	1960s	set of four, 100 pieces each, each	15	20	35
Puzzles	Doug Smith	1977	17" x 22" each, frame tray	10	16	28
Puzzles	Golden Press	1985	frame tray, Return to Oz characters	3	4	5
Puzzles	Jaymar	1960s	frame tray	10	16	25
Return to Oz Game	Golden Press	1985		8	13	20
Return to Oz Hand Puppets	Welch's Jelly	1985	Scarecrow, Gump, or Tik-Tok, Return to Oz promotion	12	18	30
Return To Oz Little Golden Books	Western	1985	Dorothy Returns to Oz, Escape from the Witch's Castle, Dorothy in the Ornament Room, Dorothy Saves the Emerald City, each	5	4	6
Rubber Stamps		1989	18 chracter stamps	12	20	30
Rubber Stamps		1989	set of 11 characters in plastic case	10	15	25
Rubber Stamps	Multi Toys	1989	12 figural stampers	4	6	10
Rusty the Tin Man Doll	Artistic Toy Company	1962	14" tall, cloth and vinyl	35	60	90
Scarecrow and the Tin Man Book	G. W. Dillingham	1904		125	275	400
Scarecrow and the Tin Man Book	Perks Publishing	1946	black and yellow pictures	20	30	50
Scarecrow Bank		1960s	ceramic	30	50	85
Scarecrow Costume	Collegeville	1989	deluxe, includes straw	20	35	50
Scarecrow Costume	Ben Cooper	1967		20	30	50
Scarecrow Costume	Ben Cooper	1968	battery-operated light-up mask	20	30	50
Scarecrow Costume	Collegeville	1989	plastic mask and vinyl bodysuit	6	12	20
Scarecrow Doll	Ideal	1984	9", Character Dolls series	20	35	50
Scarecrow Doll	Largo Toys	1989	rag doll	9	15	30
Scarecrow Doll	Presents	1988	vinyl, brown pants, green shirt, and black hat and shoes, on a yellow brick road base	25	40	60
Scarecrow Doll	Oz Doll and Toy	1924	13"	430	750	1300
Scarecrow Doll	M-D Tissue	1971	cloth, stuffed, frowning, blue pants and red and white plaid jacket	10	15	30
Scarecrow Figure	Dalen Products	1984	6' inflatable	12	20	30
Scarecrow Figure	Artisans Studio	1939	4", wood composition	75	125	275
Scarecrow Figure		1968	15", ceramic, painted or unpainted	20	35	60

TOY	COMPANY	YEAR	DESCRIPTION	GOOD	EX	MIB
Scarecrow Figure	Heart and Heart	1985	Return to Oz, 3"-4" tall, plastic jointed	30	45	75
Scarecrow Mask	Newark Mask	1939	linen, hand painted	55	90	150
Scarecrow Mask	Don Post Studios	1983	rubber	40	60	90
Scarecrow Music Box	Schmid	1983		20	35	50
Scarecrow Night Light	Hamilton Gifts	1989	7", unpainted bone china	10	15	25
Scarecrow Talkin' Patter Pillow Doll	Mattel	1968	cloth, pull-string, says 10 phrases, dark blue pants and sleeves, white gloves, black boots	40	60	120
Scarecrow Wind-Up	Durham Industries	1975	on illustrated card	15	20	35
Scarecrow-in-the-Box	Mattel	1967	jack-in-the-box	20	30	60
Showboat Play Set	Remco	1962	pink plastic showboat w/oversized central stage area, four different plays, scenery, players and scripts	40	60	110
Snack 'N Sip Pals	Multi Toys	1989	12 red and white striped straws w/detachable character figures	4	6	10
Socrates the Scarecrow Doll	Artistic	1962	14" tall, cloth and vinyl	35	55	90
Stand-Up Rub-Ons	Hasbro	1968	three full color transfer sheets, character outline sheets of 10 characters	20	30	50
Stationery	Whitman	1939	10 sheets and envelopes, w/character illustations	75	130	300
Stitch a Story Set	Hasbro	1973	two framed pictures, thread and embroidery needle	10	15	25
Strawman Doll	Ideal	1939	17", Ray Bolger, tan or pink pants, black or navy jacket	300	500	900
Tales of the Wizard of Oz Coloring Book	Whitman	1962	art from animated TV show	15	20	30
Tales of the Wizard of Oz Comic Book	Dell	1962	#1306	10	15	25
Tea Set	Ohio Art	1970s	30-piece set, red and yellow plastic	30	45	75
The Tin Woodsman and Dorothy Book	Curtis Candy	1967	candy premium	6	12	35
The Wonderful Cut-Outs of Oz Book	Crown	1985	35 figures to cut out	6	12	20
Tik Tok Figure	Heart and Heart	1985	Return to Oz, 3"-4" tall, plastic jointed	35	55	85
Tin	Multi Toys	1989	8" x 10" x 2", illustrated w/Emerald City and characters	8	12	25
Tin Man Bank		1960s	ceramic, silver	30	45	85
Tin Man Costume	Halco	1961	costume and mask	20	35	60
Tin Man Costume	Ben Cooper	1968		20	30	40
Tin Man Costume	Ben Cooper	1975	costume and mask	15	25	38
Tin Man Costume	Collegeville	1989	plastic mask and vinyl bodysuit	6	10	15
Tin Man Costume	Collegeville	1989	deluxe	20	35	50
Tin Man Doll	Oz Doll and Toy	1924	13"	390	650	1100
Tin Man Doll	Largo Toys	1989	rag doll	10	15	30
Tin Man Doll	Ideal	1984	9", Character Dolls series	18	30	48
Tin Man Doll	Presents	1988	vinyl, silver body w/a heart clock on chaint, on a yellow brick road base	20	35	50
Tin Man Doll	M-D Tissue	1971	cloth, stuffed, gray body, blue eyes, red heart	8	15	30
Tin Man Figure	Artisans Studio	1939	4", wood composition	75	150	275
Tin Man Figure		1968	15", ceramic, painted or unpainted	20	30	50
Tin Man Figure		1985	Return to Oz, 3"-4" tall, plastic jointed	20	35	60
Tin Man Mask	Newark Mask	1939	linen, hand painted	60	90	150
Tin Man Mask	Don Post Studios	1983	rubber	35	55	85
Tin Man Music Box	Schmid	1983		20	35	50

TOY	COMPANY	YEAR	DESCRIPTION	GOOD	EX	MIB
Tin Man Robot	Remco	1969	21-1/2" tall, battery operated, lifts legs and swings arms as he walks	75	125	210
Tin Man Wind-Up	Durham Industries	1975		15	25	50
Toto Doll	Presents	1988	5-1/2" plush	10	15	50
Toy Watch		1940s	tin, Scarecrow and the Tin Man on either side of non-working dial	20	40	85
Trash Can	Chein	1975	oval metal	20	35	60
Vinyl Stick-On Play Set	Multi Toys	1989	10 vinyl stickers w/Emerald City background, on header card	4	6	10
Wall Decorations	Shepard Press	1967	20 punch-out decorations	20	35	50
Water Guns	Durham	1976	heads of Scarecrow, Tin Man, or Cowardly Lion, water squirts out of nose, each	15	22	35
Wicked Witch Doll	Presents	1989	vinyl, black dress and hat, green face and hands holding broom on a yellow brick road base	25	40	60
Wicked Witch Mask	Ben Cooper	1975		6	12	20
Wicked Witch Squeak Toy	Burnstein	1939	7", hollow rubber	125	250	350
Wizard of Oz Book	Western	1975	#310-32, Little Golden Book	2	4	10
Wizard of Oz Christmas Book	Gimbel's	1968	New York department store premium	15	25	65
Wizard of Oz Color-By-Number Book	Karas Publishing	1962	#A-116, Twinkle Books series	8	15	40
Wizard of Oz Coloring Book	Playmore	1970s	#A400-10	4	6	20
Wizard of Oz Coloring Book	Saalfield	1957		15	25	50
Wizard of Oz Coloring Book	Swift	1955	advertised Oz Peanut Butter	20	50	100
Wizard of Oz Comic Book	Dell	1956	Dell Junior Treasury, #5	12	40	65
Wizard of Oz Comic Book	Dell	1957	Classic Illustrated Jr., #535	12	20	30
Wizard of Oz Costume	Halco	1961	costume and mask	20	35	50
Wizard of Oz Dart Game	Dart Board Equipment	1939	board illustrated w/yellow brick road and circular targets of Oz characters, w/three darts	200	400	750
Wizard of Oz Dolls	Effanbee	1985	11-1/2", Dorothy, Scarecrow, Tin Man, Cowardly Lion, each	15	22	35
Wizard of Oz Figures	Presents	1989	six figures on musical bases, each	10	12	15
Wizard of Oz Figures	Multiple Toymakers	1967	6" tall, bendy, several characters, on card	16	30	45
Wizard of Oz Figures	Presents	1988	3-3/4": Dorothy, Scarecrow, Tin Man, Cowardly Lion, Wicked Witch, Glinda, each	2	4	8
Wizard of Oz Figures	Multi Toys	1989	4" poseable figures, set of six	15	25	35
Wizard of Oz Figures	Just Toys	1989	several characters, bendy, each	4	6	10
Wizard of Oz Hand Puppets	Proctor and Gamble	1965	plastic	8	15	25
Wizard of Oz Hand Puppets	Presents	1989	several characters available, each	8	15	30
Wizard of Oz Hand Puppets	Multi Toys	1989	set of six on blister cards, each	6	12	20
Wizard of Oz Live! Dolls	Applause		cloth, three different sizes, each	8	15	25
Wizard of Oz Paint Book	Whitman	1939		35	125	200
Wizard of Oz Paper Dolls	Whitman	1976		5	10	20
Wizard of Oz Pocket Watch	Westclock	1980s	silver finish case, four characters on dial	20	35	65
Wizard of Oz Squeak Toy	Burnstein	1939	7" tall, hollow rubber, several characters	75	125	250

WIZARD OF OZ

TOY	COMPANY	YEAR	DESCRIPTION	GOOD	EX	MIB
Wizard of Oz Sticker Fun Book	Whitman	1976		4	6	20
Wizard of Oz Wind-Ups	Multi Toys	1989	50th anniversary editions, several characters, each	4	5	10
Wizard of Oz Wristwatch	EKO	1989	quartz, illustrated face showing Emerald City, black plastic band	15	20	35
Wizard of Oz Wristwatch	EKO	1989	child's LCD, red face in round yellow case, plastic band shows yellow brick road and Emerald City	8	12	20
Wizard Squeak Toy	Burnstein	1939	7", hollow rubber	80	150	250

WOODY WOODPECKER

TOY	COMPANY	YEAR	DESCRIPTION	GOOD	EX	MIB
Alarm Clock	Columbia Time	1959	Woody's Cafe	75	125	300
Lamp		1971	20" tall, plastic	15	35	75
Paper Dolls	Saalfield	1968	Woody Woodpecker and Andy Panda	20	35	65
Playing Cards		1950s	two decks in a carrying case	30	55	85
Woody Woodpecker Hand Puppet	Mattel	1963	pull-string voice box	35	65	100
Woody Woodpecker Nodder		1950s	plastic	50	125	175
Woody Woodpecker's Fun-o-Rama Punch-Out Book		1972		10	20	30

YOGI BEAR

TOY	COMPANY	YEAR	DESCRIPTION	GOOD	EX	MIB
Boo Boo Doll	Knickerbocker	1960s	9-1/2" tall, plush	40	50	65
Bubble Pipe	Transogram	1963	Yogi Bear figural pipe	20	35	50
Character Figures		1960	12" tall, Yogi, Boo Boo, and Ranger Smith, each	20	35	50
Cindy Bear Doll	Knickerbocker	1959	16", plush w/vinyl face	40	70	75
Coat Rack	Wolverine	1979	48", red wood, Yogi and Boo Boo cut out in front, growth chart on back	40	70	100
Hot Water Bottle		1966		25	50	75
Magic Slate		1963		15	25	40
Safety Scissors	Monogram	1973	on card	4	7	10
Snagglepuss Figure	Dakin	1970		30	55	85
Snagglepuss Soaky	Purex	1960s	9" tall, vinyl/plastic	20	40	75
Snagglepuss Sticker Fun Book	Whitman	1963		15	25	40
Yogi Bear and Cindy Push Puppet Set	Kohner	1960s	boxed set of two	45	100	225
Yogi Bear and Pixie and Dixie Game Car	Whitman		7-1/2" pile on game in car	15	30	60
Yogi Bear Bank	Dakin	1980	7", figural	6	12	25
Yogi Bear Bank	Knickerbocker	1960s	22", figural	20	35	75
Yogi Bear Cartoonist Stamp Set	Lido	1961		30	60	100
Yogi Bear Doll	Knickerbocker	1959	10" tall	45	100	200
Yogi Bear Doll	Knickerbocker	1960s	19" plush	60	75	125
Yogi Bear Doll	Knickerbocker	1959	16" plush w/vinyl face	40	85	125
Yogi Bear Doll		1962	6", soft vinyl w/movable arms and head	25	50	95
Yogi Bear Figure	Knickerbocker	1960s	9" tall, plastic	25	50	75
Yogi Bear Figure	Dakin	1970	7-3/4" tall	20	35	50
Yogi Bear Figure	Marx	1961	TV-Tinykins	20	35	50
Yogi Bear Friction Toy		1960s	Yogi in yellow tie and green hat, illustrated red box	40	75	125
Yogi Bear Ge-Tar	Mattel	1960s		55	90	160
Yogi Bear Hand Puppet	Knickerbocker			20	35	60

YOGI BEAR

TOY	COMPANY	YEAR	DESCRIPTION	GOOD	EX	MIB
Yogi Bear Paint 'em Pals	Craft Master	1978	paint-by-number set	15	20	40
Yogi Bear Push Puppet	Kohner	1960s		25	45	75
Yogi Bear Stuff and Lace Doll	Knickerbocker	1959	items to make a 13" x 5" doll	25	45	75
Yogi Bear Wristwatch		1963		40	85	150
Yogi Score-A-Matic Ball Toss Game	Transogram	1960		45	80	120
Yogi Squeeze Doll	Sanitoy	1979	12", vinyl	10	35	50
Yogi vs. Magilla for President Coloring Book	Whitman	1964		20	45	85
Yogi Wristwatch	Bradley	1967	medium base metal case, shows Yogi w/hobo sack on stick, black vinyl band	45	120	180

YOSEMITE SAM

TOY	COMPANY	YEAR	DESCRIPTION	GOOD	EX	MIB
Mini Snow Dome	Applause	1980s		9	16	25
Musical Snow Dome	Applause	1980s		15	30	45
Yosemite Sam Figure	Dakin	1971	on treasure chest	15	40	65
Yosemite Sam Figure	Dakin	1968	7" tall	15	25	50
Yosemite Sam Figure	Dakin	1978	Fun Farm	15	25	35
Yosemite Sam Nodder		1960s	6-1/4", bobbing head and spring mounted head	45	150	225

Coloring Books

Paper goods have always been popular among collectors, whether it be tickets, postcards, Valentines, display pieces or other ephemera. Coloring books can be added to that category, although collectors of specific characters are already familiar with adding these items to their collections.

Coloring books have been around for more than a century. As early as the 1880s, the McLoughlin Brothers, a 19th century giant in publishing children's books, produced The Little Folks Painting Book illustrated by Kate Greenaway. The firm continued to publish books of this type through the 1920s when it became a part of the Milton Bradley Company.

Some of the first advertising premium coloring and painting books appeared in the 1890s including Hood's Sarsaparilla Painting Book in 1894.

During the early 1900s, the Stokes Company issued some of the first true coloring books of the century with Buster's Paint Book and the Buster Brown Stocking Paint Box, a cardboard folder containing packets of pictures to color. Both booklets, starring Buster Brown, were the work of Yellow Kid comic strip artist Richard Outcault.

Among the major coloring book producers of the 20th century were Saalfield, Whitman, and Merrill Publishing. Saalfield was founded in Akron, Ohio, in the early 1900s and achieved fame with the popular Billy Whiskers series and later with the immortal Shirley Temple coloring books. Whitman Publishing was founded in Racine, Wis., in the early 1900s, and today as Western Publishing is one of the country's largest producers of children's books. Merrill Publishing came along in the 1930s, but for the next 20 years they provided a major challenge to Whitman in the field of coloring books.

Walt Disney's immortal characters were naturals for the coloring book medium, and that went for Disney's TV heroes as well, like Fess Parker as Daniel Boone.

In the early 1940s, Western film heroes burst into the scene with their own books. Gene Autry and Roy Rogers joined fictional heroes like Red Ryder and Hopalong Cassidy. Cowboy heroes continued as coloring book stars into the 1950s, as did a host

Nancy and Sluggo, 1970s, Whitman

277

of comic strip and comic book characters like Captain Marvel, Superman, Blondie, Bugs Bunny and Little Lulu. Adventures in space got an early start with coloring books too. Buck Rogers may have beat Flash Gordon to publication as a newspaper comic strip, but Flash Gordon appeared first in a 1934 painting book, followed a year later by Whitman's Buck Rogers Paint Book.

The 1960s could be called the golden age for coloring books. Television provided a wealth of worthy subjects, from sitcom to cartoon characters.

Trends

Aside from Disney and other comic classics of the 1930s, the coloring books of the 1960s tend to be among the most collectible because of the heavy following of character collectors.

Condition is very important when grading coloring books. A Mint condition coloring book should not be colored in, and the cover and pages should be in prime condition (no creases, tears or marks). Character-related books — especially Disney, Western and superheroes — tend to be the most highly sought. Generic titles generate little collector interest.

The Top 10 Coloring Books
(in Mint condition)

1. Courageous Cat and Minute Mouse, Artcraft $175
2. John Wayne Coloring Book, Saalfield, 1951 150
3. Hood's Sarsaparilla Painting Book, Hood, 1894 150
4. Gone with the Wind Paint Book, Merrill, 1940 150
5. Funny Company, Whitman, 1966 130
6. Touche Turtle, Whitman 125
7. Shirley Temple Crosses the Country, Saalfield, 1939 125
8. Draw & Paint Tom Mix, Whitman, 1935 125
9. Charlie Chaplin Up in the Air, M.A. Donahue & Co., 1914 125
10. Walt Disney's Mickey Mouse Paint Book, Whitman, 1937 110

COLORING BOOKS

NAME/COMPANY/YEAR	NO.	GOOD	EX	MINT
Superman Coloring Book (Saalfield, 1940)		100	350	550
Superman Coloring Book (Saalfield, 1941)		100	350	850
Superman Coloring Book (Whitman, 1966)		10	30	60
Superman Coloring Book (Saalfield, 1940)		100	350	850
Superman Coloring Book (Saalfield, 1955)		30	100	175
Superman Coloring Book (Saalfield, 1958)		30	100	175
ABC-TV Discovery (Saalfield)	9659	10	20	30
Addams Family, The (Artcraft)	4331	40	65	100
Alvin and the Chipmunks (Whitman)	1157	10	30	35
Amazing Chan & the Chan Clan, The (Whitman)	1063	10	25	35
Andy Griffith Show (Saalfield)	5361	15	25	50
Annie Oakley (Whitman, 1957)	1756	20	40	65
Apollo, Man on the Moon (Artcraft, 1969)		10	20	25
Archies, The (Whitman)	1135	10	15	20
Astro Boy (Saalfield)	4551	25	80	100
Astronut (Treasure, 1963)		20	30	35
Atom Ant (Whitman, 1966)	1113	15	30	70
Attack! Fighting Men in Action (Whitman, 1964)		15	20	30
Baba Looey (Watkins-Strathmore)	1853	10	20	40
Banana Splits (Whitman)	1062	30	50	70
Bat Masterson (Saalfield, 1959)	4634	20	40	50
Adventures of Batman (Whitman, 1966)		15	30	45
Beany & Cecil (Whitman)	203425	15	30	55
Beany & Cecil (Whitman)	1648	10	30	55
Beany's Coloring Book (Whitman)	112015	10	30	55
Beatles Official Coloring Book (Peerless, 1964)	5240	30	45	75
Beatles (Saalfield)	5240	30	60	75
Beaver's Big Book (Saalfield)	5327	20	45	65
Beetle Bailey (Lowe, 1961)	2860	20	30	35
Ben-Hur (Lowe)	2851	20	30	40
Bette Davis (Merrill, 1942)	4817	25	45	75
Betty Grable (Merrill, 1951)	1501	25	40	65
Beverly Hillbillies (Watkins-Strathmore, 1964)	1883	15	30	40
Beverly Hillbillies (Whitman, 1963)	1137	15	30	35
Bewitched Fun and Activity Book (Treasure)	8908	25	50	65
Blackbeard's Ghost (Whitman, 1968)		15	20	25
Blondie (Saalfield, 1968)	9961	15	25	40
Bob Hope (Saalfield, 1954)	1257	20	40	55
Bonanza (Saalfield, 1960s)	1617	12	30	35
Boo Boo Bear (Watkins-Strathmore)	1882	15	20	30
Bozo the Clown (Whitman)	1179	10	20	25
Brady Bunch (Whitman, 1974)	1657	15	30	40
Brady Bunch (Whitman)	1061	20	35	45
Brady Bunch (Whitman)	1004	20	30	40
Brenda Starr (Saalfield, 1964)	9675	25	40	50
Buccaneer, The (Saalfield)	4633	10	15	25
Bugs Bunny (Whitman)	1147	10	30	40
Bugs Bunny's Big Busy Color & Fun (Whitman)	2017	10	30	40
Bullwinkle the Moose (Whitman, 1960)		25	45	50
Camelot (Whitman)	1157	15	20	25
Captain America (Whitman, 1966)	1181	15	30	35
Captain Kangaroo (Lowe, 1977)	4967	10	20	30
Car 54, Where are You? (Whitman, 1962)	1157	20	40	55
Carmen Miranda (Saalfield)	2370	30	50	60
Ben Casey (Saalfield)	9532	10	15	35
Charge - G.I. Joe (Watkins, 1965)		25	40	45
Charlie Chan (Saalfield, 1941)	2355	30	65	90
Charlie Chaplin Up in the Air (M.A. Donahue & Co., 1914)	317	30	85	125
Chatter (Winter)	4106	10	25	35

COLORING BOOKS

NAME/COMPANY/YEAR	NO.	GOOD	EX	MINT
Choo Choo (Watkins-Strathmore)	1857	10	20	30
Circus Boy (Whitman)	1198	10	20	30
Cisco Kid (Saalfield, 1950)	2078	15	20	35
Clutch Cargo (Artcraft)	9547	50	60	75
Clutch Cargo (Whitman, 1965)		50	90	95
Combat (Saalfield, 1963)		10	30	35
Courageous Cat and Minute Mouse (Artcraft)	9540	60	140	175
Bing Crosby (Saalfield)	4840	15	25	45
Cuffy and Captain Gallant (Lowe)	2521	15	25	35
Curiosity Shop (Artcraft)	5353	10	20	25
Daktari (Whitman)	1649	15	25	35
Dastardly and Muttley (Whitman)	1023	20	40	45
Doris Day (Whitman)	1143	10	25	30
Dennis the Menace (Whitman)	1135	12	30	40
Dick Tracy (Saalfield, 1946)	2536	20	60	75
Dick Van Dyke (Saalfield/Artcraft, 1963)	9557	25	40	45
Dino the Dinosaur (Whitman)	1117	10	15	20
Diver Dan (Saalfield)	4512	30	60	75
Donald Duck (Whitman, 1959)		15	20	25
Donny and Marie (Whitman)	1641	5	12	25
Doris Day (Whitman, 1952)	1138	20	35	50
Doris Day "A Warner Brothers Star" (Whitman, 1955)	1751	20	35	50
Double Deckers (Artcraft)	3936	10	20	25
Double Deckers (Saalfield)	3836	10	20	25
Dr. Kildare Play Book (Lowe)	3092	10	15	35
Draw & Paint Tom Mix (Whitman, 1935)		30	80	125
Patty Duke (Whitman, 1964)	1122	15	25	35
Patty Duke (Whitman)	1141	15	25	40
Jimmy Durante (Funtime)	F5035	30	60	75
Edgar Bergen's Charlie McCarthy Paint Book (Whitman, 1938)	690	25	40	85
Electro Man (Lowe)	4971	7	25	35
Elizabeth Taylor (Whitman, 1950)	1119	30	60	80
Elizabeth Taylor (Whitman, 1954)	1144	30	50	75
Elmer Fudd (Western)	1878	12	25	35
Elvis (TN Mfg. & Dist. Co., 1983)		10	20	45
Emmett Kelly as Willy the Clown (Saalfield)	4533	10	20	30
Esther Williams (Merrill, 1950)	1591	20	40	70
Eve Arden Coloring Book (Saalfield, 1953)	2310	10	20	45
F-Troop (Saalfield)	9560	15	30	45
Family Affair (Whitman)	1640	7	15	25
Family Affair (Whitman, 1968)		7	20	25
Fantastic Osmonds: A Coloring Book, The (Osbro, 1973)	4622	15	35	50
Felix the Cat (Saalfield, 1959)	4655	15	35	60
Fireball XL5 (Golden, 1963)		35	50	90
Flintstones Gismos and Gadgets (Whitman, 1961)	1117	10	20	30
Flintstones Hoppy the Hopparoo, The (Whitman)	1117	15	25	35
Flintstones Pebbles & Bamm Bamm, The (Whitman)	1004	10	20	25
Flintstones with Pebbles & Bamm Bamm, The (Whitman)	1117	10	15	25
Flintstones, The (Whitman)	1138	10	20	30
Flintstones, The (Whitman, 1964)		10	20	25
Flipper Paint with Water (Whitman)	1340	5	15	25
Flying Nun (Artcraft)	4672	12	25	35
Foreign Legionnaire (Abbott)	2613	10	20	30
Frankenstein, Jr. (Whitman)	1115	20	40	50
Freddie (Whitman)	B400	10	15	20
Funky Phantom (Whitman)	1003	12	30	40
Funny Company (Whitman, 1966)		45	125	130
Gabby Hayes (Abbott, 1954)		10	25	35
Garrison's Gorillas (Whitman, 1968)	1149	10	20	35

NAME/COMPANY/YEAR	NO.	GOOD	EX	MINT
Gene Autry (Whitman, 1949)	1157	25	45	70
Gene Autry (Whitman, 1951)	1153	25	45	60
Gene Autry Cowboy Adventures to Color (Merrill, 1941)	4803	25	60	90
Gentle Ben (Whitman, 1968)	1642	10	25	30
George of the Jungle (Whitman, 1967)		25	50	100
Get Smart (Saalfield)	4519	20	40	50
Get Smart (Saalfield)	9562	20	40	50
G.I. Joe Action Coloring Book (Whitman)	1156	10	25	40
G.I. Joe (Whitman)	1412	15	30	50
Gilligan's Island (Whitman, 1965)	1135	15	30	50
Godzilla (Resource Pub.)	630	20	40	45
Grace Kelly (Whitman, 1956)	1752	30	60	75
Green Acres (Whitman)	1188	25	45	60
Green Hornet (Watkins, 1966)		15	20	50
Green Hornet (Whitman, 1966)	1190	20	35	50
Greer Garson (Merrill, 1944)	3480	25	50	70
Grizzly Adams (NcNally)	06528	5	10	20
Grizzly Adams and Ben (McNally)	06534	5	10	30
Gumby and Pokey (Whitman, 1966)	1141	10	20	40
Gunsmoke (Whitman, 1958)	1184	20	30	45
Hee Haw (Saalfield, 4538)	1970	10	20	30
Hercules (Lowe)	2838	20	40	75
Hi Mr. Jinks (Watkins-Strathmore)	1832	10	15	20
Hong Kong Phooey (Saalfield)	#H1852	10	20	30
Hood's Sarsaparilla Painting Book (Hood, 1894)		30	50	150
Hopalong Cassidy (Abbott)	1311	30	50	75
Hopalong Cassidy Starring William Boyd (Lowe, 1950)	1200	30	55	75
Hoppity Hopper (Whitman, 1965)		20	45	50
Hot Wheels (Whitman, 1969)		20	30	50
Howdy Doody (Whitman, 1952)	217625	20	35	60
Howdy Doody Fun Book (Whitman, 1951)		20	30	40
Huckleberry Hound (Whitman, 1959)	1130	10	20	40
Huckleberry Hound (Watkins-Strathmore)	1883	10	20	50
Huckleberry Hound (Whitman, 1959)		15	35	45
I Love Lucy, Lucille Ball, Desi Arnaz, Little Ricky (Western/Dell, 1955)		25	45	70
It's About Time (Whitman)	1134	15	30	50
Jack Webb's Safety Squad (Lowe)	1525	20	35	45
Jackie Gleason's TV Show (Abbott, 1956)	2614	35	45	60
Jambo (Whitman)	1173	5	10	20
Jetsons, The (Whitman, 1962)	1135	20	45	60
Jetsons, The (Whitman)	1114	15	20	40
Jetsons, The (Whitman, 1963)		15	30	35
JFK (Kanrom, 1962)		10	15	35
Jimmy Durante Cut-Out Coloring Book (Pocket Books, 1952)	F5035	20	40	55
John Wayne (Saalfield, 1951)	1238	40	100	150
Johnny Lightning (Whitman)	1057	10	20	35
Casey Jones (Saalfield)	4618	10	25	35
Josie and the Pussy Cats (Saalfield)	H1881	15	30	50
Journey to the Center of the Earth (Whitman)	1137	7	15	30
June Allyson (Whitman, 1952)	1862	20	40	55
Jungle Book (Saalfield)	9524	10	20	25
Kato's Revenge (Watkins-Strathmore)	1824	20	30	40
Kimba the White Lion (Saalfield)	4575	35	60	90
King Kong (Whitman)	1097	30	60	75
King Leonardo (Whitman)	1138	25	40	60
Korg (Saalfield)	H1853	5	10	30
Lad A Dog (Artcraft)	4526	12	20	40
Lancelot Link (Whitman)	1146	10	20	25

COLORING BOOKS

NAME/COMPANY/YEAR	NO.	GOOD	EX	MINT
Land of the Giants, The (Whitman, 1969)	1138	15	30	55
Lariat Sam (Whitman, 1962)	1133	30	60	75
Lassie (Whitman, 1969)	1656	10	20	30
Lassie (Whitman, 1969)	1642	15	25	30
Lassie (Whitman)	1114	15	25	35
Lassie (Whitman, 1958)	1039	15	25	30
Laugh-In (Saalfield)	4633	15	30	50
Laurel & Hardy (Saalfield, 1972)	3883	10	15	25
Leave It To Beaver (Saalfield/Artcraft, 1958)	5662	20	50	60
Leave It To Beaver: A Book to Color (Saalfield, 1963)	5662	15	30	60
Lennon Sisters, The (Whitman, 1958)	158	10	20	45
Lennon Sisters, The (Watkins-Strathmore)	1833	10	20	45
Shari Lewis (Saalfield)	5335	10	20	30
Shari Lewis (Artcraft)	5654	10	20	30
Li'l Abner & Daisy Mae (Saalfield, 1942)	2391	25	60	100
Li'l Abner (Saalfield, 1941)	121	30	50	75
Liddle Kiddles (Whitman)	1411	20	30	55
Liddle Kiddles (Whitman)	1648	20	40	60
Lieutenant, The (Saalfield)	9577	10	20	30
Little Lulu & Tubby (Whitman, 1959)		20	30	50
Little Orphan Annie (Saalfield, 1974)	4689	15	30	45
Little Rascals (Saalfield)	4546	10	20	35
Lone Ranger (Whitman, 1951)	1117-15	25	40	50
Loopy de Loop (Whitman)	2946	15	25	40
Loretta Young (Saalfield, 1956)	1108	25	40	50
Lucille Ball/Desi Arnaz (Whitman, 1953)	2079	25	40	60
Lucy Show Cut-Out Coloring Book, The (Golden, 1963)		25	40	75
Lucy Show, The (Funtime)	GF227	15	30	50
Magilla Gorilla (Whitman)	1113	20	30	50
Man Called Flintstone, The (Whitman)	1090	7	10	25
Man from U.N.C.L.E. (Western)	1855	15	30	45
Man from U.N.C.L.E. (Watkins-Strathmore)	1855	15	25	50
Man from U.N.C.L.E. (Whitman, 1965)	1095	15	30	40
Milton the Monster (Whitman)	1139	10	20	40
Moby Dick (Whitman)	1170	5	10	20
Monkees Big Beat Fun Book (Young World, 1986)		20	35	50
Monster Squad (McNally)	06428	7	10	25
Mister Ed the Talking Horse (Whitman, 1963)	1135	15	30	45
Munsters, The (Whitman)	1149	20	40	75
Munsters, The (Whitman)	1648	30	65	75
Mushmouse and Punkin' Puss (Whitman)	1342	20	30	45
My Mother the Car (Saalfield)	4518	20	40	50
My Three Sons (Whitman, 1967)	1113	10	20	30
N.W. Passage (Lowe)	2852	10	20	30
Nancy Drew #1 (Treasure)	16003	5	10	15
Nancy Drew #2 (Treasure)	16004	5	10	15
Nanny and the Professor (Saalfield, 1971)	3829	7	10	25
Nanny and the Professor (Artcraft)	9620	7	10	25
National Velvet (Whitman)	2975	10	20	45
National Velvet (Whitman)	1186	10	20	40
New Zoo Revue, The (Saalfield)	C1854	5	10	20
Ozzie & Harriet, David & Ricky (Saalfield)	125910	25	40	50
Partridge Family (Artcraft, 1970)	3939	20	35	50
Partridge Family, The (Saalfield)	4537	20	35	45
Partridge Family, The (Artcraft)	3937	20	30	40
Peanuts (Saalfield)	5615	15	20	25
Pebbles Flintstone (Whitman)	1117	5	10	20
Peter Potamus (Whitman, 1964)	1139	10	20	35
Petticoat Junction (Whitman)	1111	20	40	60

Adventures of Batman, 1966, Whitman

Hopalong Cassidy Starring William Boyd, 1950, Lowe

Touche Turtle, Whitman

COLORING BOOKS

NAME/COMPANY/YEAR	NO.	GOOD	EX	MINT
Pinky Lee's Health and Safety (Funtime)	DF104	30	40	55
Popeye (Lowe, 1958)	2834	20	35	45
Prince Valiant (Saalfield, 1954)		15	20	30
Jonny Quest (Whitman)	1091	20	50	75
Jonny Quest (Whitman)	1111	20	50	75
Quick Draw McGraw (Whitman, 1959)		20	35	45
Raggedy Ann & Andy (Saalfield, 1944)	2498	20	40	75
Ramar (Saalfield)	4881	10	20	30
Ramar of the Jungle (Saalfield)	2208	15	20	30
Range Rider, The (Abbott, 1956)		15	20	35
Rat Patrol (Saalfield)	2273	20	35	50
Red Ryder (Whitman, 1952)	1155	15	30	50
Donna Reed (Artcraft)	2218	15	35	40
Ricochet Rabbit (Whitman)	1142	20	40	50
Rin Tin Tin (Whitman, 1959)		10	25	30
Ripcord (Artcraft)	9529	20	30	40
Rita Hayworth (Merrill, 1942)	3483	30	60	75
Road Runner, The (Whitman)	1133	10	15	25
Rocky & Bullwinkle (Whitman, 1961)		12	20	45
Roger Ramjet (Whitman)	1115	20	50	75
Ronny Howard of the Andy Griffith Show (Artcraft)	5644	10	35	50
Roy Rogers & Dale Evans (Whitman, 1951)	2171	20	40	55
Ruff and Reddy (Watkins-Strathmore)	1856	10	20	30
Sabrina (Whitman)	1071	10	20	40
Soupy Sales (Treasure)	8907	10	15	25
Samson and Goliath (Whitman)	1113	10	15	25
Seahunt (Artcraft)	4558	15	35	45
Sgt. Bilko (Treasure, 1959)	330	15	35	45
Shari Lewis and Her Puppets (Saalfield)	4527	15	25	35
Shazan (Whitman)	1084	12	20	30
Shirley Temple (Saalfield, 1935)	1738	20	50	60
Shirley Temple Crosses the Country (Saalfield, 1939)	1779	30	110	125
Shirley Temple Drawing & Coloring Book (Saalfield, 1936)	1724	30	60	100
Skippy (Whitman, 1970)	1116	5	10	20
Snagglepuss & Yakky Doodle (Whitman, 1962)	1209	15	25	40
Space Angel (Artcraft)	9528	30	50	100
Space Ghost (Whitman)	1082	10	30	40
Speed Buggy (Saalfield)	H1860	15	30	35
Star Trek (Saalfield, 1975)	C1856	5	10	20
Steve Canyon (Saalfield, 1952)	123410	20	35	60
Stingray (Whitman, 1965)	1133	15	35	40
Super Circus (Whitman)	1251	15	25	35
Super Six (Whitman)	1181	15	30	60
Superboy (Whitman, 1967)		10	25	30
Superman (Whitman, 1964)		20	35	40
Tales of Wells Fargo (Whitman, 1957)		15	25	35
Tarzan (Whitman, 1968)	1157	10	30	40
Tarzan (Whitman)	1157	10	30	40
Tennessee Tuxedo (Whitman)	1011	15	40	60
That Girl (Saalfield, 1967)	4513	10	20	30
That Girl (Saalfield)	4510	10	20	30
Three Stooges Funny Coloring Book (Norman Maurer, 1960)	2855	20	40	55
Three Stooges, The (Whitman)	1135	10	20	35
Three Stooges, The (Lowe)	2822	25	50	80
Time Tunnel (Saalfield, 1967)		25	50	80
Tom and Jerry (Whitman, 1959)		10	20	30
Tonto (Whitman, 1957)	2953	15	25	40
Top Cat (Whitman, 1961)	1185	15	30	40
Touche Turtle (Whitman)	1185	20	50	125

COLORING BOOKS

NAME/COMPANY/YEAR	NO.	GOOD	EX	MINT
Uncle Martin the Martian (Funtime)	GF233	15	30	40
Underdog (Whitman)	1666	15	25	40
Underdog (Whitman)	1010	20	30	35
Dick Van Dyke (Artcraft)	9557	30	75	100
Voyage to the Bottom of the Sea (Whitman, 1965)	1851-B	15	30	50
Wacky Races (Whitman)	1067	15	30	40
Wacky World of the Great Grape Ape, The (McNally)	06440	10	15	20
Wally Gator (Whitman)	2975	30	50	70
Walt Disney's Alice in Wonderland Paint Book (Whitman, 1951)	2167	25	50	60
Walt Disney's Mickey Mouse Paint Book (Whitman, 1937)	1069	30	60	110
Walt Disney's Swamp Fox (Whitman, 1961)	1134	10	20	25
Where's Huddles? (Whitman)	1089	5	10	25
Whirlybirds (Whitman)	1151	15	35	60
Wild Kingdom (Whitman)	1004	10	15	20
Yakky Doodle and Chopper (Whitman)	1800	15	25	35
Yogi Bear (Whitman)	1111	15	20	35
Yosemite Sam (Watkins, 1963)		20	25	30
Sigmund and the Sea Monsters (Saalfield, 1974)		10	30	40
Wyatt Earp Coloring Book (Whitman, 1958)		20	35	55
I Love Lucy Coloring Book (Whitman, 1954)		25	50	75
Danger! with the Green Hornet (Watkins-Strathmore, 1966)		20	35	55
Archie's Pal Jughead (Whitman, 1972)		10	15	25
Tom Corbett (Saalfield, 1950)		15	30	55
Fury (Whitman, 1958)	1199	10	20	30
Convoy (Artcraft)	9637	5	10	20
Roy Rogers' Pal Pat Brady (Whitman, 1955)	1255	10	25	30
Little Lulu (Watkins-Strathmore, 1950s)	1852	15	25	50
Barney Google/Snuffy Smith (Lowe, 1950s)	2831	10	20	35
Woody Woodpecker (Whitman, 1950s)	1416	15	20	35
Rocky the Flying Squirrel (Whitman, 1960)	1134	10	20	35
Elmer Fudd & Friends (Watkins-Strathmore, 1962)	1849	10	20	30
Howdy Doody (Whitman, 1950)	2093	15	25	60
Tales of the Texas Rangers (Saalfield, 1958)	2071	10	15	25
Tales of the Vikings (Saalfield)	4566	10	15	25
Pinocchio (Whitman, 1961)	1184	10	15	25
Disneyland (Whitman, 1961)	2975	5	10	15
Lady and the Tramp (Whitman, 1954)	1139	7	15	25
Walt Disney's Spin & Marty (Whitman, 1956)	1194	5	10	20
101 Dalmatians (Watkins-Strathmore, 1960)	1864	5	15	25
Twelve O'Clock High (Artcraft, 1960s)	9636	10	20	35
Walt Disney's Annette (Whitman, 1964)	1145	10	15	40
Sonja Henie Coloring Book (Merrill, 1939)	3476	20	50	75
Margaret O'Brien Paint Book (Whitman, 1947)	1155	25	40	75
Our Gang Coloring Book (Saalfield, 1933)	966	10	20	35
Roy Rogers Paint Book (Whitman, 1944)	668	25	45	65
Roy Rogers and Dale Evans' Big Book to Color (Whitman)	1184	15	30	50
Bonny Braids Coloring Book (Saalfield, 1951)	2366	15	25	55
Mister Magoo Cut-Out Coloring Book (Golden, 1961)	GF186	12	20	30
Smitty Color Book (McLoughlin Bros., 1931)		20	40	75
Tweety Coloring Book (Whitman, 1955)	2953	10	15	25
Walt Disney's Mickey Mouse Club (Whitman)	1059	7	10	15
Walt Disney's Peter Pan (Whitman, 1952)	2186	15	30	55
Walt Disney's Snow White and the Seven Dwarfs Paint Book (Whitman, 1938)		30	50	110
Walt Disney's Zorro (Whitman)	1158	15	30	50
Walt Disney Presents Winnie the Pooh (Whitman)	1058	5	10	15
Doctor Dolittle and His Animals (Watkins-Strathmore, 1967)	1871-4	10	15	20
Chitty Chitty Bang Bang (Whitman, 1968)	1654	5	10	20
Gone with the Wind Paint Book (Merrill, 1940)	3403	30	50	150

COLORING BOOKS

NAME/COMPANY/YEAR	NO.	GOOD	EX	MINT
Buster Brown Coloring Book (, 1950s)		10	15	35
Alvin and the Chipmunks (Watkins-Strathmore, 1966)	1878-G	5	7	10
Captain Kangaroo Trace and Color (Whitman, 1960)	1413	10	15	20
Hi! I'm Mrs. Beasley Color and Read (Whitman/Western, 1972)	1364	10	20	30
Buffy and Jody Coloring Book (Whitman)	1640	5	10	15
Harlem Globetrotters (Whitman, 1971)	1085	7	10	25
Incredible Hulk at the Circus (Whitman, 1977)	1040	5	10	15
Land of the Lost (Whitman, 1975)	1045	15	25	40
My Favorite Martian (Whitman)	1148	15	20	35
Planet of the Apes Cut and Color Book (Saalfield)	C2434	10	15	35
Shadow (Saalfield, 1974)	4636	10	15	25
Sergeant Preston (Whitman, 1953)	1329	10	15	25
Six Million Dollar Man (Saalfield, 1974)	C1832	10	15	20
Six Million Dollar Man Activity Book (Rand McNally, 1977)	C2471	10	15	20
Star Trek (Saalfield, 1975)	C1862	10	15	25
Space:1999 (Saalfield)	C1881	10	20	30
Welcome Back Kotter (Whitman, 1977)	1081	5	10	15
Wild Bill Hickok and Jingles (Saalfield, 1953)	120910	15	30	45
New York World's Fair (Spertus, 1960s)		5	10	20
H.R. Pufnstuf (Whitman, 1970)	1093	10	20	50
Nancy and Sluggo (Whitman, 1970s)		15	25	40
Little Annie Rooney Paint Book (Whitman, 1930s)		25	40	75
Hey There! It's Yogi Bear (Whitman)	GF232	10	20	35

A.C. Gilbert Erector Sets

What adult doesn't recall the joy of using toys to vicariously experience adult tasks — whether it be driving a toy truck or playing house? Construction toys were designed to make kids "feel big" and exercise their imagination and creativity.

Those boxes of parts of many sizes, shapes, colors, and purpose taught basic mechanics, logic, fine motor coordination and a host of other skills — all while providing hours of fun.

Most boys can recall the colors, heft and smell of their first construction set, even if they may not remember when they received it or who gave it to them. Those unfortunates who never got one no doubt made do with sets of their own design — including wood scraps, string, old wheels and nails.

Few joys of childhood rival that of laboriously constructing some mechanical wonder, watching it work, and then gleefully tearing it all apart.

While many other construction sets have been made through the years, none has received the most collectors' attention and praise like the original A.C. Gilbert Erector sets.

A Set by Any Other Name isn't the Same

Alfred Carlton Gilbert, born in 1884, was both a product of and producer for his time, the industrial coming of age in America. He inspired legions of bright young tinkerers to grow up to become architects of the future — engineers, scientists and craftsmen of all types.

As a child, Gilbert loved magic tricks, a fascination that would later pay off almost like magic. Also an aspiring sports star, he decided on a career in health education, and worked his way through Yale medical school by performing magic shows. At Yale he also won a berth on the 1908 U.S. Olympic team and won the gold medal in the pole vault.

While at Yale, Gilbert began giving magic lessons and became frustrated by the lack of available magic props for his students. A fellow amateur magician named John Petrie was also a mechanic, and he and Gilbert began making small magic kits and selling them.

After the Olympics, Gilbert returned to medical school and the magic business, which soon grew into a mail order magic company, supplying both amateurs and professionals. Gilbert and Petrie formed the Mysto Manufacturing Company.

By 1909, the newly degreed Dr. Gilbert left his medical career to pursue his magic business — and business was good. In his promotional travels across America, Gilbert began selling to toy store buyers and soon realized the need for quality American-made toys. Deep in thought, he went home, and the result was the birth of the Erector set.

The origin of the first Erector set is the stuff of debate and myth, and even Gilbert told several versions of it during his life. What is fact is that Petrie was not impressed with Gilbert's new toy idea, and this eventually led Gilbert to buy out Petrie's interest in the Mysto Manufacturing Company.

Gilbert showed his new Mysto-Erector toy at the 1913 Toy Fair and retail orders poured in, threatening to swamp his new company. Gilbert rolled out a major national promotion for his new line, including an ingenious model building contest that provided him hundreds of new and free model configurations he promoted in future instruction manuals.

The 1913 holiday sales season was a resounding success, and Gilbert turned his sights on refining and improving the product line, upgrading the girders and providing factory-assembled motors for the 1914 kits. He also continued the model building contests with huge success, offering real cars as prizes, and those new model ideas were incorporated into instruction manuals.

A new plant in 1915 allowed Gilbert to expand the line into better motors for his Erector sets, tin toys and electric fans to fill the off-season work void.

In 1916, Gilbert renamed his firm The A.C. Gilbert Company, but kept the Mysto name for his magic sets. He also created the Gilbert Engineering Institute for Boys, a national club which became a highly successful promotional tool.

In 1917, World War I threatened to sideline the entire toy industry. Gilbert was called by the fledgling Toy Manufacturers Association, which he helped create, to lobby Congress for permission for the toy industry to continue making toys. Armed with his own toys, Gilbert triumphed and was hailed nationwide as the "Man Who Saved Christmas."

Gilbert introduced his now-famous chemistry sets in 1917 and proceeded to dramatically expand the Gilbert line in the years to come, introducing tool chests, a line of power tools and books.

It was a year of great change in 1920, with a near total overhaul of the Gilbert lines and the introduction of a series of more advanced scientific, mechanical and radio sets. That year also saw the introduction of the No. 10 Deluxe Erector sets, now by far the most highly desirable of all Gilbert construction sets.

A true overhaul came in 1924, when Gilbert introduced the new Erector line. He completely redesigned the Erector system with thinner girders and debuted curved girders and numerous other advancements. The 1924 line also saw streamlining across all other divisions, with many toys dropped from production.

In 1927, Gilbert expanded his control over the construction toy market by buying Trumodel, a line of high quality toys that were redesigned and rolled into his deluxe Erector sets.

Gilbert's promotional activities took another turn in 1929 when he entered into a number of exclusive contracts with Sears, Macy's, J.C. Penney and other national retailers. Each company was allowed to market low-end Gilbert products, but not under the Erector name. They were sold under the names Trumodel, Steel-Tech and Little Jim among others, with each retailer having a different line. These sets have since become collectible in their own right.

Also in 1929, Gilbert essentially monopolized the American construction toy market by acquiring his chief rival, Meccano. For 1930, the Erector and Meccano lines were partially merged in the New American Meccano line, now commonly called Erector-Meccano.

The Great Depression finally hit the Gilbert company, but not before the Erector series hit its all-time pinnacle with the Erector Hudson Locomotive model, which was included in the top-of-the-line sets. In 1931, Gilbert's most expansive No. 10 set was produced. In addition to containing parts to build all models from lower numbered sets (which included the White Truck model, the Steam Shovel, and the Zeppelin), it also included parts for both the Hudson Locomotive and its tender. Gilbert would never offer an Erector set this grand again.

The Depression forced major downsizing at Gilbert, but the company would survive. The Erector line was acquired by Gabriel Industries in 1967. As previously noted, the Erector line has been revived with resounding success.

Trends

While still a relatively small subset of the toy collecting field, construction set collecting, particularly of Erector and Meccano products, is enjoying moderate and steady growth. Original Gilbert sets command the highest premiums, particularly the earliest ones bearing the company's previous Mysto Manufacturing name.

Not all collecting fields have their day in the sun, but this one, rich as it is in history and variety, presents a strong case for higher visibility.

Note: All sets listed are made by The A.C. Gilbert Company. Collectors tend to identify sets by number and year, rather than name; in this book, sets are listed by set number, then by year.

Erector sets are rarely found in Mint condition, especially with all the pieces and the box intact. This section lists two grades for sets collectors may likely find — Good and Excellent. Sets that have been refurbished and reassembled as a whole may be found and can command a price 40 to 75 percent higher than a similar, unrefurbished set.

Values given are averages for the time period noted. As a general rule, older sets are worth more than newer ones; larger sets are worth more than smaller.

The Top 10 A.C. Gilbert Erector Sets
(in Excellent condition)

1. Set #10, Complete Erector in all its Glory, 1929-31, oak chest $7,875
2. Set #10, Complete Deluxe Set, 1928, nine-drawer oak chest 7,875
3. Set #10, Erector Deluxe in all its Glory, 1927, eight-drawer oak chest 7,875
4. Set #10, 1920-26, wood box 7,875
5. Set #9, Mechanical Wonders Set with 110-Volt Motor, 1929-32, wood box 4,610
6. Set #8-1/2, 1931-32, wood box 3,150
7. Set #7-1/2, Motorized Erector, 1914, wood box 1,575
8. Set #12-1/2, 1956-57, metal box 1,365
9. Set #12-1/2, 1948-50, metal box 1,365
10. Set #10093, 1959, metal box 1,265

ERECTOR SETS

A.C. GILBERT ERECTOR SETS

YEAR	BOX TYPE	GOOD	EX	YEAR	BOX TYPE	GOOD	EX
Erector Junior				**Set #4-1/2**			
1943-47	cardboard box	100	225	1935	metal box	140	235
1943-47	cardboard box	70	185	1936-42	cardboard box	50	85
1943-47	cardboard box	40	115	1946-57	metal box	140	235
Junior Erector				**Set #5**			
1949-55	cardboard box	85	225	1913	cardboard box	220	525
1949-55	cardboard box	45	100	1914	cardboard box	180	290
1949-55	cardboard box	30	75	1915	wood box	145	265
Set #0				1916	cardboard box	145	265
1913	cardboard box	80	130	1923	wood box	550	895
1914	cardboard box	60	100	1930	cardboard box	120	290
1915	cardboard box	120	290	**Set #5-1/2**			
Set #1				1936-38	metal box	95	140
1913	cardboard box	105	210	**Set #6**			
1914-34	cardboard box	80	130	1913		630	840
1945	cardboard box	80	130	1914	wood box	185	290
Set #1-1/2				1915-16	wood box	155	260
1935-42	cardboard box	40	55	1920	wood box	155	260
1950-56	cardboard box	40	55	1921	wood box	155	260
Set #10				1931	cardboard box	100	260
1920-26	wood box	4610	7875	1945	metal box	190	260
1927	eight drawer oak chest box	4610	7875	**Set #6-1/2**			
1928	nine-drawer oak chest box	4610	7875	1935-42	metal, not made in 1936 or 1937 box	50	95
1929-31	oak box	4610	7875	1946-57	metal box	50	95
Set #10-1/2				**Set #7**			
1936-42	metal box	315	470	1913	wood box	315	470
1949-57	metal box	235	395	1914-32	wood box	160	260
Set #12-1/2				1933-34	metal box	160	260
1948-50	metal box	735	1365	1945	metal box	210	315
1956-57	metal box	735	1365	**Set #7-1/2**			
Set #2				1914	wood box	655	1575
1913	cardboard box	110	220	1928-32	wood box	260	420
1914-21	cardboard box	75	115	1934-37	metal box	90	155
Set #2-1/2				1938-57	metal box	75	130
1936-42	cardboard box	45	65	**Set #8**			
1946-56	cardboard box	45	65	1913	wood box	575	945
Set #3				1914-31	wood box	575	945
1913	cardboard box	195	315	1933-34	metal box	575	945
1914-34	cardboard box	95	155	1945	metal box	260	350
1945	cardboard box	95	155	**Set #8-1/2**			
Set #3-1/2				1931-32	wood box	1900	3150
1935	cardboard box	125	165	1933	metal box	190	240
1936-42	cardboard box	65	85	1935-57	metal box	105	180
Set #4				**Set #9**			
1913	cardboard box	220	420	1929-32	wood box	2650	4610
1914	cardboard box	130	210	1945	metal box	210	315
1915	wood box	130	210	**Set #9-1/2**			
1916-34	cardboard box	130	210	1935	metal box	290	390
1945	metal box	105	185	1936-49	metal box	210	315

No. 10062, 1958

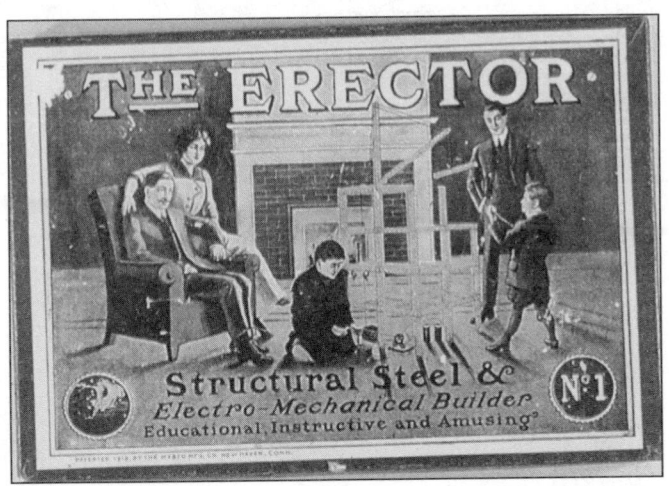

Set #1, 1913

POST 1957 SETS

NO.	YEAR	BOX TYPE	GOOD	EX
10052	1958	metal box	55	95
10072	1958	metal box	185	290
10092	1958	metal box	785	1260
10082	1958	metal box	315	525
10062	1958	metal box	77	145
10041	1958	metal box	45	85
10026	1958	cardboard box	45	85
10031	1958	cardboard box	65	105
10011	1958-61	cardboard tube box	45	70
10021	1958-61	cardboard tube box	55	95
10083	1959	metal box	315	525
10073	1959	metal box	185	290
10093	1959	metal box	735	1265
10032	1959-61	cardboard tube box	70	115
10042	1959-61	metal box	45	85
10063	1959-61	metal box	80	150
10037	1960	cardboard tube box	135	210
18030	1960-61	tube box	80	115
18040	1960-61	tube box	105	150
18020	1960-61	tube box	65	95
10084	1960-61	metal box	160	295
10074	1960-61	metal box	85	150
18010	1960-61	tube box	55	80
10094	1960-62	metal box	420	685
10221	1962	metal box	100	185
10211	1962	metal box	85	160
10231	1962	metal box	210	315
10201	1962	metal box	60	95
10161	1962-63	carton box	55	85
10171	1962-63	carton box	65	105
10181	1962-63	metal box	50	80
10129	1963-64	metal box	210	315
10128	1963-64	metal box	120	160
10127	1963-64	metal box	95	135
10251	1964	cardboard box	22	35
10252	1964	cardboard box	30	40
10253	1964	cardboard box	35	45
10254	1964	cardboard box	40	55
10351	1965-66	cardboard box	22	35
10352	1965-66	cardboard box	30	40
10353	1965-66	cardboard box	35	45
10354	1965-66	cardboard box	45	55
10601	1965-66	cardboard box	115	210
10606	1966	cardboard box	180	265

Fisher-Price Toys

The familiar sturdy wood toys with paper lithography made by Fisher-Price are colorful remnants of how toys used to be made. Collectors especially value their quality and nostalgia.

While the rest of the world suffered through the Depression, Fisher-Price set up shop in 1930 in East Aurora, N.Y. Founded by Herman Fisher, Irving Price and Helen Schelle, the company hoped to bring toys of matchless charm and inherent quality to children.

Sixteen toys were introduced in the 1931, the first production year, including Granny Doodle and Doctor Doodle, a pair of charming ducks.

Most collectors are familiar with the look of vintage Fisher-Price. Early toys featured a unique, colorful, crisp paper lithography on wood. Finding such charm today is as rare as some of the early toys.

It didn't take long for Fisher-Price to realize the value of licensing. In 1935, the company issued the Walt Disney Mickey Mouse Band, featuring Mickey and Pluto. That piece alone can command around $2,000 in Mint in Box condition. Other Disney characters and Popeye also became popular Fisher-Price toys.

Musical toys, especially items featuring bells or xylophones, became perennial favorites.

By the late 1950s, plastic was beginning to appear as accents on toys, but by the late 1960s, most of the toys' bodies were made entirely of plastic.

The common Fisher-Price Play Family Little People appeared as early as 1959 in a yellow wooden Safety School Bus. Made of wood, they could be removed from their vehicles. Their body shapes and compositions have changed throughout the years. Today the Little People are about three times the size of the originals and are made of plastic.

Today, Fisher-Price is a subsidiary of toy giant Mattel. The company continues to make Little People play sets in a variety of themes, but has expanded its line to include outdoor playground and riding toys, apparel and books.

Mickey Mouse Choo-Choo, 1938, Fisher-Price

Trends

Collecting vintage Fisher-Price, especially pre-1950s pieces, can be costly, since it is difficult to find older pieces in premium condition. Many 1930s-1940s wooden toys can command $400-$2,000 or more in Mint in Box condition.

But collectors shouldn't pass on more modern, plastic Fisher-Price toys. Many toys from the 1960s and later are gaining favor with younger collectors, especially Little People play sets and musical radios, clocks, and televisions. The musical toys are still fairly easy to find and can range from $5-$30 in general.

Some of the more common and easy-to-find toys include the Chatter Telephone, Pull-a-Tune Xylophone, Corn Popper and numerous bees and Snoopy dogs. Because of their inherent play value and lengthy history, many were and still are used as toys and are often found in less than Mint condition.

Editor's Note: Many Fisher-Price toys had several variations, which often means several different values. Also, the date found on the toy may only be a copyright date, which may be earlier than the actual date of manufacture.

The Top 10 Wooden Fisher-Price Toys
(in Mint in Box condition)

1. Skipper Sam, 1934, #155 .... $2,800
2. Popeye the Sailor, 1936, #703 2,400
3. Popeye, 1935, #700 2,200
4. Woodsy-Wee Circus, 1931, #201 2,100
5. Mickey Mouse Band, 1935, #530 2,100
6. Popeye Cowboy, 1937, #705 2,100
7. Doughboy Donald, 1942, #744 2,000
8. Drummer Bear, 1931, #102 2,000
9. Doctor Doodle, 1931, #100 2,000
10. Granny Doodle, 1931, #101 2,000

The Top 10 Plastic Fisher-Price Toys
(in Mint in Box condition)

1. Amusement Park, # 932 .... $425
2. Safety School Bus, # 984 375
3. Safety School Bus, # 983 375
4. Safety School Bus, # 990 375
5. Nifty Station Wagon, # 234 375
6. Snorkey Fire Engine, # 168 350
7. Snorkey Fire Engine, # 168 350
8. Rooms—Sears exclusive, # 909 350
9. Castle, # 993 200
10. Sesame Street Extras, # 940 125

Contributor to this section: **Plastic:** Sean, and Debbie Craig, toys96fp@aol.com

FISHER-PRICE

WOODEN FISHER-PRICE TOYS

NAME	NO.	YEAR	GOOD	EX	MINT
Allie Gator	653	1960	40	80	160
Amusement Park	932	1963	50	100	200
Baby Chick Tandem Cart	50	1953	45	65	125
Barky	462	1958	45	75	125
Barky Buddy	150	1934	400	900	1800
Barky Puppy	103	1931	550	1000	2000
Big Bill Pelican	794	1961	45	75	125
Big Performing Circus	250	1932	450	900	1800
Blackie Drummer	785	1939	400	650	1000
Bonny Bunny Wagon	318	1959	30	45	80
Boom Boom Popeye	491	1937	550	800	1600
Bossy Bell	656	1959	35	45	70
Bouncing Bunny Wheelbarrow	727	1939	450	750	1300
Bouncy Racer	8	1960	40	65	90
Bucky Burro	166	1955	95	200	550
Buddy Bronc	430	1938	200	400	800
Buddy Bullfrog	728	1959	40	65	125
Bunny Basket Cart	301	1957	30	45	80
Bunny Basket Cart	303	1960	30	45	95
Bunny Bell Cart	520	1941	125	250	550
Bunny Bell Cart	604	1954	45	75	150
Bunny Cart	5	1948	75	100	145
Bunny Drummer	512	1942	150	225	550
Bunny Drummer	505	1946	150	225	550
Bunny Egg Cart	28	1950	50	70	125
Bunny Egg Cart	404	1949	50	70	125
Bunny Engine	703	1954	45	75	135
Bunny Racer	474	1942	125	225	550
Busy Bunny Cart	719	1936	150	300	750
Butch the Pup	333	1951	45	75	125
Buzzy Bee	325	1950	40	60	80
Cash Register	972	1960	35	75	125
Chatter Monk	798	1957	45	65	145
Chatter Telephone	747	1962	30	45	65
Choo-Choo Local	517	1936	350	700	1500
Chubby Chief	110	1932	450	950	2000
Chuggy Pop-Up	616	1955	40	65	135
Circus Wagon	156	1942	125	300	650
Concrete Mixer Truck	926	1959	150	300	625
Corn Popper	785	1957	35	50	115
Corn Popper	788	1963	35	50	85
Cotton Tail Cart	525	1940	200	400	800
Cowboy Chime	700	1951	150	300	600
Dandy Dobbin	765	1941	150	325	675
Dashing Dobbin	742	1938	250	400	850
Ding-Dong Duckey	724	1949	175	225	575
Dinkey Engine	642	1959	35	50	95
Dizzy Dino	407	1931	250	400	800
Dizzy Donkey	433	1939	45	80	160
Doc & Dopey Dwarfs	770	1938	550	1000	2000
Doctor Doodle	477	1940	150	300	600
Doctor Doodle	100	1931	600	1000	2000
Dog Cart Donald	149	1936	600	1000	2000
Doggy Racer	7	1942	150	300	600
Donald Cart	469	1940	450	900	1800
Donald Duck & Nephews	479	1941	350	700	1400
Donald Duck Cart	544	1942	200	350	750
Donald Duck Cart	605	1954	125	250	500
Donald Duck Cart	500	1937	350	600	1500

FISHER-PRICE

295

WOODEN FISHER-PRICE TOYS

NAME	NO.	YEAR	GOOD	EX	MINT
Donald Duck Choo-Choo	450	1942	225	450	900
Donald Duck Choo-Choo	450	1940	350	600	1200
Donald Duck Delivery	715	1936	350	750	1500
Donald Duck Drum Major	432	1948	150	300	600
Donald Duck Drum Major	550	1940	150	300	600
Donald Duck Drummer	454	1949	175	225	550
Donald Duck Pop-Up	425	1938	325	650	1200
Donald Duck Xylophone	185	1938	325	750	1000
Donald Duck Xylophone	177	1946	150	350	700
Dopey Dwarf	770	1939	350	650	1700
Doughboy Donald	744	1942	550	1000	2000
Drummer Bear	102	1931	550	1000	2000
Ducky Cart	51	1950	45	85	145
Ducky Cart	6	1948	45	85	145
Ducky Daddles	14	1941	35	65	135
Ducky Daddles	148	1942	175	300	600
Dumbo Circus Racer	738	1941	450	1000	2000
Easter Bunny	490	1936	165	300	675
Elsie's Dairy Truck	745	1948	300	700	1400
Farm Truck	845	1954	145	300	600
Farmer in Dell Music Box	763	1962	30	40	65
Farmer in the Dell TV Radio	166	1963	25	35	75
Fido Zilo	707	1955	35	65	135
Fire Truck	630	1959	35	50	95
Fuzzy Fido	444	1941	125	200	550
Gabby Duck	767	1952	55	80	160
Gabby Goofies	777	1963	35	40	65
Gabby Goofies	775	1956	25	45	75
Gabby Goose	120	1936	35	65	95
Galloping Horse & Wagon	737	1948	150	350	750
Gold Star Stagecoach	175	1954	150	425	975
Golden Gulch Express	191	1961	65	95	165
Go'N Back Jumbo	360	1931	450	900	1800
Granny Doodle	101	1931	600	1000	2000
Granny Doodle & Family	101	1933	650	1500	2000
Happy Helicopter	498	1953	150	225	425
Happy Hippo	151	1962	35	65	145
Hot Diggety	800	1934	450	900	1800
Howdy Bunny	757	1939	300	650	1100
Huckleberry Hound Xylo	711	1961	175	225	475
Huffy Puffy Train	999	1958	55	80	175
Humpty Dump Truck	145	1963	40	65	125
Humpty Dumpty	757	1957	165	225	550
Husky Dump Truck	145	1961	30	45	95
Jack-n-Jill TV Radio	148	1959	25	45	85
Jingle Giraffe	472	1956	55	175	375
Jolly Jumper	793	1963	25	50	85
Jolly Jumper	450	1954	35	75	165
Juggling Jumbo	735	1958	150	225	425
Jumbo Jitterbug	422	1940	65	150	325
Jumbo Rolo	755	1951	65	150	295
Junior Circus	902	1963	75	200	395
Katy Kackler	140	1954	45	80	160
Kicking Donkey	175	1937	175	285	725
Kitty Bell	499	1950	65	150	275
Lady Bug	658	1961	30	45	75
Leo the Drummer	480	1952	175	225	450
Little Snoopy		1970s	3	7	10
Looky Chug-Chug	161	1949	75	175	325
Looky Fire Truck	7	1950	65	100	250
Lop-Ear Looie	415	1934	150	300	600

WOODEN FISHER-PRICE TOYS

NAME	NO.	YEAR	GOOD	EX	MINT
Lucky Monk	109	1932	350	850	1800
Merry Mousewife	662	1962	35	50	80
Merry Mutt	473	1949	45	75	145
Mickey Mouse Band	530	1935	750	1500	2100
Mickey Mouse Choo-Choo	432	1938	450	850	1800
Mickey Mouse Drummer	476	1941	150	300	625
Mickey Mouse Puddle Jumper	310	1953	150	225	395
Mickey Mouse Safety Patrol	733	1956	165	300	625
Mickey Mouse Xylophone	798	1942	275	500	925
Mickey Mouse Xylophone	798	1939	300	600	975
Mickey Mouse Zilo	714	1963	165	325	575
Mini Bus		1970s	1	3	5
Molly Moo-Moo	190	1956	65	200	400
Moo-oo Cow	155	1958	40	80	160
Mother Goose Cart	784	1955	35	70	145
Music Box Barn	764	1960	25	45	90
Music Box Sweeper	131	1961	40	65	165
Musical Elephant	145	1948	165	325	700
Musical Push Chime	722	1950	35	50	95
Musical Sweeper	225	1953	40	65	170
Musical Sweeper	100	1950	65	135	275
Musical Tick Tock Clock	997	1962	25	45	90
Nosey Pup	445	1956	45	75	155
Patch Pony	616	1963	25	40	85
Perky the Pot	686	1958	40	65	135
Peter Bunny Cart	472	1939	150	325	725
Peter Bunny Engine	721	1949	75	200	425
Peter Bunny Engine	715	1941	70	225	475
Peter Pig	479	1959	35	50	110
Pinky Pig	695	1958	35	65	145
Pinky Pig	695	1956	40	70	160
Pinocchio	494	1939	105	400	975
Pinocchio	720	1939	200	400	940
Playful Puppy	625	1961	35	60	120
Playland Express	192	1962	40	80	165
Pluto Pop-Up	440	1936	35	75	160
Pony Chime	137	1962	30	65	135
Pony Express	733	1941	65	200	445
Poodle Zilo	739	1962	30	65	145
Pop 'N Ring	809	1959	40	65	125
Popeye	700	1935	700	1500	2200
Popeye Cowboy	705	1937	650	1000	2100
Popeye Spinach Eater	488	1939	225	650	1300
Popeye the Sailor	703	1936	600	1200	2400
Prancing Horses	766	1937	175	400	900
Pudgy Pig	478	1962	35	50	110
Puffy Engine	444	1951	35	75	145
Pull-A-Tune Xylophone	870	1957	30	45	95
Pushy Doddle	507	1933	350	800	1900
Pushy Elephant	525	1934	225	600	1700
Pushy Piggy	500	1932	350	800	1800
Quacko Duck	300	1939	135	250	600
Quacky Family	799	1946	30	50	85
Queen Buzzy Bee	444	1962	25	50	80
Rabbit Cart	52	1950	35	70	140
Racing Bunny Cart	723	1938	150	350	700
Racing Ponies	760	1936	200	500	850
Racing Pony	705	1933	325	1000	1475
Racing Rowboat	730	1952	105	225	475
Raggedy Ann & Andy	711	1941	400	900	1975
Rattle Ball	682	1959	20	30	50

FISHER-PRICE

Bucky Burro, 1955, Fisher-Price

Donald Duck Cart, 1942, Fisher-Price

WOODEN FISHER-PRICE TOYS

NAME	NO.	YEAR	GOOD	EX	MINT
Riding Horse	254	1940	400	900	1475
Rock-A-Bye Bunny Cart	788	1940	175	425	825
Rock-A-Stack	627	1960	15	25	40
Roller Chime	123	1953	35	70	140
Rolling Bunny Basket	310	1961	35	65	135
Rooster Cart	469	1938	95	225	575
Safety School Bus	990	1962	50	100	175
Safety School Bus	983	1959	150	300	600
Scotty Dog	710	1933	350	850	1900
Shaggy Zilo	738	1960	40	80	160
Skipper Sam	155	1934	650	1300	2800
Sleepy Sue (Turtle)	495	1962	25	45	90
Smokie Engine	642	1960	30	40	85
Snoopy Sniffer	180	1958	50	100	195
Snoopy Sniffer	180	1938	65	200	475
Snorky Fire Engine	168	1960	50	95	195
Sonny Duck Cart	410	1941	75	200	475
Space Blazer	750	1953	175	400	850
Squeaky the Clown	777	1958	125	225	550
Stake Truck	649	1960	40	80	160
Streamline Express	215	1935	350	700	1700
Strutter Donald Duck	510	1941	125	300	700
Struttin' Donald Duck	900	1939	205	450	875
Sunny Fish	420	1955	75	200	425
Suzie Seal	460	1961	25	40	85
Tabby Ding Dong	730	1939	200	400	800
Tailspin Tabby	400	1931	125	350	700
Tailspin Tabby Pop-Up	600	1947	100	200	400
Talk-Back Telephone	747	1961	35	70	140
Talking Donald Duck	765	1955	35	70	140
Talky Parrot	698	1963	50	100	195
Tawny Tiger	654	1962	30	65	165
Teddy Bear Parade	195	1938	300	700	1700
Teddy Choo-Choo	465	1937	200	400	825
Teddy Drummer	775	1936	300	600	1200
Teddy Station Wagon	480	1942	150	300	650
Teddy Tooter	712	1957	100	225	525
Teddy Tooter	150	1940	200	400	895
Teddy Trucker	711	1949	100	225	575
Teddy Xylophone	752	1948	175	225	475
Teddy Zilo	777	1950	35	50	165
Ten Little Indians TV Radio	159	1961	25	50	75
This Little Pig	910	1963	25	40	45
Thumper Bunny	533	1942	225	400	800
Timber Toter	810	1957	50	100	175
Timmy Turtle	150	1953	40	80	160
Tiny Teddy	634	1955	40	75	145
Tiny Tim	496	1957	35	70	135
Tip-Toe Turtle	773	1962	30	45	95
Toot Toot Engine	641	1962	30	45	90
Tow Truck	615	1960	45	70	155
Toy Wagon	131	1951	125	250	500
Trotting Donald Duck	741	1937	300	650	1450
Tuggy Turtle	139	1959	45	75	165
Uncle Timmy Turtle	125	1956	50	100	195
Waggy Woofy	437	1942	100	250	500
Walt Disney's Carnival	207	1936	325	600	1200
Walt Disney's Donald Duck	208	1936	250	400	900
Walt Disney's Easter Parade	475	1936	450	1000	1900
Walt Disney's Mickey Mouse	209	1936	250	400	800
Walt Disney's Pluto-the-Pup	210	1936	225	450	800

FISHER-PRICE

WOODEN FISHER-PRICE TOYS

NAME	NO.	YEAR	GOOD	EX	MINT
Whistling Engine	617	1957	40	80	160
Wiggily Woofer	640	1957	40	95	195
Winky Blinky Fire Truck	200	1954	45	100	195
Woodsy-Wee Circus	201	1931	500	900	2100
Woofy Wagger	447	1947	45	75	185
Woofy Wowser	700	1940	100	325	825
Ziggy Zilo	737	1958	50	100	175

PLASTIC FISHER-PRICE TOYS

NAME	NO.	YEAR	GOOD	EX	MINT
Adventure Sets					
Aero-Marine Search Team	323	1979	40	50	60
Alpha Probe	325	1980	40	50	60
Alpha Star	326	1983	40	50	60
Construction Workers	352	1976	30	40	50
Cycle Racing Team	356	1977	20	25	30
Dare Devil Sport Van	318	1978	40	50	60
Daredevil Skydiver	354	1977	10	15	20
Deep Sea Diver	358	1980	20	30	40
Dune Buster	322	1979	30	40	50
Firestar 1	357	1980	20	25	30
Motocross Team	335	1983	40	50	60
Mountain Climbers	351	1976	40	50	60
Northwoods Trailblazer	312	1977	25	30	40
Rescue Copter	305	1975	20	25	30
Rescue Team	350	1976	15	20	30
Rescue Truck	303	1975	25	30	40
Safari	304	1975	60	65	70
Scuba Divers	353	1976	20	25	30
Sea Explorer	310	1977	40	50	60
Sea Shark	334	1981	40	50	60
Sport Plane	306	1975	20	25	30
Super Speed Racer	308	1976	20	25	30
T.V. Action Team	309	1977	60	70	80
Wheelie Dragster	333	1981	15	20	30
White Water Kayak	355	1977	20	25	30
Wilderness Patrol	307	1976	50	60	70
Husky Play Sets					
Bulldozer	329	1980	10	12	15
Farm Set	331	1981	15	20	30
Fire Pumper	336	1983	10	20	30
Firefighters	321	1979	20	30	35
Highway Dump Truck	328	1980	20	25	30
Hook & Ladder	319	1979	20	25	30
Load Master Dump	327	1984	10	15	20
Police Patrol Squad	332	1981	10	15	20
Power & Light Service Rig	339	1983	20	25	35
Power Tow Truck	338	1982	15	20	30
Race Car Rig	320	1979	15	20	30
Rescue Rig	337	1982	10	15	20
Rodeo Rig	330	1980	10	15	20
Little People					
3-Car Circus Train, three-car train, engine w/silver imprinted headlight, green or blue cage car w/lion litho, red caboose, light blue engineer, short ringmaster, and a red clown w/pointed yellow hat	991	1979	25	40	65

PLASTIC FISHER-PRICE TOYS

NAME	NO.	YEAR	GOOD	EX	MINT
4-Car Circus Train, four-car train, engine w/paper headlight litho, blue or green car w/giraffe litho, blue or green flat car w/lion litho, red caboose, elephant, monkey, lion, giraffe, tan bear, short, light blue engineer, red clown w/pointed yellow hat, and a short ringmaster	991	1973	25	40	60
A-Frame, A-frame house w/removable door and sidewalk, three-rung white ladder, two sets of yellow bunk beds, two yellow lounge chairs, grill, two white picnic benches, white table w/steak litho, two yellow captain chairs, four-seat jeep, dad, mom, boy, girl and Lucky the dog	990	1973	35	50	80
Airport, large fold out airport base, white/turquoise jet, orange/yellow helicopter, four-car tram front car, two luggage cars, fuel car, two white/green two seat cars w/luggage rack, two green hat boxes, two yellow pieces of luggage, cardboard hanger parts box, dad, mom, boy, girl, stewardess, African-American pilot w/turquoise base	996	1972	35	50	90
Airport, airport building, blue and yellow copter, large blue and yellow plane, four captain chairs, two orange coffee tables, green and white two-seat car w/luggage rack, one brown and one blue suitcase, three-car tram, tan bald man, short light blue blond stewardess, short pilot, mom, boy and girl	2502	1986	15	25	45
Airport Crew, green pilot, black pilot w/blue body, and a tall light blue stewardess	678		4	7	15
Amusement Park, large vinyl mat, tunnel/bridge, four-chair swing ride, single-seat swing ride, merry-go-round, four-piece train, two small single-seat cars (no holes for gas), two small single-seat boats, two small boats, straight-sided Little People including two blue boys, two mauve girls, two green boys and a black dog w/yellow or white ears	932	1963	175	250	425
Bath and Utility Sets, toilet, sink, tub, captains chair, sewing machine, washer, dryer, all wooded family consisting of a dad, mom, boy and a girl; many color variations exist	725	1972	12	35	60
Beauty Salon, small beauty salon connects w/No. 2454 and No. 2455; set comes w/one pink and white car w/a luggage rack and a girl	2453	1990	7	12	25
Boat Hauler, blue and white truck and trailer w/snap on gray boat holder, blue and white speedboat, one man w/white body and blue ca and one dark blue worker	345	1981	5	12	25
Brown Roof House, fold-open house w/a garage, green and white car, one double bed, two twin beds, four captain chairs, one round table, two lounge chairs, one coffee table, dad, mom, boy, girl, and Lucky the dog	952	1980	25	35	45
Car and Camper, white and red four-seat SUV, white and red pop-up camper w/yellow canvas tent inside, yellow clam carrier w/litho on top, green and yellow boat that sits on top of jeep, two green lounge chairs, grill, green table w/steak litho, motorcycle, dad, mom, boy and girl	992	1979	25	40	60
Castle, castle w/attached flag, pink dragon, oone brown and one black horse, white or yellow horse armor, white or yellow scalloped horse harness, castle coach, two short red or yellow thrones, two tall red or yellow thrones, two red or yellow twin beds w/ crown headboard, one red or yellow double bed w/ crwon headboard, one red or yellow round table w/ medievil-style litho, plastic knight, woodsman, king, queen, prince, princess and a cardboard parts box; reissued in 1987 w/no flag and all plastic people	993	1975	90	125	200
Change-a-Tune Carousel, three records labeled A-B-C, two boys and a girl	170	1981	25	35	55

Donald Duck Drummer, 1949, Fisher-Price

Gold Star Stagecoach, 1954, Fisher-Price

PLASTIC FISHER-PRICE TOYS

NAME	NO.	YEAR	GOOD	EX	MINT
Choo-Choo Train, small wood and plastic train engine w/three, three straight-sided Little People and a Lucky the dog	719	1963	25	35	60
Circus clowns, threee different clowns, on card	675	1984	4	7	15
Copter, green and white truck and trailer w/gray snap-on compass, gold one-seat helicopter, one tall blue pilot and one worker w/tan base	344	1981	5	12	25
Crazy Clown Brigade, large clown car, two white crooked hoses, two white crooked ladders, white hose reel, and small green bathtub w/wheels, clown feet, tall blue clown w/white or yellow tie, and a short black clown w/a red fireman hat	657	1983	35	50	80
Cruise boat, S.S. Tadpole, small ship, one-piece chair w/fishing pole, one yellow life preserver, short blue sea captain w/white beard, blond boy w/green base boy	2524	1988	15	25	35
Decorator Set, double bed, two twin beds, T.V., checkerboard litho round table, two stuffed chairs, coffee table, all wooden family consisting of a dad, mom, boy and a girl; many color variations exist	728	1970	13	35	60
Drive In Movie, small drive in movie building w/movie screen connects w/No. 2453 and No. 2455; set comes w/one white and yellow car w/a luggage rack and a boy	2454	1990	7	12	25
Dump Truckers, dumping station w/three slots for trucks, three trucks of different shape and color, three balls in wood or plastic, three light or dark blue straight-sided boys (one smiling, one frowning, and one w/freckles)	979	1965	45	70	120
Express Train, three-car train, flat car, caboose, solid yellow one-seat car w/luggage rack, one yellow and one blue suitcase, dad, mom, light blue engineer and Lucky the dog	2581	1987	10	17	25
Farm, barn base w/mooing door, silo, four pieces of fence, tractor, cart, white harness, white trough, red chicken, white chicken, horse, cow, pig, jointed dog, sheep, dad w/cowboy hat, mom, boy w/cowboy hat and a girl	2501	1986	17	25	45
Farm family on card, dark red woman w/blond hair, tall green dad w/white hat and yellow scarf, and a blue girl w/blond hair	677	1984	4	7	15
Ferris Wheel, ferris wheel base winds up plays music, three Little People and Lucky the dog; first year versions come w/straight-sided Little People	969	1966	25	45	80
Ferry Boat, w/pull string and wheels, white and blue speed boat, two yellow life preservers, two two-seat cars, orange and black man w/o mustache, blue mom w/blond hair, tall blue captain	932	1979	45	60	100
Fire Engine, wooden truck and a fireman	720	1969	7	13	30
Fire Engine, large red and white truck w/cherry picker and attached yellow hose, red fire hydrant, two firemen and one dalmatian	2361		7	12	25
Fire Station, fire house building, gray fire training tower, two yellow connecting ladders, two barricades, ambulance, fire truck w/ladder, fire chief car, two yellow truck braces, two black connecting fire hoses, two black rubber hoses, two yellow truck braces, three fireman and one dalmatian dog	928	1979	45	60	80
Fire Truck Rig, long red fire engine w/two yellow braces, w/two firemen	346	1983	5	12	25
Floating Marina, floating marina building w/two boats slips, orange seaplane, one yellow life preserver, detachable clear lighthouse dome, orange boat, red and white boat w/steering wheel, short blue captain w/white beard, boy and girl	2582	1988	10	17	25
Fun Jet, plane w/red wings and tail, one green and one yellow suitcase, w/dad, mom, boy and a girl	183	1970	5	12	20

FISHER-PRICE

PLASTIC FISHER-PRICE TOYS

NAME	NO.	YEAR	GOOD	EX	MINT
Fun Jet, Green/white yellow plane, one brown and one blue suitcase, w/dad, mom, boy, and a girl	182	1981	12	18	25
Garage, two-story building, elevator and car ramps, car grease rack, four single-seat cars in red, blue, green, yellow, and three little boys and one little girl	930	1970	20	25	30
Garage, two-story building, elevator and car ramps, fire hydrant, pay phone, gas pump, three single-seat cars, and three little boys and one little girl	2504	1986	15	25	45
Garage Squad, three workers	679		4	7	15
Gas Station, small gas station building connects w/No. 2453 and No. 2454; set comes w/one red and white car w/a luggage rack and a boy	2455	1990	7	12	25
Goldilocks, playhouse w/yellow key attached, w/mama bear, papa bear, baby bear, and blue girl w/blond braids	151	1967	35	45	75
Happy Hoppers, push toy playset w/three Little People that pop up and down as toy is pushed; value may fluctuate depending on version of Little People	121	1969	15	25	40
Hospital, building w/fold down door and elevator and white ambulance, turquoise plastic pieces include stretcher, x-ray, scale, two chairs, two beds, large sink, baby cradle; white plastic pieces include wheelchair, operating table, privacy screen; white baby without bib, white nurse w/white mask, doctor, African-American doctor, dad, mom and girl	931	1976	65	85	125
House, fold-open house w/ yellow roof and attached garage, car w/hook, one double bed, two twin beds, four captain chairs, one round table, two lounge chairs, one coffee table, yellow stairs w/closet and litho, blue cardboard moving van parts box, dad, mom, boy, girl and Lucky the dog; complete w/ moving van add $100-200 to total value	952	1969	25	35	55
Houseboat, blue base boat w/wheels and fold open lid, two yellow lounge chairs, two yellow life preservers, two red captain chairs, red lobster litho table, yellow grill, white/blue speedboat, white-bodied dad w/ blue hat, mom, boy, girl and Lucky the dog	985	1972	25	40	65
Indy Race Rig, yellow and white truck w/trailer, red Indy-type racecar, w/dad engineer and a driver w/a black body and helmet	347	1983	5	12	25
Jetliner, large yellow and blue plane, one blue and one brown suitcase, dad, mom, boy and girl	2360	1986	7	12	25
Jetport, airport building, blue and yellow copter, large blue and yellow plane, four captain chairs, two orange coffee tables, green and white two-seat car w/luggage rack, one brown and one blue suitcase, three-car tram, tan bald man, light blue short stewardess w/blond hair, short pilot, mom, boy and girl	933	1981	25	35	50
Kitchen Set, stove, sink, fridge, litho table, four captain chairs, all wooden family consisting of a dad, mom, boy and a girl; many color variations exist	729	1971	12	35	60
Lacing Shoe, shoe w/mostly brown litho and wheels, special lace, mom wearing glasses w/regular shaped body, two yellow triangle-shaped girls w/ different faces, two square red boys w/different faces, and a dog w/marshmallow-shaped base	146	1970	35	45	75
Lift & Load Depot, building, green and yellow dump truck, fork lift, scoop loader, yellow sling, four brown pallets, two brown crates, two gray crates, two black barrels, orange scoop bucket attached to building, and one African-American and two white workers w/light blue bodies and orange hardhats	942	1977	35	50	80

PLASTIC FISHER-PRICE TOYS

NAME	NO.	YEAR	GOOD	EX	MINT
Lift & Load Lumber Yard, small lumber yard building w/ yellow ramp, green and yellow lift truck, truck and trailer, six pieces of wood lumber (two square, two long rectangular, two short rectangular), four brown pallets, one white and one African-American worker w/light blue bodies and orange hardhats	944	1978	35	45	70
Lift & Load Railroad, train depot building w/track section, seven-piece track (makes a oval), two-piece train (engine winds up), orange sling, two gray crates, two black barrels, four brown pallets, orange ramp, green/yellow lift truck, one white and one Afrrican-American worker w/light blue body and orange hardhats, tall light blue train engineer w/mustache	943	1978	35	50	80
Little Mart, small shopping mart building, red tow truck w/orange hook, orange shopping cart, brown bag of groceries, two-seat car w/solid greenback, yellow pay phone, dad, mom, policewoman and Lucky the dog	2580	1987	10	17	25
Little People Construction Set, orange and yellow dump truck, scoop loader, bulldozer, two black barrels, one gold-cone barricade, one brown crate, two yellow w/black stripes road barricades, two white and one African-American construction workers	2352	1985	7	12	25
Little Riders, plane, rocking horse, tricycle, wagon, train, w/boy and girl	656	1976	4	7	15
Little Trucks, orange and yellow scoop loader, bulldozer, dump truck, lift truck, one brown pallet, one gray crate, w/two light blue construction workers and two green construction workers	398	1981	12	17	30
Main Street, large building of main street w/a pull up background, two blue ramps, yellow two-seat taxi, blue mailbox, parking meter, pay phone, red fire hydrant, red stop sign, yellow turning stop light, yellow-and-black striped road diverter, mail truck, seven plastic letters, small one-seat fire truck, shopkeeper, fireman, mom, mailman, and a little girl	2500	1986	17	25	45
McDonald's, McDonald's restaurant w/pull-out playground, one blue and white two-seat car, one brown trash can, one McDonald's sign, french fry cart, Ronald McDonald, Hamburglar, mom, yellow boy w/black molded hair and girl	2552	1990	27	45	80
Merry-Go-Round, merry-go-round playset base, w/ mom, two boys and a girl	111	1972	35	45	80
Mini Boat Set, car w/hook, boat w/two holes in bottom, V-shaped trailer, straight yellow body boy w/cap, and a straight-sided Lucky	685	1969	50	80	120
Mini Camper Set, car and trailer same as mini boat, wood camper marked "Fisher Price," straight yellow body boy w/cap, and a straight-sided Lucky the dog	686	1969	50	75	120
Mini Snowmobile, snowmobile w/detachable sled, turquoise boy red cap, turquoise girl w/red hair and Lucky the dog	705	1970	30	50	80
Mini Van, w/five Little People-dad, mom, girl, boy, and a dog	141	1969	5	10	25
Musical Shoe, wind-up musical shoe w/wheels and special lace, and three straight-sided people w/red bases, all w/different facial imprints (girl, two different boys)	991	1964	45	55	80
Neighborhood, pull apart two-piece building connected by tree, attached basketball hoop w/ball, yellow five-rung ladder, two twin beds w/teddy bear imprint, one bed w/quilt imprint, one lounge chair, modular kitchen insert, modular bathroom insert, two-seat car, turquoise pool, one round table, two captain chairs, dad, mom, boy, girl and Lucky the dog	2551	1988	17	25	45

FISHER-PRICE

305

Katy Kackler, 1954, Fisher-Price

Popeye the Sailor, 1936, Fisher-Price

PLASTIC FISHER-PRICE TOYS

NAME	NO.	YEAR	GOOD	EX	MINT
New School, school house building w/pull-out playground, red stop sign, small school bus, yellow skateboard, white flag, chalk, orange and blue jump rope, white drum, red-bodied woman teacher w/glasses, boy, African-American girl, Asian-American boy, and orange-bodied girl w/glasses	2550	1988	17	25	45
Nifty Station Wagon, wooden car w/wood top and two plastic braces on top, w/four large straight wooden figures, blue dad, green mom, yellow cone-shaped boy, and a black dog w/white ears and a ribbed body. The people from this set are similar in design to the people from the No. 990-984 Safety School Bus	234	1960	175	250	375
Nursery School, flat base w/dividing rooms and plastic edges, cardboard roof/play area, gold bus w/apple, double sink, stove, toilet, bathroom sink, slide, merry-go-round, blue easel, teeter totter, four captain chairs, round arts-and-craft table, dad, mom, African-American boy and two girls	929	1978	35	50	80
Nursery Sets, changing table, highchair, cradle, rocking horse, playpen, stroller, dad, mom, girl and a baby; many color variations exist	761	1973	8	13	20
Off-Shore Cargo Base, one large rectangular and square black floats, crane, tan cargo hold, helicopter landing pad, cargo hold cover, tug boat, helicopter, white and blue barge, two gold feed bags, two sections of pipe, two crates, mesh cargo net, two black tow chains, red diver, tall blue captain, and one white and one African-American worker w/light green bodies and yellow hardhats	945	1979	55	75	120
Pampers Promotional, yellow mini van w/family, green body boy and red cap exclusive to the set		1988 only	5	10	25
Patio Set, flowered umbrella table, pool w/imprint, four captain chairs, BBQ grill, all wooden family consisting of a dad, mom, boy and a girl; many color variations exist	726	1971	13	35	60
Play Family Camper, green flatbed truck, white removable camper, green boat w/litho inside, boat sits on top of camper, yellow/red umbrella table, four red captain chairs, grill, yellow motorcycle, red table w/hot dog litho, toilet, sink, red ladder, dad, mom, boy, girl and Lucky the dog	994	1972	25	40	65
Play Family Circus, two yellow ladders, red hoop, yellow trapeze, blue tub (base w/clown on cardboard litho), yellow elephant stand, w/bear, monkey, lion, blue elephant, giraffe, short ringmaster and red clown	135	1974	35	45	80
Play Family Farm, barn base w/mooing door, silo, four pieces of fence, tractor, cart, white harness, white trough, red chicken, white chicken, horse, cow, pig, jointed dog, sheep, dad w/cowboy hat, mom, boy w/cowboy hat, and a girl; many variations exist	915	1968	25	40	60
Play Family Lacing Shoe, shoe w/mostly black litho and blue base, special lace, w/large all-wood mom wearing glasses, two-yellow triangle-shaped girls w/different faces, two square red boys w/different faces, and a dog w/marshmallow-shaped base	136	1965	35	50	75
Play Family Tow Truck and Car, tow truck, car w/hook, and a straight body yellow boy w/cap	718	1969	35	55	115
Playground, green base playground w/spring rides and a slide, orange and yellow swing, orange and yellow merry-go-round, blue climbing cube, boy and girl	2525	1986	4	7	15
Pool, swimming pool base, black stand-up grill, diving board, slide, lifeguard stand w/white life preserver, two lounge chairs (one orange and one yellow), umbrella table w/base shaped to fit in hole, boy, and a girl	2526	1986	4	7	15

FISHER-PRICE

PLASTIC FISHER-PRICE TOYS

NAME	NO.	YEAR	GOOD	EX	MINT
Rooms—Sears exclusive, flat base w/divided rooms, yellow fridge, yellow double sink, yellow stove w/litho, green table w/formal setting, four green captain chairs, white tub, scale, toilet, sink, red or blue couch, two red or blue twin beds, red or blue T.V. w/litho puppet, red or blue coffeetable, red and blue stuffed chair, turquoise umbrella table, two yellow captain chairs, turquoise or yellow grill, white cotton drawstring bag, all wooden family consisting of a green bald man, blue mom w/blond hair, orange bald boy, red girl w/blond hair and Lucky the dog	909	1971	180	250	350
Safety School Bus, yellow school bus w/stop sign on the drivers side and a flat nose, five tall wooden people, the people from this bus are similar in design to the people from the No. 990 Safety School Bus and the No. 234 Nifty Station wagon	984	1961	150	225	375
Safety School Bus, yellow school bus w/stop sign on the drivers side and a flat nose, five tall wooden people; the people from this bus and similar in design to the people from the No. 984 Safety School Bus and the No. 234 Nifty Station wagon	990	1962	150	225	375
Safety School Bus, First version-yellow school bus w/stop sign on the drivers side and a flat nose, wooden top piece reads "Fisher Price," six removable people w/litho on wooden bodies; Second version-four removable people and two that are fixed in the back, as the bus moves the fixed people bounce up and down	983	1959	150	225	375
School, schoolhouse building w/bell and pull down sidewall w/chalkboard, four green or yellow student desks, one green or yellow teachers desk w/chair, green and yellow swing, merry-go-round, green or yellow slide, numbers tray, letter tray w/letters A-Z and extra P, S, T, N, R, I, and E letters, chalk box, eraser, blue teacher w/blond hair, two boys and two girls	923	1971	35	50	80
School Bus, five Little People kids, and one dog. There have been many variations of the School bus over the years years; all brown dog from first issue is worth $30-50 in Excellent condition	192	1965	12	25	50
Sesame Street Clubhouse, clubhouse w/bird nest and shaker board and attached tire swing, yellow slide, three barrels (red, blue, yellow), yellow cable drum, black and red jump rope, two-seat wagon, Big Bird, Roosevelt Franklin, Grover, The Count, Bert, and Ernie	937	1977	45	60	100
Sesame Street Extras, boxed set showing Sesame Street scenes comes w/Ernie, Bert, Cookie Monster, Susan, Gordon, Mr. Hooper, Big Bird and Oscar in his can	939	1976	25	45	100
Sesame Street Extras, Boxed set showing Sesame Street scenes comes w/Roosevelt Franklin, Grover, Sherlock Hemlock, Prairie Dawn, The Count, Harry Monster, and Snuffleupagus	940	1977	35	55	125
Sesame Street House, brownstone fold-out building, Sesame Street lamppost, mailbox w/litho, garbage truck, five-rung white ladder, newsstand, fire hydrant on gray triangle, soda fountain stand, T.V. showing Grover, sofa, table w/pork chop litho, two captain chairs, two twin beds marked "B" and "E," chalk box, eraser, Big Bird's nest, coffeetable, Bert, Ernie, Mr. Hooper, Big Bird, Cookie Monster, Susan, Gordon, and Oscar in his can	938	1975	45	70	125
Snorkey Fire Engine, fire truck w/white base and blue wheels and yellow boom, w/four firemen w/green bases, red arms and hats, and a black dog exclusive to this set	168	1960	150	225	350

FISHER-PRICE

Teddy Zilo, 1950, Fisher-Price

Little People, No. 932 Ferry Boat, 1979. Photo Courtesy Sean and Debbie Craig

Little People, No. 952 House, 1969. Photo Courtesy Sean and Debbie Craig

PLASTIC FISHER-PRICE TOYS

NAME	NO.	YEAR	GOOD	EX	MINT
Snorkey Fire Engine, fire truck w/red base, black wheels and a yellow boom, w/four firemen w/white bases, red arms and hats	168	1961	150	225	350
Village, large fold out village base, connecting bridge and traffic light, six letters, one yellow single bed, small fire engine, red and blue police car, mail truck, four yellow captain chairs, umbrella table, green and white one-seat car w/luggage rack, white and green back-to-back two-seat car, phone booth, yellow grill, dentist chair, barber chair, yellow couch and coffeetable, African-American doctor, white doctor, fireman, mailman w/gray base, policewoman, mom, boy, girl and Lucky the dog	997	1973	65	75	100
Western Town, building w/shaker board, tan or green buckboard, tan or green stagecoach w/removable red top, one brown and one black horse, two brown harnesses, brown saddle, gray crate, green hatbox luggage, four-pieces fence, blue sheriff w/star badge on chest, red sod-buster man w/black hat and mustache, Native American w/chest markings on front, yellow lady w/green hat	934	1982	40	50	85
Westerners, tall ringmaster, Native American w/ headdress, and a green cowboy w/ten-gallon hat, on card	676	1984	4	7	15
Zoo, zoo base, tree, orange and yellow parrots, vulture, black and orange monkeys, orange cabaña, black seal, blue elephant, yellow lion cub, hippo, gorilla, mountain goat, four food trays, two green benches, one green table, three car tram, dad, mom, girl, boy, and a zookeeper w/safari-style hat	916	1984	20	30	45

FISHER-PRICE

Games

Just a few years ago, except for a handful of visionaries, no one considered board and card games worthy of collecting, which in hindsight is itself a strong indicator of their future collectibility. Games were playthings only and were treated casually compared to thousands of other now highly-collectible items. Their entire value was in the playing, in how much fun and social interaction they afforded. They were casually played, their parts cheerfully smudged, crumpled and misplaced. Once their fun quotient was exhausted, they were just as casually tossed in closets, attics or in the trash.

While the idea of games as collectibles is a recent one in the world of antiques, the field is making up for that oversight with a vengeance. This is particularly true in the three most visible groupings — Victorian games, sports games and character/TV-related games.

Victorian games are loosely defined as those produced between the Civil War and World War I. During this period, manufacturing technologies advanced from the hand-tinted games of the pre-1860s to chromolithography, which ushered in the age of mass production.

The premier marque of Victorian games belongs to McLoughlin Bros., which progressed from hand tinting to lithography in grand style, producing many of the most beautifully illustrated — and most valuable — games ever made. In many cases, simply the McLoughlin name on the box will make a game considerably more valuable than the identical item produced by a competitor.

McLoughlin was purchased by Milton Bradley in 1920, which reissued many games under the Milton Bradley name. As would be expected, these reissues have only a fraction of the value of McLoughlin originals.

Tiddley Winks Game,
1920s, Wilder

GAMES

311

Another noteworthy game maker was Parker Brothers, which since 1883 has produced many games rivaling the beauty and collectibility of McLoughlin, Bliss, Clark & Sowdon and J.H. Singer are other names to watch for, as they also held to high standards of creativity and artistry in the execution of their games.

However, if you do come across a Victorian game in your travels, most likely it will be by Milton Bradley, by far the most prolific manufacturer of the age. While its games were generally neither as beautiful nor as valuable as those of its competitors, they are still collected for both their artwork and subject matter.

Postwar Games Also Popular

Many collectors consider World War II as the breaking point between antique and modern games. However, this turning point can be defined perhaps just as logically as either before or after the advent of TV. The fact that World War II and the rise of television took place in the same decade is a largely convenient coincidence. Which event wrought the most lasting changes on American life can make for a rousing evening's debate, but TV's impact on modern marketing and consumer habits is hard to overestimate.

Character games in particular lend themselves to the theory of television classification. Pre-TV games can be seen as evolving from Victorian nursery rhyme games like McLoughlin's Little Goldenlocks and The Three Bears (1890), numerous variations on Mother Goose and Milton Bradley's Little Jack Horner (1910) to name a few.

These were supplemented by popular comic characters like Winnie Winkle, The Katzenjammer Kids, Chester Gump, Dick Tracy and also by literary entries such as Parker Brother's classic Wonderful Game of Oz (1921) and Kerk Guild's A. A. Milne's Winnie The Pooh Game (1931).

The 1930s also saw the tapping of a limitless well of Disney character games, beginning with numerous Mickey Mouse games and following with Ferdinand the Bull, Snow White, Alice In Wonderland and many more. Disney's merchandising grew more sophisticated with each new film, setting precedents that have become today's standard practice.

Television games of the 1950s saw a general decline in the quality of materials and execution and an increasing reliance on character affiliation. Games like Lowell's Gunsmoke (1950), Milton Bradley's Annie Oakley (1950) and Parker Brothers' Bing Crosby — Call Me Lucky (1954) set a new, albeit lower, standard for game production and marketing.

TV-based games of the 1950s and '60s are currently the most eagerly sought-after of all modern games, and their values reflect that demand.

Tabletop Sports Games

Sports games, of which there are many, have enjoyed immense gains in value along with the boom in other sports memorabilia which essentially began in the late 1970s. This area also illustrates the issue of relative value across collecting fields.

In general, sports collectors assign a higher value to sports games than game collectors do, and asking prices for the same game can vary widely from a toy show to a sports show, or even from one table to another at the same show. But the point is repeatedly proven that collectors within a specialized field will often pay more for a particular item than generalized collectors in a related field.

GAMES

Still, no hobby operates in a vacuum. Increasing demand by sports collectors will also drive up prices for game collectors, just as demand by Christmas collectors for Santa games will drive up prices for both Christmas and game collectors. Game collectors might always assign a lower value to the same game than either of these more specialized groups, but whatever its origin, demand drives value. As collectors grow more sophisticated and knowledgeable about various sources of items in their special areas, these cross-field price variances begin to fade, but they will probably never disappear altogether, particularly when one field can experience a boom time when another may not.

Sports games are collected either by individual sport, like baseball or horse racing, or by personality, such as Babe Ruth's Baseball Game (1926) or Mickey Mantle's Big League Baseball (1955). Personality-based games typically have higher values than their generic counterparts, and older generic games are normally more valuable than newer ones.

Sport enthusiasts have driven up the interest in tabletop electronic games. Tudor started it all with their first electronic game — Electric Auto Races. Gotham followed suit at the 1954 International Toy Fair when introduced Gotham Electronic Magnetic Football. Other sports, such as baseball, football, hockey and horse racing were all

GAMES

Elvis Presley Game, 1957, Teen Age Games

made into electronic or vibrating games by Tudor and Gotham. Other companies, including Eagle, Munro and Coleco.

As with any collectible, there are factors to consider before purchasing a tabletop game. Make sure the game is complete. A game with a scoreboard and missing the box is considered nearly complete. A game with a box and no scoreboard is a "parts game" and carries little value. Players are the easiest pieces to replace. Do your research and stay informed. This is the easiest way to avoid making a purchase you may later regret.

Trends

Today's TV, film and cartoon character games — those from the 1960s and newer — are strong bets for future appreciation. Comic character games from the 1940s and earlier, however, are losing their nostalgic value and have to stand on artistic merit. Values of these games have been declining.

Strong bets for future investment include sports games, particularly if they are celebrity-based, and games which address current historical or cultural affairs. Also worth seeking out are the limited run products of smaller players in the game field, again, especially those with character affiliation.

Word games, generic strategy games and non-character related games have historically demonstrated little or no appreciation, and their heritage as poor investments will likely be inherited by their modern counterparts. Exceptions are games in genres like science fiction, all of which have better than normal potential as long as sci-fi remains in vogue. Another exception is in games which utilize unique, complex or intricate playing pieces and apparatus. A good example of this can be seen in Transogram's Ka-Bala (1965). This game would be moderately collectible simply by virtue of its fortune telling theme, but its board-dominating, glow-in-the-dark eyeball centerpiece is thrillingly ghoulish.

The burgeoning field of game collecting offers a wealth of benefits including investment potential, history and artistry. But the games can also be played. While most Victorian and modern character games are sought primarily for box and board art, many have been designed to fulfill the mission of fun.

Editor's Note: Since experts agree that so few Mint examples of prewar games exist, the prewar section in this edition lists only two grades, Good and Excellent, as Excellent is the highest grade generally applied to prewar games in auction catalogs and dealer price lists. This is particularly true of Victorian games.

The postwar game section lists three grades of value — Good, Excellent and Mint — as enough examples of Mint condition modern games exist to have established sales histories on which to base market values.

Games in both sections are listed alphabetically by name. Letters listed after the game denote the type of game: B - Board Games, C - Card Games, S - Skill/Action Games.

The Top 10 Prewar Games
(in Excellent condition)

1. Bulls and Bears, McLoughlin Bros., 1896 .... $13,000
2. New Parlor Game of Baseball, Sumner, 1896 10,000
3. Champion Baseball Game, Schultz, 1889 6,800
4. Little Fireman Game, McLoughlin Bros., 1897 6,000
5. Zimmer Baseball Game, McLoughlin Bros., 1885 6,000
6. Teddy's Ride from Oyster Bay to Albany, Jesse Crandall, 1899 5,500
7. Golf, Schoenhut, 1900 5,000
8. Egerton R. Williams Popular Indoor Baseball Game, Hatch, 1886 5,000
9. Great Mails Baseball Game, Walter Mails Baseball Game, 1919 4,100
10. Darrow Monopoly, Charles Darrow, 1934 4,000

The Top 10 Postwar Games
(in Mint condition)

1. Elvis Presley Game, Teen Age Games, 1957 .... $1,000
2. Red Barber's Big League Baseball Game, G & R Anthony, 1950s 900
3. Win A Card Trading Card Game, Milton Bradley, 1965 900
4. Munsters Drag Race Game, Hasbro, 1965 800
5. Munsters Masquerade Game, Hasbro, 1965 800
6. Creature From The Black Lagoon, Hasbro, 1963 750
7. Strike Three, Tone Products, 1948 725
8. Jonny Quest Game, Transogram, 1964 700
9. Munsters Picnic Game, Hasbro, 1965 700
10. Challenge the Yankees, Hasbro, 1960s 700

The Top 10 Tabletop Games
(in Mint condition)

1. Official NHL, 1969-71, Coleco $500
2. Olympic, 1964, Eagle 500
3. Hockey games, various games, 1940s-50s, Cresta 500
4. No. G-200, 1930s-1950s, Gotham 350
5. Official Hockey Night, early 1960s, Eagle 300
6. Playmaker, early 1960s, Eagle 250
7. Pee Wee, late 1950s, Eagle 250
8. Bobby Hull, 1960s, Munro 250
9. Bobby Orr, late 1960s-early 1970s, Munro 250
10. Stanley Cup, mid 1960s, Eagle 250

GAMES

Contributors to this section: **Postwar Games,** Jeff Lowe's extravaGAMEza, 9674 V Plaza #29, Omaha, NE 68127; **Prewar Games,** Paul Fink, Paul Fink's Fun and Games, P.O. Box 488, 59 South Kent Road, Kent, CT 06757. **Tabletop Games,** Steve Giannangelo, 1108 Old Crow's Way, Springfield, IL 62707

NAME	TYPE	YEAR	COMPANY	GOOD	EX
21st Century Football	B	1930s	Kerger	55	90
400 Game, The	B	1890s	J.H. Singer	100	150
400, Aristocrat of Games, The	S	1933	Morris Systems	15	25
A&P Relay Boat Race Coast-to-Coast	B	1930s	A&P	30	40
ABC	C	1900s	Parker Brothers	25	40
ABC Baseball Game	B	1910s		430	715
ABC, Game of	B	1914		60	100
Abcdarian, The	B	1899	Chaffee & Selchow	40	100
Across the Channel	B	1926	Wolverine	50	85
Across the Continent	B	1922	Parker Brothers	150	300
Across the Continent	B	1892	Parker Brothers	100	175
Across the Sea Game	B	1930	Gabriel	60	100
Across the Yalu	B	1905	Milton Bradley	75	175
Add-Too	B	1940	All-Fair	10	15
Admiral Byrd's South Pole Game Little America	B	1930s	Parker Brothers	125	300
Admirals, The Naval War Game	B	1939	Merchandisers	75	120
ADT Delivery Boy	B	1890	Milton Bradley	120	200
ADT Messenger Boy (Small Version)	B	1915	Milton Bradley	40	70
Advance And Retreat, Game of	B	1900s	Milton Bradley	95	175
Aero Ball	S	1940s	Game Makers	30	75
Aero-Chute	B	1940	American Toy Works	75	150
Aeroplane Race	B	1922	Wolverine	60	95
After Dinner	B	1937	Frederick H. Beach (Beachcraft)	10	20
Air Base Checkers	B	1942	Einson-Freeman	20	30
Air Mail, The	B	1930	Archer Toy	75	125
Air Mail, The Game of	B	1927	Milton Bradley	95	100
Air Ship Game, The	B	1912	McLoughlin Bros.	150	300
Air Ship Game, The	B	1904	McLoughlin Bros.	300	700
Airplane Speedway Game	B	1941	Lowe	20	30
Airship Game, The	C	1916	Parker Brothers	30	50
Akins Real Baseball	B	1915	Akins	450	750
Aldjemma	B	1944	Corey Games	30	45
Alee-Oop	B	1937	Royal Toy	30	50
Alexander's Baseball	B	1940s		245	400
Alice in Wonderland	B	1930s	Parker Brothers	60	150
Alice In Wonderland, Game of	B	1923	Stoll & Edwards	50	85
All American Basketball	B	1941	Corey Games	55	65
All American Football	B	1935		35	55
All-American Big Boy Baseball Game	B	1920s	Rosensteel-Pulich	200	500
All-American Football	B	1925	Parker Brothers	100	165
All-Star Baseball Game	B	1935	Whitman	100	165
Allegrando	C	1884	Theodore Presser	40	60
Allie-Patriot Game	C	1917	McDowell And Mellor	30	50
Alpha Baseball Game	B	1930s	Redlich	100	150
Alpha Football Game	B	1940s	Replica	70	115
Amateur Golf	B	1928	Parker Brothers	145	245
Ambuscade, Constellations And Bounce	B	1877	McLoughlin Bros.	150	300
America's Football	B	1939	Trojan Games	55	90
America's Yacht Race	B	1904	McLoughlin Bros.	450	750
American Boy Game	B	1920s	Milton Bradley	75	125
American Derby	B	1931	Henschel	55	90
American Football Game	B	1930	Ace Leather Goods	70	115
American History, The Game of	C	1890s	Parker Brothers	50	90
American League Fan Craze Card Game	C	1904	Fan Craze	1950	3250
American National Game Baseball	C	1909	American National Game Co.	75	200
American Revolution, The New Game of The	B	1844	Lorenzo Burge	960	1600
American Sports	B	1880s		110	180
Amusing Game of Conundrums	C	1853	John McLoughlin	750	1300
Amusing Game of Innocence Abroad, The	B	1888	Parker Brothers	135	300
Amusing Game of the Corner Grocery	C	1890s		100	150
Anagrams	C	1885	Peter G. Thompson	50	90
Ancient Game of the Mandarins, The	B	1923	Parker Brothers	45	75
Andy Gump, His Game	B	1924	Milton Bradley	60	100
Anex-A-Gram	B	1938	Embossing	20	40
Animal & Bird Lotto	B	1926	All-Fair	15	20
Animal Bingo	S		Baldwin Manufacturing	40	125
Apple Pie	C	1895	Parker Brothers	40	60

NAME	TYPE	YEAR	COMPANY	GOOD	EX
Arena	B	1896	Bliss	120	200
Armstead's Play Ball	C	1910s	Austin	200	500
Astronomy	C	1905	Cincinnati Game	40	60
Athletic Sports	B	1900	Parker Brothers	145	245
Attack, Game of	B	1889	Bliss	500	900
Auction Letters	C	1900	Parker Brothers	40	60
Authors	B	1890s	J.H. Singer	40	80
Authors	B	1861	Whipple & Smith	100	300
Authors Illustrated	C	1893	Clark & Sowdon	40	60
Authors, Game of Standard	C	1890s	McLoughlin Bros.	25	50
Authors, The Game of	C	1890s	Parker Brothers	15	35
Auto Game, The	B	1906	Milton Bradley	100	200
Auto Race Electro Game	B	1929	Knapp Electric & Novelty	125	210
Auto Race Game	B	1925	Milton Bradley	200	325
Auto Race Jr.	B	1925	All-Fair	150	200
Auto Race, Army, Navy, Game Hunt (Four game set)	B	1920s	Wilder	110	180
Auto Race, Game Of	B	1920s	Orotech	105	175
Auto-Play Baseball Game	B	1911	Auto-Play	425	700
Automobile Race, Game of the	B	1904	McLoughlin Bros.	500	1000
Avilude	C	1873	West & Lee	65	100
Aydelott's Parlor Baseball	B	1910		195	325
Babe Ruth National Game of Baseball	B	1929	Keiser-Fry	550	910
Babe Ruth's Baseball Game	B	1926	Milton Bradley	400	700
Babe Ruth's Official Baseball Game	B	1940s	Toytown	430	715
Baby Barn Yard	B	1940s	B.L. Fry Products	15	25
Bag of Fun	S	1932	Rosebud Art	15	20
Bagatelle, Game of	B	1898	McLoughlin Bros.	350	700
Bagdad, The Game of The East	B	1940	Clover Games	25	40
Balance The Budget	C	1938	Elten Game	45	75
Balloonio	S	1937	Frederick H. Beach	20	40
Bally Hoo	C	1931	Gabriel	30	65
Bambino	S	1934	Bambino Products	75	125
Bambino (Baseball, Chicago World's Fair)	B	1933	Johnson Store Equipment	295	490
Bambino Baseball Game	B	1940	Mansfield-Zesiger	145	250
Bamboozle, or The Enchanted Isle	B	1876	Milton Bradley	175	250
Bang Bird	S	1924	Doremus Schoen	20	30
Bang, Game of	B	1903	McLoughlin Bros.	100	200
Banner Lye Checkerboard	B	1930s	Geo E. Schweig & Son	15	20
Barage	B	1941	Corey Games	50	100
Barber Pole	S	1908	Parker Brothers	50	75
Barn Yard Tiddledy Winks	S	1910s	Parker Brothers	50	85
Barney Google and Spark Plug Game	B	1923	Milton Bradley	100	200
Baron Munchausen Game, The	B	1933	Parker Brothers	50	75
Base Hit	B	1944	Games	55	90
Baseball	B	1942	Lowe	15	25
Baseball & Checkers	B	1925	Milton Bradley	75	150
Baseball Dominoes	B	1910	Evans	250	400
Baseball Game	B	1930	All-Fair	125	250
Baseball Game & G-Man Target Game	B	1940	Marks Brothers	100	165
Baseball Game, New	B	1885	Clark & Martin	165	275
Baseball Wizard Game	B	1916	Morehouse	265	450
Baseball, Game of	B	1886	J.H. Singer	325	550
Baseballitis Card Game	C	1909	Baseballitis Card	125	205
Bases Full	S	1930		45	70
Basilinda	B	1890	Horsman	105	175
Basket Ball	S	1929	Russell	150	350
Basketball	B	1942	Lowe	15	25
Basketball Card Game	C	1940s	Warren/Built-Rite	20	35
Basketball Game, Official	B	1940	Toy Creations	55	90
Batter Up, Game of	C	1908	Fenner Game	150	200
Battle Checkers	B	1925	Pen Man	15	50
Battle Game, The	B	1890s	Parker Brothers	120	200
Battle of Ballots	B	1931	All-Fair	55	125
Battle of Manila	B	1899	Parker Brothers	400	650
Battles, or Fun For Boys, Game of	S	1889	McLoughlin Bros.	600	1000
Bean-Em	S	1931	All-Fair	250	600
Bear Hunt, Game of	B	1923	Milton Bradley	45	70
Beauty And The Beast, Game of	B	1905	Milton Bradley	45	75
Bee Gee Baseball Dart Target	B	1935s	Bee Gee	70	115
Bell Boy Game, The	B	1898	Chaffee & Selchow	425	700

GAMES

NAME	TYPE	YEAR	COMPANY	GOOD	EX
Belmont Park	B	1930	Marks Brothers	75	125
Bengalee	B	1940s	Advance Games	20	35
Benny Goodman Swings	B	1930s	Toy Creations	65	125
Benson Football Game, The	B	1930s	Benson	85	140
Betty Boop Coed Bridge	C	1930s		50	75
Bible ABCs and Promises	C	1940s	Judson Press	15	25
Bible Authors	C	1895	Evangelical Pub.	20	35
Bible Boys	B	1901	Zondervan	10	15
Bible Characters	B	1890s	Decker & Decker	10	25
Bible Cities	C	1920s	Nellie T. Magee	15	25
Bible Lotto	B	1933	Goodenough and Woglom	10	15
Bible Quotto	B	1932	Goodenough and Woglom	6	10
Bible Rhymes	B	1933	Goodenough and Woglom	10	15
Bicycle Cards	C	1898	Parker Brothers	150	200
Bicycle Game	B	1896	Donaldson Brothers	205	350
Bicycle Game, The New	B	1894	Parker Brothers	400	700
Bicycle Race	B	1910	Milton Bradley	85	140
Bicycle Race Game, The	B	1898	Chaffee & Selchow	430	715
Bicycle Race, A Game for the Wheelmen	B	1891	McLoughlin Bros.	700	1000
Bicycling, The Merry Game of	B	1900	Parker Brothers	100	165
Big Apple	B	1938	Rosebud Art	30	50
Big Bad Wolf Game	B	1930s	Parker Brothers	100	175
Big Business	B	1936	Parker Brothers	75	90
Big Business	B	1937	Transogram	20	50
Big League Baseball Card Game	C	1940s	State College Game Lab	35	60
Big League Basketball	B	1920s	Baumgarten	145	245
Big Six: Christy Mathewson Indoor Baseball Game	B	1922	Piroxloid	400	700
Big Ten Football Game	B	1936	Wheaties	55	90
Bike Race Game, The	B	1930s	Master Toy	35	100
Bild-A-Word	B	1929	Educational Card & Game	20	35
Billy Bump's Visit To Boston	C	1888	Parker Brothers	25	55
Billy Whiskers	B	1924	Russell	45	75
Billy Whiskers	B	1923	Saalfield	45	100
Bilt-Rite Miniature Bowling Alley	B	1930s	Atwood Momanus	70	115
Bing Miller Base Ball Game	B	1932	Ryan	750	2000
Bingo	S	1929	All-Fair	15	25
Bingo	B	1925	Rosebud Art	15	25
Bingo or Beano	B	1940s	Parker Brothers	10	15
Bird Center Etiquette	C	1904	Home Game	55	90
Bird Lotto	B	1940s	Gabriel	20	35
Birds, Game of	C	1899	Cincinnati Game	55	90
Black Beauty	B	1921	Stoll & Edwards	40	65
Black Cat Fortune Telling Game, The	C	1897	Parker Brothers	95	150
Black Falcon of The Flying G-Men, The	B	1939	Ruckelshaus	175	400
Black Sambo, Game of	B	1939	Gabriel	90	200
Blackout	B	1939	Milton Bradley	60	150
Block	C	1905	Parker Brothers	15	20
Blockade	B	1941	Corey Games	50	95
Blondie Goes To Leisureland	B	1935	Westinghouse	20	35
Blondie Playing Card Game	C	1941	Whitman	55	90
Blow Football Game	B	1912		30	50
Blox-O	B	1923	Lubbers & Bell	15	25
Bluff	B	1944	Games of Fame	15	25
Bo Bang & Hong Kong	B	1890	Parker Brothers	275	450
Bo McMillan's Indoor Football	B	1939	Indiana Game	60	125
Bo Peep Game	B	1895	McLoughlin Bros.	195	325
Bo Peep, The Game of	B	1890	J.H. Singer	200	300
Boake Carter's Star Reporter	B	1937	Parker Brothers	105	225
Bobb, Game of	S	1898	McLoughlin Bros.	200	400
Bomb The Navy	B	1940s	Pressman	20	50
Bombardment, Game of	B	1898	McLoughlin Bros.	100	350
Bomber Ball	S	1940s	Game Makers	75	125
Bombs Away	B	1944	Toy Creations	75	175
Bookie	B	1931	Bookie Games	55	90
Boston Baseball Game	B	1906	Boston Game	495	825
Boston Globe Bicycle Game of Circulation	B	1895	Boston Globe	55	90
Boston-New York Motor Tour	B	1920s	American Toy	90	150

GAMES

NAME	TYPE	YEAR	COMPANY	GOOD	EX
Botany	C	1900s	G.H. Dunston	50	100
Bottle Imps, Game of	S	1907	Milton Bradley	300	500
Bottle-Quoits	B	1897	Parker Brothers	50	85
Bottoms Up	B	1934	Embossing	20	45
Bourse, or Stock Exchange	C	1903	Flinch Card	25	40
Bow-O-Winks	S	1932	All-Fair	60	120
Bowl 'em	B	1930s	Parker Brothers	20	35
Bowling Alley	S	1921	N.D. Cass	20	35
Bowling Board Game	B	1896	Parker Brothers	350	575
Box Hockey	B	1941	Milton Bradley	35	60
Boxing Game, The	B	1928	Stoll & Edwards	85	140
Boy Hunter, The	S	1925	Parker Brothers	60	100
Boy Scouts	B	1910s	McLoughlin Bros.	125	200
Boy Scouts in Camp	B		McLoughlin Bros.	150	300
Boy Scouts Progress Game	B	1924	Parker Brothers	150	200
Boy Scouts, The Game of	C	1912	Parker Brothers	75	125
Boy Scouts, The Game of	B	1926	Parker Brothers	200	350
Boys Own Football Game	B	1900s	McLoughlin Bros.	325	750
Bradley's Circus Game	B	1882	Milton Bradley	60	150
Bradley's Telegraph Game	B	1900s	Milton Bradley	85	145
Bradley's Toy Town Post Office	B	1910s	Milton Bradley	90	150
Bringing Up Father Game	B	1920	Embee Distributing	75	175
Broadway	B	1917	Parker Brothers	150	250
Brownie Auto Race	B	1920s	Jeanette Toy & Novelty	115	195
Brownie Character Ten Pins Game	S	1890s		125	200
Brownie Horseshoe Game	B	1900s	M.H. Miller	30	50
Brownie Kick-In Top	S	1910s	M.H. Miller	35	60
Brownie Ring Toss	B	1920s	M.H. Miller	30	50
Buck Rogers and His Cosmic Rocket Wars Game	B	1934		200	350
Buck Rogers In The 25th Century	C	1936	All-Fair	160	350
Buck Rogers Siege of Gigantica Game	B	1934		400	600
Bucking Bronco	B	1930s	Transogram	30	50
Buffalo Bill, The Game of	B	1898	Parker Brothers	200	400
Buffalo Hunt	B	1898	Parker Brothers	175	250
Bugle Horn or Robin Hood	C	1850s	McLoughlin Bros.	600	1000
Bugle Horn or Robin Hood, Game of	B	1895	McLoughlin Bros.	350	650
Bugville Games	B	1915	Animate Toy	75	125
Bula	S	1943	Games Of Fame	30	45
Bull In The China Shop	S	1937	Milton Bradley	20	40
Bulls and Bears	B	1896	McLoughlin Bros.	10000	13000
Bulls and Bears	B	1936	Parker Brothers	150	250
Bunco	C	1904	Home Game	35	55
Bunker Golf	B	1932		115	195
Bunny Rabbit, Or Cottontail & Peter, The Game of	B	1928	Parker Brothers	85	145
Buried Treasure, The Game of	B	1930s	Russell	35	60
Buster Brown at Coney Island	B	1890s	J. Ottmann Lith.	225	350
Buster Brown at the Circus	C	1900s	Selchow & Righter	100	250
Buster Brown Hurdle Race	B	1890s	J. Ottmann Lith.	330	550
Buster Brown, Pin The Tail On The Tiger Game	S	1900s		60	100
Busto	S	1931	All-Fair	100	200
Buying and Selling Game	B	1903	Milton Bradley	100	200
Buzzing Around	S	1924	Parker Brothers	40	65
Cabby	B	1940	Selchow & Righter	40	75
Cabin Boy	B	1910	Milton Bradley	60	100
Cadet Game, The	B	1905	Milton Bradley	100	150
Cake Walk Game, The	B	1900s	Parker Brothers	750	1500
Cake Walk, The	B	1900s	Anglo American	600	1300
Calling All Cars	B	1938	Parker Brothers	25	50
Camelot	B	1950s	Parker Brothers	20	35
Camouflage, The Game of	C	1918	Parker Brothers	35	75
Canoe Race	B	1910	Milton Bradley	35	60
Capital Cities Air Derby, The	B	1929	All-Fair	200	350
Captain and the (Katzenjammer) Kids	B	1940s	Milton Bradley	50	100
Captain Hop Across Junior	B	1928	All-Fair	100	200
Captain Jinks	C	1900s	Parker Brothers	30	55
Captain Kidd And His Treasure	B	1896	Parker Brothers	195	350
Captain Kidd Junior	B	1926	Parker Brothers	50	75
Captive Princess	B	1880	McLoughlin Bros.	135	225
Captive Princess	B	1899	McLoughlin Bros.	65	150
Captive Princess, Tournament And Pathfinders, Games of	B	1888	McLoughlin Bros.	100	200

GAMES

A Radio Game Nebbs on the Air, 1930s, Milton Bradley

Alice in Wonderland, 1930s, Parker Brothers

Bicycle Race, 1910, Milton Bradley

NAME	TYPE	YEAR	COMPANY	GOOD	EX
Capture The Fort	B	1914	Valley Novelty Works	45	75
Car Race & Game Hunt	B	1920s	Wilder	100	165
Cargo For Victory	B	1943	All-Fair	75	125
Cargoes	B	1934	Selchow & Righter	50	95
Carl Hubbell Mechanical Baseball	B		Gotham	200	500
Carnival, The Show Business Game	B	1937	Milton Bradley	50	100
Casey on the Mound	B	1940s	Kamm Games	150	300
Cat	B	1915	Carl F. Doerr	15	25
Cat And Witch	S	1940s	Whitman	25	65
Cat, Game of	B	1900	Chaffee & Selchow	270	450
Catching Mice, Game of	B	1888	McLoughlin Bros.	200	325
Cats And Dogs	B	1929	Parker Brothers	100	225
Cavalcade	B	1930s	Selchow & Righter	40	60
Cavalcade Derby Game	S	1930s	Wyandotte	50	85
Century Ride	B	1900	Milton Bradley	100	200
Century Run Bicycle Game, The	B	1897	Parker Brothers	210	350
Champion Baseball Game, The	B	1889	Schultz	4100	6800
Champion Game of Baseball, The	B	1910s	Proctor Amusement	60	100
Champion Road Race	B	1934	Champion Spark Plugs	40	75
Championship Baseball Parlor Game	B	1914	Grebnelle Novelty	150	250
Championship Fight Game	B	1940s	Frankie Goodman	20	50
Champs, The Land of Brawno	B	1940	Selchow & Righter	30	50
Characteristics	B	1845	Ives	180	300
Characters, A Game of	C	1889	Decker & Decker	25	40
Charge, The	B	1898	E.O. Clark	180	300
Charlie Chan Game	C	1939	Whitman	30	75
Charlie Chan, The Great Charlie Chan Detective Game	B	1937	Milton Bradley	150	250
Charlie McCarthy Game of Topper	B	1938	Whitman	20	45
Charlie McCarthy Put and Take Bingo Game	B	1938	Whitman	30	45
Charlie McCarthy Question and Answer Game	C	1938	Whitman	40	65
Charlie McCarthy Rummy Game	C	1938	Whitman	20	35
Charlie McCarthy's Flying Hats	B	1938	Whitman	25	40
Chasing Villa	B	1920	Smith, Kline & French	65	180
Checkered Game of Life	B	1866	Milton Bradley	130	200
Checkered Game of Life	B	1860	Milton Bradley	200	300
Checkered Game of Life	B	1911	Milton Bradley	100	200
Checkers & Avion	B	1925	American Toy Works	30	50
Chee Chow	B	1939	Gabriel	15	25
Cheerios Bird Hunt	B	1930s	General Mills	15	25
Cheerios Hook The Fish	B	1930s	General Mills	15	25
Chessindia	B	1895	Clark & Sowdon	55	95
Chester Gump Game	B	1938	Milton Bradley	65	125
Chester Gump Hops over the Pole	B	1930s	Milton Bradley	75	125
Chestnut Burrs	C	1896	Fireside Game	35	65
Chevy Chase	B	1890	Hamilton-Myers	75	125
Chicago Game Series Baseball	B	1890s	Doan	1175	1950
Chin-Chow and Sum Flu	B	1925	Novitas Sales	6	10
China	B	1905	Wilkens Thompson	50	85
Chinaman Party	S	1896	Selchow & Righter	75	130
Ching Gong	B	1937	Gabriel	20	40
Chiromagica, or The Hand of Fate	B	1901	McLoughlin Bros.	225	350
Chivalrie Lawn Game	B	1875		60	100
Chivalry	B	1925	Parker Brothers	75	125
Chivalry, The Game of	S	1888	Parker Brothers	150	225
Chocolate Splash	B	1916	Willis G. Young	51	85
Christmas Goose	B	1890	McLoughlin Bros.	750	1500
Christmas Jewel, Game of the	B	1899	McLoughlin Bros.	250	400
Christmas Mail	B	1890s	J. Ottmann Lith.	390	650
Chutes And Ladders	B	1943	Milton Bradley	15	35
Cinderella	C	1905	Milton Bradley	50	80
Cinderella	C	1921	Milton Bradley	15	25
Cinderella	B	1923	Stoll & Edwards	40	95
Cinderella	C	1895	Parker Brothers	55	90
Cinderella or Hunt the Slipper	C	1887	McLoughlin Bros.	75	105
Circus Game	B	1914		75	125
Citadel	B	1940	Parker Brothers	40	60
Cities	B	1932	All-Fair	25	40
City Life, or The Boys of New York, The Game of	C	1889	McLoughlin Bros.	65	250
City of Gold	B	1926	Zulu Toy	150	250

GAMES

321

NAME	TYPE	YEAR	COMPANY	GOOD	EX
Classic Derby	B	1930s	Doremus Schoen	30	50
Click	S	1930s	Akro Agate	50	85
Clipper Race	B	1930	Gabriel	25	75
Clown Tenpins Game	B	1912		60	100
Clown Winks	S	1930s	Gabriel	15	25
Coast To Coast	B	1940s	Master Toy	15	25
Cock Robin	C	1895	Parker Brothers	40	75
Cock Robin and His Tragical Death, Game of	C	1885	McLoughlin Bros.	65	105
Cock-A-Doodle-Doo Game	B	1914		60	100
Cocked Hat, Game of	B	1892	J.H. Singer	150	250
College Baseball Game	B	1890s	Parker Brothers	350	700
College Boat Race, Game of	B	1896	McLoughlin Bros.	350	650
Colors, Game of	B	1888	McLoughlin Bros.	150	225
Columbia's Presidents and our Country, Game of	C	1886	McLoughlin Bros.	250	400
Columbus	B	1892	Milton Bradley	775	1300
Combination Board Games	B	1922	Wilder	40	65
Combination Tiddledy Winks	S	1910	Milton Bradley	40	65
Comic Conversation Cards	C	1890	J. Ottmann Lith.	100	200
Comic Leaves of Fortune-The Sibyl's Prophecy	C	1850s	Charles Magnus	500	900
Comical Animals Ten Pins	B	1910	Parker Brothers	185	310
Comical Game of "Who", The	C	1910s	Parker Brothers	35	50
Comical Game of Whip, The	C	1920s	Russell	20	45
Comical History of America	C	1924	Parker Brothers	40	75
Comical Snap, Game of	C	1903	McLoughlin Bros.	35	55
Commanders of our Forces, The	C	1863	E.C. Eastman	150	225
Commerce	C	1900s	J. Ottmann Lith.	60	125
Competition, or Department Store	C	1904	Flinch Card	25	35
Cones & Corns	S	1924	Parker Brothers	39	65
Conette	S	1890	Milton Bradley	45	75
Coney Island Playland Park	B	1940	Vitaplay Toy	54	90
Conflict	B	1942	Parker Brothers	100	175
Conquest of Nations, or Old Games With New Faces, The	C	1853	Willis P. Hazard	100	175
Construction Game	B	1925	Wilder	150	300
Contack	S	1939	Parker Brothers	5	15
Coon Hunt Game, The	B	1903	Parker Brothers	450	1200
Corn & Beans	B	1875	E.G. Selchow	50	85
Corner The Market	B	1938	Whitman	25	40
Cortella	B	1915	Atkins	22	35
Costumes and Fashions, Game of	C	1881	Milton Bradley	80	225
Cottontail and Peter, The Game of	B	1922	Parker Brothers	75	150
Country Club Golf	B	1920s	Hustler Toy	75	125
Country Store, The	B	1890s	J.H. Singer	100	200
County Fair, The	C	1891	Parker Brothers	45	75
Cousin Peter's Trip to New York, Game of	C	1898	McLoughlin Bros.	45	75
Covered Wagon	B	1927	Zulu Toy	55	85
Cowboy Game, The	B	1898	Chaffee & Selchow	210	425
Cows In Corn	S	1889	Stirn & Lyon	150	250
Crash, The New Airplane Game	B	1928	Nucraft Toys	30	70
Crazy Traveller	S	1920s	Parker Brothers	40	50
Crazy Traveller	B	1908	Parker Brothers	40	60
Crickets In The Grass	S	1920s	Madmar Quality	35	50
Crime & Mystery	B	1940s	Frederick H. Beach (Beachcraft)	15	25
Criss Cross Words	B	1938	Alfred Butts	90	150
Crooked Man Game	B	1914		45	75
Cross Country	B	1941	Lowe	20	30
Cross Country Marathon	B	1920s	Milton Bradley	75	150
Cross Country Marathon Game	B	1930s	Rosebud Art	100	200
Cross Country Racer	B	1940	Automatic Toy	45	75
Cross Country Racer (w/wind-up cars)	B	1940s		75	130
Crossing the Ocean	B	1893	Parker Brothers	87	175
Crow Cards	C	1910	Milton Bradley	9	15
Crow Hunt	S	1930	Parker Brothers	50	85
Crow Hunt	B	1904	Parker Brothers	40	60
Crows In The Corn	S	1930	Parker Brothers	45	75
Crusade	B	1930s	Gabriel	27	45
Crusaders, Game of the	B	1888	McLoughlin Bros.	150	300
Cuckoo, A Society Game	B	1891	J.H. Singer	40	100

GAMES

NAME	TYPE	YEAR	COMPANY	GOOD	EX
Curly Locks Game	B	1910	United Game	60	100
Cycling, Game of	B	1910	Parker Brothers	100	165
Daisy Clown Ring Game	B	1927	Schacht Rubber	9	15
Daisy Horseshoe Game	B	1927	Schacht Rubber	9	15
Danny McFayden's Stove League Baseball Game	B	1920s	National Game	295	490
Darrow Monopoly	B	1934	Charles Darrow	1500	4000
Day at the Circus, Game of	B	1898	McLoughlin Bros.	300	400
Deck Derby	B	1920s	Wolverine	36	60
Deck Ring Toss Game	S	1910		30	50
Decoy	B	1940	Selchow & Righter	45	75
Defenders of the Flag	C	1922	Stoll & Edwards	35	65
Defenders of The Flag Game	B	1920s		24	40
Democracy	B	1940	Toy Creations	50	85
Department Store, Game of Playing	B	1898	McLoughlin Bros.	520	1300
Derby Day	C	1900s	Parker Brothers	30	50
Derby Day	B	1930	Parker Brothers	45	75
Derby Steeple Chase	B	1888	McLoughlin Bros.	150	250
Detective, The Game of	B	1889	Bliss	1200	2000
Dewey at Manila	C	1899	Chaffee & Selchow	100	175
Dewey's Victory	B	1900s	Parker Brothers	120	200
Diamond Game of Baseball, The	B	1894	McLoughlin Bros.	1275	2150
Diamond Heart	B	1902	McLoughlin Bros.	150	225
Diceball	B	1938	Ray-Fair	90	145
Dicex Baseball Game, The	B	1925	Chester S. Howland	195	325
Dick Tracy Detective Game	B	1933	Einson-Freeman	45	150
Dick Tracy Detective Game	B	1937	Whitman	40	100
Dick Tracy Playing Card Game	C	1934	Whitman	50	75
Dick Tracy Super Detective Mystery Card Game	C	1937	Whitman	65	90
Dig	S	1940	Parker Brothers	2	5
Dim Those Lights	S	1932	All-Fair	300	600
Din	C	1905	Horsman	25	45
Discretion	B	1942	Volume Sprayer	30	45
Disk	S	1900s	Madmar Quality	35	55
District Messenger Boy, Game of	B	1904	McLoughlin Bros.	80	200
District Messenger Boy, Game of	B	1886	McLoughlin Bros.	250	500
Diving Fish	S	1920s	C.E. Bradley	20	30
Dixie Land, Game of	C	1897	Fireside	60	90
Doctor Busby Card Game	C	1910		35	55
Doctor Quack, Game of	C	1922	Russell	25	40
Doctors and the Quack	C	1890s	Parker Brothers	45	75
Dodging Donkey, The	S	1920s	Parker Brothers	45	75
Dog Race	B	1937	Transogram	20	40
Dog Show	B	1890s	J.H. Singer	85	140
Dog Sweepstakes	B	1935	Stoll & Einson	45	75
Donald Duck Game	C	1930s	Whitman	15	30
Donald Duck Playing Game	C	1941	Whitman	25	40
Donald Duck's Own Party Game	B	1938	Parker Brothers	80	150
Donkey Party	S	1887	McLoughlin Bros.	75	150
Double Eagle Anagrams	C	1890	McLoughlin Bros.	35	75
Double Flag Game, The	C	1904	McLoughlin Bros.	75	125
Double Game Board (Baseball)	B	1925	Parker Brothers	50	75
Double Header Baseball	B	1935	Redlich	145	250
Down and Out	S	1928	Milton Bradley	50	75
Down the Pike with Mrs. Wiggs at the St. Louis Exposition	C	1904	Milton Bradley	40	75
Dr. Busby	C	1890s	J.H. Singer	60	75
Dr. Busby	C	1900s	J. Ottmann Lith.	40	60
Dr. Busby	C	1937	Milton Bradley	20	50
Dr. Fusby, Game of	C	1890s	McLoughlin Bros.	65	125
Dreamland Wonder Resort Game	B	1914	Parker Brothers	275	700
Drive 'n Putt	B	1940s	Carrom Industries	50	90
Drummer Boy Game, The	B	1890s	Parker Brothers	100	250
Dubble Up	B	1940s	Gabriel	15	25
Dudes, Game of the	B	1890	Bliss	225	375
Durgin's New Baseball Game	B	1885	Durgin & Palmer	425	700
E-E-YAH Base Ball Game	B	1900s	National Games	600	1800
Eagle Bombsight	B	1940s	Toy Creations	100	175
East is East and West is West	B	1920s	Parker Brothers	80	200
Easy Money	B	1936	Milton Bradley	35	55
Ed Wynn The Fire Chief	B	1937	Selchow & Righter	45	75
Eddie Cantor's Tell It To The Judge	B	1930s	Parker Brothers	30	50

NAME	TYPE	YEAR	COMPANY	GOOD	EX
Egerton R. Williams Popular Indoor Baseball Game	C	1886	Hatch	2500	5000
Election	B	1896	Fireside	20	35
Electric Baseball	B	1935	Einson-Freeman	35	60
Electric Football	B	1930s	Electric Football	55	90
Electric Magnetic Baseball	B	1900		175	295
Electric Questioner	B	1920	Knapp Electric & Novelty	20	35
Electric Speed Classic	B	1930	Pressman	390	650
Electro Gameset	B	1930	Knapp Electric & Novelty	30	45
Elementaire Musical Game	B	1896	Theodore Presser	20	35
Elite Conversation Cards	C	1887	McLoughlin Bros.	35	75
Ella Cinders	B	1944	Milton Bradley	40	80
Elmer Layden's Scientific Football Game	B	1936	Cadaco	40	80
Elsie the Cow Game, The	B	1941	Selchow & Righter	50	100
Enchanted Forest Game	B	1914		120	200
Endurance Run	B	1930	Milton Bradley	60	150
Errand Boy, The	B	1891	McLoughlin Bros.	200	350
Ethan Allen's All-Star Baseball Game	B	1942	Cadaco-Ellis	60	150
Evening Parties, Game of	B	1910s	Parker Brothers	180	300
Excursion to Coney Island	C	1880s	Milton Bradley	55	75
Excuse Me!	C	1923	Parker Brothers	15	35
Faba Baga or Parlor Quiots	S	1883	Morton E. Converse	40	65
Fairies' Cauldron Tiddledy Winks Game, The	S	1925	Parker Brothers	35	50
Fairyland Game	B	1880s	Milton Bradley	60	95
Famous Authors	C	1910	Parker Brothers	40	65
Famous Authors	C	1943	Parker Brothers	10	15
Fan Craze Card Game, Generic	C	1904	Fan Craze	175	295
Fan Craze Card Game, Name Players	C	1904	Fan Craze	1500	2000
Fan-i-Tis	B	1913	C.W. Marsh	110	180
Fan-Tel	B	1937	Schoenhut	20	30
Farmer Jones' Pigs	B	1890	McLoughlin Bros.	165	200
Fascination	S	1890	Selchow & Righter	35	50
Fashionable English Sorry Game, The	B	1934	Parker Brothers	20	50
Fast Mail Game	B	1910	Milton Bradley	105	225
Fast Mail Railroad Game	B	1930s	Milton Bradley	50	85
Favorite Art, Game of	C	1897	Parker Brothers	40	65
Favorite Steeple Chase	B	1895	J.H. Singer	200	350
Ferdinand Card Game	C	1938	Whitman	25	65
Ferdinand The Bull Chinese Checkers Game	B	1930s		60	100
Fibber McGee	B	1936	Milton Bradley	25	40
Fibber McGee and The Wistful Vista Mystery	B	1940	Milton Bradley	30	45
Fiddlestix	S	1937	Plaza	10	15
Fig Mill	B	1916	Willis G. Young	25	80
Finance	B	1937	Parker Brothers	25	40
Finance And Fortune	B	1936	Parker Brothers	35	50
Fire Alarm Game	B	1899	Parker Brothers	1300	2300
Fire Department	B	1930s	Milton Bradley	80	125
Fire Fighters Game	B	1909	Milton Bradley	120	200
Fish Pond	S	1920s	Wilder	25	60
Fish Pond	S	1890	E.O. Clark	50	125
Fish Pond Game, Magnetic	S	1891	McLoughlin Bros.	175	300
Fish Pond, Game of	S	1910s	Wescott Brothers	30	50
Fish Pond, New and Improved	S	1890s	McLoughlin Bros.	75	125
Fish Pond, The Game of	S	1890	McLoughlin Bros.	100	175
Fishing Game	S	1899	Martin	30	65
Five Hundred, Game of	C	1900s	Home Game	20	35
Five Little Pigs	S	1890s	J.H. Singer	50	100
Five Wise Birds, The	S	1923	Parker Brothers	25	50
Flag Travelette	B	1895	Archarena	45	100
Flags	C	1899	Cincinnati Game	55	90
Flap Jacks	S	1931	All-Fair	80	225
Flapper Fortunes	B	1929	Embossing	30	45
Flash	S	1940s	Pressman	20	50
Flight To Paris	B	1927	Milton Bradley	150	250
Flinch	C	1902	Flinch Card	10	15
Fling-A-Ring	B	1930s	Wolverine	20	35
Flip It	B	1940	Deluxe Game	20	30

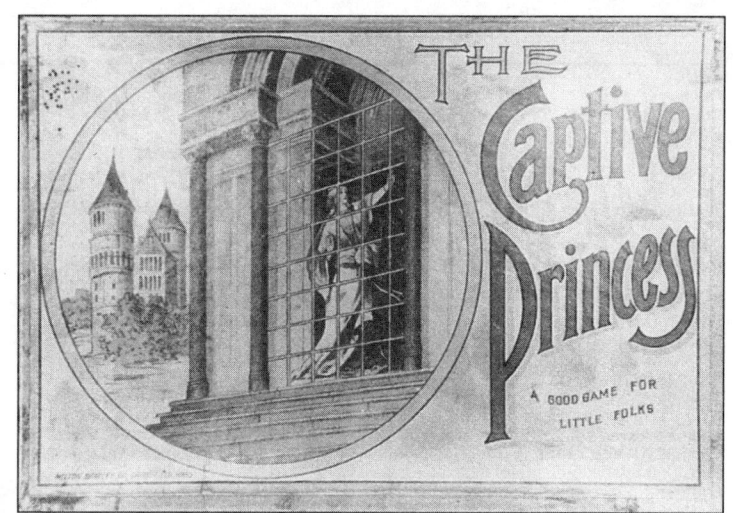

Captive Princess, 1899, McLoughlin Bros.

Finance And Fortune, 1936, Parker Brothers

Peg Baseball, 1924, Parker Brothers

NAME	TYPE	YEAR	COMPANY	GOOD	EX
Flip It	B	1925	American Toy Works	40	60
Flip It, Auto Race & Transcontinental Tour	B	1920s	Deluxe Game	35	90
Flitters	S	1899	Martin	45	75
Flivver	B	1927	Milton Bradley	150	250
Floor Croquet Game	S	1912		60	100
Flowers, Game of	B	1899	Cincinnati Game	45	75
Flying Aces	B	1940s	Selchow & Righter	50	100
Flying the Beam	B	1941	Parker Brothers	75	125
Flying the United States Airmail	B	1929	Parker Brothers	200	400
Fobaga (football)	B	1942	American Football	50	80
Follow the Stars	B	1922	Watts	225	375
Foolish Questions	C	1920s	Wallie Dorr	50	100
Foot Race, The	B	1900s	Parker Brothers	60	100
Football	B	1930s	Wilder	50	80
Football Game	B	1898	Parker Brothers	295	495
Football Knapp Electro Game Set	B	1929	Knapp Electric & Novelty	125	205
Football, The Game of	B	1895	George A. Childs	75	125
Football-As-You-Like-It	B	1940	Wayne W. Light	85	145
Fore Country Club Game of Golf	B	1929	Wilder	175	295
Fortune	B	1938	Parker Brothers	40	70
Fortune Teller, The	B	1905	Milton Bradley	20	50
Fortune Telling	C	1920s	All-Fair	40	75
Fortune Telling & Baseball Game	B	1889		85	140
Fortune Telling Game	C	1930s	Stoll & Edwards	35	55
Fortune Telling Game	B	1934	Whitman	50	100
Fortune Telling Game, The	C	1890s	Parker Brothers	40	65
Fortunes, Game of	C	1902	Cincinnati Game	55	95
Forty-Niners Gold Mining Game	B	1930s	National Games	25	40
Foto World	B	1935	Cadaco	90	150
Foto-Electric Football	B	1930s	Cadaco	35	50
Foto-Finish Horse Race	B	1940s	Pressman	30	45
Four and Twenty Blackbirds	S	1890s	McLoughlin Bros.	750	1500
Four Dare Devils, The	S	1933	Marx, Hess & Lee	40	65
Fox and Geese	B	1903	McLoughlin Bros.	60	150
Fox and Geese, The New	C	1888	McLoughlin Bros.	45	75
Fox and Hounds	B	1900	Parker Brothers	85	140
Fox Hunt	B	1930s	Lowe	20	35
Fox Hunt	B	1905	Milton Bradley	40	65
Foxy Grandpa at the World's Fair	C	1904	J. Ottmann Lith.	150	200
Foxy Grandpa Hat Party	B	1906	Selchow & Righter	55	90
Fractions	C	1902	Cincinnati Game	25	45
Frank Buck's Bring 'em Back Alive Game	C	1937	All-Fair	50	100
Frisko	B	1937	Embossing	20	30
Frog He Would a Wooing Go, The	B	1898	McLoughlin Bros.	800	1200
Frog School Game	B	1914		45	75
Frog Who Would a Wooing Go, The	B	1920s	United Game	60	125
Fun at the Circus	B	1897	McLoughlin Bros.	360	600
Fun at the Zoo, A Game	B	1902	Parker Brothers	120	200
Fun Kit	B	1939	Frederick H. Beach (Beachcraft)	15	20
Fut-Ball	B	1940s	Fut-Bal	35	60
G-Men	C	1936	Milton Bradley	35	55
G-Men Clue Games	B	1935	Whitman	60	150
Game of Baseball	B	1886	McLoughlin Bros.	750	1600
Game of Friendly Fun	B	1939	Milton Bradley	50	145
Games You Like To Play	B	1920s	Parker Brothers	75	150
Gamevelope	C	1944	Morris Systems	20	35
Gang Busters Game	B	1939	Whitman	50	100
Gang Busters Game	B	1938	Lynco	150	250
Gavitt's Stock Exchange	C	1903	W.W. Gavitt	35	65
Gee-Wiz Horse Race	S	1928	Wolverine	50	85
General Headquarters	B	1940s	All-Fair	75	100
Genuine Steamer Quoits	S	1924	Milton Bradley	15	25
Geographical Cards	C	1883	Peter G. Thompson	35	65
Geographical Lotto Game	B	1921		20	30
Geography Game	B	1910s	A. Flanagan	15	25
Geography up to Date	C	1890s	Parker Brothers	35	55
George Washington's Dream	C	1900s	Parker Brothers	45	75
Ges It Game	B	1936	Knapp Electric & Novelty	20	45

PREWAR GAMES

NAME	TYPE	YEAR	COMPANY	GOOD	EX
Get The Balls Baseball Game	B	1930		20	30
Glydor	B	1931	All-Fair	75	150
Go Bang	B	1898	Milton Bradley	100	300
Go to the Head of the Class	B	1938	Milton Bradley	15	35
Goat, Game of	C	1916	Milton Bradley	15	35
Going To The Fire Game	B	1914		90	150
Gold Hunters, The	B	1900s	Parker Brothers	105	175
Gold Rush, The	C	1930s	Cracker Jack	20	50
Golden Egg	C	1850s	McLoughlin Bros.	450	750
Golden Egg, The	C	1845	R.H. Pease	165	275
Goldenlocks & The Three Bears	B	1890	McLoughlin Bros.	320	800
Golf	B	1900	Schoenhut	2700	5000
Golf Tokalon Series, The Game of	B	1890s	E.O. Clark	350	575
Golf, A Game of	B	1930	Milton Bradley	145	245
Golf, Game of	B	1896	McLoughlin Bros.	425	715
Golf, The Game of	B	1905	Clark & Sowdon	325	550
Golf, The Game of	B	1898	J.H. Singer	100	300
Golliwogg	C	1907	Milton Bradley	200	300
Gonfalon Scientific Baseball	B	1930	Pioneer Game	110	180
Good Old Aunt, The	B	1892	McLoughlin Bros.	150	250
Good Old Game of Corner Grocery, The	C	1900s	Parker Brothers	40	60
Good Old Game of Dr. Busby	C	1900s	Parker Brothers	55	85
Good Old Game of Dr. Busby	C	1920s	United Game	25	50
Good Old Game of Innocence Abroad, The	B	1888	Parker Brothers	180	300
Good Things To Eat Lotto	B	1940s	Gabriel	15	25
Goose Goslin Scientific Baseball	B	1935	Wheeler Toy	600	1000
Goose, The Jolly Game of	B	1851	J.P. Beach	750	1250
Goosey Gander, Or Who Finds the Golden Egg, Game of	B	1890	J.H. Singer	675	1150
Goosy Goosy Gander	B	1896	McLoughlin Bros.	300	500
Graham McNamee World Series Scoreboard Baseball Game	B	1930	Radio Sports	250	400
Grand National Sweepstakes	B	1937	Whitman	20	50
Grande Auto Race	B	1920s	Atkins	75	150
Grandma's Game of Useful Knowledge	C	1910s	Milton Bradley	20	50
Grandmama's Improved Arithmetical Game	C	1887	McLoughlin Bros.	30	50
Grandmama's Improved Geographical Game	C	1887	McLoughlin Bros.	55	90
Grandmama's Sunday Game: Bible Questions, Old Testament	C	1887	McLoughlin Bros.	35	65
Graphic Baseball	B	1930s	Northwestern Products	165	275
Great American Baseball Game, The	B	1906	William Dapping	145	250
Great American Flag Game, The	B	1940	Parker Brothers	50	75
Great American Game	B	1910	Neddy Pocket Game	145	250
Great American Game of Baseball, The	B	1907	Pittsburgh Brewing	145	250
Great American Game, Baseball, The	B	1923	Hustler Toy	150	225
Great American Game, The	B	1925	Frantz	110	180
Great American War Game	B	1899	J.H. Hunter	600	1000
Great Battlefields	C	1886	Parker Brothers	150	250
Great Composer, The	C	1901	Theodore Presser	35	55
Great Family Amusement Game, The	B	1889	Einson-Freeman	20	35
Great Horse Race Game, The	B	1925	Selchow & Righter	70	115
Great Mails Baseball Game	C	1919	Walter Mails Baseball Game	2475	4100
Gregg Football Game	B	1924	Albert A. Gregg	175	285
Greyhound Racing Game	B	1938	Rex Manufacturing	15	25
Guess Again, The Game of	C	1890s	McLoughlin Bros.	75	120
Gumps at the Seashore, The	B	1930s	Milton Bradley	65	135
Gym Horseshoes	B	1930	Wolverine	30	45
Gypsy Fortune Telling Game	C	1909	McLoughlin Bros.	100	175
Gypsy Fortune Telling Game, The	B	1895	Milton Bradley	75	125
H.M.S. Pinafore	C	1880	McLoughlin Bros.	300	500
Halma	B	1885	Milton Bradley	30	45
Halma	B	1885	Horsman	35	60
Hand of Fate	B	1901	McLoughlin Bros.	1200	2000
Happitime Bagatelle	S	1933	Northwestern Products	30	45
Happy Family, The	B	1910	Milton Bradley	15	25
Happy Hooligan Bowling Type Game	B	1925		60	100
Happy Landing	S	1938	Transogram	30	45

NAME	TYPE	YEAR	COMPANY	GOOD	EX
Hardwood Ten Pins Wooden Game	B	1889		60	100
Hare & Hound	B	1895	Parker Brothers	245	400
Hare and Hounds	B	1890	McLoughlin Bros.	200	325
Harlequin, The Game of The	B	1895	McLoughlin Bros.	150	300
Harold Teen Game	B	1930s	Milton Bradley	75	150
Have-U It?	C	1924	Selchow & Righter	15	25
Heads and Tails	C	1900s	Parker Brothers	30	50
Heedless Tommy	B	1893	McLoughlin Bros.	240	400
Hel-Lo Telephone Game	B	1898	J.H. Singer	100	200
Helps to History	B	1885	A. Flanagan	20	35
Hen that Laid the Golden Egg, The	B	1900	Parker Brothers	105	175
Hendrik Van Loon's Wide World Game	B	1935	Parker Brothers	35	65
Hening's In-Door Game of Professional Baseball	B	1889	Inventor's	525	875
Hens and Chickens, Game of	C	1875	McLoughlin Bros.	125	175
Heroes of America	B	1920	Educational Card & Game	20	35
Hey What?	C	1907	Parker Brothers	20	35
Hi-Way Henry	B	1928	All-Fair	600	1500
Hialeah Horse Racing Game	B	1940s	Milton Bradley	40	65
Hickety Pickety	B	1924	Parker Brothers	20	50
Hidden Titles	C	1908	Parker Brothers	20	35
Hide and Seek, Game of	B	1895	McLoughlin Bros.	1500	2000
Hippodrome Circus Game	B	1895	Milton Bradley	200	300
Hippodrome, The	B	1900s	E.O. Clark	150	200
Historical Cards	C	1884	Peter G. Thompson	55	75
History up to Date	C	1900s	Parker Brothers	55	65
Hit and Run Baseball Game	B	1930s	Wilder	150	290
Hit That Line	B	1930s	LaRue Sales	100	165
Hockey, Official	B	1940	Toy Creations	50	75
Hokum	C	1927	Parker Brothers	10	20
Hold The Fort	B	1895	Parker Brothers	125	225
Hold Your Horses	B	1930s	Klauber Novelty	10	20
Hollywood Movie Bingo	C	1937	Whitman	50	75
Home Baseball Game	B	1897	McLoughlin Bros.	900	1700
Home Defenders	B	1941	Saalfield	15	25
Home Diamond	C	1913	Phillips	150	225
Home Diamond, The Great Baseball Game	B	1925	Phillips	175	295
Home Games	B	1900s	Martin	105	175
Home History Game	C	1910s	Milton Bradley	55	75
Home Run King	B	1930s	Selrite	275	450
Home Run with Bases Loaded	B	1935	T.V. Morrison	205	350
Honey Bee Game	B	1913	Milton Bradley	50	85
Hood's Spelling School	B	1897	C.I. Hood	20	35
Hood's War Game	C	1899	C.I. Hood	40	65
Hoop-O-Loop	B	1930	Wolverine	20	30
Hoot	C	1926	Saalfield	55	85
Hop-Over Puzzle	S	1930s	Pressman	20	35
Hornet	B	1941	Lowe	30	45
Horse Race	B	1943	Lowe	10	20
Horse Racing	B	1935	Milton Bradley	35	60
Horses	B	1927	Modern Makers	45	75
Hounds & Hares	B	1894	J.W. Keller	35	60
House that Jack Built	C	1900s	Parker Brothers	55	75
House that Jack Built, The	C	1887	McLoughlin Bros.	55	85
Household Words, Game of	C	1916	Household Words Game	50	85
How Good Are You?	B	1937	Whitman	10	15
How Silas Popped the Question	C	1915	Parker Brothers	25	40
Howard H. Jones Collegiate Football	B	1932	Municipal Service	40	100
Huddle All-American Football Game	B	1931		100	165
Hungry Willie	S	1930s	Transogram	40	70
Hunting Hare, Game of	B	1891	McLoughlin Bros.	205	350
Hunting in the Jungle	S	1920s	A. Gropper	30	45
Hunting the Rabbit	B	1895	Clark & Sowdon	70	115
Hunting, The New Game of	B	1904	McLoughlin Bros.	360	600
Hurdle Race	B	1905	Milton Bradley	75	150
Hymn Quartets	B	1933	Goodenough and Woglom	10	15
I Doubt It	C	1910	Parker Brothers	35	55
Ice Hockey	B	1942	Milton Bradley	50	75
Illustrated Mythology	C	1896	Cincinnati Game	25	50

GAMES

NAME	TYPE	YEAR	COMPANY	GOOD	EX
Improved Geographical Game, The	B	1890s	Parker Brothers	60	100
Improved Historical Cards	C	1900	McLoughlin Bros.	35	55
In and Out the Window	B	1940s	Gabriel	20	35
In-Door Baseball	B	1926	E. Bommer Foundation	100	180
India	B	1940	Parker Brothers	15	20
India Bombay	B	1910s	Cutler & Saleeby	25	40
India, An Oriental Game	B	1890s	McLoughlin Bros.	100	125
India, Game of	B	1910s	Milton Bradley	15	40
Indianapolis 500 Mile Race Game	B	1938	Shaw	350	575
Indians and Cowboys	B	1940s	Gabriel	40	65
Indoor Football	B	1919	Underwood	145	250
Indoor Golf Dice	S	1920s	W.P. Bushell	20	35
Indoor Horse Racing	B	1924	Man-O-War	70	115
Industries, Game of	C	1897	A.W. Mumford	25	55
Inside Baseball Game	B	1911	Popular Games	300	500
Intercollegiate Football	B	1923	Hustler Toy	125	245
International Automobile Race	B	1903	Parker Brothers	875	1450
International Spy, Game of	B	1943	All-Fair	75	125
Ivanhoe	C	1886	Parker Brothers	55	75
Jack and Jill	B	1890s	Parker Brothers	55	95
Jack and Jill	B	1909	Milton Bradley	60	100
Jack and the Bean Stalk	B	1895	Parker Brothers	110	175
Jack and the Bean Stalk, The Game of	B	1898	McLoughlin Bros.	550	900
Jack Spratt Game	B	1914		45	75
Jack Straws, The Game of	S	1901	Parker Brothers	25	35
Jack-Be-Nimble	B	1940s	Embossing	20	35
Jackie Robinson Baseball Game	B	1940s	Gotham	425	725
Jackpot	B	1943	B.L. Fry Products	15	25
Jamboree	S	1937	Selchow & Righter	75	150
Japan, The Game of	B	1903	J. Ottmann Lith.	180	300
Japanese Ball Game	S	1930s	Girard	35	65
Japanese Games of Cash and Akambo	B	1881	McLoughlin Bros.	150	250
Japanese Oracle, Game of	C	1875	McLoughlin Bros.	200	325
Japanola	S	1928	Parker Brothers	35	60
Jaunty Butler	S	1932	All-Fair	75	150
Jav-Lin	S	1931	All-Fair	105	225
Jeep Board, The	B	1944	Lowe	15	35
Jeffries Championship Playing Cards	B	1904		35	55
Jig Chase	B	1930s	Game Makers	35	50
Jig Race	B	1930s	Game Makers	35	50
Jockey	B	1920s	Carrom Industries	35	60
Joe "Ducky" Medwick's Big Leaguer Baseball Game	C	1930s	Johnson-Breier	125	200
John Gilpin, Rainbow Backgammon and Bewildered Travelers	B	1875	McLoughlin Bros.	175	300
Johnny Get Your Gun	B	1928	Parker Brothers	50	75
Johnny's Historical Game	C	1890s	Parker Brothers	55	95
Jolly Clown Spinette	S	1932	Milton Bradley	30	45
Jolly Pirates	B	1938	Russell	20	35
Jolly Robbers	S	1929	Wilder	50	75
Journey to Bethlehem, The	B	1923	Parker Brothers	95	160
Jumping Frog, Game of	C	1890	J.H. Singer	75	125
Jumping Jupiter	S	1940s	Gabriel	30	50
Jumpy Tinker	B	1920s	Tinker Toys	20	30
Jungle Hunt	B	1940s	Rosebud Art	30	50
Jungle Hunt	S	1940	Gotham Pressed Steel	30	45
Jungle Jump-Up Game	S	1940s	Judson Press	30	45
Junior Baseball Game	B	1915	Benjamin Seller	100	165
Junior Basketball Game	B	1930s	Rosebud Art	55	90
Junior Bicycle Game, The	B	1897	Parker Brothers	250	400
Junior Combination Board	B	1905	McLoughlin Bros.	30	50
Junior Football	B	1944	Deluxe Game	30	45
Junior Motor Race	B	1925	Wolverine	40	70
Just Like Me, Game of	C	1899	McLoughlin Bros.	55	95
Kan-Oo-Win-It	B	1893	McLoughlin Bros.	345	575
Kate Smith's Own Game America	B	1940s	Toy Creations	40	65
Katzenjammer Kids Hockey	S	1940s	Jaymar	40	65
Katzy Party	S	1900s	Selchow & Righter	70	120
Keeping Up with the Jones'	B	1921	Parker Brothers	50	85
Keeping Up with the Jones', The Game of	B	1921	Phillips	75	100
Kellogg's Baseball Game	B	1936	Kellogg's	25	35
Kellogg's Boxing Game	B	1936	Kellogg's	35	55

GAMES

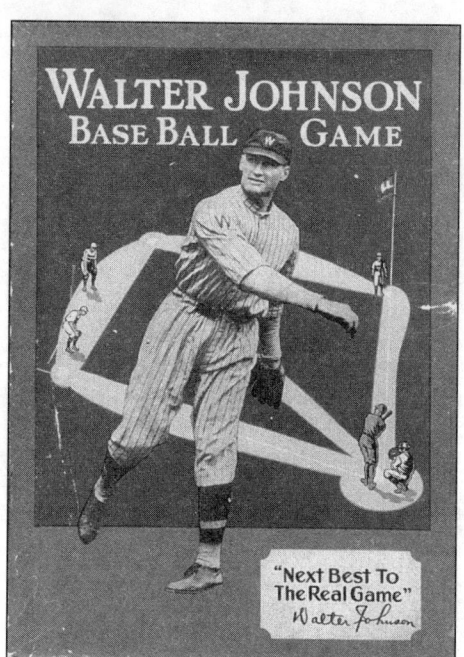

Walter Johnson Baseball Game, 1930s

We, The Magnetic Flying Game, 1928, Parker Brothers

Zippy Zepps,
1930s, All-Fair

NAME	TYPE	YEAR	COMPANY	GOOD	EX
Kellogg's Football Game	B	1936	Kellogg's	25	40
Kellogg's Golf Game	B	1936	Kellogg's	25	40
Kentucky Derby Racing Game	B	1938	Whitman	20	40
Kilkenny Cats, The Amusing Game of	B	1890	Parker Brothers	100	200
Kindergarten Lotto	S	1904	Strauss	50	80
King's Quoits, New Game of	B	1893	McLoughlin Bros.	300	450
Kings	B	1931	Akro Agate	55	95
Kings, The Game of	C	1845	Josiah Adams	150	300
Kitty Kat Cup Ball	B	1930s	Rosebud Art	50	100
Klondike Game	B	1890s	Parker Brothers	345	575
Knockout	B	1937	Scarne Games	55	90
Knockout Andy	S	1926	Parker Brothers	35	75
Knute Rockne Football Game, Official	B	1930	Radio Sports	250	400
Ko-Ko the Clown	B	1940	All-Fair	20	30
Komical Konversation Kards	C	1893	Parker Brothers	50	75
Kriegspiel Junior	B	1915	Parker Brothers	50	80
Kuti-Kuts	S	1922	Regensteiner	20	30
La Haza	B	1923	Supply Sales	10	20
Lame Duck, The	B	1928	Parker Brothers	60	100
Land and Sea War Games	B	1941	Lowe	40	65
Lasso the Jumping Ring	B	1912		60	100
Lawson's Baseball Card Game	C	1910		100	175
Lawson's Patent Game of Baseball	C	1884	Lawson's Card	500	1000
Le Choc	B	1919	Milton Bradley	50	85
League Parlor Base Ball	B	1889	Bliss	600	1000
Leap Frog Game	B	1900	McLoughlin Bros.	165	275
Leap Frog, Game of	B	1910	McLoughlin Bros.	45	75
Leaping Lena	S	1920s	Parker Brothers	100	200
Lee at Havana	B	1899	Chaffee & Selchow	150	250
Leslie's Baseball Game	B	1909	Perfection Novelty	145	250
Let's go to College	B	1944	Einson-Freeman	30	45
Let's Play Games, Golf	B	1939	American Toy Works	50	80
Let's Play Polo	B	1940	American Toy Works	45	75
Letter Carrier, The	B	1890	McLoughlin Bros.	100	200
Letters	B	1878	Horsman	30	45
Letters Improved for the Logomachist	C	1878	Noyes & Snow	50	100
Letters or Anagrams	B	1890s	Parker Brothers	30	50
Lew Fonseca Baseball Game, The	B	1920s	Carrom Industries	525	875
Library of Games	C	1939	Russell	55	75
Library of Games	B	1938	American Toy Works	15	25
Lid's Off, The	S	1937	American Toy Works	35	75
Life in the Wild West	B	1894	Bliss	300	500
Life of the Party	B	1940s	Rosebud Art	25	35
Life's Mishaps & Bobbing 'Round the Circle	B	1891	McLoughlin Bros.	300	400
Light Horse H. Cooper Golf Game	B	1943	Trojan Games	175	295
Limited Mail & Express Game, The	B	1894	Parker Brothers	200	375
Lindy Flying Game	C	1927	Parker Brothers	35	50
Lindy Flying Game, The New	C	1927	Nucraft Toys	45	75
Lindy Hop-Off	B	1927	Parker Brothers	200	400
Lion & the Eagle, or the Days of '76	C	1883	E.H. Snow	75	125
Literature Game	B	1897	L.J. Colby	15	25
Little Black Sambo, Game of	B	1934	Einson-Freeman	75	150
Little Bo-Beep Game	B	1914		60	100
Little Boy Blue	B	1910s	Milton Bradley	50	85
Little Colonel	B	1936	Selchow & Righter	75	100
Little Cowboy Game, The	B	1895	Parker Brothers	200	450
Little Fireman Game	B	1897	McLoughlin Bros.	4000	6000
Little Jack Horner Golf Course	B	1920s		145	250
Little Jack Horner, A Game	B	1910s	Milton Bradley	45	75
Little Nemo Game	B	1914		100	200
Little Orphan Annie Bead Game	S	1930s		20	35
Little Orphan Annie Game	B	1927	Milton Bradley	125	250
Little Orphan Annie Rummy Cards	C	1937	Whitman	45	75
Little Orphan Annie Shooting Game	S	1930s	Milton Bradley	30	50
Little Red Riding Hood	B	1900	McLoughlin Bros.	200	500
Little Shoppers	B	1915	Gibson Game	150	250
Little Soldier, The	B	1900s	United Game	95	160
London Bridge	B	1899	J.H. Singer	100	150
London Game, The	B	1898	Parker Brothers	165	275
Lone Ranger Game, The	B	1938	Parker Brothers	40	80
Lone Ranger Hi-Yo Silver!! Target Game	S	1939	Marx	70	115

GAMES

PREWAR GAMES

NAME	TYPE	YEAR	COMPANY	GOOD	EX
Looping the Loop	B	1940s	Advance Games	25	40
Los Angeles Rams Football Game	B	1930s	Zondine	175	295
Lost Diamond, Game of	B	1896	McLoughlin	200	300
Lost Heir, Game of the	C	1910	Milton Bradley	30	50
Lost Heir, The Game of	C	1893	McLoughlin Bros.	65	85
Lost in the Woods	B	1895	McLoughlin Bros.	660	900
Lotto	B	1932	Milton Bradley	6	10
Lou Gehrig's Official Playball	B	1930s	Christy Walsh	525	875
Lowell Thomas' World Cruise	B	1937	Parker Brothers	100	300
Luck, The Game of	B	1892	Parker Brothers	60	100
Lucky 7th Baseball Game	B	1937	All-American	100	250
Mac Baseball Game	B	1930s	Mc Dowell	145	250
Macy's Pirate Treasure Hunt	B	1942	Einson-Freeman	20	35
Madrap, The New Game of	B	1914		45	75
Magic Race	B	1942	Habob	55	90
Magnetic Jack Straws	B	1891	Horsman	27	45
Magnetic Treasure Hunt	B	1930s	American Toy Works	15	25
Mail, Express or Accommodation, Game of	B	1895	McLoughlin Bros.	600	1200
Mail, Express Or Accommodation, Game of	B	1920s	Milton Bradley	135	225
Major League Ball	B	1921	National Game Makers	325	550
Major League Base Ball Game	B	1912	Philadelphia Game	650	1000
Major League Baseball Game	C	1900s	Parker Brothers	50	150
Make A Million	C	1934	Rook Card	15	30
Mammoth Conette	S	1898	Milton Bradley	90	150
Man Hunt	B	1937	Parker Brothers	150	250
Man in the Moon	B	1901	McLoughlin Bros.	2100	3500
Mansion of Happiness	B	1843	Ives	300	400
Mansion of Happiness	B	1864	Ives	180	300
Mansion of Happiness, The	B	1895	McLoughlin Bros.	510	1000
Mar-Juck	S	1923	Regensteiner	20	30
Marathon Game, The	B	1930s	Rosebud Art	75	150
Marble Muggins	S	1920s	American Toy	100	200
Marriage, The Game of	B	1899	J.H. Singer	200	300
Match 'em	B	1926	All-Fair	12	20
Mathers Parlor Baseball Game	B	1909	McClurg	30	50
Mayflower, The	C	1897	Fireside Game	55	85
Meet the Missus	B	1937	Fitzpatrick Brothers	45	75
Mental Whoopee	B	1936	Simon & Schuster	10	15
Merry Hunt, The	B		Singer	250	400
Merry Steeple Chase	B	1890s	J. Ottmann Lith.	45	70
Merry-Go-Round	B	1898	Chaffee & Selchow	1500	2000
Messenger Boy Game	B	1910	J.H. Singer	100	200
Messenger, The	B	1890	McLoughlin Bros.	75	125
Meteor Game	S	1916	A.C. Gilbert	25	45
Mexican Pete - I Got It	B	1940s	Parker Brothers	25	50
Mickey Mouse Baseball	B	1936	Post Cereal	55	90
Mickey Mouse Big Box of Games & Things To Color	B	1930s		45	75
Mickey Mouse Bridge Game	C	1935	Whitman	35	55
Mickey Mouse Circus Game	B	1930s	Marks Brothers	180	300
Mickey Mouse Coming Home Game	B	1930s	Marks Brothers	80	200
Mickey Mouse Miniature Pinball Game	S	1930s	Marks Brothers	20	35
Mickey Mouse Old Maid Game	C	1930s	Whitman	35	65
Mickey Mouse Roll'em Game	B	1930s	Marks Brothers	90	150
Mickey Mouse Shooting Game	S	1930s	Marks Brothers	120	200
Mickey Mouse Skittle Ball Game	S	1930s	Marks Brothers	60	100
Mickey Mouse Soldier Target Set	S	1930s	Marks Brothers	60	100
Midget Auto Race	B	1930s	Cracker Jack	10	15
Midget Speedway, Game of	B	1942	Whitman	55	90
Miles at Porto Rico	B	1899	Chaffee & Selchow	100	150
Miniature Golf	B	1930s	Miniature Golf	35	60
Miss Muffet Game	B	1914		60	100
Mistress Mary, Quite Contrary	B	1905	Parker Brothers	60	105
Modern Game Assortment	B	1930s	Pressman	25	40
Moneta: "Money Makes Money", Game of	B	1889	F.A. Wright	90	150
Monkey Shines	B	1940	All-Fair	20	30
Monopolist, Mariner's Compass And Ten Up	B	1878	McLoughlin Bros.	200	500
Monopoly	B	1935	Parker Brothers	35	75
Monopoly Jr. Edition	B	1936	Parker Brothers	15	30

GAMES

332

NAME	TYPE	YEAR	COMPANY	GOOD	EX
Moon Mullins Automobile Race	B	1927	Milton Bradley	60	150
Mother Goose Bowling Game	B	1884	Charles M. Crandall	510	850
Mother Goose, Game of	B	1921	Stoll & Edwards	30	50
Mother Hubbard	C	1875	McLoughlin Bros.	75	125
Mother Hubbard Game	B	1914		60	100
Motor Boat Race, An Exciting	B	1930	American Toy Works	110	180
Motor Cycle Game	B	1905	Milton Bradley	300	600
Motor Race	B	1922	Wolverine	90	150
Movie Inn	B	1917	Willis G. Young	45	75
Movie Millions	B	1938	Transogram	100	200
Movie-Land Keeno	C	1929	Wilder	150	250
Movie-Land Lotto	B	1920s	Milton Bradley	45	75
Moving Picture Game, The	B	1920s	Milton Bradley	70	120
Mr. Ree	B	1937	Selchow & Righter	60	100
Mumbly Peg	S	1920s	All-Fair	25	50
Musical Lotto	C	1936	Tudor Metal Products	35	65
Mutuels	B	1938	Mutuels	85	150
My Word, Horse Race	B	1938	American Toy Works	60	100
Mythology	C	1900	Cincinnati Game	55	75
Mythology, Game of	B	1884	Peter G. Thompson	65	110
Napoleon LaJoie Baseball Game	C	1913	Parker Brothers	150	500
Napoleon, Game of	B	1895	Parker Brothers	775	1300
National American Baseball Game	C	1910	Parker Brothers	130	200
National Baseball Game, The	C	1913	National Baseball Playing Card	700	1200
National Derby Horse Race	B	1938	Whitman	20	35
National Game of Baseball, The	B	1900s		500	875
National Game of the American Eagle, The	B	1844	Ives	1600	3500
National Game, The	B	1889	National Game	875	1450
National League Ball Game	B	1890	Yankee Novelty	350	575
Nations or Quaker Whist, Game of	C	1898	McLoughlin Bros.	75	110
Nations, Game of	C	1908	Milton Bradley	25	45
Naughty Molly	C	1905	McLoughlin Bros.	75	100
Naval Maneuvers	B	1920	McLoughlin Bros.	600	900
Navigator	B	1938	Whitman	45	75
Navigator Boat Race	B	1890s	McLoughlin Bros.	115	195
Nebbs on the Air, A Radio Game	B	1930s	Milton Bradley	50	125
Nebbs, Game of the	B	1930s	Milton Bradley	40	75
Neck and Neck	B	1930	Wolverine	50	80
Neck and Neck	B	1929	Embossing	25	40
Nellie Bly	B	1898	J.H. Singer	150	300
New Baseball Game	B	1885	Clark & Martin	165	275
New Parlor Game of Baseball	B	1896	Sumner	5000	10000
New York Recorder Newspaper Supplement Baseball Game	B	1896		430	715
Newsboy, Game of the	B	1890	Bliss	1200	2000
NFL Strategy	B	1935	Tudor	45	70
Nine Men Morris	B	1930s	Milton Bradley	15	25
Ninteenth Hole Golf Game	B	1930s	Einson-Freeman	85	140
Nip & Tuck Hockey	B	1928	Parker Brothers	115	195
No-Joke	B	1941	Volume Sprayer	12	20
Nok-Out Baseball Game	B	1930	Dizzy & Daffy Dean	350	575
North Pole Game, The	B	1907	Milton Bradley	200	350
Nosey, The Game of	C	1905	McLoughlin Bros.	200	300
Object Lotto	B	1940s	Gabriel	15	25
Obstacle Race	B	1930s	Wilder	70	115
Ocean to Ocean Flight Game	B	1927	Wilder	55	125
Office Boy, The	B	1889	Parker Brothers	150	300
Official Radio Baseball Game	B	1930s	Toy Creations	50	75
Official Radio Basketball Game	B	1939	Toy Creations	25	50
Official Radio Football Game	B	1940	Toy Creations	25	50
Oh, Blondie!	C	1940s		30	45
Old Curiosity Shop	C	1869	Novelty Game	200	300
Old Hunter & His Game	B	1870		175	295
Old Maid	C	1890s	J.H. Singer	25	50
Old Maid	B	1898	Chaffee & Selchow	30	75
Old Maid & Old Bachelor, The Merry Game of	B	1898	McLoughlin Bros.	180	400
Old Maid Card Game	C	1889		20	50
Old Maid Fun Full Thrift Game	C	1940s	Russell	30	50
Old Maid or Matrimony, Game of	B	1890	McLoughlin Bros.	150	250
Old Maid, Game of	C	1870	McLoughlin Bros.	75	125

GAMES

PREWAR GAMES

NAME	TYPE	YEAR	COMPANY	GOOD	EX
Old Maid, with Characters from Famous Nursery Rhymes	C	1920s	All-Fair	30	50
Old Mother Goose	B	1898	Chaffee & Selchow	105	175
Old Mother Hubbard, Game of	B	1890s	Milton Bradley	60	100
Old Mrs. Goose, Game of	B	1910	Milton Bradley	50	85
Old Time Shooting Gallery	S	1940	Warren-Built-Rite	15	25
Oldtimers	B	1940	Frederick H. Beach (Beachcraft)	15	20
Oliver Twist, The Good Old Game of	C	1888	Parker Brothers	150	225
Ollo	B	1944	Games Of Fame	15	25
Olympic Runners	B	1930	Wolverine	125	175
On the Mid-Way	B	1925	Milton Bradley	90	150
One Two Button Your Shoe	B	1940s	Master Toy	15	25
Open Championship Golf Game	B	1930s	Beacon Hudson	45	75
Opportunity Hour	B	1940	American Toy Works	20	35
Ot-O-Win Football	B	1920s	Ot-O-Win Toys & Games	55	90
Ouija	B	1920	William Fuld	35	70
Our Bird Friends	C	1901	Sarah H. Dudley	20	30
Our Defenders	B	1944	Master Toy	40	65
Our Gang Tipple Topple Game	S	1930	All-Fair	160	300
Our National Ball Game	B	1887	McGill & DeLany	425	650
Our National Life	C	1903	Cincinnati Game	35	65
Our No. 7 Baseball Game Puzzle	B	1910	Satisfactory	110	180
Our Union	B	1896	Fireside Game	25	40
Outboard Motor Race, The	B	1930s	Milton Bradley	35	75
Overland Limited, The	B	1920s	Milton Bradley	75	125
Owl and the Pussy Cat, The	B	1900s	E.O. Clark	210	350
Pan-Cake Tiddly Winks	B	1920s	Russell	55	125
Pana Kanal, The Great Panama Canal Game	B	1913	Chaffee & Selchow	65	110
Panama Canal Game	B	1910	Parker Brothers	200	400
Par Golf Card Game	B	1920	National Golf Services	115	195
Par, The New Golf Game	B	1926	Russell	115	195
Parcheesi	B	1880s	H.B. Chaffee	50	75
Parker Brothers Post Office Game	B	1910s	Parker Brothers	105	175
Parlor Base Ball, Game of	B	1892	McLoughlin	1500	2100
Parlor Baseball Game	B	1908	Mathers	200	325
Parlor Croquet	B	1940	Pressman	20	35
Parlor Football Game	B	1890s	McLoughlin Bros.	525	875
Parlor Golf	B	1897	Chaffee & Selchow	55	90
Pat Moran's Own Baseball Game	B	1919	Smith, Kline & French	325	400
Patch Word	C	1938	All-Fair	15	20
Patent Parlor Bowling Alley	B	1899	Thomas Kochka	70	115
Paws & Claws	C	1895	Clark & Sowdon	60	90
Pe-Ling	B	1923	Cookson & Sullivan	25	45
Pedestrianism	B	1879		350	575
Peeza	S	1935	Toy Creations	25	45
Peg at my Heart	B	1914	Willis G. Young	20	45
Peg Baseball	B	1915	Parker Brothers	145	250
Peg Baseball	B	1924	Parker Brothers	50	100
Peg'ity	B	1925	Parker Brothers	10	25
Peggy	B	1923	Parker Brothers	35	55
Pegpin, Game of	B	1929	Stoll & Edwards	25	45
Pennant Puzzle	B	1909	L.W. Hardy	250	400
Pennant Winner	B	1930s	Wolverine	175	295
Penny Post	B	1892	Parker Brothers	150	250
Pepper	C	1906	Parker Brothers	20	35
Peter Coddle and his Trip to New York	C	1890s	J.H. Singer	35	65
Peter Coddle tells of his Trip to Chicago	C	1890	Parker Brothers	30	50
Peter Coddle's Trip to New York	C	1925	Milton Bradley	20	35
Peter Coddle's Trip to New York, The Game of	C	1888	Parker Brothers	40	50
Peter Coddle's Trip to the World's Fair	C	1939	Parker Brothers	50	85
Peter Coddle, Improved Game of	C	1900	McLoughlin Bros.	35	55
Peter Coddles	C	1890s	J. Ottmann Lith.	25	55
Peter Pan	B	1927	Selchow & Righter	100	150
Peter Peter Pumpkin Eater	B	1914	Parker Brothers	60	125
Peter Rabbit Game	B	1940s	Gabriel	45	75
Peter Rabbit Game	B	1910	Milton Bradley	55	95
Philadelphia Inquirer Baseball Game, The	B	1896		145	250
Philo Vance	B	1937	Parker Brothers	100	175

334

Barney Miller, 1977, Parker Brothers

Battle of The Planets, 1970s, Milton Bradley

Beverly Hillbillies Card Game, Set Back, 1963, Milton Bradley

NAME	TYPE	YEAR	COMPANY	GOOD	EX
Phoebe Snow, Game of	B	1899	McLoughlin Bros.	150	250
Piggies, The New Game	B	1894	Selchow & Righter	330	550
Pigskin	B	1940	Parker Brothers	20	50
Pigskin, Tom Hamilton's Football Game	B	1934	Parker Brothers	25	60
Pike's Peak or Bust	S	1890s	Parker Brothers	75	150
Pilgrim's Progress, Going To Sunday School, Tower of Babel	B	1875	McLoughlin Bros.	120	250
Pinafore	B	1879	Fuller Upham	45	75
Pinch Hitter	B	1930s		110	180
Pines, The	B	1896	Fireside Game	15	25
Ping Pong	S	1902	Parker Brothers	100	175
Pinocchio Pitfalls Marble Game	B	1940		30	50
Pinocchio Playing Card Game	C	1939	Whitman	55	95
Pinocchio Ring The Nose Game	B	1940		20	30
Pinocchio Target Game	S	1938	American Toy Works	90	150
Pinocchio the Merry Puppet Game	S	1939	Milton Bradley	55	95
Pioneers of the Santa Fe Trail	B	1935	Einson-Freeman	25	40
Pirate & Traveller	B	1936	Milton Bradley	30	65
Pirate Ship	B	1940	Lowe	15	25
Pitch Em, The Game of Indoor Horse Shoes	S	1929	Wolverine	25	35
Pla-Golf Board Game	B	1938	Pla-Golf	775	1300
Play Ball	B	1920	National Game	145	250
Play Football	B	1934	Whitman	55	90
Play Hockey Fun with Popeye & Wimpy	B	1935	Barnum	205	350
Pocket Baseball	B	1940	Toy Creations	15	25
Pocket Edition Major League Baseball Game	B	1943	Anderson	85	140
Pocket Football	B	1940	Toy Creations	25	40
Polar Ball Baseball	B	1940	Bowline Game	90	145
Pool, Game of	B	1898		700	1175
Pop the Hat	S	1930s	Milton Bradley	35	50
Posting, A Merry Game of	B	1890s	J.H. Singer	180	300
Pro Baseball	B	1940		70	115
Professional Game of Base Ball	B	1896	Parker Bros.	500	1000
Psychic Baseball	C	1927	Psychic Baseball	60	150
Psychic Baseball Game	B	1935	Parker Brothers	175	295
Quarterback	B	1914	Littlefield	100	165
Rabbit Hunt, Game of	B	1870	McLoughlin Bros.	175	400
Race for the Cup	B	1910s	Milton Bradley	125	200
Race, The Game of the	B	1860s		425	715
Races, The Game of the	B	1844	William Crosby	850	1400
Racing Stable, Game of	B	1936	D & H Games	115	195
Radio Game	B	1926	Milton Bradley	75	150
Raggedy Ann's Magic Pebble Game	B	1941	Milton Bradley	75	125
Rainy Day Golf	B	1920	Selchow & Righter	75	150
Rambles	B	1881	American	195	275
Ranger Commandos	S	1942	Parker Brothers	35	60
Razz-O-Dazz-O Six Man Football	B	1938	Gruhn & Melton	60	100
Real Baseball Card Game	C	1900	National Baseball	180	275
Realistic Baseball	B	1925	Realistic Game & Toy	205	350
Realistic Golf	B	1898	Parker Brothers	875	1450
Red Riding Hood and the Wolf, The New Game	C	1887	McLoughlin Bros.	75	120
Red Riding Hood, Game of	B	1898	Chaffee & Selchow	200	350
Red Ryder "Whirli-Crow" Target Game	S	1940s	Daisy	150	250
Red Ryder Target Game	B	1939	Whitman	75	150
Rex	C	1920s	J. Ottmann Lith.	35	65
Rex and the Kilkenny Cats Game	B	1892	Parker Brothers	45	75
Ride 'em Cowboy	S	1939	Gotham Pressed Steel	25	45
Ring My Nose	S	1926	Milton Bradley	60	100
Ring Scaling	S	1900	Martin	25	45
Ring-A-Peg	B	1885	Horsman	25	45
Rip Van Winkle	B	1890s	Clark & Sowdon	175	225
Rival Policemen	B	1896	McLoughlin Bros.	2000	4000
Road Race, Air Race (Two-game set)	B	1928	Wilder	145	250
Robinson Crusoe for Little Folks, Game of	C	1900s	E.O. Clark	35	65
Robinson Crusoe, Game of	B	1909	Milton Bradley	30	75
Roll-O Football	B	1923	Supply Sales	35	60
Roll-O Golf	B	1923	Supply Sales	35	60

GAMES

NAME	TYPE	YEAR	COMPANY	GOOD	EX
Roll-O Junior Baseball Game	B	1922	Roll-O	325	550
Roll-O-Motor Speedway	B	1922	Supply Sales	65	110
Roly Poly Game	B	1910		30	50
Roodles	C	1912	Flinch Card	30	50
Rook	C	1906	Rook Card	10	15
Roosevelt at San Juan	C	1899	Chaffee & Selchow	150	300
Rose Bowl Championship Football Game	B	1940s	Lowe	40	80
Rough Riders, The Game of	B	1898	Clark & Sowdon	400	600
Roulette Baseball Game	B	1929	W. Barthonomae	115	195
Round the World Game	B	1914	Milton Bradley	150	200
Round the World with Nellie Bly	B	1890	McLoughlin Bros.	210	350
Royal Game of Kings and Queens	B	1892	McLoughlin Bros.	375	650
Rube Bressler's Baseball Game	B	1936	Bressler	130	215
Rube Walker & Harry Davis Baseball Game	B	1905		875	1450
Rummy Football	B	1944	Milton Bradley	35	60
Runaway Sheep	B	1892	Bliss	165	275
Sabotage	C	1943	Games Of Fame	25	45
Saratoga Horse Racing Game	B	1920	Milton Bradley	40	100
Saratoga Steeple Chase	B	1900	J.H. Singer	200	500
Scout, The	B	1900s	E.O. Clark	105	175
Scouting, Game of	B	1930s	Milton Bradley	200	300
Scrambles	B	1941	Frederick H. Beach (Beachcraft)	15	20
Shadow Game, The	B	1940s	Toy Creations	500	900
Shopping, Game of	B	1891	Bliss	1500	2000
Shuffle-Board, The New Game of	S	1920	Gabriel	50	85
Shufflebug, Game of	B	1921		20	30
Siege of Havana, The	B	1898	Parker Brothers	180	300
Simba	S	1932	All-Fair	75	150
Sippa Fish	B	1936	Frederick H. Beach (Beachcraft)	20	30
Skating Race Game, The	B	1900	Chaffee & Selchow	700	1000
Skeezix and the Air Mail	B	1930s	Milton Bradley	65	125
Skeezix Visits Nina	B	1930s	Milton Bradley	65	125
Ski-Hi New York to Paris	B	1927	Cutler & Saleeby	100	150
Skippy, A Card Game	C	1936	All-Fair	45	75
Skippy, Game of	B	1932	Milton Bradley	75	150
Skirmish at Harper's Ferry	B	1891	McLoughlin Bros.	330	550
Skit Scat	C	1905	McLoughlin Bros.	50	85
Skor-It Bagatelle	B	1930s	Northwestern Products	145	250
Sky Hawks	B	1931	All-Fair	120	200
Skyscraper	B	1937	Parker Brothers	250	400
Slide Kelly! Baseball Game	B	1936	B.E. Ruth	70	115
Slugger Baseball Game	B	1930	Marks Brothers	110	180
Smitty Game	B	1930s	Milton Bradley	200	350
Smitty Speed Boat Race Game	B	1930s	Milton Bradley	50	125
Smitty Target Game	S	1930s	Milton Bradley	40	75
Snake Game	B	1890s	McLoughlin Bros.	150	300
Snap	C	1883	Horsman	20	50
Snap Dragon	B	1903	H.B. Chaffee	135	225
Snap, Game of	C	1910s	Milton Bradley	20	35
Snap, Game of	C	1892	McLoughlin Bros.	40	85
Snap, The Game of	C	1905s	Parker Brothers	25	40
Snap-Jacks	S	1940s	Gabriel	15	25
Sniff	B	1940s	The Embossing Co.	20	30
Snow White and the Seven Dwarfs	B	1938	Milton Bradley	75	150
Snow White and the Seven Dwarfs	B	1938	Parker Brothers	125	200
Snow White and the Seven Dwarfs	S	1938	American Toy Works	150	250
Snug Harbor	B	1930s	Milton Bradley	50	85
Socko the Monk, The Game of	B	1935	Einson-Freeman	15	25
Soldier Boy Game	B	1914	United Game	60	150
Soldier's Cavalry	B		McLouglin Bros.	150	300
Soldiers on Guard	B			300	500
Speculation	B	1885	Parker Brothers	40	65
Speed Boat	B	1920s	Parker Brothers	85	140
Speed Boat Race	B	1926	Wolverine	70	115
Speed King, Game Of	B	1922	Russell	115	195
Speedem Junior Auto Race Game	B	1929	All-Fair	70	125
Speedway Motor Race	B	1920s	Smith, Kline & French	145	250
Spider's Web, Game of	B	1898	McLoughlin Bros.	75	150
Spin 'em Target Game	S	1930s	All Metal Product	25	40

GAMES

PREWAR GAMES

NAME	TYPE	YEAR	COMPANY	GOOD	EX
Spin It	S	1910s	Milton Bradley	20	50
Squails	B	1870s	Adams	100	150
Squails	B	1877	Milton Bradley	50	75
Stage	C	1904	C.M. Clark	100	175
Stak, International Game of	S	1937	Marks Brothers	30	60
Stanley in Africa	B	1891	Bliss	900	1800
Star Baseball Game	C	1941	W.P. Ulrich	70	115
Star Basketball	B	1926	Star Paper Products	125	205
Star Ride	B	1934	Einson-Freeman	50	75
Stars on Stripes Football Game	B	1941	Stars & Stripes Games	55	90
Stax	S	1930s	Marks Brothers	12	20
Steeple Chase	B	1890	J.H. Singer	200	300
Steeple Chase & Checkers	B	1910	Milton Bradley	55	90
Steeple Chase, Game of	B	1900s	E.O. Clark	60	100
Steeple Chase, Game of	B	1910s	Milton Bradley	40	65
Steeple Chase, Improved Game of	B	1890s	McLoughlin Bros.	195	325
Steps to Health Coke Game	B	1938	CDN	40	70
Sto-Auto Race	B	1920s	Stough	65	110
Sto-Quoit	B	1920s	Stough	10	15
Stock Exchange	B	1936	Parker Brothers	50	100
Stock Exchange, The Game of	B	1940s	Stox	40	65
Stop & Go	B	1936	Einson-Freeman	25	50
Stop and Go	B	1928	All-Fair	100	150
Stop and Shop	B	1930	All-Fair	75	100
Stop, Look, and Listen, Game of	B	1926	Milton Bradley	40	100
Strat: The Great War Game	B	1915	Strat Game	25	45
Strategy, Game of	B	1891	McLoughlin Bros.	240	400
Strategy, Game of Armies	B	1938	Corey Games	55	100
Stratosphere	B	1930s	Parker Brothers	50	125
Stratosphere	B	1936	Whitman	100	200
Street Car Game, The	B	1890s	Parker Brothers	200	400
Strike Out	B	1920s	All-Fair	175	295
Strike-Like	B	1940s	Saxon Toy	55	90
Stubborn Pig, Game of the	B		Milton Bradley	100	200
Stunt Box	B	1941	Frederick H. Beach (Beachcraft)	12	20
Submarine Drag	B	1917	Willis G. Young	75	125
Substitute Golf	B	1906	John Wanamaker	400	700
Suffolk Downs	B	1930s	Corey Game	85	140
Superman Action Game	S	1940	American Toy Works	60	100
Superman, Adventures of	B	1942	Milton Bradley	300	400
Susceptibles, The	B	1891	McLoughlin Bros.	325	550
Sweep	B	1929	Selchow & Righter	25	40
Sweeps	B	1930s	E.E. Fairchild	25	60
Sweepstakes	B	1930s	Haras	55	90
Swing A Peg	B	1890s	Milton Bradley	30	50
T.G.O. Klondyke	B	1899	J.H. Singer	150	250
Table Croquet	S	1890s	Milton Bradley	30	75
Table Golf	B	1909	McClurg	15	25
Tackle	B	1933	Tackle Game	70	115
Tactics	S	1940	Northwestern Products	25	45
Tait's Table Golf	B	1914	John Tait	350	575
Tak-Tiks, Basketball	B	1939	Midwest Products	15	25
Take It And Double	B	1943	Frederick H. Beach (Beachcraft)	20	35
Take It or Leave It	B	1942	Zondine Game	25	45
Take-Off	C	1930s	Russell	25	45
Teddy's Bear Hunt	B	1907	Bowers & Hard	375	650
Teddy's Ride from Oyster Bay to Albany	B	1899	Jesse Crandall	3000	5500
Tee Off	B	1935	Donogof	115	195
Telegrams	B	1941	Whitman	50	100
Telegraph Boy, Game of the	B	1888	McLoughlin Bros.	250	350
Telepathy	B	1939	Cadaco-Ellis	65	110
Tell Bell, The	B	1928	Knapp Electric & Novelty	75	100
Ten Pins	B	1920	Mason & Parker	35	60
Tennis & Baseball	B	1930		70	115
Terry and the Pirates	B	1930s	Whitman	50	100
Tete-A-Tete	B	1892	Clark & Sowdon	40	100
They're Off, Race Horse Game	B	1930s	Parker Brothers	15	30
Thorobred	B	1940s	Lowe	55	90
Thorton W. Burgess Animal Game	B	1925	Saalfield	70	115
Three Bears	B	1910s	Milton Bradley	20	50

GAMES

338

NAME	TYPE	YEAR	COMPANY	GOOD	EX
Three Bears, The	C	1922	Stoll & Edwards	30	50
Three Blind Mice, Game of	B	1930s	Milton Bradley	25	45
Three Little Kittens	B	1910s	Milton Bradley	60	100
Three Little Pigs Game	B	1933	Einson-Freeman	55	95
Three Little Pigs, The Game of the	B	1933	Kenilworth Press	100	165
Three Men in a Tub	B	1935	Milton Bradley	40	65
Three Men on a Horse	B	1936	Milton Bradley	20	50
Three Merry Men	C	1865	Amsdan	75	100
Three Point Landing	B	1942	Advance Games	35	75
Thrilling Indoor Football Game	B	1933	Cronston	70	115
Through The Clouds	B	1931	Milton Bradley	75	150
Through the Locks to the Golden Gate	B	1905	Milton Bradley	125	225
Ticker	B	1929	Glow Products	50	100
Tiddledy Wink Tennis	S	1890	E.I. Horsman	45	75
Tiddledy Winks, Game of	S	1910s	Parker Brothers	35	55
Tiddley Golf Game	B	1928	Milton Bradley	80	135
Tiddley Winks Game	B	1920s	Wilder	15	35
Tiger Hunt, Game of	B	1899	Chaffee & Selchow	270	450
Tiger Tom, Game of	B	1920s	Milton Bradley	30	75
Ting-A-Ling, The Game of	B	1920	Stoll & Edwards	25	45
Tinker Toss	S	1920s	Toy Creations	25	40
Tinkerpins	B	1916	Toy Creations	55	90
Tip the Bellboy	S	1929	All-Fair	120	200
Tip Top Fish Pond	S	1930s	Milton Bradley	20	45
Tip-Top Boxing	B	1922	LaVelle	200	350
Tipit	B	1929	Wolverine	15	20
Tit for Tat Indoor Hockey	B	1920s	Lemper Novelty	45	75
Tit-Tat-Toe	B	1929	The Embossing	15	25
Tit-Tat-Toe, Three in a Row	B	1896	Austin & Craw	45	75
To the Aid of your Party	B	1942	Leister Game	15	25
Tobaggning at Christmas, Game of	B	1899	McLoughlin Bros.	1200	2000
Toboggan Slide	B	1890s	J.H. Singer	200	325
Toboggan Slide	B	1890s	Hamilton-Myers	225	385
Toll Gate, Game of	B	1890s	McLoughlin Bros.	280	700
Tom Barker Card Game	C	1913		1400	2300
Tom Hamilton's Pigskin	B	1935	Parker Brothers	50	75
Tom Sawyer and Huck Finn, Adventures of	B	1925	Stoll & Edwards	70	200
Tom Sawyer on the Mississippi	B	1935	Einson-Freeman	100	200
Tom Sawyer, The Game of	B	1937	Milton Bradley	75	150
Toonerville Trolley Game	B	1927	Milton Bradley	175	300
Toonin Radio Game	B	1925	All-Fair	150	300
Toot	C	1905	Parker Brothers	35	65
Top-Ography	B	1941	Cadaco	35	45
Topsy Turvey, Game of	B	1899	McLoughlin Bros.	150	250
Tortoise and the Hare	B	1922	Russell	45	85
Toss-O	S	1924	Lubbers & Bell	15	35
Totem	C	1873	West & Lee	45	75
Toto, The New Game	B	1925	Baseball Toto Sales	55	90
Touchdown	S	1930s	Milton Bradley	150	250
Touchdown	B	1937	Cadaco	65	110
Touchdown Football Game	B	1920s	Wilder	100	165
Touchdown or Parlor Football, Game of	B	1897	Union Mutual Life	85	140
Touchdown, The New Game	B	1920	Hartford	70	115
Touring	C	1906	Wallie Dorr	35	75
Touring	C	1926	Parker Brothers	20	40
Tourist, A Railroad Game	B	1900s	Milton Bradley	150	325
Tournament	B	1858	Mayhew & Baker	180	300
Town Hall	B	1939	Milton Bradley	20	30
Toy Town Bank	B	1910	Milton Bradley	90	150
Toy Town Conductors Game	B	1910	Milton Bradley	105	175
Toy Town Target with Repeating Pistol	S	1911	Milton Bradley	55	95
Toy Town Telegraph Office	B	1910s	Parker Brothers	75	150
Trackle-Lite	B	1940s	Saxon Toy	55	90
Traffic Hazards	B	1939	Trojan Games	30	75
Trailer Trails	B	1937	Offset Gravure	35	60
Train for Boston	B	1900	Parker Brothers	750	200
Traits, The Game of	C	1933	Goodenough and Woglom	20	35
Transatlantic Flight, Game of the	B	1925	Milton Bradley	150	400
Transport Pilot	B	1938	Cadaco	45	90
Trap-A-Tank	B	1920s	Wolverine	40	70
Traps & Bunkers	B	1926?	Milton Bradley	115	195
Traps and Bunkers, A Game of Golf	S	1930s	Milton Bradley	25	40
Travel, The Game of	B	1894	Parker Brothers	225	375

NAME	TYPE	YEAR	COMPANY	GOOD	EX
Treasure Hunt	B	1940	All-Fair	20	50
Treasure Island	B	1923	Stoll & Edwards	75	125
Treasure Island	B	1934	Stoll & Einson	60	90
Treasure Island, Game of	B	1923	Gem	40	65
Triangular Dominoes	B	1885	Frank H. Richards	35	60
Trilby	B	1894	E.I. Horsman	270	450
Trip Around the World, A	B	1920s	Parker Brothers	25	45
Trip Round the World, Game of	B	1897	McLoughlin Bros.	300	500
Trip through our National Parks: Game of Yellowstone, A	C	1910s	Cincinnati Game	20	45
Trip to Washington	B	1884	Milton Bradley	100	175
Triple Play	B	1930s	National Games	12	20
Trips of Japhet Jenkens & Sam Slick	C	1871	Milton Bradley	20	35
Trolley	C	1904	Snyder Brothers	45	75
Trolley Came Off, The	C	1900s	Parker Brothers	45	75
Trolley Ride, The Game of the	B	1890s	Hamilton-Myers	210	350
Trunk Box Lotto Game	B	1890s	McLoughlin Bros.	15	35
Tumblin Five Acrobats	B	1925	Doremus Schoen	12	20
Turn Over	B	1908	Milton Bradley	75	100
Turnover	B	1898	Chaffee & Selchow	50	85
Tutoom, Journey to the Treasures of Pharoah	B	1923	All-Fair	150	225
Twentieth Century Limited	B	1900s	Parker Brothers	90	150
Twenty Five, Game of	C	1925	Milton Bradley	10	15
Ty Cobb's Own Game of Baseball	B	1920s	National Novelty	350	650
U-Bat-It	B	1920s	Schultz Star	70	115
U.S. Postman Game	B	1914		60	100
Uncle Jim's Question Bee	B	1938	Kress	20	30
Uncle Sam at War with Spain, Great Game of	B	1898	Rhode Island Game	400	600
Uncle Sam's Baseball Game	B	1890	J.C. Bell	525	875
Uncle Sam's Mail	B	1893	McLoughlin Bros.	210	400
Uncle Wiggily's New Airplane Game	B	1920s	Milton Bradley	50	175
United States Air Mail Game, The	S	1930s	Parker Brothers	50	85
United States History, The Game of	C	1903	Parker Brothers	35	65
Van Loon Story of Mankind Game, The	B	1931	Kerk Guild	50	85
Vanderbilt Cup Race	B	1906	Bowers & Hard	800	1800
Varsity Football Game	B	1942	Cadaco-Ellis	45	75
Varsity Race	B	1899	Parker Brothers	425	725
Vassar Boat Race, The	B	1899	Chaffee & Selchow	420	700
Venetian Fortune Teller, Game of	C	1898	Parker Brothers	125	165
Verborum	C	1883	Peter G. Thompson	35	65
Vest Pocket Checker Set	B	1929	Embossing	15	25
Vest Pocket Quoits	B	1944	Colorful Creations	25	45
Victo	B	1943	Spare Time	15	25
Victory	B	1920s	Klak New Haven	105	175
Vignette Author	B	1874	E.G. Selchow	35	75
Visit of Santa Claus, Game of the	B	1899	McLoughlin Bros.	600	1000
Visit to the Farm	B	1893	Bliss	300	500
Vox-Pop	B	1938	Milton Bradley	25	45
Voyage Around the World, Game of	B	1930s	Milton Bradley	105	175
Wa-Hoo Pick-Em Up Sticks	S	1936	Doremus Schoen	15	25
Wachter's Parlor Base Ball (bagatelle)	B	1925	Wachter	145	250
Walk the Plank	B	1925	Milton Bradley	50	95
Walking the Tightrope	B	1920	Milton Bradley	50	100
Walking the Tightrope	B	1897	McLoughlin Bros.	125	250
Walt and Skeezix Gasoline Alley Game	C	1927	Milton Bradley	100	175
Walt Disney's Game Parade	B	1930s		30	50
Walt Disney's Ski Jump Target Game	S	1930s	American Toy Works	175	295
Walt Disney's Uncle Remus Game	S	1930s	Parker Brothers	60	125
Walter Johnson Baseball Game	B	1930s		195	325
Waner's Baseball Game	B	1930s	Waner's Baseball Game	350	650
Wang, Game of	B	1892	Clark & Sowdon	25	65
War and Diplomacy	C	1899	Chaffee & Selchow	85	125
War of Nations	B	1915	Milton Bradley	40	65
War of Words	C	1910	McLoughlin Bros.	35	60
Ward Cuff's Football Game	B	1938	Continental Sales	125	200
Washington's Birthday Party	S	1911	Russell	55	95
Watch on De Rind	B	1931	All-Fair	300	500
Waterloo	B	1895	Parker Brothers	325	550
Watermelon Frolic	B	1900	Horsman	135	225
Watermelon Patch	B	1940s	Craig Hopkins	25	45
Watermelon Patch Game	S	1896	McLoughlin Bros.	900	2000

GAMES

NAME	TYPE	YEAR	COMPANY	GOOD	EX
Way to the White House, The	B	1927	All-Fair	100	200
We, The Magnetic Flying Game	B	1928	Parker Brothers	100	200
West Point	B	1902	Ottoman	90	150
What Would You Do?	C	1933	Geo E. Schweig & Son	15	25
What's My Name?	B	1920s	Jaymar	15	25
When My Ship Comes In	C	1888	Parker Brothers	55	75
Where do you Live?	C	1890s	J.H. Singer	55	75
Where's Johnny?	C	1885	McLoughlin Bros.	65	110
Which is It? Speak Quick or Pay	C	1889	McLoughlin Bros.	65	110
Whip, The Comical Game of	C	1930	Russell	30	50
Whippet Race	B	1940s	Pressman	20	35
Whirlpool Game	B	1890s	McLoughlin Bros.	65	150
White Wings	B	1930s	Glevum Games	45	70
Who is the Thief?	C	1937	Whitman	35	55
Wide Awake, Game of	B	1899	McLoughlin Bros.	200	350
Wide World and a Journey Round It	B	1896	Parker Brothers	165	275
Wild West Cardboard Game	B	1914		90	150
Wild West, Game of the	B	1889	Bliss	1000	1700
Wilder's Football Game	B	1930s	Wilder	100	150
Win, Place & Show	B	1940s	3M	25	40
Winko Baseball	B	1940	Milton Bradley	45	70
Winnie Winkle Glider Race Game	B	1930s	Milton Bradley	65	150
Winnie-The-Pooh Game	B	1933	Parker Brothers	100	200
Winnie-The-Pooh Game, A. A. Milne's	B	1931	Kerk Guild	50	85
Witzi-Wits	B	1926	All-Fair	100	200
Wizard, The	B	1921	Fulton Specialty	15	25
Wogglebug Game of Conundrums, The	C	1905	Parker Brothers	200	500
Wonder Tiddley Winks	S	1899	Martin	20	35
Wonderful Game of Oz (pewter pieces)	B	1921	Parker Brothers	600	1300
Wonderful Game of Oz (wooden pieces)	B	1921	Parker Brothers	200	400
Wordy	B	1938	Pressman	25	45
World Flyers, Game of the	B	1926	All-Fair	150	300
World Series Baseball Game	B	1940s	Radio Sports	205	350
World Series Parlor Baseball	B	1916	Clifton E. Hooper	150	250
World's Championship Baseball	B	1910	Champion Amusement	175	295
World's Championship Golf Game	B	1930s	Beacon Hudson	145	250
World's Columbian Exposition, Game of the	B	1893	Bliss	450	750
World's Educator Game	B	1889	Reed	45	75
World's Fair Game	B	1939		90	150
World's Fair Game, The	B	1892	Parker Brothers	800	1400
Worth While	C	1907	Doan	25	40
WPA, Work, Progress, Action	B	1935	All-Fair	100	200
Wyhoo!	C	1906	Milton Bradley	40	60
Wyntre Golf	B	1920s	All-Fair	175	400
X-Plor-US	B	1922	All-Fair	100	150
Ya-Lo Football Card Game	B	1930s		85	140
Yacht Race	B	1930s	Pressman	150	250
Yacht Race	B	1890s	Clark & Sowdon	200	350
Yachting	B	1890	J.H. Singer	70	115
Yale Harvard Football Game	B	1922	LaVelle	200	300
Yale Harvard Game	B	1890	McLoughlin Bros.	1050	1775
Yale-Princeton Football Game	B	1895	McLoughlin Bros.	575	1100
Yankee Doodle!	B	1940	Cadaco-Ellis	30	50
Yankee Doodle, A Game of American History	B	1895	Parker Brothers	285	475
Yankee Pedlar, Or What Do You Buy	C	1850s	John McLoughlin	725	1200
Yankee Trader	B	1941	Corey Games	35	80
Yellowstone, Game of	C	1895	Fireside Game	75	100
You're Out! Baseball Game	B	1941	Corey Games	35	65
Young Athlete, The	B	1898	Chaffee & Selchow	425	700
Young Folks Historical Game	C	1890s	McLoughlin Bros.	45	85
Young Peddlers, Game of the	C	1859	Mayhew & Baker	125	175
Young People's Geographical Game	C	1900s	Parker Brothers	35	55
Yuneek Game	B	1889	McLoughlin Bros.	450	750
Zimmer Baseball Game	B	1885	McLoughlin Bros.	3000	6000
Zip-Top	B	1940	Deluxe Game	35	55
Zippy Zepps	B	1930s	All-Fair	350	600
Zoo Hoo	B	1924	Lubbers & Bell	125	200
Zoom	C	1941	Whitman	35	55
Zoom, Original Game of	B	1940s	All-Fair	45	85
Zulu Blowing Game	B	1927	Zulu Toy	50	100

GAMES

341

NAME	TYPE	YEAR	COMPANY	GOOD	EX	MINT
$25,000 Pyramid	B	1980s	Cardinal Industries	15	35	50
$64,000 Question Quiz Game	B	1955	Lowell	12	30	45
1-2-3 Game Hot Spot!	B	1961	Parker Brothers	6	15	25
1863, Civil War Game	B	1961	Parker Brothers	20	40	65
2 For The Money	B	1955	Lowell	10	25	35
20,000 Leagues Under the Sea	B	1950s	Gardner	25	55	100
25 Ghosts	B	1969	Lakeside	15	25	40
300 Mile Race	B	1955	Warren	15	35	60
36 Fits	B	1966	Watkins-Strathmore	12	30	40
4 Alarm Game	B	1963	Milton Bradley	18	40	65
4000 A.D. Interstellar Conflict Game	B	1972	House of Games	8	20	35
77 Sunset Strip	B	1960	Lowell	35	50	75
99, The Game of	B	1969	Broman-Percepta Corp.	8	20	30
A-Team	B	1984	Parker Brothers	5	10	15
Abbott & Costello Who's On First?	B	1978	Selchow & Righter	5	10	15
ABC Monday Night Football Roger Staubach Edition	B	1973	Aurora	8	20	35
ABC Sports Winter Olympics	B	1987	Mindscape	10	15	25
Acquire (plastic tiles)	B	1968	3M	12	30	45
Acquire (wood tiles)	B	1963	3M	35	75	120
Across the Board Horse Racing Game	B	1975	MPH	8	20	35
Across the Continent (cars)	B	1960	Parker Brothers	20	40	65
Across the Continent (trains)	B	1952	Parker Brothers	30	50	80
Action Baseball	B	1965	Pressman	35	45	50
Addams Family	B	1965	Ideal	65	100	175
Addams Family	C	1965	Milton Bradley	25	55	75
Addams Family	B	1973	Milton Bradley	15	35	50
Admirals	B	1973	Parker Brothers (U.K.)	10	25	35
Advance To Boardwalk	B	1985	Parker Brothers	5	15	20
Adventure in Science, An	B	1950	Jacmar	20	30	50
Agent Zero-M Spy Detector	B	1964	Mattel	30	50	80
Aggravation	B	1970	Lakeside	5	10	15
Air Assault on Crete	B	1977	Avalon Hill	3	10	15
Air Charter	B	1970	Waddington	20	50	70
Air Empire	B	1961	Avalon Hill	40	100	160
Air Race Around the World	B	1950s	Lido	12	30	50
Air Traffic Controller	B	1974	Schaper	12	30	40
Airways	S	1950s	Lindstrom Tool & Toy	30	50	75
Alfred Hitchcock "Why?"	B	1965	Milton Bradley	10	20	30
Alfred Hitchcock Presents Mystery Game "Why"	B	1958	Milton Bradley	20	35	55
Alien	B	1979	Kenner	15	45	70
All American Football	B	1969	Cadaco	5	10	20
All In The Family	B	1972	Milton Bradley	10	20	30
All My Children	B	1985	TSR	5	10	20
All Pro Baseball	B	1969	Ideal	20	35	55
All Pro Basketball	B	1969	Ideal	10	25	35
All Pro Football	B	1967	Ideal	8	20	30
All Star Baseball	B	1989	Cadaco	5	12	20
All Star Baseball	B	1970s	Cadaco-Ellis	10	25	45
All Star Baseball	B	1960s	Cadaco-Ellis	20	50	75
All Star Baseball Fame	B	1962	Cadaco-Ellis	15	25	40
All Star Basketball	B	1950s	Gardner	55	90	135
All Star Electric Baseball & Football	B	1955	Harett-Gilmar	35	60	90
All Star Football	B	1950	Gardner	20	45	65
All The King's Men	B	1979	Parker Brothers	6	10	15
All Time Greats Baseball Game	B	1971	Midwest Research	15	35	50
Alumni Fun	B	1964	Milton Bradley	8	20	30
Amazing Dunninger Mind Reading Game	B	1967	Hasbro	12	30	40
American Derby, The	B	1951	Cadaco-Ellis	15	35	50
Angry Donald Duck Game	S	1970s	Mexico	40	65	100
Animal Crackers	B	1970s	Milton Bradley	4	7	11
Annette's Secret Passage	B	1958	Parker Brothers	25	55	80
Annie Oakley (larger)	B	1955	Milton Bradley	20	50	75
Annie Oakley (smaller game)	B	1950s	Milton Bradley	12	30	40
Annie, The Movie Game	B	1981	Parker Brothers	4	6	10

GAMES

342

NAME	TYPE	YEAR	COMPANY	GOOD	EX	MINT
Anti-Monopoly	B	1973	Anti-Monopoly	8	20	30
APBA "Pro" League Football	B	1980s	APBA	12	20	30
APBA Baseball Master Game	B	1975	APBA	20	50	75
APBA Pro League Football	B	1964	APBA	25	60	85
APBA Saddle Racing Game	B	1970s	APBA	15	25	40
Apollo: A Voyage to the Moon	B	1969	Tracianne	12	30	40
Apple's Way	B	1974	Milton Bradley	15	40	60
Archie Bunker's Card Game	C	1972	Milton Bradley	6	15	25
Archies, The	B	1969	Whitman	15	35	50
Arnold Palmer's Inside Golf	B	1961	D.B. Remson	50	85	130
Around the World	B	1962	Milton Bradley	10	25	35
Around The World In 80 Days	B	1957	Transogram	15	35	50
Art Lewis Football Game	B	1955	Morgantown Game	70	115	175
Art Linkletter's House Party	B	1968	Whitman	8	20	30
Art Linkletter's People are Funny Party Game	C	1954	Whitman	5	16	25
As The World Turns	B	1966	Parker Brothers	12	30	50
ASG Baseball	B	1989	3W (World Wide Wargames)	15	35	50
ASG Baseball	B	1974	Gerney Games	35	75	100
ASG Major League Baseball	B	1973	Gerney Games	35	75	125
Assembly Line	B	1953	Selchow & Righter	18	45	65
Astro Launch	B	1963	Ohio Art	18	40	60
Astron	B	1955	Parker Prothers	50	120	150
Atom Ant Game	B	1966	Transogram	25	60	90
Aurora Pursuit! Game	B	1973	Aurora	8	25	40
Auto Dome	B	1967	Transogram	18	40	60
Autograph Baseball Game	B	1948	Philadelphia Inquirer	110	180	275
B-17 Queen of The Skies	B	1983	Avalon Hill	6	10	15
B.T.O. (Big Time Operator)	B	1956	Bettye-B	20	45	70
Babes in Toyland	B	1961	Whitman	15	35	50
Bali	C	1954	I-S Unlimited	8	20	30
Ballplayer's Baseball Game	B	1955	Jon Weber	30	50	75
Bamboozle	B	1962	Milton Bradley	20	45	65
Banana Tree	B	1977	Marx	10	15	25
Bang, A Game of the Old West	B	1956	Selchow & Righter	35	75	100
Bantu	B	1955	Parker Brothers	18	40	60
Bar-Teen Ranch Game	B	1950s	Warren Built-Rite	10	25	35
Barbapapa Takes A Trip	B	1977	Selchow & Righter	3	5	8
Barbie's Little Sister Skipper Game	B	1964	Mattel	15	40	60
Barbie, Queen of The Prom	B	1960	Mattel	30	60	85
Baretta	B	1976	Milton Bradley	10	25	40
Barnabas Collins Game	B	1969	Milton Bradley	20	50	80
Barney Miller	B	1977	Parker Brothers	10	15	25
Barnstormer	B	1970s	Marx	20	35	55
Bart Starr Quarterback Game	B	1960s		175	295	450
Baseball	S	1960s	Tudor	25	40	60
Baseball Card All Star Game	C	1987	Captoys	5	12	15
Baseball Card Game	C	1950s	Ed-U-Cards	8	20	30
Baseball Card Game, Official	C	1965	Milton Bradley	20	55	80
Baseball Challenge	B	1980	Tri-Valley Games	15	35	50
Baseball Game, Official	B	1969	Milton Bradley	100	165	250
Baseball Game, The	B	1988	Horatio	12	20	30
Baseball Strategy	B	1973	Avalon Hill	6	15	25
Baseball, A Sports Illustrated Game	B	1971-73	Time	60	150	200
Baseball, Football & Checkers	B	1957	Parker Brothers	20	50	75
Bash!	S	1967	Ideal	10	15	25
Basketball Strategy	B	1974	Avalon Hill	10	15	25
Bat Masterson	B	1958	Lowell	45	75	120
Batman	B	1978	Hasbro	15	30	50
Batman and Robin Game	B	1965	Hasbro	30	65	95
Batman Batarang Toss	S	1966	Pressman	150	250	400
Batman Card Game	C	1966	Ideal	20	65	85
Batman Game	B	1966	Milton Bradley	25	60	90
Batman Pin Ball	S	1966	Marx	55	95	150
Bats in the Belfry	S	1964	Mattel	20	55	80
Batter Up	B	1946	M. Hopper	30	50	75
Batter Up Card Game	C	1949	Ed-U-Cards	8	20	30

GAMES

Bugaloos, 1971, Milton Bradley

Dragnet, 1955, Transogram

Family Affair, 1967, Whitman

POSTWAR GAMES

NAME	TYPE	YEAR	COMPANY	GOOD	EX	MINT
Batter-Rou Baseball Game (Dizzy Dean)	B	1950s	Memphis Plastic	100	165	250
Battle Cry	B	1962	Milton Bradley	25	60	85
Battle Line	B	1964	Ideal	25	50	75
Battle Masters	B	1992	Milton Bradley	15	40	60
Battle of The Planets	B	1970s	Milton Bradley	15	25	35
Battleboard	B	1972	Ideal	10	25	35
Battleship	B	1965	Milton Bradley	10	15	25
Battlestar Galactica	B	1978	Parker Brothers	10	15	25
Battling Tops Game	B	1968	Ideal	20	45	65
Bazaar	B	1967	3M	12	30	40
Beany & Cecil Match It	B	1960s	Mattel	30	50	80
Beat Inflation	B	1975	Avalon Hill	8	20	30
Beat The Buzz	B	1958	Kenner	10	15	25
Beat The Clock	B	1960s	Milton Bradley	6	10	16
Beat The Clock	B	1954	Lowell	15	45	70
Beatles Flip Your Wig Game	B	1964	Milton Bradley	60	150	250
Beetle Bailey, The Old Army Game	B	1963	Milton Bradley	40	70	90
Behind The 8 Ball Game	B	1969	Selchow & Righter	8	20	35
Ben Casey MD Game	B	1961	Transogram	15	30	45
Bermuda Triangle	B	1976	Milton Bradley	10	15	25
Betsy Ross and the Flag	B	1950s	Transogram	18	45	70
Beverly Hillbillies Game	B	1963	Standard Toykraft	25	55	80
Beverly Hillbillies Game, "Set Back"	C	1963	Milton Bradley	10	25	40
Bewitched	B	1965	T. Cohn	50	80	120
Bewitched Stymie Game	C	1960s	Milton Bradley	15	40	60
Beyond the Stars	B	1964	Game Partners	20	45	65
Bible Baseball	B	1950s	Standard	50	75	150
Bible Quiz Lotto	C	1949	Jack Levitz	5	12	20
Big 5 Poosh-M Up	S	1950s	Knickerbocker	25	40	60
Big Foot	B	1977	Milton Bradley	5	12	20
Big Game Hunt, The	S	1947	Carrom Industries	15	25	40
Big League Baseball	B	1959	Saalfield	20	45	65
Big League Baseball Game	B	1966	3M	15	25	40
Big League Manager Football	B	1965	BLM	30	75	100
Big Payoff	B	1984	Payoff Enterprises	6	10	15
Big Six Sports Game	B	1950s	Gardner	125	295	450
Big Sneeze Game, The	S	1968	Ideal	10	25	40
Big Time Colorado Football	B	1983	B.J. Tall	6	10	15
Big Town	B	1954	Lowell	50	80	125
Billionaire	B	1973	Parker Brothers	5	15	20
Bing Crosby's Game, Call Me Lucky	B	1954	Parker Brothers	15	35	50
Bingo-Matic	B	1954	Transogram	5	10	20
Bionic Crisis	B	1975	Parker Brothers	6	15	25
Bionic Woman	B	1976	Parker Brothers	6	15	25
Bird Brain	B	1966	Milton Bradley	10	25	40
Bird Watcher	B	1958	Parker Brothers	15	35	50
Birdie Golf	B	1964	Barris	15	35	50
Black Ball Express	B	1957	Schaper	10	25	40
Black Beauty	B	1957	Transogram	15	35	50
Black Box	B	1978	Parker Brothers	5	10	15
Blade Runner	B	1982		25	60	85
Blast Off	B	1953	Selchow & Righter	35	75	100
Blast, The Game of	B	1973	Ideal	8	20	35
Blitzkrieg	B	1965	Avalon Hill	4	10	16
Blockhead	B	1954	Russell	10	15	25
Blondie	B	1970s	Parker Brothers	6	10	15
Blondie and Dagwood's Race for the Office	B	1950	Jaymar	30	45	70
Blue Line Hockey	B	1968	3M	10	25	40
Bluff	B	1964	Saalfield	10	25	40
BMX Cross Challenge Action Game	B	1988	Cross Challenge	6	10	15
Bob Feller's Big League Baseball	B	1949	Saalfield	75	150	200
Bobbsey Twins	B	1957	Milton Bradley	8	20	30
Bobby Shantz Baseball Game	B	1955	Realistic Games	80	150	225
Body Language	B	1975	Milton Bradley	2	5	10
Boggle	B	1976	Parker Brothers	3	8	12
Bonanza Michigan Rummy Game	B	1964	Parker Brothers	30	45	70

345

NAME	TYPE	YEAR	COMPANY	GOOD	EX	MINT
Bonkers!, This Game is	B	1978	Parker Brothers	3	10	15
Boob Tube Race	S	1962	Milton Bradley	2	80	30
Booby Trap	S	1965	Parker Brothers	10	15	25
Boom or Bust	B	1951	Parker Brothers	60	125	175
Booth's Pro Conference Football	B	1977	Sher-Co	10	15	25
Boots and Saddles	B	1960	Chad Valley	35	65	100
Bop Bop 'N Rebop	S	1979	Hasbro	12	30	40
Bop The Beetle	S	1963	Ideal	25	60	85
Boris Karloff's Monster Game	B	1965	Gems	75	125	200
Boston Marathon Game, Official	B	1978	Perl Products	15	25	35
Boston Red Sox Game	C	1964	Ed-U-Cards	15	35	55
Bottoms Up	B	1970s		3	5	8
Boundary	B	1970	Mattel	8	20	30
Bowl & Score	B	1974	Lowe	6	10	15
Bowl And Score	B	1962	Lowe	6	10	15
Bowl Bound!	B	1973	Sports Illustrated	15	25	40
Bowl-A-Matic	S	1963	Eldon	45	75	120
Brain Waves	B	1977	Milton Bradley	6	15	25
Branded	B	1966	Milton Bradley	30	60	90
Brass Monkey Game, The	B	1973	U.S. Game Systems	6	15	25
Break Par Golf Game	B	1950s	Warren/Built-Rite	8	20	30
Break The Bank	B	1955	Bettye-B	12	30	45
Breaker 1-9	B	1976	Milton Bradley	5	10	15
Breakthru	B	1965	3M	8	20	30
Brett Ball	B	1981	9th Inning	15	30	45
Bride Bingo	B	1957	Leister Game	5	12	20
Broadside	B	1962	Milton Bradley	35	75	100
Bruce Jenner Decathlon Game	B	1979	Parker Brothers	4	7	11
Buck Fever	B	1984	L & D Robton	12	20	30
Buckaroo	B	1947	Milton Bradley	20	35	55
Bucket Ball	B	1972	Marx	10	15	25
Bug-A-Boo	B	1968	Whitman	6	15	20
Bugaloos	B	1971	Milton Bradley	15	35	60
Bugs Bunny Game (Bagatelle)	S	1975	Ideal	15	25	40
Bugs Bunny Under The Cawit Game	B	1972	Whitman	15	25	40
Building Boom	B	1950s	Kohner	10	20	35
Built-Rite Swish Basketball Game	B	1950s	Warren/Built-Rite	10	20	35
Bullwinkle Card Game	C	1962	Ed-U-Cards	10	30	50
Bullwinkle Hide & Seek Game	B	1961	Milton Bradley	25	40	75
Bullwinkle's Super Market Game	B	1970s	Whitman	15	25	60
Buster Brown Game and Play Box	B	1950s	Buster Brown Shoes	40	75	125
C&O/B&O	B	1969	Avalon Hill	20	50	95
Cabbage Patch Kids	B	1984	Parker Brothers	5	10	15
California Raisins Board Game	B	1987	Decipher	4	16	25
Call It Golf	B	1966	Strauss	15	25	40
Call It!	S	1978	Ideal	5	12	20
Call My Bluff	B	1965	Milton Bradley	15	20	30
Calling All Cars	B	1930s-40s	Parker Brothers	25	60	85
Calling All Cars	B	1950s	Parker Brothers	15	35	50
Calling Superman	S	1955	Transogram	25	85	125
Calvin & The Colonel High Spirits	B	1962	Milton Bradley	12	30	50
Camelot	B	1955	Parker Brothers	20	30	50
Camouflage	B	1961	Milton Bradley	5	20	35
Camp Granada Game, Allan Sherman's	B	1968	Milton Bradley	20	50	75
Camp Runamuck	B	1965	Ideal	15	30	65
Campaign	B	1966	Campaign Game	8	25	40
Campaign	B	1971	Waddington	10	30	45
Campaign: The American "Go" Game	B	1961	Saalfield	15	45	65
Can You Catch It Charlie Brown?	B	1976	Ideal	10	25	35
Can't Stop	B	1980	Parker Brothers	5	12	20
Candid Camera Game	B	1963	Lowell	15	40	65
Candid Camera Target Shot	S	1950s	Lindstrom Tool & Toy	35	60	90
Candyland	B	1949	Milton Bradley	25	50	90
Candyland	B	1960s	Milton Bradley	10	25	45
Cannonball Run, The	B	1981	Cadaco	4	16	25
Caper	B	1970	Parker Brothers	20	45	65

GAMES

NAME	TYPE	YEAR	COMPANY	GOOD	EX	MINT
Capital Punishment	B	1981	Hammerhead	25	45	75
Captain America	B	1966	Milton Bradley	40	65	105
Captain America	B	1977	Milton Bradley	10	15	25
Captain Caveman and the Teen Angels	B	1981	Milton Bradley	8	20	30
Captain Gallant Desert Fort Game	B	1956	Transogram	20	40	65
Captain Kangaroo	B	1956	Milton Bradley	40	85	125
Captain Video Game	B	1952	Milton Bradley	55	125	200
Car Travel Game	B	1958	Milton Bradley	5	16	25
Carapace	B	1970	Plan B Corp.	5	16	25
Cardino	B	1970	Milton Bradley	10	15	25
Careers	B	1957	Parker Brothers	8	20	30
Careers	B	1965	Parker Brothers	6	15	25
Careful: The Toppling Tower	S	1967	Ideal	10	15	25
Cargoes	B	1958	Selchow & Righter	15	35	50
Carl Hubbell Mechanical Baseball	B	1950	Gotham	100	200	300
Carl Yastrzemski's Action Baseball	B	1968	Pressman	90	145	195
Carrier Strike	B	1977	Milton Bradley	15	25	45
Cars 'n Trucks Build-A-Game	B	1961	Ideal	15	45	80
Cartel	B	1974	Gamut of Games	18	45	65
Case of The Elusive Assassin, The	B	1967	Ideal	20	50	75
Casey Jones	B	1959	Saalfield	20	45	65
Casper The Friendly Ghost Game	B	1974	Schaper	8	18	30
Casper The Friendly Ghost Game	B	1959	Milton Bradley	5	10	20
Castle Risk	B	1986	Parker Brothers	15	35	50
Cat & Mouse	B	1964	Parker Brothers	7	15	20
Catchword	B	1954	Whitman	3	10	15
Catfish Bend Storybook Game	B	1978	Selchow & Righter	15	20	35
Cattlemen, The	B	1977	Selchow & Righter	10	15	25
Cavalcade	B	1953	Selchow & Righter	15	45	65
Caveat Emptor	B	1971	Plan B	5	16	25
Centipede	B	1983	Milton Bradley	6	10	15
Century of Great Fights	B	1969	Research Games	40	75	110
Challenge Golf at Pebble Beach	B	1972	3M	6	15	25
Challenge the Yankees	B	1960s	Hasbro	200	500	700
Challenge Yahtzee	B	1974	Milton Bradley	7	15	20
Championship Baseball	B	1966	Championship Games	8	20	30
Championship Basketball	B	1966	Championship Games	8	20	30
Championship Golf	B	1966	Championship Games	8	20	30
Changeover: The Metric Game	B	1976	John Ladell	8	20	30
Changing Society	B	1981	Phil Carter	5	16	25
Chaos	B	1971	Lakeside	8	20	30
Chaos	B	1965	Amsco Toys	5	16	25
Charge It!	C	1972	Whitman	5	15	25
Charlie Brown's All Star Baseball Game	B	1965	Parker Brothers	35	60	90
Charlie's Angels	B	1977	Milton Bradley	6	10	20
Charlie's Angels (Farrah Fawcett box)	B	1977	Milton Bradley	10	20	45
Chase, The	B	1966	Cadaco	12	30	45
Chaseback	B	1962	Milton Bradley	5	16	25
Checkpoint: Danger!	B	1978	Ideal	5	16	25
Cherry Ames' Nursing Game	B	1959	Parker Brothers	40	90	135
Chess	B	1977	Milton Bradley	3	5	8
Chevyland Sweepstakes	B	1968	Milton Bradley	25	50	100
Chex Ches Football	B	1971	Chex Ches Games	15	25	40
Cheyenne	B	1958	Milton Bradley	25	60	95
Chicago Sports Trivia Game	B	1984	Sports Trivia	6	10	15
Chicken In Every Pot, A	B	1980s	Animal Town Game	20	30	50
Chicken Lotto	S	1965	Ideal	8	25	40
Children's Hour, The	B	1946	Parker Brothers	10	30	45
CHiPS	B	1981	Ideal	7	10	20
CHiPS Game	B	1977	Milton Bradley	4	7	10
Chit Chat Game	B	1963	Milton Bradley	6	10	15
Chopper Strike	B	1976	Milton Bradley	10	25	40
Chug-A-Lug	B	1969	Dynamic	5	16	25
Chute-5	B	1973	Lowe	5	12	20
Chutes & Ladders	B	1956	Milton Bradley	10	15	25

GAMES

NAME	TYPE	YEAR	COMPANY	GOOD	EX	MINT
Chutes Away!	S	1978	Gabriel	15	45	65
Chutzpah	B	1967	Cadaco	10	25	40
Chutzpah	B	1967	Middle Earth	15	35	50
Cimarron Strip	B	1967	Ideal	35	75	125
Circle Racer Board Game	B	1988	Sport Games USA	6	10	15
Cities Game, The	B	1970	Psychology Today	8	25	40
Civil War	B	1961	Avalon Hill	15	45	65
Civilization	B	1982	Avalon Hill	7	10	20
Clash of the Titans	B	1981	Whitman	10	25	45
Class Struggle	B	1978	Bernard Ollman	10	25	35
Clean Sweep	B	1960s	Schaper	20	50	75
Clean Water	B	1972	Urban Systems	8	25	40
Clickety-Clak	S	1950s	Milton Bradley	10	30	45
Cloak & Dagger	B	1984	Ideal	8	25	40
Close Encounters of the Third Kind	B	1977	Parker Brothers	7	15	20
Clue	B	1972	Parker Brothers	4	7	11
Clue	B	1949	Parker Brothers	25	40	65
Clue Master Detective	B	1988	Parker Brothers	20	55	75
Clunk-A-Glunk	S	1968	Whitman	8	25	40
Code Name: Sector	B	1977	Parker Brothers	10	30	45
Collector, The	B	1977	Avalon Hill	5	16	25
College Basketball	B	1954	Cadaco-Ellis	10	25	35
Columbo	B	1973	Milton Bradley	6	10	15
Combat	B	1963	Ideal	25	45	70
Combat	C	1964	Milton Bradley	10	25	40
Comin' Round The Mountain	B	1954	Einson-Freeman	30	50	80
Computer Baseball	B	1966	Epoch Playtime	25	40	65
Computer Basketball	B	1969	Electric Data	10	25	35
Computerized Pro Football	B	1971	Data Prog.	15	25	40
Concentration (25th Anniversary Ed.)	B	1982	Milton Bradley	6	10	16
Concentration (3rd Ed.)	B	1960	Milton Bradley	12	20	35
Conestoga	B	1964	Washburne Research	25	65	95
Coney Island Penny Pitch	S	1950s	Novel Toy	33	55	88
Coney Island, The Game of	B	1956	Selchow & Righter	35	75	125
Conflict	B	1960	Parker Brothers	15	45	65
Confucius Say	B	1960s	Pressman	10	30	45
Conquer	B	1979	Whitman	5	16	25
Conquest of the Empire	B	1984	Milton Bradley	45	100	150
Consetta and Her Wheel of Fate	B	1946	Selchow & Righter	30	75	110
Conspiracy	B	1982	Milton Bradley	4	7	11
Contigo	B	1974	3M	7	20	35
Cootie	B	1949	Schaper	10	25	35
Count Coup	B	1979	Marcian Chronicles	10	30	45
Count Down Space Game	B	1960	Transogram	15	45	65
Countdown	B	1967	Lowe	15	40	60
Counter Point	B	1976	Hallmark	10	15	25
Cowboy Roundup	B	1952	Parker Brothers	15	25	40
Cowboys & Indians	C	1949	Ed-U-Cards	8	20	35
Cracker Jack Game	B	1976	Milton Bradley	5	16	25
Crazy Clock Game	S	1964	Ideal	35	75	100
Crazy Maze	S	1966, 1975	Lakeside	8	20	30
Creature Features	B	1975	Athol	20	50	75
Creature From The Black Lagoon	B	1963	Hasbro	150	400	750
Cribb Golf	B	1980s		10	25	40
Crosby Derby, The	B	1947	Fishlove	50	90	135
Cross Up	B	1974	Milton Bradley	2	5	10
Crosswords	B	1954	National Games	12	20	32
Crusader Rabbit TV Game	B	1960s		50	100	175
Cub Scouting, The Game of	B	1987	Cadaco	5	16	25
Curious George Game	B	1977	Parker Brothers	4	6	10
Curse of the Cobras Game	B	1982	Ideal	12	20	32
Cut Up Shopping Spree Game	B	1968	Milton Bradley	6	10	16
Dallas (TV Role Playing)	B	1980	SPI	4	7	11
Dallas Game	C	1980	Mego	3	10	15
Danger Pass	B	1964	Game Partners	15	45	65
Daniel Boone Trail Blazer	B	1964		25	60	85
Daniel Boone Wilderness Trail	C	1964	Transogram	10	40	65

GAMES

348

*Fireball XL-5, 1963,
Milton Bradley*

Get Smart Game, 1966, Ideal

Howdy Doody's TV Game, 1950s, Milton Bradley

POSTWAR GAMES

NAME	TYPE	YEAR	COMPANY	GOOD	EX	MINT
Dark Crystal Game, The	B	1982	Milton Bradley	7	20	35
Dark Shadows Game	B	1968	Whitman	18	40	60
Dark Tower	B	1981	Milton Bradley	100	175	225
Dark World	B	1992	Mattel	10	25	35
Dastardly & Muttley	B	1969	Milton Bradley	25	45	65
Dating Game, The	B	1967	Hasbro	15	25	40
Davy Crockett Adventure Game	B	1956	Gardner	45	75	120
Davy Crockett Frontierland Game	B	1955	Parker Brothers	20	50	75
Davy Crockett Radar Action Game	B	1955	Ewing Mfg. & Sales	51	85	136
Davy Crockett Rescue Race Game	B	1950s	Gabriel	20	50	75
Dawn of The Dead	B	1978	SPI	45	95	135
Daytona 500 Race Game	B	1989	Milton Bradley	10	25	35
Dead Pan	B	1956	Selchow & Righter	8	25	40
Deadlock	B	1972	American Greetings	8	20	30
Dealer's Choice	B	1972	Parker Brothers	10	25	35
Dear Abby	B	1972	Ideal	7	20	35
Decathalon	B	1972	Sports Illustrated	10	25	35
Decoy	B	1956	Selchow & Righter	12	40	60
Deduction	B	1976	Ideal	2	7	12
Deluxe Wheel of Fortune	B	1986	Pressman	5	8	13
Dennis The Menace Baseball Game	B	1960		20	50	70
Denny McLain Magnetik Baseball Game	B	1968	Gotham	115	195	295
Deputy Dawg Hoss Toss	S	1973		15	25	40
Deputy Dawg TV Lotto	B	1961		21	35	56
Deputy Game, The	B	1960	Milton Bradley	30	50	80
Derby Day	B	1959	Parker Brothers	18	45	65
Derby Downs	B	1973	Great Games	10	30	45
Detectives Game, The	B	1961	Transogram	30	50	80
Dick Tracy Crime Stopper	B	1963	Ideal	30	70	95
Dick Tracy Playing Card Game	C	1934	Whitman	25	60	100
Dick Tracy Playing Card Game	C	1939	Esquire Novelty	20	45	75
Dick Tracy Playing Card Game	C	1937	Whitman	20	45	75
Dick Tracy The Master Detective Game	B	1961	Selchow & Righter	25	65	90
Dick Van Dyke Board Game	B	1964	Standard Toykraft	45	100	175
Diet	B	1972	Dynamic	5	16	25
Diner's Club Credit Card Game, The	B	1961	Ideal	15	45	65
Dinosaur Island	B	1980	Parker Brothers	5	16	25
Diplomacy	B	1961	Games Research	21	35	56
Diplomacy	B	1976	Avalon Hill	15	25	40
Direct Hit	B	1950s	Northwestern Products	40	70	110
Dirty Water-The Water Pollution Game	B	1970	Urban Systems	8	20	30
Disney Dodgem Bagatelle	S	1960s	Marx	30	65	90
Disney Mouseketeer	B	1964	Parker Brothers	40	65	100
Disneyland Game	B	1965	Transogram	25	60	85
Dispatcher	B	1958	Avalon Hill	30	70	100
Dobbin Derby	B	1950	Cadaco-Ellis	8	25	40
Doctor Who	B	1980s	Denys Fisher	35	75	100
Dogfight	B	1962	Milton Bradley	35	75	100
Dollar A Second	B	1955	Lowell	12	30	45
Dollars & Sense	B	1946	Sidney Rogers	100	150	200
Domain	B	1983	Parker Brothers	2	3	5
Domination	B	1982	Milton Bradley	8	20	30
Don Carter's Strike Bowling Game	B	1964	Saalfield	55	90	135
Don't Break the Ice	S	1960s	Schaper	5	16	25
Don't Miss the Boat	B	1965	Parker Brothers	12	30	40
Don't Spill the Beans	S	1967	Schaper	5	16	25
Donald Duck Big Game Box	B	1979	Whitman	10	15	20
Donald Duck Pins & Bowling Game	B	1955s	Pressman	35	60	90
Donald Duck Tiddley Winks Game	B	1950s		6	10	15
Donald Duck's Party Game	B	1950s	Parker Brothers	10	35	50
Dondi Potato Race Game	B	1950s	Hasbro	15	35	50
Donkey Party Game	B	1950	Saalfield	4	10	15
Donny & Marie Osmond TV Show Game	B	1977	Mattel	8	25	40
Double Cross	B	1974	Lakeside	5	16	25

NAME	TYPE	YEAR	COMPANY	GOOD	EX	MINT
Double Trouble	B	1987	Milton Bradley	3	5	8
Doubletrack	B	1981	Milton Bradley	2	7	12
Dr. Kildare	B	1962	Ideal	25	40	65
Dracula Mystery Game	B	1960s	Hasbro	80	160	225
Dracula's "I Vant To Bite Your Finger" Game	B	1981	Hasbro	10	20	30
Dragnet	B	1955	Transogram	35	60	95
Dragon's Lair	B	1983	Milton Bradley	7	10	20
Dragonlance	B	1988	TSR	15	35	50
Dragonmaster	C	1981	Lowe	8	20	30
Dream House	B	1968	Milton Bradley	15	35	50
Driver Ed	B	1973	Cadaco	6	10	20
Duell	B	1976	Lakeside	5	16	25
Dukes of Hazzard	B	1981	Ideal	6	15	25
Dunce	B	1955	Schaper	7	20	35
Dune	B	1984	Parker Brothers	10	25	35
Dune, Frank Herbert's	B	1979	Avalon Hill	20	50	75
Dungeon Dice	B	1977	Parker Brothers	5	8	15
Dungeons & Dragons	B	1980	Mattel	6	10	15
Duplicate Ad-Lib	B	1976	Lowe	5	10	15
Duran Duran Game	B	1985	Milton Bradley	15	25	40
Dynamite Shack Game	S	1968	Milton Bradley	10	25	45
Dynomutt	B	1977	Milton Bradley	10	15	25
E.T. The Extra-Terrestrial	B	1982	Parker Brothers	6	10	15
Earl Gillespie Baseball Game	B	1961	Wei-Gill	25	40	65
Earth Satellite Game	B	1956	Gabriel	30	70	100
Ecology	B	1970	Urban Systems	7	20	35
Egg and I, The	B	1947	Capex	30	50	80
El Dorado	B	1977	Invicta	7	20	35
Electra Woman and Dyna Girl	B	1977	Ideal	10	25	45
Electric Sports Car Race	B	1959	Tudor	35	60	90
Electronic Detective Game	B	1970s	Ideal	20	30	45
Electronic Lightfight	B	1981	Milton Bradley	10	30	45
Electronic Radar Search	B	1967	Ideal	10	15	25
Eliot Ness and the Untouchables	B	1961	Transogram	30	70	100
Ellsworth Elephant Game	B	1960	Selchow & Righter	30	45	70
Elmer Wheeler's Fat Boys Game	B	1951	Parker Brothers	18	40	60
Elvis Presley Game	B	1957	Teen Age Games	300	650	1000
Emenee Chocolate Factory	B	1966		6	10	15
Emergency	B	1974	Milton Bradley	15	35	50
Emily Post Popularity Game	B	1970	Selchow & Righter	15	20	35
Emperor of China	B	1972	Dynamic	10	25	40
Empire Auto Races	B	1950s	Empire Plastics	20	30	50
Empire Builder (1sy edition)	B	1982	Mayfair Games	20	50	75
Empire Strikes Back, Hoth Ice World	B	1977	Kenner	10	20	30
Enemy Agent	B	1976	Milton Bradley	8	20	30
Energy Quest	B	1977	Weldon	5	16	25
Engineer	B	1957	Selchow & Righter	8	25	40
Entertainment Trivia Game	B	1984	Lakeside	5	10	15
Entre's Fun & Games In Accounting	B	1988	Entrepreneurial Games	4	7	12
Ergo	B	1977	Invicta	5	16	25
Escape From New York	B	1980	TSR	12	30	40
Escape from the Casbah	B	1975	Selchow & Righter	7	20	35
Escape From the Death Star	B	1977	Kenner	10	20	30
Espionage	B	1973	MPH	6	18	30
Everybody's Talking!	B	1967	Watkins-Strathmore	8	25	40
Executive Decision	B	1971	3M	5	16	25
Expanse	B	1949	Milton Bradley	15	45	65
Extra Innings	B	1975	J. Kavanaugh	30	50	75
Eye Guess	B	1960s	Milton Bradley	15	20	35
F-Troop	B	1965	Ideal	40	100	155
F.B.I.	B	1958	Transogram	35	55	90
F.B.I. Crime Resistance Game	B	1975	Milton Bradley	12	30	40
F/11 Armchair Quarterback	B	1964	James R. Hock	15	25	40
Fact Finder Fun	B	1963	Milton Bradley	10	15	25
Facts In Five	S	1967	3M	3	8	12
Fall Guy, The	B	1981	Milton Bradley	10	15	25
Falls	B	1950s	National	85	140	215

NAME	TYPE	YEAR	COMPANY	GOOD	EX	MINT
Family Affair	B	1967	Whitman	25	40	65
Family Feud	B	1977	Milton Bradley	4	12	20
Family Ties Game, The	B	1986	Apple Street	10	20	25
Famous 500 Mile Race	B	1988		8	13	20
Fang Bang	B	1966	Milton Bradley	12	25	35
Fangface	B	1979	Parker Brothers	5	8	13
Fantastic Voyage Game	B	1968	Milton Bradley	15	25	40
Fantasy Island Game	B	1978	Ideal	7	20	35
Fascination	S	1962	Remco	15	35	50
Fast 111s	B	1981	Parker Brothers	5	16	25
Fast Golf	C	1977	Whitman	8	13	20
Fastest Gun, The	B	1974	Milton Bradley	10	35	50
Fat Albert	B	1973	Milton Bradley	15	25	40
Fearless Fireman	B	1957	Hasbro	35	100	150
Feed the Elephant!	S	1952	Cadaco-Ellis	10	35	50
Feeley Meeley Game	S	1967	Milton Bradley	20	50	75
Felix the Cat Dandy Candy Game	B	1957	Warren/Built-Rite	15	35	50
Felix the Cat Game	B	1960	Milton Bradley	10	25	45
Felix the Cat Game	B	1968	Milton Bradley	8	20	30
Feudal	B	1967	3M	8	20	30
Fighter Bomber	B	1977	Cadaco	15	25	40
Finance	B	1962	Parker Brothers	10	20	35
Fire Chief	B	1957	Selchow & Righter	8	25	40
Fire Fighters!	B	1957	Russell	15	25	40
Fire House Mouse Game	B	1967	Transogram	10	35	50
Fireball XL-5	B	1963	Milton Bradley	40	100	145
Fireball XL-5 Magnetic Dart Game	S	1963	Magic Wand	75	125	200
First Class Farmer	B	1965	F & W Publishing	7	20	35
First Down	B	1970	TGP Games	50	80	125
Fish Pond	B	1950s	National Games	10	30	45
Fishbait	B	1965	Ideal	40	60	75
Flagship Airfreight: The Airplane Cargo Game	B	1946	Milton Bradley	40	70	115
Flash Gordon	B	1977	Waddington/House Of Games	10	25	35
Flash: The Press Photographer Game	B	1956	Selchow & Righter	18	50	75
Flea Circus Magnetic Action Game	S	1968	Mattel	15	25	40
Flight Captain	B	1972	Lowe	5	16	25
Flintstones	B	1980	Milton Bradley	15	20	35
Flintstones	B	1971	Milton Bradley	6	15	25
Flintstones Animal Rummy	C	1960	Ed-U-Cards	7	25	45
Flintstones Brake Ball	S	1962	Whitman	45	75	120
Flintstones Cut-Ups Game	C	1963	Whitman	15	45	75
Flintstones Dino The Dinosaur Game	B	1961	Transogram	45	75	120
Flintstones Hoppy The Hopperoo Game	B	1964	Transogram	45	75	120
Flintstones Mechanical Shooting Gallery	S	1962	Marx	75	125	200
Flintstones Mitt-Full Game	B	1962	Whitman	40	65	100
Flintstones Stone Age Game	B	1961	Transogram	20	45	65
Flip 'N Skip	B	1971	Little Kennys	5	10	15
Flip Flop Go	B	1962	Mattel	6	10	15
Flipper Flips	B	1960s	Mattel	30	50	80
Flying Nun Game, The	B	1968	Milton Bradley	20	30	50
Flying Nun Marble Maze Game, The	S	1967	Hasbro	20	30	50
Fonz Game, The	B	1976	Milton Bradley	15	25	40
Fooba-Roo Football Game	B	1955	Memphis Plastic	15	35	50
Football Fever	B	1985	Hansen	20	35	50
Football Strategy	B	1962	Avalon Hill	8	25	40
Football Strategy	B	1972	Avalon Hill	3	10	15
Football, Baseball, & Checkers	B	1948	Parker Brothers	15	45	65
Fore	B	1954	Artcraft Paper	20	35	50
Formula One Car Race Game	B	1968	Parker Brothers	18	40	60
Fortress America	B	1986	Milton Bradley	35	75	100
Fortune 500	B	1979	Pressman	8	25	40
Foto-Electric Baseball	B	1951	Cadaco-Ellis	15	35	65
Foto-Electric Football	B	1965	Cadaco	10	25	35

GAMES

POSTWAR GAMES

NAME	TYPE	YEAR	COMPANY	GOOD	EX	MINT
Four Lane Road Racing	B	1963	Transogram	15	45	65
Fox & Hounds, Game of	B	1948	Parker Brothers	10	30	45
Frank Cavanaugh's American Football	B	1955	F. Cavanaugh	25	60	90
Frankenstein Game	B	1962	Hasbro	80	160	225
Frisky Flippers Slide Bar Game	B	1950s	Warren/Built-Rite	5	10	15
Frontier Fort Rescue Game	B	1956	Gabriel	10	35	50
Frontier-6	B	1980	Rimbold	8	25	40
Fu Manchu's Hidden Hoard	B	1967	Ideal	20	50	75
Fugitive	B	1966	Ideal	60	150	225
Funky Phantom Game	B	1971	Milton Bradley	10	15	25
Funny Bones Game	C	1968	Parker Brothers	5	7	11
G.I. Joe	B	1982	International Games	15	25	40
G.I. Joe Adventure	B	1982	Hasbro	20	30	50
G.I. Joe Bagatelle Gun Action Game	S	1970s	Hasbro	7	12	15
G.I. Joe Card Game	B	1965	Whitman	10	15	25
G.I. Joe Marine Paratrooper	B	1965	Hasbro	20	50	70
G.I. Joe Navy Frogman	B	1965	Hasbro	25	60	85
Gambler's Golf	B	1975	Gammon Games	4	10	15
Games People Play Game, The	B	1967	Alpsco	7	20	35
Gammonball	B	1980	Fun-Time Products	10	16	25
Gang Way For Fun	B	1964	Transogram	25	40	65
Gardner's Championship Golf	B	1950s	Gardner	10	35	50
Garfield	B	1981	Parker Brothers	4	6	10
Garrison's Gorillas	B	1967	Ideal	45	75	120
Gay Puree	B	1962		25	40	65
Gene Autry's Dude Ranch Game	B	1950s	Warren/Built-Rite	30	70	100
General Hospital	B	1974	Parker Brothers	7	15	25
General Hospital	B	1980s	Cardinal	15	20	30
Generals, The	B	1980	Ideal	7	20	35
Gentle Ben Animal Hunt Game	B	1967	Mattel	30	70	100
Geo-Graphy	B	1954	Cadaco-Ellis	5	15	25
George of the Jungle Game	B	1968	Parker Brothers	40	90	125
Get Beep Beep: The Road Runner Game	B	1975	Whitman	15	25	35
Get Smart Game	B	1966	Ideal	40	95	130
Get That License	B	1955	Selchow & Righter	10	35	50
Get the Message	B	1964	Milton Bradley	5	16	25
Get the Picture	B	1987	Worlds Of Wonder	6	10	15
Gettysburg	B	1960	Avalon Hill	5	16	25
Ghosts	B	1985	Milton Bradley	8	20	35
Giant Wheel Thrills 'n Spills Horse Race	B	1958	Remco	30	50	75
Gidget	C	1966	Milton Bradley	15	35	50
Gil Hodges' Pennant Fever	B	1970	Research Games	35	75	100
Gilligan's Island	B	1965	Game Gems	175	350	600
Gilligan, The New Adventures of	B	1974	Milton Bradley	15	35	50
Gingerbread Man	B	1964	Selchow & Righter	10	35	50
Globe-Trotters	B	1950	Selchow & Righter	8	25	40
Globetrotter Basketball, Official	B	1950s	Meljak	60	100	150
Gnip Gnop	S	1971	Parker Brothers	5	16	25
Go For Broke	B	1965	Selchow & Righter	10	15	25
Go for the Green	B	1973	Sports Illustrated	10	25	40
Go Go Go	C	1950s	Arco Playing Card	6	20	35
Goal Line Stand	B	1980	Game Shop	12	20	30
Godfather	B	1971	Family Games	8	20	30
Godzilla	B	1978	Mattel	30	50	80
Godzilla	B	1960s	Ideal	75	250	400
Going to Jerusalem	B	1955	Parker Brothers	8	25	40
Going, Going, Gone!	B	1975	Milton Bradley	9	15	25
Gold!	B	1981	Avalon Hill	5	16	25
Golden Trivia Game	B	1984	Western	6	10	15
Goldilocks	B	1955	Cadaco-Ellis	8	25	40
Gomer Pyle Game	B	1960s	Transogram	20	45	65
Gong Hee Fot Choy	C	1948	Zondine Game	20	35	55
Gong Show Game	B	1977	American Publishing	15	25	40
Gong Show Game	B	1975	Milton Bradley	15	25	40
Good Guys 'N Bad Guys	B	1973	Cadaco	5	16	25

GAMES

353

Intrigue, 1954, Milton Bradley

Jonny Quest Game, 1964, Transogram

POSTWAR GAMES

NAME	TYPE	YEAR	COMPANY	GOOD	EX	MINT
Good Ol' Charlie Brown Game	B	1971	Milton Bradley	8	20	30
Goofy's Mad Maze	B	1970s	Whitman	6	10	15
Goonies	B	1980s	Milton Bradley	10	15	20
Gooses Wild	B	1966	CO-5	2	7	12
Gotham Professional Basketball	B	1950s	Gotham	35	50	70
Gotham's Ice Hockey	S	1960s	Gotham	25	60	85
Grab A Loop	S	1968	Milton Bradley	7	12	20
Grabitz	C	1979	International Games	2	5	7
Grand Master of Martial Arts	B	1986	Hoyle	6	10	15
Gray Ghost, The	B	1958	Transogram	30	70	100
Great Escape, The	B	1967	Ideal	8	25	40
Great Grape Ape Game, The	B	1975	Milton Bradley	15	25	40
Green Acres Game, The	B	1960s	Standard Toykraft	25	65	90
Green Ghost Game	B	1965	Transogram	40	90	135
Green Ghost Game (re-issue)	B	1997	Marx	15	35	50
Green Hornet Quick Switch Game	B	1966	Milton Bradley	180	300	475
Gremlins	B	1984	International Games	10	15	25
Greyhound Pursuit	B	1985	N/N Games	8	13	20
Grizzly Adams	B	1978	Waddington's House of Games	15	25	40
Groucho's TV Quiz Game	B	1954	Pressman	30	65	100
Groucho's You Bet Your Life	B	1955	Lowell	50	100	140
Group Therapy	B	1969	Group Therapy Assn.	3	12	20
Guinness Book of World Records Game, The	B	1979	Parker Brothers	5	9	15
Gulf Strike	B	1983	Victory Games	5	16	25
Gunsmoke Game	B	1950s	Lowell	40	65	100
Gusher	B	1946	Carrom Industries	40	90	135
Half-Time Football	B	1979	Lakeside	5	9	15
Handicap Harness Racing	B	1978	Hall of Fame Games	15	25	35
Hands Down	S	1965	Ideal	10	15	25
Hang On Harvey	B	1969	Ideal	15	20	30
Hangman	B	1976	Milton Bradley	5	8	15
Hank Aaron Baseball Game	B	1970s	Ideal	50	80	125
Hank Aaron Bases Loaded	B	1976	Twentieth Century Enterprises	45	70	100
Hank Bauer's "Be a Manager"	B	1960s	Barco Games	75	125	175
Happiness	B	1972	Milton Bradley	12	30	45
Happy Days	B	1976	Parker Brothers	8	20	30
Happy Little Train Game, The	B	1957	Milton Bradley	3	12	20
Hardy Boys Mystery Game, Secret of Thunder Mountain	B	1978	Parker Brothers	7	15	25
Hardy Boys Mystery Game, The	B	1968	Milton Bradley	6	15	25
Hardy Boys Treasure	B	1960	Parker Brothers	25	50	85
Harlem Globetrotters Game	B	1971	Milton Bradley	12	30	50
Harlem Globetrotters Official Edition Basketball	B	1970s	Cadaco-Ellis	45	75	115
Harpoon	B	1955	Gabriel	20	45	65
Harry Lorayne Memory Game, The	B	1976	Reiss	7	20	35
Harry's Glam Slam	C	1962	Harry Obst	35	60	90
Hashimoto San	B	1963	Transogram	30	45	70
Haul the Freight	B	1962	Bar-Zim	15	50	75
Haunted House Game	B	1963	Ideal	120	250	400
Haunted Mansion	B	1970s	Lakeside	60	150	200
Have Gun Will Travel Game	B	1959	Parker Brothers	30	75	100
Hawaii Five-O	B	1960s	Remco	30	90	120
Hawaiian Eye	B	1960	Transogram	50	120	160
Hawaiian Punch Game	B	1978	Mattel	5	16	25
Hector Heathcote	B	1963	Transogram	35	75	100
Hex: The Zig-Zag Game	B	1950	Parker Brothers	10	35	50
Hey Pa, There's a Goat on the Roof!	B	1965	Parker Brothers	20	50	70
Hi Pop	S	1946	Advance Games	20	35	55
Hi-Ho! Cherry-O	B	1960	Whitman	6	10	15
Hide 'N' Thief	B	1965	Whitman	7	20	35
Hide-N-Seek	B	1967	Ideal	20	50	75
High-Bid	B	1965	3M	7	20	35
Hip Flip	B	1968	Parker Brothers	6	15	25
Hippety Hop	B	1947	Corey Game	25	40	65

GAMES

355

NAME	TYPE	YEAR	COMPANY	GOOD	EX	MINT
Hippopotamus	B	1961	Remco	8	25	40
Hit The Beach	B	1965	Milton Bradley	45	85	120
Hobbit Game, The	B	1978	Milton Bradley	25	60	85
Hoc-Key	S	1958	Cadaco-Ellis	10	35	50
Hock Shop	B	1975	Whitman	3	12	20
Hocus Pocus	B	1960s	Transogram	30	45	70
Hog Tied	B	1981	Selchow & Righter	3	12	20
Hogan's Heroes Game	B	1966	Transogram	45	85	120
Holiday	B	1958	Replogle Globes	40	65	100
Hollywood Awards Game	B	1976	Milton Bradley	8	25	40
Hollywood Go	B	1954	Parker Brothers	10	25	35
Hollywood Squares	B	1974	Ideal	6	10	15
Hollywood Squares	B	1980	Milton Bradley	4	6	10
Home Court Basketball	B	1954		145	250	375
Home Game	B	1960s	Pressman	30	50	80
Home Stretch Harness Racing	B	1967	Lowe	15	35	50
Home Team Baseball Game	B	1957	Selchow & Righter	18	45	65
Honey West	B	1965	Ideal	50	85	135
Honeymooners Game, The	B	1986	TSR	7	12	20
Hoodoo	B	1950	Tryne	4	10	15
Hookey Go Fishin'	B	1974	Cadaco	8	16	25
Hopalong Cassidy Bean Bag Toss Game	S	1950s		20	40	60
Hopalong Cassidy Chinese Checkers Game	B	1950s		20	50	75
Hopalong Cassidy Game	B	1950s	Milton Bradley	40	100	145
Hoppity Hooper Pin Ball Game	S	1965	Lido	40	75	115
Horse Play	B	1962	Schaper	10	35	50
Horseshoe Derby Game	B	1950s	Built-Rite	8	20	30
Hot Property!	B	1980s	Take One Games	8	25	40
Hot Rod	B	1953	Harett-Gilmar	15	35	50
Hot Spot	B	1961	Parker Brothers	10	20	30
Hot Wheels Game	B	1982	Whitman	8	13	20
Hot Wheels Wipe-Out Game	B	1968	Mattel	15	35	50
Hotels	B	1987	Milton Bradley	15	35	50
Houndcats Game	B	1970s	Milton Bradley	8	15	25
House Party	B	1968	Whitman	10	25	35
Houston Astros Baseball Challenge Game	B	1980	Croque	15	25	35
How To Succeed In Business Without Really Trying	B	1963	Milton Bradley	6	15	25
Howard Hughes Game, The	B	1972	Family Games	10	35	50
Howdy Doody Adventure Game	B	1950s	Milton Bradley	45	75	100
Howdy Doody Card Game	C	1954	Russell	20	50	75
Howdy Doody Dominoes Game	S	1950s	Ed-U-Cards	60	100	200
Howdy Doody Quiz Show	B	1950s	Multiple Products	20	40	75
Howdy Doody's Electric Carnival Game	B		Harrett-Gilmar	15	20	35
Howdy Doody's Own Game	B	1949	Parker Brothers	40	90	135
Howdy Doody's Three Ring Circus	B	1950	Harett-Gilmar	45	75	120
Howdy Doody's TV Game	B	1950s	Milton Bradley	35	50	100
Huckleberry Hound	B	1981	Milton Bradley	10	20	35
Huckleberry Hound Bumps	B	1960	Transogram	20	50	75
Huckleberry Hound Spin-O-Game	B	1959		45	75	120
Huckleberry Hound Tiddly Winks	B	1959	Milton Bradley	15	30	60
Huckleberry Hound Western Game	B	1959	Milton Bradley	25	40	65
Huckleberry Hound's Huckle Chuck Target Game	S	1961	Transogram	25	50	100
Huggin' The Rail	S	1948	Selchow & Righter	45	65	100
Hullabaloo	B	1965	Remco	25	65	90
Humor Rumor	B	1969	Whitman	10	20	30
Humpty Dumpty Game	B	1950s	Lowell	6	10	15
Hunch	B	1956	Happy Hour	7	20	35
Hungry Ant, The	B	1978	Milton Bradley	5	16	25
Hungry Henry	S	1969	Ideal	7	20	35
Hunt For Red October	B	1988	TSR	5	15	25
Hurry Up	B	1971	Parker Brothers	5	16	25
I Dream of Jeannie Game	B	1965	Milton Bradley	30	75	105

GAMES

POSTWAR GAMES

NAME	TYPE	YEAR	COMPANY	GOOD	EX	MINT
I Spy	B	1965	Ideal	35	75	100
I Survived New York!	C	1981	City Enterprises	4	7	12
I Wanna Be President	B	1983	J.R. Mackey	5	16	25
I'm George Gobel, And Here's The Game	B	1955	Schaper	12	30	40
I-Qubes	S	1948	Capex	10	15	25
Ice Cube Game, The	B	1972	Milton Bradley	50	125	175
Identipops	B	1969	Playvalue	75	175	250
Image	B	1972	3M	3	12	20
Incredible Hulk	B	1978	Milton Bradley	6	10	15
Indiana Jones: Raiders of The Lost Ark	B	1981	Kenner	20	35	55
Indianapolis 500 75th Running Race Game	B	1991	International Games	8	13	20
Input	B	1984	Milton Bradley	4	7	15
Inside Moves	B	1985	Parker Brothers	3	12	20
Inspector Gadget	B	1983	Milton Bradley	15	25	40
Instant Replay	B	1987	Parker Brothers	8	13	20
Intercept	B	1978	Lakeside	7	20	35
International Grand Prix	B	1975	Cadaco	30	50	75
Interpretation of Dreams	B	1969	Hasbro	7	15	25
Interstate Highway	B	1963	Selchow & Righter	20	50	75
Intrigue	B	1954	Milton Bradley	12	30	40
Inventors, The	B	1974	Parker Brothers	5	12	20
Ipcress File	B	1966	Milton Bradley	20	50	75
Ironside	B	1976	Ideal	55	95	150
Is the Pope Catholic?!	B	1986	Crowley Connections	10	25	45
Isolation	B	1978	Lakeside	2	7	12
Itinerary	B	1980	Xanadu Leisure	3	12	20
Jace Pearson's Tales of The Texas Rangers	B	1955	E.E. Fairchild	20	50	75
Jack & Jill Target Game	S	1948	Cadaco-Ellis	7	20	35
Jack and The Beanstalk	B	1946	National Games	30	45	75
Jack and The Beanstalk Adventure Game	B	1957	Transogram	25	50	75
Jack Barry's Twenty One	B	1956	Lowell	20	30	50
Jackie Gleason's and AW-A-A-A-Y We Go!	B	1956	Transogram	75	125	200
Jackie Gleason's Story Stage Game	B	1955	Utopia Enterprises	100	200	300
Jackpot	B	1975	Milton Bradley	7	11	20
Jacmar Big League Electric Baseball	B	1950s	Jacmar	100	175	250
James Bond 007 Goldfinger Game	B	1966	Milton Bradley	35	75	100
James Bond 007 Thunderball Game	B	1965	Milton Bradley	35	75	100
James Bond Live and Let Die Tarot Game	C	1973	US Games Systems	20	55	85
James Bond Message From M Game	B	1966	Ideal	100	250	350
James Bond Secret Agent 007 Game	B	1964	Milton Bradley	15	35	50
James Bond You Only Live Twice	B	1984	Victory Games	5	8	13
James Clavell's Noble House	B	1987	FASA	7	20	35
James Clavell's Shogun	B	1983	FASA	7	20	35
James Clavell's Tai-Pan	B	1987	FASA	7	20	35
James Clavell's Whirlwind	B	1986	FASA	7	20	35
Jan Murray's Charge Account	B	1961	Lowell	25	40	65
Jan Murray's Treasure Hunt	B	1950s	Gardner	10	25	35
Jaws, The Game of	S	1975	Ideal	5	16	25
JDK Baseball	B	1982	JDK Baseball	20	45	65
Jeanne Dixon's Game of Destiny	B	1968	Milton Bradley	7	12	20
Jeopardy	B	1964	Milton Bradley	10	15	25
Jerry Kramer's Instant Replay	B	1970	EMD Enterprises	15	25	40
Jet World	B	1975	Milton Bradley	5	16	25
Jetsons Fun Pad Game	B	1963	Milton Bradley	40	100	145
Jetsons Game	B	1985	Milton Bradley	5	10	15
Jetsons Out of this World Game	B	1963	Transogram	85	140	225
Jimmy the Greek Oddsmaker Football	B	1974	Aurora	10	25	35
Jockette	B	1950s	Jockette	25	40	60
Joe Palooka Boxing Game	B	1950s	Lowell	35	65	100
John Drake Secret Agent	B	1966	Milton Bradley	30	45	70

GAMES

357

NAME	TYPE	YEAR	COMPANY	GOOD	EX	MINT
Johnny Apollo Moon Landing Bagatelle	S	1969	Marx	20	35	55
Johnny Ringo	B	1959	Transogram	40	90	135
Johnny Unitas Football Game	B	1970	Pro Mentor	15	35	50
Joker's Wild	B	1973	Milton Bradley	5	10	15
Jonathan Livingston Seagull	B	1973	Mattel	8	20	30
Jonny Quest Game	B	1964	Transogram	200	500	700
Jose Canseco's Perfect Baseball Game	B	1991	Perfect Game	8	13	20
Jubilee	B	1954	Cadaco-Ellis	10	25	35
Jumbo Jet	B	1963	Jumbo	18	45	65
Jumpin'	B	1964	3M	7	20	35
Jumping DJ	B	1962	Mattel	15	50	75
Junior Bingo-Matic	B	1968	Transogram	6	10	15
Junior Executive	B	1963	Whitman	7	15	30
Junior Quarterback Football	B	1950s	Warren/Built-Rite	7	20	35
Justice	B	1954	Lowell	25	55	75
Justice League of America	B	1967	Hasbro	70	150	250
Ka Bala	B	1965	Transogram	40	75	120
KaBoom!	S	1965	Ideal	10	15	25
Kar-Zoom	B	1964	Whitman	15	20	35
Karate, The Game of	B	1964	Selchow & Righter	7	20	35
Kardball	C	1946	Ajak	20	30	40
Karter Peanut Shell Game	B	1978	Morey & Neely	7	20	35
Kennedys, The	B	1962	Transogram	25	60	90
Kentucky Derby	B	1960	Whitman	15	25	40
Kentucky Jones	B	1964	T. Cohn	25	40	65
Ker-Plunk	S	1967	Ideal	5	10	15
Keyword	B	1954	Parker Brothers	3	7	10
Kick Back	S	1965	Schaper	5	16	25
Kick-Off Soccer	B	1978	Camden Products	7	20	35
Kimbo	S	1950s	Parker Brothers	10	15	25
King Arthur	S	1950s	Northwestern Products	25	40	65
King Kong Game	B	1963	Ideal	75	200	325
King Kong Game	B	1966	Milton Bradley	8	20	30
King Kong Game	B	1976	Ideal	8	20	30
King Leonardo and His Subjects Game	B	1960	Milton Bradley	18	45	65
King of the Hill	B	1965	Schaper	25	60	80
King of the Sea	B	1975	Ideal	8	25	40
King Oil	B	1974	Milton Bradley	25	55	75
King Pin Deluxe Bowling Alley	S	1947	Baldwin Mfg.	10	20	30
King Tut's Game	B	1978	Cadaco	5	16	25
King Zor, The Dinosaur Game	B	1964	Ideal	45	85	120
Kismet	B	1971	Lakeside	6	15	25
KISS On Tour Game	B	1978	Aucoin	25	60	80
Klondike	B	1975	Gamma Two	12	30	40
Knight Rider	B	1983	Parker Brothers	7	12	20
Knockout, Electronic Boxing Game	S	1950s	Northwestern Products	90	150	240
Know Your States	C	1955	Garrard Press	10	25	45
Kojak	B	1975	Milton Bradley	7	12	20
Kommisar	B	1960s	Selchow & Righter	12	30	40
Kooky Carnival	B	1969	Milton Bradley	10	35	50
Korg 70,000 BC	B	1974	Milton Bradley	7	15	25
Kreskin's ESP	B	1966	Milton Bradley	4	10	18
Krokay	S	1955	Transogram	4	10	15
Krull	B	1983	Parker Brothers	6	10	15
KSP Baseball	B	1983	Koch Sports Products	25	60	85
Kukla & Ollie	B	1962	Parker Brothers	20	45	65
Lancer	B	1968	Remco	40	90	135
Land of The Giants	B	1968	Ideal	60	125	175
Land of The Lost	B	1975	Milton Bradley	10	25	35
Land of The Lost Pinball	S	1975	Larami	10	20	30
Landslide	B	1971	Parker Brothers	5	16	25
Laramie	B	1960	Lowell	50	100	140
Las Vegas Baseball	B	1987	Samar Enterprises	8	13	20
Laser Attack Game	B	1978	Milton Bradley	7	20	35
Lassie Game	B	1965	Game Gems	10	35	50

King Kong Game, 1966, Milton Bradley

Lippy the Lion Game, 1963, Transogram

National Velvet Game, 1950s, Transogram

POSTWAR GAMES

NAME	TYPE	YEAR	COMPANY	GOOD	EX	MINT
Last Straw	B	1966	Schaper	5	10	15
Laugh-In's Squeeze Your Bippy Game	B	1968	Hasbro	35	75	100
Laurel & Hardy Game	B	1962	Transogram	12	30	40
Laverne & Shirley Game	B	1977	Parker Brothers	9	15	25
Leapin' Letters	S	1969	Parker Brothers	5	16	25
Leave It To Beaver Ambush Game	B	1959	Hasbro	20	45	70
Leave It To Beaver Money Maker	B	1959	Hasbro	20	45	70
Leave It To Beaver Rocket To The Moon	B	1959	Hasbro	20	45	70
Lee Vs Meade: Battle of Gettysburg	B	1974	Gamut of Games	7	15	25
Legend of Jesse James Game, The	B	1965	Milton Bradley	30	70	100
LeMans	B	1961	Avalon Hill	25	60	85
Let's Bowl a Game	B	1960	DMR	5	12	20
Let's Go to the Races	B	1987	Parker Brothers	7	20	35
Let's Make A Deal	B	1970s	Ideal	10	15	25
Let's Play Basketball	C	1965	D.M.R.	12	20	35
Let's Play Golf "The Hawaiian Open"	B	1968	Burlu	8	20	30
Let's Play Safe Traffic Game	B	1960s	X-Acto	25	50	90
Let's Play Tag	B	1958	Milton Bradley	5	16	25
Leverage	B	1982	Milton Bradley	4	6	10
LF Baseball	B	1980	Len Feder	18	45	65
Li'l Abner's Spoof Game	C	1950	Milton Bradley	65	95	135
Lie Detector Game	B	1961	Mattel	20	50	75
Lieutenant, The	B	1963	Transogram	30	70	100
Life, The Game of	B	1960	Milton Bradley	8	20	30
Limit Up	B	1980	Willem	6	18	30
Line Drive	B	1953	Lord & Freber	18	45	65
Linebacker Football	B	1990	Linebacker	12	20	30
Linkup	B	1972	American Greetings	5	16	25
Linus the Lionhearted Uproarious Game	B	1965	Transogram	50	85	135
Lion and the White Witch, The	B	1983	David Cook	5	16	25
Lippy the Lion Game	B	1963	Transogram	25	45	70
Little Black Sambo	B	1952	Cadaco-Ellis	50	100	140
Little Boy Blue	B	1955	Cadaco-Ellis	6	18	30
Little Creepies Monster Game	B	1974	Toy Factory	6	10	15
Little House On The Prairie	B	1978	Parker Brothers	12	30	40
Little League Baseball Game	B	1950s	Standard Toykraft	25	45	70
Little Orphan Annie	B	1981	Parker Brothers	10	20	30
Little Red Schoolhouse	B	1952	Parker Brothers	10	25	35
Lobby	B	1949	Milton Bradley	8	25	40
Lone Ranger and Tonto Spin Game, The	S	1967	Pressman	15	25	40
Long Shot	B	1962	Parker Brothers	45	75	125
Longball	B	1975	Ashburn Industries	35	75	100
Look All-Star Baseball Game	B	1960	Progressive Research	35	60	90
Looney Tunes Game	B	1968	Milton Bradley	20	40	65
Lord of the Rings, The	B	1979	Milton Bradley	40	85	110
Los Angeles Dodgers Baseball Game	B	1964	Ed-U-Cards	10	25	35
Lost Gold	B	1975	Parker Brothers	7	20	35
Lost In Space Game	B	1965	Milton Bradley	45	75	120
Lost Treasure	B	1982	Parker Brothers	7	20	35
Lottery Game	B	1972	Selchow & Righter	6	18	30
Louie the Electrician	B	ca. 1960	Hasbro	20	50	70
Love Boat World Cruise	B	1980	Ungame	5	15	20
Loving Game, The	B	1987	R.J.E. Enterprises	4	6	10
Lucan, The Wolf Boy	B	1977	Milton Bradley	5	10	15
Lucky Break	B	1975	Gabriel	10	20	30
Lucky Strike	B	1972	International Toy	5	10	15
Lucky Town	B	1946	Milton Bradley	15	50	75
Lucy Show Game, The	B	1962	Transogram	60	100	160
Lucy's Tea Party Game	B	1971	Milton Bradley	20	35	55
Ludwig Von Drake Ball Toss Game	B	1960		6	10	15
Luftwaffe	B	1971	Avalon Hill	3	8	15
M Squad	B	1958	Bell Toys	35	75	125
M*A*S*H* Game	B	1981	Milton Bradley	15	35	50

NAME	TYPE	YEAR	COMPANY	GOOD	EX	MINT
MacDonald's Farm	B	1948	Selchow & Righter	20	45	65
MAD Magazine Game, The	B	1979	Parker Brothers	4	12	20
MAD, What Me Worry?	B	1987	Milton Bradley	6	10	15
Madame Planchette Horoscope Game	B	1967	Selchow & Righter	6	18	30
Magilla Gorilla	B	1964	Ideal	40	65	100
Magnetic Fish Pond	S	1948	Milton Bradley	15	25	65
Magnetic Flying Saucers	B	1950s	Pressman	21	35	55
Magnificent Race	B	1975	Parker Brothers	10	25	40
Mail Run	B	1960	Quality Games	35	75	100
Main Street Baseball	B	1989	Main St. Toy	20	35	55
Major League Baseball	B	1965	Cadaco	10	20	30
Major League Baseball Magnetic Dart Game	B	1958	Pressman	20	45	65
Man from U.N.C.L.E. Illya Kuryakin Card Game	C	1966	Milton Bradley	10	25	40
Man from U.N.C.L.E. Napoleon Solo Game	B	1965	Ideal	25	45	70
Man from U.N.C.L.E. Pinball Game	S	1966		80	135	215
Man from U.N.C.L.E. Target Game	S	1966	Marx	130	275	550
Man from U.N.C.L.E. THRUSH Ray Gun Affair Game	B	1966	Ideal	50	85	135
Manage Your Own Team	B	1950s	Warren	10	30	40
Management	B	1960	Avalon Hill	10	25	40
Mandinka	B	1978	Lowe	3	12	20
Manhunt	B	1972	Milton Bradley	5	16	25
Maniac	B	1979	Ideal	7	15	20
Marathon Game	S	1978	Sports Games	10	20	35
Marblehead	S	1969	Ideal	5	16	25
Margie, The Game of Whoopie	B	1961	Milton Bradley	12	30	50
Mark "Three"	S	1972	Ideal	6	18	30
Marlin Perkins' Zoo Parade	B	1965	Cadaco-Ellis	12	30	40
Martin Luther King Jr.	B	1980	Cadaco	6	10	15
Marx-O-Matic All Star Basketball	S	1950s	Marx	150	250	400
Mary Hartman, Mary Hartman	B	1976	Reiss Games	10	25	35
Mary Poppins Carousel Game	B	1964	Parker Brothers	12	30	50
Masquerade Party	B	1955	Bettye-B	45	75	100
Mastermind	B	1970s	Invicta	5	10	15
Masterpiece, The Art Auction Game	B	1971	Parker Brothers	8	20	30
Match	C	1953	Garrard Press	10	15	25
Match Game (3rd Ed.), The	B	1963	Milton Bradley	15	25	40
Matchbox Traffic Game	B	1960s	Bronner	25	45	70
McDonald's Game, The	B	1975	Milton Bradley	10	20	30
McHale's Navy Game	B	1962	Transogram	30	50	80
McMurtle Turtle	B	1965	Cadaco-Ellis	8	25	40
Mechanic Mac	B	1961	Selchow & Richter	15	35	50
Mechanical Shooting Gallery	S	1950s	Wyandotte	70	135	195
Meet The Presidents	B	1953	Selchow & Righter	8	20	30
Megiddo	B	1985	Global Games	8	20	30
Melvin The Moon Man	B	1960s	Remco	50	85	135
Men Into Space	B	1960	Milton Bradley	20	60	90
Mentor	S	1960s	Hasbro	20	70	100
Merger	B	1965	Universal Games	12	30	40
Merry Milkman	B	1955	Hasbro	35	85	125
Merv Griffin's Word For Word	B	1963	Mattel	5	16	25
Miami Vice: The Game	B	1984	Pepperlane	10	25	35
Mickey Mantle's Action Baseball	B	1960	Pressman	50	125	175
Mickey Mantle's Big League Baseball	B	1958	Gardner	125	250	325
Mickey Mouse	B	1950	Jacmar	35	55	90
Mickey Mouse	B	1976	Parker Brothers	6	10	15
Mickey Mouse Basketball	B	1950s	Gardner	55	90	135
Mickey Mouse Canasta Jr.	C	1950	Russell	20	55	85
Mickey Mouse Haunted House Bagatelle	S	1950s		210	350	550
Mickey Mouse Jr. Royal Rummy	C	1970s	Whitman	5	15	30
Mickey Mouse Library of Games	C	1946	Russell	30	65	125
Mickey Mouse Lotto Game	B	1950s	Jaymar	10	15	25
Mickey Mouse Pop Up Game	B	1970s	Whitman	7	15	20

GAMES

POSTWAR GAMES

NAME	TYPE	YEAR	COMPANY	GOOD	EX	MINT
Mickey Mouse Slugaroo	B	1950s		20	30	50
Mid Life Crisis	B	1982	Gameworks	5	15	20
Mighty Comics Super Heroes Game	B	1966	Transogram	30	70	100
Mighty Hercules Game	B	1963	Hasbro	125	300	500
Mighty Heroes on the Scene Game	B	1960s	Transogram	35	75	120
Mighty Mouse	B	1978	Milton Bradley	15	20	30
Mighty Mouse Rescue Game	B	1960s	Harett-Gilmar	35	60	125
Mighty Mouse Target Game	S	1960s	Parks	30	60	90
Mille Bornes	C	1962	Parker Brothers	2	7	12
Milton The Monster	B	1966	Milton Bradley	25	45	70
Mind Maze Game	S	1970	Parker Brothers	5	16	25
Mind Over Matter	B	1968	Transogram	10	15	25
Miss America Pageant Game	B	1974	Parker Brothers	15	35	50
Miss Popularity Game	B	1961	Transogram	20	35	55
Missing Links	B	1964	Milton Bradley	6	18	35
Mission: Impossible	B	1967	Ideal	40	100	135
Mission: Impossible	B	1975	Berwick	10	15	25
Mister Ed Game	B	1962	Parker Brothers	20	50	75
Mister Football	B	1951	Alkay	30	75	100
Mob Strategy	B	1969	NBC-Hasbro	6	18	30
Monday Morning Quarterback	B	1963	Zbinden	8	25	35
Money! Money! Money!	B	1957	Whitman	15	35	50
Monkees Game	B	1968	Transogram	30	75	105
Monkeys and Coconuts	B	1965	Schaper	6	15	20
Monster Game	B	1977	Ideal	25	60	85
Monster Game, The	B	1965	Milton Bradley	15	25	40
Monster Lab	S	1964	Ideal	175	275	450
Monster Mansion	B	1981	Milton Bradley	7	12	20
Monster Old Maid	C	1964	Milton Bradley	10	40	55
Monster Squad	B	1977	Milton Bradley	10	25	40
Monsters of the Deep	B	1976	Whitman	5	16	25
Moon Blast-Off	B	1970	Schaper	12	30	40
Moon Shot	B	1960s	Cadaco	15	35	60
Moon Tag, Game of	B	1957	Parker Brothers	40	90	135
Mork and Mindy	B	1978	Milton Bradley	10	15	25
Mostly Ghostly	B	1975	Cadaco	15	20	30
Mouse Trap	S	1963	Ideal	25	45	70
Movie Moguls	B	1970	RGI	15	35	50
Movie Studio Mogul	B	1981	International Mktg.	8	25	40
Mr. Bug Goes To Town	B	1955	Milton Bradley	8	20	30
Mr. Doodle's Dog	B	1940s	Selchow & Righter	20	45	70
Mr. Machine Game	B	1961	Ideal	40	65	100
Mr. Mad Game	S	1970	Ideal	12	40	60
Mr. Magoo Maddening Misadventures Game, The	B	1970	Transogram	45	75	120
Mr. Magoo Visits The Zoo	B	1961	Lowell	25	45	70
Mr. President	B	1967	3M	8	25	40
Mr. Ree	B	1957	Selchow & Righter	10	30	45
Mr. T Game	C	1983	Milton Bradley	5	15	25
Mt. Everest	B	1955	Gabriel	18	40	60
Mug Shots	B	1975	Cadaco	7	12	20
Munsters Card Game	C	1966	Milton Bradley	20	45	65
Munsters Drag Race Game	B	1965	Hasbro	250	600	800
Munsters Masquerade Game	B	1965	Hasbro	250	600	800
Munsters Picnic Game	B	1965	Hasbro	200	500	700
Muppet Show	B	1977	Parker Brothers	10	15	25
Murder on the Orient Express	B	1967	Ideal	20	50	75
Murder She Wrote	B	1985	Warren	4	6	10
Mushmouse & Punkin Puss	B	1964	Ideal	45	75	120
MVP Baseball, The Sports Card Game	B	1989	Ideal	8	13	20
My Fair Lady	B	1960s	Standard Toykraft	15	35	50
My Favorite Martian	B	1963	Transogram	50	90	125
My First (Walt Disney Character) Game	B	1963	Gabriel	20	35	60
Mystery Checkers	B	1950s	Creative Designs	15	20	30
Mystery Date	B	1965	Milton Bradley	60	125	175
Mystery Mansion	B	1984	Milton Bradley	10	25	35

GAMES

362

NAME	TYPE	YEAR	COMPANY	GOOD	EX	MINT
Mystic Skull The Game of Voodoo	B	1965	Ideal	15	40	60
Mystic Wheel of Knowledge	B	1950s	Novel Toy	15	25	40
Name That Tune	B	1959	Milton Bradley	12	30	50
Nancy Drew Mystery Game	B	1957	Parker Brothers	35	75	110
NASCAR Daytona 500	B	1990	Milton Bradley	10	25	35
National Football League Quarterback, Official	B	1965	Standard Toykraft	12	30	40
National Inquirer	B	1991	Tyco	10	15	20
National Lampoon's Sellout	B	1970s	Cardinal	6	15	25
National Pro Football Hall of Fame Game	B	1965	Cadaco	15	25	40
National Pro Hockey	B	1985	Sports Action	15	25	40
National Velvet Game	B	1950s	Transogram	20	40	65
NBA Basketball Game, Official	B	1970s	Gerney Games	35	75	100
NBC Game of the Week	B	1969	Hasbro	10	25	35
NBC Peacock	B	1966	Selchow & Righter	20	50	75
NBC Pro Playoff	B	1969	Hasbro	10	25	35
NBC TV News	B	1960	Dadan	15	35	50
Nebula	B	1976	Nebula	4	6	10
Neck & Neck	B	1981	Yaquinto	8	13	20
Negamco Basketball	B	1975	Nemadji Game	10	16	25
New Avengers Shooting Game	B	1976	Denys Fisher	165	275	440
New Frontier	B	1962	Colorful Products	30	50	80
New York World's Fair	B	1964	Milton Bradley	20	50	75
New York World's Fair Children's Game	C	1964	Ed-U-Cards	15	35	55
Newlywed Game (1st Ed.)	B	1967	Hasbro	8	20	30
NFL Armchair Quarterback	B	1986	Trade Wind	8	13	20
NFL Football Game, Official	S	1968	Ideal	20	30	50
NFL Franchise	B	1982	Rohrwood	10	16	25
NFL Game Plan	B	1980	Tudor	6	10	15
NFL Quarterback	B	1977	Tudor	8	20	30
NFL Strategy	B	1976	Tudor	15	35	50
NHL All-Pro Hockey	B	1969	Ideal	10	16	25
NHL Strategy	B	1976	Tudor	10	35	50
Nibbles 'N Bites	S	1964	Schaper	5	16	25
Nieuchess	B	1961	Avalon Hill	12	40	60
Nightmare On Elm Street	B	1989	Cardinal	15	30	45
Nile	B	1967	Lowe	6	18	30
Nixon Ring Toss	S	1970s		20	30	50
No Respect, The Rodney Dangerfield Game	B	1985	Milton Bradley	15	25	40
No Time for Sergeants Game	B	1964	Ideal	12	40	60
Noah's Ark	B	1953	Cadaco-Ellis	8	25	40
Nok-Hockey	B	1947	Carrom	20	35	55
Noma Party Quiz	B	1947	Noma Electric	20	35	50
Northwest Passage	B	1969	Impact	8	20	30
Nuclear War	C	1965	Douglas Malewicki	25	40	75
Number Please TV Quiz	B	1961	Parker Brothers	15	25	40
Numble	B	1968	Selchow & Righter	4	10	15
Numeralogic	B	1973	American Greetings	6	18	30
Nurses, The	B	1963	Ideal	10	35	50
Nutty Mads Bagatelle	S	1963	Marx	25	45	85
Nutty Mads Target Game	S	1960s	Marx	35	70	125
NY Mets Baseball Card Game, Official	C	1961	Ed-U-Cards	20	45	65
O.J. Simpson See-Action Football	B	1974	Kenner	50	125	175
Obsession	B	1978	Mego	5	10	15
Obstruction	B	1979	Whitman	4	10	15
Octopus	B	1954	Norton Games	12	40	60
Off To See The Wizard	B	1968		10	15	25
Oh Magoo Game	B	1960s	Warren	15	30	45
Oh What a Mountain	B	1980	Milton Bradley	5	16	25
Oh, Nuts! Game	B	1968	Ideal	10	25	35
Oh-Wah-Ree	B	1966	3M	8	20	30
Oil Power	B	1980s	Antfamco	20	45	65
Old Shell Game, The	B	1974	Selchow & Righter	7	20	35
Oldies But Goodies	B	1987	Orig. Sound Record	6	18	30

GAMES

Star Trek, 1979, Milton Bradley

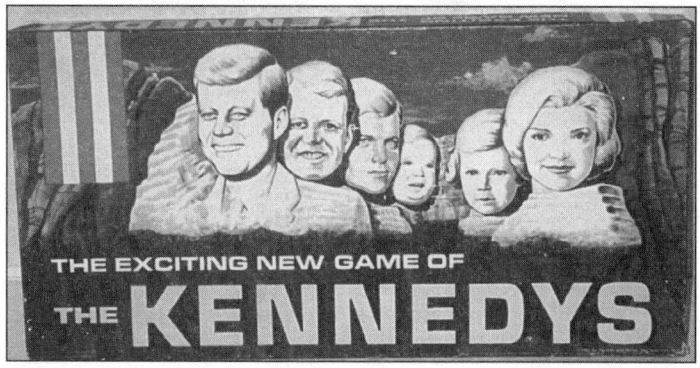

The Kennedys, 1962, Transogram

The New Adventures of Gilligan, 1974, Milton Bradley

NAME	TYPE	YEAR	COMPANY	GOOD	EX	MINT
On Guard	B	1967	Parker Brothers	6	10	15
On Target	S	1973	Milton Bradley	12	40	60
Operation	B	1965	Milton Bradley	5	12	18
Option	B	1983	Parker Brothers	2	7	12
Orbit	B	1959	Parker Brothers	10	30	50
Organized Crime	B	1974	Koplow Games	6	18	30
Orient Express	B	1985	Just Games	5	16	25
Original Home Jai-Alai Game, The	B	1984	Design Origin	15	25	35
Oscar Robertson's Pro Basketball Strategy	B	1964	Research Games	30	70	100
Our Gang Bingo	B	1958		50	85	135
Outdoor Survival	B	1972	Avalon Hill	2	6	10
Outer Limits	B	1964	Milton Bradley	80	180	275
Outlaw Trail	B	1972	Dynamic	6	18	30
Outwit	B	1978	Parker Brothers	5	10	15
Overboard	B	1978	Lakeside	3	12	18
Overland Trail Board Game	B	1960	Transogram	35	75	100
Ozark Ike's Complete 3 Game Set	B	1956	Warren Built-Rite	55	90	135
P.T. Boat 109 Game	B	1963	Ideal	18	45	65
Pac-Man	B	1980	Milton Bradley	5	15	20
Pan American World Jet Flight Game	B	1960	Hasbro	10	35	50
Panic Button	B	1978	Mego	7	15	20
Panzer Blitz	B	1970	Avalon Hill	6	12	20
Panzer Leader	B	1974	Avalon Hill	8	15	25
Par '73	B	1961	Big Top Games	15	25	40
Par Golf	B	1950s	National Games	20	50	75
Par-A-Shoot Game	S	1947	Baldwin	15	25	40
Parcheesi (Gold Seal Ed.)	B	1964	Selchow & Righter	7	12	20
Pari Horse Race Card Game	B	1959	Pari Sales	20	35	50
Paris Metro	B	1981	Infinity Games	10	16	25
Park and Shop	B	1952	Traffic Game	35	75	100
Park and Shop Game	B	1960	Milton Bradley	30	70	110
Parker Brothers Baseball Game	B	1955	Parker Brothers	25	60	85
Partridge Family	B	1974	Milton Bradley	10	25	40
Pass It On	B	1978	Selchow & Righter	3	12	20
Password	B	1963	Milton Bradley	6	15	25
Pathfinder	B	1977	Milton Bradley	5	15	20
Patty Duke Game	B	1963	Milton Bradley	18	45	65
Paul Brown's Football Game	B	1947	Trikilis	110	180	275
Paydirt	B	1979	Avalon Hill	12	30	40
Paydirt!	B	1973	Time, Inc., (Sports Illustrated)	10	25	35
Payoff Machine Game	B	1978	Ideal	5	16	25
Peanuts: The Game of Charlie Brown And His Pals	B	1959	Selchow & Righter	20	30	50
Pebbles Flintstone Game	B	1962	Transogram	20	35	55
Pee Wee Reese Marble Game	B	1956	Pee Wee Enterprises	175	295	450
Pennant Chasers Baseball Game	B	1946	Craig Hopkins	25	45	70
Pennant Drive	B	1980	Accu-Stat Game	8	13	20
People Trivia Game	B	1984	Parker Brothers	7	11	20
Perquackey	B	1970	Lakeside	4	9	12
Perry Mason Case of The Missing Suspect Game	B	1959	Transogram	20	30	50
Personalysis	B	1957	Lowell	15	25	40
Peter Gunn Dectective Game	B	1960	Lowell	25	60	90
Peter Pan	B	1953	Transogram	15	35	60
Peter Potamus Game	B	1964	Ideal	30	50	80
Peter Principle Game	B	1973	Skor-Mor	6	18	30
Peter Principle Game	B	1981	Avalon Hill	5	16	25
Petropolis	B	1976	Pressman	10	35	50
Petticoat Junction	B	1963	Standard Toykraft	25	55	90
Phalanx	B	1964	Whitman	10	30	45
Phantom Game, The	B	1965	Transogram	95	160	255
Phantom's Complete Three Game Set, The	B	1955	Built-Rite	30	75	125
Phil Silvers' You'll Never Get Rich Game	B	1955	Gardner	25	60	85
Philip Marlowe	B	1960	Transogram	20	50	75

NAME	TYPE	YEAR	COMPANY	GOOD	EX	MINT
Phlounder	B	1962	3M	6	18	30
Pig in the Garden	B	1970s	Time, Inc. (Sports Illustrated)	15	35	50
Pigskin Vegas	B	1980	Jokari/US	6	10	15
Pinbo Sport-o-Rama	B	1950s		35	60	90
Pinhead	B	1959	Remco	10	35	50
Pink Panther Game	B	1981	Cadaco	4	7	12
Pink Panther Game	B	1977	Warren	10	25	40
Pinky Lee and the Runaway Frankfurters	B	1950s	Lisbeth Whiting	30	75	105
Pinocchio	B	1977	Parker Brothers	5	8	15
Pinocchio Board Game, Disney's	B	1960	Parker Brothers	10	15	25
Pinocchio, The New Adventures of	B	1961	Lowell	25	45	70
Pirate and Traveller	B	1953	Milton Bradley	10	25	40
Pirate Raid	B	1956	Cadaco-Ellis	8	25	40
Pirate's Cove	B	1956	Gabriel	15	35	65
Pitchin' Pal	S	1952	Cadaco-Ellis	7	20	35
Pizza Pie Game	B	1974	Milton Bradley	5	16	25
Planet of the Apes	B	1974	Milton Bradley	18	45	65
Play Ball! A Baseball Game of Skill	B	1940s	Rosebud Art	50	75	150
Play Basketball with Bob Cousy	B	1950s	National Games	115	195	295
Play Your Hunch	B	1960	Transogram	8	25	40
Playoff Football	B	1970s	Crestline	20	35	50
Plaza	B	1947	Parker Brothers	7	20	35
Ploy	B	1970	3M	5	16	25
Plus One	B	1980	Milton Bradley	6	18	30
Pocket Size Bowling Card Game	B	1950s	Warren/Built-Rite	15	25	40
Pocket Whoozit	B	1985	Trivia	4	7	10
Point of Law	B	1972	3M	4	14	20
Pole Position	B	1983	Parker Brothers	8	13	20
Police Patrol	B	1955	Hasbro	40	100	150
Politics, Game of	B	1952	Parker Brothers	15	45	65
Pony Express, Game of	B	1947	Polygon	12	40	60
Pony Polo	S	1960s	Remco	10	20	35
Pooch	B	1956	Hasbro	10	35	50
Poosh-em-up Slugger Bagatelle	B	1946	Northwestern Products	30	75	105
Pop Yer Top!	B	1968	Milton Bradley	15	35	50
Pop-Up Store Game	B	1950s	Milton Bradley	12	40	60
Popeye, Adventures of	B	1957	Transogram	35	75	100
Population	B	1970	Urban Systems	6	18	30
Postman	B	1957	Selchow & Righter	8	25	40
Pothole Game, The	B	1979	Cadaco	10	25	40
Pow, The Frontier Game	B	1955	Selchow & Righter	12	40	60
Power 4 Car Racing Game	B	1960s	Manning	15	50	75
Power Play Hockey	B	1970	Romac	12	35	50
Prediction Rod	B	1970	Parker Brothers	5	16	25
Presidential Campaign	B	1979	John Hansen	6	18	30
Prince Caspian	B	1983	David Cook	5	16	25
Prince Valiant (Harold Foster's)	B	1950s	Transogram	12	40	60
Prize Property	B	1974	Milton Bradley	8	25	40
Pro Baseball Card Game	C	1980s	Just Games	6	10	15
Pro Bowl Live Action Football	S	1960s	Marx	35	65	95
Pro Draft	B	1974	Parker Brothers	15	35	45
Pro Football	B	1980s	Strat-O-Matic	6	10	15
Pro Foto-Football	B	1977	Cadaco	6	15	25
Pro Franchise Football	B	1987	Rohrwood	10	16	25
Pro Golf	B	1982	Avalon Hill	7	11	17
Pro Quarterback	B	1964	Tod Lansing	20	40	60
Probe	B	1964	Parker Brothers	2	7	12
Products and Resources, Game of	B	1962	Selchow & Righter	6	18	30
Profit Farming	B	1979	Foster Enterprises	6	18	30
Prospecting	B	1953	Selchow & Righter	25	65	90
Public Assistance	B	1980	Hammerhead	12	40	60
Pug-i-Lo	B	1960	Pug-i-Lo Games	55	90	135
Pursue the Pennant	B	1984	Pursue the Pennant	25	40	60
Pursuit!	B	1973	Aurora	8	25	40
Push Over	B	1981	Parker Brothers	3	12	18
Put and Take	B	1956	Schaper	5	16	25

GAMES

NAME	TYPE	YEAR	COMPANY	GOOD	EX	MINT
Puzzling Pyramid	B	1960	Schaper	6	18	30
Quad-Ominos	B	1978	Pressman	2	6	10
Quarterback Football Game	B	1969	Transogram	25	40	65
Qubic	B	1965	Parker Brothers	3	10	15
Quick Shoot	S	1970	Ideal	6	18	30
Quinto	B	1964	3M	6	18	30
Quiz Panel	B	1954	Cadaco-Ellis	6	18	30
Race-A-Plane	B	1947	Phon-O-Game	12	40	60
Race-O-Rama	B	1960	Warren/Built-Rite	10	25	45
Raceway	B	1950s	B & B Toy	30	50	75
Radaronics	B	1946	ARC	20	65	90
Raggedy Ann	B	1956	Milton Bradley	6	18	30
Rainy Day Golf	B	1980	Bryad	6	18	30
Raise the Titanic	B	1987	Hoyle	12	30	40
Rat Patrol Game	B	1966	Transogram	40	70	100
Rat Patrol Spin Game	S	1967	Pressman	30	65	85
Rawhide	B	1959	Lowell	75	175	300
Raymar of The Jungle	B	1952	Dexter Wayne	40	100	135
Razzle	B	1981	Parker Brothers	2	6	10
Razzle Dazzle Football Game	B	1954	Texantics Unlimited	50	80	125
React-Or	B	1979		15	25	40
Real Action Baseball Game	B	1966	Real-Action Games	20	35	50
Real Baseball Card Game	B	1990	National Baseball	110	180	275
Real Ghostbusters, The	B	1986	Milton Bradley	6	18	30
Real Life Basketball	B	1974	Gamecraft	20	50	75
Realistic Football	B	1976	Match Play	15	25	35
Rebel, The	B	1961	Ideal	50	85	135
Rebound	B	1971	Ideal	5	16	25
Record Game, The	B	1984	The Record Game	8	25	40
Red Barber's Big League Baseball Game	B	1950s	G & R Anthony	350	575	900
Red Herring	B	1945	Cadaco-Ellis	12	40	60
Red Rover Game, The	B	1963	Cadaco-Ellis	5	16	25
Reddy Clown 3-Ring Circus Game	B	1952	Parker Brothers	15	35	55
Reese's Pieces Game	B	1983	Ideal	5	8	15
Reflex	B	1966	Lakeside	5	16	25
Regatta	B	1968	3M	8	25	40
Regatta	B	1946		40	70	110
Replay Series Baseball	B	1983	Bond Sports	6	10	15
Restless Gun	B	1950s	Milton Bradley	18	40	60
Return To Oz Game	B	1985	Western	10	15	25
Reward	B	1958	Happy Hour	10	35	50
Rich Farmer, Poor Farmer	B	1978	McJay Game	5	16	25
Rich Uncle The Stock Market Game	B	1955	Parker Brothers	18	40	60
Rich Uncle, Game of	B	1946	Parker Brothers	18	40	60
Richie Rich	B	1982	Milton Bradley	3	5	10
Rickenbacker Ace Game	B	1946	Milton Bradley	60	150	200
Ricochet Rabbit Game	B	1965	Ideal	45	75	120
Rifleman Game	B	1959	Milton Bradley	20	50	75
Rin Tin Tin Game	B	1950s	Transogram	20	50	65
Ringmaster	B	1947	Cadaco-Ellis	12	40	60
Ringmaster Circus Game	B	1947	Cadaco-Ellis	15	25	40
Rio, The Game of	B	1956	Parker Brothers	10	35	50
Ripley's Believe It Or Not	B	1979	Whitman	6	10	15
Risk	B	1959	Parker Brothers	25	50	75
Riverboat Game	B	1950s	Parker Brothers/Disney	20	35	55
Road Runner Game	B	1968	Milton Bradley	10	25	35
Road Runner Pop Up Game	B	1982	Whitman	20	30	50
Robert Schuller's Possibility Thinkers Game	B	1977	Selchow & Righter	3	5	10
Robin Hood	B	1955	Harett-Gilmar	30	50	80
Robin Hood Game	B	1970s	Parker Brothers	7	15	30
Robin Hood, Adventures of	B	1956	Bettye-B	45	75	120
Robin Roberts Sports Club Baseball Game	B	1960	Dexter Wayne	100	165	250
Robocop VCR Game	B	1988	Spinnaker	7	20	35
Robot Sam the Answer Man	B	1950	Jacmar	15	35	50
Rock 'N' Roll Replay	B	1984	Baron-Scott	7	20	35

GAMES

367

NAME	TYPE	YEAR	COMPANY	GOOD	EX	MINT
Rock the Boat Game	B	1978	Milton Bradley	6	18	30
Rock Trivia	B	1984	Pressman	5	10	15
Rocket Patrol Magnetic Target Game	S	1950s	American Toy Products	45	75	120
Rocket Race	B	1958	Stone Craft	30	70	95
Rocket Race To Saturn	B	1950s	Lido	15	20	35
Rocket Sock-It Rifle and Target Game	S	1960s	Kenner	20	35	75
Rodeo, The Wild West Game	B	1957	Whitman	12	40	60
Roger Maris' Action Baseball	B	1962	Pressman	50	125	175
Rol-A-Lite	B	1947	Durable Toy & Novelty	45	75	120
Rol-It	B	1954	Parker Brothers	4	12	20
Roll And Score Poker	B	1977	Lowe	3	7	12
Roll-A-Par	B	1964	Lowe	8	20	30
Roller Derby	B	1974	Milton Bradley	70	150	225
Roman X	B	1964	Selchow & Righter	7	20	35
Route 66 Game	B	1960	Transogram	75	125	200
Roy Rogers Game	B	1950s		20	35	55
Rribit, Battle of the Frogs	B	1982	Genesis Enterprises	6	18	30
Ruffhouse	B	1980	Parker Brothers	3	10	15
Rules of the Road	B	1977	Cadaco	5	16	25
Run to Win	B	1980	Cabela	6	18	30
Russian Campaign, The	B	1976	Avalon Hill	3	5	10
S.O.S.	B	1947	Durable Toy & Novelty	40	70	110
S.W.A.T. Game	B	1970s	Milton Bradley	10	15	25
Sabotage	B	1985	Lakeside	2	6	10
Saddle Racing Game	B	1974	APBA	20	50	75
Safari	B	1950	Selchow & Righter	12	40	60
Safecrack	B	1982	Selchow & Righter	4	15	20
Sail Away	B	1962	Howard Mullen	12	30	40
Salvo	B	1961	Ideal	15	25	40
Samsonite Basketball	B	1969	Samsonite	15	35	60
Samsonite Football	B	1969	Samsonite	12	30	50
Sandlot Slugger	B	1960s	Milton Bradley	35	60	90
Saratoga: 1777	S	1974	Gamut of Games	10	25	50
Save the President	B	1984	Jack Jaffe	12	30	45
Say When!	B	1961	Parker Brothers	6	18	30
Scan	C	1970	Parker Brothers	3	10	15
Scarne's Challenge	C	1947	John Scarne Games	10	25	35
Scavenger Hunt	B	1983	Milton Bradley	3	5	10
Scooby Doo and Scrappy Doo	B	1983	Milton Bradley	3	8	16
Scooby-Doo, Where are You?	B	1973	Milton Bradley	18	40	60
Scoop	B	1956	Parker Brothers	35	75	100
Score Four	B	1968	Funtastic	3	10	15
Scotland Yard	B	1985	Milton Bradley	3	10	15
Scott's Baseball Card Game	C	1989	Scott's Baseball Cards	12	20	30
Scrabble	B	1953	Selchow & Righter	5	12	20
Screaming Eagles	B	1987	Milton Bradley	4	15	20
Screwball The Mad Mad Mad Game	B	1960	Transogram	30	75	105
Scribbage	B	1963	Lowe	3	10	15
Scrimmage	B	1973	SPI	5	15	25
Scruples	B	1986	Milton Bradley	5	10	15
Sea World Treasure Key	B	1983	International Games	4	15	20
Sealab 2020 Game	B	1973	Milton Bradley	6	10	15
Seance	B	1972	Milton Bradley	18	60	80
Secrecy	B	1965	Universal Games	12	30	40
Secret Agent Man	B	1966	Milton Bradley	25	40	65
Secret of NIMH	B	1982	Whitman	6	10	15
Secret Weapon	B	1984	Selchow & Righter	5	16	25
Seduction	B	1966	Createk	10	25	35
See New York 'Round the Town	B	1964	Transogram	8	25	40
Sergeant Preston Game	B	1950s	Milton Bradley	15	35	50
Set Point	B	1971	XV Productions	8	20	30
Seven Keys	B	1961	Ideal	12	30	40
Seven Seas	B	1960	Cadaco-Ellis	30	50	80
Seven Up	B	1960s	Transogram	7	12	20
Sha-ee, the Game of Destiny	B	1963	Ideal	20	65	90
Shadowlord!	B	1983	Parker Brothers	3	10	15
Sharpshooter	S	1962	Cadaco-Ellis	12	40	60

NAME	TYPE	YEAR	COMPANY	GOOD	EX	MINT
Shazam, Captian Marvel's Own Game	B	1950s	Reed & Associates	30	60	95
Shenanigans	B	1964	Milton Bradley	15	40	60
Sheriff of Dodge City	B	1966	Parker Brothers	8	25	40
Sherlock Holmes	B	1950s	National Games	30	75	100
Sherlock Holmes	B	1980	Whitman	5	16	25
Sherlock Holmes Game, The	B	1974	Cadaco	6	18	30
Shifty Checkers	B	1973	Aurora	8	25	40
Shifty Gear Game	B	1962	Schaper	5	16	25
Shindig	B	1965	Remco	25	65	90
Shmo	B	1960s	Remco	10	35	50
Shogun	B	1986	Milton Bradley	18	45	75
Shopping	B	1973	John Ladell	5	16	25
Shotgun Slade	B	1960	Milton Bradley	20	45	65
Show-Biz	B	1950s	Lowell	15	50	75
SI: The Sporting Word Game	B	1961	Time	10	16	25
Siege Game	B	1966	Milton Bradley	20	50	70
Silly Carnival	B	1969	Whitman	7	12	20
Silly Safari	B	1966	Topper	30	70	105
Simpsons Mystery of Life, The	B	1990	Cardinal	5	7	10
Sinbad	B	1978	Cadaco	20	30	50
Sinking of The Titanic, The	B	1976	Ideal	25	55	75
Sir Lancelot, Adventures of	B	1960s	Lisbeth Whiting	40	70	110
Situation 4	B	1968	Parker Brothers	5	16	25
Situation 7	B	1969	Parker Brothers	8	25	40
Six Million Dollar Man	B	1975	Parker Brothers	5	10	15
Skatebirds Game	B	1978	Milton Bradley	7	20	35
Skatterbug, Game of	B	1951	Parker Brothers	30	50	80
Skedaddle	B	1965	Cadaco-Ellis	8	25	40
Skeeter	C	1950s	Arco Playing Card	6	20	35
Ski Gammon	B	1962	American Publishing	8	20	30
Skill-Drive	B	1950s	Sidney Tarrson	10	35	50
Skins Golf Game, Official	B	1985	O'Connor Hall	12	20	30
Skip Bowl	S	1955	Transogram	6	18	30
Skip-A-Cross	B	1953	Cadaco	3	7	10
Skipper Race Sailing Game	B	1949	Cadaco-Ellis	25	60	90
Skirmish	B	1975	Milton Bradley	20	35	55
Skirrid	B	1979	Kenner	4	15	20
Skudo	B	1949	Parker Brothers	8	25	40
Skully	B	1961	Ideal	3	5	10
Skunk	B	1950s	Schaper	7	12	20
Sky Lanes	B	1958	Parker Brothers	35	75	120
Sky's The Limit, The	B	1955	Kohner	15	25	40
Sla-lom Ski Race Game	B	1957	Cadaco-Ellis	20	50	75
Slap Stick	S	1967	Milton Bradley	7	20	35
Slap Trap	B	1967	Ideal	8	25	40
Slapshot	B	1982	Avalon Hill	10	25	35
Slip Disc	B	1980	Milton Bradley	5	16	25
Smack-A-Roo	S	1964	Mattel	6	18	30
Smess, The Ninny's Chess	B	1970	Parker Brothers	10	35	50
Smog	B	1970	Urban Systems	8	20	30
Smokey: The Forest Fire Prevention Bear	B	1961	Ideal	30	65	105
Smurf Game	B	1984	Milton Bradley	4	7	12
Snafu	B	1969	Gamescience	7	20	35
Snagglepuss Fun at the Picnic Game	B	1961	Transogram	40	60	100
Snake Eyes	B	1957	Selchow & Righter	15	50	75
Snake's Alive, Game of	B	1967	Ideal	6	18	30
Snakes & Ladders	B	1974	Summmerville/Canada	4	7	10
Snakes In The Grass	B	1960s	Kohner	10	15	25
Snappet Catch Game with Harmon Killebrew	B	1960	Killebrew	55	90	135
Snob, A Fantasy Shopping Spree	B	1983	Helene Fox	7	20	35
Snoopy & The Red Baron	B	1970	Milton Bradley	15	35	50
Snoopy Come Home Game	B	1973	Milton Bradley	5	16	25
Snoopy Game	B	1960	Selchow & Righter	25	45	70
Snoopy's Doghouse Game	B	1977	Milton Bradley	5	16	25
Snow White and the Seven Dwarfs	B	1970s	Cadaco	6	10	15

GAMES

369

POSTWAR GAMES

NAME	TYPE	YEAR	COMPANY	GOOD	EX	MINT
Snuffy Smith Game	B	1970s	Milton Bradley	10	30	45
Sod Buster	B	1980	Santee	10	16	25
Solarquest	B	1986	Western	6	10	15
Solid Gold Music Trivia	B	1984	Ideal	6	10	15
Solitaire (Lucille Ball)	B	1973	Milton Bradley	2	5	10
Sons of Hercules Game, The	B	1966	Milton Bradley	30	70	100
Soupy Sales Sez Go-Go-Go Game	B	1960s	Milton Bradley	55	95	150
Southern Fast Freight Game	B	1970	American Publishing	8	25	40
Space Angel Game	B	1966	Transogram	25	65	85
Space Game	B	1953	Parker Brothers	25	65	85
Space Pilot	B	1951	Cadaco-Ellis	35	75	100
Space Shuttle 101	B	1978	Media-Ungame	8	20	30
Space Shuttle, The	B	1981	Ungame	8	20	30
Space: 1999 Game	B	1975	Milton Bradley	10	15	25
Special Agent	B	1966	Parker Brothers	10	25	40
Special Detective/Speedway	B	1959	Saalfield	15	40	60
Speed Circuit	S	1971	3M	15	30	45
Speedorama	B	1950s	Jacmar	30	50	80
Speedway, Big Bopper Game	B	1961	Ideal	18	40	60
Spider and the Fly	B	1981	Marx	12	20	30
Spider's Web Game, The	B	1969	Multiple Plastics	7	12	20
Spider-Man Game, The Amazing	B	1967	Milton Bradley	20	45	85
Spider-Man with The Fantastic Four	B	1977	Milton Bradley	10	15	25
Spin Cycle Baseball	B	1965	Pressman	25	40	65
Spin The Bottle	B	1968	Hasbro	8	20	30
Spin Welder	B	1960s	Mattel	7	12	20
Spiro T. Agnew American History Challenge Game	B	1971	Gabriel	20	35	55
Sporting News Baseball	B	1986	Mundo Games	8	13	20
Sports Arena No. 1	B	1954	Rennoc Games & Toys	35	60	90
Sports Illustrated All Time All Star Baseball	B	1973	Sports Illustrated	50	125	175
Sports Illustrated Baseball	B	1972	Time, Inc. (Sports Illustrated)	60	120	175
Sports Illustrated College Football	B	1971	Sports Illustrated	8	25	40
Sports Illustrated Decathlon	B	1972	Time	8	25	40
Sports Illustrated Handicap Golf	B	1971	Sports Illustrated	10	25	35
Sports Illustrated Pro Football	B	1970	Time	15	25	40
Sports Trivia Game	B	1984	Hoyle	6	10	15
Sports Yesteryear	B	1977	Skor-Mor	15	25	35
Spot Cash	B	1959	Milton Bradley	7	15	20
Spy vs. Spy	B	1986	Milton Bradley	10	15	25
Square Mile	B	1962	Milton Bradley	12	40	60
Square-It	B	1961	Hasbro	5	16	25
Squares	B	1950s	Schaper	4	15	20
Squatter: The Australian Wool Game	B	1960s	John Sands/Australia	15	25	45
St. Louis Cardinals Baseball Card Game	B	1964	Ed-U-Cards	10	25	35
Stadium Checkers	B	1954	Schaper	7	12	20
Stagecoach West Game	B	1961	Transogram	35	75	125
Stampede	B	1956	Gabriel	8	25	40
Star Reporter	B	1950s	Parker Brothers	40	90	135
Star Team Battling Spaceships	B	1977	Ideal	8	20	30
Star Trek	B	1979	Milton Bradley	18	40	60
Star Trek Adventure Game	B	1985	West End Games	8	20	30
Star Trek Game	B	1960s	Ideal	35	75	100
Star Trek: The Next Generation	B	1993	Classic Games	15	25	50
Star Wars Adventures of R2D2 Game	B	1977	Kenner	12	20	30
Star Wars Battle at Sarlacc's Pit	B	1983	Parker Brothers	10	15	25
Star Wars Escape from Death Star	B	1977	Kenner	10	15	25
Star Wars Monopoly	B	1997	Parker Brothers	15	20	35
Star Wars ROTJ Ewoks Save The Trees	B	1984	Parker Brothers	10	15	25
Star Wars Wicket the Ewok	B	1983	Parker Brothers	7	12	20
Star Wars X-Wing Aces Target Game	B	1978		20	30	50
Starship Troopers	B	1976	Avalon Hill	5	16	25

Travel with Woody Woodpecker, 1950s, Cadaco-Ellis

Veda, The Magic Answer Man, 1960s, Pressman

Bewitched Stymie Game, 1960s, Milton Bradley

Monster Old Maid, 1964, Milton Bradley

NAME	TYPE	YEAR	COMPANY	GOOD	EX	MINT
Starsky & Hutch	B	1977	Milton Bradley	5	16	25
State Capitals, Game of	B	1952	Parker Brothers	4	10	15
States, Game of the	B	1975	Milton Bradley	4	6	10
Statis Pro Football	B	1970s	Statis-Pro	25	40	65
Stay Alive	B	1971	Milton Bradley	6	15	25
Steps of Toyland	B	1954	Parker Brothers	20	35	55
Steve Allen's Qubila	B	1955	Lord & Freber	8	25	40
Steve Canyon	B	1959	Lowell	20	50	85
Steve Scott Space Scout Game	B	1952	Transogram	30	75	105
Stick the IRS!	B	1981	Courtland Playthings	5	16	25
Sting, The	B	1976	Ideal	10	25	40
Stock Car Race	B	1950s	Gardner	20	50	75
Stock Car Racing Game	B	1956	Whitman	12	30	40
Stock Car Racing Game (w/Petty/ Yarborough)	B	1981	Ribbit Toy	17	30	45
Stock Car Speedway, Game of	B	1965	Johnstone	55	90	135
Stock Market Game	B	1963, 1968	Whitman	15	35	50
Stock Market Game	B	1955	Gabriel	8	20	30
Stock Market Game	B	1970	Avalon Hill	7	12	20
Stock Market Specialist	B	1983	John Hansen	6	18	30
Stoney Burk	B	1963	Transogram	30	70	100
Stop Thief	B	1979	Parker Brothers	15	35	50
Straight Arrow	B	1950	Selchow & Righter	25	45	70
Straightaway	B	1961	Selchow & Righter	45	70	110
Strat-O-Matic Baseball	B	1961	Strat-O-Matic	100	165	250
Strat-O-Matic College Football	B	1976	Strat-O-Matic	25	55	75
Strat-O-Matic Hockey	B	1978	Strat-O-Matic	12	30	50
Strat-O-Matic Sports "Know-How"	B	1984	Strat-O-Matic	6	10	15
Strata 5	B	1984	Milton Bradley	5	16	25
Strategic Command	B	1950s	Transogram	15	35	50
Stratego (plastic pieces)	B	1962-on	Milton Bradley	6	15	25
Stratego (wood pieces)	B	1961	Milton Bradley	30	70	100
Strategy Manager Baseball	B	1967	McGuffin-Ramsey	2	6	12
Strategy Poker Fine Edition	C	1967	Milton Bradley	5	12	18
Strato Tac-tics	B	1972	Strato-Various	8	25	40
Strato-O-Matic Baseball	B	1980	Strat-O-Matic	15	35	50
Strato-O-Matic Baseball	B	1970	Strat-O-Matic	20	50	70
Strato-O-Matic Baseball (varies by season of cards)	B	1960s	Strat-O-Matic	80	150	225
Strato-O-Matic Football (varies by season of cards)	B	1986-90s	Strat-O-Matic	12	30	40
Strato-O-Matic Football (varies by season of cards)	B	1975-85	Strat-O-Matic	25	60	85
Strato-O-Matic Football (varies by season of cards)	B	1967-74	Strat-O-Matic	50	125	175
Stretch Call	B	1986	Sevedeo A. Vigil	12	20	30
Strike Three	B	1948	Tone Products	275	475	725
Stuff Yer Face	B	1982	Milton Bradley	6	20	35
Stump the Stars	B	1962	Ideal	8	25	40
Sub Attack Game	B	1965	Milton Bradley	7	20	35
Sub Search	B	1973	Milton Bradley	8	25	40
Sub Search	B	1977	Milton Bradley	6	18	30
Sudden Death!	B	1978	Gabriel	5	16	25
Suffolk Downs Racing Game	B	1947	Corey Game	40	90	135
Sugar Bowl	B	1950s	Transogram	20	45	65
Summit	B	1961	Milton Bradley	20	45	65
Sunken Treasure	B	1948	Parker Brothers	15	25	45
Sunken Treasure	B	1976	Milton Bradley	7	12	20
Super Coach TV Football	B	1974	Coleco	5	12	20
Super Market	B	1953	Selchow & Righter	10	35	50
Super Powers	B	1984	Parker Brothers	15	25	40
Super Spy	B	1971	Milton Bradley	15	25	40
Superboy Game	B	1960s	Hasbro	45	75	135
Supercar Road Race	B	1962	Standard Toykraft	45	100	140
Supercar to the Rescue Game	B	1962	Milton Bradley	20	50	75
Superheroes Card Game	C	1978	Milton Bradley	15	30	55
Superman & Superboy	B	1967	Milton Bradley	40	65	105

GAMES

372

NAME	TYPE	YEAR	COMPANY	GOOD	EX	MINT
Superman Game	B	1965	Hasbro	45	75	120
Superman Game	B	1966	Merry Manufacturing	35	55	90
Superman Game	C	1966	Whitman	35	75	110
Superman II	B	1981	Milton Bradley	10	20	35
Superman III	B	1982	Parker Brothers	4	12	20
Superman Spin Game	S	1967	Pressman	40	65	105
Superman, Adventures of	B	1940s	Milton Bradley	100	250	375
Superstar Baseball	B	1966	Sports Illustrated	30	50	75
Superstar Pro Wrestling Game	B	1984	Super Star Game	8	13	20
Superstar TV Sports	B	1980	ARC	6	10	15
Superstition	B	1977	Milton Bradley	12	30	40
Sure Shot Hockey	B	1970	Ideal	15	25	40
Surfside 6	B	1961	Lowell	30	75	125
Surprise Package, Your	B	1961	Ideal	25	60	85
Survive!	B	1982	Parker Brothers	12	30	40
Suspense	S	1950s	Northwestern Products	15	20	30
Swahili Game	B	1968	Milton Bradley	8	20	30
Swap, the Wheeler-Dealer Game	B	1965	Ideal	7	20	35
Swat Baseball	B	1948	Milton Bradley	20	35	50
Swayze	B	1954	Milton Bradley	12	30	40
Swish	B	1948	Jim Hawkers Games	45	75	115
Swoop	B	1969	Whitman	7	12	20
Sword In The Stone Game	B	1960s	Parker Brothers	18	40	60
Swords and Shields	B	1970	Milton Bradley	10	35	50
Syllable	C	1948	Garrard Press	10	15	25
T.V. Bingo	B	1970	Selchow & Richter	3	5	10
Tabit	B	1954	John Norton	25	35	75
Tactics II	B	1984	Avalon Hill	6	10	15
Taffy's Party Game	B	1960s	Transogram	10	15	25
Tales of Wells Fargo	B	1959	Milton Bradley	40	65	105
Talking Baseball	B	1971	Mattel	25	60	85
Talking Football	B	1971	Mattel	20	50	75
Talking Monday Night Football	B	1977	Mattel	10	30	50
Tally Ho!	B	1950s	Whitman	8	20	30
Tangle	B	1964	Selchow & Righter	6	18	30
Tank Battle	B	1975	Milton Bradley	15	35	50
Tank Command	B	1975	Ideal	7	20	35
Tantalizer	B	1958	Northern Signal	10	25	35
Tarzan	B	1984	Milton Bradley	5	10	15
Tarzan To The Rescue	B	1976	Milton Bradley	10	15	25
Taxi!	B	1960	Selchow & Righter	15	35	50
Tee Off by Sam Snead	B	1973	Glenn Industries	18	40	60
Teed Off!	B	1966	Cadaco	6	15	25
Teeko	B	1948	John Scarne Games	10	25	35
Telephone Game, The	B	1982	Cadaco	7	20	35
Television	B	1953	National Novelty	35	75	100
Tell It To The Judge	B	1959	Parker Brothers	12	35	60
Temple of Fu Manchu Game, The	B	1967	Pressman	20	30	50
Ten-Four, Good Buddy	B	1976	Parker Brothers	5	7	12
Tennessee Tuxedo	B	1963	Transogram	75	125	200
Tennis	B	1975	Parker Brothers	10	16	25
Tension	B	1970	Kohner	7	12	20
Terrytoons Hide N' Seek Game	B	1960	Transogram	35	75	100
Test Driver Game, The	B	1956	Milton Bradley	25	75	125
Texas Millionaire	B	1955	Texantics	25	55	75
Texas Rangers, Game of	B	1950s	All-Fair	12	40	60
That's Truckin'	B	1976	Showker	7	20	35
They're at the Post	B	1976	MAAS Marketing	12	30	40
Thing Ding Robot Game	B	1961	Schaper	35	75	100
Think Twice	B	1974	Dynamic	4	15	20
Think-Thunk	B	1973	Milton Bradley	6	18	30
Thinking Man's Football	B	1969	3M	6	15	25
Thinking Man's Golf	B	1966	3M	5	15	25
Third Reich	B	1974	Avalon Hill	3	8	15
Thirteen	B	1955	Cadaco-Ellis	4	10	15
This Is Your Life	B	1954	Lowell	15	35	50
Three Little Pigs	B	1959	Selchow & Righter	7	20	35
Three Musketeers	B	1958	Milton Bradley	35	55	90

GAMES

GAMES

NAME	TYPE	YEAR	COMPANY	GOOD	EX	MINT
Three Stooges Fun House Game	B	1950s	Lowell	100	275	400
Thunder Road	B	1986	Milton Bradley	10	16	25
Thunderbirds Game	B	1965	Waddington/England	40	70	115
Tic-Tac Dough	B	1957	Transogram	12	30	45
Tickle Bee	S	1956	Schaper	15	20	35
Tiddle Flip Baseball	B	1949	Modern Craft	20	35	50
Tiddle-Tac-Toe	B	1955	Schaper	3	10	15
Tight Squeeze	S	1967	Mattel	7	20	35
Tilt Score	B	1964	Schaper	4	15	20
Time Bomb	S	1965	Milton Bradley	35	50	75
Time Machine	B	1961	American Toy	75	150	250
Time Tunnel Game, The	B	1966	Ideal	90	150	240
Time Tunnel Spin Game, The	S	1967	Pressman	60	100	160
Tiny Tim Game of Beautiful Things, The	B	1970	Parker Brothers	25	65	90
Tip-It	S	1965	Ideal	5	16	25
Tipp Kick	S	1970s	Top Set	15	25	40
Tom & Jerry	B	1977	Milton Bradley	10	15	25
Tom & Jerry Adventure In Blunderland	B	1965	Transogram	25	45	70
Tom Seaver Game Action Baseball	B	1969	Pressman	50	125	175
Tomorrowland Rocket To Moon	B	1956	Parker Brothers	20	50	75
Toot! Toot!	B	1964	Selchow & Righter	8	25	40
Tootsie Roll Train Game	B	1969	Hasbro	20	30	50
Top Cat Game	B	1962	Transogram	50	120	175
Top Cop	B	1961	Cadaco-Ellis	35	65	105
Top Pro Basketball Quiz Game	B	1970	Ed-U-Cards	6	15	25
Top Pro Football Quiz Game	B	1970	Ed-U-Cards	6	15	25
Top Scholar	B	1957	Cadaco-Ellis	5	16	25
Top Ten College Basketball	B	1980	Top Ten Game	30	70	100
Top-ography	B	1951	Cadaco-Ellis	4	15	20
Topple	B	1979	Kenner	4	15	20
Topple Chairs	S	1962	Eberhard Faber	6	18	30
Tornado Bowl	B	1971	Ideal	5	16	25
Total Depth	B	1984	Orc Productions	12	30	40
Touch	C	1970	Parker Brothers	5	16	25
Touche Turtle Game	B	1964	Ideal	45	100	175
Tournament Labyrinth	S	1980s	Pressman	10	15	25
Town & Country Traffic Game	B	1950s	Ranger Steel	40	90	135
Track Meet	B	1972	Sports Illustrated	10	25	35
Trade Winds: The Caribbean Sea Pirate Treasure Hunt	B	1960	Parker Brothers	35	75	125
Traffic Game	B	1968	Matchbox	35	55	90
Traffic Jam	B	1954	Harett-Gilmar	15	35	50
Trail Blazers Game	B	1964	Milton Bradley	10	35	50
Trail Drive	C	1950s	Arco Playing Card	15	35	65
Trails to Tremble By	B	1971	Whitman	6	18	30
Trap Door	B	1982	Milton Bradley	3	10	15
Trap-em!	B	1957	Selchow & Righter	8	25	40
Trapped (Ellery Queen's)	B	1956	Bettye-B	30	70	100
Traps, The Game of	B	1950s	Traps	75	125	200
Travel America	B	1950	Jacmar	15	25	40
Travel-Lite	B	1946	Saxon Toy	45	75	120
Treasure Island	B	1954	Harett-Gilmar	30	50	80
Tri-Ominoes, Deluxe	B	1978	Pressman	3	5	10
Tribulation, The Game of	B	1981	Whitman	3	10	15
Triple Play	B	1978	Milton Bradley	5	10	15
Triple Yahtzee	B	1972	Lowe	4	6	10
Tripoley Junior	B	1962	Cadaco-Ellis	5	16	25
Trivial Pursuit	B	1981	Selchow & Righter	3	10	15
Troke (Castle Checkers)	B	1961	Selchow & Righter	6	18	30
Tru-Action Electric Baseball Game	B	1955	Tudor	12	30	40
Tru-Action Electric Basketball	S	1965	Tudor	25	50	75
Tru-Action Electric Harness Race Game	S	1950s	Tudor	15	40	65
Tru-Action Electric Sports Car Race	B	1959	Tudor	20	50	75
True Colors	B	1990	Milton Bradley	20	50	70
Trump, the Game	B	1989	Milton Bradley	5	16	25

NAME	TYPE	YEAR	COMPANY	GOOD	EX	MINT
Trust Me	B	1981	Parker Brothers	5	8	13
Truth or Consequences	B	1962	Lowell	10	35	50
Truth or Consequences	B	1955	Gabriel	12	40	60
Try-It Maze Puzzle Game	S	1965	Milton Bradley	7	12	20
TSG I: Pro Football	B	1971	TSG	35	55	85
Tumble Bug	B	1950s	Schaper	6	18	30
Turbo	B	1981	Milton Bradley	4	15	20
TV Guide Game	B	1984	Trivia	8	13	20
Twelve O'Clock High	B	1965	Ideal	25	60	85
Twelve O'Clock High	C	1966	Milton Bradley	20	40	65
Twiggy, Game of	B	1967	Milton Bradley	18	45	65
Twilight Zone Game	B	1960s	Ideal	75	100	200
Twinkles Trip to the Star Factory	B	1960	Milton Bradley	45	75	120
Twister	B	1966	Milton Bradley	5	15	25
Twixt	B	1962	3M	5	16	25
Two For The Money	B	1950s	Lowell	10	25	40
U.N. Game of Flags	B	1961	Parker Brothers	12	20	30
U.S. Air Force, Game of	B	1950s	Transogram	25	45	70
Ubi	B	1986	Selchow & Righter	6	18	30
Ultimate Golf	B	1985	Ultimate Golf	10	25	35
Uncle Milton's Ant Farm Game	B	1969	Uncle Milton Industries	15	35	50
Uncle Wiggly	B	1979	Parker Brothers	8	20	30
Undercover: The Game of Secret Agents	B	1960	Cadaco-Ellis	20	35	55
Underdog	B	1964	Milton Bradley	20	50	75
Underdog Save Sweet Polly	B	1972	Whitman	25	45	70
Undersea World of Jacques Cousteau	B	1968	Parker Brothers	18	40	60
Ungame	B	1975	Ungame	4	6	10
United Nations, A Game about the	B	1961	Payton Products	12	30	40
Universe	B	1966	Parker Brothers	6	18	30
Untouchables, The	S	1950s	Marx	95	160	250
Ur, Royal Game of Sumer	B	1977	Selchow & Righter	3	10	15
Uranium	B	1950s	Saalfield	18	40	60
Uranium Rush	B	1955	Gardner	30	70	100
USAC Auto Racing	B	1980	Avalon Hill	18	45	65
Vagabondo	B	1979	Invicta	5	16	25
Vallco Pro Drag Racing Game	B	1975	Zyla	15	25	35
Valvigi Downs	B	1985	Valvigi	6	18	30
Vaquero	B	1952	Wales Game Systems	15	50	75
Varsity	B	1955	Cadaco-Ellis	12	30	50
VCR Basketball Game	B	1987	Interactive VCR Games	6	10	15
VCR Quarterback Game	B	1986	Interactive VCR Games	8	13	20
Veda, The Magic Answer Man	B	1960s	Pressman	20	30	45
Vegas	B	1974	Milton Bradley	4	15	20
Verbatim	B	1985	Lakeside	3	10	15
Verdict	B	1959	Avalon Hill	15	50	75
Verdict II	B	1961	Avalon Hill	12	40	60
Verne Gagne World Champion Wrestling	B	1950	Gardner	40	90	135
Vice Versa	B	1976	Hallmark Games	5	16	25
Video Village	B	1960	Milton Bradley	10	30	40
Vietnam	B	1984	Victory Games	10	15	25
Vince Lombardi's Game	B	1970	Research Games	30	65	85
Virginian, The	B	1962	Transogram	35	80	125
Visit To Walt Disney World Game	B	1970	Milton Bradley	15	20	35
Voice of The Mummy	B	1960s	Milton Bradley	25	60	90
Voodoo Doll Game	B	1967	Schaper	18	45	65
Voyage of the Dawn Treader	B	1983	David Cook	5	16	25
Voyage to Cipangu	B	1979	Heise-Cipangu	25	55	75
Wackiest Ship In The Army	B	1964	Ideal	18	45	65
Wacky Races Game	B	1970s	Milton Bradley	15	25	40
Wagon Train	B	1960	Milton Bradley	25	40	65
Wahoo	B	1947	Zondine	15	20	30
Wally Gator Game	B	1963	Transogram	50	85	130
Walt Disney's 101 Dalmatians	B	1960	Whitman	20	35	55
Walt Disney's 20,000 Leagues Under The Sea	B	1954	Jacmar	45	75	120

NAME	TYPE	YEAR	COMPANY	GOOD	EX	MINT
Walt Disney's Jungle Book	B	1967	Parker Brothers	15	25	45
Walt Disney's Official Frontierland	B	1950s	Parker Brothers	15	35	50
Walt Disney's Sleeping Beauty Game	B	1958	Whitman	30	50	80
Walt Disney's Swamp Fox Game	B	1960	Parker Brothers	30	50	80
Waltons	B	1974	Milton Bradley	6	15	25
Wanted Dead or Alive	B	1959	Lowell	50	75	125
War At Sea	B	1976	Avalon Hill	10	20	30
War of the Networks	B	1979	Hasbro	6	18	30
Watergate Scandal, The	B	1973	American Symbolic	8	20	30
Waterloo	B	1962	Avalon Hill	10	20	45
Waterworks	C	1972	Parker Brothers	5	12	18
Weird-Ohs Game, The	B	1964	Ideal	85	145	230
Welcome Back, Kotter	B	1977	Ideal	10	25	40
Welcome Back, Kotter	C	1976	Milton Bradley	5	16	25
Welfare	B	1978	Jedco	12	40	60
Wendy, The Good Little Witch	B	1966	Milton Bradley	60	135	175
West Point Story, The	B	1950s	Transogram	10	35	50
What Shall I Be?	B	1966	Selchow & Righter	10	15	25
What Shall I Wear?	B	1969	Selchow & Righter	5	16	25
What's My Line Game	B	1950s	Lowell	15	35	50
Whatzit?	B	1987	Milton Bradley	5	16	25
Wheel of Fortune	B	1985	Pressman	5	8	13
Where's The Beef?	B	1984	Milton Bradley	6	10	15
Which Witch?	B	1970	Milton Bradley	35	75	100
Whirl Out Game	B	1971	Milton Bradley	6	18	30
Whirl-A-Ball	B	1978	Pressman	10	15	25
Whirly Bird Play Catch	B	1960s	Innovation Industries	20	35	50
White Shadow Basketball Game, The	B	1980	Cadaco	10	25	40
Who Can Beat Nixon?	B	1971	Dynamic	10	35	50
Who Framed Roger Rabbit?	B	1987	Milton Bradley	20	35	55
Who What Or Where?	B	1970	Milton Bradley	5	8	13
Who, Game of	B	1951	Parker Brothers	30	50	80
Whodunit	B	1972	Selchow & Righter	10	15	25
Whodunit?	B	1959	Cadaco-Ellis	8	25	40
Whosit?	B	1976	Parker Brothers	6	10	15
Wide World	B	1957, 1962	Parker Brothers	15	25	40
Wide World of Sports Golf	B	1975	Milton Bradley	12	30	45
Wide World Travel	B	1957	Parker Brothers	15	35	50
Wil-Croft Baseball	B	1971	Wil-Croft	10	16	25
Wild Bill Hickock	B	1955	Built-Rite	15	35	50
Wild Kingdom Game	B	1977	Teaching Concepts	20	35	50
Wild, Wild West, The	B	1966	Transogram	150	350	500
Wildlife	B	1971	Lowe	15	35	50
Willie Mays "Say Hey"	B	1954	Toy Development	200	350	525
Willie Mays "Say Hey" Baseball	B	1958	Centennial Games	190	295	450
Willie Mays Push Button Baseball	B	1965	Eldon	175	295	450
Willow	B	1988	Parker Brothers	10	25	35
Win A Card Trading Card Game	B	1965	Milton Bradley	350	575	900
Win, Place & Show	B	1966	3M	6	20	30
Wine Cellar	B	1971	Dynamic	5	16	25
Wing-Ding	S	1951	Cadaco-Ellis	8	25	40
Winko Baseball	B	1940s	Milton Bradley	45	70	95
Winky Dink Official TV Game Kit	B	1950s		35	75	100
Winnie The Pooh Game	B	1959	Parker Brothers	30	50	80
Winnie The Pooh Game	B	1979	Parker Brothers	5	8	13
Winning Ticket, The	B	1977	Ideal	6	20	30
Wiry Dan's Electric Baseball Game	B	1953	Harett-Gilmar	8	25	35
Wiry Dan's Electric Football Game	B	1953	Harett-Gilmar	8	25	35
Wise Old Owl	C	1950s	Novel Toy	20	35	55
Witch Pitch Game	B	1970	Parker Brothers	15	25	40
Wizard of Oz Game	B	1962	Lowe	20	30	50
Wizard of Oz Game	B	1974	Cadaco	6	15	25
Wolfman Mystery Game	B	1963	Hasbro	80	160	225
Woman & Man	B	1971	Psychology Today	4	15	20
Wonder Woman Game	B	1967	Hasbro	20	35	65

GAMES

376

POSTWAR GAMES

NAME	TYPE	YEAR	COMPANY	GOOD	EX	MINT
Wonderbug Game	B	1977	Ideal	8	25	35
Woody Woodpecker Game	B	1959	Milton Bradley	15	35	50
Woody Woodpecker's Crazy Mixed Up Color Factory	B	1972	Whitman	12	20	30
Woody Woodpecker's Moon Dash Game	B	1976	Whitman	12	20	30
Woody Woodpecker, Travel With	B	1950s	Cadaco-Ellis	35	65	100
World Bowling Tour	B	1979	World Bowling Tour	7	20	35
World Champion Wrestling Official Slam O' Rama	B	1990	International Games	5	8	12
World of Micronauts	B	1978	Milton Bradley	10	15	25
World of Wall Street	B	1969	NBC-Hasbro	4	15	20
World's Greatest Baseball Game	B	1977	J. Woodlock	35	75	100
Wow! Pillow Fight For Girls Game	S	1964	Milton Bradley	10	20	30
Wrestling Superstars	B	1985	Milton Bradley	8	13	20
WWF Wrestling Game	B	1991	Colorforms	5	8	12
Wyatt Earp Game	B	1958	Transogram	35	60	85
Xaviera's Game	B	1974	Dynamic	7	20	35
Yacht Race	B	1961	Parker Brothers	40	85	125
Yahtzee	B	1956	Lowe	6	10	15
Yertle, The Game of	B	1960	Revell	55	95	150
Yogi Bear Break A Plate Game	B	1960s	Transogram	50	80	130
Yogi Bear Cartoon Game	B	1980	Milton Bradley	3	5	10
Yogi Bear Game	B	1971	Milton Bradley	8	20	30
Yogi Bear Go Fly A Kite Game	B	1961	Transogram	25	60	85
Yogi Berra Pitch Kit	S	1963	Ross Products	35	50	100
Your America	B	1970	Cadaco	2	7	12
Yours For a Song	B	1962	Lowell	20	35	55
Zaxxon	B	1982	Milton Bradley	6	10	15
Zig Zag Zoom	B	1970	Ideal	10	20	30
Ziggy Game, A Day With	B	1977	Milton Bradley	15	20	30
Zingo	B	1950s	Empire Plastics	15	20	30
Zip Code Game	B	1964	Lakeside	35	55	90
Zomax	B	1988	Zomax	8	25	40
Zoography	B	1972	Amway	5	16	25
Zorro Game, Walt Disney's	B	1966	Parker Brothers	18	40	65
Zorro Target Game with Dart Gun	B	1950s	Knickerbocker	20	30	50
Zowie Horseshoe Game	S	1947	James L. Decker	20	35	55

GAMES

TABLETOP GAMES

NAME	TYPE	YEAR	COMPANY	GOOD	EX
Bobby Hull	Hockey	1970s	Munro	75	150
Bobby Hull	Hockey	1960s	Munro	125	250
Bobby Orr	Hockey	late 1960s-early 1970s	Munro	125	250
Canadian	Hockey	late 1960s	Eagle	75	135
Canadian Hockey Master	Hockey	early 1960s	Munro	100	225
City Series	Hockey	early 1970s	Coleco	100	200
Foster Hewitt	Hockey	1950s	Reliable	125	225
G-890 Dick Butkus	Football	1972	Gotham	30	60
Hockey games	Hockey	1940s-50s	Cresta	200	500
Horse and Harness Race Game	Horse Racing	1963-64	Tudor	20	45
Hot Shot	Hockey	mid 1960s	Munro	75	150
Hot Shot	Hockey	late 1960s	Munro	60	110
National	Hockey	early 1960s	Eagle	125	200
NHPLA	Hockey	1969	Tudor	75	125
No. 300 Electric Auto Racing	Auto Racing	1948-49	Tudor	50	100
No. 475 Magnetic Baseball	Basketball	1964-67	Tudor	20	40
No. 480 NBPA Game	Basketball	1971	Tudor	15	30
No. 480 NBPA Game	Basketball	1968-70	Tudor	30	60
No. 5100 Pro Stars	Hockey	mid 1960s-early 1970s	Coleco	65	125
No. 5160-80 Pro Stars	Hockey	late 1960s-early 1970s	Coleco	75	150
No. 525 Horse Race Game	Horse Racing	1959-61	Tudor	22	45
No. 525 Horse Race Game	Horse Racing	1962	Tudor	20	40
No. 525 Horse Race Game	Horse Racing	1950-58	Tudor	25	60
No. 526 Harness Race Game	Horse Racing	1962	Tudor	20	40
No. 528 Track and Field Meet	Track and Field	1963-64	Tudor	35	75
No. 528 Tru-Action Races	Track and Field	1965-67	Tudor	35	75
No. 528 Tudor Track	Track and Field	1962	Tudor	15	35
No. 530 Tru-Action Sports Car Race	Auto Racing	1959-65	Tudor	20	40
No. 550 Tru-Action Baseball	Baseball	1958-63	Tudor	25	50
No. 550 Tru-Action Baseball	Baseball	1950-58	Tudor	30	60
No. 555 Tru-Action Baseball	Baseball	1964-88	Tudor	22	45
No. 575 Tru-Action Electric Basketball	Basketball	1957-58	Tudor	30	60
No. 575 Tru-Action Electric Basketball	Basketball	1959-63	Tudor	25	50
No. 590 Mickey Mouse Electric Treasure Hunt Game	Auto Racing	1963-64	Tudor	40	80
No. G-1400	Football	1965-67	Gotham	30	60
No. G-1440	Football	1962-64	Gotham	35	70
No. G-1503	Football	1968	Gotham	33	65
No. G-1503-S NFL Big Bowl	Football	1965-67	Gotham	50	125
No. G-1506 NFL Players Association	Football		Gotham	25	50
No. G-1512 Super Dome	Football	1969-71	Gotham	45	100
No. G-1550 Yankee Stadium Grandstand	Football	1962-64	Gotham	40	80
No. G-200	Hockey	1930s-1950s	Gotham	125	350
No. G-812 Joe Namath	Football	1969-71	Gotham	35	70
No. G-812 Joe Namath	Football	1972	Gotham	35	70
No. G-818 Roman Gabriel Model	Football	1969-71	Gotham	25	50
No. G-818 Roman Gabriel Model	Football	1972	Gotham	25	50
No. G-880 Gotham All-Star Electric Football	Football	1959-61	Gotham	25	50
No. G-880 Gotham All-Star Electric Football	Football	1956-58	Gotham	30	60
No. G-882	Football	1965-67	Gotham	18	35
No. G-883	Football	1968	Gotham	15	30
No. G-883	Football	1972	Gotham	10	20
No. G-890 Gotham Official NFL Electric Football	Football	1962-64	Gotham	20	40
No. G-895 NFL Players Association	Football	1969-71	Gotham	22	45
No. G-940 Gotham Electro Magnetic Football	Football	1954-55	Gotham	38	75

GAMES

TABLETOP GAMES

NAME	TYPE	YEAR	COMPANY	GOOD	EX
No. G1200	Hockey	1950s-1960s	Gotham	75	150
Official Hockey Night	Hockey	early 1960s	Eagle	150	300
Official NHL	Hockey	1969-71	Coleco	150	500
Olympic	Hockey	1964	Eagle	200	500
Pee Wee	Hockey	late 1950s	Eagle	150	250
Playmaker	Hockey	early 1960s	Eagle	150	250
Playoff	Hockey	early 1960s	Eagle	125	200
Power Play	Hockey	late 1950s	Eagle	125	225
Power Play	Hockey	early 1960s	Eagle	125	200
Power Play	Hockey	late 1960s	Coleco	100	175
Pro Series	Hockey	mid 1950s-early 1960s	Eagle	125	225
Stanley Cup	Hockey	mid 1960s	Eagle	150	250
Stanley Cup, Beliveau	Hockey	late 1960s	Coleco	125	225
Tru-Action Races Game	Horse Racing	1965-67	Tudor	35	70

GAMES

G.I. Joe

"G.I. Joe, G.I. Joe Fighting man from head to toe. On the land, on the sea, in the air…"

This is a familiar phrase to all the now "grown-up" men who played with G.I. Joe in the 1960s. It is one of the few advertising slogans to have survived for so many years.

G.I. Joe, the twelve-inch action figure made especially for boys, was a brand new concept to the toy industry in the 1960s. Could it be sold to the public as a military action figure? Or would it be perceived as a doll for boys? Hasbro took a huge gamble and sizable investment to launch an extensive advertising campaign portraying G.I. Joe as "America's Moveable Fighting Man."

In retrospect, we can see how much G.I. Joe influenced the world of action figures. Hasbro single-handedly broke the stigma of boys playing with a doll-like figure by creating an articulated, movable man-of-action figure. G.I. Joe did for boys what his female counterpart, Barbie, did for girls — allowed them to role play any situation imaginable.

In the Beginning…

February 9, 1964 is the magical date in G.I. Joe history. This was the beginning of New York's International Toy Fair and the day Hasbro introduced G.I. Joe to a few select toy buyers. Even though Merrill Hassenfeld, president of Hasbro, was able to convince buyers that G.I. Joe was an action figure and not a doll, they were still skeptical. New York City was chosen as the initial test market for G.I. Joe; the figures sold out in a week. Hasbro put their new toy into limited national distribution in August and September of 1964. Before long, almost every young American boy had a G.I. Joe. Hasbro had a winner.

That initial year there were four figures — Action Soldier, Action Sailor, Action Marine and Action Pilot. Each figure came with that military branch's basic uniform and dog tags, and sold separately were dozens of uniform and accessory sets. The original Joes had twenty-one moveable parts and painted hair, thus the nickname "painted head G.I. Joe." Authenticity was one of Hasbro's goals with their first line of figures, and with an articulated body and an attention to detail they were able to produce a realistic fighting man. This particular style of G.I Joe was used through most of the Adventure Team years.

The military era for G.I. Joe spanned from 1964 to 1968. Action Soldiers of the World entered the G.I. Joe line-up in 1966 and Talking G.I. Joe in 1967. During that time additions were added to the core product line. Vehicles like a scaled-to-size Space Capsule and Underworld Sea Sled helped Joe get from one place to the other and defeat the enemy. In 1967, Hasbro attempted to capture the girls' market by introducing the G.I. Nurse. She gathered dust sitting on toy store shelves; she couldn't compete with Mattel's Barbie doll and boys didn't want to introduce a girl into their adventures. Because so few were sold, G.I. Joe Nurse is now one of the most valuable and sought after G.I. Joe action figures.

Joe's military heyday ended in the late 1960s due the Vietnam conflict. Many anti-war activists had protested Hasbro's production. As public sentiment turned against the military action in Southeast Asia, many parents did not want their children playing with war toys of any kind. Hasbro recognized the need for change, and G.I. Joe saw his last year of military service in 1968.

G.I. Joe became a civilian adventurer in 1969. He was an Aquanaut, an Astronaut, a Frogman and an Underwater Diver. He lead missions on spy island and searched for sunken treasure. Referred to as The Adventures of G.I. Joe, each doll came with a generic military uniform, dog tags and a booklet outlining the adventures of Joe.

The Adventure Team was the next step for G.I. Joe. Available from 1970 to 1976, this was a new line of figures sporting life-like hair along with the same the basic body as those from the 1960s. Joe's head was cast from the same mold with flocked hair. Man of Action, Talking Commander, Black Adventurer and Land, Air, and Sea Adventurers joined the G.I. Joe ranks. Hasbro introduced several new features and series during this phase—Kung-Fu Grip, Eagle Eyes, Atomic Man, Bullet Man and The Intruders.

The End of an Era

By 1976 Hasbro could no longer produce a twelve-inch action figure due to sky rocketing oil prices and thus the high cost of plastics. To utilize much of the remaining accessories on hand, Hasbro introduced The Defender, a twelve-inch figure made of

blown plastics jointed only at the shoulders, neck and hips. The Defender series was popular for a short while, but interest soon waned.

Super Joe Adventure team was Hasbro's next approach to G.I Joe. The eight-inch figures, introduced in 1977, consisted of several space-alien-type figures, known as Luminous, Darkon, Gor, King of Terrors, and, of course, the Super Joe and Super Joe Commander.

The Star Wars trilogy of the late 1970s and early 1980s triggered interest in 3-3/4-inch action figures. Their success prompted Hasbro to re-introduce G.I. Joe in a smaller format. In 1982 Joe was reborn as a 3-3/4-inch action figure. No one could have predicted the success of this new line. Over the next few years several hundred figures and vehicles were produced. Each figure had been given his own military history, vital statistics and code names. This product line consisted primarily of futuristic adventures and was tied into comic books and television cartoon series.

Old Becomes New Again

In 1991, Hasbro introduced The Hall of Fame Series, twelve-inch models of their 3-3/4-inch counterparts, with four figures — Duke, Stalker, Cobra Commander and Snake Eyes. Duke was dressed in a Desert-Storm-style fatigues, Kevlar helmet, dog tags and an MAS-62 mm combat assault rifle. The popularity of the "new" 12-inch figures prompted Hasbro to expand the Hall of Fame series to include additional figures, accessories and vehicles. Electronic Talking Battle Command Duke became part of the Hall of Fame line in 1993, the first talking G.I. Joe since the original debuted in the 1960s.

G.I. Nurse, 1967, Hasbro

GI JOE

Hasbro marked the G.I. Joe's 30th Anniversary in 1994 at New York's International Toy Fair by introducing a special line of twelve- and 3-3/4-inch action figures. G.I. Joe Action Soldier, Action Sailor, Action Marine, Action Pilot and an African-American Action Soldier were released to commemorate Joe's anniversary and to honor the four branches of military represented by the original G.I. Joe.

This same year also marked the largest G.I. Joe Collector's Convention ever. In the past Hasbro had created a special convention uniform for Joe. This year Hasbro presented attendees and dealers with, among other items, limited-edition figures representing the entire G.I Joe line.

Although the Hall of Fame series was a huge success, Hasbro has continued to release numerous G.I. Joe figures in twelve-inch scale under the Classic Collection Series and Timeless Collection Series. Both lines are created with the same attention to details as were the vintage G.I. Joes of the 1960s and 1970s.

Joe into the Next Millennium

In 1999, G.I. Joe's turned 35. He is the only action figure to have reached this milestone, and few toys have reflected changes in the United States and the rest of the world like Joe. The first change was during the Vietnam era, the second wasn't due to public reaction but because of world economics. The OPEC oil embargo of the 1970s made the production of a twelve-inch action figure an expensive endeavor. The end of the Cold War and the downfall of the Soviet Union ended the battle against the so-called Evil Empire. Joe's adventures moved away from military actions and became more futuristic and imaginary.

Adults who played with G.I. Joes in the 1960s and '70s still enjoy collecting vintage Joes. The limited-edition figures are poplar among collectors of all ages, yet the 3-3/4-inch Joes do not enjoy the same kind of mass appeal as their twelve-inch counterparts. But as the kids who played with the 3-3/4-inch G.I. Joes enter their late-20s and early 30s will they begin searching toy shows and flea markets for those figures they so fondly remember? Doubtful. So far, collectors haven't sought out the smaller Joes for their collections, and action figure collectors in their 30s are going for their childhood favorites —Transformers and Masters of the Universe to name a few.

What adventures will Joe encounter in the future? We can only wait and see.

The Top 10 G.I. Joe Figures / Sets
(All made by Hasbro. Prices are for items in Mint in Package condition)

1. Foreign Soldiers of the World, Action Soldiers of the World, 1968 .... $5,000
2. G.I. Nurse, Action Girl Series, 1967 4,000
3. Canadian Mountie Set, Action Soldier Series, 1967 4,000
4. Dress Parade Adventure Pack, Action Soldier Series, 1968 3,500
5. Crash Crew Fire Truck Set, Action Pilot Series, 1967 3,500
6. Talking Landing Signal Officer Set, Action Sailor Series, 1968 3,500
7. Talking Shore Patrol Set, Action Sailor Series, 1968 3,500
8. Adventure Pack, Army Bivouac Series, Action Soldier Series, 1968 3,500
9. Military Police Uniform Set, Action Soldier Series, 1967 3,500
10. Shore Patrol, Action Sailor Series, 1967 3,500

Contributor to this section: Dale Womer, The Joe Depot, P.O. Box 228, Kulpsville, PA 19443-0228

FIGURE SETS

NO.	NAME	DESCRIPTION	YEAR	EX	MNP	MIP
		12" HALL OF FAME FIGURES				
6837	Ace	Fighter Pilot	1993	15	20	25
6827	Cobra Commander	Cobra Leader	1992	20	30	35
6839	Destro	Weapons Manufacturer	1993	15	20	25
6826	Duke	Master Sergeant	1992	20	30	35
6019	Duke	Master Sergeant	1991	25	35	45
6111	Grunt	Infantry Squad Leader	1993	5	10	25
6849	Gung-Ho	Dress Marine	1993	15	20	25
6114	Heavy Duty	Heavy Ordinance Specialist	1993	15	20	35
6924	Rapid Fire	Commando	1993	35	50	60
6128	Rock 'n Roll	Heavy Weapons Gunner	1993	15	20	25
6828	Snake Eyes	Commando	1992	20	30	35
6829	Stalker	Ranger	1992	20	30	35
6848	Storm Shadow	Ninja	1993	15	20	25
6117	Talking Duke	Talking Battle Commander	1993	25	35	50
		30TH SALUTE SERIES				
81271	30th Salute Black Action Soldier		1994	55	100	150
81047	Action Marine		1994	45	60	80
81046	Action Pilot		1994	50	75	125
81048	Action Sailor		1994	60	80	100
81045	Action Soldier		1994	25	50	95
	Green Beret Lt. Joseph Colton	mail order	1994	75	125	175
		3-3/4" SERIES #1, COBRA				
6423	Cobra	Infantry Soldier	1982	25	55	110
	Cobra Commander	mail order; Commanding Leader	1982	25	55	110
6424	Cobra Officer	Infantry Officer	1982	25	55	110
6426	Major Bludd	mail order; Mercenary w/card	1982	10	25	50
		3-3/4" SERIES #1, GI JOE				
6403	Breaker	Communications Officer	1982	20	35	75
6406	Flash	Laser Rifle Trooper	1982	20	35	75
6409	Grunt	Infantry Trooper	1982	20	35	75
6408	Rock 'n Roll	Machine Gunner	1982	20	35	75
6407	Scarlett	Counter Intelligence	1982	40	85	175
6402	Short Fuse	Mortar Soldier	1982	20	35	75
6404	Snake Eyes	Commando	1982	40	85	175
6401	Stalker	Ranger	1982	25	35	100
6405	Zap	Bazooka Soldier	1982	20	35	75
		3-3/4" SERIES #2, COBRA				
6423	Cobra	Reissue	1983	25	50	100
6425	Cobra Commander	Reissue	1983	25	50	100
6424	Cobra Officer	Reissue	1983	25	50	100
6427	Destro	Enemy Weapons Supplier	1983	25	50	75
6426	Major Bludd		1983	15	30	65
		3-3/4" SERIES #2, GI JOE				
6411	Airborne	Helicopter Assault Trooper	1983	15	35	75
6403	Breaker	Reissue	1983	15	30	65
6415	Doc	Medic	1983	10	20	45
	Duke	mail order; Master Sergeant	1983	10	25	40
6406	Flash	Reissue	1983	15	30	65
6409	Grunt	Reissue	1983	15	30	65
6414	Gung-Ho	Marine	1983	12	30	65
6408	Rock 'n Roll	Reissue	1983	15	30	65
6407	Scarlett		1983	30	80	165
6402	Short Fuse	Reissue	1983	15	30	65
6404	Snake Eyes	Reissue	1983	40	80	165
6412	Snow Job	Arctic Trooper	1983	15	25	50
6401	Stalker	Reissue	1983	25	45	90
6413	Torpedo	Navy S.E.A.L.	1983	12	30	65

GI JOE

FIGURE SETS

NO.	NAME	DESCRIPTION	YEAR	EX	MNP	MIP
6410	Tripwire	Mine Detector	1983	15	30	65
6405	Zap	Reissue	1983	15	30	60
3-3/4" SERIES #3, COBRA						
6428	Baroness	Intelligence Officer	1983-84	40	85	175
6425	Cobra Commander	mail order; Enemy Leader with Hood	1983-84	10	20	40
6432	Fire Fly	Saboteur	1983-84	40	85	175
6431	Scrap Iron	Anti-Armor Specialist	1983-84	15	30	60
6429	Storm Shadow	Ninja	1983-84	35	75	150
3-3/4" SERIES #3, GI JOE						
6421	Blow Torch	Flamethrower	1983-84	10	20	40
6422	Duke	First Sergeant	1983-84	15	25	50
6416	Mutt	Dog Handler with Dog	1983-84	10	25	50
6420	Recondo	Jungle Trooper	1983-84	15	25	50
6418	Rip-Cord	H.A.L.O. Jumper	1983-84	10	25	50
6419	Road Block	Heavy Machine Gunner	1983-84	15	25	50
6417	Spirit	Tracker with Eagle	1983-84	15	25	50
3-3/4" SERIES #4, COBRA						
6433	Buzzer	Mercenary	1984	10	25	50
6450	Crimson Guard	Elite Trooper	1984	15	30	60
6448	Eel	Frogman	1984	15	30	60
6434	Ripper	Mercenary	1984	15	30	60
6449	Snow Serpent	Polar Assault Trooper	1984	15	30	60
6447	Tele-Viper	Communications Trooper	1984	15	30	60
6063	Tomax	Crimson Guard Commander with Xamot	1984	30	65	125
6435	Torch	Mercenary	1984	15	30	60
3-3/4" SERIES #4, GI JOE						
6439	Air Tight	Hostile Environment Trooper	1984	20	40	85
6443	Alpine	Mountain Trooper	1984	15	25	50
6445	Barbecue	Fire Fighter	1984	10	25	50
6438	Bazooka	Missile Specialist	1984	10	25	50
6442	Dusty	Desert Trooper	1984	10	25	50
6436	Flint	Warrant Officer	1984	10	25	50
6444	Footloose	Infantry Trooper	1984	10	25	50
6440	Lady Jaye	Covert Operations Officer	1984	25	50	100
6441	Quick Kick	Silent Weapons Martial Artist	1984	20	40	85
6446	Shipwreck	Sailor and Parrot	1984	15	25	50
6437	Snake Eyes	Commando and Wolf	1984	30	60	125
6102	Tripwire	Mine Detector	1984	20	35	75
3-3/4" SERIES #5, COBRA						
6456	B.A.T.	Battle Android Trooper	1985	10	15	35
6461	Dr. Mindbender	Master of Mind Control	1985	10	15	35
6460	Monkey Wrench	Mercenary	1985	10	15	35
6473	Viper	Infantry Trooper	1985	10	15	35
6457	Zandar	Zartan's Brother Mercenary	1985	10	15	35
6472	Zarana	Reissue w/earrings	1985	30	65	125
6472	Zarana	Zartan's Sister Mercenary	1985	10	15	35
3-3/4" SERIES #5, GI JOE						
6463	Beach Head	Ranger	1985	10	15	30
6471	Dial Tone	Communications Expert	1985	10	15	30
6468	Hawk	Commander	1985	10	15	30
6466	Ice Berg	Snow Trooper	1985	10	15	30
6458	Leather Neck	Marine Gunner	1985	10	15	30
6465	Life Line	Rescue Trooper	1985	10	15	30
6459	Low-Light	Night Spotter	1985	10	15	30
6462	Main Frame	Computer Specialist	1985	10	15	30
6467	Road Block	Heavy Machine Gunner	1985	10	15	30
6469	Sci-Fi	Laser Trooper	1985	10	15	30
	Sgt. Slaughter	Mail order; Drill Instructor	1985	10	15	30
6470	Wet-Suit	Navy S.E.A.L.	1985	15	20	40

GI JOE

384

NO.	NAME	DESCRIPTION	YEAR	EX	MNP	MIP
		3-3/4" SERIES #6, COBRA				
6484	Big Boa	Troop Trainer	1986-87	5	10	20
6474	Cobra Commander	Cobra Leader with Battle Armor	1986-87	10	15	30
6154	Cobra-La Team	Three-figure set	1986-87	20	40	75
6487	Crocmaster	Reptile Trainer	1986-87	10	15	30
6479	Crystal Ball	Hypnotist	1986-87	5	10	20
6485	Raptor	Falconer	1986-87	5	10	20
6490	Techno-Viper	Battlefield Technician	1986-87	5	10	20
		3-3/4" SERIES #6, GI JOE				
6482	Chuckles	Undercover M.P.	1986-87	3	5	10
6475	Crazy Legs	Air Assault Trooper	1986-87	10	15	30
6476	Falcon	Green Beret	1986-87	10	15	30
6488	Fast Draw	Mobile Missile Specialist	1986-87	10	15	25
6486	Gung-Ho	Marine in Dress Blues	1986-87	10	15	25
6480	Jinx	Ninja Intelligence Officer	1986-87	10	15	25
6478	Law & Order	M.P. with Dog	1986-87	10	15	25
6483	Outback	Survivalist	1986-87	5	10	20
6477	Psych-Out	Deceptive Warfare Trooper	1986-87	5	10	20
	Secret Mission: Brazil	Toys R Us set w/four figures	1986-87	75	150	300
6153	Sgt. Slaughter Set	Three-figure set	1986-87	10	25	50
6491	Sneak Peek	Advanced Recon Trooper	1986-87	10	15	30
6481	Tunnel Rat	Underground Explosive Expert	1986-87	5	10	20
		35TH ANNIVERSARY GIFT SET				
	Then and Now	1964 figure, 1999 figure, set of two	1999	25	50	75
		ACTION ASSORTMENT				
	Salute to the Millennium Marine		1999	5	15	25
		ACTION GIRL SERIES				
8060	G.I. Nurse	Red Cross hat and arm band, white dress, stockings, shoes, crutches, medic bag, stethescope, plasma bottle, bandages and splints.	1967	1750	2000	4000
		ACTION MARINE SERIES				
7700	Action Marine	Fatigues, green cap, boots, dog tags, insignias and manual	1964	125	145	375
90711	Marine Medic Series	Red Cross helmet, flag and arm bands, crutch, bandages, splints, first aid pouch, stethoscope, plasma bottle, stretcher, medic bag, belt with ammo pouches	1967	325	425	3250
7790	Talking Action Marine		1967	175	200	850
90711	Talking Adventure Pack and Tent Set		1968	275	325	3250
90712	Talking Adventure Pack w/Field Pack Equipment		1968	275	325	3250
		ACTION PILOT SERIES				
7800	Action Pilot	Orange jumpsuit, blue cap, black boots, dog tags, insignias, manual, catalog and club application	1964	130	165	600
7890	Talking Action Pilot		1967	190	245	1500
		ACTION SAILOR SERIES				
7600	Action Sailor	White cap, denim shirt and pants, boots, dog tags, navy manual and insignias	1964	125	225	350
7643-83	Navy Scuba Set	Adventure Pack	1968	300	450	3250
7690	Talking Action Sailor		1967	200	330	1250
90621	Talking Landing Signal Officer Set	Talking Adventure Pack	1968	325	350	3500
90612	Talking Shore Patrol Set	Talking Adventure Pack	1968	200	450	3500

GI JOE

FIGURE SETS

NO.	NAME	DESCRIPTION	YEAR	EX	MNP	MIP
		ACTION SOLDIER SERIES				
7500	Action Soldier	Fatigue cap, shirt, pants, boots, dog tags, army manual and insignias, helmet, belt with pouches, M-1 rifle	1964	100	175	350
7900	Black Action Soldier		1965	450	800	2500
5904	Canadian Mountie Set	Sears' exclusive	1967	850	1500	4000
8030	Desert Patrol Attack Jeep Set	Desert Fighter figure, jeep with steering wheel, spare tire, tan tripod, gun and gun mount and ring, black antenna, tan jacket and shorts, socks, goggles	1967	400	1250	2000
5969	Forward Observer Set	Sears' exclusive	1966	200	375	750
7536	Green Beret	Field radio, bazooka rocket, bazooka, green beret, jacket, pants, M-16 rifle, grenades, camo scarf, belt pistol and holster	1966	275	400	3000
7531	Machine Gun Emplacement Set	Sears' exclusive	1965	150	275	1250
7590	Talking Action Soldier		1967	85	135	825
90513	Talking Adventure Pack, Bivouac Equipment		1968	275	325	3000
90517	Talking Adventure Pack, Command Post Equip.		1968	275	375	3000
7557-83	Talking Adventure Pack, Mountain Troop Series		1968	375	650	3500
90532	Talking Adventure Pack, Special Forces Equip.		1968	275	500	3500
		ACTION SOLDIERS OF THE WORLD				
8105	Australian Jungle Fighter	action figure with jacket, shorts, socks, boots, bush hat, belt, "Victoria Cross" medal, knuckle knife, flamethrower, entrenching tool, bush knife and sheath	1966	250	400	2500
8205	Australian Jungle Fighter	Standard set with action figure uniform, no equipment	1966	150	275	1200
8104	British Commando	Deluxe set with action figure, helmet, night raid green jacket, pants, boots, canteen and cover, gas mask and cover, belt, Sten sub machine gun, gun clip and "Victoria Cross" medal	1966	300	425	2500
8204	British Commando	Standard set with no equipment	1966	150	275	1750
8111-83	Foreign Soldiers of the World	Talking Adventure Pack	1968	750	825	5000
8103	French Resistance Fighter	Deluxe set with figure, beret, short black boots, black sweater, denim pants, "Croix de Guerre" medal, knife, shoulder holster, pistol, radio, sub machine gun and grenades	1966	200	250	2250
8203	French Resistance Fighter	Standard set with action figure and equipment	1966	125	225	1250
8200	German Storm Trooper	Standard set with no equipment	1966	275	325	1300
8100	German Storm Trooper	Deluxe set with figure, helmet, jacket, pants, boots, Luger pistol, holster, cartridge belt, cartridges, "Iron Cross" medal, stick grenades, 9MM Schmeisser, field pack	1966	275	425	2500
8101	Japanese Imperial Soldier	Deluxe set with figure, Arisaka rifle, belt, cartridges, field pack, Nambu pistol, holster, bayonet, "Order of the Kite" medal, helmet, jacket, pants, short brown boots	1966	425	675	2700
8201	Japanese Imperial Soldier	Standard set with equipment	1966	300	325	1425

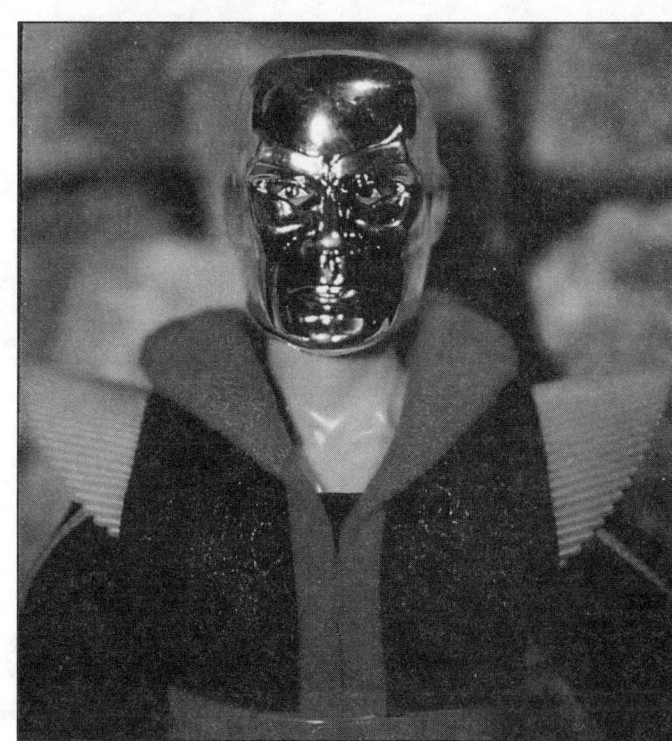

Destro, 1993, Hasbro

Scarlett, 1982, Hasbro

GI JOE

NO.	NAME	DESCRIPTION	YEAR	EX	MNP	MIP
8102	Russian Infantry Man	Deluxe set with action figure, fur cap, tunic, pants, boots, ammo box, ammo rounds, anti-tank grenades, belt, bipod, DP light machine gun, "Order of Lenin" medal, field glasses and case	1966	275	400	2250
8202	Russian Infantry Man	Standard set with no equipment	1966	315	400	1250
5038	Uniforms of Six Nations		1967	750	950	2500
		ADVENTURE TEAM				
7403	Air Adventurer	includes figure with Kung Fu grip, orange flight suit, boots, insignia, dog tags, rifle, boots, warranty, club insert	1970	120	375	300
7282	Air Adventurer	life-like body figure, uniform and equipment	1976	75	100	200
7282	Air Adventurer	with Kung Fu grip	1974	95	125	325
7404	Black Adventurer	includes figure, shirt with insignia, pants, boots, dog tags, shoulder holster with pistol	1970	100	150	375
7283	Black Adventurer	With life-like body and Kung Fu grip	1976	85	125	225
8026	Bulletman		1976	50	75	150
7278	Eagle Eye Black Commando		1976	85	125	250
7276	Eagle Eye Land Commander		1976	65	80	150
7277	Eagle Eye Man of Action		1976	65	80	165
8050	Intruder Commander		1976	50	75	150
8051	Intruder Warrior		1976	50	75	175
7280	Land Adventurer		1976	35	50	150
7270	Land Adventurer		1976	20	50	180
7280	Land Adventurer	with life-like body and Kung Fu grip and uniform set	1974	50	65	225
7401	Land Adventurer	includes figure, camo shirt and pants, boots, insignia, shoulder holster and pistol, dog tags and team inserts	1970	45	75	200
7284	Man of Action	figure with life-like body and Kung Fu grip	1974	45	75	200
7274	Man of Action		1976	25	45	175
7500	Man of Action	includes figure, shirt and pants, boots, insignia, dog tags, team inserts	1970	50	75	225
8025	Mike Powers/Atomic Man	figure with "atomic" flashing eye, arm that spins hand-held helicopter	1975	20	45	150
7402	Sea Adventurer	includes figure, shirt, dungarees, insignia, boots, shoulder holster and pistol	1970	45	70	245
7271	Sea Adventurer		1976	40	75	250
7281	Sea Adventurer	with life-like body and Kung Fu grip and uniform with equipment	1974	55	75	225
7281	Sea Adventurer		1976	55	85	200
8040	Secret Mountain Outpost		1975	50	85	150
7291	Talking Adventure Team Black Commander	with Kung Fu grip	1974	85	350	750
7406	Talking Adventure Team Black Commander		1973	150	225	600
7290	Talking Adventure Team Commander	with Kung Fu grip	1974	75	200	500
7400	Talking Adventure Team Commander	includes figure, 2-pocket green shirt, pants, boots, insignia, instructions, dog tag, shoulder holster and pistol	1970	65	125	400
7590	Talking Astronaut		1970	90	175	650
7291	Talking Black Commander		1976	125	300	600
7290	Talking Commander		1976	75	115	500
7292	Talking Man of Action	with life-like body and Kung Fu grip	1974	75	200	650
7292	Talking Man of Action		1976	75	120	525
7590	Talking Man of Action	shirt, pants, boots, dog tags, rifle, insignia, instructions	1970	75	125	350

FIGURE SETS

NO.	NAME	DESCRIPTION	YEAR	EX	MNP	MIP
	ADVENTURES OF G.I. JOE					
	Challenge at Hawk River	Recreations of Adventure Team series	1999	5	10	20
	Peril of the Raging Inferno		1999	5	10	20
	Save the Tiger		1999	5	10	20
	ADVENTURES OF GI JOE					
7910	Aquanaut		1969	175	550	3000
7905	Negro Adventurer	Sears' exclusive, includes painted hair figure, blue jeans, pullover sweater, shoulder holster and pistol, plus product letter from Sears	1969	450	750	2750
7980	Sharks Surprise Set w/ Frogman	with figure, orange scuba suit, blue sea sled, air tanks, harpoon, face mask, treasure chest, shark, instructions and comic	1969	125	300	750
7615	Talking Astronaut	hard-hand figure with white coveralls with insignias, white boots, dog tags	1969	85	275	1000
	ARMED FORCES ASSORTMENT					
	Army National Guard		1998	10	20	30
	Navy Serviceman		1998	10	20	30
	U.S. Marine Corps Recruit		1998	10	20	30
	US Korean Soldier		1998	10	20	30
	USAF Crew Chief		1998	10	20	30
	ARMED FORCES SERVICE COLLECTION					
	Police Officer		1999	5	10	20
	U.S. Army Infantry Desert Soldier		1999	5	10	20
	U.S. Army Pacific Forces		1999	5	10	20
	U.S. Navy SEAL		1999	5	10	20
	USAF Korean War Fighter Pilot		1999	5	10	20
	Vietnam Marine		1999	5	10	20
	ASTRONAUT ASSORTMENT					
	Mercury Astronaut		1997	15	30	40
	Space Shuttle Astronaut		1997	15	30	40
	BATTLE CORPS					
81089	Alley-Viper		1994	3	5	10
81088	Beach-Head		1994	3	5	10
81002	Dialtone		1994	3	5	10
81001	Flint		1994	3	5	10
81004	Ice-Cream Soldier		1994	3	5	10
81007	Life-Line		1994	3	5	10
81012	Major Bludd		1994	3	5	10
81005	Metal-Head		1994	3	5	10
81098	Night Creeper Leader		1994	3	5	10
81003	Shipwreck		1994	3	5	10
81097	Snow Storm		1994	3	5	10
81008	Stalker		1994	3	5	10
81006	Viper		1994	3	5	10
	CLASSIC COLLECTION					
	442nd Americans of Japanese Descent Combat So		1998	10	20	30
	CORE FIGURE COLLECTION					
	U.S. Army Nurse, Vietnam		1999	5	10	20
	U.S. Coast Guard Boarding Party		1999	5	10	20
	FOURTH OF JULY EDITION					
	D-Day Salute		1997	15	30	40

GI JOE

389

FIGURE SETS

NO.	NAME	DESCRIPTION	YEAR	EX	MNP	MIP
GI JOE EXTREME						
81209	Ballistic		1995	7	8	10
81168	Ballistic		1995	5	6	8
81176	Freight		1995	5	6	8
81179	Inferno		1995	5	6	8
81177	Iron Klaw		1995	5	6	8
81208	Iron Klaw (Deluxe)		1995	7	8	10
81161	Lt. Stone		1995	5	6	8
81207	Lt. Stone (Deluxe)		1995	7	8	10
81295	Lt. Stone vs. Iron Klaw	Super Deluxe	1995	10	15	20
81167	Metalhead		1995	5	6	8
81206	Metalhead (Deluxe)		1995	7	8	10
81162	Sgt. Savage		1995	5	6	8
GREATEST HEROES						
	Buzz Aldrin		1999	10	20	30
	Ted Williams		1999	10	20	30
	Theodore Roosevelt		1999	10	20	30
	WWII Flame Thrower Soldier		1999	10	20	30
HISTORICAL COMMANDERS ASSORTMENT						
	Colin Powell		1998	20	45	60
	Dwight Eisenhower		1997	20	35	50
	General Patton		1997	20	35	50
	Omar Bradley		1998	20	45	60
HOLIDAY SALUTE						
	George Washington		1998	20	45	60
HOLLYWOOD HEROES						
	Bob Hope		1998	15	25	35
MILITARY SPORTS ASSORTMENT						
	Army Football		1998	10	20	30
	Navy Football		1998	10	20	30
MODERN FORCES ASSORTMENT						
	82nd Airborne Division	Female figure	1998	15	25	35
	Belgium Para Commando		1997	15	40	45
	French Foreign Legion Legionnaire		1997	15	30	40
	Navy Blue Angel		1998	15	30	40
	U.S. Army Drill Sergeant		1997	10	20	30
	U.S. Army Helicopter Pilot	Female figure	1997	15	30	55
	U.S. Army M-1 Tank Commander		1997	10	20	30
	U.S. Marine Coprs Sniper		1997	10	20	35
	U.S. Navy Flight Deck Fuel Handler		1997	10	20	30
	US Army Coldweather		1998	10	20	30
	USMC Force Recon		1998	10	20	30
SHADOW NINJA						
81147	Bushido		1994	5	10	25
81146	Night Creeper		1994	5	10	25
81145	Nunchuck		1994	5	10	25
81144	Slice		1994	5	10	25
81141	Snake-Eyes		1994	5	10	25
81142	Storm Shadow		1994	5	10	25
STAR BRIGADE/COBRA						
81105	Cobra Astro-Viper		1993	5	10	25
81057	Cobra Blackstar		1994	5	10	25
81056	Cobra Commander		1994	5	10	25
81106	Cobra TARGAT		1993	5	10	25

FIGURE SETS

NO.	NAME	DESCRIPTION	YEAR	EX	MNP	MIP
		STAR BRIGADE/GI JOE				
81061	Carcass		1994	5	10	25
81102	Countdown		1993	5	10	25
81119	Countdown		1994	5	10	25
81052	Duke		1994	5	10	25
81054	Effects		1994	5	10	25
81058	Lobotomaxx		1994	5	10	25
81103	Ozone		1993	5	10	25
81127	Ozone		1994	5	10	25
81101	Payload		1993	5	10	25
81117	Payload		1994	5	10	25
81059	Predacon		1994	5	10	25
81104	Roadblock		1993	5	10	25
81118	Roadblock		1994	5	10	25
81053	Sci-Fi		1994	5	10	25
81055	Space Shot		1994	5	10	25
		SUPER JOE				
7510	Gor		1977	40	70	130
7506	Luminos		1977	45	70	130
7503	Super Joe		1977	20	35	70
7504	Super Joe (Black)		1977	35	50	100
7501	Super Joe Commander		1977	25	45	75
7505	The Shield		1977	40	65	125
		WWII COLLECTION				
	B-17 Bomber Crewman		1998	15	25	35
	Congressional Medal of Honor	Mitchell Paige	1998	15	30	40
	PT Boat Commander		1998	15	25	35
		WWII FORCES ASSORTMENT				
	Congressional Medal of Honor	Francis Currey	1997	15	30	40
	Tuskegee B-25 Bomber Pilot	Black figure	1997	10	20	30
	Tuskegee Fighter Pilot	Black figure	1997	10	20	30

UNIFORM/EQUIPMENT SETS

NO.	NAME	DESCRIPTION	YEAR	EX	MNP	MIP
		3-3/4" SERIES #1, GI JOE				
6075	F.L.A.K.	Attack Cannon	1982	20	45	90
6052	H.A.L.	Heavy Artillery Laser with Grand Slam	1982	20	45	90
6071	J.U.M.P.	Jet Pack with Platform	1982	20	45	90
6054	M.M.S.	Mobile Missile System with Hawk	1982	20	45	90
		3-3/4" SERIES #2, COBRA				
6200	Headquarters Missile-Command Center	with three figures	1983	65	125	250
6083	S.N.A.K.E.	One-Man Battle Armor	1983	10	25	50
		3-3/4" SERIES #2, GI JOE				
6088	Battle Gear Accessory Pack #1		1983	10	20	40
6020	Headquarters Command Center		1983	40	85	175
6065	Jump	Jet Pack and Platform with Grand Slam	1983	25	50	100
6086-1	Pac/Rats Flamethrower	Remote Control Weapon	1983	10	25	50
6086-2	Pac/Rats Machine Gun	Remote Control Weapon	1983	10	25	50
6086-3	Pac/Rats Missile Launcher	Remote Control Weapon	1983	10	25	50
6074	Whirlwind	Twin Battle Gun	1983	10	25	45

GI JOE

Australian Jungle Fighter, 1966, Hasbro

Japanese Imperial Soldier, 1966, Hasbro

Air Adventurer, 1974, Hasbro

Super Joe, 1977, Hasbro

UNIFORM/EQUIPMENT SETS

NO.	NAME	DESCRIPTION	YEAR	EX	MNP	MIP
		3-3/4" SERIES #3, COBRA				
6070	A.S.P.	Assault System Pod	1983	15	30	60
6081-1	C.L.A.W.	Cobra Covert Light Aerial Weapons	1983	15	30	60
6081-2	S.N.A.K.E.	One-Man Armored Suit (white)	1983	10	25	50
		3-3/4" SERIES #3, GI JOE				
6092	Battle Gear Accessory Pack #2		1983	10	20	40
6125-1	Bivouac	Battle Station	1983	10	25	35
6129-2	Machine Gun Defense Unit		1983	10	20	40
	Manta	mail order; Marine Assault Nautical Air Driven Transport	1983	10	20	35
6129-1	Missile Defense Unit		1983	10	15	25
6129-3	Mortar Defense Unit		1983	10	15	25
6125-3	Mountain Howitzer		1983	10	15	25
	Parachute	mail order; Parachute Pack with Working Parachute	1983	5	10	20
6125-2	Watchtower		1983	10	15	25
		3-3/4" SERIES #4, COBRA				
6125	Cobra Bunker		1984	5	15	25
6081	Flight Pod	One-Man Bubble Pod	1984	5	15	25
6085	Night Landing	Mini Battlefield Vehicles Assortment	1984	5	15	25
6129	Rifle Range		1984	5	15	25
		3-3/4" SERIES #4, GI JOE				
6125-2	Air Defense		1984	10	15	25
6129-1	Ammo Dump		1984	10	15	25
6092	Battle Gear Accessory Pack #3		1984	5	10	15
6085-2	Bomb Disposal		1984	10	15	25
6125-1	Check Point		1984	10	15	25
6129-2	Forward Observer		1984	10	15	25
6021	Tactical Battle Platform		1984	10	20	40
6085-1	Weapon Transport	Battlefield	1984	10	15	25
		3-3/4" SERIES #5, COBRA				
6096	Battle Gear Accessory Pack #4		1985	5	10	15
6130	Surveillance Port Playset		1985	15	30	75
6003	Terror Drome	Armored Headquarters with Fireball Jet and A.V.A.C.	1985	75	150	300
		3-3/4" SERIES #5, GI JOE				
6130	Outpost Defender Mini Playset		1985	5	10	15
		3-3/4" SERIES #6, COBRA				
6133-3	Earth Borer		1986	5	10	15
6133-7	Mountain Climber		1986	5	10	15
6133-8	Pom-Pom Gun Pack		1986	5	10	15
6133-5	Rope Crosser		1986	5	10	15
		3-3/4" SERIES #6, GI JOE				
6133-1	Antiaircraft Gun		1986	5	10	15
6677	Battle Gear Accessory Pack #5		1986	5	10	15
6133-2	Helicopter Pack		1986	5	10	15
6006	Mobile Command Center Play Set		1986	25	50	100
6133-4	Rope Walker		1986	5	10	15
6172	S.L.A.M.	Strategic Long-Range Artillery Machine	1986	10	15	30
6098	Vehicle Gear Accessory Pack #1		1986	5	10	15

GI JOE

393

GI JOE

NO.	NAME	DESCRIPTION	YEAR	EX	MNP	MIP
		ACTION MARINE SERIES				
7713	Beachhead Assault Field Pack Set	M-1 rifle, bayonet, entrenching shovel and cover, canteen w/cover, belt, mess kit w/cover, field pack, flamethrower, first aid pouch, tent, pegs and poles, tent camo and camo	1964	100	175	325
7711	Beachhead Assault Tent Set	Tent, flamethrower, pistol belt, first-aid pouch, mess kit with utensils and manual	1964	100	200	475
7715	Beachhead Fatigue Pants		1964	15	30	200
7714	Beachhead Fatigue Shirt		1964	20	30	225
7712	Beachhead Field Pack	Cartridge belt, rifle, grenades, field pack, entrenching tool, canteen and manual	1964	40	65	150
7718	Beachhead Flamethrower Set		1964	15	30	125
7718	Beachhead Flamethrower Set	Reissue	1967	15	30	225
7716	Beachhead Mess Kit Set		1964	25	40	275
7717	Beachhead Rifle Set	Reissue	1967	30	50	225
7717	Beachhead Rifle Set	Bayonet, cartridge belt, hand grenades and M-1 rifle.	1964	30	50	150
7703	Communications Field Radio/Telephone Set	Reissue	1967	35	60	275
7703	Communications Field Set		1964	35	50	175
7704	Communications Flag Set	Flags for Army, Navy, Air Corps, Marines and United States.	1964	200	250	475
7702	Communications Poncho		1964	35	50	250
7701	Communications Post and Poncho Set	Field radio and telephone, wire roll, carbine, binoculars, map, case, manual, poncho	1964	125	175	475
7710	Dress Parade Set	Marine jacket, trousers, pistol belt, shoes, hat, M-1 rifle and manual	1964	125	225	450
7710	Dress Parade Set	Reissue	1968	125	225	750
7732	Jungle Fighter Set	Bush hat, jacket w/emblems, pants, flamethrower, field telephone, knife and sheath, pistol belt, pistol, holster, canteen w/cover and knuckle knife	1967	450	700	3500
7732	Jungle Fighter Set	Reissue	1968	450	700	2750
7726	Marine Automatic M-60 Machine Gun Set		1967	35	75	325
7722	Marine Basics Set		1966	55	85	275
7723	Marine Bunk Bed Set	Reissue	1967	55	80	475
7723	Marine Bunk Bed Set		1966	55	80	375
7730	Marine Demolition Set	Reissue	1968	50	100	450
7730	Marine Demolition Set	mine detector and harness, land mine	1966	50	100	350
7721	Marine First Aid Set	Reissue	1967	45	85	225
7721	Marine First Aid Set	First-aid pouch, arm band and helmet	1964	45	85	125
7720	Marine Medic Set	Reissue	1967	25	40	225
7720	Marine Medic Set	with crutch, etc.	1965	25	40	125
7719	Marine Medic Set w/ stretcher	First-aid shoulder pouch, stretcher, bandages, arm bands, plasma bottle, stethoscope, Red Cross flag, and manual	1964	175	300	850
7725	Marine Mortar Set		1967	60	80	350
7727	Marine Weapons Rack Set		1967	75	145	625
7708	Paratrooper Camouflage Set	netting and foliage	1964	20	35	65
7707	Paratrooper Helmet Set		1964	20	40	85
7709	Paratrooper Parachute Pack		1964	30	80	125
7706	Paratrooper Small Arms Set	Reissue	1967	30	75	225

UNIFORM/EQUIPMENT SETS

NO.	NAME	DESCRIPTION	YEAR	EX	MNP	MIP
7731	Tank Commander Set	includes faux leather jacket, helmet and visor, insignia, radio with tripod, machine gun, ammo box	1967	325	500	1750
7731	Tank Commander Set	Reissue	1968	325	500	1525
		ACTION PILOT SERIES				
7822	Air Academy Cadet Set	Reissue	1968	225	450	1150
7822	Air Academy Cadet Set	deluxe set with figure, dress jacket, shoes, and pants, garrison cap, saber and scabbard, white M-1 rifle, chest sash and belt sash	1967	225	450	1250
7814	Air Force Basics Set		1966	30	55	200
7814	Air Force Basics Set	Reissue	1967	30	55	275
7816	Air Force Mae West Air Vest & Equipment Set		1967	85	125	325
7813	Air Force Police Set		1965	70	150	250
7813	Air Force Police Set	Reissue	1967	70	150	325
7815	Air Force Security Set	Air Security radio and helmet, cartridge belt, pistol and holster	1967	275	350	590
7825	Air/Sea Rescue Set	includes black air tanks, rescue ring, buoy, depth gauge, face mask, fins, orange scuba outfit	1967	325	550	2500
7825	Air/Sea Rescue Set	Reissue	1968	325	550	2500
7824	Astronaut Set	Helmet w/visor, foil space suit, booties, gloves, space camera, propellant gun, tether cord, oxygen chest pack, silver boots, white jumpsuit and cloth cap	1967	100	200	3000
7824	Astronaut Set	Reissue	1968	100	200	1250
7812	Communications Set		1964	55	100	225
7820	Crash Crew Set	fire proof jacket, hood, pants and gloves, silver boots, belt, flashlight, axe, pliers, fire extinguisher, stretcher, strap cutter	1966	125	250	450
7804	Dress Uniform Jacket Set		1964	40	65	250
7805	Dress Uniform Pants		1964	20	35	200
7803	Dress Uniform Set	Air Force jacket, trousers, shirt, tie, cap and manual	1964	225	450	3000
7806	Dress Uniform Shirt & Equipment Set		1964	25	40	200
7823	Fighter Pilot Set	Reissue	1968	400	650	2650
7823	Fighter Pilot Set	working parachute and pack, gold helmet, Mae West vest, green pants, flash light, orange jump suit, black boots	1967	400	650	2500
7812	Scramble Communications Set	Reissue	1967	35	75	250
7812	Scramble Communications Set	Poncho, field telephone and radio, map w/case, binoculars and wire roll	1965	35	75	175
7810	Scramble Crash Helmet	Reissue	1967	65	90	225
7810	Scramble Crash Helmet	helmet, face mask, hose, tinted visor	1964	65	90	125
7808	Scramble Flight Suit	gray flight suit	1964	50	300	225
7808	Scramble Flight Suit		1967	50	75	400
7809	Scramble Parachute Set	Reissue	1967	20	40	250
7811	Scramble Parachute Set		1964	20	40	150
7807	Scramble Set	Deluxe set, gray flight suit, orange air vest, white crash helmet, pistol belt w/ .45 pistol, holster, clipboard, flare gun and parachute w/insert	1964	125	225	950
7802	Survival Life Raft Set	Raft with oar and sea anchor	1964	45	90	325
7801	Survival Life Raft Set	Raft with oar, flare gun, knife, air vest, first-aid kit, sea anchor and manual	1964	75	125	550
		ACTION SAILOR SERIES				
7624	Annapolis Cadet	Garrison cap, dress jacket, pants, shoes, sword, scabbard, belt and white M-1 rifle	1967	275	375	1350

GI JOE

UNIFORM/EQUIPMENT SETS

NO.	NAME	DESCRIPTION	YEAR	EX	MNP	MIP
7624	Annapolis Cadet	Reissue	1968	275	375	1350
7625	Breeches Buoy	yellow jacket and pants, chair and pulley, flare gun, blinker light	1967	325	425	1500
7625	Breeches Buoy	Reissue	1968	325	425	1450
7623	Deep Freeze	Reissue	1968	250	375	1500
7623	Deep Freeze	White boots, fur parka, pants, snow shoes, ice axe, snow sled w/rope and flare gun	1967	250	375	1600
7620	Deep Sea Diver Set	Reissue	1968	325	425	2000
7620	Deep Sea Diver Set	Underwater uniform, helmet, upper and lower plate, sledge hammer, buoy w/rope, gloves, compass, hoses, lead boots and weight belt	1965	325	425	2000
7604	Frogman Scuba Bottoms		1964	20	35	100
7606	Frogman Scuba Tank Set		1964	25	40	100
7603	Frogman Scuba Top Set		1964	25	45	125
7602	Frogman Underwater Demolition Set	Headpiece, face mask, swim fins, rubber suit, scuba tank, depth gauge, knife, dynamite and manual	1964	175	250	1500
7621	Landing Signal Officer	jumpsuit, signal paddles, goggles, cloth head gear, headphones, clipboard (complete), binoculars and flare gun.	1966	225	350	575
7610	Navy Attack Helmet Set	shirt and pants, boots, yellow life vest, blue helmet, flare gun binoculars, signal flags	1964	35	75	150
7611	Navy Attack Life Jacket		1964	20	45	120
7607	Navy Attack Set	life jacket, field glasses, blinker light, signal flags, manual	1964	60	125	425
7609	Navy Attack Work Pants Set		1964	25	40	150
7608	Navy Attack Work Shirt Set		1964	25	40	175
7628	Navy Basics Set		1966	25	55	125
7619	Navy Dress Parade Rifle Set		1965	35	65	125
7619	Navy Dress Parade Set	Billy club, cartridge belt, bayonet and white dress rifle	1964	45	80	175
7626	Navy L.S.O. Equipment Set	helmet, headphones, signal paddles, flare gun	1966	40	80	150
7627	Navy Life Ring Set	U.S.N. life ring, helmet sticker	1966	25	45	150
7618	Navy Machine Gun Set	MG and ammo box	1965	40	80	175
7601	Sea Rescue Set	life raft, oar, anchor, flare gun, first-aid kit, knife, scabbard, manual	1964	95	135	500
7622	Sea Rescue Set	Reissued with life preserver	1966	95	135	500
7612	Shore Patrol	dress shirt, tie and pants, helmet, white belt, .45 and holster, billy club, boots, arm band, sea bag	1964	500	1000	2000
7612	Shore Patrol	Reissued with radio and helmet and shoes	1967	1000	2000	3500
7613	Shore Patrol Dress Jumper Set		1964	75	125	225
7614	Shore Patrol Dress Pant Set		1964	40	75	175
7616	Shore Patrol Helmet and Small Arms Set	white belt, billy stick, white helmet, .45 pistol	1964	40	75	150
7615	Shore Patrol Sea Bag Set		1964	25	50	125
	ACTION SOLDIER SERIES					
8006.83	Adventure Pack with 12 items	Adventure Pack Footlocker	1968	75	125	600
8005.83	Adventure Pack with 12 items	Adventure Pack Footlocker	1968	75	125	600
8008.83	Adventure Pack with 14 pieces	Adventure Pack Footlocker	1968	75	125	600
8007.83	Adventure Pack with 16 items	Adventure Pack Footlocker	1968	75	125	600

Green Beret Machine Gun Outpost Set, 1966, Hasbro

Sky Dive to Danger, 1975, Hasbro

GI JOE

NO.	NAME	DESCRIPTION	YEAR	EX	MNP	MIP
7549-83	Adventure Pack, Army Bivouac Series		1968	225	450	3500
7813	Air Police Equipment	gray field phone, carbine, white helmet and bayonet	1964	40	95	200
8000	Basic Footlocker	wood tray with cardboard wrapper	1964	35	75	125
7513	Bivouac Deluxe Pup Tent Set	M-1 rifle and bayonet, shovel and cover, canteen and cover, mess kit, cartridge belt, machine gun, tent, pegs, poles, camoflage, sleeping bag, netting, ammo box	1964	115	225	450
7514	Bivouac Machine Gun Set	machine gun set and ammo box	1964	25	40	125
7514	Bivouac Machine Gun Set	Reissue	1967	25	40	225
7515	Bivouac Sleeping Bag	zippered bag	1964	20	30	125
7512	Bivouac Sleeping Bag Set	mess kit, canteen, bayonet, cartridge belt, M-1 rifle, manual	1964	25	30	150
7511	Combat Camouflaged Netting Set	foliage and posts	1964	25	40	85
7572	Combat Construction Set	orange safety helmet, work gloves, jack hammer	1967	325	400	575
7573	Combat Demolition Set		1967	65	100	525
7571	Combat Engineer Set	pick, shovel, detonator, dynamite, tripod and transit with grease gun	1967	125	175	625
7504	Combat Fatigue Pants Set		1964	15	25	110
7503	Combat Fatigue Shirt Set		1964	20	30	125
7505	Combat Field Jacket		1964	45	65	325
7501	Combat Field Jacket Set	Jacket, bayonet, cartridge belt, hand grenades, M-1 rifle and manual	1964	65	100	525
7506	Combat Field Pack & Entrenching Tool		1964	25	45	125
7502	Combat Field Pack Deluxe Set	field jacket, pack, entrenching shovel w/cover, mess kit, first-aid pouch, canteen w/cover	1964	75	125	325
7507	Combat Helmet Set	with netting and foliage leaves	1964	20	35	75
7509	Combat Mess Kit	plate, fork, knife, spoon, canteen, etc.	1964	20	45	85
7510	Combat Rifle and Helmet Set	bayonet, M-1 rifle, belt and grenades	1967	55	100	325
7508	Combat Sandbags Set	three bags per set	1964	10	40	85
7520	Command Post Field Radio and Telephone Set	Field radio, telephone with wire roll and map	1964	35	70	135
7520	Command Post Field Radio and Telephone Set	Reissue	1967	35	70	400
7519	Command Post Poncho	on card	1964	30	45	225
7517	Command Post Poncho Set	Poncho, field radio and telephone, wire roll, pistol, belt and holster, map and case and manual	1964	85	125	400
7518	Command Post Small Arms Set	Holster and .45 pistol, belt, grenades	1964	30	60	100
8009.83	Dress Parade Adventure Pack	Adventure Pack with 37 pieces	1968	750	1250	3500
7533	Green Beret and Small Arms Set	Reissue	1967	85	100	425
7533	Green Beret and Small Arms Set		1966	85	110	300
5978	Green Beret Machine Gun Outpost Set	Sears' exclusive w/two figures and equipment	1966	225	450	1500
7538	Heavy Weapons Set	mortar launcher and shells, M-60 machine gun, grenades, flak jacket, shirt and pants	1967	175	325	1750
7538	Heavy Weapons Set	Reissue	1968	175	325	1500
7523	Military Police Duffle Bag Set		1964	25	40	85
7526	Military Police Helmet and Small Arms Set	Reissue	1967	35	75	250
7526	Military Police Helmet and Small Arms Set		1964	35	75	125
7524	Military Police Ike Jacket	Jacket with red scarf and arm band	1964	40	60	125

UNIFORM/EQUIPMENT SETS

NO.	NAME	DESCRIPTION	YEAR	EX	MNP	MIP
7525	Military Police Ike Pants	Matches Ike jacket	1964	20	30	100
7539	Military Police Uniform Set	Reissue	1968	450	900	3000
7521	Military Police Uniform Set	includes Ike jacket and pants, scarf, boots, helmet, belt with ammo pouches, .45 pistol and holster, billy club, armband, duffle bag	1964	450	1650	3000
7539	Military Police Uniform Set	includes green or tan uniform, black and gold MP Helmet, billy club, belt, pistol and holster, MP armband and red tunic	1967	450	1650	3500
7530	Mountain Troops Set	snow shoes, ice axe, ropes, grenades, camoflage pack, web belt, manual	1964	90	175	350
7516	Sabotage Set	Reissued in photo box	1968	125	250	1700
7516	Sabotage Set	dingy and oar, blinker light, detonator w/strap, TNT, wool stocking cap, gas mask, binoculars, green radio and .45 pistol and holster	1967	125	250	2000
7531	Ski Patrol Deluxe Set	White parka, boots, goggles, mittens, skis, poles and manual	1964	170	350	1250
7527	Ski Patrol Helmet and Small Arms Set		1965	35	75	135
7527	Ski Patrol Helmet and Small Arms Set	Reissue	1967	75	125	250
7529	Snow Troop Set	Reissue	1967	20	45	225
7529	Snow Troop Set	snow shoes, goggles and ice pick	1966	20	45	150
7528	Special Forces Bazooka Set	Reissue	1967	35	45	325
7528	Special Forces Bazooka Set		1966	35	45	225
7532	Special Forces Uniform Set		1966	200	375	1000
7537	West Point Cadet Uniform Set	Dress jacket, pants, shoes, chest and belt sash, parade hat w/plume, saber, scabbard and white M-1 rifle	1967	250	475	1500
7537	West Point Cadet Uniform Set	Reissue	1968	250	375	1200
ACTION SOLDIERS OF THE WORLD						
8305	Australian Jungle Fighter Set		1966	25	50	250
8304	British Commando Set	Sten submachine gun, gas mask and carrier, canteen and cover, cartridge belt, rifle, "Victoria Cross" medal, manual	1966	125	200	325
8303	French Resistance Fighter Set	shoulder holster, Lebel pistol, knife, grenades, radio, 7.65 submachine gun, "Croix de Guerra" medal, counter-intelligence manual	1966	25	50	275
8300	German Storm Trooper		1966	125	175	325
8301	Japanese Imperial Soldier Set	field pack, Nambu pistol and holster, Arisaka rifle with bayonet, cartridge belt, "Order of the Kite" medal, counter-intelligence manual	1966	175	275	625
8302	Russian Infantry Man Set	DP light machine gun, bipod, field glasses and case, anti-tank grenades, ammo box, "Order of Lenin" medal, counter-intelligence medal	1966	175	220	325
ADVENTURE TEAM						
7490	Adventure Team Headquarters Set	Adventure Team playset	1972	50	125	200
7495	Adventure Team Training Center Set	rifle rack, logs, barrel, barber wire, rope ladder, 3 tires, 2 targets, escape slide, tent and poles, first aid kit, respirator and mask, snake, instructions	1973	75	125	225

GI JOE

GI JOE

NO.	NAME	DESCRIPTION	YEAR	EX	MNP	MIP
7345	Aerial Reconnaissance Set	jumpsuit, helmet, aerial recon vehicle with built-in camera	1971	75	125	225
7420	Attack at Vulture Falls	Super Deluxe Set	1975	75	150	275
7414	Black Widow Rendezvous	Super Deluxe Set	1975	125	200	350
7328-5	Buried Bounty	Deluxe Set	1975	10	25	85
7437	Capture of the Pygmy Gorilla Set		1970	100	175	325
8032	Challenge of Savage River	Deluxe Set	1975	100	175	350
7313	Chest Winch Set		1972	10	15	40
7313	Chest Winch Set	Reissue	1974	10	15	75
8033	Command Para Drop	Deluxe Set	1975	200	300	550
7308-3	Copter Rescue Set	blue jumpsuit, red binoculars	1973	15	20	30
7412	Danger of the Depths Set		1970	100	175	325
7338-1	Danger Ray Detection	magnetic ray detector, solar communicator with headphones, two-piece uniform, instructions and comic	1975	45	90	225
7309-2	Dangerous Climb Set		1973	20	35	75
7608-5	Dangerous Mission Set	green shirt, pants, hunting rifle	1973	20	35	75
7370	Demolition Set	armored suit, face shield, bomb, bomb disposal box, extension grips	1971	20	45	125
7371	Demolition Set	with land mines, mine detector and carrying case with metallic suit	1971	75	100	250
7309-5	Desert Explorer Set		1973	20	40	80
7308-6	Desert Survival Set		1973	20	40	80
8031	Dive to Danger	Mike Powers set, orange scuba suit, fins, mask, spear gun, shark, buoy, knife and scabbard, mini sled, air tanks, comic	1975	150	250	450
7328-6	Diver's Distress		1975	35	70	125
7364	Drag Bike Set	three-wheel motorcycle brakes down to backpack size	1971	25	65	125
7422	Eight Ropes of Danger Set		1970	125	225	375
7374	Emergency Rescue Set	shirt, pants, rope ladder and hook, walkie talkie, safety belt, flashlight, oxygen tank, axe, first aid kit	1971	45	75	150
7319-5	Equipment Tester Set		1972	15	20	40
7360	Escape Car Set		1971	30	60	85
7319-1	Escape Slide Set		1972	15	25	40
8028-2	Fangs of the Cobra	Deluxe Set	1975	125	200	375
7423	Fantastic Freefall Set		1970	125	200	375
7308-2	Fight for Survival Set	brown shirt and pants, machete	1973	20	30	45
7431	Fight For Survival Set	with blue parka	1970	300	550	2500
7982	Fight for Survival Set w/ Polar Explorer		1969	250	450	850
7351	Fire Fighter Set		1971	20	30	55
7361	Flying Rescue Set		1971	35	60	85
7425	Flying Space Adventure Set		1970	400	600	1000
8000	Footlocker	green plastic with cardboard wrapper	1974	35	70	225
7328-4	Green Danger		1975	30	45	60
7415	Hidden Missile Discovery Set		1970	100	200	450
7308-1	Hidden Treasure Set	shirt, pants, pick axe, shovel	1973	15	25	40
7342	High Voltage Escape Set	net, jumpsuit, hat, wrist meter, wire cutters, wire, warning sign	1971	40	75	150
7343	Hurricane Spotter Set	slicker suit, rain measure, portable radar, map and case, binoculars	1971	55	80	175
7421	Jaws of Death	Super Deluxe Set	1975	325	500	650
7339-2	Jettison to Safety	infrared terrain scanner, mobile rocket pack, two-piece flight suit, instructions and comic	1975	85	200	275
7309-3	Jungle Ordeal Set		1973	15	25	45
7373	Jungle Survival Set		1971	15	25	45

UNIFORM/EQUIPMENT SETS

NO.	NAME	DESCRIPTION	YEAR	EX	MNP	MIP
7372	Karate Set		1971	35	70	125
7311	Laser Rescue Set	Reissue	1974	20	35	100
7311	Laser Rescue Set	hand-held laser with backpack generator	1972	20	35	45
7353	Life-Line Catapult Set		1971	15	25	40
7328-3	Long Range Recon	Deluxe Set	1975	10	20	35
7319-2	Magnetic Flaw Detector Set		1972	10	20	30
7339-3	Mine Shaft Breakout	sonic rock blaster, chest winch, two-piece uniform, netting, instructions, comic	1975	70	125	250
7340	Missile Recovery Set		1971	40	55	85
	Mystery of the Boiling Lagoon	Sears', pontoon boat, diver's suit, diver's helmet, weighted belt and boots, depth gauge, air hose, buoy, nose cone, pincer arm, instructions	1973	150	200	225
7338-2	Night Surveillance	Deluxe Set	1975	35	45	90
7416	Peril of the Raging Inferno	fireproof suit, hood and boots, breathing apparatus, camera, fire extinguisher, detection meter, gaskets	1975	85	150	275
7309-4	Photo Reconnaissance Set		1973	20	30	45
8028-1	Race for Recovery		1975	20	35	125
7341	Radiation Detection Set	jumpsuit with belt, "uranium ore", goggles, container, pincer arm.	1971	30	50	85
7339-1	Raging River Dam Up		1975	60	90	150
7350	Rescue Raft Set		1971	15	20	65
7413	Revenge of the Spy Shark	Super Deluxe Set	1975	50	175	400
7312	Rock Blaster	sonic blaster with tripod, backpack generator, face shield	1972	10	20	35
7315	Rocket Pack Set		1972	10	20	75
7315	Rocket Pack Set	Reissue	1974	10	20	50
7319-3	Sample Analyzer Set		1972	10	20	45
7439.16	Search for the Abominable Snowman Set	Sears, white suit, belt, goggles, gloves, rifle, skis and poles, show shoes, sled, rope, net, supply chest, binoculars, Abominable Snowman, comic book	1973	110	175	350
7375	Secret Agent Set		1971	30	55	175
7328-1	Secret Courier		1975	45	65	135
8030	Secret Mission Set	Deluxe Set	1975	65	95	200
7309-1	Secret Mission Set		1973	45	65	135
7411	Secret Mission to Spy Island Set	comic, inflatable raft with oar, binoculars, signal light, flare gun, TNT and detonator, wire roll, boots, pants, sweater, black cap, camera, radio with earphones, .45 submachine gun	1970	75	125	250
7308-4	Secret Rendezvous Set	parka, pants, flare gun	1973	10	20	35
7319-6	Seismograph Set		1972	10	20	35
7338-3	Shocking Escape	escape slide, chest pack climber, jumpsuit with gloves and belt, high voltage sign, instructions and comic	1975	25	65	125
7362	Signal Flasher Set	large back pack type signal flash unit	1971	15	30	50
7440	Sky Dive to Danger	Super Deluxe Set	1975	90	150	325
7314	Solar Communicator Set	Reissue	1974	10	20	95
7314	Solar Communicator Set		1972	10	20	35
7312	Sonic Rock Blaster Set	Reissue	1974	10	20	35
7312	Sonic Rock Blaster Set		1972	10	20	35
8028-3	Special Assignment	Deluxe Set	1975	30	55	135
7319-4	Thermal Terrain Scanner Set		1972	25	35	50
7480	Three-in-One Super Adventure Set	Danger of the Depths, Secret Mission to Spy Island and Flying Space Adventure Packs	1971	550	975	1250

401

Windboat Set, 1971, Hasbro

Heavy Artillery Laser (HAL),
1983, Hasbro

Motorized Battle Tank
(MOBAT), 1983, Hasbro

UNIFORM/EQUIPMENT SETS

NO.	NAME	DESCRIPTION	YEAR	EX	MNP	MIP
7480	Three-in-One Super Adventure Set	Cold of the Arctic, Heat of the Desert and Danger of the Jungle	1971	250	400	750
7328-2	Thrust into Danger	Deluxe Set	1975	45	55	175
59289	Trouble at Vulture Pass	Sears' exclusive, Super Deluxe Set	1975	75	125	325
7363	Turbo Copter Set	strap-on one man helicopter	1971	15	35	65
7309-6	Undercover Agent Set	trenchcoat and belt, walkie-talkie	1973	15	30	35
7310	Underwater Demolition Set	hand-held propulsion device, breathing apparatus, dynamite	1972	15	20	40
7310	Underwater Demolition Set	Reissue	1974	10	20	75
7354	Underwater Explorer Set	self propelled underwater device	1971	15	30	60
7344	Volcano Jumper Set	jumpsuit with hood, belt, nylon rope, chest pack, TNT pack	1971	45	80	250
7436	White Tiger Hunt Set	hunter's jacket and pants, hat, rifle, tent, cage, chain, campfire, white tiger, comic	1970	80	125	275
7353	Windboat Set	back pack, sled with wheels, sail	1971	10	25	55
7309-4	Winter Rescue Set	Replaced Photo Reconnaissance Set	1973	40	75	150

ADVENTURES OF GI JOE

NO.	NAME	DESCRIPTION	YEAR	EX	MNP	MIP
7940	Adventure Locker	Footlocker	1969	80	165	350
7941	Aqua Locker	Footlocker	1969	90	180	375
7942	Astro Locker	Footlocker	1969	90	180	375
7920	Danger of the Depths Underwater Diver Set		1969	140	275	500
7950	Eight Ropes of Danger Set	diving suit, treasure chest, octopus	1969	110	225	525
7951	Fantastic Freefall Set	includes figure with parachute and pack, blinker light, air vest, flash light, crash helmet with visor and oxygen mask, dog tags, orange jump suit, black boots	1969	150	325	675
7982.83	Flight for Survival Set w/o Polar Explorer	Reissue	1969	150	300	500
7952	Hidden Missile Discovery Set		1969	70	135	400
7953	Mouth of Doom Set		1969	125	250	550
7921	Mysterious Explosion Set	basic	1969	60	125	425
7923	Perilous Rescue Set	basic	1969	150	300	500
7922	Secret Mission to Spy Island Set	basic	1969	110	225	450

GI JOE ACTION SERIES, ARMY, NAVY, MARINE AND AIR FORCE

NO.	NAME	DESCRIPTION	YEAR	EX	MNP	MIP
8000	Basic Footlocker		1965	50	75	175
8000.83	Footlocker Adventure Pack	16 pieces	1968	65	135	450
8002.83	Footlocker Adventure Pack	15 pieces	1968	65	135	450
8001.83	Footlocker Adventure Pack	15 pieces	1968	65	135	450
8002.83	Footlocker Adventure Pack	22 pieces	1968	70	145	450

SUPER JOE

NO.	NAME	DESCRIPTION	YEAR	EX	MNP	MIP
7528-1	Aqua Laser		1977	10	20	30
7518-2	Edge of Adventure		1977	10	20	35
7518-3	Emergency Rescue		1977	10	20	30
7528-3	Fusion Bazooka		1977	10	20	30
7538-2	Helipak		1977	10	20	30
7518-1	Invisible Danger		1977	10	20	35
7538-1	Magna Tools		1977	10	20	30
7518-4	Path of Danger		1977	10	20	30
7538-3	Sonic Scanner		1977	10	20	30
7528-2	Treacherous Dive		1977	10	20	30

GI JOE

VEHICLE SETS

NO.	NAME	DESCRIPTION	YEAR	EX	MNP	MIP
		3-3/4" SERIES #1, COBRA				
	C.A.T.	Motorized Crimson Attack Tank	1982	15	25	55
		3-3/4" SERIES #1, GI JOE				
6000	M.O.B.A.T.	Motorized Battle Tank with Steeler	1982	30	65	125
6073	R.A.M.	Rapid Fire Motorcycle	1982	15	25	55
6050	V.A.M.P.	Multi-Purpose Attack Vehicle with Clutch	1982	20	35	70
		3-3/4" SERIES #2, COBRA				
6097	Cobra Glider	Attack Glider with Viper	1983	35	75	150
6077	F.A.N.G.	Fully Armed Negator Gyro Copter	1983	10	20	45
6051	H.I.S.S.	High Speed Sentry Tank with H.I.S.S.	1983	25	50	100
		3-3/4" SERIES #2, GI JOE				
6093	A.P.C.	Amphibious Personnel Carrier	1983	15	25	50
4025	Dragon Fly XH-1	Assault Copter with Wild Bill	1983	25	50	100
6097	Falcon	Attack Glider with Grunt	1983	30	75	150
6072	Polar Battle Bear	Sky Mobile	1983	15	25	50
6010	Sky Striker XP-14F	F-14 Jet and Parachute with Ace	1983	35	75	150
6048	Wolverine	Armored Missile Vehicle with Cover Girl	1983	25	50	100
		3-3/4" SERIES #3, COBRA				
6027	Rattler	Ground Attack Jet with Wild Weasel	1983-84	25	50	100
6055	Stinger	Night Attack Jeep with Cobra Officer	1983-84	20	40	80
6064	Swamp Skier	Chameleon Vehicle with Zartan	1983-84	30	55	125
6058	Water Moccasin	Swamp Boat with Copperhead	1983-84	20	40	80
		3-3/4" SERIES #3, GI JOE				
7444-3	Attack Cannon (FLAK)		1983	5	10	15
7444-1	Attack Vehicle (VAMP)		1983	15	35	70
7444-2	Heavy Artillery Laser (HAL)		1983	10	15	25
6005	Killer W.H.A.L.E.	Armored Hovercraft with Cutter	1983	30	65	125
7444-5	Mobile Missile System (MMS)		1983	10	15	30
7444-4	Motorized Battle Tank (MOBAT)		1983	15	25	50
74450	RAM, HAL & VAMP	three-piece, die-cast set	1983	10	20	40
7444-6	Rapid-Fire Motorcycle (RAM)		1983	15	20	30
6049	S.H.A.R.C.	Submersible High-Speed Attack & Recon Craft with Deep Six	1983	25	50	100
6079	Sky Hawk	V.T.O.L. Jet	1983	10	15	30
6056	Slugger	Self-Propelled Cannon with Thunder	1983	15	25	50
6680	Vamp Jeep with H.A.L.	Attack Vehicle with Heavy Artillery Laser Cannon	1983	20	35	75
6055	Vamp Mark II	Desert Jeep with Clutch	1983	25	40	80
		3-3/4" SERIES #4, COBRA				
6069	Ferret	All-Terrain Vehicle	1984	10	15	30
6024	Moray	Hydrofoil with Lamprey	1984	15	25	50
6687	Motorized Crimson Attack Tank	MOBAT Tank	1984	30	60	125
6686	Sentry and Missile System	Sears', with H.I.S.S. Tank, Cobra Commander, Officer and Soldier	1984	75	150	250
		3-3/4" SERIES #4, GI JOE				
6053	A.W.E. Striker	All-Weather Environment Jeep with Crankcase	1984	15	25	50
6078	Armadillo	One-Man Mini-Tank	1984	10	15	35
6023	Bridge Layer	Bridge Laying Trank with Toll Booth	1984	15	25	50
6015	Mauler	Motorized Tank with Heavy Metal	1984	15	25	50
6076	Silver Mirage	Motorcycle with Sidecar	1984	10	15	35
6057	Snowcat	Snow Half-Track Vehicle with Frost-Bite	1984	15	25	50
6001	U.S.S. Flagg	Aircraft Carrier with Admiral Keel Haul	1984	125	250	500

GI JOE

404

VEHICLE SETS

NO.	NAME	DESCRIPTION	YEAR	EX	MNP	MIP
		3-3/4" SERIES #5, COBRA				
	Air Assault	Air Vehicle	1985	10	15	25
6062	Air Chariot	Vehicle with Serpentor "Cobra Emperor"	1985	15	20	55
	Ground Assault	Land Vehicle	1985	10	20	25
6099-2	Hydro Sled		1985	10	15	25
6099j-1	Jet Pack	One-Man Jet Set	1985	10	15	25
6014	Night Raven S-3P	Surveillance Jet with Drone Pod and Strato Viper	1985	20	35	70
6041	Stun	Split Attack Vehicle with Motor Viper	1985	10	20	35
6068	Swamp Fire	Air/Swamp Transforming Vehicle with Color-Change	1985	10	15	30
6042	Thunder Machine	Compilation Vehicle of Spare Parts with Thrasher	1985	10	20	35
		3-3/4" SERIES #5, GI JOE				
6031	Conquest X-30	Super-Sonic Jet with Slip Stream	1985	15	30	65
6066	Devil Fish	High-Speed Attack Boat	1985	10	15	30
6030	H.A.V.O.C.	Heavy Artillery Vehicle Ordinance Carrier with Cross-Country	1985	10	15	35
6067	L.V.C. Recon Sled	Low-Crawl Vehicle Cycle	1985	10	15	30
6022	Tomahawk	Troop Transit Helicopter with Lift Ticket	1985	15	30	65
6061	Triple T	One-Man Tank with Sgt. Slaughter	1985	10	25	50
		3-3/4" SERIES #6, COBRA				
6087-3	Buzz Boar	Underground Attack Vehicle	1986-87	5	10	15
6070	Dreadnok Air Skiff	Mini-set with Zanzibar	1986-87	10	20	30
6171	Dreadnok Cycle	Compilation Cycle with Gunner Station	1986-87	5	10	20
6029	Maggot	three-in-one tank vehicle with W.O.R.M.S. driver	1986-87	10	15	35
6026	Mamba	Attack Copter with removable pods with Gyro-Viper	1986-87	10	15	30
6170	Pogo	Ballistic Battle Ball	1986-87	5	10	20
6040	Sea Ray	Combination Submarine/Jet with Sea Slug	1986-87	10	20	40
6039	Wolf	Arctic Terrain Vehicle with Ice Viper	1986-87	10	20	45
		3-3/4" SERIES #6, GI JOE				
6087-2	Coastal Defender	Mini-Vehicle with accessories	1986-87	5	10	15
6004-1	Crossfire-Alfa	Radio Control Vehicle with Rumbler	1986-87	25	50	100
6004-2	Crossfire-Delta	Radio Control Vehicle with Rumbler	1986-87	25	50	100
6002	Defiant Space Shuttle Complex	Space shuttle, space station, crawler	1986-87	75	350	525
6038	Persuader	Laser Tank with Backstop	1986-87	10	15	35
6133-3	Radar Station		1986-87	5	10	15
6087-1	Road Toad	Tow Vehicle with accessories	1986-87	5	10	15
		ACTION PILOT SERIES				
8040	Crash Crew Fire Truck Set		1967	950	1700	3500
8020	Official Space Capsule Set	space capsule, record, space suit, cloth space boots, space gloves, helmet with visor	1966	175	225	350
5979	Official Space Capsule Set w/ flotation	Sears' exclusive with collar, life raft and oars	1966	200	325	700
		ACTION SAILOR SERIES				
5979	Official Sea Sled and Frogman Set	Sears, with figure and underwater cave, orange scuba suit, fins, mask, tanks, sea sled in orange and black	1966	175	325	650
8050	Official Sea Sled and Frogman Set	without cave	1966	150	300	550
		ACTION SOLDIER SERIES				
5693	Amphibious Duck	Irwin, 26" long	1967	175	375	700
5397	Armored Car	Irwin, friction powered, 20" long	1967	150	300	500
5395	Helicopter	Irwin, friction powered, 28" long	1967	150	300	500

GI JOE

Official Sea Sled and Frogman Set, 1966, Hasbro

Recovery of the Lost Mummy Adventure Set, 1971, Hasbro

NO.	NAME	DESCRIPTION	YEAR	EX	MNP	MIP
5396	Jet Fighter Plane	Irwin, friction powered, 30" long	1967	225	475	800
5652	Military Staff Car	Irwin, friction powered, 24" long	1967	200	400	750
5651	Motorcycle and Sidecar	Irwin, 14" long, khaki, with decals	1967	75	150	325
7000	Official Combat Jeep Set	Trailer, steering wheel, spare tire, windshield, cannon, search light, shell, flag, guard rails, tripod, tailgate and hood, without Moto-Rev Sound	1965	200	375	550
7000	Official Jeep Combat Set	With Moto-Rev sound	1965	225	400	650
5694	Personnel Carrier/Mine Sweeper	Irwin, 26" long	1967	300	350	700

ADVENTURE TEAM

NO.	NAME	DESCRIPTION	YEAR	EX	MNP	MIP
	Action Sea Sled	J.C. Penney, 13", Adventure Pack	1973	25	40	85
7005	Adventure Team Vehicle Set		1970	50	75	225
23528	All Terrain Vehicle	14" vehicle	1973	50	75	125
59158	Amphicat	Irwin, scaled to fit two figures	1973	35	55	125
	Avenger Pursuit Craft	Sears' exclusive	1976	100	175	275
7498	Big Trapper	without action figure	1976	75	105	325
7494	Big Trapper Adventure with Intruder	with action figure	1976	100	150	425
7480	Capture Copter	without action figure	1976	80	175	325
7481	Capture Copter Adventure with Intruder	with action figure	1976	110	200	350
59114	Chopper Cycle	15" vehicle, J.C. Penney's	1973	30	50	100
59751	Combat Action Jeep	18" vehicle, J.C. Penney's	1973	50	65	125
7000	Combat Jeep and Trailer		1976	80	135	550
7439	Devil of the Deep		1974	80	135	325
7460	Fantastic Sea Wolf Submarine		1975	60	100	175
7450	Fate of the Troubleshooter		1974	50	125	225
59189	Giant Air-Sea Helicopter	28" vehicle, J.C. Penney's	1973	50	125	225
7380	Helicopter	14"; yellow; with working winch	1973	50	90	150
7380	Helicopter		1976	50	90	300
7499	Mobile Support Vehicle Set		1972	85	150	325
	Recovery of the Lost Mummy Adventure Set	Sears' exclusive	1971	125	250	425
7493	Sandstorm Survival Adventure		1974	125	200	300
7418	Search for the Stolen Idol Set		1971	120	225	350
7441	Secret of the Mummy's Tomb Set	with Land Adventurer figure, shirt, pants, boots, insignia, pith helmet, pick, shovel, Mummy's tomb, net, gems, vehicle with winch, comic	1970	175	300	600
7442	Sharks Surprise Set w/ Sea Adventurer		1970	175	325	550
	Signal All Terrain Vehicle	J.C. Penney's, 12" vehicle	1973	30	65	125
7470	Sky Hawk	5-3/4-foot wingspan	1975	65	100	175
7445	Spacewalk Mystery Set w/ Astronaut		1970	225	300	550
79-59301	Trapped in the Coils of Doom	J.C. Penney's exclusive	1974	250	300	550

ADVENTURES OF GI JOE

NO.	NAME	DESCRIPTION	YEAR	EX	MNP	MIP
7980	Sharks Surprise Set w/ Frogman		1969	175	325	650
7980.83	Sharks Surprise Set without Frogman		1969	150	300	550
7981	Spacewalk Mystery Set w/ Spaceman		1969	150	375	650
7981.83	Spacewalk Mystery Set without Spaceman	Reissue	1969	125	275	550

SUPER JOE

NO.	NAME	DESCRIPTION	YEAR	EX	MNP	MIP
7571	Rocket Command Center	Super Adventure Set including Gor	1977	60	115	225
7570	Rocket Command Center		1977	50	100	200

GI JOE

Toy Guns

Remember the toy guns of your childhood? Baby boomers who grew up watching TV Westerns and space operas have been largely responsible for the increased interest in toy gun collecting. This, plus the increasing interest in related Western and cowboy hero collectibles, has brought prices and demand into new realms.

The first cap gun patent dates back to 1860. The preferred material of toy construction until World War II was cast iron. Most early cap guns, exploders and figural guns were made of cast iron, though variations of plastic, tin and stamped metal also appear.

Metal toy gun production ceased around 1940. The companies that survived after 1946 experimented with a variety of materials and methods of production, the most successful of which was die casting. This involved injecting an alloy mixture into a mold, which resulted in fine detail, lower costs and a much lighter gun.

Die-cast guns dominated the 1950s and '60s marketplace. Television brought little buckaroos daily installments of the thrilling adventures of cowboy heroes such as Roy Rogers, Gene Autry and Hopalong Cassidy. Manufacturers such as the George Schmidt Company, Classy Products, Marx, Hubley, Nichols, Kilgore and Wyandotte all scrambled to arm these cowpokes and compete for a piece of the market. This, by some standards, was the golden age of die-cast guns.

Mattel, a relative newcomer to the business, introduced its first Western-style cap gun, the Fanner 50, in 1957. This shiny, oversized gun would, by its incredible success, drive many manufacturers out of the toy gun market and some out of business entirely.

The bottom line of toy making has always been cost. Mattel produced a line of low priced plastic and die-cast cap guns, rifles and machine guns that arrived on the market at a time when TV Western heroes such as Maverick, The Lawman, Sugarfoot, Bronco and Matt Dillon were replacing the older serial cowboys.

Cap guns would never be the same. All major producers added plastic to their lines, and the race was on to lower production costs and remain competitive. As far as most collectors are concerned, things went downhill from there. Each year toy guns seemed to decrease in quality and detail.

While cap guns sold in the American market were largely produced by American manufacturers in both the prewar and postwar periods, other toy guns came from overseas producers. Tin lithography became an art form in postwar Japan. The same Japanese companies that produced the robots and tin cars so widely sought by today's collectors also produced space ray guns, cowboy, G-men and military-style tin litho guns for the American market.

While prewar Japanese toy guns are rare, postwar sparkling ray guns, pop guns, water and clicker guns abound. These guns were generally cheaper than their American competition and provided a profitable low end product for American retailers.

As the postwar Japanese economy grew and workers demanded more money, toy gun manufacturing moved from Japan to Hong Kong to Taiwan to Korea and eventually to mainland China, currently one of the major producers of toy guns and caps.

Where to Begin Collecting?

What do you want to collect, and why do you want to collect it? Most toy gun collectors are buying back a bit of their childhood. They played with these guns in countless childhood fantasies, and holding them again unlocks memories. Some collectors are searching only for the toy guns they had (or wish they had) as children. These folks may actually fire their guns and may not be as interested in condition and packaging as collectors on the other side of the spectrum who collect for the investment. Investment collectors seek only the highest grade Mint in Box guns that will appreciate in value. They never play with their guns, and the idea of firing caps in a gun gives them shivers. Most collectors fall between these two extremes.

Some collectors amass guns by a specific manufacturer, like Hubley, Mattel or Nichols, while others search for the shootin' irons that bear the names of their cowboy heroes. Some specialize in military-style toy weapons, bullet-firing machine guns, rocket-firing bazookas and cap-firing hand grenades. Recently, space guns have increased in popularity. Collectors needn't limit collections to guns only. Some people collect toy gun advertising, catalogs, store displays or other accessories.

Another point to consider is condition. It may be a Holy Grail quest to collect only Mint In Box pieces. Many times guns came off the assembly line in less than perfect condition, due to bad batches of metal, lack of quality control or poor design. Toy guns are, after all, just that — toys. They were meant to be played with, used and then discarded. To expect them to exist in pristine condition for decades is often wishful thinking.

The high acid content of the paper pulp used to make toy gun boxes has damaged the finish of many guns. Mattel's Fanner guns are especially prone to this problem. Some guns have inherent problems that surface with age, such as flaking or lifting of their finishes. This occurs because the gun was not properly prepared before being plated or the particular batch of plating wasn't properly mixed. The big Nichols Stallion .45s suffered from this problem. Sometimes a better quality of nickel just wasn't available and the production line had to use what was on hand. Any grading system used should be flexible and take this into consideration.

Watch for Variations

Variations enhance quality and expand the depth of a collection, but they can also drive collectors crazy. Forced by economic considerations, most companies would continue production of a popular gun for years with only minor changes to the molds or packaging. Each of these changes, no matter how minor, is technically a variation.

A good example of production variations can be found in Hubley's Texan cap guns. The Texan began life in the golden age of cast iron, the mid-1930s. It was a large, well-designed, sturdy pistol that fired roll caps and had a revolving cylinder and a Western look. The initial cast-iron version was offered in a cap-firing version and a dummy version. (Most manufacturers offered dummy versions in states and cities where caps were prohibited as fireworks.) The dummy version had a different hammer than the standard version, so it couldn't fire caps.

For a while, Hubley boosted sales appeal by obtaining a license to use the famous Colt firearms rearing horse logo instead of the traditional Hubley star. This variation is a must for any complete Texan collection. After World War II, the Texan reappeared in a nearly identical die-cast version that was offered in nickel, gold, gray or blue finishes with both standard or dummy hammers.

To further complicate matters, Hubley redesigned the gun and issued it as a Texan, offering it in nickel, gold and metal finishes. All these guns had the familiar Hubley longhorn steer head plastic grips. These vary by being either all white or white with a black steer.

Hubley also produced a smaller version of the Texan, called the Texan Jr., in many variations and box styles. As far as variations go, an enthusiast could amass quite a collection of variations on just one gun. This is why deciding what you want to collect is so important.

GUNS

Beware of Reproductions

Reproductions and misrepresentations are common in any collecting field and a hazard for both the novice and experienced collector. Reproductions of highly-sought toy guns have yet to appear on the scene, mainly because the production and tooling costs for the potential market demand would be too high. But this has not stopped many small-time entrepreneurs from producing reproduction hammers, grips and laser-copy boxes.

Toy restoration and repair is not a concern as imperative as reproduction. As certain pieces become more difficult to find, restoration is a logical approach to fill the collecting demand. But restored or repaired pieces should always be presented as such and should be priced accordingly lower than an unrestored version.

Most reproduction boxes are easy to spot. The inside cardboard is usually whiter than an original and many times flaws, tears and dirt from the original are visible.

Reproduction hammers are usually easy to spot, especially when placed next to an original. The original usually tends to be cleaner and more detailed. Clues such as a Mint hammer and pitted pan or anvil (striking surface) are also dead giveaways.

Misrepresentations are sometimes the most difficult situations to unmask. Many dealers misrepresent pieces simply from lack of knowledge and experience, and many beginning collectors fall victim for the same reasons. Simple mistakes include listing incorrect dates or manufacturer. Beware the dealer who doesn't know the difference between cast iron and die cast.

Experience will show you that an "H" in a diamond or oval on the side of a gun is usually the trademark of either Leslie-Henry (the Diamond H brand) or the Halco (J. Halpern) Company, not Hubley. Hubley guns are usually marked "Hubley" somewhere on the gun. Knowing trademarks and distinguishing styles is learned through experience.

Stallion .38 Cap Pistol, 1950s, Nichols

What Gun...What Holster?

One area of major confusion seems to be centered around the question of "What gun went in what holster?" Holster makers were often not the same companies that made the guns. The cowboy cap gun craze of the 1940s through the 1950s supported the growth of many small production leather holster manufacturers. Companies such as Halco, Classy Products and Pilgrim Leather Goods produced holsters for major manufacturers and at the same time produced empty holsters. These empty sets were sold to jobbers who would buy quantities of guns — the cheaper the better — from different manufacturers to fill them. They would then sell the gun/holster sets to individual retailers.

Large chain stores such as Toys R Us and Kmart didn't exist at this time. Every local department store, hardware store, hobby shop, and sporting goods store was a potential customer. Years later, it's not uncommon to find a Leslie Henry Gene Autry Pistols in a Lasso 'Em Bill Holster set by Keyston Bros. What is this set? It's not really a Gene Autry set, no matter how nice it looks, and it shouldn't be represented as such. Most character holster sets were produced by major companies that paid hefty licensing fees to use cowboy names on both guns and holsters. Though there were a number of exceptions, most of these sets were sold with matching guns and holsters. The Gunsmoke set would have Marshal Matt Dillon guns in it, the Have Gun, Will Travel set would have Paladin guns, and so forth. Beware of the Mint In Box character set with a photo of the cowboy star on the box cover, his name on the holsters paired with common, no-name guns.

Trends

Toy guns are among the most passionately sought collectibles in the world. There are collectors who would trade or give anything for that gun they had as a child.

Auction and show prices for classic Western holster sets such as Hopalong Cassidy, Lone Ranger and Roy Rogers have remained strong.

The Top 10 Toy Guns / Sets
(in Mint in Box condition)

1. Man From U.N.C.L.E. THRUSH Rifle, Ideal, 1966 .... $3,000
2. Lost In Space Roto-Jet Gun Set, Mattel, 1966 2,500
3. Hopalong Cassidy Double Holster Set, Wyandotte, 1940s 2,500
4. Hopalong Cassidy Holster/Gun Set, Schmidt, 1950s 2,300
5. Man From U.N.C.L.E. Attache Case, Ideal, 1965 1,500
6. Roy Rogers Double Gun & Holster Set, Classy, 1950s 1,200
7. Roy Rogers Double Holster Set, Classy, 1950s 1,150
8. Roy Rogers Double Holster Set, Classy 1,100
9. Dale Evans D-26, Schmidt, 1950s 1,000
10. Flash Gordon Radio Repeater Clicker Pistol, Marx, 1937 1,000

Contributor to this section: John Snyder Jr., Diamond International Galleries, 1966 Greenspring Dr., Suite 401, Timonium, MD 21093.

GUNS

GUNS

NAME	COMPANY/DESCRIPTION	YEAR	GOOD	EX	MIP
Benton Harbor Novelty					
Dick Cap Pistol	4-3/4", automatic, side loading, black finish	1950s	20	37	75
Edison					
Sharkmatic Cap Gun	6" automatic, style pistol, fires "Supermatic System" strip caps	1980s	10	15	20
Hubley					
Dick Cap Pistol	4-1/8" cast iron automatic style, side loading, nickel finish, Dick oval in red paint	1930	75	125	250
Dick Cap Pistol	die-cast, 4-1/4" automatic style, side loading w/nickel finish	1950s	25	60	120
Ideal					
Man From U.N.C.L.E. Attache Case	15" x 10" x 2-1/2", comes w/cap firing pistol and clip, ID card, wallet, cap grenade, badge, passport and secret message sender	1965	525	975	1500
Man From U.N.C.L.E. Illya K. Special Lighter Gun	cigarette lighter gun shoots caps, has radio compartment concealed behind fake cigs, in window box	1966	125	225	350
Man From U.N.C.L.E. Illya Kuryakin Gun Set	includes clip loading, cap firing plastic pistol, badge, wallet, ID card, in window box	1966	210	390	600
Man From U.N.C.L.E. Napoleon Solo Gun Set	clip loading, cap firing plastic pistol w/rifle attachments, badge, ID card, in window box	1965	280	520	800
Man From U.N.C.L.E. Pistol and Holster	7" long pistol and plastic holster, both w/orange ID sticker	1965	45	85	125
Man From U.N.C.L.E. Stash Away Guns	three cap firing guns, holsters, two straps, ID card and badge, in window box	1966	210	390	600
Man From U.N.C.L.E. THRUSH Rifle	36" long	1966	875	1600	3000
Knickerbocker					
Dragnet Badge 714 Triple Fire Comb. Game	tin litho stand-up target has four plastic spinners, includes two 6" black plastic guns, one fires darts, the other cork gun, includes four plastic darts and three corks	1955	90	150	275
Dragnet Snub Nose Cap Pistol	plastic/die-cast works, 6-3/4", black plastic w/gold "Dragnet" and "714" badge on grip, on card	1960s	30	100	200
Dragnet Water Gun	6" black plastic, .38 Special-style w/gold "714" shield on grip	1960s	15	65	175
Lone Star					
Girl From U.N.C.L.E. Garter Holster	"gang buster" metal gun fires plastic bullets from metal shells, checker design vinyl holster and bullet pouch, on card	1966	80	145	225
Man From U.N.C.L.E. Attache Case	vinyl case w/pistol, holster, walkie talkie, cigarette box gun, badge, passport, invisible cartridge pen, handcuffs	1966	265	475	750
Man From U.N.C.L.E. Attache Case	vinyl covered cardboard, 9mm automatic Luger, shoulder stock, sight, silencer, belt, holster, secret wrist holster and pistol, grenade, wallet, passport, money	1966	300	550	850
Man From U.N.C.L.E. Attache Case	small cardboard briefcase, contains die-cast Mauser and parts to assemble U.N.C.L.E. Special	1966	140	260	400
Marx					
G-Man Gun Wind-Up Machine Gun	23" tin-litho, red, black, orange and gray litho, round drum magazine, wind-up mechanism makes sparks from muzzle, uses cigarette flint, wooden stock	1948	145	200	375
Man From U.N.C.L.E. Pistol Cane	25" long, cap firing, bullet shooting aluminum cane w/eight bullets and one metal shell, on card	1966	175	325	500
Mattel					
Agent Zero M Snap-Shot Camera Pistol	7-1/2" extended, camera turns into pistol at press of a button	1964	25	50	75
Agent Zero W Potshot	3" die-cast potshot derringer, gold finish, has brown vinyl armband holster holds two Shootin' Shell cartridges, gold buckle w/Agent Zero W logo	1965	40	85	125

DETECTIVE/SPY

NAME	COMPANY/DESCRIPTION	YEAR	GOOD	EX	MIP
Official Detective Shootin' Shell Snub-Nose	.38 die-cast chrome w/brown plastic grips, black vinyl shoulder holster, wallet, badge, ID card, Pistol Range Target and bullets	1959	95	175	250
Official Detective Shootin' Shell Snub-Nose	.38 die-cast 7" chrome finish, gold cylinder, brown plastic grips, Private Detective badge and Shootin' Shell bullets	1960	60	100	165
Official Dick Tracy Shootin' Shell Snub-Nose .38	die-cast chrome .38 w/brown plastic grips, chrome finish w/Shootin' Shell bullets and Stick-m caps	1961	75	125	210

Nichols

NAME	COMPANY/DESCRIPTION	YEAR	GOOD	EX	MIP
Detective Shell Firing Pistol	5-1/2" snub-nose pistol chambers and fires six three-piece cap cartridges, cut-out badge, bullet cartridges, extra red plastic bullet heads	1950s	100	175	275

Unknown

NAME	COMPANY/DESCRIPTION	YEAR	GOOD	EX	MIP
Man From U.N.C.L.E. Secret Service Pop Gun	bagged luger pop gun on header card w/unlicensed art of Napoleon and Illya	1960s	4	10	20

MILITARY/AUTOMATICS

NAME	COMPANY/DESCRIPTION	YEAR	GOOD	EX	MIP

Buddy L

NAME	COMPANY/DESCRIPTION	YEAR	GOOD	EX	MIP
Spitfire Cap Firing Machine Gun	biped stand attached to muzzle, black plastic stock and grip w/cap or clicker firing	1950	80	130	175

Coibel

Official James Bond 007 Thunderball Pistol	4-1/2" Walther PPK style, single shot fires plastic caps, Secret Agent ID	1985	15	25	50

Daisy

Model 12 SoftAir Gun	machine gun style, loads "SoftAir" pellets in plastic cartridge, ten rounds, spring fired, can be cocked by barrel grip or bolt	1990	35	50	75
SA Automatic Burp Gun	10" w/stock, black plastic, burp-gun style, removeable clip, loads and fires white plastic bullets	1970s	20	35	50

Edison

Matic 45 Cap Gun	24", plastic gun w/stock, fires "Supermatic System" strip caps	1980s	10	15	20

Esquire Novelty

7580 UZI Automatic	10-1/2", battery-operated, black plastic uses 250-shot roll caps, shoulder strap	1986	20	45	60

Hubley

Army .45 Cap Pistol	6-1/2" automatic, dark gray finish, white plastic grips, pop-up cap	1950s	45	125	250
Automatic Cap Pistol No. 290	die-cast, 6-1/2", nickel finish, brown checkered grips, magazine pops up when slider is pulled back		85	150	300

Larami

9mm Z-Matic Uzi Cap Gun	8" replica, removeable cap storage magazine, black finish, small orange plug in barrel	1984	5	10	15

Maco

Molotov Cocktail Tank Buster Cap Bomb	6" plastic and die-cast, insert caps in head and throw	1964	10	15	25
MP Holster Set	plastic pistol has removeable magazine, loads and ejects bullets, white leather belt and holster	1950s	65	120	175
Paratrooper Carbine	24" carbine, removeable magazine, fires plastic bullets, bayonet and target	1950s	75	115	165
USA Machine Gun	12" tripod-mounted gun fires plastic bullets, red and yellow plastic	1950s	65	130	200

GUNS

NAME	COMPANY/DESCRIPTION	YEAR	GOOD	EX	MIP

Main Machine

Mustang Toy Machine Gun	25" long chrome and hard plastic paper firing gun	1950s	75	125	175

Marx

Anti Aircraft Gun	mechanical, sparks, tin litho, 16-1/2" long, 1941		50	135	275
Army Automatic Pistol	2-1/2" automatic, (ACP style), black w/white grips, small leather holster w/flaps (Marx Miniature)	1950s	10	20	40
Army Pistol with Revolving Cylinder	tin litho		35	60	125
Army Sparking Pop Gun	1940-50		45	75	150
Desert Patrol Machine Pistol	plastic, 11" long		30	45	75
Green Beret Tommy Gun	sparkles, trigger action, on card	1960s	35	55	95
Mini-M.A.G. Combat Gun	cap pistol, miniature scale, die-cast		20	30	40
Siren Sparkling Airplane Pistol	heavy-gauge enamel steel, 9-1/2" wingspan, 7" long		50	75	100
Sparkling Siren Machine Gun	26" long	1949	45	75	150
Special Mission Tommy Gun			20	35	45
Tommy Gun	sparks and makes noise	1939	65	100	200

Mattel

Burp Gun	17" plastic w/die-cast works, perforated roll caps fired by cranking the handle	1957	25	50	75
Mattel-O-Matic Air Cooled Machine Gun	16" machine gun fires perforated roll caps by cranking handle, plastic w/die-cast, tripod-mounted, plastic/die-cast works, red and black plastic, box	1955	45	85	125
Wind-Up Burp Gun	plastic/pressed steel, 24", "Grease Gun", fires perforated roll caps, fold-over wire stock, cap storage in magazine, boxed	1955	50	90	150

National

Automatic Cap Pistol	4-1/4" automatic style, grip swivels to load, black finish	1925	45	100	200
Automatic Cap Pistol	6-1/2" silver finish w/simulated walnut grip	1950s	35	65	90

Nichols

Army 45 Automatic	4-1/4" all metal, side loading automatic, olive	1959	15	25	50

Parris

M-1 Kadet Training Rifle	32" wood/metal M-1 carbine, clicker action, metal barrel, trigger guard, bolt	1960s	20	35	50

Redondo

Revolver Mauser Cap Pistol	6-1/4", Mauser style automatic pop-up magazine, silver finish, brown plastic grips	1960s	4	10	20

Stevens

Spitfire Automatic Cap Pistol	4-5/8" cast iron, side loading, silver finish, "flying airplanes" white plastic grips	1940	60	125	250

Topper/Deluxe

Johnny Seven One Man Army-OMA	36" multi-purpose seven guns in one, removeable pistol fires caps, rifle fires white plastic bullets, bolt spring fired machine gun "tommy gun" sound, rear launcher fires grenades, forward diff. shell	1964	125	225	350

Unknown

MM Automatic Carbine	24" recoil red slide in muzzle and flashing light, brown and black plastic	1960s	15	30	45

GUNS

414

MISCELLANEOUS

NAME	COMPANY/DESCRIPTION	YEAR	GOOD	EX	MIP
Ambrit Industries					
Spud Gun	case aluminum, pneumatic all-metal gun shoots pellets	1950s	15	35	50
Atomic Industries					
Dynamic Automatic Repeating Bubble Gun	8" black plastic pistol projects bubbles		25	40	65
Buddy L					
Paper Cracker Rifle	26" steel and machined aluminum mechanism, barrel, trigger and operating lever, uses 1000 shot paper roll, brown plastic stock	1940s	95	165	225
Daisy					
Buzz Barton Special, No. 195	blue metal finish, wood stock w/ring sight	1930s	85	125	200
Jack Armstrong Shooting Propeller Plane Gun	5-1/2" gun, shoots flying disk, pressed tin	1933	35	125	250
Model No. 25 Pump Action BB Gun	plastic stock	1960s	35	65	125
Targeteer No. 18 Target Air Pistol	10" gun metal finish, push barrel to cock, Daisy BB tin w/special BBs, spinner target	1949	50	85	125
Water Pistol No. 17	5-1/4" tin	1940	25	40	65
Water Pistol No. 8	5-1/4" tin	1930s	25	50	80
EMU Rififi					
Automatic Sparkling Pistol	6-1/2", plastic/metal, uses cigarette lighter flints to make sparks, available in green-red, yellow-green, red or white colors	1960s	15	30	45
Esquire Novelty					
Hideaway Derringer	3-1/2" single shot, loads solid metal bullet, grip is removeable to store two more bullets, gold finish, white plastic grips	1950s	65	90	110
Hong Kong					
Potato Gun	Spud Gun, plastic, pneumatic action fires potato pellet from muzzle	1991	3	7	10
Hubley					
Midget Cap Pistol	5-1/2" long, die-cast, all metal flintlock w/silver finish	1950s	20	35	50
Pirate Cap Pistol	9-1/2" side-by-side flintlock style w/die-cast frame and cast double hammers and trigger, chrome finish, white plastic grips feature Pirate in red oval	1940s	50	200	400
Tiger Cap Pistol	6 7/8", single action, mammoth caps, metal finish	1935	35	100	200
Trooper Cap Pistol	6-1/2" all metal, pop up cap magazine, nickel finish, black grips	1950	30	85	175
Winner Cap Pistol	4-3/8" automatic style, pop-up magazine release in front of trigger guard, nickel finish	1940	45	100	200
Kilgore					
Clip 50 Cap Pistol	4-1/4", unusual automatic style, black Bakelite plastic frame, removeable cap magazine clip	1940	75	110	200
Mountie Automatic Cap Pistol	6", double action, automatic style w/pop-up magazine, unusual nickel finish, black plastic grips		20	30	60
Presto Cap Pistol	5-1/8", pop up cap magazine nickel finish brown plastic grips	1940	65	120	225
Rex Automatic Cap Pistol	3-7/8", blue metal finish cast iron, small size automatic style, side loading, white pearlized grips	1939	45	100	200
Langson					
Nu-Matic Paper Popper Gun	pressed steel, 7" squeeze grip trigger, mechanism pops roll of paper (reel at top of gun) to make loud noise, black finish	1940s	30	50	75

GUNS

415

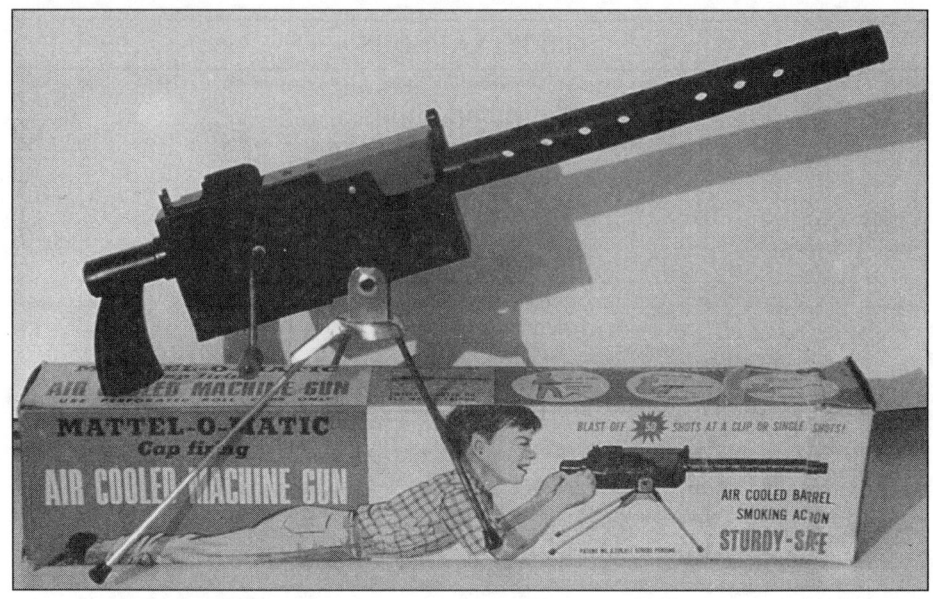

Mattel-O-Matic Air Cooled Machine Gun, 1955, Mattel

Popeye Pirate Click Pistol, Marx

MISCELLANEOUS

Marx

NAME	COMPANY/DESCRIPTION	YEAR	GOOD	EX	MIP
Automatic Repeater Paper Pop Pistol	7-3/4" long		35	65	125
Blastaway Cap Gun	50 shooter repeater		25	35	75
Burp Gun	20" battery-operated, green and black plastic	1960s	20	35	75
Click Pistol	pressed steel, 7-3/4" long		20	50	100
Click Pistol	tin litho		20	50	100
Famous Firearms Deluxe Edition Collectors Album	set of four rifles, five pistols and four holsters miniature series, includes: Mare's Laig, Thompson machine gun, Sharps rifle, Winchester saddle rifle, Derringer, .38 snub-nose, Civil War pistol, six shooter/Flint	1959	50	100	200
Marx Miniatures Famous Gun Sets	Four-gun set features tommy gun, Civil War revolver, "Mare's Laig" and western saddle rifle	1958	25	50	100
Marxman Target Pistol	plastic, 5-1/2" long		35	50	100
Popeye Pirate Click Pistol	tin litho, 10" long, 1930s, with box		200	500	850
Repeating Cap Pistol	aluminum		20	30	50
Sparkling Pop Gun			25	50	100
Streamline Siren Sparkling Pistol	tin litho		25	50	100

Meldon

NAME	COMPANY/DESCRIPTION	YEAR	GOOD	EX	MIP
P-38 Clicker Pistol	7-1/2" black finish, automatic style	1950s	35	50	100

Midwest

NAME	COMPANY/DESCRIPTION	YEAR	GOOD	EX	MIP
Long Tom Dart Gun	11" pressed steel	1950s	35	50	100

Palmer Plastics

NAME	COMPANY/DESCRIPTION	YEAR	GOOD	EX	MIP
Airplane Clicker Pistol	4-1/2" yellow and black plane, red pilot and guns	1950s	25	45	65

Park Plastics

NAME	COMPANY/DESCRIPTION	YEAR	GOOD	EX	MIP
Atomee Water Pistol	4-1/4" black plastic	1960s	10	20	35

Rosvi

NAME	COMPANY/DESCRIPTION	YEAR	GOOD	EX	MIP
Revolver Aquila Pop Pistol	10" green finish, pop gun breaks to cock, fires cork from barrel, sparks from mechanism under barrel	1960s	15	20	50

Stevens

NAME	COMPANY/DESCRIPTION	YEAR	GOOD	EX	MIP
25 Jr. Cap Pistol	4-1/8" automatic, side loading, silver finish	1930	25	50	100
6 Shot Cap Pistol	6-3/4", six separate triggers revolve to deliver caps to hammer, metal finish		85	135	250
Model 25-50	4-1/2" nickel finish	1930	35	65	135
Pluck Cap Pistol	3-1/2" cast iron, single shot single action	1930	15	50	100

Unknown

NAME	COMPANY/DESCRIPTION	YEAR	GOOD	EX	MIP
Double Holster Set	black leather, large size, steer head conches, lots of red jewels, fringe, holsters only, no guns	1950s	65	100	200

Welco

NAME	COMPANY/DESCRIPTION	YEAR	GOOD	EX	MIP
Spud Gun (Tira Papas)	6" all-metal gun	1960s	10	20	35

POLICE

Acme Novelty

NAME	COMPANY/DESCRIPTION	YEAR	GOOD	EX	MIP
G-Boy Pistol	7" automatic (ACP) style entire left rear side of gun swings down to load	1950s	15	35	65

Hubley

NAME	COMPANY/DESCRIPTION	YEAR	GOOD	EX	MIP
Mountie Automatic Cap Pistol	die-cast, 7-1/4" automatic style, pop up lever-release magazine, blue finish	1960s	20	35	65

GUNS

POLICE

NAME	COMPANY/DESCRIPTION	YEAR	GOOD	EX	MIP

Kilgore

NAME	COMPANY/DESCRIPTION	YEAR	GOOD	EX	MIP
Machine Gun Cap Pistol	5-1/8", long cast iron crank-fired gun	1938	100	175	250

Marx

NAME	COMPANY/DESCRIPTION	YEAR	GOOD	EX	MIP
.38 Cap Pistol	w/caps, miniature scale, die-cast		35	75	125
Detective Snub-Nose Special	die-cast, 5-3/4" top release break, unusual revolving cylinder, fires Kilgore style disc caps, chrome finish w/black plastic grips	1950s	65	100	150
Dick Tracy Click Pistol			35	100	150
Dick Tracy Jr. Click Pistol	aluminum	1930s	100	150	250
Dick Tracy Siren Pistol	pressed steel, 8-1/2" long	1935	40	125	250
Dick Tracy Sparkling Pop Pistol	tin litho		35	100	150
G-Man Automatic Silent Arm Pistol	tin		35	55	100
G-Man Automatic Sparkling Pistol	pressed steel, 4" long	1930s	45	85	175
G-Man Machine Gun	tin miniature, wind-up	1940s	25	35	65
G-Man Sparkling Sub-Machine Gun			50	75	150
G-Man Tommy Gun	sparkles when wound	1936	55	80	175
Gang Buster Crusade Against Crime Sub-Machine Gun	litho, metal w/wooden stock, 23" long	1938	95	180	375
Marx Miniatures Detective Set	miniature cap firing brown and gray tommy gun, chrome pistol and holster on card w/wood grain frame border	1950s	25	45	75
Sheriff Signal Pistol	plastic, 5-1/2" long	1950	20	30	60
Siren Sparkling Pistol	tin litho		20	30	60

Mattel

NAME	COMPANY/DESCRIPTION	YEAR	GOOD	EX	MIP
Official Dick Tracy Tommy Burst Machine Gun	25" Thompson style machine gun fire perforated roll caps, single shot or in full burst when bolt is pulled back, brown plastic stock and black plastic body, lift up rear sight, Dick Tracy decal on stock	1960s	100	200	375

Pilgrim Leather

NAME	COMPANY/DESCRIPTION	YEAR	GOOD	EX	MIP
Peter Gunn Private Eye Revolver & Holster Set	36" die-cast Remington w/six two-piece bullets, badge and wallet, Peter Gunn business cards, black leather shoulder holster	1959	200	325	450

T. Cohn

NAME	COMPANY/DESCRIPTION	YEAR	GOOD	EX	MIP
Sparkling "Sure-Shot" Machine Gun	long body tin multicolored red/yellow/blue tin noise making gun, great box graphics show boy shooting sparks as pigtailed blond girl looks	1950s	50	75	150

WESTERN

NAME	COMPANY/DESCRIPTION	YEAR	GOOD	EX	MIP

Actoy

NAME	COMPANY/DESCRIPTION	YEAR	GOOD	EX	MIP
Pony Cap Pistol	single shot, all-metal, nickel finish w/eagle on grip	1950s	25	45	100
Wells Fargo Buntline Cap Pistol	11" long barrel, break-to-front, cream plastic stag grips	1950s	85	135	275
Wyatt Earp Buntline Special	11" barrel, die-cast, friction break-to-front, white plastic grips, nickel finish	1950s	95	175	350

Buzz-Henry

NAME	COMPANY/DESCRIPTION	YEAR	GOOD	EX	MIP
Lone Rider Cap Pistol	8" die-cast, white plastic inset rearing horse grips	1950s	35	75	150

Carnell

NAME	COMPANY/DESCRIPTION	YEAR	GOOD	EX	MIP
Maverick Cap Pistol	9" break-to-front, lever release, nickel finish, Maverick on sides, cream and brown swirl colored grips features notch bar w/extra set of black plastic grips	1960	40	100	200

WESTERN

NAME	COMPANY/DESCRIPTION	YEAR	GOOD	EX	MIP
Maverick Two Gun Holster Set	9" break-to-front, lever release, nickel finish, Maverick on sides, cream/brown swirl grips features notch bar, black leather dbl. holster set w/silver plates, studs and white trim, six loops, buckle	1960	175	375	650

Classy

NAME	COMPANY/DESCRIPTION	YEAR	GOOD	EX	MIP
Dale Evans Holster Set	brown and yellow leather, white fringe on holsters, stylized blue butterflies are also "DE" logo, if buckled in front, holsters are backwards; holsters only, no guns		55	150	300
Double Holster Set	imitation alligator-texture brown leather, steer-head conches on holsters, lots of studs, yellow felt backing, holsters only, no guns	1950s	100	200	400
Rebel Holster & Pistol	12" die-cast long barrel pistol, brown plastic grips, black leather single holster left side, Rebel insignia on holster flap,	1960s	195	375	650
Roy Rogers Double Gun & Holster Set	die-cast two 8-1/2" nickel finish pistols w/copper figural grips, holster is brown and black leather w/raised detail, plastic play bullets and leather tie-downs	1950s	325	750	1200
Roy Rogers Double Holster Set	10" guns w/plain nickel finish and copper grips, lever release, brown and cream leather set, silver studs, gold fleck jewels and four wooden bullets		300	650	1100
Roy Rogers Double Holster Set	black and white leather set, silver studs and conches, 9" Roy Rogers pistols w/plain nickel finish and copper figural grips, friction release	1950s	310	700	1150

Daisy

NAME	COMPANY/DESCRIPTION	YEAR	GOOD	EX	MIP
760 Rapid Fire Shotgun Air Rifle	31" pump shotgun, gray metal one piece frame, brown plastic stock and slider grip, fires blast of air	1960s	65	95	150
Red Ryder BB Rifle	carved wooden stock	1980	25	50	100
Spittin Image Peacemaker BB Pistol	10-1/2" die-cast, spring fired, single action, BBs load into spring fed magazine under barrel		25	60	120

Edison

NAME	COMPANY/DESCRIPTION	YEAR	GOOD	EX	MIP
Susanna 90 12 Shot Cap Pistol	9" uses ring caps, wind out cylinder, black finish, plastic wood grips	1980s	10	15	25

Esquire Novelty

NAME	COMPANY/DESCRIPTION	YEAR	GOOD	EX	MIP
Authentic Derringer	classic miniature Series #10, 2" cap firing, copper finish, twin swivel barrel	1960	15	25	45
Authentic Derringer	die-cast, 2" cap firing, copper finish, twin swivel barrel	1960	15	25	45
Johnny Ringo, Adventure of, Gun & Holster	10-3/4" long barrel Actoy, friction break, black/gold plastic stag grips, black leather two-gun holster, felt backing, loops hold four to six bullets, silver buckle	1960	200	400	600
Pony Boy Double Holster Set	brown leather double holster w/bucking broncs and studs, cuffs, spurs and spur leathers, guns are Actoy "Spitfires", die-cast 8-1/2" copper finish, white plastic grips	1950s	175	300	500

Haig

NAME	COMPANY/DESCRIPTION	YEAR	GOOD	EX	MIP
Western Buntline Pistol	13", pistol fires single caps and/or BBs, BBs are propelled down barrel sleeve by cap explosion	1963	75	120	165

Hubley

NAME	COMPANY/DESCRIPTION	YEAR	GOOD	EX	MIP
2 Guns in 1 Cap Pistol	die-cast, 8" w/long barrel, twist-off barrels to change from long to short, side loading, white plastic grips	1950s	75	125	200
Colt .38 Detective Special	4-1/2" Colt .38 pistol single shot caps and loads six play bullets w/suspenders chest holster	1959	35	75	150
Colt .45 Cap Pistol	die-cast, 13", revolving cylinder produced w/open or closed chamber ends, loads six two-piece cap-firing bullets, white plastic grips, red felt box	1959	100	200	400

GUNS

NAME	COMPANY/DESCRIPTION	YEAR	GOOD	EX	MIP
Cowboy Cap Pistol	8" friction break-to-front nickel finish cast iron, rose swirl plastic grips w/Colt logo	1940	85	175	300
Cowboy Cap Pistol	12", die-cast, swing-out revolving cylinder, release on barrel, nickel finish, black plastic steer grips	1950s	100	200	350
Cowboy Cap Pistol	die-cast, 12" swing out revolving cyclinder, release on barrel, nickel or aluminum finish, white plastic steer grips w/black steer head	1950s	95	185	325
Cowboy Jr. Cap Pistol No. 225	9" die-cast, revolving cylinder, side loading, release on barrel, silver finish, white plastic cow grips, lanyard ring and cord	1950s	65	130	275
Dagger Derringer	7", unusual over and under pistol has hidden red plastic dagger that slides out from between barrels, rotating barrels load and fire two-piece bullets	1958	55	100	145
Davy Crockett Buffalo Rifle	25" die-cast and plastic, unusual flintlock style, fires single cap under pan cover, brown plastic stock, ammo storage door in stock	1950s	75	145	200
Deputy Cap Pistol	10" die-cast, front breaking, release on barrel, ornate scroll work, nickel finish	1950s	45	85	175
Flintlock Jr. Cap Pistol	7-1/2" single shot, double action, brown swirl plastic stock	1955	10	30	65
Flintlock Pistol	9-1/4", two shot cap shooting single action double barrel, over and under style, brown swirl plastic stock, nickel finish	1954	50	95	160
Frontier Repeating Cap Rifle	35-1/4" rifle nickel finish w/brown plastic stock and forestock, blue metal barrel, red plastic choke and front sight, pop down magazine, released by catch in front of trigger, scroll work	1950s	75	165	210
Lone Ranger Rifle	29" long	1973	55	100	150
Marshal Cap Pistol	9-3/4" die-cast, side loading, nickel finish w/scrollwork, w/brown and white plastic stag grips w/a clip on left grip	1960	35	75	150
Model 1860 Cal .44 Cap Pistol	13", revolving cylinder w/closed chamber ends, six two-piece bullets, flat aluminum finish, white plastic grips, complete w/wooden display plaque	1959	125	250	400
Panther Pistol	die-cast, 4" derringer style pistol snaps out from secret spring-loaded wrist holster	1958	85	130	185
Remington .36 Cap Pistol	8" long, nickel finish, black plastic grips, revolving cylinder chambers two-piece bullets	1950s	75	145	225
Rex Trailer Two Gun & Holster Set	9-1/2" side loading, nickel finish, stag plastic grips, brown textured tooled leather w/white holsters and trim, six bullet loops w/plastic silver bullets, plain buckle	1960	90	200	375
Ric-O-Shay .45 Cap Pistol	13" die-cast, nickel chrome finish, large frame, revolving cylinder, fires rolled caps, chambers brass bullets and fires caps, black plastic grips, makes a twang sound when fired	1959	85	125	275
Ric-O-Shay .45 Cap Pistol Holster Set	13", die-cast, revolving cylinder swings out to chamber six brass bullets, six loaded in gun and 12 on holster, 1" flake in nickel finish at heel, holster black leather w/separate belt, horse-head emblem, rawhide tiedown		200	400	750
Rifleman Flip Special Cap Rifle	3' long rifle, resembles classic Winchester w/ring lever, brown plastic stock, pop down cap magazine	1959	125	275	400
Rodeo Cap Pistol	7-1/2" single shot, white plastic steer grips	1950s	20	50	100
Roy Rogers Tiny Tots Double Holster Set			55	100	150
Texan .38 Cap Pistol	10" long, revolving cylinder gun chambers six solid brass bullets (caps go into cylinder first), top release front break automatically ejects shells, plastic steer grips	1950s	100	165	300

GUNS

Flintlock Pistol, 1954, Hubley

Hawkeye Cap Pistol, 1950s, Kilgore

Johnny Ringo Gun & Holster Set, 1960, Marx

Mare's Laig Rifle Pistol, Marx

NAME	COMPANY/DESCRIPTION	YEAR	GOOD	EX	MIP
Texan Cap Pistol	9-1/4" cast iron revolving cylinder lever release, white plastic steer grips, nickel finish, Colt rearing horse logo on grips	1940	90	175	375
Texan Cap Pistol	die-cast, nickel finish, white plastic steer grips, star logo on grips	1950s	75	145	275
Texan Cap Pistol No. 285	9-1/4", cast iron, revolving cylinder, lever release, white plastic steer grips, nickel finish w/star logo in grip	1940	85	185	400
Texan Dummy Cap Pistol	9-1/4" revolving cylinder, lever release, white plastic steer grips, nickel finish, Colt rearing horse logo	1940	65	110	250
Texan Dummy Cap Pistol	9-1/4", revolving cylinder, lever release, white plastic steer grips, nickel finish, star logo on grip	1950s	90	165	300
Texan Jr. Cap Pistol	10", spring button release on side of cylinder, break-to-front, nickel finish white plastic grips w/black steers	1950s	65	90	200
Texan Jr. Cap Pistol	die-cast, release under cylinder, nickel finish, white plastic Longhorn grips	1954	50	75	185
Texan Jr. Gold Plated Cap Pistol	9", gold finish w/black longhorn steer grips, break-to-front release from cylinder	1950s	85	130	275
Western Cap Pistol	9" die-cast, friction break, nickel finish w/white plastic steer grips w/black steer	1950s	40	55	120
Wyatt Earp Double Holster Set	black and white leather holster w/silk screened "Marshal Wyatt Earp" logo, two No. 247 Hubley Wyatt Earp Buntline Specials, 10-3/4" nickel finish, purple swirl grips	1950s	175	400	750

Ideal

NAME	COMPANY/DESCRIPTION	YEAR	GOOD	EX	MIP
Yo Gun	7-1/4" red plastic gun releases yellow plastic ball which snaps back when trigger is pulled, functions like a yo-yo	1960s	30	45	60

John Henry Products

NAME	COMPANY/DESCRIPTION	YEAR	GOOD	EX	MIP
Matt Dillon Marshal Set	gun and holster set w/jail keys, handcuffs and badge		55	100	200

Kenton

NAME	COMPANY/DESCRIPTION	YEAR	GOOD	EX	MIP
Gene Autry Cap Pistol	8-3/8" cast iron, long barrel, dark gray gunmetal finish w/white plastic grips w/signature, (Best/Logan G3.1.1)	1939	175	250	450
Gene Autry Cap Pistol	6-1/2" cast iron, nickel finish, red plastic grips w/etched signature (Best/Logan G3.2.1)	1940	125	175	400
Gene Autry Dummy Cap Pistol	cast iron, 8-3/8", long barrel, dark gray, gunmetal finish, white plastic grips	1939	100	175	400
Lawmaker Cap Pistol	8-3/8", break-to-front friction break, unusual dark gray gunmetal finish, white plastic raised grips	1941	100	175	400

Kilgore

NAME	COMPANY/DESCRIPTION	YEAR	GOOD	EX	MIP
Big Horn Cap Pistol	7" all metal revolving cylinder, break-to-front, disk caps, silver finish	1950s	85	125	250
Bronco Cap Pistol	8-1/2", revolving swing-out cylinder fires Kilgore disc caps, silver finish, black plastic "Bronco" grips	1950s	50	100	225
Champion Quick Draw Timer Cap Pistol	silver finish, side loading, wind up mechanism in grip records elapsed time of draw, black plastic grips	1959	65	150	300
Cheyenne Cap Pistol	9-3/4" side loading, "Sure-K" plastic stag grips, silver finish	1974	10	15	35
Fastest Gun Electronic Draw Game	die-cast, wire plug into "Rangers" gun grips, gun that shoots first lights eye of plastic battery-operated steer head, red and blue plastic holsters w/matching cowboy gun grips, plastic belts	1958	80	145	250
Grizzly Cap Pistol	10" revolving cylinder fires disc caps, swing out cylinder, black plastic grips w/grizzly bear	1950s	95	165	350
Hawkeye Cap Pistol	4-1/4" all metal, automatic style, side loading, silver finish	1950s	20	35	65
Lone Ranger Cap Pistol	8-1/4" cast iron, small hammer, nickel finish, friction break, purple plastic "Hi-Yo Silver" grips	1938	95	200	400

GUNS

WESTERN

NAME	COMPANY/DESCRIPTION	YEAR	GOOD	EX	MIP
Lone Ranger Cap Pistol	8-1/2" cast iron, large hammer, nickel finish, spring release on side for break, red-brown, Hi-Yo Silver grips	1940	85	200	350
Long Boy Cap Gun	11-1/2" long, cast iron		65	125	200
Mustang Cap Pistol	9-1/2" chrome finish w/"stag" plastic grips	1960s	20	35	75
Ranger Cap Pistol	8-1/2" nickel finish, brown swirl plastic grips, spring release on right side, break-to-front	1950s	90	125	200
Roy Rogers Cap Pistol	10" revolving cylinder swings out to load, fires disc caps, white plastic horse-head grips w/"RR" logo	1950s	125	225	450

Langson

NAME	COMPANY/DESCRIPTION	YEAR	GOOD	EX	MIP
Cody Colt Paper Buster Gun	7-3/4", paper popper, nickel finish, white plastic steer grips fires Cody Colt ammunition	1950s	35	65	100

Leslie-Henry

NAME	COMPANY/DESCRIPTION	YEAR	GOOD	EX	MIP
Gene Autry 44 Cap Pistol	11" lever release, side loading, long barrel, loads solid metal bullets, nickel finish, brown translucent plastic horse-head grips	1950s	125	300	650
Gene Autry 44 Cap Pistol	11" lever release, side loading, long barrel, nickel finish, white plastic horse-head grips	1950s	85	200	400
Gene Autry Cap Pistol	9", break-to-front lever release, nickel finish, white plastic horse-head grips	1950s	80	175	350
Gene Autry Cap Pistol	9" break-to-front lever release, copper finish, white plastic horse-head grips	1950s	80	175	350
Gene Autry Cap Pistol	7-3/4" die-cast, small size, lever release, break-to-front, nickel finish w/extension scroll work, black plastic horse-head grips	1950s	80	175	350
Gene Autry Cap Pistol	9" break-to-front, lever release, nickel finish, black plastic horse-head grips	1950s	80	175	350
Gunsmoke Double Holster Set	w/copper clad grips		200	350	650
Longhorn Cap Pistol	10" die-cast, release in front of trigger guard, scroll work, white plastic horse head grips, unusual pop-up cap magazine	1950s	85	125	225
Marshal Cap Pistol	10" revolving cylinder chambers, Nichols-style bullets, white plastic grips w/star ovals	1950s	35	75	150
Marshal Matt Dillon "Gunsmoke" Cap Pistol	10" pop-up cap magazine, release in front of trigger guard, scroll work, bronze steer-head grips	1950s	50	100	200
Maverick Derringer	3-1/4" w/removeable cap-shooting bullets, tan vinyl holster w/two bullets	1958	35	55	85
Ranger Cap Pistol	7-3/4" derringer w/removeable cap, shooting bullets, tan vinyl holster w/two bullets	1950s	85	110	150
Texas Ranger Cap Pistol	8-1/4" die-cast, lever release break to front, nickel finish, scroll work, vasoline colored plastic grips		65	95	175
Wagon Train Complete Western Cowboy Outfit	plastic flip ring lever rifle and wagon train pistol (late model L-H pistol) and leather holster	1960	75	185	375
Wild Bill Hickok 44 Cap Pistol Set	11" nickel finish, swing-out side loading action, revolving cylinder chambers six metal bullets, amber plastic horse-head grips, single holster black and brown leather w/silver studs, diamond conches	1950s	200	325	550
Wild Bill Hickok Cap Pistol	10" pop-up cap magazine, release in front of trigger guard, scroll work, translucent brown plastic grips w/oval star inserts	1950s	90	135	250
Wild Bill Hickok Gun & Holster	single gun and holster set		100	200	400
Young Buffalo Bill Cowboy Outfit	black and white leather holster set w/pistol, white grip, holster bands read Texas Ranger		100	175	300

Lone Star

NAME	COMPANY/DESCRIPTION	YEAR	GOOD	EX	MIP
Gunfighter Holster Set	9" Frontier Ace, lever release, break-to-front, silver finish, brown plastic grips, white and red leather "Laramie" single holster w/separate belt	1960s	55	85	200

GUNS

WESTERN

NAME	COMPANY/DESCRIPTION	YEAR	GOOD	EX	MIP
Pecos Kid Cap Pistol	9" silver chrome finish, brown plastic grips, lever release	1970s	10	15	50
Pepperbox Derringer Cap Pistol	die-cast, 6-1/4" rotating barrel holds four cap loads, silver finish w/black plastic grips	1960	75	110	185

Long Island Die Casting

Texas Cap Pistol	die-cast, 8-1/2" friction break, Circle "T" logo, scroll work on barrel	1950s	45	85	150

Marx

NAME	COMPANY/DESCRIPTION	YEAR	GOOD	EX	MIP
Bonanza Guns Outfit	25" cap firing saddle rifle, magazine pulls down to load, 9-1/2" Western pistol fires two-piece Marx shooting bullets, wood plastic stocks and gun metal gray plastic body, tan vinyl holster	1960s	75	145	300
Buffalo	50 shooter repeater		70	100	140
Centennial Rifle	w/big sound		25	35	65
Cork-Shooting Rifle			25	40	60
Double Holster Set	10" two pistols similar to 1860s Remington, fires roll caps by use of a lanyard that is pulled from the bottom of the grip, internal hammer, white plastic horse and steer grips, silver, brown vinyl holster	1960	70	120	300
Double-Barrel Pop Gun Rifle	28" long	1935	50	85	175
Double-Barrel Pop Gun Rifle	22" long	1935	45	75	150
Hi-Yo Silver Lone Ranger Pistol	tin gun		45	125	275
Historic Guns Derringer	Marx Historic Guns series, derringer w/plastic presentation case, 4-1/2" long, on card	1974	15	25	30
How the West Was Won Gun Rifle	deep gray Winchester model w/tan stock, in box		55	85	145
Johnny Ringo Gun & Holster Set	die-cast gun, white plastic head grips, vinyl quick draw holster has rawhide tie, gun is fired by lanyard which passes through grip butt and attaches to belt, when pulled lanyard trips internal hammer	1960	80	150	275
Lone Ranger 45 Flasher Flashlight Pistol			25	50	85
Lone Ranger Carbine	26" gray plastic repeater-style rifle has pull down cap magazine, western trim and Lone Ranger signature on stock	1950s	65	100	165
Lone Ranger Clicker Pistol	8", nickel finish, red jewels, inlaid white plastic grip w/the Lone Ranger, Hi-Yo Silver and LR head embossed, brown leather holster	1938	60	200	300
Lone Ranger Double Target Set	9-1/2" square stand up target, tin litho, wire frame holds target upright, backed w/bulls-eye target, 8" metal dart gun fires wooden shaft dart	1939	95	210	375
Mare's Laig Rifle Pistol	13-1/2" brown plastic, black plastic body, pull down magazine		60	95	135
Official Wanted Dead or Alive Mare's Laig Rifle	19" bullet loading, cap firing saddle rifle-pistol ejects plastic bullets, w/holster		100	195	300
Ranch Rifle	plastic, repeater		30	45	60
Roy Rogers Carbine	26" gray plastic repeater-style rifle has pull down cap magazine, western trim and Roy Rogers signature on stock	1950s	80	120	250
Side-By Double Barrel Pop Gun Rifle	9" long		20	35	45
Tales of Wells Fargo Double Barrel Shotgun	26" long double barrel shotgun, two toy shotgun shells, decal on the butt of the gun	1950s	100	200	300
Thundergun Cap Pistol	12-1/2" single action,"Thundercaps" perforated roll cap system, silver finish, brown plastic grips	1950s	100	175	250

GUNS

424

NAME	COMPANY/DESCRIPTION	YEAR	GOOD	EX	MIP
Wanted Dead or Alive Miniature Mare's Laig	Marx Miniatures series miniature cap rifle on "wood frame" card	1959	20	35	50
Wild West Rifle	30" long w/sight, cap rifle		40	75	125
Zorro Flintock Pistol			30	45	100
Zorro Rifle			60	90	150

Mattel

NAME	COMPANY/DESCRIPTION	YEAR	GOOD	EX	MIP
Fanner 50 "Swivelshot Trick Holster" Set	die-cast bullet loading Fanner 50, leather swivel style holster, attaches to any belt, gun fires in holster when swiveled, string included for last ditch draw	1958	85	165	325
Fanner 50 Cap Pistol	later version 11" fires perforated roll caps, black finish, white plastic antelope grips	1960s	30	65	150
Fanner 50 Cap Pistol	11" fanner non-revolving cylinder, stag plastic grips, nickel finish, black vinyl "Durahyde" holster	1960s	50	75	200
Fanner 50 Smoking Cap Pistol	10-1/2" w/revolving cylinder, first version w/grapefruit cylinder does not chamber bullets	1957	75	150	350
Fanner 50 Smoking Cap Pistol	10-1/2" w/ revolving cylinder, chambers six metal play bullets, die-cast	1958	55	120	300
Shootin' Shell .45 Fanner Cap Pistol	11" revolving cylinder pistol shoots Mattel Shootin' Shell cartridges, shell ejector	1959	250	400	650
Shootin' Shell Buckle Gun	cap and bullet shooting copy of Remington Derringer pops out from belt buckle, two brass cartridges and six bullets	1958	45	80	125
Shootin' Shell Fanner	9" die-cast chrome finish, revolving cylinder chambers six Shootin' Shell bullets	1958	65	175	350
Shootin' Shell Fanner & Derringer Set	small size Shooting Shell Fanner w/chrome finish, revolving cylinder, chambers six Shootin' Shell bullets, brown leather holster	1958	75	175	350
Shootin' Shell Fanner Single Holster	cowhide holster takes small size Shootin' Shell Fanner w/six brass play bullets and tie-downs	1959	80	175	350
Shootin' Shell Indian Scout Rifle	29-1/2" plastic/metal Sharps rolling block rifle, chambers two-piece Shootin' Shell bullets, secret compartment in stock for ammo storage, plastic stock and metal barrel	1958	100	145	250
Shootin' Shell Potshot Remington Derringer	3" derringer, on card	1959	35	60	90
Shootin' Shell Winchester Rifle	26" long		55	100	150
Showdown Set with Three Shootin' Shell Guns	30" single shot rifle w/metal barrel, die-cast w/plastic stock, Shootin' Shell Fanner sm. size, revolving cylinder, chrome finish and imitation stag plastic grips, tan holster w/bullet loops	1958	300	600	950
Winchester Saddle Gun Rifle	33" die-cast and plastic, perforated roll caps and chambers eight play bullets loaded through side door	1959	45	95	350

National Metal & Plastic Toy

NAME	COMPANY/DESCRIPTION	YEAR	GOOD	EX	MIP
The Plainsman Cap Pistol	10-1/2" revolving cylinder loads Kilgore-style disk caps, lever holds cylinder forward for loading, scroll work, white plastic grips	1950s	125	175	300

Nichols

NAME	COMPANY/DESCRIPTION	YEAR	GOOD	EX	MIP
Cap Gun Store Display	24" x 14" wood board, derringer and two strips of Nichols bullets	1950s	300	600	950
Dyna-Mite Derringer	3-1/4" die-cast, loads single cap cartridge, silver finish, white plastic grips	1955	15	30	45
Dyna-Mite Derringer in Clip	3-1/2" die-cast, fires single cap in Nichols cartridge, nickel finish, white plastic grips w/small leather holster		25	45	65

GUNS

Ranger Cap Pistol, 1950s, Kilgore

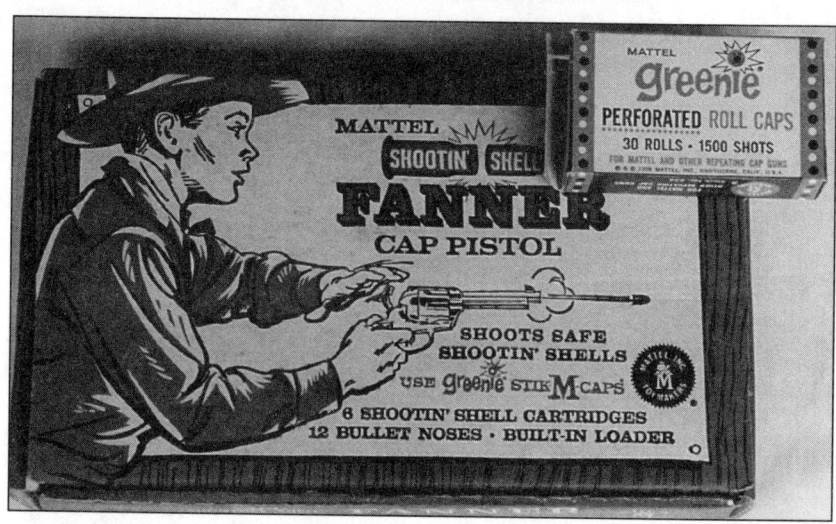

Shootin' Shell .45 Fanner Cap Pistol, 1959, Mattel

GUNS

Stallion 41-40 Cap Pistol, 1950s, Nichols

WESTERN

NAME	COMPANY/DESCRIPTION	YEAR	GOOD	EX	MIP
Model 95 Shell Firing Rifle	35-1/2" rifle uses shell firing cartridges, holds five in removeable magazine and one chamber, lever action ejects cartridges, open frame box holds six bullets and twelve additional red bullet heads	1961	200	350	550
Pinto Cap Pistol	3-1/2", chrome finish, black plastic grips, flip out cylinder, white plastic "Pinto" holster in leather holster clip	1950s	20	35	75
Silver Pony Cap Pistol	7-1/2" single shot, silver metal grip and one replacement black plastic grip, silver finish	1950s	30	45	100
Spitfire Hip Gun No. 100	9" cap cartridge loading mini rifle, chrome finish, tan plastic stock	1950s	15	20	35
Spitfire with Clip	9" mini rifle, chrome finish, plastic stock, plastic holders w/two extra cartridges	1950s	12	25	35
Stallion .22 Cap Pistol	7" revolving cylinder chambers five two-piece cartridges, single action, black plastic stag grips, never came in box	1950s	30	65	125
Stallion .22 Double Action Cap Pistol	7" double action, pull trigger to fire, white plastic grips, nickel finish, cylinder revolves	1950s	45	120	250
Stallion .38 Cap Pistol	9-1/2", chambers six two-piece cap cartridges, nickel finish, white plastic grips	1950s	75	150	300
Stallion .45 MK I Cap Pistol	die-cast, 12" chrome finish, revolving cylinder, chambers six two-piece bullets, shell ejector, white "pearlescent" plastic grips w/rearing stallion, red jewels and 6 bullets and Stallion caps	1950	100	250	450
Stallion .45 MK II Cap Pistol	12" pistol, chrome finish, revolving cylinder, chambers six two-piece, bullets, shell ejector, extra set of white grips to replace black grips on gun and box of Stallion caps	1956	100	185	300
Stallion 32 Six Shooter	8" revolving cylinder chambers six two-piece cartridges, nickel finish, black plastic grips	1955	75	110	250
Stallion 41-40 Cap Pistol	10-1/2" revolving cylinder chrome finish pistol, swing out cylinder that chambers six two-piece cap cartridges, shell ejector, scroll work on frame, cream-purple swirl colored plastic grips	1950s	150	250	375
Tophand 250 Cap Pistol	9-1/2" break-to-front, lever release, black finish, brown plastic grips w/a roll of "Tophand 250" caps	1960	45	85	165

Ohio Art

NAME	COMPANY/DESCRIPTION	YEAR	GOOD	EX	MIP
Sheriff's Derringer Pocket Pistol	3-1/4" silver finish derringer chambers two-piece, Nichols-style cartridge, red plastic grips w/an "A" logo, on card	1960s	10	20	25

Pilgrim Leather

NAME	COMPANY/DESCRIPTION	YEAR	GOOD	EX	MIP
Ruff Rider Western Holster Set	brown leather double holster, variety of studs and red jewels, twelve plastic silver bullets, tie-downs		100	250	400

Product Engineering

NAME	COMPANY/DESCRIPTION	YEAR	GOOD	EX	MIP
45 Smoker	10" single cap, shoots talcum-like powder by use of bellows when trigger is pulled, aluminum finish	1950s	45	75	150
Frontier Smoker	9-1/2" cap pistol, die-cast, pop up magazine shoots white powder from internal bellows, all metal, black grips, silver finish, gold magazine, hammer and trigger		85	135	210

Ralston-Purina

NAME	COMPANY/DESCRIPTION	YEAR	GOOD	EX	MIP
Tom Mix Wooden Gun	three all-wood versions w/leather holster, came in mailer, each	1930s	125	250	350

Schmidt

NAME	COMPANY/DESCRIPTION	YEAR	GOOD	EX	MIP
Buck 'n Bronc Marshal Cap Pistol	10" long barrel revolver style, lever release, break-to-front, plain silver finish, copper color metal grips	1950s	90	150	350
Dale Evans D-26	initials in butterfly symbol	1950s	400	750	1000
Hopalong Cassidy Cap Pistol	9" pull hammer to release, scroll work, nickel finish w/black plastic grips w/white bust of Hopalong Cassidy	1950	150	375	650

GUNS

WESTERN

NAME	COMPANY/DESCRIPTION	YEAR	GOOD	EX	MIP
Hopalong Cassidy Holster/Gun Set	black holster; black grips on gun w/bust of Hoppy	1950s	400	1200	2300

Smart Style

Real Texan Outfit with Nichols Stallion .22	brown/white leather double holsters have silver conches w/red reflectors, silver horses at top of holster, belt w/three bullet loops, guns are a pair of double action .22s	1950s	95	200	400

Stevens

49er Cap Pistol	cast iron, 9", unusual internal hammer w/revolving steel cylinder, nickel finish, white plastic figural grips	1940	100	275	450
Billy The Kid Cap Pistol	8" long, cap pistol		55	100	200
Buffalo Bill Cap Pistol	7-3/4", silver nickel finish, side loading magazine door, white "tenite" plastic horse and cowboy grips, red jewels	1940	65	110	225
Colt Cap Pistol	6-1/2", revolver-style double action	1935	15	50	100
Cowboy Cap Pistol	3-1/2" cast iron, single shot single action, sold loose	1935	20	50	100
Cowboy King Cap Pistol	9" break-to-front release, gold finish cast iron, black plastic grips, yellow jewels	1940	85	175	375

Topper/Deluxe

Johnny Eagle Red River Bullet Firing	over 12" double action revolving cylinder pistol, die-cast hammer, trigger, blue plastic overall w/wood plastic grips w/gold horse, side loading, shell ejector, fires two-piece plastic bullets	1965	65	95	175

Unknown

Davy Crockett Frontier Fighter Cork Gun	21" pop gun shoots cork on string and has cigarette flint mechanism at muzzle that makes sparks when fired, wood stock, leather sling	1950s	65	135	225
Gene Autry Champion Single Holster Set	leather and cardboard, red, yellow and green "jewels," four white wooden bullets, silver buckle	1940s	125	175	300
Lone Ranger Holster	9", leather/pressboard, Hi-Yo Silver and Lone Ranger printed, red jewel, belt loop		35	60	125
Wagon Train Gun & Holster Set	two 5" plastic guns, vinyl holster w/plastic bullets and metal badge	1950s	25	35	65
Wyatt Earp Double Holster Set	med. size, reflectors, black leather w/brown rawhide fringe, holsters only	1950s	50	70	95

USA

Bobcat Saddle Gun	5-1/2" black finish, imprinted w/"Official Wanted Dead or Alive "Mare's Laig" logo, brown plastic stock	1960s	10	20	30

Wyandotte

Hopalong Cassidy Double Holster Set	w/two guns; gold guns w/black grips;holster has silver studs w/Hoppy's name in belt	1940s	800	1650	2500
Red Ranger Jr. Cap Pistol	7-1/2" lever release, break-to-front, silver finish, white plastic horse grips	1950s	55	85	120

Young Premiums

Official Wyatt Earp Buntline Clicker Pistol	18-1/2" plastic		35	60	125

GUNS

Lunch Boxes

Remember carrying your lunch to school in a colorful metal lunch box?

Lunch kits have been manufactured since the 1920s, but the boxes that are most collectible today are those bearing illustrations of popular licensed characters.

It took the power of television to launch the lunch box industry out of the domed steel domain of workmen into the colorful art boxes generations of children carried to school each day.

As World War II ended, Aladdin Industries returned to providing millions of workmen with sturdy, if uninspired, lunch kits designed to take the beating of the workplace. Great change occurred in 1950 when Aladdin released a pair of rectangular steel boxes, one red and one blue, sporting scalloped color decals of the TV western hero of the day, Hopalong Cassidy. Soon, 600,000 Hoppy boxes were being carried to school by proud young owners. The youth market had been found, and it would never be ignored again.

The envious classmates of those first Hoppy boxers would not be denied. American Thermos, Aladdin's chief competitor, went one up on Aladdin by introducing the 1953 Roy Rogers box in full-color lithography. Aladdin responded by issuing a new 1954 Hoppy box in full color litho, and the lunch box era officially began.

Throughout the latter 1950s, the box wars were fought in earnest between Aladdin and American Thermos, with occasional challenges by Adco Liberty, Ohio Art and Okay Industries.

The smaller firms produced some classic boxes, notably Mickey Mouse and Donald Duck (1954), Howdy Doody (1954) and Davy Crockett (1955) from Adco Liberty; and Captain Astro (1966), Bond XX (1967), Snow White (1980) and Pit Stop (1968) from Ohio Art. Okay Industries weighed in briefly later on with the now highly prized Wake Up America (1973) and Underdog (1974) boxes, but from the beginning it had always been a two-horse race.

The popular boxes of each year mirrored the stars, heroes, and interests of the times. From the Westerns and space explorations of the late 1950s through the 1960s, Americans enjoyed a golden age of cartoon and film heroes such as the Flintstones (1962), Dudley Do-Right (1962), Bullwinkle and Rocky (1962) and Mary Poppins (1965). As the decade progressed, America grew more aggressive, turning toward such violent heroes as the Man From U.N.C.L.E. (1966) and G.I. Joe (1967) before Vietnam changed the national consciousness.

The early 1970s brought us such innocuous role models as H.R. Pufnstuf (1970), The Partridge Family (1971) and Bobby Sherman (1972), and by decade's end we were greeting both the promise and the threat from beyond in Close Encounters (1978) and Star Wars (1978).

Bonanza, 1965, Aladdin

Charlie's Angels Brunch Bag, 1978, Aladdin

The metal box reigned supreme through the mid-1980s when parental groups began calling for a ban on metal boxes as "deadly weapons." The industry capitulated, and by 1986, both Aladdin and American Thermos were producing all their boxes in plastic.

The switch to plastic was not nearly as abrupt as might be expected. Aladdin and Thermos had been making plastic and vinyl boxes since the late 1950s. These included many character boxes that had no counterparts in metal, which is presently their major saving grace in the collector market.

Vinyl boxes were made of lower cost materials, consisting basically of cardboard sheathed in thin vinyl. They were not as popular as metal boxes, and their poor construction combined with lower unit sales have resulted in a field with higher rarity factors than the metal box arena. Additionally, vinyl was more affordable to small companies, which produced numerous limited-run boxes for sale or use as premiums.

Vinyl box collecting is an emerging field with few firmly established prices compared to the relative maturity of the metal box market, so any price guide such as this will be more open to debate. As the field matures, the pricing precedents of sales and time will build into a stronger body of knowledge. In this book, for ease of searching, boxes are listed alphabetically by box composition — plastic, steel and vinyl.

Trends

Lunch boxes are still visible at toy and collectors' shows, but generalized dealers don't feature them quite as much. Specialized dealers still exist, however, dealing in good numbers. Character related boxes — from Superman to Western heroes to the Munsters — remain popular, rounding out character toy collections. Boxes aren't made like they used to be, and vintage ones hold a true nostalgia and make great display items.

Editor's note: An n/a in the bottle column means the box did not come with a bottle.

The Top 10 Lunch Boxes
(in Near Mint condition)

1. 240 Robert, steel, Aladdin, 1978 .... $2,500
2. Toppie Elephant, steel, American Thermos, 1957 1,600
3. Home Town Airport Dome, steel, King Seeley Thermos, 1960 1,000
4. Underdog, steel, Okay Industries, 1974 900
5. Knight in Armor, steel, Universal, 1959 825
6. Ballerina, vinyl, Universal, 1960s 800
7. Superman, steel, Universal, 1954 800
8. Dudley Do-Right, steel, Universal, 1962 800
9. Bullwinkle & Rocky, steel, Universal, 1962 800
10. Little Friends, vinyl, Aladdin, 1982 760

PLASTIC

NAME, YEAR, COMPANY, DESCRIPTION	BOX NM	BOTTLE NM
101 Dalmatians, 1990, Aladdin	18	8
18 Wheeler, 1978, Aladdin	30	10
ALF, unknown, red plastic	20	n/a
Animalympics Dome, 1979, Thermos	35	10
Astronauts, 1986, Thermos	30	15
Atari Missile Command Dome, 1983, Aladdin	35	10
Back to School, 1980, Aladdin	60	20
Back to the Future, 1989, Thermos	30	12
Bang Bang, 1982, Thermos	45	n/a
Barbie with Hologram Mirror, 1990, Thermos	25	8
Batman (dark blue), 1989, Thermos	20	10
Batman (light blue), 1989, Thermos	40	10
Batman Returns, 1991, Thermos	15	5
Beach Bronto, 1984, Aladdin, no bottle	40	n/a
Beach Party (blue/pink), 1988, Deka, w/generic plastic bottle	15	5
Bear with Heart (3-D), 1987, Servo	12	n/a
Beauty & the Beast, 1991, Aladdin	20	5
Bee Gees, 1978, Thermos	40	20
Beetlejuice, 1980, Thermos	10	4
Big Jim, 1976, Thermos	80	30
Bozostuffs, 1988, Deka	25	10
C.B. Bears, 1977, Thermos	20	n/a
Care Bears, 1986, Aladdin	10	5
Centurions, 1986, Thermos	15	8
Chiclets, 1987, Thermos, no bottle	40	n/a
Chipmunks, Alvin and the, 1983, Thermos	20	10
CHiPs, 1977, Thermos	45	15
Cinderella, 1992, Aladdin	25	10
Civil War, The, 1961, Universal, generic "Thermax" bottle	200	25
Colonial Bread Van, 1984, Moldmark Industries	60	20
Crestman Tubular!, 1980, Taiwan	50	20
Days of Thunder, 1988, Thermos	30	10
Deka 4 x 4, 1988, Deka, generic plastic bottle	25	5
Dick Tracy, 1989, Aladdin	20	10
Dino Riders, 1988, Aladdin	20	10
Dinobeasties, 1988, Thermos	15	n/a
Dinorocker with Radio & Headset, 1986, Fundes	45	n/a
Disney on Parade, 1970, Aladdin, plastic bottle, glass liner	30	15
Disney's Little Mermaid, 1989, Thermos, w/generic plastic bottle	10	5
Duck Tales (4 X 4/Game), 1986, Aladdin	15	5
Dukes of Hazzard, 1981, Aladdin	45	10
Dukes of Hazzard Dome, 1981, Aladdin	45	10
Dune, 1984, Aladdin	45	20
Dunkin Munchkins, 1972, Thermos	25	15
Ecology Dome, 1980, Thermos	45	20
Ed Grimley, 1988, Aladdin	20	5
Entenmann's, 1989, Thermos	15	n/a
Ewoks, 1983, Thermos	20	5
Fame, 1972, Thermos	35	15
Fievel Goes West, 1991, Aladdin	10	4
Fire Engine Co. 7, 1985, D.A.S., w/generic plastic bottle	30	5
Fisher-Price Mini Lunch Box, 1962, Fisher-Price, red w/barnyard scenes, matching bottle	20	5
Flash Gordon Dome, 1979, Aladdin	60	20
Flintstones, unknown, premium, Denny's Restaurants	30	n/a
Flintstones Kids, 1987, Thermos	40	10
Food Fighters, 1988, Aladdin	20	10
Fraggle Rock, 1987, Thermos	15	5
Frito Lay's, 1982, Thermos, no bottle	50	n/a
G.I. Joe (Space Mission), 1989, Aladdin	25	10
G.I. Joe, Live the Adventure, 1986, Aladdin	25	10
Garfield (food fight), 1979, Thermos	25	10
Garfield (lunch), 1977, Thermos	20	10
Geoffrey, 1981, Aladdin	30	10
Get Along Gang, 1983, Aladdin	10	5

NAME, YEAR, COMPANY, DESCRIPTION	BOX NM	BOTTLE NM
Ghostbusters, 1986, Deka	15	5
Go Bots, 1984, Thermos	10	5
Golden Girls, 1984, Thermos	10	5
Goonies, 1985, Aladdin	20	5
Gumby, 1986, Thermos	60	20
Hot Wheels, 1984, Thermos	50	20
Howdy Doody Dome, 1977, Thermos	80	35
Incredible Hulk Dome, 1980, Aladdin	30	10
Incredible Hulk, The, 1978, Aladdin, plastic bottle	30	10
Inspector Gadget, 1983, Thermos	20	8
It's Not Just the Bus - Greyhound, 1980, Aladdin	60	20
Jabber Jaw, 1977, Thermos	50	20
Jetsons (3-D), 1987, Servo	75	30
Jetsons (paper picture), 1987, Servo	110	30
Jetsons, The Movie, 1990, Aladdin	30	15
Kermit the Frog, Lunch With, 1988, Thermos	18	5
Kermit's Frog Scout Van, 1989, Superseal, no bottle	15	n/a
Kool-Aid Man, 1986, Thermos	20	10
Lisa Frank, 1980, Thermos	10	5
Little Orphan Annie, 1973, Thermos	50	20
Looney Tunes Birthday Party, 1989, Thermos, blue or red	20	10
Looney Tunes Dancing, 1977, Thermos	20	10
Looney Tunes Playing Drums, 1978, Thermos	20	10
Looney Tunes Tasmanian Devil, 1988, Thermos, w/generic plastic bottle	15	10
Los Angeles Olympics, 1984, Aladdin	20	5
Lucy's Luncheonette, 1981, Thermos, Peanuts characters	15	5
Lunch 'N Tunes Safari, 1986, Fun Design, w/built-in radio, no bottle	35	n/a
Lunch 'N Tunes Singing Sandwich, 1986, Fun Design, w/built-in radio, no bottle	35	n/a
Lunch Man with Radio, 1986, Fun Design, w/built-in radio, no bottle	35	n/a
Lunch Time with Snoopy Dome, 1981, Thermos	15	5
Mad Balls, 1986, Aladdin	25	10
Marvel Super Heroes, 1990, Thermos	20	10
Max Headroom (Coca-Cola), 1985, Aladdin	50	25
McDonald's Happy Meal, 1986, Fisher-Price	15	n/a
Menudo, 1984, Thermos	12	5
Mickey & Minnie Mouse in Pink Car, 1988, Aladdin	10	5
Mickey Mouse & Donald Duck, 1984, Aladdin	10	5
Mickey Mouse & Donald Duck See-Saw, 1986, Aladdin	10	5
Mickey Mouse at City Zoo, 1985, Aladdin	10	5
Mickey Mouse Head, 1989, Aladdin	20	5
Mickey on Swinging Bridge, 1987, Aladdin	10	5
Mickey Skateboarding, 1980, Aladdin	18	5
Mighty Mouse, 1979, Thermos	35	10
Miss Piggy's Safari Van, 1989, Superseal, no bottle	15	n/a
Monster in My Pocket, 1990, Aladdin	30	5
Movie Monsters, 1979, Universal	35	12
Mr. T, 1984, Aladdin	20	10
Munchie Tunes Bear with Radio, 1986, Fun Design, w/built-in radio	35	5
Munchie Tunes Punchie Pup w/Radio, 1986, Fun Design, w/built-in radio	35	5
Munchie Tunes Robot with Radio, 1986, Fun Design, w/built-in radio	35	5
Muppets (blue), 1982, Thermos	12	5
Muppets Dome, 1981, Thermos, plastic red box w/matching bottle	20	5
New Kids on the Block (pink/orange), 1990, Thermos	10	5
Nosy Bears, 1988, Aladdin	12	5
Official Lunch Football, 1974, unknown, football shaped box, red or brown	100	n/a
Peanuts, Wienie Roast, 1985, Thermos	10	4
Pee Wee's Playhouse, 1987, Thermos, w/generic plastic bottle	20	5
Peter Pan Peanut Butter, 1984, Taiwan	85	20
Pickle, 1972, Fesco, no bottle	140	n/a
Popeye & Son, 1987, Servo, plastic red box, flat paper label, w/matching bottle	65	12
Popeye & Son (3-D), 1987, Servo, plastic box, red or yellow, w/matching bottle	50	12
Popeye Dome, 1979, Aladdin	35	15
Popeye, Truant Officer, 1964, King Seeley Thermos, plastic red box, matching metal bottle (Canada)	150	35
Punky Brewster, 1984, Deka	20	10

PLASTIC

NAME, YEAR, COMPANY, DESCRIPTION	BOX NM	BOTTLE NM
Q-Bert, 1983, Thermos	15	12
Race Cars, 1987, Servo	20	n/a
Raggedy Ann & Andy, 1988, Aladdin	45	20
Rainbow Bread Van, 1984, Moldmark Industries	60	20
Rainbow Brite, 1983, Thermos	10	5
Robot Man and Friends, 1984, Thermos	20	10
Rocketeer, 1990, Aladdin	10	5
Rocky Roughneck, 1977, Thermos	25	10
Roller Games, 1989, Thermos	25	10
S.W.A.T. Dome, 1975, Thermos	45	15
Scooby Doo, 1973, Thermos	30	20
Scooby Doo, 1984, Aladdin	40	20
Scooby-Doo, A Pup Named, 1988, Aladdin	20	10
Sesame Street, 1985, Aladdin/Canada	10	5
Shirt Tales, 1981, Thermos	10	5
Sky Commanders, 1987, Thermos, generic plastic bottle	15	5
Smurfette, 1984, Thermos	10	5
Smurfs, 1984, Thermos	15	5
Smurfs Dome, 1981, Thermos	20	5
Smurfs Fishing, 1984, Thermos	15	5
Snak Shot Camera, 1987, Hummer, camera-shaped box, blue or green, w/generic plastic bottle	30	2
Snoopy Dome, 1978, Thermos	20	5
Snorks, 1984, Thermos	12	5
Snow White, 1980, Aladdin	40	15
Spare Parts, 1982, Aladdin, w/generic plastic bottle	35	10
Sport Billy, 1982, Thermos	20	10
Sport Goofy, 1986, Aladdin	30	10
Star Com. U.S. Space Force, 1987, Thermos	20	10
Star Trek Next Generation, 1989, Thermos, red box, Picard, Data, Wesley, matching bottle	50	20
Star Trek Next Generation, 1988, Thermos, blue box, group picture, matching bottle	35	10
Star Wars, Droids, 1985, Thermos	30	10
Strawberry Shortcake, 1980, Aladdin	10	5
Superman II Dome, 1986, Aladdin	40	20
Superman, This is a Job For, 1980, Aladdin, no bottle	25	n/a
Tail Spin, 1986, Aladdin	10	5
Tang Trio, 1988, Thermos, red or yellow box w/generic plastic bottle	35	5
Teenage Mutant Ninja Turtles, 1990, Thermos, w/generic plastic bottle	12	5
Thundarr the Barbarian Dome, 1981, Aladdin, plastic dome box w/matching bottle	25	10
Timeless Tales, 1989, Aladdin	10	5
Tiny Toon Adventures, 1990, Thermos	10	5
Tom & Jerry, 1989, Aladdin	30	10
Transformers, 1985, Aladdin	15	5
Transformers Dome, 1986, Aladdin/Canada, dome box, generic plastic bottle	35	8
Tweety & Sylvester, 1986, Thermos	45	20
Wayne Gretzky, 1980, Aladdin	100	30
Wayne Gretzky Dome, 1980, Aladdin	120	30
Where's Waldo, 1990, Thermos	10	5
Who Framed Roger Rabbit, 1987, Thermos, red or yellow, w/matching bottle	20	10
Wild Fire, 1986, Aladdin	15	8
Wizard of Oz, 50th Anniversary, 1989, Aladdin	60	20
Woody Woodpecker, 1972, Aladdin, yellow box, red bottle	50	40
World Wrestling Federation, 1986, Thermos	10	5
Wrinkles, 1984, Thermos	10	5
Wuzzles, 1985, Aladdin	10	5
Yogi's Treasure Hunt, 1987, Servo, flat paper label, w/matching bottle	25	30
Yogi's Treasure Hunt (3-D), 1987, Servo, 3-D box, green or pink, w/matching bottle	55	30

STEEL

NAME, YEAR, COMPANY, DESCRIPTION	BOX NM	BOTTLE NM
240 Robert, 1978, Aladdin	2500	300
A-Team, 1985, King Seeley Thermos, plastic bottle	20	15

LUNCH BOXES

Geoffrey, 1981, Aladdin

Jabber Jaw, 1977, Thermos

The Incredible Hulk, 1978, Aladdin

Astronauts, 1969, Aladdin

Beverly Hillbillies, 1963, Aladdin

Gremlins, 1984, Aladdin

NAME, YEAR, COMPANY, DESCRIPTION	BOX NM	BOTTLE NM
Action Jackson, 1973, Okay Industries, matching steel bottle	600	200
Adam-12, 1973, Aladdin, matching plastic bottle	60	20
Addams Family, 1974, King Seeley Thermos, matching plastic bottle	100	30
Airline, 1969, Ohio Art, no bottle	80	n/a
All American, 1954, Universal, steel/glass bottle	350	65
America on Parade, 1976, Aladdin, matching plastic bottle	40	20
Americana, 1958, King Seeley Thermos, steel/glass bottle	325	125
Animal Friends, 1978, Ohio Art, yellow or red background behind name	35	n/a
Annie Oakley & Tagg, 1955, Aladdin, matching steel bottle	300	110
Annie, The Movie, 1982, Aladdin, plastic bottle	25	15
Apple's Way, 1975, King Seeley Thermos, plastic bottle	75	20
Archies, 1969, Aladdin, matching plastic bottle	70	30
Astronaut Dome, 1960, King Seeley Thermos, steel/glass bottle	250	60
Astronauts, 1969, Aladdin, matching plastic bottle	65	40
Atom Ant/Secret Squirrel, 1966, King Seeley Thermos, matching steel bottle	200	110
Auto Race, 1967, King Seeley Thermos, matching steel bottle	60	30
Back in '76, 1975, Aladdin, plastic bottle	55	25
Barbie Lunch Kit, 1962, King Seeley Thermos, steel/glass bottle	250	90
Basketweave, 1968, Ohio Art, no bottle	60	n/a
Batman, 1966, Aladdin, matching steel bottle	150	80
Battle Kit, 1965, King Seeley Thermos, matching steel bottle	85	50
Battle of the Planets, 1979, King Seeley Thermos, matching plastic bottle	45	25
Battlestar Galactica, 1978, Aladdin, matching plastic bottle	45	15
Beatles, 1966, Aladdin, blue, matching bottle	400	150
Bedknobs & Broomsticks, 1972, Aladdin, plastic bottle	40	25
Bee Gees, 1978, King Seeley Thermos, Barry on back, matching plastic bottle	35	15
Bee Gees, 1978, King Seeley Thermos, Maurice on back, matching plastic bottle	35	15
Bee Gees, 1978, King Seeley Thermos, Robin on back, matching plastic bottle	35	15
Berenstain Bears, 1983, American Thermos, matching plastic bottle	35	10
Beverly Hillbillies, 1963, Aladdin, matching steel bottle	180	80
Bionic Woman, with Car, 1977, Aladdin, plastic bottle	35	20
Bionic Woman, with Dog, 1978, Aladdin, matching plastic bottle	35	25
Black Hole, 1979, Aladdin, matching plastic bottle	60	30
Blondie, 1969, King Seeley Thermos, matching steel bottle	150	50
Boating, 1959, American Thermos, matching steel bottle	400	125
Bobby Sherman, 1972, King Seeley Thermos, matching steel bottle	75	50
Bonanza, 1965, Aladdin, brown rim box, steel bottle	120	60
Bonanza, 1963, Aladdin, green rim box, steel bottle	140	60
Bonanza, 1968, Aladdin, black rim box, steel bottle	160	90
Bond XX, 1967, Ohio Art, no bottle	150	n/a
Boston Bruins, 1973, Okay Industries, steel/glass bottle	525	250
Bozo the Clown Dome, Aladdin, steel bottle	280	100
Brady Bunch, 1970, King Seeley Thermos, matching steel bottle	250	75
Brave Eagle, 1957, American Thermos, red, blue, gray or green band, matching steel bottle	220	120
Bread Box Dome, 1968, Aladdin, Campbell's Soup bottle	250	160
Buccaneer Dome, 1957, Aladdin, matching bottle	200	125
Buck Rogers, 1979, Aladdin, matching plastic bottle	35	20
Bugaloos, 1971, Aladdin, matching plastic bottle	125	45
Bullwinkle & Rocky, 1962, Universal, blue box, steel bottle	800	220
Cabbage Patch Kids, 1984, King Seeley Thermos, matching plastic bottle	15	5
Cable Car Dome, 1962, Aladdin, steel/glass bottle	600	125
Campbell's Kids, 1973, Okay, matching steel bottle	180	100
Campus Queen, 1967, King Seeley Thermos, matching steel bottle	50	25
Canadian Pacific Railroad, 1970, Ohio Art, no bottle	60	n/a
Captain Astro, 1966, Ohio Art, no bottle	325	n/a
Care Bear Cousins, 1985, Aladdin, matching plastic bottle	10	5
Care Bears, 1984, Aladdin, plastic bottle	10	5
Carnival, 1959, Universal, matching steel bottle	550	250
Cartoon Zoo Lunch Chest, 1962, Universal, steel/glass bottle	325	125
Casey Jones, 1960, Universal, steel dome box, steel/glass bottle	650	125
Chan Clan, The, 1973, King Seeley Thermos, plastic bottle	110	35
Charlie's Angels, 1978, Aladdin, matching plastic bottle	35	10

LUNCH BOXES

NAME, YEAR, COMPANY, DESCRIPTION	BOX NM	BOTTLE NM
Chavo, 1979, Aladdin, matching plastic bottle	140	50
Children's, 1984, Ohio Art, no bottle	60	n/a
Children, Blue, 1974, Okay Industries, plastic bottle	160	40
Children, Yellow, 1974, Okay Industries, plastic bottle	210	40
Chitty Chitty Bang Bang, 1969, King Seeley Thermos, matching steel bottle	125	60
Chuck Wagon Dome, 1958, Aladdin, matching bottle	180	90
Circus Wagon Dome, 1958, King Seeley Thermos, steel/glass bottle	350	150
Clash of the Titans, 1981, King Seeley Thermos, matching plastic bottle	30	12
Close Encounters of the Third Kind, 1978, King Seeley Thermos, plastic bottle	80	20
Color Me Happy, 1984, Ohio Art, no bottle	110	n/a
Corsage, 1958, American Thermos, matching steel bottle	50	20
Cowboy in Africa, Chuck Connors, 1968, King Seeley Thermos, matching steel bottle	190	75
Cracker Jack, 1969, Aladdin, matching plastic bottle	55	20
Curiosity Shop, 1972, King Seeley Thermos, matching steel bottle	45	30
Cyclist Dirt Bike, 1979, Aladdin, plastic bottle	40	20
Daniel Boone, 1955, Aladdin, matching steel bottle	350	110
Daniel Boone, 1965, Aladdin, matching steel bottle	140	90
Dark Crystal, 1982, King Seeley Thermos, matching plastic bottle	20	10
Davy Crockett, 1955, Kruger, no bottle	350	n/a
Davy Crockett, 1955, Holtemp, matching steel bottle	140	75
Davy Crockett/Kit Carson, 1955, Adco Liberty	200	n/a
Debutante, 1958, Aladdin, matching steel bottle	110	75
Denim Diner Dome, 1975, Aladdin, matching plastic bottle	60	20
Dick Tracy, 1967, Aladdin, matching steel bottle	150	80
Disco, 1979, Aladdin, matching plastic bottle	50	15
Disco Fever, 1980, Aladdin, matching plastic bottle	55	15
Disney Express, 1979, Aladdin, matching plastic bottle	10	5
Disney Fire Fighters Dome, 1974, Aladdin, matching plastic bottle	150	60
Disney School Bus Dome, 1968, Aladdin, steel/glass bottle	75	30
Disney World, 1972, Aladdin, matching plastic bottle	30	10
Disney's Magic Kingdom, 1980, Aladdin, plastic bottle	15	10
Disney's Rescuers, The, 1977, Aladdin, plastic bottle	35	20
Disney's Robin Hood, 1974, Aladdin, plastic bottle	55	25
Disney, Wonderful World of, 1982, Aladdin, plastic bottle	15	10
Disneyland (Castle), 1957, Aladdin, matching steel bottle	160	115
Disneyland (Monorail), 1968, Aladdin, matching steel bottle	200	115
Donald Duck, 1980, Cheinco, no bottle	30	n/a
Double Decker, 1970, Aladdin, matching plastic bottle	60	40
Dr. Dolittle, Aladdin, steel/glass bottle	100	50
Dr. Seuss, 1970, Aladdin, matching plastic bottle	150	50
Drag Strip, 1975, Aladdin, matching plastic bottle	45	25
Dragon's Lair, 1983, Aladdin, matching plastic bottle	25	15
Duchess, 1960, Aladdin, steel/glass bottle	85	30
Dudley Do-Right, 1962, Universal, matching steel bottle	800	350
Dukes of Hazzard, 1983, Aladdin, matching plastic bottle	45	20
Dutch Cottage Dome, 1958, King Seeley Thermos, steel/glass bottle	450	150
Dyno Mutt, 1977, King Seeley Thermos, plastic bottle	45	20
E.T., The Extra-Terrestrial, 1982, Aladdin, matching plastic bottle	30	10
Early West Indian Territory, 1982, Ohio Art	60	n/a
Early West Oregon Trail, 1982, Ohio Art, no bottle	60	n/a
Early West Pony Express, 1982, Ohio Art, no bottle	60	n/a
Emergency!, 1973, Aladdin, plastic bottle	50	30
Emergency! Dome, 1977, Aladdin, plastic bottle	160	30
Evel Knievel, 1974, Aladdin, plastic bottle	60	25
Exciting World of Metrics, The, 1976, King Seeley Thermos, plastic bottle	40	25
Fall Guy, 1981, Aladdin, matching plastic bottle	20	15
Family Affair, 1969, King Seeley Thermos, matching steel bottle	70	30
Fat Albert and the Cosby Kids, 1973, King Seeley Thermos, plastic bottle	45	20
Fess Parker, 1965, King Seeley Thermos, matching steel bottle	160	90
Fireball XL5, 1964, King Seeley Thermos, steel/glass bottle	185	85
Firehouse Dome, 1959, American Thermos, steel/glass bottle	350	150
Flag-O-Rama, 1954, Universal, steel/glass bottle	475	110

NAME, YEAR, COMPANY, DESCRIPTION	BOX NM	BOTTLE NM
Flintstones, 1962, Aladdin, orange, 1st issue, matching bottle	150	80
Flintstones, 1973, Aladdin, matching plastic bottle	130	50
Flintstones, 1963, Aladdin, yellow, 2nd issue, matching bottle	160	80
Flipper, 1966, King Seeley Thermos, matching steel bottle	160	75
Floral, 1970, Ohio Art, no bottle	40	n/a
Flying Nun, 1968, Aladdin, matching steel bottle	150	80
Fonz, The, 1978, King Seeley Thermos, plastic bottle	40	20
Fox and the Hound, 1981, Aladdin, plastic bottle	30	10
Fraggle Rock, 1984, King Seeley Thermos, matching plastic bottle	15	5
Fritos, 1975, King Seeley Thermos, generic bottle	90	5
Frontier Days, 1957, Ohio Art, no bottle	210	n/a
Frost Flowers, 1962, Ohio Art, no bottle	70	n/a
Fruit Basket, 1975, Ohio Art, no bottle	35	n/a
Funtastic World of Hanna-Barbera, 1977, King Seeley Thermos, Huck Hound, plastic bottle	65	30
Funtastic World of Hanna-Barbera, 1978, King Seeley Thermos, Flintstones & Yogi, plastic bottle	75	30
G.I. Joe, 1982, King Seeley Thermos, plastic bottle	25	15
G.I. Joe, 1967, King Seeley Thermos, steel/glass bottle	100	60
Gene Autry, 1954, Universal, steel/glass bottle	425	125
Gentle Ben, 1968, Aladdin, plastic bottle, glass liner	95	30
Get Smart, 1966, King Seeley Thermos, steel/glass bottle	175	85
Ghostland, 1977, Ohio Art, spinner game, no bottle	35	n/a
Globe-Trotter Dome, 1959, Aladdin, steel dome box, matching steel/glass bottle	240	120
Gomer Pyle USMC, 1966, Aladdin, matching steel bottle	145	90
Goober and the Ghostchasers / Inch High, 1974, King Seeley Thermos, matching plastic bottle	35	15
Great Wild West, 1959, Universal, matching steel bottle	425	180
Green Hornet, 1967, King Seeley Thermos, matching steel bottle	375	150
Gremlins, 1984, Aladdin, matching plastic bottle	20	5
Grizzly Adams Dome, 1977, Aladdin, plastic bottle	80	25
Guns of Will Sonnett, The, 1968, King Seeley Thermos, steel/glass bottle	160	90
Gunsmoke, 1972, Aladdin, mule splashing box w/matching bottle	130	55
Gunsmoke, 1973, Aladdin, stagecoach box, matching bottle	130	55
Gunsmoke, 1959, Aladdin, plastic bottle	160	80
Gunsmoke, Double L Version, 1959, Aladdin, double L error version, matching bottle	550	80
Gunsmoke, Marshal Matt Dillon, 1962, Aladdin, matching steel bottle	180	75
H.R. Pufnstuf, 1970, Aladdin, matching plastic bottle	100	50
Hair Bear Bunch, The, 1972, King Seeley Thermos, plastic bottle	45	35
Hansel and Gretel, 1982, Ohio Art, no bottle	80	n/a
Happy Days, 1977, American Thermos, matching plastic bottle	40	20
Hardy Boys Mysteries, 1977, King Seeley Thermos, matching plastic bottle	40	30
Harlem Globetrotters, 1971, King Seeley Thermos, steel bottle, blue or purple uniforms	50	35
Have Gun, Will Travel, 1960, Aladdin, matching bottle	250	150
He-Man & Masters of the Universe, 1984, Aladdin, matching plastic bottle	5	5
Heathcliff, 1982, Aladdin, matching plastic bottle	20	10
Hector Heathcote, 1964, Aladdin, matching steel bottle	250	90
Hee Haw, 1971, King Seeley Thermos, matching steel bottle	70	50
Highway Signs, 1972, Ohio Art, no bottle	70	n/a
Hogan's Heroes Dome, 1966, Aladdin, steel/glass bottle	280	110
Holly Hobbie, 1979, Aladdin, matching plastic bottle	15	5
Holly Hobbie, 1973, Aladdin, matching plastic bottle	15	10
Holly Hobbie, 1968, Aladdin, red rim, matching plastic bottle	15	5
Home Town Airport Dome, 1960, King Seeley Thermos, steel/glass bottle	1000	275
Hong Kong Phooey, 1975, King Seeley Thermos, steel/glass bottle	40	15
Hopalong Cassidy, 1954, Aladdin, black rim, steel/glass bottle	250	125
Hopalong Cassidy, 1952, Aladdin, full litho, matching steel bottle	210	70
Hopalong Cassidy, 1950, Aladdin, red or blue, steel/glass bottle	160	75
Hot Wheels, 1969, King Seeley Thermos, matching steel bottle	70	25
How the West Was Won, 1979, King Seeley Thermos, matching plastic bottle	45	35
Howdy Doody, 1954, Adco Liberty	500	n/a
Huckleberry Hound, 1961, Aladdin, steel/glass bottle	175	60
Indiana Jones, 1984, King Seeley Thermos, matching plastic bottle	20	15

LUNCH BOXES

437

Hee Haw, 1971, King Seeley Thermos

Hopalong Cassidy Thermos, 1950, Aladdin

Huckleberry Hound Thermos, 1961, Aladdin

Mork & Mindy, 1979, American Thermos

NAME, YEAR, COMPANY, DESCRIPTION	BOX NM	BOTTLE NM
Indiana Jones Temple of Doom, 1984, King Seeley Thermos, matching plastic bottle	20	15
It's About Time Dome, 1967, Aladdin, matching bottle	220	125
Jack and Jill, 1982, Ohio Art	400	n/a
James Bond 007, 1966, Aladdin, matching steel bottle	260	135
Jet Patrol, 1957, Aladdin, matching steel bottle	360	150
Jetsons Dome, 1963, Aladdin, matching bottle	675	175
Joe Palooka, 1949, Continental Can, no bottle	90	n/a
Johnny Lightning, 1970, Aladdin, plastic bottle	75	30
Jonathan Livingston Seagull, 1973, Aladdin, matching plastic bottle	50	25
Julia, 1969, King Seeley Thermos, matching steel bottle	110	45
Jungle Book, 1968, Aladdin, matching steel bottle	65	60
Junior Miss, 1978, Aladdin, matching plastic bottle	30	20
Kellogg's, 1969, Aladdin, plastic bottle	150	60
King Kong, 1977, King Seeley Thermos, plastic bottle	55	25
KISS, 1977, King Seeley Thermos, plastic bottle	100	30
Knight in Armor, 1959, Universal, matching steel bottle	825	250
Knight Rider, 1984, King Seeley Thermos, matching plastic bottle	20	10
Korg, 1975, King Seeley Thermos, matching plastic bottle	50	30
Krofft Supershow, 1976, Aladdin, matching plastic bottle	85	35
Kung Fu, 1974, King Seeley Thermos, matching plastic bottle	65	25
Lance Link, Secret Chimp, 1971, King Seeley Thermos, matching steel bottle	110	65
Land of the Giants, 1968, Aladdin, plastic bottle	150	50
Land of the Lost, 1975, Aladdin, matching plastic bottle	80	35
Laugh-In (Helmet), 1969, Aladdin, helmet on back, matching plastic bottle	90	40
Laugh-In (Tricycle), 1969, Aladdin, trike on back, matching plastic bottle	140	40
Lawman, 1961, King Seeley Thermos, generic bottle	140	60
Legend of the Lone Ranger, 1980, Aladdin, plastic bottle	45	20
Lidsville, 1971, Aladdin, matching plastic bottle	90	45
Little Dutch Miss, 1959, Universal, matching steel bottle	110	60
Little Friends, 1982, Aladdin, matching plastic bottle	760	260
Little House on the Prairie, 1978, King Seeley Thermos, matching plastic bottle	80	35
Little Red Riding Hood, 1982, Ohio Art, no bottle	25	n/a
Lone Ranger, 1955, Adco Liberty, red rim, blue band, no bottle	450	n/a
Looney Tunes TV Set, 1959, King Seeley Thermos, steel/glass bottle	220	120
Lost in Space Dome, 1967, King Seeley Thermos, steel/glass bottle	600	60
Ludwig Von Drake, 1962, Aladdin, steel/glass bottle	190	90
Luggage Plaid, 1955, Adco Liberty, no bottle	75	n/a
Luggage Plaid, 1957, Ohio Art, no bottle	50	22
Magic of Lassie, 1978, King Seeley Thermos, matching plastic bottle	65	30
Major League Baseball, 1968, King Seeley Thermos, matching bottle	70	30
Man from U.N.C.L.E., 1966, King Seeley Thermos, matching steel bottle	140	90
Marvel Super Heroes, 1976, Aladdin, black rim, matching plastic bottle	35	5
Mary Poppins, 1965, Aladdin, steel/glass bottle	75	50
Masters of the Universe, 1983, Aladdin, matching plastic bottle	10	5
Mickey Mouse & Donald Duck, 1954, Adco Liberty, matching steel bottle	280	200
Mickey Mouse Club, 1963, Aladdin, yellow, steel/glass bottle	65	30
Mickey Mouse Club, 1976, Aladdin, white, matching steel bottle	65	30
Mickey Mouse Club, 1977, Aladdin, red rim, sky boat, matching bottle	35	15
Miss America, 1972, Aladdin, matching plastic bottle	55	30
Mod Floral Dome, 1975, Okay Industries, matching steel bottle	250	220
Monroes, 1967, Aladdin, matching steel bottle	160	110
Mork & Mindy, 1979, American Thermos, matching plastic bottle	25	15
Mr. Merlin, 1982, King Seeley Thermos, matching plastic bottle	25	10
Munsters, 1965, King Seeley Thermos, matching steel bottle	275	125
Muppet Babies, 1985, King Seeley Thermos, matching plastic bottle	12	5
Muppet Movie, 1979, King Seeley Thermos, matching plastic bottle	30	10
Muppet Show, 1978, King Seeley Thermos, plastic bottle	20	10
Muppets, 1979, King Seeley Thermos, back shows Animal, Fozzie or Kermit, matching plastic bottle	20	10
My Lunch, 1976, Ohio Art, no bottle	30	n/a
Nancy Drew, 1978, King Seeley Thermos, plastic bottle	40	20
NFL, 1978, King Seeley Thermos, blue rim, matching plastic bottle	25	15

LUNCH BOXES

NAME, YEAR, COMPANY, DESCRIPTION	BOX NM	BOTTLE NM
NFL, 1976, King Seeley Thermos, red rim, matching plastic bottle	30	15
NFL, 1975, King Seeley Thermos, yellow rim, plastic bottle	30	15
NFL, 1972, Okay, black rim, steel/glass bottle	160	130
NFL Quarterback, 1964, Aladdin, matching steel bottle	150	60
NHL, 1970, Okay Industries, plastic bottle	525	225
Orbit, 1963, King Seeley Thermos, matching steel bottle	250	90
Osmonds, The, 1973, Aladdin, matching plastic bottle	70	30
Our Friends, 1982, Aladdin, matching plastic bottle	575	180
Pac-Man, 1980, Aladdin, matching plastic bottle	10	5
Para-Medic, 1978, Ohio Art, no bottle	65	n/a
Partridge Family, 1971, King Seeley Thermos, plastic or steel bottle	50	30
Pathfinder, 1959, Universal, matching steel bottle	525	180
Patriotic, 1974, Ohio Art, no bottle	45	n/a
Peanuts, 1976, King Seeley Thermos, red pitching box, plastic bottle	25	5
Peanuts, 1980, King Seeley Thermos, pitching box, yellow face, green band, matching bottle	20	5
Peanuts, 1966, King Seeley Thermos, orange rim, matching steel bottle	35	15
Peanuts, 1973, King Seeley Thermos, red rim psychiatric box, plastic bottle	40	10
Pebbles & Bamm-Bamm, 1971, Aladdin, matching plastic bottle	55	40
Pele, 1975, King Seeley Thermos, matching plastic bottle	80	40
Pennant, 1950, Ohio Art, basket type box, no bottle	30	n/a
Pete's Dragon, 1978, Aladdin, matching plastic bottle	35	20
Peter Pan, 1969, Aladdin, matching plastic bottle, Disney	80	30
Pets 'n Pals, 1961, King Seeley Thermos, matching steel bottle	75	30
Pigs In Space, 1977, King Seeley Thermos, matching plastic bottle	20	10
Pink Gingham, 1976, King Seeley Thermos, matching plastic bottle	45	20
Pink Panther & Sons, 1984, King Seeley Thermos, matching plastic bottle	45	20
Pinocchio, 1971, Aladdin, plastic bottle	80	50
Pinocchio, 1938, unknown, steel round tin w/handle	150	n/a
Pinocchio, 1938, unknown, square	150	n/a
Pit Stop, 1968, Ohio Art	175	n/a
Planet of the Apes, 1974, Aladdin, matching plastic bottle	85	45
Play Ball, 1969, King Seeley Thermos, game on back, steel bottle	70	35
Police Patrol, 1978, Aladdin, plastic bottle	140	30
Polly Pal, 1975, King Seeley Thermos, matching plastic bottle	20	10
Pony Express, 1982, Ohio Art	90	n/a
Popeye, 1980, Aladdin, "arm wrestling" box, plastic bottle	40	25
Popeye, 1964, King Seeley Thermos, "Popeye in boat" box w/matching steel bottle	120	80
Popeye, 1962, Universal, "Popeye socks Bluto" box, matching bottle	450	300
Popples, 1986, Aladdin, plastic bottle	10	5
Porky's Lunch Wagon Dome, 1959, King Seeley Thermos, steel/glass bottle	375	110
Pro Sports, 1974, Ohio Art, no bottle	50	n/a
Psychedelic Dome, 1969, Aladdin, plastic bottle	335	85
Racing Wheels, 1977, King Seeley Thermos, plastic bottle	40	25
Raggedy Ann & Andy, 1973, Aladdin, plastic bottle	30	10
Rambo, 1985, King Seeley Thermos, matching plastic bottle	15	5
Rat Patrol, 1967, Aladdin, steel/glass bottle	100	60
Red Barn Dome, 1972, Thermos, matching steel/glass bottle	65	45
Red Barn Dome, 1957, King Seeley Thermos, closed door version, plain Holtemp bottle	80	20
Red Barn Dome, 1958, King Seeley Thermos, open door version, matching steel bottle	75	30
Rifleman, The, 1961, Aladdin, steel/glass bottle	330	140
Road Runner, 1970, King Seeley Thermos, lavender or purple rim, steel or plastic bottle	65	35
Robin Hood, 1956, Aladdin, matching bottle	190	120
Ronald McDonald, Sheriff, 1982, Aladdin, plastic bottle	30	10
Rose Petal Place, 1983, Aladdin, plastic bottle	15	5
Rough Rider, 1973, Aladdin, plastic bottle	55	30
Roy Rogers & Dale Double R Bar Ranch, 1955, American Thermos, eight-scene box, red or blue band, matching bottle	150	85
Roy Rogers & Dale Double R Bar Ranch, 1955, American Thermos, cowhide back box, red or blue band, matching bottle	160	80
Roy Rogers & Dale Double R Bar Ranch, 1954, American Thermos, blue or red band, woodgrain tall bottle	150	75

LUNCH BOXES

STEEL

NAME, YEAR, COMPANY, DESCRIPTION	BOX NM	BOTTLE NM
Roy Rogers & Dale Double R Bar Ranch, 1953, King Seeley Thermos, steel/glass bottle	130	75
Roy Rogers & Dale on Rail, 1957, American Thermos, red or blue band, matching bottle	180	80
Roy Rogers Chow Wagon Dome, 1958, King Seeley Thermos, steel/glass bottle	250	80
Saddlebag, 1977, King Seeley Thermos, generic plastic bottle	120	30
Satellite, 1960, King Seeley Thermos, steel bottle	110	60
Satellite, 1958, American Thermos, matching bottle	110	60
Scooby Doo, 1973, King Seeley Thermos, yellow or orange rim, plastic bottle	45	25
Secret Agent T, 1968, King Seeley Thermos, matching bottle	95	45
Secret of NIMH, 1982, Aladdin, plastic bottle	30	10
Secret Wars, 1984, Aladdin, plastic bottle	45	20
See America, 1972, Ohio Art, no bottle	50	n/a
Sesame Street, 1983, Aladdin, yellow rim, plastic bottle	10	5
Sigmund and the Sea Monsters, 1974, Aladdin, plastic bottle	95	40
Six Million Dollar Man, 1978, Aladdin, plastic bottle	40	25
Six Million Dollar Man, 1974, Aladdin, plastic bottle	40	25
Skateboarder, 1977, Aladdin, plastic bottle	40	20
Sleeping Beauty, 1960, General Steel Ware/Canada, generic steel bottle	450	55
Smokey Bear, 1975, Okay Industries, plastic bottle	350	200
Smurfs, 1983, King Seeley Thermos, blue box, plastic bottle	45	20
Snoopy Dome, 1968, King Seeley Thermos, yellow, "Have Lunch w/Snoopy", matching bottle	60	25
Snow White, Disney, 1975, Aladdin, orange rim, plastic bottle	55	25
Snow White, with Game, 1980, Ohio Art, no bottle	45	n/a
Space Explorer Ed McCauley, 1960, Aladdin, matching steel bottle	250	110
Space Ship, 1950, unknown, Decoware, dark blue square	250	n/a
Space Shuttle Orbiter Enterprise, 1977, King Seeley Thermos, plastic bottle	80	45
Space:1999, 1976, King Seeley Thermos, plastic bottle	55	25
Speed Buggy, 1974, King Seeley Thermos, red rim, plastic bottle	40	15
Spider-Man & Hulk, 1980, Aladdin, Captain America on back, plastic bottle	30	10
Sport Goofy, 1983, Aladdin, yellow rim, plastic bottle	25	10
Sport Skwirts, 1982, Ohio Art, several variations	35	n/a
Sports Afield, 1957, Ohio Art, no bottle	130	n/a
Star Trek Dome, 1968, Aladdin, matching bottle	700	375
Star Trek, The Motion Picture, 1980, King Seeley Thermos, matching bottle	80	40
Star Wars, 1978, King Seeley Thermos, cast or stars on band, matching plastic bottle	60	30
Star Wars, Empire Strikes Back, 1980, King Seeley Thermos, plastic bottle	40	10
Star Wars, Return of the Jedi, 1983, King Seeley Thermos, plastic bottle	40	10
Stars and Stripes Dome, 1970, King Seeley Thermos, matching plastic bottle	90	30
Steve Canyon, 1959, Aladdin, steel/glass bottle	260	150
Strawberry Shortcake, 1980, Aladdin, plastic bottle	10	5
Strawberry Shortcake, 1981, Aladdin, plastic bottle	10	5
Street Hawk, 1985, Aladdin, plastic bottle	160	90
Submarine, 1960, King Seeley Thermos, steel/glass bottle	110	60
Super Friends, 1976, Aladdin, matching plastic bottle	55	35
Super Powers, 1983, Aladdin, plastic bottle	65	30
Supercar, 1962, Universal, steel/glass bottle	325	150
Superman, 1967, King Seeley Thermos, red rim, "under fire" art on back, matching steel/glass bottle	155	85
Superman, 1954, Universal, blue rim	800	n/a
Superman, 1978, Aladdin, red rim, Daily Planet Office on back, matching bottle	35	20
Tapestry, 1963, Ohio Art, no bottle	60	n/a
Tarzan, 1966, Aladdin, steel/glass bottle	100	40
Teenager, 1957, King Seeley Thermos, generic bottle	85	10
Teenager Dome, 1957, King Seeley Thermos, generic bottle	140	10
Three Little Pigs, 1982, Ohio Art, red rim, generic/plastic bottle	70	n/a
Thundercats, 1985, Aladdin, plastic bottle	20	5
Tom Corbett Space Cadet, 1952, Aladdin, blue or red paper decal box, steel/glass bottle	250	95
Tom Corbett Space Cadet, 1954, Aladdin, full litho, matching bottle	475	95
Toppie Elephant, 1957, American Thermos, yellow, matching bottle	1600	800
Track King, 1975, Okay Industries, matching steel bottle	260	180
Train, 1971, Ohio Art, no bottle	60	n/a
Transformers, 1986, Aladdin, red box, matching plastic bottle	10	5

LUNCH BOXES

441

Munsters Thermos, 1965, King Seeley Thermos

Space:1999, 1976, King Seeley Thermos

Superman, 1967, King Seeley Thermos

Roy Rogers & Dale Double R Bar Ranch, 1955, American Thermos

Wild Bill Hickok, 1955, Aladdin

STEEL

NAME, YEAR, COMPANY, DESCRIPTION	BOX NM	BOTTLE NM
Traveler, 1962, Ohio Art, no bottle	85	n/a
Trigger, 1956, King Seeley Thermos, no bottle	225	n/a
U.S. Mail Dome, 1969, Aladdin, plastic bottle	65	20
U.S. Space Corps, 1961, Universal, plastic rocket bottle	350	110
UFO, 1973, King Seeley Thermos, plastic bottle	90	30
Underdog, 1974, Okay Industries, plastic bottle	900	350
Universal's Movie Monsters, 1980, Aladdin, plastic bottle	70	25
Voyage to the Bottom of the Sea, 1967, Aladdin, steel/glass bottle	300	140
VW Bus Dome, 1960, Omni, plastic bottle	500	220
Wagon Train, 1964, King Seeley Thermos, matching steel bottle	160	50
Wags 'n Whiskers, 1978, King Seeley Thermos, matching plastic bottle	30	10
Wake Up America, 1973, Okay Industries, matching steel bottle	600	250
Waltons, The, 1973, Aladdin, plastic bottle	50	20
Washington Redskins, 1970, Okay Industries, steel bottle	260	140
Wee Pals Kid Power, 1974, American Thermos, matching plastic bottle	40	10
Welcome Back Kotter, 1977, Aladdin, flat or embossed face, red rim, matching plastic bottle	40	15
Western, 1963, King Seeley Thermos, tan or red rim, steel/glass bottle	140	55
Wild Bill Hickok, 1955, Aladdin, steel/glass bottle	165	80
Wild Frontier, 1977, Ohio Art, spinner game on back, no bottle	45	n/a
Wild, Wild West, 1969, Aladdin, plastic bottle	165	80
Winnie the Pooh, 1976, Aladdin, blue rim, plastic bottle	190	70
Yankee Doodles, 1975, King Seeley Thermos, plastic bottle	40	20
Yellow Submarine, 1968, King Seeley Thermos, steel/glass bottle	375	175
Yogi Bear, 1974, Aladdin	95	45
Yogi Bear & Friends, 1961, Aladdin, black rim, matching steel bottle	140	100
Zorro, 1958, Aladdin, black band, steel/glass bottle	170	120
Zorro, 1966, Aladdin, red band, steel/glass bottle	200	120

VINYL

NAME, YEAR, COMPANY, DESCRIPTION	BOX NM	BOTTLE NM
Alice in Wonderland, 1972, Aladdin, matching plastic bottle	200	45
All American, 1976, Bayville, Styrofoam bottle	160	20
All Dressed Up, 1970s, Bayville, Styrofoam bottle	90	20
All Star, 1960, Aladdin	450	60
Alvin and the Chipmunks, 1963, King Seeley Thermos, matching plastic bottle	400	140
Annie 1, 1981, Aladdin, matching plastic bottle	75	20
Bach's Lunch, 1975, Volkwein Bros., red Styrofoam bottle	130	20
Ballerina, 1960s, Universal, black, Thermax bottle	800	150
Ballerina, 1962, Aladdin, pink, steel/glass bottle	200	60
Ballet, 1961, Universal, red, plastic generic bottle	500	20
Banana Splits, 1969, King Seeley Thermos, matching steel/glass bottle	500	150
Barbarino Brunch Bag, 1977, Aladdin, zippered bag, plastic bottle	250	30
Barbie & Francie, 1965, King Seeley Thermos, black, matching steel/glass bottle	120	65
Barbie & Midge, 1965, King Seeley Thermos, black, matching steel/glass bottle	110	65
Barbie & Midge Dome, 1964, King Seeley Thermos, matching glass/steel bottle	530	65
Barbie Softy, 1988, King Seeley Thermos, generic plastic bottle	45	15
Barbie, World of, 1971, King Seeley Thermos, blue box, matching steel/glass bottle	90	25
Barbie, World of, 1971, King Seeley Thermos, pink box, matching steel/glass bottle	75	25
Barnum's Animals, 1978, Adco Liberty, no bottle	60	n/a
Beany & Cecil, 1963, King Seeley Thermos, steel/glass bottle	560	150
Beatles, 1965, Air Flite, no bottle	525	n/a
Beatles Brunch Bag, 1966, Aladdin, zippered bag, matching bottle	650	150
Beatles Kaboodles Kit, 1965, Standard Plastic Products, no bottle	600	n/a
Betsey Clark, 1977, King Seeley Thermos, yellow box, matching plastic bottle	110	15
Betsey Clark Munchies Bag, 1977, King Seeley Thermos, zippered bag, plastic bottle	90	10
Blue Gingham Brunch Bag, 1975, Aladdin, zippered box and plastic bottle	45	30
Bobby Soxer, 1959, Aladdin	300	n/a
Boston Red Sox, 1960s, Universal	30	20
Boy on the Swing, Abeama Industries	80	20
Buick 1910, 1974, Bayville, Styrofoam bottle	90	20

NAME, YEAR, COMPANY, DESCRIPTION	BOX NM	BOTTLE NM
Bullwinkle, 1963, King Seeley Thermos, yellow, generic steel bottle	450	60
Bullwinkle, 1963, King Seeley Thermos, blue steel/glass bottle	650	200
Calico Brunch Bag, 1980, Aladdin, zippered bag, plastic bottle	70	30
Captain Kangaroo, King Seeley Thermos, steel/glass bottle	500	150
Carousel, 1962, Aladdin, matching steel/glass bottle	425	130
Cars, 1960, Universal	140	n/a
Casper the Friendly Ghost, 1966, King Seeley Thermos, blue box, orange steel bottle	550	150
Challenger, Space Shuttle, 1986, Babcock, puffy box, no bottle	175	n/a
Charlie's Angels Brunch Bag, 1978, Aladdin, zippered bag, plastic bottle	170	30
Coca-Cola, 1947, Aladdin, Styrofoam bottle	160	20
Coco the Clown, 1970s, Gary, Styrofoam bottle	110	20
Combo Brunch Bag, 1967, Aladdin, zippered bag, steel/glass bottle	180	80
Corsage, 1970, King Seeley Thermos, steel/glass bottle	120	30
Cottage, 1974, King Seeley Thermos	130	n/a
Cowboy, 1960, Universal, plain plastic bottle	170	20
Dateline Lunch Kit, 1960, Hasbro, blue/pink, no bottle	250	n/a
Dawn, 1972, Aladdin, matching plastic bottle	140	35
Dawn, 1971, Aladdin, matching plastic bottle	140	35
Dawn Brunch Bag, 1971, Aladdin, zippered bag, plastic bottle	180	35
Denim Brunch Bag, 1980, Aladdin, zippered bag, plastic bottle	80	15
Deputy Dawg, 1964, Thermos, no bottle	550	n/a
Deputy Dawg, King Seeley Thermos, steel/glass bottle	550	120
Donny & Marie, 1977, Aladdin, long hair version, matching plastic bottle	110	20
Donny & Marie, 1978, Aladdin, short hair version, matching plastic bottle	120	20
Donny & Marie Brunch Bag, 1977, Aladdin, zippered bag, plastic bottle	125	20
Dr. Seuss, 1970, Aladdin, plastic bottle	575	60
Dream Boat, 1960, Feldco, Styrofoam bottle	275	20
Eats 'n Treats, King Seeley Thermos, blue steel/glass bottle	200	40
Fess Parker Kaboodle Kit, 1960s, Aladdin, matching steel bottle	425	90
Fishing, 1970, Universal, Styrofoam bottle	120	20
Frog Flutist, 1975, Aladdin, matching plastic bottle	75	20
Fun to See'n Keep Tiger, 1960, unknown, no bottle	175	n/a
G.I. Joe, 1989, King Seeley Thermos, generic plastic bottle	55	10
Gigi, 1962, Aladdin, matching steel/glass bottle	280	80
Girl & Poodle, 1960, Universal, Styrofoam bottle	140	20
Glamour Gal, 1960, Aladdin, steel/glass bottle	150	35
Go-Go Brunch Bag, 1966, Aladdin, plastic bottle	245	60
Goat Butt Mountain, 1960, Universal, Styrofoam bottle	140	20
Happy Powwow, 1970s, Bayville, red or blue, w/Styrofoam bottle	60	20
Highway Signs Snap Pack, 1988, Avon	20	n/a
Holly Hobbie, 1972, Aladdin, white bag, matching plastic bottle	85	10
I Love a Parade, 1970, Universal, Styrofoam bottle	130	20
Ice Cream Cone, 1975, Aladdin, matching plastic bottle	55	20
It's a Small World, 1968, Aladdin, matching steel/glass bottle	250	110
Jonathan Livingston Seagull, 1974, Aladdin, matching plastic bottle	160	35
Junior Deb, 1960, Aladdin, steel/glass bottle	175	50
Junior Miss Safari, 1962, Prepac, no bottle	140	n/a
Junior Nurse, 1963, King Seeley Thermos, steel/glass bottle	320	90
Kaboodle Kit, 1960s, Aladdin, pink or white, no bottle	160	n/a
Kewtie Pie, Aladdin, steel/glass bottle	125	60
Kodak Gold, 1970s, Aladdin	85	20
Kodak II, 1970s, Aladdin	85	20
L'il Jodie (Puffy), 1985, Babcock	90	n/a
Lassie, 1960s, Universal, Styrofoam bottle	120	20
Liddle Kiddles, 1969, King Seeley Thermos, matching steel/glass bottle	250	60
Linus the Lion-Hearted, 1965, Aladdin, steel/glass bottle	550	110
Little Ballerina, 1975, Bayville, Styrofoam bottle	75	20
Little Old Schoolhouse, 1974, Dart	80	n/a
Love, 1972, Aladdin, matching plastic bottle	160	45
Lunch 'n Munch, 1959, King Seeley Thermos, steel/glass bottle	450	50
Lunch 'n Munch, 1959, American Thermos, corsage bottle	400	75
Mam'zelle, 1971, Aladdin, plastic bottle	180	60

Bach's Lunch, 1975, Volkwein Bros.

The Pussycats, 1968, Aladdin

VINYL

NAME, YEAR, COMPANY, DESCRIPTION	BOX NM	BOTTLE NM
Mardi-Gras, 1971, Aladdin, matching plastic bottle	80	20
Mary Ann, 1960, Aladdin, matching steel/glass bottle	75	25
Mary Ann Lunch 'N Bag, 1960, Universal, no bottle	110	n/a
Mary Poppins, 1973, Aladdin, matching plastic bottle	90	50
Mary Poppins Brunch Bag, 1966, Aladdin, steel/glass bottle	150	50
Mod Miss Brunch Bag, 1969, Aladdin, plastic bottle	110	30
Monkees, 1967, King Seeley Thermos, matching steel/glass bottle	380	125
Moon Landing, 1960, Universal, Styrofoam bottle	180	20
Mr. Peanut Snap Pack, 1979, Dart, snap close bag, no bottle	110	n/a
Mushrooms, 1972, Aladdin, matching plastic bottle	125	45
New Zoo Revue, 1975, Aladdin, plastic bottle	210	60
Pac-Man (Puffy), 1985, Aladdin	65	n/a
Peanuts, 1973, King Seeley Thermos, white "piano" box, steel bottle	90	30
Peanuts, 1971, King Seeley Thermos, green "baseball" box, steel bottle	150	30
Peanuts, 1969, King Seeley Thermos, red "baseball" box, steel bottle	90	30
Peanuts, 1967, King Seeley Thermos, red "kite" box, steel/glass bottle	90	30
Pebbles & Bamm-Bamm, 1973, Gary, matching plastic bottle	250	55
Penelope & Penny, 1970s, Gary, yellow box w/Styrofoam bottle	120	20
Peter Pan, 1969, Aladdin, white box, matching plastic bottle	210	65
Pink Panther, 1980, Aladdin, matching plastic bottle	95	20
Pony Tail, 1960s, Thermos, white box, original art w/gray border added, no bottle	200	n/a
Pony Tail, 1965, King Seeley Thermos, white box, fold over lid, steel/glass bottle	200	30
Pony Tail Tid-Bit-Kit, 1962, King Seeley Thermos, steel/glass satellite bottle	200	30
Ponytails Poodle Kit, 1960, King Seeley Thermos, steel/glass bottle	150	20
Princess, 1963, Aladdin, steel/glass bottle	190	55
Psychedelic, 1969, Aladdin, yellow, matching steel/glass bottle	150	30
Pussycats, The, 1968, Aladdin, plastic bottle	220	80
Ringling Bros. Circus, 1970, King Seeley Thermos, orange box w/matching steel/glass bottle	425	140
Ringling Bros. Circus, 1971, King Seeley Thermos, puffy blue box, steel/glass bottle	110	40
Robo Warriors, 1970, unknown, no bottle	35	n/a
Roy Rogers Saddlebag, 1960, King Seeley Thermos, brown, steel/glass bottle	250	95
Roy Rogers Saddlebag, 1960, King Seeley Thermos, cream, steel/glass bottle	650	95
Sabrina, 1972, Aladdin, yellow box w/matching plastic bottle	230	85
Sesame Street, 1979, Aladdin, orange, matching plastic bottle	35	10
Sesame Street, 1981, Aladdin, yellow, matching plastic bottle	85	15
Shari Lewis, 1963, Aladdin, matching steel/glass bottle	470	120
Sizzlers, Hot Wheels, 1971, King Seeley Thermos, matching steel/glass bottle	225	60
Skipper, 1965, King Seeley Thermos, steel/glass bottle	220	60
Sleeping Beauty, Disney, 1970, Aladdin, white box, matching plastic bottle	240	80
Smokey the Bear, 1965, King Seeley Thermos, steel/glass bottle	450	110
Snoopy Munchies Bag, 1977, King Seeley Thermos, plastic bottle	45	10
Snoopy Softy, 1988, King Seeley Thermos, matching plastic bottle	20	10
Snow White, 1975, Aladdin, white box w/matching plastic bottle	285	45
Snow White, Disney, 1967, unknown, fold-over lid, tapered box, no bottle	400	n/a
Soupy Sales, 1966, King Seeley Thermos, blue box, no bottle	600	n/a
Spirit of '76, unknown, red	110	n/a
Sports Kit, 1960, Universal	350	40
Stewardess, 1962, Aladdin, steel/glass bottle	650	110
Strawberry Shortcake, 1980, Aladdin, matching plastic bottle	40	15
Tammy, 1964, Aladdin, matching steel/glass bottle	240	85
Tammy & Pepper, 1965, Aladdin, matching steel/glass bottle	240	85
Tinker Bell, Disney, 1969, Aladdin, plastic bottle	260	90
Twiggy, 1967, Aladdin, matching steel/glass bottle	225	80
Twiggy, 1967, King Seeley Thermos, steel/glass bottle	225	80
U.S. Mail Brunch Bag, 1971, Aladdin, zippered bag, plastic bottle	160	80
Winnie the Pooh, Aladdin, steel/glass bottle	450	110
Wonder Woman (blue), 1977, Aladdin, matching plastic bottle	150	35
Wonder Woman (yellow), 1978, Aladdin, matching plastic bottle	200	35
Wrangler, 1982, Aladdin, steel/glass bottle	325	95
Yosemite Sam, 1971, King Seeley Thermos, matching steel/glass bottle	560	140
Ziggy's Munch Box, 1979, Aladdin, plastic bottle	140	40

Marx Play Sets

For all practical purposes, play sets could have been invented by Louis Marx . . . at least as far as boys growing up in the 1950s and 1960s were concerned.

The words "Marx" and "play set" just went together, and they still go together today for many dedicated collectors.

A typical Marx play set included buildings, figures and lots of realistic accessories that helped bring the miniature world to life. The Fort Apache Stockade, for example, came with a hard plastic log fort, a colorful lithographed tin cabin, and, of course, pioneers and Indians locked in deadly combat. It was no wonder millions of kids had a burning desire for these toys. The play scenarios were almost endless.

This modern version of an age-old toy was a tribute to the marketing and manufacturing talents and whimsical genius of Louis Marx, the modern-day king of toys.

Not only was he responsible for developing the play set, but he popularized the yo-yo and produced some of the most innovative tin wind-ups, guns, dolls, trains, trikes, trucks and other toys that were commercially feasible. In 1955, Marx sold more than $30 million worth of toys, easily making it the largest toy manufacturer in the world.

What makes Marx's domination even more impressive was the fact that he rose from humble beginnings. He was born in Brooklyn in 1896 and didn't learn to speak English until he started school. At age 16, Marx went to work for Ferdinand Strauss, a toy manufacturer who produced items for Abraham & Strauss Department Stores. By the age of 20, Marx was managing the company's New Jersey factory.

After being fired by Strauss, Marx contracted with manufacturers to produce toys he designed. By the mid-1920s, Marx had three plants in the United States. By 1955, there were more than 5,000 items in the Marx toy line with plants worldwide.

Mass production and mass marketing through stores such as Sears and Montgomery Ward allowed Marx to keep prices low and quality high. Marx was also a master at producing new toys from the same basic components. Existing elements could be modified slightly, and new lithography would produce a new building from standard stock.

Part of Marx's repackaging genius included using popular TV or movie tie-ins to breathe new life into existing products. The Rifleman Ranch, Roy Rogers Ranch, Wyatt Earp and Wagon Train play sets were examples of repackaging existing parts to capture the fad of the day.

Marx sold his company to the Quaker Oats Company in 1972 for $31 million. Quaker Oats sold the company four years later for $15 million after losing money every year of its ownership.

Medieval Castle Fort

The Marx Toy Company is in existence once again making favorite Marx toys from original molds.

With the passing of a few short decades, once affordable children's toys have become highly prized collectibles. Play sets are among the price leaders in today's market for childhood treasures. And the figures that accompanied the play sets are also highly desired for their craftsmanship and detail.

A play set listed as MIB (Mint In Box) should be untouched and unassembled in the original box. Excellent condition means a complete set, but the buildings are assembled and the box may be worn or damaged. Good condition means the play set shows wear and may have a few minor pieces missing.

Trends

The play set market continues on a strong course, with several sets now commanding prices as high as some of their "classic" Marx tin wind-up counterparts. As it becomes increasingly difficult to find complete sets, individual pieces should sell well as collectors try to complete sets.

The Top 10 Marx Play Sets
(in Mint in Box condition)

1. Johnny Ringo Western Frontier Set,#4784 .... $2,500
2. Johnny Tremain Revolutionary War, #3402 2,000
3. Gunsmoke Dodge City, #4268 2,000
4. Fire House, #4820 2,000
5. Civil War Centennial, #5929 2,000
6. Sears Store, #5490 1,800
7. Custer's Last Stand, #4670 1,800
8. Ben Hur, #4701 1,800
9. World War II European Theatre, #5949... 1,500
10. Wagon Train, #4888 1,500

MARX PLAY SETS

MINIATURE PLAY SETS

NAME	DESCRIPTION	NO.	GOOD	EX	MIB
101 Dalmatians	1961, "The Wedding Scene"		75	300	450
20 Minutes to Berlin	1964, 174 pieces		100	300	500
Alice in Wonderland	New series, 1961		100	225	350
Attack on Fort Apache	stable, cowboys, Indians	HK-8078	85	225	500
Babes In Toyland	six different scenes, each		25	65	100
Battleground	1963, 170 pieces	HK-6111	20	60	200
Blue and Gray	1960s, 101 individual pieces	HK-6109	90	175	325
Border Battle	Mexican-American War		145	350	700
Charge of the Bengal Lancers	British/Turks		125	325	500
Charge of the Light Brigade	Sears, 216 pieces, Lancers/Cossacks		175	325	400
Charge of the Light Brigade	2nd version, photo box art, Lancers/Turks		110	300	400
Charge of the Light Brigade	smaller version, Lancers/Russians		75	225	325
Cinderella	New series		100	225	350
Covered Wagon Attack			85	200	400
Custer's Last Stand	1964, 181 pieces		125	325	600
Disney 3-in-1 Set	original series		75	225	350
Disney Circus Parade	Super Circus performers, Disneykins		85	225	350
Disney See and Play Castle	1st and 2nd series Disneykins	48-24388	150	350	450
Disney See and Play Doll House	1st series Disneykins		100	265	350
Donald Duck	original series; Donald, Daisy, Louie, Goofy		45	100	150
Dumbo's Circus	original series		50	100	150
Fairykin	six different, each		30	80	125
Fairykin TV Scenes	12 different, each		8	20	30
Fairykin TV Scenes Gift Set	two different, each w/six scenes, each		65	165	250
Fairykins 3-in-1 Diorama Set			100	265	400
Fairykins Gift Set	34 in window box		40	175	250
Fairykins TV Scenes Boxed Set of Eight			45	200	250
Fort Apache	1963, 90 pieces, Indians	HK-7526	55	80	165
Fort Apache	large set, HQ bldg., cavalry/cowboys/ Indians		115	295	375
Guerrilla Warfare	1960s, Viet Cong		275	350	450
Huckleberry Hound Presents	two different, each		75	115	175
Invasion Day	1964, 304 pieces		65	200	400
Jungle	smaller than Jungle Safari		50	85	175
Jungle Safari	260 pieces, hunters/natives		55	100	200
Knights and Castle	1963, 132 pieces	HK-7563	130	200	300
Knights and Castle	1964, 64 pieces	HK-7562	95	175	275
Knights and Vikings	1964, 143 pieces		145	275	425
Lady and the Tramp	New series, 1961		100	225	350
Lost Boys	second series, 1961		40	120	200
Lost Boys	New series		100	225	350
Ludwig Von Drake	RCA premium set		65	130	200
Ludwig Von Drake	1962, "The Professor Misses"		50	100	150
Ludwig Von Drake	1962, "The Nearsighted Professor"		50	100	150
Mickey Mouse and Friends	original series, display box		50	100	150
Munchville	vegetable characters		65	165	250
Noah's Ark	1968, 100 pieces		25	65	100
Noah's Ark	Ward's version, soft plastic figures		20	50	75
Over The Top	WWI, Germans/Doughboys		200	600	950
Panchito Western	original series, display box		50	100	150
Pinocchio	six different sets, each original series, display box		65	165	250

MINIATURE PLAY SETS

NAME	DESCRIPTION	NO.	GOOD	EX	MIB
Pinocchio 3-in-1 Set			115	295	450
Quick Draw McGraw	two different, each		75	115	200
Revolutionary War	British/Colonials		95	250	500
Sands of Iwo Jima	1964, 296 pieces		150	295	450
Sands of Iwo Jima	1963, 205 pieces		115	210	325
Sands of Iwo Jima	1963, 88 pieces		75	145	225
See and Play Dollhouse	American Beauties/Campus Cuties		75	175	350
Sleeping Beauty	new series, 1961		75	175	275
Snow White and the Seven Dwarfs	original series, display box		50	100	150
Sunshine Farm Set	farmers and animals		45	115	175
Sword in the Stone	British only Disney release		300	1000	1500
Ten Commandments	Montgomery Ward		150	395	600
Three Little Pigs	new series		100	225	350
Tiger Town	ENCO-like tigers, 1960s		75	175	300
Top Cat	three different, each		75	115	200
Troll Village			80	300	350
TV-Tinykins Gift Set	set of 34 figures		115	350	550
TV-Tinykins TV Scenes	12 different, each		12	35	50
Western Town	over 170 pieces	48-24398	50	150	250
Wooden Horse of Troy	British only issue		125	600	800

PLAY SETS

NAME	DESCRIPTION	NO.	GOOD	EX	MIB
Adventures of Robin Hood	1956, Richard Greene TV series	4722	250	750	1250
Alamo	1960, for 54mm figures	3534	140	250	400
Alamo	only two cannons	3546	100	300	500
Alaska Frontier	1959, 100 pieces	3708	275	525	800
American Airlines Astro Jet Port		4822	150	250	450
American Airlines International Jet Port	1962, 98 pieces	4810	150	250	450
Arctic Explorer	1960, Series 2000	3702	250	450	700
Army Combat Set	Sears, 411 pieces	6019	100	300	500
Army Combat Training Center		2654	20	55	90
Babyland Nursery		3379	125	225	350
Bar-M Ranch		3956	50	100	150
Battle of Iwo Jima	1964, 247 pieces	4147	80	240	400
Battle of Iwo Jima	1964, 128 pieces	6057	35	105	175
Battle of Little Big Horn	1972	4679MO	125	250	400
Battle of the Blue & Gray	Series 1000, small set, no house	2646	80	240	400
Battle of the Blue & Gray	1959, Series 2000, 54mm	4745	175	375	600
Battle of the Blue & Gray	Series 2000, large set	4658	250	700	1200
Battle of the Blue & Gray	1963, Centennial edition	4744	200	700	1200
Battlefield	1958, Series 5000	4756	25	95	150
Battleground	1963, Montgomery Ward	3745	80	240	400
Battleground	U.S. and Nazi troops	4169	30	90	150
Battleground	1971, Montgomery Ward	4752	90	275	450
Battleground	1962, 200 pieces	4754	35	110	185
Battleground	1959, 180 pieces	4751	35	110	185
Battleground	1958, largest of military sets	4750	130	395	650
Battleground	1963, Sears, 160 pieces		70	210	350
Battleground	1970s	4756	40	125	250
Beach Head Landing Set	U.S. and Nazi Troops	4939	15	65	100
Ben Hur	Series 5000, large set	4701	350	1075	1800
Ben Hur	1959, Series 2000, medium set	4702	250	750	1250
Ben Hur	blister card	2648	25	95	150
Ben Hur	1959, 132 pieces	4696	170	510	850
Big Inch Pipeline	1963, 200 pieces	6008	80	240	400
Big Top Circus	1952	4310	80	325	500

Alaska Frontier, 1959

Battleground, 1970s

Fort Apache, 1965

NAME	DESCRIPTION	NO.	GOOD	EX	MIB
Boot Camp	tin box set	4645	30	130	200
Boy Scout			115	600	900
Boys Camp	1956	4103	130	395	650
Cape Canaveral	1960	4524	85	195	300
Cape Canaveral	1959, Sears set	5963	80	325	500
Cape Canaveral Missile Center	1959	4528	80	240	400
Cape Canaveral Missile Center	1959	2656	50	150	250
Cape Canaveral Missile Center		4525	50	195	300
Cape Canaveral Missile Set	1958	4526	55	225	350
Cape Kennedy Carry All	1968, tin box set	4625	35	45	75
Captain Gallant of the Foreign Legion	1956	4729/ 4730	200	600	1000
Captain Space Solar Academy	1954	7018	65	260	400
Captain Space Solar Academy		7026	80	325	500
Castle and Moat Set	Sears exclusive	4734	65	260	400
Cattle Drive	mid-1970s	3983	60	245	375
Civil War Centennial	1961	5929	400	1200	2000
Comanche Pass	1976	3416	30	130	200
Complete Happitime Dairy Farm	Sears	5957	80	325	500
Complete U.S. Army Training Center	1954	4145	70	210	350
Construction Camp	1956, 54mm, Series 1000	4442	110	325	550
Construction Camp	1954	4439	90	275	450
Cowboy And Indian Camp	1953	3950	90	275	450
Custer's Last Stand	1956, Series 500	4779	80	325	500
Custer's Last Stand	1963, Sears, 187 pieces	4670	195	1200	1800
D-Day Army Set	U.S. and Nazi troops	6027	100	300	500
D.E.W. Defense Line Arctic Satellite Base		4802	100	300	500
Daktari	1967, 110 pieces	3717	100	300	500
Daktari	1967, 140 pieces	3720	130	395	650
Daktari		3718	80	325	500
Daniel Boone Frontier		1393	60	230	350
Daniel Boone Wilderness Scout	1964	0631	75	225	375
Daniel Boone Wilderness Scout	1964	0670	75	225	375
Daniel Boone Wilderness Scout	1964	2640	120	360	600
Davy Crockett at the Alamo		3442	120	360	600
Davy Crockett at the Alamo	1955, official Walt Disney, 100 pieces, first set	3530	65	260	400
Davy Crockett at the Alamo	1955, official Walt Disney, biggest set	3544	160	500	800
Desert Fox	1966, 244 pieces	4177	90	275	450
Desert Patrol	1967, U.S., Nazi troops	4174	60	175	300
Farm Set		6050	45	180	275
Farm Set	deluxe, 1969	3953	75	225	375
Farm Set		6006	50	195	300
Farm Set		5942	40	160	250
Farm Set	1958, 100 pieces, Series 2000	3948	80	250	400
Farm Set	Lazy Day, 1960, 100 pieces	3945	55	165	275
Fighting Knights Carry All	1966-68	4635	45	135	225
Fire House	w/two friction vehicles	4820	500	1500	2000
Fire House		4819	180	715	1100
Fort Apache		3616	30	90	150

NAME	DESCRIPTION	NO.	GOOD	EX	MIB
Fort Apache	1965, Sears, 335 pieces	6063	105	315	525
Fort Apache		3681A	30	90	150
Fort Apache			40	120	200
Fort Apache	1965, Sears, 147 pieces	59093C	30	90	150
Fort Apache	1972, Sears, over 100 pieces	6068	35	100	165
Fort Apache		6059	11	35	55
Fort Apache	Sears	4202	15	50	80
Fort Apache	1970s	3685	140	425	700
Fort Apache	giant set	3682	15	50	85
Fort Apache		3681	45	135	225
Fort Apache	1967	3681	40	120	200
Fort Apache	1976	4685	15	45	75
Fort Apache Carry All		3627	100	300	450
Fort Apache Rin Tin Tin	early, 60mm	3658	90	275	350
Fort Apache Rin Tin Tin	54mm	3957	90	275	350
Fort Apache Rin Tin Tin	mixed scale set	3610	70	210	350
Fort Apache Stockade	1951		55	165	275
Fort Apache Stockade	1961, Series 5000	3660	75	225	375
Fort Apache Stockade	1960, Series 2000, 60mm figures	3612	50	155	255
Fort Apache Stockade	1953	3636	55	165	270
Fort Apache with Famous Americans					
Fort Dearborn	1952, w/metal walls	3510	85	255	375
Fort Dearborn	larger set	3514	20	60	100
Fort Dearborn	w/plastic walls	3688	80	240	400
Fort Mohawk	British, Colonials, Indians, 54mm	3751	80	325	500
Fort Pitt	1959, Series 750, 54mm	3741	65	260	400
Fort Pitt	1959, Series 1000, 54mm	3742	70	290	450
Four-Level Allstate Service Station		6004	80	325	500
Four-Level Parking Garage		3502	40	120	200
Four-Level Parking Garage		3511	40	200	300
Freight Trucking Terminal	plastic trucks	5220	30	90	150
Freight Trucking Terminal	friction trucks	5422	30	90	150
Galaxy Command	1976	4206	10	30	50
Gallant Men	official set from TV series	4634	70	290	450
Gallant Men Army	U.S. troops	4632	65	260	400
Gunsmoke Dodge City	1960, official, Series 2000, 80 pieces	4268	245	1200	2000
Happitime Army and Air Force Training Center	1954, 147 pieces	4159	50	150	250
Happitime Civil War Centennial	1962, Sears	5929	115	455	700
Happitime Farm Set		3480	25	95	150
Happitime Roy Rogers Rodeo Ranch	1953	3990	60	180	300
Heritage Battle of the Alamo	1972, Heritage Series	59091	80	240	400
History in the Pacific	1972	4164	90	275	450
Holiday Turnpike	battery-operated w/HO scale vehicles	5230	10	30	45
I.G.Y. Arctic Satellite Base	1959, Series 1000	4800	235	700	1175
Indian Warfare	Series 2000	4778	65	260	400
Irrigated Farm Set	working pump	6021	7	20	35
Johnny Apollo Moon Launch Center	1970	4630	45	135	225
Johnny Ringo Western Frontier Set	1959, Series 2000	4784	1200	1800	2500
Johnny Tremain Revolutionary War	1957, official Walt Disney, Series 1000	3402	400	1200	2000
Jungle	metal trading post, Series 500	3705	110	325	550
Jungle	1960, 48 pieces, Sears, large animals	3716	25	95	150

MARX PLAY SETS

453

Lone Ranger Ranch, 1957

Navarone Mountain Battleground Set, 1976

PLAY SETS

NAME	DESCRIPTION	NO.	GOOD	EX	MIB
Jungle Jim	1957, official, Series 1000	3706	280	850	1400
Knights and Vikings	1972	4743	50	150	250
Knights and Vikings	1973	4733	50	150	250
Knights and Vikings		4773	30	90	150
Little Red School House	1956	3381	90	270	450
Lone Ranger Ranch	1957, Series 500	3969	85	250	425
Lone Ranger Rodeo Set	1953	3696	30	90	150
Medieval Castle	1960, metallic knights	4700	75	290	450
Medieval Castle	Sears, w/knights and Vikings	4734	75	290	450
Medieval Castle	w/knights and Vikings	4733	30	130	200
Medieval Castle	1954	4709	25	95	150
Medieval Castle	1959, Sears, Series 2000	4708	120	350	600
Medieval Castle	1964, gold knights, moat	4704	30	90	150
Medieval Castle	w/knights and Vikings	4707	35	110	180
Medieval Castle Fort	1953	4710	30	130	200
Midtown Service Station	1960	3420	50	150	250
Midtown Shopping Center		2644	30	90	150
Military Academy		4718	90	350	500
Modern Farm Set	1951, 54mm	3931	50	150	250
Modern Farm Set	1967	3932	60	180	300
Modern Service Center	1962	3471	70	210	350
Modern Service Station	1966	6044	35	105	175
Navarone Mountain Battleground Set	1976	3412	40	115	195
New Car Sales and Service		3466, 3465	75	290	450
One Million, B.C.	1970s		40	115	195
Operation Moon Base	1962	4654	90	270	450
Pet Shop		4209	60	230	350
Pet Shop	1953	4210	60	230	350
Prehistoric	1969	3398	35	105	175
Prehistoric Dinosaur	1978	4208	35	105	175
Prehistoric Times		3391	20	55	95
Prehistoric Times		2650	30	130	200
Prehistoric Times	Series 500	3389	35	105	175
Prehistoric Times	1957, Series 1000, big set	3390	60	230	350
Prehistoric Times		3388	25	75	125
Prince Valiant Castle	1955	4705	90	270	450
Prince Valiant Castle	1955, has figures	4706	100	300	500
Project Apollo Cape Kennedy		4523	25	75	125
Project Apollo Moon Landing		4646	50	150	250
Project Mercury Cape Canaveral	1959	4524	90	270	450
Raytheon Missile Test Center	1961	603-A	60	180	300
Real Life Western Wagon		4998	15	45	75
Red River Gang	1970s, mini set w/cowboys	4104	35	105	175
Revolutionary War	Series 1000	3404	120	490	750
Revolutionary War	1959, 80 pieces, Sears	3408	100	390	600
Revolutionary War	1957, Series 500	3401	200	500	1000
Rex Mars Planet Patrol		7040	100	300	500
Rex Mars Space Drome	1954	7016	130	395	650
Rifleman Ranch, The	1959	3998	130	395	650
Rifleman Ranch, The	1959	3997	115	455	700
Rin Tin Tin at Fort Apache	1956, Series 5000	3686R	240	725	1200
Rin Tin Tin at Fort Apache	1956, Series 500, 60mm	3628	160	475	800
Robin Hood Castle	60mm	4717	120	360	600
Robin Hood Castle	1958, 54mm	4718	80	325	500

NAME	DESCRIPTION	NO.	GOOD	EX	MIB
Roy Rogers Double R Bar Ranch	1962	3982	100	300	500
Roy Rogers Mineral City	1958, 95 pieces	4227	100	300	500
Roy Rogers Ranch	w/ranch kids	3980	200	300	500
Roy Rogers Rodeo		3689	20	60	100
Roy Rogers Rodeo Ranch	1952	3979	55	165	275
Roy Rogers Rodeo Ranch	1958	3986R	250	750	1250
Roy Rogers Rodeo Ranch	54mm	3988	65	195	325
Roy Rogers Rodeo Ranch	Series 2000	3996	130	395	650
Roy Rogers Rodeo Ranch	1952, 60mm	3985	45	135	225
Roy Rogers Western Town	1952, large set	4258	160	475	800
Roy Rogers Western Town	official, Series 5000	4259	80	235	395
Roy Rogers Western Town		4216	80	240	400
Sears Store	1961, Allstate box	5490	350	1200	1800
Service Station		5459	15	45	75
Service Station	w/parking garage	3485	105	315	525
Service Station	w/elevator	3495	30	90	150
Service Station	deluxe	3501	50	150	250
Shopping Center		3755	40	120	200
Silver City Western Town	has Custer, Boone, Carson, Buffalo Bill, Sitting Bull	4220	50	150	250
Skyscraper	working elevator	5449	155	800	1200
Skyscraper	working elevator and light	5450	155	800	1200
Sons of Liberty	Sears	4170	50	150	250
Star Station Seven	1970s		10	30	50
Strategic Air Command		6013	130	520	800
Super Circus	1952, over 70 pieces	4319	80	240	400
Super Circus	1952, w/character figures	4320	75	290	450
Tactical Air Command	1970s	4106	15	40	65
Tales of Wells Fargo		4262	150	450	750
Tales of Wells Fargo		4263	80	240	400
Tales of Wells Fargo	Series 1000	4264	150	450	750
Tales of Wells Fargo Train Set	1959, w/electric train	54752	240	600	800
Tank Battle	Sears, U.S., Nazi troops	6056	40	120	200
Tank Battle	U.S., Nazi troops	6060	40	120	200
Turnpike Service Center	1961	3460	100	300	500
U.S. Air Force		4807	30	90	160
U.S. Armed Forces		4151	70	210	350
U.S. Armed Forces Training Center	1955, Series 500	4149	85	255	425
U.S. Armed Forces Training Center	Marines, soldiers, sailors, airmen, tin litho building	4144	40	160	250
U.S. Armed Forces Training Center	1956	4158	110	330	550
U.S. Armed Forces Training Center		4150	50	150	250
U.S. Army Mobile Set	1956, flat figures	3655	20	60	100
U.S. Army Training Center		4153	15	55	85
U.S. Army Training Center		4123	25	75	125
U.S. Army Training Center		4122	20	60	100
U.S. Army Training Center		3378	20	55	95

Rin Tin Tin at Fort Apache, 1956

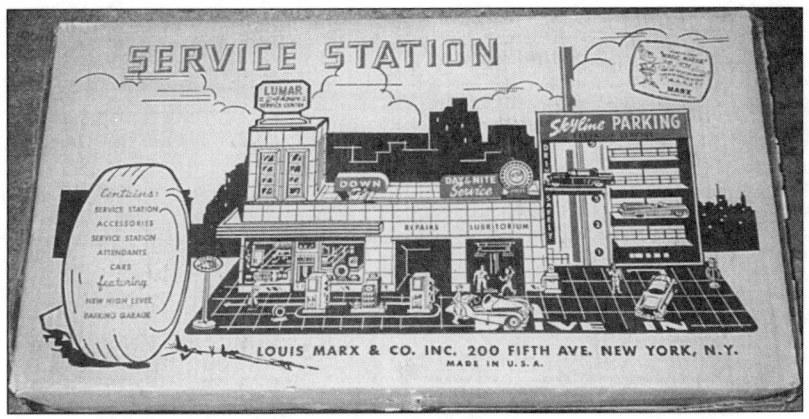

Service Station

Walt Disney's Zorro, 1958

PLAY SETS

NAME	DESCRIPTION	NO.	GOOD	EX	MIB
U.S. Army Training Center		3146	20	55	95
Untouchables	1961, 90 pieces	4676	245	975	1500
Vikings and Knights		6053	60	180	300
Wagon Train	Series 1000, X Team	4805	160	480	800
Wagon Train	official, Series 5000	4888	245	975	1500
Wagon Train	official, Series 2000	4788	120	360	600
Walt Disney Television Playhouse	1953	4352	120	360	600
Walt Disney Television Playhouse	1953	4350	100	300	500
Walt Disney Television Playhouse	1953, Peter Pan figures	4352	105	420	650
Walt Disney's Zorro	1958, official, Series 1000	3754	260	775	1300
Walt Disney's Zorro	1958, official, Series 500	3753	230	695	1150
Walt Disney's Zorro	1958, official	3758	240	725	1200
Walt Disney's Zorro	1972, official, Series 1000	3758	160	500	800
Ward's Service Station	1959	3488	80	240	400
Western Frontier Set			90	275	450
Western Mining Town	1950s	4265	135	400	675
Western Mining Town	1950s	4266	135	405	675
Western Ranch Set		3954	35	105	175
Western Ranch Set		3980	35	105	175
Western Stagecoach	1965	1395	20	60	100
Western Town	1952, bi-level town	4229	120	490	650
Western Town	single level	2652	60	180	400
Westgate Auto Center	1968		40	120	200
White House	house w/eight figures		15	40	70
White House & Presidents	house & figures, 1/48 scale presidents	3920	15	40	70
White House & Presidents	house & figures	3921	15	40	70
Wild Animal Jungle	large animals	3716	10	30	50
World War II Battleground	1970s	4204	30	90	150
World War II European Theatre	rare big set	5949	245	1200	1500
World War II European Theatre	Sears	5939	155	465	775
World War II Set	U.S., Nazi troops	5938	25	75	125
Wyatt Earp Dodge City Western Town	1957, Series 1000	4228	150	450	750

MARX PLAY SETS

458

Model Kits

Model kits have always been popular toys for boys, and in recent years the kits have found a new following among older collectors, primarily men recapturing a part of their youth.

Plastic model kits were first produced shortly before World War II, but it wasn't until after the war that plastic kit building really began to take off. Automobiles, aircraft and ships all became subject matter for the miniature replicas popularized by such companies as Aurora, Revell, Monogram and Lindberg.

Each type of model kit has its own enthusiastic following, but probably the most collectible kits today are the figure and character kits produced in the 1960s. These kits have seen dramatic increases in collector values over the past 10 years.

The company that did the most to popularize the figure kit was Aurora, with its early 1960s kits representing the monsters from Universal Pictures. Aurora had been producing figure kits prior to that, but the monster craze of the period was responsible for a highly successful line of kits. These kits have become the backbone of the hobby, as our Top 10 listing at the end of this article shows.

Starting with the Frankenstein monster in 1961, Aurora produced kits of many memorable movie monsters before moving into more general monstrosities, such as its famous working guillotine kit. Such toys offended the sensibilities of some groups, who brought about political pressure that spelled the end of these kits. The firm also produced kits based on popular television shows, comic characters and sports celebrities. Some of the kits originally made by Aurora were later reissued by Monogram and Revell. Resin copies of the harder-to-find Aurora kits are still being produced and sold today by independent garage kit makers.

Other popular monster kits were also a fad in the 1960s. These weren't the traditional movie monsters, but rather an assortment of strange characters that often came in wild hot rods. Among the more popular were Revell kits based on Ed "Big Daddy"

No. 1305 Rat Fink, 1963, Revell

Roth's Rat Fink concept. Other firms, most notably Hawk, also produced kits of this new type of monster.

Even popular celebrities of the day became the subject of model kits. Revell, for example, issued figure kits of each of the four Beatles.

Figure kits began to enjoy new popularity in the 1980s as new large-scale kits of rather limited production runs were being made in vinyl and resin. Billiken, a Japanese company, produced vinyl kits of the classic movie monsters, some of which have become highly collectible. Screamin' and Horizon are two leaders in a burgeoning "garage kit" field of large-scale vinyl and resin kits of movie, monster, and comic book characters. This area bears watching as limited runs of these garage kits will no doubt translate into collectibility in the future.

The prices indicated provide general guidelines as to what these kits would sell for today at retail. MIB refers to a kit that is Mint in Box, in original condition in the original Mint box with instructions. The box may not be in the original factory seal, but if the kit pieces were contained in bags inside the box, the bags have not been opened. Kits that remain in pristine condition in factory seals may command a slight premium. Near Mint (NM) refers to a kit that is like new, complete and unassembled. The box may show some shelf wear and the interior bags may have been opened. B/U refers to a kit that has been assembled or built up. These price guidelines assume a neatly built, cleanly painted, complete kit.

Trends

The model kit market may have softened somewhat, but collectors are now seeking to upgrade their collections with Mint in Box kits, especially those that are still factory sealed. Aurora figure kits from the 1960s continue to be the cream of the figure model crop.

Figural kits from the 1960s are so popular that reissues have become popular.

The top end of the market remains firm, as do licensed kits like Star Trek. The true Aurora rarities like Godzilla's Go-Cart and those kits with cult and crossover followings like Lost In Space, continue to post steadily increasing values.

The Top 10 Figural Model Kits
(in Mint in Box condition)

1. Godzilla's Go-Cart, Aurora, 1966 .... $6,520
2. Lost In Space, large kit w/chariot, Aurora, 1966 1,485
3. Frankenstein, Gigantic 1:5 scale, Aurora, 1964 1,430
4. Munsters Living Room, Aurora, 1964 1,430
5. King Kong's Thronester, Aurora, 1966 1,375
6. Lost In Space, small kit, Aurora, 1966 1020
7. Lost In Space, The Robot, Aurora, 1968 880
8. Addams Family Haunted House, Aurora, 1964 880
9. Bride of Frankenstein, Aurora, 1965 825
10. Penguin (Batman), Aurora, 1967 578

ADDAR

NO.	NAME	YEAR	B/U	NM	MIP
106	Caesar, Planet of the Apes	1974	15	42	55
101	Cornelius, Planet of the Apes	1974	12	31	55
216	Cornfield Roundup, Planet of the Apes	1975	15	42	55
102	Dr. Zaius, Planet of the Apes	1974	10	26	44
105	Dr. Zira, Planet of the Apes	1974	10	26	44
152	Evil Knievel	1974	12	26	55
154	Evil Knievel's Sky Cycle	1974	12	26	55
104	Gen. Aldo, Planet of the Apes		10	26	33
103	Gen. Ursus, Planet of the Apes		12	31	38
217	Jail Wagon, Planet of the Apes	1975	15	42	49
270	Jaws	1975	35	57	110
270	Jaws in a Bottle	1975	20	52	66
227	Spirit in a Bottle	1975	10	21	49
107	Stallion & Soldier, Planet of the Apes	1974	25	78	110
215	Tree House, Planet of the Apes	1975	15	42	49

AIRFIX

NO.	NAME	YEAR	B/U	NM	MIP
3542	Anne Boleyn	1974	7	15	22
2502	Black Prince	1973	10	26	33
212	Boy Scout	1965	7	15	22
211	Charles I	1965	10	21	27
2501	Henry VIII	1973	4	8	11
M401F	James Bond and Odd Job		30	68	220
823	James Bond's Aston Martin DB-5	1965	60	210	247
2504	Julius Caesar	1973	10	26	33
2508	Napoleon	1978	4	8	11
3546	Queen Elizabeth I	1980	7	15	22
3544	Queen Victoria	1976	7	15	22
203	Richard I	1965	10	26	33
2507	Yeoman of the Guard	1978	4	8	11

AMAZING FIGURE MODELER

NO.	NAME	YEAR	B/U	NM	MIP
	London After Midnight	1998	30	60	90

AMT

NO.	NAME	YEAR	B/U	NM	MIP
7701	Bigfoot	1978	20	63	82
611	Brute Farce	1960s	5	10	16
610	Cliff Hanger	1960s	5	10	16
905	Drag-U-La, Munsters	1965	40	183	275
497	Flintstones Rock Crusher	1974	20	52	66
495	Flintstones Sports Car	1974	20	57	71
913	Girl From U.N.C.L.E. Car	1974	75	262	330
309	Graveyard Ghoul Duo (Munsters cars)	1970	50	105	165
2501	KISS Custom Chevy Van	1977	20	52	82
462	Laurel & Hardy '27 T Roadster	1976	20	52	66
461	Laurel & Hardy '27 T Touring Car	1976	20	52	66
912	Man From U.N.C.L.E. Car	1966	75	183	247
956	Mr. Spock, large box	1973	15	78	192
	Mr. Spock, small box	1973	20	105	165
901	Munster Koach	1964	50	105	220
904	My Mother The Car	1965	15	36	44
	Sonny & Cher Mustang		75	262	330
612	Threw'd Dude	1960s	5	10	16
614	Touchdown?	1960s	5	10	16
	UFO Mystery Ship		15	63	82
950	USS Enterprise Bridge, Star Trek	1975	10	26	38
921-200	USS Enterprise w/lights, Star Trek	1967	40	210	275
951-250	USS Enterprise, Star Trek	1966	40	131	165

MODEL KITS

Barnabas Vampire Van, MPC

No. 278 Wyatt Earp, Pyro

No. 152 Evil Knievel, 1974, Addar

NO.	NAME	YEAR	B/U	NM	MIP
805	Addams Family Haunted House	1964	300	630	880
409	American Astronaut	1967	15	63	82
402	American Buffalo	1964	10	21	27
402	American Buffalo, reissue	1972	8	12	16
401	Apache Warrior on Horse	1960	175	315	495
K-10	Aramis, Three Musketeers	1958	20	78	110
582	Archie's Car	1969	25	89	110
819	Aston Martin Super Spy Car		40	157	220
K-8	Athos, Three Musketeers	1958	20	78	110
832	Banana Splits Banana Buggy	1969	150	420	550
811	Batboat	1968	150	315	495
810	Batcycle	1967	125	262	440
467	Batman	1964	15	78	275
187	Batman, Comic Scenes	1974	15	42	66
486	Batmobile	1966	100	204	357
487	Batplane	1967	50	105	275
407	Black Bear and Cubs	1962	15	31	44
407	Black Bear and Cubs, reissue	1969	15	21	27
400	Black Fury	1958	10	26	33
400	Black Fury, reissue	1969	10	13	16
K-3	Black Knight	1956	10	31	38
473	Black Knight, reissue	1963	10	13	16
463	Blackbeard	1965	75	210	247
K-2	Blue Knight	1956	10	36	55
472	Blue Knight, reissue	1963	10	17	22
414	Bond, James	1966	250	315	495
482	Bride of Frankenstein	1965	300	525	825
863	Brown, Jimmy	1965	75	157	192
409	Canyon, Steve	1958	75	183	275
480	Captain Action	1966	100	288	330
476	Captain America	1966	85	199	330
192	Captain America, Comic Scenes	1974	30	84	137
464	Captain Kidd	1965	25	52	88
738	Cave Bear	1971	15	26	44
416	Chinese Girl	1957	10	21	27
415	Chinese Mandarin	1957	12	26	33
213	Chinese Mandarin & Girl	1957	75	105	330
828	Chitty Chitty Bang Bang	1968	30	89	165
402	Confederate Raider	1959	150	210	385
426	Creature From The Black Lagoon	1963	65	315	467
483	Creature From The Black Lagoon, Glow Kit	1972	65	105	220
483	Creature From The Black Lagoon, Glow Kit	1969	65	105	247
653	Creature, Monsters of Movies	1975	75	105	247
730	Cro-Magnon Man	1971	10	31	49
731	Cro-Magnon Woman	1971	7	26	38
K-7	Crusader	1959	75	157	220
410	D'Artagnan, Three Musketeers	1966	50	157	192
861	Dempsey vs Firpo	1965	20	78	82
631	Dr. Deadly	1971	25	73	88
632	Dr. Deadly's Daughter	1971	25	68	82
460	Dr. Jekyll as Mr. Hyde	1964	45	262	385
482	Dr. Jekyll, Glow Kit	1969	45	105	192
482	Dr. Jekyll, Glow Kit	1972	45	68	88
462	Dr. Jekyll, Monster Scenes	1971	40	94	137
654	Dr. Jekyll, Monsters of Movies	1975	25	63	77
424	Dracula	1962	25	236	330
466	Dracula's Dragster	1966	125	315	440
454	Dracula, Frightning Lightning	1969	30	315	550
454	Dracula, Glow Kit	1969	20	78	165
454	Dracula, Glow Kit	1972	20	63	82
641	Dracula, Monster Scenes	1971	75	105	220
656	Dracula, Monsters of Movies	1975	75	105	275
413	Dutch Boy	1957	10	26	33

MODEL KITS

No. 408 Jesse James, 1966,
Aurora

No. 418 Lost In Space, The Robot, 1968,
Aurora

No. 420 Lost In Space, Large kit with
chariot, 1966, Aurora

NO.	NAME	YEAR	B/U	NM	MIP
209	Dutch Boy & Girl	1957	75	210	330
414	Dutch Girl	1957	10	21	27
817	Flying Sub	1968	35	183	220
254	Flying Sub, reissue	1975	35	89	110
422	Forgotten Prisoner	1966	65	367	440
453	Forgotten Prisoner, Frightning Lightning	1969	65	341	495
453	Forgotten Prisoner, Glow Kit	1972	65	157	192
453	Forgotten Prisoner, Glow Kit	1969	65	183	220
423	Frankenstein	1961	30	210	330
449	Frankenstein, Frightning Lightning	1969	30	315	440
470	Frankenstein, Gigantic 1:5 scale	1964	300	945	1430
449	Frankenstein, Glow Kit	1969	20	68	165
449	Frankenstein, Glow Kit	1972	20	52	82
633	Frankenstein, Monster Scenes	1971	50	78	110
651	Frankenstein, Monsters of Movies	1975	100	210	275
465	Frankie's Flivver	1964	150	367	440
451	Frog, Castle Creatures	1966	75	210	275
658	Ghidrah	1975	95	273	330
643	Giant Insect, Monster Scene	1971	95	367	440
469	Godzilla	1964	85	420	577
485	Godzilla's Go-Cart	1966	650	2310	3520
466	Godzilla, Glow Kit	1969	75	236	357
466	Godzilla, Glow Kit	1972	75	157	192
475	Gold Knight of Nice	1957	125	262	330
475	Gold Knight of Nice	1965	125	262	302
413	Green Beret	1966	75	157	192
489	Green Hornet Black Beauty	1966	125	367	550
634	Gruesome Goodies	1971	25	84	110
800	Guillotine	1964	125	367	440
637	Hanging Cage	1971	20	84	110
481	Hercules	1965	100	210	302
184	Hulk, Comic Scenes	1974	25	78	93
421	Hulk, Original	1966	75	262	330
460	Hunchback of Notre Dame	1964	45	210	330
481	Hunchback of Notre Dame, Glow Kit	1972	45	68	82
481	Hunchback of Notre Dame, Glow Kit	1969	45	94	165
417	Indian Chief	1957	40	94	110
212	Indian Chief & Squaw	1957	60	131	165
418	Indian Squaw	1957	15	39	49
411	Infantryman	1957	20	78	110
813	Invaders UFO	1968	35	89	110
256	Invaders UFO	1975	25	68	82
853	Iwo Jima	1966	75	183	220
408	Jesse James	1966	60	105	220
851	Kennedy, John F.	1965	50	73	165
885	King Arthur	1973	50	105	220
825	King Arthur of Camelot	1967	30	68	82
468	King Kong	1964	75	315	495
484	King Kong's Thronester	1966	370	840	1375
468	King Kong, Glow Kit	1972	75	131	192
468	King Kong, Glow Kit	1969	75	183	275
830	Land of the Giants Space Ship	1968	150	304	440
816	Land of the Giants, Diorama	1968	150	367	495
808	Lone Ranger	1967	75	105	192
188	Lone Ranger, Comic Scenes	1974	20	42	55
420	Lost In Space, Large kit w/chariot	1966	450	1050	1485
419	Lost In Space, Small kit	1966	300	735	1012
418	Lost In Space, The Robot	1968	250	630	880
455	Mad Barber	1972	45	105	165
457	Mad Dentist	1972	45	105	165
456	Mad Doctor	1972	45	105	165
412	Man From U.N.C.L.E., Illya Kuryakin	1966	75	105	220
411	Man From U.N.C.L.E., Napoleon Solo	1966	75	236	286

MODEL KITS

MODEL KITS

NO.	NAME	YEAR	B/U	NM	MIP
412	Marine	1959	20	84	110
860	Mays, Willie	1965	100	210	330
421	Mexican Caballero	1957	75	94	165
422	Mexican Senorita	1957	50	94	165
583	Mod Squad Wagon	1970	35	131	192
463	Monster Customizing Kit #1	1964	35	115	137
464	Monster Customizing Kit #2	1964	65	157	192
828	Moon Bus from 2001	1968	100	288	330
655	Mr. Hyde, Monsters of Movies	1975	25	68	82
922	Mr. Spock	1972	25	105	148
427	Mummy	1963	30	262	357
459	Mummy's Chariot	1965	200	341	550
452	Mummy, Frightning Lightning	1969	30	210	440
452	Mummy, Glow Kit	1969	20	94	192
452	Mummy, Glow Kit	1972	20	42	66
804	Munsters, Living Room	1964	400	945	1430
729	Neanderthal Man	1971	15	42	55
802	Neuman, Alfred E.	1965	100	288	440
806	Nutty Nose Nipper	1965	45	183	220
415	Odd Job	1966	200	367	495
635	Pain Parlor	1971	25	105	137
636	Pendulum	1971	25	52	82
416	Penguin	1967	200	420	577
428	Phantom of the Opera	1963	30	262	330
451	Phantom of the Opera, Frightning Lightning	1969	20	262	385
451	Phantom of the Opera, Glow Kit	1969	20	94	165
451	Phantom of the Opera, Glow Kit	1972	20	63	88
409	Pilot USAF	1957	75	152	192
K-9	Porthos, Three Musketeers	1958	25	78	110
814	Pushmi-Pullyu, Dr. Dolittle	1968	30	78	93
340	Rat Patrol	1967	30	78	104
474	Red Knight	1963	15	42	55
K-4	Red Knight	1957	15	78	110
488	Robin	1966	40	78	110
193	Robin, Comic Scenes	1974	20	73	99
657	Rodan	1975	125	210	385
405	Roman Gladiator with sword	1959	75	131	192
406	Roman Gladiator with Trident	1964	75	136	192
216	Roman Gladiators	1959	100	210	275
862	Ruth, Babe	1965	100	236	357
419	Scotch Lad	1957	10	26	33
214	Scotch Lad & Lassie	1957	60	89	110
420	Scotch Lassie	1957	10	21	27
707	Seaview, Voyage to the Bottom of Sea	1966	100	210	330
253	Seaview, Voyage to the Bottom of Sea	1975	100	168	209
K-1	Silver Knight	1956	15	42	55
471	Silver Knight	1963	15	21	33
881	Sir Galahad	1973	15	42	55
826	Sir Galahad of Camelot	1967	25	94	192
882	Sir Kay	1973	20	42	55
883	Sir Lancelot	1973	20	42	55
827	Sir Lancelot of Camelot	1967	25	94	137
884	Sir Percival	1973	20	47	55
405	Spartacus (Gladiator/sword reissue)	1964	85	157	275
477	Spider-Man	1966	85	210	330
182	Spider-Man, Comic Scenes	1974	50	73	93
923	Star Trek, Klingon Cruiser	1972	20	68	82
921	Star Trek, USS Enterprise	1972	20	89	110
478	Superboy	1964	75	210	275
186	Superboy, Comic Scenes	1974	35	52	66
462	Superman	1963	25	288	374
185	Superman, Comic Scenes	1974	20	42	66
735	Tarpit	1972	50	94	137

AURORA

NO.	NAME	YEAR	B/U	NM	MIP
820	Tarzan	1967	25	105	220
181	Tarzan, Comic Scenes	1974	15	26	38
207	Three Knights Set	1959	50	105	192
398	Three Musketeers Set	1958	95	210	385
809	Tonto	1967	20	105	220
183	Tonto, Comic Scenes	1974	15	21	33
818	Tracy, Dick	1968	60	105	275
819	Tracy, Dick, Space Coupe	1968	50	105	165
408	U.S. Marshal	1958	50	73	110
864	Unitas, Johnny	1965	75	131	192
410	United States Sailor	1957	10	26	33
452	Vampire, Castle Creatures	1966	60	183	275
638	Vampirella	1971	75	131	220
632	Victim	1971	20	68	82
K-6	Viking	1959	65	105	275
831	Voyager, Fantastic Voyage	1969	100	210	495
807	Wacky Back-Whacker	1965	50	105	275
852	Washington, George	1965	25	52	82
865	West, Jerry	1965	50	105	165
401	White Stallion	1964	10	26	33
401	White Stallion, reissue	1969	10	15	22
403	White-tailed Deer	1962	10	26	33
403	White-tailed Deer, reissue	1969	10	15	22
204	Whoozis, Alfalfa	1966	25	52	82
203	Whoozis, Denty	1966	25	52	82
202	Whoozis, Esmerelda	1966	25	52	82
205	Whoozis, Kitty	1966	25	52	82
206	Whoozis, Snuffy	1966	25	52	82
201	Whoozis, Susie	1966	25	52	82
483	Witch	1965	75	210	330
470	Witch, Glow Kit	1969	50	105	220
470	Witch, Glow Kit	1972	75	105	137
425	Wolfman	1962	35	210	330
458	Wolfman's Wagon	1965	175	315	467
450	Wolfman, Frightning Lightning	1969	35	315	440
450	Wolfman, Glow Kit	1969	20	52	165
450	Wolfman, Glow Kit	1972	20	52	82
652	Wolfman, Monsters of Movies	1975	100	210	275
479	Wonder Woman	1965	150	315	550
801	Zorro	1965	125	210	330

BILLIKEN

NO.	NAME	YEAR	B/U	NM	MIP
	Batman, type A	1989	35	89	110
	Batman, type B	1989	35	94	137
	Bride of Frankenstein		75	105	247
	Colossal Beast	1986	20	31	44
	Creature From Black Lagoon	1991	50	89	137
	Cyclops		75	105	220
	Dracula		60	105	165
	Frankenstein		60	94	137
	Joker	1989	40	94	165
	Mummy	1990	60	105	165
	Phantom of the Opera		100	210	302
	Predator		25	52	71
	Saucer Man		20	31	44
	She-Creature		25	42	55
	Syngenor		100	157	275
	The Thing		150	210	330
	Ultraman		20	31	44

MODEL KITS

No. 475 Gold Knight of Nice, 1957, Aurora

No. 476 Captain America, 1966, Aurora

No. 488 Robin, 1966, Aurora

No. 478 Superboy, 1964, Aurora

468

BOWEN DESIGNS

NO.	NAME	YEAR	B/U	NM	MIP
	Kongzilla	1998	15	30	50

GEOMETRIC DESIGN

NO.	NAME	YEAR	B/U	NM	MIP
	Son of Frankenstein	1998	15	30	50

HAWK

NO.	NAME	YEAR	B/U	NM	MIP
542	Beach Bunny	1964	25	68	82
532	Daddy the Way-Out Suburbanite	1963	30	78	99
531	Davy the Way-Out Cyclist	1963	30	78	99
530	Digger and Dragster	1963	30	78	99
	Drag Hag	1963	30	78	99
537	Endsville Eddie	1963	20	52	82
535	Francis The Foul	1963	15	36	49
548	Frantic Banana	1965	20	84	137
550	Frantic Cats	1965	20	73	110
547	Frantics Steel Pluckers	1965	20	73	110
549	Frantics Totally Fab	1965	20	84	110
533	Freddy Flameout	1963	20	68	88
543	Hidad Silly Surfer	1964	20	68	88
541	Hot Dogger Hangin' Ten	1964	20	68	88
538	Huey's Hut Rod	1963	20	47	60
	Killer McBash	1963	40	131	165
534	Leaky Boat Louie	1963	25	84	104
	Riding Tandem		25	68	82
637	Sling Rave Curvette	1964	15	26	49
547	Steel Pluckers	1965	20	68	93
550	Totally Fab	1965	25	78	110
636	Wade A Minute	1963	15	26	38
	Weird-Oh Customizing Kit	1964	75	262	330
545	Wild Woodie Car		20	52	66
540	Woodie on a Surfari	1964	25	89	110

LINDBERG

NO.	NAME	YEAR	B/U	NM	MIP
6422	Bert's Bucket	1971	30	84	110
277	Big Wheeler	1965	30	84	110
280	Blurp	1964	10	21	49
273	Creeping Crusher	1965	20	42	60
6420	Fat Max	1971	30	84	99
281	Glob	1964	10	21	55
274	Green Ghoul	1965	20	36	55
272	Krimson Terror	1965	20	42	60
275	Mad Mangler	1965	20	42	60
276	Road Hog	1964	30	84	99
	Satan's Crate	1964	75	131	165
	Scuttle Bucket	1964	30	84	99
6421	Sick Cycle	1971	30	84	99
283	Voop	1964	10	21	55
282	Zopp	1964	10	21	55

MONOGRAM

NO.	NAME	YEAR	B/U	NM	MIP
6028	Battlestar Galactica	1979	15	36	44
6008	Dracula	1983	20	26	44
105	Flip Out	1965	50	157	220

MODEL KITS

MONOGRAM

NO.	NAME	YEAR	B/U	NM	MIP
6007	Frankenstein	1983	20	31	44
6300	Godzilla	1978	40	68	88
6010	Mummy	1983	20	31	44
	Snoopy & Motorcycle	1971	15	26	33
6779	Snoopy & Sopwith Camel	1971	20	31	38
	Snoopy as Joe Cool	1971	25	52	110
MM106	Speed Shift	1965	70	105	220
	Super Fuzz	1965	80	105	247
6301	Superman	1978	20	31	44
6012	UFO, The Invaders	1979	15	36	44
6009	Wolfman	1983	20	31	38

MPC

NO.	NAME	YEAR	B/U	NM	MIP
1-1961	Alien	1979	25	78	110
0303	Ape Man Haunted Glow Head	1975	10	31	55
	AT-AT, Empire Strikes Back	1980	15	21	38
	Barnabas Vampire Van		75	105	275
1550	Barnabas, Dark Shadows	1968	100	341	440
1702	Batman	1984	20	31	38
612	Beverly Hillbillies Truck	1968	60	105	220
0609	Bionic Bustout, Six Million Dollar Man	1975	15	26	38
0610	Bionic Repair, Bionic Woman	1976	15	26	38
5003	Condemned to Chains Forever	1974	20	42	60
103	Curl's Gurl	1960s	25	68	88
	Darth Vader Bust	1977	20	42	60
	Darth Vader with Light Saber	1977	15	31	44
5005	Dead Man's Raft	1974	20	84	110
5001	Dead Men Tell No Tales	1974	20	42	55
1983	Encounter With Yoda Diorama	1981	15	21	38
5053	Escape From the Crypt	1974	20	42	55
604	Evil Rider, Six Million Dollar Man	1975	15	21	44
5004	Fate of the Mutineers	1974	20	42	55
602	Fight for Survival, Six Million Dollar Man	1975	15	21	44
0635	Fonzie & Dream Rod	1976	10	26	38
0634	Fonzie & Motorcycle		10	15	27
5007	Freed in the Nick of Time	1974	20	63	82
5006	Ghost of the Treasure Guard	1974	20	36	55
5051	Grave Robber's Reward	1974	20	42	55
402	Hogan's Heroes Jeep	1968	30	78	137
5002	Hoist High the Jolly Roger	1974	20	42	55
101	Hot Curl	1960s	20	42	55
	Hot Shot		20	42	55
1932	Hulk	1978	20	31	44
	Jabba's Throne Room	1983	20	31	49
603	Jaws of Doom, Six Million Dollar Man	1975	15	21	44
1925	Millennium Falcon with Light	1977	35	89	137
605	Monkeemobile	1967	70	183	247
1-0702	Muldowney, Shirley, Drag Kit		20	52	71
304	Mummy Haunted Glow Head	1975	20	31	55
	Night Crawler Wolfman Car	1971	45	78	137
622	Paul Revere & The Raiders Coach	1970	40	73	137
5052	Play It Again Sam	1974	35	84	110
1906	Raiders of the Lost Ark Chase Scene	1982	15	31	44
	Road Runner Beep Beep		20	52	82
1931	Spider-Man	1978	20	26	38
0902	Strange Changing Mummy	1974	15	31	44
0903	Strange Changing Time Machine	1974	20	42	55

MODEL KITS

Candy Shooter

Pinocchio B

Space Gun, 1950s

Left to Right: Orange, Mary Poppins, Psychedelic Eye, Green Hornet, Bride, Pear, Cowboy

Aliens Alien vs. Predator, 1993, Kenner

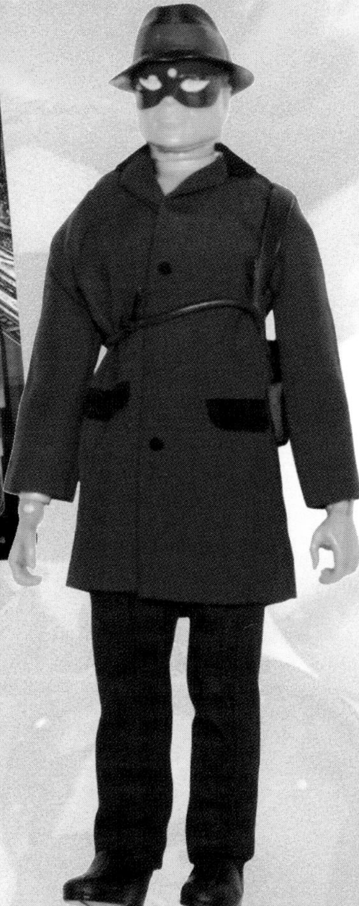

Captain Action Green Hornet, 1967, Ideal

Movie Maniacs II Norman Bates from Psycho, 1999, McFarlane

Beatles Yellow Submarine, 1999, McFarlane

Planet of the Apes Galen, 1975, Mego

Marx's Major Matt Mason action figure, circa 1967-1970. Left to Right: Scorpio, 7"; Callisto, 6"

Geronimo, 1967, Marx

Bob Mackie Jewel Essence
Ruby Radiance, 1997

Ponytail Barbie #4,
brunette, 1960

Ponytail Barbie
#3, blond, 1960

Byron Lars In the
Limelight, 1997

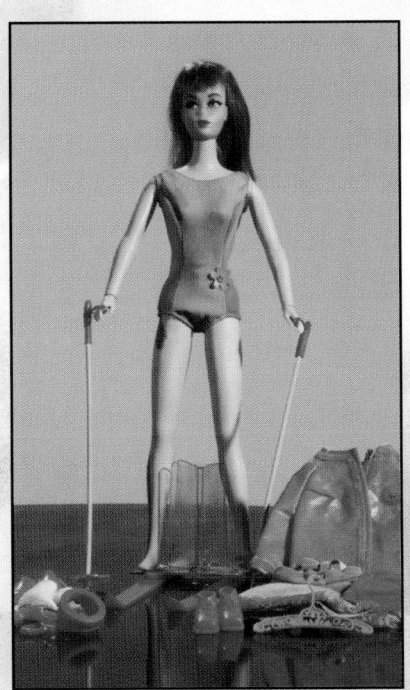

**Living Barbie Action Accents
Gift Set, 1970**

Millennium Bride, 1999

**Lucy Ricardo
"Job Switching," 1999**

**Elvis Presley #2
The Army Years, 1999**

'33 Willys, Monopoly, Johnny Lightning / Playing Mantis

Classic '36 Ford Coupe, 1969, Hot Wheels

Custom El Camino, 1969, Johnny Lightning / Topper *Photo courtesy Dennis Seleman*

Deora, 1968, Hot Wheels

Red Baron, 1970, Hot Wheels

Vega Bomb, 1975, Hot Wheels

Twinmill, 1969, Hot Wheels

Playing Mantis Internet Car, Com cars (Internet program), Johnny Lightning / Playing Mantis

Arby's Little Miss Figures, 1981.
Copyright Museum of Science and Industry, Chicago

White Castle Fat Albert and the Cosby Kids, 1990. *Copyright Museum of Science and Industry, Chicago*

Kentucky Fried Chicken Pokémon, 1998

McDonald's Walt Disney Home Video Masterpiece Collection—Toy Story and Three Caballeros, 1997

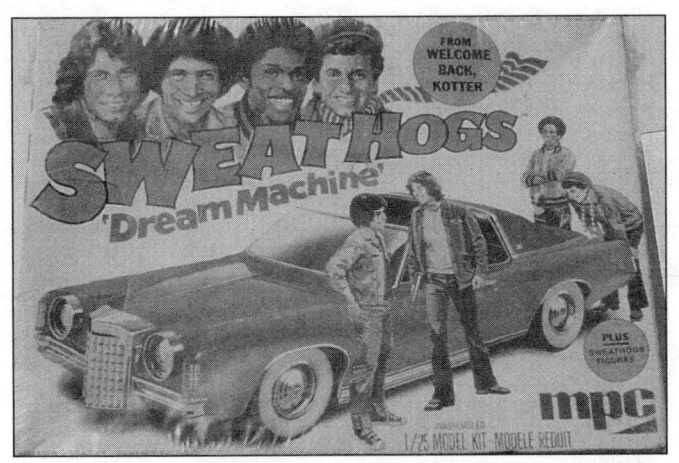

No. 641 Sweathog Dream Machine, 1976, MPC

No. 813 Invaders UFO, 1968, Aurora

MPC

NO.	NAME	YEAR	B/U	NM	MIP
0901	Strange Changing Vampire	1974	20	42	55
100	Stroker McGurk & Surf Rod	1960s	30	84	137
102	Stroker McGurk Tall T		30	84	137
1701	Superman	1984	15	21	27
641	Sweathog Dream Machine	1976	10	15	33
301	Vampire Haunted Glow Head	1975	15	21	49
5050	Vampire's Midnight Madness	1974	20	47	55
302	Werewolf Haunted Glow Head	1975	20	36	49
1552	Werewolf, Dark Shadows	1969	75	199	275
2651	Wile E. Coyote		20	52	71
617	Yellow Submarine	1968	70	178	275

MULTIPLE TOYMAKERS

NO.	NAME	YEAR	B/U	NM	MIP
955	Automatic Baby Feeder	1965	25	63	82
958	Back Scrubber	1965	25	63	82
981	Iron Maiden	1966	35	105	165
956	Painless Tooth Extractor	1965	25	63	82
957	Signal for Shipwrecked Sailors	1965	25	63	82
980	Torture Chair	1966	35	94	165
979	Torture Wheel	1966	35	94	165

PARK

NO.	NAME	YEAR	B/U	NM	MIP
803	Castro, Born Losers	1965	35	68	137
802	Hitler, Born Losers	1965	35	68	192
801	Napoleon, Born Losers	1965	35	68	137

PLAYING MANTIS

NO.	NAME	YEAR	B/U	NM	MIP
	Creature from the Black Lagoon	1998	10	20	30
	KISS, Ace Frehley	1998	10	20	30
	KISS, Gene Simmons	1998	10	20	30
	KISS, Paul Stanley	1998	10	20	30
	KISS, Peter Criss	1998	10	20	30
	Lost in Space Cyclops w/Chariot	1998	10	20	30
	The Wolf Man	1998	50	100	200

PRECISION

NO.	NAME	YEAR	B/U	NM	MIP
402	Cap'n Kidd the Pirate	1959	25	63	82
501	Crucifix		20	42	55

PYRO

NO.	NAME	YEAR	B/U	NM	MIP
166	Der-Baron	1958	50	78	110
175	Gladiator Show Cycle		20	42	55
281	Indian Chief		20	52	66
282	Indian Medicine Man		20	52	66
283	Indian Warrior	1960	20	52	66
168	Li'l Corporal	1970	25	68	82
276	Rawhide, Gil Favor	1958	20	52	66
277	Restless Gun Deputy	1959	20	52	66
176	Surf's Up	1970	15	36	44
286	U.S. Marshal		20	52	66
278	Wyatt Earp		20	52	66

MODEL KITS

REMCO

NO.	NAME	YEAR	B/U	NM	MIP
452	Flintstones Motorized Paddy Wagon	1961	30	105	220
450	Flintstones Motorized Sports Car & Trailer	1961	30	105	220
451	Flintstones Motorized Yacht	1961	30	105	220

REVELL

NO.	NAME	YEAR	B/U	NM	MIP
1307	Angel Fink	1965	40	105	154
1353	Beatles, George Harrison	1965	75	157	275
1352	Beatles, John Lennon	1965	75	157	275
1350	Beatles, Paul McCartney	1965	75	157	220
1351	Beatles, Ringo Starr	1965	75	157	220
	Birthday Bird	1959	40	157	275
1931	Bonanza	1965	50	105	165
1304	Brother Rat Fink	1963	20	52	71
	Busby the Tasselated Afghan Spaniel Yak	1960	50	131	275
2000	Cat in the Hat	1960	45	105	165
2050	Cat in the Hat with Thing 1 and Thing 2	1960s	45	105	247
1397	Charlie's Angels Van	1977	10	21	33
	Dr. Seuss Zoo Kit #1	1959	50	236	440
	Dr. Seuss Zoo Kit #2	1960	50	367	550
1303	Drag Nut	1963	20	52	71
1310	Fink-Eliminator	1965	30	105	220
1450	Flash Gordon & Martian	1965	60	105	165
1930	Flipper	1965	75	105	165
	Gowdy the Dowdy Grackle	1959	40	78	192
	Grickily the Gractus	1960	50	131	275
	Horton the Elephant	1960	150	210	440
323	McHale's Navy PT-73	1965	25	63	82
1302	Mother's Worry	1963	20	63	110
1301	Mr. Gasser	1963	30	78	110
3181	Mr. Gasser BMR Racer	1964	30	78	110
	Norval the Bashful Blinket	1959	40	78	192
1451	Phantom & Voodoo Witch Doctor	1965	50	105	220
1305	Rat Fink	1963	25	63	82
	Rat Fink Lotus Racer	1964	25	63	82
	Robbin' Hood Fink	1965	200	315	440
2004	Roscoe the Many-Footed Lion	1960s	30	78	181
1309	Scuz-Fink with Dingbat	1965	275	367	495
	Superfink	1964	150	262	385
1306	Surfink	1965	35	89	110
	Tingo the Noodle-Topped Stroodle	1960s	50	78	192
1271	Tweedy Pie with Boss-Fink	1965	200	315	440

TOY BIZ

NO.	NAME	YEAR	B/U	NM	MIP
48660	Ghost Rider	1996	7	12	27
48656	Hulk	1996	5	10	22
48640	Onslaught	1997	7	12	27
48653	Silver Surfer	1996	5	10	22
48651	Spider-Man	1996	5	10	22
48658	Spider-Man, with wall	1996	5	10	22
48659	Storm	1996	5	10	22
48652	Thing	1996	5	10	22
48654	Venom	1996	5	10	22
48657	Wolverine	1996	5	10	22

MODEL KITS

481

PEZ Candy Dispensers

In 1952, Americans saw the inauspicious introduction of an Austrian mint in a handy dispenser. Long popular in the homeland, the pocket candy lost something in the translation. The marketing cure for this was successful beyond all expectations.

PEZ was created in Austria in 1927 as a peppermint candy and breath mint sold in a clever package which dispensed the candies one at a time. Highly successful in Europe, it became the fashionable adult candy of its time. But its launch in America found a disinterested public.

Soon PEZ would be reinvented for the American market as a children's candy with fruit-flavored candies replacing the staid pfefferminz of old. The dispensers were redesigned and given colorful heads in the shapes of popular cartoon characters, and American children quickly claimed the new candy as their own.

Today PEZ is available everywhere from the local Kmart to the corner convenience store, and few Americans can see a dispenser without it evoking a few childhood memories. This ability to reconnect us, either with our own childhoods or with our national past, is central to collectibility in any field, and a PEZ dispenser holds a rich postwar legacy in its tiny plastic container.

PEZ collectors nationwide have formed clubs, published newsletters and held national conventions. Long ago, kids threw away the dispensers, but these once lowly candy holders have grown in popularity and respect to the point that rare dispensers are now highly-prized collectibles and have even been sold by internationally-known auction houses like Christie's.

The PEZ market has developed some noteworthy variations on standard collecting procedures. In many fields, a toy still in the original package commands a premium over the same toy with no package. This is not usually the case in PEZ collecting. Before blister cards, PEZ dispensers were packaged in boxes or cellophane bags, which did not allow for either display or handling of the toys themselves.

Since dispenser stems are easily interchangeable, PEZ authorities hold that only variations in head configuration or coloring affect value. There is no difference in value between dispensers with different colored stems but the same head.

Finally, there is the matter of feet and no feet. This refers to the presence or absence of a flattened rounded base on the stem resembling flat shoes. PEZ dispensers released in America before 1987 were all of the no-feet variety, so a dispenser with feet was made after that year. However, certain older molds continued to be produced with no feet after 1987 as well, but these are common dispensers with little variance in value between feet and no-feet varieties. The major difference in value here applies to older, no-feet dispensers that were discontinued and perhaps reissued after 1987 with feet.

Trends

PEZ dispensers have seen mixed performance at shows, but values are on the rise, with the most sought after dispensers being the Bridge, Mueslix, Pineapple, Vucko and Make-A-Face. Two PEZ items fast on the rise in popularity are Vucko from the 1984 Sarajevo Olympics and advertising regulars. The latter look like a regular non-headed PEZ with a company's name on the side.

PEZ

Low-end common dispensers have been selling in large quantities, but many new collectors are hedging at the price points of dispensers in the $75 and up range, indicating this is still a strongly collector-based market. The top of the market appears healthy, with reports of dispensers achieving two and three times prior estimates at auction.

The Top 10 PEZ Dispensers
(in Mint condition)

1. Make-A-Face $3,400
2. Elephant 3,200
3. Witch Regular 3,200
4. Make-A-Face 3,000
5. Lion's Club Lion 3,000
6. Mueslix 2,950
7. Pineapple 2,850
8. Space Trooper 2,000
9. Make-A-Face 2,000
10. Bride 2,000

Contributors to this section: John Devlin, 5541 Oakville Center, Suite 119, St. Louis, MO 63129-3554; Richard Belyski, PEZ Collector's News, P.O. Box 124, Sea Cliff, NY 11579

PEZ

PEZ

NAME	DESCRIPTION	EX	MINT
Advertising Regular	no feet, no head, advertising printed on side MUST be complete	650	1200
Air Spirit	no feet, reddish triangular fish face	175	250
Alpine	1972 Munich Olympics, no feet, green hat w/beige plume, black mustache	700	900
Angel A	no feet, hair and halo	60	75
Arithmetic Regular	no feet, headless dispenser w/white top, side of body has openings w/columns of numbers	450	550
Arlene	w/feet, pink head, Garfield's girlfriend	2	5
Asterix	no feet, blue hat w/wings, yellow mustache, European	800	1400
Asterix (1998 foreign issue)	head different than old	3	5
Astronaut A	no feet, helmet, yellow visor, small head	410	565
Astronaut B	no feet, green stem, white helmet, yellow visor, large head	115	165
Baloo	no feet, Jungle Book	20	40
Baloo	w/feet, Jungle Book	12	25
Bambi	w/feet	20	50
Barney Bear	w/feet, brown head, white cheeks and snout, black nose	15	30
Barney Bear	no feet, brown head, white cheeks and snout, black nose	30	45
Barney Rubble	Flintstones	1	2
Baseball Dispenser Set	no feet, baseball glove w/ball, bat, white home plate marked "PEZ"	500	750
Baseball Glove	no feet, brown baseball glove w/white ball	165	220
Batgirl	Soft Head Superhero, no feet, blue mask, black hair	130	175
Batman	w/feet, blue	3	6
Batman	no feet, blue cape, mask and hat	75	100
Batman	Soft Head Superhero, no feet, blue mask	125	175
Betsy Ross	no feet, dark hair and white hat, Bicentennial issue	130	175
Big Top Elephant	no feet, orange head w/blue pointed hat	70	85
Big Top Elephant	no feet, gray-green head, red flat hat	70	85
Big Top Elephant With Hair	no feet, yellow head and red hair	125	250
Bouncer Beagle		5	6
Boy	no feet, brown hair	20	35
Boy with Cap	no feet, white hair, blue cap	85	100
Bozo the Clown	die-cut Bozo and Butch on stem, no feet, white face, red hair and nose	140	200
Bride	no feet, white veil, light brown, blond or red hair	950	2000
Brutus	no feet, black beard and hair	145	250
Bugs Bunny		1	3
Bugs Bunny	no feet, gray head w/white cheeks	5	10
Bugs Bunny	w/feet, gray head w/white cheeks	2	4
Bullwinkle	no feet, brown head, yellow antlers	200	250
Bunny		1	3
Bunny 1990	w/feet, long ears, white face	1	3
Bunny 1999		1	3
Bunny Original A	no feet, narrow head and tall ears	275	275
Bunny Original B	no feet, tall ears and full face, smiling buck teeth	275	375
Bunny w/Fat Ears	no feet, wide ear version, yellow	20	15
Bunny w/Fat Ears	no feet, wide ear version, pink	20	25
Camel	w/feet, brown face w/red fez hat	35	50
Candy Shooter	black gun w/PEZ monogram on stock	85	135
Candy Shooter	red body, white grip, w/German license and double PEZ candy	50	75
Captain (Paul Revere)	no feet, blue hat, Bicentennial issue	130	125
Captain America	no feet, blue cowl, black mask w/white letter A	95	150
Captain America	blue mask	75	100
Captain Hook	no feet, black hair, flesh face winking w/right eye open	65	95
Casper The Friendly Ghost	no feet, white face	100	200
Casper The Friendly Ghost	die-cut	165	225
Cat with Derby		50	100
Charlie Brown	w/feet, crooked smile, blue cap	1	2
Charlie Brown	w/feet, blue cap, smile w/red tongue at corner	15	10

NAME	DESCRIPTION	EX	MINT
Charlie Brown	w/feet, blue cap, eyes closed	45	75
Chick in Egg	no feet, yellow chick in egg shell, red hat	15	25
Chick in Egg	no feet, yellow chick in egg shell, no hat	80	125
Chip	no feet, black top hat, tan head w/white sideburns, brown nose, foreign issue	80	100
Clown	w/feet, green hat, foreign issue (Merry Music Makers)	3	6
Clown with Chin	no feet, long chin, hat and hair	50	80
Clown with Collar	no feet, yellow collar, red hair, green hat	45	80
Cockatoo	no feet, yellow beak and green head, red head feathers	45	75
Cocoa Marsh Spaceman	no feet, clear helmet on small male head, w/Cocoa Marsh embossed on side	155	225
Cool Cat	w/feet, orange head, blue snout, black ears	35	60
Cow A	no feet, cow head, separate nose	60	95
Cow B	no feet, blue head, separate snout, horns, ears and eyes	50	90
Cowboy	no feet, human head, brown hat	225	300
Creature From Black Lagoon	no feet, green head and matching stem, w/copyright	225	275
Crocodile	no feet, dark green head w/red eyes	60	120
Daffy Duck		1	3
Daffy Duck A	no feet, black head, yellow beak, removable white eyes	10	15
Daffy Duck B	w/feet, black head, yellow beak	3	5
Dalmatian Pup	w/feet, white head w/left ear cocked, foreign issue	35	55
Daniel Boone	no feet, light brown hair under dark brown hat, Bicentennial issue	150	215
Dewey	no feet, blue hat, white head, yellow beak, small black eyes	20	35
Diabolic	no feet, soft orange monster head	150	225
Dino the Dinosaur		1	2
Dinosaurs	PEZasaurs line, four different dinosaurs, each	1	3
Doctor	no feet, white hair and mustache, gray reflector on white band, black stethoscope	145	210
Donald Duck	die-cut	135	185
Donald Duck A	no feet, blue hat, one-piece head and bill, open mouth	12	25
Donald Duck B	w/feet, blue hat, white head and hair w/large eyes, removable beak	1	3
Donkey	w/feet, gray head w/pink nose, whistlehead	5	10
Donkey Kong Jr.	no feet, blond monkey face, dark hair, white cap w/"J" on it, w/box	350	650
Dopey	no feet, flesh colored die cut face w/wide ears, orange cap	175	225
Dr. Skull B	no feet, black collar	10	15
Droopy Dog	w/feet	5	6
Droopy Dog A	w/feet, white face, flesh snout, black movable ears and red hair	5	25
Droopy Dog B	w/feet	5	6
Duck	w/feet, brown head w/yellow beak, whistlehead	25	50
Duck	no feet, brown head w/yellow beak, whistlehead	30	55
Duckie with Flower	no feet, flower, duck head w/beak	60	100
Dumbo	w/feet, blue head w/large ears, yellow hat	30	50
Dumbo	no feet, gray head w/large ears, red hat	50	85
Easter Bunny Die Cut	no feet, die cut	450	575
Elephant	gold or black	2600	3200
Engineer	no feet, blue hat	100	175
Fireman	no feet, red hat w/gray #1 insignia	75	95
Foghorn Leghorn	w/feet, brown head, yellow beak, red wattle	60	85
Foghorn Leghorn	no feet, brown head, yellow beak, red wattle	75	95
Football Player	no feet, white stem, red helmet w/white stripe	100	150
Fozzie Bear	w/feet, brown head, bow tie, small brown hat	1	2
Frankenstein	no feet, black hair, gray head	180	300
Fred Flintstone	Flintstones	1	2
Frog	w/feet, yellow and green head w/black eyes, foreign issue	35	45
Frog	no feet, yellow and green head w/black eyes, foreign issue	40	50
Garfield	w/feet, orange head	1	2
Garfield w/teeth	w/feet, orange head, wide painted toothy grin	1	2
Garfield w/visor	w/feet, orange face, green visor	1	2

PEZ

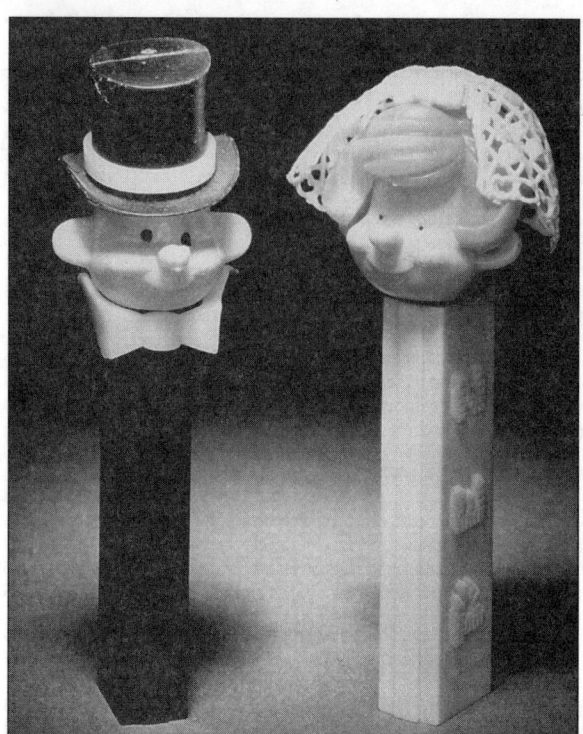

Bride & Groom, PEZ

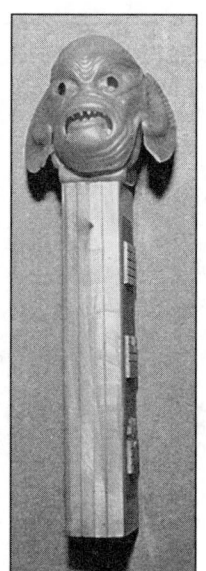

Creature From
Black Lagoon,
PEZ

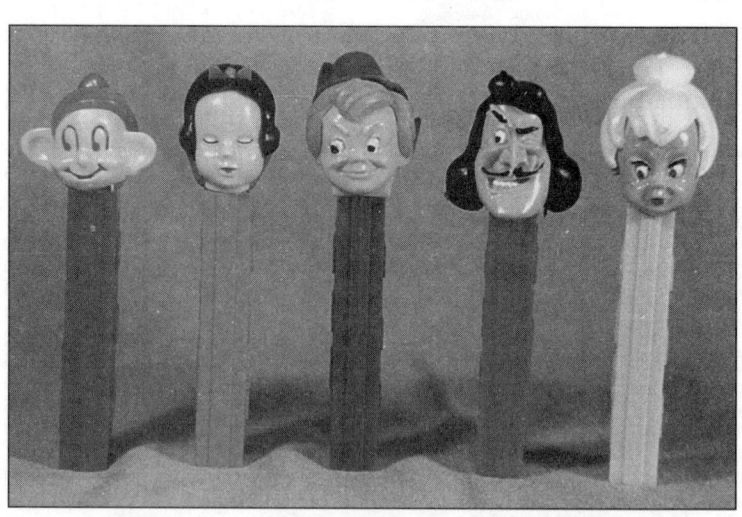

Dopey, Snow White, Peter Pan, Captain Hook, Tinkerbelle, PEZ

NAME	DESCRIPTION	EX	MINT
Giraffe	no feet, orange head w/horns, black eyes	125	200
Girl	no feet, blond pigtails	25	35
Girl	w/feet, pigtails	1	3
Golden Glow	no feet, no head, gold stem and top	80	150
Gonzo	w/feet, blue head, yellow eyelids, bow tie	1	3
Goofy B	no feet, red hat, painted nose, removable white teeth	35	50
Goofy C	same as version B except teeth are part of head	15	25
Goofy D	w/feet, beige snout, green hat	1	3
Gorilla	no feet, black head w/red eyes and white teeth	50	80
Green Hornet	no feet, green mask and hat; two hat styles exist	175	255
Groom	no feet, black top hat, white bow tie	250	425
Gyro Gearloose		5	6
Henry Hawk	w/feet	55	80
Henry Hawk	no feet, light brown head, yellow beak	60	95
Hippo	no feet, green stem w/"Hippo" printed on side, foreign issue	700	925
Huey	no feet, red hat, white head, yellow beak, small black eyes	20	35
Huey, Dewey or Louie Duck	w/feet, red, blue, or green stem and matching cap, white head and orange beak	5	10
Hulk A	no feet, dark green head, black hair	30	60
Hulk B	no feet, light green head, dark green hair	25	30
Hulk B	w/feet, light green head, tall dark green hair	3	6
Hulk C		1	2
Indian	w/feet, black hair and green headband w/feather, foreign issue (Merry Music Makers)	10	15
Indian Brave	no feet, small human head, Indian headband w/one feather, Bicentennial issue	100	200
Indian Chief	no feet, war bonnet, Bicentennial issue	100	110
Indian Chief	no feet, marbleized headress	110	155
Indian Woman	no feet, black hair in braids w/headband	95	175
Jerry (Tom & Jerry)	no feet, brown face, pink lining in ears	100	200
Jerry (Tom & Jerry)	w/feet, brown face, multiple piece head	8	10
Jiminy Cricket	no feet, green hatband and collar, flesh face, black top hat	180	260
Joker	Soft Head Superhero, no feet, green painted hair	125	175
Kermit the Frog	w/feet, green head	1	2
King Louie	w/feet, brown hair and 'sideburns' over light brown head	10	15
Knight	no feet, gray helmet w/plume	200	325
Koala	w/feet, brown head w/a black nose, foreign issue, whistlehead	25	35
Lamb	no feet, white head w/a pink bow	7	15
Lamb	no feet, pink stem, white head, whistle	10	25
Li'l Bad Wolf	no feet, black ears, white face, red tongue	15	25
Li'l Bad Wolf	w/feet, black ears, white face, red tongue	12	20
Lion with Crown	no feet, black mane, green head w/yellow cheeks and red crown	45	100
Lion's Club Lion	no feet, stem imprinted "1962 Lion's Club Inter'l Convention," yellow roaring lion head	2000	3000
Little Lion	no feet, yellow head w/brown mane	40	60
Little Orphan Annie	no feet, light brown hair, flesh face w/black painted features	100	160
Louie	no feet, green hat, white head, yellow beak, small black eyes	10	30
Lucy	w/feet, black hair	1	2
Maharajah	no feet, green turban w/red inset	35	50
Make-A-Face	no card, feet, oversized head w/18 facial parts	1700	2000
Make-A-Face	German "Super Spiel" card	2000	3000
Make-A-Face	American card	2400	3400
Mary Poppins	no feet, flesh face, reddish hair, lavender hat	900	1100
Merlin Mouse	w/feet, gray head w/flesh cheeks, green hat	10	15
Merlin Mouse	no feet, gray head w/flesh cheeks, green hat	17	25
Mexican	no feet, yellow sombrero, black beard and mustache, two earrings	140	185
Mickey Mouse A	no feet, black head and ears, pink face, mask w/cut out eyes and mouth, nose pokes through mask	60	85

NAME	DESCRIPTION	EX	MINT
Mickey Mouse B	no feet, painted face, non-painted black eyes and mouth	85	140
Mickey Mouse C	no feet, flesh face, removable nose, painted eyes	10	15
Mickey Mouse D	no feet, flesh face, mask embossed white and black eyes	5	10
Mickey Mouse Die-Cut	no feet, die-cut stem w/Minnie, die cut face mask	120	175
Mickey Mouse Die-Cut	no feet, die-cut stem w/Minnie, painted face	125	225
Mickey Mouse E	w/feet, flesh face, bulging black and white eyes, oval nose	1	3
Mimic the Monkey	no feet, wearing baseball cap, white eyes	35	45
Miraculix (1998 foreign issue)		3	5
Miss Piggy	w/eyelashes	10	15
Miss Piggy	w/feet, pink face, yellow hair	1	2
Miss Piggy B		1	3
Monkey	whistle head	10	25
Monkey	w/feet, tan monkey face in brown head, foreign issue	10	25
Monkey Sailor	no feet, cream face, brown hair, white sailor cap, whistlehead	40	50
Mowgli	w/feet, black hair over brown head, Jungle Book	5	20
Mowgli	no feet, black hair over brown head, Jungle Book	20	35
Mr. Ugly	no feet, black hair, many color variations	35	50
Mueslix	no feet, white beard, moustache and eyebrows, European	2800	2950
Nermal	w/feet, gray stem and head	1	3
Nintendo, Diddy Dong		4	6
Nintendo, Koopa Trooper		4	6
Nintendo, Mario		4	6
Nintendo, Yoshi		4	6
Nurse	no feet, hair color variations, white nurse's cap	100	165
Obelix	no feet, red mustache and hair, blue hat, European	800	1400
Obelix (1998 foreign issue)	head different than old	3	5
Octopus	no feet; black; orange or black head	35	75
Octopus	no feet, red head	70	90
Olive Oyl	no feet, black hair and flesh painted face	125	225
One-Eyed Monster	no feet, gorilla head w/one eye missing	75	95
Orange	no feet, orange (fruit) head w/face and leaves on top	160	200
Panda A	no feet, white head w/black eyes and ears	15	20
Panda A	no feet, yellow head w/black eyes and ears	150	300
Panda B	w/feet, white head w/black eyes and ears	1	3
Panther	no feet, blue head w/pink nose	100	200
Papa Smurf	w/feet, red hat, white beard, blue face	2	5
Parrot	w/feet, red hair, yellow beak and green eyes, whistle head	5	6
Pear	no feet, yellow pear face, green visor	800	1000
Pebbles Flintstone	Flintstones	1	2
Penguin	w/feet, penguin head w/yellow beak and red hat, foreign issue, whistle head	5	6
Penguin (Batman villain)	Soft Head Superhero, no feet, yellow top hat, black painted monocle, whistlehead	130	175
Personalized Regular	no feet, no head, paper label for monogramming	175	250
Peter Pan	no feet, green hat, flesh face, orange hair	100	175
Peter PEZ	no feet, blue top hat that says "PEZ," white face, yellow hair	50	65
Peter PEZ	1990s remake w/feet	1	2
Petunia Pig	w/or without feet, black hair in pigtails	25	35
Phone		5	10
Pig	w/feet, pink head, whistlehead	25	50
Pilgrim	no feet, pilgrim hat, blond hair, hat band	125	160
Pilot	no feet, blue hat, gray headphones	150	225
Pineapple	no feet, pineapple head w/greenery and sunglasses	2350	2850
Pinocchio A	no feet, red or yellow cap, pink face, black painted hair	145	180
Pinocchio B	no feet, black hair, red hat	110	175
Pirate	no feet, red cap, patch over right eye	50	60
Pluto A	no feet, yellow head, long black ears, small painted eyes	5	20
Pluto C	w/feet, yellow head, long painted black ears, large white and black decal eyes	1	5
Policeman	no feet, blue hat w/gray badge	40	50

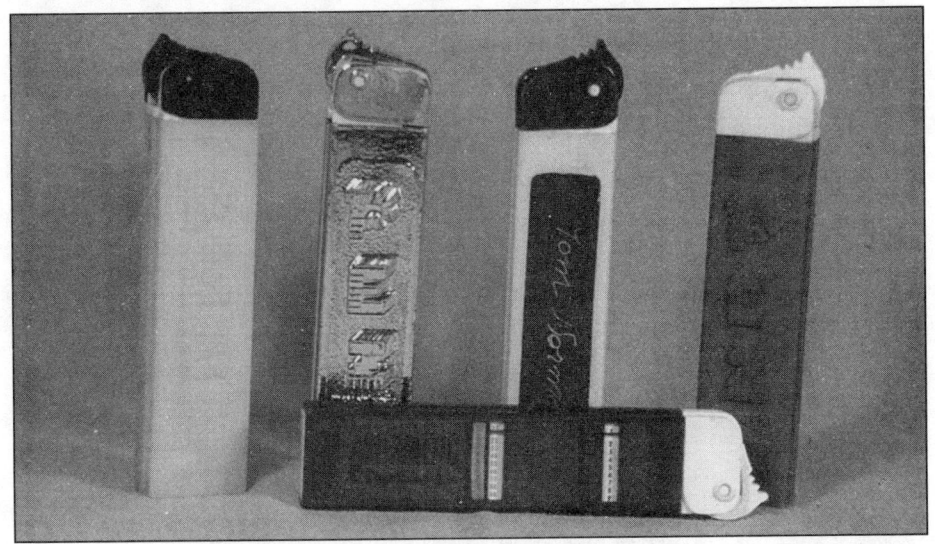

Left to Right: Regular, Golden Glow, Personalized Regular. Front: Arithmetic Regular, PEZ

Make-A-Face, PEZ

NAME	DESCRIPTION	EX	MINT
Pony-Go-Round	no feet, orange head, white harness, blue hair	60	75
Popeye A	no feet, yellow face, painted hat	95	125
Popeye B	no feet, removable white sailor cap	65	100
Popeye C	no feet, one eye painted, removeable pipe and cap	65	100
Practical Pig A	no feet, rounded blue hat, round snout	25	30
Practical Pig B	no feet, crooked blue hat	10	25
Psychedelic Eye	no feet, decal design on stem, beige or black hands; many color variations	200	450
Psychedelic Eye (1998 limited-edition)	limited-edition; has 1967 copyright date	10	20
Psychedelic Flower	no feet, stem w/decal on side, many color variations	225	500
Pumpkin A	no feet, green stem, carved face	10	15
Pumpkin B	black facial features	1	3
Pussy Cat	no feet, cat head w/hat	45	95
Raven	no feet, black head, beak, and glasses	35	60
Regular	no feet, no head, stem w/top only; assorted colors; 1990s issues	2	3
Regular	no feet, no head, stem w/top only; 1950s	80	160
Rhino	w/feet, green head, red horn, foreign issue, whistle head	5	6
Ringmaster	no feet, white bow tie, white hat w/red hatband, and black handlebar moustache	200	325
Road Runner A	no feet, purple head, yellow beak	25	35
Road Runner B	w/feet, purple head, yellow beak	15	20
Roman Soldier (1998 foreign issue)		4	6
Rooster	no feet, yellow head, comb and wattle	25	45
Rooster	no feet, white head, comb	20	40
Rudolph	no feet, brown deer head, red nose	35	60
Sailor	no feet, blue hat, white beard	110	160
Santa	full body stem w/painted Santa suit and hat	135	200
Santa Claus A	no feet, ivory head w/painted hat	80	125
Santa Claus B	no feet, small head w/flesh painted face, black eyes, red hat	85	150
Santa Claus C	no feet, large head w/white beard, flesh face, red open mouth and hat	5	10
Santa Claus C	w/feet, removable red hat, white beard	1	2
Scarewolf	no feet, soft head w/orange hair and ears	150	225
Scrooge McDuck A	no feet, white head, yellow beak, black top hat and glasses, white sideburns	15	30
Scrooge McDuck B	w/feet, white head, removable yellow beak, tall black top hat and glasses, large eyes	5	6
Sheik	no feet, white head drape, headband	40	60
Sheriff	no feet, brown hat w/badge	110	165
Smurf	no feet, blue face, white hat	3	6
Smurfette	w/feet, blue face, yellow hair, white hat	3	8
Snoopy	w/feet, w/white head and black ears	1	2
Snow White	no feet, flesh face, black hair w/ribbon and matching collar	170	220
Snowman	no feet, black hat, white face	5	10
Space Gun 1950s	various colors	275	425
Space Gun 1980s	red or silver, on blister pack	150	200
Space Gun 1980s	red or silver, loose	55	85
Space Trooper	full bodied robot w/backpack; blue, red, or yellow	250	375
Space Trooper	gold	1400	2000
Spaceman	no feet, clear helmet over flesh-color head	90	150
Sparefroh (foreign issue)	no feet, green stem, red triangle hat, coin glued on stem	575	1200
Speedy Gonzales	no feet, brown head, yellow sombrero	25	35
Speedy Gonzales	w/feet, brown head, yellow sombrero	15	20
Spider-Man A	no feet, red head w/black eyes	10	15
Spider-Man B	w/feet, bigger head	1	2
Spider-Man C		1	2
Spike	w/feet, brown face, pink snout	5	6
Spook	blue head w/horns, soft head	150	225
Stand By Me	dispenser packed w/mini film poster and candy	140	185

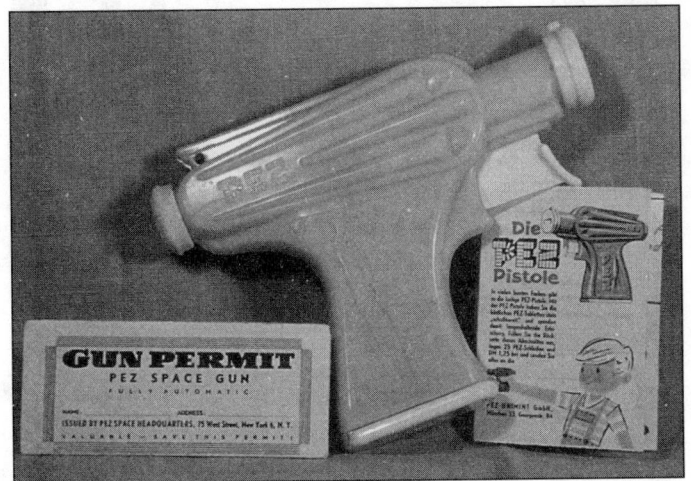

Space Gun 1950s, PEZ

Uncle Sam, Wounded Soldier, Betsy Ross, Captain (Paul Revere), Daniel Boone, PEZ

NAME	DESCRIPTION	EX	MINT
Stewardess	no feet, light blue flight cap, blond hair	150	225
Sylvester		1	3
Sylvester	w/feet, black head, white whiskers, red nose	1	3
Sylvester	no feet, black head, white whiskers, red nose	10	15
Taz		1	3
Teenage Mutant Ninja Turtles	four different characters	1	3
Thor	no feet, yellow hair, gray winged helmet	225	325
Thumper	w/feet, no Disney logo	30	50
Thumper	no feet, orange face, w/logo	200	300
Tiger	w/feet, tiger head w/white snout, whistle head	5	6
Tinkerbelle	no feet, pale pink stem, white hair, flesh face w/blue and white eyes	180	230
Tom A (Tom & Jerry)	no feet, gray cat head w/painted black features	25	35
Tom B (Tom & Jerry)	w/feet, gray cat head w/removable facial features	10	15
Truck A	cab, stem body, single rear axle	50	90
Truck B	cab, stem body, dual rear axle and dual arch fenders	40	65
Truck C	cab, stem body, dual rear wheels w/single arch fender, movable wheels	15	30
Truck D	cab, stem body, dual rear wheels, single arch fender, nonmovable wheels	1	2
Tweety		1	3
Tweety 1999		1	3
Tweety Bird	w/feet, yellow head	1	3
Tweety Bird	no feet, yellow head	10	17
Tyke	w/feet, brown head	10	25
Uncle Sam	no feet, stars and stripes on hat band, white hair and beard, Bicentennial issue	150	225
Valentine Heart		1	2
Vamp	no feet, light gray head on black collar, green hair and face, red teeth	225	280
Vucko Wolf	1984 Sarajevo Olympics issue, w/feet, gray or brown face w/bobsled helmet	650	775
Vucko Wolf	1984 Sarajevo Olympics issue, w/feet, gray or brown face w/ski hat	650	775
Vucko Wolf	1984 Sarajevo Olympics issue, w/feet, gray or brown face	650	750
Whistles	no feet; police whistles on top	25	40
Wile E. Coyote	no feet, brown head	60	75
Wile E. Coyote	w/feet, brown head	30	40
Winnie the Pooh	w/feet, yellow head	60	70
Winter Olympics Snowman	1976 Innsbruck, red nose and hat, white head w/arms extended, black eyes, blue smile	375	425
Witch 1 Piece	no feet, black stem w/witch embossed on stem, orange one-piece head	225	300
Witch 3 Piece A	w/feet, red head and hair, green mask, black hat	3	7
Witch 3 Piece B	no feet, chartreuse face, black hair, orange hat	70	120
Witch Regular	orange stem w/black witch graphics, no head	1700	3200
Wolf Man	no feet, black stem, gray head	200	275
Wolverine		1	2
Wonder Woman	Soft Head Superhero, no feet, black hair and yellow band w/star	100	165
Wonder Woman	w/feet, red stem	1	3
Wonder Woman	no feet, black hair and yellow band w/red star	5	10
Woodstock	w/painted feathers	5	10
Woodstock	w/feet, yellow head	1	2
Wounded Soldier	no feet, white bandage, brown hair, Bicentennial issue	135	170
Yappy Dog	no feet, black floppy ears and nose, green or orange head	60	70
Zombie	no feet, burgundy and black soft head	175	250
Zorro	no feet, black mask and hat	55	65
Zorro with Logo	no feet, black mask and hat, says "Zorro" on stem	65	85

Restaurant Premiums

Collecting restaurant premiums — fast food toys — is a recent but already highly-developed area for collectors, with many clubs and conventions in existence. It offers collectors an entry into the field at relatively inexpensive prices, compared to other collectible toys.

The typical child's meal customer is under age twelve, an age range not known for gentle play habits. Thus, condition of toys is critical to value. Only very rare toys hold any value at all if found in less than perfect condition. This price guide lists two grading classifications — Excellent and Mint. Excellent toys are rarely played with and exhibit no scratches or other imperfections.

Rarity is also a primary factor in determining value. The age of a toy plays a role in this, as does popularity and cross collectibility. Modern Disney movie tie-in toys are frequently worth more than older toys because of the strong Disneyana collector market. The same holds true for popular cartoon or comic character items.

Another factor affecting rarity is distribution. Some restaurant premiums were offered only in certain regions of the country. The toys of these campaigns are known as "regionals" and command higher than average prices due to their limited release areas.

Several years back some toys had to be recalled, resulting in the design of special one-piece toys for younger children, commonly called "Under 3" or U3 toys. Under 3 toys are not produced for each campaign, and are not normally advertised in the in-store displays. Lower numbers of these toys are released, again resulting in premiums typically twenty percent higher than regular toys of the same campaign.

One more factor deserves mention — international toys. Major film and comic character toy campaigns sometimes run worldwide with little or no changes from country to country. Sometimes only the package printing is changed. But occasionally foreign market toys are never released in America. These toys are highly valued by some collectors simply due to their foreign status. Other collectors also consider aspects such as popular character affiliation when calculating the value of these toys. Again, as the market matures, these values and item inventories will establish a track record.

The ten-year-old McDonald's customer of 1979 turns thirty years this year 1999, and it seems likely that nostalgia will accompany this generation into their middle years, as it has for baby boomers. As McDonald's is the first global restaurant, and popular film and TV tie-ins are now the rule of the day, the future of this field looks secure.

Gargoyles II, 1995, Burger King

Muppet Babies III,
1991, McDonald's

Trends

McDonald's continues to lead the way. Across fast food companies, character toys lead all others, with certain series standing heads above their peers. Characters from Disney films continue to lead the pack. They have set the standard for fast food toy mania with their Beanie Baby promotions, their most successful Happy Meal promotion ever. Their third Beanie Baby promotion, featuring four over-the-counter international Beanie Baby bears — Britannia, Glory, Erin and Maple — surpassed their expectations.

Over all, the restaurant premium market shows no sights of fatigue and continues on a strong course.

Editor's Note: Unless otherwise noted, prices listed are for **each** piece in a set, not the entire set.

The Top 10 Restaurant Premiums
(in Mint condition)

1. Big Boy Nodder, Big Boy, 1960s $1,500
2. Black History, McDonald's, sold in six Detroit stores, 1988................................ 500
3. Big Boy Bank, Large, Big Boy, 1960s.. 300
4. Metrozoo Happy Meal, McDonald's, distributed only in south Florida area, 1987... 250
5. High Flying Kite Happy Meal, McDonald's distributed in New England area, 1986... 225
6. Big Boy Bank, Medium, Big Boy, 1960s 165
7. Colonel Sanders Nodder, Kentucky Fried Chicken, 1960s 150
8. Transformers/My Little Pony, McDonald's distributed in St. Louis, Missouri area, 1985.. 140
9. Barbie/Hot Wheels, McDonald's distributed in Savanah, Ga., 1990 125
10. Big Boy Board Game, Big Boy,1960s.. 120

RESTAURANT PREMIUMS

ARBY'S

NAME	DESCRIPTION	YEAR	EX	MINT
Babar's World Tour at the Beach Summer Sippers	set of three squeeze bottles: orange, yellow or purple top	1991	1	5
Babar's World Tour Finger Puppets	set of four: King Babar, Queen Celeste, Alexander & Zephyr, Pom	1990	3	5
Babar's World Tour License Plates	set of four: Paris, Brazil, USA, North Pole	1990	1	2
Babar's World Tour Puzzles	set of four: Cousin Arthur's New Camera, Babar's Gondola Ride, Babar, the Haunted Castle, Babar's Trip to Greece	1990	2	4
Babar's World Tour Racers	set of three pull-back racers: King Babar, Cousin Arthur, Queen Celeste	1992	2	4
Babar's World Tour Squirters	set of three		1	3
Babar's World Tour Stampers	set of three: Babar, Flora, Arthur	1990	2	4
Babar's World Tour Storybooks	set of three: Read Get Ready, Set, Go, Calendar-Read and Have Fun-Read, Grow and Grow	1991	1	2
Babar's World Tour Vehicles	set of three vehicles: Babar in helicopter, Arthur on trike, Zephyr in car	1990	2	4
Classic Fairy Tales	set of three: Jack and the Beanstalk, The 3 Little Pigs, Hansel and Gretel	1993	4	5
Little Miss Figures	set of eight: Little Miss Giggles, Little Miss Helpful, Little Miss Shy, Little Miss Splendid, Little Miss Late, Little Miss Naughty, Little Miss Star, Little Miss Sunshine	1981	3	10
Looney Tunes Car-Tunes	set of six: Sylvester's Cat-illac, Daffy's Dragster, Yosemite Sam's Rackin Frackin Wagon, Taz's Slush Musher, Bugs' Buggy, Road Runner's Racer	1989	3	6
Looney Tunes Christmas Ornament	set of three: Bugs as Santa, Porky Pig as toy soldier, Tweety as elf	1989	3	8
Looney Tunes Figures	set of seven figures on oval base: Tasmanian Devil, Tweetie, Porky, Bugs Bunny, Yosemite Sam, Sylvester, Pepe Le Pew	1987	4	10
Looney Tunes Figures	set of six free-standing figures: Bugs Bunny, Daffy Duck, Taz, Elmer Fudd, Road Runner, Wile E. Coyote	1988	3	6
Looney Tunes Flicker Rings	set of four rings: Bugs Bunny, Yosemite Sam, Porky Pig, Daffy Duck	1987	20	40
Looney Tunes Fun Figures	set of three: Tazmanian Devil as pilot, Daffy as student, Sylvester as fireman	1989	3	6
Looney Tunes Pencil Toppers	set of six: Sylvester, Yosemite, Porky Pig, Bugs Bunny, Taz, Daffy Duck, Tweety Bird	1988	5	10
Megaphone, Minnesota Twins 25th Anniversary		1986	1	2
Mr. Men Figures	set of ten: Mr. Bounce, Mr. Bump, Mr. Daydream, Mr. Funny, Mr. Greedy, Mr. Mischeif, Mr. Nosey, Mr. Rush, Mr. Strong, Mr. Tickle	1981	3	10
Polar Swirl Penguins	set of four: penguin with mask and snorkle, penguin with headphones, penguin with sunglasses, penguin with surfboard	1987	15	40
Yogi & Friends Fun Squirters	set of three: Yogi, Cindy, Boo-Boo	1994	4	5
Yogi & Friends Mini-Disk	set of four: Ranger Smith, Yogi, Cindy, Snagglepus	1993	1	2
Yogi & Friends Winter Wonderland Crazy Cruisers	Yogi, Snagglepuss, Cindy	1995	4	5

BIG BOY

NAME	DESCRIPTION	YEAR	EX	MINT
Action Figures	complete set of four: skater, pitcher, surfer, race driver	1990	2	4
Big Boy Bank, Large	produced from 1966-1976, 18" tall, full color	1960s	125	300
Big Boy Bank, Medium	produced from 1966-1976, 9" tall, brown	1960s	50	165

RESTAURANT PREMIUMS

495

BIG BOY

NAME	DESCRIPTION	YEAR	EX	MINT
Big Boy Bank, Small	produced from 1966-1976, 7" tall, painted red/white	1960s	40	100
Big Boy Board Game		1960s	50	120
Big Boy Kite	kite with image of Big Boy	1960s	10	25
Big Boy Nodder	papier-mâché	1960s	900	1500
Big Boy Playing Cards	produced in four designs	1960s	15	45
Big Boy Stuffed Dolls	set of three: Big Boy, girlfriend Dolly, both 12" tall, and dog Nuggets, 7" tall	1960s	40	80
Helicopters	set of plastic vehicles: Ambulance, Police, Fire Department	1991	1	3
Monster In My Pocket	various secret monster packs	1991	2	4
Racers	set of three cars: yellow, orange, purple	1992	2	5
Sport Poses	set of four: surfing, baseball, racing, roller skating	1990	3	5

BURGER CHEF

NAME	DESCRIPTION	YEAR	EX	MINT
Fun Village Funmeal Boxes	set of 24 featuring Burger Chef characters	1973-74	25	60
Funmeal Boxes	set of 24 village buildings: Antique Shop, Bakery Shop, Barn, Beauty Shop, Bike Shop, Burger Chef, Cape Cod, Castle, Cottage (2), Colonial, Gas Station, Grocery Shop, Hardware Store, Haunted House, Pirate Ship, Ranch (2), Toy Shop, Two Story (2), Shoe Shop	1975	20	30
Star Wars Funmeal Boxes	set of seven: Darth Vader's Card Game, Tie Fighter, X-Wing Fighter, Land Speeder, R2D2 Droid Puppet, C3PO Droid Puppet, Flight Game	1978	25	40
Triple Play Funmeal Boxes	set of 24 featuring Major League Baseball teams: Astros, A's, Braves, Brewers, Cubs, Cards, Dodgers, Expos, Giants, Indians, Orioles, Padres, Rangers, Reds, Red Sox, Tigers, Twins, White Sox, Mets, Yankees, Angels, Phillies, Pirates, Royals	1978	20	90
Vacuform Race Cars		1981	20	30

BURGER KING

NAME	DESCRIPTION	YEAR	EX	MINT
Adventure Kits	set of four activity kits with crayons; Passport, African Adventure, European Escapades, Worldwide Treasure Hunt	1991	1	3
Aladdin	set of five figures: Jafar and Iago, Genie in lamp, Jasmine and Rajah, Abu, Aladdin and the Magic Carpet	1992	1	3
Aladdin Hidden Treasures	set of four: Jasmine, Aladdin, Abu, Iago	1994	2	5
Alf	set of four: joke and riddle disk, door knob card, sand mold, refrigerator magnet	1987	1	2
Alf Puppets	set of four puppets with records: Sporting with Alf, Cooking with Alf, Born to Rock, Surfing with Alf	1987	3	8
Alvin and the Chipmunks	set of three: super ball, stickers, pencil topper	1987	1	2
Anastasia	set of six: Bouncing Bartok, Fiendish Flyer, Fall-Apart Rasputin, Beanie Bat Bartok, Collision Course Dimitri, Anya & Pooka	1997	2	5
Aquaman Tub Toy	green	1987	3	5
Archie Cars	set of four: Archie in red car, Betty in aqua car, Jughead in green car, Veronica in purple car	1991	1	3
Barnyard Commandos	set of four: Major Legger Mutton in boat, Sgt. Shoat & Sweet in plane, Sgt. Wooley Pullover in sub, Pvt. Side O'Bacon in truck	1991	1	2
Batman Toothbrush Holder		1987	4	10
Beauty & the Beast	set of four PVC figures: Belle, Beast, Chip, Cogsworth	1991	2	5
Beetlejuice	set of six figures: Uneasy Chair, Head Over Heels, Ghost to Ghost TV, Charmer, Ghost Post, Peek A Boo Doo	1990	1	2

BURGER KING

NAME	DESCRIPTION	YEAR	EX	MINT
Bicycle Safety Fun Booklet			1	2
BK Kids Club Action Figures	set of four: Boomer, I.Q., Jaws, Kid Vid	1991	1	3
BK Kids Club All-Stars	set of five: All-Stars Boomer, All-Stars I/Q, All-Stars Jaws, All-Stars Kid Vid, All-Stars Snaps	1994	2	5
BK Kids Club Bugs	set of five: I/Q Caterpillar, Snaps Cricket, Lingo Spider, Boomer Fire Eye, Kid Vid Scorpian	1998	1	3
BK Kids Club Coolers	set of five: Kid Vid, blue; Jaws, turquoise; Snaps, yellow; I/Q, red; Boomer, purple	1995	2	4
BK Kids Club Glo Force	set of five glow-in-the-dark figures with costumes: Jaws as scubdiver, Snaps with safari gear, I/Q as surgeon, Kid Vid as astronaut, Boomer with ski gear	1996	1	2
BK Kids Club Mini Sports Games	set of four games: two catcher mitts with ball, football, basketball hoop with ball, inflatable soccer ball	1993	1	2
BK Kids Club Planet Patrol	Space Commander Jaws, I.Q.'s Planet Pacer, Boomer's Lightspeed Spacetop, Kid Vid's Glo Chopper, J.D. Shuttle Launch	1997	2	1
BK Kids Club Pranks	set of five: Boomer's Joy Buzzer, Jaw's Spider, Kid Vid's Squirting Remote Control, Longo's Gumballs, I/Q's Whoopee Cushion	1994	3	5
BK Kids Club Transporters	set of six: Snaps and her Camera Car, Boomer and her Super Shoe, I/Q and his World Book Mobile, Kid Vid and his SEGA Video Gamester	1990	4	6
BK Kids Club World Travel Adventure Kits	set of four: Kid Vid's Mystery Treasure Map, Lingo's South American Quest, Jaw's African Adventure, Snap's Eu015ropean Escapade	1991	3	5
Bone Age Skeleton Kit	set of four dinos: T-Rex, Dimetron, Mastadon, Similodon	1989	3	6
Bonkers Crash-Apart Cars	set of five: Toots, Jitters, Fall-apart Rabbit, Piquel, Bonkers	1993	1	2
Burger King Clubhouse	full size for kids to play in		15	35
Burger King Socks	rhinestone accents		2	5
Calendar "20 Magical Years" Walt Disney World		1992	2	4
Capitol Critters	set of four: Hemmet for Prez in White House, Max at Jefferson Memorial, Muggle at Lincoln Memorial, Presidential Cat	1992	1	2
Capitol Critters Cartons	punch-out masks: dog, chicken, duck, panda, rabbit, tiger, turtle	1992	2	4
Captain Planet	set of four flip-over vehicles: Captain Planet & Hoggish Greedily, Linka, Ma-Ti & Dr. Blight ecomobile, Verminous Skumm & Kwane helicopter, Wheeler and Duke Nukem snowmobile	1991	1	2
Captain Power	set of four plastic vacuform boxes: Powerjet Xt-7, Bio-Dread Patroller, Power Base, Phantom Striker	1988	8	10
Cartoon King Doll	16" tall; cloth	1972	20	30
Cartoon Network Racing Team	set of five: Speeding Bomber, Jeff Gordon Car, Scooby Doo Car, Burger King Race Car, Stoneage Rocker	1997	1	2
CatDog	set of five: Souped-up Skateboard, Crazy Catch Up, Gourmet Garbage Chaser, Key Catchin' Clock, Wacy Walker Upper	1999	1	3
Chicago Bull Bendies	set of four figures: Stacey King #21, John Paxson #5, Scotti Pippen #33, BJ Armstrong #10	1994	3	6
Chipmunk Adventure	set of four: bicycle licence plate; Alvin pencil topper, Alvin rubber ball, Sick 'Ems	1987	4	6
Christmas Crayola Bear	set of four bears: blue, red, yellow, red	1986	5	8
Christmas Crayola Bear Plush Toys	set of four: red, yellow, blue or purple	1986	3	6
Christmas Sing-A-Long Cassette Tapes	set of three Christmas sing-a-long tapes: Joy to the World/Silent Night, We Three Kings/O Holy Night, Deck the Halls/Night Before Christmas	1989	2	4

RESTAURANT PREMIUMS

497

BURGER KING

NAME	DESCRIPTION	YEAR	EX	MINT
Crayola Coloring Books	set of six books: Boomer's Color Chase, I.Q.'s Computer Code, Kids Club Poster, Jaws' Colorful Clue, Snaps' Photo Power, Kid Vid's Video Vision	1990	2	4
Crayola World Travel Adventure Kits	set of four: Kid Vid's Tresure Map, Lingo's South American Quest, Jaw's African Adventure, Snap's European Escape	1991	2	5
Dino Crawlers	set of five: blue, red, yellow, green, purple	1994	1	2
Dino Meals	punch-out sheets: Stegosaurus, Woolly Mammoth, T-Rex, Triceratops	1987	3	6
Disney 20th Anniversary Figures	set of four wind-up vehicles with connecting track: Minnie, Donald, Roger Rabbit, Mickey	1992	3	5
Disney Afternoon	set of four: Shovel, Treasure Chest, Sunshoes, Beach Balls	1994	2	5
Disney Collector Series Tumblers	set of eight: Snow White, Jungle Book, Lion King, Peter Pan, Beauty and the Beast, Pinocchio, Dumbo, Aladdin	1994	2	4
Disney Parade Figures	set of four: Mickey, Minnie, Donald, Roger Rabbit	1991	3	5
Fairy Tale Cassette Tapes	set of four fairy tale cassettes: Goldilocks, Jack and the Beanstalk, Three Little Pigs, Hansel and Gretel	1989	1	3
Food Miniatures		1983	3	5
Freaky Fellas	set of four: blue, green, red, yellow; each came with a roll of Life Savers candy	1992	2	4
Gargoyles I	set of four: Spin to Life Goliath, Color Mutation Broadway, Gargoyles Pop-up book	1995	3	5
Gargoyles II	set of five: Spectroscope, Sparkling Spinner, Mini-viewer, Spin-attack Broadway, Bronx Launcher	1995	4	5
Go-Go Gadget Gizmos	set of four: Copter Gadget, Inflated Gadget, Scuba Gadget, Surfer Gadget	1992	4	6
Golden Junior Classic Books	set of four: Roundabout Train, The Circus Train, Train to Timbucktoo, My Little Book of Trains		1	2
Good Gobblin'	set of three: Frankie Steen, Zelda Zoombroom, Gordy Goblin	1989	4	6
Goof Troop Bowlers	set of four: Goofy, Pete, PJ Max	1992	3	4
Goofy and Max's Adventure Toys	set of five: Water Raft, Water Skis, Goofy on Bucking Bronco, Row Boat, Runaway Car	1995	2	5
Hunchback of Notre Dame	set of eight figures: Laverne, Clopin, Hugo, Frollo, Pheobus, Victor, Quasimodo, Esmerelda and Djali the Goat	1996	1	2
Hunchback of Notre Dame Puppets	four finger: Quasimodo, Esmeralda, Gargoyle, Jester	1996	2	4
It's Magic	set of four: Magic Trunk, Disappearing Food, Magic Frame, Remote Control	1992	1	2
Jet Age Meal	set of three: Widebody Glider, X-2000 Gilder, Magellan Glider	1982	10	12
Kid's Choice Awards	set of six: Slimed Again, Big Bold Blimp, Winning Wiggle Writer, Pop Goes the Rosie, Give the Winner a Hand, Heeeeere's Rosie	1999	1	3
Land Before Time	set of six: Littlefoot, Spike, Perle, Chomper, Cera, Duckey	1997	3	6
Lickety Splits	set of seven: Carbo Cooler, Carsan'which, Chicken Chassis, Expresstix, Flame Broiled Buggy, Indianapolis Racer, Spry Fries	1990	3	5
Lifesaver Funsters	set of four: red, yellow, green, blue	1992	2	5
Lion King Collectible Kingdom	set of seven figures: Mufasa, Young Nala, Young Simba, Scar, Rafiki, Ed the Hyena, Pumbaa and Timon	1994	2	3
Lion King Finger Puppets	set of six: Mufasa, Simba, Rafiki, Pumbaa and Timon, Ed the Hyena, Scar	1995	1	2
Lion King's Timon & Pumbaa	set of four: Timon, Pumbaa, Bug Munchin' Pumbaa, Super Secret Compass	1996	2	3
Little Mermaid Splash Collection	set of four: Ariel wind-up, Flounder squirter, Sebastian wind-up, Urchin squirter	1993	2	4
M & M's	set of five: red, orange, yellow, blue, green	1997	2	5
M & M's Minis	set of five: Chomping Teeth Swarm, Giggle Stick, Crazy Pull-back Swarm, Secret Swarm Squirter, Scoop & Shoot Buggy	1997	1	2

BURGER KING

NAME	DESCRIPTION	YEAR	EX	MINT
Masters of the Universe Cups	set of four: Thunder Punch He-Man Saves the Day, He-Man and Roboto to the Rescue, He-Man Takes on the Evil Horde, Spydor—Stalking Enemies of Skeletor	1985	3	5
Matchbox Cars	set of four vehicles: blue Mountain Man 4x4, yellow Corvette, red Ferrari, Ford LTD police car	1987	5	7
Meal Bots	paper masks with 3-D lenses: Broil Master, red; Winter Wizard, blue; Beta Burger, gray; Galactic Guardians, yellow	1986	4	8
Men in Black	set of twelve: Squishy Worm Guy, Squirting Worm Guy, Globe Space Spinner, Building Space Spinner, Split Apart Light Up Zed, Split Apart Rotating Zed, Red Button Building Blaster, Red Button Loop Blaster, Slimed Out Kay, Slimed Out Jay, MIB Alien Detector, MIB Neitralyzer	1998	1	3
Mickey's Toontown	set of four: Mickey and Minnie, Goofy, Donald, Chip 'n Dale; each comes with map section	1993	5	7
Mr. Potato Head	set of five: Fry Fighter, Gotta Get 'Em Mr. Potato Head, Fry Jumper, Smashed Potato, Light Up Mr. Potato Head	1999	1	3
Mr. Potato Head	set of five: Speedster, Hats Off, Fry Flyer, Spinning Spud, Basket Shoot	1998	1	3
Nerfuls	set of four: Bitsy Ball, Fetch, Officer Bob, Scratch; rubber characters, interchangeable	1989	5	7
Nickel-O-Zone	set of five: Action League Now, Hay Arnold Football, Alien Strange Pod, Cruising Skeeter, Thornberry Comvee	1998	1	3
Nightmare Before Christmas Wristwatches	set of four different styles		15	30
Oliver & Co.	set of four: Dashing Dodger, Desot Launcher, Skateway Tito, Oliver Viewer; the second Oliver & Co. set was released to coincide with home video release	1996	2	5
Oliver & Company	set of four: Sneak-A-Peek Oliver, Dashing Dodger, Surprise Attack DeSoto, Skateaway Tito	1996	1	2
Pilot Paks	set of four Styrofoam airplanes: two-seater, sunburst, lightning, one unknown example	1988	4	8
Pinocchio Inflatables	set of four: Pinocchio, Jiminy Cricket, Monstro the Whale, Figaro	1992	3	5
Pocahontas Figures	set of eight: Meeko, Governor Radcliffe, Pocahontas, Flit, Captain John Smith, Grandmother Willow, Chief Powhatan, Percy	1995	1	3
Pocahontas Pop-Up Puppets	set of six: Peek-a-Boo Pocahontas, Meeko's Hideout, Pampered Percy, Ruthless Radcliffe, John Smith's Lookout, Busy Body Flit	1996	1	2
Pocahontas Tumblers	set of four: Chief Powhatan, Meeko, Governor Radcliffe, John Smith and Pocahontas	1995	3	5
Purrtenders	set of four: Free Wheeling Cheese Rider, Flip-Top Car, Radio Bank, Storybook	1988	2	5
Purrtenders Plush	set of four: Hop-purr, Flop-purr, Scamp-purr, Romp-purr	1988	2	4
Record Breakers	set of six cars: Aero, Indy, Dominator, Accelerator, Fastland, Shockwave	1990	3	6
Rodney & Friends	set of four plush toys: Rodney, Rhonda, Romona, Randy	1986	5	8
Rugrats	set of five: Reptar Alive, Hero on the Move Tommy, Jumpin' Chuckle, Wind Blown Angelica, Tandem Phil & Lil	1998	1	3
Rugrats, The Movie	set of twelve: Okeydokey Tommy; Reptar Wagon; Aqua Reptar; Monkey Mayhem; Phil & Lil: Reptar Mine!; Chuckie's Treasure Hunt; Spike to the Rescue; Shirley Lock Angelica; Dactar Glider; Scooting Susie; Baby Dil Awakened; Clip-On Tommy with Baby Dil	1998	1	3
Save the Animals	set of four: Mammals, Birds, Reptiles and Amphibians, Fish	1993	3	5

RESTAURANT PREMIUMS

Beetlejuice, 1990, Burger King

Capitol Critters, 1992, Burger King

NAME	DESCRIPTION	YEAR	EX	MINT
Scooby Doo	set of five: Scrappy-Doo, Scooby and Shaggy, Scooby Coffin, Scoby-Doo, Mystery Machine	1996	1	3
Sea Creatures	set of four terrycloth wash mitts: Stella Starfish, Dolly Dolphin, Sammy Seahorse, Ozzie Octopus	1989	2	3
Silverhawks	set of four: Sticker, Name Plate, Decoder Ring, Pencil Topper	1987	5	10
Simpsons Cups	set of four	1991	1	2
Simpsons Dolls	set of five soft plastic dolls: Bart, Homer, Lisa, Marge, Maggie	1990	2	4
Simpsons Figures	set of five: Bart with backpack, Homer with skunk, Lisa with saxaphone, Marge with birds, Maggie with turtle	1991	2	5
Small Soldiers	set of twelve: Chip Hazard, Slamfist Soft 'n Cuddly, Rip Roarin' Kip Killigan, Butch's Battle, Bobbling Insaniac, Levitating Lens Ocula, Morning Brake Brick Bazooka, Nick Nitro, Freedom Firing Archer, Laughing Insaniac, Boulder Blasting Punchit & Scratchit, Crawling Link Static	1998	1	3
Spacebase Racers	set of five plastic vehicles: Moon Man Rover, Skylab Cruiser, StarshipViking, Super Shuttle, Cosmic Copter	1989	2	4
Spacebase Racers	set of four: Super Shuttle, Moonman Rover, Starship Viking, Cosmic Copter	1989	5	10
Super Hero Cups	set of four cups with figural handles: Batman, Wonder Woman, Darkseid, Superman	1984	4	8
Super Powers	set of four: Superman coin, Batman toothbrush holder, Aquaman toy, Super Powers door nameplate	1987	7	15
Teenage Mutant Ninja Turtles Bike Gear	set of eleven: pouch, horn, water bottle, four spike buttons, three license plates	1993	3	5
Teenage Mutant Ninja Turtles Poster		1991	2	4
Teenage Mutant Ninja Turtles Rad Badges	set of six: Michaelangelo, Leonardo, Raphael, Donatello, Heroes in a Half Shell, Shredder	1990	3	5
Teletubbies	set of six: Laa-Laa, Tinky Winky, Dipsy, Po, Bunny, Noo-Noo	1999	1	3
Thundercats	set of four: cup/bank, Snarf strawholder, light switch plate, secret message ring	1986	3	8
Toonsylvania	set of five: Gurney Getaway, Phil's Teddy Cruiser, Vic's Walkaway Bride, Monster Maker, Screaming Screetch	1998	1	3
Top Kids	set of four spinning tops with figural heads: Wheels, Kid Vid, Jaws, Boomer	1993	1	2
Toy Story	set of eight: Stroll 'n Scope Lenny, Jawbreaker Scud, Speedy Deposit Hamm, Round 'em Up Woody, Spin-Top Bo Peep, Blast-away Buzz, Spaced Out Alien, Slinky Dog	1996	2	3
Toy Story	set of six: Hopping Mr. Potato Head, Woody, Action Wing Buzz, Racing R.C. Car, Squash 'N Go Rex, Green Army Men Recon Squad	1995	2	4
Toy Story Puppets	set of four: Woody, Buzz Lightyear, Rex, Hamm	1995	2	3
Toy Story Talking Puppets	set of four: R.C. Racer, Talking Woody, Talking Buzz	1995	3	5
Tricky Treaters Boxes	Monster Manor, Creepy Castle, Haunted House	1989	1	3
Tricky Treaters Figures	set of three PVC figures: Frankie Steen, Gourdy Goblin, Zelda Zoom Broom	1989	3	10
Trolls Dolls	set of four Kids Club characters with neon hair: Snaps, I.Q. Jaws, Kid Vid	1993	1	2
Universal Monsters	set of four: Wolf Man, Frankenstein, Dracula, Creature	1997	2	4
Watermates	set of four: Lingo's Jet Ski, Snaps in Boat, Wheels on raft, I.Q. on dolphin	1991	1	2
Wild Wild West		1999	1	3
Z-bots	set of five: Bugeye, Buzzsaw, Jawbreaker, Skyviper, Turbine	1994	2	5

RESTAURANT PREMIUMS

CARL'S JR.

NAME	DESCRIPTION	YEAR	EX	MINT
50th Anniversary	set of four: Happy Star baseball, Happy Star plastic puzzle, Cruisin booklet, Groovy 60's jigsaw puzzle	1991	3	5
Addams Family Figure	set of five: Thing pencil topper, Lurch stamper, Cousin Itt Bubbles, The Addams Family Mansion and Stickers	1993	2	5
Camp California	set of four: Bear Squirter, Lil' Bro Disk, Mini Volleyball, Spinner; similar to set issued by Hardee's	1992	3	5
Camping with Woody Woodpecker	set of two: Andy Panda container, pen knife utensil kit	1991	5	10
Fender Bender 500	set of five: Yogi and Boo Boo, Huckleberry Hound and Snagglepuss, Magilla Gorilla and Wally Gator, Quick Draw McGraw and Baba Looey, Dick Dasterdly and Muttley; also issued by Hardee's	1990	3	5
Life Savers Roll 'Em	set of five: Pineapple, Cherry, Orange, Lemon, Lime	1995	1	2
Life Savers Roll 'Em	set of five: Pineapple, Cherry, Orange, Lemon, Lime	1990	4	8
Muppet Parade of Stars	set of four: Miss Piggy, Kermit Gonzo, Fozzy	1995	4	6
Starnaments	set of five: Angel star, Mouse star, Toy Soldier star, Caroler star, Snow star	1992	4	6
Starnaments	set of four: Anniversary star, Moose star, Holly star, Twinkle star	1991	4	6
Starnaments	set of seven: Yellow star, Reindeer star, Snowman star, Elf Star, Chimney Sweep star, Toy Soldier star	1990	4	6

CHICK-FIL-A

NAME	DESCRIPTION	YEAR	EX	MINT
Adventures in Odyssey Books	set of seven: Mike Makes Right, The Treasure of La Monde, Isaac the Courageous, All's Well with Boswell, A Matter of Obedience, Last Great Adventure of Summer	1991	2	4
Adventures in Odyssey Cassette Tapes	set of six: The Ill-Gotten Deed, This is Chad Pearson?, Wishful Thinking, A Test for Robin, Suspicious Minds, Father's Day	1993	3	6
On the Go	set of six foam vehicles: car, airplane, train, truck, boat, helicopter	1993	1	2
Wonderful World of Kids		1995	2	5

DAIRY QUEEN

NAME	DESCRIPTION	YEAR	EX	MINT
Circus Train		1994	4	5
Dennis the Menace	set of four: Dennis in fire truck, Margaret in astronaut suit, Ruff in dinosaur costume, Joey in race car	1993	4	6
Dennis the Menace	set of four: Dennis, Margaret, Joey, Ruff; each cup featured images of individual character and a 3-D molded plastic cup lid	1993	4	6
Funbunch Flyer	each featured a different animal with the Dairy Queen logo		3	5
Holiday Bendies	set of four: Santa with open eyes, Santa with closed eyes, Reindeer with bell, Reindeer with scarf	1993	3	5
Rock-A-Doodles	set of six: Chanticleer, Patou, Edmund, Peepers, Peepers, The Grand Duke of Owl	1992	6	10
Rockin' Toppers	set of four pencil toppers: blue, yellow, green, red; rubber toppers with clingy surface allowing them to walk down walls	1993	1	2
Supersaurus Puzzles	set of three	1993	2	3
Tom and Jerry figures	set of six: Tom Squirter, Jerry Squirter, Tom Summer Cruiser, Jerry Summer Cruiser, Tom Stamper, Jerry Stamper	1993	4	6

DENNY'S

NAME	DESCRIPTION	YEAR	EX	MINT
Dino-Makers	set of six: including blue dino, purple elephant, orange bird	1991	1	2
Flintstones Dino Racers	set of six: Fred, Bamm-Bamm, Dino, Pebbles, Barney, Wilma	1991	3	6
Flintstones Fun Squirters	set of six: Fred with telephone, Wilma with camera, Dino with flowers, Bam Bam with soda, Barney, Pebbles	1991	2	4
Flintstones Glacier Gliders	set of six: Bamm-Bamm, Barney, Fred, Dino, Hoppy, Pebbles	1990	2	4
Flintstones Mini Plush	set of four, in packages of two: Fred/Wilma, Betty/Barney, Dino/Hoppy, Pebbles/Bamm-Bamm	1989	2	4
Flintstones Rock 'n Rollers	set of six: Fred with guitar, Barney with sax, Bam Bam, Dino with piano, Elephant, Pebbles	1990	3	6
Flintstones Stone-Age Cruisers	set of six: Fred in green car, Wilma in red car, Dino in blue car, Pebbles in in purple bird, Bam Bam in orange car, Barney in yellow car with sidecar	1991	2	4
Flintstones Vehicles	set of six: Fred, Wilma, Pebbles, Dino, Barney, Bamm-Bamm	1990	2	4
Jetsons Crayon Fun Game	set of six booklets with crayon game: George in Leisurly George, Jane in Jane Gets Decorated, Judy in Dream Date, Elroy What a Sport, Astro in Every Dog has his Daydream, Rosie in I Need Some Space		2	4
Jetsons Game Packs	set of six: George, Elroy, Judy, Astro, Rosie, Jane	1992	2	4
Jetsons Go Back to School	set of six school tools: mini dictionary, folder, message board, pencil and topper, pencil box, triangle and curve	1992	2	4
Jetsons Puzzle Ornaments	set of six: Saturn with George, Earth with Jane, Jupiter with Judy, Mars with Elroy, Moon with Astro, Neptune with Rosie	1992	2	4
Jetsons Space Balls (Planets)	set of six: Jupiter, Neptune, Earth, Saturn, Mars, glow-in-the-dark Moon	1992	2	4
Jetsons Space Cards	set of five: Spacecraft, Phenomenon, Astronomers, Constellations, Planets	1992	2	4
Jetsons Space Travel Coloring Books	set of six books: each with four crayons	1992	2	4

DOMINO'S PIZZA

NAME	DESCRIPTION	YEAR	EX	MINT
Noids	set of seven figures: Boxer, Clown, He Man, Holding Bomb, Holding Jack Hammer, Hunchback, Magician	1987	2	4
Quarterback Challenge Cards	pack of four cards	1991	1	2

HARDEE'S

NAME	DESCRIPTION	YEAR	EX	MINT
Apollo 13		1995	2	5
Beach Bunnies	set of four: girl with ball, boy with skateboard, girl with skates, boy with frisbee	1989	2	4
California Raisins	third set: Alotta Stile in pink boots, Anita Break with package under her arm, Benny bowling, Buster with skateboard	1991	2	6
California Raisins	set of four: dancer with blue and white shoes, singer with mike, sax player, raisin with sunglasses	1987	2	8
California Raisins	set of six: Waves Weaver, F.F. Strings, Captain Toonz, Rollin' Rollo, Trumpy Tru-Note, S.B. Stuntz	1988	2	4
California Raisins	set of four: Berry, Anita Break, Alotta Stile, Buster	1991	3	5
California Raisins Plush	set of four: lady in yellow shoes, dancer in yellow hat, with mike in white shoes, in sunglasses with orange hat; each 6" tall	1988	3	6

HARDEE'S

NAME	DESCRIPTION	YEAR	EX	MINT
Camp California	set of four: Bear Squirter, Lil' Bro Disk, Mini Volleyball, Spinner; similar to set issued by Carl's Jr.	1993	3	5
Days of Thunder Racers	set of four cars: Mello Yello #51, Hardee's #18 orange, City Chevrolet #46, Superflo #46 pink/white	1990	3	6
Dinosaur in My Pocket	set of four: Stegosaurus, Triceratops, Bronotsaurus, Tyrannosaurus	1993	2	5
Disney's Animated Classics Plush Toys	Pinocchio, Bambi		3	5
Fender Bender 500	set of five: Yogi and Boo Boo, Huckleberry Hound and Snagglepuss, Magilla Gorilla and Wally Gator, Quick Draw McGraw and Baba Looey, Dick Dasterdly and Muttley; also issued by Carl's Jr.	1990	2	3
Finger Crayons	set of four: two Crayons included in each package; not marked Hardee's	1992	2	3
Flintstones First 30 Years	set of five: Fred with TV, Barney with grill, Pebbles with phone, Dino with jukebox, Bamm Bamm with pinball	1991	3	6
Food Squirters	set of four: cheeseburger, hot dog, shake, fries	1990	2	4
Ghostbuster Beepers	set of four: red, white, black, gray	1989	10	12
Gremlin Adventures	set of five book and record sets: Gift of the Mogwai, Gismo & the Gremlins, Escape from the Gremlins, Gremlins Trapped, The Late Gremlin	1989	2	4
Halloween Hideaways	set of four: goblin in blue cauldron, ghost in yellow bag, cat in pumpkin, bat in stump	1989	3	6
Hardee's Racer	blue or green		4	6
Home Alone 2	set of four cups: Kevin, The Pigeo Lady, Marv, Harry	1992	1	2
Homeward Bound	set of five: Chance, Riley, Sassy, Delilah, Shadow		2	5
Kazoo Crew Sailors	set of four: bear, monkey, rabbit, rhino	1991	1	2
Little Little Golden Books	set of four: The Little Red Caboose, The Three Bears, Old MacDonald Had a Farm, Three Little Kittens	1988	2	4
Little Little Golden Books	set of four: The Poky Little Puppy, Little Red Riding Hood, The Three Little Pigs, The Little Red Hen	1987	5	7
Marvel Super Heroes	set of three: She Hulk, Hulk, Captain America, Spider-Man	1990	3	6
Muppet Christmas Carol Finger Puppets	set of four: Miss Piggy, Kermit, Gonzo, Fozzy Bear	1994	3	5
Nicktoons	set of eight: Ren, Stimpy, Angelica Pickles, Tommy Pickles, Porkchop, Doug Funnie, Rocko, Spunky	1994	4	6
Pound Puppies	set of four: black, white with black, tan with black, gray with black	1986	5	10
Pound Puppies and Pur-r-ries	set of four: white cat with gray stripes, brown cat, gray bulldog, Damlatian	1987	5	10
Shirt Tales Plush Dolls	set of five: Bogey, Pammy, Tyg, Digger, Rick; each 7" tall		3	6
Smurfin' Smurfs	set of four: Papa Smurf with red board, boy with orange board, girl with purple board, dog with blue board	1990	2	4
Smurfs figures	Hardee's issued over 100 Smurfs in the promotion; No list is available	1987	3	5
Speed Bunnies	set of four: Cruiser, Dusty, Sunny, Stretch	1994	2	4
Super Bowl Cloisonné Pins	set of twenty-five NFL Super Bowl pins	1991	2	6
Swan Princess	set of four: Prince Derek, Princess Odette/Swan, Jean-Bob, Puffin, Rothbart	1994	3	5
Tang Mouth Figures	set of four: Lance, Tag, Flap, Awesome Annie	1989	2	4
Waldo and Friends Holiday Ornaments	in sets of three: Waldo with Woof, Waldo Watchers, Snowman; Waldo with camping gear, Wenda, Woof; Reindeer in sleigh, Wizard, Waldo with books	1991	3	5

HARDEE'S

NAME	DESCRIPTION	YEAR	EX	MINT
Waldo's Straw Buddies	set of four: Waldo, Wenda, Wizard, Woof	1990	2	3
Waldo's Travel Adventure	set of four: Adventure Travel Journal, Postcards, Fold 'N Solve Travel Pictures, Space Puzzle	1992	2	3
X-Men	set of three, in sets of two: Cyclops vs. Commando; Phantasia vs. Storm; The Blob vs. Wolverine; Rogue vs. Wolverine	1995	3	6

INTERNATIONAL HOUSE OF PANCAKES

NAME	DESCRIPTION	YEAR	EX	MINT
Pancake Kid dolls	set of three cloth dolls: Bonnie Blueberry, Susie Strawberry, Chocolate Chip Charlie	1992	7	10
Pancake Kids	set of ten: Cynthis Cinnamon Apple, Susie Strawberry, Bonnie Blueberry, Harvey Harvest, Betty Buttermilk, Frenchy, Rosana Banana Nut, Peter Potato, Von der Gus	1991	4	6
Pancake Kids Cruisers	set of eight: Von der Gus, Bonnie Blueberry, Susie Strawberry, Harvey Harvest, Chocolate Chip Charlie, Frenchy, Cynthia Cinnamon Apple, Betty Buttermilk	1993	4	6

JACK IN THE BOX

NAME	DESCRIPTION	YEAR	EX	MINT
Bendables		1992	n/a	0
Bendables		1991	n/a	0
Bendables	set of five: Jack the Clown, Onion Ring Thing, Hamburger Meister, Secret Soft Agent, Small Fry	1980s	10	15
Jack Pack Finger Puppets		1993	n/a	0

KENTUCKY FRIED CHICKEN

NAME	DESCRIPTION	YEAR	EX	MINT
Alvin and the Chipmunks	Canadian issues; Alvin and Simon	1992	2	4
Alvin and the Chipmunks	Canadian issues; Alvin and Theodore	1991	3	5
Animorphs	set of five: Animorphs Puzzle Cube, DNA Transfer Cards, Animorphing Box, Tobias Hawk Glider, Thought Speak Revealer	1998	2	3
Beakman's World	set of six: Lester Reverser, Penguin TV, Optical Illusion Top, Diver Don, Beakman's Balancer, Dancing Liza	1998	2	3
Carmen Sandiego	set of six: Jr. Sleuth Pocket Pack, Carmen's Mystery Decoder, Carmen's World Map Puzzle, Carmen's Breakaway Escape Care, Carmen's Undercover Case with Stickers, Magic Answer Globe	1997	2	3
Colonel Sanders Figure	9" tall	1960s	35	50
Colonel Sanders Nodder	7" tall; papier-mâché	1960s	50	150
Colonel Sanders Nodder	7" tall; plastic	1960s	15	40
Cool Summer Stuff featuring Chester Cheetah	set of five: Fast Flyin' Disk, Spotted Summer Shades, Mini Wrist-Pack, Totally Fun Visor, Inflatable Wobble Ball	1996	2	3
Extreme Ghostbusters	set of six: Haunted Cube, Ghost Trap Challenge, Screamin' Scrambler, Ecto1 Haunted Hauler, Ghostbusters Keychain Keeper, Slimer Squirter	1997	2	3
Garfield Catmobiles	set of six: Arlene finger puppet, Pookie finger puppet, Nermal Freewheeler, Jon Freewheeler, Garfield Pullback, Odie Pullback	1996	2	3
Garfield Racers	set of six	1996	2	4
Ghostly Glowing Squirters	set of six: Casper, Spooky, Stretch, Fatso, Poil, Stinkie	1996	2	3
Giga Pets	set of four: Digipooch, Cyberkitty, Micropup, Bitty Kitty; over the counter promotion	1997	2	3

RESTAURANT PREMIUMS

Simpsons Figures, 1991, Burger King

Toy Story Puppets, 1995, Burger King

Flintstones Dino Racers, 1991, Denny's

KENTUCKY FRIED CHICKEN

NAME	DESCRIPTION	YEAR	EX	MINT
Jim Henson's Scary Scary Monsters	set of five: Flip-A-Mungo, Super Stretch Norbert, Zuzu Zoomer, Monster Shoelace Munchers, Scary Scary Stick-Ons	1999	2	3
Koosh	set of three: Zipper Pull, Bookmark, Pencil Topper	1995	2	3
Linkbots	set of six Transformers	1995	2	3
Marvel Super Heroes	set of six: Spider-Man Symbol Clip, Invisible Woman Escape Launcher, Incredible Hulk Pencil Twirler, Spider-Man Wall Walker, Fantastic Four Terra Craft, Wolverine Press 'n Go	1997	2	3
Masked Rider to the Rescue	set of six: Masked Rider Super Gold, Magno the Super Car, Press & Go Super Chopper, Glow-in-the-Dark X-Ray Cyclopter, Ecto Viewer Wrist Band, Bump & Go Ferbus	1997	2	3
Matchbox	set of six: BMW, Ambulance, Fire Engine, Mustang, Jeep, Ferrari	1995	2	3
NCAA March Madness	set of three: 2-Hoop Game, Wacky Wrist Toss, Final Four Basketball	1999	2	3
Pokémon	set of six: Pokémon Monster Blocks, Go Pokémon Card Game, Pokémon Monster Matcher, Pokémon Tattoos, Ivysaur Squirter, Pikachu Treasure Keeper	1998	2	3
Pokémon Beanbags	set of four: Seel, Vulpix, Dratini, Zubat; over-the-counter promotion	1998	2	5
Secret Files of the Spy Dogs	set of five: The Evil Cat Astrophe, Fidgety Scribble, Mitzy Rolling Stamper, Eye Popping Space Slug, Agent Ralph's Marble Game	1999	2	3
SI for Kids	set of four: Dunk It In Fun Book, Slam Dunk! Flipbook, Kick it in Fun Book, Kick! Flipbook	1998	2	3
Slimamander	set of six: Slimamander Wrist Squirter, Slimamander's Glowing Goo, Slimamander and Leap the Frog Tattoos, Leap the Frog Launcher, Slimamander Bubble Wand, Slimamander Spraying Top	1998	2	3
Timon and Pumbaa's World of Bugs	set of six: Snail Snackin' Timon, Bug Munchin' Pumbaa, Out-to-Lunch Timon, Hawaiian Luau Pumbaa, Jungle River-Riding Timon, Bug Bath Pumbaa	1997	2	3
Treeples	set of six: Dress-Up Rachel, Stevie's Acorn Searcher, Tangled Treeples, Othello Yo-Yo, Miranda's Banana-mated Theater, Linky Lurker	1999	2	3
Ultimate Eekstravaganza	set of five: Eek! Balancing Act, Sharky's Dog House Launcher, Ka-Boooom! Annabelle, Cool Moves Doc, Kutler Copter	1996	2	3
Wallace & Gromit	set of six: The Wrong Trousers, Gromit's Rollalong Sidecar, Wallace Bendable, Wallace & Gromit Character Card Set, Sheep-on-a-String, Blinking Feathers McGraw	1998	2	3
Winter Wonderpals	set of five: Wallace the Walrus Paper Puncher, Roley Poley Polar Ball, Sippy the Penguin Play Straw, Slick the Sled Dog Igloo Launcher, Howl E. Wolf	1999	2	4
WWF Stampers	set of four: Canadian issues		2	4

LEE'S FRIED CHICKEN

NAME	DESCRIPTION	YEAR	EX	MINT
Cartoon Viewers	set of six: Mighty Mouse, Woody Woodpecker, Popeye, Superman, Bugs Bunny, Porky Pig	1980s	20	50

LONG JOHN SILVER'S

NAME	DESCRIPTION	YEAR	EX	MINT
Adventure on Volcano Island	paint with water activity book	1991	2	4
Berenstain Bear books		1995	2	5
Fish Cars	fish-shaped cars done in red, yellow and blue, each with different peel-off stickers and details	1986	8	12

LONG JOHN SILVER'S

NAME	DESCRIPTION	YEAR	EX	MINT
Once Upon a Forest	set of five straw huggers: Abigail, Michelle, Cornelius, Edgar, Russell; done in two mold colors	1993	3	6
Sea Walkers	set of four packaged with string: Parrot, Penguin, Turtle, Sylvia	1990	3	8
Sea Watchers Kaleidoscopes	set of three: orange, yellow, pink	1991	2	4
Superstar Baseball Cards	eight sets of five cards: Don Mattingly, Mark McGwire, Mark Grace, Wade Boggs, Darryl Strawberry, Nolan Ryan, Bobby Bonilla, Bret Saberhagen	1990	10	15
Treasure Trolls	set of six: yellow hair, red hair, pink hair, blue hair, purple hair, green hair	1992	1	3
Water Blasters	set of four: Billy Bones, Captain Flint, Ophelia Octopus, Parrot	1990	3	5

MCDONALD'S

NAME	DESCRIPTION	YEAR	EX	MINT
101 Dalmatians	set of four: Lucky, Pongo, Sergeant Tibbs, Cruella	1991	1	2
101 Dalmatians	101 different PVC dogs. Premiums were randomly distributed in opaque bag and were un-named. Values for each dog can vary due to the haphazzard distribution.	1996	3	10
101 Dalmatians Snow Globes	set of four: Snoman's Best Friend (snowman), Snow Furries (dome with red ribbon), Dog Sledding (sleigh), Dalmatian Celebration (number 101)	1996	2	5
101 Dalmatians the Series	set of eight flip cars: Perdita/Scorch, Two-Tone/Lt. Pug, Lucky/Cruella, Rolly/Ed Pig, Steven/Sydney, Tripod/Dumpling, Cadpig/Spot, Pongo/Swamprat	1997	1	2
3-D Happy Meal	set of four cartons with 3-D designs and 3-D glasses inside: Bugsville, High Jinx, Loco Motion, Space Follies	1981	20	40
A Bug's Life Figures	set of eight wind-ups: Dim, Rosie, Dot, Flik, Francis, Heimlich, Hopper, Atta	1998	1	2
A Bug's Life Watches	set of three: Leafy Ant-icks with 3-D face, Pop Topper with flip-top lid, Bug Eye Spy with two floating characters	1998	2	3
Adventures of Ronald McDonald	set of seven rubber figures: Ronald, Birdie, Big Mac, Captain Crook, Mayor McCheese, Hamburglar, Grimace	1981	5	10
Airport Happy Meal	set of five: Birdie Bentwing Blazer, Fry Guy Flyer, Grimace Bi-Plane, Big Mac Helicopter, Ronald Sea Plane	1986	5	10
Airport Happy Meal	set of two U3 toys: Fry Guy Friendly Flyer, Grimace Smiling Shuttle	1986	3	5
Aladdin and the King of Theives	one U3 toy: Abu squirter	1996	2	5
Aladdin and the King of Thieves	set of eight: Cassim, Abu, Jasmine, Iago, Genie, Sa'luk, Aladdin, Maitre d'Genie	1996	1	3
Alvin and The Chipmunks	one U3 toy: Alvin leaning on jukebox	1991	10	20
Alvin and The Chipmunks	set of four figures: Simon with movie camera, Theodore with rap machine, Brittany with juke box, Alvin with guitar	1991	3	6
Amazing Wildlife	set of eight plush animals: Asiatic Lion, Chimpanzee, Koala Bear, African Elephant, Dromedary Camel, Galapagos Tortoise, Siberian Tiger, Polar Bear	1995	2	3
An American Tail	set of four books: Fievel and Tiger, Fievel's Friends, Fievel's Boat Trip, Tony and Fievel	1986	2	3

MCDONALD'S

NAME	DESCRIPTION	YEAR	EX	MINT
Animal Kingdom	set of thirteen: triceratops, toucan, gorilla and baby, elephant, dragon, iguanodon, lion, cheetah, zebra, rhino, crocodile, ringtail lemur, tortoise (only available at McDonald's in Wal-Mart stores); four special collector's cups were available with super sized combo meal	1998	1	2
Animal Pals	set of six plush toys: Panda, Rhinoceros, Yak, Moose, Brown Bear, Gorilla	1997	1	2
Animal Riddles	set of eight rubber figures: condor, snail, turtle, mouse, anteater, alligator, pelican, dragon, in various colors	1979	2	4
Animaniacs	set of four U3 toys: Bicycle Built for Trio, Goodskate Goodfeathers, Yakko Ridin' Ralph, Mindy and Buttons Wild Ride	1995	3	5
Animaniacs	set of eight: Bicycle Built for Trio, Goodskate Goodfeathers, Upside-Down Wakko, Slappy and Skipper's Chopper, Dot's Ice Cream Machine, Midy and Buttons Wild RideYakko Ridin' Ralph, Pink and the Brain Mobile,	1994	2	3
Animaniacs	set of eight: Pinky & the Brain, Goodfeathers, Dot & Ralph, Wacko & Yakko, Slappy & Skippy, Mindy & Buttons, Wakko, Yakko & Dot, Hip Hippos	1995	1	2
Astrosnick Spacemobile	9-1/2" rocket ship available with four Happy Meal Cosmic Coupons	1984	30	60
Astrosnicks I	set of eight: eight different 3" rubber space creatures: Scout, Thirsty, Robo-Robot, Laser, Snickapotamus, Sport, Skater, Astralia	1983	4	20
Astrosnicks II	set of six: Copter, Drill, Ski, Racing, Perfido, Commander	1984	5	20
Astrosnicks III	set of eleven figures: C.B., Banner, Commander, Junior, Jet, Laser, Perfido, Pyramido, Robo-Robot, Astralia, Snikapotamus; regionally distributed in the Oklahoma area, many are the same as other Astroniks but without "m" marking	1985	5	40
Attack Pack/Polly Pocket	one U3 toy: Truck	1995	2	3
Attack Pack/Polly Pocket	set of four: Ruck, Battle Bird, Lunar Invader, Sea Creature; joint promotion with Polly Pocket	1995	1	2
Babe	set of seven plush toys: Babe, Ferdinand, Fly, Maa, Cow, Mouse, Dutchess	1996	1	2
Back to the Future	set of four: Doc's DeLorean, Verne's Jukebox, Marty's Hoverboard, Einstein's Traveling Train	1992	1	2
Bambi	set of four figures: Owl, Flower, Thumper, Bambi	1988	2	4
Bambi	set of three U3 toys: Bambi with butterfly on tail, Bambi, Thumper	1988	5	10
Barbie and Friends/World of Hot Wheels	set of eleven: Bicyclin' Barbie, Jewel and Glitter Shani, Camp Barbie, Camp Teresa, Locket Surprise Ken, African-American or Caucasian, Locket Surprise Barbie, African-American or Caucasian, Jewel and Glitter Barbie, Bridesmaid Skipper; joint promotion with Hot Wheels	1994	2	5
Barbie/Hot Wheels	set of five: Dutch Barbie, Kenyan Barbie, Japanese Barbie, Mexican Barbie, USA Barbie; joint promotion with Hot Wheels	1996	1	3
Barbie/Hot Wheels	set of five: Wedding Rapunzel Barbie, Rapunzel Barbie, Angel Princess Barbie, Blossom Beauty Barbie, Happy Holidays Barbie; joint promo with Hot Wheels	1997	1	3
Barbie/Hot Wheels	one U3 toy: Barbie slide puzzle	1996	2	3
Barbie/Hot Wheels	set of four: Barbie, Teen Skipper, Eating Fun Kelly, Bead Blast Christie; joint promo with NASCAR Hot Wheels	1998	1	3

RESTAURANT PREMIUMS

MCDONALD'S

NAME	DESCRIPTION	YEAR	EX	MINT
Barbie/Hot Wheels	set of ten: Hot Skatin' Barbie, Dance Moves Barbie, Butterfly Princess Teresa, Cool Country Barbie, Caucasian Lifeguard Ken, African-American Lifeguard Ken, Caucasian Lifeguard Barbie, African-American Lifeguard Barbie, Bubble Angel Barbie, Ice Skatin' Barbie; joint promotion with Hot Wheels	1995	2	3
Barbie/Hot Wheels	set of eight: Ice Capades, All American, Lights & Lace, Hawaiian Fun, Happy Birthday, Costume Ball, Wedding Day Midge, My First Barbie	1991	2	3
Barbie/Hot Wheels	set of two U3 toys: Costume Ball Barbie, Wedding Day Midge; joint promotion with Hot Wheels	1991	2	4
Barbie/Hot Wheels	one U3 toy: figurine of blond girl wearing green dress	1995	2	3
Barbie/Hot Wheels	set of four Barbie figures with dioramas: Movie Star with SuperStar Barbie; In Concert with Solo in the Spotlight Barbie; Tea Party with Enchanted Evening Barbie; Moonlight Ball with 1989 Happy Holiday Barbie. Test Market Happy Meal, regionally distributed in Savanah, Georgia; joint promotion with Hot Wheels	1990	90	125
Barbie/Hot Wheels	set of eight: My First Ballerina, Birthday Party, Western Stamping, Romantic Bride, Hollywood Hair, Paint 'n Dazzle, Twinkle Lights, Secret Hearts; joint promotion with Hot Wheels	1993	2	3
Barbie/Hot Wheels Mini-Streex	set of eight dolls: Sparkle Eyes, Roller Blade, Rappin' Rockin', My First Ballerina, Snap 'N PLay, Sun Sensation, Birthday Surprise, Rose Bride; joint promotion with Hot Wheels Mini-Streex	1992	1	2
Barbie/Hot Wheels Mini-Streex	one U3 toy: Sparkle Eyes Babie	1992	2	5
Batman	set of four: Batmobile, Batmissle, Catwoman Cat Coupe, Penguin Roto-Roadster	1992	1	2
Batman Cups	set of six cups; offered in conjunction with Happy Meal	1992	1	2
Batman, the Animated Series	set of eight: Batman with removable cape, Robin, Batgirl, Two Face, Poison Ivy, Joker, Catwoman with leopard, Riddler	1993	2	3
Batman, the Animated Series	one U3 toy: Batman without removable cape	1993	2	5
Beach Ball	set of three inflatables: Ronald waving, red; Birdie with sandcastle, blue; Grimace with beach umbrella, yellow. Regionally distributed in Washington, New York and Colorado	1986	10	15
Beach Ball Characters	set of three: Grimace in kayak, Ronald holding flag and beachball, Birdie in sailboat	1985	5	8
Beach Toy II	set of eight: Ronald and Grimace sand pail with yellow lid and shovel, Birdie Seaside Submarine, Fry Kid Super Sailor, Fry Kids Sand Castle Pail, Grimace Beach Ball, Birdie Shovel, Ronald Squirt Gun Rake, Ronald Fun Flyer	1990	2	3
Beach Toys I	set of four: Birdie Seaside Submarine, Grimace Bouncin' Beachball, Fry Kid Super Sailor, Ronald Fun Flyer; test market Happy Meal	1989	10	15
Beachcomber Happy Meal ·	set of three sand pails with shovels: Grimace, Mayor McCheese, Ronald	1986	5	10
Bedtime	set of four: Ronald toothbrush with tube of Crest toothpaste, Ronald bath mitt, Ronald Nite Stand Star Figure, Ronald cup	1989	4	8
BeetleBorgs Metallix	set of six: Stinger Drill, Beetle Bonder, Hunter Claw, Platinum Purple BeetleBorg Covert Compact, Chromuim Gold BeetleBorg Covert Compact, Titanium Silver BeetleBorg Covert Compact	1997	1	2
Behind the Scenes	set of four: Cartoon Wheel, Rainbow Viewer, Rub 'N' Draw, Balance Builder	1992	2	3

RESTAURANT PREMIUMS

NAME	DESCRIPTION	YEAR	EX	MINT
Berenstain Bears I	set of four figures: Papa with wheelbarrow, Mama with shopping cart, Brother with scooter, Sister with sled; test market set, distributed in Evansville, Indiana	1986	30	75
Berenstain Bears II	set of two U3 toys with paper punch outs: Mama, Papa	1987	5	10
Berenstain Bears II	set of four figures with flocked heads: Papa with wheelbarrow, Mama with shopping cart, Brother with scooter, Sister with wagon	1987	2	4
Berenstain Bears Story Books	set of eight books: Attic Treasure Story Book, Attic Treasure Activity Book, Substitute Teacher Story Book, Substitute Activity Book, Eager Beavers Story Book, Eager Beavers Activity Book, Life with Papa Story Book, Life with Papa Activity Book	1990	2	4
Bigfoot	set of eight Ford trucks: Bronco, green or orange; Pickup, purple or orange; Ms. Pickup, turquoise or pink; Shuttle, red or black; without McDonald's "M" logo on back window	1987	5	10
Bigfoot	set of eight Ford trucks: Bronco, green or orange; Pickup purple or orange; Ms. Pickup, turquoise or pink; Shuttle, red or black; each had McDonald's "M" logo on back window	1987	3	5
Birdie Bike Horn	Japanese		4	9
Birdie Magic Trick	green or orange		2	5
Black History	two coloring books: Little Martin Jr. Coloring Book Volume One, Little Martin Jr. Coloring Book Volume Two; sold in six Detroit stores	1988	200	500
Boats 'n Floats	set of four vaccuform boats with stickers: Chicken McNugget lifeboat, Birdie float, Fry Guys raft, Grimace ski boat	1987	5	10
Bobby's World	set of four: Wagon-Race Car, Innertube-Submarine, Three Wheeler-Space Ship, Skates-Roller Coaster	1994	1	2
Bobby's World	one U3 toy: Bobby in intertube	1994	1	3
Bobby's World	one U3 toy: inner tube	1994	2	3
Breakfast Happy Meal	squeeze bottle with Minute Maid logo	1991	1	3
Cabbage Patch	one U3 toy: Anne Louise "Ribbons & Bows"	1992	1	2
Cabbage Patch Kids/Tonka	one U3 toy: SaraJane	1994	2	3
Cabbage Patch Kids/Tonka	set of four: Mimi Kristina, Abigail Lynn, Kimberly Katherine, Michelle Elyse; joint promotion with Tonka	1994	1	3
Cabbage Patch Kids/Tonka	set of five: Tiny Dancer, Holiday Pageant, Holiday Dreamer, Fun On Ice, All Dressed Up; joint promotion with Tonka	1992	2	3
Camp McDonaldland	set of four: Grimace Canteen, Birdie Mess Kit, Fry Kid Utensils, Ronald Collapsible Cup (also U3 premium)	1990	2	3
Captain Crook Bike Reflector	blue plastic, Canada	1988	1	3
Castlemaker	set of four vacuuform molds: dome, square, cylinder, rectangle; regionally distributed in Michigan and Houston, Texas	1987	20	40
Changeables	set of six figures that change into robots: Big Mac, Milk Shake, Egg McMuffin, Quarter Pounder, French Fries, Chicken McNuggets	1987	4	8
Chip 'N Dale's Rescue Rangers	set of four figures: Chip's Whirly-Cuptor, Dale's Roto-Roadster, Gadgets Rescue Racer, Monteray Jack's Propel-A-Phone	1989	2	4
Chip 'N Dale's Rescue Rangers	set of two U3 toys: Gadget's Rockin', Chip's Rockin Racer	1989	2	4
Christmas Ornaments	Fry Guy and Fry Girl, cloth, 3-1/2" tall	1987	3	6
Christmas Stocking	plastic, "Merry Christmas to My Pal"	1981	3	6

RESTAURANT PREMIUMS

Funny Fry Friends II, 1990, McDonald's

Hook Figures, 1991, McDonald's

NAME	DESCRIPTION	YEAR	EX	MINT
Circus	set of nine: Fun House Mirror with Ronald; Fun House Mirror with Hamburglar; Acrobatic Ronald, French Fry Faller; Strong Gong with Grimace; Punchout Midway: The Ronald Midway; Punchout Midaway: Fun House; Punchout Tent with Grimace; Punchout Tent with Birdie	1983	15	25
Circus Parade	set of four: Ringmaster Ronald McDonald, Bareback Rider Birdie, Grimace Playing Caliope, Elephant Trainer Fry Guy	1991	2	4
Circus Wagon	set of four rubber toys: poodle, chimp, clown, horse	1979	2	3
Colorforms Happy Meal	set of five: Beach set, Grimace; Farm set, Ronald; Camping set, Professor; Play set, Birdie; Picnic, Hamburglar	1986	10	15
Colorforms Happy Meal	two U3 sticker sets: Beach set, Grimace; Farm set, Ronald	1986	10	15
Colorful Puzzles-Japan	set of three: Dumbo, Mickey & Minnie, Dumbo & Train		5	10
Coloring Stand-Ups	characters and backgrounds to color, punch out and stand	1978	4	8
Combs	set of four: Capt. Crook, red; Grimace, yellow; Ronald, yellow, blue or purple; Grimace Groomer, green	1988	1	2
Commandrons	set of four robots: Solardyn, Magna, Motron, Velocitor	1985	5	15
Connectables	set of four: Birdie on tricycle, Grimace in wagon, Hamburglar in airplane, Ronald in soapbox racer	1991	3	5
Construx	set of four: axle, wing, body cylinder, canopy; spaceship could be built from all four preiums	1986	10	25
CosMc Crayola	one U3 toy: two fluorescent crayons with coloring page	1988	5	10
CosMc Crayola	set of five coloring kits: four crayons with coloring page, thin red marker with coloring page, four chalk with chalkboard, washable thin marker with coloring page, three paints and brush with paint-by-number page	1988	5	10
Crayola Happy Meal	set of three kits: triangle stencil with green marker, rectangular stencil with four fluorescent crayons, triangle stencil with orange marker, traingle stencil with thin blue marker, triangle stencil with thin red marker	1986	10	15
Crayola II	set of four stencils: Grimace with four fluorescent crayons, Hamburglar with four crayons, Birdie with thick orange or green marker, Ronald with thin blue or red marker	1987	2	5
Crayola II	one U3 stencil: Ronald on fire engine with four crayons	1987	5	10
Crayola Squeeze Bottle, Kay Bee	set of four: regional promotion		3	6
Crayon Squeeze Bottle	set of four: blue, green, yellow, red; regionally distributed in New York state and Connecticut	1992	3	5
Crazy Creatures with Popoids	set of four made up of two bellows and one connector: red and blue bellows with wheel joint; yellow and blue connectors with ball joint; yellow and red bellows with cube joint; red and yellow with seven-sided joint	1985	6	12
Crazy Vehicles	set of four: Ronald in red car, Hamburglar in yellow train engine, Grimace in green car, Birdie in pink airplane	1991	3	5
Design-O-Saurs	set of four: Ronald on Tyrannosaurus, Grimace on Pterodactyl, Fry Guy on Brontosaurus, Hamburglar on Triceratops	1987	5	10
Dink the Little Dinosaur	set of six figures with diorama and description: Dink, Flapper, Amber, Crusty, Scat, Shyler	1990	4	8
Dino-Motion Dinosaurs	set of six: Baby, Grandma, Robbie, Earl, Fran, Charlene	1993	1	2

RESTAURANT PREMIUMS

NAME	DESCRIPTION	YEAR	EX	MINT
Dino-Motion Dinosaurs	one U3 toy: Baby squirter	1993	2	4
Dinosaur Days	set of six rubber dinos: Pteranodon, Triceratops, Stegosaurus, Dimetrodon, T-Rex, Ankylosaurus	1981	1	2
Dinosaur Talking Storybook	set of four books and tape: The Dinosaur Baby Boom, Danger Under the Lake, The Creature in the Cave, The Amazing Birthday Adventure	1989	5	10
Discover the Rain Forest	set of four activity books with punch out figures: Sticker Safari, Wonders in the Wild, Paint It Wild, Ronald and the Jewel of the Amazon Kingdom	1991	2	4
Disney Favorites	set of four activity books: Lady and the Tramp, Dumbo, Cinderella, The Sword in the Stone	1987	3	4
Disney Masterpiece Collection	figures in video-shaped box	1996	1	2
Disney Video Favorites	set of six: The Spirit of Mickey, Lady & the Tramp, Pocahontas: Journey to a New World, Mary Poppins, The Black Cauldron, Flubber	1998	1	3
Disneyland 40th Anniversary Viewers	set of nine: Brer on Space Mountain; Aladdin & Jasmine at Aladdin's Castle; Roger Rabbit in Mickey's Toontown; Winnie the Pooh on Big Thunder Mountain with viewer, green cab; Winnie the Pooh on Big Thunder Mountain with viewer, black cab; Simba in The Lion King Celebration; Mickey Mouse on Space Mountain; Peter Pan in Fantasmic!; King Louie on the Jungle Cruise	1995	2	3
Disneyland 40th Anniversary Viewers	one U3 toy: Winnie the Pooh on Big Thunder Mountain without viewer (green cab)	1995	2	3
Double Bell Alarm Clock	wind-up alarm clock with silver bells, hammer ringer, silver feet, image of Ronald on face with head tilted over folded hands, as if asleep		20	40
Duck Tales I	one U3 toy: Motion Magic Map	1988	2	5
Duck Tales I	set of four toys: Telescope, Duck Code Quacker, Magnifying Glass, Wrist Decoder	1988	2	4
Duck Tales II	one U3 toy: Huey on skates	1988	15	20
Duck Tales II	set of four toys: Uncle Scrooge in red car; Launchpad in plane; Huey, Dewey and Louie on jet ski; Webby on blue trike	1988	3	6
Dukes of Hazzard	set of five vaccuform container vehicles, Boss Hogg's Caddy, Daisy's Jeep, Sheriff Roscoe's Police Car, Uncle Jesse's Pickup, General Lee; each container came with sticker sheet; regionally distributed in Missouri	1982	20	50
Dukes of Hazzard	set of six white plastic cups: Luke, Boss Hogg, Bo, Sheriff Roscoe, Daisy, Uncle Jesse	1982	3	6
E.T.	set of four posters: E.T. with boy and girl in front of spaceship, E.T. with boy and bike, E.T. with glowing finger, E.T. with radio	1985	8	12
Earth Days	set of four: birdfeeder, globe terrarium, binoculars, tool carrier with shovel	1994	1	2
Earth Days	one U3 toy: tool carrier with shovel	1994	1	2
Earth Days	one U3 toy: tool carrier with shovel	1994	1	2
Eric Carle Finger Puppets	set of six puppets: The Very Quiet Crickett, The Very Lonely Firefly, A House for Hermit Crab, The Grouchy Ladybug, The Very Hungry Caterpillar, The Very Busy Spider	1996	1	2
Fast Macs I	set of four pull-back action cars: Big Mac in white police car, Ronald in yellow Jeep, Hamburglar in red racer, Birdie in pink convertible	1984	3	5
Fast Macs II	set of four pull-back action cars: Big Mac in white police car, Ronald in yellow Jeep, Hamburglar in red racer, Birdie in pink convertible	1985	3	5
Favorite Friends	set of seven character punch-out cards	1978	2	5
Feeling Good	set of six grooming toys: Grimace soap dish, Fry Guy sponge, Birdie mirror, Ronald toothbrush, Hamburglar toothbrush, Captain Crook comb	1985	1	3
Feeling Good	set of two U3 floating toys: Grimace in Tub, Fry Guys on Duck	1985	5	8

MCDONALD'S

NAME	DESCRIPTION	YEAR	EX	MINT
Field Trip	one U3 toy: Nature Viewer	1993	1	2
Field Trip	set of four: Kaleidoscope, Leaf Printer, Nature Viewer, Explorer Bag	1993	1	2
Fisher-Price U3 Toys	set of twenty-four: Balls in ball, Barn Puzzle, Bear in Train, Birdie in Poppity-Pop Car, Bus, Clock, Corn Popper, Cow Book, Dog Squeek, Dog Roll-A-Rounds, Dog in House, Dog on Red Wheels, Grimace Roll-A-Rounds, Horse, Jeep, Key Ring, Man in Poppity-Pop Car, Truck, Fun Sounds Ball, Puzzle Maze, Ronald McDonald in Drive-thru, Pig in Barrel, Radio Rattle, Chatter Telephone; In 1996, McDonald's began offering generic Fisher-Price toys as the U3 premium for Happy Meals.	1996	3	5
Flintstone Kids	set of four figures in animal vehicles: Betty, Barney, Fred, Wilma	1988	4	8
Flintstone Kids	one U3 toy: Dino figure	1988	10	15
Flintstones	one U3 toy: Rocking Dino	1994	3	5
Flintstones	set of five: Fred at Bedrock Bowl-O-Rama, Betty and Bamm Bamm at Roc Donald's, Wilma at the Flinstone's house, Barney at the Fossil Fill-Up, Pebbles and Dino at Toy-S-Aurus	1994	1	2
Florida Beach Ball	set of three with Florida logo: Grimace in kayak, Ronald holding flag and beachball, Birdie in sailboat	1985	20	25
Food Fundamentals	set of four: Slugger the steak; Otis the sandwhich, Milly the milk carton, Ruby the apple	1993	1	2
Food Fundamentals	one U3 toy: Dunkan the ear of corn	1993	1	2
Fraggle Rock I	set of four: Gobo Fraggle, Bulldoozer and Friends, Cotterpin Doozer and Friends, Cotterpin Doozer; test market Happy Meal, regionally distributed in West Virginia	1987	20	30
Fraggle Rock II	set of four: Gobo in carrot car, Red in radish car, Mokey in eggplant car, Wembly and Boober in pickle car	1988	1	2
Fraggle Rock II	set of two U3 toys: Gobo holding carrot, Red holding radish	1988	4	6
French Fry Radio	large red fry container with fries	1977	12	25
Friendly Skies	set of two: Ronald in white plane, Grimace in white plane	1991	5	10
Friends of Barbie/World of Hot Wheels	one U3 toy: Barbie Ball	1994	2	3
Fry Benders	set of four figures: Grand Slam with baseball glove, Froggy with scuba tanks, Roadie with bicycle, Freestyle with rollerskates	1990	5	10
Fry Guy Cookie Cutter	Fry Guy on unicycle, green or orange	1987	1	3
Fun Ruler	white platic ruler featuring Mayor McCheese, Fry Guys, Birdie, Ronald, Grimace, Hamburglar	1983	3	5
Fun To Go	set of seven cartons with games and activities	1977	2	4
Fun with Food	set of four: Hamburger Guy, Fry Guy, Soft Drink Guy, Chicken McNugget Guys	1989	3	6
Funny Fry Friends	two U3 toys: Lil' Chief, Little Darling	1990	3	5
Funny Fry Friends II	set of eight: Too Tall, Tracker, Rollin' Rocker, Sweet Cuddles, Zzz's, Gadzooks, Matey, Hoops	1990	2	4
Funny Fry Guys	set of four: Gadzooks, Matey, Zzz's, Tracker; test market Happy Meal, regionally distributed in California, Pennsylvania, Maryland	1989	15	25
Furby	eight different designs done in ten different color combinations; there are a total of eighty diffferent Furby toys available. Each toy comes packaged in opage bags so the collector doesn't know which Furby they have	1999	5	10
Garfield	set of four: Garfield on skateboard, Garfield on tricycle, Garfield in car, Garfield on scooter; test market Happy Meal, regionally distributed in Erie, Pennsylvania and Charlston, South Carolina	1988	20	50

NAME	DESCRIPTION	YEAR	EX	MINT
Garfield II	set of four: Garfield on Scooter, Garfield on Skateboard, Garfield in Jeep, Garfield with Odie on Motorscooter	1989	3	6
Garfield II	set of two U3 toys: Garfield Skating, Garfield with Pooky	1989	2	5
Glo-Tron Spaceship	set of four vacuform spaceships: red, blue, green, gray; each spaceship came with set of glow-in-the-dark stickers	1986	25	50
Glow in the Dark Yo-Yo	no markings or dates	1978	2	5
Going Places/Hot Wheels	set of fourteen: Corvette Stingray, Jeep CJ-7, 3-Window '34, Baja Breaker, Chevy Citation, Firebird Funny Car, Land Lord, Malibu Grand Prix, 380-SEL, Minitrek, P-928, Sheriff Patrol, Split Window '63, Turismo	1983	12	15
Golf Ball	marked with McDonald's logo		1	3
Good Morning	set of four: Ronald toothbrush, McDonaldland comb, Ronald clock, white plastic cup	1991	1	2
Good Sports	set of six puffy stickers: Hamburglar, Mayor McCheese, Ronald, Sam the Olympic Eagle, Birdie, Grimace	1984	8	12
Good Times Great Taste Record			2	4
Gravedale High	set of four mechanical Halloween figures: Cleofatra, Frankentyke, Vinnie Stoker, Sid the Invisible Kid	1991	2	3
Gravedale High	one U3 toy: Cleofatra	1991	3	5
Grimace Bank	purple ceramic, 9" tall	1985	10	20
Grimace Pin	enamel		6	12
Grimace Ring		1970	8	15
Grimace Sponge	Grimace, Grimace Car Wash		2	4
Halloween	one U3 toy: pumpkin with pop-up Grimace	1995	2	3
Halloween	set of four figures: Hamburglar with witch costume, Grimace with ghost costume, Ronald with Frankenstein soctume, Birdie with pumpkin costume	1995	2	3
Halloween	set of four cassete tapes: Ronald Makes it Magic, Travel Tunes, Silly Sing-Along, Scary Sound Affects	1995	1	2
Halloween Buckets	set of three pumpkin-shaped pails: McGoblin, McPumpkin, McBoo	1986	2	4
Halloween Buckets	set of three pumpkin-shaped pails: McBoo, McGoblin, McPunk'n	1987	2	3
Halloween Buckets	set of three: Ghost, Witch, Pumpkin	1989	1	3
Halloween Buckets	set of three pumpkin-shaped pails with cut-out lids: Ghost, Witch, Pumpkin	1992	1	2
Halloween Buckets	set of three with cookie-cutter lids: Ghost, Whitch, Pumpkin	1994	1	3
Halloween Buckets	set of threepumpkin-shaped pails: orange pumpkin, white glow-in-dark ghost, Green witch	1990	2	4
Halloween Happy Meal	set of five pumpkin-shaped pails: McGoblin, McPunk'n, McPunky, McBoo, McBoo; regionally distributed in the northeast, marked with 1985 copyright	1985	12	15
Halloween McNugget Buddies	set of six: Dragon, Spider, Fairy Princess, Alien Monster, Rock Star, Ronald	1996	2	3
Halloween McNugget Buddies	set of six: Pumpkin McNugget, McBoo McNugget, Monster McNugget, McNuggula McNugget, Witchie McNugget, Mummie McNugget	1993	1	3
Halloween McNugget Buddies	one U3 toy: McBoo McNugget	1993	3	5
Halloween Pumpkin Ring	orange pumpkin face		1	3
Hamburglar Doll	7" stuffed doll by Remco; one of set of seven, sold on blister card	1976	12	25
Hamburglar Hockey		1979	2	4
Happy Holidays	set of two cards with stickers: Gingerbread House, Train	1984	15	20

NAME	DESCRIPTION	YEAR	EX	MINT
Happy Meal From the Heart	set of two scratch-and-sniff Valentines: Grimace—Valentine Your Shake Me Up!; Ronald—Valentine You Warm My Heart!	1990	2	3
Happy Pail	set of two scratch pail with purple shovel, shows Ronald and Mayor McCheese under umbrella with purple shovel; white pail with yellow shovel, shows Ronald in intertube; white pail with slotted yellow shovel, shows airplane pulling banner; distributed in the New York state and New England area only	1983	25	35
Happy Pail III	set of five sand pails with either yellow shovel or red rake: Beach with blue lid, Parade with orange lid, Treasure Hunt with red lid, Vacation with green lid, Picnic with yellow lid	1986	5	10
Happy Pails, Olympics	set of four with shovels: Swimming, blue; Cycling, yellow; Athletics, beige; Olympic Games, white	1984	1	3
Happy Teeth	set of two: Reach toothbrush, tube of toothpaste	1983	15	20
Hat Happy Meal	set of four: Birdie green derby, Fry Guy orange safari hat, Grimace yellow construction hat, Ronald red fireman hat	1990	10	15
Hercules	set of ten: Wind Titan & Hermes, Rock Titan & Zeus, Hydra & Hercules, Lava Titan & Baby Pegasus, Cyclops & Pain, Fates & Panic, Pegasus & Megara, Ice Tita & Calliope, Nessus & Phil, Cerberus & Hades	1997	1	2
Hercules Plates	set of six: Hercules, Megara, Pegasus, Zeus, Muses, Phil; offered by McDonald's for $1.99 with purchase and $2.99 without purchase	1997	3	5
Hercules Sports Toys	set of eight: Zeus football, Hades stopwatch, Hercules sport bottle, Eye of Fates foot bag, Pain and Panic sound stick, Hercules medal, Phil megaphone, Whistling Discus	1998	1	2
High Flying Kite Happy Meal	set of three kites: Hamburglar, Birdie, Ronald; regionally distributed in New England area	1986	200	225
Hobby Box	set of four plastic boxes: yellow, green, red, blue; regionally distributed in the Southern United States	1985	10	15
Honey, I Shrunk the Kids Cups	set of three white 20 oz. plastic cups: Giant Bee, On the Dog's Nose, Riding the Ant	1988	1	2
Hook Figures	set of four: Peter Pan, Mermaid, Rufio, Hook	1991	1	2
Hot Wheels Mini-Streex/ Barbie	one U3 toy: Orange Arrow car	1992	3	6
Hot Wheels Mini-Streex/ Barbie	set of eight: Flame-Out, Quick Flash, Turbo Flyer, Black Arrow, Hot Shock, Racer Tracer, Night Shadow, Blade Burner; joint promotion with Barbie	1992	2	4
Hot Wheels/Barbie	set of eight: Quaker State Racer #62, McDonald's Dragster, McDonald's Thunderbird #23, Hot Wheels Dragster, McDonald's Funny Car, Hot Wheels Funny Car, Hot Wheels Camaro #1, Duracell Racer #88; joint promotion with Barbie	1993	2	3
Hot Wheels/Barbie	set of twelve: Streat Beast, silver or red; P-911, white or black; Split Window '63, silver or black; '57 T-Bird, turquoise or white; 80's Firebird, blue or black; Sheriff Patrol; Fire Patrol	1988	10	15
Hot Wheels/Barbie	set of four: Corvette, white; Ferrari, red; Hot Bird, silver; Camaro, turquoise; test market Happy Meal, regionally distributed in Savanah, Georgia; joint promotion with Barbie	1990	50	75
Hot Wheels/Barbie	Ronald NASCAR, Mac Tonight NASCAR, Hot Wheels NASCAR, 50th Anniversary NASCAR; joint promo with Barbie	1998	1	2
Hot Wheels/Barbie	set of eight cars: '55 Chevy, white or yellow; '63 Corvette, green or black; Camaro Z-28, purple or orange; '57 T-Bird, turquoise or red; joint promotion with Barbie	1991	2	3
Hot Wheels/Barbie	one U3 tool set: yellow wrench and red hammer	1991	2	3

RESTAURANT PREMIUMS

517

Super Mario Brothers, 1990, McDonald's

Tale Spin, 1990, McDonald's

NAME	DESCRIPTION	YEAR	EX	MINT
Hot Wheels/Barbie	set of five: Tow Truck, Taxi, Police Car, Ambulance, Fire Truck; joint promotion with Barbie	1997	1	2
Hot Wheels/Barbie	one U3 tool set: blue wrench and yellow hammer	1993	3	6
Hot Wheels/Barbie	set of eight: Lightning Speed, Shock Force, Blue Bandit, Power Circuit, Twin Engine, Radar Racer, Back Burner, After Blast; joint promotion with Barbie	1995	2	3
Hot Wheels/Barbie	set of five: Flame Series, Roarin' Road Series, Dark Rider Series, Hot Hubs Series, Krakel Car Series; joint promotion with Barbie	1996	1	2
Hot Wheels/Barbie	one U3 toy: Hot Wheels squeek toy	1996	1	3
Hot Wheels/Barbie	one U3 toy: Key Force car	1995	2	3
Hunchback of Notre Dame	set of eight: Esmeralda Amulet, Scepter, Clopin Mask, Hugo Horn, Clopin Puppet Drum, Juggling Balls, Tambourine, Quasimodo Bird Catcher	1997	1	2
I Like Bikes	set of four bike accessories: Ronald Basket, Grimace mirror, Birdie spinner, Fry Guy Horn	1990	10	20
Jungle Book	set of four wind-up figures: Baloo the bear, Shere Kahn the tiger, King Louie the orangutan, Kaa the snake	1990	1	3
Jungle Book	set of two U3 toys: Junior, Mowgli	1990	3	6
Jungle Book	set of six: Baloo, Junior, Bagheera, King Louie, Kaa, Mowgli	1997	1	2
Kissyfur	set of four non-flocked figures: Floyd, Gus, Kissyfur, Jolene; the flocked and non-flocked figres make up one complete set	1987	5	10
Kissyfur	set of four flocked figure: Beehonie, Duane, Toot, Lennie	1987	20	40
Lego Building Set III	four different sets: tanker boat, blue; airplane, green; roadster, red; helicopter, yellow	1986	3	5
Lego Building Sets	set of four: ship, helicopter, truck, airplane	1983	25	40
Lego Building Sets	set of four Duplo U3 toys: blue blocks, Bird, red blocks, green Duplo blocks	1983	5	10
Lego Building Sets II	set of two U3 toys: Duplo bird, Duplo boat with sailor	1984	4	8
Lego Building Sets II	set of four: ship, truck, helicopter, airplane	1984	3	5
Lego Building Sets III	set of two U3 toys: Duplo bird, Duplo boat	1986	3	5
Lego Motion IV	set of two U3 Duplo toys: Giddy the Gator, Tuttle the Turtle	1989	2	5
Lego Motion IV	set of eight kits: Gyro Bird, Lightning Striker, Land Laser, Sea Eagle, Wind Whirler, Sea Skimmer, Turbo Force, Swamp Stinger	1989	3	6
Linkables	set of four: Birdie on tricycle, Ronald in soap-box racer, Grimace in wagon, Hamburglar in airplane; regionally distributed in New England area	1993	2	4
Lion Circus	set of four rubber figures: bear, elephant, hippo, lion	1979	2	3
Little Engineer	set of five vacuform train engines: Birdie Sunshine Special, Fry Girl's Express, Fry Guy's Flyer, Grimace Streak, Ronald Railway	1987	4	8
Little Engineer	set of four floating toys: Grimace Happy Taxi, green or yellow; Birdie, green or yellow	1987	2	6
Little Gardener	set of four: Ronald Water Can, Birdie Shovel with Marigold seeds, Grimace Rake with radish seeds, Fry Guy Planter	1989	1	2
Little Gardener	one U3 toy: Birdie shovel	1989	5	10
Little Golden Books	set of five books: Country Mouse and City Mouse, Tom & Jerry, Pokey Little Puppy, Benji, Monster at the End of This Block	1982	2	4
Little Mermaid	set of four: Flounder, Ursula, Prince Eric, Ariel with Sebastian	1989	1	2
Little Mermaid	set of eight: Ursula, Flounder, Scuttle, Ariel, Max, Glut, Eric, Sebastian	1997	1	2

RESTAURANT PREMIUMS

NAME	DESCRIPTION	YEAR	EX	MINT
Little Mermaid, Gold	set of eight: Ursula, Flounder, Scuttle, Ariel, Max, Glut, Eric, Sebastian; one out of every ten toys distributed with Happy Meal was a gold toy; compete sets of gold Little Mermaid premiums could be ordered for $12.99 plus shipping with forms available at McDonald's	1997	5	10
Little Travelers with Lego Building Sets	set of four: airplane, boat, helicopter, car; regionally distributed in Oklahoma; similar to Lego Building Set Happy Meal	1985	20	30
Littlest Pet Shop/ Transformers Beast Wars	set of four: Swan, Unicorn, Dragon, Tiger; joint promotion with Transformers Beast Wars	1996	1	2
Littlest Pet Shop/ Transformers Beast Wars	one U3 toy: Hamster Wheel.	1996	1	2
Looney Tunes Christmas Dolls-Canada	set of four: Sylvester in nightgown and cap, Tasmanian Devil in Santa hat, Bugs in winter scarf , Tweetie dressed as Elf		3	6
Looney Tunes Quack Up Cars	set of five: Taz Tornado Tracker, Porky Ghost Catcher, Bugs Super Stretch Limo in red or orange, Daffy Splittin' Sportster	1993	3	5
Looney Tunes Quack Up Cars	one U3 toy: Bugs Bunny Swingin' Sedan in red or orange	1993	3	5
Luggage Tags	set of four: Birdie, Hamburglar, Grimace, Ronald	1988	3	5
Lunch Box	set of four lunch boxes: Grimace at bat, Ronald playing football, Ronald on rainbow, Ronald flying spaceship	1987	5	10
Mac Tonight	set of six: Mac in Jeep, Mac in sports car, Mac on Surf Ski (with or without wheels), Mac on Motorcycle (red or black), Mac in Airplane (wearing blue or black sunglasses), Mac on Scooter; given out from 1988 to 1990, Surf Ski with wheels and Airplane with dark sunglasses were distributed in 1990	1988	8	15
Mac Tonight Pin	Moonface and slogan enamel pin	1988	2	4
Mac Tonight Puppet	Fingertronic foam puppet	1988	6	15
Mac Tonight Sunglasses	adult size	1988	2	5
Magic School Bus	one U3 toy: Undersea Adventure Game without yellow tab	1994	1	2
Magic School Bus	set of four: Collector Card Kit, Space Tracer, Geo Fossil Finder, Undersea Adventure Game with yellow tab	1994	1	2
Magic Show	set of five tricks: String Trick, Disappearing Hamburger Patch, Magic Tablet, Magic Picture—Ronald, Magic Picture—Grimace	1985	3	6
Makin' Movies	set of four: Sound Effects Machine, Movie Camera, Clapboard with chalk, Megaphone	1994	1	2
Makin' Movies	one U3 toy: Sound Effects Machine	1994	1	2
Marvel Super Heroes	set of eight: Spider-Man, Storm, Wolverine, Jubilee, Color Change Invisible Woman, Thing, Hulk, Human Torch	1996	1	2
Marvel Super Heroes	one U3 Toy: Spider-Man Ball	1996	1	2
Matchbox Mini-Flexies	set of eight rubber cars: Cosmobile, Hairy Hustler, Planet Scout, Hi-Tailer, Datsun, Beach Hopper, Baja Buggy	1979	2	4
McBoo Bags	set of six: three McBoo bags: Witch, Ghost, Monster; three pails: McBoo, McGoblin, witch	1991	3	5
McBunny Easter Pails	set of three: Pinky, Fluffy, Whiskers	1989	3	6
McCharacters on Bikes	set of four: Ronald on red tricycle, Grimace on blue tricycle, Hamburglar on yellow tricycle, Birdie on pink tricycle	1991	3	5
McDino Changeables	set of three U3 toys: Bronto Cheeseburger, Small Fry Ceratops with yellow arches, Small Fry Ceratops with red arches	1991	2	3

NAME	DESCRIPTION	YEAR	EX	MINT
McDino Changeables	set of eight: Happy Meal-o-don, Quarter Pounder Chees-o-saur, Big Mac-o-saurus Rex, McNugget-o-saurus, Hotcakes-o-dactyl, Large Fry-o-saur, Tri-shak-atops, McDino cone	1991	2	3
McDonald Sun Glasses	set of four: Grimace, Birdie, Ronald, Hamburglar; over-the-counter premium, sold for 99 cents, each	1989	5	7
McDonaldland Band	set of eight music toys: Grimace saxophone, Fry Guy trumpet, Fry Guy boat whistle, Ronald harmonica, Ronald train whistle, Ronald pan pipes, Birdie kazoo, Hamburglar whistle	1987	1	3
McDonaldland Carnival	set of four: Birdie on swing, Grimace in turn-around, Hamburglar on ferris wheel, Ronald on carousel	1990	3	5
McDonaldland Carnival	one U3 floaty toy: Grimace	1990	10	15
McDonaldland Dough	set of eight, each included can of modeling clay and mold: red with Ronald star mold, yellow with Ronald square mold, green with Fry Girl octagon mold, blue with Fry Guy hexagon mold, purple with Grimace square mold, orange with Grimace triangle mold, pink with Birdie heart mold, white with Birdie circle mold; sold in the Southern United States only	1990	3	5
McDonaldland Express	set of four train car containers: Ronald engine, caboose, freight car, coach car	1982	25	50
McDonaldland Junction	set of four snap-together train cars: red Ronald Engine, yellow Birdie Parlor car, green Hamburger Flat Car, purple Grimace caboose	1983	5	10
McDonaldland Junction	set of four regionally distributed cars: blue Ronald Engine, pink Birdie Parlor Car, white Hamburger Flat Car, orange Grimace Caboose	1983	20	30
McDonaldland Play-Doh	set of eight colors: white, orange, yellow, purple, pink, red, green, blue	1986	2	4
McDonaldland TV Lunch Box	set of four lunch boxes: blue, green, yellow, red; each box came with a sheet of stickers; regionally distributed in New England area	1987	5	10
McDonald's All-Star Race Team (MAXX) '91	complete set of cards	1991	4	5
McDonald's All-Star Race Team (MAXX) '92	complete set of 36 cards	1992	4	5
McDonald's Playing Cards	two decks to a set		2	5
McDonald's Spinner Top-Holland			2	4
McDrive Thru Crew	set of four: fries in potato roadster, shake in milk carton, McNugget in egg roadster, hamburger in ketchup bottle; regionally distributed in Ohio and Illinois	1990	20	40
McNugget Buddies	set of ten rubber figures and accessories: Sparky, Volley, Corny, Drummer, Cowpoke, Sarge, Snorkel, First Class, Rocker, Boomerang	1989	1	2
McNugget Buddies	set of two U3 toy: Slugger, Daisy	1989	1	2
McNugget Buddies	set of ten: Cowpoke, First-Class, Sarge, Drummer, Corny, Sparky, Boomerang, Volley, Snorkel, Rocker	1988	4	6
Metrozoo Happy Meal	set of four: Elephant, Chimp, Flamingo, Tiger; distributed only in South Florida area	1987	25	250
Michael Jordan Fitness	set of eight toys: soccer ball, squeeze bottle, stopwatch, basketball, football, baseball, jump rope, flying disc	1992	2	4
Michael Jordan Fitness Fun Challenge	set of eight: baseball, basketball, flying disc, football, jump rope, soccer ball, squeeze bottle, stop watch; all premiums are marked with Michael Jordan logo	1992	2	4
Mickey and Friends Epcot Center '94 Adventure	set of eight: Donald in Mexico, Daisy in Germany, Mickey in U.S.A., Minnie in Japan, Chip in China, Pluto in France, Dale in Moroco, Goofy in Norway	1994	2	3

RESTAURANT PREMIUMS

NAME	DESCRIPTION	YEAR	EX	MINT
Mickey and Friends Epcot Center '94 Adventure	one U3 toy: Mickey in U.S.A.	1994	2	3
Mickey's Birthdayland	set of five characters in vehicles: Minnie's Convertible, Donald's Train, Goofy's Jalopy, Mickey's Roadster, Pluto's Rumbler	1989	1	3
Mickey's Birthdayland	set of four U3 vehicles: Mickey's Convertible, Goofy's Car, Minnie's Convertible, Donald's Jeep	1989	5	10
Micro Machines/Sky Dancers	set of four: Evac Copter, Polar Explorer, Ocean Flyer, Deep Sea Hunter; joint promotion with Sky Dancers	1997	1	2
Mighty Duck Pucks	set of four: Wildwing, Nosedive, Mallory, Duke L'Orange	1997	1	2
Mighty Mini 4x4s	set of four: Cargo Climber, Dune Buster, L'il Classic, Pocket Pickup	1991	1	2
Mighty Mini 4x4s	one U3 toy: Pocket Pickup	1991	3	5
Mighty Morphin Power Rangers	one U3 toy: Power Flute	1995	1	2
Mighty Morphin Power Rangers	set of four: Power Com, Powermorpher Buckle, Alien Detector, Power Siren	1995	1	2
Minnesota Twins Baseball Glove	Twins logo on side, Coca-Cola inside glove, McDonald's satin logo on back, given to the first 100 kids at 1984 Twins game	1984	40	75
Mix 'em Up Monsters	set of four: Thuggle, Blibble, Corkle, Gropple; regionally distributed in St. Louis, Missouri and Northern California	1989	2	5
Moveables	set of six vinyl bendies: Birdie, Captain Crook, Fry Girl, Hamburglar, Professor, Ronald; regionally distributed in St Louis, Missouri area	1988	4	12
M-Squad	set of four: Spystamper, Spytracker, Spynocular, Spycoder	1993	2	4
M-Squad	one U3 toy: Spytracker watch	1993	1	2
Mulan	set of eight: Mulan, Kahn, Little Brother, Shan-Yu, Mushi, Shan-Li, Cri-Kee, Chien-Po, Ling, Yao	1998	1	2
Muppet Babies holiday promotion	set of four stuffed toys: Miss Piggy, Kermit, Fozzie; over-the-counter premium sold with food purchase for for $1.99	1988	2	5
Muppet Babies I	set of four: Kermit with skateboard, Miss Piggy with car and flat hair ribbon, Gonzo with tricycle and no shoes, Fozzie with horse; test market Happy Meal, regionally distributed in Savannah, Georgia	1986	25	50
Muppet Babies II	set of four: Kermit with skateboard, Miss Piggy with pink car, Gonzo with tricycle and shoes, Fozzie with horse	1987	2	4
Muppet Babies II	set of two U3 toys: Kermit on skates, Miss Piggy on Skates	1987	3	5
Muppet Babies III	set of four: Miss Piggy on tricycle, Gonzo in airplane, Fozzie in wagon, Kermit on soapbox racer	1991	2	4
Muppet Kids	set of four: Kermit with red tricycle, Miss Piggy with pink tricycle, Gonzo with yellow tricycle, Fozzie with green tricycle	1989	15	25
Muppet Treasure Island	set of four: Miss Piggy, Kermit, Gonzo, Fozzy Bear	1996	2	3
Muppet Treasure Island	one U3 toy: Bath Book "The Muppet Treasure Island"	1996	1	2
Muppet Workshop	set of four: Bird, Dog, What-Not, Monster	1995	1	2
Muppet Workshop	one U3 toy: What-Not	1995	1	2
Music Happy Meal	set of four 33-1/3 RPM records: If You're Happy/ Little Bunny Foo Foo; Do the Hokey Pokey/ Eensy Weensy Spider; Boom, Boom, Ain't it Great to Be Crazy; She'll be Comin' 'Round the Mountain, Head, Shoulders, Knees and Toes	1985	3	5
My Little Pony (joint promotion w/ Transformers)	set of six: Minty, Snuzzle, Blossom, Cotton Candy, Blue Belle, Butterscotch; regionally distributed in St. Louis, Missouri area	1985	20	80
My Little Pony/ Transformers	set of three: Ivy, Sundance, Light Heart; split promo with Transformers	1998	1	2

MCDONALD'S

NAME	DESCRIPTION	YEAR	EX	MINT
Mystery Happy Meal	set of five: Detective Kit, Crystal Ball, Ronald Magni-Finder, Birdie Mangi-Finder, Fry Guys Magni-Finder	1983	20	35
Mystery of the Lost Arches	set of five: Phone/Periscope, Flashlight/Telescope in red and blue or red and yellow, Magic Lens Camera, Microcaste/Magnifier	1992	1	2
Mystery of the Lost Arches	set of four: mini-cassette, phone, telescope, camera	1992	1	2
Mystic Knights of Tir na Nog	set of eight: Rohan, Queen Maeve, Angus. Tore, Deirdre, mider, Ivar, Lugad; a bonus toy can be built from Queen Maeve, Tore, Mider and Lugad	1999	1	3
NASCAR Hot Wheels/ Barbie	set of four: Ronald Happy Meal NASCAR, Mac Tonight, Hot Wheels, 50th Anniversary NASCAR; split promo with Barbie;	1998	1	3
Nature's Helpers	set of five: Double Digger with cucumber seeds, Bird Feeder, Watering Can, Terrarium with coleus seeds, Rake with marigold seeds	1991	1	2
Nature's Watch	one U3 toy: double shovel-rake	1992	1	2
Nature's Watch	set of four: Bird Feeder, Double Shovel-Rake, Greenhouse, Sprinkler	1992	1	2
New Archies	set of six figures in bumper cars: Moose, Reggie, Archie, Veronica, Betty, Jughead; regionally distributed in St. Louis, Missouri area	1988	5	15
New Food Changeables	set of eight: Krypto Cup, Fry Bot, Turbo Cone, Macro Mac, Gallacta Burger, Robo Cakes, C2 Cheeseburger, Fry Force	1989	2	4
Nickelodeon	one U3 toy: Blimp squirter	1993	1	2
Nickelodeon	set of four: Blimp Game, Loud-Mouth Mike, Gotcha Gusher, Applause Paws	1993	1	2
Nickelodeon's Tangle Toy	set of eight Twist-a-zoids	1997	1	2
Norman Rockwell Brass Ornament	50th Annivesary Norman Rockwell design, gift packaged with McDonald and Coca-Cola logos	1983	3	7
Norman Rockwell Ornament	clear acrylic, "Christmas Trio," gift boxed	1978	3	7
Old McDonald's Farm	set of six figures: farmer, wife, rooster, pig, sheep, cow; regionally distributed in Missouri and Tennessee	1986	10	15
Old West	set of six rubber figures: cowboy, frontiersman, lady, Indian, Indian woman, sheriff	1981	7	14
Oliver & Company	set of four finger puppets: Oliver, Georgette, Francis, Dodger	1988	3	5
Olympic Beach Ball	set of three: Grimace in kayak, green; Ronald holding flag and beachball, red; Birdie in sailboat, blue	1984	15	20
Olympic Sports	set of five Guess'n'Glow puzzles: Guess Which Guy Comes in Under the Wire (Grimace and Hamburglar), Guess Who Makes the Biggest Splash (Ronald, Birdie and Captain); Guess Who Finished Smiles Ahead (Hamburglar and Birdie); Who Do You Know That Can Help them Row? (Ronald and Fry Guy); Guess Who Stole the Winning Goal (Grimace); this promotion replaced the original Olympics Sports Happy Meal	1984	15	30
Olympic Sports	set of five zip-action toys: Ronald on bicycle, roller skating Birdie, Grimace, Birdie and Captain rowing, running Grimace; prototypes only. The Olympic sports Happy Meal was cancelled after the toys failed safety tests. It was replaced by Guess'n'Glow puzzles	1984	30	60
Olympic Sports II	set of six clip-on buttons: Birdie/gymnastics, Hamburglar/track and field, CosMc/basketball, Fry Girl/diving, Ronald/bicyclling, Grimace/ soccer	1988	5	8
On the Go I	set of five: On the Go Bead Game, Stop & Go Bead Game, Ronald Magic Slate, Hamburglar Magic Slate, On the Go Transfers	1985	10	15

*Eureeka's Castle
Puppets, 1991,
Pizza Hut*

Land Before Time Puppets, 1988, Pizza Hut

Fast Food Racers, 1990, Wendy's

NAME	DESCRIPTION	YEAR	EX	MINT
On the Go Lunch Box II	set of four: red lunch box with bulliten board and stickers, green lunch box with bulliten board and stickers, yellow lunch bag with Ronald, white lunch bag with Grimace	1988	2	4
Out of Fun Happy Meal	set of four: Balloon Ball, Ronald Bubble Shoe Wand, Sunglasses, Sand Pail	1993	1	2
Paint with Water	paintless coloring board with self contained frame and easel	1978	5	10
Peanuts	set of two U3 toys: Charlie Brown's egg basket or Snoopy's potato sack	1990	2	4
Peanuts	set of four: Snoopy's Hay Hauler, Charlie Brown's Seed Bag 'N Tiller, Lucy's Apple Cart, Linus' Milk Mover	1990	2	4
Pencil Puppets	six different pencil toppers in shapes of McDonaldland characters	1978	2	4
Peter Pan	set of seven: Peter Pan Glider, Tic Tock Croc, Captain Hook Spyglass, Tinker Bell Lantern Clip, Smee Light, Wendy & Michael Magnifier, Activity Tool	1998	1	2
Peter Rabbit	set of four books: The Tale of Benjamin Bunny, The Tale of Peter Rabbit, The Tale of the Flopsy Bunnies, The Tale of Squirrel Nutkin; regionally distributed in Pennsylvania and New York	1988	10	25
Picture Perfect	set of four Crayola products: coloring (thin) marker, red or blue; drawing (thick) marker, orange or green; box of three fluorescent Cayons; box of six Crayons	1985	5	10
Piggsburg Pigs	set of four: Rembrandt, Huff & Puff, Piggy & Crackers, Portly & Pighead; regionally distributed in Florida, Colorado and Ohio	1991	3	5
Play-Doh	set of four containers of Play-Doh: blue, red, yellow, white; regionally distributed in the New England area; containers did not have any McDonald's markings	1983	15	20
Play-Doh II	set of two containers of Play-Doh: pink and green	1985	15	20
Play-Doh III	set of eight containers of Play-Doh: pink, blue, purple, green, red, yellow, white, orange	1986	5	8
Playmobile	set of five toys and accesories: farmer, sheriff, Indian, umbrella girl, horse and saddle	1982	10	20
Polly Pocket/Attack Pack	one U3 toy: watch	1995	2	3
Polly Pocket/Attack Pack	set of four: Ring, Locket, Watch, Bracelet; joint promotion with Attack Pack	1995	1	2
Popoids	set of six made up of two to three bellows and one joint piece: blue and dark blue bellows with one ball joint; blue and white bellows with cube joint; blue and dark blue bellows with one cube joint; red and yellow bellows with pentahedron joint; red and yellow bellows with wheel joint; blue, dark blue and yellow bellows without joint; regionally distributed in the St. Louis, Missouri area	1984	40	50
Potato Head Kids I	set of twelve: Lumpy, Potato Dumpling, Big Chip, Smarty Pants, Dimples, Spike, Potato Puff, Tulip, Spud, Lolly, Slugger, Slick; regionally distributed in Texas, Oklahoma and New Mexico	1987	5	25
Potato Head Kids II	set of eight: Dimples, Spike, Potato Dumpling, Slugger, Slick, Tulip, Potato Puff, Spud	1992	3	6
Punkin' Makins	character cutouts to decorate pumpkins: Ronald, Goblin, Grimace	1977	7	15
Raggedy Ann and Andy	set of four: Raggedy Andy with slide, Raggedy Ann with swing, Grouchy Bear merry-go-round, Camel with Wrinkled Knees with teeter totter	1989	5	10
Raggedy Ann and Andy	one U3 toy: Camel with Wrinkled Knees	1989	8	12
Read Along with Ronald	set of four books and tapes: Grimace Goes to School, The Day Birdie the Early Bird Learned to Fly, The Mystery of the Missing French Fries, Dinosaur in McDonaldland	1989	5	10

RESTAURANT PREMIUMS

RESTAURANT PREMIUMS

NAME	DESCRIPTION	YEAR	EX	MINT
Real Ghostbusters	set of five school tools: pencil case, notepad, ruler, pencil with pencil topper, pencil sharpener	1987	3	5
Real Ghostbusters II	set of four: Ecto Siren, Egon Spinner, Slimer horn, water bottle; regionally distributed in Kansas City, Kansas	1992	3	5
Real Ghostbusters II	one U3 toy: Slimer squirter	1992	3	5
Recess	set of seven: TJ, Spinelli, Vince, Mikey, Gretchen, Gus, School Teacher	1998	1	2
Records	set of four 45-RPM records in sleeves with different songs and colored labels	1985	3	6
Rescuers Down Under	set of four slide-viewing movie camera toys: Jake, Wilbur, Bernard and Bianca, Cody	1990	2	4
Rescuers Down Under	One U3 toy: Bernard	1990	3	6
Rescuers Down Under Christmas Ornament	set of two: Miss Bianca, Bernard	1990	3	6
Rings	set of five rings with character heads: Big Mac, Captain Crook, Grimace, Hamburglar, Ronald	1977	5	10
Roger Rabbit Scarf-Japan	McDonald's logo, Japanese writing on scarf	1988	10	20
Ronald and Pals Haunted Halloween	set of six: Birdie, Gramace, Iam Hungry, Hamburglar, Ronald, McNugget Buddy	1998	1	2
Ronald McDonald Celebrates Happy Birthday	one U3 toy: Ronald McDonald	1994	3	5
Ronald McDonald Celebrates Happy Birthday	set of sixteen: Ronald McDonald, Barbie, Hot Wheels, E.T., Sonic the Hedgehog, Berenstain Bears, Tonka, Cabbage Patch Kids, 101 Dalmatians, Little Mermaid, Muppet Babies with white tie, Muppet Babies with or blue tie, Peanuts, The Little Mermaid, Tiny Toons, Happy Meal Guys	1994	3	5
Ronald McDonald Cookie Cutter	Ronald with balloons, green or orange	1987	1	3
Ronald McDonald Doll	14" vinyl head with a soft body by Dakin		15	35
Ronald McDonald Doll	7" doll by Remco		18	25
Ronald McDonald Maze	lift up mystery game	1979	4	10
Ronald McDonald Pin	enamel, Ronald in Christmas wreath		6	12
Ronald McDonald Plastic Flyers	Ronald with legs and arms extended, red or yellow		1	3
Ronald McDonald Shoe & Sock Game-Japan	plastic with ball and string, with Japanese writing		5	10
Ronald McDonald Tote Bag-Japan	writing in Japanese		5	10
Runaway Robots	set of six: Skull, Jab, Flame, Beak, bolt, Coil; regionally distributed in Nebraske, Maine, Massachusettes, Tenessee and Alabama	1987	15	20
Safari Adventure	six different rubber animals: alligator, monkey, gorilla, tiger, hippo, rhinoceros	1980	2	4
Sailors	set of two U3 floating toys: Grimace in speedboat, Fry Guy on intertube	1988	4	8
Sailors	set of four floating toys: Hamburglar Sailboat, Ronald Airboat, Grimace Submarine, Fry Kids Ferry	1988	5	10
Santa Claus: The Movie	set of four books: The Elves at the Top of the World, Sleighful of Surprises, Workshop of Surprises	1985	1	3
School Days	set of twelve: Ronald pencil, Grimace pencil, Hamburglar Pencil, Ronald eraser, Grimace eraser, Hamburglar eraser, Captain Crook eraser, Birdie eraser, Grimace pencil sharpener, Ronald pencil sharpener, Ronald and Birdie ruler, Ronald and Birdie pencil case	1984	5	10
Sea World of Ohio	set of three figures: Dolly Dolphin, Penny Penguin, Shamu the whale; regionally distributed in Clevland, Ohio area	1988	20	40
Sea World of Texas	set of four stuffed toys: dolphin, penguin, walrus, whale; regionally distributed in San Antonio, Texas area	1988	20	30

NAME	DESCRIPTION	YEAR	EX	MINT
Sea World of Texas II	set of five: sea otter stuffed toy, dolphin stuffed toy, whale stuffed toy, penguin sunglasses, whale sunglasses	1989	25	50
Serving Trays	set of six white plastic wedge-shaped trays: Ronald, Big Mac, Mayor McCheese, Hamburglar, Grimace, Captain Crook		3	7
Ship Shape I	set of four vacuform boat containers with stickers: Tubby Tugger, Splash Dasher, Rub-a-Dub Sub, Riverboat	1983	10	15
Ship Shape II	set of four vacuform boat containers with stickers: Tubby Tugger, Splash Dasher, Rub-a-Dub Sub, Riverboat; similar to 1983 Ship Shape Happy Meal but with redesigned stickers	1985	10	20
Ship Shape II	set of two U3 floating toys: Grimace in Tub, Fry Guys on Duck	1985	5	8
Sindy Doll	dressed in older McDonald's uniform	1970	4	8
Sky Dancers/Micro Machines	set of four dancing dolls: Rosemerry, Swan Shimmer, Princess Pegasus, Flutter Fly; split promo with Micro Machines	1997	1	2
Sky-Busters	set of six rubber airplanes: Skyhawk AAF, Phantom, Mirage F1, United DC-10, MIG-21, Tornado	1982	3	5
Sleeping Beauty	set of six: Sleeping Beauty, Maleficent, Prince Philip, Flora, Dragon, Raven	1997	1	2
Smart Duck	set of six rubber figures: duck, cat, donkey, chipmunk, two rabbits	1979	2	3
Snow White and the Seven Dwarfs	set of nine: Snow White with wishing well, Prince on horse with green base, Prince on horse without base, Queen/Witch, Bashful, Dopey and Sneezy, Doc, Happy and Grumpy, Sleepy	1993	3	6
Snow White and the Seven Dwarfs	one U3 toy: Dopey and Sleepy	1993	2	3
Sonic 3 The Hedgehog	one U3 toy: Sonic Ball	1994	3	6
Sonic 3 The Hedgehog	set of four: Sonic the Hedgehog, Miles "Tails" Power, Knuckles & Dr. Ivo Robotnik	1994	2	4
Space Aliens	set of eight rubber monsters: Lizard Man, Vampire Bat, Gill Face, Tree Monster, Winged Fish, Cyclops, Veined Brain, Insectman	1979	2	3
Space Jam	set of eight interlocking pieces: Lola Bunny, Bugs Bunny, Taz, Marvin the Martian, Daffy Duck, Monstar, Sylvester & Tweety, Nerdlucks	1996	2	4
Space Jam Plush	set of six: Lola Bunny, Bugs Bunny, Taz, Daffy Duck, Monstar, Nerdlucks	1996	3	5
Space Raiders	set of eight rubber aliens: Drak, Dard, flying saucer, Rocket Kryoo-5, Horta, Zama, Rocket Ceti-3, Rocket Altair-2	1979	2	3
Space Rescue	one U3 toy: Astro-Viewer	1995	1	2
Space Rescue	set of four: Astro Viewer, Tele-Communicator, Space Slate, Lunar Graber	1995	1	2
Spider-Man	one U3 toy: The Amazing Spider-man	1995	3	5
Spider-Man	set of eight: The Amazing Spider-Man, Dr. Octopus with moving tentacles, Mary Jane Watson with clip-on costumes, Spider-Sense Peter Parker, Scorpion Stingstriker, Spider-Man Webrunner, Venom Transport, Hobgoblin Landglider	1995	3	5
Spinner Baseball Game	green plastic with four characters	1983	2	4
Spinner Bicycle Game	pink or green game with two bicyclists	1984	2	5
Sports Ball	set of gour: white baseball, brown football, orange basketball, red and yellow soccer ball; regionally distributed in Kansas City and Indiana	1991	2	5
Sports Balls	set of four: basketball, baseball, football and tennis ball; test market Happy Meal, regionally distributed in Springfield, Missouri	1988	20	40
Sports Balls	set of four: baseball, football, basketball, soccer	1990	2	4
Sports Balls	one U3 toy: hard plastic baseball	1988	30	40
Star Trek	Starfleet game	1979	10	15

RESTAURANT PREMIUMS

NAME	DESCRIPTION	YEAR	EX	MINT
Star Trek	set of five video viewers, each with different story	1979	15	30
Star Trek	rings: Kirk, Spock, Starfleet insignia, Enterprise	1979	15	20
Star Trek	set of four glitter iron-ons: Kirk, Spock, McCoy, Ilia; packaged in pairs	1979	10	20
Star Trek	navigation bracelet with decals	1979	10	25
Sticker Club	set of five different sticker sheets: shiny, scratch and sniff, action stickers, puffy stickers, paper	1985	5	10
Stomper Mini 4x4	set of sixteen: Toyota Tercel, blue or gray; AMC Eagle, black or orange; Chevy S-10 pickup, black or yellow; Chevy van, red or yellow; Chevy Blazer, yellow or red; Ford Ranger, orange or red; Jeep Renegade, maroon or orange; Dodge Rampage, blue or white	1986	5	10
Stomper Mini 4x4 I	set of six push toys: Jeep Renegade, Dodge Rampage, white; Dodge Rampage, blue; Chevy S-10 Pick-up, blue; Chevy S-10 Pick-up, yellow; Chevy Van	1985	5	10
Stomper Mini 4x4 I	set of six: Chevy S-10 Pick-Up, blue; Chevy S-10 Pick-up, white; Chevy Van; Dodge Rampage, white; Dodge Rampage, blue; Jeep Renegade	1985	5	10
Story of Texas	set of eight books: Austin series—The Beginning, Independence, The Frontier, The 20th Century; Houston series—The Beginning, Independence, The Frontier, The 20th Century; regionally distributed in Texas	1986	75	100
Storybook Muppet Babies	set of three books: Baby Piggy, the Living Doll; The Legend of Gimmee Gulch; Just Kermit and Me!	1988	2	5
Super Looney Tunes	one U3 toy: Bat Duck in rocking boat	1991	2	4
Super Looney Tunes	set of four figures with costumes: Super Bugs, Bat Duck, Taz Flash, Wonder Pig	1991	2	4
Super Mario Brothers	one U3 toy: Super Mario	1990	2	4
Super Mario Brothers	set of four action figures: Mario, Luigi, Little Goomba, Koopa	1990	2	4
Super Sticker Squares	nine scenes and over 100 reusable stickers	1987	1	3
Super Summer	set of three: sailboat, watering can, beachball; test market Happy Meal, distributed in Fresno, California	1987	20	30
Super Summer II	set of six: sand castle pail with shovel, sand pail with rake, fish sand mold, inflatable sailboat, beach ball, watering can	1988	2	4
Tale Spin	set of U3 toys: Baloo's seaplane, Wildcat's jet	1990	2	4
Tale Spin	set of four characters in airplanes: Wildcat's Flying Machine, Baloo's Seaplane, Molly's Biplane, Kit's Racing Plane	1990	2	4
Tamagotchi Key Chains	set of nine: yellow, purple, green, red, blue with yellow figure inside, white with red figure inside, red/orange flip action, blue flashlight, purple #9 (only available at McDonald's in Wal-Mart stores)	1998	2	4
Teenie Beanie Babies	set of twelve plush toys: Doby the Doberman, Bongo the Monkey, Twigs the Giraffe, Inch the Worm, Pinchers the Lobster, Happy the Hippo, Mel the Koala, Scoop the Pelican, Bones the Dog, Zip the Cat, Waddle the Penguin, Peanut the Elephant	1998	4	8
Teenie Beanie Babies	set of twelve: Freckles the Leopard, Smoochy the Frog, Rocket the Blue Jay, Strut the Rooster, Claude the Crab, 'Nook the Husky, Antsy the Anteater, Spunk the Cocker Spaniel, Iggy the Iguana, Nuts the Squirrel, Stretchy the Ostrich, Chip the Cat	1999	2	4
Teenie Beanie Babies	set of ten plush toys: Patti the Platypus, Pinky the Flamingo, Chops the Lamb, Chocolate the Moose, Goldie the Goldfish, Speed the Turtle, Seamore the Seal, Snort the Bull, Quack the Duck, Lizz the Lizard	1997	10	20

NAME	DESCRIPTION	YEAR	EX	MINT
Teenie Beanie Babies International Bears	set of four: Britania, Glory, Erin, Maple; over-the-counter promotion available for $1.99 with food purchase	1999	1	2
The Busy World of Richard Scarry	one U3 toy: Lowly Worm, rubber	1995	1	2
The Busy World of Richard Scarry	set of four: Lowly Worm and Post Office, Huckle Cat and School, Mr. Fumble and Fire Station, Bananas Gorilla and Grocery Store	1995	1	2
The Legend of Mulan	set of ten figures: Mulan, Khan, Mushu, Shanyu, Shang, Chein Po, Ying, Yao, Little Brother, Cri-Kee	1998	1	2
The Lion King II Simba's Pride	set of eight: Kovu, Zazu, Timon, Simba, Kiara, Zira, Rafiki, Pumbaa	1998	1	2
Tic Toc Mac Game	yellow base, Grimace is X, Ronald is O	1981	2	5
Tinosaurs	set of eight figures: Link the Elf, Baby Jad, Merry Bones, Dinah, Time Traveller Fern, Tiny, Grumpy Spell, Kave Kolt Kobby; regionally distributed in St. Louis, Missouri	1986	5	10
Tiny Toon Adventures Flip Cars	set of two U3 toys: Gogo Dodo in bathtub, Plucky Duck in red boat	1991	3	5
Tiny Toon Adventures Flip Cars	set of four cars, each with two characters: Montana Max/Gobo Dodo, Babs/Plucky Duck, Hampton/Devil, Elmyra/Buster Bunny	1991	1	2
Tiny Toon Adventures Wacky Rollers	set of eight: Buster Bunny, Babs Bunny, Elmyra, Dizzy Devil, Gogo Dodo, Montana Max, Plucky Duck, Sweetie	1992	1	3
Tiny Toon Adventures Wacky Rollers	one U3 toy: Sweetie	1992	2	4
Tiny Toons Adventures Wacky Rollers				
Tom & Jerry Band	one U3 toy: Droopy	1990	5	8
Tom & Jerry Band	set of four characters with musical instruments: Tom at keyboard, Jerry on drums, Spike on bass, Droopy at the mike	1990	4	8
Tonka/Cabbage Patch Kids	one U3 toy: Dump Truck	1992	1	2
Tonka/Cabbage Patch Kids	set of five: Fire Truck, Loader, Cement Mixer, Dump Truck, Backhoe; joint promotion with Cabbage Patch Kids	1992	1	2
Tonka/Cabbage Patch Kids	set of four: Crane, Loader, Grader, Bulldozer; joint promotion with Cabbage Patch Kids	1992	1	3
Tonka/Cabbage Patch Kids	one U3 toy: Dump Truck	1994	2	3
Toothbrush Happy Meal	set of three Ronald toothbrushes: red, yellow, blue	1985	20	40
Tops	set of three: red, blue and green	1978	3	7
Totally Toy Holiday	set of two U3 toys: Magic Nursery Boy, Magic Nursery Girl, Key Force Car	1995	3	5
Totally Toy Holiday	set of eight: Great Adventures Knight figurine with green dragon, Holiday Barbie, Hot Wheels Vehicle with ramp (came with red or green vehicle), "Once Upon a Dream" Princess figurine, Polly Pocket Playset, Mighty Max Playset, Cabbage Patch Playset, South Pole Explorer Vehicle	1995	1	2
Totally Toy Holiday	set of eleven: Lil' Miss Candistripes, Magic Nursery Boy, Magic Nursery Girl, Polly Pocket, Key Force Truck, Key Force Car, Mighty Max, Tattoo Machines, Attack Pack Vehicles, Sally Secrets, Caucasian, Sally Sercets, African-American	1993	2	3
Totally Toy Holiday	set of three U3 toys: Keyforce Car, Magic Nursery Boy, Magic Nursery Boy	1993	2	3
Totally Toy Holiday	Holiday Barbie snow dome; recalled	1993	25	50
Transformers Beast Wars/ Littlest Pet Shop	set of four Transformer Beast Wars: Manta Ray, Beetle, Panther, Rhino; joint promotion with Littlest Pet Shop	1996	1	2
Transformers Beast Wars/ Littlest Pet Shop	one U3 toy: Lion's Head Transformer	1996	1	2

RESTAURANT PREMIUMS

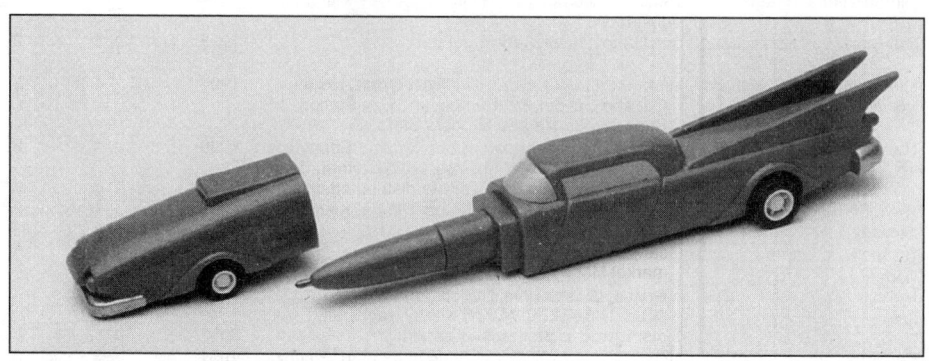

Speed Writers, 1991, Wendy's

Yogi Bear & Friends, 1990, Wendy's

530

NAME	DESCRIPTION	YEAR	EX	MINT
Transformers/My Little Pony	set of three: Scorponok, Dinobot, Blackarachnia; split promo with My Little Pony	1998	1	2
Transformers/My Little Pony	set of twenty-six: Brawn—green/blue, blue/yellow, red/green, red/blue, red/yellow, green/yellow; Cliffjumper—red/black, burgundy/black, yellow/black, black/green, violet/blue, teal/black, black/blue; Bumblebee—black/red, burgundy/black, teal/black, violet/blue, black/green, yellow/black; Gears—green/yellow, green/blue, red/yellow, red/green, blue/yellow, red/blue; joint promotion with My Little Pony; regionally distributed in St. Louis, Missouri area	1985	50	140
Turbo Macs I	set of four: Birdie in pink car, Hamburglar in yellow car, Grimace in white car, Ronald in red car; test market Happy Meal	1988	5	10
Turbo Macs I	one U3 toy: Ronald in red car with yellow wheels	1988	5	10
Turbo Macs II	one U3 toy: Ronald in red car with yellow wheels	1990	5	10
Turbo Macs II	set of four: Ronald in red car, Grimace in white car, Birdie in pink car, Hamburglar in yellow car	1990	3	6
Under Sea	set of six cartons with undersea art: Alligator, Dolphin, Hammerhead Shark, Sea Turtle, Seal, Walrus	1980	2	3
VR Troopers	one U3 toy: Sphere	1996	1	2
VR Troopers	set of four: Visor, Wrist Spinner, Virtualizer, Kaleidoscope	1996	1	2
Walt Disney Home Video Masterpiece Collection	set of eight video cases with figure: Bambi with Bambi figure, The Lion King with Simba figure, Pete's Dragon with Elliot figure, Oliver and Company with Dodger figure, Toy Story with Woody figure, Sleeping Beauty with Sleeping Beauty figure, The Three Caballeros with Donald Duck figure, Winnie the Pooh with Tigger figure	1997	2	3
Walt Disney Home Video Masterpiece Collection	one U3 toy: Dumbo water squirter	1996	3	5
Walt Disney Home Video Masterpiece Collection	set of eight: Cinderella, Robin Hood, Pocahontas, Return to Jafar, Snow White, Sword and the Stone, Alice in Wonderland, Aristocats	1996	1	2
Water Friends	one U3 toy: soft rubber Giant Panda	1992	3	5
Water Games	one U3 toy: Grimace with squirting camera	1992	15	20
Water Games	set of four: Birdie sorts eggs, Grimace juggles shakes, Ronald catches fries, Hamburglar stacks burgers	1992	3	5
What is It?	set of six rubber animals: Skunk, Squirrel, Bear, Owl, Baboon, Snake	1979	1	3
Wild Friends	set of four animals on mini-comic books: Crocodile, Gorilla, Elephant, Panda; regionally distributed in Indiana and southern California	1992	3	5
Winnie the Pooh Sing a Song with Pooh Bear	set of eight: Eeyore, Owl, Winnie the Pooh, Rabbit, Roo, Piglet, Gopher, Tigger	1999	5	10
Winter World	set of five flat vinyl tree ornaments: Ronald, Hamburglar, Grimace, Mayor McCheese, Birdie	1983	5	10
World of Hot Wheels/ Friends of Barbie	set of eight: Turbine 4-2, Flame Rider, 2-Cool, Bold Eagle, Black Cat, Gas Hog, X21J Cruiser, Street Shocker; joint promotion with Barbie	1994	2	3
World of Hot Wheels/ Friends of Barbie	one U3 toy: Fast Forward	1994	2	3
Wrist Wallets	set of four watch-type bands with coin-holding dial: Ronald, Captain Crook, Big Mac, Hamburglar	1977	5	10
Yo Yogi	set of four: Yogi Bear on wave jumper, Cindy Bear on scooter, Huckleberry Hound in race car, Boo Boo Bear on skate board	1992	3	5
Young Astronauts	one U3 toy: Ronald in lunar rover	1992	2	4
Young Astronauts	set of four vehicles: Space Shuttle & Space Walker, Command Module, Lunar Rover, Satalite Dish & Space Walker	1992	2	4

RESTAURANT PREMIUMS

MCDONALD'S

NAME	DESCRIPTION	YEAR	EX	MINT
Young Astronauts	set of four snap-together models: Apollo Command Module, Argo Land Shuttle, Space Shuttle, Cirrus Vtol	1986	5	20
Yo-Yo	half red, half yellow	1979	2	5
Zoo Face I	set of four masks: Alligator, Monkey, Tiger, Toucan; test market Happy Meal, distributed in Evansville, Indiana	1987	20	30
Zoo Face II	set of four rubber noses and makeup kits: Alligator, Monkey, Tiger, Toucan	1988	5	10

PIZZA HUT

NAME	DESCRIPTION	YEAR	EX	MINT
Air Garfield	figure of Garfield attached to either a parachute or suspended in a spaceball	1993	2	4
Air Garfield Cups	set of two: each cup featured Garfield and Odie	1993	1	4
Beauty & the Beast Puppets	set of four: Belle, Beast, Chip, Cogsworth	1992	4	8
Color Your World	set includes erasable calendar board with four Crayons, poster with four Crayons; each meal came with plastic cup	1993	4	6
Dinosaurs!	set of four 16 oz. cups with 3-D lids and sticker books: Brachiosaurus, Tyrannosaurus, Stegosaurus, Brachiosaurus	1993	4	8
Eureeka's Castle Puppets	set of three: Batly, Eureeka, Magellan	1991	3	6
Fievel Goes West cups	set of three: Fievel with cowboy hat, Cat R. Waul with red top hat, Wylie Burp with tan hat	1991	4	6
Land Before Time Puppets	set of six: Spike, Sharptooth, Pteri, Little Foot, Cera, Ducky	1988	4	8
Marsupilami Houba Douba	set of three: yo-yo, jump rope, glow ball	1994	4	6
Universal Monster Cups	set of three: holographic cards with 3-D cups		10	20
Young Indiana Jones Chronicles		1993	4	6

ROY ROGERS

NAME	DESCRIPTION	YEAR	EX	MINT
Critters	set of eight: blue eyes-yellow; blue eyes-orange; blue eyes-purple; blue eyes-red; yellow eyes-orange; yellow eyes-yellow; pink eyes-orange; pink eyes-purple	1990	1	2
Cup Critters	Elephant/Alligator/Frog/Bear/Pig/Beaver/Lion/Duck/Turtle	1994	2	5
Gator Tales	set of four: AV Gator, Investi-Gator, Flora Gator, Skater Gator	1989	4	6
Hide 'n Keep Dinos	set of three: Brontosaurus, Triceratops, Stegosaurus	1989	3	5
Ickky Stickky Bugs	set of sixteen: Centipede, Grasshopper, Worm, Spider	1989	2	3
Skateboard Kids Figures	set of four: Boy with red skateboard; Boy with orange skateboard, Boy with purple, Girl with blue skateboard	1989	3	5
Snorks	set of thirty version of the four characters: Allstar, Case, Dimmy, Tooter	1988	3	5
Star Searchers	set of four: Saucer, Robot, Vehicle, Shuttle	1990	2	3
Tatoo Heads		1995	2	5

SONIC DRIVE-IN

NAME	DESCRIPTION	YEAR	EX	MINT
Bag-A-Wag	set of four: man with bag of burgers in hamburger car, man with bag of burgers walking, man with bag of burgers rollerblading, man with hamburger	1990	3	6
Brown Bag Bowlers	set of four brown bag figures holding ball: yellow ball, red ball, blue ball, orange ball	1994	3	5

SONIC DRIVE-IN

NAME	DESCRIPTION	YEAR	EX	MINT
Brown Bag Buddies	set of four brown bag figures with sports equipment: sled, skiis, surfboard, intertube	1993	2	5
Brown Bag Juniors	set of four brown bag figures: Too Cool, Bookworm, Sure Shot, Marbles	1989	4	6
Bump and Go	series of 2" metal cars	1993	2	5
Custom Cruisers	set of four: Mercury, Chevy Convertible, Chevy Nomad, Cadillac Convertible	1993	3	5
Dino Makers		1994	2	5
Sonic Super Kids	set of four with comic book: Steve, Rick, Corky, Brin	1989	5	8
Sonic Turbo Racers	set of four: pink, yellow, orange, green	1993	2	5
Wacky Sackers	set of six: pink with bug-eyes, green with sunglasses, yelow, pink with three eyes, blue	1994	3	5

TACO BELL

NAME	DESCRIPTION	YEAR	EX	MINT
Chihuahua Plush	set of four talking dogs:standing, says "Yo Quiero Toca Bell"; sitting with Free Tacos sign, says "Here Lizard, Lizard"; sitting wearing beret, says: "Viva Gorditas"; lying down wearing Santa hat, says: "Feliz Navidad Amigos"	1999	3	7
Happy Talk Sprites	set of two: Spark, yellow; Twink, white		2	4
Hugga Bunch Plush Dolls			2	4

TASTEE FREEZE

NAME	DESCRIPTION	YEAR	EX	MINT
Roy Campanella Figure			20	35

WENDY'S

NAME	DESCRIPTION	YEAR	EX	MINT
Alf Tales	set of six: Sleeping Alf, Alf Hood, Little Red Riding Alf, Alf of Arabia, Three Little Pigs, Sir Gordon of Melmac	1990	2	4
Alien Mix-Ups	set of six: Crimsonoid, Bluezoid, Limetoid, Spotasoid, Yellowboid, Purpapoid	1990	1	2
All Dogs Go To Heaven	set of six: Anne Marie, Carface, Charlie, Flo, Itchy, King Gator	1989	2	4
Definitely Dinosaurs	set of four: blue Apatosaurus, gray T-Rex, yellow Anatosaurus, green Triceratops	1988	3	6
Definitely Dinosaurs	set of five: green Ankylosaurus, blue Parasaurolophus, green Ceratosaurus, yellow Stegosaurus, pink Apatosaurus	1989	2	4
Fast Food Racers	set of five: hamburger, fries, shake, salad, kid's meal	1990	2	4
Felix the Cat		1995	2	5
Fun Flyers	3-1/2" wide in red, yellow or blue		1	3
Furskins Plush Dolls	set of three: Boone in plaid shirt and red pants, Farrell in plaid shirt and blue jeans, Hattie in pink and white dress; all 7" tall	1988	4	8
Glass Hangers	set of four: yellow turtle, yellow frog, yellow penguin and purple gator		3	5
Glo Friends	set of twelve: Book Bug, Bop Bug, Butterfly, Clutter Bug, Cricket, Doodle Bug, Globug, Granny Bug, Skunk Bug, Snail Bug, Snug Bug	1988	2	4
Good Stuff Gang	set of six: Cool Stuff, Cat, Hot Stuff, Overstuffed, Bear, Penguin	1985	2	4
Jetsons Figures	set of six figures in spaceships: George, Judy, Jane, Elroy, Astro, Spacely	1989	2	4
Jetsons: The Movie Space Gliders	set of six PVC figures on wheeled bases: Astro, Elroy, Judy, Fergie, Grunchee, George	1990	2	4
Micro Machines Super Sky Carriers	set of six kits: connect to form Super Sky Carrier	1990	2	4

RESTAURANT PREMIUMS

WENDY'S

NAME	DESCRIPTION	YEAR	EX	MINT
Mighty Mouse	set of six: Bat Bat, Cow, Mighty Mouse, Pearl Pureheart, Petey, Scrappy	1989	3	5
Play-Doh Fingles	set of three finger puppet molding kits: green dough with black mold, blue dough with green mold, yellow dough with white mold	1989	3	6
Potato Head Kids	set of six: Captain Kid, Daisy, Nurse, Policeman, Slugger, Sparky	1987	4	8
Speed Writers	set of six car-shaped pens: black, blue, fuchsia, green, orange, red	1991	2	4
Summer Fun	float pouch, sky saucer	1991	1	2
Teddy Ruxpin	set of five: Professor Newton Gimmick, Teddy, Wolly Whats-It, Fob, Grubby Worm	1987	3	8
Too Kool for School	set of five		2	4
Tricky Tints	set of four		2	4
Wacky Wind-Ups	set of five: Milk Shake, Biggie French Fry, Stuff Potato, Hamburger, Hamburger in box	1991	2	3
Where's the Beef Stickers	set of six	1984	1	3
World Wildlife Foundation	set of four plush toys: Panda, Snow Leopard, Koala, Tiger	1988	5	10
World Wildlife Foundation	set of four books: All About Koalas, All About Tigers, All About Snow Leopards, All About Pandas	1988	2	4
Yogi Bear & Friends	set of six: Ranger Smith in kayak, Boo Boo on skateboard, Yogi on skates, Cindy on red scooter, Huckleberry in inner tube, Snagglepuss with surfboard	1990	2	4

WHITE CASTLE

NAME	DESCRIPTION	YEAR	EX	MINT
Ballerina's Tiara			3	6
Bendy Pens	set of five: Wilfred, Wobbles, Woofles, Woozy Wizard, Willis	1993	3	6
Camp White Castle			2	4
Camp White Castle Bowls	orange plastic		3	6
Castle Creatures			2	5
Castle Friends Bubble Makers	set of four	1992	3	5
Castle Meal Family	set of five: Wilfred, King Wooly and Queen Winnevere, Wally, Wobbles and Woody, Friar Wack	1992	4	6
Castle Meal Family	set of six: Princess Wilhelmina, Wendell, Sir Wincelot, Willis, Woozy Wizard, Woofles	1989	4	6
Castle Meal Friends	set of six	1989-90	4	10
Castleburger Dudes Figures	set of four: Castleburger Dude, Castle Fry Dudette, Castle Drink Dude, Castle Cheeseburger Dude	1991	3	6
Castleburger Dudes Wind-Up Toys	set of four: Castleburger Dude, Castle Fry Dudette, Castle Drink Dude, Castle Cheeseburger Dude	1991	2	4
Easter Pals	set of two: rabbit with carrot, rabbit with purse		3	5
Fat Albert and the Cosby Kids	set of four: Fat Albert, Dumb Donald, Russely, Weird Harold	1990	8	15
Food Squirters	set of three: Castle Fry Dudette, Castle Drink Dude, Castleburger Dude	1994	2	4
Glow in the Dark Monsters	set of three: Wolfman, Frankenstein, Mummy	1992	3	6
Godzilla Squirter			3	6
Halloween PEZ	set of three PEZ dispensers: Pumpkin, Witch, Skull	1990	n/a	0
Holiday Huggables	Candy Canine, Kitty Lights, Holly Hog		2	5
Nestle's Quik Rabbit	set of four: straw holder, spoon, cup, plush toy	1990	2	4
Puppy in My Pocket	set of twelve, two per package	1995	2	3
Silly Putty	set of three molds with Silly Putty: orange mold, yellow mold, green mold	1994	2	4
Stunt Grip Geckos	set of four figures: turquoise, pink, purple, blue	1992	2	4

RESTAURANT PREMIUMS

WHITE CASTLE

NAME	DESCRIPTION	YEAR	EX	MINT
Super Balls	set of four: Castleburger Dude, Castle Cheeseburger Dude, Castle Fry Dudette, Castle Drink Dude	1994	2	3
Swat Kats	set of three figures with launchers: Razor, T-Bone, Callie	1994	2	3
Tootsie Roll Express	set of four train cars: Engine, Gondola, Hopper, Caboose	1994	3	5
Totally U Back To School	set of two: pencil, pencil case		2	4
Triastic Take-a-Parta	set of four: Megasaur, Spinasaur, Coolasaur, Sorasaur; also distributed by Carl's Jr.	1994	2	3
Water Balls	set of four: Castleburger Dude, Castle Cheeseburger Dude, Castle Fry Dudette, Castle Drink Dude	1993	2	3
Willis the Dragon	Christmas giveaway		3	6
Willis the Dragon Sunglasses			2	4

RESTAURANT PREMIUMS

Robots

Take several hunks of metal, fashion them into a barrel-chested automaton with a blank stare and you've got yourself a robot.

The word "robot" is derived from the Czech word "robota" meaning forced labor or drudgery. The word quickly gained usage in English after 1920.

The style, look, composition and purpose of robots has changed quite a bit throughout the past sixty years, since the time when the earliest toy robots were made. But collectors have remained enamored of the artistry, design and function of these otherworldly pieces of pop culture.

Think of a toy robot, and it's likely you'll think of Japan. As early as the 1940s, Japan was making somewhat crude walking robots. Among the earliest is Atomic Robot Man, made in Occupied Japan in the late 1940s. The small robot, a mere five inches tall, featured clunky red feet, a blank facial expression and oversized gauges. Its value, like many early robots, can soar to four figures or more in Mint in Box condition.

The 1950s was the true golden age of robots and space toys. Science fiction exploded into the pop culture sensibilities with TV shows and movies catering to space themes. The lithographed tin toymakers in Japan responded accordingly, setting the world awash in a sea of spacemen robots. One of the world's major Japanese makers of robots at the time was Alps.

Notable entries to the robot field in the 1950s included Ideal's Robert the Robot, unusual because it was made of plastic, unlike Japan's tin litho giants. Louis Marx's Japanese subsidiary, Linemar, also brought many Japanese-made robots to the United States.

Easily the most popular robots ever to be made are what is known as the Gang of Five — a series of five skirted robots made in the mid-1950s by Masudaya of Japan. These stunningly colorful robots (the most familiar is the Lavender Robot) have easily commanded five to six-figure prices at top-of-the-line space auctions.

According to *Vintage Toys* (Krause Publications, 1999), "Japan had dominated the 1950s robot and space toy category with innovation, creativity, and perhaps most important, low price points.

"Yet their success was also their undoing, because as the Japanese saw their standard of living grow,

Cragstan's Mr. Robot, 1960s, Cragstan

536

the costs associated with their successful industries also rose, reducing their marketplace competitiveness . . . Most Japanese toymakers fought this losing battle well into the decade, but by the end of 1960s, most had either vanished or constricted precipitously. In fact, as the 1970s dawned, it was becoming difficult to find playthings on American toy shelves marked 'Made in Japan.' "

By the mid-1970s, interest in robots and space toys had waned. Japan's reign in the space toys arena had fallen. Items made in Hong Kong and Taiwan were more readily available.

By the late-1970s, the space toy world would turn its focus from robots and space men to *Star Wars* and other licensed realms.

The exciting historic and artistic world of robot toys would be gone, but those toys remain valuable vintage icons.

The Top 10 Robots
(in Mint condition)

1. Mr. Atomic, 1960s, Cragstan $15,000
2. Radar Robot, 1950s, ASC Japan 7,000
3. Thunder Robot, 1950s, Japan 6,500
4. Space Scout, 1950s 5,000
5. Door Robot, 1950s, Japan 3,000
6. Big Loo, 1960s, Marx 2,600
7. Ranger Robot, Japan, 1950s 2,250
8. Mechanized Robot, 1950s 2,000
9. Cragstan Great Astronaut, 1960s, ALPS 2,000
10. Frankenstein Robot, 1960s, Marx 2,000

Contributor to this section: Edwin Price Jr., 105 Wellington Rd., Easley, SC 29642-3411

ROBOTS

NAME	COMPANY	YEAR	DESCRIPTION	GOOD	EX	MIB
Action Robot	Hong-Kong	1970s	10", yellow/blue plastic, battery-operated, multiple functions	15	35	55
Answer Game Machine	Japan	1960s	14", tin, battery-operated, performs math tricks	350	675	950
Apollo 2000 Robot	Japan	1960s	12", tin, battery-operated, red and blue, w/chest guns	125	300	550
Apollo 2000X	Japan	1970s	6", blue and red tin wind-up w/ spark	35	55	100
Astro Captain	Daiya	1970s	6", red/white/blue tin wind-up sparker, NASA on helmet	35	65	100
Astronaut Robot	AN-Japan	1950s	8", tin, wind-up, tanks on back, gun in hand	500	1250	2000
Atomic Robot Man	Japan	1948	6", all tin, wind-up	325	900	1550
Attacking Martian	S.H.	1970s	10", tin/plastic, battery-operated, guns in chest	85	150	250
Attacking Martian	S.H.	1960s	12", tin, battery-operated, green lens on chest doors	100	200	300
Big Loo	Marx	1960s	36", plastic, battery-operated, water squirter, w/rockets and tools	450	1300	2600
Big Max & His Electronic Conveyor	Remco	1958	8 x 7", battery-operated, plastic, w/truck and coins	100	185	300
Captain the Robot	MTU-Korea	1970s	6", gray plastic wind-up, sparking	15	35	50
Chief Robotman	KO-Japan	1960s	12", tin and plastic, battery-operated, bump and go	450	900	1550
Colonel Hap Hazard	Marx	1960s	11", tin and plastic, rotating antenna on head	250	575	1200
Construction Robot	Japan	1960s	12", yellow tin, battery-operated, with forklift	450	100	1650
Countdown-Y	Cragstan	1960s	9"	100	145	225
Cragstan Great Astronaut	ALPS	1960s	11", red tin, battery-operated, w/video scene, key in head	500	1250	2000
Cragstan's Mr. Robot	Cragstan	1960s	10-1/2" tin, battery-operated, red or white body, clear dome head	300	500	900
Dino Robot	SH-Japan	1960s	11", tin, battery-operated, head opens to reveal dinosaur	450	950	1600
Directional Robot	Yonezawa	1950s	10", blue tin, battery-operated, rotates, bump and go action	225	650	1200
Door Robot	Japan	1950s	9 1/2", tin, battery-operated, remote cont, revolving head	700	1650	3000
Electric Robot	Marx	1950s	15", blk and red plastic, battery-operated, w/morse code	125	250	500
Engine Robot	SH-Japan	1960s	9", tin and plastic, battery-operated, w/chest gears	125	250	500
Engine Robot	SH-Japan	1970s	10", plastic, battery-operated	75	150	300
Excavator Robot	SH-Japan	1960s	10", tin and plastic, battery-operated, w/drill type hands	275	550	875
Fighting Robot	SH-Japan	1960s	11", tin and plastic, battery-operated, single chest gun, flashing light on head	125	350	600
Forbidden Planet Robby	Masudaya	1985	16", plastic, battery-operated, talks	65	125	200
Forbidden Planet Robby	Masudaya	1985	5", plastic, wind-up	10	20	35
Frankenstein	Marx	1960s	6", metal and plastic, wind-up walker	100	250	450
Frankenstein Robot	Marx	1960s	14", tin and plastic, battery-operated, wired remote control	575	1250	2000
Gear Robot	SH	1960s	9", wind-up, visible gears	125	275	450
Gear Robot	SH	1960s	11 1/2", battery-operated, tin w/ plastic gears in chest, antennae on shoulders	225	500	850
High-Wheel Robot	Japan	1950s	9", blue, tin and plastic, battery-operated, remote control	325	750	1250

Attacking Martian, 1970s, S.H.

*Big Max & His Electronic
Conveyor, 1958, Remco*

ROBOTS

NAME	COMPANY	YEAR	DESCRIPTION	GOOD	EX	MIB
Jupiter Robot	KO-Japan	1970s	6 1/2", red plastic, wind-up, w/ two antennae	65	125	225
King-Ding Robot	Topper	1970	12", plastic, battery-operated, separate brain robot goes in head	110	275	500
Laughing Robot	Waco-Japan	1960s	13", plastic, battery-operated, mouth opens, laughs loudly	125	275	500
Launching Robot	S.H.	1975	10"	25	35	55
Lunar Robot	Yonezawa	1960s	7", wind-up, sparks, companion to Thunder Robot	225	550	800
Lunar Spaceman		1978	12", battery operated	20	30	45
Machine Robot	Japan	1960s	11", tin and plastic, battery-operated, w/shoulder antennae	125	275	450
Magnor	Cragstan	1975	9", plastic	23	35	50
Man from Mars	Irwin	1950s	11", red tin, wind-up, "space boy"	100	250	450
Mars Explorer	Japan	1950s	9 1/2", red tin, battery-operated, w/wheels, face doors open	450	1000	1750
Marvelous Mike	Saunders	1950s	battery-operated, plastic robot on tin bulldozer	110	225	395
Maxx Steele Robot	Ideal	1984	30", plastic, programmable servant, w/charger	100	250	425
Mechanical Interplanetary Explorer		1950s	8", wind-up	180	260	400
Mechanical Television Spaceman	ALPS	1960s	7", tin and plastic, wind-up, w/ chest scene and antenna	95	185	325
Mechanized Robot		1950s	13",tin and plastic, battery-operated, "Robby" type	500	1200	2000
Mighty Zogg the Leader Zeroid	Ideal	1960s	6", plastic, battery-operated, w/ Motorific motors	60	110	225
Moon Creature	Marx	1960s	5 1/2", Bug-eyed, mechanical, tin, wind-up	95	165	275
Moon Explorer	Yoshiya	1960s	12", tin, battery-operated, w/ clock in chest	475	1000	1850
Moon Scout	Marx	1968	11", tin and plastic, shoots balls from chest	500	1050	2000
Mr. Atom	Advance Toys	1960s	18", red and silver plastic, battery-operated	125	300	650
Mr. Atomic	Cragstan	1960s	rare, 8", tin and plastic, battery-operated, bump and go action	n/a	n/a	15000
Mr. Atomic	Mikes Toy House	1990s	Limited reproduction	95	200	350
Mr. Brain	Remco	1970	13", plastic, battery-operated, programmable memory	75	150	250
Mr. Hustler	Orikawa	1960s	11 1/2", tin and plastic, battery-operated, center chest light	100	225	400
Mr. LEM Astronaut Robot	Cragstan	1970	13", all plastic, battery-operated, rotates	150	310	475
Mr. Machine	Ideal	1961	18", plastic, wind-up, w/bell and key, disassembles	85	210	425
Mr. Machine	Ideal	1977	18", plastic, wind-up, whistles, does not disassemble	10	25	55
Mr. Mercury	Marx	1960s	14", tinand plastic, battery-operated, bending action	175	450	1000
Mr. Patrol	Japan	1960s	11", tin and plastic, battery-operated, meter in chest	150	350	575
Mr. Zerox	SH-Japan	1960s	9", tin and plastic, battery-operated, w/blinking, shooting actions	100	210	350
Myrobo		1970s	9", battery operated	25	35	55
New Astronaut Robot	Japan	1970s	9", tin and plastic, battery-operated, w/three firing chest guns	45	85	135
Omnibot 2000	Tomy	1980s	2 ft., plastic, battery-operated, remote control, programmable servant	175	400	675

Left to Right: Apollo 2000 Robot, 1960s, Japan; Space Fighter, 1960s, SH-Japan; Video Robot, 1960s, SH-Japan, 1960s, Japan

Moon Creature, 1960s, Marx

Robot Commando, 1960s, Ideal

Piston Robot, 1970s, Japan

ROBOTS

NAME	COMPANY	YEAR	DESCRIPTION	GOOD	EX	MIB
Piston Action Robot	Japan	1950s	8 1/2", tin and plastic, battery-operated, remote cont, "Robby" type	500	1200	2000
Piston Robot	Japan	1970s	10", tin and plastic, battery-operated, lighted chest pistons	60	110	225
Piston Robot	Japan	1980s	10", plastic, battery-operated, lighted chest pistons	35	65	125
Piston Robot	Horikawa	1960s	10", tin/plastic, battery-operated, lighted pistons in square head	200	450	750
R-35 Robot	Japan	1950s	7 1/2", tin litho, battery-operated, remote cont, eyes lite up	150	400	650
Radar Hunter	Hong-Kong	1970s	5", plastic, wind-up, red/silver or orange	15	35	55
Radar Robot	ASC Japan	1950s	11", orange tin, wind-up, rotating antenna, chest sparks	1500	4000	7000
Radar Scope Space Scout	SH-Japan	1960s	10", tin and plastic, battery-operated, TV screen w/ noise	65	125	210
Raid "Bug" Robot	1960s	Korea	Large plastic, battery-operated, remote control, ad promo	75	150	250
Ranger Robot	1950s	Japan	11", battery-operated, clear body, w/smoke and sound	500	1200	2250
Rendezvous 7.8	Yanoman		15"	170	245	375
Ro-Gun "It's A Robot"	Arco	1984	robot changes into a rifle	11	16	25
Robbie Robot	Hong-Kong	1970s	9", blue/red/yellow, all plastic, battery-operated, blinks	25	45	85
Robert the Wonder Toy	Ideal	1960	14", plastic, battery-operated, remote cont crank on back	100	195	425
Robot 2500	Durham	1970s	10", tin/plastic, battery-operated, "cyclops"	25	45	65
Robot Commando	Ideal	1960s	19", blue/red plastic, battery-operated, remote cont, fires rockets and balls	135	325	575
Robot Tank-Z	TN-Japan	1960s	10", battery-operated, tin and plastic, bumpandgo	175	395	575
Robot YM-3	Masudaya	1985	5", wind-up, "Lost in Space B9" type	10	20	35
Roto-Robot	Japan	1960s	9", tin and plastic, battery-operated, w/chest guns, rotates 360 degrees	95	185	325
Rudy the Robot	Remco	1967	16", orange plastic, battery-operated	50	165	375
Singing Robot	Japan	1970s	10", plastic, battery-operated, missiles in head	35	75	100
Sky Robot	S.H.	1970s	8", yellow/red plastic, battery-operated	20	45	65
Smoking Engine Robot	SH-Japan	1970s	10", plastic, battery-operated, piston action, w/sound and smoke	45	85	135
Son of Garloo	Marx	1960s	6", green metal and plastic, monster wind-up walker	100	225	425
Sounding Robot	Hong-Kong	1970s	8", plastic, battery-operated, three push buttons on head	25	50	75
Space Command Robot	TN-Japan	1950s	7 1/2", all tin, wind-up, w/gun in hand	375	1000	1650
Space Commander Robot	SH-Japan	1960s	10", tin and plastic, tank type base, bumpandgo, w/guns	500	1200	2000
Space Explorer Robot	Japan	1950s	9", tin, wind-up, w/O2 gauge on chest	450	1000	1650
Space Explorer Robot	Japan	1960s	12", tin and plastic, battery-operated, rotating shoulder antenna	450	1000	1650
Space Explorer Robot	Horikawa	1960s	11", tin and plastic, battery-operated, drop down chest cover reveals video	95	200	325

Sparky Robot, 1950s,
KO-Japan

Super Astronaut, 1981, S.J.M.

ROBOTS

NAME	COMPANY	YEAR	DESCRIPTION	GOOD	EX	MIB
Space Fighter	SH-Japan	1960s	9", tin and plastic, battery-operated, w/chest doors and guns	95	200	325
Space Guard Pilot	Asak	1975	8"	20	30	45
Space Man Robot	SY Japan	1950s	7 1/2" tin litho windup, w/floppy arms	150	400	700
Space Ranger	Japan	1970s	10", battery-operated, all plastic, R/C, fires balls from chest	50	110	165
Space Robot X-70	Japan	1960s	12", tin and plastic, battery-operated, lights, noise, and "Tulip Head"	450	1000	1650
Space Scout		1950s	Rare 10", tin wind-up, w/ radiation meter in chest	1000	2250	5000
Sparking Robot	Hong-Kong	1970s	6", black plastic, wind-up	20	35	50
Sparking Robot	SY Japan	1960s	7", all tin, silver w/litho, keywound	100	225	350
Sparky Robot	Japan	1960s	7", green cylindrical body, tin wind-up	45	65	100
Sparky Robot	KO-Japan	1950s	8 1/2", silver and red, all tin, wind-up, w/head spring	150	295	500
Star Robot	Hong-Kong	1970s	10", plastic, battery-operated, Star Wars Trooper head	25	45	70
Super Astronaut	S.J.M.	1981	10", battery-operated, tin and plastic, man's face, w/chest guns	12	20	30
Super Astronaut	Japan	1960s	10", battery-operated, mostly tin, man's face, w/chest guns	65	145	250
Super Giant Rotate-a-Matic	SH-Japan	1970s	16", battery-operated, plastic, w/chest guns	85	150	250
Super Robot Tank	SH-Japan	1950s	9" long, tin, friction powered w/ two guns	80	175	295
Talking Robot	Cragstan	1960s	10 1/2", battery-operated, tin and plastic, three functions	375	650	1000
Television Space Man	Alps	1950s	11", tin and plastic, battery-operated, chest video, key in head operates	125	350	800
Thunder Robot	Japan	1950s	11", tin and plastic, battery-operated, w/antenna and guns in palms of hands	1200	3500	6500
Tobor	Schaper	1978	7", black plastic, battery-operated, radio control	15	30	45
Venus Robot	KO-Japan	1960s	8", blue/red, tin and plastic, battery-operated, remote control	210	455	725
Verbot	Tomy	1984	8", plastic, battery-operated, radio control, programmable	15	35	60
Video Robot	SH-Japan	1960s	9", blue tin and plastic, battery-operated, w/chest video	75	155	250
Walking W Robot	N-Japan	1960s	7", tin wind-up sparker, plastic antenna on head	100	225	350
Zerak the Blue Destroyer Zeroid	Ideal	1968	6", plastic, battery-operated, w/ Motorific motors	50	100	200
Zintar the Silver Explorer Zeroid	Ideal	1960s	6", plastic, battery-operated, w/ Motorific motors	50	100	200
Zobor the Bronze Transporter Zeroid	Ideal	1960s	6", plastic, battery-operated, w/ Motorific motors	50	100	200
Zoomer Robot	Japan	1950s	7", blue or silver w/red, tin, battery-operated, w/wrench	295	525	900

ROBOTS

Rock and Roll

It's true that rock and roll is here to stay. That's easily evidenced by the number of toys and memorabilia avidly sought by collectors today.

The beginnings of rock and roll took root with the rhythm and blues music popularized after World War II. In the 1950s, Elvis Presley revolutionized the rock sound. But it wasn't until Liverpool's four young men swept America in the early 1960s that the rock and roll boom began. The Beatles' impact was so strong, in fact, it resonated not only in the music world, but in the merchandising and collectibles arena as well.

Because of the group's charm and popularity, companies soon learned the marketing potential of John, Paul, George and Ringo. Millions of young fans swooned over the Beatles, so it was only natural that licensees would immediately attach themselves to their success. Soon, and for decades following their debut, images of the Fab Four would appear on lunch boxes, wallets, clothing, toiletries, knickknacks, toys and more.

Not only were the Beatles' images used to endorse products, but many toys were made to help kids recreate the frenzy at home. Toy guitars, drums and dolls brought the Beatles to life to a younger audience. Today, collectors are thrilled to find such remnants of rock and roll history. And while Beatles collectibles aren't particularly difficult to find, those in the best condition are treasured.

After the success companies enjoyed marketing Beatles toys, rock and roll continued to be a successful font for merchandisers. Although their musical talent was scrutinized, both the Monkees and the Partridge Family enjoyed added exposure on television. That exposure created much interest in related memorabilia, especially for young fans.

In the 1970s, KISS stormed onto the rock scene in wild face makeup and costumes unlike anything previously seen. Armies of KISS fans rocked and rolled all night, and in 1979, Mego made 12-inch dolls of band members Paul Stanley, Gene Simmons, Ace Frehley and Peter Criss. Dozens of KISS toys followed to the delight of eager fans. McFarlane Toys continues the KISS craze today with new action figures (see **Action Figures** chapter for values).

But KISS was one of the last rock and roll groups featured on numerous toys and memorabilia. While 1980s and 1990s icons like Michael Jackson and Madonna have been the subjects of some toys and collectibles, the trend has, for the most part, ended. The Spice Girls are the only recent performers to be personified as toys. Their outrageous "girl power" style is perfect for 11-1/2-inch fashion dolls.

Why? In their heyday, the Beatles were a clean-cut group with non-threatening personas. The Monkees and the Partridge Family were rather wholesome, humorous groups (see **TV Toys** chapter for values). KISS flaunted their distinctive look and image. But today's rockers (and rappers) do not lend themselves as well to having their images represented on toys. Their lyrics, images and attitudes are often sexual, violent or anti-establishment — not exactly the sweet, non-threatening images of the past.

Trends

Beatles toys lead the pack of rock and roll memorabilia. The market remains active with growth each year, particularly with renewed interest in the group since the release of the 1996 Beatles Anthology albums.

Non-toy items such as ticket stubs, recordings and posters are consistent sellers, but toys bearing the images of revered rockers seem to always be in vogue.

Beatles Bobbin' Head Dolls, 1960s

These licenses, although 30 years old, haven't lost their power. In fact, many new limited-edition collectibles (like plates, dolls and ornaments) have continued to satisfy the public's hunger for Beatles and Elvis items. Even the new toys of 1998 embraced these vintage rockers. New toys based on Elvis and KISS were represented at 1998's Toy Fair.

Toys featuring minor or fleeting rock phenomenons (like New Kids on the Block, MC Hammer or others) will likely see no future increase in collectibility. But collectors can't really go wrong picking up items featuring major players in rock and roll history.

One caveat, however. Reproductions and unlicensed items are rampant, so collectors should educate themselves about items before purchasing.

The Top 10 Rock and Roll Toys
(in Mint in Box condition)

1. Beatles Banjo, Mastro, 1964 .... $800
2. Beatles Bobbin' Head Dolls, 1960s 750
3. Beatles Guitar, Selcol, 1960s 550
4. Beatles Magic Slate, Merit 500
5. Beatles Cartoon Kit, Colorforms, 1966 500
6. Beatles Jr. Guitar, Mastro, 1960s 425
7. Beatles Costume, Ben Cooper, 1960s 400
8. Paint Your Own Beatle Kit, Artistic Creations, 1960s 400
9. Yellow Submarine Halloween Costume, Collegeville, 1960s 375
10. Partridge Family Bus, Remco, 1973 300

ROCK AND ROLL

BEATLES

NAME	COMPANY	YEAR	DESCRIPTION	GOOD	EX	MIB
Beatles Banjo	Mastro	1964		200	400	800
Beatles Cartoon Kit	Colorforms	1966		150	300	500
Beatles Coloring Book	Saalfield	1964		25	60	110
Beatles Costume	Ben Cooper	1960s	child's costume and mask; John, Paul, George, or Ringo, each	100	200	400
Beatles Forever Cloth Dolls	Applause	1987	22" tall, each	55	75	100
Beatles Guitar	Selcol	1960s	23", plastic	200	300	550
Beatles in Pepperland Puzzles	Jaymar		many variations and sizes, each	25	60	90
Beatles Jr. Guitar	Mastro	1960s	14" red/pink plastic guitar w/ Beatles graphics	100	225	425
Beatles Magic Slate	Merit		British	150	300	500
Beatles Notebook Binder		1960s	binder from Beatles Fan Club	30	75	125
Beatles Toy Watches		1960s	four, tin w/plastic bands, on card	30	75	150
Beatles Wig	Lowell Toy			65	90	130
Bobbin' Head Dolls		1960s	8" tall, ceramic, four in set	300	500	750
Disk Go Case	Charter	1966	45 rpm carrying case; several colors	70	100	200
George Harrison Doll	Remco	1964		50	100	250
Harmonica	Hohner		in Beatles box	35	50	75
Inflatable Dolls		1966	Lux promotional; 13" tall; each	25	35	50
John Lennon Doll	Remco	1964		50	100	250
Paint Your Own Beatle Kit	Artistic Creations	1960s	oil painting kit; John, Paul, George, or Ringo, each	150	300	400
Paul McCartney Doll	Remco	1964		50	100	250
Paul McCartney Soaky	Colgate	1965	red plastic	70	120	250
Ringo Starr Doll	Remco	1964		50	100	250
Ringo Starr Soaky	Colgate	1965	blue plastic	70	120	250
Yellow Submarine Halloween Costume	Collegeville	1960s	Blue Meanie costume and mask	100	200	375
Yellow Submarine Water Color Set	Craft Master	1960s	pictures and paints	35	75	140

ELVIS PRESLEY

NAME	COMPANY	YEAR	DESCRIPTION	GOOD	EX	MIB
Elvis Presley Doll	World Dolls	1984	21" tall	50	100	200
Elvis Presley Doll	Eugene	1984	12" tall	20	40	80
Elvis Presley Wristwatch	Bradley	1983	white plastic case, quartz, stainless back, face shows a young Elvis, white vinyl band	20	35	75
Jigsaw Puzzle	Milton Bradley	1992	Elvis postage stamp	5	10	20

KISS

NAME	COMPANY	YEAR	DESCRIPTION	GOOD	EX	MIB
Jigsaw Puzzles	Milton Bradley	1970s		10	20	35
KISS Rub n' Play Magic Transfer Set	Colorforms	1979		20	40	80
KISS Van Model Kit	AMT	1977		35	70	140
KISS Your Face Make-Up Kit	Remco	1978		30	65	115
Trading Cards Set	Donruss	1978	set of 132 cards	25	35	70
View-Master Set	GAF	1978		10	20	35
Wastebasket		1978	metal, cylindrical	20	45	65

MICHAEL JACKSON

NAME	COMPANY	YEAR	DESCRIPTION	GOOD	EX	MIB
Michael Jackson AM Radio	Ertl	1984		12	25	50
Michael Jackson Doll	LJN	1984	several styles	12	25	60

ROCK AND ROLL

Beatles Dolls, 1964, Remco

Beatles Wig, Lowell Toy

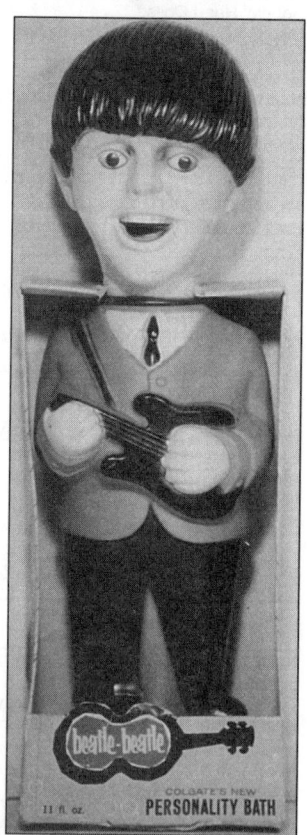

Paul McCartney Soaky, 1965, Colgate

Rick Nelson Paper Dolls, 1959, Whitman

548

MICHAEL JACKSON

NAME	COMPANY	YEAR	DESCRIPTION	GOOD	EX	MIB
Michael Jackson Dress-Up Set	Colorforms	1984		10	15	25
Michael Jackson Microphone	LJN	1984	cordless, electronic	10	20	35
Michael's [Jackson] Pets	Ideal	1987	plush animals, 10 kinds, each	7	15	25

MISCELLANEOUS

NAME	COMPANY	YEAR	DESCRIPTION	GOOD	EX	MIB
Andy Gibb Doll	Ideal	1979	7" tall	15	30	60
Boy George Doll	LJN	1980s	15", polka dot shirt	20	40	75
Boy George Doll	LJN	1980s	12", poseable in alphabet shirt	30	60	120
Cher Doll	Mego	1976	12", w/growing hair	35	75	140
Cher Doll	Mego	1976	12"	25	45	80
Debby Boone Doll	Mattel		10" tall	20	40	80
Dolly Parton Doll	Goldberger	1970s	12" tall	20	40	80
Pat Boone Paper Dolls	Whitman	1959	two cardboard dolls plus clothes	20	45	70
Pinky Lee Costume		1950s	hat, pants, and shirt	35	75	145
Pinky Lee Xylophone	Emenee			35	70	120
Rick Nelson Paper Dolls	Whitman	1959		20	45	70
Sonny & Cher Play Set	Mego	1976		20	45	80
Toni Tennile Doll			12" tall	8	15	30

OSMONDS

NAME	COMPANY	YEAR	DESCRIPTION	GOOD	EX	MIB
Donny & Marie TV Show Play Set	Mattel	1976		15	35	55
Donny Osmond Doll	Mattel	1976	12" tall	15	25	45
Donny Osmond String Puppet	Madison	1978		20	35	60
Marie Osmond Doll	Mattel	1976	12" tall	10	25	40
Marie Osmond Modeling Doll	Mattel	1976	30" tall	20	40	80
Marie Osmond String Puppet	Madison	1978		25	35	65
Osmonds Colorforms Dress-Up Set	Colorforms	1976		10	25	45

Space/Science Fiction Toys

Some would trace the modern age of science fiction to 1956 and *Forbidden Planet*. Undoubtedly, the toy world would be poorer for the lack of the movie's Robby the Robot. But through one medium or another, science fiction has enthralled millions for many years, back to Jonathan Swift's *Gulliver's Travels*.

The first universally acclaimed work of science fiction was Mary Shelley's *Frankenstein or The Modern Prometheus*, and her vision made way for Verne, Wells, Burroughs, Lovecraft, Heinlein, Asimov, Clarke and a host of others, whose collective imaginations led us up to today and through tomorrow.

Even with its classical pedigree, science fiction is almost exclusively a product of the 20th century, as the hard foundation of science

Battlestar Galactica Colorforms Adventure Set, 1978, Colorforms

had to exist before fiction writers could extrapolate upon it. In particular, science fiction is a phenomenon of the atomic age. World War II, more than any other event this century, opened our eyes to the wondrous and horrific potential of applied science.

Just as science fiction has captivated readers of all ages, so have toys. Buck Rogers made his first appearance in 1928, but in 1929, Buck Rogers went from pulp to newsprint, becoming the first science fiction comic strip. Flash Gordon followed Buck Rogers into print in 1934 and was an immediate success. Within two years, Flash was on the silver screen, portrayed by Buster Crabbe. Buck Rogers finally made it to the screen in 1939, also played by Crabbe.

During this period, Marx produced numerous toys in support of each character, including two ships that have become classics of the space toy field. Opinions vary as to which wind-up is better executed, Buck Rogers' 25th Century Rocket Ship or Flash Gordon's Rocket Fighter. Both are considered superb examples of tin character space toys.

From Ray Guns to *Star Wars*

No discussion of space toys would be complete without mention of ray guns. Here again Marx is a major player, producing numerous generic and character space guns. Daisy, Hubley and Wyandotte, among others, all made memorable contributions as well.

Space toys have been made continuously for most of the 20th century. The 1930s and 1940s saw Buck Rogers and Flash Gordon. The 1950s saw fiction become reality with the growth of television. *Captain Video* was the first space series on TV, appearing in the summer of 1949. *Buzz Correy and his Space Patrol* and *Tom Corbett, Space Cadet* would feed the appetite for adventure until 1956 when the heavens took on a visual scale and grandeur never seen before — in the panoramic wonder of *Forbidden Planet*.

In 1966, when the low budget *Star Trek* went on the air, few dreamed that for millions of people, life would never be the same. Even though the original show ran only three seasons, its impact and legacy are undeniable. The phenomenon of *Star Trek* has grown far beyond cult status, and the extraordinary success of *Star Trek: The Next Generation* has only broadened its reach.

Star Trek may be big; however, the king of space toys has to be *Star Wars*. The array of books, models, figures, play sets and other items released since its debut in 1977 continued unabated until 1988. The license gained a new lease in 1987 with the opening of Star Tours at Disneyland and Disney World, generating still more new merchandise.

In terms of diversity of toys, the universe of *Star Wars* is easily the most fully realized and diversely populated in all science fiction. Star Wars figures, vehicles and play sets are the most widely-traded science fiction toys on the market today.

Today, store shelves are again seeing new Star Wars toys thanks to the highly successful 1997 re-release of the *Star Wars* trilogy and 1999's *Episode I The Phantom Menace*. Star Wars' longevity and international name recognition are excellent assurances of the continuing popularity of its toys. (See **Star Wars** chapter for values.)

Trends

In general, the field of science fiction toys is one with particular growth potential, given the prevalence of science fiction in today's culture and the exceptional strength of franchises like Star Trek and Star Wars. Recent generations have been weaned on Luke Skywalker, Han Solo, Mr. Spock and Captain Picard. Newer incarnations such as *Star Trek: Voyager* only fuel the series' popularity. Toys from older, nostalgic series such as *Lost in Space*

Lost in Space Trading Cards, 1966, Topps

and *Buck Rogers in the 25th Century* continue to top lists of the most sought-after space/science fiction toys, and their values are soaring, particularly at auction.

Editor's Note: Several abbreviations are used in this section to denote *Star Trek* movies. Key is as follows ST:TMP: Star Trek, The Motion Picture; ST:TNG: Star Trek, The Next Generation.

The Top 10 Space / Science Fiction Toys
(in Mint in Package condition)

1. Lost in Space, Doll Set, Marusan/Japanese $7,000
2. Buck Rogers, Solar Scouts Patch, Cream of Wheat, 1936 7,000
3. Buck Rogers, Cut-Out Adventure Book, 1933 6,000
4. Lost in Space, Roto-Jet Gun Set, Mattel, 1966 6,000
5. Space Patrol, Monorail Set, Toys of Tomorrow, 1950s 4,200
6. Buck Rogers, Roller Skates, Marx, 1935 3600
7. Buck Rogers, Pocket Watch, E. Ingraham, 1935 3,500
8. Buck Rogers, Costume, Sackman Bros., 1934 2,500
9. Lost in Space, Switch-and-Go Set, Mattel, 1966 2,300
10. Buck Rogers, 25th Century Scientific Laboratory, Porter Chemical, 1934 2,200

Contributors to this section: Edwin Price Jr., 105 Wellington Rd., Easley, SC 29642-3411; **Space: 1999**, Corey LeChat, P.O. Box 40135, Pittsburgh, PA 15201; **Buck Rogers**, John Snyder Jr., 1966 Greenspring Dr. Suite 401, Timonium, MD 21093.

SPACE/SCIENCE FICTION TOYS

ALIEN/ALIENS

NAME	COMPANY	YEAR	DESCRIPTION	GOOD	EX	MIB
Alien Blaster Target Game	H.G. Toys	1979	set features large free standing cardboard Alien target and plastic dart shooting rifle, gun has large block letters "Alien" on side, based on the movie	55	110	175
Alien Blaster Target Set	HG Toys		larger set	75	170	250
Alien Chase Target Set	HG Toys		dart pistol, cardboard target	50	165	200
Alien Costume	Ben Cooper		black/white	50	65	100
Alien Model Kit	Tsukuda	1980s	vinyl, 1/6 scale	60	225	350
Alien Warrior Model Kit	Halcyon		base and egg	20	30	50
Aliens Colorforms Set	Colorforms			10	20	40
Aliens Computer Game	Commodore	1985		5	15	30
Glow Putty	Laramie		unlicensed art, carded	10	15	20
Movie Viewer	Kenner		"Alien Terror" film clip	40	75	100

BATTLESTAR GALACTICA

NAME	COMPANY	YEAR	DESCRIPTION	GOOD	EX	MIB
Battlestar Galactica Model Kit	Monogram	1979	No. 6028	15	25	40
Colonial Viper Model Kit	Monogram	1979		15	25	40
Colorforms Adventure Set	Colorforms	1978		12	20	30
Cylon Base Star Model Kit	Monogram	1979	silver plastic	15	30	45
Cylon Helmet Radio	Vanity Fair	1979		20	40	75
Cylon Raider Model Kit	Monogram	1979		15	25	40
Cylon Warrior Costume		1978	boxed	10	15	25
Galactic Cruiser	Larami	1978	die-cast	5	8	12
Game of Starfighter Combat	FASA	1978	role playing game	10	15	25
L.E.M. Lander	Larami	1978	die-cast	5	8	12
Lasermatic Pistol	Mattel	1978		15	30	45
Lasermatic Rifle	Mattel	1978		25	40	65
Muffit the Daggit Halloween Costume	Collegeville	1978		7	15	35
Poster Art Set	Craft Master	1978		6	10	15
Puzzles	Parker Brothers	1978	The Rag-Tag Fleet, Starbuck, Interstellar Battle, price for each	6	10	15
Space Alert Game	Mattel	1978	hand-held electronic game	10	20	45
Viper Vertibird	Mattel	1979		50	100	200

BUCK ROGERS

NAME	COMPANY	YEAR	DESCRIPTION	GOOD	EX	MIB
25th Century Police Patrol Rocket	Marx	1935	tin wind-up, 12" long	300	800	1500
25th Century Scientific Laboratory	Porter Chemical	1934	w/three manuals	800	1300	2200
Adventures of Buck Rogers Book	Whitman	1934	All Pictures Comics edition, Big Big Book	25	90	150
Battle Cruiser Rocket	Tootsietoy	1937	two grooved wheels to run on string	75	190	300
Battle for the 25th Century Game	TSR	1988	role playing board game	15	25	50
Buck and Wilma Masks	Einson-Freeman	1933	paper litho, each	120	200	325
Buck Rogers 25th Century Rocket	Marx	1939	Buck and Wilma in window, 12" long, tin wind-up	225	550	1100
Buck Rogers and the Children of Hopetown Book	Golden Press	1980s	Little Golden Book	4	7	15
Buck Rogers and the Depth Men of Jupiter Book	Whitman	1935	Big Little Book	50	90	150

SPACE/SCIENCE FICTION TOYS

NAME	COMPANY	YEAR	DESCRIPTION	GOOD	EX	MIB
Buck Rogers and the Doom Comet Book	Whitman	1935	Big Little Book	50	90	150
Buck Rogers and the Overturned World Book	Whitman	1941	Big Little Book	50	75	120
Buck Rogers and the Planetoid Plot Book	Whitman	1936	Big Little Book	50	90	150
Buck Rogers and the Super Dwarf of Space Book	Whitman	1943	Big Little Book	50	75	120
Buck Rogers Figure	Tootsietoy	1937	1-3/4" tall, cast, gray	100	150	250
Buck Rogers Films	Irwin	1936	set of six	110	190	285
Buck Rogers Holster for U-238 Atomic Pistol	Daisy	1946	leather holster only	40	125	250
Buck Rogers Holster for XZ-35 Pop Gun	Daisy	1934	embossed leather, attached to belt by two short riveted straps	40	125	250
Buck Rogers in the 25th Century Book	Whitman	1933	Big Little Book, Cocomalt premium	50	80	150
Buck Rogers in the 25th Century Book	Whitman	1933	Big Little Book	75	120	200
Buck Rogers in the 25th Century Button		1935	pinback, color Buck bust profile on blue background, w/small ray gun and rocket ship at his shoulders	30	75	150
Buck Rogers in the 25th Century Pistol Set	Daisy	1930s	holster is red, yellow and blue leather gun is 9-1/2" pressed steel pop gun	200	300	600
Buck Rogers in the 25th Century Star Fighter	Mego	1979	vehicle for 3-3/4" figures	20	35	60
Buck Rogers in the 25th Century XZ-35 Rocket Pistol	Daisy	1934	holster is red, yellow and blue leather, gun is 9-1/2" pressed steel Rocket Pistol w/single cooling fin at barrel base	155	260	575
Buck Rogers in the City Below The Sea Book	Whitman	1934	Big Little Book	75	150	250
Buck Rogers in the City of Floating Globes Book	Whitman	1935	Cocomalt premium, paperback Big Little Book	125	250	500
Buck Rogers in the War With the Planet Venus Book	Whitman	1938	Big Little Book	45	70	120
Buck Rogers on the Moons of Saturn Book	Whitman	1934	premium, paperback Big Little Book	75	150	250
Buck Rogers Rubber Band Gun	Unknown	1930s	cut-out paper gun, on card, advertising premium item	30	50	75
Buck Rogers Sonic Ray Flashlight Gun	Norton-Honer	1955	7-1/4" black, green and yellow plastic w/code signal screw	70	125	250
Buck Rogers U-235 Atomic Pistol	Daisy	1946	9-1/2" long, pressed steel, makes pop noise and flash in window when trigger is pulled	105	225	400
Buck Rogers vs. The Fiend of Space Book	Whitman	1940	Big Little Book	45	70	120
Buck Rogers Wristwatch	E. Ingraham	1935		400	650	1250
Buck Rogers Wristwatch	Huckleberry Time	1970s		50	100	200
Buck Rogers XZ-31 Rocket Pistol	Daisy	1934	10-1/2" long, heavy blued metal, grip pumps the action, gun pops when trigger is pulled	135	250	500
Buck Rogers XZ-35 Space Gun	Daisy	1934	7" long, heavy blued metal ray gun, the grip pumps the action and the gun pops when trigger is pulled, single cooling fin at barrel base, also called "Wilma Gun"	105	225	400

NAME	COMPANY	YEAR	DESCRIPTION	GOOD	EX	MIB
Buck Rogers XZ-38 Disintegrator Pistol	Daisy	1936	10-1/2" long, polished copper or blued finish, four flutes on barrel, spark is produced in the window on top of the gun when the trigger is pulled	115	250	450
Buck Rogers XZ-44 Liquid Helium Water Gun	Daisy	1936	7-1/2" long, red and yellow lightning bolt design stamped metal body w/a leather bladder to hold water; a later version was available in copper finish	145	300	600
Century of Progess Medallion		1934	metal, reverse shows Buck silhouette profile	100	175	350
Century of Progress Button		1934	pinback, I Saw Buck Rogers 25th Century Show, color litho	135	250	500
Chemistry Set	Grooper	1937	beginners	300	600	1200
Chemistry Set	Grooper	1937	advanced	300	700	1500
Chief Explorer Badge		1936	gold	150	350	750
Chief Explorer Badge		1936	red enamel	90	210	375
Chief Explorer Folder		1936		70	125	250
Clock	Huckleberry Time	1970s		30	50	80
Colorforms Set	Colorforms	1979		10	15	40
Comet Socker Paddle Ball	Lee-Tex	1935		35	75	150
Communicator Set		1970s	w/silver Twiki figure	10	15	30
Costume	Sackman Bros.	1934		850	1400	2500
Cut-Out Adventure Book		1933	Cocomalt premium	1000	3000	6000
Electric Caster Rocket	Marx	1930s		125	210	350
Flash Blast Attack Ship Rocket	Tootsietoy	1937	Flash Blast Attack Ship 4-1/2", Venus Duo-Destroyer w/two grooved wheels to run on string	90	150	250
Galactic Play Set	HG Toys	1980s		17	30	55
Helmet and Rocket Pistol Set	Einson-Freeman	1933	set of paper partial-face "helmet" mask and paper pop gun, in envelope	115	250	500
Helmet XZ-34	Daisy	1935	leather	285	475	725
Interplanetary Games Set		1934	three game boards in box: Cosmic Rocket Wars, Secrets of Atlantis, Siege of Gigantica, set	235	390	650
Interplanetary Space Fleet Model Kit		1935	six different kits, including instructions and poster, in box, each	100	165	300
Lite-Blaster Flashlight		1936		155	260	450
Martian Wars Game	TSR	1980s	role playing game	15	25	50
Official Utility Belt	Remco	1970s	in window box, w/decoder glasses, wristwatch, disk-shooting ray gun, intruder detection badge, city decoder map, secret message	20	35	75
Paint By Number Set	Craft Master	1980s		8	15	30
Pencil Box	American Pencil	1930s		75	125	250
Pendant Watch	Huckleberry Time	1970s		115	185	285
Pocket Knife	Adolph Kastor	1934	red, green, blue	450	900	2000
Pocket Watch	Huckleberry Time	1970s		90	150	250
Pocket Watch	E. Ingraham	1935	round, face shows Buck and Wilma, lightning bolt hands	450	1500	3500
Punching Bag	Morton Salt	1942	balloon w/characters	50	75	150
Puzzle	Milton Bradley	1952	space station scene, 14" x 10"	20	35	75
Puzzle	Milton Bradley	1979	two versions showing TV scenes, each	6	10	20

SPACE/SCIENCE FICTION TOYS

Battlestar Galactica Cylon Base Star Model Kit, 1979, Monogram

Buck Rogers in the 25th Century Star Fighter, 1979, Mego

BUCK ROGERS

NAME	COMPANY	YEAR	DESCRIPTION	GOOD	EX	MIB
Puzzle	Puzzle Craft	1945	Buck Rogers and His Atomic Bomber	60	100	150
Puzzle	Milton Bradley	1950		20	35	75
Repeller Ray Ring			brass w/inset green stone	200	600	1000
Rocket Rangers Iron-On Transfers		1940s	set of three	30	50	100
Rocket Rangers Membership Card				45	75	150
Rocket Ship	Marx	1934	12" tall, wind-up	250	425	650
Roller Skates	Marx	1935		1400	2350	3600
Rubber Band Gun		1930s	cut-out paper gun, on card	35	75	125
Satellite Pioneers Button		1950s	green or blue	20	35	75
Satellite Pioneers Map of Solar System		1958		20	35	75
Satellite Pioneers Membership Card		1950s		30	50	100
Satellite Pioneers Starfinder		1950s	paper	20	40	60
Saturn Ring	Post Corn Toasties	1946	red stone, glow-in-the-dark white plastic on crocodile base	300	500	850
School Bag				60	100	200
Solar Scouts Member Badge		1935	gold	60	100	160
Solar Scouts Patch	Cream of Wheat	1936	three colors	1500	5000	7000
Solar Scouts Radio Club Manual		1936		125	250	500
Space Glasses	Norton-Honer	1955		40	75	200
Space Ranger Halolight Ring	Sylvania	1953		400	800	1500
Space Ranger Kit	Sylvania	1952	11" x 15" premium, envelope w/six punch-out sheets	50	100	200
Spaceship Commander		1930s	stationary	50	100	200
Spaceship Commander Banner		1936		100	250	500
Spaceship Commander Whistling Badge		1930s		50	85	175
Strange Adventures in the Spider Ship Pop-Up Book		1935		110	200	350
Strato-Kite	Aero-Kite	1946		20	35	75
Super Foto Camera	Norton-Honer	1955		40	70	150
Super Scope Telescope	Norton-Honer	1955	9" plastic telescope	40	70	150
Superdreadnought SD51X Model Kit		1936	6-1/2" long, balsa wood, one of Interplanetary Space Fleet kit set	100	170	275
Toy Watch	GLJ Toys	1978		15	25	50
Two-Way Transceiver	DA Myco	1948		80	130	200
View-Master Set	View-Master	1979	three-reel set, in envelope or on blister card	5	8	15
Walkie Talkies	Remco	1950s		60	125	175
Wilma Deering Figure	Tootsietoy	1937	1-3/4" tall, cast, gold	70	125	185

CAPTAIN MIDNIGHT

NAME	COMPANY	YEAR	DESCRIPTION	GOOD	EX	MIB
Air Heroes Stamp Album		1930s	12 stamps	35	75	150
Captain Midnight Medal		1930s	gold medal pin w/centered wings and words "Flight Commander"; Capt. is embossed on top w/ medal dangling beneath	65	125	175
Cup	Ovaltine		plastic, 4" tall, "Ovaltine-The Heart of a Hearty Breakfast"	25	50	75

CAPTAIN MIDNIGHT

NAME	COMPANY	YEAR	DESCRIPTION	GOOD	EX	MIB
Membership Manual		1930s	Secret Squadron official code and manual guide	30	55	100
Secret Society Decoder w/key		1949		80	175	300

CAPTAIN VIDEO

NAME	COMPANY	YEAR	DESCRIPTION	GOOD	EX	MIB
Captain Video and Ranger Photo		1950s	premium	25	45	75
Captain Video Game	Milton Bradley	1952		75	125	250
Captain Video Rite-O-Lite Flashlight Gun	Power House Candy	1950s	3" long, red plastic gun w/bulb, space map, paper, directions and order form, in mailing envelope	20	50	85
Captain Video Rocket Launcher	Lido	1952		65	175	350
Comic Book, Captain Video No. 1	Fawcett	1951		100	375	1000
Flying Saucer Ring		1950s	w/two saucers and papers	500	1000	1500
Galaxy Spaceship Riding Toy		1950s		250	425	650
Interplantary Space Men Figures		1950s	in die cut box	55	90	150
Kukla, Fran and Ollie Puppet Show	Milton Bradley	1962	cardboard stage, puppets, props	50	200	375
Mysto-Coder		1950s	w/photo	65	175	375
Rite-O-Lite Flashlight Gun	Power House Candy	1950s		40	80	160
Rocket Tank	Lido	1952		55	95	145
Secret Seal Ring		1950s	w/initials CV, gold or copper	250	400	600
Space Port Play Set	Superior	1950s		250	425	650
Troop Transport Ship	Lido	1950s	in box	55	95	145

DEFENDERS OF THE EARTH

NAME	COMPANY	YEAR	DESCRIPTION	GOOD	EX	MIB
Defenders Claw Copter	Galoob	1985		11	16	25
Flash Gordon Battle Action Figure	Galoob	1985	5-1/2" tall	7	10	15
Flash Swordship	Galoob	1985		11	16	25
Garax Battle Action Figure	Galoob	1985	5-1/2" tall	11	16	25
Garax Swordship	Galoob	1985		11	16	25
Gripjaw Vehicle	Galoob	1985		11	16	25
Mongor Figure	Galoob	1985		16	23	35
Phantom Skull Copter	Galoob	1985		7	10	15
Puzzle			frame tray	9	13	20

DEFENDERS OF THE UNIVERSE

NAME	COMPANY	YEAR	DESCRIPTION	GOOD	EX	MIB
Battling Black Lion Voltron Vehicle	LJN	1986		9	13	20
Coffin of Darkness Voltron Vehicle	LJN	1986		7	10	15
Doom Blaster Voltron Vehicle	LJN	1986	mysterious flying machine	9	13	20
Doom Commander Figure	Matchbox	1985		5	7	10
Green Lion Voltron Vehicle	LJN	1986		9	13	20
Hagar Figure	Matchbox	1985		5	7	10
Hunk Figure	Matchbox	1985		5	7	10
Keith Figure	Matchbox	1985		5	7	10
King Zarkon Figure	Matchbox	1985		5	7	10

DEFENDERS OF THE UNIVERSE

NAME	COMPANY	YEAR	DESCRIPTION	GOOD	EX	MIB
Lance Figure	Matchbox	1985		5	7	10
Motorized Lion Force Voltron Vehicle Set	LJN	1986	black lion w/blazing sound	9	13	20
Pidge Figure	Matchbox	1985		5	7	10
Prince Lothar Figure	Matchbox	1985		5	7	10
Princess Allura Figure	Matchbox	1985		5	7	10
Robeast Mutilor Figure	Matchbox	1985		5	7	10
Robeast Scorpious Figure	Matchbox	1985		5	7	10
Skull Tank Voltron Vehicle	LJN	1986		9	13	20
Vehicle Team Assembler	LJN	1986	forms Voltron	9	13	20
Voltron Lion Force & Vehicle Team Assemblers Gift Set	LJN	1986		9	13	20
Voltron Motorized Giant Commander	LJN	1984	plastic 36", multicolor body w/ movable head, arms and wings, wire remote control, battery operated	15	25	35
Zarkon Zapper Voltron Vehicle	LJN	1986	w/galactic sound	11	16	25

DOCTOR WHO

NAME	COMPANY	YEAR	DESCRIPTION	GOOD	EX	MIB
Ace Figure	Dapol	1986		11	16	25
Anniversary Set	Dapol	1986	Doctor Who, Melanie, K-9, Tardis, base and five-sided console	275	390	600
Cyberman	Dapol	1986		11	16	25
Cyberman Robot Doll	Denys Fisher	1970s	10"	250	350	550
Dalek Army Gift Set	Dapol	1976	seven color varieties of Dapol Dalek plus Dalek Leader, Davros	46	60	95
Dalek Bagatelle	Denys Fisher	1976		70	100	150
Dalek Shooting Game	Marx	1965	8" x 20", four-color tin litho stand up target and generic cork rifle	225	325	500
Dalek's Oracle Question & Answer Board Game		1965	magnetized Dalek that spins	115	165	250
Davros Figure	Dapol	1986	villain w/left arm	11	16	40
Doctor Who Card Set	Denys Fisher	1976	24 cards	18	26	40
Doctor Who Card Set		1970s	12 octagon cards	14	20	30
Doctor Who Doll	Denys Fisher	1976	10" tall w/scarf and screwdriver	90	130	200
Doctor Who Tardis Play Set	Denys Fisher	1970s		205	295	450
Doctor Who Trump Card Game		1970s		9	13	20
Doctor Who...Dodge the Daleks Board Game		1965		115	165	250
Ice Warrior	Dapol	1986		9	13	20
K-9 Figure	Dapol	1986	the Doctor's dog	7	10	15
Mel Figure	Dapol	1976	pink or blue jacket	9	13	20
Seventh Doctor Figure	Dapol	1976	gray or brown jacket	9	13	20
Tardis Figure	Denys Fisher	1976	the Doctor's transporter	225	325	500

FLASH GORDON

NAME	COMPANY	YEAR	DESCRIPTION	GOOD	EX	MIB
Adventure on the Moons of Mongo Game	House of Games	1977		15	25	35
Arak Figure	Mattel	1979	3-3/4", carded	17	30	45
Battle Rocket with Space Probing Action		1976		6	10	15
Beastman Figure	Mattel	1979	3-3/4", carded	15	25	40
Book Bag		1950s	12" wide, three-color art on flap	17	30	45

SPACE/SCIENCE FICTION TOYS

Doctor Who Cyberman, 1986, Dapol

Doctor Who...Dodge the Daleks Board Game, 1965

NAME	COMPANY	YEAR	DESCRIPTION	GOOD	EX	MIB
Candy Box		1970s	eight illustrated boxes, each	4	7	10
Captain Action Outfit	Ideal	1967	all accessories and videomatic ring	185	310	475
Captain Action Outfit	Ideal	1966	w/space suit, helmet, mask, belt w/ray gun, air tank, boots	165	275	425
Dr. Zarkov Figure	Mattel	1979	3-3/4" figure, on card	15	25	40
Flash and Ming Button		1970s	shows Flash and Ming crossing swords	4	7	10
Flash Figure	Galoob	1986	Defenders of the Earth series	6	10	15
Flash Figure	Mattel	1979	3-3/4" figure, on card	10	16	25
Flash Gordon Air Ray Gun	Budson	1950s	10" unusual air blaster, handle on top cocks mechanism, pressed steel	215	350	550
Flash Gordon and Alien Model Kit	Revell	1965	#1450	60	100	150
Flash Gordon and the Ape Men of Mor Book	Dell	1942	196 pages, Fast Action Story	70	115	175
Flash Gordon and the Fiery Desert of Mongo Book	Whitman	1948	Big Little Book	30	50	80
Flash Gordon and the Monsters of Mongo Book	Whitman	1935	hardback Big Little Book	50	80	125
Flash Gordon and the Perils of Mongo Book	Whitman	1940	Big Little Book	35	60	90
Flash Gordon and the Power Men of Mongo Book	Whitman	1943	Big Little Book	35	55	85
Flash Gordon and the Red Sword Invaders Book	Whitman	1945	Big Little Book	30	50	80
Flash Gordon and the Tournaments of Mongo Book	Whitman	1935	paperback Big Little Book	45	70	110
Flash Gordon and the Tyrant of Mongo Book	Whitman	1941	Big Little Book, w/flip pictures	35	60	95
Flash Gordon and the Witch Queen of Mongo Book	Whitman	1936	Big Little Book	45	70	110
Flash Gordon Arresting Ray Gun	Marx	1939	picture of Flash on handle, 12" long	175	295	450
Flash Gordon Costume	Esquire Novelty	1951		90	145	225
Flash Gordon Figure		1944	wood composition, 5" tall	115	195	300
Flash Gordon Game	House of Games	1970s		15	25	35
Flash Gordon Hand Puppet		1950s	rubber head	90	145	225
Flash Gordon in the Forest Kingdom of Mongo Book	Whitman	1938	Big Little Book	40	65	100
Flash Gordon in the Ice World of Mongo Book	Whitman	1942	Big Little Book, w/flip pictures	35	60	90
Flash Gordon in the Jungles of Mongo Book	Whitman	1947	Big Little Book	35	55	85
Flash Gordon in the Water World of Mongo Book	Whitman	1937	Big Little Book	35	60	95
Flash Gordon Kite		1950s	21" x 17", paper	55	90	135
Flash Gordon on the Planet Mongo Book	Whitman	1934	Big Little Book	55	95	145
Flash Gordon Paint Book		1930s		60	100	150
Flash Gordon Radio Repeater Clicker Pistol	Marx		10" long, 1930s	175	500	1000

SPACE/SCIENCE FICTION TOYS

FLASH GORDON

NAME	COMPANY	YEAR	DESCRIPTION	GOOD	EX	MIB
Flash Gordon Signal Pistol	Marx	1930s	7", siren sounds when trigger is pulled, tin/pressed steel, green w/red trim	195	430	850
Flash Gordon Space Water Gun	Nasta	1976	water ray gun on illustrated card	6	15	30
Flash Gordon Three Color Ray Gun	Nasta	1976	battery-operated	8	25	50
Flash Gordon vs. the Emperor of Mongo Book	Dell	1936	244 pages, Fast Action Story	70	115	175
Flash Gordon Water Pistol	Marx	1940s	plastic w/whistle in handle, 7-1/2" long	80	200	400
Flash Gordon Wristwatch	Bradley	1979	medium chrome case, back and sweep seconds, Flash in foreground w/city behind	70	115	175
Flash Gordon, The Movie Buttons		1980	set of five, each	2	3	5
Home Foundry Casting Set		1935	lead casting set w/molds of Flash and other characters	575	975	1500
Lizard Woman Figure	Mattel	1979	3-3/4", carded	15	25	35
Medals and Insignia	Larami	1978	set of five on blister card	3	5	8
Ming Figure	Mattel	1979	3-3/4", carded	12	20	30
Ming's Space Shuttle	Mattel			15	25	35
Pencil Box		1951		70	120	185
Puzzle	Milton Bradley	1951	frame tray	45	80	120
Puzzle		1930s	Featured Funnies	55	95	145
Puzzles	Milton Bradley	1951	set of three	105	180	275
Rocket Fighter	Marx	1939	tin wind-up, 12" long	175	295	450
Rocket Ship	Mattel	1979	inflatable, 3' long, w/plastic nose, rocket and gondola attachments	20	35	50
Rocket Ship		1975	3" die cast metal	10	16	25
Solar Commando Set	Premier Products	1950s		65	105	165
Space Compass		1950s	ornately housed compass on illustrated watchband	25	40	65
Space Water Gun	Nasta	1976	water ray gun on illustrated card	6	10	15
Sunglasses	Ja-Ru	1981	plastic w/emblem on bridge, carded	3	5	8
Three-Color Ray Gun	Nasta	1976		8	13	20
Thun, Lion Man Figure	Mattel	1979	3-3/4", carded	15	25	40
Two-Way Telephone	Marx	1940s		60	100	175
View-Master Set	View-Master	1963	three reels in envelope	20	35	50
View-Master Set	View-Master	1976	three reels, In the Planet Mongo	6	10	15
Vultan Figure	Mattel	1979	3-3/4", carded	15	30	45
Wallet		1949	w/zipper	70	115	175
Water Pistol	Marx	1950s	7-1/2" plastic	155	260	425

LAND OF THE GIANTS

NAME	COMPANY	YEAR	DESCRIPTION	GOOD	EX	MIB
Annual Book	World Dist./ UK	1969	two volumes, set	30	50	75
Colored Pencil Set	Hasbro	1969		60	100	150
Colorforms Set	Colorforms	1968		30	50	75
Costumes	Ben Cooper	1968	Steve Burton, Giant Witch, or Scientist, each	35	60	150
Double Action Bagatelle Game	Hasbro	1969	pinball game, cardboard back	35	65	150
Flight of Fear Book	Whitman		hardcover	8	15	25
Flying Saucer	Remco	1968	flying disk	60	100	150
Land of the Giants Book	Pyramid		paperback by Murray Leinster	8	13	20
Land of the Giants Coloring Book	Whitman	1968		20	35	50

LAND OF THE GIANTS

NAME	COMPANY	YEAR	DESCRIPTION	GOOD	EX	MIB
Land of the Giants Comic Book #1	Gold Key	1968		10	15	25
Land of the Giants Comic Books #2-#5	Gold Key	1968	each	8	13	20
Motorized Flying Rocket	Remco	1968	plastic airplane w/motor, LOTG logo on wings	80	130	200
Movie Viewer	Acme	1968	film strip viewer, on card	30	45	70
Painting Set	Hasbro	1969		40	65	100
Puzzle	Whitman	1968	round floor puzzle w/cartoon illustration	35	55	85
Rub-Ons	Hasbro	1969		30	50	75
Shoot & Stick Target Rifle Set	Remco	1968	western rifle w/logo decals	90	145	225
Signal Ray Space Gun	Remco	1968	ray gun w/logo decals	70	115	175
Space Sled	Remco	1968	Supercar refitted w/LOTG decals--Mike Mercury still sits behind the wheel	195	325	500
Spaceship Control Panel	Remco	1968	Firebird 99 dashboard w/a cardboard cut-out of logo on top	195	325	500
Spindrift Interior Model Kit	Lunar Models	1989	#Sf029, interior for 16" model shell	35	55	85
Spindrift Model Kit	Aurora	1968	box shows model under a branch w/logo on the side	275	450	700
Spindrift Model Kit	Aurora	1975	reissue, box shows ship in space and features the words Rocket Transport	115	195	300
Spindrift Toothpick Kit	Remco	1968	box of toothpicks w/a few cardboard pieces to build ship	30	50	80
Target Set	Hasbro	1969	small guns w/darts	60	100	150
The Hot Spot Book	Pyramid		paperback, #2 in series, by Leinster	12	20	30
Trading Card Wrapper	Topps/A & BC	1968		60	100	150
Trading Cards	Topps USA	1968	55 cards	275	450	700
Trading Cards	A & BC/ England	1968	55 cards	275	450	700
Trading Cards Box	Topps/A & BC	1968	display box only	395	650	1000
Unknown Danger Book	Pyramid		paperback #3 by Leinster	12	20	30
View-Master Set	GAF	1968	three reels, first episode	20	35	50
Walkie Talkies	Remco	1968	generic walkie talkies w/LOTG decals added	80	130	200
Wrist Flashlight	Bantam Lite	1968		30	50	75

LOST IN SPACE

NAME	COMPANY	YEAR	DESCRIPTION	GOOD	EX	MIB
3-D Fun Set	Remco	1966	three levels w/small cardboard figures	500	775	1200
Chariot Model Kit	Marusan/ Japanese		figures and motor	625	975	1500
Chariot Model Kit	Lunar Models	1987	#SF009, 1/35 scale, w/clear vacuform canopy and dome, plastic body, treads, roof rack	35	50	80
Costume	Ben Cooper	1965	silver spacesuit w/logo	85	130	200
Diorama Model Kit	Aurora	1966	figures, Cyclops, mountain and boulders	150	300	1000
Doll Set	Marusan/ Japanese		dressed in spacesuits w/their own freezing tubes w/a cardboard insert w/color photos and description	2900	4500	7000
Fan Cards		1960s	promo cards mailed to fans; color photo	20	35	50
Fan Cards		1960s	promo cards mailed to fans; black/ white photo	15	25	35

Land of the Giants Colored Pencil Set, 1969, Hasbro

Land of the Giants Spindrift Toothpick Kit, 1968, Remco

LOST IN SPACE

NAME	COMPANY	YEAR	DESCRIPTION	GOOD	EX	MIB
Helmet and Gun Set	Remco	1967	child size helmet w/blue flashing light and logo decals, blue/red molded gun	325	525	800
Jupiter Model Kit	Marusan/ Japanese	1966	large version	425	650	1000
Jupiter-2 Model Kit	Comet/ England		2" diameter, solid metal	8	13	20
Jupiter-2 Model Kit	Marusan/ Japanese	1966	6" molded in green plstic w/wheels and wind-up motor	425	650	1000
Laser Water Pistol			5" long, first season pistol style	30	50	75
Lost In Space Helmet and Gun Set	Remco	1967	child size helmet w/blue flashing light and logo decals, blue and red molded gun	310	525	850
Lost In Space Laser Water Pistol	Unknown		5" long, first season pistol style	30	50	75
Lost In Space Roto-Jet Gun Set	Mattel	1966	TV tie-in, modular gun can be reconfigured into different variations, shoots discs	775	1300	2500
Lost In Space Saucer Gun	Ahi	1977	disk shooting gun	30	50	100
Note Pad			June Lockhart on front	25	40	65
Puzzles	Milton Bradley	1966	frame tray; three poses w/Cyclops	40	65	100
Robot	Aurora	1968	6" high w/base	150	300	1000
Robot	Remco	1966	12" high, motorized w/blinking lights	175	300	600
Robot	K-mart/Ahi	1977	10", plastic w/green dome, battery-operated	85	185	295
Robot YM-3	Masudaya	1985	4" high, wind-up	20	30	45
Robot YM-3	Masudaya	1986	16" high, speaks English and Japanese	85	130	200
Roto-Jet Gun Set	Mattel	1966	gun can be turned into different variations of weapons that shot off small round discs	750	1500	6000
Saucer Gun	AHI	1977	toy gun w/discs to shoot	30	50	75
Space Family Robinson Comic Book	Gold Key	1960s		15	25	40
Switch-and-Go Set	Mattel	1966	figures, Jupiter and chariot that ran around track	975	1500	2300
Trading Cards	Topps	1966	55 black and white cards, no wrappers or box	175	260	400
Tru-Vue Magic Eyes Set	GAF	1967	rectangular reels	30	50	75
View-Master Set	GAF	1967	Condemned of Space	25	40	60
Walkie Talkies	AHI	1977	small card	30	50	75

MISCELLANEOUS

NAME	COMPANY	YEAR	DESCRIPTION	GOOD	EX	MIB
Astro Base	Ideal	1960	22" tall, red/white astronaut base, control panel opens lock door, extends crane and lowers astronaut in scout car	225	325	500
Astro Boy Mask/ Glasses		1960s	blue glasses w/Astro boy hair on top	20	45	65
Astronaut Costume	Collegeville	1960		18	25	40
Astronaut Costume	Ben Cooper	1962		18	25	40
Astronaut Space Commander Play Suit	Yankeeboy	1950s	green outfit and cap (military style) w/gold piping on collar and pants	35	50	80
Fireball XL-5 Space City Play Set	MPC	1963	includes ship, base and figures	500	1000	2000
Fireball XL-5 Spaceship	MPC	1963	plastic, 20" ship w/figures	200	450	1200
Martian Bobbing Head		1960s	7" tall, blue vinyl martian w/ bobbing eyes and exposed brain	23	35	50
Men into Space Astronaut Space Helmet	Ideal	1960s	plastic helmet w/visor	35	50	75

MISCELLANEOUS

NAME	COMPANY	YEAR	DESCRIPTION	GOOD	EX	MIB
Puzzle	Selchow & Righter	1970	10" x 14", picture of the moon's surface	14	20	30
Rex Mars Atomix Pistol Flashlight	Marx	1950s	plastic	50	75	100
Space Safari Planetary Play Set		1969	four battery operated space vehicles, 3" tall astronaut figures in silver plastic, 2" hard plastic aliens	45	65	95
TV Space Riders Coloring Book	Abbott	1952	14" X 15"	7	10	15
V-Enemy Visitor Doll	LJN	1984	12"	16	23	35
Voyage to the Bottom of the Sea Scout Play Set	Remco	1964	includes mini-sub, sea crawler and divers	250	600	1250
Voyage to the Bottom of the Sea Seaview Play Set	Remco	1964	includes plastic sub, sea monster and divers	300	650	1500

MONSTERS

NAME	COMPANY	YEAR	DESCRIPTION	GOOD	EX	MIB
Creature from the Black Lagoon Aquarium Figure	Japan	1950s	3 1/2" Lead figure	85	150	n/a
Creature from the Black Lagoon Aquarium Figure	Penn-Plax	1971	6" Moving Figure	150	250	450
Creature from the Black Lagoon Figure	AHI	1973, 74	5", hard rubber like bendy	40	65	100
Creature from the Black Lagoon Figure	Marx	1963	5", hard plastic blue or orange	10	20	35
Creature from the Black Lagoon Figure	Remco	1980	8", official Universal Studios figure	90	130	200
Creature from the Black Lagoon Figure	AHI	1974	8", plastic, bendable joints	295	425	700
Creature from the Black Lagoon Halloween Costume	Ben Cooper	1973	Child's Mask and Costume	35	70	100
Creature from the Black Lagoon Motionette	Telco	1992	24", Electric, w/sound	100	200	350
Creature from the Black Lagoon Motionette	Telco	1992	17", Batt op, w/sound	10	15	25
Creature from the Black Lagoon Robot	Robot House	1991	9", tin/plastic, w/u	35	65	110
Creature from the Black Lagoon Soaky	Colgate-Palmolive	1960s	10", plastic, bubble bath bottle	45	85	125
Creature from the Black Lagoon Sparky	Hong Kong	1970s	3 1/2", plastic, w/u	10	20	35
Creature from the Black Lagoon Wiggle Ick Figure	Japan	1960s	7", rubbery plastic, bobbin' head	50	85	150
Creature from the Lagoon Glow-in-the-Dark Mini Monsters	Remco	1980	3 3/4", action fig	8	15	30
Creature from the Lagoon Mini Monsters	Remco	1980	3 3/4", action fig	10	20	40
Deadly Grell Figure	LJN	1983	bendable	5	7	10
Dracula Action Figure	AHI		w/Aurora head	65	125	200
Dracula Figure	Remco	1980	8", official Universal Studios figure	30	45	70
Dracula Glow-in-the-Dark Mini Monsters	Remco			23	30	45
Dwarves of the Mountain Human/Monster Figure	LJN	1983		5	7	10
Evil Monster Figure Bugbear & Goblin	LJN	1983	Orcs of the Broken Bone	5	7	10

MONSTERS

NAME	COMPANY	YEAR	DESCRIPTION	GOOD	EX	MIB
Frankenstein Figure	Remco	1978	poseable, glow-in-the-dark features and removable cloth costumes	23	35	50
Frankenstein Figure	Remco	1980	8", official Universal Studios figure	27	40	60
Frankenstein Figure	AHI		w/Aurora head	65	125	200
Frankenstein Glow-in-the-Dark Mini Monsters	Remco			20	30	45
Godzilla Combat Joe Set		1984	vinyl, w/12" tall combat Joe figure, poseable	450	650	1000
Godzilla Figure	Imperial	1985	6-1/2" tall, arms, legs and tail movable	5	10	15
Godzilla Figure	Imperial	1985	13" tall, arms, legs and tail movable	15	23	35
Godzilla Figure	Mattel	1977	19" tall	20	30	55

MOON MCDARE

NAME	COMPANY	YEAR	DESCRIPTION	GOOD	EX	MIB
Action Communication Set	Gilbert	1966		25	35	55
Moon Explorer Set	Gilbert	1966		35	50	75
Moon McDare Figure	Gilbert	1966	12" tall astronaut w/blue jumpsuit	55	80	125
Moon McDare Space Gun Set	Gilbert	1966		25	50	100
Space Accessory Pack	Gilbert	1966		25	35	55
Space Gun Set	Gilbert	1966		30	40	65
Space Mutt Set	Gilbert	1966		30	45	70

OTHER WORLDS, THE

NAME	COMPANY	YEAR	DESCRIPTION	GOOD	EX	MIB
Castle Zendo	Arco	1983		20	30	45
Fighting Glowgons Figure Set	Arco	1983		18	25	40
Fighting Terrans Figure Set	Arco	1983		20	30	45
Kamaro Figure	Arco	1983		8	12	18
Sharkoss Figure	Arco	1983		8	12	18

PLANET OF THE APES

NAME	COMPANY	YEAR	DESCRIPTION	GOOD	EX	MIB
Color-Vue Set	Hasbro	1970s	eight pencils and nine 12" x 13" pictures to color	30	45	65
Dr. Zaius Bank	Play Pal	1967	figural, vinyl, 11"	20	25	45
Fun-Doh Modeling Molds	Chemtoy	1974	molds of Zira, Cornelius, Zaius, and Aldo	20	30	45
Galen Bank	Play Pal	1960s		25	35	55
Planet of the Apes Activity Book	Saalfield	1974	#C3031	15	30	40
Planet of the Apes Coloring Book	Saalfield	1974	#C1531	15	30	40
Planet of the Apes Coloring Book	Artcraft	1974	#C1837	15	30	40
Puzzles	H.G. Toys		96-piece canister puzzles, each	7	10	20
View-Master Set	GAF	1967	#B507, three reels	10	25	40
Wagon	AHI		friction powered prison wagon	20	45	65
Wastebasket	Chein	1967	oval, tin	25	35	60
Zaius, Zera, or Cornelius W/U Walkers	Hong Kong	1970s	3 1/2" plastic, windups	20	40	75

SPACE/SCIENCE FICTION TOYS

Lost in Space 3-D Fun Set, 1966, Remco

Lost in Space Robot, 1966, Remco

ROCKY JONES, SPACE RANGER

NAME	COMPANY	YEAR	DESCRIPTION	GOOD	EX	MIB
Rocky Jones, Space Ranger Coloring Book	Whitman	1951	14" x 16"	25	40	60
Space Ranger Button		1954		17	30	45
Wings Pin		1954		17	30	45
Wristwatch		1954	in illustrated box	80	130	200

SPACE GUNS

NAME	COMPANY	YEAR	DESCRIPTION	GOOD	EX	MIB
4-Barrel Waist Space Dart Gun Belt	Knickerbocker	1950s	11" wide gun system on belt, designed to be worn on waist or chest and aimed w/periscope sight, red plastic belt	30	50	75
888 Space Gun	Japan	1955	3" long, tin, shoots caps, painted blue body and grip w/stars, planets and spaceship, red barrel w/"888" above grip	30	50	100
Astro Ray Gun	Shudo/Japan	1968	9" long, friction spark action, tin litho body w/clear red plastic barrel, red on yellow "ASTRO RAY GUN" lettering	25	40	65
Astro Ray Gun	Shudo/Japan	1960s	5-7/8" long, silver finish body w/ red, yellow and black detailing, friction sparkling action, single large spark window near muzzle, prominent "Astro Ray Gun" in center of body	15	30	45
Astro Ray Laser Lite Beam Dart Gun	Ohio Art	1960s	10" red and white plastic flashlight lights target w/four darts	70	115	175
Astro-Ray Space Gun			10"	20	30	45
Atom Bubble Gun	Unknown	1940s	red tubular barrel w/handle attached, two sets of silver finish fins--at barrel base and muzzle, wire loop projects from muzzle for bubble blowing, handle embossed "Atom Trade Mark"	75	130	200
Atom Buster Mystery Gun	Webb Electric	1950s	11" long yellow plastic gun w/inner bladder, fires blast of air at tissue paper atomic mushroom target, w/instructions, atomic explosion cover art on box	105	180	275
Atom Ray Gun	Hiller	1949	5-1/2" long, sleek red body gun of aluminum and brass w/bulbous water reservoir on top of gun, reads "Atom Ray Gun" between two lightning bolts on reservoir	135	250	400
Atomee Water Pistol	Park Plastics	1960s	4-1/4" black plastic	15	25	35
Atomic Disintegrator Ray Gun	Hubley	1954	8" long, die-cast metal w/red handles, ornately embellished w/ dials and other equipment outcroppings, shoots caps	150	300	650
Atomic Flash Gun	Chein	1955	7-1/2" long, tin, sparkling action seen through tinted elongated oval plastic muzzle, w/yellow and red on turquoise body w/red lettered "Atomic Flash" over trigger	40	65	125
Atomic Gun	Haji	1969	9" long, red, gray and yellow tin litho gun w/plastic muzzle, friction sparkling action, large hollow letter "ATOMIC GUN" on body	15	30	60
Atomic Gun	Japan	1960s	5" long, gold, blue, white and red tin litho, friction sparkling action, "Atomic Gun" on body sides	20	35	65
Atomic Jet Gun	Stevens	1954	8-1/2" long, gold chromed die-cast metal, cap shooting, "Atomic Jet" and large circular "S" logo on grip	90	145	250

SPACE/SCIENCE FICTION TOYS

NAME	COMPANY	YEAR	DESCRIPTION	GOOD	EX	MIB
Atomic Ray Gun	Marx	1957	30" long, "Captain Space Solar Scout," blue plastic w/oversized telescope sight flashlight and "electric buzzer" sound	75	130	250
Baby Space Gun	Daiya/Japan	1950s	6" friction siren and spark action	35	60	125
Batman Ray Gun	Unknown	1960s	cap pistol w/bat symbol for the sight	35	55	125
Battlestar Galactica Lasermatic Pistol	Mattel	1978		15	30	50
Battlestar Galactica Lasermatic Rifle	Mattel	1978		25	40	75
Bee-Vo Bell Gun	Beaver Toys	1950s	#204, 6-1/2" long, red plastic, fires trapped marble at bell in muzzle, in box	25	40	75
Bicycle Water Cannon Ray Gun	Unknown	1950s	10", red plastic, swivel mount attached to bicycle handles, fired by lever	30	75	125
Cherilea Space Gun	Marx		miniature scale, die cast	27	40	60
Clicker Ray Gun	Irwin	1960	9" long, red plastic w/deep blue cooling fins on barrel base	30	45	70
Clicker Ray Gun	Unknown	1950s	5" red, blue or gray hard plastic, no boxes, sold loose	15	25	35
Clicker Whistle Ray Gun	Unknown	1950s	5" plastic, blue/green or olive/green swirl plastic, imprinted spacemen and rocket ships, back of gun is a whistle	15	25	35
Daisy Rocket Dart Pistol	Daisy	1954	7" long, red, blue and yellow sheet metal gun w/blue body, blue grips w/yellow trim, blue and yellow barrel stripes, same body as Zooka Pop Pistol but w/connecting rod from gun to barrel	60	150	275
Daisy Zooka Pop Pistol	Daisy	1954	7" long, colorful red, blue and yellow sheet metal gun w/blue body, red grips w/yellow trim and litho star reading "It's a Daisy Play Gun," yellow barrel w/red stripes, and wide red muzzle, handle cock	80	150	275
Dan Dare & the Aliens Ray Gun		1950s	21", tin litho gun	105	155	235
Dune Fremen Tarpel Gun	LJN	1984	8" long, battery-operated w/internal light, light beam and chirping sound, plastic	25	40	65
Dune Sardaukar Laser Gun	LJN	1984	7" black plastic w/flashing lights, battery-operated	20	35	50
Flash-O-Matic, The Safe Gun	Royal Plastics	1950s	7" long red and yellow plastic battery-operated light beam gun	60	100	150
Floating Satellite Target Game	S. Horikawa/Japan	1958	6-1/2" x 9", includes a pistol and three rubber tipped darts, a blower supports the styrofoam ball on a column of air and the players shoot darts to knock it down	175	295	450
Ideal Flash Gun	Ideal	1957	9" long, plastic three-color flashlight gun w/red or blue body and bulbous contrasting-color blue or red rimmed flash unit, trigger switch and tail battery compartment cover, w/color switch at top of flash unit	80	130	200
Jack Dan Space Gun	Metamol/Spain	1959	7-1/2" long, in black, red or blue painted die-cast metal cap gun w/"Jack Dan" over trigger	105	180	275

NAME	COMPANY	YEAR	DESCRIPTION	GOOD	EX	MIB
Jet Gun	Japan	1957	6" long, tin, sparkling action, red body w/three small red tinted spark windows near muzzle, grip shows silver-suited astronaut in modern helmet and wording "JET GUN" at top of grip near trigger	35	60	120
Jet Jr. Cap Gun	Stevens	1950s	6-1/2" long, fires roll caps, side loading door, silver finish, rear jet "Blast Off Fins"	135	225	350
Jet Plane Missile Gun	Hasbro	1968	jet shaped handgun shoots darts, targets supplied on box back	35	60	95
Jupiter 4 Color Signal Gun	Remco	1950s	9" long black, red and yellow plastic gun that lights up in four colors, red telescoping sight	35	55	85
Over and Under Ray Gun	Haji	1960s	8-1/2" long, red, yellow, white and black tin litho gun w/two over and under reciprocating plastic muzzles, friction sparkling action	30	50	75
Planet Clicker Bubble Gun	Mercury Toys	1953	8" long, plastic, red body w/yellow accents, dip the barrel in bubble solution and pull trigger to make bubbles and produce click sound, in illustrated box	40	65	100
Planet Patrol Saucer Gun	Unknown	1950s	w/spaceman motif	40	65	100
Pop Gun	Chemtoy	1967	4-1/2" long red hard plastic gun w/ space designs on handle	25	35	75
Pop Ray Gun	Wyandotte	1930s	red pressed steel body w/five widely spaced vertical round fins, unpainted trigger and muzzle w/ large gunsight, rod connects body to pop mechanism in muzzle	70	115	175
Radar Gun	Unknown	1956	5-1/2" long, mauve or silver/gray swirl plastic body w/green or yellow spaceman sight and trigger, Saturn and star embossed above grip and "Radar Gun" embossed above that	20	35	55
Ratchet Sound Space Gun	Ideal	1950s	7" long, red plastic w/silver trim, flywheel ratchet on top of gun	30	50	75
Ratchet Water Pistol Ray Gun	Hong Kong	1960s	6-1/2" unusual pull back mechanism loads pistol, ratchet forces water out when trigger is pulled	25	40	65
Ray Dart Gun	Tarrson	1968	9-1/2" long, blue plastic body w/ yellow muzzle, w/three darts, storage compartment in red handle base	15	25	50
Ray Gun	Wyandotte	1936	7" stamped metal pop gun that uses a captive cork to make the pop, red body, unpainted muzzle, w/connecting rod from body to barrel tip	35	75	150
Ray Gun	Japan	1957	6-1/2" long, tin, sparkling action w/ two red tinted plastic tapered rectangle windows at muzzle, "Ray Gun" in red at top of body w/ rocket exhaust encircling green/ blue planet against deep blue star studded background	30	50	120
Ray Gun Water Pistol	Palmer Plastics	1950s	5-1/2" many color variations: green, orange, translucent blue, royal blue, black, yellow and red	10	15	20
Ray Gun Water Pistols	Palmer Plastics	1950s	5-1/2" many color variations green, orange, translucent blue, royal blue, black, yellow and red	8	13	20

SPACE/SCIENCE FICTION TOYS

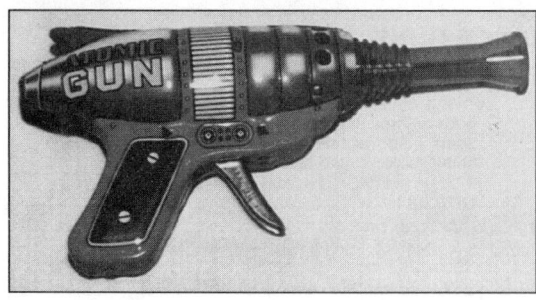

Atomic Gun, 1969, Haji

Daisy Zooka Pop Pistol, 1954, Daisy

Jupiter 4 Color Signal Gun, 1950s, Remco

SPACE GUNS

NAME	COMPANY	YEAR	DESCRIPTION	GOOD	EX	MIB
Razer Ray Gun	H.Y. Mfg./ Hong Kong	1972	plastic bronze finish body w/five large cooling fins near red plastic barrel, friction sparkling action, chrome finish muzzle tip, "Razer Ray Gun" embossed on rear of barrel	10	15	25
Rex Mars Planet Patrol 45 Caliber Machine Gun	Marx	1950s	22" long, tin and plastic, wind-up	60	100	250
Ro-Gun "It's A Robot"	Arco	1984	Shogun-type robot transforms into a rifle, in window box	8	13	20
Robot Raiders Space Signal Gun	TNT/Hong Kong	1980s	6" long flashlight gun w/ interchangeable lenses and click sound	6	10	15
Robotech Water Pistol	Matchbox	1985		6	10	15
Rocket Gun	Jak-Pak	1958	7" hard yellow/green plastic w/ spring loaded plunger that shoots corks up to 50 feet	9	13	20
Rocket Jet Water Pistol	U.S. Plastics	1957	5" long, red, orange or yellow clear plastic body, fill plug at top of gun, large integral gunsight fin at rear, small sight fin at front	12	20	50
Rocket Pop Gun	Unknown	1955	wood, green and red horizontal striped body w/black tri-fin pump base, cork and string stopper in nose, pump fins into body to make it pop	25	40	65
Rocket Signal Pistol	Marx	1930s	same bulbous teardrop metal body as Flash Gordon Signal Pistol and Siren sparkling Airplane Pistol but without siren hole or wings; same rear fin, red w/litho of three horizontally stacked finned orange/yellow bombs	135	250	500
S-58 Space Gun	Japan	1957	12" long, tin litho, deep metallic blue body w/friction sparkling action, "S-58" on muzzle, w/ ringed planet graphic on front sight	35	55	120
Satellite & Rocket Pistol	Hong Kong	1960s	5" long, green plastic gun fires either yellow plastic darts or saucers, on card	12	20	50
Secret Squirrel Ray Gun	Unknown	1960s		25	40	75
Signal Flash Gun	Unknown	1957	6" long, plastic flashlight, black body w/translucent white plastic light housing at muzzle and pearl finish plastic grip plates, modern missile type sight on top of barrel, large "SIGNAL FLASH" above trigger	20	35	65
Smoke Ring Gun	Nu-Age Products	1950s	large, sleek gray finished breakfront pistol w/red barrel and muzzle ring, used rocket shaped matches to produce smoke, trigger fired smoke rings, small engraved "Smoke Ring Gun" logo on gunsight fin	175	295	450
Space Atomic Gun	Japan	1955	5-1/2" long, tin, sparkling action seen through red tinted plastic window, two-tone blue body w/ red/white atomic symbol on grip, "Space Atomic Gun" letters around oval spaceship-and-stars logo above trigger	30	50	120

SPACE/SCIENCE FICTION TOYS

NAME	COMPANY	YEAR	DESCRIPTION	GOOD	EX	MIB
Space Atomic Gun	T/Japan	1960	4" long, tin litho, friction sparkling action, silver gray finish w/yellow and red trim, w/"SPACE" on body in white small all caps and large yellow lower caps "atomic gun", small "T/Made in JAPAN" logo above trigger	25	40	65
Space Atomic Gun	Unknown	1960s	4" silver, orange/red tin litho, sparking action	25	40	65
Space Control Ray Gun	Unknown	1956	5-1/2" long, red plastic w/yellow trigger, clicks	25	40	75
Space Control Space Gun	Nomura/ Japan	1954	3" long, tin sparkling gun w/green body, red sights, decorated all over w/stars and planets, red and yellow "Space Control" letters over trigger and spacemen firing gun and rocket flying overhead on grips	30	50	75
Space Dart Gun	Unknown	1950s	6" long, gun has one white side and one black side, both w/star and lightning motif, eight thin cooling fins on barrel	30	50	85
Space Dart Gun	Arliss	1950s	4" solid color plastic gun, shoots standard rubber tipped darts	12	20	60
Space Gun	TN/Japan	1960s	8" long, battery-operated, reciprocating barrel shaft has red and blue lenses that flash when fired, makes rat-a-tat noise, large circular "8" over handgrip, winged eagle over trigger, large block letter "SPACE GUN" on barrel	70	115	175
Space Gun	San/Japan	1955	3-1/4" long, tin, sparkling action, aqua blue body w/red and yellow highlights and "Space" in script lettering over grip, grip shows rocket shooting toward planets, circular San/Japan logo behind trigger	30	50	75
Space Gun	Yoshiya/ Japan	1957	7" long, tin w/sparkling action, shows a realistic white rocket blasting off over lunar terrain on side of body and atomic symbol on grip center w/diamond-shaped "SY" logo and "Made in Japan" at bottom of grip	40	65	100
Space Gun	Daiya/Japan	1957	6" long, tin, sparkling action, metallic teal finish w/red grooves and muzzle, green spaceship on body above "Space Gun," small Daiya logo inside red/yellow burst on grip w/"577001" at bottom of grip	35	60	125
Space Gun	Japan	1957	9" long, friction sparkling action w/ three red tinted plastic spark windows and clear red plastic barrel, body in metallic blue w/ large red "SPACE GUN" letters on yellow background	35	55	120
Space Gun	Hero Toy/ Japan	1960	7" long, tin litho, friction sparkling action, yellow body w/blue and red trim, small Hero Toy logo by trigger	35	55	85

SPACE GUNS

NAME	COMPANY	YEAR	DESCRIPTION	GOOD	EX	MIB
Space Gun	Shudo/Japan	1967	4" tin litho, friction sparkling action, red body w/blue inset and grips, yellow block letter "SPACE GUN," large yellow and white vertical painted fins, six red tinted plastic sparkling windows, oval Shudo logo by grip	20	35	65
Space Jet Gun	KO/Japan	1957	9" long, tin, sparkling action w/ black body, orange "Space Jet" on body w/orange and red atomic symbol on grip, clear green plastic finned barrel base, clear blue plastic finned muzzle	35	60	110
Space Jet Water Pistol	Knickerbocker	1957	4" long, black plastic w/white "Space Jet" lettering and spaceship line art on sides, fill plug in gunsight	15	30	60
Space Navigator Gun	Asahitoy/ Japan	1953	3-1/2" long, tin, looks like sawed off military .45, colorfully trimmed blue body w/smiling spaceman, blasting winged rocketship and "Space Navigator" logo on grips, planets and star on body	35	60	125
Space Outlaw Ray Gun	B.C.M.	1965	10" long, chrome plated, die-cast metal, recoiling barrel action, "Cosmic", "Sonic" or "Gamma" power levels, large red clear plastic teardrop shaped window	115	250	450
Space Rocket Gun	M & L Toy	1950s	9" gray plastic, modern police-style pistol grip and shell chamber body w/oversized barrel and muzzle sights, spring loaded, shoots rocket projectiles, in box w/two "rockets"	55	95	175
Space Scout Spud Gun	Mil Jo	1960s	7" black and white plastic	15	30	45
Space Ship Flashlight Gun	Irwin	1950s	7-1/4", blue plastic ray gun has cockpit w/orange spaceman, nose unscrews for AAA batteries, pulling trigger lights nose and moves guns and spaceman	60	100	150
Space Target Game	T. Cohn	1952	24" tall, metal target w/rubber tipped darts and dartgun to shoot down all the jet rockets and missiles	40	65	150
Space Water Gun	Palmer Plastics	1957	5-1/2" long, clear red plastic body w/embossed Ringed planet and star, four cooling fins at barrel base, hollow telescope sight, yellow plastic trigger, white plastic stopper attached by loop to red knob at gun back	15	30	45
Space Water Gun	Park Plastics	1960	6" long, red transparent plastic, stopper at rear of gun, finned trigger guard, zeppelin-shaped reservoir w/single embossed lightning bolt running its length, tiny "Park Plastics" imprinted along lateral reservoir fin	15	25	35
Space Water Pistol	Nasta	1976		7	10	15
Space X-Ray Gun	Lido	1970s	#46598, 8-1/2" long, plastic, friction sparkling action, same body as Razer Ray Gun but w/ more futuristic handgrip and noisemaker at rear, sold in bag w/header card	15	25	35
Sparking Atom Buster Pistol	Marx		aluminum	30	50	75
Sparking Space Gun Rifle	Marx			50	80	150

*Space Patrol Non-Fall Space Patrol X-16,
1950s, Matsudaya*

Space Patrol Rocket Lite Flashlight, 1950s, Rayovac

SPACE GUNS

NAME	COMPANY	YEAR	DESCRIPTION	GOOD	EX	MIB
Sparkling Ray Gun	Nasta	1976		6	10	15
Star Team Ionization Nebulizer	Ideal	1969	9" water gun fires water mist, red, white, blue and black plastic, Star Team decal	30	50	75
Strato Gun	Futuristic Products	1950s	9" long, gray finish die-cast, cap firing, internal hammer, top of gun lifts to load	70	115	175
Strato Gun	Futuristic Products	1950s	9" long, chrome finish die-cast, red cooling fins, cap firing, internal hammer, top of gun lifts to load	100	165	300
Super Sonic Gun	Endoh/Japan	1957	9" long, tin, sparkling action w/ three red plastic spark windows and clear red plastic barrel, blue body w/red lightning bolt beneath yellow "Super Sonic" on rounded gun body, small ENDOH logo printed above grips	40	75	150
Super Sonic Space Gun	Daiya/Japan	1957	7-1/2" long, tin litho, metallic gray body w/red gunsight fin, friction siren and sparkling action, large oval center art w/outstanding lunar scene of rockets, mountains and Earth in sky, red helmeted spaceman on grip	40	75	150
Super Space Gun	Japan	1960	6" long, tin litho, friction sparkling action, blue on blue body w/ white/yellow/red highlights, large red on white "SUPER SPACE" lettering on side	25	40	90
Superior Rocket Gun	Unknown	1956	8" long, dark gray plastic, embossed "Superior Rocket Gun" on grip	30	50	75
Tomi Space Gun	Shawnee	1950s	solid red plastic w/yellow barrel plug, modelled after modern .45 caliber pistol w/rounded reservoir lined w/two horizontal fins over grip; embossed logo and circular Shawnee logos on grip	50	80	125
Universe Gun	T/Japan	1960s	4" long, blue, yellow and red tin litho gun w/friction sparkling action, large all caps italic "Universe" on body side, sold in bag w/header card	15	25	35
Visible Sparkling Ray Gun	Hong Kong		8-1/2" long, plastic, mechanism visible, bagged w/header card	15	25	60
Wham-O Air Blaster	Wham-O	1960s	10" long plastic gun uses rubber diaphragm to shoot air; styling is reminiscent of Budson Flash Gordon Air Ray Gun	70	115	175
X100 Mystery Dart Gun	Arliss	1956	3-3/4" long, yellow or gray plastic gun on cardboard display card, w/two yellow and blue talcum impregnated darts which create a smoke effect when striking any target	25	40	75

SPACE PATROL

NAME	COMPANY	YEAR	DESCRIPTION	GOOD	EX	MIB
Atomic Pistol Flashlight Gun	Marx	1950s	plastic	85	150	250
Cosmic Cap		1950s		125	200	375
Cosmic Gun	Nomura/Japan	1970	12" long, plastic, battery-operated w/a small electric motor that runs reciprocating light in clear red plastic barrel, dark blue body, red and orange lettered "COSMIC GUN" decal	35	55	85

SPACE/SCIENCE FICTION TOYS

NAME	COMPANY	YEAR	DESCRIPTION	GOOD	EX	MIB
Cosmic Ray Gun	Ranger Steel Products	1954	9" long, tin body w/plastic barrel, boldly painted in blue, yellow and red lightning bolts	50	80	125
Cosmic Ray Gun #249	Ranger Steel Products	1953	8" long, plastic, blue body, yellow barrel, red tip, in box showing two space kids in bubble helmets and backpacks shooting at spaceships	40	65	100
Cosmic Rocket Launcher Set		1950s		300	500	800
Cosmic Smoke Gun		1950s	red	110	170	300
Cosmic Smoke Gun		1950s	green	120	325	650
Drink Mixer		1950s	boxed	60	100	200
Emergency Kit		1950s	w/rations, plastic w/yellow insert	500	1200	2000
Handbook		1950s		55	100	175
Hydrogen Ray Gun Ring		1950s	glow-in-the-dark, fires caps	75	125	250
Interplanetary Space Patrol Credits Coins			different denominations and colors: Terra, Moon and Saturn, each	10	16	30
Jet Glow Code Belt		1950s	gold-finish metal, spaceship-shaped buckle, decoder ring behind buckle	120	200	350
Lunar Fleet Base		1950s	premium punch-outs in mailing envelope	500	1700	300
Man From Mars Totem Head Mask		1950s	paper, several styles	65	105	165
Monorail Set	Toys of Tomorrow	1950s		1650	3000	4200
Non-Fall Space Patrol X-16	Matsudaya	1950s		50	150	300
Outer Space Helmet Mask		1950s	paper helmet w/plastic one-way visor	110	170	300
Project-O-Scope		1950s	rocket-shaped film viewer w/ filmstrips	175	300	750
Puzzle	Milton Bradley	1950s	frame tray	40	75	150
Rocket Gun and Holster Set		1950s	w/darts	200	300	500
Rocket Gun Set		1950s	w/darts, without holster	110	185	350
Rocket Lite Flashlight	Rayovac	1950s	in box	140	250	350
Rocket Port Set	Marx	1950s		125	200	350
Rocket-Shaped Pen		1950s		120	185	350
Space Binoculars		1950s	black plastic, logo on sides	80	125	200
Space Binoculars		1950s	green plastic, large logo on top	120	190	300
Space Holster with oval badge		1950	w/unmarked blue gun	200	400	600
Space Patrol Atomic Flashlight Pistol	Marx	1950s	gold/bronze finish pistol w/seven large cooling fins on barrel and three smaller ones at back of gun, large clear plastic diffuser on muzzle, white "Official Space Patrol" on handgrip	135	225	500
Space Patrol Badge		1950s	metal oval on card	125	350	750
Space Patrol Badge		1950s	plastic, w/ship and crest	75	125	250
Space Patrol Cadet Membership Card		1950s		25	40	150
Space Patrol Commander Helmet		1950s	plastic, in box	140	250	400
Space Patrol Cosmic Smoke Gun	Unknown	1950s	solid color red or green plastic w/ "Space Patrol" on body above grip, TV show tie-in, shoots baking powder, on card	135	275	500
Space Patrol Hydrogen Ray Gun Ring	Unknown	1950s	glow-in-the-dark ring	70	125	250
Space Patrol Periscope		1950s	paper w/mirrors	75	160	350

SPACE/SCIENCE FICTION TOYS

SPACE PATROL

NAME	COMPANY	YEAR	DESCRIPTION	GOOD	EX	MIB
Space Patrol Rocket Gun	U.S. Plastics	1954	black or red plastic pistol body w/ red trigger, grip embossed w/ vertically printed "Space Patrol" in irregular oval grip design showing rocket, stars and ringed planet, shoots rubber tipped darts	145	250	450
Space Patrol Rocket Gun and Holster Set	Unknown	1950s	w/darts	185	310	500
Space Patrol Rocket Gun Set	Unknown	1950s	w/darts, sold without holster	105	180	375
Space Patrol Wristwatch		1950s	illustrated box w/"Terra" compass	275	450	675
Space Pistol	Unknown	1954	plastic ray gun that shoots rubber tip darts	20	35	50
Space Pistol	Ranger Steel Products		large yellow and orange flint gun	40	65	100
Space Police Neutron Blaster Cap Pistol	Stevens	1949	7-3/4" die-cast, cap firing ray gun, lock mechanism pulls out through the top of the gun, silver finish	185	310	475
Space-A-Phones		1950s		175	400	600

SPACE:1999

NAME	COMPANY	YEAR	DESCRIPTION	GOOD	EX	MIB
Adventure Play Set	Amsco/Milton Bradley	1976		30	50	75
Astro Popper Gun	Larami	1976	on card	6	10	35
Colorforms Adventure Set	Colorforms	1975		10	16	25
Commander Koenig	Mattel	1976		n/a	30	60
Commander Koenig Figure	Mattel	1976		17	30	45
Cut and Color Book	Saalfield	1975		6	10	20
Dr. Russell	Mattel	1976		n/a	30	60
Dr. Russell Figure	Mattel	1976		17	30	45
Eagle Freighter	Dinky	1975	No. 360, die cast	25	50	150
Eagle One Model Kit	MPC	1976		50	80	100
Eagle One Spaceship	Mattel	1976		100	300	500
Eagle Transport	Dinky	1975	No. 359, die cast	25	50	100
Eagle Transporter Model Kit	Airfix	1976		12	20	75
Film Viewer TV Set	Larami	1976		8	20	55
Galaxy Time Meter	Larami	1976		6	10	15
Moon Base Alpha Model Kit	MPC	1976		15	30	50
Moonbase Alpha Play Set	Mattel	1976		30	50	150
Professor Bergman	Mattel	1976		n/a	30	60
Professor Bergman Figure	Mattel	1976		17	30	45
Puzzle	HG Toys	1976		6	10	25
Space Expedition Dart Set	Larami	1976	carded	6	10	15
Space:1999 Astro Popper Gun	Mattel	1976	on card	6	10	15
Space:1999 Utility Belt Set	Remco	1976	w/disc shooting stun gun, watch and compass	12	20	50
Stamping Set	Larami	1976		8	13	20
Superscope	Larami	1976		6	10	15
Talking View-Master Set	View-Master	1975	three reels	6	20	40
Utility Belt Set	Remco	1976		12	40	100
View-Master Set	View-Master	1975	three reels	10	16	25
Walking Spaceman	Azrak Hamway	1975		50	150	400
Zython Figure	Mattel	1976		40	80	150

SPACE/SCIENCE FICTION TOYS

Space:1999 Adventure Play Set, 1976, Amsco/Milton Bradley

Space:1999 Eagle One Spaceship, 1976, Mattel

SPACESHIPS

NAME	COMPANY	YEAR	DESCRIPTION	GOOD	EX	MIB
Eagle Lunar Module		1960s	9"	80	115	175
Friendship 7			9-1/2", friction	35	50	75
Inter-Planet Toy Rocketank Patrol	Macrey	1950	10"	30	45	70
Jupiter Space Station	TN/Japan	1960s	8"	90	125	195
Moon-Rider Spaceship	Marx	1930s	tin wind-up	125	200	250
Mystery Spaceship	Marx	1960s	35mm astronauts and moonmen, rockets, launchers	50	75	100
Rocket Fighter	Marx	1950s	w/tail fin and sparking action, tin wind-up	250	375	500
Rocket Fighter Spaceship	Marx	1930s	celluloid window, tin wind-up, 12" long	125	200	250
Satellite X-107	Cragstan	1965	9"	90	130	200
Sky Patrol Jet	TN/Japan	1960s	5" x 13" x 5", battery operated, working taillights	295	425	650
Solar-X Space Rocket	TN/Japan		15"	45	65	100
Space Bus			tin helicopter, battery operated w/ wired remote	350	500	750
Space Pacer		1978	7", battery operated	20	29	45
Space Survey X-09			battery operated, tin and plastic flying saucer w/clear bubble	175	350	525
Space Train		1950s	9" long, engine and three metallic cars	18	26	40
Spaceship	Marx		bronze plastic	40	60	90
Super Space Capsule		1960s	9-1/2"	70	100	150
X-3 Rocket Gyro		1950s		25	35	50

STAR TREK

NAME	COMPANY	YEAR	DESCRIPTION	GOOD	EX	MIB
Action Toy Book	Random House	1976		7	10	15
Beanbag Chair, ST:TMP				25	35	55
Bowl, ST:TMP	Deka	1979	plastic	3	4	10
Bridge Punch-Out Book, ST:TMP	Wanderer	1979		7	10	15
Bulletin Board, ST:TMP	Milton Bradley	1979	w/four pens	6	8	12
Clock		1989	Enterprise orbiting planet, rectangular	23	33	50
Clock		1986	white wall clock, red 20th anniversary logo on face, Official Star Trek Fan Club	14	20	30
Colorforms Set	Colorforms	1975		15	20	35
Comb & Brush Set		1977	6" x 3", blue, oval brush	14	20	30
Command Bridge Model Kit	AMT	1975	#S950-601	40	50	75
Communicators	Mego	1976	blue plastic walkie talkies	70	100	155
Communicators	McNerney	1989	black plastic walkie talkies	35	50	75
Communicators, ST:TMP	Mego	1980	plastic wristband walkie talkies belt pack, battery operated	90	130	200
Controlled Space Flight	Remco	1976	plastic Enterprise, battery operated	80	115	200
Digital Travel Alarm	Lincoln Enterprises			15	20	30
Dinnerware Set, ST:TMP	Deka	1979	plate, bowl, glass and cup	15	25	35
Enterprise Make-A-Model, ST:TNG	Chatham River Press	1990		4	5	8
Enterprise Model Kit	AMT	1966	#S921-200, 15" x 10" box, lights	200	350	500
Enterprise Model Kit	Mego/Grand Toys	1980	#91232/B, Canadian issue, ST:TMP	90	100	130
Enterprise Punch-Out Book, ST:TMP	Wanderer	1979		9	13	20

SPACE/SCIENCE FICTION TOYS

SPACE/SCIENCE FICTION TOYS

NAME	COMPANY	YEAR	DESCRIPTION	GOOD	EX	MIB
Enterprise Wristwatch, ST:TMP	Rarities Mint	1989	gold-plated silver	55	80	125
Enterprise Wristwatch, ST:TMP	Bradley			20	30	45
Enterprise, ST:III	Ertl	1984	4" long, die cast w/black plastic stand	10	12	25
Enterprise, ST:IV	Sterling	1986	24", silver plastic, inflatable	20	30	45
Enterprise, ST:TMP	South Bend	1979	20" long, white plastic, battery powered lights and sound w/ stand	80	115	175
Excelsior, ST:III	Ertl	1984	4" long, die cast w/black plastic stand	7	10	25
Ferengi Costume, ST:TNG	Ben Cooper	1988		7	10	20
Figurine Paint Set	Milton Bradley	1979		14	20	30
Flashlight		1976	battery operated, small phaser shape	6	8	12
Flashlight, ST:TMP	Larami	1979		6	8	12
Galileo Shuttle Model Kit	AMT	1974	#S959-602	80	95	175
Giant in the Universe Pop-Up Book	Random House	1977		14	20	30
Golden Trivia Game	Western	1985		20	30	45
Helmet	Remco	1976	plastic, w/sound and red lights	55	80	130
Kirk & Spock Wristwatch, ST:TMP	Bradley		LCD rectangular face display, Enterprise on blue face w/Kirk and Spock	25	35	55
Kirk Bank	Play Pal	1975	12" plastic	25	35	55
Kirk Costume	Ben Cooper	1975	plastic mask, one-piece jumpsuit	9	13	20
Kirk Doll, ST:TMP	Knickerbocker	1979	13" tall, soft body w/plastic head	16	23	35
Kirk or Spock Costumes	Ben Cooper	1967	tie-on jumpsuit, mask	11	16	25
Kirk Puzzle, ST:TMP	Larami	1979	15-piece sliding puzzle	5	7	10
Kite	Hi-Flyer	1975	TV Enterprise or Spock	14	20	30
Kite, ST:III	Lever Bros.	1984	pictures Enterprise	14	20	30
Kite, ST:TMP	Aviva	1976	picture of Spock	11	16	25
Klingon Bird of Prey, ST:III	Ertl	1984	3-1/2", die cast w/black plastic stand	7	10	25
Klingon Costume	Ben Cooper	1975	plastic mask, one piece jumpsuit	9	13	25
Klingon Costume, ST:TNG	Ben Cooper	1988		7	10	15
Klingon Cruiser Model Kit	AMT	1968	#S952-802	135	155	225
Klingon Cruiser Model Kit	Matchbox/ AMT		#PK-5111, ST:TMP	45	60	80
Light Switch Cover	American Tack & Hardware	1985	ST:TMP	6	8	12
Magic Slates	Whitman	1979	four designs: Spock, Kirk, Kirk and Spock	7	10	15
Make-a-Game Book	Wanderer	1979		7	10	15
Metal Detector	Jetco	1976	U.S.S. Enterprise decal	100	145	225
Mirror		1966	2" x 3" metal, w/black and white photo of crew	2	4	6
Mix 'N Mold		1975	Kirk, Spock or McCoy, molding compound, paint and brush	35	50	75
Movie Viewer	Chemtoy	1967	3" red and black plastic	10	16	30
Needlepoint Kit	Arista	1980	Kirk	16	23	35
Needlepoint Kit	Arista	1980	14" x 18", "Live Long and Prosper"	16	23	35
Paint-By-Numbers Set	Hasbro	1972	large	35	50	75
Paint-By-Numbers Set	Hasbro	1972	small	20	35	50
Pen & Poster Kit	Open Door	1976	four versions; each	11	16	25
Pen & Poster Kit, ST:III	Placo	1984	3-D poster "Search for Spock" w/ overlay, 3-D glasses and four felt tip pens	9	13	20

Star Trek Colorforms Set,
1975, Colorforms

Star Trek Dolls,
1979, Knickerbocker

STAR TREK

NAME	COMPANY	YEAR	DESCRIPTION	GOOD	EX	MIB
Pennant	Image Products	1982	12" x 30" triangle, The Wrath of Khan	6	8	12
Pennant	Universal Studios	1988	Paramount Pictures Adventure	5	7	10
Pennant	Image Products	1982	12" x 30" triangular, black, yellow and red on white w/"Spock Lives"	6	8	12
Phaser	Remco	1975	black plastic, shaped like pistol, electronic sound, flashlight projects target	35	50	80
Phaser Battle Game	Mego	1976	black plastic, 13" high battery operated electronic target game, LED scoring lights, sound effects and adjustable controls	195	275	450
Phaser Gun	Remco	1967	Astro Buzz-Ray Gun w/three-color flash beam	80	115	200
Phaser Gun, ST:III	Daisy	1984	white and blue plastic gun w/light and sound effects	35	50	80
Phaser Gun, ST:TNG	Galoob	1988	gray plastic light and sound hand phaser	14	20	35
Pinball Game, ST:TMP	Azrak-Hamway		12", plastic, Kirk or Spock	23	35	75
Pinball Game, ST:TMP	Bally	1979	electronic	200	295	600
Pocket Flix	Ideal	1978	battery operated movie viewer and film cartridge	18	25	40
Pop-Up Book, ST:TMP	Wanderer	1980		11	16	30
Puzzle	Aviva	1979	551 pieces	9	13	20
Puzzle	Whitman	1978	8-1/2" x 11" tray, Spock in spacesuit	2	3	8
Puzzle	H.G. Toys	1974	150 pieces, Battle on the Planet Romulon	5	7	10
Puzzle	H.G. Toys	1976	150 pieces; Kirk, Spock, and McCoy	4	6	10
Puzzle	Mind's Eye Press	1986	551 pieces, ST:IV, "The Voyage Home"	14	20	30
Puzzle	H.G. Toys	1976	150 pieces, "Force Field Capture"	4	6	10
Puzzle	H.G. Toys	1974	150 pieces, Attempted Hijacking of U.S.S. Enterprise	6	8	12
Puzzle	Milton Bradley	1979	ST:TMP, 50 pieces	5	7	10
Puzzle	H.G. Toys	1974	150 pieces, Battle on the Planet Klingon	5	7	10
Puzzle	H.G. Toys	1974	150 pieces, Kirk and officers beaming down	5	7	10
Puzzle	Larami	1979	ST:TMP, 15-piece sliding puzzle	5	7	10
Role Playing Game, 2001 Deluxe Edition	FASA		Star Trek Basic Set and the Star Trek III Combat Game	20	30	45
Role Playing Game, 2004 Basic Set	FASA		three books outlining Star Trek Universe	7	10	15
Role Playing Game, Second Deluxe Edition	FASA			14	20	30
Romulan Bird of Prey Model Kit	AMT	1975	#S957-601	100	120	130
Shuttlecraft Galileo, ST:TNG	Galoob	1989	white plastic w/movable doors and sensor unit	16	23	40
Space Design Center, ST:TMP	Avalon	1979	blue plastic tray, paints, pens, crayons, project book and crew member cut-outs	70	100	150
Spock & Enterprise Wristwatch, ST:TMP	Lewco	1986	20th anniversary, digital	9	13	30
Spock Bank	Play Pal	1975	12" plastic	25	35	55
Spock Bop Bag		1975	plastic, inflatable	55	80	125
Spock Chair, ST:TMP		1979	inflatable	16	23	35
Spock Costume	Ben Cooper	1973	plastic mask, one-piece jumpsuit	11	16	30
Spock Doll, ST:TMP	Knickerbocker	1979	13" tall, soft body, plastic head	16	23	35
Spock Ears, ST:TMP	Aviva	1979		7	10	15
Spock Model Kit	AMT	1973	#S956-601, Spock w/snake	120	130	175

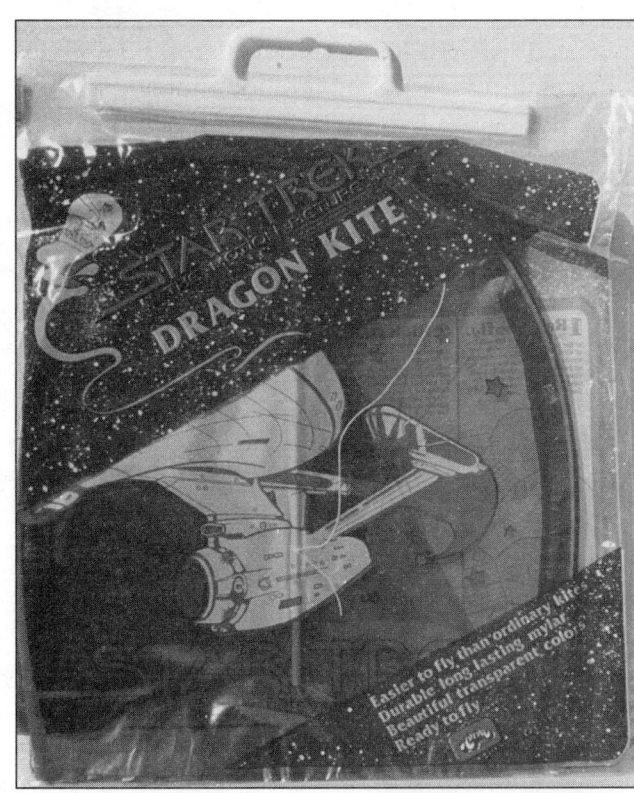

*Star Trek Kite, 1976,
Aviva*

*Star Trek Paint-By-
Numbers Set, 1972, Hasbro*

STAR TREK

NAME	COMPANY	YEAR	DESCRIPTION	GOOD	EX	MIB
Spock Tray	Aviva	1979	17-1/2" metal lap tray	9	13	20
Spock Wristwatch	Bradley		ST:TMP	20	30	45
Star Trek Cartoon Puzzle	Whitman	1978		4	5	8
Star Trek Color & Activity Book	Whitman	1979		4	5	8
Star Trek Coloring Book	Saalfield	1979		7	10	15
Star Trek Costume	'Collegeville	1979	one-piece outfit, Spock, Kirk, Ilia or Klingon, each	11	16	25
Star Trek II U.S.S. Enterprise Ship	Corgi	1982	3" die cast	9	13	20
Star Trek Phaser	Remco	1967	Astro Buzz-Ray Gun w/three color flash beam	50	80	150
Star Trek Phaser	Remco	1975	black plastic shaped like pistol, electronic sound, flashlight projects target	30	50	85
Star Trek Phaser Flashlight	Unknown	1976	battery-operated, small phaser shape	8	13	30
Star Trek Tracer Gun	Rayline	1966	6-1/2" plastic firing tracer gun	40	65	125
Star Trek Tracer Scope	Rayline	1968	rifle w/disks	50	80	150
Star Trek Water Pistol	Azrak-Hamway	1976	white plastic, shaped like U.S.S. Enterprise	15	30	60
Star Trek Wristwatch	Bradley	1979	Spock on dial w/revolving Enterprise and Shuttle craft hands	45	65	100
Star Trek:III Phaser	Daisy	1984	white and blue plastic gun w/light and sound effects	30	100	150
Star Trek:TMP Water Pistol	Aviva	1979	gray plastic, early pistol-grip phaser design	10	20	50
Telescreen	Mego	1976	plastic, battery operated target game w/light and sound effects	70	100	155
Tracer Gun	Rayline	1966	plastic pistol w/colored plastic discs	45	65	125
Tricorder	Mego	1976	blue plastic tape recorder, battery operated w/shoulder strap	70	100	150
Trillions of Trilligs Pop-Up Book	Random House	1977		16	25	35
U.S.S. Enterprise Action Play Set	Mego	1975	8" dolls, stools, console, captain's chair, three scenes w/blue plastic fold-out w/picture of U.S.S. Enterprise	125	180	300
U.S.S. Enterprise Bridge, ST:TMP	Mego	1980	white plastic	70	100	200
Utility Belt	Remco	1975	black plastic phaser miniature, tricorder, communicator and belt w/Star Trek buckle	45	65	120
Vulcan Shuttle Model Kit	Ertl	1984	#6679, ST:TMP	18	20	30
Vulcan Shuttle Model Kit	Mego/Grand Toy	1980	#91231, ST:TMP	100	120	130
Vulcan Shuttle Model Kit	Ertl	1984	#6679, ST:III	20	25	40
Wastebasket	Chein	1977	black metal	35	50	80
Wastebasket, ST:TMP	Chein	1979	13" high, metal rainbow painting w/photograph of Enterprise surrounded by smaller pictures	11	16	35
Water Pistol	Azrak-Hamway	1976	white plastic, shaped like U.S.S. Enterprise	20	30	45
Water Pistol, ST:TMP	Aviva	1979	gray plastic, early phaser	11	16	25
Writing Tablet		1967	8" x 10"	11	16	25
Yo-Yo	Aviva	1979	ST:TMP, blue sparkle plastic	7	10	20

SPACE/SCIENCE FICTION TOYS

Star Trek Space Design
Center, 1979, Avalon

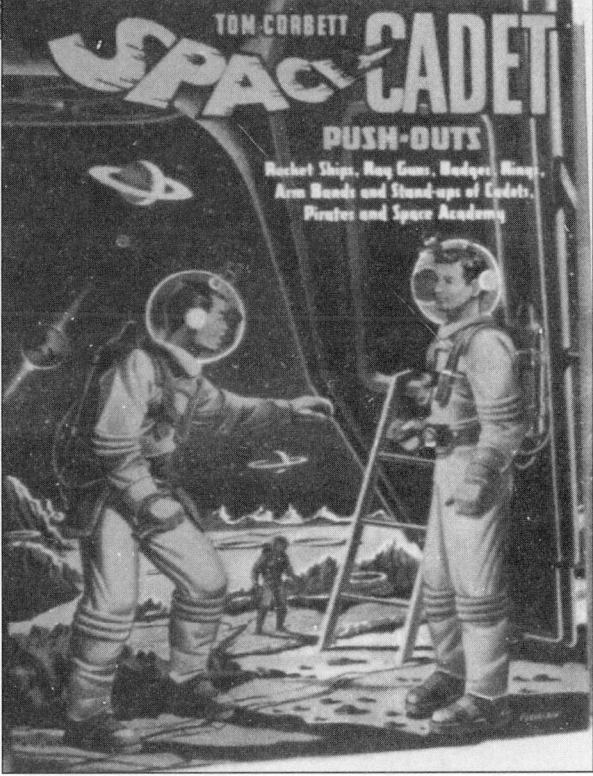

*Tom Corbett Space
Cadet Push-Outs Book,
1952, Saalfield*

TOM CORBETT

NAME	COMPANY	YEAR	DESCRIPTION	GOOD	EX	MIB
Binoculars				60	100	150
Flash X-1	Shudo/Japan	1967	4" long, tin litho, friction sparkling action, red body w/blue and yellow inset and grips, large white "Flash X-1" on body, four red tinted plastic sparkling windows	15	25	50
Flash X-1 Space Gun			5" long	55	95	145
Model Craft Molding Super Set	Kay Standley	1950s	various characters	100	165	250
Official Space Pistol	Marx	1950s		50	80	125
Official Sparking Space Gun	Marx		21" long, w/numerous apparatus on body	80	130	200
Polaris Wind-Up Spaceship	Marx	1952	12" long, 1952	195	325	500
Push-Outs Book	Saalfield	1952		30	50	75
Puzzles	Saalfield	1950s	frame tray, three versions, each	17	30	45
Rocket Scout Ring		1950s		10	16	25
Signal Siren Flashlight	Usalite	1950s		70	115	175
Space Academy Play Set	Marx	1950s	#7020	185	310	475
Space Academy Play Set	Marx	1952	#7010, 45mm figures	185	310	475
Space Cadet 2 Spaceship	Marx	1930s	tin wind-up, 12" long	225	375	575
Space Cadet Atomic Rifle		1950s		100	165	250
Space Cadet Belt		1950s		65	105	165
Space Gun		1950s	9-1/2" long light blue and black sparking	70	120	185
Space Suit Ring		1950s		10	16	25
Tom Corbett Coloring Book	Saalfield	1950s	two versions, each	25	40	70
Tom Corbett Official Space Cadet Gun	Marx	1950s	poorly designed composite rifle w/ modern military plastic stock and front grip at ends of long tin litho gun body w/litho bombs and "Ray Adjuster" scale	135	300	500
Tom Corbett Portrait Ring		1950s		20	35	50
Tom Corbett Space Cadet Atomic Flashlight Pistol	Marx	1950s	identical to Space Patrol Atomic Flashlight Pistol except for body colors and "Tom Corbett Space Cadet" printed upside down on handgrip	135	300	500
Tom Corbett Space Cadet Gun	Marx	1952	10-1/2" long, sheet metal clicker based on Flash Gordon Radio repeater molds, red body, blue barrel reads "Space Cadet," handgrips show bust of Tom in front of planet w/rocket ship symbol above	125	350	700
Tom Corbett Wristwatch	Ingraham	1950s	round dial, embossed band w/ship and planets, on illustrated rocket shaped card	250	425	650
View-Master Set	Sawyer's	1950s	three reels, Tom Corbett Secret from Space	30	50	75

SPACE/SCIENCE FICTION TOYS

Star Wars

Star Wars trilogy — the top grossing trilogy of all time — spawned a line of toys that changed the face of the industry. Before *Star Wars*, large-sized action figures were produced of superheroes or perhaps television characters — anywhere from six to twelve inches tall. But Lucasfilm along with Kenner (the major licensee of Star Wars toys) decided that smaller was better. The 3-3/4-inch size became the industry standard, making larger action figures seem bulky in comparison.

Why this change in size was made is open to speculation, but here's something to consider — how big would your Millennium Falcon have to be to fit your twelve-inch Han Solo action figure into the cockpit? (And how many kids would it take to lift it?) While Kenner's plastic Millennium Falcon was not produced to true scale, it still allowed a figure to sit in the cockpit with room for more in the main hold.

Star Wars also set the stage for what has become the staple of the toy industry movie tie-ins. Licensing is now the name of the game for most toy companies, so if a movie is expected to do well at the box office, then there will assuredly be a line of toys and collectibles associated with it. The next time you wander through the aisles of your favorite toy store and shake your head over the number of toys dedicated to that latest blockbuster movie, blame *Star Wars*.

Toy Line of the Millennium?

But what makes *Star Wars* toys so great? If you're not impressed with their smaller size or the way they revolutionized the licensing market, then consider their position as one of the most venerable toy lines of the millennium. While there was a period between 1984 and 1995 when Star Wars toys seemed to cool and few if any new items appeared on the market, the news that George Lucas would update the old movies and would soon begin scripting the three prequels renewed industry interest in this merchandising gold mine. New lines of Star Wars action figures were released by Kenner in July 1995, and Galoob began issuing Star Wars Micro Machines in 1996. While neither line of toys has reached the level of the original toys of the late 1970s and early 1980s, they still helped bring Star Wars toys to a new generation of fans.

Jawa with cloth cape, Star Wars, 1977

Cantina Adventure Set, Sears Exclusive, Star Wars, 1977

Star Wars Staying Power

But how collectible are these new toys? Well, remember that the main reason the original toys are so collectible is because they were taken out of the package — children enamored with the latest Star Wars movie were not going to leave their Luke Skywalker with telescoping lightsaber in his blisterpack. As is the case with most hobbies, items are collectible because they are rare. While children will play with their Darth Maul and Jar Jar Binks action figures, their parents will stash Mint, unopened toys in the attic. But since ninety percent of all collectors will be doing the same thing, don't expect your Obi-Wan action figure put your kids through college.

That doesn't mean these toys weren't desirable or hard-to-find. Before *Episode I* was released, Lucasfilm began the unpopular information and product embargo strategy. Ostensibly, part of the idea behind this strategy was to build consumer demand before the toys were released. In 1998, licensees of the movie tie-ins for Godzilla attempted the same strategy and in essence slit their own throats. Godzilla toys grew dusty on shelves as consumers and collectors passed them by. In the case of *Star Wars*, however, the strategy may have also been an attempt to keep people from getting sick of the movie — and everything associated with it — before the release date. Considered to be the most anticipated movie of all time, *Episode I* also had the dubious potential to cause the largest backlash of any movie in history.

Market Update

The new toys don't have great collectible value — all of the *Episode I* toys can be found on the secondary market. Darth Maul — the new cult favorite — is the most popular character, and could easily have eclipsed Boba Fett as the current favorite character of true fans if Hasbro hadn't overproduced the new toys. Some characters, namely Jar-Jar Binks, were so unpopular among collectors that their toys have no secondary market value..

What may eventually ruin the Star Wars market is the new breed of Star Wars collector. He'll buy all the figures and all the vehicles, and he'll tuck them away, awaiting the day when he can put them up for sale on an auction site. But since so many collectors will be stashing away their Mint on Card figures, the new toys won't bring thousands of dollars at an auction. With any luck, the toy will make its way into the hands of a child who will play with it. Then, and only then, will the long-term value increase.

As we move into the new millennium, *Star Wars* will eventually fade from the memories of collectors, just as it did through the late 1980s and early 1990s. But since there are two more movies planned tentatively for release in 2002 and 2005, it will be some time before this fade-out occurs. On average, prices on early Star Wars toys will never vary much from their current levels and the collectible value of the new crop of toys is uncertain, although expect the values of *Episode I* toys (and any toys from the other prequels) to stay low. That's not to say that people will stop buying into the Star Wars merchandising craze. While certain prequel products have languished on the shelves, new licensees such as Lego have been hard-pressed to keep up with demand. *Star Wars* and its toys will endure, even if the movies are considered financial failures, but the days of the $8,000 action figure are long gone.

Top Ten Star Wars Action Figures
(in Mint in Package condition)

1. Luke w/Telescoping Saber, Original 12, 3", 1977 .... $4,500
2. Jawa, Vinyl Cape, Original 12, 3",1977 2,570
3. Anakin Skywalker, Power of the Force, 3", 1985 2,330
4. Yak Face w/coin, Power of the Force, 3", 1985 1,500
5. Boba Fett, 3", 1978 970
6. Droids, Boba Fett, 3", 1985 670
7. IG-88, 12", Empire Strikes Back box, 1980 660
8. AT-AT Driver w/coin, Power of the Force, 3" 550
9. Early Bird Figures — Luke, Leia, R2-D2, Chewbacca,
   3", 1977 550
10. Nikto, Power of the Force, 3" 550

Top Ten Star Wars Toys (non-action figures)
(in Mint in Package condition)

1. Star Wars Mylar (advance) Poster $750
2. Star Wars Birthday Poster 700
3. Star Wars X-Wing Aces Target Game, 1978 500
4. Star Wars Action Figure Display Stand, 1977 300
5. Revenge of the Jedi (without date) Poster 250
6. C-3PO Cookie Jar, ceramic, 1977 250
7. Blue Harvest Cap, Cast & Crew Item, 1983 250
8. May the Force Be With You, lucite star, Cast & Crew Item, 1977 200
9. Star Wars lucite star, Cast & Crew Item, 1977 200
10. Empire Strikes Back, lucite star, Cast & Crew Item, 1980 200

Contributors to this section: Chris Fawcett, cfawcett@ix.netcom.com; Gus Lopez, 4756 University Plaza NE #134, Seattle, WA 98105, lopez@halcyon.com.

ACTION FIGURES, 12"

NAME	YEAR	MNP	MIP
COLLECTOR'S SERIES			
Admiral Akbar	1997	15	30
AT-AT Driver	1998	15	22
Barquin D'an	1998	15	22
Boba Fett	1997	15	70
C-3PO	1997	15	30
Cantina Band Aliens		15	35
Chewbacca	1997	15	75
Chewbacca (Chained)	1998	15	35
Darth Vader	1996	15	20
Emperor Palpatine	1998	15	18
Grand Moff Tarkin and Imperial Gunner		30	60
Grand Moff Tarkin w/Interrogation Droid	1998	15	22
Greedo	1998	15	22
Han and Luke in Stormtrooper Disguise		30	55
Han in Carbonite	1998	15	35
Han in Hoth Gear	1998	15	18
Han in Hoth Gear w/Tauntaun		25	45
Han Solo	1996	15	20
Jawa	1998	15	12
Lando Calrissian	1997	15	20
Leia as Jabba's Prisoner and R2-D2		30	60
Leia in Hoth Gear	1999	15	20
Luke as Jedi Knight	1998	15	18
Luke as Jedi Knight and Bib Fortuna		30	60
Luke as X-Wing Pilot	1997	15	30
Luke in Bespin Outfit	1997	15	35
Luke in Ceremonial Garb	1998	15	15
Luke in Hoth Gear	1998	15	18
Luke in Hoth Gear w/Wampa		30	80
Luke Skywalker	1996	15	20
Luke w/Poncho (Tatooine), Han w/Flight Jacket, Leia in Boushh Disguise		20	65
Obi-Wan Kenobi	1996	15	35
Princess Leia	1997	15	45
R2-D2	1998	15	12
R2-D2	1998	10	15
R5-D4	1998	10	15
Sandtrooper	1998	15	15
Snowtrooper	1998	15	18
Stormtrooper	1997	15	36
TIE Fighter Pilot	1997	15	28
Tusken Raider	1997	15	35
Wedge Antilles and Biggs Darklighter		30	60
Wicket	1998	10	15
Yoda	1998	15	20
EMPIRE STRIKES BACK			
Boba Fett	1979	155	420
IG-88	1980	240	660
EPISODE ONE			
Anakin Skywalker	1999	6	10
Battle Droid	1999	6	15
Darth Maul	1999	10	25
Jar Jar Binks	1999	6	20
Obi-Wan Kenobi	1999	6	15

ACTION FIGURES, 12"

NAME	YEAR	MNP	MIP
Pit Droids	1999	6	10
Qui-Gon Jinn	1999	6	20
R2-A6	1999	6	10
Watto	1999	6	15
PRINCESS LEIA COLLECTION			
Princess Leia in Cermonial Gown	1999	10	25
QUEEN AMIDALA COLLECTION			
Padme (Beautiful Braids)	2000	8	16
Queen Amidala (Black Travel Dress)	1999	10	40
Queen Amidala (Hidden Majesty)	1999	8	16
Queen Amidala (Red Senate Gown)	1999	10	40
Queen Amidala (Return to Naboo)	2000	10	45
Queen Amidala (Royal Elegance)	1999	8	16
Queen Amidala (Ultimate Hair)	1999	8	16
STAR WARS			
Boba Fett	1979	160	410
C-3PO	1979	45	125
Chewbacca	1979	55	175
Darth Vader	1978	70	195
Han Solo	1979	170	380
Jawa	1979	80	175
Luke Skywalker	1979	90	240
Obi-Wan Kenobi	1979	115	220
Princess Leia	1979	90	260
R2-D2	1979	45	110
Stormtrooper	1979	90	260

ACTION FIGURES, 3"

NAME	YEAR	MNP	MIP
DROIDS			
A-Wing Pilot	1985	25	170
Boba Fett	1985	17	670
C-3PO	1985	45	125
Jann Tosh	1985	8	20
Jord Dusat	1985	8	20
Kea Moll	1985	10	30
Kez-Iban	1985	10	25
R2-D2	1985	40	85
Sise Fromm	1985	35	85
Thall Joben	1985	8	20
Tig Fromm	1985	30	75
Uncle Gundy	1985	8	19
EMPIRE STRIKES BACK			
2-1B	1980	7	85
4-LOM		9	105
AT-AT Commander	1980	6	50
AT-AT Driver	1981	8	65
Bespin Security Guard, black	1980	8	55
Bespin Security Guard, white	1980	8	60
Bossk	1980	9	95
C-3PO w/Removable Limbs	1982	7	55
Cloud Car Pilot	1982	12	70
Dengar	1980	7	65
FX-7	1980	6	60
Han in Bespin Outfit	1981	10	105
Han in Hoth Gear	1980	8	85
Hoth Rebel Soldier	1980	6	55
IG-88	1980	10	115
Imperial Commander	1981	6	45

Boba Fett, Star Wars,
1979

Jawa, Star Wars,
1979

ACTION FIGURES, 3"

NAME	YEAR	MNP	MIP
Imperial TIE Fighter Pilot	1982	10	100
Lando Calrissian		8	70
Leia in Bespin Gown	1980	12	125
Leia in Hoth Gear	1981	15	100
Lobot	1981	5	50
Luke in Bespin Outfit	1980	15	150
Luke in Hoth Gear	1982	8	70
R2-D2 with Sensorscope		9	60
Rebel Commander	1980	6	50
Snowtrooper	1980	8	70
Ugnaught	1981	6	55
Yoda	1981	16	140
Zuckuss	1982	7	85
EPISODE ONE			
Adi Gallia	1999	3	8
Anakin Skywalker (Naboo Pilot)	2000	3	8
Anakin Skywalker (Naboo)	1999	3	8
Anakin Skywalker (Tatooine)	1999	3	8
Battle Droid (four versions)	1999	3	8
Boss Nass	1999	3	8
C-3PO	1999	3	8
Captain Panaka	2000	3	9
Captain Tarpals	1999	3	8
Chancellor Valorum	1999	3	8
Darth Maul	1999	3	10
Darth Maul (Jedi Duel)	1999	3	9
Darth Maul (Sith Lord)	2000	3	8
Darth Maul (Tatooine)	1999	3	8
Darth Sidious	1999	3	8
Darth Sidious (Holograph)	2000	3	8
Destroyer Droid	1999	3	8
Destroyer Droid (Battle Damaged)	2000	3	8
Gasgano	1999	3	8
Jar Jar Binks	1999	3	8
Jar Jar Binks (Swamp)	2000	3	8
Ki-Adi-Mundi	1999	3	8
Mace Windu	1999	3	8
Mosespa Encounter - Sebulba, Jar Jar, Anakin	1999	6	12
Naboo Royal Guard	2000	3	8
Naboo Royal Security	2000	3	9
Obi-Wan Kenobi	1999	3	10
Obi-Wan Kenobi (Jedi Duel)	1999	3	8
Obi-Wan Kenobi (Jedi Knight)	2000	3	8
Obi-Wan Kenobi (Naboo)	1999	3	8
Ody Mandrell w/Pit Droid	1999	3	8
OOM-9	1999	3	8
Padme Naberrie	1999	3	8
Pit Droids	2000	3	8
Queen Amidala (Battle)	2000	3	8
Queen Amidala (Coruscant)	1999	3	10
Queen Amidala (Naboo) w/Blaster Pistols	1999	3	8
Qui-Gon Jinn	1999	3	10
Qui-Gon Jinn (Jedi Duel)	1999	3	8
Qui-Gon Jinn (Jedi Master)	2000	3	8
Qui-Gon Jinn (Naboo)	1999	3	8
R2-B1	2000	3	8
Ric Olie	1999	3	8
Senator Palpatine	1999	3	8
Sio Bibble	2000	3	8

ACTION FIGURES, 3"

ACTION FIGURES, 3"

NAME	YEAR	MNP	MIP
Tatooine Showdown - Darth Maul, Qui-Gon, Anakin	1999	6	15
TC-14	2000	3	8
Watto	1999	3	9
Watto's Box - Watto, Graxol Kelvyyn, Shakka	2000	6	20
Yoda	1999	3	8
EWOKS			
Dulok Scout	1985	8	18
Dulok Shaman	1985	8	19
King Gornesh	1985	8	18
Logray	1985	10	20
Urgah	1985	8	18
Wicket	1985	11	35
POTF			
A-Wing Pilot, w/coin	1985	45	80
Amanaman, w/coin	1985	105	230
Anakin Skywalker, w/coin	1985	20	2330
AT-AT Driver, w/coin		4	550
AT-ST Driver, w/coin		5	50
B-Wing Pilot, w/coin	1985	4	30
Barada, w/coin	1985	35	105
Biker Scout, w/coin	1985	6	90
C-3PO w/Removable Limbs, w/coin		4	70
Chewbacca, w/coin		5	100
Darth Vader, w/coin		6	115
Emperor Palpatine, w/coin	1985	5	60
EV-9D9, w/coin	1985	60	140
Gamorrean Guard, w/coin		4	240
Han in Carbonite, w/coin	1985	80	195
Han in Trenchcoat, w/coin		6	490
Imperial Dignitary, w/coin	1985	40	70
Imperial Gunner, w/coin	1985	60	130
Jawa, w/coin	1985	7	85
Lando as General Pilot, w/coin	1985	55	105
Leia in Battle Poncho		10	80
Luke as Jedi Knight w/Green Saber, w/coin		18	195
Luke as X-Wing Pilot, w/coin	1985	6	85
Luke in Battle Poncho, w/coin		50	115
Luke in Stormtrooper Disguise, w/coin	1985	125	380
Lumat, w/coin	1985	8	45
Nikto, w/coin		6	590
Obi-Wan Kenobi, w/coin	1985	7	95
Paploo, w/coin	1985	8	50
R2-D2 with pop-up Lightsaber, w/coin	1985	85	155
Romba, w/coin	1985	30	55
Stormtrooper, w/coin		7	190
Teebo, w/coin		6	135
Warok, w/coin	1985	30	65
Wicket, w/coin	1985	8	135
Yak Face, w/coin	1985	175	1500
Yoda, w/coin		12	340
POTF2			
2-1B Medic Droid	1997	2	8
4-LOM	1997	3	10
8-D8 Droid	1998	3	10
Admiral Ackbar	1997	3	10
Admiral Motti	2000	5	9

*Princess Leia, Star Wars,
1979*

*Kea Moll,
Droids, 1985*

595

ACTION FIGURES, 3"

NAME	YEAR	MNP	MIP
Anakin Skywalker	1999	3	12
ASP-7 Droid	1997	3	8
AT-AT Driver	1998	3	20
AT-ST Driver	1997	3	10
Aunt Beru	1999	3	14
B'omarr Monk		10	15
Ben (Obi-Wan) Kenobi	1997	5	9
Bib Fortuna	1997	3	10
Biggs Darklighter	1998	3	14
Boba Fett	1997	5	10
Boba Fett	1996	4	15
Boba Fett vs. IG-88	1996	6	25
Bossk	1997	3	10
C-3PO	1995	3	10
C-3PO w/Removable Limbs and Backpack	1998	3	16
C-3PO, Shop Worn	1999	3	8
C-3PO, w/Millennium Minted Coin		5	10
Cantina Aliens—Labria, Nabrun Leids, Takeel		6	12
Cantina Greedo	1999	3	7
Cantina Han Solo	1999	3	7
Cantina Showdown—Obi-Wan Kenobi, Ponda Baba, Dr. Evazan		6	12
Captain Piett	1998	3	14
Chewbacca	1995	3	12
Chewbacca (Hoth)	1998	3	8
Chewbacca as Boushh's Bounty	1998	3	18
Chewbacca in Bounty Hunter Disguise	1996	3	6
Chewbacca, w/Millennium Minted Coin		5	10
Clone Emperor	1998	3	18
Crowd Control Stormtrooper	1996	5	9
Dagobah w/Yoda	1998	6	12
Darktrooper	1998	3	30
Darth Vader	1998	3	8
Darth Vader	1997	5	9
Darth Vader	1995	4	13
Darth Vader w/Interrogation Droid	1999	5	7
Darth Vader w/Removable Helmet	1998	4	24
Dash Rendar	1996	3	8
Death Star Droid w/Mouse Droid	1998	3	20
Death Star Escape—Luke and Han in Stormtrooper Disguise, Chewbacca		6	22
Death Star Gunner	1996	3	18
Death Star Trooper	1998	3	26
Death Star w/Darth Vader	1998	6	12
Dengar	1997	3	10
Droopy McCool and Barquin D'an		6	20
Emperor Palpatine	1998	3	8
Emperor Palpatine	1997	3	10
Emperor Palpatine, w/Millennium Minted Coin		5	10
Emperor's Royal Guard	1997	3	12
Emporer Palpatine	1997	5	9
Endor Rebel Soldier	1998	3	14
Endor w/Wicket	1998	10	22
EV-9D9	1997	3	10
Falcon w/Han Solo	1998	6	8
Falcon w/Luke Skywalker	1998	6	8

ACTION FIGURES, 3"

NAME	YEAR	MNP	MIP
Figrin D'an (Cantina Band Member)		10	15
Final Jedi Duel—Darth Vader, Luke, Emperor Palpatine		6	24
Gamorrean Guard	1997	3	10
Garindan (Long Snoot)	1997	3	10
Grand Admiral Thrawn	1998	3	20
Grand Moff Tarkin	1997	3	10
Greedo	1996	3	18
Han in Bespin Outfit	1997	3	10
Han in Bespin Outfit, w/Millennium Minted Coin		5	10
Han in Carbonite	1996	3	6
Han in Endor Gear	1997	3	12
Han in Hoth Gear	1996	3	12
Han in Stormtrooper Disguise		10	20
Han Solo	1995	3	12
Han Solo w/Smuggler's Flight Pack	1996	5	9
Hoth Rebel Soldier	1997	3	10
Imperial Probe Droid	1997	5	9
Imperial Sentinel	1998	3	18
Ishi Tib	1998	3	14
Jabba the Hutt's Dancers— Rystall, Greeata, Lyn Me		6	16
Jabba's Skiff Guards - Klaatu, Barada, Nikto	1999	8	35
Jawa & Gonk Droid	1999	3	7
Jawas	1996	3	20
Jedi Knight Luke Skywalker	1997	5	9
Jedi Spirits—Anakin Skywalker, Yoda, Obi-Wan Kenobi		6	10
Kyle Katarn	1998	3	35
Lak Sivrak	1998	3	12
Lando as General	1998	3	14
Lando as Skiff Guard	1997	3	10
Lando Calrissian	1996	3	10
Leia and Han	1998	6	12
Leia and Luke	1998	6	12
Leia and R2-D2	1998	6	12
Leia and Wicket the Ewok	1998	6	12
Leia as Jabba's Prisoner	1997	3	10
Leia in Boushh Disguise	1996	3	6
Leia in Endor Gear, w/Millennium Minted Coin		5	10
Leia in Ewok Celebration Outfit	1998	3	14
Leia in Hoth Gear	1998	3	22
Leia w/All-New Likeness	1998	3	16
Lobot	1998	3	14
Luke as X-Wing Pilot	1996	3	14
Luke in Battle Poncho, w/ Millennium Minted Coin		5	10
Luke in Bespin Outfit	1998	3	16
Luke in Ceremonial Garb	1997	3	12
Luke in Dagobah Fatigues	1996	3	12
Luke in Hoth Gear	1997	3	11
Luke in Imperial Guard Disguise	1996	3	8
Luke in Stormtrooper Disguise	1996	4	24
Luke Skywalker	1998	3	18
Luke Skywalker	1995	4	12
Luke Skywalker	1998	3	8
Luke Skywalker w/T16	1999	3	7

596

Imperial Commander, Empire Strikes
Back, 1981

Lobot, Empire Strikes
Back, 1981

ACTION FIGURES, 3"

NAME	YEAR	MNP	MIP
Luke Skywalker's Desert Sport Skiff	1996	5	10
Luke w/Blast Shield Helmet	1998	3	16
Mace Windu		5	10
Malakili (Rancor Keeper)	1997	3	8
Mara Jade	1998	3	35
Max Rebo and Doda Bodonawieedo		6	25
Momaw Nadon (Hammerhead)	1996	2	16
Mon Mothma	1998	3	16
Muftak and Kabe		10	16
Mynock Hunt—Han, Leia, Chewbacca		6	32
Nien Nunb	1997	3	10
Obi-Wan Kenobi	1995	4	12
Obi-Wan Kenobi	1998	3	8
Obi-Wan Kenobi Spirit		10	10
Oola and Salacious Crumb		10	14
Orrimaarko (Prune Face)	1998	3	22
Ponda Baba	1997	3	10
Pote Snitkin	1998	3	20
Prince Xizor	1996	3	6
Prince Xizor vs. Darth Vader	1996	6	15
Princess Leia	1998	3	8
Princess Leia	1995	3	13
Princess Leia (Hood Up)	2000	5	9
Princess Leia Organa Solo	1998	3	18
Purchase of the Droids—Luke, C-3PO, Uncle Owen		6	18
R2-D2	1998	3	8
R2-D2	1995	3	12
R2-D2	1997	5	9
R2-D2 w/Datalink and Sensorscope	1998	3	14
R2-D2 w/Holographic Princess Leia	1999	5	9
R5-D4	1996	3	11
Rebel Fleet Trooper	1997	3	11
Rebel Pilots—Wedge Antilles, B-Wing Pilot (Ten Nunb), Y-Wing Pilot		6	26
Ree-Yees	1998	3	26
Saelt-Marae (Yak Face)	1997	3	10
Sandtrooper	1996	3	12
Snowtrooper	1997	5	9
Snowtrooper	1997	3	10
Snowtrooper, w/Millennium Minted Coin		5	10
Spacetrooper	1998	3	25
STAP and Battle Droid		10	12
Stormtrooper	1995	3	11
Stormtrooper	1999	5	7
Sy Snootles and Joh Yowza		6	20
Tatooine w/Luke Skywalker	1998	10	25
Theater Edition Jedi Knight Luke Skywalker	1996	10	65
TIE Fighter Pilot	1996	3	11
Tie Fighter w/Darth Vader	1998	6	15
Tusken Raider	1996	3	13
Ugnaught	1998	3	10
Weequay Skiff Guard	1997	3	10
Wicket and Logray	1998	3	10
Yoda	1996	3	11

ACTION FIGURES, 3"

NAME	YEAR	MNP	MIP
Yoda	1998	3	12
Zuckuss	1998	3	14
RETURN OF THE JEDI			
8D8	1983	7	25
Admiral Ackbar	1983	8	30
AT-ST Driver		9	25
B-Wing Pilot		7	25
Bib Fortuna		10	30
Biker Scout	1983	10	45
Chief Chirpa	1983	8	30
Emperor Palpatine	1983	8	40
Emperor's Royal Guard		8	35
Gamorrean Guard	1983	7	35
General Madine	1983	7	30
Han in Trenchcoat	1984	11	35
Klaatu	1983	9	25
Klaatu in Skiff Guard Outfit	1983	9	25
Lando Calrissian, Skiff Guard Outfit	1983	9	35
Leia in Battle Poncho	1984	20	45
Leia in Boushh Disguise	1983	12	40
Logray	1983	7	25
Luke as Jedi Knight, Blue Saber	1983	35	145
Luke as Jedi Knight, Green Saber	1983	25	90
Lumat	1983	14	35
Nien Nunb	1983	6	30
Nikto	1984	10	30
Paploo		14	40
Pruneface	1984	8	30
Rancor Keeper	1984	9	25
Rebel Commando	1983	8	25
Ree-Yees	1983	7	25
Squid Head	1983	8	35
Sy Snootles and the Rebo Band	1984	25	150
Teebo	1984	10	35
Weequay		10	30
Wicket	1984	13	50
STAR WARS			
Boba Fett	1978	25	970
C-3PO	1977	10	195
Chewbacca	1977	9	230
Darth Vader	1977	11	280
Death Squad Commander	1977	9	185
Death Star Droid	1978	8	140
Early Bird Figures — Luke, Leia, R2-D2, Chewbacca	1977	220	550
Greedo	1978	7	150
Hammerhead	1978	7	165
Han Solo, Large Head	1977	20	510
Han Solo, Small Head	1977	25	450
Jawa, Cloth Cape	1977	10	200
Jawa, Vinyl Cape	1977	230	2570
Luke as X-Wing Pilot	1978	8	140
Luke Skywalker	1977	25	400
Luke w/Telescoping Saber	1977	195	4850
Obi-Wan Kenobi	1977	11	250
Power Droid	1978	6	110
Princess Leia	1977	30	330
R2-D2	1977	9	165
R5-D4	1978	8	110

A-Wing Pilot with coin, POTF, 1985

Barada with coin,
POTF, 1985

ACTION FIGURES, 3"

NAME	YEAR	MNP	MIP
Snaggletooth, Blue Body, Sears Exclusive	1978	185	n/a
Snaggletooth, Red Body	1978	7	160
Stormtrooper	1977	12	200
Tusken Raider	1977	9	220
Walrus Man	1978	7	125

BEASTS

NAME	YEAR	MNP	MIP
EMPIRE STRIKES BACK			
Taun Taun, solid belly		14	40
Taun Taun, split belly		13	45
Wampa		14	35
RETURN OF THE JEDI			
Rancor		30	60
STAR WARS			
Partol Dewback		20	75

CARRYING CASES

NAME	YEAR	MNP	MIP
EMPIRE STRIKES BACK			
Darth Vader	1982	n/a	40
Mini Figure	1980	n/a	30
RETURN OF THE JEDI			
C-3PO	1983	n/a	25
Darth Vader	1983	n/a	220
Laser Rifle	1984	n/a	25
STAR WARS			
24-Figure		n/a	30

COINS

NAME	YEAR	MNP	MIP
2-1B	1985	n/a	120
63rd Coin, lightsaber	1985	n/a	500
A-Wing Pilot	1985	n/a	5
Amanaman	1985	n/a	5
Anakin Skywalker	1985	n/a	75
AT-AT	1985	n/a	75
AT-ST Driver	1985	n/a	10
B-Wing Pilot	1985	n/a	10
Barada	1985	n/a	5
Bib Fortuna	1985	n/a	75
Biker Scout	1985	n/a	10
Boba Fett	1985	n/a	75
C-3PO	1985	n/a	10
Chewbacca	1985	n/a	10
Chief Chirpa	1985	n/a	50
Creatures	1985	n/a	75
Darth Vader	1985	n/a	10
Droids	1985	n/a	75
Emperor	1985	n/a	10
Emperor's Royal Guard	1985	n/a	50
EV-9D9	1985	n/a	5
FX-7	1985	n/a	120
Gamorrean Guard	1985	n/a	10
Greedo	1985	n/a	75
Han Carbonite	1985	n/a	5
Han Hoth	1985	n/a	75
Han Original	1985	n/a	120

COINS

NAME	YEAR	MNP	MIP
Han Solo Rebel (trenchcoat)	1985	n/a	10
Hoth Stormtrooper	1985	n/a	120
Imperial Commander	1985	n/a	75
Imperial Dignitary	1985	n/a	5
Imperial Gunner	1985	n/a	5
Jawas	1985	n/a	10
Lando General	1985	n/a	5
Lando with Cloud City	1985	n/a	75
Logray	1985	n/a	50
Luke Jedi	1985	n/a	10
Luke on Dagobah	1985	n/a	120
Luke original	1985	n/a	50
Luke Poncho	1985	n/a	5
Luke Stormtrooper	1985	n/a	5
Luke with Tauntaun	1985	n/a	75
Luke X-Wing	1985	n/a	10
Luke X-Wing, small	1985	n/a	30
Lumat	1985	n/a	10
Millennium Falcon	1994	n/a	5
Millennium Falcon	1985	n/a	75
Obi-Wan Kenobi	1985	n/a	10
Paploo	1985	n/a	10
Princess Leia Rebel Leader (poncho)	1985	n/a	10
Princess Leia, Boushh	1985	n/a	120
Princess Leia, Original	1985	n/a	120
R2-D2 Pop-Up Lightsaber	1985	n/a	5
Romba	1985	n/a	5
Sail Skiff	1985	n/a	120
Star Destroyer Commander	1985	n/a	75
Stormtrooper	1985	n/a	10
Teebo	1985	n/a	10
TIE Fighter	1994	n/a	5
TIE Fighter Pilot	1985	n/a	50
Tusken Raider	1985	n/a	120
Warok	1985	n/a	5
Wicket	1985	n/a	10
X-Wing	1994	n/a	5
Yak Face	1985	n/a	75
Yoda	1985	n/a	10
Yoda	1985	n/a	10
Zuckuss	1985	n/a	120

MICRO SERIES

NAME	YEAR	MNP	MIP
Bespin Control Room	1982	11	25
Bespin Freeze Chamber	1982	20	60
Bespin Gantry	1982	11	25
Bespin World	1982	40	90
Death Star Compactor	1982	20	45
Death Star Escape	1982	17	40
Death Star World	1982	40	100
Hoth Generator Attack	1982	14	30
Hoth Ion Cannon	1982	17	40
Hoth Turret Defense	1982	15	30
Hoth Wampa Cave	1982	14	30
Hoth World	1982	60	120
Imperial TIE Fighter	1982	25	60
Millennium Falcon	1982	140	320
Snowspeeder	1982	90	175

600

Gamorrean Guard, Return
of the Jedi, 1983

Leia in Boushh Disguise,
Return of the Jedi, 1983

MICRO SERIES

NAME	YEAR	MNP	MIP
X-Wing Fighter	1982	20	45

MINI RIGS

NAME	YEAR	MNP	MIP
AST-5	1983	7	20
CAP-2 Captivator	1982	9	25
Desert Sail Skiff	1984	7	20
Endor Forest Ranger	1984	12	25
INT-4 Interceptor	1982	9	25
ISP-6 Imperial Shuttle Pod	1983	9	20
MLC-3 Mobile Laser Cannon	1981	10	30
MTV-7 Multi-Terrain Vehicle	1981	9	30
PDT-8 Personal Deployment Transport	1981	10	30
Radar Laser Cannon	1982	8	19
Tri-Pod Laser Cannon	1982	8	17
Vehicle Maintenance Energizer	1982	8	17

PLAY SETS

NAME	YEAR	MNP	MIP
EMPIRE STRIKES BACK			
Cloud City Play Set, Sears Exclusive	1981	100	270
Dagobah	1982	18	75
Darth Vader's Star Destroyer		35	115
Hoth Ice Planet	1980	35	85
Imperial Attack Base	1980	25	80
Rebel Command Center	1980	60	155
Turret and Probot	1980	35	80
EWOKS			
Ewoks Treehouse	1985	16	35
POTF			
Jabba's Dungeon, w/Amanaman, EV-9D9, Barada	1983	220	310
RETURN OF THE JEDI			
Ewok Village	1983	30	75
Jabba the Hutt Playset		25	55
Jabba's Dungeon, w/Nikto, 8D8, Klaatu	1983	30	90
STAR WARS			
Cantina Adventure Set, Sears Exclusive	1977	180	510
Creature Cantina	1977	35	95
Death Star Space Station	1977	60	250
Droid Factory	1977	35	115
Land of the Jawas	1977	40	140

VEHICLES

NAME	YEAR	MNP	MIP
DIE-CAST			
Darth Vader's TIE Fighter	1979	11	55
Land Speeder	1979	13	60
Millennium Falcon	1979	30	110
Slave I	1979	25	75
Snowspeeder	1979	25	80
Star Destroyer	1979	45	125
TIE Bomber	1979	250	670
TIE Fighter	1979	15	45

VEHICLES

NAME	YEAR	MNP	MIP
Twin-Pod Cloud Car	1979	25	75
X-Wing Fighter	1979	18	70
Y-Wing Fighter	1979	40	145
DROIDS			
A-Wing Fighter, Droids Box	1983	195	400
ATL Interceptor	1985	15	45
Imperial Side Gunner	1985	18	60
EMPIRE STRIKES BACK			
AT-AT	1980	75	190
Rebel Transport	1980	45	100
Scout Walker	1982	30	65
Slave I	1980	35	100
Snowspeeder		35	75
Twin-Pod Cloud Car	1980	30	70
EWOKS			
Ewoks Fire Cart	1985	7	18
Ewoks Woodland Wagon	1985	7	40
POTF			
Ewok Battle Wagon	1985	65	220
Imperial Sniper Vehicle	1985	30	70
One-Man Sand Skimmer	1985	25	65
Security Scout Vehicle	1985	30	80
Tatooine Skiff		280	570
RETURN OF THE JEDI			
B-Wing Fighter	1984	65	125
Ewok Combat Glider	1984	7	18
Imperial Shuttle	1984	165	330
Speeder Bike	1983	11	30
TIE Interceptor	1984	50	110
Y-Wing Fighter	1983	55	135
STAR WARS			
Darth Vader's TIE Fighter	1977	45	105
Imperial TIE Fighter	1977	30	120
Imperial Trooper Transport		30	70
Jawa Sand Crawler, battery-operated	1977	210	540
Land Speeder, battery-operated	1977	16	60
Millennium Falcon	1977	70	210
Sonic Land Speeder, JC Penney Exclusive	1977	140	470
X-Wing Fighter	1977	30	110

WEAPONS

NAME	YEAR	MNP	MIP
DROIDS			
Droids Lightsaber	1985	75	190
EMPIRE STRIKES BACK			
Laser Pistol	1980	20	80
Lightsaber	1980	16	40
Lightsaber	1980	16	45
RETURN OF THE JEDI			
Biker Scout's Laser Pistol	1984	20	55
Lightsaber		20	40
STAR WARS			
Han Solo's Laser Pistol		20	90
Inflatable Lightsaber	1977	30	135
Three-Position Laser Rifle	1980	75	240

Gamorrean Guard, Return
of the Jedi, 1983

Leia in Boushh Disguise,
Return of the Jedi, 1983

STAR WARS TOYS
(NON-ACTION FIGURES)

NAME	YEAR	MNP	MIP
BANKS			
C-3PO, ceramic, Roman	1977	50	65
Chewbacca, Sigma	1983	25	35
Darth Vader, Adam Joseph	1983	9	13
Darth Vader, ceramic, Roman	1977	50	75
Darth Vader, silver plated, Leonard Silver	1981	45	65
Emperor's Royal Guard, Adam Joseph	1983	9	13
Gamorrean Guard, Adam Joseph	1983	75	100
Jabba the Hutt, Sigma	1983	25	35
Kneesaa Bank, Adam Joseph	1983	7	10
R2-D2, Adam Joseph	1983	7	10
R2-D2, ceramic, Roman	1977	25	35
Wicket, Adam Joseph	1983	7	10
Yoda, Sigma	1983	25	35
Yoda, lithographed tin w/ combination dials		11	16
BISQUE FIGURES			
Boba Fett, bisque, Towle/Sigma	1983	30	45
Darth Vader, bisque, Towle/ Sigma	1983	30	45
Galactic Emperor, bisque, Towle/ Sigma	1983	20	30
Gamorrean Guard, bisque, Towle/ Sigma	1983	20	30
Han Solo, bisque, Towle/Sigma	1983	25	35
Lando Calrissian, bisque, Towle/ Sigma	1983	30	45
Luke Skywalker, bisque, Towle/ Sigma	1983	30	45
BOARD GAMES			
Star Wars Adventures of R2D2 Game, Kenner	1977	10	20
Star Wars Battle at Sarlacc's Pit, Parker Brothers	1983	10	20
Star Wars Escape from Death Star, Kenner	1977	15	25
Star Wars Monopoly, Parker Brothers	1997	15	25
Star Wars ROTJ Ewoks Save The Trees, Parker Brothers	1984	10	15
Star Wars Wicket the Ewok, Parker Brothers	1983	10	15
Star Wars X-Wing Aces Target Game	1978	150	500
BOOKS			
Burger Chef Fun Book	1978	3	3
Chewbacca and C-3PO Coloring Book, Kenner		2	4
Chewbacca and Leia Coloring Book, Kenner		2	4
Chewbacca's Activity Book, Random House		3	5
Chewbacca, Han, Leia and Lando Coloring Book, Kenner		2	4
Darth Vader and Stormtroopers Coloring Book, Kenner		2	4
Empire Strikes Back Coloring Book	1980	5	7
Empire Strikes Back Panorama Book, Random House		15	20
Empire Strikes Back Pop-Up Book, Random House	1980	10	15

STAR WARS TOYS
(NON-ACTION FIGURES)

NAME	YEAR	MNP	MIP
Empire Strikes Back Sketchbook, Ballantine	1980	14	20
Escape from the Monster Ship Book, Random House	1985	6	8
Ewoks Coloring Book, Kenner	1983	7	10
Fuzzy as an Ewok, Random House	1985	6	8
How the Ewoks Saved the Trees, Random House	1985	6	8
Jedi Master's Quiz, Random House	1985	6	8
Lando Fighting Skiff Guard Coloring Book, Kenner	1983	2	4
Lando in Falcon Cockpit Coloring Book, Kenner	1983	2	4
Learn-to-Read Activity Book, Random House	1985	6	8
Luke Skywalker Coloring Book, Kenner	1983	2	4
Max Rebo Coloring Book, Kenner	1983	3	5
My Jedi Journal, Ballantine		7	10
R2-D2 Coloring Book, Kenner		2	4
Return of the Jedi Activity Book, Happy House	1983	5	7
Return of the Jedi Coloring Book	1984	2	4
Return of the Jedi Maze Book, Happy House	1983	2	4
Return of the Jedi Monster Activity Book, Happy House	1983	2	4
Return of the Jedi Picture Puzzle Book, Happy House	1983	2	4
Return of the Jedi Pop-Up Book, Random House	1983	10	12
Return of the Jedi Punch-Out Book, Random House		10	12
Return of the Jedi Sketchbook, Ballantine	1983	11	16
Return of the Jedi Word Puzzle Book, Happy House	1983	5	7
Star Wars Pop-Up Book, Random House	1978	10	16
Star Wars Poster Art Coloring Set, Craft Master	1978	9	13
Star Wars Questions and Answers About Space Book, Random House	1979	5	7
Star Wars Sketchbook, Ballantine	1977	10	12
Sticker Book, 256 stickers, Panini	1977	23	35
Yoda Coloring Book, Kenner		2	4
CANDLES			
Chewbacca Birthday Candle, Wilton		6	8
Darth Vader Birthday Candle, Wilton		6	8
R2-D2 Birthday Candle, Wilton		6	8
CAST & CREW ITEMS			
"The Star Wars" large sticker	1977	n/a	10
Blue Harvest cap	1983	n/a	250
Blue Harvest stationery	1983	n/a	10
Blue Harvest t-shirt	1983	n/a	75
Dancing Probot t-shirt	1980	n/a	50
Empire Srikes Back Norwegian unit patch	1980	n/a	75
Empire Strikes Back logo coaster	1980	n/a	20
Empire Strikes Back lucite star	1980	n/a	200
Empire Strikes Back paperweight	1980	n/a	150

STAR WARS TOYS
(NON-ACTION FIGURES)

NAME	YEAR	MNP	MIP
Empire Strikes Back R2-D2 coaster	1980	n/a	20
Empire Strikes Back Vader flames patch	1980	n/a	75
Intergalactic Passport, stamped	1980	n/a	150
Intergalactic Passport, unstamped	1980	n/a	75
May the Force Be With You lucite star	1977	n/a	200
McQuarrie lettering Star Wars patch	1977	n/a	75
Revenge of the Jedi paperweight	1983	n/a	150
Revenge of the Jedi t-shirt	1983	n/a	50
Revenge of the Jedi Yoda patch	1983	n/a	50
Revenge of the Jedi Yoda sticker	1983	n/a	10
Star Wars lucite star	1977	n/a	200

CEREAL BOXES

NAME	YEAR	MNP	MIP
Apple Jacks, w/Droids comic, Kellogg's	1995	n/a	15
Apple Jacks, w/Star Wars comic, Kellogg's	1995	n/a	10
Boo Berry, w/card offer, General Mills	1978	n/a	150
Boo Berry, w/sticker offer, General Mills	1978	n/a	150
C-3PO's, w/C-3PO mask, Kellogg's	1984	n/a	30
C-3PO's, w/Chewbacca mask, Kellogg's	1984	n/a	30
C-3PO's, w/Darth Vader mask, Kellogg's	1984	n/a	30
C-3PO's, w/Luke mask, Kellogg's	1984	n/a	30
C-3PO's, w/Rebel Rocket, Kellogg's	1984	n/a	30
C-3PO's, w/Stick R Card, Kellogg's	1984	n/a	30
C-3PO's, w/Stormtrooper mask, Kellogg's	1984	n/a	30
Cheerios, w/poster offer, General Mills	1978	n/a	50
Cheerios, w/tumbler offer, General Mills	1979	n/a	50
Chocolate Crazy Cow, w/card offer, General Mills	1978	n/a	150
Cocoa Puffs, w/card offer, General Mills	1978	n/a	75
Cocoa Puffs, w/sticker offer, General Mills	1978	n/a	75
Corn Pops, w/Making of Star Wars, Kellogg's	1995	n/a	10
Count Chocula, w/card offer, General Mills	1978	n/a	150
Count Chocula, w/sticker offer, General Mills	1978	n/a	150
Franken Berry, w/card offer, General Mills	1978	n/a	150
Franken Berry, w/sticker offer, General Mills	1978	n/a	150
Froot Loops, w/Han Stormtrooper offer, Kellogg's	1995	n/a	10
Lucky Charms, w/hang glider offer, General Mills	1978	n/a	75
Lucky Charms, w/sticker offer, General Mills	1978	n/a	75
Raisin Bran, w/Star Wars video ad, Kellogg's	1995	n/a	10
Strawberry Crazy Cow, w/card offer, General Mills	1978	n/a	150

STAR WARS TOYS
(NON-ACTION FIGURES)

NAME	YEAR	MNP	MIP
Trix, w/hang glider offer, General Mills	1978	n/a	75
Trix, w/sticker offer, General Mills	1978	n/a	75

CEREAL PREMIUMS

NAME	YEAR	MNP	MIP
card, set of eighteen, General Mills	1978	n/a	3
Han Stormtrooper, Kellogg's	1995	n/a	10
hang glider, set of four, General Mills	1978	n/a	8
kite, General Mills	1978	n/a	30
Making of Star Wars video, Kellogg's	1995	n/a	5
Micro Collection figures, Kellogg's	1984	n/a	10
poster, set of four, General Mills	1978	n/a	2
Rebel Rocket, set of four, Kellogg's	1984	n/a	10
Star Wars comic, Kellogg's	1995	n/a	5
Stick R Card, set of ten, Kellogg's	1984	n/a	2
Stickers, set of sixteen, General Mills	1978	n/a	4
Tumbler, General Mills	1978	n/a	15

CLOCKS

NAME	YEAR	MNP	MIP
3-D, electronic, quartz, Bradley	1982	16	23
C-3PO and R2-D2 Alarm Clock, Bradley	1980	15	25
Droid, wall clock, Bradley		20	30
Empire Strikes Back, wall clock, Bradley		20	30
Portable Clock/Radio, Bradley	1984	11	16

CLOTHING

NAME	YEAR	MNP	MIP
Chewbacca Bandolier Strap	1983	n/a	15
Darth Vader Belt Buckle, Leather Shop	1977	14	20
R2-D2 and C-3PO Belt Buckles, Leather Shop	1977	14	20
R2-D2 Belt Buckle, Leather Shop	1977	14	20
Return of the Jedi Belt, Leather Shop	1977	5	7
Yoda Backpack, Sigma		14	20

COOKIE JARS

NAME	YEAR	MNP	MIP
C-3PO Cookie Jar, ceramic, Roman	1977	150	250
Darth Vader, R2-D2 and C-3PO Cookie Jar, hexagon, Sigma		55	80
R2-D2 Cookie Jar, ceramic, Roman	1977	90	150

DISPLAYS

NAME	YEAR	MNP	MIP
Action Figure Display Stand	1977	n/a	300
Display Arena	1980	n/a	105

ELECTRONICS

NAME	YEAR	MNP	MIP
Darth Vader Speaker Phone, ATC	1983	40	60
Duel Racing Set, Lionel	1978	40	75
Give-A-Show Projector, w/ filmstrips, Kenner	1979	25	35
Luke Skywalker AM Headset Radio		95	150
Movie Viewer, Kenner	1978	15	20

FAST FOOD

NAME	YEAR	MNP	MIP
Boba Fett toy, Taco Bell	1997	n/a	2
Cloud City toy, Taco Bell	1997	n/a	2
Death Star Spinner toy, Taco Bell	1997	n/a	2
Empire Strikes Back glasses, Burger King	1980	n/a	8

Walrus Man, Star Wars, 1978

Cloud City Play Set, Sears Exclusive, Empire Strikes Back, 1981

STAR WARS TOYS
(NON-ACTION FIGURES)

NAME	YEAR	MNP	MIP
Empire Strikes Back Sticker Album, Burger King	1980	n/a	20
Fun Trays, Burger Chef		n/a	10
Glasses, Burger King	1977	n/a	10
Millennium Falcon toy, Taco Bell	1997	n/a	2
Mirror Cube toy, Taco Bell	1997	n/a	2
Puzzle Cube, Taco Bell	1997	n/a	2
R2-D2 toy, Taco Bell	1997	n/a	2
Return of the Jedi glasses, Burger King	1983	n/a	5
Star Wars poster, Pizza Hut	1997	n/a	5
Transforming playsets, small, set of sixteen, Pizza Hut	1998	n/a	3
Yoda toy, Taco Bell	1997	n/a	2
FRAMES			
Darth Vader Picture Frame, Sigma		30	45
R2-D2 Picture Frame, Sigma		30	45
HALLOWEEN COSTUME			
Admiral Ackbar, Ben Cooper	1983	n/a	10
Boba Fett, Ben Cooper	1979	n/a	10
C-3PO, Ben Cooper	1977	n/a	10
Chewbacca, Ben Cooper	1977	n/a	10
Darth Vader, Ben Cooper	1977	n/a	10
Gamorrean Guard, Ben Cooper	1983	n/a	10
Klaatu, Ben Cooper	1983	n/a	10
Leia, Ben Cooper	1977	n/a	10
Luke, Ben Cooper	1977	n/a	10
Luke X-Wing pilot, Ben Cooper	1977	n/a	10
R2-D2, Ben Cooper	1977	n/a	10
Stormtrooper, Ben Cooper	1977	n/a	10
Wicket, Ben Cooper	1983	n/a	10
Yoda, Ben Cooper	1980	n/a	10
KITS			
Flying R2-D2 Rocket Kit, Estes	1978	9	13
TIE Fighter Rocket Kit, Estes	1978	11	16
X-Wing Fighter Rocket Kit, Estes	1978	11	16
X-Wing with Maxi-Brutel Rocket Kit, Estes	1978	18	25
MEDALS			
Chewbacca, W. Berrie	1980	6	8
X-Wing, W. Berrie	1980	6	8
MISCELLANEOUS			
Chewbacca/Darth Vader Bookends, Sigma		25	35
Darth Vader Duty Roster		5	7
Darth Vader SSP Van, Kenner	1978	20	25
Empire Strikes Back Dinnerware Set		15	25
Intergalactic Passport and Stickers, Ballantine	1983	7	10
Original Fan Club Kit	1977	10	15
Original Press Kit	1977	25	45
Return of the Jedi Candy Containers, figural, set of eighteen, Topps	1983	25	35
Star Wars Dinnerware Set		20	30
Sticker Set and Album, Burger King		7	10
Yoda Hand Puppet		14	20
Yoda Jedi Master Fortune Teller Ball		20	30

STAR WARS TOYS
(NON-ACTION FIGURES)

NAME	YEAR	MNP	MIP
MUGS			
C-3PO, ceramic, Sigma		16	23
Chewbacca, ceramic, Sigma		18	25
Darth Vader, ceramic, Sigma		16	23
Gamorrean Guard, ceramic, Sigma		10	20
Han Solo, ceramic, Sigma		23	35
Lando Calrissian, ceramic, Sigma		16	23
Leia, ceramic, Sigma		20	30
Luke Skywalker, ceramic, Sigma		20	30
PAINTS			
Admiral Ackbar Figurine Paint Set, Craft Master		9	13
C-3PO Figurine Paint Set, Craft Master		9	13
Darth Vader Paint Set, glow-in-the-dark		9	13
Han Solo Figurine Paint Set, Craft Master		16	23
Leia and Han Solo Paint Set, glow-in-the-dark		9	13
Leia Figurine Paint Set, Craft Master		11	16
Luke and Tauntaun Figurine Paint Set, Craft Master		14	20
Luke Skywalker Paint Set, glow-in-the-dark		9	13
Wicket Figurine Paint Set, Craft Master		9	13
Yoda Figurine Paint Set, Craft Master		9	13
Yoda Paint Set, glow-in-the-dark		9	13
PEZ			
Boba Fett, PEZ	1999	1	2
C-3PO, PEZ	1997	1	3
Chewbacca, PEZ	1997	1	3
Darth Vader, PEZ	1997	1	3
Ewok, PEZ	1999	1	3
Luke Skywalker, PEZ	1999	1	3
Princess Leia, PEZ	1999	1	3
Stormtrooper, PEZ	1997	1	3
Yoda, PEZ	1997	1	3
PLAY-DOH			
Ewoks Play-Doh Set		11	16
Ice Planet Hoth Play-Doh Set		16	23
Jabba the Hutt Play-Doh Set		11	16
Star Wars Action Play-Doh Set		20	30
POSTERS			
Ben Kenobi/Darth Vader, Proctor & Gamble	1978	9	13
Chewbacca, Burger King	1978	5	7
Dagobah, Burger King	1980	5	7
Darth Vader, Proctor & Gamble	1980	5	8
Darth Vader, Nestea	1980	5	7
Darth Vader, Burger King	1978	5	7
Death Star, Proctor & Gamble	1978	5	8
Empire Strikes Back 1981 re-release		n/a	40
Empire Strikes Back 1982 re-release		n/a	40
Empire Strikes Back advance		n/a	65
Empire Strikes Back Poster Album Vol. 1		10	15

Twin-Pod Cloud Car,
Empire Strikes Back, 1979

Tatooine Skiff, POTF

C-3PO Cookie
Jar, ceramic,
1977, Roman

STAR WARS TOYS (NON-ACTION FIGURES)

NAME	YEAR	MNP	MIP
Empire Strikes Back Radio Program Poster		15	20
Empire Strikes Back Special Edition		n/a	20
Hoth Poster, Burger King	1980	5	7
Luke Skywalker, Nestea	1980	5	7
Luke Skywalker, Proctor & Gamble	1980	5	8
Luke Skywalker, Burger King	1978	5	7
R2-D2 and C-3PO Poster, Proctor & Gamble	1980	5	8
R2-D2 Poster, Burger King	1978	5	7
Return of the Jedi 1985 re-release		n/a	40
Return of the Jedi Special Edition		n/a	20
Revenge of the Jedi w/date		n/a	175
Revenge of the Jedi without date		n/a	250
Star Destroyer, General Mills	1978	5	10
Star Wars 1982 re-release		n/a	65
Star Wars Birthday		n/a	700
Star Wars Mylar Advance		n/a	750
Star Wars Radio Program, Golden		23	35
Star Wars second advance		n/a	100
Star Wars Special Edition		n/a	20
Star Wars: Episode I ó The Phantom Menace		n/a	20
TIE Fighter and X-Wing Poster, General Mills	1978	30	40

PUNCHING BAGS

NAME	YEAR	MNP	MIP
Chewbacca, Kenner	1977	20	40
Darth Vader, Kenner	1977	15	30
Jawa, Kenner	1977	45	65
R2-D2, Kenner	1977	15	30

PUZZLES

NAME	YEAR	MNP	MIP
Attack of the Sand People, 140 pieces, Kenner		5	7
Cantina Band, 500 pieces, Kenner		6	8
Han Solo and Chewbacca, 140 pieces, Kenner		6	8
Jabba the Hutt, Craft Master	1983	4	7
Jabba the Hutt, Craft Master	1983	4	7
Jawas capture R2-D2, 140 pieces, Kenner		4	6
Luke and Leia leap for their lives, 500 pieces, Kenner		6	8
Luke Skywalker, 500 pieces, Kenner		6	10
Space Battle, 500 pieces, Kenner		7	10
Stormtroopers stop the Landspeeder, 140 pieces, Kenner		5	7
Trapped in the Trash Compactor, 140 pieces, Kenner		5	7
Victory Celebration, 500 pieces, Kenner		6	8
X-Wing Fighters Prepare to Attack, 500 pieces, Kenner		6	8

RINGS

NAME	YEAR	MNP	MIP
Darth Vader, W. Berrie	1980	6	8

STAR WARS TOYS (NON-ACTION FIGURES)

NAME	YEAR	MNP	MIP
SCHOOL SUPPLIES			
C-3PO Pencil Tray, Sigma		23	35
C-3PO Tape Dispenser, Sigma		23	35
R2-D2 String Dispenser with Scissors, Sigma		20	30
Yoda Tumbler/Pencil Cup, Sigma		20	30
STAR WARS BUDDIES			
C-3PO, Hasbro	1998	n/a	6
Cantina Band Member, Hasbro	1998	n/a	6
Chewbacca, first version, Hasbro	1998	n/a	10
Chewbacca, second version, Hasbro	1998	n/a	6
Darth Vader Pillow	1983	9	13
Jabba the Hutt, Hasbro	1998	n/a	6
Jawa, Hasbro	1998	n/a	6
Max Rebo, Hasbro	1998	n/a	6
R2-D2, Hasbro	1998	n/a	6
Salacious Crumb, Hasbro	1998	n/a	6
Wampa, Hasbro	1998	n/a	6
Wicket, Hasbro	1998	n/a	6
Yoda, Hasbro	1998	n/a	6
Yoda Sleeping Bag		16	23
TOOTHBRUSHES & ACC.			
Electric Toothbrush, Kenner	1978	16	23
Snow Speeder Toothbrush Holder, Sigma		25	35
Wicket Toothbrush, battery-operated	1984	9	13
WATCHES			
C-3PO and R2-D2, digital, Bradley	1970s	55	80
C-3PO and R2-D2, digital, rectangular, Bradley	1970s	30	45
C-3PO and R2-D2, digital, round face, Bradley	1970s	45	65
C-3PO and R2-D2, digital, round, musical, Bradley	1970s	70	100
C-3PO and R2-D2, vinyl band, Bradley	1970s	45	60
C-3PO and R2-D2, vinyl band, photo, Bradley	1970s	30	45
C-3PO and R2-D2, white border, photo, Bradley	1970s	45	65
Darth Vader, digital, Bradley	1970s	30	45
Darth Vader, star and planet on face, Bradley	1970s	45	65
Darth Vader, vinyl band, Bradley	1970s	30	45
Droids, digital, Bradley	1970s	30	45
Ewoks, vinyl band, Bradley	1970s	30	45
Jabba the Hutt, digital, Bradley	1970s	30	45
Wicket the Ewok Wristwatch, Bradley	1970s	30	45
Yoda, Bradley	1970s	30	45
Yoda, Bradley	1970s	30	45

Classic Tin Toys

Today's toys may be durable, but most are made of plastic, which just doesn't hold the charm and nostalgia of yesterday's tin creations. Those tin toys, made in large numbers mainly before World War II, are among the priciest collectible toys today.

Metal toys produced before World War I can be considered true works of art, especially since tin toys were often painstakingly hand painted.

But the advent of chromolithography changed the way most toys were produced. Chromolithography was actually developed late in the 19th century. The technique allowed multicolor illustrations to be printed on flat tin plates which were molded into toys.

Starting in the 1920s, lithographed tin toys began to dramatically change toy production. American manufacturers could produce these colorful toys more inexpensively than the classic European toys that had dominated the toy market until this time.

With mass production came mass appeal. New tin mechanical toys were based on the characters and celebrities that were popular at the time. Newspaper comic strips and Walt Disney movies provided already popular subject matter for toy marketers.

Among the most well-known makers of mechanical tin toys were Marx, Chein, Lehmann and Strauss. Others included Courtland, Girard, Ohio Art, Schuco, Unique Art and Wolverine.

Many of these manufacturers had business relationships with each other. Over the years, some would be found working together, producing toys for others, distributing others' toys or being absorbed by other companies. There even appeared to be some pilfering and reproducing others' ideas.

One of the advantages of lithography was that it allowed old toys to be recycled in many ways. When a character's public appeal began to wane, a new image could be printed on the same body to produce a new toy. Or when a toy company was absorbed by another, older models could be dusted off and dressed up with new lithography. Many of the mechanical tin wind-up toys show up in surprisingly similar versions with another manufacturer's name on them.

Of the companies listed here, Marx was no doubt the most prolific. The company's founder, Louis Marx, at one time was employed by another leading toy maker, Ferdinand Strauss. He left Strauss in 1918 to start his own company. Some of his first successes were new versions of old Strauss toys like the Climbing Monkey and Alabama Coon Jigger.

Many of the popular Marx tin wind-ups were based on popular characters. One of the most sought-after is the Merrymakers

Disneyland Ferris Wheel, Chein

Band, a group of mouse musicians. Some of the other highly valued character toys are the Amos 'N Andy Walkers, the Donald Duck Duet, Popeye the Champ, Li'l Abner and his Dogpatch Band and the Superman Rollover Airplane.

While Marx went on to produce many different kinds of toys, other companies, such as Chein, specialized in inexpensive lithographed tin. And like Marx, Chein also capitalized on popular cartoon characters, producing several Popeye toys, among others. J. Chein and Company, which was founded in 1903, was best known for its carnival-themed mechanical toys. Its Ferris wheel is fairly well known among toy collectors and was made in several lithographed versions, including one with a Disneyland theme. Chein also produced a number of affordable tin banks.

Girard was founded shortly after Chein, but didn't start producing toys until 1918. It subcontracted toys for Marx and Strauss in the 1920s. In fact, several Girard and Marx toys are identical, having been produced in the same plant with different names on them. Marx later took over the company in the 1930s.

New Jersey-based Unique Art isn't known for an extensive line of toys, but it produced some that are favorites among tin toy collectors. It, too, reportedly was acquired by Marx at some point.

There are many other companies that produced lithographed tin toys not included in this section, particularly German and Japanese companies. Lehmann and Schuco, both German firms, are the only non-American toy makers listed in this guide. More lithographed tin toys can be found in the vehicles section of this book.

Prices listed are for toys in Good, Excellent and Mint conditions. Toys will usually command a premium over the listed price if they are in their original boxes.

Trends

Older tin litho toy values are holding their own. However, due to the scarcity that has been created by collectors building and maintaining their collections, the values will continue to rise during 1998.

Remember, the better the condition, the better the value, especially with tin. Any character toys in Excellent condition or better are certain winners. Those with the original box are true treasures.

The Top 10 Tin Toys
(in Mint condition)

1. Popeye the Heavy Hitter, Chein $6,500
2. Popeye Acrobat, Marx 5,500
3. Popeye the Champ, Marx 4,600
4. Mikado Family, Lehmann 3,900
5. Red the Iceman, Marx 3,500
6. Mortimer Snerd Hometown Band, Marx 2,500
7. Popeye with Punching Bag, Chein 2,500
8. Lehmann's Autobus, Lehmann 2,500
9. Popeye Express, Marx 2,400
10. Hott and Trott, Unique Art 2,300

CHEIN

NAME	DESCRIPTION	GOOD	EX	MINT

Banks

NAME	DESCRIPTION	GOOD	EX	MINT
2nd National Duck Bank	1954, 3-1/2" high, Disney characters	90	145	225
Cash Box	1930, 2" high, round trap	30	50	75
Child's Safe Bank	1900's, 5-1/2" high	40	65	100
Child's Safe Bank	1910, 4" high, sailboat on front of door	35	60	90
Child's Safe Bank	1910, 3" high, dog on front of door	35	60	95
Church	1930s, 4" high	35	60	90
Church	1954, 3-1/2" high	70	115	175
Clown	1931, 5" high	70	115	175
Clown	1949, 5" high, says bank on front	35	60	95
Drum	1930s, 2-1/2" high	35	60	95
Elephant	1950s, 5" high	55	90	135
God Bless America	1930s, 2-1/2" high, drum shaped	30	50	75
Happy Days Cash Register	1930s, 4" high	45	80	120
Humpty Dumpty	1934, 5-1/4" high	60	100	150
Log Cabin	1930s, 3" high	80	130	200
Mascot Safe	1914, 5" high	35	60	95
Mascot Safe	1914, 4" high	35	55	85
Monkey	1950s, 5-1/4" high	55	90	135
New Deal	1930s, 3-1/4" high	50	80	125
Prosperity Bank	1930s, 2-1/4" high, pail shaped, w/band	35	60	95
Prosperity Bank	1930s, 2-1/4" high, pail shaped, without band	30	50	75
Roly Poly	1940s, 6" high	135	230	350
Scout	1931, 3-1/4" high, cylinder	100	165	250
Three Little Pigs	1930s, 3" high	60	100	150
Treasure Chest	1930s, 2" high	35	60	90
Uncle Sam	1934, 4" high, hat shaped	50	75	100
Uncle Wiggly	1950s, 5" high	50	75	100

Miscellaneous Toys

NAME	DESCRIPTION	GOOD	EX	MINT
Army Drummer	1930s, 7" high, plunger-activated	70	115	175
Disneyland Tea Set	15-piece set featuring Disney characters	100	175	500
Dolly's Washer	washing machine	65	100	300
Easter Basket	nursery rhyme figures	35	55	100
Easter Egg	1938, 5-1/2", tin, chicken on top, opens to hold candy	35	55	85
Helicopter, Toy Town Airways	1950s, 13" long, friction drive	55	90	135
Indian in Headdress	1930s, 5-1/2" high	75	125	200
Marine	hand on belt	60	100	150
Melody Organ Player		75	125	175
Musical Top Clown	1950s, 7" high, clown head handle	75	125	195
Player Piano	eight rolls	195	325	500
Sand Toy	7" high, monkey bends and twists	30	50	75
Sand Toy Set	duck mold, sifter, frog on card	30	45	70
Scuba Diver	10" long	70	120	185
See-Saw Sand Toy	1930s, bright colors, boy and girl on see-saw move	55	90	135
See-Saw Sand Toy	1930s, pastel colors, boy and girl on see-saw move	70	120	185
Space Ride	tin litho, boxed, lever action w/music	135	230	350
Sparkler Toy	5", on original card	30	50	75

Wind-up Toys

NAME	DESCRIPTION	GOOD	EX	MINT
Airplane, square-winged	early tin, 7" wingspan	90	145	225
Army Cargo Truck	1920s, 8" long	235	390	600
Army Plane	11" wingspan	135	230	350
Army Sergeant		70	120	185
Army Truck	8-1/2" long, cannon on back	50	80	125
Army Truck	8-1/2" long, open bed	40	65	100
Barnacle Bill	1930s, looks like Popeye, waddles	330	550	850
Bear	1938, w/hat, pants, shirt, bow tie	55	90	135
Bunny	1940s	35	60	100
Cabin Cruiser	1940s, 9" long	35	55	85

Acrobatic Marvel Monkey, Marx

*B.O. Plenty
Walker, Marx*

CHEIN

NAME	DESCRIPTION	GOOD	EX	MINT
Cat	w/wood wheels	40	65	100
Chick	4" high, bright colored clothes, polka dot bow tie	35	55	85
Chicken Pushing Wheelbarrow	1930s	35	60	100
China Clipper	10" long	135	225	350
Clown Boxing	8" tall, tin	235	390	600
Clown in Barrel	1930s, 8" high, waddles	175	295	450
Clown with Parasol	1920s, 8" tall	105	180	275
Dan-Dee Dump Truck		115	195	300
Disneyland Ferris Wheel	1940s	400	650	1200
Disneyland Roller Coaster		400	620	1200
Doughboy	1920s, 6" high, tin litho, WWI soldier w/rifle	145	245	375
Drummer Boy	1930s, 9" high, w/shako	100	150	225
Duck	1930, 4" high, waddles	50	75	100
Duck	1930, 6" high, waddles	50	80	150
Ferris Wheel	1930s, 16-1/2" high, six compartments, ringing bell	250	425	1000
Ferris Wheel, The Giant Ride	16" high	100	250	500
Greyhound Bus	6" long, wood tires	90	155	235
Handstand Clown		75	125	200
Handstand Clown	1930s, 5" tall	75	125	200
Happy Hooligan	1932, 6" high, tin litho	195	325	500
Hercules Ferris Wheel		145	245	400
Indian in Headdress	4" high, red, 1930s	50	80	125
Jumping Rabbit	1925	100	165	250
Junior Bus	9" long, yellow	70	115	175
Mack Hercules Motor Express	19-1/2" long, tin litho	235	385	595
Mack Hercules Truck	7-1/2" long	165	275	425
Mark 1 Cabin Cruiser	1957, 9" long	35	60	95
Mechanical Aquaplane, No. 39	1932, 8-1/2" long, boat-like pontoons	100	165	250
Mechanical Fish	1940s, 11" long	30	50	75
Merry-Go-Round	11" w/swan chairs	475	775	1200
Motorboat	1950s, 7" long, crank action	35	60	90
Motorboat	1950s, 9" long	40	65	100
Musical Aero Swing	1940s, 10" high	295	490	750
Musical Merry-Go-Round	small version	155	260	400
Musical Toy Church	1937, crank music box	90	145	225
Peggy Jane Speedboat		50	75	100
Pelican		100	165	250
Penguin in Tuxedo	1940s	50	100	125
Pig		35	60	95
Playland Merry-Go-Round	1930s, 9-1/2" high	500	850	1200
Playland Whip, No. 340	four bump cars, driver's head wobbles	500	850	1250
Popeye in Barrel		380	625	1000
Popeye the Heavy Hitter	bell and mallet	2550	4225	6500
Popeye with Punching Bag		975	1625	2500
Ride-A-Rocket Carnival Ride	1950s, 19" high, four rockets	510	845	1300
Roadster	1925, 8-1/2" long	50	80	125
Roller Coaster	1950s, includes two cars	300	450	700
Roller Coaster	1938, includes two cars	255	425	650
Royal Blue Line Coast to Coast Service		410	685	1050
Sandmill	beach scene on side	90	145	225
Santa's Elf	1925, 6" high, boxed	235	390	600
Sea Plane	1930s, silver, red, and blue	115	195	300
Seal	balancing barbells	90	145	225
Ski-Boy	1930s, 6" long	200	300	450
Ski-Boy	1930s, 8" long	200	300	450
Speedboat	14" long	90	145	225
Touring Car	7" long	60	100	150
Turtle with Native on Its Back	1940s	165	275	425
Woody Car	1940s, 5" long, red	100	165	250
Yellow Cab	7" long	200	300	400
Yellow Taxi	6" long, orange and black	135	225	350

Butter and Egg Man,
Unique Art

Clown in Barrel,
Chein

TIN TOYS

LEHMANN

NAME	DESCRIPTION	GOOD	EX	MINT
Aha Truck		470	780	1200
Ajax Acrobat	does somersaults, 10" tall	850	1425	2200
Alabama Jigger	wind-up tap dancer on square base, 1920s	490	825	1500
Auton Boy & Cart		195	325	495
Captain of Kopenick	early 1900s	625	1050	1600
Crocodile	walks, mouth opens	285	475	725
Dancing Sailor		585	975	1500
Delivery Van	"Huntley & Palmers Biscuits"	650	1075	1650
Express Man & Cart		335	550	850
Flying Bird		295	475	750
Galop Race Car	1920s	235	390	600
Gustav The Climbing Miller		390	650	1000
Ito Sedan and Driver		525	875	1350
KADI	Chinese men carrying box	600	975	2000
Lehmann's Autobus		975	1625	2500
Li-La Car	driver in rear, women passengers	725	1200	1850
Mikado Family		1525	2550	3900
Minstrel Man	early 1900s	335	550	1000
New Century Cycle	driver and black man w/umbrella	700	1175	1800
Ostrich Cart		380	650	975
Paddy Riding Pig		700	1175	1800
Quack Quack	duck pulling babies	295	495	750
Rooster and Rabbit	rooster pulls rabbit on cart	380	625	975
Sea Lion		145	250	375
Sedan and Garage		335	550	850
Shenandoah Zeppelin		155	255	395
Skier	wind-up, 1920s	510	850	1300
Taxi	10" long, 1920s	450	750	1150
Tut-Tut Car	driver has horn	850	1430	2200
Wild West Bucking Bronco		525	875	1350
Zebra Cart "Dare Devil"	1920s	400	600	800
Zig-Zag	handcar-type vehicle on oversized wheels	780	1300	2000

MARX

NAME	DESCRIPTION	GOOD	EX	MINT

Buildings and Rooms

NAME	DESCRIPTION	GOOD	EX	MINT
Airport	1930s	115	195	300
Automatic Car Wash		135	225	350
Automatic Firehouse with Fire Chief Car	friction car, firehouse w/plastic doors, 1940s	115	195	300
Automatic Garage	family car	145	245	375
Blue Bird Garage	1937	135	225	350
Brightlite Filling Station	pump w/round top says "Fresh Air," 1930s	250	425	650
Brightlite Filling Station	rectangular shaped pumps, battery-operated, late 1930s	255	425	650
Brightlite Filling Station	bottle-shaped gas pumps, battery-operated, 1930s	255	425	650
Bus Terminal	1937	175	295	450
Busy Airport Garage	1936	195	325	500
Busy Parking Lot	five heavy gauge streamline autos, 1937	235	390	600
Busy Street	six vehicles, 1935	145	310	475
City Airport	w/two metal planes, 1938	115	195	300
Crossing Gate House		115	195	300
Crossover Speedway	1941	100	165	250
Crossover Speedway	litho buildings on bridge, two cars, litho drivers, 1938	115	190	295
Dick Tracy Automatic Police Station	station and car	375	625	950
Gas Pump Island		115	195	300
General Alarm Fire House	wind-up alarm bell, steel chief car and patrol truck, 1938	175	295	450
Greyhound Bus Terminal	1938	115	195	300
Gull Service Station	1940s	185	310	475
Hollywood Bungalow House	1935	165	275	425

TIN TOYS

Dancing Sailor, Lehmann

Daredevil Motor Cop, Unique Art

NAME	DESCRIPTION	GOOD	EX	MINT
Home Town Drug Store	1930s	175	295	450
Home Town Favorite Store	1930s	175	295	450
Home Town Fire House	1930s	175	295	450
Home Town Grocery Store	1930s	165	275	425
Home Town Meat Market	1930s	180	300	465
Home Town Movie Theatre	1930s	145	245	375
Home Town Police Station	1930s	145	245	375
Home Town Savings Bank	1930s	145	245	375
Honeymoon Garage	1935	165	275	425
Lincoln Highway Set	pumps, oil-grease rack, traffic light and car, 1933	350	585	900
Loop-the-Loop Auto Racer	1-3/4", 1931	155	260	400
Magic Garage	w/friction town car, 1934	145	250	375
Magic Garage	litho garage, wind-up car, 1934	145	250	375
Main Street Station	litho garage, 4" wind-up steel vehicles	165	275	425
Metal Service Station	1949-50	165	275	425
Military Airport		105	180	275
Model School House	1960s	50	80	125
Mot-O-Run 4 Lane Hi-Way	cars, trucks, buses move on 27" electric track, 1949	105	180	275
New York World's Fair Speedway	litho track, two red cars, 1939	295	495	750
Newlyweds' Bathroom	1920s	100	165	500
Newlyweds' Bedroom	1920s	100	165	500
Newlyweds' Dining Room	1920s	100	165	500
Newlyweds' Kitchen	1920s	100	165	500
Newlyweds' Library	1920s	100	165	500
Roadside Rest Service Station	Laurel and Hardy at counter, w/stools in front, 1935	625	1050	1600
Roadside Rest Service Station	Laurel and Hardy at counter, no stool in front, 1938	550	950	1450
Service Station	two pumps, two friction vehicles, 1929	295	495	750
Service Station Gas Pumps	wind-up, 9"	125	210	325
Sky Hawk Flyer	wind-up, two planes, tower, 7-1/2" tall	125	210	325
Stunt Auto Racer	two blue racers, 1931	135	225	350
Sunnyside Garage	1935	255	425	650
TV and Radio Station		135	225	350
Universal Motor Repair Shop	tin, 1938	255	425	650
Used Car Market	base, several vehicles and signs, 1939	255	425	650
Whee-Whiz Auto Racer	four 2" multicolored racers w/litho driver, 1925	295	495	750

Miscellaneous Toys

NAME	DESCRIPTION	GOOD	EX	MINT
Army Code Sender	pressed steel	20	35	50
Baby Grand Piano	w/piano-shaped music books	50	100	250
Big Shot		75	100	150
Cat Pushing Ball	lever action, wood ball, 1938	75	100	150
Hopping Rabbit	metal and plastic, 4" tall, 1950s	40	65	100
Jumping Frog		40	65	100
Jungle Man Spear		100	150	200
King Kong	on wheels, w/spring-loaded arms, 6-1/2" tall	35	60	95
Mysterious Woodpecker		50	80	125
Pathe Movie Camera	6" tall, 1930s	55	90	135
Rooster		60	100	150
Searchlight	3-1/2" tall	40	65	100
Toto the Acrobat		100	165	250

Trains

NAME	DESCRIPTION	GOOD	EX	MINT
Commodore Vanderbilt Train	track, wind-up	75	125	190
Crazy Express Train	plastic and litho, wind-up, 12" long, 1960s	115	195	300
Disneyland Express	locomotive and three tin cars, wind-up, 21-1/2" long, 1950s	255	425	650
Disneyland Express, Casey Jr. Circus Train	wind-up, 12" long	100	165	250
Disneyland Train	Goofy drives locomotive w/three tin cars, wind-up, 1950	135	225	350

TIN TOYS

Disneyland Roller Coaster, Chein

Flippo the Jumping Dog, Marx

MARX

NAME	DESCRIPTION	GOOD	EX	MINT
Engine Train	ten cars, no track, HO, 1960s	65	110	170
Flintstones Choo Choo Train "Bedrock Express"	wind-up, 13" long, 1950s	235	390	600
Glendale Depot Railroad Station Train	1930s	235	390	600
Mickey Mouse Express Train Set	1952	235	390	900
Mickey Mouse Meteor Train	four cars/engine, wind-up, 1950s	255	425	650
Musical Choo-Choo	1966	35	60	90
Mystery Tunnel	wind-up	90	145	225
New York Central Engine Train	four cars	195	325	500
New York Circular with Train, with airplane	wind-up, 1928	490	825	1250
New York Circular with Train, without airplane	wind-up, 1928	410	695	1050
Popeye Express	1936, version of Honeymoon Express, w/ airplane	925	1550	2400
Railroad Watch Tower	electric light, 9" tall	35	60	90
Scenic Express Train Set	wind-up, 1950s	60	105	160
Subway Express	w/plastic tunnel, 1954	185	310	475
Train Set	plastic locomotive, tin cars, wind-up, 6" long, 1950s	60	100	150
Trolley No. 200	headlight, bell, tin wind-up, 9" long, 1920s	195	325	500

Wagons and Carts

NAME	DESCRIPTION	GOOD	EX	MINT
Bluto, Brutus, Horse and Cart	celluloid figure, metal, 1938	350	585	900
Busy Delivery	open three-wheel cart, wind-up, 9" long, 1939	295	475	750
Farm Wagon	horse pulling wagon, 10" long, 1940s	60	100	150
Horse and Cart	wind-up, 7" long, 1934	80	130	200
Horse and Cart	w/driver, 9-1/2" long, 1950s	40	65	100
Horse and Cart with Clown Driver	wind-up, 7-5/8" long, 1923	135	225	350
Pinocchio Busy Delivery	on unicycle facing two-wheel cart, wind-up, 7-3/4" long, 1939	275	475	750
Popeye Horse and Cart	wind-up	335	550	850
Rooster Pulling Wagon	1930s	135	225	350
Toyland's Farm Products Milk Wagon	wind-up, 10-1/2" long, 1930s	145	245	375
Two Donkeys Pulling Cart	w/driver, wind-up, 10-1/4" long, 1940s	105	180	275
Wagon with Two-Horse Team	late 1940s, wind-up	90	145	225

Wind-up Toys

NAME	DESCRIPTION	GOOD	EX	MINT
Acrobatic Marvel Monkey	balances on two chairs, 1930s	100	165	250
Amos 'n Andy Walkers	11" tall, 1930, each	650	1075	1800
B.O. Plenty Walker	8-1/2" tall, holds Sparkle Plenty, 1940s	185	310	475
Balky Mule	8-3/4" long, 1948	100	175	250
Ballerina	6" tall	90	145	225
Barney Rubble Riding Dino	8" long, 1960s	185	310	475
Bear Cyclist	5-3/4" tall, 1934	70	115	175
Bear Waddler	4" tall, 1960s	50	80	125
Beat! The Komikal Kop	1930s	125	210	325
Big Parade	1928	410	685	1050
Big Three Aerial Acrobats	1920	235	390	600
Boy on Trapeze		90	145	225
Busy Bridge	vehicles on bridge, 24" long, 1937	350	575	895
Busy Miners	miner's car, 16-1/2" long, 1930s	175	295	450
Butter and Egg Man	wind-up walker	700	1175	1800
Captain America	5" tall, 1968	55	90	140
Carter Climbing Monkey	8-1/2" tall, 1921	115	190	290
Charleston Trio	man, boy and dog dancers on roof, 9" tall, 1926	525	875	1350
Charlie McCarthy Bass Drummer	1939	450	750	1150
Charlie McCarthy Walker	1930s	335	550	850

Gobbling Goose, Marx

Handstand Clown, Chein

Hoky Poky, 1930s, Wyandotte

MARX

NAME	DESCRIPTION	GOOD	EX	MINT
Chipmunk		50	80	125
Chompy the Beetle	w/action and sound, 6" tall, 1960s	60	100	150
Clancy	11" tall wind-up walker, 1931	195	325	500
Climbing Fireman	tin and plastic, 1950s	135	225	350
Coast Defense Revolving Airplane	circular w/three cannons, 1929	390	650	1000
Cowboy on Horse	6" tall, 1925	70	115	175
Cowboy Rider	black horse version, 7", 1930s	165	275	425
Cowboy Rider	w/lariat on black horse, 1941	145	245	375
Crazy Dora		165	275	425
Dapper Dan Coon Jigger	10" tall, 1922	600	900	1300
Dapper Dan the Jigger Porter	9-1/2" tall, 1924	600	900	1300
Dippy Dumper		135	225	350
Donald Duck and Scooter	1960s	90	145	225
Donald Duck Duet	Donald and Goofy, 10-1/2" tall, 1946	470	780	1200
Donald Duck Walker	w/three nephews	100	165	250
Donald the Drummer	10" tall, 1940s	135	225	350
Donald the Skier	plastic, metal skis, 10-1/2" tall, 1940s	165	275	425
Dopey	walker, 8" tall, 1938	310	525	1000
Doughboy Walker		215	360	550
Drummer Boy	1939	275	475	725
Dumbo	rollover action, 4" tall, 1941	175	295	450
Easter Rabbit	holds Easter basket, 5" tall	70	115	175
Ferdinand the Bull	tail spins, 4" tall, 1938	250	400	600
Ferdinand the Bull and the Matador	5-1/2" tall, 1938	300	500	800
Figaro (Pinocchio)	rollover action, 5" long, 1940	135	225	350
Fireman on Ladder	24" tall	165	275	425
Flipping Monkey		80	130	200
Flippo the Jumping Dog	3" tall, 1940	165	275	425
Flutterfly	3" long, 1929	90	145	225
George the Drummer Boy	moving eyes, 9" tall, 1930s	195	325	500
George the Drummer Boy	stationary eyes, 9" tall, 1930s	175	295	450
Gobbling Goose	lays golden eggs, 1940s	125	210	325
Golden Pecking Goose	9-1/2" long, 1924	135	225	350
Goofy	tail spins, plastic, 9" tall, 1950s	125	210	325
Goofy the Walking Gardener	holds a wheelbarrow, 9" tall, 1960	250	425	650
Hap/Hop Ramp Walker	2-1/2" tall, 1950s	40	65	100
Harold Lloyd Funny Face	walker, 11" tall, 1928	275	475	725
Hey Hey the Chicken Snatcher	1926, 8-1/2", black man w/chicken	850	1450	2200
Hi-Yo Silver and the Lone Ranger	8" tall, 1938	195	325	650
Honeymoon Cottage, Honeymoon Express 7	square base	115	195	300
Honeymoon Express	1940s, circular train and plane	215	360	550
Honeymoon Express	1927, old-fashioned train on circular track	225	375	575
Honeymoon Express	1947, streamlined train on circular track	185	310	475
Hoppo the Monkey	plays cymbals, 8" tall, 1925	100	165	250
Howdy Doody	plays banjo and moves head, 5" tall, 1950	250	425	800
Howdy Doody	does jig and Clarabell sits at piano, 5-1/2" tall, 1950	525	875	1350
Jazzbo Jim	9" tall, 1920s	375	625	1200
Jetsons Figure	4" tall, 1960s	75	130	200
Jiminy Cricket Pushing Bass Fiddle	walker	85	145	220
Jiving Jigger	1950	135	225	350
Joe Penner and His Duck Goo-Goo	7-1/2" tall, 1934	375	625	1000
Jumbo The Climbing Monkey	9-3/4" tall, 1923	135	225	425
Knockout Champs Boxing Toy	1930s	175	295	450
Leopard	growls and walks, 1950	65	105	165
Little King Walkers	3" tall, 1963	50	80	125
Little Orphan Annie and Sandy	1930s	275	475	725
Little Orphan Annie Skipping Rope		165	275	425

Honeymoon Express, Marx

Indian in Headdress, Chein

NAME	DESCRIPTION	GOOD	EX	MINT
Little Orphan Annie's Dog Sandy	tin litho	105	180	275
Mad Russian Drummer	7" tall	225	375	575
Main Street	street scene w/moving cars, traffic cop, 1927	340	575	875
Mammy's Boy	wind-up walker, 11" tall, 1929	310	525	795
Merrymakers Band	w/marquee, mouse band, 1931	700	1200	1900
Merrymakers Band	without marquee, mouse band, 1931	600	1000	1600
Mickey Mouse	7" tall	200	400	600
Minnie Mouse	7" tall	200	400	600
Minnie Mouse in Rocker	1950s	275	450	695
Minstrel Figure	11" tall	175	295	450
Monkey Cyclist	9-3/4" tall, 1923	105	180	275
Moon Creature	5-1/2" tall	135	225	350
Moon Mullins and Kayo on Handcar	6" long, 1930s	335	550	850
Mortimer Snerd Bass Drummer	1939	850	1450	2200
Mortimer Snerd Hometown Band	1935	925	1550	2500
Mortimer Snerd Walker	1939	185	310	475
Mother Goose	7-1/2" tall, 1920s	150	250	500
Mother Penguin with Baby Penguin on Sled	3" long, 1950s	35	55	85
Musical Circus Horse	pull toy, metal drum rolls w/chimes, 10-1/2" long, 1939	80	130	200
Mystery Cat	8-1/2" long, 1931	100	165	250
Mystery Pluto	8" long, 1948	100	165	250
Nodding Goose		75	120	150
Pecos Bill	twirls rope, plastic, 10" tall, 1950s	80	130	200
Pikes Peak Mountain Climber	vehicle on track	325	525	800
Pinched	square based, open circular track, 1927	275	450	695
Pinocchio	5" tall, 1950s	250	425	650
Pinocchio	9" tall, 1938	275	450	700
Pinocchio the Acrobat	16" tall, 1939	335	550	850
Pinocchio Walker	stationary eyes, 1930s	250	425	650
Pinocchio Walker	animated eyes, 8-1/2" tall, 1930s	275	450	700
Pluto Drum Major		235	390	595
Pluto Watch Me Roll-Over	8" long, 1939	165	275	425
Poor Fish	8-1/2" long, 1936	70	115	175
Popeye Acrobat		2150	3600	5500
Popeye and Olive Oyl Jiggers	10" tall, 1936	700	1175	1800
Popeye Express	w/trunk and wheelbarrow	200	500	800
Popeye Handcar	1935	775	1300	2000
Popeye the Champ	tin and celluloid, 7" long, 1936	1800	3000	4600
Popeye the Pilot		100	300	500
Porky Pig Cowboy with Lariat	8" tall, 1949	280	475	725
Porky Pig with Rotating Umbrella	8" tall, 1939, w/or without top hat	310	525	800
Red Cap Porter		375	625	950
Red the Iceman		1350	2275	3500
Ride 'Em Cowboy		90	145	225
Ring-A-Ling Circus	7-1/2" diameter base, 1925	475	775	1200
Rodeo Joe	1933	200	300	450
Running Scottie	12-1/2" long, 1938	70	115	175
Smitty Riding a Scooter	8" tall, 1932	500	850	1300
Smokey Joe the Climbing Fireman	1930s, 7-1/2" tall	225	375	575
Smokey Sam the World Fireman	7" tall, 1950s	125	210	325
Snappy the Miracle Dog	w/dog house, 3-1/2" long, 1931	80	130	200
Spic and Span	10" tall, black drummer and dancer, 1924	500	850	1300
Stop, Look and Listen	1927, circular track toy	295	490	750
Streamline Speedway	two racers on track	80	130	200
Subway Express	1950s	65	110	170

TIN TOYS

KADI, Lehmann

Little Orphan Annie Skipping Rope, Marx

TIN TOYS

MARX

NAME	DESCRIPTION	GOOD	EX	MINT
Superman Holding Airplane	6" wingspan on airplane, 1940	875	1450	2250
Tidy Tim Streetcleaner	pushes wagon, 8" tall, 1933	175	295	450
Tom Tom Jungle Boy	7" tall	100	150	200
Tumbling Monkey	4-1/2" tall, 1942	75	125	190
Tumbling Monkey and Trapeze	5-3/4" tall, 1932	135	225	350
Walking Popeye	carrying parrots in cages, 8-1/4" tall, 1932	400	700	1000
Walking Porter	carries two suitcases, 8" tall, 1930s	205	340	525
Wee Running Scottie	5-1/2" long, 1952	35	50	100
Wee Running Scottie	5-1/2" long, 1930s	65	110	165
Wise Pluto		100	165	250
WWI Soldier	prone position w/rifle	50	80	125
Xylophonist	5" long	20	35	50
Zippo Monkey	9-1/2", 1938	100	150	200

MATTEL

NAME	DESCRIPTION	GOOD	EX	MINT

Jack in the Boxes

NAME	DESCRIPTION	GOOD	EX	MINT
Flipper		45	75	125
Mother Goose		10	15	25
Porky Pig		40	75	150
Super Chief		50	200	300
Tom & Jerry		25	45	100
Woody Woodpecker		40	75	150

Musical Toys

NAME	DESCRIPTION	GOOD	EX	MINT
Hickory Dickory Dock Clock	crank; mouse climbs clock	10	25	40
Man on the Flying Trapeze	tin base, two metal rods holding trapeze man on top	75	100	145
Sing a Song of Sixpence	pie-shaped tin music box	20	35	65

OHIO ART

NAME	DESCRIPTION	GOOD	EX	MINT
Automatic Airport	two planes circle tower	195	325	500
Circus Shooting Gallery	1960s; w/gun and darts	50	100	200
Coast Guard Plane		50	75	100
Coney Island Roller Coaster	1950s	125	200	300
Doll Stroller	teddy bear design	40	60	80
Donald Duck Carpet Sweeper	red w/Disney litho	60	100	250
Jungle Eyes Shooting Gallery	1960s; w/gun and darts	50	75	150
Little Red Riding Hood Tea Set	seven-piece set	100	200	350
Mexican Boy Tea Set	nine-piece set	55	100	200
Mickey Mouse Tray		50	100	200
Mother Goose Tea Set	seven-piece set	90	150	250
Ten Little Indians Spinning Top		15	25	35
Three Little Pigs Spinning Top		15	25	35
Watering Cans	many variations, each	25	30	40

SCHUCO

NAME	DESCRIPTION	GOOD	EX	MINT
1917 Ford		50	80	125
Airplane and Pilot	friction toy, oversized pilot, 1930s	135	225	350
Bavarian Boy	tin and cloth boy w/beer mug, 5" tall, 1950s	115	195	295
Bavarian Dancing Couple	tin & cloth, 5" high	105	180	275
Black Man	tin & cloth, 5" high	250	425	650
Clown Playing Violin	tin and cloth, 4-1/2" tall, 1950s	135	225	350

626

Merrymakers Band, Marx

Rodeo Joe Crazy Car,
1950s, Unique Art

Tom Tom Jungle Boy, Marx

TIN TOYS

SCHUCO

NAME	DESCRIPTION	GOOD	EX	MINT
Combinato Convertible	7-1/2" long, 1950s	100	165	250
Curvo Motorcycle	5" long, 1950s	135	225	350
Dancing Boy and Girl	tin and cloth, 1930s	115	195	300
Dancing Mice	large and small mouse, tin and cloth, 1950s	135	225	350
Dancing Monkey With Mouse	tin and cloth, 1950s	125	210	325
Drummer	tin and cloth, 5" tall, 1930s	125	210	325
Examico 4001 Convertible	maroon tin wind-up, 5-1/2"	145	250	375
Flic 4520	traffic cop type figure	135	225	350
Fox And Goose	tin and cloth, fox holding goose in cage, 1950s	145	250	375
Juggling Clown	tin and cloth, 4-1/2" tall	135	225	350
Mauswagen	tin & cloth mice and wagon	195	325	500
Mercer Car #1225	7-1/2" long, 1950s	100	150	225
Mickey & Minnie Dancing	tin & cloth	675	1150	1750
Monk Drinking Beer	tin & cloth, 5" high	115	195	300
Monkey Drummer	tin and cloth, 1950s	115	195	300
Monkey in Car	1930s	335	550	850
Monkey on Scooter	tin and cloth, 1930s	115	195	300
Monkey Playing Violin	tin and cloth, 1950s	125	210	325
Schuco Turn Monkey on Suitcase	tin and cloth, 1950s	115	195	300
Studio #1050 Race Car		125	175	250
Tumbling Boy	tin and cloth, 1950s	100	165	250
Yes-No Monkey		165	275	425

UNIQUE ART

NAME	DESCRIPTION	GOOD	EX	MINT
Artie the Clown in his Crazy Car		235	390	595
Bombo the Monk		115	195	295
Butter and Egg Man		475	825	1250
Capitol Hill Racer		125	210	325
Casey The Cop		350	575	895
Dandy Jim		500	750	1000
Daredevil Motor Cop		300	450	600
Finnegan the Porter		200	300	400
Flying Circus		490	825	1250
G.I. Joe and His Jouncing Jeep	1940s, wind-up, 7"	200	275	400
G.I. Joe and His K-9 Pups		150	225	300
Gertie the Galloping Goose		115	190	295
Hee Haw	donkey pulling milk cart	150	225	300
Hillbilly Express		135	225	350
Hobo Train		175	295	450
Hott and Trott		900	1500	2300
Howdy Doody & Buffalo Bob at Piano		750	1300	2000
Kid-Go-Round		155	260	400
Kiddy Go-Round		155	260	400
Krazy Kar		200	335	515
Li'l Abner and His Dogpatch Band		400	700	1200
Lincoln Tunnel		235	375	595
Motorcycle Cop		300	400	500
Musical Sail-Way Carousel		175	295	450
Pecking Goose, Witch and Cat		175	295	450
Rodeo Joe Crazy Car		150	250	400
Rollover Motorcycle Cop		300	400	500
Sky Rangers		300	400	625

Wind-up Toys

NAME	DESCRIPTION	GOOD	EX	MINT
Artie the Clown in his Crazy Car		235	390	595
Bombo the Monk		115	195	295

UNIQUE ART

NAME	DESCRIPTION	GOOD	EX	MINT
Butter and Egg Man		475	825	1250
Capitol Hill Racer		125	210	325
Casey The Cop		350	575	895
Dandy Jim		500	750	1000
Daredevil Motor Cop		300	450	600
Finnegan the Porter		200	300	400
Flying Circus		490	825	1250
G.I. Joe and His Jouncing Jeep	1940s, wind-up, 7"	200	275	400
G.I. Joe and His K-9 Pups		150	225	300
Gertie the Galloping Goose		115	190	295
Hee Haw	donkey pulling milk cart	150	225	300
Hillbilly Express		135	225	350
Hobo Train		175	295	450
Hott and Trott		900	1500	2300
Howdy Doody & Buffalo Bob at Piano		750	1300	2000
Jazzbo Jim		375	625	1200
Kid-Go-Round		155	260	400
Kiddy Go-Round		155	260	400
Krazy Kar		200	335	515
Li'l Abner and His Dogpatch Band		400	700	1200
Lincoln Tunnel		235	375	595
Motorcycle Cop		300	400	500
Musical Sail-Way Carousel		175	295	450
Pecking Goose, Witch and Cat		175	295	450
Rodeo Joe Crazy Car		150	250	400
Rollover Motorcycle Cop		300	400	500
Sky Rangers		300	400	625

WOLVERINE

NAME	DESCRIPTION	GOOD	EX	MINT
Arithmetic Quiz Toy	1950s; math quiz machine	30	50	75
Battleship	14" long, 1930s	70	120	185
Crane	red and blue, 18" high	40	65	100
Drum Major		100	150	300
Drum Major	round base, 13"	100	165	250
Express Bus		125	210	325
Jet Roller Coaster	21" long	125	200	300
Merry-Go-Round		235	390	595
Mystery Car		100	165	250
Sandy Andy Fullback	kicking fullback, 8" tall	175	295	450
Snow White Stove		20	35	50
Submarine	13" long	100	165	250
Sunny and Tank	yellow and green, 14-1/2" long	75	130	200
Sunny Suzy Deluxe Washing Machine		50	95	200
Yellow Taxi	13" long, 1940s	150	225	350
Zilotone	clown on xylophone, w/musical discs, 1920s	450	750	1150

WYANDOTTE

NAME	DESCRIPTION	GOOD	EX	MINT
Airplane Carousel	1930s	100	200	375
Carnival Set	1930s; diorama w/several rides on tin base	300	500	1000
Hoky Poky	1930s; clowns on railcar	150	250	350
Model Shooting Gallery	1930s	85	200	300
Mother Duck with Baby Ducks	two baby ducks on wheels pulled behind mother ducks	50	90	125
Trapeze Artist	1930s	95	200	325

TIN TOYS

TV Toys

What is your favorite television show of all time? *The Rifleman*? *The Munsters*? *Welcome Back, Kotter*?

Whatever the era, these television programs shared an important component — licensed merchandise. Licensed toys based on television shows have been around for more than fifty years. And collectors have been fond of them ever since.

Among the earliest toys based on a television license were those based on The Howdy Doody Show from the 1950s.

Making toys based on TV characters was an effective way of marketing the program to a target audience. The popularity of the shows, for example, fueled interest in the toys — and often vice versa. For example, young aspiring cowpokes were thrilled to carry their lunches to school in a Gunsmoke or Bonanza lunch box. Young musicians, perhaps, sought the toys from *Josie & the Pussycats* and *The Monkees*. Space freaks couldn't get their hands on enough Lost in Space or Land of the Giants toys. Toys transported yesterday's kids (and collectors today) into the virtual worlds represented in the shows.

Trends

Within the last 10 years, TV toys have enjoyed a surge in popularity and collectibility — particularly the toys from the 1950s, '60s and '70s. Adults who grew up watching TV shows from those eras now seek to recapture the pleasant memories with trading cards, board games, dolls, lunch boxes and more.

Often those memories don't come cheaply. The steel lunch boxes that once sold for $5 or less now may sell for $200 or more. Board games that survived without missing pieces or dinged boxes might bring $25 to $50 or more.

5 Family Affair Paper Dolls, Whitman

Today, TV toys still exist, but fewer 1990s shows bear examples. Recent examples include *The X-Files*, *Buffy the Vampire Slayer* and *The Simpsons*.

Children's diversified interests — like video and computer games — have somewhat replaced TV shows. Toys based on the latest action-packed games are now sharing shelf space with the more popular licensed movie toys.

Will there be a return to licensed TV toys? As tastes change and topics become more adult, it is unlikely many toy manufacturers will take expensive risks.

But collectors needn't worry. Their vintage favorites remain tangible memories of a simpler time and place.

The Top 10 TV Toys
(in Mint condition)

1. Green Hornet Dashboard, 1966, Remco...$2,000
2. Green Hornet Seal Ring, 1940, General Mills 1,650
3. Gilligan's Island Trading Cards, 1965, Topps 1,550
4. Counterspy Outfit Store Display, 1966, Marx 1,250
5. Fan Club Photos, 1938, Golden Jersey Milk 1,200
6. New Adventures of Gilligan Dip Dots Painting Set, 1975, Kenner 1,200
7. Cereal Box, 1954, Kellogg's 1,000
8. Howdy Doody Periscope, 1950s 1,000
9. Crime Buster Gift Set, 1966, Corgi...1050
10. Brady Bunch Trading Cards, 1971, Topps 800

Contributor to this section: Romper Room, Shawn Brecka, P.O. Box 441, Plover, WI 54467.

TV TOYS

Howdy Doody Wristwatch, 1954, Ingraham

Flintstones Great Big Punch-Out Book, 1961, Whitman

A-TEAM

TOY	COMPANY	YEAR	DESCRIPTION	GOOD	EX	MIB
A-Team Rocket Ball Target Set		1983	gumballs w/gun and target	5	10	20
A-Team Shrinky Dinks Set		1980s		5	10	20

ADDAMS FAMILY

TOY	COMPANY	YEAR	DESCRIPTION	GOOD	EX	MIB
Gomez Hand Puppet	Ideal	1965		50	120	250
Lurch Figure	Remco	1964		80	175	350
Morticia Figure	Remco	1964		100	200	675
Morticia Halloween Costume	Ben Cooper	1964	painted hair	40	100	200
Morticia Halloween Costume	Ben Cooper	1964	w/hair	50	125	250
Morticia Hand Puppet	Ideal	1965		50	130	260
Thing Bank		1964	plastic, battery-operated	40	150	225
Uncle Fester Figure	Remco	1964		100	250	600

BANANA SPLITS

TOY	COMPANY	YEAR	DESCRIPTION	GOOD	EX	MIB
4 The Banana Splits Puzzle	Whitman	1969	frame tray	25	55	85
Banana Band	Larami	1973	horn, sax, mouth harp	25	60	120
Banana Buggy Model Kit	Aurora	1968		60	200	325
Banana Splits Bingo Costume	Ben Cooper	1968		60	175	300
Banana Splits Doll	Sutton	1960s	12" tall Drooper	50	100	200
Banana Splits Kut-Up Kit	Larami	1973		20	40	75
Banana Splits Mug		1969	plastic yellow dog mug	20	40	65
Banana Splits Record	Kellogg's	1969		20	90	175
Paint-By-Number Set	Hasbro	1969		45	80	150
Talking Telephone	Hasbro	1969		70	175	350

BEANY AND CECIL

TOY	COMPANY	YEAR	DESCRIPTION	GOOD	EX	MIB
Beany and Cecil and Their Pals Record Player	Vanity Fair	1961		80	200	375
Beany and Cecil Carrying Case		1960s	9" diameter w/strap, vinyl-covered cardboard	40	85	100
Beany and Cecil Gun	Mattel	1961	w/propeller disks	30	150	200
Beany and Cecil Puzzle	Playskool	1961	wooden frame tray	25	65	100
Beany and Cecil Skill Ball		1960s	colorful tin w/wood frame	30	80	120
Beany and Cecil Travel Case		1960s	8" tall, round, red vinyl w/zipper and strap	25	55	95
Beany and Cecil Travel Case		1960s	square, 4-1/2" x 3-1/2" x 3" red vinyl, carrying strap, illustrated w/characters	30	70	100
Beany and His Magic Set Book		1953	Tell-a-Tale Book	10	20	50
Beany Doll	Mattel	1963	15", non-talking	20	100	150
Beany Figure	Caltoy	1984	8" tall	8	20	40
Beany Talking Doll	Mattel	1950s	17" tall, stuffed cloth, vinyl head w/pull string	90	250	425
Bob Clampetts' Beany Coloring Book	Whitman	1960s		15	75	150
Captain Huffenpuff Puzzle		1961	large	25	85	120
Cecil and His Disguise Kit	Mattel	1962	17" tall plush Cecil w/disguise wigs, mustaches, etc.	30	90	175
Cecil in the Music Box	Mattel	1961	jack-in-the-box	80	225	375
Cecil Soaky			8-1/2" tall, plastic	25	85	150
Leakin' Lena Boat	Irwin	1962	plastic and wood	50	110	225
Leakin' Lena Pound 'N Pull Toy	Pressman	1960s	wood	60	125	250

BEN CASEY

TOY	COMPANY	YEAR	DESCRIPTION	GOOD	EX	MIB
Ben Casey Pencils	Hassenfeld Bros.	1962	10 red/white pencils on card	15	30	65

BEWITCHED

TOY	COMPANY	YEAR	DESCRIPTION	GOOD	EX	MIB
Bewitched Samantha Doll	Ideal	1967	12-1/2" tall	175	400	750
Bewitched Tabitha Paper Doll Set	Magic Wand	1966	11" cardboard doll, clothes	30	75	150

BOZO

TOY	COMPANY	YEAR	DESCRIPTION	GOOD	EX	MIB
Bozo the Clown Beach Towel		1960s	16" x 24"	8	15	35
Bozo the Clown Doll		1970s		10	30	60
Bozo the Clown Figure		1970s	vinyl, 5" tall	5	15	30
Bozo the Clown Push Button Marionette	Knickerbocker	1962		25	45	85
Bozo the Clown Puzzle	Whitman	1965	#4516	10	25	50
Bozo the Clown Slide Puzzle		1960s		15	40	75
Bozo the Clown Soaky	Palmolive	1960s		15	45	75
Bozo Trick Trapeze		1960s	red base	15	35	65

BRADY BUNCH

TOY	COMPANY	YEAR	DESCRIPTION	GOOD	EX	MIB
Brady Bunch Halloween Costume	Collegeville	1970s	smock reads "One of The Brady Bunch"	40	90	150
Brady Bunch Kite Fun Book	Pacific Gas and Electric	1976		15	35	75
Brady Bunch Paper Dolls Cut-Out Book	Whitman	1973		30	85	150
Brady Bunch Puzzle			frame tray	25	45	80
Brady Bunch Trading Cards	Topps	1971	55 cards	250	550	800
Kitty Karry-All Doll	Remco	1969		80	160	325

CAPTIAN KANGAROO

TOY	COMPANY	YEAR	DESCRIPTION	GOOD	EX	MIB
Captain Kangaroo Presto Slate	Fairchild	1960s	slate on illustrated card, several versions	15	25	40
Captain Kangaroo Puzzle	Whitman	1960	#4446, frame tray	10	30	60

DR. KILDARE

TOY	COMPANY	YEAR	DESCRIPTION	GOOD	EX	MIB
Dr. Kildare Photo Scrapbook		1962		10	25	50

DRAGNET

TOY	COMPANY	YEAR	DESCRIPTION	GOOD	EX	MIB
Dragnet Badge 714	Knickerbocker	1955	2-1/2" bronze finish badge in yellow box w/illustration of Jack Webb, box bottom has ID card	10	40	80

FAMILY AFFAIR

TOY	COMPANY	YEAR	DESCRIPTION	GOOD	EX	MIB
5 Family Affair Paper Dolls	Whitman			25	40	55
Buffy Halloween Costume	Ben Cooper	1970		20	40	80
Buffy Make-Up and Hairstyling Set	Amsco	1971		20	40	80
Buffy with Mrs. Beasley Dolls	Mattel	1967	6" Buffy w/smaller Mrs. Beasley	30	65	115
Family Affair Cartoon Kit	Colorforms	1970		12	25	50

FAMILY AFFAIR

TOY	COMPANY	YEAR	DESCRIPTION	GOOD	EX	MIB
Family Affair Puzzle	Whitman	1970		12	30	60
Mrs. Beasley Paper Dolls	Whitman	1970s	several variations	12	30	60
Mrs. Beasley Rag Doll	Mattel	1973	14"	12	25	45
Talking Mrs. Beasley Doll	Mattel	1967		50	95	210

FLINTSTONES

TOY	COMPANY	YEAR	DESCRIPTION	GOOD	EX	MIB
Baby Puss Figure	Knickerbocker	1961	10" tall, vinyl	35	75	135
Bamm-Bamm Bank		1960s	11" tall, hard plastic figure sitting on turtle	20	45	75
Bamm-Bamm Bubble Pipe	Transogram	1963	figural pipe on illustrated card	12	25	50
Bamm-Bamm Doll	Ideal	1962	15" tall	50	115	225
Bamm-Bamm Figure	Dakin	1970	7" tall	20	40	75
Bamm-Bamm Finger Puppet	Knickerbocker	1972		5	15	25
Bamm-Bamm Soaky	Purex	1960s		20	40	70
Barney Bank		1973	solid plastic, Barney holding a bowling ball	15	35	60
Barney Doll		1962	6" tall, soft vinyl doll, movable arms and head	25	45	80
Barney Figure	Knickerbocker	1961	10" tall, vinyl	40	55	160
Barney Figure	Flintoys	1986		5	10	15
Barney Figure	Dakin	1970	7-1/4" tall	20	40	75
Barney Finger Puppet	Knickerbocker	1972		8	15	25
Barney Night Light	Electricord	1979	figural	8	15	25
Barney Policeman Figure	Flintoys	1986		4	8	12
Barney Riding Dino Toy	Marx	1960s	8" long, metal and vinyl, wind-up	110	300	550
Barney Soaky	Roclar	1970s		6	15	35
Barney Wind-Up Toy	Marx	1960s	3-1/2" tall figure, tin	85	190	375
Barney's Car	Flintoys	1986		8	15	30
Betty Figure	Knickerbocker	1961	10" tall, vinyl	50	100	200
Betty Figure	Flintoys	1986		4	7	10
Dino Bank			china, Dino carrying a golf bag	45	95	185
Dino Bank		1973	hard vinyl, blue w/Pebbles on his back	18	35	75
Dino Bath Puppet Sponge		1973	bath mitt	10	18	35
Dino Doll			movable head and arms	15	25	45
Dino Figure	Flintoys	1986		4	7	15
Dino Figure	Dakin	1970	7-3/4" tall	25	50	100
Dino Wind-Up Toy	Marx	1960s	3-1/2" tall, tin	90	180	360
Fang Figure	Dakin	1970	7" tall	25	50	95
Flintmobile	Flintoys	1986		10	18	40
Flintmobile with Fred Figure	Flintoys	1986		18	33	60
Flintstones Ashtray		1960	ceramic w/Wilma	25	70	100
Flintstones Bank		1971	19" tall w/Barney and Bamm Bamm	25	50	85
Flintstones Car	Remco	1964	battery operated car w/Barney, Fred, Wilma and Betty	85	200	385
Flintstones Figure Set	Spoontiques	1981	eight figures	35	50	90
Flintstones Figures	Empire	1976	three-inch solid figures of Fred, Barney, Wilma and Betty	10	40	85
Flintstones Figures	Imperial	1976	eight acrylic figures: Fred, Barney, Wilma, Betty, Pebbles, Bamm Bamm, Dino and Baby Puss	15	35	65
Flintstones House	Flintoys	1986		12	25	35
Flintstones Lamp			9-1/2" tall, plastic Fred w/ lampshade picturing characters	50	120	210
Flintstones Paint Box	Transogram	1961		18	35	60
Flintstones Party Place Set	Reed	1969	tablecloth, napkins, plates, cups	10	20	40
Flintstones Roto Draw	British	1969		30	70	100
Flintstones Tru-Vue Film Card	Tru-Vue	1962	#T-37, w/strips of Fred	30	70	100
Fred Bubble Blowing Pipe			soft vinyl w/curved stem	6	12	20

4 The Banana Splits Puzzle,
1969, Whitman

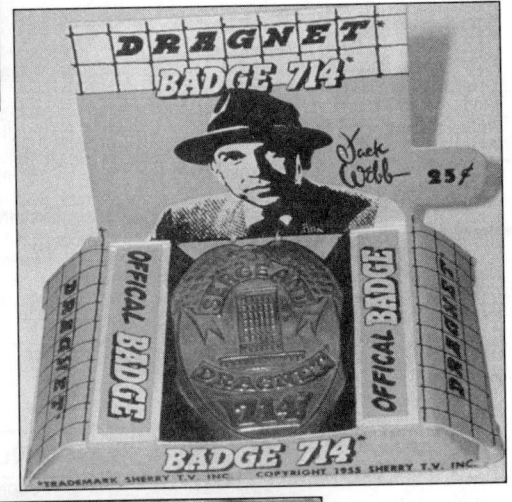

Dragnet Badge 714, 1955,
Knickerbocker

Captain Kangaroo Presto Slate, 1960s, Fairchild

FLINTSTONES

TOY	COMPANY	YEAR	DESCRIPTION	GOOD	EX	MIB
Fred Doll		1960	13" soft vinyl doll w/movable head	45	100	225
Fred Doll	Perfection Plastic	1972	11" tall	15	35	60
Fred Figure	Knickerbocker	1960	15" tall	40	85	200
Fred Figure	Knickerbocker	1961	10" tall, vinyl	32	75	150
Fred Figure	Flintoys	1986		4	8	12
Fred Figure	Dakin	1970	8-1/4" tall	22	45	85
Fred Finger Puppet	Knickerbocker	1972		8	15	22
Fred Flintstone's Bedrock Bank	Alps	1962	9", tin and vinyl, battery operated	175	310	325
Fred Flintstone's Lithograph Wind-Up	Marx	1960s	3-1/2" tall figure, metal	85	170	385
Fred Gumball Machine		1960s	plastic, shaped like Fred's head	20	32	60
Fred Loves Wilma Bank			ceramic	50	110	185
Fred Night Light		1970	figural	6	12	25
Fred Policeman Figure	Flintoys	1986		4	8	15
Fred Push Puppet	Kohner	1960s		10	25	45
Fred Riding Dino	Marx	1962	18" long battery operated w/ Fred in Howdah	175	350	675
Fred Riding Dino	Marx	1962	8" long, tin and vinyl, wind-up	175	350	675
Great Big Punch-Out Book	Whitman	1961		20	50	125
Motorbike	Flintoys	1986		6	12	20
Pebbles Bank			9" tall vinyl w/Pebbles sitting in chair	10	25	50
Pebbles Doll	Ideal	1963	15" tall	55	115	225
Pebbles Doll	Mighty Star	1982	vinyl head, arms and legs, cloth stuffed body 12" tall	15	25	45
Pebbles Figure	Dakin	1970	8" tall w/blonde hair and purple velvet shirt	25	45	85
Pebbles Finger Puppet	Knickerbocker	1972		5	13	20
Pebbles Flintstone Cradle	Ideal	1963	for a 15" doll	40	75	150
Pebbles Soaky	Purex	1960s		20	35	65
Police Car	Flintoys	1986		8	15	30
Wilma Figure	Knickerbocker	1961	10" tall, vinyl	50	100	190
Wilma Figure	Flintoys	1986		4	7	15
Wilma Friction Car	Marx	1962	metal	90	175	375

FLYING NUN

TOY	COMPANY	YEAR	DESCRIPTION	GOOD	EX	MIB
Flying Nun Chalkboard	Screen Gems	1967		22	45	80
Flying Nun Doll	Hasbro	1960s	4"	22	125	200
Flying Nun Doll	Hasbro	1967	11"	30	85	175
Flying Nun Halloween Costume	Ben Cooper	1967		20	60	100
Flying Nun Paint-By-Number Set	Hasbro	1960s	two scenes and 10 paint vials	15	30	60
Flying Nun Paper Doll Set	Saalfield	1969	five dolls and costumes	16	40	80

GILLIGAN'S ISLAND

TOY	COMPANY	YEAR	DESCRIPTION	GOOD	EX	MIB
Gilligan's Floating Island Play Set	Playskool	1977		75	190	350
Gilligan's Island Notepad	Whitman	1965	Gilligan and Skipper on cover	12	30	60
Gilligan's Island Trading Cards	Topps	1965	set of 55 cards	400	800	1550
New Adventures of Gilligan Dip Dots Painting Set	Kenner	1975	book w/paints and brush	220	570	1200

GIRL FROM U.N.C.L.E.

TOY	COMPANY	YEAR	DESCRIPTION	GOOD	EX	MIB
1967 British Annual Book	World Distributors	1967	hardcover, 95 pages, photo cover	10	30	60
1968 British Annual Book	World Distributors	1968	hardcover, 95 pages, photo cover	10	30	60

GIRL FROM U.N.C.L.E.

TOY	COMPANY	YEAR	DESCRIPTION	GOOD	EX	MIB
1969 British Annual Book	World Distributors	1969	hardcover, 95 pages, photo cover	10	30	60
Costume	Halco	1967	transparent or painted mask, dress-style costume has show logo and silhouette image of Girl spy holding smoking gun, in illustrated window box	55	115	250
Garter Holster	Lone Star	1966	metal pistol fires small plastic bullets from metal shells, checker design vinyl holster and bullet pouch, on card	60	125	275
Girl From U.N.C.L.E. Doll	Marx	1967	11" tall w/30 accessories in illustrated box	250	500	1000
Music from the Television Series	M.G.M. Records	1966	photo cover shows Stephanie against a wall	9	20	40
Secret Agent Wristwatch	Bradley	1966	watch has pink face w/April Dancer image, in case	85	200	400

GREEN HORNET

TOY	COMPANY	YEAR	DESCRIPTION	GOOD	EX	MIB
Assistant Badge	Don Howard Associates	1966		45	95	200
Bike Badge	Burry Cookies	1966	premium; w/Vari-Vue flasher	85	175	350
Black Beauty Balloon Toy	Oak Rubber	1966		70	145	275
Black Beauty Slot Car	Aurora	1966	clear box w/insert	85	200	400
Black Beauty Slot Car	BZ Industries	1966	large scale	160	380	775
Captain Action Flasher Ring	Vari-Vue	1966	blue	10	18	30
Captain Action Flasher Ring	Vari-Vue	1966	chrome	13	25	40
Charm	Cracker Jack	1966	hornet-shaped	10	30	50
Charms	Folz Vending	1966	hornet-shaped	10	15	25
Comic Strip Stickers	Folz Vending	1966	7" long, from vending machines, each	25	50	100
Electric Drawing Set	Lakeside	1966		90	190	275
Fan Club Photos	Golden Jersey Milk	1938	set of four; radio premium	400	800	1200
Flasher Button	Vari-Vue	1966	pinback, 3"	15	30	45
Flasher Button	Vari-Vue	1966	no pinback, 3"	10	20	35
Flasher Button	Vari-Vue	1966	no pinback, 7"	25	45	80
Flasher Rings	Vari-Vue	1960s	chrome base, each	10	20	40
Flasher Rings	Vari-Vue	1960s	blue plastic base, each	5	10	30
Flashlight Whistle	Bantamlight	1966		40	90	175
Frame Tray Puzzles	Whitman	1966	box of four	40	90	175
Green Hornet Bendy Figure	Lakeside	1966		40	80	175
Green Hornet Bubble Gum Ring	Frito Lay		rubber ring, in cello pack	25	45	90
Green Hornet Candy/Toy Box	Phoenix Candy	1966	several variations	40	90	150
Green Hornet Charm Bracelet		1966	gold finish chain w/five charms: Hornet, Van, Kato, Pistol, Black Beauty, on 3" x 7-1/2" illustrated card	50	125	200
Green Hornet Colorforms Set	Colorforms	1966		60	125	250
Green Hornet Dashboard	Remco	1966		300	1000	2000
Green Hornet Mini Walkie Talkies	Remco	1966		75	150	300
Green Hornet Print Putty	Colorforms	1966		20	50	95
Green Hornet Seal Ring	General Mills	1940	cereal premium	225	780	1650
Green Hornet Soundtrack Record	20th Century Fox	1966		25	100	200
Green Hornet Troll Figure	Uneeda Wishnik	1966	7" tall	55	100	250
Green Hornet Troll Figure	Damm	1966	3" tall	45	75	150
Green Hornet TV Guide		1966	Cover features Van Williams and Bruce Lee	50	125	250

TV TOYS

GREEN HORNET

TOY	COMPANY	YEAR	DESCRIPTION	GOOD	EX	MIB
Green Hornet Utensils	Imperial Knife	1966	fork and spoon	30	75	150
Green Hornet Walkie Talkies	Remco	1966		50	100	175
Green Hornet Wallet		1966	green vinyl, Hornet or Kato	25	50	100
Green Hornet Wrist Radios	Remco	1966	battery-operated	150	250	525
Halloween Costume	Ben Cooper	1966	several variations	100	200	350
Hand Puppet	Ideal	1966	w/hat	80	175	300
Inflatable Raft	Ideal	1966		160	350	700
Instant Squeeze Candy	Dre's Inc.	1966	toothpaste-type container w/ hornet-shaped plug	40	90	175
Kato and Black Beauty Glass	Golden Jersey Milk	1938	radio premium	100	300	500
Kite	Roalex	1966		30	75	150
Magic Eyes Movie Viewer Slides	Sawyers	1966		75	150	300
Magic Rub-On Set	Whitman	1966		70	150	275
Magic Slate	Watkins-Strathmore	1966	three variations	35	90	175
Mini Movie Viewer	Chemtoy	1971	w/filmstrips	25	45	90
Mini Movie Viewer	Acme/Chemtoy	1966	w/filmstrips	50	100	200
Numbered Pencil and Paint Set	Hasbro	1966		75	160	300
Paint By Number Set	Hasbro	1966		65	130	260
Pencil Case	Hasbro	1966		30	65	120
Pencils	Empire Pencil	1966	five on card	30	80	150
Pennant	RMS	1966	blue or orange	35	100	175
Playing Cards	Ed-U-Cards	1966		10	75	150
Postcard	Golden Jersey Milk	1936	radio premium	150	300	400
Punch-Out Book	Whitman	1966		100	200	375
Secret Agent Badge	Don Howard Associates	1966		20	35	50
Stardust Craft Kit	Hasbro	1966		35	75	150
The Case of the Disappearing Doctor Book	Whitman	1966		20	30	45
The Green Hornet Cracks Down Book	Whitman	1942	Better Little Books	25	60	120
The Green Hornet Returns Book	Whitman	1941	Better Little Books	25	60	120
The Green Hornet Strikes Book	Whitman	1940	Better Little Books	25	60	120
Thingmaker Mold and Accessories	Mattel	1966		100	175	325
Trading Cards	Donruss	1966	set of 44	85	100	325
Trading Cards Display Box	Donruss	1966		100	250	500
Trading Cards Wrapper	Donruss	1966		15	30	60
Trading Stickers	Topps	1966	set of 44	85	160	325
Trading Stickers Display Box	Topps	1966		100	250	500
Trading Stickers Wrapper	Topps	1966		10	25	50
Wrist Signal Light	Bantamlight	1966		40	80	175

HOWDY DOODY

TOY	COMPANY	YEAR	DESCRIPTION	GOOD	EX	MIB
Cereal Box	Kellogg's	1954	Rice Krispies, Howdy Mask on back	250	650	1000
Clarabell Bank	Strauss	1976	flocked plastic, 9"	20	40	85
Clarabell Jumping Toy	Linemar	1950s	7" tall tin litho, squeeze lever to make figure hop forward and squeak	200	450	825
Clarabell Marionette	Peter Puppet	1950s		100	210	425
Flub-a-Dub Figure	TeeVee Toys	1950s	4" x 4" painted plastic, movable mouth	40	90	150
Flub-a-Dub Flip A Ring Game	Flip-A-Ring	1950s	9", ring toss game	25	45	75

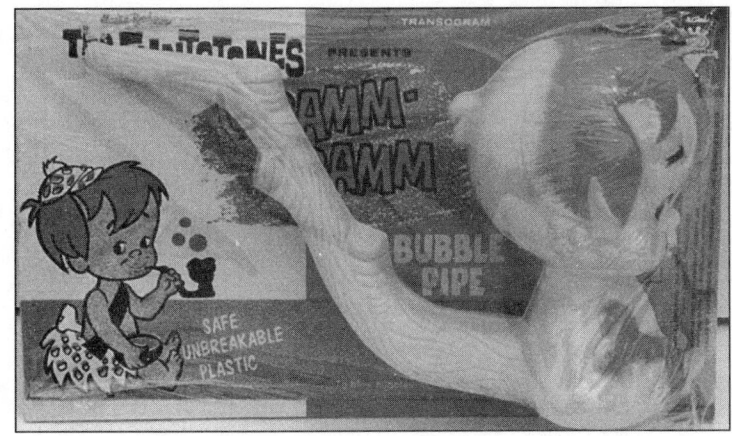

Flintstones Bamm-Bamm Bubble Pipe, 1963, Transogram

*Flintstones Bamm-Bamm
Doll, 1962, Ideal*

TV TOYS

TOY	COMPANY	YEAR	DESCRIPTION	GOOD	EX	MIB
Flub-a-Dub Marionette	Peter Puppet	1950s		100	225	450
Flub-a-Dub Puppet	Gund	1950s		40	75	150
Howdy Doody Acrobat	Arnold	1950s	tin, plastic, Howdy swings on high bar	15	25	60
Howdy Doody Air Doodle Beanie	Kellogg's	1950s	Rice Krispies premium	75	200	300
Howdy Doody Air-O-Doodle Circus Train	Plasticraft/ Kagran	1950s	red/yellow plastic train, boat and plane toy on card w/cut out character passengers	40	100	160
Howdy Doody and Clarabell Book	Simon and Schuster	1952	Little Golden Book	12	22	50
Howdy Doody and Clarabell Coloring Book	Whitman	1955		15	75	185
Howdy Doody and Clarabell Puppet Mitten Kit	Connecticut Leather	1950s		30	75	110
Howdy Doody and his Magic Hat Book	Whitman	1953	Little Golden Book	10	22	40
Howdy Doody and Mr. Bluster Book	Whitman	1954	Little Golden Book	10	22	40
Howdy Doody and the Musical Forest Record	RCA	1950s	45 rpm	20	50	80
Howdy Doody and the Princess Book	Whitman	1952	Little Golden Book	10	25	45
Howdy Doody and You Record	RCA	1950s	45 rpm	18	40	65
Howdy Doody Bank	Vandor		ceramic figural head	25	55	100
Howdy Doody Bank		1950s	ceramic bank, all color, bust of Howdy	300	500	850
Howdy Doody Bank		1950s	7" tall, ceramic, Howdy riding a pig	70	160	300
Howdy Doody Bank	Strauss	1976	flocked plastic, 9"	20	40	85
Howdy Doody Bubble Pipe	Lido	1950s	4" long, Howdy or Clarabell	30	160	285
Howdy Doody Button	New York Sunday News	1949	reads "New Color Comic -- Sunday News"	30	55	100
Howdy Doody Coin	Kellogg's	1950s	plastic, silver, raised bust on Howdy on front	20	40	75
Howdy Doody Color TV Set	American Plastic		plastic, w/films	130	275	500
Howdy Doody Coloring Books	Whitman	1955	boxed set of six	42	150	300
Howdy Doody Comic Book	Dell	1949	Issue No. 1	110	420	1200
Howdy Doody Cookbook	Welch's	1952		30	110	225
Howdy Doody Cookie-Go-Round	Luce/Krispy Kan	1950s	lithographed cookie tin	75	160	285
Howdy Doody Costume	Collegeville	1950s		50	100	200
Howdy Doody Crayon Set	Milton Bradley	1950	16 crayons w/pictures	45	100	200
Howdy Doody Doll	Applause	1988	11" cloth doll	10	40	75
Howdy Doody Doll	Goldberger	1976	12" vinyl ventriloquist doll	25	50	95
Howdy Doody Doll		1950s	7" tall vinyl squeeze toy, Howdy in blue pants and red shirt	40	90	160
Howdy Doody Doll	Goldberger	1970s	30", vinyl ventriloquist doll	40	90	160
Howdy Doody Doll	Ideal	1950s	eyes and mouth move	40	90	160
Howdy Doody Dominoes		1950s		20	40	80
Howdy Doody Figure	Stahlwood		5" x 7" rubber squeeze figure on airplane	175	360	725
Howdy Doody Fingertronic Puppet Theater	Sutton	1970s		25	45	85
Howdy Doody Flasher Rings	Nabisco	1950s	set of eight plastic character rings	90	175	400
Howdy Doody Flicker Ring	Nabisco	1950s		10	20	50
Howdy Doody in Funland Book	Whitman	1953	Little Golden Book	10	25	50
Howdy Doody Kiddie Pool	Ideal	1950s	40" diameter, yellow/blue vinyl	80	150	275
Howdy Doody Marionette	Peter Puppet	1950s		85	190	375

TOY	COMPANY	YEAR	DESCRIPTION	GOOD	EX	MIB
Howdy Doody Mug	Ovaltine	1950s	red plastic w/Howdy decal (Be Keen, Drink Chocolate Flavored Ovaltine)	35	50	100
Howdy Doody Music Box	Vandor		Howdy playing piano	40	55	90
Howdy Doody Newspaper #1	Poll Parrot	1950	premium	200	400	500
Howdy Doody Night Light	Leco	1950s	figural, Howdy's face	35	75	140
Howdy Doody Outdoor Sports Box		1950s	tin litho box w/colorful graphics	30	60	110
Howdy Doody Paint Set	Milton Bradley	1950s		40	80	160
Howdy Doody Paint Set	Marx	1950s	plaster figures, paint	35	100	185
Howdy Doody Pencil Case		1950s	vinyl; smiling Howdy on front	20	90	160
Howdy Doody Periscope		1950s	Wonder Bread premium	350	700	1000
Howdy Doody Phono Doodle	Sharatone Products			120	260	350
Howdy Doody Pumpmobile	Nylint		tin vehicle	110	275	525
Howdy Doody Puppet Show Set		1950s	includes plastic figures of Howdy, Clarabell, Mr. Bluster, Flub, Dilly Dally	80	170	325
Howdy Doody Puzzle	Whitman	1950s	frame tray, Howdy Goes Fishing	25	45	90
Howdy Doody Puzzle Set	Milton Bradley	1950s	set of three	40	75	150
Howdy Doody Ranch House Tool Box	Liberty Steel	1950s	14" x 6" x 3" illustrated steel box w/handle	45	110	185
Howdy Doody Salt and Pepper Shakers	Peter Puppet	1950s	shape of Howdy's head; removable blue vinyl neckerchief	75	160	300
Howdy Doody Sand Forms	Ideal/Kagran	1952	on card	40	80	150
Howdy Doody Songs Record	Take Two	1974	record, cut-outs, coloring book	20	50	75
Howdy Doody Sticker Fun Book	Whitman	1952		15	30	60
Howdy Doody Swim Ring	Ideal	1950s	inflatable, 20" diameter	20	40	75
Howdy Doody Talking Alarm Clock	Janex	1974		30	90	185
Howdy Doody Television	Lido	1950s	filmstrips w/TV box	25	110	250
Howdy Doody Ukulele	Emenee	1950s	plastic, white or yellow, 17"	40	65	110
Howdy Doody Umbrella	Holllander	1950s	Howdy head for handle	30	80	160
Howdy Doody Wall Walker	Tigrett			25	50	100
Howdy Doody Wristwatch	Ingraham	1954	deep blue band w/blue and white dial showing character faces	140	350	750
Howdy Doody Wristwatch	Ever Tick/ Kagran	1950s	glow-in-the-dark	100	300	600
Howdy Doody Xylo-Doodle		1950s	yellow plastic piano/xylophone w/colorful graphics	75	375	675
Howdy Doody's Animal Friends Book	Whitman	1956	Little Golden Book	10	20	50
Howdy Doody's Circus Book	Whitman	1950	Little Golden Book	10	20	50
Howdy Doody's Electric Carnival Game	Harett-Gilmar	1950s		60	120	225
Howdy Doody's Laughing Circus Record Set	RCA	1950s	two 78 rpm records	35	70	135
Howdy Doody's Lucky Trip Book	Whitman	1953	Little Golden Book	12	25	50
Howdy Doody's One-Man Band	Trophy Products/ Kagran		musical instruments	100	225	500
Merchandise Manual		1955	list of toys	100	350	600
Merchandise Manual		1954	list of toys	150	450	650
Mr. Bluster Bank	Strauss	1976	flocked plastic, 9"	20	35	65
Princess Summerfall Winterspring Doll	Beehler Arts	1950s	8", hard plastic, braided black hair	100	190	350
Princess Summerfall Winterspring Sewing Cards	Milton Bradley	1950s	four cards, thread, plastic needle	30	65	135
Puppets	Gund	1950s	Howdy, Bluster, Clarabell, Dilly or Princess	20	50	90

HOWDY DOODY

TOY	COMPANY	YEAR	DESCRIPTION	GOOD	EX	MIB
Sparkle Gun	Ja-Ru	1987	plastic gun	6	20	45
Spinning Top	Lorenz Bolz	1970s	tin top w/characters	30	60	110

I DREAM OF JEANNIE

TOY	COMPANY	YEAR	DESCRIPTION	GOOD	EX	MIB
I Dream of Jeannie Costume	Ben Cooper	1970s		8	20	50
I Dream of Jeannie Doll	Ideal	1965	18"	45	120	225
I Dream of Jeannie Doll	Remco	1977	6"	25	50	110
I Dream of Jeannie Play Set	Remco	1977	w/6" doll	40	120	250

KNIGHT RIDER

TOY	COMPANY	YEAR	DESCRIPTION	GOOD	EX	MIB
Knight Rider Impossibles Stunt Set	LJN	1982		45	95	150
Knight Rider Wrist Communicator	Larami	1982		10	20	40

MAN FROM U.N.C.L.E.

TOY	COMPANY	YEAR	DESCRIPTION	GOOD	EX	MIB
1966 British Annual	World Distributors	1966	hardcover, 95 pages, photo cover	20	50	75
1967 British Annual	World Distributors	1967	hardcover, 95 pages, photo cover	15	35	65
1968 British Annual	World Distributors	1968	hardcover, 95 pages, photo cover	15	30	60
1969 British Annual	World Distributors	1969	hardcover, 95 pages, photo cover	15	25	55
Action Figure Apparel Set	Gilbert	1965	bullet proof vest, three targets, three shells, binoculars, and bazooka	50	100	210
Action Figure Armament Set	Gilbert	1965	for 12" figures: jacket, cap firing pistol w/barrel extension, bipod stand, telescopic sight, grenade belt, binoculars, accessory pouch and beret	50	90	180
Action Figure Arsenal Set #1	Gilbert	1965	tommy gun, bazooka, three shells, cap firing pistol and attachments, in shallow window box	40	80	175
Action Figure Arsenal Set #2	Gilbert	1965	cap firing THRUSH rifle w/ telescopic sight, grenade belt and four grenades, on wrapped header card	40	80	175
Action Figure Jumpsuit Set	Gilbert	1965	for 12" figures: jumpsuit w/ boots, helmet w/chin strap, 28" parachute and pack, cap firing tommy gun w/scope, instructions	50	100	225
Action Figure Pistol Conversion Kit	Gilbert	1965	binoculars and pistol w/ attachments, for 12" figures, on wrapped header card	22	45	90
Action Figure Scuba Set	Gilbert	1965	for 12" Gilbert dolls: swim trunks, air tanks, tank bracket, tubes, scuba jacket and knife	65	130	260
Affair of the Gentle Saboteur Book	Whitman	1966	hardcover	8	15	35
Affair of the Gunrunners' Gold Book	Whitman	1967	hardcover	8	15	35
Alexander Waverly Figure	Marx	1966	blue plastic, 5-3/4" tall, stamped w/character's name and U.N.C.L.E. logo on the bottom of base	8	15	30
Arcade Cards		1960s	postcards w/b/w photo fronts, Napoleon or Illya	5	10	30

Green Hornet Wrist Radios, 1966, Remco

Green Hornet Halloween Costume, 1966, Ben Cooper

Green Hornet Hand Puppet, 1966, Ideal

TV TOYS

TOY	COMPANY	YEAR	DESCRIPTION	GOOD	EX	MIB
Attache Case	Lone Star	1966	small cardboard briefcase, contains die-cast Mauser and parts to assemble U.N.C.L.E. Special	130	230	500
Attache Case, British	Lone Star	1966	cardboard covered in vinyl, 9mm automatic luger, shoulder stock, sight, silencer, belt, holster, secret wrist holster and pistol that fires cap and cork, grenade, wallet w/passport, play money	250	500	950
Attache Case, British	Lone Star	1965	15" x 8" x 2" vinyl case w/a pistol, holster, walkie talkie, cigarette box gun, U.N.C.L.E. badge, international passport, invisible cartridge pen and handcuffs	225	450	900
Bagatelle Game	Hong Kong	1966	8" x 14" pinball game	75	155	325
Bicycle License Plates	Marx	1967	four different, metal: Man from U.N.C.L.E., The Girl from U.N.C.L.E., Napoleon Solo, Illya Kuryakin, each	15	30	50
Calcutta Affair Book	Whitman	1967	254 pages, Big Little Book	5	10	30
Candy Cigarette Box	Cadet Sweets	1966	candy and trading card, illustrated box	25	60	125
Candy Cigarette Counter Display Box	Cadet Sweets	1966	holds 72 candy cigarette boxes, illustrated	30	90	200
Coin of El Diablo Affair Book	Wonder Books	1965	softcover, 48 pages	10	20	40
Counter Spy Water Gun	Hong Kong	1960s	luger water gun w/unlicensed Napoleon Solo illustration header card	5	15	40
Counterspy Outfit	Marx	1966	contains trench coat w/secret pockets, pistol, shoulder holster, launcher barrel, silencer, scope sight, two pair of glasses, beards, eye patch, badge case, etc., in box	125	230	475
Counterspy Outfit Store Display	Marx	1966	35" x 36" wide cardboard display w/one piece of each item in Counterspy Outfit	320	650	1250
Crime Buster Gift Set	Corgi	1966	set includes Man from U.N.C.L.E. car, James Bond Aston Martin and Batmobile w/Batboat on trailer, in window box	275	525	1050
Die-Cast Car	Playart	1968	2-3/4" long, die-cast metal, metallic purple	90	200	425
Die-Cast Metal Gun	Lone Star	1965	die-cast automatic cap pistol w/ plastic grips, plus cut-out badge, on card	75	150	325
Diving Dames Affair Book	Souvenir Press/ England	1967	#10 in series	4	8	20
Doomsday Affair Book	Souvenir Press	1965	#2 in series	4	8	20
Fingerprint Kit		1966	ink pad, roller, code book, magnifier, fingerprint records and pressure plate, in illustrated window box	125	250	500
Flicker Ring		1965	silver plastic ring w/b/w photos, each	10	20	50
Flicker Ring		1966	blue plastic w/"changing portrait" of Napoleon or Illya, each	10	20	40
Foto-Fantastiks Coloring Set	Eberhard Faber	1965	six colored pencils, paint brush, and six 8" x 10" photos, came in four different versions, each	40	85	175

TOY	COMPANY	YEAR	DESCRIPTION	GOOD	EX	MIB
Generic Spies Figures	Marx	1966	six different solid plastic, unpainted figures 5-3/4" tall, each	8	15	20
Handkerchief	England	1966	U.N.C.L.E. logo, Illya and Napoleon	30	65	150
Headquarters Transmitter	Cragstan	1965	molded gold colored plastic transmitter, amplifier and under cover case, silver ID card, 20-foot wire, in box	80	160	325
Illya Kuryakin Action Figure	Gilbert	1965	12" tall, plastic, black sweater, pants and shoes, spring loaded arm for firing cap pistol, folding badge, ID card and instruction sheet, in photo box	80	225	425
Illya Kuryakin Action Puppet	Gilbert	1965	13" tall, soft vinyl hand puppet of Illya holding a communicator, on 10" x 16" card	80	175	375
Illya Kuryakin Costume	Halco	1967	painted mask, rayon costume in three colors showing Illya holding a gun, in illustrated window box	45	90	200
Illya Kuryakin Figure	Marx	1966	blue or gray plastic figure, 5-3/4" tall, stamped w/character's name and U.N.C.L.E. logo on the bottom of base	15	30	70
Illya, That Man From U.N.C.L.E. Book	Pocket Books	1966	6" x 9" paperback, 100 pages of David McCallum	10	30	70
Invisible Writing Cartridge Pen	Platinum/England	1965	pen, two vials of ink and two invisible ink vials	125	230	475
Magic Slates	Watkins-Strathmore	1965	9" x 14" slate w/two punch-out figures of either Napoleon or Illya, each	45	100	200
Man from the U.N.C.L.E. Record	Capitol Records	1965	45 rpm w/The Man from U.N.C.L.E. theme song and "The Vagabond"	25	60	120
Man from U.N.C.L.E. and other TV Themes Record	Metro Records	1965	photo cover, has three songs from U.N.C.L.E. plus theme songs from Dr. Kildare, Mr. Novak, Bonanza and other shows	8	25	50
Man from U.N.C.L.E. Button	Button World	1965	3-1/2" diam. round button w/portrait of Napoleon or Illya, each	10	17	30
Man from U.N.C.L.E. Card Game	Japan	1966	small artwork cards in illustrated box	40	75	160
Man from U.N.C.L.E. Code Board		1966	chalkboard w/line art illustrations	70	150	300
Man from U.N.C.L.E. Finger Puppets	Dean	1966	vinyl; THRUSH agent, Solo, Kuryakin, Waverly and two female agents; window box	140	300	600
Man from U.N.C.L.E. Playing Cards	Ed-U-Cards	1965	standard 54-card deck w/action photo illustrations, on card	20	35	70
Man from U.N.C.L.E. Playing Cards Display Box	Ed-U-Cards	1965	holds 12 packs	130	250	525
Man from U.N.C.L.E. Puzzles	Jaymar	1965	frame tray; three versions; each	25	40	75
Man from U.N.C.L.E. Record	Crescendo Records	1965	by the Challengers, cover shows blonde female spy w/gun	5	15	35
Man from U.N.C.L.E. Record	Union/Japan	1966	45 rpm w/photo sleeve	35	75	150
Man from U.N.C.L.E. Sheet Music	Hastings Music Corp.	1964	six pages, theme song and a brief description of the TV show	15	50	100
Man from U.N.C.L.E. Trading Cards	Topps	1965	set of 55 b/w photo cards	45	90	160

TV TOYS

TV TOYS

TOY	COMPANY	YEAR	DESCRIPTION	GOOD	EX	MIB
Man from U.N.C.L.E. Trading Cards	Cadet Sweets	1966	set of 50 cards, color photos, set	22	45	90
Man from U.N.C.L.E. Trading Cards	ABC/England	1966	25 cards	22	45	90
Mystery Jigsaw Series Puzzles	Milton Bradley	1965	14" x 24" puzzle, 250 pieces plus story booklet, The Loyal Groom, The Vital Observation, The Impossible Escape, The Micro-Film Affair, each	25	50	100
Napoleon Solo Costume	Halco	1965	transparent plastic "mystery mask," costume has line art shirt, tie, shoulder holster and U.N.C.L.E. logo, in illustrated box	50	95	185
Napoleon Solo Credentials and Passport Set	Ideal	1965	silver ID card, badge, identification wallet, slide window passport, on header card	35	65	150
Napoleon Solo Credentials and Secret Message Sender	Ideal	1965	message sender, badge, and silver ID, on card	40	80	175
Napoleon Solo Doll	Gilbert	1965	11" tall, plastic, white shirt, black pants and shoes, spring loaded arm for firing cap pistol, folding badge, ID card and instruction sheet	70	145	350
Napoleon Solo Figure	Marx	1966	blue or gray plastic figure, 5-3/4" tall stamped w/character's name and U.N.C.L.E. logo on the bottom of base	10	25	65
Pinball Affair Game	Marx	1966	12" x 24" tin litho pinball game	75	150	300
Pistol Cane Gun	Marx	1966	25" long, cap firing, bullet shooting aluminum cane w/ eight bullets and one metal shell, on illustrated card	125	250	600
Power Cube Affair Book	Souvenir	1968	#15 in series, British	5	10	25
Puzzle	Milton Bradley	1966	10" x 19", 100 pieces, Illya's Battle Below	15	35	70
Puzzle	Milton Bradley	1966	10" x 19", 100 pieces, Illya Crushes THRUSH	15	40	70
Puzzles	England	1966	four 11" x 17" puzzles, each w/ 340 pieces: The Getaway, Solo in Trouble, The Frogman Affair, Secret Plans, each	40	80	165
Secret Agent Wristwatch	Bradley	1966	gray watch face shows Solo holding a communicator, came w/either plain "leather" or "mod" watch band, in case	115	250	500
Secret Code Wheel Pinball	Marx	1966	10" x 22" x 6" tin litho pinball game	80	170	325
Secret Message Pen	American Character	1966	6-1/2" long double tipped pen for writing invisible messages, on header card	100	200	325
Secret Print Putty	Colorforms	1965	putty in a gun shaped container, print paper, display cards of Kuryakin and Solo and a book of spy and weapons illustrations, on card	20	45	95
Secret Service Gun	Ideal	1965	pistol, holster, badge and silver ID card, in window box	160	310	650
Secret Service Pop Gun		1960s	bagged Luger pop gun on header card w/unlicensed illustration of Illya and Napoleon on header	10	15	50
Secret Weapon Set	Ideal	1965	clip loading cap firing pistol, holster, ID wallet, silver ID card, U.N.C.L.E. badge, two demolition grenades and holster, in window box	190	400	775

Howdy Doody Color TV Set, American Plastic

*Howdy Doody Puzzle Set,
1950s, Milton Bradley*

Howdy Doody Ranch House Tool Box, 1950s, Liberty Steel

Howdy Doody Swim Ring, 1950s, Ideal

Man From U.N.C.L.E. Illya Kuryakin Action Figure, 1965, Gilbert

MAN FROM U.N.C.L.E.

TOY	COMPANY	YEAR	DESCRIPTION	GOOD	EX	MIB
Shirt		1965	has secret pocket, glow-in-the-dark badge and ID, photo package	190	375	725
Shoot Out! Game	Milton Bradley	1965	skill and action game for two players, plastic marble game in illustrated box	80	160	325
Shooting Arcade Game	Marx	1966	tin litho arcade w/mechanical wind-up THRUSH agent targets for pellet shooting pistol, scope and stock attachments	200	400	850
Shooting Arcade Game	Marx	1966	smaller version w/THRUSH spinner targets	150	275	525
Spy Magic Tricks	Gilbert	1965	mystery gun, Illya playing cards, tricks	125	250	525
Television Picture Story Book	P.B.S. Limited	1968	hardcover, 62 pages, Gold Key reprints	15	20	60
THRUSH Agent Figures	Marx	1966	three different blue plastic figures, 5-3/4" tall stamped w/ titles and U.N.C.L.E. logo on the bottom of each base, each	10	20	35
THRUSH Ray-Gun Affair Game	Ideal	1966	four U.N.C.L.E. agent pieces, Area Decoder cards, 3-D THRUSH hideouts, THRUSH vehicles, crayons, dice and a rotating "ray gun," in illustrated box	55	110	225
THRUSH-Buster Display Box	Corgi	1966	large display box w/graphics, holds 12 cars	170	330	700
U.N.C.L.E. Badges Store Display	Lone Star	1965	illustrated card holds 12 triangular black plastic badges w/gold lettering, w/ badges	50	120	225

MONKEES

TOY	COMPANY	YEAR	DESCRIPTION	GOOD	EX	MIB
Flip Movies	Topps	1967	each	5	10	20
Halloween Costumes	Bland Charnas	1967	each	60	125	250
Jigsaw Puzzle	Fairchild	1967		15	25	45
Monkees Dolls	Remco	1967	4", rubber, each	35	80	175
Monkees Finger Puppets	Remco	1969		15	25	45
Talking Hand Puppet	Mattel	1966	cloth w/heads of Monkees on fingertips	50	100	200
Tambourine	Raybert	1967		45	100	200
Toy Guitar	Mattel	1966	20"	60	125	250
Toy Guitar	Mattel	1966	14", wind-up crank	40	90	175

MORK AND MINDY

TOY	COMPANY	YEAR	DESCRIPTION	GOOD	EX	MIB
Mork and Mindy Colorforms	Colorforms	1979		10	15	30

MR. ED

TOY	COMPANY	YEAR	DESCRIPTION	GOOD	EX	MIB
Mr. Ed Talking Horse Puppet	Mattel	1962		35	75	150

MUNSTERS, THE

TOY	COMPANY	YEAR	DESCRIPTION	GOOD	EX	MIB
Grandpa Doll	Remco	1964		150	325	610
Herman Munster Doll	Remco	1964		155	350	720
Lily Baby Doll	Ideal	1965	unlicensed "monster baby"	45	85	170
Lily Doll	Remco	1964		150	325	625
Puzzle	Whitman	1960s	frame tray	30	50	100
Puzzle	Whitman	1965	100 pieces, boxed	35	60	150
The Last Resort Book	Whitman	1964		13	30	50

PARTRIDGE FAMILY

TOY	COMPANY	YEAR	DESCRIPTION	GOOD	EX	MIB
David Cassidy Dress-Up Kit	Colorforms	1972		20	40	75
Laurie Partridge Doll	Remco	1973	20" tall	55	120	225
Partridge Family Bus	Remco	1973	plastic, 14" long	55	160	300
Partridge Family Guitar	Carnival	1970s	19" plastic, decal of David Cassidy on body	35	75	150
Partridge Family Paper Dolls	Saalfield	1970s	several styles	20	40	75
Patti Partridge Doll	Ideal	1971		50	110	200

PEE WEE HERMAN

TOY	COMPANY	YEAR	DESCRIPTION	GOOD	EX	MIB
Ball Dart Set				5	10	15
Billy Baloney Doll	Matchbox	1988	18" tall	12	20	45
Chairry Figure	Matchbox	1988	5" tall	3	5	10
Chairry Figure	Matchbox		15" tall	12	20	45
Conky Wacky Wind-Up	Matchbox	1988		3	5	10
Cowboy Curtis Figure	Matchbox			8	15	35
Globey with Randy	Matchbox	1988		8	15	35
King of Cartoons Figure	Matchbox	1988	5" tall	8	15	35
Magic Screen Figure	Matchbox	1988	5" tall poseable	8	15	35
Magic Screen Wacky Wind-Up	Matchbox	1988	6" tall	3	5	10
Miss Yvonne Doll	Matchbox	1988	poseable 5" tall	8	15	45
Pee Wee Herman Deluxe Colorforms	Colorforms	1980s		7	10	35
Pee Wee Herman Doll	Matchbox	1988	poseable 5" tall	4	10	25
Pee Wee Herman Doll	Matchbox		15" tall, non talking	10	20	65
Pee Wee Herman Play Set	Matchbox	1989	20" x 28" x 8" for use w/5" figures, Pee Wee's bike, folds into large carrying case	12	28	60
Pee Wee Herman Slumber Bag	Matchbox	1988		10	20	35
Pee Wee Herman Ventriloquist Doll	Matchbox	1980s		30	65	135
Pee Wee with Scooter and Helmet	Matchbox	1988		4	7	10
Pee Wee Yo-Yo				3	10	20
Pterri Doll	Matchbox		13" tall	15	25	45
Pterri Wacky Wind-Ups	Matchbox	1988		3	5	10
Reba Figure	Matchbox	1988	poseable	5	10	30
Ricardo Figure	Matchbox	1988		5	10	30
Vance the Talking Pig Figure	Matchbox	1987		20	40	85
View-Master Gift Set	View-Master	1980s		6	12	20

ROMPER ROOM

TOY	COMPANY	YEAR	DESCRIPTION	GOOD	EX	MIB
Bo Dee Iron On Transfer	Hasbro			2	3	5
Bop-A-Loop Toy (MIB)	Hasbro			3	5	10
Build & Play Discs	Hasbro			3	6	12
Can You Guess? Wonder Book	Hasbro			4	9	8
Ceramic Mug – Jack-in-the-Box	Hasbro			8	15	34
Chalkboard	Hasbro			4	8	15
Digger the Dog (MIB)	Hasbro			8	15	32
Do Bee Dough Machine	Hasbro			8	15	34
Do Bee Rider	Hasbro			12	25	55
Do Bees Little Golden Book of Manners	Hasbro			4	9	18
Dump Truck (Do Bee hubcaps)	Hasbro			2	3	6
Fitness Fun 45 RPM	Hasbro			1	2	4
Fun Time Puzzle Clock	Hasbro			3	5	10
G.E. Show 'N Tell Phonoviewer	Hasbro			6	12	28

ROMPER ROOM

TOY	COMPANY	YEAR	DESCRIPTION	GOOD	EX	MIB
G.E. Show 'N Tell Picturesound Refill Programs (each)	Hasbro			1	2	4
Happy Jack and Mr. Do Bee hand puppets	Hasbro			10	20	40
Happy Jack Magnetic Puzzle	Hasbro			4	8	16
Happy Jack Punching Clown	Hasbro			4	9	18
Inchworm	Hasbro			15	30	60
Moe the Monkey Game	Hasbro			2	5	10
Mr. Bo-Dee Miniature Poly-Blocks	Hasbro			2	5	10
Mr. Do Bee Bank	Hasbro			8	15	35
Mr. Stacking Man	Hasbro			4	8	15
Musical Block Clock	Hasbro			10	20	45
Musical Jack in the Box	Hasbro			15	35	75
Official TV Bo Dee Dance Record	Hasbro			4	8	16
Peg Town Railroad	Hasbro			2	5	10
Preschool Super Fun Pad	Hasbro			2	3	6
Sew Easy Sewing Machine	Hasbro			3	6	12
Snoopy Counting Camera	Hasbro			5	10	20
Snoopy Play Telephone	Hasbro			2	5	10
Squirt, Squirt, Squirt the Animals Tub Toy	Hasbro			2	5	10
Super Mr. Potato Head	Hasbro			3	7	14
Talk 'N Chalk Board	Hasbro			8	15	30
Tambourine	Hasbro			5	10	22
Toy Ring – Gold Plated Plastic	Hasbro			10	20	40
Weebles Playground	Hasbro			20	50	110
Willie the Weather Man	Hasbro			10	20	45

ROOKIES, THE

TOY	COMPANY	YEAR	DESCRIPTION	GOOD	EX	MIB
Rookie Chris Doll	LJN	1973	8" tall	10	20	40
Rookie Mike Doll	LJN	1973	8" tall	10	20	40
Rookie Terry Doll	LJN	1973	8" tall	10	20	40
Rookie Willy Doll	LJN	1973	8" tall	10	20	40

SCOOBY DOO

TOY	COMPANY	YEAR	DESCRIPTION	GOOD	EX	MIB
Scooby Doo and the Pirate Treasure Book	Golden	1974	Little Golden Book	5	10	15
Scooby Doo Hand Puppet	Ideal	1970s	vinyl head	20	40	75
Scooby Doo Paint with Water Book		1984		5	10	20
Scooby Doo Squeak Toy	Sanitoy	1970s	6" tall	20	35	50

SGT. PRESTON

TOY	COMPANY	YEAR	DESCRIPTION	GOOD	EX	MIB
Sgt. Preston of the Yukon Punch-Out Cards	Quaker	1950s	"Big Game Trophy" cardboard cut-outs, set of nine	30	100	175

SOUPY SALES

TOY	COMPANY	YEAR	DESCRIPTION	GOOD	EX	MIB
Soupy Sales Card Game	Jaymar	1960s	Slap Jack, Old Maid, Funny Rummy, or Hearts/Crazy 8s	20	40	60
Soupy Sales Doll	Remco	1960s	5" doll	40	150	250
Soupy Sales Doll	Knickerbocker	1966	12" plush, vinyl head	25	60	150

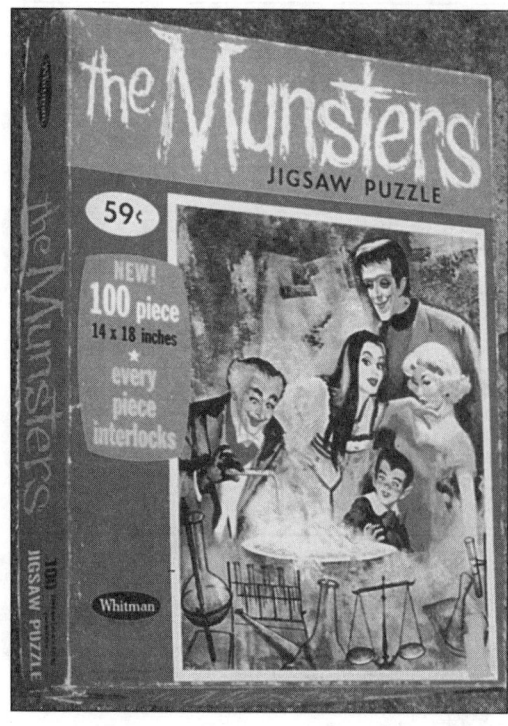

The Munsters Dolls, 1964, Remco

The Munsters Puzzle, 1965, Whitman

STARSKY AND HUTCH

TOY	COMPANY	YEAR	DESCRIPTION	GOOD	EX	MIB
Starsky and Hutch Puzzle	HG Toys	1970s		15	30	50
Starsky and Hutch Shoot-Out Target Set	Berwick	1970s		25	45	95

UNDERDOG

TOY	COMPANY	YEAR	DESCRIPTION	GOOD	EX	MIB
Kite Fun Book	Pacific Gas and Electric	1970s		10	35	85
Puzzle	Whitman	1975	100 pieces	10	20	30
Underdog Costume	Ben Cooper	1969		55	85	125
Underdog Dot Funnies Kit	Whitman	1974		10	20	40
Underdog Figure	Dakin	1976	plastic, Cartoon Theater	35	100	150

WELCOME BACK, KOTTER

TOY	COMPANY	YEAR	DESCRIPTION	GOOD	EX	MIB
Halloween Costume	Collegeville	1976	several styles	10	20	25
Sweathogs Dolls	Mattel	1976	Epstein, Washington, Barbarino, Kotter, Horshack; each	10	25	60
Sweathogs Grease Machine Cars	Ahi	1977	3" long, plastic cars; various styles, each	15	30	60
Welcome Back, Kotter Classroom	Mattel	1976	play set	25	45	100
Welcome Back, Kotter Colorforms Set	Colorforms	1976		10	20	50

WINKY DINK AND YOU

TOY	COMPANY	YEAR	DESCRIPTION	GOOD	EX	MIB
When Winky Winks at You Record	Decca	1956		45	60	80
Winky Dink Book	Golden	1956	Little Golden Book	9	16	25
Winky Dink Comic Book	Dell	1950s	#663	20	40	90
Winky Dink Magic Crayons		1960s		20	35	50
Winky Dink Official TV Game Kit		1950s		30	50	100
Winky Dink Secret Message Game	Lowell	1950s		75	130	225
Winky Dink Winko Magic Kit		1950s		20	35	50

Vehicle Toys

Modern man has always had a love affair with machines that move. Partial evidence of this is the amazing number of toy vehicles that have been produced in the 20th century. In fact, it could be reasonably argued that toy vehicles are collected more than any other type of toy.

With the dawn of the modern industrial age, the mass production of full-size automobiles and their toy counterparts seemed to go hand-in-hand. As cars rolled off assembly lines, their miniature replicas were not far behind.

Cars and trucks weren't the only toy vehicles, however. Any sort of vehicle — including boats, planes and horse-drawn wagons — was a natural for miniaturization. The types and manufacturers of toy vehicles were as varied as the real things too. Toy makers crafted them from everything from cast iron and tin to wood and plastic.

The earliest toy automobiles came along soon after their big daddy originals in the late 19th century and were produced in cast iron. But it wasn't until after World War I that toy automobile production really began to hit its stride.

The Early Days

Firms such as Arcade and Hubley are among the most well-known and sought-after manufacturers of early cast-iron vehicles.

Cars, trucks, and buses produced by Arcade Manufacturing of Freeport, Ill., are highly valued to toy vehicle collectors. Arcade actually began producing toys in the late 1800s, but it wasn't until around 1920 when the company reportedly issued its first toy vehicle, a replica of a Chicago Yellow Cab. After that came more realistic models of actual cars, trucks, and buses. The company's slogan was "They Look Real."

Hubley is another name associated with quality toy vehicles. This Pennsylvania company began manufacturing cast-iron toys in the 1890s, mostly horse-drawn wagons, trains and guns. By the 1930s, Hubley was producing the cast-iron cars that became their most well-known products. Many were patterned after actual automobiles of the day, while others were apparently looser interpretations of reality. Some of the Hubley vehicles also included company names, and some of the most interesting pieces had separate nickel-plated grilles.

One of the more skilled makers of smaller scale cast-iron vehicles was A.C. Williams. The Ohio company began producing toys in the late 1800s. The smaller cars and airplanes produced by A.C. Williams were intended for the five-and-dime market of the time. Williams' toys are difficult for the novice collector to identify since the toys bear no markings.

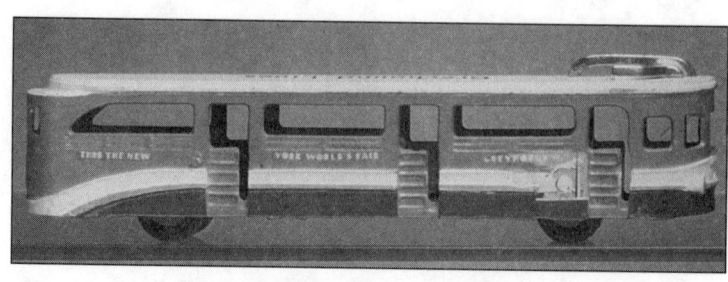

New York World's Fair Bus, No. 3780, 1939, Arcade

While heavy cast-iron toys ruled at the turn of the century, lithographed tin toys began stealing a large part of the market in the 1920s. One of the world's leading producers of these toys was Louis Marx. Over the years, Marx produced an extensive line of toy cars, trucks, airplanes, and farm equipment, not only in tin, but also in steel and later in plastic.

Marx capitalized on the popularity of certain celebrities and comic strip characters, incorporating them into its toy vehicles. With lithography, it was easy to put a new character into a car and create a brand new toy ready for market. Characters such as Mickey Mouse, Donald Duck, Dick Tracy, Blondie and Dagwood, Charlie McCarthy, Amos 'N Andy and Milton Berle show up in Marx cars.

Steel Takes Over

One of the most famous manufacturers of toy cars and trucks was Buddy "L." These large pressed-steel toys were not the kind of toys bought for display or quiet play on the living room floor. These were big trucks (around two feet long) designed for tough play.

Buddy "L" toys grew out of the Moline Pressed Steel Company of Moline, Ill. The company was named for the son of the company's owner, reportedly for whom the first toys were produced. The Buddy "L" toys most sought by collectors were produced in the 1920s and 1930s and were of very heavy-duty construction. Starting in the early 1930s, the company began to use lighter-weight materials.

The Buddy "L" name has remained, but its post-World War II toys are not considered in the same league as its early issues, which command high collector prices today.

Buddy "L" is best remembered for its heavy duty trucks, but another name that was synonymous with trucks was Smith-Miller. Founded by Bob Smith and Matt Miller, the company specialized in "famous trucks in miniature." Smith-Miller was later known as Miller-Ironson Corporation, but is more commonly referred to as Smitty Toys. It produced large cast-metal and aluminum trucks.

Because of their outstanding quality, some of the Mack trucks made by Smith-Miller are very highly regarded among toy collectors. The Smith-Miller name continues today, with new limited-edition trucks produced for collectors.

Wyandotte is another company associated with pressed steel vehicles. Known as both Wyandotte Toys or All Metal Products, this Michigan company produced several large steel vehicles with baked enamel finishes in the 1930s. Not all Wyandotte toys are marked, which tends to cause some confusion among collectors, but the vehicles can often be identified by their art deco-type styling and wooden wheels.

Another company that produced large steel toys was Structo. The company originally produced metal construction sets, but developed a line of vehicles in the 1920s.

While major toy companies were producing vehicles in cast iron, tin, and steel, others made toys in rubber. Probably the best-known manufacturer of rubber toys is the Auburn Rubber Company of Auburn, Ind. From the mid-1930s into the 1950s, Auburn produced rubber cars, trucks, tractors, motorcycles, airplanes, trains and boats.

Other popularly-collected vehicles are smaller die-cast models, generally three to six inches long. Probably the leading producer of this type of vehicle was Tootsietoy.

The company dates back to before the turn of the century to Samuel Dowst of Chicago. The trade name, which would eventually become the firm's mainstay, originates with Dowst's daughter, Tootsie. Although a few toy cars were produced by the firm before 1920, it was during the Roaring Twenties when the name Tootsietoy began to appear regularly. By the 1930s, the company was producing a wide line of toys, many of which are highly prized by collectors today. Tootsietoy's Federal vans from the 1920s are among the most sought-after toys, particularly those with company logos.

Being mass produced and economically priced, Tootsietoys were widely available in the five-and-dime arena. The success of these products no doubt led to several competitors.

One of those competitors was Barclay, which also manufactured die-cast vehicles, although most were generally considered of lesser quality than Tootsietoys. The first Barclay vehicles had metal tires, but in the mid-1930s, white rubber tires on wooden axles were introduced. Metal axles soon replaced the wood, and black tires replaced white after World War II.

Another competitor soon emerged from Europe — Dinky Toys were manufactured from 1933 through the 1970s in England and France. Their vehicles were high quality die cast, at least until the mid-1960s, generally in 1:43-scale.

Another competitor in this classification of small die-cast vehicles is Corgi, which came on the scene in the late 1950s. Corgi was the trade name for the die-cast toys which were produced by England's Mettoy Company.

One of the best known series of toy cars today is Matchbox. These die-cast beauties are roughly three inches in length. However Lesney, the company that produced them, did produce several larger cars before it began the Matchbox line. Some of these early Lesney vehicles are valued at up to $2,000 each.

The Lesney company originated in England after World War II. The name came from the combination of parts of the two founders' first names, LESlie and RodNEY Smith. After tinkering with several products, including a few larger vehicles, the company hit paydirt with small cars that would eventually be dubbed "Matchbox." Soon the

VEHICLES

No. 370 Rail Rodder (1996 First Editions), Hot Wheels Numbered Packs

656

company began issuing 75 models each year, called the 1-75 Series. Lesney also issued a larger series of four- to six-inch cars called Models of Yesteryear.

Matchbox vehicles were immensely popular, so much so that in the United States, Mattel introduced a similar line called Hot Wheels. The California-based company gave its cars a California-type appeal, focusing on colorful hot rods that appealed to youngsters.

In the head-to-head battle that followed, Lesney at one time was producing 5.5 million toys a week. Eventually, Lesney lost the battle and went into receivership. Matchbox was restructured and sold twice, eventually landing with Tyco Toys. In 1996, Mattel purchased Tyco, bringing Matchbox cars to their company.

Matchbox has strong name recognition, but Hot Wheels are beyond hot. Introduced in 1968 by Mattel, Hot Wheels changed the world of die-cast. Made to be raced, these 1:64-scale cars took the world by storm. The original sixteen Hot Wheels had a look of California cool, and a strong advertising campaign ensured that kids of all ages wanted the new car.

Over the past thirty-two years, Hot Wheels have remained a constant toy for kids and collectible for adults. By the late 1980s, Mattel began making Numbered Packs making it easier for enthusiasts to collect the little cars. Still going strong, Numbered Packs have become the darling of die-cast attracting collectors of all ages.

The popularity of Hot Wheels forced the already-established manufacturers to take note. It also encouraged others to duplicate Hot Wheels success. Johnny Lightnings, made by Topper Toys, went head to head with Hot Wheels for a few years before Topper went under in 1971. Re-introduced by Playing Mantis, new Johnny Lightnings were made with the collector in mind. Produced in limited quantities, the new Johnnies have become popular among die-cast enthusiasts.

There are many other toy cars collected today than are listed in this book. For example, a wide variety of tin toy cars came out of Japan after World War II. Many Japanese toy companies emerged during that period; Bandai is listed separately. Other Japanese tin vehicles are listed under a general "Japanese" heading including numerous, and sometimes unmarked, manufacturers.

Tips on Grading

Since the universe of vehicle toys is diverse, grading condition must also take into consideration such differences. For example, when grading a much older cast-iron vehicle such as a Hubley or Arcade, one must consider the age and sturdiness of the vehicle. While any imperfections or scratches always lessen a vehicle's value, such things are more likely to deflate prices on vehicles such as Hot Wheels or Matchbox cars. On the latter two, any defect will bring the value down about 25 percent.

Editor's Note: Several vehicle listings may feature an n/a in the MIP column. This means either the car did not come in a package, or it is ultimately too rare to be found in original packaging.

The Top 10 Vehicle Toys
(in Mint condition)

1. Packard Straight 8, Hubley...$15,000
2. Checker Cab, No. 175, Arcade 12,000
3. Elgin Street Sweeper, Hubley.. 11,500
4. World's Greatest Circus Truck, Keystone... 10,000

*Custom Mustang,
1968, Hot Wheels*

5. Ingersoll-Rand Compressor, Hubley 10,000
6. Motorized Sidecar Motorcycle, Hubley... 10,000
7. Ahrens-Fox Fire Engine, Hubley 8,000
8. Seven Man Fire Patrol, Hubley 7,500
9. Tractor Dredge (on Treads), Buddy L.. 7,500
10.White Bus, No. 319, Arcade 7,400

The Top 10 Mattel Classic Hot Wheels
(in Mint in Package condition)

1. Volkswagen Beach Bomb, surf boards in rear window, 1969 .... $7,000
2. Custom Camaro, 1968, white enamel 2,500
3. Snake, 1973, white/yellow 1,500
4. Mongoose, 1973, red/blue 1,400
5. Carabo, 1974, yellow 1,400
6. Baja Bruiser, light green, 1976 1,300
7. Baja Bruiser, yellow, magenta in tampo, 1974 1,200
8. Mustang Stocker, 1975, white 1,200
9. Custom Mustang, 1968 1,200
10. Mercedes C-111, 1973 1,200

The Top 10 Mattel Hot Wheels Numbered Packs
(in Mint in Package condition)

1. No. 51 '40s Woodie $700
2. No. 355 '67 Camaro, 1995 Treasure Hunt Series 600
3. No. 714 Talbot Lago 350
4. No. 672 #35-Dodge Concept Car, 1998 First Editions 350
5. No. 12 Jeep 275
6. No. 50 Rolls Royce Phantom II 250
7. No. 271 Side Splitter 250
8. No. 88 Thunderbird Stocker 250
9. No. 89 Mini Truck 250
10.No. 75 Pontiac Banshee 200

Contributors to this section: **Corgi,** Dr. Douglas Sadecky, Medical Arts Plaza, 1619 Union Ave., Natrona Heights, PA 15065; **Hot Wheels,** Andrew Dudek, adudak@aol.com; Jim Wilson, jw1962pw@aol.com; and Steve and Anna Cinnamon, cinman@provide.net; They can all be reached at: P.O. Box 55, Belleville, MI 48112-0055; **Johnny Lightning / Topper,** Tom Brown, tmbrown@edgenet.net; Ray Falcoa, johnnylray@aol.com.

VEHICLES

NAME	DESCRIPTION	GOOD	EX	MINT
A.C.F. Bus	1927, 11-1/2" long	1200	2200	3500
Allis-Chalmers "WC" Tractor	1941, 7-3/4" long	180	350	600
Allis-Chalmers Tractor and Dump Trailer	1937, No. 2657, 12-3/4" long w/trailer	200	345	460
Allis-Chalmers Tractor and Dump Trailer	1937, No. 2660, 8-1/4" long	150	200	300
Allis-Chalmers Tractor and Trailer	1936, No. 2650, total length 13" long	175	300	400
Allis-Chalmers Tractor Trailer	1937, No. 2650, 13" long w/trailer	250	375	500
Ambulance	1932, No. 187, 7-3/4" long	400	700	1200
Ambulance	1932, No. 188, 6" long	370	550	740
Ambulance	1936, white-painted version of No. 2620 Chevrolet Panel Delivery Truck, 4" long	340	510	680
Andy Gump and Old 348	bright red car, red green, green disc wheels w/red hubcaps, cast iron, 7-1/4" long	800	1400	1900
Anthony Dump Truck	1927, 8-1/8" long	700	1500	2400
Austin "Roll-A-Plane"	8" long	450	675	900
Austin Autocrat Road Roller	1928, No. 291, 7" long	200	300	450
Austin Delivery Truck	1932, No. 173, 3-3/4" long	40	75	100
Austin Racer	1932, No. 175X, 3-3/4" long	50	90	135
Austin Roadster	1932, No. 174, 3-3/4" long	90	140	190
Austin Stake Truck	1932, No. 176X, 3-3/4" long	90	140	200
Austin Wrecker	1932, No. 177X, 3-3/4" long	100	150	225
Avery Tractor	1923, stack, no hood, 4-1/2" long	50	75	110
Avery Tractor	1926, has hood, no stack, 4-1/2" long	125	200	325
Borden's Milk Bottle Truck	1936, No. 2640X, 6-1/4" long	750	1200	2500
Buick Opera Coupe	1927, 8-1/2" long	1900	2900	4900
Buick Sedan	1927, 8-1/2" long	1500	2500	4000
Bus, Double-Decker	1929, No. 316X, 8-1/2" long	350	600	900
Bus, Double-Decker	1936, No. 317, "Chicago Motor Coach" stamp, 8-1/4" long	350	600	900
Car Carrier	1932, No. 296, Ford AA truck carries all options of 5" and 6" Ford Model A cars and trucks, 24-1/2" long	2000	3500	5000
Car Carrier	1930, No. 238, Ford AA truck w/5" Ford Model A cars or three 6" Ford Model A cars, 24-1/2" long	2000	3500	5000
Car Transport	1937, No. 2977, holds two sedans and two trucks, 11-1/2" long	427	640	855
Car Transport	1937, No. 3107, came w/two No. 1501 sedans, No. 1502 stake truck and No. 1503 wrecker, 18-1/2" long	900	1350	1800
Carry Car Truck and Trailer Set	1934, No. 2970, carries three Austins, 14-1/4" long	650	1000	1500
Caterpillar Tractor	1931, No. 266X, 3" long	50	75	100
Caterpillar Tractor	1936, No. 270Y, later 2700Y, 7-3/4" long	700	1200	2200
Caterpillar Tractor	1931, No. 269X, 6-7/8" long	375	650	1100
Caterpillar Tractor	1931, No. 268X 5-5/8" long	350	600	900
Caterpillar Tractor	1930, No. 271, 7-1/2" long	450	800	1300
Caterpillar Tractor	1931, No. 267X, 3-7/8" long	150	250	400
Century of Progress Bus	1933, No. 3220, 10-1/2" long	150	250	350
Century of Progress Bus	1933, No. 3230, 7-5/8" long	100	175	250
Century of Progress Bus	1933, No. 3250, 1934, 14-1/2" long	250	350	525
Century of Progress Bus	1933, No. 3210, 12" long	200	300	400
Century of Progress Yellow Cab	6-3/4" long	750	1000	1600
Checker Cab	1932, No. 157, (came w/ and w/o "Checker" on visor), 9-1/4" long	5000	8000	12000
Chevrolet Coupe	1929, No. 121X, 8-1/4" long	700	1200	1800
Chevrolet Coupe	1934, rumble seat, No. 1150X, 4-3/8" long	150	250	350
Chevrolet Panel Delivery Truck	1936, No. 2620X, 4" long	100	150	200
Chevrolet Sedan	1929, No. 122X, 8-1/4" long	800	1300	2200

VEHICLES

Andy Gump and Old 348, 1923, Arcade

Bus, Double-Decker, No. 317, 1936, Arcade

VEHICLES

Century of Progress Bus, No. 3220, 1933, Arcade

NAME	DESCRIPTION	GOOD	EX	MINT
Chevrolet Sedan	1934, No. 1170X, 4-1/4" long	70	110	180
Chevrolet Stake Truck	1925, 9" long	800	1400	2300
Chevrolet Stake Truck	1936, No. 2610, 4-1/4" long	90	120	200
Chevrolet Superior Roadster	1925, 7" long	550	7500	1100
Chevrolet Superior Sedan	1925, 7" long	450	650	950
Chevrolet Superior Touring Car	1925, 7" long	500	700	1000
Chevrolet Utility Coupe	1925, 7" long	500	700	900
Chevrolet Wrecker Truck	1936, No. 2630X, 4-1/4" long	100	200	300
Chief Fire Chief Coupe	1934, No. 1240, 5" long	500	800	1400
Chief Fire Chief Coupe	1934, No. 1230, 6-3/4" long	1500	2500	3400
Coast to Coast GMC Transcontinental Bus	1937, No. 4378X, 9" long	212	320	425
Corn Harvester	1939, No. 702, 6-1/2" long	150	250	400
Corn Harvester	1939, No. 4180, 5" long	100	175	250
Corn Planter	1939, 4-1/2" long	40	80	125
Coupe	"1922" on spare tire, 9" long	800	1500	4000
Coupe	1932, No. 109, no Arcade markings, rumble seat opens, 6" long	300	450	650
Deluxe Sedan	1941, No. 1590X, same as Yellow Cab No. 1590Y, but w/top lights and sun roof ground off, 8-1/2" long	500	825	1200
DeSoto Sedan	1936, No. 1460X, 4" long	90	150	250
Double Decker Bus	1939, No. 3180, 8" long	300	450	750
Dump Truck	1936, No. 2320, 4-1/2" long	90	130	200
Dump Truck	1941, No. 3910X, 7" long	300	450	600
Dump Truck Trailer	1931, No. 234, 12-7/8" long	700	1150	1900
Dump Wagon	1923, driver, no cab, 7" long	300	550	850
Express Truck	1929, No. 207X, 8" long	300	600	900
Express Truck	1929, No. 209X, 6" long	200	300	500
Express Truck	1929, No. 214X, 5" long	150	250	400
Fageol Bus	1925, 12" long	200	350	500
Fageol Bus	5" long	80	150	300
Fageol Bus	8" long	150	250	400
Farm Mower	1939, No. 4210X, 4" long	40	70	100
Farmall "A" Tractor	1941, No. 7050, 7-1/2" long	475	850	1200
Farmall "M" Tractor	1941, No. 7070, 7-1/4" long	300	450	700
Farmall Tractor	1929, No. 279, 6" long	225	400	800
Fire Chief Car	1941, 5-5/8" long	160	300	450
Fire Engine	1941, No. 6990, 13-1/2" long	500	950	1525
Fire Engine	1936, No. 2340, 4-1/2" long	90	150	250
Fire Engine	1923, pumper, 7-1/2" long	200	375	500
Fire Engine	1936, No. 1740, pumper, 9" long	400	700	1150
Fire Ladder Truck	1936, No. 1820, 7" long	150	250	400
Fire Trailer Truck	1934, No. 1940, 16-1/4" long	600	900	1200
Ford Coupe,	1934, No. 1610X, rumble seat opens, 6-3/4" long	300	550	950
Ford Dump Truck	1929, No. 219X, 7-1/2" long	285	425	700
Ford Express Truck	1929, No. 210X, 8-1/4" long	700	1100	1900
Ford Model A Coupe	1928, No. 113X, 4-1/8" long	200	300	400
Ford Model A Coupe	1928, No. 106, rumble seat, 6-3/4" long	550	950	1400
Ford Model A Coupe	1928, No. 116X, rumble seat, 5" long	350	550	700
Ford Model A Fordor	1928, No. 207, 6-3/4" long	350	500	750
Ford Model A Tudor	1928, No. 108, 6-3/4" long	550	850	1200
Ford Model A Wrecker	1930, No. 218, 4-1/2" long	125	200	300
Ford Model A Wrecker	1929, No. 215, w/"weaver" host	550	850	1400
Ford Model T Coupe	1924, 6-1/2" long	290	435	750
Ford Model T Coupe	1923, 6" long	175	300	450
Ford Model T Fordor Sedan	1924, removable chauffeur, 6-1/2" long	250	350	650
Ford Model T Sedan	center door, 1923, 6-1/2" long	325	490	650
Ford Model T Stake Truck	1934, No. 2010X, 7" long	300	600	950
Ford Model T Stake Truck	1927, 5-3/4" long	250	350	450
Ford Model T Stake Truck	1927, 9" long	600	925	1250

*Checker Cab, No. 157,
1932, Arcade*

*Chevrolet Utility
Coupe, 1925, Arcade*

*Farmall Tractor, No. 279,
1929, Arcade*

VEHICLES

ARCADE

NAME	DESCRIPTION	GOOD	EX	MINT
Ford Model T Stake Truck	1925, 8-3/4" long	800	1100	1600
Ford Model T Touring Car	1923, 6-1/2" long	250	300	700
Ford Model T Touring Car Bank	1923, 6-1/2" long	800	1100	1900
Ford Model T Tudor	1928, No. 118, 5" long	350	550	700
Ford Model T Wrecker	1927, 11" long	700	1200	2000
Ford Sedan	1934, "Century of Progress," 4-3/4" long	200	600	900
Ford Sedan	1933, No. 1620X, 6-7/8" long	350	600	850
Ford Sedan	1934, "Century of Progress," 6-7/8" long	800	1500	2400
Ford Sedan w/Trailer	1937, "Covered Wagon," No. 1970, 12" long, trailer 5-1/2" long	650	120	2500
Ford Tractor and Plow	1941, No. 7220, tractor 6-1/2" long, overall length 8-3/4"	350	550	850
Ford Truck	1923, cab, one ton, 8-1/2" long	600	850	1500
Ford Tudor	1937, 5-1/4" long	550	950	1500
Fordson Tractor	1923, 5-3/4" long	138	225	325
Fordson Tractor	1928, No. 273, 3 -7/8" long	90	150	200
Fordson Tractor	1928, No. 274, 4-3/4" long	112	190	250
Fordson Tractor	1934, rubber wheels, No. 2730X, 3-1/2" long	75	125	175
Greyhound Cruiser Coach Bus	1941, No. 4400, 9-1/8" long	200	325	450
Greyhound Lines Bus	GMC, 1933, one-piece casting, 6"	100	200	300
Greyhound Lines Bus	1937, No. 3850 SP, 7-3/4" long	175	275	400
Greyhound Lines Great Lakes Exposition	1936, No. 437, 11" long	375	650	1000
Greyhound Lines Great Lakes Exposition	1936, No. 436, 6-3/4" long	300	500	750
Greyhound Super Coach	1937, No. 4380, 9" long	300	500	750
Ice Truck	circa 1941, No. 1933, 6-3/4" long	270	355	540
International Delivery Truck	1936, No. 3020, 9-1/2" long	750	1900	1500
International Delivery Truck	1932, No. 226, 9-3/4" long	1500	2400	3500
International Dump Truck	1937, No. 3710, 9-1/2" long	400	550	950
International Dump Truck	1940, No. 1670, chassis and dump box are steel, 11-5/8" long	500	1000	1650
International Dump Truck	1941, No. 7100, 11-1/8" long	500	900	1400
International Dump Truck	1936, No. 3030, 10-1/2" long	800	1600	2200
International Dump Truck	1931, No. 236-0, 10-3/4" long	750	1200	1750
International Harvester	Trac Tractor, 1941, No. 7120, 7-1/2" long	800	1400	2000
International Pickup Truck	1941, No. 7000, 9-1/2" long	450	850	1280
International Stake Truck	1931, No. 237-0, 12" long	600	900	1400
International Stake Truck	1941, No. 7090, 11-1/2" long	800	1100	2000
International Stake Truck	1936, No. 3090, 12" long	800	1100	2000
International Stake Truck	1937, No. 2600, 9-1/2" long	700	1000	2800
International Wrecker	1940, No. 1650, wrecker crane body and crane are steel, 13" long	500	800	1100
Ladder Truck	1936, No. 1700, w/ladders 12-1/2" long	475	715	950
Ladder Truck	1936, No. 2350, 4-3/4" long	90	150	200
Mack Bus	1929, No. 318, 13-1/4" long	950	1500	3000
Mack Cement Mixer	1931, 6-11/16" long, drum revolves	700	900	1200
Mack Chemical Truck	1929, fire ladder truck, 15" long	800	1500	2000
Mack Chemical Truck	1928, fire engine No. 245R, has ladders, 15" long	1500	2500	4000
Mack Chemical Truck	1929, fire engine w/ladders, 10" long	350	650	100
Mack Dump Truck	1925, 12" long	1400	2400	3400
Mack Dump Truck	1929, No. 248X, 8-1/2" long	600	950	1600
Mack Fire Apparatus Truck	1929, No. 242, ladder truck, 21" long	850	1350	2000
Mack High Dump Truck	1931, No. 244X, 10" long	900	1600	2300
Mack High Dump Truck	1931, No. 259X, 8-1/2" long	700	1150	1700
Mack Hoist Truck	1932, No. 198, body 8" long	900	1500	2130
Mack Ice Truck	1932, No. 257, w/driver, glass "ice" and tongs, 10-3/4" long	1200	2500	4000
Mack Ice Truck	1930, No. 257, w/driver, glass "ice" and tongs, 10-5/8" long	375	600	1000

VEHICLES

International Pickup Truck, No. 7000, 1941, Arcade

Mack Tank Truck, 1925, Arcade

Mack Wrecker, No. 255, 1930, Arcade

NAME	DESCRIPTION	GOOD	EX	MINT
Mack Ice Truck	1931, No. 226, 8-1/2" long	300	500	800
Mack Side Dump Truck	1932, No. 1960, 9" long	1200	2000	2800
Mack Stake Truck	1929, No. 246X, 12" long	1400	2800	4000
Mack Stake Truck	1929, No. 253, 8-3/4" long	800	1600	2200
Mack Tank Truck	1925, "American Gasoline," 13-1/4" long	1200	1850	2800
Mack Tank Truck	1930, No. 241, sheet metal tank, marked "Gasoline" and "Mack," 13" long	1200	1800	2800
Mack Tank Truck	1925, 13-1/4" long	1000	1600	2800
Mack Tank Truck	1925, "Lubrite," 13-1/4" long	1200	1800	2800
Mack Wrecker	1930 No. 255, 12-1/2" long	1500	2400	3500
McCormick-Deering Farmall Tractor	1937, 6-1/4" long	250	400	600
McCormick-Deering Thresher	1927, 12" long	250	400	600
McCormick-Deering Thresher	1930, 9-1/2" long	200	300	400
McCormick-Deering Tractor	1925, No.10-20, 6-3/4" long	300	425	600
Mullins Red Cap auto trailer		225	338	450
Nash Coupe	1943, 4-1/2" long	250	400	650
Nash Panel Delivery	1934, 4"	150	250	400
Nash Wrecker	1936, 4-1/2" long	250	375	500
National Trailways Bus	1937, No. 3870, 9-1/4" long	650	1200	1700
New York World's Fair Bus	1939, No. 3780, 10-1/2" long	450	650	900
New York World's Fair Bus	1939, No. 3750, 7" long	150	200	300
New York World's Fair Bus	1939, No. 3770, 8-1/2" long	300	400	550
New York World's Fair Tractor-Train	1939, No. 7290, same as above w/three cars	350	600	900
New York World's Fair Tractor-Train	1939, No. 7270, tractor and one car, tractor 3-1/4" long, car 4-1/4" long	200	300	450
Oliver Plow	1923, 6-1/2" long	250	375	500
Oliver Plow	1941, No. 4230X, 6-1/4" long	150	225	300
Oliver Superior Spreader	No. 7140, 1941, 10-1/4" long	350	550	950
Oliver Tractor	1937, No. 356, 7-1/2" long	300	500	675
Oliver Tractor	1941, No. 3560, 7-1/2" long	300	500	700
Pierce "Silver Arrow"	1934, 7-1/4" long	300	450	750
Plymouth Coupe	1933, No. 1340, 4-3/4" long	300	500	800
Plymouth Sedan	1933, No. 1330, 4-3/4" long	300	450	750
Plymouth Stake Truck	1933, No. 1840, 4-3/4" long	250	325	450
Plymouth Wrecker	1933, No. 1830, 4-3/4" long	175	250	350
Pontiac Sedan	1935, 6-1/2" long	350	525	800
Pontiac Sedan	1935, No. 1350, 4-1/4" long	150	250	375
Pontiac Stake Truck	1936, No. 2780, 4-1/4" long	150	250	350
Pontiac Stake Truck	1935, No. 2390, 6-1/4" long	300	450	600
Pontiac Wrecker	1936, No. 2000, 4-1/4" long	125	188	250
Racer	1932, No. 137, 5-5/8" long	120	180	240
Racer	1937, No. 1457, 5-3/4" long	150	250	350
Racer	Bullet Racer, 1931, No. 139, 7-5/8" long	950	1500	2300
Racer	pre-1923, 7-3/4" long	400	600	800
Racer	1931, No. 138, 6-3/4" long	200	300	450
Red Baby "Weaver" Wrecker	1929, 12" long	900	1500	2300
Red Baby Dump Truck	1923, No. 2, 10-3/4" long	900	1500	2500
Red Baby Dump Truck	1923, No. 1, 10-3/4" long	900	1500	2500
Reo Coupe	1932, No. 1247, 9-3/8" long	1100	2500	4500
Reo Coupe	1931, 7-1/2"	1000	1700	3000
Sand Loading Shovel	1932, No. 298 (later No. 299)	300	650	900
Scraper	1929, No. 287, 8-1/4" long	100	200	300
Sedan	1937, No. 1501X, 4-3/4" long	100	200	300
Sedan and Trailer	1937, No. 1497X, car 5-5/8" long, trailer 2-1/2" long	300	500	800
Side Dump Trailer	1932, No. 290, fastens to trucks or tractors, 7" long	100	200	350
Stake Trailer Truck	1931, No. 233, 11-5/16" long	200	450	600
Stake Truck	1929, No. 208X, 6" long	220	330	440

VEHICLES

NAME	DESCRIPTION	GOOD	EX	MINT
Stake Truck	1932, No. 208, no Arcade markings, 6" long	300	500	750
Stake Truck	1937, No. 1502, 4-1/4" long	125	200	300
Stake Truck	1929, No. 213, 5" long	125	200	325
Steam Shovel	1932, No. 292 Industrial Derrick, body 6" long	500	750	1100
Tandem Disc Harrow	1939, No. 704, 6-3/4" long	50	100	200
Tank, Army	1937, No. 400, 8" long	400	700	950
Tank, Army	1941, No. 3960, shoots, 4" long	100	200	300
Texas Centennial Bus	1936, 10-3/4" long	1300	2200	3000
Trac-Tractor	1937, No. 277, 8-1/4" long	600	950	1300
Tractor	1941, No. 4060, black rubber wheels, 6-1/4" long	180	300	450
Tractor	1941, No. 7200, 6-1/2" long	180	270	360
Tractor	1941, No. 7240, rubber wheels, 3-1/8" long	100	150	200
Tractor	1941, No. 7341, wood wheels, 6-1/4" long	200	350	550
Tractor and Dump Trailer	1941, No. 7300, 15-1/2" long	600	950	1300
Trailer, Farm	1929, No. 289, 3-3/4" long	75	150	250
Trailer, Farm	1929, No. 288, 4-5/8" long	150	150	250
Trailer, Farm	1929, No. 286, 6-3/8" long	150	200	325
Transport Trailer Truck	1934, No. 1800, 7-1/2" long	385	580	770
Two-Wheeled Jack	1932, No. 216, 5-1/2" long	75	125	200
W&K Truck Trailer	1923, 8-1/2" long	200	300	450
White Bus	No. 319, 1928, 13-1/4" long	2800	5500	7400
White Delivery Truck	1929, No. 252X, 8-1/4" long	2000	3000	6000
White Tank Truck	1931, No. 254, "Gasoline," 14-1/8" long	850	1500	2000
Wrecker	1929, No. 217, 1928, body 8" long	500	850	1400
Wrecker	1932, No. 225, no Arcade markings	600	950	1500
Wrecker	1934, No. 2020, 7" long	600	950	1500
Wrecker	1937, No. 1493, 6-1/2" long	150	250	350
Wrecker	1937, No. 1503, 4-3/4" long	100	150	200
Wrecker	1941, No. 3900, 8-1/2" long	150	250	350
Yellow Baby Dump Truck	1923, 10-1/2" long	900	1500	2500
Yellow Baby Wrecker	1929, 12" long	650	1100	1600
Yellow Cab	1925, No. 3, 5-1/4" long	400	700	1100
Yellow Cab	No. 1350, 1935, 4-1/4" long	200	300	450
Yellow Cab	1941, No. 1590Y, 8-1/2" long	350	650	1000
Yellow Cab	1936, No. 1580Y, 8-1/4" long	1400	2800	4000
Yellow Cab	1927, No. 5, 8-1/2" long	500	800	1000
Yellow Cab	1925, No. 2, 8" long	600	900	1400
Yellow Cab	1922, No. 2, 8" long	500	800	1200
Yellow Cab	1922, No. 1, 9" long	600	900	1400
Yellow Cab	1934, Ford Sedan, 6-7/8" long	1200	2200	3500
Yellow Cab Bank	1923, 8" long	700	1100	1500
Yellow Cab Bank	1927, "Flat Top"	1200	2800	4000
Yellow Cab Panel Delivery Truck	1925, 8-1/4" long, w/driver	900	1800	2500
Yellow Coach Double-Decker Bus	1925, 14" long	1500	2500	4000
Yellow Parlor Coach Bus	1926, 9-1/2" long	325	550	750
Yellow Parlor Coach Bus	1926, 13" long	800	1400	2200

VEHICLES

McCormick-Deering Farmall Tractor, 1937, Arcade

Minneapolis Moline Tractor, 1950, Auburn

AUBURN

NAME	DESCRIPTION	GOOD	EX	MINT

Airplanes

NAME	DESCRIPTION	GOOD	EX	MINT
Clipper Plane	rubber, 7" wingspan, 1941	10	20	25
Dive Bomber	rubber, 4" wingspan, 1937	10	20	25
Pursuit Ship Plane	4" wingspan, 1941	10	20	25
Two-Engine Transport Plane	1937	10	20	27

Boats and Ships

NAME	DESCRIPTION	GOOD	EX	MINT
Battleship	rubber, 8-1/4" long, 1941	15	25	30
Cruiser	rubber	15	25	30
Freighter	rubber, 8" long, 1941	15	25	30
Submarine	rubber, 6-1/2" long, 1941	10	20	27

Cars

NAME	DESCRIPTION	GOOD	EX	MINT
1947 Buick Coupe	#100 on license plate, 7" long	75	115	150
Airport Limousine	rubber, 8" long	25	40	50
Fire Chief's Car	red, yellow wheels	7	10	15
Ford	rubber, 1930s	10	20	25
Race Car	red, rubber, 6" long	40	65	85
Race Car	rubber, 6" long, 1930s	15	25	30
Race Car With Goggled Driver	rubber, 10" long	50	75	100
Racer	red vinyl w/white plastic tires	25	40	50
Racer	rubber	20	30	40
Sedan	cast iron driver	25	40	50
Sedan	green, rubber, license #500R	15	25	30

Emergency Vehicles

NAME	DESCRIPTION	GOOD	EX	MINT
Fire Engine	red, rubber, 8" long	15	25	30
Fire Truck	black rubber wheels	7	10	15
Rescue Truck	dark army green	15	25	30

Farm and Construction Equipment

NAME	DESCRIPTION	GOOD	EX	MINT
Allis-Chalmers Tractor	red and silver plastic, 1/16 scale, 1950	25	40	50
Earthmover	red front, yellow back, plastic wheels	15	25	30
Giant Tractor	red tractor, silver motor, black tires, 7" long, 1950s	30	45	60
John Deere Tractor	plastic, 1/20 scale	25	40	50
Minneapolis Moline Tractor	red, large rubber tires, rubber, 1/16 scale, 1950	25	40	50
Tractor and Wagon	orange tractor, silver motor, black tires, red spreader wagon, yellow spoke tires	75	115	150

Motorcycles

NAME	DESCRIPTION	GOOD	EX	MINT
Motorcycle		20	30	40
Police Cycle	red rubber, drive chain, 6" long, 1950s	50	75	100

Trucks

NAME	DESCRIPTION	GOOD	EX	MINT
2-1/2 Ton Truck		20	30	40
Army Jeep	olive drab	5	7	10
Army Recon Half Truck	bright green	10	15	20
Stake Truck	rubber	15	25	30
Telephone Truck	6-1/2" long	35	55	75

BANDAI

NAME	DESCRIPTION	GOOD	EX	MINT

Buses

NAME	DESCRIPTION	GOOD	EX	MINT
Volkswagen Bus	red and white, battery-operated, 9-1/2" long, 1960s	65	150	275

Cars

NAME	DESCRIPTION	GOOD	EX	MINT
1915 Ford Touring Car	7" long	90	135	180
1955 MG TF Convertible	8-1/2" aqua blue, aqua green, or black, friction	85	195	275
1956 Buick	6" green, battery-operated	35	60	85
1956 Chevrolet Convertible	10" cream, friction	135	315	450
1958 Chevrolet Convertible	8" light blue, friction	65	140	200

BANDAI

NAME	DESCRIPTION	GOOD	EX	MINT
1958 Chrysler Imperial Convertible	8-1/2" maroon, friction	195	245	350
1958 Chrysler Imperial HT	8-1/2" two-tone green, friction	90	125	175
1958 Ford Station Wagon	8" two-tone green, friction	60	85	125
1958 Plymouth Station Wagon	8-1/2" green/white, friction	55	85	125
1960 Rolls-Royce Silver Cloud	blue body, white top, electric lights, 12" long	350	525	700
1961 Buick Station Wagon	blue, friction	50	85	125
1961 Plymouth Valiant	8" blue	45	105	150
1964 Chevrolet Malibu Fire Chief Car	8" red, friction	45	55	75
1964 Ford Fairlane	8" metallic red, friction	35	50	85
1965 Chrysler Four-Door HT	8-1/2" two-tone green, friction	40	55	75
1965 Ford Mustang	11" cream/black, friction	50	90	125
1967 Chevrolet Camaro	13-1/2" red battery-operated w/lighted engine and turning fan	85	100	140
Cadillac	gold, hardtop, friction powered, 17" long, 1960s	195	350	550
Cadillac	gold fins, black top, tin, 11-1/2" long, 1959	150	225	300
Cadillac	8" long	100	175	275
Cadillac	white, hardtop, friction powered, 11" long, 1959	100	175	275
Cadillac	copper, hardtop, friction powered, 11" long, 1960	75	125	175
Cadillac Convertible	white, red interior, friction powered, 17" long, 1963	200	400	600
Cadillac Convertible	black, friction powered, 11" long, 1960	180	275	380
Cadillac Convertible	red, green interior, friction powered, 11" long, 1959	175	300	400
Chevrolet Corvette	white and black, battery-operated, 8" long, 1962	75	125	175
Chevrolet Corvette	red, friction powered, 8" long, 1963	75	125	175
Chevrolet Impala Convertible	white, friction powered, 11" long, 1961	250	400	550
Chevrolet Impala Sedan	cream, friction powered, 11" long, 1961	225	350	500
Citroen	blue and white, friction powered, 12" long, 1958	300	650	1000
Citroen DS-19 Sedan	8-1/2" metallic red/white, friction, 1950s	130	300	425
Corvair Bertone	white, battery-operated, tin, 12" long, 1963	70	120	175
Cougar	white, battery-operated, tin	100	150	200
D.K.W. Sedan	8-1/2" grey/black, friction, 1950s	175	245	350
Excalibur Roadster	white body, red fenders, black top, battery-operated, rubber wheels, motor sparks, 11" long	135	200	275
Ferrari	silver w/red interior, battery-operated, tin, gearshift on floor, working lights, horn, and engine noise, 11" long, 1958	300	550	850
Fiat 600	7" blue, friction, opening sun roof, 1950s	35	70	100
Ford Convertible	green, friction powered, 12" long, 1955	350	650	900
Ford Convertible	red/black or two-tone green, friction powered, 12" long, 1957	150	275	375
Ford Country Sedan	blue and white, friction powered, 10-1/2" long, 1961	65	100	140
Ford F.B.I. Mustang	black and white, friction powered, 11" long, 1965	75	100	140
Ford Flower Delivery Wagon	blue, friction powered, 12" long, 1955	275	400	650
Ford GT	red, battery-operated, 10" long, 1960s	100	150	200
Ford Mustang	silver and black, battery-operated, 11" long, 1965	65	100	145
Ford Mustang	red, battery-operated, 11" long, 1965	125	200	275
Ford Mustang	red, battery-operated, 13" long, 1967	80	125	175
Ford Ranchero	two-tone blue, friction powered, 12"long, 1955	175	250	350
Ford Ranchero	black and red, friction powered, 12" long, 1957	175	250	350
Ford Standard Fresh Coffee Wagon	black and orange, friction powered, 12" long, 1955	350	625	975
Ford Station Wagon	cream and black, two-tone green, or red and black, friction powered, 12" long, 1955	75	125	200
Ford Thunderbird	red or red and black, friction powered, 8" long, 1962	65	100	150
Ford Thunderbird	red and black, friction powered, 10-3/4" long, 1965	100	175	225
Ford Wagon	green body, black top, 12" long	300	450	600
Ford Wagon	blue and white, friction powered, 12" long, 1957	90	150	200
GT-40	blue, hood and trunk open, rubber tires, tin, battery-operated, 11" long	100	150	200
Isetta	white and two-tone green, three wheels, friction powered, 6-1/2" long, 1950s	200	300	400
Jaguar 3.4 Sedan	8-1/2" light green, friction, 1960s	85	125	175
Jaguar XK 140 Convertible	various colors, 9-1/2" long, 1950s	125	200	275
Jaguar XK-E	red, battery-operated, 10" long, 1960s	100	150	250

NAME	DESCRIPTION	GOOD	EX	MINT
Lincoln Continental	turquoise and white, matching interior, 1958	150	250	375
Lincoln Continental Convertible	white, red interior, 1958	200	300	425
Lincoln Mark III	turquoise and white, friction powered, 11" long, 1958	150	275	375
Lotus	blue, battery-operated, 9-1/2" long	110	175	225
Lotus Elite	red and black, friction powered, 8-1/2" long, 1950s	75	100	150
Mazda 360 Coupe	blue, friction powered, 7" long, 1960	65	100	125
Mercedes-Benz 219 Convertible	8" blue, wrap around windshield, friction	85	125	175
Mercedes-Benz 220 Sedan	"Scale Model Series", 10-1/2", red, battery-operated w/working headlights	85	125	175
Mercedes-Benz 300 SL Coupe	silver and black, friction powered, 8" long, 1950s	160	245	325
Mercedes-Benz Taxi	black, battery-operated, 10" long, 1960s	125	250	350
MG 1600 Mark II	red, friction powered, 8-1/2" long, 1950s	75	125	175
MG TF	green, friction powered, 8" long, 1955	75	125	175
MGA-1600 Coupe	8-1/2" silver/red, friction, 1950s	85	125	175
Old Timer Police Car	battery-operated, 8" long	60	95	125
Olds Toronado	gold, battery-operated, 11" long, 1966	30	50	65
Oldsmobile	surrey top, friction, 1900's	75	115	150
Plymouth Valiant	blue, wind-up, 8" long	50	75	100
Pontiac Firebird	red, battery-operated, 9-1/2" long, 1967	75	125	175
Porsche 911	white, battery-operated, 10" long, 1960s	90	150	200
Racer with Hand Control		85	130	175
Rolls-Royce Convertible	several colors available, 12" long, friction, 1950s	200	300	450
Rolls-Royce Hardtop Sedan	blue, black, white, rare version w/working headlights, battery-operated, 12" long, 1950s	275	400	600
Subaru 360	red, friction powered, 8" long, 1959	75	125	175
Taxi	friction, 1950s	75	115	150
Triumph TR-4	8" red/white battery-operated w/signal lights, 1950s	50	100	140
Volkswagen	red, battery-operated, 8" long, 1960s	35	75	100
Volkswagen	blue, battery-operated, 10-1/2" long, 1960s	75	125	175
Volkswagen	red, battery-operated, 15" long, 1960s	95	150	225
Volkswagen	red, w/sun roof, battery-operated, 15" long, 1960s	90	150	225
Volkswagen Convertible	white, battery-operated, 7-1/2" long, 1960s	50	95	125

Emergency Vehicles

NAME	DESCRIPTION	GOOD	EX	MINT
Plymouth Ambulance	white, red cross on doors, friction powered, 12" long, 1961	35	50	75
Rambler Ambulance	white, friction powered, 11" long, 1962	40	75	100

Motorcycles

NAME	DESCRIPTION	GOOD	EX	MINT
Police Auto Cycle	battery-operated, hard plastic, 10" long, 1970s	100	150	200

Sets

NAME	DESCRIPTION	GOOD	EX	MINT
Ferrari and Speed Boat	white car, red and white speed boat w/white trailer, tin, overall 23" long, 1958	350	650	900
Lincoln Continental and Cabin Cruiser	turquoise and white car and cruiser, red car interior and cruiser trailer, overall 23" long, 1958	300	550	800
Rambler Wagon and Cabin Cruiser	green and white Rambler wagon, red trailer, friction powered rambler, electric boat motor, overall 23" long, 1959	200	400	600
Rambler Wagon and Shasta Trailer	green and white Rambler wagon, yellow and white trailer, 11" long wagon, 12" long trailer, 1959	200	400	600
Rambler, Trailer and Cabin Cruiser	turquoise and white Rambler, red trailer, cruiser color varies, overall 35" long, 1959	350	650	1000

Trucks

NAME	DESCRIPTION	GOOD	EX	MINT
1958 Ford Ranchero Pickup Truck	8" long	110	175	225
Land Rover	red, friction powered, 7-1/2" long, 1960	75	100	150
Land Rover	maroon, 8" long	125	185	250
Volkswagen Truck	blue, open flatbed cargo section, battery-operated, 8" long, 1960s	90	150	200

VEHICLES

BARCLAY

NAME	DESCRIPTION	GOOD	EX	MINT

Airplanes

NAME	DESCRIPTION	GOOD	EX	MINT
Dirigible Plane	4-3/8" long, 1930s	7	10	15
Lindy-Type Plane	4" wingspan, 1930s	7	10	15
Monoplane	single engine plane, red propeller, red metal wheels	15	30	40
Monoplane	single engine plane	15	28	35
U.S. Army Single Engine Transport Plane	white rubber wheels, 1940	10	15	20
U.S. Army Small Pursuit Plane	lead, rubber wheels, 1941	10	15	20

Buses

Double-Decker Bus	4" long	20	30	40

Cannons

Cannon	spoked wheels, 3" long	10	15	20
Cannon	silver w/black rubber wheels, 7-3/4" long	20	30	40
Cannon	very large wheels, 4" long	15	20	25
Cannon	1931	20	30	40
Cannon	barrel elevated, 2-1/2" long	15	25	35
Coast Defense Rifle Cannon	4-1/2" long	25	40	50
Howitzer Cannon	vertical loop hitch, four wheels, 3" long	15	25	35
Howitzer Cannon	horizontal loop hitch, four wheels, 3" long	15	25	35
Mortar Cannon	swivels on base, 3" long	20	30	40
Spring-Firing Cannon	spoked wheels, 4" long	20	25	35

Cars

1930s Sedan and Tourist Trailer	white rubber tires, 6-1/2"	35	55	75
Armoured Car	1937	15	25	35
Car Carrier	w/two cars	25	40	55
Coupe	3" long, 1930s	15	25	35
Race Car	white tires, 4" long	25	40	55
Tow Car #205	white rubber tires, red wood wheels, 3"	25	35	50

Farm Equipment

Fordson Tractor #203	white rubber tires, red wood wheels, 2-1/8"	15	20	25

Trucks

Beer Truck	slush metal, 4" long	15	25	35
Mack Pickup Truck	3-1/2" long	25	40	55
Milk Truck #377	w/milk cans	25	40	55
Open Truck	3-1/2" long	10	20	25
Stake Truck	slush metal, 5" long	15	25	35
White Horse Milk Van Delivery Truck	2-7/8", white rubber tires	25	35	50

BROOKLIN

NAME	DESCRIPTION	GOOD	EX	MINT

Cars

1932 Packard Light 8 Coupe		35	50	70
1933 Pierce Arrow	silver	35	50	70
1934 Chrysler Airflow Sedan	four door	35	50	70
1935 Dodge "City Ice Delivery" Van		40	60	80
1935 Dodge "Dr. Pepper" Van		45	70	90
1935 Dodge "Sears Roebuck" Van		40	60	80
1940 Ford Sedan Delivery "Ford Service"		40	60	80
1941 Packard Clipper" Van		40	60	80
1948 Tucker Torpedo		35	50	70

VEHICLES

BROOKLIN

NAME	DESCRIPTION	GOOD	EX	MINT
1949 Buick Roadmaster		35	55	75
1949 Mercury Coupe	two door	30	45	65
1952 Hudson Hornet Convertible	1:43 scale	30	45	65
1952 Studebaker Champion Starlight Coupe		40	60	80
1953 Buick Skylark		35	50	70
1953 Pontiac Sedan Delivery Gulf Oil Truck	1:43 scale	30	45	60
1953 Pontiac Sedan Delivery Mobil Oil Truck	1:43 scale	30	45	60
1953 Studebaker Commander	1:43 scale	30	45	60
1953 Studebaker Indiana State Police	1:43 scale	50	75	100
1954 Dodge 500 Indy Pace Car	1:43 scale	50	75	100
1955 Chrysler 300		30	45	60
1956 Ford Fairline Victoria	two door	25	40	55
1956 Ford Thunderbird 500	hardtop	30	45	65
1956 Lincoln Continental		30	45	60
1956 Lincoln Continental Mark II Coupe		30	45	65
1956 Lincoln Continental MKII		30	45	65
1957 Ford Fairlane Skyliner Police	1:43 scale	30	45	60
1958 Edsel Citation	two-door hardtop	30	45	30
1958 Pontiac Bonneville		30	45	65
1960 Ford Sunliner Convertible	1:43 scale	30	45	60
1963 Chevrolet Corvette Stingray Coupe		35	55	75
1968 Shelby Mustang GT 500		35	55	75
Lincoln Mark	1:43 scale	30	45	60
Mini Marquee Packard Convertible	1:43 scale	50	75	100
Tucker	1:43 scale	30	45	60

BUDDY L

NAME	DESCRIPTION	GOOD	EX	MINT

Airplanes

NAME	DESCRIPTION	GOOD	EX	MINT
5000 Monocoupe "The Lone Eagle"	orange wing, black fuselage and tail w/tailskid, all steel high wind cabin monoplane, 9-7/8" wingspan, 1929	250	300	400
Army Tank Transport Plane	low-wing monoplane, two small four-wheel tanks that clip beneath wings, 27" wingspan, 1941	250	350	400
Catapult Airplane and Hangar	5000 Monocoupe w/tailwheel, 9-7/8" wingspan, olive/gray hangar, black twin-spring catapult, 1930	950	1200	1500
Four Motor Air Cruiser	white, red engine cowlings, yellow fuselage and twin tails, four engine monoplane, 27" wingspan, 1952	200	300	350
Four-Engine Transport	green wings, white engine cowlings, yellow fuselage and twin tails, four engine monoplane, 27" wingspan, 1949	200	300	400
Hangar and Three 5000 Monocoupes	olive/gray hangar, windows outlined in red or orange, planes 9-7/8" wingspan, all steel high wing cabin monoplanes, 1930	750	1000	2000
Transport Airplane	white wings and engine cowlings, red fuselage and twin tails, four engine monoplane, 27" wingspan, 1946	200	300	400

Cars

NAME	DESCRIPTION	GOOD	EX	MINT
Army Staff Car	olive drab body, 15-3/4" long, 1964	100	150	200
Bloomin' Bus	chartreuse body, white roof and supports, similar to VW minibus, 10-3/4" long, 1969	90	135	180

BUDDY L

NAME	DESCRIPTION	GOOD	EX	MINT
Buddywagon	red body w/white roof, 10-3/4" long, 1966	100	150	200
Buddywagon	red body w/white roof, no chrome on front, 10-3/4" long, 1967	95	145	190
Colt Sportsliner	red open body, white hardtop, off-white seats and interior, 10-1/4" long, 1967	35	50	70
Colt Sportsliner	light blue-green open body, white hardtop, pale tan seats and interior, 10-1/4" long, 1968	30	45	65
Colt Utility Car	red open body, white plstic seats, floor and luggage space, 10-1/4" long, 1967	35	50	70
Colt Utility Car	light orange body, tan interior, 10-1/4" long, 1968	30	45	65
Country Squire Wagon	off-white hood fenders, end gate and roof, brown woodgrain side panels, 15-1/2" long, 1963	85	130	175
Country Squire Wagon	red hood fenders, end gate and roof, brown woodgrain side panels, 15" long, 1965	75	115	150
Deluxe Convertible Coupe	metallic blue enamel front, sides and deck, cream top retracts into rumble seat, 19" long, 1949	300	450	600
Desert Rats Command Car	light tan open body, light beige interior, black .50-caliber machine gun swivels on post between seats, 10-1/4" long, blackwall tires, 1968	45	65	90
Desert Rats Command Car	light tan open body, light beige interior, black .50-caliber machine gun swivels on post between seats, 10-1/4" long, 1967	50	75	100
Flivver Coupe	black w/red eight-spoke wheels, black hubs, aluminum tires, flat, hardtop roof on enclosed glass-window-style body, 11" long, 1924	775	1100	1550
Flivver Roadster	black w/red eight-spoke wheels, black hubs, aluminum tires, simulated soft, folding top, 11" long, 1924	750	1000	1500
Jr. Camaro	metallic blue body, white racing stripes across hood nose, 9" long, 1968	50	75	100
Jr. Flower Power Sportster	purple hood, fenders and body, white roof and supports, white plastic seats, lavender and orange five-petal blossom decals on hood top, roof, and sides, 6" long, 1969	35	55	75
Jr. Sportster	blue hood and open body, white hardtop and upper sides, 6" long, 1968	35	55	75
Mechanical Scarab Automobile	red radically streamlined body, bright metal front and rear bumpers, 10-1/2" long, 1936	200	300	500
Police Colt	deep blue open body, white hardtop, "POLICE" across top of hood, "POLICE 1" on sides, 10-1/4" long, 1968	50	75	100
Ski Bus	white body and roof, similar to VW minibus, 10-3/4" long, 1967	75	115	150
Station Wagon	light blue/green body and roof, 15-1/2" long, 1963	75	115	150
Streamline Scarab	red, radically streamlined body, non-mechanical, 10-1/2" long, 1941	145	225	290
Suburban Wagon	powder blue or white body and roof, 15-1/2" long, 1963	75	115	150
Suburban Wagon	gray/green body and roof, 15-3/4" long, 1964	70	100	140
Town and Country Convertible	maroon front, hood, rear deck and fenders, gray top retracts into rumble seat, 19" long, 1947	300	450	600
Travel Trailer and Station Wagon	red station wagon, two-wheel trailer w/red lower body and white steel camper-style upper body, 27-1/4" long, 1965	150	225	300
Yellow Taxi with Skyview	yellow hood, roof and body, red radiator front and fenders, 18-1/2" long, 1948	200	400	600

Emergency Vehicles

NAME	DESCRIPTION	GOOD	EX	MINT
Aerial Ladder and Emergency Truck	red w/white ladders, bumper and steel disc wheels, three 8-rung steel ladders, no rear step, no siren or SIREN decal, 22-1/4" long, 1953	225	345	450
Aerial Ladder and Emergency Truck	red w/white ladders, bumper and steel disc wheels, three 8-rung steel ladders, 22-1/4" long, 1952	200	300	400
Aerial Ladder Fire Engine	red tractor, wraparound bumper and semi-trailer, two aluminum 13-rung extension ladders on sides, swivel-base aluminum central ladder, 26-1/2" long, 1960	125	185	250
Aerial Ladder Fire Engine	red tractor and semi-trailer, white plastic bumper w/integral grille guard, two aluminum 13-rung extension ladders on sides, swivel-base aluminum central ladder, 26-1/2" long, 1961	125	185	250

VEHICLES

NAME	DESCRIPTION	GOOD	EX	MINT
Aerial Ladder Fire Engine	red tractor and semi-trailer, chrome one-piece wraparound bumper, slotted grille, two aluminum 13-rung extension ladders on sides, swivel-base aluminum central ladder, 26-1/2" long, 1966	125	185	250
Aerial Ladder Fire Engine	red cab-over-engine tractor and semi-trailer units, two 13-rung white sectional ladders and swivel-mounted aerial ladder w/side rails, 25-1/2" long, 1968	100	150	200
Aerial Ladder Fire Engine	snub-nose red tractor and semi-trailer, white swivel-mounted aerial ladder w/side rails, two white 13-rung sectional ladders, 27-1/2" long, 1970	100	150	200
Aerial Truck	red w/nickel ladders, black hand wheel, brass bell, and black hubs, 39" long w/ladder down, 1925	850	1300	1700
American LaFrance Aero-Chief Pumper	red cab-over-engine and body, white underbody, rear step and simulated hose reels, black extension ladders on right side, 25-1/2" long, 1972	90	150	200
Brute Fire Pumper	red cab-over-engine body and frame, two yellow 5-rung sectional ladders on sides of open body, 5-1/4" long, 1969	30	50	75
Brute Hook-N-Ladder	red cab-over-engine tractor and detachable semi-trailer, white elevating, swveling aerial ladder w/side rails, 10" long, 1969	30	40	55
Extension Ladder Fire Truck	red w/silver ladders and yellow removable rider seat, enclosed cab, 35" long, 1945	200	300	400
Extension Ladder Rider Fire Truck	duo-tone slant design, tractor has white front, lower hood sides and lower doors, red hood top, cab and frame, red semi-trailer, white 10-rung and 8-rung ladders, 32-1/2" long, 1949	150	225	300
Extension Ladder Trailer Fire Truck	red tractor w/enclosed cab, boxy fenders, red semi-trailer w/fenders, two white 8-rung side ladders, 10-rung central extension ladder, 29-1/2" long, 1955	200	300	400
Extension Ladder Trailer Fire Truck	red tractor unit and semi-trailer, enclosed cab, two white 13-rung side extension ladders on sides, white central ladder on swivel base, 29-1/2" long, 1956	125	185	250
Fire and Chemical Truck	duo-tone slant design, white front, lower hood sides and lower doors, rest is red, bright-metal or white eight-rung ladder on sides, 25" long, 1949	125	185	250
Fire Department Emergency Truck	red streamlined body, enclosed cab, chrome one-piece grille, bumper, and headlights, 12-3/4" long, 1953	100	150	200
Fire Engine	red w/nickel-plated upright broiler, nickel rims and flywheels on dummy water pump, brass bell, 23-1/4" long, 1925-29	500	800	1600
Fire Engine	red w/nickel rim flywheels on dummy pump, brass bell, dim-or-bright electric headlights, 25-1/2" long, 1933	500	750	1500
Fire Hose and Water Pumper	red w/two white five-rung ladders, one red/white removable fire extinguisher, enclosed cab, 12-1/2" long, 1952	100	150	200
Fire Hose and Water Pumper	red w/two white five-rung ladders, two removable fire extinguishers, enclosed cab, 12-1/2" long, 1950	100	150	200
Fire Pumper	red cab-over-engine and open body, 11-rung white 10" ladder on each side, 16-1/4" long, 1968	100	150	200
Fire Pumper with Action Hydrant	red wraparound bumper, hood cab and cargo section, aluminum nine-rung ladders, white hose reel, 15" long, 1960	75	115	150
Fire Truck	bright red w/black inverted L-shaped crane mounted in socket on seat back, red floor, open driver's seat, 26" long, 1925	450	800	1600
Fire Truck	red w/two white ladders, enclosed cab, bright metal grille and headlights, 25" long, 1948	125	200	250
Fire Truck	duo-tone slant design, yellow front, bumper, hood sides and skirted fenders, rest is red, nickel ladders, 28-1/2" long, 1939	500	700	1000
Fire Truck	duo-tone slant design, yellow front, single-bar bumper, hood sides and removable rider seat, rest is red, 25-1/2" long, 1936	170	250	500
Fire Truck	red w/nickel or white ladders, bright-metal radiator grille and black removable rider saddle, 25-1/2" long, 1935	250	375	500
Fire Truck	bright red, red floor, open driver's seat, 26" long, 1928	450	800	1200

VEHICLES

NAME	DESCRIPTION	GOOD	EX	MINT
Fire Truck	bright red w/black inverted L-shaped crane mounted in socket on seat back, open driver's seat, 26" long, 1924	500	900	1850
Fire Truck	duo-tone slant design, tractor has white front, lower hood sides and lower doors, red hood top, cab and frame, red semi-trailer, rubber wheels w/black tires, 32-1/2" long, 1953	200	300	400
Fire Truck	red w/white ladders, black rubber wheels, enclosed cab, 12" long, 1945	75	115	150
Fire Truck	red w/black solid-rubber Firestone tires on red seven-spoke embossed metal wheels, two 18-1/2" red steel sectional ladders, 26" long, 1930	800	1000	1600
GMC Deluxe Aerial Ladder Fire Engine	white tractor and semi-trailer units, golden 13-rung extension ladder on sides, golden central aerial ladder, black and white DANGER battery case w/two flashing lights, 28" long, 1959	225	345	450
GMC Extension Ladder Trailer Fire Engine	red w/chrome GMC bar grille, red semi-trailer, white 13-rung extension ladders on sides, white swiveling central ladder w/side rails, 27-1/4" long, 1957	100	250	400
GMC Fire Pumper with Horn	red w/aluminum-finish 11-rung side ladders and white reel of black plastic hose in open cargo section, chrome GMC bar grille, 15" long, 1958	150	200	300
GMC Hydraulic Aerial Ladder Fire Engine	red tractor unit w/chrome GMC bar grille, red semi-trailer, white 13-rung extension ladders on sides, white swiveling central ladder, 26-1/2" long, 1958	125	185	250
GMC Red Cross Ambulance	all white, removable fabric canopy w/a red cross and "Ambulance" in red, 14-1/2" long, 1960	150	250	400
Hook & Ladder Fire Truck	medium-dark red, w/black inverted L-shaped crane mounted in socket on seat back, open driver's seat, 26" long, 1923	1200	1800	2400
Hose Truck	red w/two white hose pipes, white cord hose on reeland brass nozzle, electric headlights w/red bulbs, 21 3/4" long, 1933	500	750	1000
Hydraulic Aerial Truck	duo-tone slant design, yellow front, single-bar bumper, chassis, radiator, front fender, lower sides and removable rider saddle, rest is red, 40" long w/ladders down, 1936	550	825	1100
Hydraulic Aerial Truck	red w/brass bell on cowl, nickel ladders mounted on 5-1/2" turntable rotated by black hand wheel, 39" long, 1927	850	1300	1700
Hydraulic Snorkel Fire Pumper	red cab-over-engine and open rear body, white 11-rung 10" ladder on each side, snorkel pod w/solid sides, 21" long, 1969	100	150	200
Hydraulic Water Tower Truck	red w/nickel water tower, dim/bright electric headlights, brass bell, added-on bright-metal grille, 44-7/8" long w/tower down, 1935	600	900	1500
Hydraulic Water Tower Truck	duo-tone slant design, yellow bumper, hood sides, front fenders, rest is red, electric headlights, added-on bright-metal grille, 44-7/8" long w/tower down, 1936	600	1000	1500
Hydraulic Water Tower Truck	red w/nickel water tower, dim/bright electric headlights, brass bell, 44-7/8" long w/tower down, 1933	800	1000	1700
Hydraulic Water Tower Truck	duo-tone slant design, yellow front, single-bar bumper and hood sides, red hood top, enclosed cab and water tank, brass bell, nickel water tower, 46" long w/tower down, 1939	900	1200	1700
Jr. Fire Emergency Truck	red cab-over-engine and body, one-piece chrome wraparound narrow bumper and 24-hole grille w/plastic vertical-pair headlights, 6-3/4" long, 1968	50	75	100
Jr. Fire Emergency Truck	red cab-over-engine and body, wider one-piece chrome wraparound narrow bumper and four-slot grille w/two square plastic headlights, 6-3/4" long, 1969	50	75	100
Jr. Fire Snorkel Truck	red cab-over-engine and body, chrome one-piece narrow wraparound bumper and 24-hole grille w/plastic vertical-pair headlights, 11-1/2" long, 1968	100	150	200
Jr. Fire Snorkel Truck	red cab-over-engine and body, full-width chrome one-piece bumper and four-slot grille w/two square plastic headlights, 11" long, 1969	60	150	200

VEHICLES

NAME	DESCRIPTION	GOOD	EX	MINT
Jr. Hook-n-Ladder Aerial Truck	red cab-over-engine tractor w/one-piece four-slot grille and two square plastic headlights, red semi-trailer, white high-sides ladder, plastic vertical-pair headlights, 17" long, 1969	75	115	150
Jr. Hook-n-Ladder Aerial Truck	red cab-over-engine tractor and semi-trailer, white high-sides ladder, chrome one-piece wraparound bumper and 24-hole grille, plastic veritcal-pair headlights, 17" long, 1967	100	150	200
Jr. Hook-n-Ladder Aerial Truck	red cab-over-engine tractor and semi-trailer, white high-sides ladder, one-piece chrome four-slot grille, two square plastic headlights, 17" long, 1969	75	115	150
Ladder Fire Truck	red w/bright-metal V-nose radiator, headlights and ladder, black wooden wheels, 12" long, 1941	125	200	250
Ladder Truck	modified duo-tone slant design, white front, front fenders and lower doors, white ladders, bright-metal grille, no bumper, 17-1/2" long, 1941	200	300	400
Ladder Truck	red w/two yellow sectional ladders, enclosed square cab, 22-3/4" long, 1933	120	250	500
Ladder Truck	red w/two white ladders, bright-metal radiator grille and headlights, 24" long, 1941	125	200	250
Ladder Truck	red w/yellow severely streamlined, skirted fenders and lower doors, white ladders, bright-metal grille, no bumper, 17-1/2" long, 1940	200	300	400
Ladder Truck	red w/bright-metal grille and headlights, two white ladders, 24" long, 1939	100	200	300
Ladder Truck	duo-tone slant design, white front, hood sides, fenders and two ladders, rest is red, square enclosed cab w/sharply protruding visor, no headlights, 22-3/4" long, 1937	135	200	275
Ladder Truck	duo-tone slant design, white front, hood sides, fenders and two ladders, rest is red, square enclosed cab w/sharply protruding visor, 22-3/4" long, 1936	150	225	300
Ladder Truck	red w/two yellow ladders, enclosed square cab w/sharply protruding visor, bright-metal radiator front, 22-3/4" long, 1935	250	375	500
Ladder Truck	red w/two yellow ladders, enclosed square cab w/sharply protruding visor, 22-3/4" long, 1934	200	300	400
Police Squad Truck	yellow front and front fenders, dark blue-green body, yellow fire extinguisher, 21-1/2" long over ladders, 1947	150	300	550
Pumping Fire Engine	red w/nickel stack on boiler, nickel rims on pump flywheels, nickel-rim headlights and searchlight, 23-1/2" long, 1929	3000	3500	4000
Rear Steer Trailer Fire Truck	red w/two white 10-rung ladders, chrome one-piece grille, headlights and bumper, 20" long, 1952	65	100	200
Red Cross Ambulance	all white, removable fabric canopy w/a red cross and "Ambulance" in red, 14-1/2" long, 1958	60	95	125
Suburban Pumper	red station wagon body, white plastic wraparound bumpers, one-piece grille and double headlights, 15" long, 1964	100	150	175
Texaco Fire Chief American LaFrance Pumper	promotional piece, red rounded-front enclosed cab and body, white one-pice underbody, running boards and rear step, 25" long, 1962	200	300	400
Trailer Ladder Truck	duo-tone slant design, tractor unit has yellow front, lower hood sides and lower doors, red hood top, enclosed cab and semi-trailer, nickel 10-rung ladders, 30" long w/ladders, 1940	200	300	400
Trailer Ladder Truck	all red w/cream removable rider saddle, three bright metal 10-rung ladders, 20" long over ladders, 1941	150	225	300
Water Tower Truck	red w/nickel two-bar front bumper, red nickel-rim headlights plus searchllight on cowl, nickel latticework water tower, 45-1/2" long w/tower down, 1929	3000	4500	6000

Farm and Construction Equipment

Aerial Tower Tramway	two tapering dark green 33-1/2" tall towers and 12" square bases, black hand crank, 1928	1000	1300	2700
Big Derrick	red mast and 20" boom, black base, 24" tall, 1921	600	900	1200

VEHICLES

NAME	DESCRIPTION	GOOD	EX	MINT
Brute Articulated Scooper	yellow front-loading scoop, cab, articulated frame and rear power unit, black radiator, exhaust, steering wheel and driver's seat, 5-1/2" long, 1970	50	75	100
Brute Double Dump Train	yellow hood, fenders and back on tractor unit, yellow coupled bottom-dumping earth carriers, 9-1/2" long, 1969	50	75	100
Brute Dumping Scraper	yellow hood, fenders and back on two-wheel tractor unit, yellow scraper-dump unit, 7" long, 1970	50	75	100
Brute Farm Tractor-n-Cart	bright blue tractor body and rear fenders, green plastic radiator, engine, exhaust and driver's seat, bright blue detachable, square, two-wheel open cart, 6-1/4" long, 1969	30	40	55
Brute Road Grader	yellow hood, cab, frame and adjustable blade, black radiator, driver's seat and steering wheel, 6-1/2" long, 1970	50	75	100
Cement Mixer on Treads	medium gray w/black treads and water tank, 16" tall, 1929-31	2500	3500	4500
Cement Mixer on Wheels	medium gray w/black cast steel wheels and water tank, 14-1/2" tall, 1926-29	700	900	1500
Concrete Mixer	green w/black cast-steel wheels, crank, gears, and band mixing drum, 10-1/2" long, 1930	175	265	350
Concrete Mixer	yellow/orange frame and base, red hopper and drum, black crank handle, 10-1/2" long, 1936	110	175	225
Concrete Mixer	red frame and base, cream/yellow hopper, drum and crank handle, 10-1/2" long, 1941	125	185	250
Concrete Mixer	green frame, base, crank, crank handle and bottom of mixing drum, gray hopper and top of drum, 9-5/8" long, 1949	100	150	200
Concrete Mixer	medium gray w/black cast-steel wheels, black water tank, w/wood-handle, steel-blade scoop shovel, 17-3/4" long w/tow bar up, 1926	500	700	1000
Concrete Mixer with Motor Sound	green frame, base, crank, crank handle and bottom of mixing drum, gray hopper and top of drum, w/sound when crank rotates drum, 9 5/8" long, 1950	75	115	150
Dandy Digger	yellow main frame, operators, seat and boom, brown shovel, arm, under frame and twin skids, 27" long, 1941	95	145	195
Dandy Digger	yellow seat, lower control lever and main boom, black underframe, skids, shovel, arm and control lever, 38-1/2" long w/shovel arm extended, 1953	75	115	150
Dandy Digger	yellow main frame, operators, seat and boom, green shovel, arm, under frame and twin skids, 27" long, 1936	85	130	175
Dandy Digger	yellow seat lower control lever and main boom, black underframe, skids, shovel and arm, 38-1/2" long w/shovel arm extended, 1953	75	115	150
Dandy Digger	red main frame, operators, seat and boom, black shovel, arm, under frame and twin skids, 27" long, 1931	100	160	215
Digger	red main frame, operators, seat and boom, black shovel, arm, lower frame and twin skids, curved connecting rod, boom tilts down for digging, 11-1/2" long w/shovel arm extended, 1935	100	150	200
Dredge	red corrugated roof and base w/four wide black wheels, red hubs, black boiler, floor, frame boom and clamshell bucket, 19" long, 1924	750	1000	1500
Giant Digger	red main frame, operators, seat and boom, black shovel, arm, lower frame and twin skids, boom tilts down for digging, 42" long w/shovel arm extended, 1931	275	415	550
Giant Digger	red main frame, operators, seat and boom, black shovel, arm, lower frame and twin skids, curved connecting rod, boom tilts, 31" long w/shovel arm extended, 1933	265	395	525
Giant Digger	yellow main frame, operators, seat and boom, green shovel, arm, lower frame and twin skids, boom tilts, 11-1/2" long w/shovel arm extended, 1936	85	130	175

VEHICLES

NAME	DESCRIPTION	GOOD	EX	MINT
Giant Digger	yellow main frame, operators, seat and boom, brown shovel, arm, lower frame and twin skids, boom tilts, 11-1/2" long w/shovel arm extended, 1941	75	115	155
Gradall	bright yellow truck and superstructure, black plastic bumper and radiator, 32" long w/digging arm extended, 1965	350	750	1000
Hauling Rig with Construction Derrick	duo-tone slant design tractor, yellow bumper, lower hood and cab sides, white upper hood and cab, white trailer w/yellow loading ramp, overall 38-1/2" long, 1953	175	250	400
Hauling Rig with Construction Derrick	yellow tractor unit, green semi-trailer, winch on front of trailer makes sound, 36-3/4" long, 1954	110	175	225
Hoisting Tower	dark green, hoist tower and three distribution chutes, 29" tall, 1928-31	1500	2000	2500
Husky Tractor	bright blue body and large rear fenders, black engine block, exhaust, steering wheel and driver's seat, 13" long, 1969	40	60	80
Husky Tractor	bright yellow body, red large rear fenders and wheels, black engine block, exhaust, steering wheel and driver's seat, 13" long, 1970	30	45	65
Husky Tractor	bright yellow body and large rear fenders, black engine block, exhaust, steering wheel and driver's seat, 13" long, 1966	50	75	100
Improved Steam Shovel	black w/red roof and base, 14" tall, 1927-29	100	150	200
Junior Excavator	red shovel, arm, underframe, control lever and twin skids, yellow boom, rear lever, frame and seat, 28" long, 1945	75	115	150
Mechanical Crane	orange removable roof, boom and wheels in black cleated rubber crawler treads, olive green enclosed cab and base, hand crank w/rat-tat motor noise, 20" tall, 1950	175	265	350
Mechanical Crane	orange removable roof, boom, yellow wheels in white rubber crawler treads, olive green enclosed cab and base, hand crank w/rat-tat motor noise, 20" tall, 1952	150	225	300
Mobile Construction Derrick	orange laticework main mast, swiveling base, yellow latticework boom, green clamshell bucket and main platform base, 25-1/2" long w/boom lowered, 1953	150	250	350
Mobile Construction Derrick	orange laticework main mast, swiveling base, yellow latticework boom, gray clamshell bucket, green main platform base, 25-1/2" long w/boom lowered, 1955	150	250	350
Mobile Construction Derrick	orange laticework main mast, swiveling base, yellow latticework boom, gray clamshell bucket, orange main platform base, 25-1/2" long w/boom lowered, 1956	150	250	350
Mobile Power Digger Unit	clamshell dredge mounted on 10-wheel truck, orange truck, yellow dredge cab on swivel base, 31-3/4" long w/boom lowered, 1955	125	185	250
Mobile Power Digger Unit	clamshell dredge mounted on six-wheel truck, orange truck, yellow dredge cab on swivel base, 31-3/4" long w/boom lowered, 1956	100	150	250
Overhead Crane	black folding end frames and legs, braces, red crossbeams and platform, 45" long, 1924	1500	2000	3000
Pile Driver on Wheels	black w/red roof and base, 22-1/2" tall, 1924-27	800	1800	2600
Polysteel Farm Tractor	orange molded plastic four-wheel tractor, silver radiator front, headlights, and motor parts, 12" long, 1961	75	115	150
Pull-n-Ride Horse-Drawn Farm Wagon	red four-wheel steel hopper-body wagon, detailed litho horse, 22-3/4" long, 1952	150	225	300
Road Roller	dark green w/red roof and rollers, nickel plated steam cylinders, 20" long, 1929-31	3000	4000	5000
Ruff-n-Tuff Tractor	yellow grille, hood and frame, black plastic engine block and driver's seat, 10-1/2" long, 1971	50	75	100
Sand Loader	warm gray w/12 black buckets, 21" long, 18" high, 1924	150	200	450
Sand Loader	warm gray w/12 black buckets, chain-tension adjusting device at bottom of elevator side frames, 21" long, 1929	175	300	500

VEHICLES

Travel Trailer and Station Wagon, 1965, Buddy L

Hose Truck, 1933, Buddy L

Coca-Cola Delivery Truck, 1960, Buddy L

NAME	DESCRIPTION	GOOD	EX	MINT
Sand Loader	yellow w/12 black buckets, chain-tension adjusting device at bottom of elevator side frames, 21" long, 1931	200	250	350
Scoop-n-Load Conveyor	cream body frame, red loading scoop and chute, bright-plated circular crank operates black rubber cleated conveyor belt, "PORTABLE" decal in white, 18" long, 1955	60	95	125
Scoop-n-Load Conveyor	cream body frame, red loading scoop and chute, bright-plated circular crank operates black rubber cleated conveyor belt, "PORTABLE" decal in yellow, 18" long, 1956	55	85	115
Scoop-n-Load Conveyor	cream body frame, green loading scoop, black circular crank operates black rubber cleated conveyor belt, "PORTABLE" decal in red, 18" long, 1954	65	100	135
Scoop-n-Load Conveyor	cream body frame, green loading scoop, black circular crank operates black rubber cleated conveyor belt, 18" long, 1953	75	115	150
Side Conveyor Load-n-Dump	all steel yellow cab, hood, bumper and frame, white dump body and tailgate, red conveyor frame w/chute, 21-1/4" long, 1954	65	100	135
Side Conveyor Load-n-Dump	all steel yellow cab, hood, bumper and frame, deep blue dump body, white tailgate, red conveyor frame w/chute, 21-1/4" long, 1955	60	95	125
Side Conveyor Load-n-Dump	yellow plastic front end including cab, yellow steel bumper, green frame and dump body, red conveyor frame w/chute, 20-1/2" long, 1953	70	125	145
Small Derrick	red 20" movable boom and three angle-iron braces, black base and vertical mast, 21-1/2" tall, 1921	500	750	1000
Steam Shovel	black w/red roof and base, 25-1/2" tall, 1921-22	125	250	500
Traveling Crane	red crane, carriage, and long cross beams, hand wheel rotates crane boom, 46" long, 1928	1275	1900	2550
Trench Digger	yellow main frame, base, and motor housing, red elevator and conveyor frame and track frames, 20" tall, 1928-31	2000	3500	5000

Sets

NAME	DESCRIPTION	GOOD	EX	MINT
Army Combination Set	searchlight repair-it truck, transport truck and howitzer, ammunition conveyor, stake delivery truck, ammo, soldiers, 1956	300	400	500
Army Commando Set	14-1/2" truck, searchlight unit, two-wheel howitzer, soldiers, 1957	125	185	250
Big Brute 3-Piece Highway Set	bulldozer, dump truck, yellow four-wheel trailer, 1971	100	150	200
Big Brute 3-Piece Road Set	cement mixer truck, scooper, dump truck, 1971	125	185	250
Big Brute 4-Piece Freeway Set	scraper, grader, scooper and dump truck, 1971	125	185	250
Brute Fire Department Set	semi-trailer aerial ladder truck, fire pumper, fire wrecker, brute tow truck, 1970	75	115	150
Brute Five-Piece Highway Set	bulldozer, grader, scraper, dumping scraper and double dump train, 1970	50	75	100
Brute Fleet Set	car carrier w/two plastic coupes, dump truck, pickup truck, cement mixer truck, tow truck, 1969	85	130	175
Delivery Set Combination	16-1/2" long wrigley express truck, 15" long sand and stone dump truck, 14-1/4" long freight conveyor and 14-1/4" long stake delivery truck, 1955	175	265	350
Family Camping Set	Camper/cruiser truck, 15-1/2" long maroon suburban wagon, and brown/light gray/beige folding teepee camping trailer, 1963	60	95	125
Family Camping Set	blue camping trailer and suburban wagon, blue camper-n-cruiser, 1964	50	75	100
Farm Combination Set	cattle transport stake truck w/six plastic steers, hydraulic farm supplies trailer dump truck, trailer and three farm machines and farm machinery trailer hauler truck, 1956	100	150	200
Fire Department Set	aerial ladder fire engine, fire pumper w/action hydrant that squirts water, two plastic hoses, two plastic firemen, fire chief's badge, 1960	250	375	500

VEHICLES

NAME	DESCRIPTION	GOOD	EX	MINT
Freight Conveyor and Stake Delivery Truck	blue frame 14-1/4" long conveyor, red, white and yellow body 14-3/4" long truck, 1955	125	185	250
GMC Air Defense Set	15" long, GMC army searchlight truck, 15" long, GMC signal corps truck, two four-wheel trailers, plastic soliders, 1957	300	500	700
GMC Brinks Bank Set	silver gray, barred windows on sides and in double doors, coin slot and hole in roof, brass padlock w/two keys, pouch, play money, two gray plastic guard figures, 16" long, 1959	300	350	450
GMC Fire Department Set	red GMC extension ladder trailer and GMC pumper w/ladders and hose reel, four-wheel red electric searchlight trailer, warning barrier, red plastic helmet, firemen, policeman, 1958	300	500	750
GMC Highway Maintenance Fleet	orange maintenance truck w/trailer, sand and stone dump truck, scoop-n-load conveyor, sand hopper, steel scoop shovel, four white steel road barriers, 1957	300	500	700
GMC Livestock Set	red fenders, hood, cab and frame, white flatbed cargo section , six sections of brown plastic rail fencing, five black plastic steers, 14-1/2" long, 1958	300	400	500
GMC Western Roundup Set	blue fenders, hood, cab and frame, white flatbed cargo section, plastic six sections of rail fencing w/swinging gate, rearing and standing horse, cowboys, calf, steer, 1959	300	400	500
Highway Construction Set	orange and black bulldozer and driver, truck w/orange pickup body, orange dump truck, 1962	200	300	400
Highway Maintenance Mechanical Truck & Concrete Mixer	20" truck plus movable ramp, w/duo-tone slant design, blue lower hood sides, yellow hood top and cab, 10-3/4" blue and yellow mixer, overall 36" long, 1949	160	245	325
Interstate Highway Set	orange, parks department dumper, landscape truck, telephone truck, accessories include trees, drums, workmen and traffic cones, scoop shovel, 1959	250	400	500
Interstate Highway Set	orange, husky dumper, contractor's truck and ladder, utility truck, plastic pickaxe, spade, shovel, nail keg, 1960	250	350	500
Jr. Animal Farm Set	6-1/2" long Jr. Giraffe Truck, 6-1/4" long Jr. Kitty Kennel, 11-1/4" long Jr. Pony Trailer w/Sportster, 1968	125	185	250
Jr. Fire Department	17" long Jr. hook-n-ladder aerial truck, 11-1/2" long Jr. fire snorkel, 6-3/4" long truck, all have 24-hole chrome grilles, 1968	125	185	250
Jr. Fire Department	17" long Jr. hook-n-ladder aerial truck, 11-1/2" long Jr. fire snorkel, 6-3/4" long truck, all have four-slot grilles and two square plastic headlights, 1969	125	185	250
Jr. Highway Set	yellow and black Jr. scooper tractor, yellow and white Jr. cement mixer truck, yellow Jr. dump truck, 1969	200	300	400
Jr. Sportsman Set	Jr. camper pickup w/red cab and body and yellow camper, towing 6" plastic runabout on yellow two-wheel boat trailer, 1971	50	75	100
Loader, Dump Truck, and Shovel Set	conveyor, green body sand and gravel dump truck, 8-3/4" long green-enameled steel scoop shovel, 1954	100	150	200
Loader, Dump Truck, and Shovel Set	conveyor, blue body sand and gravel dump truck, 8-3/4" long blue-enameled steel scoop shovel, 1955	85	130	175
Mechanical Hauling Truck and Concrete Mixer	truck w/duo-tone slant design, red/orange lower hood sides, dark green upper hood, cab, ramp, yellow trailer, 9-5/8" green mixer, gray hopper, 38" long w/ramps, 1951	150	225	300
Mechanical Hauling Truck and Concrete Mixer	truck w/duo-tone slant design, red-orange lower hood sides, dark green upper hood, cab, trailer and ramp, 9-5/8" green mixer, gray hopper, 38" long w/ramps, 1950	160	245	325
Polysteel Farm Set	blue milkman truck w/rack and nine milk bottles, red and gray milk tanker, orange farm tractor, 1961	75	115	150
Road Builder Set	green/white cement mixer truck, yellow/black bulldozer, red dump truck, husky dumper, 1963	200	300	400
Truck with Concrete Mixer Trailer	22" truck w/duo-tone slant design, green fenders and lower sides, yellow squarish cab and body, 10" mixer w/yellow frame and red hopper, overall 34-1/2" long, 1937	175	265	350

VEHICLES

BUDDY L

NAME	DESCRIPTION	GOOD	EX	MINT
Truck with Concrete Mixer Trailer	22" truck w/duo-tone slant design, green front and lower hood sides, yellow upper hood, cab and body, 10" mixer w/yellow frame and red hopper, overall 32-1/2" long, 1938	165	250	330
Warehouse Set	Coca-Cola truck, two hand trucks, eight cases Coke bottles, store-door delivery truck, lumber, sign, two barrels, forklift, 1958	175	265	350
Warehouse Set	Coca-Cola truck, two hand trucks, eight cases Coke bottles, store-door delivery truck, sign, two barrels, forklift, 1959	150	225	300
Western Roundup Set	turquoise fenders, hood, cab and frame, white flatbed cargo section, six sections of rail fencing w/swinging gate, rearing and standing horse, cowboys, calf, steer, 1960	175	250	400

Trucks

NAME	DESCRIPTION	GOOD	EX	MINT
Air Force Supply Transport	blue w/blue removable fabric canopy, rubber wheels, decals on cab doors, 14-1/2" long, 1957	125	250	350
Air Mail Truck	black front, hood fenders, enclosed cab and opening doors, red enclosed body and chassis, 24" long, 1930	675	1000	1400
Allied Moving Van	tractor and semi-trailer van, duo-tone slant design, black front and lower sides, orange hood top, cab and van body, 29-1/2" long, 1941	600	900	1200
Army Electric Searchlight Unit	shiny olive drab flatbed truck, battery-operated searchlight, 14-3/4" long, 1957	125	225	325
Army Half-Track and Howitzer	olive drab w/olive drab carriage, 12-1/2" truck, 9-3/4" gun, overall 22-1/2" long, 1953	100	150	200
Army Half-Track with Howitzer	olive drab steel, red firing knob on gun, 17" truck, 9-3/4" gun, overall 27" long, 1955	100	150	200
Army Medical Corps Truck	white, black rubber tires on white steel disc wheels, 29-1/2" long, 1941	125	185	250
Army Searchlight Repair-It Truck	shiny olive drab truck and flatbed cargo section, 15" long, 1956	125	175	225
Army Supply Truck	shiny olive drab truck and removable fabric cover, 14-1/2" long, 1956	100	150	175
Army Transport Truck and Trailer	olive drab truck, 20-1/2" long, trailer 34-1/2" long, 1940	250	350	450
Army Transport with Howitzer	olive drab steel, 17" truck, 9-3/4" gun, overall 27" long, 1955	150	250	350
Army Transport with Howitzer	olive drab steel, re-firing knob on gun, 17" truck, 9-3/4" gun, overall 27" long, 1954	115	175	230
Army Transport with Howitzer	olive drab, 12" truck, 9-3/4" gun, overall 28" long, 1953	100	150	200
Army Transport with Tank	olive drab, 15-1/2" long truck, 11-1/2" long detachable two-wheel trailer, overall 26-1/2" long, 7-1/2" long tank, 1959	100	150	200
Army Troop Transport with Howitzer	dark forest green truck and gun, canopy mixture of greens, 14" long truck, 12" long, gun, overall 25-3/4" long, 1965	100	150	200
Army Truck	olive drab, 20-1/2" long, 1939	110	175	225
Army Truck	olive drab, 17" long, 1940	150	200	250
Atlas Van Lines	green tractor unit, chrome one-piece toothed grille and headlights, green lower half of semi-trailer van body, cream upper half, silvery roof, 29" long, 1956	200	300	400
Auto Hauler	yellow cab-over-engine tractor unit and double-deck semi-trailer, three 8" long vehicles, 25-1/2" long, 1968	75	115	150
Auto Hauler	snub-nose medium blue tractor unit and double-deck semi-truck trailer, three plastic coupes, overall 27-1/2" long, 1970	65	95	130
Baggage Rider	duo-tone horizontal design, green bumper, fenders and lower half of truck, white upper half, 28" long, 1950	250	175	500
Baggage Truck	green hood, fenders, and cab, yellow cargo section, no bumper, 17-1/2" long, 1945	175	265	350

VEHICLES

682

NAME	DESCRIPTION	GOOD	EX	MINT
Baggage Truck	duo-tone slant design, yellow skirted fenders and cargo section, green hood top, enclosed cab, 27-3/4" long, 1938	300	600	1000
Baggage Truck	black front, hood, and fenders, enclosed cab w/opening doors, nickel-rim, red-shell headlights, yellow stake body, 26-1/2" long, 1930-32	3000	5000	7000
Baggage Truck	green front, hood, and fenders, non-open doors, yellow cargo section slat or solid sides, metal grille, 26-1/2" long, 1935	350	500	650
Baggage Truck	black front, hood, and fenders, doorless cab, yellow four-post stake sides, two chains across back, 26-1/2" long, 1927	800	1000	2000
Baggage Truck	duo-tone slant design, yellow fenders, green hood top, cab, and removable rider seat, 26-1/2" long, 1936	350	750	1000
Big Brute Dumper	yellow cab-over-engine, frame and tiltback dump section w/cab shield, striped black and yellow bumper, black grille, 8" long, 1971	50	75	100
Big Brute Mixer Truck	yellow cab-over-engine, body and frame, white plastic mixing drum, white plastic seats, 7" long, 1971	35	50	70
Big Fella Hydraulic Rider Dumper	duo-tone slant design, yellow front and lower hood, red upper cab, dump body and upper hood, rider seat has large yellow sunburst-style decal, 26-1/2" long, 1950	110	175	225
Big Mack Dumper	off-white front, hood cab and chassis, blue-green tiltback dump section, white plastic bumper, 20-1/2" long, 1964	75	115	150
Big Mack Dumper	yellow front, hood cab, chassis and tiltback dump section, black plastic bumper, 20-1/2" long, 1967	70	100	140
Big Mack Dumper	yellow front, hood cab, chassis and tiltback dump section, black plastic bumper, single rear wheels, 20-1/2" long, 1968	65	95	130
Big Mack Dumper	yellow front, hood cab, chassis and tiltback dump section, black plastic bumper, heavy-duty black balloon tires on yellow plastic five-spoke wheels, 20-1/2" long, 1971	60	90	120
Big Mack Hydraulic Dumper	red hood, cab and tiltback dump section w/cab shield, white plastic bumper, short step ladder on each side, 20-1/2" long, 1968	50	75	100
Big Mack Hydraulic Dumper	white hood, cab and tiltback dump section w/cab shield, white plastic bumper, short step ladder on each side, 20-1/2" long, 1969	45	65	90
Big Mack Hydraulic Dumper	red hood, cab and tiltback dump section w/cab shield, dump body sides have a large circular back, white plastic bumper, short step ladder on each side, 20-1/2" long, 1970	40	60	80
Boat Transport	blue flatbed truck carrying 8" litho metal boat, boat deck white, hull red, truck 15" long, 1959	300	550	750
Borden's Milk Delivery Van	white upper cab-over-engine van body and sliding side doors, yellow lower body, metal-handle yellow plastic tray and six white milk bottle w/yellow caps, 11-1/2" long, 1965	125	200	275
Brute Car Carrier	bright blue cab-over-engine tractor unit and detachable double-deck semi-trailer, two plastic cars, 10" long, 1969	60	95	125
Brute Cement Mixer Truck	sand-beige cab-over-engine body and frame, white plastic mixing drum, white plastic seats, 5-1/4" long, 1968	35	55	75
Brute Cement Mixer Truck	blue cab-over-engine body and frame, white plastic mixing drum, white plastic seats, white-handled crank rotates drum, 5-1/4" long, 1969	30	45	65
Brute Dumper	red cab-over-engine body and cab shield on tiltback dump section, wide chrome wraparound bumper, 5" long, 1968	35	55	75
Brute Monkey House	yellow cab-over-engine body, striped orange and white awning roof, cage on back, two plastic monkeys, 5" long, 1968	50	75	100

VEHICLES

NAME	DESCRIPTION	GOOD	EX	MINT
Brute Monkey House	yellow cab-over-engine body, red and white awning roof, cage on back, two plastic monkeys, 5" long, 1969	40	60	80
Brute Sanitation Truck	lime green cab-over-engine and frame, white open-top body, wide chrome wraparound bumper, 5-1/4" long, 1969	50	75	100
Buddy L Milk Farms Truck	white body, black roof, short hood w/black wooden headlights, 13-1/2" long, 1945	150	300	450
Buddy L Milk Farms Truck	light cream body, red roof, nickel glide headlights, sliding doors, 13" long, 1949	170	300	500
Camper	bright medium blue steel truck and camper body, 14-1/2" long, 1964	60	95	125
Camper	medium blue truck and back door, white camper body, 14-1/2" long, 1965	50	75	100
Camper-N-Cruiser	bright medium blue camper w/matching boat trailer and 8-1/2" long plastic sport cruiser, overall 27" long, 1964	50	75	100
Camper-N-Cruiser	powder blue pickup truck and trailer, pale blue camper body, 24-1/2" long, 1963	60	95	125
Campers Truck	turquoise pickup truck, pale turquoise plastic camper, 14-1/2" long, 1961	55	85	110
Campers Truck with Boat	green/turquoise pickup truck, lime green camper body, red plastic runabout boat on camper roof, 14-1/2" long, 1962	50	100	150
Campers Truck with Boat	green/turquoise pickup, no side mirror, lime green camper body w/red plastic runabout boat on top, 14-1/2" long, 1963	50	100	150
Camping Trailer and Wagon	bright medium blue suburban wagon, matching teepee trailer, overall 24-1/2" long, 1964	60	95	125
Cattle Transport Truck	red w/yellow stake sides, 15" long, 1956	75	115	150
Cattle Transport Truck	green and white w/white stake sides, 15" long, 1957	75	115	150
Cement Mixer Truck	red body, tank ends, and chute, white side ladder, water tank, mixing drum and loading hopper, 15-1/2" long, 1965	75	115	150
Cement Mixer Truck	snub-nosed yellow body, cab, frame and chute, white plastic mixing drum, loading hopper and water tank w/yellow ends, 16" long, 1970	35	50	70
Cement Mixer Truck	red body, tank ends, and chute, white water tank, mixing drum and loading hopper, black wall tires, 15-1/2" long, 1967	60	95	125
Cement Mixer Truck	turquoise body, tank ends, and chute, white side ladder, water tank, mixing drum and loading hopper, 16-1/2" long, 1964	60	95	125
Cement Mixer Truck	red body, tank ends, and chute, white water tank, mixing drum and loading hopper, whitewall tires, 15-1/2" long, 1968	50	75	100
Charles Chip Delivery Truck Van	tan/beige body, decal on sides has brown irregular center resembling a large potato chip, 1966	125	200	275
City Baggage Dray	duo-tone slant design, green front and skirted fenders, yellow hood top, enclosed cab and cargo section, 20-3/4" long, 1938	150	200	350
City Baggage Dray	green front, hood, and fenders, non-open doors, yellow stake-side cargo section, 19" long, 1934	150	300	400
City Baggage Dray	cream w/aluminum-finish grille, no bumper, black rubber wheels, 20-3/4" long, 1940	100	200	300
City Baggage Dray	light green w/aluminum-finish grille, no bumper, black rubber wheels, 20-3/4" long, 1939	95	250	300
City Baggage Dray	duo-tone slant design, green front and fenders, yellow hood top and cargo section, dummy headlights, 19" long, 1937	150	300	400
City Baggage Dray	green front, hood, and fenders, non-open doors, yellow stake-side cargo section, bright metal grille, 19" long, 1935	150	300	400
City Baggage Dray	duo-tone slant design, green front and fenders, yellow hood top and cargo section, 19" long, 1936	150	300	400
Coal Truck	black hopper body and fully enclosed cab w/opening doors, red wheels, 25" long, 1930	900	1500	2000

VEHICLES

NAME	DESCRIPTION	GOOD	EX	MINT
Coal Truck	black front, hood, fenders, doorless cab, red chassis and disc wheels, 25" long, 1926	700	1000	2000
Coal Truck	black front, hood, fenders, sliding discharge door on each side of hopper body, red chassis and disc wheels, 25" long, 1927	800	1000	2000
Coca-Cola Bottling Route Truck	bright yellow, w/small metal hand truck, six or eight yellow cases of miniature green Coke bottles, 14-3/4" long, 1955	125	175	250
Coca-Cola Bottling Route Truck	bright yellow, w/two small metal hand trucks and eight yellow cases of miniature green Coke bottles, 14-3/4" long, 1957	110	175	225
Coca-Cola Delivery Truck	orange/yellow cab and double-deck, open-side cargo, two small hand trucks, four red and four green cases of bottles, 15" long, 1963	75	100	150
Coca-Cola Delivery Truck	orange/yellow cab and double-deck, open-side cargo, two small hand trucks, four red and four green cases of bottles, 15" long, 1964	60	95	125
Coca-Cola Delivery Truck	red lowercab-over-engine and van body, white upper cab, left side of van lifts to reveal 10 miniature bottle cases, 9-1/2" long, 1971	25	40	55
Coca-Cola Delivery Truck	orange/yellow cab and double-deck, open-side cargo, two small hand trucks, four red and four green cases of bottles, 15" long, 1960	100	150	200
Coke Coffee Co. Delivery Truck Van	black lower half of body, orange upper half, roof and sliding side doors, 1966	85	130	175
Colt Vacationer	blue/white Colt sportsliner w/trailer carrying 8-1/2" long red/white plastic sport cruiser, overall 22-1/2" long, 1967	60	95	125
Curtiss Candy Trailer Van	blue tractor and bumper, white semi-trailer van, blue roof, chrome one-piece toothed grille and headlights, white drop-down rear door, 32-3/4" long w/tailgate/ramp lowered, 1955	250	400	500
Dairy Transport Truck	duo-tone slant design, red front and lower hood sides, white hood top, cab and semi-trailer tank body, tank opens in back, 26" long, 1939	150	225	300
Deluxe Auto Carrier	turquoise tractor unit, aluminum loading ramps, three plastic cars, overall 34" long including, 1962	100	175	250
Deluxe Camping Outfit	turquoise pickup truck and camper, and 8-1/2" long plastic boat on pale turquoise boat trailer, overall 24" long, 1961	60	95	125
Deluxe Hydraulic Rider Dump Truck	duo-tone slant design, red front and lower hood sides, white upper cab, dump body and chassis, red or black removable rider saddle, 26" long, 1948	175	265	350
Deluxe Motor Market	duo-tone slant design, red front, curved bumper, lower hood and cab sides, white hood top, body and cab, 22-1/4" long, 1950	250	350	500
Deluxe Rider Delivery Truck	duo-tone horizontal design, deep blue lower half, gray upper half, red rubber disc wheels, black barrel skid, 22-3/4" long, 1945	135	200	270
Deluxe Rider Delivery Truck	duo-tone horizontal design, gray lower half, blue upper half, red rubber disc wheels, black barrel skid, 22-3/4" long, 1945	135	200	270
Deluxe Rider Dump Truck	various colors, dual rear wheels, no bumper, 25-1/2" long, 1945	75	115	150
Double Hydraulic Self-Loader-N-Dump	green front loading scoop w/yellow arms attached to cab sides, yellow hood and enclosed cab, orange frame and wide dump body, 29" long w/scoop lowered, 1956	85	130	175
Double Tandem Hydraulic Dump and Trailer	truck has red bumper, hood, cab and frame, four-wheel trailer w/red tow and frame, both w/white tiltback dump bodies, 38" long, 1957	85	130	175
Double-Deck Boat Transport	light blue steel flatbed truck carrying three 8" white plastic boats w/red decks, truck 15" long, 1960	150	250	400
Dr. Pepper Delivery Truck Van	red, white, and blue, 1966	85	130	175
Dump Body Truck	black front, hood, open driver's seat and dump section, red chassis, crank windlass w/ratchet raises dump bed, 25" long, 1921	800	1400	2000

NAME	DESCRIPTION	GOOD	EX	MINT
Dump Body Truck	black front, hood, open driver's seat and dump section, red chassis, chain drive dump mechanism, 25" long, 1923	1200	1800	2500
Dump Truck	duo-tone slant design, red lower cab, lower hood, front and dump body, yellow upper hood, upper cab and chassis, no bumper, 22-1/4" long, 1939	250	375	500
Dump Truck	duo-tone slant design, red front, fenders and dump body, yellow hood top, upper sides, upper cab and chassis, no bumper, 22-1/2" long, 1948	125	185	250
Dump Truck	various colors, black rubber wheels, 12" long, 1945	50	75	100
Dump Truck	red hood top and cab, white or cream dump body and frame, no bumper, 17-1/2" long, 1945	75	115	150
Dump Truck	white upper hood, enclosed cab, wide-skirt fenders and open-frame chassis, orange dump body, bright-metal grille, no bumper, 17-3/8" long, 1941	85	130	175
Dump Truck	green w/cream hood top and upper enclosed cab, no bumper, bright-metal headlights and grille, 22-1/4" long, 1941	85	130	175
Dump Truck	duo-tone slant design, red front, fenders and lower doors, white upper, bright radiator grille and headlights, no bumper, 22-1/4" long, 1939	250	375	500
Dump Truck	duo-tone slant design, yellow enclosed cab and hood, red front and dump body, no bumper, bright-metal headlights, 20" long, 1936	250	375	500
Dump Truck	yellow enclosed cab, front and hood, red dump section, no bumper, bright-metal radiator, 20" long, 1935	325	485	650
Dump Truck	yellow enclosed cab, front and hood, red dump section, no bumper, 20" long, 1934	275	415	550
Dump Truck	black enclosed cab and opening doors, front and hood, red dump body and chassis, simple lever arrangement lifts dump bed, 24" long, 1930	650	975	1300
Dump Truck	black enclosed cab and opening doors, front and hood, red dump body and chassis, crank handle lifts dump bed, 24" long, 1931	750	1125	1500
Dump Truck	yellow upper hood and enclosed cab, red wide-skirt fenders and open-frame chassis, blue dump body, no bumper, 17-1/4" long, 1940	85	130	175
Dump Truck	duo-tone slant design, yellow enclosed cab and hood, red front and dump body, no bumper, dummy headlights, 20" long, 1937	250	375	500
Dump Truck-Economy Line	dark blue dump body, remainder is yellow, bright-metal grille and headlights, no bumper or running boards, 12" long, 1941	75	115	150
Dump-n-Dozer	orange husky dumper truck and orange flatbed four-wheel trailer carrying orange bulldozer, 23" long including trailer, 1962	75	115	150
Dumper with Shovel	medium green body, frame and dump section, white one-piece bumper and grille guard, no side mirror, large white steel scoop shovel, spring suspension on front axle only, 15" long, 1964	75	115	150
Dumper with Shovel	orange body, frame and dump section, chrome one-piece grille, no bumper guard, no side mirror, large white steel scoop shovel, no spring suspension, 15-3/4" long, 1965	75	115	150
Dumper with Shovel	medium green body, frame and dump section, white one-piece bumper and grille guard, no side mirror, large white steel scoop shovel, 15" long, 1963	75	115	150
Dumper with Shovel	turquoise body, frame and dump section, white one-piece bumper and grille guard, large white steel scoop shovel, 15" long, 1962	75	115	150
Express Trailer Truck	red tractor unit, hood, fenders and enclosed cab, green semi-trailer van w/removable roof and drop-down rear door, bright-metal dummy headlights, 23-3/4" long, 1934	350	525	700
Express Trailer Truck	red tractor unit, hood, fenders and enclosed cab, green semi-trailer van w/removable roof and drop-down rear door, 23-3/4" long, 1933	350	525	700

VEHICLES

BUDDY L

NAME	DESCRIPTION	GOOD	EX	MINT
Express Truck	all black except red frame, enclosed cab w/opening doors, nickel-rim, red-shell headlights, six rubber tires, double bar front bumper, 24-1/2" long, 1930-32	3000	4500	6000
Farm Machinery Hauler Trailer Truck	blue tractor unit, yellow flatbed semi-trailer, 31-1/2" long, 1956	125	185	250
Farm Supplies Automatic Dump	duo-tone slant design, blue curved bumper, front, lower hood sides and cab, yellow upper hood, cab and rest of body, 22-1/2" long, 1950	125	185	250
Farm Supplies Dump Truck	duo-tone slant design, red front, fenders and lower hood sides, yellow upper hood, cab and body, 22-3/4" long, 1949	125	185	250
Farm Supplies Hydraulic Dump Trailer	green tractor unit, long cream body on semi-trailer, 14 rubber wheels, 26-1/2" long, 1956	100	150	200
Fast Delivery Pickup	yellow hood and cab, red open cargo body, removable chain across open back, 13-1/2" long, 1949	100	150	200
Finger-Tip Steering Hydraulic Dumper	powder blue bumper, fenders, hood, cab and frame, white tiltback dump body, 22" long, 1959	75	115	150
Fisherman	sage gray/green and white pickup truck w/steel trailer carrying plastic 8-1/2" long sport cruiser, overall 25" long, 1965	65	95	130
Fisherman	metallic sage green pickup truck w/boat trailer carrying plastic 8-1/2" long sport cruiser, overall 25" long, 1964	70	100	140
Fisherman	pale blue/green station wagon w/four-wheel boat trailer carrying plastic 8-1/2" long boat, overall 27-1/2" long, 1963	75	115	150
Fisherman	light tan pickup truck w/tan steel trailer carrying plastic 8-1/2" long sport crusier, overall 24-1/4" long, 1962	80	120	160
Flivver Dump Truck	black w/red eight-spoke wheels, black hubs, aluminum tires, flat, open dump section w/squared-off back w/latching, drop-down endgate, 11" long, 1926	700	1000	1500
Flivver Scoop Dump Truck	black w/red eight-spoke wheels, 12-1/2" long, 1926-27, 1929-30	1500	2500	3500
Flivver Truck	black w/red eight-spoke wheels w/aluminum tires, black hubs, 12" long, 1924	800	1000	1500
Ford Flivver Dump Cart	black w/red eight-spoke wheels, black hubs, aluminum tires, flat, short open dump section tapers to point on each side, 12-1/2" long, 1926	1500	2500	3500
Frederick & Nelson Delivery Truck Van	medium green body, roof and sliding side doors, 1966	125	200	275
Freight Delivery Stake Truck	red hood, bumper, cab and frame, white cargo section, yellow three-post, three-slat removable stake sides, 14-3/4" long, 1955	75	125	150
Front Loader Hi-Lift Dump Truck	red scoop and arms attached to white truck at rear fenders, green dump body, 17-3/4" long w/scoop down and dump body raised, 1955	85	130	175
Giant Hydraulic Dumper	red bumper, frame, hood and cab, light tan tiltback dump body and cab shield 23-3/4" long, 1960	125	185	250
Giant Hydraulic Dumper	overall color turquoise, dump lever has a red plastic tip, 22-3/4" long, 1961	135	200	275
Giraffe Truck	powder blue hood, white cab roof, high-sided open-top cargo section, two orange/yellow plastic giraffes, 13-1/4" long,1968	60	95	125
GMC Air Force Electric Searchlight Unit	all blue flatbed, off white battery-operated searchlight swivel mount, decals on cab doors, 14-3/4" long, 1958	200	300	400
GMC Airway Express Van	green hood, cab and van body, latching double rear doors, shiny metal drum coin bank and metal hand truck, 17-1/2" long w/rear doors open, 1957	250	350	450
GMC Anti-Aircraft Unit with Searchlight	15" truck w/four-wheel trailer, battery-operated, over 25-1/4" long, 1957	250	350	450
GMC Army Hauler with Jeep	shiny olive drab tractor unit and flatbed trailer, 10" long jeep, overall 31-1/2" long, 1958	200	300	400
GMC Army Transport with Howitzer	shiny olive drab, 14-1/2" long, truck, overall w/gun 22-1/2" long, 1957	200	300	400

VEHICLES

687

NAME	DESCRIPTION	GOOD	EX	MINT
GMC Brinks Armored Truck Van	silver gray, barred windows on sides and in double doors, coin slot and hole in roof, brass padlock w/two keys, pouch, play money, three gray plastic guard figures, 16" long, 1958	300	350	450
GMC Coca-Cola Route Truck	lime/yellow, w/small metal hand truck and eight cases of miniature green Coke bottles, 14-1/8" long, 1957	200	300	400
GMC Coca-Cola Route Truck	orange/yellow, w/two small metal hand trucks and eight cases of miniature green Coke bottles, 14-1/8" long, 1958	200	300	400
GMC Construction Company Dumper	pastel blue including control lever on left and dump section w/cab shield, hinged tailgate, chrome GMC bar grille, six wheels, 16" long, 1958	200	300	400
GMC Construction Company Dumper	pastel blue including control lever on left and dump section w/cab shield, hinged tailgate, chrome GMC bar grille, four wheels, 16" long, 1959	150	250	350
GMC Highway Giant Trailer	blue tractor, blue and white van, chrome GMC bar grille and headlights, blue roof on semi-trailer, white tailgate doubles as loading ramp, 18-wheeler, 31-1/4" long, 1957	250	350	450
GMC Highway Giant Trailer Truck	blue tractor, blue and white van, chrome GMC bar grille and headlights, blue roof on semi-trailer, white tailgate doubles as loading ramp, 14-wheeler, 30-3/4" long, 1958	200	300	400
GMC Husky Dumper	red hood, bumper, cab and chassis, chrome GMC bar grille and nose emblem, white oversize dump body, red control lever on right side, 17-1/2" long, 1957	150	250	350
GMC Self-Loading Auto Carrier	yellow tractor and double-deck semi trailer, three plastic cars, overall 33-1/4" long, 1959	200	300	400
GMC Signal Corps Unit	both olive drab, 14-1/4" long truck w/removable fabric canopy, 8" long four-wheel trailer, 1957	150	200	250
Grocery Motor Market Truck	duo-tone slant design, yellow front, lower hood sides, fenders and lower doors, white hood top, enclosed cab and body, no bumper, 20-1/2" long, 1937	275	415	550
Grocery Motor Market Truck	duo-tone slant design, yellow front, lower hood sides, skirted fenders and lower doors, white hood top, cab and body, no bumper, 21-1/2" long, 1938	275	415	550
Heavy Hauling Dumper	red hood, bumper, cab and frame, cream tiltback dump body, 20-1/2" long, 1955	75	125	150
Heavy Hauling Dumper	red hood, bumper, cab and frame, cream oversize dump body, hinged tailgate, 21-1/2" long, 1956	70	125	140
Heavy Hauling Hydraulic Dumper	green hood, cab and frame, cream tiltback dump body, and cab shield, raising dump body almost to vertical, 23" long, 1956	70	105	140
Hertz Auto Hauler	bright yellow tractor and double-deck semi-trailer, three plastic vehicles, 27" long, 1965	100	150	200
Hi-Lift Farm Supplies Dump	red plastic front end including hood and enclosed cab, yellow dump body, cab shield and hinged tailgate, 21-1/2" long, 1953	100	175	225
Hi-Lift Farm Supplies Dump	all steel, red front end including hood and enclosed cab, yellow dump body, cab shield and hinged tailgate, 23-1/2" long, 1954	100	175	225
Hi-Lift Scoop-n-Dump Truck	orange truck w/deeply fluted sides, dark green scoop on front rises to empty load into hi-lift light cream dump body, 16" long, 1953	80	125	165
Hi-Lift Scoop-n-Dump Truck	orange truck w/deeply fluted sides, dark green scoop on front rises to empty load into deep hi-lift slightly orange dump body, 16" long, 1955	75	115	155
Hi-Lift Scoop-n-Dump Truck	orange hood, fenders and cab, yellow front loading scoop and arms attached to fenders, white frame, dump body and cab shield, 17-3/4" long, 1956	70	125	145
Hi-Lift Scoop-n-Dump Truck	blue hood, fenders and cab, yellow front loading scoop and arms attached to fenders, white frame, dump body, cab shield, and running boards, 17-3/4" long, 1957	65	100	135
Hi-Lift Scoop-n-Dump Truck	orange truck w/deeply fluted sides, dark green scoop on front rises to empty load into hi-lift cream/yellow dump body, 16" long, 1952	85	130	175

VEHICLES

NAME	DESCRIPTION	GOOD	EX	MINT
Hi-Tip Hydraulic Dumper	orange hood, cab and frame, cream tiltback dump body, and cab shield, raising dump body almost to vertical, 23" long, 1957	75	115	150
Highway Hawk Trailer Van	bronze cab tractor, chrome metallized plastic bumper, grille, air cleaner and exhaust, 19-3/4" long, 1985	50	75	100
Highway Maintenance Truck with Trailer	orange w/black rack of four simulated floodlights behind cab, 19-1/2" long including small two-wheel trailer, 1957	100	150	200
Husky Dumper	yellow hood, cab, fram and tiltback dump section w/cab shield, crome one-piece wraparound bumper, 14-1/2" long, 1969	50	75	100
Husky Dumper	orange wraparound bumper, body, frame and dump section, hinged tailgate, plated dump lever on left side, 15-1/4" long, 1960	75	115	150
Husky Dumper	snub-nose red body, tiltback dump section, cab shield, full-width chrome bumperless grille, deep-tread whitewall tires, 14-1/2" long, 1970	45	70	90
Husky Dumper	snub-nose red body, tiltback dump section snda cab shield, full-width chrome bumperless grille, white-tipped dump-control lever on left, deep-tread whitewall tires, 14-1/2" long, 1971	40	60	80
Husky Dumper	white plastic wraparound bumper, tan body, frame and dump section, hinged tailgate, plated dump lever on left side, 15-1/4" long, 1961	70	125	140
Husky Dumper	red hood, cab, chassis and dump section, chrome one-piece bumper and slotted grille w/double headlights, 14-1/2" long, 1968	60	95	125
Husky Dumper	bright yellow, chrome one-piece bumper, slotted rectangular grille and double headlights, 14-1/2" long, 1966,	75	115	150
Hydraulic Auto Hauler with Four GMC Cars	powder blue GMC tractor, 7" long plastic cars, overall 33-1/2" long including loading ramp, 1958	250	350	450
Hydraulic Construction Dumper	red front, cab and chassis, large green dump section w/cab shield, 15-1/4" long, 1962	65	100	135
Hydraulic Construction Dumper	tan/beige front, cab and chassis, large green dump section w/cab shield, 15-1/4" long, 1963	60	95	125
Hydraulic Construction Dumper	bright blue front, cab and chassis, large green dump section w/cab shield, 15-1/2" long, 1964	50	75	100
Hydraulic Construction Dumper	bright green front, cab and chassis, large green dump section w/cab shield, 14" long, 1965	50	75	100
Hydraulic Construction Dumper	medium blue front, cab and chassis, large green dump section w/cab shield, 15-1/4" long, 1967	50	75	100
Hydraulic Dump Truck	black front, hood, fenders, open seat, and dump body, red chassis and disc wheels w/aluminum tires, 25" long, 1926	500	800	1000
Hydraulic Dump Truck	duo-tone slant design, red hood sides, dump body and chassis, white upper hood, cab and removable rider seat, electric headlights, 24-3/4" long, 1936	300	500	700
Hydraulic Dump Truck	black front, hood, fenders, dark reddish maroon dump body, red chassis and disc wheels w/seven embossed spokes, black hubs, 25" long, 1931	675	900	1300
Hydraulic Dump Truck	black front, hood, fenders and enclosed cab, red dump body, chassis and wheels w/six embossed spokes, bright hubs, 24-3/4" long, 1933	325	485	650
Hydraulic Dumper	green, plated dump lever on left side, large hooks on left side hold yellow or off-white steel scoop shovel, white plastic side mirro and grille guard, 17" long, 1961	125	185	250
Hydraulic Dumper with Shovel	green, plated dump lever on left side, large hooks on left side hold yellow or off-white steel scoop shovel, 17" long, 1960	125	185	250
Hydraulic Hi-Lift Dumper	duo-tone slant design, green hood nose and lower cab sides, remainder white w/chrome grille, enclosed cab, 24" long, 1953	75	115	150
Hydraulic Hi-Lift Dumper	green hood, fenders, cab, and dump-body supports, white dump body w/cab shield, 22-1/2" long, 1954	85	130	175
Hydraulic Hi-Lift Dumper	blue hood, fenders, cab, and dump-body supports, white dump body w/cab shield, 22-1/2" long, 1955	75	115	150

VEHICLES

*Ice Truck,
1926, Buddy L*

*U.S. Mail Truck,
1953, Buddy L*

*Wild Animal Circus,
1966, Buddy L*

NAME	DESCRIPTION	GOOD	EX	MINT
Hydraulic Highway Dumper	orange w/row of black square across scraper edges, one-piece chrome eight-hole grille and double headlights, no scraper blade, 17-3/4" long over blade and raised dump body, 1959	50	75	100
Hydraulic Highway Dumper with Scraper Blade	orange w/row of black square across scraper edges, one-piece chrome eight-hole grille and double headlights, 17-3/4" long over blade and raised dump body, 1958	75	115	150
Hydraulic Husky Dumper	red body, frame, dump section and cab shield, 15-1/4" long, 1962	65	100	135
Hydraulic Husky Dumper	red body, white one-piece bumper and grille guard, heavy side braces on dump section, 14" long, 1963	50	75	100
Hydraulic Rider Dumper	duo-tone slant design, yellow front and lower hood, red upper cab, dump body and upper hood, 26-1/2" long, 1949	175	265	350
Hydraulic Sturdy Dumper	lime green hood, cab, frame and tiltback dump section, green lever on left side controls hydraulic dumping, 14-1/2" long, 1969	50	75	100
Hydraulic Sturdy Dumper	yellow hood, cab, fram and tiltback dump section, green lever on left side controls hydraulic dumping, 14-1/2" long, 1969	50	75	100
Hydraulic Sturdy Dumper	snub-nose green/yellow body, cab and tiltback dump section, white plastic seats, 14-1/2" long, 1970	45	60	80
Ice Truck	black front, hood, fenders and doorless cab, yellow open cargo section, canvas sliding cover, 26-1/2" long, 1926	700	900	1600
Ice Truck	black front, hood, fenders and enclosed cab, yellow open cargo section, canvas, ice cakes, miniature tongs, 26-1/2" long, 1930	700	900	1500
Ice Truck	black front, hood, fenders and enclosed cab, yellow ice compartment, canvas, ice cakes, tongs, 26-1/2" long, 1933-34	700	900	1300
Ice Truck	black front, hood, fenders and enclosed cab, yellow ice compartment, 26-1/2" long, 1933	700	900	1500
IHC "Red Baby" Express Truck	red w/black hubs and aluminum tires, 24-1/4" long, 1929	800	1300	1900
IHC "Red Baby" Express Truck	red doorless roofed cab, open pickup body, chassis and fenders, 24-1/4" long, 1928	750	1000	2000
Insurance Patrol	red w/open driver's seat and body, brass bell on cowl and full-length handrails, 27" long, 1925	650	1000	1300
Insurance Patrol	red w/open driver's seat and body, brass bell on cowl and full-length handrails, no CFD decal, 27" long, 1928	625	950	1250
International Delivery Truck	red w/removable black rider saddle, black-edged yellow horizontal strip on cargo body, 24-1/2" long, 1935	225	350	450
International Delivery Truck	duo-tone slant design, red front, bumper and lower hood sides, yellow hood top, upper sides, cab and open cargo body, 24-1/2" long, 1936	200	300	400
International Delivery Truck	duo-tone slant design, red front, bumper and lower hood sides, yellow hood top, upper sides, cab and open cargo body, bright metal dummy headlights, 24-1/2" long, 1938	150	225	300
International Dump Truck	red w/bright-metal radiator grille, and black removable rider saddle, 25-3/4" long, 1935	325	485	650
International Dump Truck	duo-tone slant design, yellow radiator, fenders, lower hood and detachable rider seat, rest of truck is red, 25-3/4" long, 1936	315	475	630
International Dump Truck	red, w/red headlights on radiator, black removable rider saddle, 25-3/4" long, 1938	125	185	250
International Railway Express Truck	duo-tone slant design, yellow front, lower hood sides and removable top, green hood top, enclosed cab and van body, electric headlights, 25" long, 1937	350	525	700

VEHICLES

NAME	DESCRIPTION	GOOD	EX	MINT
International Railway Express Truck	duo-tone slant design, yellow front, lower hood sides and removable top, green hood top, enclosed cab and van body, dummy headlights, 25" long, 1938	345	525	690
International Wrecker Truck	duo-tone slant design, yellow upper cab, hood, and boom, red lower cab, fenders, grille and body, rubber tires, removable rider seat, 32" long, 1938	600	900	1800
Jewel Home Service Truck Van	dark brown body and sliding side doors, 1967	125	200	275
Jewel Home Shopping Truck Van	pale mint green upper body and roof, darker mint green lower half, no sliding doors, 1968	125	200	275
Jolly Joe Ice Cream Truck	white w/black roof, black tires and wooden wheels, 17-1/2" long, 1947	225	350	450
Jolly Joe Popsicle Truck	white w/black roof, black tires and wooden wheels, 17-1/2" long, 1948	275	425	550
Jr. Animal Ark	fuchsia lapstrake hull, four black tires, 10 pairs of plastic animals, 5" long, 1970	40	60	80
Jr. Auto Carrier	yellow cab-over-engine tractor unit and double-deck semi-trailer, two red plastic cars, 15-1/2" long, 1967	50	75	100
Jr. Auto Carrier	bright blue cab-over-engine tractor unit and double-deck semi-trailer, two plastic cars, 17-1/4" long, 1969	60	95	125
Jr. Beach Buggy	yellow hood, fenders and topless jeep body, red plastic seats, white plastic surfboard that clips to roll bar and windshield, truck 6" long, 1969	45	65	90
Jr. Beach Buggy	lime green hood, fenders and topless jeep body, red plastic seats, lime green plastic surfboard that clips to roll bar and windshield, truck 6" long, 1971	35	50	70
Jr. Buggy Hauler	fuchsia jeep body w/orange seats, orange two-wheel trailer tilts to unload sandpiper beach buggy, 12" long including jeep and trailer, 1970	35	55	75
Jr. Camper	red cab and pickup body wih yellow camper body, 7" long, 1971	50	75	100
Jr. Canada Dry Delivery Truck	green/lime cab-over-engine body, hand truck, 10 cases of green bottles, 9-1/2" long, 1968	100	150	200
Jr. Canada Dry Delivery Truck	green/lime cab-over-engine body, hand truck, 10 cases of green bottles, 9-1/2" long, 1969	85	130	170
Jr. Cement Mixer Truck	blue cab-over-engine body, frame and hopper, white plastic mixing drum, white plastic seats, wide one-piece chrome bumper, 7-1/2" long, 1969	35	50	70
Jr. Cement Mixer Truck	blue cab-over-engine body, frame and hopper, white plastic mixing drum, white plastic seats, 7-1/2" long, 1968	50	75	100
Jr. Dump Truck	red cab-over-engine, frame and tiltback dump section, plastic vertical headlights, 7-1/2" long, 1967	50	75	100
Jr. Dumper	avocado cab-over-engine, frame and tiltback dump section w/cab shield, one-piece chrome bumper and four-slot grille, 7-1/2" long, 1969	335	55	75
Jr. Giraffe Truck	turquoise cab-over-engine body, white cab roof, plastic giraffe, 6-1/2" long, 1968	50	75	100
Jr. Giraffe Truck	turquoise cab-over-engine body, white cab roof, plastic giraffe, 6-1/4" long, 1969	40	60	80
Jr. Kitty Kennel	pink cab-over-engine body, white cab roof, four white plastic cats, 6-1/4" long, 1969	55	85	115
Jr. Kitty Kennel	pink cab-over-engine body, white cab roof, four colored plastic cats, 6-1/4" long, 1968	60	95	125
Jr. Sanitation Truck	blue cab-over-engine, white frame, refuse body and loading hopper, 10" long, 1968	75	115	150
Jr. Sanitation Truck	yellow cab-over-engine and underframe, refuse body and loading hopper, full width bumper and grille, 10" long, 1969	75	115	150
Junior Line Air Mail Truck	black enclosed cab, red chassis and body, headlights and double bar bumper, six rubber tires, 24" long, 1930-32	400	650	1200

VEHICLES

BUDDY L

NAME	DESCRIPTION	GOOD	EX	MINT
Kennel Truck	turquoise pickup body and cab, clear plastic 12-section kennel w/12 plastic dogs fits in cargo box, 13-1/2" long, 1965	60	95	125
Kennel Truck	snub-nosed red/orange body and cab, plastic kennel section in back, six kennels w/six plastic dogs, 13-1/4" long, 1970	60	95	125
Kennel Truck	red/orange pickup body and cab, yellow roof, six section kennel w/six plastic dogs fits in cargo box, 13-1/4" long, 1969	65	100	135
Kennel Truck	cream/yellow pickup body and cab, clear plastic 12-section kennel w/12 plastic dogs fits in cargo box, 13-1/4" long, 1968	80	120	160
Kennel Truck ,	bright blue pickup body and cab, clear plastic 12-section kennel w/12 plastic dogs fits in cargo box, 13-1/4" long, 1967	85	130	175
Kennel Truck	medium blue pickup body and cab, clear plastic 12-section kennel w/12 plastic dogs fits in cargo box, 13-1/2" long, 1964	60	90	120
Kennel Truck	bright blue pickup body and cab, clear plastic 12-section kennel w/12 plastic dogs fits in cargo box, 13-1/4" long, 1966	95	145	190
Lumber Truck	black front, hood, fenders, cabless open seat and low-sides cargo bed, red bumper, chassis and a pair of removable solid stake sides, load of lumber pieces, 24" long, 1924	750	1000	1500
Lumber Truck	black front, hood, fenders, doorless cab and low-sides cargo bed, red bumper, chassis and a pair of removable solid stake sides, load of lumber, 25-1/2" long, 1926	650	1300	2700
Mack Hydraulic Dumper	red front, hood, cab, chassis and tiltback dump section w/cab shield, white plastic bumper, 20-1/2" long, 1965	60	95	125
Mack Hydraulic Dumper	red front, hood, cab, chassis and tiltback dump section w/cab shield, white plastic bumper, short step ladder on each side, 20-1/2" long, 1967	50	75	100
Mack Quarry Dumper	orange front, hood cab and chassis, blue-green tiltback dump section, white plastic bumper, 20-1/2" long, 1965	75	115	150
Mammoth Hydraulic Quarry Dumper	deep green hood, cab and chassis, red tiltback dump section, black plastic bumper, 23" long, 1962	50	100	175
Mammoth Hydraulic Quarry Dumper	deep green hood, red cab, chassis and tiltback dump section, black plastic bumper, 22-1/2" long, 1963	60	90	125
Marshall Field's Delivery Truck Van	hunter green body, sliding doors and roof, 1966	125	200	275
Milkman Truck	lime yellow hood, cab and flatbed body, white side rails, 14 3" white plastic milk bottles, 14-1/4" long, 1964	75	115	150
Milkman Truck	light blue hood, cab and flatbed body, white side rails, 14 3" white plastic milk bottles, 14-1/4" long, 1963	85	130	175
Milkman Truck	deep cream hood, cab and flatbed body, white side rails, 14 3" white plastic milk bottles w/red caps, 14-1/4" long, 1962	100	150	200
Milkman Truck	medium blue hood, cab and flatbed body, white side rails, eight 3" white plastic milk bottles, 14-1/4" long, 1961	110	175	225
Milkman Truck	light yellow hood, cab and flatbed body, white side rails, 14 3" white plastic milk bottles, 14-1/4" long, 1964	75	115	150
Milkman Truck	light blue hood, cab and flatbed body, white side rails, 14 3" white plastic milk bottles, 14-1/4" long, 1963	85	130	175
Milkman Truck	medium blue hood, cab and flatbed body, white side rails, eight 3" white plastic milk bottles, 14-1/4" long, 1961	50	100	200
Milkman Truck	deep cream hood, cab and flatbed body, white side rails, fourteen 3" white plastic milk bottles w/red caps, 14-1/4" long, 1962	50	100	200

VEHICLES

693

NAME	DESCRIPTION	GOOD	EX	MINT
Mister Buddy Ice Cream Truck	white cab-over-engine van body, pale blue or off-white plastic underbody and floor, 11-1/2" long, 1964	45	60	100
Mister Buddy Ice Cream Truck	white cab-over-engine van body, red plastic underbody and floor, 11-1/2" long, 1966	45	75	100
Mister Buddy Ice Cream Truck	white cab-over-engine van body, red plastic underbody and floor, red bell knob, 11-1/2" long, 1967	55	85	115
Model T Flivver Truck	black w/red eight-spoke wheels w/aluminum tires, black hubs, 12" long, 1924	1000	1500	2000
Motor Market Truck	duo-tone horizontal design, white hood top, upper cab and high partition in cargo section, yellow-orange grille, fenders, lower hood and cab sides, 21-1/2" long, 1941	200	350	550
Moving Van	black front, hood and seat, red chassis and disc wheels w/black hubs, green van body, roof extends forward above open driver's seat, 25" long, 1924	1200	2000	3000
Overland Trailer Truck	yellow tractor, enclosed cab, red semi-trailer and four-wheel full trailer w/removable roofs, 39-3/4" long, 1935	350	525	700
Overland Trailer Truck	duo-tone slant design, green and yellow tractor unit w/yellow cab, red semi-trailer and four-wheel full trailer w/yellow removable roofs, 39-3/4" long, 1936	325	485	650
Overland Trailer Truck	duo-tone slant design, green and yellow semi-streamlined tractor and green hood sides, yellow hood, chassis, enclosed cab, 40", 1939	350	550	700
Overland Trailer Truck	duo-tone horizontal design, red and white tractor has red front, lower half chassis, chassis, enclosed cab, 40", 1939	350	550	700
Pepsi Delivery Truck	powder blue hood and lower cab, white upper cab and double-deck cargo section, two hand trucks, four blue cases of red bottles, four red cases of blue bottles, 15" long, 1970	60	95	125
Polysteel Boat Transport	medium blue soft plastic body, steel flatbed carrying 8" white plastic runabout boat w/red deck, truck 12-1/2" long, 1960	75	115	150
Polysteel Coca-Cola Delivery Truck	yellow plastic truck, slanted bottle racks, eight red Coke cases w/green bottles, small metal hand truck, 12-1/2" long, 1961	50	75	100
Polysteel Coca-Cola Delivery Truck	yellow plastic truck, slanted bottle racks, eight green Coke cases w/red bottles, small metal hand truck, 12-1/4" long, 1962	60	90	120
Polysteel Dumper	medium blue soft molded plastic front, cab and frame, off-white steel dump body w/sides rounded at back, hinged tailgate, 13" long, 1960	87	130	175
Polysteel Dumper	orange plastic body and tiltback dump section w/cab shield, "Come-Back Motor", 13" long, 1961	75	115	150
Polysteel Dumper	green soft molded plastic front, cab and frame, yellow steel dump body w/sides rounded at back, hinged tailgate, 13" long, 1959	100	150	200
Polysteel Dumper	orange plastic body and tiltback dump section w/cab shield, no "Come-Back Motor", no door decals, 13-1/2" long, 1962	60	95	125
Polysteel Highway Transport	red soft plastic tractor, cab roof lights, double horn, radio antenna and side fuel tanks, white steel semi-trailer van, 20-1/2" long, 1960	100	150	200
Polysteel Hydraulic Dumper	beige soft molded-plastic front, cab and frame, off-white steel dump section w/sides rounded at rear, 13" long, 1959	60	95	125
Polysteel Hydraulic Dumper	red soft molded-plastic front, cab and frame, light green steel dump section w/sides rounded at rear, 13" long, 1960	80	120	160
Polysteel Hydraulic Dumper	yellow soft plastic body, frame and tiltback ribbed dump section w/cab shield, 13" long, 1961	75	115	150
Polysteel Hydraulic Dumper	red soft plastic body, frame and tiltback ribbed dump section w/cab shield, 13" long, 1962	65	100	130

VEHICLES

NAME	DESCRIPTION	GOOD	EX	MINT
Polysteel Milk Tanker	red soft plastic tractor unit, light blue/gray semi-trailer tank w/red ladders and five dooms, 22" long, 1961	60	95	125
Polysteel Milk Tanker	turquoise soft plastic tractor unit, light blue/gray semi-trailer tank w/red ladders and five dooms, 22" long, 1961	60	95	125
Polysteel Milkman Truck	turquoise soft plastic front, cab and frame, light blue steel open cargo section w/nine oversized white plastic milk bottles w/red caps, 11-3/4" long, 1962	35	50	70
Polysteel Milkman Truck	light blue soft plastic front, cab and frame, light yellow steel open cargo section w/nine oversized white plastic milk bottles, 11-3/4" long, 1960	65	100	130
Polysteel Milkman Truck	light blue soft plastic front, cab and frame, light blue steel open cargo section w/nine oversized white plastic milk bottles, 11-3/4" long, 1961	60	95	125
Polysteel Supermarket Delivery	medium blue soft molded-plastic front, hood, cab and frame, steel off-white open cargo section, 13" long, 1959	75	115	150
Pull-N-Ride Baggage Truck	duo-tone horizontal design, light cream upper half, off-white lower half and bumper, 24-1/4" long, 1953	150	225	300
R E A Express Truck	dark green cab-over-engine van body, sliding side doors, double rear doors, white plastic one-piece bumper, 11-1/2" long, 1964	200	300	400
R E A Express Truck	dark green cab-over-engine van body, sliding side doors, double rear doors, white plastic one-piece bumper, no spring suspension, 11-1/2" long, 1965	130	195	260
R E A Express Truck	dark green cab-over-engine van body, sliding side doors, double rear doors, white plastic one-piece bumper, no spring suspension, side doors are embossed "BUDDY L", 11-1/2" long, 1966	125	185	250
Railroad Transfer Rider Delivery Truck	duo-tone horizontal design, yellow upper half, hood top, cab and slatted caro sides, green lower half, small hand truck, two milk cans w/removable lids, 23-1/4" long, 1949	70	100	140
Railroad Transfer Store Door Delivery	duo-tone horizontal design, yellow hood top, cab and upper body, red lower half of hood and body, small hand truck, two metal drums w/coin slots, 23-1/4" long, 1950	90	135	180
Railway Express Truck	dark green or light green screen body, double-bar nickel front bumper, brass radiator knob, red wheels, 25" long, 1930	500	1000	2000
Railway Express Truck	green all-steel hood, cab, frame and high-sides open bady, sides have three horizontal slots in upper back corners, 22" long, 1954	75	115	150
Railway Express Truck	green plastic hood and cab, green steel high-sides open body, frame and bumper, small two-wheel hand truck, steel four-rung barrel skid, 20-3/4" long, 1953	125	185	250
Railway Express Truck	deep green plastic "Diamond T" hood and cab, deep green steel frame and van body w/removable silvery roof, small two-wheel hand truck, steel four-rung barrel skid, 21" long, 1952	200	300	400
Railway Express Truck	yellow and green tractor unit has white skirted fenders and hood sides, green hood top, enclosed cab and chassis, green semi-trailer w/yellow removable roof, 25" long, 1940	330	495	660
Railway Express Truck	black front hood, fenders, seat and low body sides, dark green van body, red chassis, 25" long, 1926	400	800	1600
Railway Express Truck	duo-tone slant design, tractor has silvery and hood sides, green hood top, enclosed cab, green semi-trailer, "Wrigley's Spearmint Gum" poster on trailer sides, 23" long, 1935	400	600	800
Railway Express Truck	duo-tone slant design, tractor unit has white skirted fenders and hood sides, green hood top, enclosed cab and chassis, green semi-trailer w/white removable roof, 25" long, 1939	350	475	700

VEHICLES

NAME	DESCRIPTION	GOOD	EX	MINT
Railway Express Truck	red tractor unit, enclosed square cab, green 12-1/4" long two-wheel semi-trailer van w/removable roof, "Wrigley's Spearmint Gum" poster on trailer sides, 23" long, 1935	375	565	750
Railway Express Truck	duo-tone horizontal design, tractor unit has yellow front, lower door and chassis, green hood top and enclosed upper cab, semi-trailer has yellow lower sides, 25" long, 1941	325	485	650
Ranchero Stake Truck	medium green, white plastic one-piece bumper and grille guard, four-post, four-slat fixed stake sides and cargo section, 14" long, 1963	50	75	100
Rider Dump Truck	duo-tone horizontal design, yellow hood top, upper cab and upper dump body, red front, hood sides, lower doors and lower dump body, no bumper, 21-1/2" long, 1945	160	245	325
Rider Dump Truck	duo-tone horizontal design, yellow hood top, upper cab and upper dump body, red front, hood sides, lower doors and lower dump body, no bumper, 23" long, 1947	75	115	150
Rival Dog Food Delivery Van	cream front, cab and boxy van body, metal drum coin bank w/"RIVAL DOG FOOD" label in blue, red, white and yellow, 16-1/2" long, 1956	160	245	325
Robotoy	black fenders and chassis, red hood and enclosed cab w/small visor, green dump body's front and back are higher than sides, 21-5/8" long, 1932	575	900	1200
Rockin' Giraffe Truck	powder blue hood, cab, and high-sided open-top cargo section, two orange and yellow plastic giraffes, 13-1/4" long, 1967	75	115	150
Ruff-n-Tuff Cement Mixer Truck	yellow snub-nosed cab-over-engine body, frame and water-tank ends, white plastic water tank and mixing drum, white seats, 16" long, 1971	35	55	75
Ruff-n-Tuff Log Truck	yellow snub-nose cab-over-engine, frame and shallow truck bed, black full-width grille, 16" long, 1971	50	75	100
Ryder City Special Delivery Truck Van	duo-tone horizontal design, yellow upper half including hood top and cab, brown removable van roof, warm brown front and lower half of van body, 24-1/2" long, 1949	150	225	300
Ryder Van Lines Trailer	duo-tone slant design, black front and lower hood sides and doors, deep red hood top, enclosed cab and chassis, 35-1/2" long, 1949	350	525	700
Saddle Dump Truck	duo-tone slant design, yellow front, fenders and removable rider seat, red enclosed square cab and dump body, no bumper, 19-1/2" long, 1937	200	300	400
Saddle Dump Truck	duo-tone slant design, yellow front, fenders, lower hood and cab, and removable rider seat, rest of body red, no bumper, 21-1/2" long, 1939	125	185	250
Saddle Dump Truck	duo-tone horizontal design, deep blue hood top, upper cab and upper dump body, orange fenders radiator front lower two-thirds of cab and lower half of dump body, 21-1/2" long, 1941	85	130	175
Sand and Gravel Rider Dump Truck	duo-tone horizontal design, blue lower half, yellow upper half including hoop top and enclosed cab, 24" long, 1950	350	525	700
Sand and Gravel Truck	black body, doorless roofed cab and steering wheel, red chassis and disc wheels w/black hubs, 25-1/2" long, 1926	600	1000	1200
Sand and Gravel Truck	dark or medium green hood, cab, roof lights and skirted body, white or cream dump section, 13-1/2" long, 1949	100	150	200
Sand and Gravel Truck	duo-tone horizontal design, red front, bumper, lower hood, cab sides, chassis and lower dump body sides, white hood top, enclosed cab and upper dump body, 23-3/4" long, 1949	350	525	700
Sand and Gravel Truck	black w/red chassis and wheels, nickel-rim, red-shell headlights, enclosed cab w/opening doors, 25-1/2" long, 1930-32	2000	3000	5000

NAME	DESCRIPTION	GOOD	EX	MINT
Sand Loader and Dump Truck	duo-tone horizontal design, yellow hood top and upper dump blue cab sides, frame and lower dump body, red loader on dump w/black rubber conveyor belt, 24-1/2" long, 1950	175	265	350
Sand Loader and Dump Truck	duo-tone horizontal design, yellow hood top and upper dump blue cab sides, frame and lower dump body, red loader on dump w/black rubber conveyor belt, 24-1/2" long, 1952	60	95	125
Sanitation Service Truck	blue front fenders, hood, cab and chassis, white encllosed dump section and hinged loading hopper, one-piece chrome bumper, no plastic windows in garbage section, 16-1/2" long, 1968	75	115	150
Sanitation Service Truck	blue snub-nose hood, cab and frame, white cargo dump body and rear loading unit, two round plastic headlights, 17" long, 1972	75	115	150
Sanitation Service Truck	blue front fenders, hood, cab and chassis, white encllosed dump section and hinged loading hopper, one-piece chrome bumper, plastic windows in garbage section, 16-1/2" long, 1967	75	150	200
Sears Roebuck Delivery Truck Van	gray/green and off-white, no side doors, 1967	125	200	275
Self-Loading Auto Carrier	medium tan tractor unit, three plastic cars, overall 34" long including loading ramp, 1960	85	130	175
Self-Loading Boat Hauler	pastel blue tractor and semi-trailer w/three 8-1/2" long boats, overall 26-1/2" long, 1962	150	225	350
Self-Loading Boat Hauler	pastel blue tractor and semi-trailer w/three 8-1/2" long boats, no side mirror on truck, overall 26-1/2" long, 1963	150	225	350
Self-Loading Car Carrier	lime green tractor unit, three plastic cars, overall 33-1/2" long including, 1963	75	115	150
Self-Loading Car Carrier	beige/yellow tractor unit, three plastic cars, overall 33-1/2" long including, 1964	60	95	125
Shell Pickup and Delivery	yellow/orange hood and body, open cargo section w/three curved slots toward rear in sides, red coin-slot oil drum w/Shell emblem and lettering, 13-1/4" long, 1953	110	175	225
Shell Pickup and Delivery	reddish orange hood and body, open cargo section w/solid sides, chain across back, red coin-slot oil drum w/Shell emblem and lettering, 13-1/4" long, 1950	135	200	275
Shell Pickup and Delivery	yellow/orange hood and body, open cargo section, three curved slots toward rear in sides, chains across back, red coin-slot oil drum w/Shell emblem and lettering, 13-1/4" long, 1952	125	185	250
Smoke Patrol	lemon yellow body, six wheels, garden hose attaches and water squirts through large chrome swivel-mount water cannon on rear deck, 7" long, 1970	50	75	100
Sprinkler Truck	black front, hood, fenders and cabless open driver's seat, red bumper and chassis, bluish/gray/green water tank, 25" long, 1929	800	1500	2000
Stake Body Truck	black cabless open driver's seat, hood, front fenders and flatbed body, red chassis and five removable stake sections, 25" long, 1921	1000	1500	2000
Stake Body Truck	black cabless open driver's seat, hood, front fenders and flatbed body, red chassis and five removable stake sections, cargo bed w/low sidesboards, drop-down tailgate, 25" long, 1924	1000	1500	2000
Standard Coffee Co. Delivery Truck Van	1966	125	200	275
Standard Oil Tank Truck	duo-tone slant design, white upper cab and hood, red lower cab, grille, fenders and tank, rubber wheels, electric headlights, 26" long, 1936-37	350	500	1000
Stor-Dor Delivery	red hood and body, open cargo body w/four horizontal slots in sides, plated chains across open back, 14-1/2" long, 1955	65	100	175

NAME	DESCRIPTION	GOOD	EX	MINT
Street Sprinkler Truck	black front, hood, front fenders and cabless open driver's seat, red bumper and chassis, bluish/gray/green water tank, 25" long, 1929	700	900	1800
Street Sprinkler Truck	black front, hood, and fenders, open cab, nickel-rim, red-shell headlights, double bar front bumper, bluish/gray/green water tank, six rubber tires, 25" long, 1930-32	800	1000	1900
Sunshine Delivery Truck Van	bright, yellow cab-over-engine van body and opening double rear doors, off-white plastic bumper and under body, 11-1/2" long, 1967	125	200	275
Super Motor Market	duo-tone horizontal design, white hood top, upper cab and high partition in cargo section, yellow/orange lower hood and cab sides, semi-trailer carrying supplies, 21-1/2" long, 1942	300	500	700
Supermarket Delivery	all white w/rubber wheels, enclosed cab, pointed nose, bright metal one-piece grille, 13-3/4" long, 1950	125	185	250
Supermarket Delivery	blue bumper, front, hood, cab and frame, one-piece chrome four-hole grille and headlights, 14-1/2" long, 1956	75	115	150
Tank and Sprinkler Truck	black front, hood, fenders, doorless cab and seat, dark green tank and side racks, black or dark green sprinkler attachment, 26-1/4" long w/sprinkler attachment, 1924	700	900	1700
Teepee Camping Trailer and Wagon	maroon suburban wagon, two-wheel teepee trailer and its beige plastic folding tent, overall 24-1/2" long, 1963	75	175	250
Texaco Tank Truck	red steel GMC 550-series blunt-nose tractor and semi-trailer tank, 25" long, 1959	175	250	400
Tom's Toasted Peanuts Delivery Truck Van	light tan/beige body, no seat or sliding doors, blue bumpers, floor and underbody, 11-1/2" long, 1973	125	200	275
Trail Boss	red, square-corner body w/sloping sides, open cockpit, white plastic seat, 7" long, 1970	40	60	80
Trail Boss	lime green, square-corner body w/sloping sides, open cockpit, yellow plastic seat, 7" long, 1971	35	55	75
Trailer Dump Truck	cream tractor unit w/enclosed cab, dark blue semi-trailer dump body w/high sides and top-hinged opening endgate, no bumper, 20-3/4" long, 1941	75	115	155
Trailer Van Truck	red tractor and van roof, blue bumper, white semi-trailer van, chrome one-piece toothed grille and headlights, white drop-down rear door, 29" long w/tailgate/ramp lowered, 1956	150	225	300
Trailer Van with Tailgate Loader	green high-impacted styrene plastic tractor on steel frame, cream steel detachable semi-trailer van w/green roof and crank operated tailgate, 33" long w/tailgate lowered, 1953	125	185	250
Trailer Van with Tailgate Loader	green steel tractor, bumper, chrome one-piece toothed grille and headlights, cream van w/green roof and tailgate loader, 31-3/4" long, w/tailgate down, 1954	125	185	250
Traveling Zoo	red high side pickup w/yellow plastic triple-cage unit, six compartments w/plastic animals, 13-1/4" long, 1965	85	130	175
Traveling Zoo	snub-nosed yellow body and cab, six red plastic cages w/six plastic zoo animals, 13-1/4" long, 1970	60	95	125
Traveling Zoo	yellow high side pickup w/red plastic triple-cage unit, six compartments w/plastic animals, 13-1/4" long, 1969	65	95	130
Traveling Zoo	red high side pickup w/yellow plastic triple-cage unit, six compartments w/plastic animals, 13-1/4" long, 1967	75	115	150
U.S. Army Half-Track and Howitzer	olive drab, 12-1/2" truck, 9-3/4" gun, overall 22-1/2" long, 1952	125	200	275
U.S. Mail Delivery Truck	blue cab, hood, bumper, frame and removable roof on white van body, 23-1/4" long, 1956	150	300	500

NAME	DESCRIPTION	GOOD	EX	MINT
U.S. Mail Delivery Truck	white upper cab-over-engine, sliding side doors and double rear doors, red belt-line stripe on sides and front, blue lower body, 11-1/2" long, 1964	65	100	200
U.S. Mail Truck	shiny olive green body and bumper, yellow-cream removable van roof, enclosed cab, 22-1/2" long, 1953	225	400	575
United Parcel Delivery Van	duo-tone horizontal design, deep cream upper half w/brown removable roof, chocolate brown front and lower half, 25" long, 1941	250	450	650
Utility Delivery Truck	duo-tone slant design, blue front and lower hood sides, gray hood top, cab and open body w/red and yellow horizontal stripe, 22-3/4" long, 1940	250	450	650
Utility Delivery Truck	duo-tone horizontal design, green upper half including hood top, dark cream lower half, green wheels, red and yellow horizontal stripe, 22-3/4" long, 1941	125	185	250
Utility Dump Truck	duo-tone slant design, red front, lower doord and fenders, gray chassis and enclosed upper cab, royal blue dump body, yellow removable rider seat, 25-1/2" long, 1940	125	185	250
Utility Dump Truck	duo-tone slant design, red front, lower door and fenders, gray chassis, red upper hood, upper enclosed cab and removable rider seat, yellow body, 25-1/2" long, 1941	85	130	175
Van Freight Carriers Trailer	bright blue streanlined tractor and enclosed cab, cream/yellow semi-trailer van, removable silvery roof, 22" long, 1949	65	100	135
Van Freight Carriers Trailer	red streamlined tractor, bright blue enclosed cab, cream/yellow semi-trailer van, white removable van roof, 22" long, 1952	55	85	115
Van Freight Carriers Trailer	red streamlined tractor, bright blue enclosed cab, light cream/white semi-trailer van w/removable white roof, 22" long, 1953	125	185	250
Wild Animal Circus	red tractor unit and semi-trailer, three cages w/plastic elephant, lion, tiger, 26" long, 1966	150	225	300
Wild Animal Circus	red tractor unit and semi-trailer, three cages w/six plastic animals, 26" long, 1967	110	175	225
Wild Animal Circus	red tractor unit and semi-trailer, trailer cage doors lighter than body, 26" long, 1970	100	150	200
Wrecker Truck	black front, hood, and fenders, open cab, four rubber tires, red wrecker body, 26-1/2" long, 1930	800	1000	2500
Wrecker Truck	duo-tone slant design, red upper cab, hood, and boom, white lower cab, grille, fenders, body, rubber wheels, electric headlights, removable rider seat, 31" long, 1936	250	450	700
Wrecker Truck	black open cab, red chassis and bed, disc wheels, 26-1/2" long, 1928-29	700	1000	2000
Wrigley Express Truck	forest green w/chrome one-piece, three-bar grille and headlights, "Wrigley's Spearmint Gum" poster on sides, 16-1/2" long, 1955	135	200	275
Zoo-A-Rama	greenish yellow four-wheel trailer cage, matching Colt Sportsliner w/white top, three plastic animals, 20-3/4" long, 1969	85	130	175
Zoo-A-Rama	lime green Colt Sportsliner w/four-wheel trailer cage, cage contains plastic tree, monkeys and bears, 20-3/4" long, 1967	100	150	200
Zoo-A-Rama	sand yellow four-wheel trailer cage, matching Colt Sportsliner w/white top, three plastic animals, 20-3/4" long, 1968	100	150	200

VEHICLES

NAME	DESCRIPTION	GOOD	EX	MINT
Adams Drag-Star	orange body, red nose, gold engines, chrome pipes and hood panels, Whizz Wheels, 4-3/8"	20	30	45
Adams Probe 16	one-piece body, blue sliding canopy; metallic burgundy, or metallic lime/gold w/and without racing stripes, Whizz Wheels, 3-5/8"	15	25	40
Agricultural Set	1962-64 issue: #55 Fordson Tractor, #51 Tipping Trailer, #438 Land Rover, #101 Flat Trailer w/#1487 Milk Churns; 1965-66 issue: #60 Fordson Tractor, #62 Tipping Trailer, #438 Land Rover, red #100 Dropside Trailer w/#1487 Milk Churns	280	450	1000
Agricultural Set	No. 69 Massey Ferguson tractor, No. 62 trailer, No. 438 Land Rover, No. 484 Livestock Truck w/pigs, No. 71 harrow, No. 1490 skip and churns; with accessories: four calves, farmland, dog and six sacks	120	180	400
Agricultural Set	No. 55 Tractor, No. 56 Tipping Trailer, Silo and mustard yellow conveyor	60	90	130
Alfa Romeo P33 Pininfarina	white body, gold or black spoiler, red seats, Whizz Wheels, 3-5/8"	16	24	45
All Winners Set	first issue: #310 Corvette, #312 Jaguar XKE, #314 Ferrari 250LM, #324 Marcos, #325 Mustang; second issue: #312 Jaguar XKE, #314 Ferrari 250LM, #264 Toronado, #327 MGB, #337 Corvette	100	240	450
Allis-Chalmers AFC 60 Fork Lift	yellow body, white engine hood, w/driver, tan pallets and red conatiners, 4-3/8"	15	20	45
AMC Pacer	metallic red body, white Pacer X decals, working hatch, clear windows, light yellow interior, chrome bumpers and wheels, 4-3/4"	15	20	50
AMC Pacer Rescue Car	chrome roll bars and red roof lights, white w/black engine hood; w/or without Secours decal, 4-7/8"	10	15	30
American LaFrance Ladder Truck	first issue: red cab, trailer, ladder rack and wheels; chrome decks and chassis, yellow plastic three-piece operable ladder, rubber tires, six firemen figures, issued 1968-70; second issue: same as first issue except for unpainted wheels, issued 1970-72;	60	90	150
AMX 30D Recovery Tank	olive body w/black plastic turret and gun, accessories and three figures, 6-7/8"	35	50	80
Army Heavy Equipment Transporter	olive cab and trailer w/white U.S. Army decals w/red interior and driver, 9-1/2"	70	105	325
Army Troop Transporter	olive w/white U.S. Army decals, 5-1/2"	70	105	175
Aston Martin DB4	white top w/aqua green sides, yellow plastic interior, racing Nos. 1, 3 or 7, 3-3/4"	50	75	125
Aston Martin DB4	red or yellow body w/working hood, detailed engine, clear windows, plastic interior, silver lights, grille, license plate and bumpers, red taillights, rubber tires, smooth or cast spoked wheels; working scoop on early models, 3-3/4"	45	65	110
Austin A40	one-piece light blue or red body w/black roof and clear windows, smooth wheels, rubber tires, 3-1/8"	35	50	100
Austin A40-Mechanical	friction motor, red body w/black roof, 3-1/8"	55	75	170
Austin A60 Driving School	medium blue body w/silver trim, left hand drive steering wheel, steering control on left; came with five lanquage leeflet (US version of No. 236), 3-3/4"	45	65	160
Austin A60 Motor School	light blue body w/silver trim, red interior, single body casting, right hand drive steering wheel, two figures, steering control on roof; came with "Highway Patrol leaflet, 3-3/4"	45	65	120
Austin Cambridge	available in gray, green/gray, silver/green, aqua, green/cream, two-tone green, smooth wheels, 3-1/2"	40	60	120
Austin Cambridge-Mechanical	fly-wheel motor, available in orange, cream, light or dark gray, cream, or silver over metallic blue, smooth wheels, 3-1/2"	50	75	150
Austin Healey	blue body w/cream seats, shaped hubs	75	125	250
Austin London Taxi	black body w/yellow plastic interior, w/or without driver, shaped hubs, smooth or rubber tires, 3-7/8"	36	55	90
Austin London Taxi	black body w/two working doors, light brown interior, Whizz Wheels, 4-5/8"	15	20	35
Austin London Taxi/Reissue	updated version w/Whizz Wheels, black or maroon body, 3-7/8"	15	20	35

NAME	DESCRIPTION	GOOD	EX	MINT
Austin Mini Countryman	turquoise body, jeweled headlights, opening rear doors, chrome roofrack w/two surfboards, shaped or cast wheels, w/surfer figure, 3-1/8"	55	80	150
Austin Mini Van	w/two working rear doors, clear windows, metallic deep green body, 3-1/8"	40	60	100
Austin Mini-Metro	blue or red body w/plastic interior, working rear hatch and doors, clear windows, folding seats, chrome headlights, or ange taillights, black plastic base, grille, bumpers, Whizz Wheels, 3-1/2"	18	27	45
Austin Mini-Metro Datapost	white body, blue roof, hood and trim, red plastic interior, hepolite and #77 decals, working hatch and doors, clear windows, folding seats, chrome headlights, orange taillights, Whizz Wheels, 3-1/2"	15	18	30
Austin Police Mini Van	dark blue body w/policeman and dog figures, white police decals, opening rear doors, gray plastic antenna, 3-1/8"	50	75	175
Austin Seven Mini	red or yellow body, yellow interior, silver bumpers, grille and headlights, orange taillights, 2-3/4"	50	75	125
Austin Seven Mini	primrose yellow, red interior, rare, 2-3/4"	100	200	325
Austin-Healey	cream body w/red seats or red body w/cream seats, 3-1/4"	50	75	125
Avengers Set	white Lotus, red or green Bentley; Jonathan Steed and Emma Peel figures w/three umbrellas	260	390	800
Basil Brush's Car	red body, dark yellow chassis, gold lamps and dash, Basil Brush figure, red plastic wheels, plastic tires; w/"Laugh Tapes" and soundbox, 3-5/8"	70	105	200
Batbike	black body, one-piece body, black and red plastic parts, gold engine and exhaust pipes, clear windshield, chrome stand, black plastic five-spoked wheels, Batman figure and decals, 4-1/4"	40	60	125
Batboat	black plastic boat, red seats, fin and jet, blue windshield, Batman and Robin figures, gold cast trailer, tinplate fin cover, cast wheels, plastic tires, w/plastic towhook for Batmobile, 5-1/8"	60	90	175
Batboat	black plastic boat w/Batman and Robin figures, small decals on fin and on side of boat, chain link Whizz Wheels on trailer, 5-1/8"	30	45	100
Batcopter	black body w/yellow/red/black decals, red rotors, Batman figure, operable winch, 5-1/2"	26	39	95
Batman Set	three vehicle set: No. 267 Batmobile, No. 107 Batboat w/trailer and No. 925 Batcopter, Whizz Wheels on trailer	150	300	800
Batmobile	chrome hubs w/black plastic tires, red bat logos on door, light red interior, regular wheels, gold tow hook, plastic rockets, gold headlights and rocket control, tinted canopy w/chrome support, 5"	80	120	200
Batmobile	matte black (rare) or gloss black body, gold hubs, bat logos on door, maroon interior, black body, plastic rockets, gold headlights and rocket control, tinted canopy, working front chain cutter, no tow hook, rubber tires, 5"	200	300	550
Batmobile	same as first issue except for gloss black body, gold towhook	200	300	500
Batmobile	chrome hubs w/red bat logos on door, maroon interior, red plastic tires, gold tow hook, plastic rockets, gold headlight and rocket control, tinted canopy w/chrome support, chain cutter, 5"	140	200	400
Batmobile, Batboat and Trailer	first and second versions: red bat hubs on wheels, 1967-72; red tires and chrome wheels	240	360	650
Batmobile, Batboat and Trailer	third and fourth versions: 1973; black tires, big decals on boat, 1974-76; chrome wheels, boat decals, Whizz Wheels on trailer	120	175	350
Beach Buggy & Sailboat	purple No. 381 buggy, yellow trailer and red/white boat	20	30	55
Beast Carrier Trailer	red chassis, yellow body and tailgate, four plastic calves, red plastic wheels, black rubber tires, 4-1/2"	24	36	60
Beatles' Yellow Submarine	yellow and white body, working red hatches w/two Beatles in each, 5"	180	270	700
Beatles' Yellow Submarine	yellow and white hatches, red pinstripes, 5"	200	500	1000

VEHICLES

NAME	DESCRIPTION	GOOD	EX	MINT
Bedford AA Road Service Van	dark yellow body in two versions: divided windshield, 1957-59; single windshield, 1960-62, 3-5/8"	50	75	125
Bedford Army Tanker	olive cab and tanker, w/white U.S. Army and "No Smoking" decals, 7-3/8"	140	210	375
Bedford Articulated Horse Box	cast cab, lower body and three working ramps, yellow interior, plastic upper body, w/horse and Newmarket Racing Stables decals, dark metallic green or light green body w/orange or yellow upper, four horses, 10"	32	48	80
Bedford Car Transporter	black die cast cab base w/blue "S" cab, yellow semi trailer, blue lettering decals, 10-1/4"	100	200	350
Bedford Car Transporter	red "TK" cab w/blue lower and light green upper trailer, working ramp, yellow interior, clear windows, white wording and Corgi dog decals, 10-5/8"	60	90	150
Bedford Car Transporter	red cab, pale green upper and blue lower semi-trailer, white decals, lower tailgate, clear windshield, 10-1/4" long^	70	105	175
Bedford Carrimore Low Loader	red or yellow "S" cab, metallic blue semi trailer and tailgate; smooth and/or shaped wheels, 8-1/2"	60	90	150
Bedford Carrimore Low Loader	yellow "TK" cab and working tailgate, red trailer, clear windows, red interior, suspension, shaped wheels, rubber tires, 9-1/2"	90	190	325
Bedford Corgi Toys Van	yellow upper/blue lower body, 3-1/4" long^	100	225	400
Bedford Corgi Toys Van	Corgi Toys decals, w/either yellow body/blue roof, 3-1/4"	60	90	175
Bedford Daily Express Van	dark blue body w/white Daily Express decals, divided windshield, smooth wheels, rubber tires, 3-1/4"	60	90	150
Bedford Dormobile	two versions and several colors: divided windshield w/cream, green or metallic maroon body; or single windshield w/yellow body/blue roof w/shaped or smooth wheels, 3-1/4"	50	75	125
Bedford Dormobile-Mechanical	friction motor, dark metallic red or turquoise body, smooth wheels, 3-1/4"	60	90	175
Bedford Evening Standard Van	black body/silver roof or black lower body/silver upper body and roof, Evening Standard decals, smooth wheels, 3-1/4"	55	80	130
Bedford Fire Tender	divided windshield, red or green body, each w/different decals, smooth or shaped hubs, 3-1/4"	60	90	175
Bedford Fire Tender	single windshield version, red body w/either black ladders and smooth wheels or unpainted ladders and shaped wheels, 3-1/4"	60	90	150
Bedford Fire Tender-Mechanical	friction motor, red body w/Fire Dept. decals, diveided whinshield. Silver or black ladder, smooth or shaped hubs, 3-1/4"	70	105	175
Bedford KLG Van-Mechanical	w/friction motor, in either red body w/KLG Spark Plugs decals, smooth hubs, 3-1/4"	70	125	285
Bedford Military Ambulance	clear front and white rear windows, olive body w/Red Cross decals, w/or without suspension, 3-1/4"	56	84	140
Bedford Milk Tanker	light blue "S" cab and lower semi, white upper tank, w/blue/white milk decals, shaped wheels, rubber tires, 7-1/2"	100	150	275
Bedford Milk Tanker	light blue "TK" cab and lower semi, white upper tank w/blue/white milk decals, 7-3/4"	110	165	375
Bedford Mobilgas Tanker	red "TK" cab and tanker w/red, white and blue Mobilgas decals, shaped wheels, rubber tires, 7-3/4"	100	175	350
Bedford Mobilgas Tanker	red "S" cab w/Mobilgas decals, shaped wheels, rubber tires, 7-5/8"	100	150	250
Bedford Tanker	red cab w/black chassis, plastic tank w/chrome catwalk, Corgi Chemco decals, 7-1/2"	15	20	35
Bedford TK Tipper Truck	red cab and chassis w/yellow tipper, side mirrors, 4-1/8"	26	39	65
Bedford Utilecon Ambulance	divided windshield, cream body w/red/white/blue decals, smooth wheels, 3-1/4"	50	75	125
Beep Beep London Bus	battery-operated working horn, red body, black windows, BTA decals, 4-3/4"	26	39	65
Belgian Police Range Rover	white body, working doors, red interior, Belgian Police decal; includes policeman, evergency signs, 4"	22	33	55

VEHICLES

NAME	DESCRIPTION	GOOD	EX	MINT
Bell Army Helicopter	two-piece olive/tan camo body, clear canopy, olive green rotors, U.S. Army decals, 5-1/4"	24	36	60
Bell Rescue Helicopter	two-piece blue body w/working doors, red interior, yellow plastic floats, black rotors, white N428 decals, 5-3/4"	20	30	50
Bentley Continental	two-tone green or black and silver bodies, w/red interior, clear windows, chrome grille and bumpers, jewel headlights, red jeweled taillights, suspension, shaped wheels, gray rubber tires, 4-1/4"	45	65	110
Bentley T Series	red body, cream interior; working hood, trunk and doors; clear windows, folding seats, chrome bumper/grille, jewel headlights, Whizz Wheels, 4-1/2"	36	55	90
Berliet Articulated Horse Box	bronze cab and lower semi body, cream chassis, white upper body, black interior, three working ramps, National Racing Stables decals, horse figures, chrome wheels, 10-7/8"	30	45	75
Berliet Container Truck	blue cab and semi fenders; white cab chassis and semi flatbed; each with United States Lines label	30	45	75
Berliet Dolphinarium Truck	yellow and blue cab and trailer, clear plastic tank; includes two dolphins and a girl trainer	56	84	175
Berliet Fruehauf Dumper	yellow cab, fenders and dumper; black cab and semi chassis; plastic orange dumper body; or dark orange, black interior, 11-1/4"	30	45	75
Berliet Holmes Wrecker	red cab and bed, blue rear body, white chassis, black interior, two gold booms and hooks, yellow dome light, driver, amber lenses and red/white/blue stripes, 5"	30	45	75
Bertone Barchetta Runabout	yellow and black body, black interior, amber windows, die cast air foil, suspension, red/yellow Runabout decals, Whizz Wheels, 3-1/4"	15	22	45
Bertone Shake Buggy	clear windows, green interior, gold engine, four variations: yellow upper/white lower body or metallic mauve upper/white lower body w/spoked or solid chrome wheels, 3-3/8"	15	22	45
BL Roadtrain and Trailers	white and orange cab, dark blue freighter semi body w/Yorkie Chocolate labels and tanker semi body w/Gulf label; includes playmat	16	24	40
Bloodhound Launching Ramp	military green ramp	34	51	85
Bloodhound Loading Trolley	white and yellow missle, red rubber nose cone	40	60	100
Bloodhound Missile	white and yellow missle, red rubber nose cone	70	105	175
Bloodhound Missile on Trolley	white and yellow missle, red rubber nose cone; military green trolley, rubber tires	120	180	300
Bloodhound Missle and Launching Platform	white and yellow missle, red rubber nose cone; military green ramp	110	165	275
BMC Mini-Cooper	white body, black working hood, trunk, two doors, red interior, clear windows, orange/black stripes and #177 decals, suspension, Whizz Wheels, 3"	30	45	95
BMC Mini-Cooper Magnifique	metallic blue or olive green body w/working doors, hood and trunk, clear windows and sunroof, cream interior w/folding seats, jewel headlights, cast detailed wheels, plastic tires, 2-7/8"	34	65	115
BMC Mini-Cooper S	bright yellow body, red plastic interior, chrome plastic roof rack w/two spare wheels, clear windshield, one-piece body silver grille, bumpers, headlights, red taillights, suspension, Whizz Wheels, 3"	45	65	110
BMC Mini-Cooper S "Sun/RAC" Rally Car	red body, white roof w/six jewel headlights, RAC Rally and #21 decals, 2-7/8"	90	180	350
BMC Mini-Cooper S Rally	red body, white roof, chrome roof rack w/two spare tires, Monte Carlo Rally and #177 decals, w/shaped wheels/rubber tires or cast detailed wheels/plastic tires, 2-7/8"	40	90	180
BMC Mini-Cooper S Rally Car	red body, white roof, five jewel headlights, Monte Carlo Rally decals w/either #52 (1965) or #2 (1966); rare w/drivers' autographs on roof, 2-7/8"	100	275	500
BMW M1	yellow body, black plastic base, rear panel and interior, white seats, clear windshield, multicolored stripes, lettering and #25 decal, Goodyear label, 5"	15	20	35

NAME	DESCRIPTION	GOOD	EX	MINT
BMW M1 BASF	red body, white trim w/black/white BASF and #80 decals, 4-7/8"	15	18	30
Breakdown Truck	red body, black plastic boom w/gold hook, yellow interior, amber windows, black/yellow decals, Whizz Wheels, 3-7/8"	15	18	30
British Leyland Mini 1000	red interior, chrome lights, grille and bumper, #8 decal; three variations: silver body w/decals, 1978-82; silver body, no decals; orange body w/extra hood stripes, 1983, 3-1/4"	16	24	40
British Leyland Mini 1000	metallic blue body, working doors, black base, clear windows, white interior, silver lights, grille and bumper, Union Jack decal on roof, Whizz Wheels, 3-3/8"	18	27	45
British Racing Cars	set of three cars, three versions: blue No. 152 Lotus, green No. 151 BRM, green No. 150 Vanwall, all w/smooth wheels, 1959; same cars w/shaped wheels, 1960-61; red Vanwall, green BRM and blue Lotus, 1963, each set	140	210	475
BRM Racing Car	silver seat, dash and pipes, smooth wheels, rubber tires, in three versions: dark green body, 1958-60; light green body w/driver and various number decals 1961-65; light green body, no driver, 3-1/2"	50	75	145
Buck Rogers Starfighter	white body w/yellow plastic wings, amber windows, blue jets, color decal, Buck and Wilma figures, 6-1/2"	32	48	90
Buick and Cabin Cruiser	three versions: light blue, dark metallic blue or gold metallic No. 245 Buick, red boat trailer, dolphin cabin cruiser w/two figures	80	120	280
Buick Police Car	metallic blue body w/white stripes and Police decals, chrome light bar w/red lights, orange taillights, chrome spoke wheels, w/two policemen, 4-1/8"	18	27	45
Buick Riviera	metallic gold, dark blue, pale blue or gold body, red interior, gray steering wheel, and tow hook, clear windshield, chrome grille and bumpers, suspension, Tan-o-lite tail and headlights, spoked wheels and rubber tires, 4-1/4"	30	45	75
Cadillac Superior Ambulance	battery-operated warning lights, red lower/cream upper body, 4-1/2"	60	90	150
Cadillac Superior Ambulance	battery-operated warning lights, white lower body/blue upper body, 4-1/2" long^	60	90	150
Cafe Racer Motorcycle		15	18	30
Campbell Bluebird	blue body, red exhaust, clear windshield, driver, in two versions: black plastic wheels, 1960; metal wheels and rubber tires, 5-1/8"	56	84	175
Canadian Mounted Police Set	blue No. 421 Land Rover w/Police sign on roof and RCMP decals, No. 102 trailer; includes mounted Policeman	30	50	100
Captain America Jetmobile	6" white body, metallic blue chassis, black nose cone, red shield and jet, red-white-blue Captain America decals, light blue seats and driver, chrome wheels, red tires	24	36	60
Captain Marvel Porsche	white body, gold parts, red seat, driver, red/yellow/blue Captain Marvel decals, black plastic base, gold wheels, 4-3/4"	20	30	60
Car Transporter & Cars	Scammell tri-deck transporter w/six cars: Ford Capri, the Saint's Volvo, Pontiac Firebird, Lancia Fulvia, MGC GT, Marcos 3 Litre, each with Whizz Wheels; value is for complete set	200	400	900
Car Transporter and Four Cars	two versions: No. 1105 Bedford TK Transposter w/Fiat 1800, Renault Floride, Mercedes 230SE and Ford Consul, 1963-65; No. 1105 Bedford TK Transposter w/Chevy Corvair, VW Ghia, Volvo P-1800 and Rover 2000, 1966 only; value is for individual complete set	200	300	700
Carrimore and Cars	Ford "H" series Transporter and six cars; there are several car variations; sold by mail order only	240	360	700
Carrimore Car Transporter	three versions: No. 1101 Bedford Carrimore Transporter w/Riley, Jaguar, Austin Healey and Triumph, 1957-60; No. 1101 Bedford Carrimore Transporter w/four American cars, 1959; No. 1101 Bedford Carrimore Transporter w/Triumph, Mini, Citroen and Plymouth, 19	300	450	800

VEHICLES

CORGI

NAME	DESCRIPTION	GOOD	EX	MINT
Caterpillar Tractor	lime green body w/black or gray rubber treads, gray plastic seat, driver figure, controls, stacks, 4-1/4"	70	105	250
Centurion Mark III Tank	tan and brown camouflage or olive drab body, rubber tracks; includes twelve shells	30	45	75
Centurion Tank and Transporter	No. 901 olive tank and No. 1100 transporter	55	80	130
Chevrolet Astro I	dark metallic green/blue body w/working rear door, cream interior w/two passengers, in two versions: gold wheels w/red plastic hubs or Whizz wheels, 4-1/8"	18	40	85
Chevrolet Camaro SS	metallic gold body w/two working doors, black roof and stripes, red interior, take-off wheels, 4"	30	45	75
Chevrolet Camaro SS	blue or turquoise body w/white stripe, cream interior, working doors, white plastic top, clear windshield, folding seats, silver air intakes, red taillights, black grille and headlights, suspension, Whizz Wheels, 4"	30	45	95
Chevrolet Caprice Classic	working doors and trunk, whitewall tires, two versions: light metallic green body w/green interior or silver on blue body w/brown interior, 5-7/8"	24	36	60
Chevrolet Caprice Classic	white upper body, red sides w/red/white/blue stripes and #43 decals, tan interior, STP labels, 6"	24	36	60
Chevrolet Caprice Fire Chief Car	red body, red-white-orange decals, chrome roof bar, opaque black windows, red dome light, chrome bumpers, grille and headlights, orange taillights, Fire Dept. and Fire Chief decals, chrome wheels; includes working siren and dome light, 5-3/4"	28	42	70
Chevrolet Caprice Police Car	black body w/white roof, doors and trunk, red interior, silver light bar, Police decals, 5-7/8"	20	30	50
Chevrolet Caprice Taxi	orange body w/red interior, white roof sign, Taxi and TWA decals, 5-7/8"	20	30	50
Chevrolet Charlie's Angels Van	light rose-mauve body w/Charlie's Angels decals, in two versions: either solid or spoked chrome wheels, 4-5/8"	15	30	55
Chevrolet Coca-Cola Van	red body, white trim, w/Coca Cola logos, 4-5/8"	15	20	35
Chevrolet Corvair	either blue or pale-blue body w/yellow interior and working hood, detailed engine, clear windows, silver bumpers, headlights and trim, red taillights, rear window blind, shaped wheels, rubber tires, 3-3/4"	36	55	90
Chevrolet Impala	pink body, yellow plastic interior, clear windows, silver headlights, bumpers, grille and trim, suspension, die cast base w/rubber tires; a second version has a blue body w/red or yellow interior and smooth or shaped hubs, 4-1/4"	50	75	125
Chevrolet Impala	tan body, cream interior, gray steering wheel, clear windshields, chrome bumpers, grille, headlights, suspension, red taillights, shaped wheels and rubber tires, 4-1/4"	50	75	125
Chevrolet Impala Fire Chief	w/Fire Chief decal on hood, yellow interior w/driver, red on white body w/either round or recangular "Fire Chief" decals on doors, spun or cast wheels, 4"	55	80	130
Chevrolet Impala Fire Chief	red body, yellow interior, w/four white doors, w/round either shield or rectangular decals on two doors; includes two fireman, 4-1/8"	55	80	130
Chevrolet Impala Police Car	black lower body and roof, white upper body, yellow interior w/two policemen, Police and Police Patrol decals on doors and hood, 4"	55	80	130
Chevrolet Impala Taxi	light orange body, base w/hexagonal panel under rear axle and smooth wheels, or two raised lines and shaped wheels, one-piece body, clear windows, plastic interior, silver grille, headlights and bumpers; smooth or shaped spun wheels w/rubber tires, 4-1	50	75	125
Chevrolet Impala Yellow Cab	red body, yellow upper, red interior w/driver, white roof sign, red decals, 4"	80	120	200
Chevrolet Kennel Club Van	white upper, red lower body, working tailgate and rear windows, green interior, four dog figures, kennel club decals; shaped spun or detailed cast wheels, rubber tires, 4"	56	84	140

VEHICLES

Beatles' Yellow Submarine, No. 803-A, Corgi, 1969-70

Cadillac Superior Ambulance, No. 437-A, 1962-68, Corgi. Photo Courtesy Mark Arruda

Chevrolet Charlie's Angels Van, No. 434-B, 1977-80, Corgi

NAME	DESCRIPTION	GOOD	EX	MINT
Chevrolet Rough Rider Van	yellow body w/working rear doors, cream interior, amber windows, Rough Rider decals, 4-5/8"	15	18	30
Chevrolet Spider-Van	dark blue body w/Spider-Man decals, in two versions: w/either spoke or solid wheels, 4-5/8"	26	39	65
Chevrolet State Patrol Car	black body, State Patrol decals, smooth wheels w/hexagonal panel or raised lines and shaped wheels, yellow plastic interior, gray antenna, clear windows, silver bumpers, grille, headlights and trim, rubber tires, 4"	50	75	125
Chevrolet Superior Ambulance	white body, orange roof and stripes, two working doors, clear windows, red interior w/patient on stretcher and attendant, Red Cross decals, 4-3/4"	30	45	75
Chevrolet Vanatic Van	off white body w/Vanatic decals, 4-5/8"	10	15	25
Chevrolet Vantastic Van	black body w/Vantastic decals, 4-5/8"	10	15	25
Chieftain Medium Tank	olive drab body, black tracks, Union Jack labels; includes twelve shells	30	45	75
Chipperfield Bedford Giraffe Transporter	red "TK" Bedford truck w/blue giraffe box w/Chipperfield decal, two giraffes, shaped or detailed wheels	60	90	175
Chipperfield Circus Cage Wagon	red body, yellow chassis, smooth or spun hubs; includes lions, tigers or polar bears	56	84	140
Chipperfield Circus Chevrolet Performing Poodles Van	blue upper body and tailgate, red lower body and base, clear windshield, pale blue interior w/poodles in back and ring of poodles and trainer, plastic tires, 4"	160	240	550
Chipperfield Circus Crane and Cage	No. 114 crane truck, cage w/rhinocerous, red and blue trailer w/three animal cages and animals; very rare gift set	400	700	2000
Chipperfield Circus Crane and Cage Wagon	No. 1121 crane truck, No. 1123 cage wagon and accessories	150	225	375
Chipperfield Circus Horse Transporter	red Bedford "TK" cab, red cover, blue upper horse trailer, three wheel variations; includes six horses	80	120	235
Chipperfield Circus Karrier Booking Office	red body, light blue roof, clear windows, tin lithographed interior, circus decals, smooth or shaped wheels, rubber tires, 3-5/8"	105	165	325
Chipperfield Circus Land Rover and Elephant Cage	red No. 438 Range Rover w/blue canopy, Chipperfields Circus decal on canopy, burnt orange No. 607 elephant cage on red bed trailer	90	135	275
Chipperfield Circus Menagerie Transporter	Scammell Handyman MKIII red/blue cab, blue trailer w/three animal cages, two lions, two tigers and two bears	120	180	350
Chipperfield Circus Scammell Crane Truck	red upper cab and rear body, light blue lower cab, crane base and winch crank housing, red interior, tow hook, jewel headlights, 8"	175	275	450
Chipperfield Circus Set	vehicle and accessory set in two versions: w/No. 426 Booking Office	380	600	1300
Chipperfield Circus Set	vehicle and accessory set w/#503 Giraffe Truck	340	500	1000
Chipperfield Land Rover Circus Vehicle	red body, yellow interior, blue rear and speakers, revolving clown, chimp figures, Chipperfield decals, 3-1/2"	60	90	175
Chitty Chitty Bang Bang	metallic copper body, dark red interior and spoked wheels, four figures, black chassis w/silver running boards, silver hood, horn, brake, dash, tail and headlights, gold radiator, red and orange wings, handbrake operates side wings, 6-1/4"	180	270	425
Chopper Squad Helicopter	blue and white body, Sure Rescue decals	20	30	50
Chopper Squad Rescue Set	blue No. 919 Jeep w/Chopper Squad decal and red/white boat w/Surf Rescue decal, No. 927 Helicopter	40	60	100
Chrysler Imperial Convertible	red body w/gray base, working hood, trunk and doors, golf bag in trunk, detailed engine, clear windshield, aqua interior, driver, chrome bumpers, 4-1/4"	50	90	160
Chrysler Imperial Convertible	red body w/gray base, working hood, trunk and doors, golf bag in trunk, detailed engine, clear windshield, aqua interior, driver, chrome bumpers, 4-1/4"	45	65	110
Chubb Pathfinder Crash Tender	red body, Emergency Unit decals, working water pump	45	65	110

VEHICLES

NAME	DESCRIPTION	GOOD	EX	MINT
Chubb Pathfinder Crash Truck	red body w/either "Airport Fire Brigade" or "New York Airport" decals, upper and lower body, gold water cannon unpainted and sirens, clear windshield, yellow interior, black steering wheel, chrome plastic deck, silver lights; w/working pump and siren, 9	60	90	150
Circus Crane Truck	red body, embossed blue logo, tinplate boom, blue wheels	80	120	225
Circus Human Cannonball Truck	red and blue body; w/Marvo figure	30	45	75
Circus Land Rover and Trailer	yellow/red No. 421 Land Rover w/Pinder-Jean Richard decals; accessories include blue loudspeakers and figures	30	50	90
Citroen 2CV Charleston	yellow/black or maroon/black body versions w/opening hood, 4-1/8"	15	18	30
Citroen Alpine Rescue Safari	white body, light blue interior, red roof and rear hatch, yellow roof rack and skis, clear windshield, man and dog, gold die cast bobsled, Alpine Rescue decals, 4"	80	150	375
Citroen DS 19 Rally	light blue body, white roof, yellow interior, four jewel headlights, Monte Carlo Rally and #75 decals, w/antena, 4"	70	105	175
Citroen DS19	one-piece body in several colors, clear windows, silver lights, grille and bumpers, smooth wheels, rubber tires: colors: red, metallic green w/black roof, yellow w/red roof, 4"	56	84	140
Citroen Dyane	metallic yellow or green body, black roof and interior, working rear hatch, clear windows, black base and tow bar, silver bumpers, grille and headlights, red taillights, marching duck and French flag decals, suspension, chrome wheels, 4-1/2"	15	18	30
Citroen ID-19 Safari	orange body w/red/brown or red/green luggage on roof rack, green/brown interior, working hatch, two passengers, Wildlife Preservation decals, 4"	40	60	100
Citroen Le Dandy Coupe	metallic maroon body and base, yellow interior, working trunk and two doors, clear windows, plastic interior, folding seats, chrome grille and bumpers, jewel headlights, red taillights, suspension, spoked wheels, rubber tires, 4"	50	75	125
Citroen Le Dandy Coupe	metallic dark blue hood, sides and base, plastic aqua interior, white roof and trunk lid, clear windows, folding seats, chrome grille and bumpers, jewel headlights, red taillights, suspension, spoked wheels, rubber tires, 4"	70	105	175
Citroen SM	metallic lime gold w/chrome wheels or mauve body w/spoked wheels, pale blue interior and lifting hatch cover, working rear hatch and two doors, chrome inner drs., window frames, bumpers, grille, amber headlights, red taillights, Whizz Wheels, 4-3/16"	16	24	40
Citroen Tour de France Car	red body, yellow interior and rear bed, clear windshield and headlights, driver, black plastic rack w/four bicycle wheels, swiveling team manager figure w/megaphone in back of car, Paramount and Tour de France decals, Whizz Wheels, 4-1/4"	40	60	100
Citroen Winter Olympics Car	white body, blue roof and hatch, blue interior, red roof rack w/yellow skis, gold sled w/rider, skier, gold Grenoble Olympiade decals on car roof, 4-1/8"	70	105	200
Citroen Winter Sports Safari	white body in three versions: two w/Corgi Ski Club decals and either w/or without roof ski rack, or one w/1964 Winter Olympics decals, 4"	56	84	140
Coast Guard Jaguar XJ12C	blue and white body, Coast Guard laels, 3-1/4"	18	27	45
Combine, Tractor and Trailer	set of three: #1111 combine, #50 Massey Ferguson tractor, and #51 trailer	110	185	350
Commer 3/4 Ton Police Bus	battery operated working dome light, in several color combinations of dark or light metallic blue or green bodies, various foreign issues, 3-1/2"	45	65	110
Commer 3/4-Ton Ambulance	in either white or cream body, red interior, blue dome light, red Ambulance decals, shaped wheels, 3-1/2"	36	55	90
Commer 3/4-Ton Milk Float	white cab w/either light or dark blue body, w/CO-OP decals, 3-1/2"	40	80	160

VEHICLES

NAME	DESCRIPTION	GOOD	EX	MINT
Commer 3/4-Ton Milk Float	white cab w/either light or dark blue body, 3-1/2"	32	48	80
Commer 3/4-Ton Pickup	either red cab w/orange canopy, yellow interior, Trans-o-Lites, 3-1/2"	30	45	75
Commer 3/4-Ton Van	either dark blue body w/Hammonds decals (1971) or white body w/CO-OP decals (1970), both with cast spoked wheels w/plastic tires, 3-1/2"	45	90	180
Commer 5-Ton Dropside Truck	either blue or red cab, both w/cream rear body, sheet metal tow hook, smooth or shaped wheels, rubber tires, 4-5/8"	40	60	110
Commer 5-Ton Platform Truck	either yellow or metallic blue cab w/silver body, smooth or shaped wheels, 4-5/8"	40	60	120
Commer Holiday Mini Bus	white upper body w/orange lower body, white interior, clear windshield, silver bumpers, grille and headlights, Holiday Camp Special decal, roof rack, two working rear doors, 3-1/2"	30	60	110
Commer Military Ambulance	olive drab body, blue rear windows and dome light, driver, Red Cross decals, 3-5/8"	50	75	125
Commer Military Police Van	olive drab body, barred rear windows, white MP decals, driver, 3-5/8"	55	80	130
Commer Mobile Camera Van	metallic blue lower body and roof rack, white upper body, two working rear doors, black camera on gold tripod, cameraman, 3-1/2"	60	90	175
Commer Refrigerator Van	either light or dark blue cab, both w/cream bodies and red/white/blue Wall's Ice Cream decals, smooth wheels, 4-5/8"	80	120	225
Commuter Dragster	maroon body w/Ford Commuter, Union Jack and #2 decals, cast silver engine, chrome plastic suspension and pipes, clear windshield, driver, spoke wheels, 4-7/8"	30	45	75
Concorde-First Issues	BOAC decals	20	30	50
Concorde-First Issues	Air France decals	20	45	85
Concorde-First Issues	Air Canada decals	80	120	200
Concorde-First Issues	Japan Airlines decals	280	420	700
Concorde-Second Issues	BOAC and Air France models on display stands	15	20	35
Constructor Set	one red and one white cab bodies, w/four different interchangeable rear units; van, pickup, milk truck, and ambulance; various accessories include a milkman figure	48	72	140
Cooper-Maserati Racing Car	yellow/white body w/yellow/black stripe and #3 decals, driver tilts to steer car, 3-3/8"	18	27	45
Cooper-Maserati Racing Car	blue body w/red/white/blue Maserati and #7 decals, unpainted engine and suspension, chrome plastic steering wheel, roll bar, mirrors and pipes, driver, cast eight-spoke wheels, plastic tires, 3-3/8"	26	39	65
Corgi Flying Club Set	blue/orange No. 438 Land Rover w/red dome light, blue trailer w/either orange/yellow or orange/white plastic airplane	24	45	90
Corgi Junior James Bond SPECTRE Bobsled	orange body w/wild boar decals, 2-7/8"	75	140	295
Corgi Juniors James Bond Bobsled	yellow body, silver base, Bond figure, 007 decals, Whizz Wheels, 2-7/8"	75	140	295
Corgie Junior Popeye's Paddle Wagon Jr.	smaller version of No. 802 w/Whizz Wheels	70	105	200
Corporal Missile & Erector Vehicle	white missle, red rubber-nose cone, olive green body on erector body	240	360	600
Corporal Missile Launching Ramp	sold in temporary pack	36	55	90
Corporal Missile on Launching Ramp	white missle, red rubber-nose cone	80	120	200
Corporal Missile Set	No. 1112 missile and No. 1113 ramp, erector vehicle and No. 1118 army truck	340	510	850
Corvette Sting Ray	metallic green or red body, yellow interior, black working hood, working headlights, clear windshield, amber roof panel, gold dash, chrome grille and bumpers, decals, gray die cast base, Golden jacks, cast wheels, plastic tires, 4"	40	90	185

VEHICLES

NAME	DESCRIPTION	GOOD	EX	MINT
Corvette Sting Ray	metallic silver or red body, two working headlights, clear windshield, yellow interior, silver hood panels, four jewel headlights, suspension, chrome bumpers, w/spoked or shaped wheels, rubber tires, 3-3/4"	60	90	175
Corvette Sting Ray	yellow body, red interior, suspension, #13 decals, 3-3/4"	30	55	95
Corvette Sting Ray	metallic gray body w/black hood, Go-Go-Go labels, Whizz Wheels, 3-5/8"	40	65	100
Corvette Sting Ray	either dark metallic blue or metallic mauve-rose body, chrome dash, Whizz Wheels, 3-7/8"	40	65	100
Country Farm Set	#50 Massey Ferguson tractor, red No. 62 hay trailer w/load, fences, figures	30	45	75
Country Farm Set	same as 4-B but without hay load on trailer	30	45	75
Daily Planet Helicopter	red and white body, rocket launcher w/ten spare missles	24	36	60
Daimler 38 1910	orange-red body, gray and yellow chassis, yellow spoked wheels; with four figures	20	30	50
Daktari Set	two versions: No. 438 Land Rover, green w/black stripes, cast wheels, 1968-73; Whizz Wheels, 1974-75, each set	50	75	150
Datsun 240Z	red body w/#11 and other decals, two working doors, white interior, orange roll bar and tire rack; one version also has East Africa Rally decals, 3-5/8"	15	20	35
Datsun 240Z	white body w/red hood and roof, #46 and John Morton labels, Whizz Wheels, 3-5/8"	15	20	35
David Brown Combine	No. 55 Tractor, red and yellow combines, white JF labels	30	45	75
David Brown Tractor	white body w/black/white David Brown #1412 decals, red chassis and plastic engine, 4-1/8"	15	25	45
David Brown Tractor & Trailer	two-piece set; #55 tractor and #56 trailer	30	45	75
De Tomaso Mangusta	metallic dark green body w/gold stripes and logo on hood, silver lower body, clear front windows, cream interior, amber rear windows and headlights, gray antenna, spare wheel, Whizz Wheels, 3-7/8"	26	39	65
De Tomaso Mangusta	white upper/light blue lower body/base, black interior, clear windows, silver engine, black grille, amber headlights, red taillights, gray antenna, spare wheel, gold stripes and black logo decal on hood, suspension, removable gray chassis, 5"	32	48	80
Decca Airfield Radar Van	cream body w/four or five vertical bands, working rotating scanner and aerial	120	180	350
Decca Radar Scanner	w/either orange or custard colored scanner frame, silver scanner face, w/gear on base for turning scanner, 3-1/4"	34	51	85
Dick Dastardly's Racing Car	dark blue body, yellow chassis, chrome engine, red wings, Dick and Muttley figures, 5"	40	60	150
Dodge Kew Fargo Tipper	white cab and working hood, blue tipper, red interior, clear windows, black hydraulic cylinders, cast wheels, plastic tires, 5-1/4"	34	51	85
Dodge Livestock Truck	tan cab and hood, green body, working tailgate and ramps, five pigs, 5-3/8"	34	51	85
Dolphin Cabin Cruiser	white hull, blue deck plastic boat w/red/white stripe decals, driver, blue motor w/white cover, gray prop, cast trailer w/smooth wheels, rubber tires, 5-1/4"	24	36	70
Dougal's Magic Roundabout Car	yellow body, red interior, clear windows, dog and snail, red wheels w/gold trim, Magic Roundabout decals, 4-1/2"	70	105	175
Drax Jet Helicopter	white body, yellow rotors and fins, yellow/black Drax decals, 5-7/8"	24	36	75
Dropside Trailer	cream body, red chassis in five versions: smooth wheels 1957-61; shaped wheels, 1962-1965; white body, cream or blue chassis; or silver gray body, blue chassis, each, 4-3/8"	10	21	45
Ecurie Ecosse Racing Set	metallic dark or light blue No. 1126 transporter w/three cars in two versions: BRM, Vanwall and Lotus XI, 1961-64; BRM, Vanwall and Ferrari, 1964-66, value is for individual complete set	140	210	450

VEHICLES

NAME	DESCRIPTION	GOOD	EX	MINT
Ecurie Ecosse Transporter	in dark blue body w/either blue or yellow lettering, or light blue body w/red or yellow lettering, working tailgate and sliding door, yellow interior, shaped wheels, rubber tires, 7-3/4"	70	105	200
Emergency Set	three-vehicle set w/figures and accessories, No. 402 Ford Cortina Police car, No. 921 Police Helicopter, No. 481 Range Rover Ambulance	40	60	100
Emergency Set	No. 339 Land Rover Police Car and No. 921 Police Helicopter w/figures and accessories	30	50	80
ERF 44G Dropside Truck	yellow cab and chassis, metallic blue bed, smooth or shaped wheels	36	55	110
ERF 44G Moorhouse Van	yellow cab, red body, Moorhouse Lemon Cheese decals, smooth wheels, rubber tires, 4-5/8"	100	150	295
ERF 44G Platform Truck	light blue cab w/either dark blue or white flatbed body or yellow cab and blue flatbed, smooth hubs, 4-5/8"	36	55	110
ERF Dropside Truck and Trailer	#456 truck and #101 trailer w/#1488 cement sack load and #1485 plank load	60	90	200
ERF Neville Cement Tipper	yellow cab, gray tipper, cement decal, plastic or metal filler caps, w/either smooth or shaped wheels, 3-3/4"	32	48	80
ERG 64G Earth Dumper	red cab, yellow tipper, clear windows, unpainted hydraulic cylinder, spare tire, smooth wheels, rubber tires, 4"	30	45	85
Euclid Caterpillar Tractor	TC-12 lime green body w/black or pale gray rubber treads, gray plastic seat, driver figure, controls, stacks, silver grille, painted blue engine sides and Euclid decals, 4-1/4"	50	100	190
Euclid TC-12 Bulldozer	lime green body w/black or pale gray treads, silver blade surface, gray plastic seat controls and stacks, silver grille and lights, painted blue engine sides, sheet metal base, rubber treads and Euclid decals, 5"	80	120	225
Euclid TC-12 Bulldozer	yellow or pale lime-green body, metal control rod, driver, black rubber treads, 6-1/8"	80	120	200
Ferrari 206 Dino	black interior and fins, in either red body w/#30 and gold hubs or Whizz Wheels, or yellow body w/#23 and gold hubs or Whizz Wheels, 4-1/8"	24	36	60
Ferrari 308GTS	red or black body w/working rear hood, black interior w/tan seats, movable chrome headlights, detailed engine, 4-5/8"	15	20	35
Ferrari 308GTS Magnum	red body w/solid chrome wheels, 4-5/8"	24	36	60
Ferrari 312 B2 Racing Car	red body, white fin, gold engine, chrome suspension, mirrors and wheels, Ferrari and #5 decals, 4"	16	24	40
Ferrari Berlinetta 250LM	red body w/yellow stripe, blue windshields, chrome interior, grille and exhaust pipes, detailed engine, #4 Ferrari logo and yellow stripe decals, spoked wheels and spare, rubber tires, 3-3/4"	30	45	75
Ferrari Daytona	apple green body, black tow hook, red-yellow-silver black Daytona #5 and other racing decals, amber windows, headlights, black plastic interior, base, four spoke chrome wheels, 5"	15	20	35
Ferrari Daytona	white body w/red roof and trunk, black interior, two working doors, amber windows and headlights, #81 and other decals, 4-3/4"	15	30	55
Ferrari Daytona and Racing Car	blue/yellow No. 323 Ferrari and No. 150 Surtees on yellow trailer	25	40	85
Ferrari Daytona JCB	orange body w/#33, Corgi and other decals, chrome spoked wheels, 4-3/4"	15	25	50
Ferrari Racing Car	red body, chrome plastic engine, roll bar and dash, driver, silver cast base and exhaust, Ferrari and #36 decals, shaped or spoked wheels, 3-5/8"	24	36	75
Fiat 1800	one-piece body in several colors, clear windows, plastic interior, silver lights, grille and bumpers, red taillights, smooth wheels, rubber tires, colors: blue body w/light or bright yellow interior, light tan, mustard, light blue or two-tone blue body, 3	24	40	80
Fiat 2100	light two-tone mauve body, yellow interior, purple roof, clear windows w/rear blind, silver grille, license plates and bumpers, red taillights, shaped wheels, rubber tires, 3-3/4"	22	33	75

VEHICLES

NAME	DESCRIPTION	GOOD	EX	MINT
Fiat X 1/9 & Powerboat	green and white automobile, w/white and gold boat, Carlsberg decals	30	45	75
Fiat X1/9	metallic blue body and base, white Fiat #3, multicolored lettering and stripe decals, black roof, trim, interior, rear panel, grille, bumpers and tow hook, chrome wheels and detailed engine, 4-3/4"	15	20	35
Fiat X1/9	metallic light green or silver body w/black roof, trim and interior, two working doors, rear panel, grille, tow hook and bumpers, detailed engine, suspension, chrome wheels, 4-1/2"	15	20	35
Fire Bug	orange body, Whizz Wheels	20	30	50
Flying Club Set	green and white No. 419 Jeep w/Corgi Flying Club decals, green trailer, blue/white airplane	36	55	90
Ford 5000 Super Major Tractor	blue body/chassis w/Ford Super Major 5000 decals, gray cast fenders and rear wheels, gray plastic front wheels, black plastic tires, driver, 3-3/4"	30	45	75
Ford 5000 Tractor with Scoop	blue body/chassis, gray fenders, yellow scoop arm and controls, chrome scoop, black control lines, 3-1/8"	55	80	130
Ford Aral Tank Truck	light blue cab and chassis, white tanker bodym Aral labels	20	30	50
Ford Capri	orange-red or dark red body, gold wheels w/red hubs, Whizz Wheels, two working doors, clear windshield and headlights, black interior, folding seats, black grille, silver bumpers, 4"	40	80	145
Ford Capri 3 Litre GT	white and black body, racing number 5	15	20	35
Ford Capri 30 S	Silver or yellow body, black markings, opening doors and hatchback	15	20	35
Ford Capri S	white body, red lower body and base, red interior, clear windshield, black bumpers, grille and tow hook, chrome headlights and wheels, red taillights, #6 and other racing decals, 4-3/4"	15	20	35
Ford Capri Santa Pod Gloworm	white and blue body w/red, white and blue lettering and flag decals, red chassis, amber windows, gold-based black engine, gold scoop, pipes and front suspension, w/driver, plasitc wheels, 4-3/8"	18	27	45
Ford Car Transporter	metallic lime green or metallic cab and semi, cream cab chassis, deck and ramp	20	30	60
Ford Car Transporter	white cab, red chassis and trailer, white decals and ramps	20	30	50
Ford Cobra Mustang	white, black, red and blue body and chassis, Mustang decal	15	18	30
Ford Consul	one-piece body in several colors, clear windows, silver grille, lights and bumpers, smooth wheels, rubber tires, 3-5/8"	45	65	120
Ford Consul Classic	cream or gold body and base, yellow interior, pink roof, clear windows, gray steering wheel, silver bumpers, grille, opening hood, 3-3/4"	35	55	90
Ford Consul-Mechanical	same as model 200-A but w/friction motor and blue or green body	55	85	160
Ford Cortina Estate Car	red body and base or metallic charcoal gray body and base, cream interior, chrome bumpers and grille, jewel headlights, 3-3/4"	35	55	90
Ford Cortina Estate Car	3-1/2" metallic dark blue body and base, brown and cream simulated wood panels, cream interior, chrome bumpers and grille, jewel headlights	35	55	90
Ford Cortina GXL	tan or metallic silver blue body, black roof and stripes, red plastic interior, working doors, clear windshield, 4"	30	45	75
Ford Cortina Police Car	white body, red or pink and black stripe labels, red interior, folding seats, blue dome light, clear windows, chrome bumpers, Police labels, opening doors, 4"	15	25	45
Ford Covered Semi-Trailer	blue cab and trailer, black cab chassis and trailer fedners, yellow covers	15	25	50
Ford Escort 13 GL	red, blue or yellow body, opening doors	8	15	25
Ford Escort Police Car	blue body and base, tan interior, white doors, blue dome lights, red Police labels, black grille and bumpers, 4-3/16"	8	15	30

VEHICLES

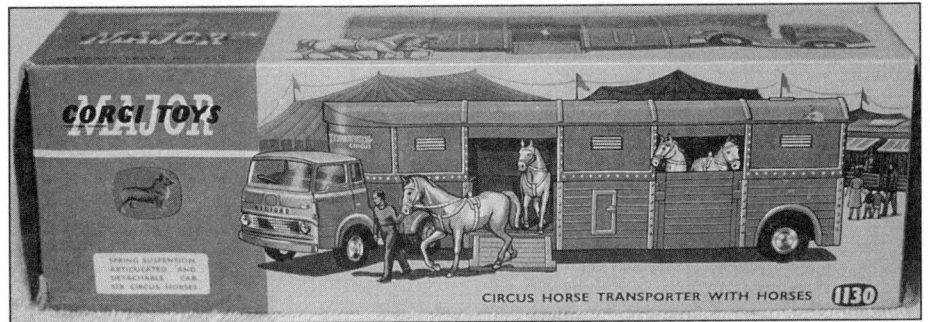

Chipperfield Circus Horse Transporter, No. 1130-A, 1962-72, Corgi

Chipperfield Circus Set, No. 23-A, 1963-65, Corgi

Chitty Chitty Bang Bang, No. 266-A, 1968-72, Corgi. Photo Courtesy Mark Arruda

VEHICLES

NAME	DESCRIPTION	GOOD	EX	MINT
Ford Esso Tank Truck	white cab and tank, red tanker chassis and fenders, chrome wheels, Esso labels	15	30	60
Ford Express Semi-Trailer	metallic blue cab and trailer, silver roof on trailer, chrome doors marked "Express Service," shaped or detailed cast wheels	60	110	225
Ford Exxon Tank Truck	white cab and tank, red tanker chassis and fenders, chrome wheels, Exxon labels	15	30	60
Ford GT 70	green and black body, white interior, number 32 label	10	25	45
Ford Guinness Tanker	orange, tan, black cab, tan tankers body, Guinness labels	20	30	50
Ford Gulf Tank Truck	white cab w/orange chassis, blue tanker body, Gulf labels, chrome wheels	15	25	40
Ford Holmes Wrecker	whie upper cab, black roof, red rear body and lower cab, mirrors, unpainted or gold booms	60	90	200
Ford Michelin Container Truck	blue cab and trailer, white cab chassis and trailer fenders, yellow containers; includes Michelin Man figure	15	25	50
Ford Mustang Fastback	metallic lilac, metallic dark blue, silver or light green body, spoked or detailed cast wheels	30	45	95
Ford Mustang Fastback	white body w/double red stripe, blue interior, spun, detailed cast, wire or cast alloy wheels	25	45	85
Ford Mustang Mach 1	green upper body, white lower body and base, cream interior, folding seat backs, chrome headlights and rear bumper, 4-1/4"	25	35	60
Ford Sierra	many body color versions w/plastic interior, working hatch and two doors, clear windows, folding seat back, lifting hatch cover, 5"	8	15	25
Ford Sierra and Caravan Trailer	blue #299 Sierra, two-tone blue/white #490 Caravan	15	20	35
Ford Sierra Taxi	cream body	8	15	20
Ford Thames Airborne Caravan	various color versions of body and plastic interior w/table, white blinds, silver bumpers, grille and headlights, two doors, 3-3/4"	35	55	95
Ford Thames Wall's Ice Cream Van	light blue body, cream pillar, chimes, chrome bumpers and grille, crank at rear to operate chimes, no figures, 4"	55	110	225
Ford Thunderbird 1957	cream body, dark brown, black or orange plastic hardtop, black interior, open hood and trunk, chrome bumpers, 5-3/16"	10	20	35
Ford Thunderbird 1957	white body, black interior and plastic top, amber windows, white seats, chrome bumpers, headlights and spare wheel cover, 5-1/4"	10	20	35
Ford Thunderbird Hardtop	light green body, cream roof, clear windows, silver lights, grille and bumpers, red taillights, rubber tires, 4-1/8"	50	80	130
Ford Thunderbird Hardtop-Mechanical	same as 214-A but w/friction motor and pink or light green body and cream or black roof, 4-1/8"	70	105	195
Ford Thunderbird Roadster	clear windshield, silver seats, lights, grille and bumpers, red taillights, rubber tires, white body, 4-1/8"	50	75	125
Ford Torino Road Hog	orange-red body, yellow and gray chassis, gold lamps, chrome radiator shell, windows and bumpers, one-piece body, working horn, 5-3/4"	15	20	35
Ford Tractor and Beast Carrier	No. 67 Ford 5000 tractor and No. 58 Beast Carrier	60	90	150
Ford Tractor and Conveyor	No. 67 tractor, conveyor w/trailer, figures and accessories	60	90	175
Ford Tractor with Trencher	blue body/chassis, gray fenders, cast yellow trencher arm and controls, chrome trencher, black control lines, 5-5/8"	50	75	125
Ford Transit Milk Float	white one-piece body, blue hood and roof, tan interior, chrome and red roof lights, open compartment door and milk cases, 5-1/2"	15	25	40
Ford Transit Tipper	orange cab and chassis, tan tipper, chrome wheels	10	15	25
Ford Transit Wrecker	white cab and rear body, red roof, silver bed, "24-hour Service" labels	25	35	60

NAME	DESCRIPTION	GOOD	EX	MINT
Ford Wall's Ice Cream Van	light blue body, dark cream pillars, plastic striped rear canopy, white interior, silver bumpers, grille and headlights; includes salesman and boy figures, 3-1/4"	80	160	325
Ford Zephyr Estate Car	light blue one-piece body, dark blue hood and stripes, red interior, silver bumpers, grille and headlights, red taillights, 3-7/8"	30	45	75
Ford Zephyr Patrol Car	white or cream body, blue and white Politie/Rijkspolitie decals, red interior, blue dome light, silver bumpers; import	60	125	225
Ford Zephyr Patrol Car	white or cream body, blue and white Police red interior, blue dome light, silver bumpers, 3-3/4"	35	50	85
Fordson Power Major Halftrack Tractor	blue body/chassis, silver steering wheel, seat and grille, three versions: orange cast wheels, gray treads, lights in radiator or on sides of radiator, 3-1/2"	90	135	225
Fordson Power Major Tractor	blue body/chassis w/Fordson Power Major decals, silver steering wheel, seat, exhaust, grille and lights, 3-1/4"	45	65	110
Fordson Power Major Tractor	blue body w/Fordson Power Major decals, driver, blue chassis and steering wheel, silver seat, hitch, exhaust, 3-3/8"	50	75	125
Fordson Tractor and Plow	No. 60 tractor and No. 61 four-furrow plow	55	85	140
Fordson Tractor and Plow	#55 Fordson Tractor and No. 56 Four Furrow plow	55	85	140
Four Furrow Plow	red frame, yellow plastic parts, 3-5/8"	15	20	35
Four Furrow Plow	blue frame w/chrome plastic parts, 3-3/4"	15	20	35
German Life Saving Set	red/white No. 421 Land Rover and lifeboat, white trailer, German decals	30	45	75
Ghia L64 Chrysler V8	metallic light blue, green, copper or yellow, plastic interior, hood, trunk and two doors working, detailed engine, clear windshield, shaped or detailed cast wheels, 4-1/4"	25	40	75
Ghia-Fiat 600 Jolly	light or dark blue body, red and silver canopy, red seats, two figures, windshield, chrome dash, floor, steering wheels, 3-1/4"	45	75	130
Ghia-Fiat 600 Jolly	dark yellow body, red seats, two figures and a dog, clear windshield, silver bumpers and headlights, red taillights, 3-1/4"	80	175	325
Giant Daktari Set	black and green No. 438 Land Rover, tan No. 503 Giraffe truck, blue and brown No. 484 Dodge Livestock truck, figures	225	350	650
Giant Tower Crane	white body, orange cab and chassis	35	50	85
Glider Set	two versions: white No. 345 Honda, 1981-82; yellow Honda, 1983, value is for individual complete sets	30	45	75
Golden Eagle Jeep	tan and brown or white and gold body, tan plastic top, chrome plastic base, bumpers and steps, chrome wheels, 3-3/4"	8	15	25
Golden Guinea Set	three vehicle set, gold plated No. 224 Bentley Continental, No. 229 Chevy Corvair and No. 234 Ford Consul	90	150	325
GP Beach Buggy	metallic blue or orange-red body, two durfboards, flower label, Whizz Wheels	15	20	35
Grand Prix Racing Set	four vehicle set includes: No. 490 Volkswagen Breakdown Truck w/#330 Porsche (1969), Porsche #371(1970-72), No. 155 Lotus, No. 156 Cooper-Maserati, red trailer	135	210	425
Grand Prix Set	sold by mail order only; kit version of No. 151 Yardley, No. 154 JPS, No. 152 Surtees and No. 153 Surtees	60	125	275
Green Hornet's Black Beauty	black body, green window/interior, two figures, working chrome grille and panels w/weapons, green headlights, red taillights, 5"	175	275	550
Green Line Bus	green body, white interior and stripe, TDK labels, six spoked wheels, 4-7/8"	10	15	25
Half Track Rocket Launcher & Trailer	two rocket launchers and single trailer castings, gray plastic roll cage, man w/machine gun, front wheels and hubs, 6-1/2"	20	35	55
Hardy Boys' Rolls-Royce	red body w/yellow hood, roof and window frames, band figures on roof on removable green base, 4-5/8"	70	105	200

NAME	DESCRIPTION	GOOD	EX	MINT
HDL Hovercraft SR-N1	blue superstructure, gray base and deck, clear canopy, red seats, yellow SR-N1 decals	60	90	150
Hesketh-Ford Racing Car	white body w/red/white/blue Hesketh, stripe and #24 decals, chrome suspension, roll bar, mirrors and pipes, 5-5/8"	15	18	30
HGB-Angus Firestreak	chrome plastic spotlight and ladders, black hose reel, red dome light, white water cannon, in two interior versions, electronic siren and lights, 6-1/4"	35	50	85
Hi-Speed Fire Engine	red body, yellow plastic ladder	16	24	40
Hillman Hunter	blue body, gray interior, black hood, white roof, unpainted spotlights, clear windshield, red radiator screen, black equipment, Golden Jacks wheels; came with Kangaroo figure, 4-1/4"	45	65	125
Hillman Husky	one-piece tan or metallic blue/silver body, clear windows, silver lights, grille and bumpers, smooth wheels, 3-1/2"	40	70	125
Hillman Husky-Mechanical	same as 206-A but w/friction motor, black base and dark blue, gray or cream body, 3-1/2"	50	90	125
Hillman Imp	metallic copper, blue, dark blue or gold one-piece bodies, w/white/yellow interior, silver bumpers, headlights, 3-1/4"	30	45	85
Hillman Imp Rally	in various metallic body colors, w/cream interior, Monte Carlo Rally and #107 decals, 3-1/4"	30	65	110
Honda Ballade Driving School	red body/base, tan interior, clear windows, tow hook, mirrors, bumpers, 4-3/4"	10	15	25
Honda Prelude	dark metallic blue body, tan interior, clear windows, folding seats, sunroof, chrome wheels, 4-3/4"	8	15	20
Hughes Police Helicopter	red interior, dark blue rotors, in several international imprints, Netherlands, German, Swiss, in white or yellow, 5-1/2"	20	30	50
Hyster 800 Stacatruck	clear windows, black interior w/driver, 8-1/2"	35	50	85
Incredible Hulk Mazda Pickup	metallic light brown body, gray or red plastic cage, black interior, Hulk decal on hood, chrome wheels; inludes green and red Hulk figure, 5"	20	30	75
Inter-City Mini Bus	orange body w/brown interior, clear windows, green/yellow/black decals, Whizz Wheels, 4-3/16"	8	15	25
International 6x6 Army Truck	olive drab body w/clear windows, red/blue decals, six cast olive wheels w/rubber tires, 5-1/2"	70	105	225
Iso Grifo 7 Litre	metallic blue body, light blue interior, black hood and stripe, clear windshield, black dash, folding seats, chrome bumpers, Whizz Wheels, 4"	15	18	30
Jaguar 1952 XK120 Rally	cream body w/black top and trim, red interior, Rally des Alps and #414 decals, 4-3/4"	8	15	25
Jaguar 2.4 Litre	one-piece white body w/no interior 1957-59, or yellow body w/red interior 1960-63, clear windows, smooth hubs, 3-7/8"	50	80	130
Jaguar 2.4 Litre Fire Chief's Car	red body w/unpainted roof signal/siren, red/white fire and shield decals on doors, in two versions, smooth or spun hubs, 3-3/4"	60	90	150
Jaguar 2.4 Litre-Mechanical	same as 208-A but w/friction motor and metallic blue body, 3-7/8"	60	90	180
Jaguar E Type	maroon or metallic dark gray body, tan interior, red and clear plastic removeable hardtop, clear windshield, folded top, spun hubs, 3-3/4"	45	65	110
Jaguar E Type 2+2	red or blue body and chassis, working hood, doors and hatch, black interior w/folding seats, copper engine, pipes and suspension, spoked wheels, 4-3/16"	40	60	120
Jaguar E Type 2+2	in five versions: red or yellow w/nonworking doors; or w/V-12 engine in yellow body or metallic yellow body, Whizz Wheels, 4-1/8"	35	55	90
Jaguar E Type Competition	gold or chrome plated body, black interior, blue and white stripes and black #2 decals, no top, clear windshield, headlights, w/driver, 3-3/4"	45	65	110
Jaguar Mark X Saloon	several different color versions w/working front and rear hood castings, clear windshields, plastic interior, gray steering wheel; includes suitcase in trunk, 4-1/4"	35	55	110

VEHICLES

NAME	DESCRIPTION	GOOD	EX	MINT
Jaguar XJ12C	five different metallic versions, working hood and two doors, clear windows, tow hook, chrome bumpers, grille and headlights, 5-1/4"	10	15	35
Jaguar XJ12C Police Car	white body w/blue and pink stripes, light bar w/blue dome light, tan interior, police decals, 5-1/8"	15	18	45
Jaguar XJS	metallic burgundy body, tan interior, clear windows, working doors, spoked chrome wheels, 5-3/4"	10	15	25
Jaguar XJS Motul	black body w/red/white Motul and #4, chrome wheels, 5-3/4"	8	15	25
Jaguar XJS-HE Supercat	black body w/silver stripes and trim, red interior, dark red taillights, light gray antenna, no tow hook, clear windshield, 5-1/4"	8	15	25
Jaguar XK120 Hardtop	red body, black hardtop, working hood and trunk, detailed engine, cream interior, clear windows, chrome wheels, 4-3/4"	8	15	25
James Bond Aston Martin	metallic silver body, red interior, two figures, working roof hatch, ejector seat, bullet shield and guns, chrome bumpers, spoked wheels, 4"	100	150	325
James Bond Aston Martin	metallic silver body and die cast base, red interior, two figures, clear windows, passenger seat raises to eject, 5"	30	45	90
James Bond Aston Martin DB5	metallic gold body, red interior, working roof hatch, clear windows, two figures, left seat ejects, spoked wheels, accessory pack, 3-3/4"	70	105	275
James Bond Citroen 2CV6	dark yellow body and hood, red interior, clear windows, chrome headlights, red taillights, black plastic grille, 4-1/4"	15	35	70
James Bond Lotus Esprit	white body and base, black windshield, grille and hood panel, white plastic roof device that triggers fins and tail, rockets, 4-3/4"	30	45	95
James Bond Moon Buggy	white body w/blue chassis, amber canopy, yellow tanks, red radar dish, arms and jaws, yellow wheels, 4-3/8"	175	275	525
James Bond Mustang Mach 1	red and white body w/black hood and opening doors, 4-3/8"	100	150	300
James Bond Set	set of three: No. 271 Lotus Esprit, No. 649 Space Shuttle and No. 269 Aston Martin	80	135	295
James Bond Space Shuttle	white body w/yellow/black Moonraker decals, 5-7/8"	30	45	75
James Bond Toyota 2000GT	white body, black interior w/Bond and passenger, working trunk and gun rack, spoked wheels, plastic tires, accessory pack, 4"	115	180	375
JCB 110B Crawler Loader	white cab, yellow body, working red shovel, red interior w/driver, clear windows, black treads, JCB decals, 6-1/2"	20	30	50
Jean Richard Circus Set	yellow and red Land Rover and cage trailer w/Pinder-Jean Richard decals, No. 426 office van and trailer, No. 1163 Human Cannonball truck, ring and cut-out "Big Top" circus tent	90	135	275
Jeep & Horse Box	metallic painted No. 441 Jeep and No. 112 trailer; accessories include girl on pony, three jumps and three hay bales	15	30	50
Jeep and Motorcycle Trailer	red working No. 441 Jeep w/two blue/yellow bikes on trailer	15	20	40
Jeep CJ-5	dark metallic green body, removable white top, white plastic wheels, spare tire, 4"	8	15	30
Jeep FC-150 Covered Truck	four versions: blue body, rubber tires (1965-67); yellow/brown body; rubber tires w/spun hubs (1965-67); blue body, plastic tires w/cast spoked hubs	30	45	75
Jeep FC-150 Pickup	blue body, clear windows, sheet metal tow hook, in two wheel versions: smooth or shaped wheels, 3-1/2"	35	55	90
Jeep FC-150 Pickup with Conveyor Belt	red body, yellow interior, orange grille, two black rubber belts, shaped wheels, black rubber tires; accessories farmland figure and sacks, 7-1/2"	45	65	130
Jeep FC-150 Tower Wagon	metallic green body, yellow interior and basket w/workman figure, clear windows, w/either rubber or plastic wheels, 4-5/8"	40	60	100
Jet Ranger Police Helicopter	white body w/chrome interior, red floats and rotors, amber windows, Police decals, 5-7/8"	25	40	65

VEHICLES

NAME	DESCRIPTION	GOOD	EX	MINT
JPS Lotus Racing Car	black body, scoop and wings w/gold John Player Special, Texaco and #1 decals, gold suspension, pipes and wheels, 10-1/2"	30	45	75
Karrier Bantam Two Ton Van	blue body, red chassis and bed, clear windows, smooth wheels, rubber tires, 4"	35	55	95
Karrier Butcher Shop	white body, blue roof, butcher shop interior, Home Service decals, in two versions: w/or without suspension, smooth hubs, 3-5/8"	65	100	165
Karrier Dairy Van	light blue body w/Drive Safely on Milk decals, white roof, w/either smooth or shaped wheels, 4-1/8"	50	75	145
Karrier Field Kitchen	olive body, white decals, w/figure, 3-5/8"	60	90	175
Karrier Ice Cream Truck	cream upper, blue lower body and interior, clear windows, sliding side windows, Mister Softee decals, figure inside, 3-5/8"	90	150	275
Karrier Lucozade Van	yellow body w/gray rear door, Lucozade decals, rubber tires, w/either smooth or shaped wheels, 4-1/8"	70	120	225
Karrier Mobile Canteen	blue body, white interior, amber windows, roof knob rotates figure, working side panel counter, Patates Frites label, Belgium issue	90	150	325
Karrier Mobile Canteen	blue body, white interior, amber windows, roof knob rotates figure, working side panel counter, Joe's Diner label, 3-5/8"	60	90	150
Karrier Mobile Grocery	light green body, grocery store interior, red/white Home Service decals, smooth hubs, rubber tires, 3-5/8"	70	110	185
King Tiger Heavy Tank	tan and rust body, working turret and barrel, tan rollers and treads, German decals, 6-1/8"	30	45	75
Kojak's Buick Regal	metallic bronze brown body, off-white interior, two opening doors, clear windows, chrome bumpers, grille and headlights, red taillights; accessories include Kojak and Crocker figures, 5-3/4"	25	55	95
Lamborghini Miura	silver body, black interior, yellow/purple stripes and #7 decal, Whizz Wheels, 3-3/4"	30	45	75
Lamborghini Miura P400	w/red or yellow body, working hood, detailed engine, clear windows, jewel headlights, bull, Whizz Wheels, 3-3/4"	40	60	100
Lancia Fulvia Zagato	metallic blue body, metallic green or yellow and black body, light blue interior, working hood and doors, folding seats, amber lights, cast wheels, 3-5/8"	25	35	70
Lancia Fulvia Zagato	orange body, black working hood and interior, Whizz Wheels, 3-5/8"	15	25	40
Land Rover & Horse Box	blue/white Land Rover w/horse trailer in two versions: cast wheels {1968-74) and Whizz Wheels (1975-77); accessories include a mare and a foal; value is for an individual and complete set	50	75	125
Land Rover 109WB	working rear doors, tan interior, spare on hood, plastic tow hook, 5-1/4"	15	18	30
Land Rover and Ferrari Racer	red and tan No. 438 Land Rover and red No. 154 Ferrari F1 on yellow trailer	60	90	150
Land Rover and Pony Trailer	two versions: green No. 438 Land Rover and a red and black No. 102 Pony trailer (1958-62); tan/cream No. 438 Land Rover and a pony trailer (1963-68); value given is for an individual and complete set	50	90	175
Land Rover Breakdown Truck	red body, yellow canopy, chrome revolving spotlight, Breakdown Service decals, shaped hubs or Whizz Wheels, 4-3/8"	25	35	60
Land Rover Breakdown Truck	red body w/silver boom and yellow canopy, revolving spotlight, Breakdown Service decals, 4-3/8"	35	55	90
Land Rover Pickup	yellow, green or metallic blue body, spare on hood, clear windows, sheet metal tow hook, smooth hubs, rubber tires, 3-3/4"	45	70	100
Land Rover with Canopy	long, one-piece body w/clear windows, plastic interior, spare on hood, issued in numerous colors, 3-3/4"	35	55	90
Lincoln Continental	metallic gold or light blue body, black roof, maroon plastic interior, working hood, trunk and doors, clear windows; accessories include TV w/picture strips for TV, 5-3/4"	60	90	150

VEHICLES

NAME	DESCRIPTION	GOOD	EX	MINT
Lions of Longleat	black/white No. 438 Land Rover pickup w/lion cages and accessories, two versions: cast wheels, 1969-73; Whizz Wheels, 1974, each	60	90	200
London Set	orange No. 226 Mini, Policeman, No. 418 London Taxi and No. 468 Outspan Routemaster bus, Whizz Wheels	50	75	125
London Set	No. 425 London Taxi and No. 469 Routemaster B.T.A. bus in two versions: w/mounted Policeman (1980-81); without Policeman, (1982-on); value is for an individual and complete set	25	35	60
London Set	No. 418 taxi and No. 468 bus w/policeman, in two versions: "Corgi Toys" on bus (1964-66); "Outspan Oranges" on bus (1967-68); values for an individual and complete set	55	85	150
London Transport Routemaster Bus	clear windows w/driver and conductor, released w/numerous advertiser logos, shaped or cast spoked wheels, 4-1/2"	35	50	85
London Transport Routemaster Bus	long, clear windows, interior, some models have driver and conductor, released w/numerous advertiser logos, Whizz Wheels, 4-7/8"	25	35	60
Lotus Elan S2 Hardtop	cream interior w/folding seats and tan dash, working hood, separate chrome chassis, issued in blue body with white top or red body with white top, 2-1/4"	30	45	75
Lotus Elan S2 Roadster	working hood, plastic interior w/folding seats, shaped wheels and rubber tires, issued in metallic blue, "I've got a Tigger on my Back" decal on trunk, 3-3/8"	30	50	110
Lotus Eleven	red, green or light green body, clear windshield and plastic headlights, smooth wheels, rubber tires, racing decals, 2-1/4"	60	95	160
Lotus Elite	red body, white interior, two working doors, clear windshield, black dash, hood panel, grille, bumpers, base and tow hook, 5-1/8"	15	18	35
Lotus Elite 22	dark blue body w/silver trim, Whizz Wheels, 4-3/4"	15	18	35
Lotus Racing Car	black body and base, gold cast engine, roll bar, pipes, dash and mirrors, driver, gold cast wheels, in two versions, 5-5/8"	25	35	60
Lotus Racing Set	three versions: "3" on No. 301 Elite and "JPS" on No. 154 Lotus racer; "7" on No. 301 Elite and "JPS" on racer; "7" on No. 301 Elite and "Texaco" on No. 154 Lotus racer; value is for an individual and complete set	30	45	95
Lotus Racing Team Set	490 VW Breakdown Truck, red trailer w/#318 Lotus Elan Open Top, #319 Lotus Elan Hard Top, #155 Lotus Climax; includes pack of cones, sheet of racing number labels	125	200	375
Lotus-Climax Racing Car	green body and base w/black/white #1 and yellow racing stripe decals, unpainted engine and suspension, w/driver, 3-5/8"	25	35	65
Lotus-Climax Racing Car	orange/white body w/black/white stripe and #8 decals, unpainted cast rear wing, cast eight-spoke wheels, w/driver, 3-5/8"	15	25	50
Lunar Bug	white body w/red roof, blue interior and wings, clear and amber windows, red working ramp, Lunar Bug decals, 5"	25	40	95
M60 A1 Medium Tank	green/tan camo body, working turret and barrel, green rollers, white decals, 4-3/4"	30	45	75
Mack Container Truck	yellow cab, red interior, white engine, red suspension, white ACL decals, 11-3/8"	30	50	80
Mack Esso Tank Truck	white cab and tank w/Esso labels, red tank chassis and fenders, 10-3/4"	20	40	80
Mack Exxon Tank Truck	white cab and tank, red tank chassis and fenders, red interior, chrome catwalk, Exxon labels, 10-3/4"	15	35	75
Mack Trans Continental Semi	orange cab body and semi chassis and fenders, metallic light blue semi body, unpainted trailer rests, 10"	35	55	90
Mack-Priestman Crane Truck	red truck, yellow crane cab, red interior, black engine, Hi Lift and Long Vehicle or Hi-Grab labels, 9"	50	75	125

VEHICLES

James Bond Citroen 2CV6, No. 272, 1981-86, Corgi. Photo Courtesy Mark Arruda

James Bond Lotus Esprit, No. 269-B, 1977, Corgi. Photo Courtesy Mark Arruda

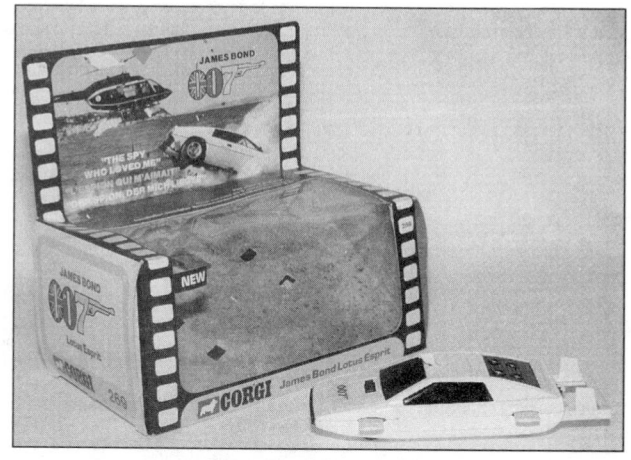

VEHICLES

James Bond Toyota 2000GT, No. 336, 1967-69, Corgi

NAME	DESCRIPTION	GOOD	EX	MINT
Magic Roundabout Musical Carousel	plastic roundabout w/Swiss musical movement, w/Dylan, Rosalie, Paul, Florence and Basil figures, rare	275	425	750
Magic Roundabout Playground	contains No. 851 Train, No. 852 Carousel, six figures, seesaw, park bench, shrubs and fowers, rare	295	500	900
Magic Roundabout Train	red and blue plastic three-piece train; accessoires include figures og Mr. Rusty, Basil, Rosaile, Paul and Dougal	70	195	350
Man From U.N.C.L.E. THRUSH-Buster	plastic interior, blue windows, two figures, two spotlights, dark metallic blue body, w/3-D Waverly ring, 4-1/8"	80	120	250
Man From U.N.C.L.E. THRUSH-Buster	plastic interior, blue windows, two figures, two spotlights, cream body, w/3-D Waverly ring, 4-1/8"	100	350	550
Marcos 3 Litre	working hood, detailed engine, black interior, Marcos decal, Whizz Wheels, issued in orange or metallic blue-green, 3-3/8"	20	30	55
Marcos Mantis	metallic red body, opening doors, cream interior and headlights, silver gray lower body base, bumpers, hood panel, spoked wheels, 4-1/4"	20	35	55
Marcos Volvo 1800 GT	issued w/either white body w/two green stripes or blue body w/two white stripes, plastic interior w/driver, spoked wheels, rubber tires, 3-5/8"	25	40	70
Massey Ferguson 165 Tractor	gray engine and chassis, red hood and fenders w/black/white Massey Ferguson 165 decals, white grille, red cast wheels; makes engine sound, 3"	35	55	90
Massey Ferguson 165 Tractor with Saw	red hood and fenders, gray engine and seat, cast yellow arm and control, chrome circular saw, 3-1/2"	55	85	140
Massey Ferguson 165 Tractor with Shovel	gray chassis, red hood, fenders and shovel arms, unpainted shovel and cylinder, red cast wheels, black plastic tires, w/figure, 5-1/8"	45	65	120
Massey Ferguson 50B Tractor	yellow body, black interior and roof, red plastic wheels w/black plastic tires, widows, 4"	15	18	75
Massey Ferguson 65 Tractor	silver metal or plastic steering wheel, seat and grille, red engine hood, red metal or plastic wheels w/black rubber tires, 3"	40	60	100
Massey Ferguson 65 Tractor And Shovel	two versions: Red bonnet w/either cream or gray chassis, red metal or orange plastic wheels; value is for each, 4-3/4"	55	85	140
Massey Ferguson Combine	red body w/yellow metal blades, metal tines, black/white decals, yellow metal wheels, 6-1/2"	70	105	175
Massey Ferguson Combine	red body, plastic yellow blades, red wheels, 6-1/2"	60	90	150
Massey Ferguson Tipping Trailer	two versions: red chassis w/either yellow or gray tipper and tailgate, red metal or platic wheels, value is for each, 3-5/8"	10	18	35
Massey Ferguson Tractor and Tipping Trailer	No. 50 tractor and No. 51 trailer, no driver	50	75	125
Massey Ferguson Tractor and Tipping Trailer	No. 50 MF tractor w/driver, No. 51 trailer	50	75	125
Massey Ferguson Tractor with Fork	red cast body and shovel, arms, cream chassis, red plastic wheels, black rubber tires, Massey Ferguson 65 decals, w/driver, 4-7/8"	60	90	150
Massey Ferguson Tractor with Shovel	two versions: either yellow and red or red and white body colors; value is for each, 6"	20	30	50
Massey Ferguson Tractor with Shovel & Trailer	No. 54 MF tractor w/driver and shovel, No. 62 trailer	30	75	150
Matra & Motorcycle Trailer	red No. 57 Talbot Matra Rancho w/two yellow and blue bikes on trailer	15	20	35
Matra and Racing Car	black/yellow No. 457 Talbot Matra Rancho and No. 160 Hesketh yellow car w/Team Corgi trailer and decals	15	35	65
Mazda 4X4 Open Truck	blue body, white roof, black windows, no interior, white plastic wheels, 4-7/8"	15	20	35
Mazda B-1600 Pickup Truck	issued in either blue and white or blue and silver bodies w/working tailgate, black interior, chrome wheels, 4-7/8"	15	20	35
Mazda Camper Pickup	red truck and white camper w/red interior and folding supports, 5-3/8"	15	25	451
Mazda Custom Pickup	orange body w/red roof, United States flag label, 4-7/8"	15	18	30

VEHICLES

NAME	DESCRIPTION	GOOD	EX	MINT
Mazda Motorway Maintenance Truck	deep yellow body w/red base, black interior and hydraulic cylinder, yellow basket w/workman figure, 6-1/8"	18	25	45
Mazda Pickup and Dinghy	two versions: red No. 493 Mazda w/"Ford" decals; or w/"Sea Spray" decals, dinghy and trailer	25	35	60
McLaren M19A Racing Car	white body, orange stripes, chrome engine, exhaust and suspension, black mirrors, driver, Yardley McLaren #55 decals, Whizz Wheels, 4-5/8"	15	25	40
McLaren M23 Racing Car	large 1:18-scale red and white body and wings w/red, white and black Texaco-Marlboro #5 decals, chrome pipes, suspension and mirrors, removable wheels, 10-1/4"	30	60	110
Mercedes-Benz 220SE Coupe	metallic maroon or blue body, cream plastic interior, medium gray base, clear windows, silver bumpers, headlights, grille and license; accessories include plastic luggage and spare wheel in boot, 4"	40	60	100
Mercedes-Benz 220SE Coupe	cream, black or dark red body, red plastic interior, clear windows, working trunk, silver bumpers, grille and plate, spare wheel in boot, 3-3/4"	40	60	100
Mercedes-Benz 240D	silver, blue or copper/beige bpdy, working trunk, two doors, clear windows, plastic interior, two hook, chrome bumpers, grille and headlights, Whizz Wheels, 5-1/4"	10	15	25
Mercedes-Benz 240D Rally	cream or tan body, black, red and blue lettering and dirt, red plastic interior, clear windows, black radiator guard and roof rack, opening doors, racing #5, 5-1/8"	10	15	25
Mercedes-Benz 240D Taxi	orange body, orange interior, black roof sign w/red and white Taxi labels, black on door, 5"	15	18	30
Mercedes-Benz 300SC Convertible	black body, black folded top, white interior, folding seat backs, detailed engine, chrome grille and wheels, lights, bumpers, 5"	8	12	25
Mercedes-Benz 300SC Hardtop	maroon body, tan top and interior, open hood and trunk, clear windows, folding seat backs, top w/chrome side irons, 5"	8	15	25
Mercedes-Benz 300SL	red body and base, tan interior, open hood and two gullwing doors, black dash, detailed engine, clear windows, chrome bumpers, 5"	8	15	25
Mercedes-Benz 300SL	silver body, tan interior, black dash, clear windows, open hood and two gullwing doors, detailed engine, chrome bumpers, 4-3/4"	8	15	25
Mercedes-Benz 300SL Coupe	chrome body, red hardtop, red stripe, clear windows, '59-60 smooth wheels no suspension, '61-65 racing stripes, 3-3/4"	45	65	130
Mercedes-Benz 300SL Roadster	blue or white body, yellow interior, plastic interior, smooth, shaped or cast wheels, racing stripes and number, driver, 3-3/4"	45	75	140
Mercedes-Benz 350SL	white body, spoke wheels or metallic dark blue body solid wheels, pale blue interior, folding seats, detailed engine, 3-3/4"	15	30	60
Mercedes-Benz 600 Pullman	metallic maroon body, cream interior and steering wheel, clear windshields, chrome grille, trim and bumpers, working windshield operators; includes instruction sheet, 4-1/4"	40	60	100
Mercedes-Benz Ambulance	white body and base, red stripes and taillights, Red Cross and black and white ambulance labels, open rear door, white interior, no figures, 5-3/4"	15	20	35
Mercedes-Benz Ambulance	four different foreign versions, white interior, open rear and two doors, blue windows and dome lights, chrome bumpers, grille and headlights, various labels; accessories include two attendat figures, 5-3/4"	15	20	35
Mercedes-Benz and Caravan	truck and trailer in two versions: w/blue No. 285 Mercedes truck and No. 490 Caravan (1975-79); w/brown No. 285 Mercedes and No. 490 Caravan (1980-81); value is for each set	15	30	50
Mercedes-Benz C-111	orange main body w/black lower and base, black interior, vents, front and rear grilles, silver headlights, red taillights, Whizz Wheels, 4"	15	20	45

VEHICLES

NAME	DESCRIPTION	GOOD	EX	MINT
Mercedes-Benz Fire Chief	light red body, black base, tan plastic interior, blue dome light, white Notruf 112 decals, red taillights, no tow hook, German export model, 5"	15	25	40
Mercedes-Benz Police Car	white body w/two different hood versions, brown interior, polizei or police lettering, blue dome light, 5"	15	18	30
Mercedes-Benz Refrigerator	yellow cab and tailgate, red semi-trailer, two-piece lowering tailgate and yellow spare wheel base, red interior, clear window, 8"	15	18	30
Mercedes-Benz Semi-Trailer	red cab and trailer, black chassis	15	18	30
Mercedes-Benz Semi-Trailer Van	black cab and plastic semi trailer, white chassis and airscreen, red doors, red-blue and yellow stripes, white Corgi lettering, 8-1/4"	15	18	30
Mercedes-Benz Tanker	tan cab, plastic tank body, black chassis, black and red Guinness labels, w/chrome or black plastic catwalk, clear windows, 7-1/4"	15	18	30
Mercedes-Benz Tanker	two different versions, white cab and tank, green chassis, chrome or black plastic catwalk, red/white/green 7-Up labels or Corgi Chemo labels, 7-1/4"	15	18	30
Mercedes-Benz Unimog & Dumper	yellow cab and tipper, red fenders and tipper chassis, charcoal gray cab chassis, black plastic mirrors or without, 6-3/4"	25	35	60
Mercedes-Benz Unimog 406	yellow body, red and green front fenders and bumpers, metallic charcoal gray chassis w/olive or tan rear plastic covers, red interior, 3-3/4"	18	25	45
Mercedes-Faun Street Sweeper	orange body w/light orange or brown figure, red interior, black chassis and unpainted brushing housing and arm castings, 5"	15	25	40
Metropolis Police Car	metallic blue body, off white interior, white roof/stripes, two working doors, clear windows, chrome bumpers, grille and headlights, two roof light bars, City of Metropolis labels, 6"	20	30	50
MG Maestro	yellow body, black trim, opaque black windows, black plastic grille, bumpers, spoiler, trim and battery hatch, clear headlights, AA Service label, 4-1/2"	15	20	35
MGA	red or metallic green body, cream seats, black dash, clear windshield, silver bumpers, grille and headlights, smooth or shaped wheels, 3-3/4"	60	90	150
MGB GT	dark red body, pale blue interior, open hatch and two doors, jewel headlights, chrome grille and bumpers, orange taillights, spoked wheels, w/suitcase, 3-1/2"	50	75	110
MGC GT	red body, black hood and base, black interior, open hatch and two doors, folding seat backs, luggage, orange taillights, Whizz Wheels, 3-1/2"	50	75	125
MGC GT	bright yellow body and base, black interior, hood and hatch, folding seats, luggage, jewel headlights, red taillights, 3-1/2"	50	75	125
Midland Red Express Coach	red one-piece body, black roof w/shaped or smooth wheels, yellow interior, clear windows, silver grille and headlights, 5-1/2"	70	105	225
Military Set	set of three, No. 904 Tiger tank, No. 920 Bell Helicopter, No. 906 Saladin Armored Car	60	90	150
Milk Truck and Trailer	blue and white No. 456 milk truck w/No. 101 trailer and milk churns	60	130	250
Mini Camping Set	cream Mini, w/red/blue tent, grille and two figures	25	40	65
Mini-Marcos GT850	white body, red-white-blue racing stripe and #7 labels, clear headlights, Whizz Wheels, opening doors and hood, 2-1/8"	20	30	50
Mini-Marcos GT850	metallic maroon body, white name and trim decals, cream interior, open hood and doors, clear windows and headlights, Golden Jacks wheels, 3-1/4"	30	45	75
Minissima	cream upper body, metallic lime green lower body w/black stripe centered, black interior, clear windows, headlights, 2-1/4"	15	20	35
Monkeemobile	red body/base, white roof, yellow interior, clear windows, four figures, chrome grille, headlights, engine, orange taillights, 4-3/4"	145	225	450

VEHICLES

NAME	DESCRIPTION	GOOD	EX	MINT
Monte Carlo Rally Set	three vehicle set, No. 326 Citroen, No. 318 Mini and No. 322 Land Rover rally cars	295	450	900
Morris Cowley	long, one-piece body in several colors, clear windows, silver lights, grille and bumper, smooth wheels, rubber tires, 3-1/8"	45	75	140
Morris Cowley-Mechanical	long, same as 202-A but w/friction motor, available in off-white or green body, 3-1/8"	55	95	170
Morris Marina 1.8 Coupe	metallic dark red or lime green body, cream interior, working hood and two doors, clear windshield, chrome grille and bumpers, Whizz Wheels, 3-3/4"	15	30	60
Morris Mini-Cooper	yellow or blue body and base and/or hood, white roof and/or hood, two versions, red plastic interior, jewel headlights, flag, No. 1 and No. 7 decals, 2-3/4"	80	150	300
Morris Mini-Cooper	red body and base, white roof, yellow interior, chrome spotlight, No. 37 and Monte Carlo Rally decals, 2-7/8"	60	125	250
Morris Mini-Cooper Deluxe	black body/base, red roof, yellow and black wicker work decals on sides and rear, yellow interior, gray steering wheel, jewel headlights, 2-3/4"	45	65	120
Morris Mini-Minor	one-piece body in dark or metallic blue or orange body, plastic interior, silver lights, grille and bumpers, red taillights, Whizz Wheels, 2-7/8"	30	45	75
Morris Mini-Minor	light blue or red body w/shaped and/or smooth wheels, plastic interior, silver bumpers, grille and headlights, 2-3/4"	40	60	100
Morris Mini-Minor	sky blue body w/shaped and/or smooth wheels, plastic interior, silver bumpers, grille and headlights	100	175	350
Motorway Ambulance	white body, dark blue interior, red-white-black Accident and Red Cross labels, dark blue windows, clear headlights, red die cast base and bumpers, 4"	10	15	30
Mr. McHenry's Trike	red and yellow trike and trailer; accessories include Mr. McHenry and Zebedee figures	70	105	175
Muppet Vehicles	Kermit's Car	15	35	60
Muppet Vehicles	Miss Piggy's Sports Coupe	15	30	50
Muppet Vehicles	Fozzie Bear's Truck	15	30	50
Muppet Vehicles	Animal's Percussionmobile	15	30	50
Mustang Organ Grinder Dragster	yellow body w/green/yellow name, #39 and racing stripe decals, black base, green windshield, red interior, roll bar, w/driver, 4"	20	30	50
NASA Space Shuttle	white body, two open hatches, black plastic interior, jets and base, unpainted retracting gear castings, black plastic wheels, w/satalite, 6"	30	45	75
National Express Bus	variety of colors and label variations	8	15	25
Noddy's Car	second issue: same as first issue except Master Tubby is substituted for Golliwog, 3-3/4"	100	200	350
Noddy's Car	first issue: yellow body, red chassis and fenders, figures of Noddy, Big-Ears, and black, gray, or light tan face Golliwog, 3-3/4"	200	400	600
Noddy's Car	yellow body, red chassis, Noddy alone, closed trunk w/spa	n/a	n/a	n/a
NSU Sport Prinz	metallic burgundy or maroon body, yellow interior, one-piece body, silver bumpers, headlights and trim, shaped wheels, 3-1/4"	30	45	75
Off Road Set	No. 5 decal on No. 447 Jeep, blue boat, trailer	15	20	45
Olds Toronado and Speedboat	blue No. 276 Toronado, blue and yellow boat and chrome trailer, w/swordfish decals and three figures	60	90	165
Oldsmobile 88 Staff Car	olive drab body, four figures, white decals, 4-1/4"	50	75	125
Oldsmobile Sheriff's Car	black upper body w/white sides, red interior w/red dome light and County Sheriff decals on doors, single body casting, 4-1/4"	50	75	125
Oldsmobile Super 88	three versions: light blue, light or dark metallic blue body w/white stripes, red interior, single body casting, 4-1/4"	40	60	100
Oldsmobile Toronado	metallic copper, metallic blue or red one-piece body, cream interior, Golden jacks, gray tow hook, clear windows, bumpers, grille, headlights, 4-3/16"	35	55	90

VEHICLES

NAME	DESCRIPTION	GOOD	EX	MINT
Oldsmobile Toronado	metallic medium or dark blue body, cream interior, one-piece body, clear windshield, chrome bumpers, grille, headlight covers, shaped or cast spoked wheels, 4-1/8"	35	55	90
Opel Senator Doctor's Car		10	15	25
Open Top Disneyland Bus	yellow body, red interior and stripe, Disneyland labels, eight spoked wheels or orange body, white interior and stripe, 4-3/4"	30	50	95
OSI DAF City Car	orange/red body, light cream interior, textured black roof, sliding left door, working hood, hatch and two right doors, Whizz Wheels, 2-3/4"	18	25	45
Penguinmobile	white body, black and white lettering on orange-yellow-blue decals, gold body panels, seats, air scoop, chrome engine, w/penguin figure, 3-3/4"	20	30	65
Pennyburn Workmen's Trailer	blue body w/working lids, red plastic interior, three plastic tools, shaped wheels, plastic tires, 3-1/8"	15	35	50
Peugeot 505 STI	red body and base, red interior, blue-red-white Taxi labels, black grille, bumpers, tow hook, chrome headlights and wheels, opening doors, 4-7/8"	8	15	25
Peugeot 505 Taxi	cream body, red interior, red, white and blue taxi decals, 4-7/8"	8	15	25
Platform Trailer	in five versions: silver body, blue chassis; silver body, yellow chassis; blue body, red chassis; blue body, yellow chassis, 4-3/8"	10	20	45
Plymouth Sports Suburban	dark cream body, tan roof, red interior, die cast base, red axle, silver bumpers, trim and grille and rubber tires, 4-1/4"	40	60	100
Plymouth Sports Suburban	pale blue body w/silver trim, red roof, yellow interior, gray die cast base without rear axle bulge, shaped wheels, 4-1/4"	40	60	100
Plymouth Suburban Mail Car	white upper, blue lower body w/red stripes, gray die cast base without rear axle bulge, silver bumpers and grille, U.S. Mail decals, 4-1/4"	55	85	140
Police Land Rover	white body, red and blue police stripes, black lettering, open rear door, opaque black windows, blue dome light, working roof light and siren, 5"	15	25	50
Police Land Rover and Horse Box	white No. 421 Land Rover w/police decals and mounted policeman, No. 112 Horse Box	30	45	75
Police Vigilant Range Rover	white body, red interior, black shutters, blue dome light, two chrome and amber spotlights, black grille, silver headlights, Police decals, w/police figure, 4"	25	35	60
Pontiac Firebird	metallic silver body and base, red interior, black hood, stripes and convertible top, doors open, clear windows, folding seats, Golden Jacks wheels, 4"	50	75	125
Pony Club Set	brown/white No. 421 Land Rover w/Corgi Pony Club decals, horse box, horse and rider	30	45	75
Pop Art Mini-Motest	light red body and base, yellow interior, jewel headlights, orange taillights, yellow-blue-purple pop art and "Motest" decals; very rare, 2-3/4"	1000	1500	2700
Popeye's Paddle Wagon	yellow and white body, red chassis, blue rear fenders, bronze and yellow stacks, white plastic deck, blue lifeboat w/Swee' Pea; includes figures of Popeye, Olive Oyl, Bluto and Wimpey, 4-7/8"	195	300	525
Porsche 917	red or metallic blue body, black or gray base, blue or amber tinted windows and headlights, open rear hood, headlights, Whizz Wheels, 4-1/4"	15	20	45
Porsche 92 Turbo	black body w/gold trim, yellow interior, four chrome headlights, clear windshield, taillight-license plate decal, opening doors and hatchback, 4-1/2"	15	20	35
Porsche 924	bright orange body, dark red interior, black plastic grille, multicolored stripes, swivel roof spotlight, 4-1/2"	10	15	25
Porsche 924	red or metallic light brown or green body, dark red interior, two doors open and rear window, chrome headlights, black plastic grille, racing #2, 4-7/8"	10	25	50
Porsche 924 Police Car	white body w/different hood and doors versions, blue and chrome light, Polizei white on green panels or Police labels, "1" or "20" decals, 4-1/4"	15	25	40

VEHICLES

NAME	DESCRIPTION	GOOD	EX	MINT
Porsche Carrera 6	white upper body, red front hood, doors, upper fins and base, black interior, purple rear window, tinted engine cover, racing #60 decals, 3-3/4"	25	35	60
Porsche Carrera 6	white body, red or blue trim, blue or amber tinted engine covers, black interior, clear windshield and canopy, red jewel taillights, #1 or #20 decals, 3-7/8"	30	45	75
Porsche Targa 911S	metallic blue, silver-blue or green body, black roof w/or without stripe, orange interior, open hood and two doors, chrome engine and bumpers, Whizz Wheels, 3-1/2"	25	35	60
Porsche Targa Police Car	white body and base, red doors and hood, black roof and plastic interior also comes w/an orange interior, unpainted siren, Polizei labels, 3-1/2"	25	35	60
Porsche-Audi 917	white body, red and black No. 6, L and M, Porsche Audi and stripe labels or orange body, orange, two-tone green, white No. 6, racing driver, 4-3/4"	15	20	35
Powerboat Team	white/red No. 319 Jaguar w/red/white boat on silver trailer, Team Corgi Carlsberg, Union Jack and #1 decals on boat	25	35	60
Priestman Cub Crane	orange body, red chassis and two-piece bucket, unpainted bucket arms, lower boom, knobs, gears and drum castings, clear window, Hi-Grab labels, 9"	50	75	125
Priestman Cub Power Shovel	orange upper body and panel, yellow lower body, lock rod and chassis, rubber or plastic treads, pulley panel, gray boom, w/figure of driver, 6"	40	60	100
Priestman Shovel and Carrier	No. 1128 cub shovel and No. 1131 low loader machinery carrier	90	135	225
Professionals Ford Capri	metallic silver body and base, red interior, black spoiler, grille, bumpers, tow hook and trim, blue windows, chrome wheels; inlcudes figures of Cowley, Bodie and Doyle, 5"	30	45	85
Psychedelic Ford Mustang	light blue body and base, aqua interior, red-orange-yellow No. 20 and flower decals, cast eight spoke wheels, plastic tire, 3-3/4"	30	45	95
Public Address Land Rover	green No. 438 Land Rover body, yellow plastic rear body and loudspeakers, red interior, clear windows, silver bumper, grille and headlights; includes figure w/microphone and girl figure w/pamphlets, 4"	50	75	145
Quartermaster Dragster	long, dark metallic green upper body w/green/yellow/black #5 and Quartermaster decals, light green lower body, w/driver, 5-3/4"	30	45	75
RAC Land Rover	light or dark blue body, plastic interior and rear cover, gray antenna, RAC and Radio Rescue decals, 3-3/4"	60	90	150
Radio Luxembourg Dragster	long, blue body w/yellow, white and blue John Wolfe Racing, Radio Luxembourg and #5 decals, silver engine, w/driver, 5-3/4"	30	45	85
Radio Roadshow Van	white body, red plastic roof and rear interior, opaque black windows, red-white-black Radio Tele Luxembourg labels, gray plastic loudspeakers and working radio in van, 4-3/4"	25	35	60
RAF Land Rover	blue body and cover, one-piece body, sheet metal rear cover, RAF rondel decal, w/or without suspension, silver bumper, 3-3/4"	60	90	150
RAF Land Rover & Bloodhound	set of three standard colored, No, 351 RAF Land Rover, No. 1115 Bloodhound Missile, No. 1116 Ramp and No. 1117 Trolley	150	300	600
RAF Land Rover and Thunderbird	Standard colors, No. 350 Thunderbird Missile on Trolley and 351 RAF Land Rover	100	150	300
Rambler Marlin Fastback	red body, black roof and trim, cream interior, clear windshield, folding seats, chrome bumpers, grille and headlights, opening doors, 4-1/8"	35	55	90
Rambler Marlin with Kayak and Trailer	blue No. 263 Marlin w/roof rack, blue/white trailer, w/two kayaks	100	150	250
Range Rover Ambulance	two different versions of body sides, red interior, raised roof, open upper and lower doors, black shutters, blue dome light, Ambulance label; includes stretcher and two ambulance attendants, 4"	20	30	50

VEHICLES

Open Top Disneyland Bus, No. 470-B, 1977-78, Corgi

Saint's Volvo P-180, No. 258, 1965-69, Corgi. Photo Courtesy Mark Arruda

Spider-Buggy, No. 261-B, 1979-81, Corgi. Photo Courtesy Mark Arruda

NAME	DESCRIPTION	GOOD	EX	MINT
Raygo Rascal Roller	dark yellow body, base and mounting, green interior and engine, orange and silver roller mounting and castings, clear windshield, 4-7/8"	15	25	45
Red Wheelie Motorcycle	red plastic body and fender w/black/white/yellow decals, black handlebars, kickstand and seat, chrome engine, pipes, flywheel-powered rear wheel, 4"	10	15	25
Reliant Bond Rug 700 E.S.	bright orange or lime green body, off white seats, black trim, silver headlights, red taillights, Bug label, 2-1/2"	15	25	50
Renault 11 GTL	light tan or maroon body and base, red interior, opening doors and rear hatch, lifting hatch cover, folding seats, grille, 4-1/4"	15	25	40
Renault 16	metallic maroon body, dark yellow interior, chrome base, grille and bumpers, clear windows, opening bonnet and hatch cover, Renault decal, 3-3/4"	25	35	60
Renault 16TS	metallic blue body w/Renault decal on working hatch, clear windows, detailed engine, yellow interior, 3-7/8"	20	25	50
Renault 5 Police Car	white body, red interior, blue dome light, black hood, hatch and doors w/white Police labels, orange taillights, aerial, 3-7/8"	15	20	35
Renault 5 Turbo	bright yellow body, red plastic interior, black roof and hood, working hatch and two doors, black dash, chrome rear engine, racing #8Cibie and other sponsor decals, 3-3/4"	15	18	25
Renault 5 Turbo	white body, red roof, red and blue trim painted on, No. 5 lettering, blue and white label on windshield, facom decal, 4"	15	18	25
Renault 5TS	light blue body, red plastic interior, dark blue roof, dome light, S.O.S. Medicine lettering, working hatch and two doors, French issue, 3-3/4"	20	35	70
Renault 5TS	metallic golden orange body, black trim, tan plasic interior, working hatch and two doors, clear windows and headlights, 3-3/4"	15	18	30
Renault 5TS Fire Chief	red body, tan interior, amber headlights, gray antenna, black/white Sapeurs Pompiers decals, blue dome light, French export issue, 3-3/4"	15	25	40
Renault Alpine 5TS	dark blue body, off white interior, red and chrome trim, clear windows and headlights, gray base and bumpers, black grille, opening doors and hatchback, 3-3/4"	15	25	40
Renault Floride	one-piece dark red, maroon or lime green body, clear windows, silver bumper, grille, lights and plates, red taillights, smooth or shaped hubs, rubber tires, 3-5/8"	35	55	95
Renegade Jeep	dark blue body w/no top, white interior, base and bumper, white plastic wheels and rear mounted spare, 4"	8	15	25
Renegade Jeep with Hood	yellow body w/removeable hood, red interior, base, bumper, white plastic wheels, side mounted spare, No. 8, 4"	8	15	25
Rice Beaufort Double Horse Box	long, blue body and working gates, white roof, brown plastic interior, two horses, cast wheels, plastic tires, 3-3/8"	15	30	50
Rice Pony Trailer	cast body and chassis w/working tailgate, horse, in six color variations, smooth or shaped hubs, cast or wire drawbar, 3-3/8"	20	30	50
Riley Pathfinder	red or dark blue one-piece body, clear windows, silver lights, grille and bumpers, smooth wheels, rubber tires, 4"	45	65	125
Riley Pathfinder Police Car	black body w/blue/white Police lettering, unpainted roof sign, gray antenna, 4"	50	75	135
Riley Pathfinder-Mechanical	w/friction motor and either red or blue body, 4"	60	95	170
Riot Police Quad Tractor	white body and chassis, brown interior, red roof w/white panel, gold water cannons, gold spotlight w/amber lense, Riot Police and No. 6 labels, 3-3/4"	15	20	35
Road Repair Unit	dark yellow Land Rover w/battery hatch and trailer w/red plastic interior w/sign and open panels, stripe and Roadwork labels, 10"	15	25	40

VEHICLES

NAME	DESCRIPTION	GOOD	EX	MINT
Rocket Age Set	set of eight standard models including: No. 350 Thunderbird Missile on Trolley, No. 351 RAF Land Rover, No. 352 RAF Staff Car, No. 353 Radar Scanner, No. 1106 Decca Radar Van and No. 1108 Bloodhound missle w/ramp	325	650	1400
Rocket Launcher and Trailer	steel blue and red launcher, fires rocket	25	35	60
Roger Clark's Capri	white body, black hood, grille and interior, open doors, folding seats, chrome bumpers, clear headlights, red taillights, Racing #73, decal sheet, Whizz Wheels, 4"	15	25	55
Rolls-Royce Corniche	different color versions w/light brown interior, working hood, trunk and two doors, clear windows, folding seats, chrome bumpers, 5-1/2"	10	20	40
Rolls-Royce Silver Ghost	silver body/hood, charcoal and silver chassis, bronze interior, gold lights, box and tank, clear windows, dash lights, radiator, 4-1/2"	15	30	60
Rolls-Royce Silver Shadow	metallic blue or gold body, bright blue interior, working hood, trunk and two doors, clear windows, folding seats, spare wheel, 4-3/4"	25	40	65
Rolls-Royce Silver Shadow	metallic white upper/dusty blue lower body, working hood, trunk and two doors, clear windows, folding seats, chrome bumpers, Golden Jacks wheels, 4-3/4"	30	50	95
Rolls-Royce Silver Shadow	metallic silver upper and metallic blue lower body, light brown interior, no hole in trunk for spare tire, Whizz Wheels, 4-3/4"	25	40	65
Rolls-Royce Silver Shadow	metallic silver upper and metallic blue lower body, light brown interior, hole in trunk for spare tire mounting, Whizz Wheels, 4-3/4"	25	40	65
Routemaster Bus-Promotionals	different body and interior versions and labels promotional, 4-7/8"	15	25	40
Rover 2000	metallic blue w/red interior or maroon body w/yellow interior, gray steering wheel, clear windshields, 3-3/4"	30	45	75
Rover 2000 Rally	two different versions, metallic dark red body, white roof, shaped wheels, No. 136 and Monte Carlo Rally decal, 3-3/4"	50	95	175
Rover 2000 Rally	white body, red interior, black bonnet, #21 decal, spoked wheels, 3-3/4"	55	100	200
Rover 2000TC	metallic olive green or maroon one-piece body, light brown interior, chrome bumpers/grille, jewel headlights, red taillights, Golden Jacks wheels, 3-3/4"	30	45	75
Rover 2000TC	metallic purple body, light orange interior, black grille, one-piece body, amber windows, chrome bumpers and headlights, Whizz Wheels, 3-3/4"	25	35	60
Rover 3500	three different body and interior versions, plastic interior, open hood, hatch and two doors, lifting hatch cover, 5-1/4"	8	15	25
Rover 3500 Police Car	white body, light red interior, red stripes, white plastic roof sign, blue dome light, red and blue Police and badge label, 5-1/4"	8	15	25
Rover 3500 Triplex	white sides and hatch, blue roof and hood, red plastic interior and trim, detailed engine, red-white-black no. 1, 5-1/4"	8	15	20
Rover 90	one-piece body in several colors, silver headlights, grille and bumpers, smooth wheels, rubber tires; mulitple colors available, 3-7/8"	50	75	145
Rover 90-Mechanical	w/friction motor and red, green, gray or metallic green body, 3-7/8"	60	90	170
Safari Land Rover and Trailer	black and white No. 341 Land Rover in two versions: w/chrome wheels, 1976; w/red wheels, 1977-80; came with Waren and Lion figures	20	30	60
Saint's Jaguar XJS	white body, red interior, black trim, Saint figure hood label, opening doors, black grille, bumpers and tow hook, chrome headlights, 5-1/4"	30	45	85
Saint's Volvo P-1800	one-piece white body w/red Saint decals on hood, gray base, clear windows, black interior w/driver, Whizz Wheels, 3-5/8"	55	95	200

VEHICLES

NAME	DESCRIPTION	GOOD	EX	MINT
Saint's Volvo P-1800	three versions of white body w/silver trim and different colored Saint decals on hood, driver, one-piece body, 3-3/4"	55	85	175
Saladin Armored Car	olive drab body, swiveling turret and raising barrel castings, black plastic barrel end and tires, olive cast wheels, w/twelve shells, fires shells, 3-1/4"	30	45	75
Scammell Carrimore Tri-deck Car Transporter	orange lower cab, chassis and lower deck, white upper cab and middle deck, blue top deck (three decks), red interior, black hydraulic cylinders, detachable rear ramp, 11"	35	60	130
Scammell Coop Semi-Trailer Truck	white cab and trailer fenders, light blue semi-trailer, red interior, gray bumper base, jewel headlights, black hitch lever, spare wheel, 9"	135	210	350
Scammell Ferrymasters Semi-Trailer Truck	white cab, red interior, yellow chassis, black fenders, clear windows, jewel headlights, cast wheels, plastic tires, 9-1/4"	60	90	150
Scania Bulk Carrier	white cab, orange and white silos, clear windows, orange screen, black/orange Spillers Flour decals, Whizz Wheels, 5-5/8"	7	15	30
Scania Bulk Carrier	white cab, blue and white silos, ladders and catwalk, amber windows, blue British Sugar decals, Whizz Wheels, 5-5/8"	7	15	30
Scania Container Truck	yellow truck and box w/red Ryder Truck rental decals, clear windows, black exhaust stack, red rear doors, six-spoke Whizz Wheels, 5-1/2"	7	15	30
Scania Container Truck	blue cab w/blue and white box and rear doors, white deck, Securicor Parcels decals, in red or white rear door colors, 5-1/2"	7	15	30
Scania Container Truck	white cab and box w/BRS Truck Rental decals, blue windows, red screen, roof and rear doors, 5-1/2"	7	15	30
Scania Dump Truck	yellow truck and tipper w/black Wimpey decals, in two versions: either clear or green windows; six-spoked Whizz Wheels, 5-3/4"	7	15	30
Scania Dump Truck	white cab w/green tipper, black/green Barratt decals, black exhaust and hydraulic cylinders, six-spoked Whizz Wheels, 5-3/4"	7	15	30
Security Van	black body, blue mesh windows and dome light, yellow/black Security decals, Whizz Wheels, 4"	7	15	25
Service Ramp	metallic blue and silver operable ramp	30	45	95
Shadow-Ford Racing Car	black body and base w/white/black #17, UOP and American flag decals, cast chrome suspension and pipes, Embassy Racing label, 5-5/8"	10	20	50
Shadow-Ford Racing Car	white body, red stripes, driver, chrome plastic pipes, mirrors and steering wheel, in two versions, Jackie Collins driver figure, 5-5/8"	10	20	45
Shell or BP Garage	gas station/garage w/pumps and other accessories including five different cars; in two versions: Shell or B.P., rare; value is for each set	295	550	1200
Shelvoke and Drewry Garbage Truck	long, orange or red cab, silver body w/City Sanitation decals, black interior, grille and bumpers, clear windows, 5-7/8"	15	25	40
Sikorsky Skycrane Army Helicopter	olive drab and yellow body w/Red Cross and Army decals, 5-1/2"	15	20	40
Sikorsky Skycrane Casualty Helicopter	red and white body, black rotors and wheels, orange pipes, working rear hatch, Red Cross decals, 6-1/8"	15	20	40
Silo & Conveyor Belt	w/yellow conveyor and Corgi Harvesting Co. decal on silo	35	50	85
Silver Jubilee Landau	Landua w/four horses, two footmen, two riders, Queen and Prince figures, and Corgi dog, in two versions	15	25	40
Silver Jubilee London Transport Bus	silver body w/red interior, no passengers, decals read "Woolworth Welcomes the World" and "The Queen's Silver, 4-7/8"	15	18	30
Silver Streak Jet Dragster	metallic blue body w/Firestone and flag decals on tank, silver engine, orange plastic jet and nose cone, 6-1/4"	15	25	45
Silverstone Racing Layout	seven-vehicle set w/accessories; Vanwall, Lotus XI, Aston Martin, Mercedes 300SL, BRM, Ford Thunderbird, Land Rover Truck; another version has a No. 154 Ferrari substituted for Lotus XI	400	700	1500

VEHICLES

CORGI

NAME	DESCRIPTION	GOOD	EX	MINT
Simca 1000	chrome plated body, #8 and red-white-blue stripe decals, one-piece body, clear windshield, red interior, 3-1/2"	30	45	75
Simon Snorkel Fire Engine	red body w/yellow interior, blue windows and dome lights, chrome deck, black hose reels and hydraulic cylinders, 10-1/2"	30	45	75
Simon Snorkel Fire Engine	red body w/yellow interior, two snorkle arms, rotating base, five firemen in cab and one in basket, various styles of wheels, 9-7/8"	35	55	90
Skyscraper Tower Crane	red body w/yellow chassis and booms, gold hook, gray loads of block, black/white Skyscraper decals, black tracks, 9-1/8" tall^	30	45	75
Spider-Bike	medium blue body, one-piece body, dark blue plastic front body and seat, blue and red Spider-Man figure, amber windshield, black or white wheels, 4-1/2"	40	60	85
Spider-Buggy	red body, blue hood, clear windows, dark blue dash, seat and crane, chrome base w/bumper and steps, silver headlights; includes Spider-Man and Green Goblin figures, 5-1/8"	50	75	150
Spider-Copter	blue body w/Spider-Man decals, red plastic legs, tongue and tail rotor, black windows and main rotor, 5-5/8"	30	45	85
Spider-Man Set	set of three: No. 266 Spider-Bike, No. 928 Spider-Copter and No. 261 Spider-Buggy	80	160	350
Standard Vanguard	one-piece red and pale green body, clear windows, silver lights, grille and bumpers, smooth wheels, rubber tires, 3-5/8"	50	75	125
Standard Vanguard RAF Staff Car	blue body, RAF decals, 3-3/4"	55	85	140
Standard Vanguard-Mechanical	w/friction motor and yellow or off-white body w/black or gray base, or cream body w/red roof, 3-5/8"	55	90	170
Starsky and Hutch Ford Torino	red one-piece body, white trim, light yellow interior, clear windows, chrome bumpers, grille and headlights, orange taillights; includes Starsky, Hutch and Bandit figures, 5-3/4"	35	55	100
STP Patrick Eagle Racing Car	red body w/red, white and black STP and #20 decals, chrome lower engine and suspension, black plastic upper engine; includes Patrick Eagle driver figure, 5-5/8"	20	30	50
Stromberg Jet Ranger Helicopter	black body w/yellow trim and interior, clear windows, black plastic rotors, white/blue decals, 5-5/8"	30	45	85
Studebaker Golden Hawk	second issue: gold painted body, shaped hubs	60	180	180
Studebaker Golden Hawk	first issue: gold plated body, white flashing, shaped hubs	55	85	140
Studebaker Golden Hawk	one-piece body in blue and gold or white and gold, clear windows, silver lights, grille and bumpers, smooth wheels, rubber tires, 4-1/8"	55	85	140
Studebaker Golden Hawk-Mechanical	w/friction motor and white body w/gold trim, 4-1/8"	70	105	175
Stunt Motorcycle	made for Corgi Rockets race track, gold cycle, blue rider w/yellow helmet, clear windshield, plastic tires, 3"	70	105	175
SU-100 Medium Tank	olive and cream camo upper body, gray lower, working hatch and barrel, black treads, red star and #103 decals; twelve shells included, fires shells, 5-5/8"	30	50	80
Sunbeam Imp Police Car	three versions, white or light blue body, tan interior, driver, black or white hood and lower doors, dome light, Police decals, cast wheels, 3-1/4"	25	45	85
Sunbeam Imp Rally	metallic blue body w/white stripes, Monte Carlo Rally and #77 decals, cast wheels, 3-3/8"	20	45	85
Super Karts	two karts, orange and blue, Whizz Wheels in front, slicks on rear, silver and gold drivers	15	18	30
Superman Set	set of three: No. 265 Supermobile, No. 925 Daily Planet Helicopter and No. 260 Metropolis Police Car	70	120	225
Supermobile	blue body, red, chrome or gray fists, red interior, clear canopy, driver, chrome arms w/removeable "striking fists", 5-1/2"	30	45	75

VEHICLES

NAME	DESCRIPTION	GOOD	EX	MINT
Supervan	silver van w/Superman decals, working rear doors, chrome spoked wheels, 4-5/8"	15	25	50
Surtees TS9 Racing Car	black upper engine, chrome lower engine, pipes and exhaust, driver, Brook Bond Oxo-Rob Walker decals, eight-spoke Whizz Wheels, 4-5/8"	15	20	40
Surtees TS9B Racing Car	red body w/white stripes and wing, black plastic lower engine, driver, chrome upper engine, pipes, suspension, eight-spoke wheels, 4-3/8"	15	20	40
Talbot-Matra Rancho	red and black, green and black or white and blue body, working tailgate and hatch, clear windows, plastic interior, black bumpers, grille and tow hook, 4-3/4"	10	15	25
Tandem Disc Harrow	yellow main frame, red upper frame, working wheels linkage, unpainted linkage and cast discs, black plastic tires, 3-5/8"	15	20	45
Tarzan Set	metallic green No. 421 Land Rover w/trailer and Dinghy; cage, five figures and other accessories	100	150	275
Thunderbird Bermuda Taxi	white body w/blue, yellow or green plastic canopy w/red fringe, yellow interior, driver, yellow and black labels, 4"	50	75	125
Thunderbird Missile and Trolley	ice blue or silver missile, RAF blue trolley, red rubber nose cone, plastic tow bar, steering front and rear axles, 5-1/2"	55	85	165
Thwaites Tusker Skip Dumper	yellow body, chassis and tipper, driver and seat, hydraulic cylinder, red wheels, black tires two sizes, name labels, Whizz Wheels, 3-1/8"	10	20	40
Tiger Mark I Tank	tan and green camouflage finish, German emblem, swiveling turret and raising barrel castings, black plastic barrel end, antenna; includes thwelve shells, fires shells, 6"	30	45	75
Tipping Farm Trailer	cast chassis and tailgate, red plastic tipper and wheels, black tires, in two versions, 5-1/8"	10	15	25
Tipping Farm Trailer	red working tipper and tailgates, yellow chassis, red plastic wheels, black tires, w/detachable raves, 4-1/4"	10	15	30
Tour de France Set	white and black body Renault w/Paramount Film roof sign, rear platform w/cameraman and black camera on tripod, plus bicycle and rider	60	90	200
Tour de France Set	w/white No. 373 Peugeot, red and yellow Raliegh and Total logos, Racing cycles, includes manager figures	25	45	90
Touring Caravan	white body w/blue trim, white plastic open roof and door, pale blue interior, red plastic hitch and awning, 4-3/4"	15	25	40
Tower Wagon and Lamp Standard	red No. 409 Jeep Tower wagon w/yellow basket, workman figure and lamp post	40	60	120
Toyota 2000 GT	metallic dark blue or purple body, cream interior, one-piece body, red gear shift and antenna, two red and two amber taillights, Whizz Wheels, 4"	15	30	55
Tractor and Beast Carrier	No. 55 Fordson tractor, figures and No. 58 beast carrier	65	100	165
Tractor with Shovel and Trailer	standard colors, No. 69 Massey Ferguson Tractor and No. 62 Tipping Trailer	65	100	165
Tractor, Trailer and Field Gun	tan tractor body and chassis, trailer body, base and opening doors, gun chassis and raising barrel castings, brown plastic interior; twelve shells included, fires shells, 10-3/4"	30	50	80
Transporter & Six Cars	Scammell transporter w/six cars: No. 180 Mini DeLuxe, No. 204 Mini, No. 339 Mini Rally, No. 201 The Saint's Volvo, No. 340 Sunbeam Imp, No. 378 MGC GT; includes bag of cones and leaflet	250	450	900
Transporter and Six Cars	first issue: #1138 Ford 'H' Series Transporter w/six cars, #252 Rover 2000, blue #251 Hillman Imp, #440 Ford Cortina Estate, #180 Mini w/'wickerwork', metallic maroon #204 Mini, and #321 Mini Rally ('1966 Monte Carlo Rally') racing No. 2; second issue: s	225	365	700
Triumph Acclaim Driving School	yellow or red body/base, Corgi Motor School decals, black roof mounted steering wheel steers front wheels, clear windows, 4-3/4"	15	25	50

CORGI

NAME	DESCRIPTION	GOOD	EX	MINT
Triumph Acclaim Driving School	dark yellow body w/black trim, black roof mounted steering wheel steers front wheels, clear windows, mirrors, bumpers, 4-3/4"	15	25	40
Triumph Acclaim HLS	metallic peacock blue body/base, black trim, light brown interior, clear windows, mirrors, bumpers, vents, tow hook, 4-3/4"	15	18	30
Triumph Herald Coupe	blue or gold top and lower body, white upper body, red interior, clear windows, silver bumpers, grille, headlights, shaped hubs, 3-1/2"	35	65	110
Triumph TR2	cream body w/red seats, light green body w/white or cream seats, one-piece body, clear windshield, silver grille, 3-1/4"	70	105	175
Triumph TR3	metallic olive or cream body, red seats, one-piece body, clear windshield, silver grille, bumpers and headlights, smooth or shaped hubs, 2-1/4"	60	90	150
Trojan Heinkel	issued in mauve, red, orange or lilac body, plastic interior, silver bumpers and headlights, red taillights, suspension, smooth spun or detailed cast wheels, 2-1/2"	35	55	95
Tyrrell P34 Racing Car	without yellow decals, First National Bank labels, w/driver in red or orange helmet	20	30	55
Tyrrell P34 Racing Car	dark blue body and wings w/yellow stripes, #4 and white Elf and Union Jack decals, chrome plastic engine, w/driver in red or blue helmet, 4-3/8"	20	30	55
Tyrrell-Ford Racing Car	dark blue body w/blue/black/white Elf and #1 decals, chrome suspension, pipes, mirrors, Jackie Stewart driver figure, 4-5/8"	18	25	50
U.S. Racing Buggy	white body w/red/white/blue stars, stripes and USA #7 decals, red base, gold engine, red plastic panels, driver, 3-3/4"	18	25	50
Unimog Dump Truck	yellow cab, chassis, rear frame and blue tipper, fenders and bumpers, red interior, no mirrors, gray tow hook, hydraulic cylinders, 4"	20	30	50
Unimog Dump Truck	blue cab, yellow tipper, fenders and bumpers, metallic charcoal gray chassis, red interior, black mirrors, gray tow hook, 3-3/4"	20	30	50
Unimog Dumper & Priestman Cub Shovel	standard colors, #1145 Mercedes-Benz unimog w/Dumper and 1128 Priestman Cub Shovel	70	105	175
Unimog with Snowplow (Mercedes-Benz)	6" four different body versions, red interior, cab, rear body, fender-plow mounting, lower and charcoal upper chassis, rear fenders	30	45	75
Vanwall Racing Car	clear windshield, unpainted dash, silver pipes and decals, smooth wheels, rubber tires, in three versions: green body or red body w/silver or yellow seats, 3-3/4"	35	55	120
Vauxhall Velox	one-piece body in red, cream, yellow or yellow and red body, clear windows, silver lights, grille and bumpers, smooth wheels, rubber tires, 3-3/4"	50	75	150
Vauxhall Velox-Mechanical	w/friction motor; orange, red, yellow or cream body, 3-3/4"	60	90	170
Vegas Ford Thunderbird	orange/red body and base, black interior and grille, open hood and trunk, amber windshield, white seats, driver, chrome bumper, 5-1/4"	25	40	75
VM Polo Mail Car	bright yellow body, black DBP and Posthorn labels, German issue	25	35	60
Volkswagen 1200	dark yellow body, white roof, red interior and dome light, unpainted base and bumpers, black and white ADAC Strassenwacht, Whizz Wheels, 3-1/2"	60	90	150
Volkswagen 1200	seven different color and label versions, plastic interior, one-piece body, silver headlights, red taillights, die cast base and bumpers, 3-1/2"	20	45	85
Volkswagen 1200 Driving School	metallic red or blue body, yellow interior, gold roof mounted steering wheel that steers, silver headlights, red taillights, 3-1/2"	25	35	60
Volkswagen 1200 Police Car	two different body versions made for Germany, Netherlands and Switzerland, blue dome light in chrome collar, Polizei or Politie decals, 3-1/2"	40	60	100

VEHICLES

733

NAME	DESCRIPTION	GOOD	EX	MINT
Volkswagen 1200 Rally	light blue body, off-white plastic interior, silver headlights, red tailights, suspension, Whizz Wheels, 3-1/2"	20	30	50
Volkswagen Breakdown Van	tan or white body, red interior and equipment boxes, clear windshield, chrome tools, spare wheels, red VW emblem, no lettering, 4"	50	75	125
Volkswagen Delivery Van	white upper and red lower body, plastic red or yellow interior, silver bumpers and headlights, red VW emblem, shaped wheels, 3-1/4"	55	85	140
Volkswagen Driving School	metallic blue body, yellow interior, gold roof mounted steering wheel that steers, silver headlights, red taillights, 3-1/2"	25	40	70
Volkswagen East African Safari	light red body, brown interior, working front and rear hood, clear windows, spare wheel on roof steers front wheels, jewel headlights, w/rhinocerous figure, 3-1/2"	60	130	285
Volkswagen Kombi Bus	off-green upper and olive green lower body, red interior, silver bumpers and headlights, red VW emblem, shaped wheels, 3-3/4"	50	75	125
Volkswagen Military Personnel Carrier	olive drab body, white decals, driver, 3-1/2"	55	95	180
Volkswagen Pickup	dark yellow body, red interior and rear plastic cover, silver bumpers and headlights, red VW emblem, shaped wheels, 3-1/2"	45	65	110
Volkswagen Police Car/Foreign Issues	five different versions, one-piece body, red interior, dome light, silver headlights, red taillights, clear windows, Whizz Wheels, 3-1/2"	60	90	150
Volkswagen Tobler Van	light blue body, plastic interior, silver bumpers, Trans-o-lite headlights and roof panel, shaped wheels, rubber tires, 3-1/2"	55	85	140
Volvo Concrete Mixer	yellow or orange cab, red or white mixer w/yellow and black stripes, rear chassis, chrome chute and unpainted hitch casings, 8-1/4"	30	45	75
Volvo P-1800	one-piece body light brown, dark red, pink or dark red body, clear windows, plastic interior, shaped wheels, rubber tires, 3-1/2"	40	60	100
VW 1500 Karmann-Ghia	cream, red or gold body, plastic interior and taillights, front and rear working hoods, clear windshields, silver bumpers; includes spare wheel and plastic suitcase in trunk, 3-1/2"	35	55	90
VW Polo	apple green or bright yellow body, black DBP and posthorn (German Post Office) decals, off white interior, black dash, 3-3/4"	25	40	65
VW Polo	metallic light brown body, off-white interior, black dash, clear windows, silver bumpers, grille and headlights, 3-3/4"	15	18	30
VW Polo Auto Club Car	yellow body, white roof, yellow dome light, ADAC Strassenwacht labels	15	25	40
VW Polo German Auto Club Car	yellow body, off-white interior, black dash, silver bumpers, grille and headlights, white roof, yellow dome light, 3-1/2"	25	35	60
VW Polo Police Car	white body, green hood and doors, black dash, silver bumpers, grille and headlights, white roof, blue dome light, 3-1/2"	15	25	40
VW Polo Turbo	cream body, red interior w/red and orange trim, working hatch and two door castings, clear windshield, black plastic dash, 3-3/4"	15	18	30
VW Racing Tender and Cooper	white No. 490 VW breakdown truck w/racing decals, blue No. 156 Cooper on trailer	50	75	150
VW Racing Tender and Cooper Maserati	two versions: tan or whiteNo. 490 VW breakdown truck, and No. 159 Cooper-Maserati on trailer; value is for each set	50	75	150
Warner & Swasey Crane	yellow cab and body, blue chassis, blue/yellow stripe decals, red interior, black steering wheel, silver knob, gold hook, 8-1/2"	30	45	75
White Wheelie Motorcycle	white body w/black/white police decals, 4"	15	20	35
Wild Honey Dragster	yellow body w/red/yellow Wild Honey and Jaguar Powered decals, green windows and roof, black grille, driver, Whizz Wheels, 3"	25	40	65

VEHICLES

NAME	NO.	YEAR	GOOD	EX	MINT

Aircraft

NAME	NO.	YEAR	GOOD	EX	MINT
A.W. Ensign, forty-seat airliner, olive/dark green, G-AZCA	62x	1945-49	95	275	350
A.W. Ensign, camouflaged, dark variation	68a	1940	150	300	450
A.W. Ensign, A.W. Airliner, silver, G-ADSV	62P	1945-49	65	145	175
Airspeed Envoy, King's Aeroplane, red, blue, and silver, G-AEXX	62k	1938-40	70	200	300
Airspeed Envoy, silver, G-ACVI	62m	1938-41	55	175	250
Airspeed Envoy, light transport, red, G-ATMH	62m	1945-49	40	125	200
Amiot 370	64a	1939-48	70	130	200
Arc-en-Ciel	60a	1935-40	200	375	450
Armstrong Whitworth Ensign, silver, G-ADSR	62p	1938-41	90	175	250
Atalanta, camouflaged, dark variation	66a	1940	200	450	650
Atalanta (Imperial Airways Liner), gold, G-ABTI	60a	1934-41	150	375	500
Autogyro, gold, blue rotor, w/pilot	60f	1934-41	90	180	250
Autogyro, Army cooperation, silver, RAF roundels	66f	1940	125	250	350
Avro Vulcan Delta Wing Bomber	749/992	1955-56	800	1500	4500
Avro York, silver, G-AGJC	70a/704	1946-59	45	155	200
Beechcraft Baron	715	1968-76	25	60	90
Beechcraft Bonanza	710	1965-76	20	55	80
Beechcraft T42A	712	1972-77	30	75	110
Bell 47 Police Helicopter	732	1974-80	10	30	55
Bloch 220	64b	1939-48	75	150	250
Boeing 737	717	1970-75	20	45	90
Boeing Flying Fortress, "Long Range Bomber" under wings	62g	1945-48	50	125	225
Boeing Flying Fortress, silver, USAAC stars on wings	62g	1939-41	100	200	300
Breguet Corsair	60d	1935-40	100	200	300
Bristol 173 Helicopter, turquoise, red rotors, G-AUXR	715	1956-63	20	60	95
Bristol Blenheim	62B		60	85	130
Bristol Blenheim, medium bomber; silver, red, and blue roundels	62B	1945-48	35	95	120
Bristol Blenheim, silver, roundels w/outer yellow ring	62b/62d	1940-41	60	140	175
Bristol Brittania, silver, blue line, CF-CZA	998	1959-65	50	250	500
Cierva Autogyro	60f	1935-40	100	250	250
Clipper III Flying Boat, silver, NC16736	60w	1938-41	150	250	400
Clipper III Flying Boat, silver, no registration	60w	1945-49	75	175	250
D.H. Albatross, camouflaged, dark variation	68b	1940	150	300	450
D.H. Albatross, silver, G-AEVV	62r	1939-41	75	275	400
D.H. Albatross, Frobisher Class Liner, silver, G-AFDI	62w	1939-41	75	275	400
D.H. Albatross, four-engine liner; gray, G-ATPV	62R	1945-49	75	170	250
D.H. Comet Jetliner, silver wings, G-ALYX	702/999	1954-65	35	100	200
D.H. Comet Racer, yellow, G-RACE	60g	1946-49	50	110	155
D.H. Comet Racer, silver, G-ACSR	60g	1935-40	60	125	225
D.H. Sea Vixen, gray, white undersides	738	1960-65	30	65	110
Dewoitine 500	60e	1935-40	100	200	300
Dewoitine D338	61a/64	1937-46	225	350	500
Douglas DC3, silver, PH-ALI	60t	1938-41	125	300	650
Empire Flying Boat, silver, G-ADUV, solid front to hull	60r	1937-41	150	325	450
Empire Flying Boat, MAIA, silver, G-AVKW	700	1937-41	150	275	350
Empire Flying Boat, Atlantic Flying Boat, blue, cream wings, G-AZBP	60x	1938-40	350	600	1000
Empire Flying Boat, silver, G-ADUV, hollowed out front to hull	60r	1945-49	90	175	250
Fairy Battle, camouflaged, one roundel, light variation	60s	1937-41	50	125	200
Fairy Battle, silver, "Fairy Battle Bomber" under wing	60n	1937-41	40	100	140
General Monospar, camouflaged, dark	66e	1940	90	300	350
General Monospar, silver, blue wing tips	60e	1934-41	75	225	300
Gloster Gladiator, silver, RAF roundels, no words under wing	60p	1937-40	90	175	225

VEHICLES

NAME	NO.	YEAR	GOOD	EX	MINT
Gloster Javelin, green/gray camouflage	735	1956-65	15	50	90
Gloster Meteor, silver, RAF roundels	70e/732	1946-62	10	25	35
Hanriot 180M	61e	1937-40	90	150	225
Hawker Harrier	722	1970-80	25	65	95
Hawker Hunter, green/gray camouflage	736	1955-63	15	45	85
Hawker Hurricane, three-blade prop; red, white, and blue roundels	62S	1945-49	40	95	130
Hawker Hurricane, silver, no undercarriage	62h	1939-41	30	70	115
Hawker Hurricane IIc	718	1972-75	50	95	155
Hawker Siddeley HS 125	723/728	1970-75	20	50	75
Hawker Tempest II, silver, RAF roundels, flat spinner	70b/730	1946-55	15	45	75
Henriot 180T	60c	1935-40	110	170	225
Junkers JU87B Stuka	721	1969-80	40	75	145
Junkers JU89, high speed monoplane, green/dark green, D-AZBK	62y	1938-41	100	275	350
Junkers JU89, high speed monoplane, silver, G-ATBK	62Y	1945-49	70	160	225
Junkers JU89 Heavy Bomber, black, German cross	67a	1941	100	400	600
Junkers JU90 Airliner, silver, D-AIVI	62n	1938-40	90	250	325
Leopard Moth, light green, G-ACPT	60b	1934-41	50	140	180
Leopard Moth, camouflaged, dark	66b	1940	70	225	300
Lockheed Constellation	60c/892	1956-63	90	200	350
Lockheed P-80 Shooting Star, silver, USAF stars	701/733	1947-62	10	20	30
M.D. F-4 Phantom	725/727/73	1972-77	70	125	175
Mayo Composite	63	1939-41	200	450	750
ME BI 109, motorized	726	1972-76	50	100	175
Mercury Seaplane, silver, G-AVKW	700	1949-57	35	75	110
Mercury Seaplane, silver, G-ADHJ	63b	1939-41	50	100	175
Mitsubishi A65M Zero, motorized	739	1975-78	75	150	225
MRCA Tornado	729	1974-76	35	90	155
Mystere IV	60a/800	1957-63	30	75	110
Nord Noratlas	804	1960-64	125	250	400
P1B Lightning, silver, RAF roundels	737	1959-69	20	55	100
Percival Gull, white, blue wing tips	60c	1934-41	70	150	225
Percival Gull, Light Tourer, light green	66c	1945-48	65	125	150
Percival Gull, camouflaged, dark	66c	1940	100	225	275
Potez 56	61b	1937-40	125	200	270
Potez 58	60b/61d	1935-40	100	260	350
Potez 58 Sanitaire	61d	1937-40	110	175	250
Potez 63	64c	1939-48	150	250	400
Potez 662	64d	1939-40	125	250	400
Republic P47 Thunderbolt, motorized	734	1975-78	75	175	250
S.E. Caravelle Airliner, Air France, F-BGNY, starboard wing	997	1962-69	70	150	250
Sea King Helicopter, motorized	724/736	1971-79	15	35	85
SEPCAT Jaguar	731	1973-76	25	70	115
Short Shetland Flying Boat, silver, G-AGVD	701	1947-49	200	550	750
Sikorsky S58 Helicopter	60d/802	1957-61	45	135	190
Singapore Flying Boat, four-engine, silver, G-EUTG	60m	1936-41	125	400	550
Singapore Flying Boat, silver, RAF roundels	60h	1936-41	100	300	400
Spitfire, silver, large canopy, roundels red, white, and blue	62A	1945-49	30	75	125
Spitfire, silver, small canopy, roundels red, white, and blue	62e/62a	1940-41	35	150	200
Spitfire II, chrome	700	1979	65	165	250
Spitfire II, non-motorized	741	1978-80	40	80	135
Sud Est Caravelle	60f/891	1959-62	40	165	225
Supermarine Spitfire II, motorized	719	1969-78	60	95	175
Supermarine Swift, green/gray camouflage	734	1955-63	10	45	85
Twin Engined Fighter, silver, no registration	70d/731	1946-55	10	25	35

VEHICLES

Rolls-Royce, No. 30B, 1946-50, Dinky

Blaw Knox Bulldozer, No. 561, Dinky

Road Grader, No. 963, 1973-75, Dinky

DINKY

NAME	NO.	YEAR	GOOD	EX	MINT
Vautour	60b/801	1957-63	30	80	125
Vickers Jockey, camouflaged, dark	66d	1940	75	175	225
Vickers Jockey, red, cream wing tips	60d	1934-41	75	110	150
Vickers Viking, silver, G-AGOL, flat spinners	70c/705	1947-63	15	40	65
Vickers Viscount, BEA, G-AOJA	706	1956-65	40	125	200
Vickers Viscount, Air France, F-BGNL	708	1956-65	40	125	200
Viscount	60e/803	1957-60	75	125	195
Vulcan Bomber, silver, RAF roundels	749/707/99	1955-56	500	1500	4000
Westland Sikorsky Helicopter, red/cream, G-ATWX	716	1957-63	30	75	125
Whitley Bomber, silver, RAF roundels	60v	1937-41	95	150	225
Whitley Bomber, camouflaged, light variation	62t	1937-41	95	300	350

Buses and Taxis

NAME	NO.	YEAR	GOOD	EX	MINT
Austin Taxi	40H/254	1951-62	60	95	135
Austin/London Taxi	284	1972-79	25	35	75
Autobus Parisien	F29D	1948-51	80	135	200
Autocar Chausson	F29F/571	1956-60	70	120	200
B.O.A.C. Coach	283	1956-63	55	80	115
Continental Touring Coach	953	1963-66	135	200	350
Ford Vedette Taxi	F24XT	1956-59	60	95	150
Observation Coach	29F/280	1954-60	50	75	100
Peugeot 404 Taxi	F1400	1967-71	50	75	100
Plymouth Plaza Taxi	266	1960-67	60	95	150
Routemaster Bus, Tern Shirts	289	1964-80	75	100	150
Silver Jubilee Bus	297	1977	25	35	70

Cars

NAME	NO.	YEAR	GOOD	EX	MINT
Armstrong Siddeley, blue or brown	36A	1937-40	85	130	225
Austin Atlantic Convertible, blue	106/140A	1954-58	60	95	150
Austin Mini-Moke	342	1967-75	20	30	55
Cadillac Eldorado	131	1956-62	60	95	135
Chrysler Airflow	32/30A	1935-40	130	250	450
Chrysler Saratoga	F550	1961-66	70	100	190
Citroen 2 CV	F535/24T	1959-63	50	70	90
Citroen DS-19	F522/24C	1959-68	60	90	135
DeSoto Diplomat, green	F545	1960-63	70	100	190
DeSoto Diplomat, orange	F545	1960-63	60	85	125
Dodge Royal	191	1959-64	75	115	150
Estate Car	27D/344	1954-61	45	70	115
Ford Cortina Rally Car	212	1967-69	35	55	75
Ford Fairlane, South African Issue, bright blue	148	1962-66	150	300	700
Ford Fairlane, pale green	148	1962-66	30	55	80
Ford Thunderbird, South African Issue, blue	F565		120	250	600
Ford Thunderbird, (Hong Kong)	57/005	1965-67	50	70	100
Jaguar D-Type	238	1957-65	60	86	125
Jaguar XK 120, white	157	1954-62	120	200	400
Jaguar XK 120, green, yellow, red	157	1954-62	50	95	135
Jaguar XK 120, turquoise, cerise	157	1954-62	80	125	250
Jaguar XK 120, yellow/gray	157	1954-62	80	125	250
Lotus Racing Car	241	1963-70	20	30	50
Maserati Race Car	231	1954-64	45	75	110
Mustang Fastback	161	1965-73	35	55	75
Panhard PL17	F547	1960-68	45	80	120
Peugeot 403 Sedan	F521/24B	1959-61	50	90	135
Plymouth Fury Sports	115	1965-69	35	55	80
Renault Dauphine	F524/24E	1959-62	50	80	125
Rolls-Royce	30B	1946-50	65	100	125

10 Ton Army Truck, No. 622, 1954-63, Dinky

Missile Servicing Platform, No. 667, Dinky

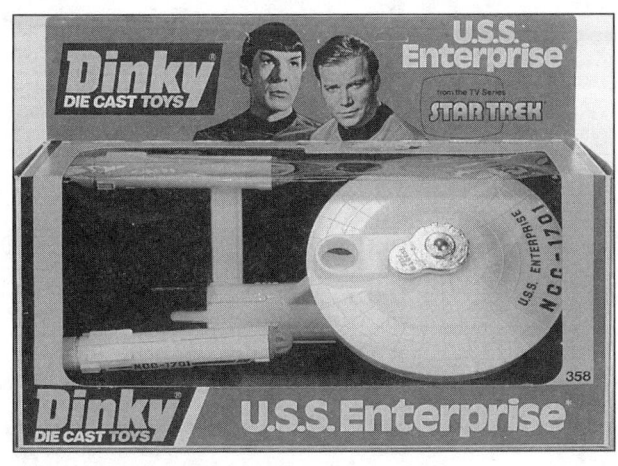

U.S.S. Enterprise, No. 371/803, 1980, Dinky

NAME	NO.	YEAR	GOOD	EX	MINT
Rolls-Royce Phantom V	198	1962-69	50	75	100
Singer Vogue	145	1962-67	50	75	100
Standard Vanguard	153	1954-60	60	85	120
Studebaker Commander	F24Y/540	1959-61	65	90	150
Town Sedan	24C	1934-40	85	130	200
Triumph TR-2, gray	105	1957-60	60	85	135
Triumph TR-2, yellow	105	1957-60	75	120	200
Volkswagen 1300 Sedan	129	1965-76	20	35	75
VW Karmann-Ghia	187	1959-64	45	80	125

Emergency Vehicles

NAME	NO.	YEAR	GOOD	EX	MINT
Ambulance	30F		100	160	275
Bedford Fire Escape	956	1969-74	75	110	175
Citroen DS19 Police Car	F501	1967-70	75	95	175
Citroen Fire Van	F25D/562	1959-63	80	110	250
Commer Fire Engine	955	1955-69	60	85	135
Delahaye Fire Truck	F32D/899	1955-70	120	190	375
Fire Chief Land Rover			35	50	85
Ford Police Car	F551	1960s	50	100	150
Mersey Tunnel Police Land Rover	255	1955-61	60	85	135
Plymouth Police Car	244	1977-80	25	35	50
Range Rover Ambulance	268	1974-78	25	35	50
Streamlined Fire Engine	25H/25	1946-53	75	100	175
Superior Criterion Ambulance	263	1962-68	50	75	100
USA Police Car (Pontiac)	251		35	50	85
Vauxhall Victor Ambulance	278	1964-70	55	85	115

Farm and Construction

NAME	NO.	YEAR	GOOD	EX	MINT
Atlas Digger	984		30	45	70
Blaw Knox Bulldozer	561		45	75	115
David Brown Tractor	305	1966-75	35	50	75
Euclid Dump Truck			45	75	115
Field Marshall Tractor	37N/301	1954-65	60	85	150
Garden Roller	105A		15	25	35
Hayrake	324	1954-71	30	40	60
Massey-Harris Tractor	27A/300		50	75	120
Moto-Cart	27G/342	1954-60	35	50	75
Muir Hill Two-Wheel Loader	437	1962-78	30	40	60
Richier Road Roller	F830	1959-69	75	100	150
Road Grader	963	1973-75	30	45	70
Salev Crane	F595	1959-61	65	100	175

Military

NAME	NO.	YEAR	GOOD	EX	MINT
10 Ton Army Truck	622	1954-63	30	50	75
5.5 Medium Gun	692		15	30	50
AEC with Helicopter	618		50	85	125
AMX Bridge Layer	F883		75	110	200
AMX Tank	F80C/817		50	75	100
Armoured Command Vehicle	677		50	85	125
Austin Covered Truck	30SM/625		85	135	275
Austin Paramoke	601		25	35	50
Bedford Military Truck	25WM/60		80	125	250
Berliet Missile Launcher	620		75	100	175
Berliet Wrecker	F806		60	90	140
Centurian Tank	651		30	50	75
Commando Jeep	612		25	35	50
Daimler Ambulance	30HM/624		80	125	250

VEHICLES

Bedford Van, No. 482, 1956-58, Dinky

Leland Comet Cement Truck, No. 419/933, 1956-59, Dinky

American LaFrance Aerial Ladder Truck, No. 2008, 1950-52, Doepke

NAME	NO.	YEAR	GOOD	EX	MINT
Dodge Command Car	F810		40	60	85
Ferret Armoured Car	630		25	35	50
GMC Tanker	F823		125	250	500
Jeep	F816		50	75	115
Military Ambulance	F80F/820		50	75	100
Military Ambulance	626		25	45	75
Missile Servicing Platform	667		80	115	225
Reconnaisance Car	152B		40	60	100
Recovery Tractor	661		60	90	140
Searchlight, prewar	161A		125	250	500
Tank Transporter	660		75	100	175
Three Ton Army Wagon	621	1954-63	50	85	125

Motorcycles and Caravans

NAME	NO.	YEAR	GOOD	EX	MINT
A.A. Motorcycle Patrol	270/44B	1946-64	30	45	70
Caravan	190	1956-64	30	45	60
Caravan, postwar	30G		40	60	85
Caravan, prewar	30G		55	85	150
Caravane Caravelair			75	150	250
Police Motorcycle Patrol	42B	1946-53	30	45	70
Police Motorcycle Patrol	42B	1936-40	50	75	125
Police Motorcyclist	37B	1946-48	30	45	70
Police Motorcyclist	37B	1938-40	50	75	125
Touring Secours Motorcycle Patrol, Swiss version	271	1960s	70	110	200

Space Vehicles

NAME	NO.	YEAR	GOOD	EX	MINT
Galactic War Chariot	361	1979-80	30	45	70
Joe's Car	102	1969-75	60	90	140
Klingon Battle Cruiser	357	1976-79	30	45	70
Lady Penelope's Fab 1, shocking pink version	100	1966-76	115	200	340
Lady Penelope's Fab 1, pink version	100	1966-76	80	135	220
Pathe News Camera Car			65	100	175
Prisoner Mini-Moke			115	200	340
Renault Sinpar	F1406	1968-71	80	135	220
Santa Special Model T Ford	485	1964-68	65	100	150
Tiny's Mini-Moke	350	1970-73	60	85	120
U.S.S. Enterprise	371/803	1980	30	45	70

Trucks

NAME	NO.	YEAR	GOOD	EX	MINT
A.E.C. Hoynor Transporter	974	1969-75	60	90	130
Atco Delivery Van, type 3	28N	1935-40	135	200	350
Atco Delivery Van, type 2	28N	1935-40	200	375	850
Austin Van, Shell/BP	470	1954-56	60	110	175
Austin Van, Nestle's	471	1955-63	60	110	175
Austin Van, Raleigh	472	1957-60	60	110	175
B.E.V. Truck	14A/400	1954-60	15	30	70
Bedford Van, Dinky Toys	482	1956-58	60	115	200
Bedford Van, Heinz	923	1955-59	100	165	300
Berliet Transformer Carrier	F898	1961-65	100	200	450
Big Bedford, maroon, fawn	408/922		80	120	185
Big Bedford, blue, yellow	408/922		90	135	210
Chevrolet El Camino	449	1961-68	35	65	100
Citroen Cibie Delivery Van	F561	1960-63	90	150	350
Citroen Milk Truck	F586	1961-65	145	275	600
Citroen Wrecker	F35A/582	1959-71	75	120	250
Coles Mobile Crane	971	1955-66	40	70	110
Covered Wagon, Carter Paterson	25B		150	300	750

DINKY

NAME	NO.	YEAR	GOOD	EX	MINT
Covered Wagon, green, gray	25B		65	115	160
Electric Articulated Vehicle	30W/421		60	85	120
Ensign Delivery Van, type 1	28E	1934	300	500	1000
Foden Flat Truck w/ Tailboard 1, red/black	503/903		140	210	450
Foden Flat Truck w/ Tailboard 2, blue/yellow, orange or blue	503/903		90	150	275
Foden Flat Truck w/Tailboard 1, gray/blue	503/903		140	210	450
Foden Mobilgas Tanker	941	1954-57	145	350	750
Foden Regent Tanker	942		135	300	550
Ford Transit Van	417	1978-80	15	20	30
Forward Control Wagon	25R	1948-53	45	65	90
Guy Van, Slumberland	514		135	300	575
Guy Van, Lyons	514		275	550	1600
Guy Van, Spratts	514		135	300	575
Guy Warrior 4 Ton	431	1958-64	150	270	450
Johnston Road Sweeper	449/451	1970s	25	50	75
Leland Comet Cement Truck	419/933	1956-59	85	150	250
Leland Tanker, Corn Products			700	1200	3000
Leland Tanker, Shell/BP	944	1963-69	125	215	450
Market Gardeners Wagon, yellow	25F		65	115	160
Midland Bank	280	1966-68	60	85	120
Mighty Antar with Propeller	986	1956-64	125	215	400
Mini Minor Van, R.A.C.	273	1960s	65	115	150
Mini Minor Van, Joseph Mason Paints	274		150	300	500
Motor Truck, red, blue	22C		150	350	650
Motor Truck, red, green, blue	22C		80	120	200
Panhard Esso Tanker	F32C	1954-59	75	120	170
Panhard Kodak Semi Trailer	F32AJ	1952-54	140	250	450
Panhard SNCF Semi Trailer	F32AB	1954-59	100	165	280
Petrol Wagon, Power	25D		150	300	500
Pickfords Delivery Van, type 1	28B	1934-35	300	500	1000
Pickfords Delivery Van, type 2	28B	1934-35	200	375	600
Pullmore Car Transporter	982	1954-63	75	125	175
Renault Estafette	F561		50	85	150
Royal Mail Van	260	1955-61	65	115	150
Saviem Race Horse Van	F571	1969-71	125	225	400
Simca Glass Truck, gray, green	F33C/579		75	120	170
Simca Glass Truck, yellow, green	F33C/579		100	150	250
Studebaker Mobilgas Tanker	440	1954-61	70	100	175
Thames Flat Truck	422/30R	1951-60	45	75	110
Trojan Dunlop Van	31B/451	1952-57	70	110	185
Unic Bucket Truck	F38A/895	1957-65	75	120	225
Willeme Log Truck	F36A/897	1956-71	75	120	200
Willeme Semi Trailer Truck	F36B/896	1959-71	85	130	225

VEHICLES

DOEPKE

NAME	DESCRIPTION	GOOD	EX	MINT
Adams Road Grader	26" long, yellow, #2006	210	295	395
Adams Road Grader	26" long, orange, #2006	160	255	355
American LaFrance Aerial Ladder Truck	33-1/2" long, red, #2008	245	325	400
American LaFrance Improved Aerial Ladder Truck	33-1/2" long, red, w/outriggers and cast aluminum ladder, #2014	290	375	450
American LaFrance Pumper	19" long, red, #2010	255	340	425
American LaFrance Searchlight Truck	white w/battery-operated search light, #2023	950	1650	2100
Barber-Greene Bucket Loader	on tracks, 18" tall, early model w/swivel chute, green, #2001	430	510	625
Barber-Greene Bucket Loader	on tracks, 18" tall, later model w/out swivel chute, green, #2001	300	375	500
Barber-Greene Bucket Loader	on tracks; 18" tall, later model w/out swivel chute, orange, #2001	350	425	550
Barber-Greene Bucket Loader	on wheels, 22" long, green, #2013	325	400	525
Bulldozer	15" long, yellow, #2012	425	550	650
Clark Airport Tractor and Trailers Set	26-1/2" long; three pieces: red tractor, green trailer, yellow trailer, #2015	375	450	550
Euclid Truck	27" long, olive green, #2009	250	330	425
Euclid Truck	27" long, forest green, #2009	250	325	400
Euclid Truck	27" long, orange, #2009	225	300	375
Heiliner Scraper	29" long, red, #2011	295	300	375
Jaeger Concrete Mixer	15" long, yellow w/black drum, #2002	225	310	450
Jaguar	18" long, kit or built, light blue or red, #2018	450	550	650
MG Auto	15-1/2" long, kit, aluminum body; red, yellow, or gray primer, #2017	360	450	525
Unit Crane	11" long, without boom, orange, w/finger wheel, #2007	250	325	400
Unit Crane	11" long, without boom, orange, w/out finger wheel, #2007	225	300	375
Wooldridge Earth Hauler	25", yellow, #2000	225	300	425

HESS

NAME	DESCRIPTION	GOOD	EX	MINT
1965 Gasoline Tanker		400	1000	2000
1966 Voyager Ship		500	1300	2500
1967 Mack Gasoline Tanker		400	900	1500
1968 Mack Gasoline Tanker	reissue of 1967	50	250	500
1969 Amerada Hess Tanker		650	1500	3500
1969 Mack Gasoline Tanker	reissue of 1968	50	250	500
1970 Fire Truck		100	350	700
1971 Fire Truck	reissue of 1970	75	300	600
1972 Gasoline Tanker	reissue of 1968-1969	50	100	250
1974 Gasoline Tanker	reissue of 1968-1969	50	100	250
1975 Fuel Oils Truck	tractor trailer	75	250	400
1976 Fuel Oils Truck	reissue of 1975 w/unlabeled oil drums	100	200	400
1977 Gasoline Tanker		50	100	225
1978 Gasoline Tanker	reissue of 1977	50	100	225
1980 Training Van		100	200	400
1982 Oil Delivery Truck	1934 Chevy Oil Tanker	25	40	80
1983 Oil Delivery Truck Bank	reissue of 1982 as bank	25	45	75
1984 Gasoline Tanker Bank	reissue of 1977 as a bank	25	35	70
1985 Oil Delivery Truck Bank		25	40	70
1986 Fire Truck	w/ladder	25	40	85
1987 Tractor Trailer Truck	w/three labeled barrels	25	40	75
1988 Car Hauler	w/race car	25	40	75
1989 Fire Truck	w/ladder	25	40	60
1990 Gasoline Tanker		20	30	50
1991 Car Hauler	w/race car	15	20	35
1992 Car Hauler	w/race car	20	30	40
1993 Police Car		15	25	35
1994 Rescue Truck		15	25	35
1995 Helicopter Transporter	w/helicopter	25	35	60

VEHICLES

744

American LaFrance Pumper, No. 2010, 1951-56, Doepke

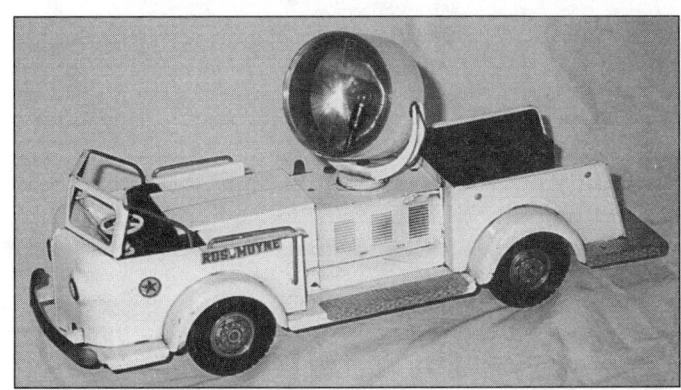

American LaFrance Searchlight Truck, No. 2023, 1955-56, Doepke

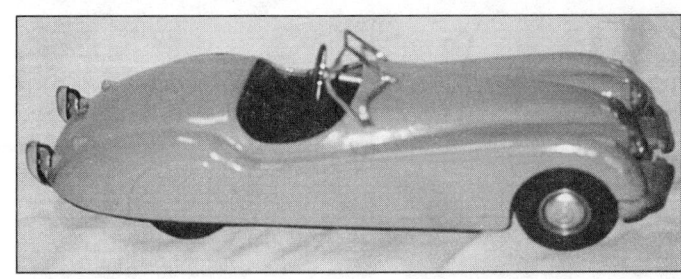

Jaguar, No. 2018, 1955-56, Doepke

Wooldridge Earth Hauler, No. 2000, 1946-49, Doepke

VEHICLES

HOT WHEELS NUMBERED PACK WHEEL ABBREVIATIONS

3sp: 3-spoke
5d: chrome 5-dot or Lamborghini wheel
5sp: 5-spoke
6sp: 6-spoke
7sp: 7-spoke
b7sp: black 7-spoke
g7sp: gold 7-spoke
8d: 8-dot
bbs/2: new wire wheel (found on #669 First Edition and #28 Chaparral 2)
bbs: chrome wire wheel
bbw: black basic wheel
bk or b: black
bl: blue
bw: blackwall (basic wheel)
cct: construction tire (8-dot)
ccts: chrome construction tire spoke

crr: chrome Real Rider
ct/b: chrome tri-blade/sawblade
ct: construction (8-dot)
cw: construction wheels
gbbs: gold wire wheel
gd: gold
gn: green
ho: Hot Ones
hoc: chrome Hot Ones
lw: lace wheels
o: orange
t/b: tri-blades (sawblades/directional)
uh: Ultra Hots
w: white
w5d: white 5-dot
ww: whitewalls
yrr: yellow Real Rider
yt/b: yellow tri-blade/sawblade

HOT WHEELS NUMBERED PACK WHEEL IDENTIFICATION

Here are examples of the most common current wheel styles. Many of these styles are available in silver, gold, black and sometimes other colors.

Sawblade

Hot Ones

5-Dot

5-Spoke

3-Spoke

Lace

Fat Lace

Real Riders

7-Spoke

Ultra Hots

Whitewalls

Blackwall

6-Spoke (Pro Circuit)

8-Dot Construction

8-Spoke Construction

Sawblade Construction

VEHICLES

HOT WHEELS LIMITED EDITIONS

NAME	DESCRIPTION	MIP
1995 ASA Chevy Lumina	white, 7,000 made	16
1999 National Balloon Rally – Dairy Delivery	blue, white	18
55 Candy Apple Chevy	red, white, 5,000 made	42
55 Chevy – Tim Flock	black	12
56 Flashsider	black	20
99 Mustang	Hot Wheels colors, Mexico exclusive, 10,000 made	14
Airwalk – '57 Chevy (Nordstroms)	black	32
Auburn-Cord – Duesenberg Museum	1936 Cord 810, black, 25,000 made	12
Barbie – '93 Camaro	dark pink, 2nd ed., 8,000 made	50
Barbie – '93 Camaro	light pink, 1st ed., 7,000 made	70
Barbie – Highway Hauler	pink, white	65
Blue Angels – Fat Fendered	40, blue, 20,000 made	20
Blue Angels – VW Bus	blue, 20,000 made	55
Bobs Toy Show – Delivery Van	red, #13, on collector number card, 8,000 made	22
Boise Roadster Show – '33 Ford Roadster	black, 12,000 made	20
Carefree Gum – '70 Funny Car	Mongoose, blue, 10,000 made	16
Carefree Gum – '70 Funny Car	Snake, yellow, 10,000 made	16
Carroll Shelby – '65 Shelby Cobra 427 SC	gray	35
Chicago Cubs – white '65 Camaro/gray 69 Mustang	10,000 made, on one card	80
Colorado Rockies – Hot Wheels 500	10, 000 made	42
Corvette Central – '58 Corvette	blue	20
Corvette Central – '63 Corvette	gray, 10,000 made	16
Corvette Central – '75 Corvette	yellow, 10,000 made	16
Corvette Central – '88 Corvette	white, 10,000 made	18
Davis Printing – Highway Hauler	black, white, 7,000 made	13
Don Garlits – Custom Dodge Ram Truck	black, 10,000 made	22
Early Times – '32 Ford Delivery	white, purple fen, on collector number card, #135	80
Early Times – '32 Ford Vicky	10,000 made	15
Early Times – 3-Window '34	yellow, 7,000 made	37
Early Times – Fat Fendered '40	black, yellow, 7,000 made	35
Early Times – Tail Dragger	orange, red, 10,000 made	18
Early Times – Way 2 Fast	10,000 made	18
Edelbrock – '63 Corvette Sting Ray	blue	18
Edelbrock – '68 Trans Am Camaro	black, brown	22
Firebird Raceway – '32 Ford Hot Rod Coupe	red, 15,000 made	14
Firebird Raceway – Ignitor Sedan	10,000 made	12
Fisher-Price – '65 Mustang Conv	white, 8,000 made	18
Full Grid – TE – Dairy Delivery	blue, silver, #1004, on collector number card, 15,000 made	20
Full Grid – TE – Dodge Ram 1500	blue, #1059, on collector number card, 15,000 made	18
Full Grid – TE – SCTA '40 Ford Pickup	orange, white, on collector number card, 15,000 made	20
Full Grid – TE – Way 2 Fast	red, #994, on collector number card, 15,000 made	18
Funny Car – Mongoose	red, 10,000 made	18
Funny Car – Snake	white, 10,000 made	22
Golden Knights	VW Bus, black	15
Grand National Roadster Show	33 Ford Roadster, red, 15,000 made	16
Grand National Roadster Show	33 Ford Roadster, maroon, 1,000 made	28
Hills – '58 Corvette Conv	5,000 made	70
Hills – '67 Camaro – blue/white	7,500 made	60
Hills – '67 GTO		24
Hills – '70 Mustang Mach I	red	24
Hills – '70 Plymouth Barracuda		22
Hot Rod Magazine – '70 Plymouth Barracuda	purple, 2,000 made	180
Hot Rod Power Tour – '70 Mustang	Hot Wheels colors, 10,000 made	24
Hot Rod Tour Edition – '70 Mustang	Hot Wheels colors, 5,000 made	30
Hot Wheels Championship Auto Shows – Way 2 Fast	white, 10,000 made	24
Houston Astros – '65 Mustang Conv	white, Coca-Cola	42
HW Newsletter – '57 Chevy	turq, in bag, #2	50
HW Newsletter – '59 Cadillac Conv	white, in bag, #3	16

VEHICLES

747

HOT WHEELS LIMITED EDITIONS

NAME	DESCRIPTION	MIP
HW Newsletter – '65 Mustang	turq, black int, in bag, #1	90
HW Newsletter – '65 Mustang	turq, tan int, in bag, 500 made, #1	45
HW Newsletter – Delivery Van	white	22
HW Newsletter – Delivery Van	black	20
HW Newsletter – Highway Hauler	red, white, #9, on collector number card, 7,000 made	22
HW Newsletter – Passion	black, 1999 Hot Wheels Convention, in bag, 1,200 made	100
JC Whitney – '32 Ford Delivery	turq, white, in bag	90
JC Whitney – '40s Ford Truck	black	18
JC Whitney – '40s Woodie	red	25
JC Whitney – '55 Chevy	teal, white	30
JC Whitney – '56 Flashsider	white	13
JC Whitney – Baja Bug	yellow	25
JC Whitney – Chevy Nomad	green	15
JC Whitney – Chevy Nomad	yellow	15
JC Whitney – Custom Camper Van	green	15
JC Whitney – Dairy Delivery	red, white	14
JC Whitney – Ford F-150 Truck	green	12
JC Whitney – Jeep	white	15
JC Whitney – Roadrunner	purple	18
JC Whitney – Scorchin Scooter	black, silver	30
JC Whitney – Scorchin Scooter	red, white, blue	30
JC Whitney – VW Bug	red	22
JC Whitney – VW Bus	white	135
Jiffy Lube – '65 Impala	white	15
Jiffy Lube – '67 Pontiac GTO	black	15
Jiffy Lube – Dairy Delivery	red	14
Jiffy Lube – Scorchin Scooter	black	18
Jiffy Lube – Tail Dragger	white, red, 25,000 made	15
Jiffy Lube – Viper RT/10	black	12
Jiffy Lube – VW Bus	yellow	28
Jurassic Park – Helicopter	red	100
Jurassic Park – Helicopter	aqua	42
LAPD – Police 'B' Wagon	black with white top, 1,000 made	46
LAPD – Police 'B' Wagon	black, 10,000 made	32
LAPD – Police Cruiser	10,000 made	32
LAPD – Police Helicopter		26
Lexmark – '67 Mustang Fastback	white	25
Lexmark – 3-Window '34	black	22
Lexmark – 3-Window '34	white	22
Lexmark – AMX – red/white/blue		25
Lexmark – Fat Fendered '40	red	20
Lexmark – Passion	white	20
Lexmark – Tail Dragger	black	25
Los Angeles Dodgers – Dodge Viper –	blue, white, 10,000 made	14
M&D Toys – '32 Ford Delivery	black, 10,000 made	22
M&D Toys – '55 Chevy	Fireball Roberts, white, 12,000 made	15
M&D Toys – '55 Chevy	Smokey Yunick, black, 12,000 made	15
M&D Toys – '55 Chevy	Smokey Yunick, blue, 12,000 made	15
M&D Toys – '58 Corvette Conv	red, #14, on collector number card, 7,000 made	30
M&D Toys – Deep Purple Nomad	purple, rr, 6,000 made	20
M&D Toys – Deep Purple Nomad	purple, ww, 6,000 made	20
M&D Toys – Golden '59 Caddy	gold, red int, 5,000 made	16
M&D Toys – Golden '59 Caddy	gold, white int, 5,000 made	16
M&D Toys – Old No. 5	yellow, 7,000 made	20
M&D Toys – Pearl Passion	white, #48, on collector number card, 8,000 made	30
M&D Toys – Pink Passion	pink, 8,000 made	48
M&D Toys – Rail Dragster	Mongoose,' blue, #90, on collector number card, 8,000 made	16
M&D Toys – Rail Dragster	Snake,' yellow #90, on collector number card, 8,000 made	16

VEHICLES

HOT WHEELS LIMITED EDITIONS

NAME	DESCRIPTION	MIP
M&D Toys – Red Passion	red, 7,000 made	36
Malleco Tower Cranes – VW Bus	red	30
Mervyns California – Custom 50 Buick	blue	16
Mervyns California – Scorchin Scooter	black	20
Minnesota Street Rod Ass. – '40s Woodie	black, beige, 10,000 made	18
Museum of Heritage – '35 Caddy	blue fen, 5,000 made	12
Museum of Heritage – '35 Caddy	red fen, 5,000 made	12
Navy Seals – VW Bus	blue	20
New York Mets – Dodge Viper	blue, same as pack #1006 but has commemorative sticker, on collector number card, 10,000 made	18
Norwalk Raceway Park – '57 Chevy –	red, 12,000 made	20
Oakland As – Ford Taurus	green, yellow	25
Penske Auto Center – '70 Mustang Mach 1	red	16
Racing Through the Years – High-way Hauler	gold, black, 8,000 made	25
Randy's Stuff – VW Bug	pink, 3,000 made	100
Randy's Stuff – VW Bug	purple, 7,000 made	33
Rebel Run – Passion	black, 7,000 made	40
Redline – SCool Bus	white, 10,000 made	20
Rod & Custom – Passion	red, 7,000 made	26
Rod & Custom – T-Bucket	black, 7,000 made	30
Seattle Toy Show – '65 Mustang Conv	black	20
Seattle Toy Show – '67 Camaro Z-28	black, 8,000 made	28
Seattle Toy Show – '70 Olds 442	black, 7,000 made	30
Seattle Toy Show – '70 Olds 442	black, 7,000 made	33
Seattle Toy Show – Custom Mustang	blue, 10,000 made	20
Seattle Toy Show – Nomad	blue, 7,000 made	20
Steadly Tudor (Fat Fendered '40)	white, 7,000 made	36
Thunderbirds – VW Bus	blue, 30,000 made	28
Tomart – '53 Corvette	red	14
Toy Cars & Vehicles – '65 Mustang	red, 10,000 made	15
Toy Cars & Vehicles – '70 Plymouth Barracuda	purple, 10,000 made	18
Toy Shop – '32 Ford	red, 10,000 made	15
Toy Shop – '63 T-Bird	black, 10,000 made	15
Toys for Tots – Scorchin Scooter	white	25
U.S. Camaro Club – '67 RS/SS Camaro	red	20
U.S. Charities Racing Team – Hummer	black, U.S. flag	24
Viper Club – Dodge Viper	black, 9,999 made	22
White's Guide – '56 Flashsider	gold	16
White's Guide – '56 Flashsider	yellow	16
White's Guide – Scorchin Scooter	black	16
White's Guide – Scorchin Scooter	gold	16
YamaHauler – Go Kart	blue, silver chrome, 10,000 made	18
YamaHauler – Golden Go-Cart	blue, gold chrome, 10,000 made	28
YamaHauler – Highway Hauler	white	14
YamaHauler – Highway Hauler	blue	18

HOT WHEELS NUMBERED PACKS

NO.	NAME	YEAR	DESCRIPTION	MIP
1	Old No. 5			110
2	Sol-Aire CX4		black, no side tampo, yellow interior, uh	120
2	Sol-Aire CX4		black, side tampo 33, yellow interior, uh	10
2	Sol-Aire CX4		black, ho	25
3	Wheel Loader		yellow, yellow interior, yct	5
4	XT3		purple, chrome bw	6
5	Good Humor Truck		white, w/new larger tampos, blue interior, 5sp	3
5	Good Humor Truck		white, small window, blue interior, 7sp	4
5	Good Humor Truck		white, small window, blue interior, 5sp	3
5	Good Humor Truck		white, small window, blue interior, t/b	4
5	Good Humor Truck		white, small window, blue interior, bw	10
5	Good Humor Truck		white, large window, blue, interior bw	12
6	Blazer 4X4		black, ct	90

VEHICLES

749

NO.	NAME	YEAR	DESCRIPTION	MIP
6	Blazer 4X4		blue, ct-bs	25
6	Blazer 4X4		black, ct-8s	80
6	Blazer 4X4		blue, ct-8d	25
7	Troop Convoy			175
8	Vampyra		dark Purple, tampo on wing, chrome interior, bw	10
8	Vampyra		light Purple, tampo on wing, chrome interior, uh	15
9	unreleased			n/a
10	Baja Breaker		white, ct	60
11	'31 Doozie		maroon, w/tan top, maroon interior, ww	60
12	Jeep			275
13	Delivery van		red rrgyc	25
14	'58 Vette		red pc	30
15	Peterbilt Tank Truck		yellow, bw	45
16	Earth Mover		yellow, black seat, yct-8d	40
17	Suzuki Quadracer		yellow, blue seat, yct-8d	30
18	Mercedes 540K		black, w/tan top, tan interior, bw	20
19	Shadow Jet		yellow, w/red interiorcooled, blue in tampo, smoked window, bw	35
19	Shadow Jet		yellow, w/red interiorcolled, maroon in tampo, smoked window, bw	50
20	Rocket Tank		olive	8
21	Nissan Hardbody		white, black interior, clear window, ct	35
21	Nissan Hardbody		white, black interior, clear window, cts	45
22	Talbot Lago		white, chrome interior, smoked window, ww	12
23	'80's Firebird		yellow, red interior, bw	15
23	'80's Firebird		black, red interior, bw	10
24	Hiway Hauler Ocean Pacific		turquoise, tan interior, blue window, bw	12
24	Hiway Hauler Pepsi		(long) red cab, smoked window, bw	18
25	unreleased			n/a
26	'65 Mustang convertible		metallic blue, tan interior, ww	20
26	'65 Mustang convertible		light blue, tan interior, ww	30
26	'65 Mustang conv.		white, tan interior, ww	150
27	Command Tank		green camo	22
28	'37 Bugatti		yellow and red, w/yellow fenders, chrome interior, ww	30
28	'37 Bugatti		blue and gray, w/yellow fenders, chrome interior, ww	15
28	'37 Bugatti		blue/gray, chrome interior, ww	15
28	'37 Bugatti		blue/gray, chrome interior, bw	35
28	'37 Bugatti		blue/gray, chrome interior, 7sp	10
29	Tail Gunner		green camo, black window, bct	85
30	'80s Corvette		blue, gho	150
31	Classic Cobra		red, w/metal base, black interior, 7sp	4
31	Classic Cobra		red, w/metal base, black interior, bw	4
31	Classic Cobra		red, w/black metal base, black interior, 3sp	3
31	Classic Cobra		red, w/black plastic base, black interior, 7sp	2
31	Classic Cobra		red, w/black metal base, black interior, 7sp	5
32	Sharkruiser		lavender, uh	6
32	Sharkruiser		lavender, ho	12
33	Camaro Z28		red, w/metal base, black window, uh	6
33	Camaro Z28		red, w/black plastic base, black window, uh	15
33	Camaro Z28		red, w/black plastic base w/skids, black window, bw	15
33	Camaro Z28		orange, w/black plastic base, black window, bw	8
33	Camaro Z28		orange, w/black plastic base, black window, uh	75
33	Camaro Z28		purple, w/black plastic base, black window, bw	8
34	Bulldozer		yellow, yellow rubber treads	30
35	Ferrari Testarossa		red, tan and red interior, uh	3
35	Ferrari Testarossa		black, black interior, gbbs	2
35	Ferrari Testarossa		black, tan interior, guh	2
35	Ferrari Testarossa		black, tan interior, g3sp	3
35	Ferrari Testarossa		black, tan interior, all small/gbbs	2

VEHICLES

HOT WHEELS NUMBERED PACKS

NO.	NAME	YEAR	DESCRIPTION	MIP
35	Ferrari Testarossa		red, black interior, uh	3
35	Ferrari Testarossa		black, tan interior, gbbs	2
36	Baja Bug		white w/flames, red interior, bw	22
37	Hot Bird		black, red interior, gho	20
37	Hot Bird		black, tan interior, gho	80
37	Hot Bird		white, red interior, uh	10
37	Hotbird		blue, tan interior, gho	35
37	Hotbird		white, tan interior, ho	17
37	Hotbird		white, red interior, guh	150
37	Hotbird		white, tan interior, gho	28
37	Hotbird		white, tan interior, uh	30
37	Hotbird		blue, tan interior, uh	20
38	Dump Truck		yellow w/plastic box, yct	5
38	Dump Truck		yellow w/metal box, yct-8d	10
39	Monster Vette		yellow, ct-8s	75
39	Monster Vette		yellow, ct-8d	75
39	Monster Vette		purple w/red flames, black window, ct-8d	20
39	Monster Vette		purple, ct-8d	25
40	Power Plower		black, ct-bd	12
41	unreleased			n/a
42	Oshkosh Snow Plow		green, ct-8s	17
42	Oshkosh Snow Plow		orange, oct-8d	18
42	Oshkosh Snow Plow		orange, 0ct-8s	18
42	Oshkosh Snow Plow		green, plastic cab, green interior, ct	12
43	Tall Ryder		gray, ct-8d	20
43	Tall Ryder		gray, cts	40
44	Classic Caddy		blue w/black fenders, tan interior, ww	8
44	Classic Caddy		blue, w/black fenders, tan interior, t/b	3
44	Classic Caddy		blue w/black fenders, tan interior, 5sp	6
45	Rescue Ranger		red, bw	12
46	Rig Wrecker			45
47	'57 Chevy		turquoise, gho	175
47	57 Chevy		turquoise, uh	100
48	Passion		white, 5sp	28
49	Gulch Stepper		red, black window, ct	12
50	Rolls Royce Phantom II		blue, ww	250
51	'40s Woodie		yellow, ww	700
52	Delivery Truck		Larry's Mobile Tune-up, white, red interior, bw	25
53	Zombot		gold, chrome pink gun, uh	8
53	Zombot		gold, chrome pink gun, hoc	8
54	Nissan 300ZX		metallic red, tan interior, uh	20
54	Nissan 300ZX		white, uh	15
54	Nissan 300ZX		white, gw	100
55	Road Roller		yellow, black seat	8
56	Bronco 4-Wheeler		light blue, red interior, ct	20
56	Bronco 4-Wheeler		white, red interior, ct	75
57	3-Window '34		purple, chrome interior, bw	30
58	Blown Camaro Z28		turquoise, bw	65
58	Blown Camaro Z28		turquoise, gray interior, uh	55
58	Blown Camaro Z28		turquoise, gho	90
59	Sheriff Patrol		blue and white, black interior, bw	10
59	Sheriff Patrol		black and white, tan interior, bw	4
59	Sheriff Patrol		black and white, tan interior, 7sp	8
60	Lamborghini Countach		white w/tampo, smoked window, uh	10
61	unreleased			n/a
62	Alien		light red, smoked window, silver interior 7sp	2
62	Alien		dark red, silver interior, uh	3
62	Alien		light red, silver interior, 5sp	2
62	Alien		light red, silver interior, uh	3
63	Radar Ranger		chrome dish, metallic silver black interior, t/b	2
63	Radar Ranger		gray dish, metallic silver black interior, t/b	2
63	Radar Ranger		chrome dish, metallic silver black interior ct	7
63	Radar Ranger		chrome dish, metallic silver black interior, cts	15

VEHICLES

No. 1051 '65 Mustang, Hot Wheels
Numbered Packs

No. 1064 Lakester, Hot Wheels
Numbered Packs

HOT WHEELS NUMBERED PACKS

NO.	NAME	YEAR	DESCRIPTION	MIP
63	Radar Ranger		chrome dish, metallic silver black interior, ctb	30
64	unreleased			n/a
65	VW Bug		turquoise, bw	25
65	VW Bug		red, blue flame outline, bw	22
65	VW Bug		red, green flame outlien, bw	27
66	Custom Corvette		metallic red, black base, tan interior, uh	30
67	'32 Delivery		yellow w/Delivery in blue, yellow interior, bw	20
68	T-Bucket		yellow, red interior, bw	10
68	T-Bucket		yellow, red interior, 5sp	8
69	Ferrari F40		red, tan interior, guh	4
69	Ferrari F40		red, tan interior, g3sp	3
69	Ferrari F40		red, tan interior, g5sp	4
69	Ferrari F40		red, tan interior, gbbs	2
69	Ferrari F40		red, tan interior, cuh	4
70	Chevy Stocker		black, five tam, bw	30
70	Chevy Stocker		black, three tam, bw	15
71	Ambulance		white, white interior, bw	5
71	Ambulance		white, white interior, 7sp	4
71	Ambulance		white, white interior, t/b	4
71	Ambulance/Rescue		yellow, yellow interior, 7sp	4
71	Ambulance/Rescue		yellow, yellow interior, 5sp	3
71	Ambulance/Rescue		yellow, yellow interior, 5dot	2
72	Bus Prisoner Transport		black w/gray plastic base, blue interior, w/o bar windows, 5dot	35
72	Bus Prisoner Transport		black w/gray plastic base, blue interior, w/bared windows, 5dot	2
72	School Bus		yellow, black interior, bw	4
73	Street Roader		white, black interior, ct	15
73	Street Rodder		white, cts	50
74	GT Racer		purple w/o "V" decal and metal base, smoked window, bw	15
74	GT Racer		purple w/"V" decal and metal base, smoked window, uh	10
75	Pontiac Banshee		red, black window, uh	3
75	Pontiac Banshee		red, guh	200
75	Pontiac Banshee		red, black window, 5sp	3
75	Pontiac Banshee		red, black window, 7sp	3
76	Kenworth Big Rig		black, w/red,orange and blue tampo, gray window, bw	5
76	Kenworth Big Rig		black, w/red,orange and blue tampo, gray window, t/b	3
76	Kenworth Big Rig		black, w/red, orange and blue tampo, gray window, 7sp	3
77	Bywayman		black, red interior, ct	10
77	Bywayman		maroon, ct-8d	15
77	Bywayman		blue, ct-8d	75
77	Bywayman		maroon, wct-8d	150
78	Peterbilt Cement Truck		red, bw	25
79	Big Bertha		olive	17
80	Porsche 959		metallic red, tan interior, clear window, uh	12
80	Porsche 959		red w/No. 59, gray interior, uh	10
80	Porsche 959		red w/#7, gray interior, uh	12
81	Ratmobile		white, chrome motor, uh	3
81	Ratmobile		white w/metal base, chrome motor, hoc	7
82	Fire-Eater		red, blue interior, 7sp	3
82	Fire-Eater		yellow w/red insert, black interior, 5sp	2
82	Fire-Eater		yellow w/red insert, black interior, smoked window, t/b	2
82	Fire-Eater		red, blue interior, 5sp	2
82	Fire-Eater		red, blue interior, bw	7
83	Tank Gunner		olive, bbw	60
84	Probe Funny Car Motorcraft		red, metal interior, bw	35
85	unreleased			n/a

VEHICLES

NO.	NAME	YEAR	DESCRIPTION	MIP
86	Propper Chopper		white, news chopper 2, blue interior, blue window	10
86	Proper Chopper		white, news chopper 2, w/triangle, blue interior, blue window	25
87	Purple Passion		purple w/scallops, red interior, ww	15
87	Purple Passion		purple w/flames, tan interior, ww	12
88	Thunderbird Stocker		black and white, uh	20
88	Thunderbird Stocker		black and white, bw	250
88	Thunderbird Stocker		red w/Motorcraft, black interior, bw	25
88	Thunderbird Stocker		black and white w/Valvoline, black interior, bw	8
89	Mini Truck		turquoise w/light tampo, blue interior, uh	8
89	Mini Truck		turquoise w/dark tampo, blue interior, hoc	250
90	unreleased			n/a
91	unreleased			n/a
92	Mercedes 380SEL		black, tan interior/clear window, hoc	12
92	Mercedes 380SEL		black, tan interior, clear window, uh	8
93	unreleased			n/a
94	Auburn 852		red, red interior, ww	10
94	Auburn 852		red, bw	140
95	'55 Chevy		yellow, purple window, bw	15
95	'55 Chevy		white, purple window, bw	20
96	unreleased			n/a
97	unreleased			n/a
98	Nissan Custom Z		red, uh	8
98	Nissan Custom Z		red, guh	200
98	Nissan Custom Z		red, tan interior, uh	6
99	Ford Stake Truck		blue, chrome interior, bw	8
100	Peterbuilt Dump Truck		red, metal interior, bw	7
100	Peterbuilt Dump Truck		red, metal interior, 7sp	3
100	Peterbuilt Dump Truck		red, metal interior, wbw	70
100	Peterbuilt Dump Truck		red, metal interior, 3sp	3
101	unreleased			n/a
102	Surf Patrol		yellow, red interior, ct	3
102	Surf Patrol		yellow, red/smoked window, ct/b	2
103	Range Rover		white, tan interior, ct	6
104	Turbostreak		fl. Red, metal interior, bw	12
104	Turbostreak		fl. red, w/pink in tampo, metal interior, bw	75
105	Peugot 205		white, bw	75
106	VW Golf		white w/pink base, pink interior, clear window, bw	65
106	VW Golf		red, tan interior, bw	10
107	unreleased			n/a
108	Ramp Truck		white, clear window, bw	20
108	Ramp Truck		white, black window, bw	15
109	unreleased			n/a
110	Trailbuster		turquoise, pink interior, w/blue in tampo, ct	10
110	Trailbuster		turquoise, pink interior, black in tampo, ct	20
111	Street Beast		teal and white, teal interior, ww	5
112	Limozeen		white, white interior, ww	8
113	Speed Shark		purple, pink interior, bw	4
113	Speed Shark		black, red interior, bw	3
113	Speed Shark		black, 5sp	3
114	Pontiac Fiero		black, red interior, sho	20
114	Pontiac Fiero		black, red interior, uh	8
114	Pontiac Fiero		black, red interior, bw	15
115	Roll Patrol Army		green w/cammo on hood, black interior, bct	15
116	Mazda MX-5 Miata		red, no tampo on hood, tan interior, bw	10
116	Mazda MX-5 Miata		red, no tampo, tan interior, bw	15
117	Ferrari 250		yellow w/chrome base and pipes, black interior, bw	12
117	Ferrari 250		yellow w/yellow base and chrome pipes, black interior, bw	8

VEHICLES

NO.	NAME	YEAR	DESCRIPTION	MIP
117	Ferrari 250		yellow w/yellow base and black pipes, black interior, bw	4
117	Ferrari 250		yellow w/yellow base and black pipes, black interior, 7sp	4
118	Ferrari 348		yellow, black and yellow interior, hoc	13
118	Ferrari 348		yellow, black and yellow interior, uh	6
119	unreleased			n/a
120	unreleased			n/a
121	unreleased			n/a
122	Toyota MR2 Rallye		white w/chrome lights, red interior, uh	10
122	Toyota MR2 Rallye		white w/chrome lights, red interior, sho	15
122	Toyota MR2 Rallye		white w/black lights, red interior, uh	25
123	Lamborghini Diablo		red tan interior, uh	5
124	unreleased			n/a
125	Zender Fact 4		metallic silver, black interior, sho	15
125	Zender Fact 4		metallic silver, black interior, uh	6
126	Lumina Minivan		red, tan interior, small Bw	6
126	Lumina Minivan		red, tan interior, large Bw	20
127	Power Plower		metallic purple, yellow interior, ct	15
127	Power Plower		purple enamel, yellow interior, ct	10
128	Baja Breaker		metallic purple and yellow, w/blue tint base, red interior, bw	5
129	Suzuki Quadracer		white, blue seat, yct	10
129	Suzuki Quadracer		white, blue seat, ct	6
130	unreleased			n/a
131	Nissan Hardbody		black, yellow interior, ct	5
131	Nissan Hardbody		red w/checkered flag, black interior, ct/b	3
131	Nissan Hardbody		black, dark tampo, yellow interior, bct	5
131	Nissan Hardbody		white w/black base, pink interior, ct	50
131	Nissan Hardbody		black, pink interior, ct	10
131	Nissan Hardbody		black, yellow interior, ct/b	5
132	unreleased			n/a
133	Shadow Jet		purple, purple interior bw	6
133	Shadow Jet		purple, yellow interior, bw	20
134	Mercedes 540K		white, w/tan top, red interior, bw	10
135	'32 Ford Delivery		white w/turquoise, pink and blue tampo, turquoise interior, bw	10
135	'32 Ford Delivery		white w/turquoise, pink and blue tampo, 7sp	7
136	'56 Flashsider		turquoise, chrome window, c5dot	18
136	'56 Flashsider		turquoise, black window, sho	20
136	'56 Flashsider		turquoise, black window, uh	8
136	'56 Flashsider		turquoise, black window, 5sp	4
136	'56 Flashsider		turquoise, black window, c5dot	3
137	Goodyear Blimp		gray w/rev it up, white gondola	5
138	unreleased			n/a
139	unreleased			n/a
140	Flashfire		black, red interior, w5dot	4
140	Flashfire		black, red interior, hoc	15
140	Flashfire		black, red interior, uh	4
140	Flashfire		black, red interior, t/b	3
140	Flashfire		black, red interior, 5sp	3
140	Flashfire		black, red interior, c5dot	6
141	Shock Factor		black and bright pink, pink interior, ct	4
141	Shock Factor		black and med. pink, pink interior, ct	4
141	Shock Factor		black and red, red interior, ct	45
141	Shock Factor		black and dark pink, pink interior, ct	4
142	Hyway Hauler		red w/Kool-Aid, thick ribbon (B), black window, bw	10
142	Hyway Hauler		red w/Kool-Aid, thin ribbon (A), black window, bw	10
143	Recycling Truck		lime green, black window, 7sp	3
143	Recycling Truck		lime green, black window, 5sp	2
143	Recycling Truck		lime green, black window, t/b	2

VEHICLES

NO.	NAME	YEAR	DESCRIPTION	MIP
143	Recycling Truck		orange, black window, bw	4
143	Recycling Truck		orange, black window, 7sp	4
144	Oshkosh Cement Mixer		red, white and blue, blue seat, bw	4
145	Tractor		yellow, yellow seat, ytt	8
145	Tractor		red, red seat, ctt	4
145	Tractor		red, red seat, t/b front/ctt rear	4
145	Tractor		red w/black cab and hydr. red seat, t/b front/ctt rear	25
145	Tractor		green w/yellow cab and hydr. green seat, yt/b front/ytt rear	2
145	Tractor		short exhaust pipe, green w/yellow cab and hydr. green seat, yt/b front/ytt rear	4
146	Bulldozer		yellow, black seat	5
147	Tank Truck		red, chrome window, 7sp	5
147	Tank Truck		red w/matching red base, chrome window, bw	7
147	Tank Truck		orange, chrome window, 7sp	3
147	Tank Truck		Dust Control, white, w/orange base, black tank, 3sp	3
147	Tank Truck		Dust Control, white w/orange base, black tank, 5sp	3
147	Tank Truck		orange, chrome window, t/b	3
147	Tank Truck		red w/dark red base, chrome window, bw	7
148	Porsche 930		purple, black interior, bw	60
148	Porsche 930		red, black interior, bw	10
148	Porsche 930		fluorescent green, bw	80
148	Porsche 930		red, black interior, 5sp	3
149	BMW 850i		light blue, tan interior, gr	8
149	BMW 850i		light blue, tan interior, uh	3
149	BMW 850i		light blue, tan interior, hoc	15
150	BMW 323		black w/black base, tan interior, hoc	15
150	BMW 323		black, tan interior, uh	5
150	BMW 323		w/BMW, rear plate black, tan interior, bw	5
151	Ford Aerostar		purple, chrome window, bw	8
152	unreleased			n/a
153	Thunderstreak		blue and green, green interior, bw	5
153	Thunderstreak		blue and green w/No. 1, green interior, bw	7
153	Thunderstreak		yellow w/Pennzoil, yellow interior, bw	10
154	'59 Caddy		white, red interior, ww	7
155	Turboa		yellow, chrome interior, uh	5
155	Turboa		yellow w/metal base, chrome interior, hoc	10
156	Rodzilla		light purple w/light purple plastic base, uh	5
156	Rodzilla		redish purple w/redish purple metal base, uh	10
157	'57 Chevy		yellow w/flames, blue interior, uh	15
157	'57 Chevy		yellow w/flames, blue interior, hoc	25
158	Mercedes Unimog		white and red, red interior, ct	7
159	Big Bertha		gray camo, n/a	6
160	Cammand Tank		white camo	6
161	Roll Patrol		gray camo, black interior, bct	10
162	'65 Mustang Conv		light red, tan interior, 7sp	5
162	'65 Mustang Conv		light red, tan interior, 5sp	4
162	'65 Mustang Conv		dark red, tan interior, ww	15
162	'65 Mustang Conv		light red, tan interior, ww	6
163	Talbot Lago		metalflake red, orange window, chrome interior, ww	10
164	Mercedes 540K		metalflake blue, red interior, 5dot	3
164	Mercedes 540K		metalflake blue, red interior, t/b	3
164	Mercedes 540K		metalflake blue, red interior, 5sp	3
164	Mercedes 540K		metalflake blue, red interior, 3sp	3
164	Mercedes 540K		metalflake blue, red interior, bw	4
165	Suzuki Quadracer		dull pink w/dark gray painted base, blue seat, ct	10
165	Suzuki Quadracer		bright pink w/dark gray painted base, blue seat, ct	10
166	Vampyra		black, no tampo on wing, uh	10

VEHICLES

HOT WHEELS NUMBERED PACKS

NO.	NAME	YEAR	DESCRIPTION	MIP
166	Vampyra		black, yellow, green and purple on wing, bw	8
166	Vampyra		black, yellow, green and purple on the wing reversed	25
167	'80's Firebird		orange, purple interior, bw	15
167	'80's Firebird		orange, purple interior, extra tampo, bw	20
168	GT Racer		black, silver window, bw	5
169	Sol-Aire CX-4		blue, w/metal base, chrome interior, uh	15
169	Sol-Aire CX4		blue, w/black plastic base, black interior, sho	15
170	Chevy Stocker		metalflake pink, yellow interior, bw	10
171	VW Bug		purple, red interior, 3sp	4
171	VW Bug		purple, red interior, bw	10
172	Mazda MX-5 Miata		metallic burgundy w/yellow and red side stripe, tan interior, 3sp	3
172	Mazda MX-5 Miata		yellow, pink interior, gr	10
172	Mazda MX-5 Miata		metallic burgundy, tan interior, 7sp	4
172	Mazda MX-5 Miata		metallic burgundy w/yellow and red side stripe, tan interior, 5sp	3
172	Mazda MX-5 Miata		yellow, pink, bw	4
172	Mazda MX-5 Miata		yellow, pink, 7sp	45
173	unreleased			n/a
174	Limozeen		metalflake light blue, yellow interior, ww	5
175	Ferrari 348		white, red and white interior, sho	15
175	Ferrari 348		pearl white w/pink strips, red letters, red and white interior, uh	45
176	Lamborghini Diablo		metalflake blue, red interior, uh	6
177	Zender Fact 4		metalflake purple, orange interior, sho	15
177	Zender Fact 4		metalflake Purple, orange interior, uh	6
178	Hot Bird		metalflake black, pink interior, uh	8
179	Porsche 959		metallic purple, chrome window, sho	15
179	Porsche 959		metallic purple, chrome window, uh	7
180	unreleased			n/a
181	Pontiac Fiero 2M4		light green flake, yellow interior, sho	15
181	Pontiac Fiero 2M4		light green flake, yellow interior, uh	7
182	Shadow Jet		green w/blue in tampo and blue metal base, smoked canopy, green interior, bw	5
182	Shadow Jet		green w/yellow in tampo and metal base, smoked canopy, green interior, bw	5
182	Shadow Jet		green w/yellow in tampo and metal base, smoked canopy, green, interior 5sp	3
183	VW Golf		metalflake green w/chrome base, yellow interior, bw	20
183	VW Golf		metalflake pink w/chrome base, yellow interior, bw	15
183	VW Golf		metalflake pink w/black base, yellow interior, bw	6
184	Mercedes 380SEL		metalflake blue, yellow interior, sho	15
184	Mercedes 380SEL		metalflake blue, yellow interior, uh	6
185	Propper Chopper		white and black, black interior, blue window, none	5
185	Propper Chopper Search & Rescue		yellow w/black base, black window, none	6
185	Propper Chopper Search & Rescue		yellow w/red base, black window, none	10
186	Ford Aerostar Speedie Pizza		w/phone number, white, chrome window, bw	10
186	Ford Aerostar Speedie Pizza		w/o phone number, white, chrome window, bw	6
187	Ramp Truck		yellow, black window, bw	5
187	Ramp Truck		yellow, black window, t/b	8
187	Ramp Truck		yellow, black window, 7sp	3
188	Hummer		plastic body, tan camo, no hood, tampo, black window, cct	4
188	Hummer		white w/metal base, small antenna, black window, t/b	4
188	Hummer		white w/silver base, small antenna, black window, t/b	3

VEHICLES

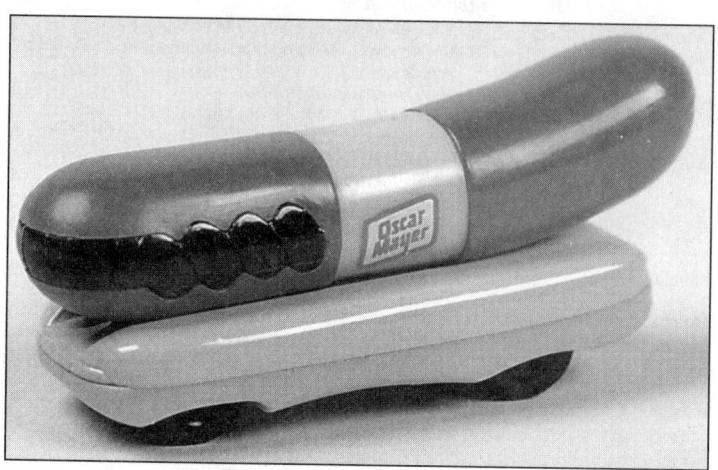

No. 204 Oscar Mayer Wienermoble, Hot Wheels Numbered Packs

No. 242 '93 Camaro, Hot Wheels Numbered Packs

VEHICLES

HOT WHEELS NUMBERED PACKS

NO.	NAME	YEAR	DESCRIPTION	MIP
188	Hummer		white w/silver base, big antenna, black window, t/b	3
188	Hummer		plastic body, tan camo, no gun, black window, t/b	4
188	Hummer		plastic body, pink camo, black window, cct	4
188	Hummer		metal body, tan camo, black window, cct	8
189	Gleamer Patrol		dark silver/chrome texture, tan interior, bw	6
189	Gleamer Patrol		med.silver/chrome texture, tan interior, bw	6
190	'57 T-Bird		med. gold chrome texture, black interior, bw	5
190	'57 T-Bird		dark gold chrome texture, black interior, bw	5
190	'57 T-Bird		light gold chrome texture, black interior, bw	5
191	Aeroflash		dark pink chrome texture, black window, guh	15
191	Aeroflash		dark pink chrome texture, black window, uh	6
192	Corvette Stingray		silver chrome texture, black interior, bw	6
192	Corvette Stingray		green chrome texture, black interior, bw	20
192	Corvette Stingray		silver chrome texture, black interior, uh	5
193	Porsche 959		pink chrome texture, dark smoked window, uh	5
193	Porsche 959		silver chrome texture, dark smoked window, uh	10
194	Goodyear Blimp		gray, silver gondola	2
194	Goodyear Blimp		gray, white gondola	3
195	Troop Convoy		tan, tan bbw	5
196	3-Window '34		white w/pink fenders, black interior, bw	25
196	3-Window '34		white w/purple fenders, black interior, bw	10
196	3-Window '34		light metallic Green, black interior, bw	150
197	Corvette Split Window		light blue w/gray base, red interior, 5sp	3
197	Corvette Split Window		light blue w/chrome base, red interior, ww	5
197	Corvette Split Window		light blue w/chrome base, red interior, bw	4
197	Corvette Split Window		light blue w/gray base, one rivet, red interior, ww	5
198	Path Beater		fl. yellow, gray interior, bct	15
198	Path Beater		fl. yellow, gray interior, cct	6
198	Path Beater		fl. yellow, gray interior, t/b	2
199	Double Deamon		yellow and green, chrome interior, uh	4
199	Double Deamon		yellow and black, black interior, uh	5
200	Custom Corvette		dark metallic purple, light gray interior, 7sp	5
200	Custom Corvette		dark metallic purple, light gray interior, cbbs	3
200	Custom Corvette		dark metallic purple, light gray interior, 5sp	3
200	Custom Corvette		dark metallic purple, light gray interior, uh	3
200	Custom Corvette		white, red interior, uh	5
201	Oshkosh Snowplow		orange, orange interior, oct	4
201	Oshkosh Snowplow		orange, orange interior, ot/b	10
201	Oshkosh Snowplow/Grain & Feed		burgundy and gray, burgundy interior, t/b	3
202	'93 Camaro		(long pipe) purple, smoked window, gray interior, uh	4
202	'93 Camaro		(short pipe) purple, clear window, white interior, uh	4
202	'93 Camaro		(short pipe) purple, smoked window, white interior, uh	4
203	Jaguar XJ220		silver, metallic black interior, uh	8
203	Jaguar XJ220		light /dark blue, metallic black interior, clear window, gbbs	3
203	Jaguar XJ220		light /dark blue, metallic gray interior, clear window, gbbs	3
203	Jaguar XJ220		dark blue, metallic gray interior, clear window, gbbs	3
203	Jaguar XJ220		light /dark blue, metallic gray interior, clear window, four small gbbs	3
203	Jaguar XJ220		dark blue w/metallic black base, black interior, clear window, guh	15
203	Jaguar XJ220		dark blue w/metallic black base, black interior, clear window, uh	3
203	Jaguar XJ220		silver, metallic black interior, guh	20
204	Oscar Mayer Wienermobile		tan and light red, smoked window, 5dot	3

HOT WHEELS NUMBERED PACKS

NO.	NAME	YEAR	DESCRIPTION	MIP
204	Oscar Mayer Wienermobile		tan and light red, smoked window, 7sp	3
204	Oscar Mayer Wienermoble		tan and light red, smoked window, 5sp	3
204	Oscar Meyer Wienermobile		tan and dark red, smoked window, bbw	3
204	Oscar Meyer Wienermobile		tan and light red, smoked window, bw	3
205	Treadator		neon green and purple, logo on front wing	2
205	Treadator		red and chrome	2
205	Treadator		green enamel, purple logo on front wing	2
205	Treadator		neon green and purple, no logo	2
206	Pipe Jammer		yellow, chome interior, uh	3
207	Vector Avtech WX-3		lavender w/black base, white interior, smoked window, 5sp	4
207	Vector Avtech WX-3		lavender w/black base, white interior, smoked window, uh	4
207	Vector Avtech WX-3		dark lavender w/black base, white interior, smoked window, uh	4
208	Avus Quatro		metallic silver, red interior, 5sp	3
208	Avus Quatro		metallic silver, red interior, uh	3
209	Lexus SC 400		metallic black, white interior, uh	4
210	Viper R/T 10		red, black interior, bbs	8
210	Viper R/T 10		red, black interior, 5sp	65
210	Viper R/T 10		yellow w/logo on windshield, black interior, guh	7
210	Viper R/T 10		green, gray interior, guh	4
210	Viper R/T 10		green, gray interior, g3sp	4
210	Viper R/T 10		green, gray interior, g5sp	4
210	Viper R/T 10		green, gray interior, gbbs	4
210	Viper R/T 10		red, black interior, guh	4
210	Viper R/T 10		yellow, black interior, guh	7
210	Viper R/T 10		red, black interior, uh	4
211	Twin Mill II		neon yellow w/black base, black window, uh	30
211	Twin Mill II		neon yellow w/chrome base, black window, uh	10
211	Twin Mill II		neon yellow w/gray base, black window, uh	4
212	Silhoutte II		metallic purple w/chrome base, white interior, uh	3
212	Silhoutte II		metallic purple w/gray base, white interior, 5dot	3
212	Silhoutte II		metallic purple w/gray base, white interior, uh	3
213	'57 Chevy		(no '57 on base) turquoise, smoked window, black interior, 5sp	4
213	'57 Chevy		turquoise, blue interior, uh	4
213	'57 Chevy		turquoise w/tampo on door, blue interior, uh	7
213	'57 Chevy		turquoise, blue window, blue interior, guh	12
213	'57 Chevy		(large '57 on base) turquoise, blue window, blue interior, 5sp	4
213	'57 Chevy		(small '57 on base) turquoise, blue window, blue interior, 5sp	4
213	'57 Chevy		(no '57 on base) turquoise, blue window, blue interior, 5sp	4
214	Swingfire		blue and white, white interior, 5sp	3
214	Swingfire		blue and white, white interior, ww	6
214	Swingfire		blue and white, white interior, 7sp	3
215	Auburn 852		red w/blackk fenders, black interior, clear window, 5sp	3
215	Auburn 852		red w/black fenders, black interior, ww	8
215	Auburn 852		red w/black fenders and 30th logo, black interior, clear window, 5sp	3
216	Fat Fendered '40		purple, black interior, bw	15
217	'40's Woodie		turquoise and black, clear window, yellow interior, 5sp	3
217	'40's Woodie		turquoise and black, clear window, yellow interior, bw	3
217	'40's Woodie		turquoise and black, clear window, yellow interior, 5dot	3
217	'40's Woodie		turquoise and black, clear window, yellow interior, 7sp	3

HOT WHEELS NUMBERED PACKS

NO.	NAME	YEAR	DESCRIPTION	MIP
218	Street Roader		green, silver interior, ct	4
219	Gulch Stepper		fl. yellow, black window, ct	4
220	Bywayman		white, blue interior, t/b	3
220	Bywayman		white w/blue metal base, blue interior, clear window, ct	3
220	Bywayman		white,w/metal base, black interior, clear window, ct	3
220	Bywayman		white w/metal base blue, interior/clear window, ct	3
221	Range Rover		black, tan interior, ct	4
221	Range Rover		black, tan interior, t/b	4
222	Blazer 4X4		metalflake blue, yellow interior, ct	4
222	Blazer 4X4		metalflake Blue, yellow interior, ctb	15
223	Baja Bug		metalflake red, black interior, bw	18
224	Zombot		blue, chrome, pink gun uh	2
224	Zombot		dark gray, chrome, orange gun, uh	2
224	Zombot		chrome, orange gun, 7sp	2
224	Zombot		dark gray, chrome, pink gun, uh	2
225	Limozeen		metalflake Black, red interior, ww	5
226	Ferrari 348		fl. pink, black and red, interior, 5sp	3
226	Ferrari 348		fl. pink, black and red, interior, uh	3
226	Ferrari 348		fl. pink, smoked window, black and red interior, uh	3
226	Ferrari 348		black, black and red interior, 5sp	3
226	Ferrari 348		black, black and red interior, 7sp	7
227	Lamborghini Diablo		metallic purple, purple interior, 5sp	5
227	Lamborghini Diablo		yellow, silver interior, uh	5
227	Lamborghini Diablo		yellow, silver interior, 5sp	5
227	Lamborghini Diablo		pearl purple, purple interior, 5sp	5
227	Lamborghini Diablo		pearl purple, purple interior, t/b	5
228	Zender Fact 4		lime green, w/orange tampo, black interior, uh	20
228	Zender Fact 4		metallic blue, black window, black interior, uh	2
228	Zender Fact 4		maroon w/black and gold tampo, tan interior, clear window, 5sp	2
228	Zender Fact 4		metallic dark blue, smoked window, black interior, uh	3
228	Zender Fact 4		lime green w/orange tamp, black window, uh	10
228	Zender Fact 4		metallic blue, clear window, gray interior, uh	15
228	Zender Fact 4		lime green, w/yellow tampo, black interior, uh	5
228	Zender Fact 4		metallic blue, smoked window, black interior, uh	5
229	Mercedes 380SEL		metalflake pink, black interior, uh	4
230	XT-3		metalflake blue, blue window, 5sp	3
230	XT-3		metalflake blue, blue window, bw	5
230	XT-3		white, red window, bw	3
230	XT-3		white, blue window, bw	40
231	Mini Truck		orange, blue interior, clear window, uh	3
231	Mini Truck		orange, blue interior, clear window, 5sp	3
231	Mini Truck		orange, blue interior, clear window, t/b	3
231	Mini Truck		orange, blue interior, clear window, c5dot	3
231	Mini Truck		orange, blue interior, clear window, w5dot	10
232	Lamborghini Countach		red w/seperate wing, tan interior, dark smoked window, uh	3
232	Lamborghini Countach		red w/molded wing, tan interior, smoked window, guh	3
232	Lamborghini Countach		white w/flush wing support, red interior, smoked window, 5dot	3
232	Lamborghini Countach		white w/inset wing support, red interior, smoked window, 5dot	3
232	Lamborghini Countach		white w/inset wing support, red interior, clear window, 5dot	6
232	Lamgoghini Countach		red w/molded wing, tan interior, dark smoke window, uh	3
233	Toyota MR2 Rallye		white, red interior, clear window, t/b	5
233	Toyota MR2 Rallye		black, red interior, clear window, 3sp	40

VEHICLES

NO.	NAME	YEAR	DESCRIPTION	MIP
233	Toyota MR2 Rallye		white w/purple, green, blue enamel graffics, purple interior, cbbs	2
233	Toyota MR2 Rallye		white w/purple, green, metallic blue, graffics, purple interior, cbbs	2
233	Toyota MR2 Rallye		black, red interior, clear window, 5sp	90
233	Toyota MR2 Rallye		black, red interior, clear window, uh	100
233	Toyota MR2 Rallye		white, red interior, clear window, 5dot rear, 5sp front	4
233	Toyota MR2 Rallye		white, red interior, clear window, uh	4
233	Toyota MR2 Rallye		white, red interior, clear window, 3sp	4
233	Toyota MR2 Rallye		white, red interior, clear window, 5dot	4
234	Nissan Custom Z		metallic purple, black interior, gbbs	3
234	Nissan Custom Z		metallic purple, black interior, g5sp	3
234	Nissan Custom Z		metallic purple, black interior, g3sp	3
234	Nissan Custom Z		metallic purple, black interior, guh	3
234	Nissan Custom Z		metallic purple, black interior, uh	3
235	Turbo Streak		neon yellow, metal interior, bw	3
236	Ford Aerostar		black, chrome window, bw	8
237	Ford Stake Rack Truck		red w/chrome base, smoked window, chrome interior, 7sp	3
237	Ford Stake Rack Truck		red w/chrome base, clear window, chrome interior, 7sp	3
237	Ford Stake Rack Truck		red w/chrome base, clear window, chrome interior, bw	3
237	Ford Stake Rack Truck		red w/chrome base, smoked window, chrome interior, 3sp	3
237	Ford Stake Rack Truck		red w/chrome base, smoked window, chrome interior, 5sp	3
237	Ford Stake Rack Truck		red w/bright yellow tampo, chrome base, clear window, chrome interior, bw	3
237	Ford Stake Rack Truck		red, gray base, smoked window, chrome interior 7sp	3
238	Hyway Hauler		purple, black window, bw	8
239	Mercedes Unimog		tan/cammo, tan interior, bct	3
239	Mercedes Unimog		tan/cammo, tan interior, wt/b	3
239	Mercedes Unimog		tan/cammo, tan interior, wct	3
239	Mercedes Unimog		tan/cammo, tan interior,, ct	10
240	unreleased			n/a
241	unreleased			n/a
242	'93 Camaro		blue, white interior, bw	3
242	'93 Camaro		blue, white interior, t/b	3
242	'93 Camaro		blue enamel, white interior, bw	25
242	'93 Camaro		blue, white interior, 5sp	3
242	'93 Camaro		blue enamel, white interior, uh	125
242	'93 Camaro		blue, white interior, uh	160
243	unreleased			n/a
244	Hot Wheels 500		w/o No Fear or Racer, black w/black metal base, black driver, 5dot	3
244	Hot Wheels 500		No Fear, black w/black metal base, black driver, 5dot	3
244	Hot Wheels 500		w/o No Fear black, w/black metal base, black driver, 5dot	3
244	No Fear Race Car		black, black interior, bw	5
244	No Fear Race Car		black, black interior, 7sp	3
245	Driven To The Max		neon yellow, yellow interior, large 5sp	2
245	Driven To The Max		orange, gray interior, bw	8
246	Shadow Jet II		dark chrome, chrome interior, uh	3
246	Shadow Jet II		dark chrome, chome interior, 5sp	3
247	Rigor Motor		maroon, chrome interior, bw	4
248	Splittn' Image II		dark blue w/white logo, chrome window, puh	4
248	Splittn' Image II		dark purple, chrome window, 7sp	4
248	Splittn' Image II		dark purple, pink window, 7sp	4
248	Splittn' Image II		dark blue, pink window, o7sp	4
248	Splittn' Image II		dark blue, pink window, puh	6

VEHICLES

NO.	NAME	YEAR	DESCRIPTION	MIP
248	Splittn' Image II		dark blue w/pink logo, chrome window, puh	6
248	Splittn' Image II		dark blue, chrome window, uh	6
249	Fuji Blimp		white and green	3
250	Talbot Lago		black chrome interior, 7sp	3
250	Talbot Lago		black chrome interior, ww	5
251	Gulch Stepper		red, black window, ct	5
251	Gulch Stepper		black, black window, ct	3
251	Gulch Stepper		black, black window, w/reverse tampo, ct/b	40
252	Street Roader		Suzuki in grill white w/blue and pink, blue interior, ct	4
252	Street Roader		white w/blue and pink, blue interior, ct	3
252	Street Roader		white w/blue and pink, blue interior, ct/b	3
253	Mercedes 380SEL		maroon w/metal base, tan interior, clear window, uh	2
253	Mercedes 380SEL		maroon w/metal base, tan interior, clear window, t/b	2
253	Mercedes 380SEL		maroon w/metal base, tan interior, clear window, 5sp	2
253	Mercedes 380SEL		maroon w/metal base, tan interior, clear window, 7sp	2
254	Sol-Aire CX-4		metallic blue, white interior, guh	5
254	Sol-Aire-CX-4		metallic blue, white interior, 7sp	2
254	Sol-Aire-CX-4		metallic blue, white interior, gbbs	2
255	BMW 850i		dark blue w/black base and red logo, red interior, smoked window uh	2
255	BMW 850i		dark blue w/black base and red logo, red interior, smoked window guh	2
255	BMW 850i		dark blue w/black base and red logo, red interior, clear window guh	2
255	BMW 850i		dark blue w/black base and black logo, red interior, clear window guh	2
255	BMW 850i		dark blue w/black base and black logo, red interior, clear window g3sp	2
255	BMW 850i		dark blue w/black base and black logo, red interior, clear window gbbs	2
256	'80's Firebird		fl. Red, yellow interior, bw	10
257	3 Window '34		silver w/flames, silver interior, 3sp	5
257	3 Window '34		silver w/flames, silver interior, small rear bw	10
257	3 Window '34		silver w/flames, silver interior, large rear bw	10
257	3 Window '34		silver w/flames, silver interior, 7sp	5
258	Blazer 4x4		light blue, w/logo on front fender, silver interior, ct	3
258	Blazer 4x4		light blue, silver interior, bct	15
258	Blazer 4x4		light blue w/logo on window, silver interior, ct	3
259	Lumina Minivan/taxi		yellow, black interior, bw	5
259	Lumina Minivan/taxi		yellow, black interior, 5sp	5
260	Twinmill II		dark blue, red window, 5dot	3
260	Twinmill II		dark blue, red window, 5sp	3
260	Twinmill II		dark blue, red window, w5dot	3
260	Twinmill II		dark blue, red window, uh	3
261	Cybercruiser		purple w/black base, purple chrome, uh	12
261	Cybercruiser		purple w/metal base, purple chrome, uh	3
262	'93 Camaro		red, tan interior, 5sp	3
262	'93 Camaro		red, tan interior, uh	3
262	'93 Camaro		red white, interior, uh	3
262	'93 Camaro		dark blue and white, white interior, guh	3
262	'93 Camaro		metallic blue and white, white interior, guh	4
263	Mean Green Passion		green, tan interior, ww	12
264	Lexus SC400		maroon metallic w/black base, tan interior, clear window, 5sp	2
264	Lexus SC400		maroon metallic w/black base, tan interior, clear window, w5dot	6
264	Lexus SC400		maroon metallic w/black base, tan interior, clear window, c5dot	2

VEHICLES

No. 269 Oshkosh Cement Mixer, Hot Wheels Numbered Packs

No. 452 Ferrari 250, Hot Wheels Numbered Packs

NO.	NAME	YEAR	DESCRIPTION	MIP
264	Lexus SC400		maroon metallic w/black base, tan interior, clear window, t/b	2
264	Lexus SC400		maroon metallic w/black base, tan interior, clear window, 3sp	2
264	Lexus SC400		maroon metallic w/black base, tan interior, clear window, 7sp	2
264	Lexus SC400		dark maroon metallic w/black base, cream interior, clear window, uh	2
264	Lexus SC400		dark maroon metallic w/black base, tan interior, clear window, uh	2
264	Lexus SC400		maroon metallic w/black base, tan interior, clear window, uh	2
265	Oldsmobile Aurora		police tampo, gray interior, b7sp	3
265	Oldsmobile Aurora		turquoise w/smoked window, gray interior, bw	20
265	Oldsmobile Aurora		turquoise, gray interior, bw	15
266	'59 Caddy conv.		pearl lavender, white interior ww	3
266	'59 Caddy conv.		pearl lavender, white interior 7sp	3
266	'59 Caddy conv.		light pearl lavender, white interior 7sp	4
266	'59 Caddy conv.		blue black interior, smoked window, gbbs	3
267	Olds 442 W-30		yellow, chrome base, black interior, 5dot	4
267	Olds 442 W-30		yellow, black interior, bw	8
267	Olds 442 W-30		yellow, black interior, 7sp	4
267	Olds 442 W-30		yellow, new casting, black interior 7sp	4
267	Olds 442 W-30		yellow w/chrome, base black interior 5sp	4
267	Olds 442 W-30		yellow w/gray base, black interior 7sp	4
267	Olds 442 W-30		yellow w/gray base, black interior 5sp	4
268	GM Lean Machine		neon yellow and black, black window 7sp	2
268	GM Lean Machine		neon yellow and black, smoked window 5sp	2
268	GM Lean Machine		neon yellow and black, smoked window tri/bl	2
268	GM Lean Machine		neon yellow and black, smoked window 3sp	2
268	GM Lean Machine		neon yellow and black, smoked window, 5dot	2
268	GM Lean Machine		neon yellow and black, smoked window, uh	2
269	Oshkosh Cement Mixer		yellow/black yellow interior, bw	2
269	Oshkosh Cement Mixer		yellow/black yellow interior, 7sp	2
269	Oshkosh Cement Mixer		yellow/black yellow interior, t/b	2
269	Oshkosh Cement Mixer		yellow/black yellow interior, 5sp	2
270	Chevy Stocker		metalflake pink, yellow interior, guh	3
270	Chevy Stocker		metallic gold, red interior, guh	40
270	Chevy Stocker		metalflake pink, red interior, guh	50
271	Side Splitter			250
273	Tail Gunner		white cammo, black window, wct	7
274	Super Cannon		green cammo, black window, w5sp	5
274	Super Cannon		green cammo, black window, wbw	5
440	Monte Carlo Stocker		race team blue, white interior, no letter, b7sp	4
440	Monte Carlo Stocker		race team blue, white interior, b7sp	4
441	Chevy Stocker		black, red interior, 7sp	2
442	Ferrari F40		white, smoked window, w5dot	2
442	Ferrari F40		white, smoked window, 7sp	2
442	Ferrari F40		white, smoked window, 5sp	2
443	Ferrari 348		black, red interior, clear window, 5dot	2
443	Ferrari 348		black, red interior, clear window, 7sp	2
443	Ferrari 348		black, red interior, clear window, 5sp	2
444	Aeroflash		white w/green and yellow tampo, orange base and window, gsp	
445	Jaguar		green, gray interior, 5sp	4
445	Jaguar		green, gray interior, 7sp	6
446	'32 Ford Delivery		dark blue, black interior, 7sp	10
446	'32 Ford Delvery		dark blue, black interior, 3sp	15
447	'63 Split Window		green, tan interior, 7sp	2
447	'63 Split Window		green, w/gray base, tan interior, 3sp	2
447	'63 Split Window		green, tan interior, 5sp	2
447	'63 Split Window		green, tan interior, 3sp	2
447	'63 Split Window		green w/gray base, tan interior, 7sp	2

VEHICLES

765

NO.	NAME	YEAR	DESCRIPTION	MIP
448	'67 Camaro		(no origin) yellow w/black stripes smoked window, black interior, 5sp	7
448	'67 Camaro		(Malaysia) yellow w/black stripes smoked window, black interior, 5sp	5
448	'67 Camaro		yellow w/blk stripes, smoked window, blk interior, 3sp	150
448	'67 Camaro		(Malaysia) yellow w/black stripes, smoked window, black interior, 5dot	3
449	Camaro Z-28		orange, black interior, 5sp	3
449	Camaro Z-28		orange, black interior, 3sp	3
450	Corvette Stingray		pearl white, chrome interior, 3sp	2
450	Corvette Stingray		pearl white, chrome interior, 7sp	2
450	Corvette Stingray		pearl white, chrome interior, all small 3sp	2
450	Corvette Stingray		pearl white, chrome interior, 5sp	2
451	3 Window '34		pink, pink interior, 7sp	5
451	3 Window '34		pink, pink interior, 3sp	5
452	Ferrari 250		green, tan interior, 7sp	3
452	Ferrari 250		green, tan interior, 5dot	2
452	Ferrari 250		green, tan interior, 5sp	2
453	Audi Avus		red, tan interior, smoked window, 7sp	2
453	Audi Avus		red, tan interior, smoked window, 5sp	2
453	Avus Quattro		red, tan interior, smoked window, 5sp	2
453	Avus Quattro		red, tan interior, smoked window, 7sp	2
453	Avus Quattro		red, tan interior, smoked window, t/b	2
454	Zender Fact 4		white, silver interior, blue window, 5sp	2
454	Zender Fact 4		white, silver interior, blue window, 7sp	2
455	'65 Mustang convertible		gold, white interior, 5sp	5
455	'65 Mustang convertible		dark metallic blue, metal China base, white interior, clear window, 5sp	3
455	'65 Mustang convertible		gold, white interior, 7sp	3
455	'65 Mustang convertible		gold, white interior, 3sp	7
457	Pontiac Banshee		black, neon yellow interior, 5sp	1
457	Pontiac Banshee		black, neon yellow interior, bbs	2
457	Pontiac Banshee		purple w/metal China base black interior, clear window, 5sp	1
458	Speed Shark		lavender, purple interior, 5sp	2
460	Zombot		black over silver, orange base and gun, 5sp	2
461	Enforcer		deep purple, silver-painted window 5sp	2
462	'80's Firebird		blue, tan interior, 5sp	2
462	'80's Firebird		blue, tan interior, bbs	2
463	Fiero 2M4		neon yellow, black interior, bbs	3
463	Fiero 2M4		neon yellow, black interior, 5sp	3
464	Blazer 4X4		metallic blue w/blue tint, China base, yellow interior, blue tint window, cts	3
464	Blazer 4X4		metallic blue w/blue tint, China base, yellow interior, blue tint window, ct	3
467	Peugeot 405		green, tan interior, 5sp	2
467	Peugeot 405		silver w/checks and orange stripe, black interior, 5sp	2
467	Peugeot 405		silver w/checks and orange stripe, black interior, bbs	2
467	Peugeot 405		silver w/orange stripe only, black interior, bbs	2
468	GT Racer		neon orange w/tampo, black window, 5sp	2
468	GT Racer		neon orange w/tampo, black window, bbs	2
468	GT Racer		neon orange, black window, 5sp	2
469	Hot Bird		gold, tan interior, 5sp	2
469	Hot Bird		gold, w/hood bird, black interior, 5sp	2
469	Hot Bird		gold w/hood bird, black interior, bbs	2
470	Turbo Streak		blue and white, white driver, 5sp	2
470	Turbo Streak		blue and white w/purple tampo, white driver, 5sp	2
471	Velocitor		blue and white, orange interior, 5sp	2
471	Velocitor		black w/Hot Wheels logo, red interior, 5sp	2
471	Velocitor		black w/Hot Wheels logo, red interior, bbs	2
472	Buick Stocker		neon yellow, red tampos, black interior, 5sp	2

VEHICLES

NO.	NAME	YEAR	DESCRIPTION	MIP
472	Buick Stocker		neon yellow, red tampos, black interior, bbs	2
472	Buick Stocker		neon yellow, black interior, 5sp	2
473	BMW M1		silver and gray two-tone, black interior, 5sp	2
473	Street Beast		silver and gray two-tone, black interior, 5sp	2
473	Street Beast		green, gray interior, 5sp	2
474	VW Golf		black, red interior, 5sp	3
474	VW Golf		black w/fahrvergnugen, red interior, 5sp	3
474	VW Golf		black w/fahrvergnugen, red interior, bbs	3
475	Fork lift		yellow, black seat, bw front/5sp rear	2
477	Double Demon		green, purple chrome, 5sp	2
478	Dragon Wagon		neon yellow w/green base, 5sp	2
479	Computer Warrior		black over blue w/orange base, 5sp	2
481	Tall Ryder		pearl yellow w/silver China base, black window, cts	2
481	Tall Ryder		pearl gold w/silver China base, black window, cts	2
481	Tall Ryder		green w/chrome China base, chrome window, cts	2
482	Earth Mover		yellow, black seat, cts	3
483	Thunder Roller		maroon, tan interior, bw rear/5sp front	4
484	Grizzlor		white, metal base, orange engine, 5sp	2
484	Grizzlor		white, black spots, red base, metal engine, 5sp	2
485	Evil Weevil		light orange, neon orange base, 5sp	2
486	Command Tank		black, purple Nite Force	2
487	Troop Convoy		green, transparent canopy, 5sp	4
487	Troop Convoy		metallic gray, neon orange w/black canopy, 5sp	4
488	Sting Rod		metallic gray, neon orange base, ct	2
489	Big Bertha		metallic gray, orange turret	3
489	Big Bertha		Nite Force, black, purple black turret	2
489	Tough Customer		Nite Force, black, purple black turret	2
491	Rocket Shot		metallic gray orange top, gray rocket	4
491	Rocket Shot		candy purple, black cammo and top purple rocket	2
492	Swingfire		neon orange, gray interior, 5sp	2
492	Swingfire		white w/blue snow patrol tampo, blue interior 5sp	2
493	Porsche 911 Targa		neon yellow, black China base, black interior, clear window, all lg 5sp	2
493	Porsche 911 Targa		neon yellow, black China base, black interior, clear window, all small 5sp	2
494	Mercedes 500SL		metallic gray, red interior, 5sp	2
496	Ferrari 308GT		red w/black base, black interior, tinted window, 5sp	2
496	Ferrari 308GT		red w/black base, black interior, tinted window, bbs	2
497	Ferrari Testarossa		pearl white, black interior, bbs	2
497	Ferrari Testarossa		pearl white, black interior, 5sp	2
498	BMW 850i		metallic silver, red interior, 5sp	2
498	BMW 850i		metallic silver, red interior, bbs	2
499	Corvette Coupe		metallic green, red interior, bbs	2
499	Corvette Coupe		metallic green, red interior, 5sp	2
502	Chevy Nomad		red, tan interior, closed wheel, g7sp	2
502	Chevy Nomad		red, tan interior, open wheel, g7sp	2
503	'80's Corvette		red, gray interior, 3sp	2
503	'80's Corvette		red, gray interior, t/b	2
503	'80's Corvette		red, gray interior, 5sp	2
503	'80's Corvette		red, gray interior, bbs	2
504	Camaro Z28		pearl white, blue window, 3sp	2
504	Camaro Z28		pearl white, blue window, 5sp	2
505	1993 Camaro		black, tan interior, 5sp	2
505	1993 Camaro		black, tan interior, t/b	2
505	1993 Camaro		black, tan interior, bbs	2
505	1993 Camaro		black, tan interior, yellow letter, b7sp	2
506	Nissan 300ZX		purple w/gold tampo, purple interior, 5sp	2

VEHICLES

HOT WHEELS NUMBERED PACKS

NO.	NAME	YEAR	DESCRIPTION	MIP
507	Peugot 205		black, blue, purple w/gray interior, red painted base, 5s	10
523	Barracuda		sublime w/chrome base, black interior and tinted windows, 5s	10
524	GMC Motor Home		metallic blue w/gray India base, white interior, bw	15
525	Trail Buster Jeep		black and red stripes, India base, red interior, lg.bw	2
526	Neet Streater		yellow w/metal India base, black interior, bw	2
527	Second Wind		white w/# 6, India base, blue interior, bw	2
528	Beach Blaster		white w/gray India base, red interior, bw	2
577	Police Cruiser		white w/Fire Chief tampo, black interior, 3sp	5
577	Police Cruiser		white w/Fire Chief tampo, black interior, 5sp	5
577	Police Cruiser		black and white, tan interior, b7sp	5
590	Porsche 911		red, smoked window, black interior, large rear t/b	2
590	Porsche 911		red, smoked window, black interior, t/b	2
590	Porsche 911		red, smoked window, black interior, large rear 5sp	2
590	Porsche 911		red, smoked window, black interior, 5sp	2
590	Porsche 911		red, smoked window, black interior, large rear 5dot	2
591	Porsche 959		silver, blue, smoked window t/b	2
591	Porsche 959		silver, blue w/metal Malaysia base, smoked window, 5sp	2
591	Porsche 959		silver, blue w/metal China base, smoked window, 5sp	2
592	Porsche 930		blue, smoked window, black interior, t/b	2
592	Porsche 930		blue, smoked window, black interior, 5sp	2
593	Skullrider		light pink tint chrome, metal base, black interior, 5sp	3
593	Skullrider		dark pink chrome, metal base, black interior, 5sp	3
594	GM Ultralite		Police white and black, black window, 7sp	4
594	GM Ultralite		no tampo, white and black, black window, 3sp	2
594	GM Ultralite		no tampo, white and black, black window, 7sp	2
594	Police Car		white and black, black window, 3sp	2
595	Corvette Sting Ray III		metallic blue, white interior, smoked window, 3sp	2
595	Corvette Sting Ray III		metallic purple, gray interior, clear window, 5sp	2
595	Corvette Sting Ray III		metallic purple, gray interior, clear window, 7sp	2
596	Pontiac Salsa		orange, metallic silver window, gray interior 7sp	2
596	Pontiac Salsa		orange, metallic silver window, gray interior t/b	2
596	Pontiac Salsa		orange, metallic silver window, gray interior 3sp	2
597	Buick Wildcat		red enamel, black motor, black window, 7sp	2
597	Buick Wildcat		red enamel, black motor, black window, 3sp	2
597	Buick Wildcat		candy red, black motor, black window, 7sp	5
597	Buick Wildcat		dark metallic green, chrome motor, black window, 3sp	2
597	Buick Wildcat		light metallic green, gray motor, black window, 3sp	2
597	Buick Wildcat		dark metallic green, gray motor, black window, 3sp	2
598	Turboa		butterscotch w/metal China base, gold motor and seat, 5sp	2
599	Camaro Wind		white w/flames, pink chrome window, bbs	3
600	Nissan Custom Z		metallic dark blue, metal China base, black interior, clear window, 5sp	2
600	Nissan Custom Z		metallic dark blue, metal China base, black interior, clear window, bbs	2
600	Nissan Custom Z		light blue enamel, metal China base black interior, clear window, bbs	2
601	Commando		bronze w/metal base, black interior, clear window, ccts	3
602	Sharkruiser		black w/gray base and red chrome, bbs	2

NO.	NAME	YEAR	DESCRIPTION	MIP
603	BMW 325i		yellow and red w/silver painted China base, black interior, clear window, bbs	2
604	Ferrari 308 GTS		yellow and black, black interior, 5sp	2
605	Mercedes 2.6		gold w/black plastic base, black interior, bbs	2
606	Mercedes 300TD		green w/gray plastic base, gray interior, 5sp	2
607	Fat Fendered '40		aqua w/yellow, orange and purple tampo, black interior, 5sp	8
608	Porsche 911		metalflake silver w/black plastic base, black interior, 5sp	2
609	Jaguar XJ40		dark metallic blue, white interior, blue tint window, bbs	2
610	Land Rover MkII		orange w/blue and white tampo, black interior, 5sp	2
611	Fire Eater II		red, blue tint window, 5sp	2
612	T-Bird		turquoise, white interior, bw	9
613	London Bus		red, black window, 5sp	5
615	Ford XR4Ti		metalflake silver w/butterscotch and purple stripe, red interior, 5sp	2
616	'80's Corvette		white w/yellow and blue tampo, blue interior, black dash, bbs	2
617	Flame Stopper II		red w/gray boom, black interior, 5sp	2
618	Chevy Stocker		white and silver, red No. 1, purple interior, 5sp	5
619	London Taxi		yellow, black interior, 5sp	2
620	Ford Transit Wrecker		light blue enamel w/white and red tampos, black window, 5sp	2
622	City Police		black and white Pontiac, gray interior, and bumpers, b5sp	2
623	Mustang Cobra		pearl pink and black, black interior, bbs	2
624	Assault Crawler		green camo, green interior, treads	2
625	Classic Packard		black, black interior, 5sp	3
641	Wheel Loader		orange w/China metal base, bk cage, gray scoop, ct	2
642	Forklift		white w/metal China base, blue cage, black forks, rear5sp/ front bw	2
643	Digger		yellow w/yellow China base, w/o HW logo, gray boom and scoop, 5sp	2
643	Digger		yellow w/yellow China base, w/HW logo, gray boom and scoop, 5sp	2
700	Shock Factor		yellow and blue w/metal China base, blue interior, all large bw	2
702	Lumina Van		dark metallic green w/black China base, tan interior, smoked window, bbs	2
702	Lumina Van		dark metallic green w/black China base, tan interior, smoked window, 5sp	2
712	Tipper		dark blue w/black China base, white tip box, black window, 5sp	2
714	Talbot Lago		blue w/bk fender, black metal base	350
715	1996 Mustang GT		white w/metal China base, red interior, clear window, 5sp	2
761	Flame Stopper		red w/gray boom, black window, t/b	2
765	Oshkosh P-Series		blue and white body w/metal base and gray plow, blue seats, t/b	2
767	Mercedes 380SEL		white w/gold base, tan interior, clear window, t/b	2
768	Lamborghini Countach		black w/black base, red interior, clear window, 5dot	2
770	Lexus SC400		metallic blue w/black base, white interior, clear window, bbs	2
770	Lexus SC400		metallic blue w/black base, white interior, smoked window, bbs	2
770	Lexus SC400		metallic purple w/black base, white interior, smoked window, bbs	2
771	'56 Flashsider		yellow pearl w/pink and blue tampo, black window, 5dot	2
771	'56 Flashsider		yellow pearl w/pink and blue tampo, black window, all small 5dot	2
773	Hot Wheels 500		neon yellow w/metal base, black driver, b/7sp	1

VEHICLES

No. 770 Lexus SC400, Hot Wheels Numbered Packs

No. 781 Lamborghini Diablo, Hot Wheels Numbered Packs

HOT WHEELS NUMBERED PACKS

NO.	NAME	YEAR	DESCRIPTION	MIP
774	Ramp Truck		metallic green w/metallic gray ramp and metal China base, smoked window, 5sp	1
778	Speed Blaster		metallic maroon w/orange tampo, black base, chrome window, 3sp	1
778	Speed Blaster		metallic blue w/orange tampo, black base, chrome window, 3sp	1
778	Speed Blaster		metallic purple w/red tampo black base, chrome window, 3sp	1
779	Big Chill		blue w/white flames and white Thialand base, chrome driver, black front wheel, white skis	2
779	Big Chill		blue w/white flames and white China base, chrome driver, white front wheel, white skis	2
780	'58 Corvette		powder blue enamel w/motor chrome interior, smoked window, 5dot	2
780	'58 Corvette		powder blue enamel w/motor chrome interior, smoked window, all small 5dot	2
780	'58 Corvette		powder blue enamel w/hood chrome interior, smoked window, 5dot	2
780	'58 Corvette		powder blue w/hood and small rear plate chrome interior, smoked window, 5dot	2
781	Lamborghini Diablo		dark red w/black-painted base, tan interior, tinted window, 5dot	1
782	Radar Ranger		gold w/metal base black seat, clear canopy, large ct/b	1
783	Twinn Mill II		metallic silver w/black base, black window, all large bbs	1
784	Ferrari F512M		metallic silver w/black painted base, black interior, clear window, 5dot	1
784	Ferrari F512M		metallic silver w/black painted base, black interior, clear window, 5sp	1
784	Ferrari Testarossa		metallic silver w/black painted base, black interior, clear window, 5dot	1
784	Ferrari Testarossa		metallic silver w/black painted base, black interior, clear window, 5sp	1
787	'57 Chevy		(metal) purple w/chrome base black interior, smoked window, t/b	1
788	Mercedes 540K		metallic purple w/blue top and tampo, black interior, clear window, large bbs	2
788	Mercedes 540K		metallic purple w/blue top and tampo, black interior, clear window, small bbs	2
788	Mercedes 540K		metallic purple w/blue top and tampo, black interior, clear window, 3sp	2
791	Treadator		metallic blue w/black base, no white side tampo, chrome canopy, black treads	1
792	Camaro Race Car		white w/orange tampo and black base, black interior, clear window, 5sp	1
793	Auburn 852		black w/gold fenders and metal base, gold interior, tinted window, gbbs	1
795	Tractor		silver w/black base black cab and hydrolics, c/tt rear/ct/b front	1
796	'96 Camaro Conv.		white w/orange stripes and gray base orange interior, smoked window, w5sp	1
797	Dodge Ram 1500		red w/white China base, yellow interior, tinted window, 5sp	1
797	Dodge Ram 1500		red w/white Maylasia base, yellow interior, smoked window, 5dot	1
798	Propper Chopper POLICE		blue w/black base, black interior, blue tint window, n/a	1
802	Flashfire		metallic gold w/green logo and gold base black spoiler and interior, smoked window, four large 5dot	1
802	Flashfire		metallic gold w/no logo and gold base, black spoiler and interior, smoked window, 5dot	1
802	Flashfire		metallic gold w/green logo and gold base, black spoiler and interior, smoked window, 5dot	1
803	'40 Woodie		white, black interior, 5s	4

NO.	NAME	YEAR	DESCRIPTION	MIP
808	Driven To The Max		pearl white w/metal base, hot pink driver and spoiler, 5sp	2
812	GM Lean Machine		green and gold w/metal base gold seat, smoked window, t/b	1
813	Ferrari 355		black w/metal base, yellow interior, yellow window, 3sp	1
813	Ferrari 355		black w/metal base, yellow interior, yellow window, 5sp	1
814	Speed-A-Saurus		teal w/orange base, large rear 5sp	2
814	Speed-A-Saurus		teal w/orange base, medium rear 5sp	2
815	Mercedes 500SL		dark metallic green w/black base tan interior, smoked window, 3sp	1
816	Ferrari 308		metallic brown w/black metal base, tan interior, smoked window, 5dot	2
816	Ferrari 308		metallic brown w/black base, tan interior, smoked window, gray rear, 5sp/5dot front	1
816	Ferrari 308		metallic brown w/black metal base, tan interior, smoked window, 5sp	2
817	Porsche 928		pearl white w/metal base, black window, bbs	1
818	Porsche Carrera		dark metallic red w/o flames, g5s	2
818	Porsche Carrera		dark metallic red w/flames, g5s	30
820	Zender Fact 4		metallic green w/black China base, black interior, clear window, bbs	1
821	'96 Mustang Conv.		white w/metal China base, red interior, clear window, 5sp	2
822	Camaro Z-28		teal w/metal base gray interior, clear window, 3sp	2
823	Sol-Aire CX4		race team blue, white base, white interior, clear window, gbbs	1
827	Radio Flyer Wagon		red w/metal Malaysia base, chrome motor, black seat, 5sp	2
829	Porsche Carrera		metallic silver w/metal base red interior, clear window, t/b	1
834	Ferrari Testarossa		black w/black painted India base, tan and black interior, clear window, bw	1
835	Baja Bug		red w/black and mustard tampo and metal India base, tan interior, large rear bw	2
835	Baja Bug		dark blue race team colors w/metal India base, white interior, all small Hbw	3
835	Baja Bug		light blue race team colors w/metal India base, white interior, all small bw	3
837	Radio Flyer		blue, white interior, 5s	2
850	Rail Rodder		gray w/gold chrome and metal Mayaysia base, b5sp	2
851	Treadator		light pearl purple w/neon green Thailand base, chrome window, white scoops	2
851	Treadator		light pearl blue w/neon green Thailand base, chrome window, white scoops	2
852	Rigor Motor		purple w/metal base and gold motor, yellow canopy, all med.g5sp	2
852	Rigor Motor		purple w/metal base and gold motor, yellow canopy, large rear/g5sp	2
853	Camaro Z28		neon yellow plastic body w/black metal base, black window, 5dot	2
853	Camaro Z28		neon yellow plastic body w/black metal base, black window, 5sp	2
853	Camaro Z28		neon yellow plastic body w/metal base, black window, 5dot	2
854	Porsche 959		white w/metal base and orange tampo, black interior, smoked window, 3sp	1
854	Porsche 959		white w/metal China base and pink tampo, black interior, smoked window, bbs	1
854	Porsche 959		white w/metal base and pink tampo, black interior, smoked window, t/b	1
854	Porsche 959		white w/metal base and orange tampo, black interior, smoked window, t/b	1

VEHICLES

NO.	NAME	YEAR	DESCRIPTION	MIP
855	Ferrari F50		purple w/black base black interior, smoked window, t/b	1
856	Porsche 930		metallic red w/metal Thailand base, black interior, smoked window, 3sp	1
857	T-Bird Stocker		orange plastic body w/black metal base, black window, 5dot	1
858	Hummer		white w/black stripes and orange Hummer Racer, red-tinted window, ct/b	2
858	Hummer		white w/black stripes and red Hummer Racer, red-tinted window, ct/b	2
859	Bronco		red w/blue tint, metal base black interior, smoked window, ct/b	2
860	Road Rocket		white and dark blue and metal base, white seat, 3sp	1
861	Twinn Mill II		gold w/black base, black window, bbs	1
862	Pontiac Salsa		dark metallic red, chrome base, black interior, black window, 5dot	1
863	Oshkosh Cement Mixer		neon yellow w/silver fenders, black base, silver interior, 3sp	2
864	Tank Truck		metallic black w/chrome tank, black base, chrome window, 5dot	1
864	Tank Truck		dark metallic burgundy w/chrome tank, black Malaysia base, chrome window, 5dot	1
865	Ford F150		white w/black base and orange tampo, chrome interior, smoked window, 3sp	2
866	Ferrari 250		gold metallic w/black base and chrome pipes black interior, smoked window, bbs	1
867	'97 Corvette		metallic blue w/red base, white interior, smoked window, 5sp	2
867	'97 Corvette		dark metallic blue w/red base, white interior, smoked window, 5sp	2
868	Range Rover		green metallic w/chrome base, tan interior, smoked window, ct/b	1
868	Range Rover		dark green metallic w/chrome base, tan interior, smoked window, ct/b	1
869	Power Pipes		black w/orange painted base, chrome interior, orange canopy, ot/b	1
870	Chevy Stocker		purple enamel w/black metal base, black window, gt/b	1
871	Olds 442 Race Team		colors w/chrome base white interior, smoked window, 5sp	4
872	Rig Wrecker		white w/black base and red boom, chrome interior, tinted window, 5dot	2
873	Hydroplane		white w/red Harbor Patrol, black base, smoked canopy	2
874	Pit Crew Truck		silver w/red plastic base, red interior, blue-tinted window, 5dot	1
876	Bywayman		red w/metal base, white interior, tinted window, ct/b	2
877	Chevy 1500		silver w/black metal base, black interior, clear window, small t/b	2
881	'95 Camaro		black enamel w/black base, red interior, smoked window, t/b	2
884	Gulch Stepper		pearl yellow and purple, blue-tinted base, black window, large ct/b	2
889	Mercedes 380SEL		black enamel w/gold base and trim, tan interior, tinted window, gbbs	2
890	BMW Roadster		white w/metal base, red interior, smoked window, 3sp	1
894	Toyota MR2		white w/black base, white interior, smoked window, bbs	1
899	'56 Flashsider		metallic silver w/chrome base, black window, 5sp	2
908	Ford F Series CNG		P/U metallic purple w/black base, chrome interior, smoked window, 5sp	5
991	Rodzilla		chrome w/metal base, gbbs	2

VEHICLES

No. 803 '40s Woodie, Hot Wheels
Numbered Packs

No. 854 Porsche 959, Hot
Wheels Numbered Packs

NO.	NAME	YEAR	DESCRIPTION	MIP
992	Ferrari F512M		red enamel w/black metal base, tan interior, smoked window, 5sp	2
993	Ferrari 348		yellow w/black Malaysia base, black and yellow interior, smoked window, 5sp	2
994	Way 2 Fast		black w/gold metal base, chrome interior, g5sp	2
995	Porsche 911		yellow w/metal base, silver interior, black tint, 5sp	1
995	Porsche 911		yellow w/metal base, black interior, black tint, 5sp	1
996	'32 Ford Delivery		pearl blue w/black fenders and metal base, black interior, clear window, bbs	2
997	Jaguar D-Type		red enamel, gray interior, smoked window, bbs	2
998	Firebird Funny Car		metallic red w/metal base, metal interior, tinted window, g5sp	2
999	Hot Seat		chrome w/metal base, red seat and plunger, 5sp	2
1000	'59 Impala		white w/chrome base, black interior, black tint, gbbs	4
1001	Slideout		metallic blue w/yellow, white Malaysia base, 5sp	2
1003	Ferrari F40		black w/metal base red interior, smoked window, 5sp	2
1009	Peterbilt Dump Truck		blue w/white box and metal base, blue-tinted window, 5sp	2
1010	Ford Stake Bed Truck		teal w/gray stake bed chrome interior, blue-tinted window, 5dot	2
1012	Flame Stopper		white w/black base, black window, ct/b	2
1015	Mercedes C-Class		yellow w/black base, red interior, clear window, bbs	2
1018	'32 Ford Coupe		white w/black base, black interior, black interior, 5sp	2
1022	'63 T-Bird		gold and black w/metal base, white interior, balck tint, bbs	2
1024	Classic Cobra		white w/metal base, black interior, black tint, 5sp	2
1025	Mercedes SLK		metallic blue w/metal base, white interior, black tint, t/b	2
1026	Dodge Carvan		metallic orange w/black base, white interior, black tint, 5sp	2
1027	Custom C3500		magenta w/black base, black interior, blue tint 5sp	2
1028	'56 Flashsider		yellow w/chrome base, black tint, 3sp	2
1029	'40 Ford		red w/chrome base, white interior, clear window, 5sp	2
1030	Porsche 959		silver w/metal base, black interior, blue tint, 5dot	2
1031	Aeroflash		green w/black metal base, black interior, clear window, 3sp	2
1032	Ford GT90		yellow w/metal base, black interior, clear window, 3sp	2
1035	'70 Cuda		purple w/chrome base, black interior, black tint, 3sp	2
1038	Dodge Viper		silver w/black base, black interior, clear window, 3sp	2
1040	Panoz GTR-1		metallic green w/black base, black interior, black tint, 3sp	2
1041	Supercomp		silver w/chrome base, black interior, 5sp	2
1043	Rail Rodder		white w/metal base, blue chrome interior, bk5sp	2
1044	Whatta Drag		black w/metal base, gold chrome interior, red tint, 5dot	2
1045	Dodge Ram		black and white w/white base, white interior, clear window, 5sp	2
1046	Police Cruiser		white w/black base, black interior, blue tint, 3sp	2
1047	Olds Aurora		black and white w/black base, tan interior, clear window, 5dot	2
1048	Rescue Ranger		white w/chrome base, blue tint interior, blue tint, 5sp	2
1049	Treadator		black w/blue base, chrome window	2
1051	'65 Mustang		black w/metal base, tan interior, black tint, g5sp	2
1052	Rigormotor		red w/metal base, chrome interior, black tint, 5sp	2

VEHICLES

No. 725 '67 Camaro (Race
Team Series IV), Hot Wheels
Numbered Packs

No. 731 VW Bug (Artistic License
Series), Hot Wheels Numbered Packs

HOT WHEELS NUMBERED PACKS

NO.	NAME	YEAR	DESCRIPTION	MIP
1053	Hydroplane		black w/black base, chrome interior, yellow tint,	2
1054	Porsche 959		black w/metal tan interior, clear window, bbs	2
1055	School Bus		black w/black base, black interior, red tint, 5 dot	2
1056	Corvette Stingray		mustard yellow w/metal base, clear window, gbbs	2
1057	Thunder Streak		metallic red and blue w/metal base, blue interior, bk7sp black	2
1058	'96 Mustang		metallic red w/metal base, black interior, black tint, gbbs	2
1059	Dodge Ram 1500		metallic green w/gray base, chrome interior, clear window, 5dot	2
1060	Ramp Truck		black and yellow w/metal base, black window, 5dot	2
1061	Rescue Ranger		white w/red base, red interior, red tint, 5dot	2
1062	Rail Rodder		dark blue w/metal base, gold interior	2
1063	'70 Cuda		orange w/chrome base, black interior, black tint, 3sp	2
1064	Lakester		metallic silver w/silver base, chrome interior, blue tint, 5sp	2
1065	Firebird		white w/gray base, black interior, black tint, gy-bk7sp	2
1066	Mustang Cobra		metallic gold w/black base, black interior clear window, 5sp	2
1067	Express Lane		orange w/metal base, red interior, 5sp	2
1068	Dodge Concept		metallic silver w/metal base, black interior, clear window, gbbs	2
1069	'40 Ford		yellow w/black base, black interior, black tint, 5dot	2
1069	'40 Ford Trailer Edition		white and orange w/chrome base, orange interior, clear window, chrr	20
1070	'32 Ford Coupe		metallic red w/gray base, black interior, clear window, 5 dot	3
1071	Panoz GTR-1		black w/black base, red interior, clear window, 3sp	2
1073	Ford GT90		red w/metal base, black interior, black tint, t/b	2
1074	Blimp		black and red w/red canopy	2
1075	Scorchin Scooter		red w/metal base, black seat	3
1076	'59 Caddy		metallic blue w/chrome base, white interior, blbbs	2
1077	'57 Chevy		red w/chrome base, black interior, black tint, gbbs	2
1078	Camaro Z28		metallic blue w/metal base, black windows, 3sp	2
1079	'63 Split-Window		metallic gray w/black base, black interior, clear, 5dot	2
1080	Hummer		metallic green w/metal base, silver windows, ct/b	2
1081	Power Plower		metallic green w/metal base, lime interior, yellow tint, ct/b	2
1082	Jaguar XJ220		metallic gold w/black base, tan interior, black tint, g3sp	2
1083	Blown Camaro		metallic aqua w/metal base, black interior, black tint, bbs	2
1085	Porsche 928		metallic gold w/metal base, black window, 5dot	2
1086	Toyota MR2		metallic purple w/black base, gray interior, clear window, 3sp	2
1087	Rig Wrecker		yellow w/chrome base, blue interior, clear window, 5 dot	2
1088	Speed Machine		black w/metal base, white interior, yellow tint, 5dot gold	2
1089	25th Ann. Countach		metallic silver w/black base, black interior, clear window, 5 dot	2
1090	'97 Corvette		black w/black base, white interior, blue tint, 3sp	2
1091	Power Rocket renamed X-ploder		black w/metal base, chrome interior, red tint, t/b	2
1092	58 Corvette		black w/black base, chrome interior, black tint, bbs	2

VEHICLES

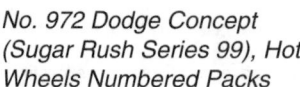

No. 961 '40's Woodie (Surf N Fun Series), Hot Wheels Numbered Packs

No. 972 Dodge Concept (Sugar Rush Series 99), Hot Wheels Numbered Packs

NO.	NAME	YEAR	DESCRIPTION	MIP
1093	BMW 850i		metallic gold w/gold base, black interior, black tint, gbbs	2
1094	Ferrari Berlinetta		red w/metal base, black interior, clear window, 5sp	2
1095	Mercedes SLK		metallic silver w/black metal base, black interior, black tint, t/b	2
1096	Avis Quattro		chrome w/black base, black interior, black tint, 5sp	2
1097	'31 Doozie		metallic red w/metal base, black interior, clear window, bbs	2
1098	'37 Bugatti		black and yellow w/metal base, chrome interior, clear window, bbs	2
1099	Road Rocket		red and black w/metal base, red interior, bbs	2
1100	Power Pipes		white w/metal orange base, gold chrome interior, red tint, 5dot	2
1101	Randa Range		metallic aqua w/metal base white interior, clear window, ct/b	2
1102	Mini Truck		black w/black base, red interior, black tint, gbbs	2
1103	80's Corvette		gold w/metal base, black interior, black tint, bbs	2
1104	Twang Thang		metallic orange w/purple base, gold chrome interior, black tint, g5sp	2
1105	Mustang Mach 1		metallic blue w/black base, black interior, clear window, bbs	2
1106	Go Cart		orange w/orange metal base, black interior, 5 dot	3
1107	Chrysler Thunderbolt		metallic blue w/black base, white interior, black tint, 3sp	2
1115	Ferrari F355		Challenge silver w/metal base, black interior, black tint, 5sp	2
1118	Ferrari 456M		red w/metal base, tan interior, clear window, 5sp	2
1119	Ferrari Spider		red w/metal base, tan interior, clear window, 5sp	2
1120	Ferrari F50		red w/black metal, black interior, clear window, 5sp	2
1121	Chevy 1500		orange w/silver base, black interior, clear window, 5dot	2

1995 Model Series

NO.	NAME	YEAR	DESCRIPTION	MIP
341	#3-'58 Corvette		pearl purple, no chrome, gray interior, 7sp	4
341	#3-'58 Corvette		pink, chrome interior, bw	6
341	#3-'58 Corvette		pink, chrome interior, 7sp	4
341	#3-'58 Corvette		light pearl purple, chrome interior, 7sp	4
341	#3-'58 Corvette		pearl purple, chrome interior, 5sp	4
341	'58 Corvette		pearl purple, chrome interior, 5dot; not on Model Series pack	2
341	'58 Corvette		pearl purple, chrome interior, 5sp; not on Model Series pack	2
341	#3-'58 Corvette		pearl purple, chrome interior, 7sp	20
342	#2-Mercedes SL		red w/dark red plastic base, tan interior, uh	3
342	Mercedes SL		black and gray, red interior, bbs; not on Model Series pack	2
342	#2-Mercedes SL		red w/matching base, tan interior, uh	3
342	#2-Mercedes SL		red w/dark red plastic base, tan interior, 5sp	3
342	#2-Mercedes SL		black and gray, tan interior, 5sp	30
342	#2-Mercedes SL		black and gray, red interior, bbs	2
342	#2-Mercedes SL		red w/matching base, tan interior, 5sp	3
342	#2 Mercedes SL		black and gray, red interior, 5sp	3
342	#2-Mercedes SL		black and gray, red interior, 7sp	3
343	#1-Speed Blaster		blue, pink chrome, uh	4
343	#1-Speed Blaster		blue, chrome window, uh	4
343	Speed Blaster		green, chrome window, 5dot; not on Model Series pack	2
343	#1-Speed Blaster		green, chrome window, t/b	5
343	#1-Speed Blaster		green, chrome window, 3sp	3
343	#1-Speed Blaster		green w/gray base, gray window, 5dot	3
343	#1-Speed Blaster		green, chrome window, 5dot	2

VEHICLES

NO.	NAME	YEAR	DESCRIPTION	MIP
343	#1-Speed Blaster		green, chrome window, 5sp	3
343	#1-Speed Blaster		blue, pink chrome, 5sp	3
343	#1-Speed Blaster		blue, long gas tank, pink chrome, uh	50
344	#8-Camaro conv.		red black interior, clear window, 5sp	3
344	Camaro conv.		red, black interior, 5sp; not on Model Series pack	2
344	Camaro conv.		red w/India base, '98 black interior, clear window, 5sp; not on Model Series pack	2
344	#8-Camaro conv.		red black interior, clear window, 3sp	5
344	#8-Camaro conv.		red w/black Maylasia base, black interior, clear window, g7sp	5
344	#8-Camaro conv.		red w/China base, black interior, clear window, 5sp	3
344	#8-Camaro conv.		red, black interior, t/b	3
344	#8-Camaro conv.		green, gray interior, uh	5
344	#8-Camaro conv.		green, gray interior, 5sp	3
344	#8-Camaro conv.		green, gray interior, 3sp	3
345	#4-Speed-a-Saurus		purple, chrome engine, 5sp	2
345	#4-Speed-a-Saurus		green, chrome engine, 5sp	2
345	#4-Speed-a-Saurus		green, chrome engine, bw	3
345	Speed-a-Saurus		purple, chrome engine, 5sp; not on Model Series pack	2
346	#6-Hydroplane		blue and white race team colors, chrome interior	3
347	#5-Power Pistons		burgundy, gray interior, 7sp	18
347	#5-Power Pistons		burgundy, gray interior, 5sp	4
347	Power Pistons		burgundy, w/painted base, gray interior, t/b; not on Model Series pack	2
347	#5-Power Pistons		bronze, gray interior, 7sp/rear-5sp/fr	3
347	#5-Power Pistons		bronze, gray interior, uh	3
347	#5-Power Pistons		bronze, gray interior, 5sp	3
347	Power Pistons		burgundy, w/painted base, gray interior, 3sp; not on Model Series pack	2
347	#5-Power Pistons		burgundy, gray interior, 3sp	4
348	#7-Dodge Ram		green, chrome interior, w5dot	3
348	#7-Dodge Ram		green, chrome interior, 5sp	2
348	#7-Dodge Ram		green, chrome interior, 5dot	3
348	Dodge Ram		green, chrome interior, 5dot; not on Model Series pack	2
349	#9-Power Pipes		dark blue w/silver base, chrome interior, 7sp	7
349	Power Pipes		dark blue w/silver base, chrome interior, purple window 5dot; not on Model Series pack	2
349	#9-Power Pipes		dark blue w/silver base, chrome interior, 3sp	3
349	#9-Power Pipes		dark blue w/silver base, chrome interior, 5sp	2
349	Power Pipes		dark blue w/silver base, chrome interior, purple window 5sp; not on Model Series pack	2
350	#10-Ferrari 355		yellow w/black stripe, black window, 5sp	5
350	#10-Ferrari 355		yellow, black interior, 3sp	2
350	#10-Ferrari 355		yellow, black interior, t/b	2
350	#10-Ferrari 355		yellow, black interior, 5sp	2
350	#10-Ferrari 355		yellow, black interior, 7sp	3
350	#10-Ferrari 355		yellow, black interior, c5dot	2
350	#10-Ferrari 355		yellow, black interior, w5dot	3
351	#11-Power Rocket		purple w/silver base, black interior, 3sp	4
351	#11-Power Rocket		purple w/silver base, black interior, t/b	4
351	#11-Power Rocket		purple w/silver base, black interior, c5dot	5
351	#11-Power Rocket		purple w/silver base, black interior, w5dot	5
351	Power Rocket		purple w/silver painted base, chrome interior, 5dot; not on Model Series pack	2
351	#11-Power Rocket		purple w/metal base, black interior, 5sp	4
352	#12-Big Chill		white, chrome canopy, pink ski	2
352	#12-Big Chill		white, chrome canopy, orange ski	4
352	#12-Big Chill		white, w/blue and orange tampo, chrome canopy, orange ski	3

VEHICLES

NO.	NAME	YEAR	DESCRIPTION	MIP
352	#12-Big Chill		white, w/black tampo, chrome canopy, orange ski	3
352	Big Chill		white w/black tampo, chrome canopy, orange ski; not on Model Series pack	2

1995 Treasure Hunt Series

NO.	NAME	YEAR	DESCRIPTION	MIP
353	#1-Olds 442		metallic blue w/white scoops, white interior, clear window, rl/rr	50
354	Passion		gold, gold and black rr-gd w/white lines	100
355	'67 Camaro		white, rr-gy-gr	200
355	'67 Camaro		white, rr-gy-gr front, rr-gy-ch in rear	600
356	'57 T-Bird		rr-gr w/white lines	45
357	VW Bug		lime, t5 purple	100
358	'63 Split Window		blue, rr-gr	80
359	#7-Stutz Blackhawk		black red interior, clear window, rl/rr	120
360	#8-Rolls-Royce		dark metallic red w/tan top red interior, clear window, r6sp	65
361	#9-Classic Caddy		metallic green w/green fenders, tan interior, g6sp	70
363	Classic Cobra		green, g6s	120
364	#12-'31 Doozie		yellow w/black fenders, black interior, clear window, y6sp	60

1996 First Editions

NO.	NAME	YEAR	DESCRIPTION	MIP
367	#2-Chevy 1500 Pick Up		silver w/metal base, silver interior, smoked window, lg b7sp	6
367	#2-Chevy 1500 Pick Up		silver w/metal base, silver interior, smoked window, small b7sp	2
367	#2-Chevy 1500 Pick Up		silver w/silver painted base, silver interior, smoked window, small b7sp	2
367	#2-Chevy 1500 Pick Up		silver w/metal base (China), silver interior, clear window, 5sp	2
368	'70 Dodge Daytona		red, t/b; not on First Edition pack	2
369	#8-Sizzlers (Turbo Flame)		red and white w/gray motor and metal base, 5sp	3
369	#8-Sizzlers (Turbo Flame)		red and white w/painted silver base, 5sp	2
369	#8-Sizzlers (Turbo Flame)		red and white, 5dot	3
369	#7-Road Rocket		transparent green, gbbs	2
369	#8-Turbo Flame		red and white, 5sp	3
370	#5-Rail Rodder		(China) black, chrome engine and wheels, large rear 5sp	3
370	#5-Rail Rodder		black, chrome engine and wheels, small rear 5sp	3
370	#5-Rail Rodder		black, chrome engine and wheels, large rear 5sp	3
370	#5-Rail Rodder		black, no chrome engine or wheels, large rear 5sp	3
370	Rail Rodder		black w/chrome engine and wheels, small rear 5sp; not on First Edition pack	3
372	#6-VW Bus Funny Car		blue, front 5sp	60
373	#4-Street Cleaver		yellow flame tampo, 5sp	2
373	#4-Street Cleaver		yellow, no tampo, w5dot	2
373	#4-Street Cleaver		yellow, no tampo, all large 5dot	2
373	#4-Street Cleaver		yellow, no tampo, 5dot	2
373	#4-Street Cleaver		yellow, no tampo, t/b	2
373	#4-Street Cleaver		yellow, no tampo, all large 5sp	2
373	#4-Street Cleaver		yellow, no tampo, 5sp	3
373	#4-Street Cleaver		yellow/no tampo, gray engine, all large 5dot	3
373	#4-Street Cleaver		yellow flame tampo, 3sp	2
374	#9-Radio Flyer Wagon		red w/painted silver base, 5sp	8
374	#9-Radio Flyer Wagon		red, 5sp	2
374	#9-Radio Flyer Wagon		red w/metal China base, bw	3
374	#9-Radio Flyer Wagon		red w/metal China base, bw rear/5sp front	2
375	#10-Dog Fighter		dark red, t/b	2
375	#10-Dog Fighter		dark red, unchromed engine and suspension, 5sp	2

VEHICLES

Cockney Cab, 1971, Hot Wheels

Custom El Dorado, 1968, Hot Wheels

HOT WHEELS NUMBERED PACKS

NO.	NAME	YEAR	DESCRIPTION	MIP
375	#10-Dog Fighter		dark red, 5sp	2
375	#10-Dog Fighter		dark red, 5dot	5
376	#11-Twang-Thang (Guitar Car)		silver, 5sp	3
377	#12-Ferrari F50		red, bbs	2
377	#12-Ferrari F50		(new casting) red w/gray plastic base (China), black interior, bbs	2
377	Ferrari F50		red w/gray plastic India base, '98 black interior, clear window bbs; not on First Edition pack	2
378	#1-'96 Mustang		dark red silver, lights, tan interior, t/b	6
378	#1-'96 Mustang		dark red silver, lights, tan interior, 7sp	7
378	#1-'96 Mustang		dark red silver, lights, tan interior, 3sp	12
378	#1-'96 Mustang		dark red silver, lights, tan interior,. c5dot	15
378	#1-'96 Mustang		dark red silver, lights, tan interior,. 5sp	6
382	#3-'70 Dodge Daytona		red, tan interior, gbbs	2
382	#3-'70 Dodge Daytona		red, tan interior, g7sp	2
382	#3-'70 Dodge Daytona		red, tan interior, t/b	2

1996 Treasure Hunt Series

NO.	NAME	YEAR	DESCRIPTION	MIP
428	#1-'40's Woodie		yellow, yrr w/yellow lines	30
428	#1-'40s Woodie		yellow, rr-y w/gold lines	65
428	#1-'40s Woodie		yellow, rr-y w/white lines	70
428	'40s Woodie		rr-y w/white lines	75
428	'40s Woodie		yellow, rr-y w/gold lines	70
429	#10-Lamborghini Countach		fluorescent orange, c6sp	20
430	#3-Ferrari 250		gray, rr	20
431	#4-Jaguar XJ 220		green, g6sp	20
432	#5-'59 Caddy		red, rr	25
433	#6-Dodge Viper RT/10		red, bbs	10
433	#6-Dodge Viper RT/10		white, w6sp	40
434	#7-'57 Chevy		purple, rr	35
435	#8-Ferrari 355		white, gold star	18
436	#9-'58 Corvette		silver, rr	30
437	#2-Auburn 852		olive, grr	20
438	#11-Dodge Ram 1500		maroon, rr	25
439	#12-'37 Bugatti		blue, c6sp	25

1997 First Editions

NO.	NAME	YEAR	DESCRIPTION	MIP
509	#1-Firebird		funny car, dark blue, metal interior, 5sp	3
510	#12-25th. Countach		pearl yellow, clear window, black interior, 5dot	2
512	#3-Excavator		white w/blue tampo, black treads	18
513	#2-Ford 150		red smoked window, 5sp	2
514	#7-Way 2 Fast		orange enamel, w/Malaysia base, chrome interior, 5sp	2
514	#7-Way 2 Fast		orange enamel, w/Thialand base, ('98) chrome interior, 5sp	2
514	#7-Way 2 Fast		orange enamel, w/Malaysia base, no chrome interior, 5sp	2
514	#7-Way 2 Fast		orange enamel w/painted Thialand base chrome interior, 5sp	2
515	#11-'97 Corvette		metallic dark green smoked window, tan interior, bbs	3
515	#11-'97 Corvette		metallic light green smoked window, tan interior, bbs	3
516	#10-Mercedes C-Class		black w/gray plastic base, gray interior, gbbs	2
517	#5-'59 Chevy Impala		light pearl purple, white interior, g7sp	6
517	#5-'59 Chevy Impala		light pearl purple, white interior, gbbs	6
518	#6 BMW M Roadster		metallic silver, metal base, red interior, 3sp	2
518	#6-BMW M Roadster		metallic silver, black painted base, red interior, 5sp	2
518	#6-BMW M Roadster		metallic silver, metal base, red interior, 5sp	2
518	#6-BMW Z3 Roadster		metallic silver, metal base, red interior, 5sp	2

VEHICLES

NO.	NAME	YEAR	DESCRIPTION	MIP
519	#9-Scorchin' Scooter (A)		purple w/silver, orange and blue flames, black seat	4
519	#9-Scorchin' Scooter (A)		purple w/blue chrome engine, silver, orange and blue flames, black seat	4
519	#9-Scorchin' Scooter		purple w/silver and blue flames, black seat	4
520	#4-Saltflat Racer		light red w/silver painted Malaysia base ('97), 5sp	2
520	#4-Saltflat Racer		dark red w/silver painted Thailand base ('98), 5sp	2
523	1970 Plymouth Barracuda		w/chrome base black interior, tinted window, 5sp	6

1997 Treasure Hunt Series

NO.	NAME	YEAR	DESCRIPTION	MIP
578	#1-'56 Flashsider		metallic green, chrome window, 5sp	26
579	#2-Silhouette II		white, blue tint window, white interior, w3sp	15
580	#3-Mercedes 500SL		black, clear window, white interior, 5sp	15
581	#4-Street Cleaver		black w/red and gold tampo, gold base, all large 5sp	22
582	#5-GM Lean Machine		chrome and metallic dark red, chrome window, 5sp	25
583	#6-Hot Rod Wagon		yellow, gold-tinted engine y5sp	36
584	#7-Olds Aurora		purple, gray interior, 5sp	15
585	#8-Dogfighter		metallic green, yellow base, orange prop, 5sp	15
586	#9-Buick Wildcat		metalflake silver, black window, 3sp	15
587	#10-Blimp		blue, white Gondola	15
588	#11-Avus Quattro		gold, white interior, t/b	15
589	#12-Rail Rodder		white	20

1998 First Editions

NO.	NAME	YEAR	DESCRIPTION	MIP
633	#4-Dodge Caravan		dark red, metallic w/gray base, white interior, smoked window, t/b	3
633	#4-Dodge Caravan		brown, metallic w/gray base, white interior, smoked window, t/b	3
633	#4-Dodge Caravan		dark red, metallic w/gray base, white interior, smoked window, 5sp	3
634	#3-Dodge Sidewinder		neon orange w/gray base, purple interior, smoked window, 5sp	3
635	#8-'65 Impala		purple w/yellow and orange tampo, tan interior, clear window, gbbs	5
636	#7-'32 Ford		black w/mostly yellow flames (w/post), red interior, clear window, 5sp	15
636	#7-'32 Ford		black w/yellow and red flames (no post), red interior, clear window, t/b	2
636	#7-'32 Ford		black w/mostly yellow flames (no post), red interior, clear window, 5sp	10
637	#1-Escort Rally		pearl white w/pearl blue trim, red interior, smoked window, bbs	3
637	#1-Escort Rally (Ford)		pearl white w/prl.blue trim, red interior, smoked window, bbs	3
638	#6-Jaguar D-type		metallic blue, gray interior, clear window, bbs	3
638	#6-Jaguar D-type		metallic blue, gray interior, clear window, 5sp	3
638	#6-Jaguar D-type		metallic blue, gray interior, clear window, small front 5sp	3
638	#6-Jaguar D-type		metallic blue, gray interior, clear window, t/b	3
639	#5-Jaguar XK8		pearl green, white interior, clear window, bbs	75
639	#5-Jaguar XK8		pearl green, black interior, clear window, bbs	3
640	#2-Slideout		purple and orange w/gray base, 5sp	4
644	#9-'63 T-Bird		teal w/metal base, white interior, clear window, 5dot	4
644	#9-'63 T-Bird		teal w/metal base, white interior, clear window, new 5dot	4
645	#10-Dairy Delivery		white w/bright pink tampo and straight top stripe aqua interior/clear window, 5sp	2
645	#10-Dairy Delivery		white w/dark pink tampo and curved top stripe, aqua interior, clear window, 5sp	2

VEHICLES

Power Pad, 1970, Hot Wheels

Racing Team Van, 1981, Hot Wheels

Ramblin' Wrecker, 1975, Hot Wheels

Ranger Rig, 1975, Hot Wheels

Rear Engine Snake, 1972, Hot Wheels

Rescue Squad, 1982, Hot Wheels

VEHICLES

NO.	NAME	YEAR	DESCRIPTION	MIP
645	#10-Dairy Delivery		white w/bright pink tampo and curved top stripe, aqua interior/clear window, 5sp	2
646	#11-Mercedes SLK		yellow pearl w/silver side painterior, tan interior, smoked window, 5dot	2
646	#11-Mercedes SLK		yellow w/white side painterior, black interior, smoked window, 5dot	10
646	#11-Mercedes SLK		yellow pearl w/silver side painterior, tan interior, smoked window, 5sp	2
647	#12-Lakester		red w/chrome headers, chrome interior, clear window, 5sp	2
648	#13-Hot Seat		white w/black seat, blue metal engine and base, 5sp	2
648	#13-Hot Seat		white w/black seat, metal engine and base, 5sp	2
650	#23-Solar Eagle III		yellow w/blue cells and black base, black window	2
651	#21-Go Kart		neon green w/black and orange tampo, black seat, 5sp	5
652	#15-Pikes Peak Celica		yellow w/purple tampo and black base, red interior, smoked window, gbbs	3
652	#15-Pikes Peak Celica		yellow w/lavender tampo and black base, red interior, smoked window, gbbs	6
653	#16-IROC Firebird		gold w/gray base, light gray interior, tinted window, b5sp	2
654	#20-'40 Ford Pick-up		dark blue w/chrome base, gray interior, blue window, 5sp	2
654	#20-'40 Ford Pick-up		pearl blue w/chrome base, gray interior, blue window, 5sp	15
655	#22-Super Comp Dragster		black w/five decals and chrome base, gray cage, 5sp	2
655	#22-Super Comp Dragster		black w/three decals and chrome base, gray cage, 5sp	10
657	#19-Panoz GTR-1		white w/black base, bright red stripes, and small logo, blue interior, clear window, bbs	2
657	#19-Panoz GTR-1		white w/black base, dark red stripes and lg.logo, blue interior, clear window, bbs	2
657	#19-Panoz GTR-1		white w/black Malaysia base, black interior, clear window, bbs	3
658	#25-Tow Jam		red w/chrome base, black window, small logo, 3sp	2
659	#24-Tail Dragger		metallic purple w/no logo or side tampo, white interior, clear window, bbs	2
659	#24-Tail Dragger		metallic purple w/metal base, white interior, clear window, bbs	2
661	#17-'70 Roadrunner		Hemi Orange w/chrome base, black interior, clear window, 5sp	2
661	#17-'70 Roadrunner		light Hemi Orange w/chrome base, black interior, clear window, 5sp	2
662	#33-Bad Mudder		white w/dark blue V, black wedge, light red stripe w/logo and no roof tampo, ct/b	2
662	#33-Bad Mudder		white w/light blue V, dark blue wedge, light red stripe, no roof tampo or logo, ct/b	50
662	#33-Bad Mudder		white w/dark blue V, black wedge, dark red stripe w/logo and roof tampo, ct/b	2
662	#33-Bad Mudder		white w/dark blue V, black wedge, light red stripe w/logo and roof tampo, ct/b	2
663	#26-Customized C3500		teal w/long white, blue and purple stripe, gray interior smoked window, 5dot	20
663	#26-Customized C3500		teal w/short blue and white stripe, gray interior, smoked window, 5dot	2
664	#27-Super Modified		black w/metal base, chrome wing, pink seat, bbs	2
665	#18-Mustang Cobra		black w/brown Mustang and gray base, gray interior, clear window, gbbs	2
665	#18-Mustang Cobra		black w/no Cosen and gray base, gray interior, clear window, gbbs	2
665	#18-Mustang Cobra		black w/orange Mustang and gray base, gray interior, clear window, gbbs	2

VEHICLES

HOT WHEELS NUMBERED PACKS

NO.	NAME	YEAR	DESCRIPTION	MIP
667	#34-At-A-Tude		metallic blue w/black base, chrome interior, orange window, all small/bbs	2
667	#34-At-A-Tude		metallic blue w/black base, chrome interior, orange window, large rear/bbs	2
667	#34-At-A-Tude		metallic blue w/black base, chrome interior, orange window, all large/bbs	2
668	#14-Ford GT-90		white w/metal base, white interior, dark blue window, 3sp	2
669	#28-Chaparral 2		white w/black metal base, black interior, clear window, bbs/2	2
670	#29-Mustang Mach 1		mustard yellow w/black base, black interior, tinted window, 5sp	2
670	#29-Mustang Mach 1		dayglo orange w/black base black interior, blue-tinted window, 5sp	25
671	#32-Chrysler Thunderbolt		silver w/black base, white interior, purple window, 5dot	2
672	#35-Dodge Concept Car		pearl orange w/metal base, smoked window, black interior, 5sp	2
672	#35-Dodge Concept Car		pearl orange w/metal base, smoked window, purple interiorer, 5sp	350
673	#36-Whatta Drag		metallic red and chrome w/metal base, chrome interior, orange window, 3sp	2
674	#30-Sweet 16 II		dark purple w/dark purple base, purple window, 5sp	2
677	#31-Callaway C-7		silver w/black base, black interior, clear window, 5sp	2
678	#37-Express Lane		red w/metal base, black seat, 5sp	2
681	#38-Cat-A-Pult		red enamel w/black logo and metal base, black interior orange window, 5sp	2
681	#38-Cat-A-Pult		red enamel w/red logo and metal base, black interior, orange window, 5sp	20
682	#39-Fathom This		white w/black and white props, orange window	2
684	#40-Double Vision		metallic red w/gray base, gray seat clear canopy, gbbs	2

1998 Treasure Hunt Series

749	#1-Twang Thang		black w/blue chrome guitars, chrome interior, 5sp	15
750	#2-Scorchin' Scooter		red w/yellow and black tampo, black forks, black spokes	30
751	#3-Kenworth T600A		dark purple w/chrome base, black window, 3sp	17
752	#4-3 Window '34		orange w/yellow and red flames, chrome interior, 5dot	19
753	#5-Turbo Flame		chrome w/black base chrome interior, green window, 5sp	15
754	#6-Saltflat Racer		black w/gold base and chrome, red window, 5sp	15
755	#7-Streat Beast		red and white w/metal base, white interior, red-tinted window, gbbs	15
756	#8-Road Rocket		chrome w/clear top and metal base, black roll bar and engine, 3sp	15
757	#9-Sol-Aire CX4		white w/flag tampo and blue base, blue interior, clear window, wbbs	15
758	#10-'57 Chevy		light metallic green w/gold tint base, yellow interior, yellow window, 3sp	20
760	#12-Way 2 Fast		metallic olive w/metal base, chrome interior, 5sp	15

1999 First Editions

1113	#21 Ferrari 360 Modena		red w/black base black interior, clear window, 5sp	2
1113	#21 Ferrari 360 Modena		red no HW tampo w/black base, black interior, clear window, 5sp	5
649	#1-1936 Cord		metallic dark red w/chrome base, purple interior, clear window, bbs	2
656	#3-'38 Phantom Corsair		black w/metal base gray interior, clear window, ww5sp	2

VEHICLES

HOT WHEELS NUMBERED PACKS

NO.	NAME	YEAR	DESCRIPTION	MIP
656	#3-'38 Phantom Corsair		black w/metal base, gray interior, clear window, 5sp	25
656	#3-'38 Phantom Corsair		blue w/metal base, gray interior, clear window, ww5sp	20
675	#7-Pontiac Rageous		metallic red w/black base, gray interior, smoked top, 3sp	4
675	#7-Pontiac Rageous		metallic red w/black base, gray interior, smoked top, black roof, 3sp	4
676	#25 Porsche 911 GT1-98		white w/black base, black interior, clear window bbs	2
680	#24 Baby Boomer		blue w/metal base, blue interior, 5sp	2
683	#9-Tee'd Off		blue w/metal base, gray interior, 5sp	2
683	#9-Tee'd Off		pearl white w/metal base, gray interior, 5sp	10
683	#9-Tee'd Off		pearl white w/metal base, maroon interior, 5sp	3
909	#2-'99 Mustang		blue w/black base tan interior, clear window, 5sp	20
909	#2-'99 Mustang		dark purple w/black base, tan interior, clear window, 3sp	2
909	#2-'99 Mustang		dark purple w/black base, red interior, clear window, 5sp	25
909	#2-'99 Mustang		purple w/black base, tan interior, clear window, 5sp	2
909	#2-'99 Mustang		dark purple w/black base, tan interior, clear window, 5sp	2
910	#6-Monte Carlo Concept Car		metallic red w/silver painted base, gray interior, smoked window, 5sp	4
910	#6-Monte Carlo Concept Car		red w/silver painted base, gray interior, smoked window, 5sp	2
911	#5-Olds Aurora GTS-1		metalflake silver w/black base, black interior, clear window, gbbs	3
911	#5-Olds Aurora GT3		white and blue w/black base, black interior, clear window, gbbs	5
911	#5-Olds Aurora GTS-1		red w/black base, black interior, clear window, gbbs	5
911	#5-Olds Aurora GTS-1		white and blue w/black base, black interior, clear window, gbbs	3
912	#10 Porsche 911 gt3		purple w/black base, orange interior, blue tint, bbs	2
912	#10 Porsche 911 gt3		metallic silver w/white HW logo, w/black base, orange interior, blue tinted window, yelllow spoiler, bbs	5
912	#10 Porsche 911 gt3		metallic silver w/red HW logo w/black base, orange interior, blue tint, bbs	5
912	#10 Porsche 911 gt3		silver w/black base, orange interior, blue black spoiler	2
913	#13 Popcycle		metallic red w/metal base, chrome interior, orange window, 3sp	20
913	#13 Popcycle		purple w/metal base, chrome interior, orange window, 3 sp	2
914	#8-Semi Fast		red w/metal base and both chrome grilles, smoked window, 5sp	2
914	#8-Semi Fast		red w/metal base and one chrome grille, smoked window, 5sp	4
914	#8-Semi Fast		black and red w/metal base, both chrome grilles, smoked window, 5sp	2
915	#4-1970 Chevelle SS		dark blue pin stripe hood and metal base, white interior, blue-tinted window, 5sp	2
915	#4-1970 Chevelle SS		gold metal base white interior, blue-tinted window	12
915	#4-1970 Chevelle SS		dark blue no pin stripe and metal base, white interior, blue-tinted window, 5sp	2
916	#14 Phaeton		aqua w/metal base, tan interior, black tint, 5sp	2
917	#12 Track T		black w/metal base, metal interior, 5sp	2
918	#15 Screamin Hauler		w/metal base, metal interior, blue tint, 5 sp	2
919	#11 Fiat 500C		metallic purple w/metal base gray interior, chrome window, 5sp	2

VEHICLES

788

HOT WHEELS NUMBERED PACKS

NO.	NAME	YEAR	DESCRIPTION	MIP
921	#16 Ford GT-40		metallic blue w/gray plastic base, gray interior, blue tint, 5sp	2
921	#16 Ford GT-40		metallic blue w/gray plastic base, gray interior, blue tint, wide 5sp	2
922	#17 Jeepster		red w/metal base, black interior, black tint, 5sp	2
923	#18 Turbolence		black w/metal base gold chrome interior, gold chrome window, g5d	2
924	#19 Pikes Peaks Tacoma		yellow w/black base black interior, clear window, gbbs	2
925	#20 Shadow MKIIA		black w/gray plastic base, gray interior, 5sp	2
925	#20 Shadow MKIIA		black w/gray plastic base, gray interior, wide 5sp	2
926	#26 Mercedes CLK-LM		silver w/black base, black interior, clear window, gbbs	2
927	#22 '56 Ford Truck		light blue w/gray base, chrome interior, blue tint, wide 5sp	3
928	#23 Chrysler Pronto		yellow w/black base gray interior black tint, 5sp	2

1999 Treasure Hunt Series

NO.	NAME	YEAR	DESCRIPTION	MIP
929	Mercedes 540K		red, 5sp	13
930	T-Bird Stocker		purple, 5sp	12
931	'97 Corvette		purple, 5sp	14
932	Rigor Mortor		yellow, g5sp	14
933	Ferrari F512M		black base, 5sw	50
933	Ferrari F512M		5sw	16
934	'59 Impala		purple, gbbs	18
935	Hot Wheel 500		black, bk5sp	16
936	Jaguar D-Type		black, 5sp	16
937	'32 Ford Delivery		gold, g5sp	30
938	Hot Seat		clear, 5sp	15
939	'70 Mustang		green, 5s	30
940	Express Lane		purple, g5sp	20

Artistic License Series

NO.	NAME	YEAR	DESCRIPTION	MIP
729	Alien		white pearl w/metal base, large Alien, white interior, tinted window, 3sp	2
729	Alien		white enamel w/metal base, small Alien white interior, tinted window, 3sp	2
730	'57 Chevy		(plastic) silver w/metal base, smoked window, t/b	2
731	VW Bug		pearl white w/roof tampo only and metal base, black interior, blue tint, window, 5dot	2
731	VW Bug		pearl white w/metal base, black interior, blue-tinted, window, all small 5dot	2
731	VW Bug		pearl white w/metal base, black interior, blue-tinted window, 5dot	2
732	1970 Barracuda		black w/chrome China base, orange logo, light orange interior, clear window, 5sp	2
732	1970 Barracuda		black w/chrome China base, blue logo, light orange interior, clear window, 5sp	2
732	1970 Barracuda		black w/chrome Maylasia base, orange logo, dark orange interior, smoked window, 3sp	2
732	1970 Barracuda		black w/chrome Maylasia base blue logo, dark orange interior, smoked window, 3sp	2

Biff! Bam! Boom! Series

NO.	NAME	YEAR	DESCRIPTION	MIP
541	Mini Truck		red, black interior, smoked window, t/b	6
541	Mini Truck		red, black interior, smoked window, 5dot rear/3sp. front	3
541	Mini Truck		red, black interior, smoked window, 5sp	3
541	Mini Truck		red, black interior, smoked window, 3sp	3
542	Limozeen		blue, white interior, smoked window, 5sp	2
542	Limozeen		light blue w/no bullet holes in front fender, white interior, smoked window, 5sp	2
543	VW Bug		green w/logo, black interior, 5sp	4
543	VW Bug		green w/o logo, black interior, 5sp	4

VEHICLES

NO.	NAME	YEAR	DESCRIPTION	MIP
543	VW Bug		green w/o logo, black interior, 7sp	18
544	Range Rover		pearl purple, gray interior, t/b	2

Biohazard Series

NO.	NAME	YEAR	DESCRIPTION	MIP
717	Hydroplane		bright neon green w/black Malaysa base, black interior, smoked canopy	2
717	Hydroplane		dark neon green w/black Thailand base, black interior, clear canopy	2
717	Hydroplane		neon green w/black Thailand base, black interior, smoked canopy	2
718	Flame Stopper		neon pink w/black base, black window and boom, yt/b	2
719	Recycling Truck		neon yellow w/orange tampo, black window, t/b	2
719	Recycling Truck		neon yellow w/black tampo, black base, black window, t/b	2
720	Rescue Ranger		black w/chrome base, yellow tint window and interior, 5dot	2
720	Rescue Ranger		black w/chrome base yellow tint window and interior, 5sp	2

Blue Streak Series

NO.	NAME	YEAR	DESCRIPTION	MIP
573	Olds 442		candy blue, black interior, 3sp	3
574	Nissan Truck		candy blue, black interior, t/b	14
575	'55 Chevy		candy blue, black window, 3sp	3
576	Speed Blaster		candy blue, w/black base, chrome window, 3sp	2
576	Speed Blaster		candy blue, w/chrome base, chrome window, 3sp	15

Buggin' Out Series

NO.	NAME	YEAR	DESCRIPTION	MIP
941	Treadator		red w/black chrome and yellow scoops, chrome window, black treads	2
941	Treadator		red w/dull chrome and yellow scoops, chrome window, black treads	2
941	Treadator		red w/chrome fenders and yellow scoops, chrome window, black treads	2
942	Shadow Jet II		gray w/green and yellow tampo and metal base, yellow interior, green window, 5sp	2
943	Radar Ranger		metallic purple w/black dish and metal base, blue tint window, blue interior, ct/b	2
944	Baja Bug		blue w/metal base, orange interior, 5sp	2

Car-toon Friends

NO.	NAME	YEAR	DESCRIPTION	MIP
985	Salt Flat Racer		purple w/silver metal base, chrome interior, clear window, 5sp	2
986	XT3		orange w/black metal, black tint window, g5sp	2
987	Double Vision		black w/black base, gray interior, clear window, gbbs	2
988	Lakester		white w/black metal base, chrome interior, red tint, 5sp	2

Classic Games Series

NO.	NAME	YEAR	DESCRIPTION	MIP
981	Super Modified		blue w/metal base, black interior, gbbs	2
982	Silhouette II		light blue w/black base, white interior, blue tint window, 5dot	2
983	Sol-aire		white w/black base, black interior, clear window, 3sp	2
984	Escort Rally		red w/gray base, black interior, clear, window, bbs	2

Dark Rider Series

NO.	NAME	YEAR	DESCRIPTION	MIP
297	Splittin Image		black, dark chrome interior, 6sp	3
297	Splittin Image		black, dark chrome interior, 7sp	3
298	Twin Mill II		black, black interior, 6sp	3
298	Twin Mill II		black, black interior, 7sp	3
299	Silhouette II		black, w/black plastic base, black interior, clear window, 6sp	3

VEHICLES

790

HOT WHEELS NUMBERED PACKS

NO.	NAME	YEAR	DESCRIPTION	MIP
299	Silhouette II		black, w/dark chrome base, black interior, 6sp	3
299	Silhouette II		black, w/black plastic base, black interior, 7sp	3
300	Rigor Motor		black, chrome interior, 5sp	3
300	Rigor Motor		black, w/metal base (China), red chrome engine, bbs	2
300	Rigor Motor		black, chrome interior, 7sp	3
300	Rigor Motor		black, chrome interior, 6sp	3

Dark Rider Series II

NO.	NAME	YEAR	DESCRIPTION	MIP
400	Big Chill		black, dark chrome canopy, black ski	2
400	Big Chill		(China) metalflake silver, chrome canopy, orange ski	2
401	Street Beast		dark chrome, black interior, 7sp	2
402	Thunderstreak		dark chrome, black, dark chrome 7sp	2
402	Thunderstreak		dark chrome, black, dark chrome, 5sp/rear-7sp/front	2
403	Power Pistons		dark chrome, black interior, 7sp	2

Dash 4 Cash Series

NO.	NAME	YEAR	DESCRIPTION	MIP
721	Jaguar XJ220		silver w/only side tampo and Malaysia base, light purple interior, clear window, t/b	2
721	Jaguar XJ220		silver w/black tampo and Malaysia base, light purple interior, clear window, t/b	2
721	Jaguar XJ220		silver w/black tampo and Malaysia base, dark purple interior, clear window, 3sp	2
721	Jaguar XJ220		silver w/black tampo and Malaysia base, light purple interior, clear window, 3sp	2
721	Jaguar XJ220		silver w/black tampo and Malaysia base, dark purple interior, clear window, bbs	2
721	Jaguar XJ220		silver w/black tampo and Malaysia base, light purple interior, clear window, bbs	2
722	Ferrari F40		gold w/metal Malaysia base, tan interior, tinted window, gbbs	2
723	Audi Avus		black w/black Thailand base, white interior, smoke and gold window, gbbs	2
724	Dodge Viper		white w/black Thialand base, red interior, smoked window, t/b	2

Dealer's Choice Series

NO.	NAME	YEAR	DESCRIPTION	MIP
565	Silhoutte II		pearl blue w/black Malaysia base, gold interior, clear window, 5dot	2
565	Silhoutte II		pearl blue w/black Malaysia base, gold interior, clear window, rear 5sp/ front 5dot	2
566	Street Beast		white and gold, gold interior, 7sp	3
566	Street Beast		white and gold, gold interior, 5dot	3
567	Baja Bug		metallic red w/metal base, white interior, 5sp	3
567	Baja Bug		metallic red w/silver base, white interior, 5sp	3
567	Baja Bug		metallic red w/metal base, white interior, all small 5sp	2
568	'63 Corvette		black w/red '63 Corvette base, red interior, clear window, 5dot	3
568	'63 Corvette		black w/red base red interior, clear window, 5dot	3

Extreme Speed

NO.	NAME	YEAR	DESCRIPTION	MIP
965	Dodge Sidewinder		white w/black base, purple interior, black tint, 5sp	2
966	Callaway C7		green w/black base black interior, clear window, 5sp	2
967	Porsche Carrera		silver w/metal base white interior, black tint, gold 5sp	2
968	Mazda MX-5 Miata		blue w/blue metal base, green interior, clear window, bbs	2

Fast Food Series

NO.	NAME	YEAR	DESCRIPTION	MIP
416	Pizza Vette		black window, 3sp	3
416	Pizza Vette		black window, 5sp	10

VEHICLES

791

NO.	NAME	YEAR	DESCRIPTION	MIP
417	Pasta Pipes		chrome interior, 3sp	3
418	Sweet Stocker		yellow interior, 3sp	18
419	Crunch Chief		yellow interior, 7sp	15
419	Crunch Chief		yellow interior, 3sp	4

Fire Rescue Series

NO.	NAME	YEAR	DESCRIPTION	MIP
424	Ambulance		bright green, ribbed rear step, white interior, 7sp	4
424	Ambulance		red w/black logo, ribbed rear step, white interior, 7sp	2
424	Ambulance		red w/white logo, ribbed rear step, white interior, 7sp	2
424	Ambulance		red w/black logo, ribbed rear step, white interior, 5sp	2
424	Ambulance		bright green, smooth rear step, white interior, 5sp	3
424	Ambulance		bright green, smooth rear step, white interior, 7sp	4
425	Rescue Ranger		yellow, black interior, 5sp	2
426	Flame Stopper		yellow, black window, yt/b	2
426	Flame Stopper		(China) yellow, black window, cts	2
427	Fire Eater		red, blue interior, 7sp	3
427	Fire Eater		red, blue interior, 5sp	3

Flamethrower Series

NO.	NAME	YEAR	DESCRIPTION	MIP
384	'57 T-Bird		white w/light pink flame, quarter logo, window logo, four-flame trunk, 7sp	2
384	'57 T-Bird		white w/fade pink flame, logo in window, five-flame trunk w/two on quarter panel, 7sp	2
384	'57 T-Bird		white w/copper flame, two-flames on quarter panel, five-flame trunk, window logo, 7sp	3
384	'57 T-Bird		white w/full bright pink flame, logo on quarter panel, five-flame trunk, 7sp	2
384	'57 T-Bird		white w/fade pink flame, logo on quarter panel, four-flame trunk, 7sp	2
384	'57 T-Bird		white w/light pink flame, two flame quarter, four-flame trunk, window logo, 7sp	2
385	Hydroplane		yellow w/gold and green flames, chrome, n/a	2
385	Hydroplane		yellow w/gold and green flames backwards on spoiler, n/a	2
386	Range Rover		red w/gold flames, tampo on quarter panel, tan interior, ct	2
386	Range Rover		red w/gold flames, window tampo, tan interior, ct	2
387	Oshkosh Snowplow		black w/yellow and blue flames, black interior, bct	14
387	Oshkosh Snowplow		black w/yellow and blue flames, black interior, ct	4

Flyn' Aces Series

NO.	NAME	YEAR	DESCRIPTION	MIP
737	'70 Dodge Daytona		metallic green w/tan base, black interior, clear window, 5sp	2
737	'70 Dodge Daytona		metallic green w/tan base, black interior, clear window, 5dot	2
738	Dogfighter		black w/yellow base, chrome seat and suspension, 5dot	2
739	Sol-air CX4		yellow, black base, black interior, clear window, 5sp	2
740	XT-3		metallic silver w/orange base, black window, 5sp	2

Game Over Series

NO.	NAME	YEAR	DESCRIPTION	MIP
957	#1-Lean Machine		purple, black tint window, 5sp	2
958	#2-Shadow Jet		yellow w/metal base, yellow interior, smoked canopy, 5sp	2
959	#3-Speed Blaster		green, lime base, gt/b	2
960	#4-Twin Mill		red w/black base black interior, black tint, bbs	2

VEHICLES

Seasider, 1970, Hot Wheels

Shelby Turbine, 1969, Hot Wheels

Short Order, 1971, Hot Wheels

Sidekick, 1972, Hot Wheels

Super Van, 1977,
Hot Wheels

VEHICLES

Team Trailer, 1971, Hot Wheels

NO.	NAME	YEAR	DESCRIPTION	MIP

Heet Fleet Series

NO.	NAME	YEAR	DESCRIPTION	MIP
537	Police Cruiser		green w/flames, clear window, purple interior, 3sp	4
537	Police Cruiser		green w/flames, clear window, purple interior, 5sp	2
537	Police Cruiser		green w/flames, clear window, purple interior, 5dot	4
537	Police Cruiser		green w/flames, clear window, purple interior, 7sp	14
537	Police Cruiser		green w/flames, clear window, purple interior, 7sp.rear/5sp. front	4
538	School Bus		green w/flames, clear window, white interior, 7sp	2
538	School Bus		(China) green w/flames, clear window, white interior, 5sp	2
538	Peterbilt Tank Truck		metallic maroon w/flames, chrome window, 5sp	14
538	School Bus		green w/flames, clear window, white interior, 5sp	2
538	School Bus		green w/flames, clear window, white interior, 3sp	14
539	Peterbilt Tank Truck		metallic maroon w/flames, no HW logo, chrome window, 7sp	2
539	Peterbilt Tank Truck		metallic maroon w/flames, chrome window, 7sp	2
540	Ramblin' Wrecker		black w/flames, smoked window, chrome 7sp	2
540	Ramblin' Wrecker		black w/flames, smoked window, chrome, t/b	2

Hot Hubs Series

NO.	NAME	YEAR	DESCRIPTION	MIP
307	Cyber Cruiser		burgundy, purple chrome, blue and orange, hh	6
308	Vampyra		purple, gold interior, green and blue 6 sp	5
308	Vampyra		purple w/black metal base (China), gold interior, bbs	2
310	Shadow Jet		green, green interior, yellow and purple, yhh	6
311	Suzuki Quadracer		(China) yellow, purple seat, cts	4
311	Suzuki Quadracer		neon yellow, purple seat, Tiger Paw	40
311	Suzuki Quadracer		yellow, purple seat, yellow and black	6
311	Suzuki Quadracer		neon yellow, purple seat, yellow and black	30

Krackle Car Series

NO.	NAME	YEAR	DESCRIPTION	MIP
280	Sharkruiser		lime and blue w/metal base, lime interior, 7sp	3
280	Sharkruiser		lime and blue w/painted base, lime interior, uh	3
280	Sharkruiser		lime and blue w/metal base, lime interior, uh	3
281	Turboa		purple and red w/painted base, red interior, uh	4
281	Turboa		purple and red w/metal base, red interior, 7sp	10
282	'63 Split		aqua and orange w/chrome base, two rivet, white interior, orange window, 5sp	4
282	'63 Split		aqua and orange w/gray base, two rivet, white interior, orange window 5sp	4
282	'63 Split		aqua and orange w/chrome base, two rivet, white interior, orange window, bw	3
282	'63 Split		aqua and orange w/gray base, two rivet, white interior, orange window, bw	3
282	'63 Split		aqua and orange w/chrome base, one rivet, white interior, orange window, bw	3
284	Flashfire		purple and orange, orange interior, 5sp	9
284	Flashfire		purple and yellow, yellow interior, 7sp	3
284	Flashfire		purple and yellow, yellow interior, 5sp	3
284	Flashfire		purple and yellow, yellow interior, uh	4

Low 'N Cool Series

NO.	NAME	YEAR	DESCRIPTION	MIP
697	Mini Truck		dayglo yellow w/black base, gray, pink and blackk tampo, black interior, g3sp	2
698	'59 Impala		pearl green w/light pearl purple tampo, white interior, smoked window, gbbs	2
698	'59 Impala		pearl green w/dark purple tampo, white interior, smoked window, gbbs	2

VEHICLES

HOT WHEELS NUMBERED PACKS

NO.	NAME	YEAR	DESCRIPTION	MIP
699	'59 Caddy		red w/yellow and blue tampo, white interior, snoked window, gbbs	2
716	Limozeen		black metalflake w/gold base white interior, smoked window, gbbs	2

Mega Graphics Series

NO.	NAME	YEAR	DESCRIPTION	MIP
973	Funny Car		fluorescent yellow w/metal base metal interior, yellow tint, 5sp	3
974	Mustang Cobra		white w/black base black interior, clear window t/b	2
975	Turbo Flame		black w/metallic red base, black interior, yellow tint, g5sp	2
976	Firebird Funny Car		metallic purple w/metal base metal interior, clear window, bk5sp	3

Mixed Signals Series

NO.	NAME	YEAR	DESCRIPTION	MIP
733	Street Roader		white and yellow w/metal base, yellow interior, smoked window, t/b	2
734	'80's Corvette		green w/metal base, black interior, smoked window, bbs	2
735	Nissan Truck		light pearl orange w/black base, black interior, clear window, large ct/b	2
736	School Bus		yellow w/black Thailand base, logo on side, black interior, clear window, 5dot	2
736	School Bus		yellow w/black Thailand base, logo on door, black interior, clear window, 5dot	2
736	School Bus		yellow w/black Malaysia base, logo on side, black interior, clear window, 5dot	2
736	School Bus		yellow w/black Malaysia base, logo on door, black interior, clear window, 5dot	2

Mod Bod Series

NO.	NAME	YEAR	DESCRIPTION	MIP
396	Hummer		pink, green window, ct	5
396	Hummer		pink, green window, t/b	8
397	School Bus		purple, yellow interior, 7sp	5
398	VW Bug		blue, yellow interior, 7sp	5
399	'67 Camaro		bright green, red interior, clear window, all small 5sp	40
399	'67 Camaro		bright green, red interior, clear window, 7sp	50
399	'67 Camaro		bright green, red interior, tinted window, 5sp	35
399	'67 Camaro		bright, green, red interior, clear window, 5sp	5

Pearl Driver Series

NO.	NAME	YEAR	DESCRIPTION	MIP
292	Pearl Passion		lavender, yellow interior, ww	4
292	Pearl Passion		lavender, yellow interior, 7sp	4
293	VW Bug		pink, gray interior, 5sp	10
293	VW Bug		pink, gray interior, bw	6
293	VW Bug		pink, gray interior, 7sp	6
295	Talbot Lago		blue, blue interior, 7sp	3
295	Talbot Lago		blue, blue interior, ww	3
296	Jaguar XJ220		white, tan interior, 3sp	3
296	Jaguar XJ220		white, tan interior, uh	3
296	Jaguar XJ220		white, tan interior, 5sp	3
296	Jaguar XJ220		white, tan interior, 7sp	5

Phantom Racers Series

NO.	NAME	YEAR	DESCRIPTION	MIP
529	Power Rocket		transparent green w/pink canopy, chrome interior, 3sp	2
529	Power Rocket		transparent green w/orange canopy, chrome interior, 3sp	2
530	Power Pistons		transparent red, gray interior, 3sp	2
530	Power Pistons		transparent red, gray interior, 5sp	3
531	Power Pipes		transparent blue w/purple canopy, chrome interior, 3sp	2
531	Power Pipes		transparent blue w/purple canapy, chrome interior,5sp-rear/3sp- front	2

VEHICLES

NO.	NAME	YEAR	DESCRIPTION	MIP
532	Road Rocket		transparent orange and lime, orange interior, t/b	4
532	Road Rocket		transparent orange and lime, orange interior, 3sp	2

Photo Finish Series

NO.	NAME	YEAR	DESCRIPTION	MIP
331	Aerostar		white, silver window, 7sp	3
332	Flying Aces Blimp		gray, black, n/a	3
333	Tank Truck		blue, chrome window, 7sp	3
335	Hiway Hauler		green, black window, 7sp	4

Pinstripe Series

NO.	NAME	YEAR	DESCRIPTION	MIP
953	'34 3 Window		purple w/metal base, black interior, blue tint window, 5sp	2
954	Tail Dragger		black w/metal base, tan interior, clear window, bbs	2
955	'65 Impala		green w/chrome plastic base, tan interior, black tint window, gbbs	2
956	Auburn 852		black and silver w/metal base, white interior, clear window, bbs	2

Quicksilver Series

NO.	NAME	YEAR	DESCRIPTION	MIP
545	Chevy Stocker		red w/silver painted base, black window, four small 3sp	3
545	Chevy Stocker		red w/metal base, black window, four small 3sp	3
546	Aeroflash		purple w/white base, white window, four small 3sp	2
546	Aeroflash		purple w/white base, white window, 3sp	2
547	Ferrari 308		pearl white w/black metal base, black window, 5dot	2
548	T-Bird Stock Car		blue enamel w/silver painted base, black window, 5sp	2
548	T-Bird Stock Car		blue enamel w/metal base, black window, 5sp	2

Race Team Series

NO.	NAME	YEAR	DESCRIPTION	MIP
275	Lumina Stocker		dark metallic blue, white interior, uh	6
275	Lumina Stocker		light metallic blue, white interior, uh	4
275	Lumina Stocker		dark metallic blue, white interior, 7sp	4
276	Hot Wheels 500		dark metallic blue, gray interior, uh	25
276	Hot Wheels 500		dark metallic blue, gray interior, bw	5
276	Hot Wheels 500		light metallic blue, gray interior, bw	3
276	Hot Wheels 500		dark metallic blue, gray interior, 7sp	10
277	Side Splitter		dark metallic blue, metal interior, 5sp	4
277	Side Splitter		light metallic blue, metal interior, bw	4
277	Side Splitter		dark metallic blue, metal interior, bw	4
278	Dragster		dark metallic blue, white interior, bw	3
278	Dragster		dark metallic blue, white interior, 5sp	3
278	Dragster		light metallic blue, white interior, bw	3
392	Ramp Truck		(China) blue and white, smoked front window w/HW Logo, 5sp	3
392	Ramp Truck		blue and white, clear window, 7sp	3
392	Ramp Truck		blue and white, clear window, 5sp	2
393	Baja Bug		blue and white, white interior, 5sp	5
394	'57 Chevy		blue and white, blue interior, 5sp	5
394	'57 Chevy		blue and white, blue interior, lg.3sp.rear/5sp front	5
395	Bywayman		blue and white, white interior, ct	3
395	Bywayman		blue and white, white interior, t/b	3

Race Team Series III

NO.	NAME	YEAR	DESCRIPTION	MIP
533	Hummer		blue w/silver base and big antenna, gray windows, t/b	3
533	Hummer		blue w/metal base and small antenna, gray windows, t/b	3
533	Hummer		blue w/metal base and big antenna, gray windows, t/b	3

VEHICLES

796

HOT WHEELS NUMBERED PACKS

NO.	NAME	YEAR	DESCRIPTION	MIP
534	Chevy 1500 Pickup		blue race team colors, white interior, smoked window, 5sp	2
534	Chevy 1500 Pickup		blue race team colors, white interior, smoked window, 3sp	4
534	Chevy 1500 Pickup		team colors/silver base, white interior, smoked window, 5sp	2
534	Chevy 1500 Pickup		blue/race team colors, white interior, smoked window, 5dot	4
534	Chevy 1500 Pickup		blue/race team colors, white interior, smoked window, 7sp	12
535	3-Window '34		blue/race team colors, blue interior, 5sp	3
536	'80's Corvette		blue/race team colors, transparent blue roof, white interior, 5sp	2
536	'80's Corvette		blue race team colors, dark blue roof, white interior, 5sp	4
536	'80's Corvette		blue/race team colors, transparent blue roof, white interior, 5dot	4

Race Team Series IV

NO.	NAME	YEAR	DESCRIPTION	MIP
725	'67 Camaro		race team colors w/metal base, white interior, tinted window, 5sp	2
726	Mercedes C-Class		race team colors w/black base, white interior, clear window, 5sp	2
727	Shelby Cobra 427 S/C		race team colors, metal base, white interior, smoked window, 5sp	2
728	'63 Corvette		race team colors, chrome base, white interior, tinted window, 5sp	2

Race Truck Series

NO.	NAME	YEAR	DESCRIPTION	MIP
380	Dodge Ram 1500		(China) gray red interior, smoked window, 5sp	2
380	Dodge Ram 1500		red w/no hood or roof tampo, red interior, b7sp	4
380	Dodge Ram 1500		red, red interior, b7sp	8
380	Dodge Ram 1500		red, red interior, no letter, b7sp	3
381	Kenworth T600		silver, blue interior, b7sp	4
381	Kenworth T600 (Ford LTL pack)		silver, blue interior, b7sp	8
382	'56 Flashsider		black side logo, chrome window, b7sp	3
382	'56 Flashsider		black side logo, chrome window, no letter, b7sp	3
382	'56 Flashsider		black rear logo, chrome window, b7sp	3
383	Nissan Truck		dark blue, gray interior, bct	7
383	Nissan Truck		dark blue, gray interior, ct	3

Racing Metals Series

NO.	NAME	YEAR	DESCRIPTION	MIP
336	Race Truck		chrome, smoked window, red interior, cct	3
337	Ramp Truck		pink chrome, black window, 7sp	6
337	Ramp Truck		purple chrome, black window, 7sp	4
337	Ramp Truck		blue chrome, black window, 7sp	4
338	Camaro Racer		light blue chrome, no Baldwin, white interior, 5sp	3
338	Camaro Racer		light blue chrome w/Baldwin, white interior, 5sp	7
340	Dragster		light blue chrome, white interior, 5sp	4

Real Rider Series

NO.	NAME	YEAR	DESCRIPTION	MIP
317	Dump Truck		neon yellow, black interior, yrr	20
318	Mercedes Unimog		orange and gray, orange interior, orr	20
320	'59 Caddy convertible		red, white interior, crr	35
321	Corvette Stingray		green, gray interior, grr	45

Roarin Rods Series

NO.	NAME	YEAR	DESCRIPTION	MIP
302	Mini Truck		tan, tan interior, smoked window, 7sp	5
302	Mini Truck		tan, tan interior, smoked window, 5sp	3
302	Mini Truck		tan w/orange base, tan interior, smoked window, 5sp	20
302	Mini Truck		tan, tan interior, smoked window, uh	3
303	Street Roader		orange and black, black interior, oct	10
304	Roll Patroll		white and black, black interior, yct	4

VEHICLES

NO.	NAME	YEAR	DESCRIPTION	MIP
304	Roll Patroll		white and black, black interior, cct	8
305	Cobra		neon yellow, black plastic base, olive interior, 7sp	4
305	Cobra		yellow, 5s	90
305	Cobra		neon yellow, black metal base, olive interior, 7sp	4

Rockin' Rods Series

NO.	NAME	YEAR	DESCRIPTION	MIP
569	Twang Thang		metallic red chrome interior, 5sp	3
570	Ferrari 355		black, purple interior, 5sp	2
570	Ferrari 355		black, purple interior, 3sp	4
571	Turbo Flame		purple w/black base, yellow window, 5sp	2
572	Porsche 930		metallic green w/metal base, black interior, smoked window, 5dot	4
572	Porsche 930		metallic green w/metal base, black interior, smoked window, 5sp	2

Silver Series

NO.	NAME	YEAR	DESCRIPTION	MIP
322	Fire Eater		chrome, blue interior, 7sp	4
322	Fire Eater		chrome, blue interior, bw	5
323	Rodzilla		chrome, gold engine, 7sp	3
323	Rodzilla		chrome, gold engine, uh	3
325	Propper Chopper		chrome black interior, blue window, n/a	4
328	School Bus		chrome, white interior, bw	6
328	School Bus		chrome, white interior, 3sp	4
328	School Bus		chrome, white interior, 5sp	4
328	School Bus		chrome, tinted windows, bw	15
328	School Bus		chrome, white interior, 7sp	5

Silver Series II

NO.	NAME	YEAR	DESCRIPTION	MIP
420	Dump Truck		chrome, black box, ct/b	12
420	Dump Truck		chrome, chrome box, ct/b	2
421	'40's Woodie		logo in side window, chrome black interior, 7sp	3
421	'40's Woodie		logo in side window, chrome black interior, 5sp	3
421	'40's Woodie		logo in rear window, chrome black interior, 5sp	3
422	'57 Chevy		chrome, orange window, 5sp	3
423	Oscar Mayer Wienermobile		chrome, b5sp	3

Space Series

NO.	NAME	YEAR	DESCRIPTION	MIP
388	Radar Ranger		white and orange, orange interior, cct	3
389	GM Lean Machine		blue and white, no taillights, orange HWSA, b5sp	3
389	GM Lean Machine		blue and white w/metal base, orange HWSA, b5sp	3
390	Alien		blue and white, black, 5sp	3
391	Treadator		white pearl and orange, blue chrome	10
391	Treadator		light blue pearl and orange, blue chrome	3

Speed Gleamer Series

NO.	NAME	YEAR	DESCRIPTION	MIP
312	3 Window '34		green, chrome aqua interior, 7sp	6
313	T-Bucket		purple, white interior, purple window, 5sp	4
313	T-Bucket		purple white interior, purple window, 7sp	7
313	T-Bucket		purple white interior, clear window, 5sp	25
315	Ratmobile		black, chrome interior, uh	4
315	Ratmobile		black, chrome interior, 7sp	6
316	Limozeen		gold, white interior, ww	10
316	Limozeen		gold, white interior, 7sp	8

Speed Spray Series

NO.	NAME	YEAR	DESCRIPTION	MIP
549	Hydroplane		white w/aqua blue tampo, blue base, chrome interior	2
550	Street Roader		white, brown tampo, red interior, ct/b	2
551	XT-3		blue, white base, orange canopy, 5sp	2
552	Funny Car		pearl magenta, metal interior, 5sp	3

VEHICLES

NO.	NAME	YEAR	DESCRIPTION	MIP

Splatter Paint Series

NO.	NAME	YEAR	DESCRIPTION	MIP
408	Rescue Ranger		orange, blue interior, t/b	2
408	Rescue Ranger		orange, blue interior, 5sp	2
408	Rescue Ranger		orange, black interior, 5sp	2
409	Side Splitter Funny Car		white, metal interior, 5sp	3
410	'55 Chevy		yellow, red interior, t/b	4
410	'55 Chevy		yellow, red interior, 5sp	3
411	'80's Camaro		white, white interior, 5sp	3

Sports Car Series

NO.	NAME	YEAR	DESCRIPTION	MIP
404	Porsche 930		silver, black interior, 7sp	3
405	Custom Corvette		purple w/logo on windshield and fender, gray interior, 7sp	35
405	Custom Corvette		purple w/logo on front fender, gray interior, 7sp	3
405	Custom Corvette		purple w/logo on windshield, gray interior, 5sp	3
405	Custom Corvette		purple w/logo on windshield, gray interior, 7sp	3
405	Custom Corvette		purple w/logo on windshield, red interior, 7sp	35
406	Cobra 427 S/C		pearl white w/metal base black interior, clear window, 7sp	3
406	Cobra 427 S/C		pearl white w/metal base black interior, clear window, 5sp	55
407	'59 Caddy		black, white interior, 7spww-rear/7sp-fr	75
407	'59 Caddy		black, white interior, 7sp	3

Spy Print Series

NO.	NAME	YEAR	DESCRIPTION	MIP
553	Stealth		purple w/metal base, purple window, t/b	2
553	Stealth		purple w/silver painted base, purple window, t/b	2
553	Stealth		purple w/silver painted base, purple window, 3sp	2
553	Stealth		purple w/metal base, purple window, 3sp	2
554	Alien		blue and white w/smoked window, white and blue, interior t/b	2
554	Alien		blue and white w/smoked window, white and blue interior, 3sp	2
555	Sol-Aire CX4		metallic maroon w/white sides, black window, t/b	2
555	Sol-Aire CX4		metallic maroon w/white sides, black window, 3sp	2
556	Custom Corvette		black w/yellow, red and white tampo, gray interior, 3sp	2

Steel Stamp Series

NO.	NAME	YEAR	DESCRIPTION	MIP
285	Steel Passion		black and rose, red interior, ww	4
285	Steel Passion		black and rose, red interior, clear window, ww	4
285	Steel Passion		black and rose, red interior, 7sp	4
287	Zender Fact 4		black, white interior, clear window, 5sp	8
287	Zender Fact 4		black, white interior, 3sp	4
287	Zender Fact 4		black, white interior, uh	4
287	Zender Fact 4		black, white interior, 5sp	4
289	'56 Flashsider		burgundy, chrome window, 5sp	4
289	'56 Flashsider		burgundy, chrome window, 7sp	4
289	56 Flashsider		burgundy, chrome window, uh	4
290	'57 Chevy		blue, blue interior, blue window, uh	4
290	'57 Chevy		blue, black interior, smoked window, 5sp	8
290	'57 Chevy		blue, blue interior, blue window, 5sp	15
290	'57 Chevy		blue, blue interior, blue window, 7sp	4

Street Art Series

NO.	NAME	YEAR	DESCRIPTION	MIP
850	Propper Chopper		pearl green w/black base, black interior, yellow window	2
949	Mini Truck		black w/black base, black interior, clear window, t/b	2
951	Ambulance		purple w/chrome base, purple interior, orange tint window, 5sp	2

VEHICLES

NO.	NAME	YEAR	DESCRIPTION	MIP
951	Ambulance		purple w/chrome base, purple interior, orange tint window, 3sp	2
952	School Bus		silver w/black base, yellow interior, red tint, 5dot	3
952	School Bus		yellow w/black base, yellow interior, red tint window, 5dot	2

Street Beast Series

557	Mercedes-Benz Unimog		red and black, w/tan top, red interior, ct/b	3
558	Jaguar XJ220		orange w/black side tampo, black interior, yt/b	3
558	Jaguar XJ220		orange w/no side tampo, black interior, yt/b	3
559	Blown Camaro		yellow w/metal Malaysia base, black interior, ot/b	3
559	Blown Camaro		yellow w/metal black base, black interior, ot/b	3
560	Corvette Stingray		white, blue interior, yt/b	3

Street Eaters Series

412	Speed Machine		light green, red interior, 7sp	5
412	Speed Machine		light green, red interior, 5sp	2
413	Silhoutte II		tampo on rear, purple, orange interior, 5sp	2
413	Silhoutte II		tampo on front, purple, orange interior, 5sp	2
414	Propper Chopper		(China) blue w/orange base, orange interior, blue window	2
414	Propper Chopper		blue w/orange base, orange interior, clear window	2
414	Propper Chopper		blue w/orange base, orange interior, blue window	2
415	Roll Patrol		brown w/orange base, dark orange, interior, yct	5
415	Roll Patrol		brown w/orange base, dark orange, interior, ytb	3
415	Roll Patrol		brown w/orange base, light orange interior, ytb	3
415	Roll Patrol		brown w/orange base, light orange, interior, yct	5

Sugar Rush Series 98

741	Mazda MX-5 Miata		orange w/orange base, Reese's, black interior, smoked window, 5sp	2
742	Funny Car		white w/metal base, Hershey's, black window, 5sp	2
743	'95 Camaro		dark metallic blue w/black base, Crunch, black interior, clear window, 5sp	2
744	'96 Mustang Convertible		yellow w/metal base Butterfinger, black interior, clear window, 5sp	2

Sugar Rush Series 99

969	'70 Road Runner		yellow w/chrome plastic base, black interior, clear window, 5dot	2
970	Jaguar XK8		red w/black base, tan interior, black tint, gbbs	2
971	Pikes Peak Celica		white w/black base, black interior, clear window, bbs	2
972	Dodge Concept		white w/metal base, blue interior, clear window, 5dot	2

Surf N Fun Series

961	'40's Woodie		purple, visible JcWhitney tampo on sides of hood, w/metal base, black interior, blue tint, 5sp	10
961	'40's Woodie		purple w/metal base black interior, blue tint, 5sp	2
962	VW Bug		metallic blue w/metal base, white interior, black tint, 5sp	2
963	'55 Chevy		metallic red w/chrome base, black tint windows, 3sp	2
964	'55 Nomad		white w/metal base, white interior, black tint, g5sp	2

Tattoo Machines

685	'57 T-Bird		metallic blue/chrome base, blue interior, blue tint window, 3sp	2
686	'93 Camaro		dayglo green/black base, white interior, smoked window, 3sp	2

VEHICLES

Torino Stocker,
1977, Hot Wheels

Yellow Cab, Hubley

Elgin Street Sweeper,
Hubley

NO.	NAME	YEAR	DESCRIPTION	MIP
686	'93 Camaro		dayglo green/black base, white interior, smoked window, t/b	2
687	Stutz Blackhawk		metallic red w/white cove, white interior, tinted window, 3sp	2
687	Stutz Blackhawk		brown w/white cove, white interior, tinted window, 3sp	2
687	Stutz Blackhawk		rootbeer w/white cove white interior, tinted window, 3sp	2
688	Corvette Stingray		orange, metal base black interior, smoked window, 3sp	2
688	Corvette Stingray		orange w/metal base black interior, smoked window, t/b	2

Techno Bits Series

NO.	NAME	YEAR	DESCRIPTION	MIP
689	Shadow Jet II		black w/red tampo and metal base, chrome interior, green window, b5sp	2
689	Shadow Jet II		black w/brown and red tampo, metal base, chrome interior, green window, b5sp	2
689	Shadow Jet II		black w/brown tampo and metal base, chrome interior, green window, b5sp	2
690	Power Pistons		purple w/yellow tampo, yellow interior and window, t/b	2
690	Power Pistons		dark purple w/yellow tampo, yellow interior and window, t/b	2
690	Power Pistons		purple w/yellow tampo, yellow interior and window, bbs	2
690	Power Pistons		purple w/yellow tampo, yellow interior and window, 3sp	2
691	Shadow Jet		metallic black w/gold trim and metal base, black interior, smoked window, 5sp	10
691	Shadow Jet		blue w/metal base, black interior, smoked window, 5sp	2
691	Shadow Jet		purple w/metal base, black interior, smoked window, 5sp	2
692	Radar Ranger		dayglo green w/black base, purple window, t/b	2

Terrorific Series

NO.	NAME	YEAR	DESCRIPTION	MIP
977	At-a-tude		green w/black base, chrome interior, green tint, bk5sp	3
978	Cat-a-pult		orange w/metaql base, black interior black tint window, 5sp	2
979	Sweet 16 II		black w/metal base gold chrome interior, yellow tint window, 5sp	2
980	Splittin' Image II		gold w/black base, pink chrome window, 3sp	2

Tropicool Series

NO.	NAME	YEAR	DESCRIPTION	MIP
693	Ice Cream Truck		white w/black base, white logo, green interior, 5sp	2
693	Ice cream Truck		white w/black base, black logo, green interior, 5sp	2
693	Ice cream Truck		white w/black base, w/o Fruits and Veggies, black logo, green interior, 5sp	2
694	Baja Bug		white w/metal base, flat red in tampo, red interior, large rear, 5sp	2
694	Baja Bug		white w/metal base, red enamel in tampo, red interior, all small 5sp	2
695	Classic Caddy		red w/black fenders red, yellow, gray, white and black stripes, gray interior, 3sp	2
695	Classic Caddy		red w/black fenders red, yellow, gray, white and black stripes, gray interior 5sp	2
695	Classic Caddy		red w/black fenders red, yellow, gray, white and black stripes, gray interior, bbs	2
696	Corvette Convertible		neon green, black Custom Corvette base, blue interior, smoke window, 3sp	2
696	Corvette Convertible		neon green, black base w/o CC, blue interior, smoke window, 3sp	2
696	Corvette Convertible		neon green, black Custom Corvette base, blue interior, smoke window, bbs	2

VEHICLES

HOT WHEELS NUMBERED PACKS

NO.	NAME	YEAR	DESCRIPTION	MIP

White Ice Series

NO.	NAME		DESCRIPTION	MIP
561	Speed Machine		pearl white, red window, 3sp	2
562	Shadow Jet		pearl white, yellow window, 5sp	2
563	Splittn' Image II		pearl white, chrome windows, 3sp	2

X-Ray Cruiser Series

NO.	NAME		DESCRIPTION	MIP
1114	63 Split Window		black w/chrome base white interior, black tint, g5sp	3
945	Mercedes C-Class		black w/light tampo and black bas,e white interior, yellow window, gbbs	4
945	Mercedes C-Class		black w/dark tampo and black base, white interior, yellow window, gbbs	4
946	Lamborghini Diablo		teal w/black painted base, gray interior, smoked window, 5sp	2
947	'67 Camaro		blue enamel w/metal Malaysia base, white interior, tinted window, 5sp	2
947	'67 Camaro		blue enamel w/metal Malaysia base, white interior, tinted window, 3sp	2
948	Jaguar XJ220		yellow w/black base blue interior, clear window, 3sp	2

HOT WHEELS VINTAGE

NAME	NO.	DESCRIPTION	YEAR	MNP	MIP
#43-STP		petty blue, gray rollbars, blackwalls	1992	10	30
'31 Doozie	9649	orange, redline	1977	15	60
'31 Doozie	9649	orange, blackwall	1977	8	15
'32 Ford Delivery		white/pink, Early Times logo, blackwalls	1993	25	35
'40 Ford Two-Door	4367	black w/white hubs, Real Rider	1983	30	50
'55 Chevy		blue #92, Real Rider	1992	10	30
'55 Chevy		black #92, Real Rider	1992	10	30
'55 Nomad		purple, Real Rider	1993	10	30
'55 Nomad		purple, blackwalls	1992	10	30
'56 Hi Tail Hauler	9647	orange, redline	1977	15	60
'56 Hi Tail Hauler	9647	orange, blackwall	1977	10	35
'57 Chevy	9638	red, blackwall	1977	10	30
'57 Chevy		white #22, Real Rider	1992	15	30
'57 Chevy	9638	red, redline	1977	20	85
'57 T-Bird	9522	black w/white hubs, Real Rider	1986	30	150
'59 Caddy		pink, Canadian, cal custom w/w	1990	35	65
'59 Caddy		gold, blackwalls	1993	10	30
3 Window '34	4352	black, Real Rider	1984	300	750
A-OK		red, Real Rider	1981	75	275
Alien		blue	1988	10	20
Alive '55	9210	chrome, redline	1977	15	55
Alive '55	6968	green	1974	50	110
Alive '55	6968	assorted	1973	125	600
Alive '55	6968	blue	1974	90	350
Alive '55	9210	chrome, blackwall	1977	15	30
Ambulance	6451	assorted	1970	30	50
American Hauler	9118	blue	1976	25	65
American Tipper	9089	red	1976	25	65
American Victory	7662	light blue	1975	20	60
AMX/2	6460	assorted	1971	40	150
Aw Shoot	9243	olive	1976	15	25
Backwoods Bomb	7670	light blue	1975	40	125
Backwoods Bomb	7670	green, redline or blackwall	1977	30	120
Baja Bruiser	8258	orange	1974	30	75
Baja Bruiser	8258	light green	1976	400	1300
Baja Bruiser	8258	blue, redline or blackwall	1977	25	85
Baja Bruiser	8258	yellow, blue in tampo	1974	300	1200
Baja Bruiser	8258	yellow, magenta in tampo	1974	300	1200

VEHICLES

NAME	NO.	DESCRIPTION	YEAR	MNP	MIP
Beatnik Bandit	6217	assorted	1968	15	45
Black Passion		black	1990	15	45
Boss Hoss	6406	assorted	1971	125	300
Boss Hoss	6499	chrome, Club Kit	1970	50	160
Brabham-Repco F1	6264	assorted	1969	20	65
Bronco 4-Wheeler	1690	Toys R Us	1981	75	150
Bugeye	6178	assorted	1971	30	75
Buzz Off	6976	assorted	1973	110	500
Buzz Off	6976	blue	1974	30	90
Buzz Off	6976	gold plated, redline or blackwall	1977	15	30
Bye Focal	6187	assorted	1971	125	400
Bywayman	2509	Toys R Us	1979	75	150
Bywayman	2196	blue, red interior	1989	60	120
Cadillac Seville		gold, Mexican, Real Rider	1987	80	140
Cadillac Seville		gray, French, Real Rider	1983	80	140
Captain America	2879	white, Heroes	1979	90	175
Carabo	7617	yellow	1974	500	1400
Carabo	7617	light green	1974	35	100
Carabo	6420	assorted	1970	35	80
Cement Mixer	6452	assorted	1970	30	60
Chaparral 2G	6256	assorted	1969	20	45
Chevy Monza 2+2	7671	orange	1975	40	110
Chevy Monza 2+2	9202	light green	1975	200	800
Chief's Special Cruiser	7665	red	1975	30	75
Chief's Special Cruiser	7665	red, redline	1977	25	65
Chief's Special Cruiser	7665	red, blackwall	1977	10	20
Circus Cats	3303	white	1981	75	150
Classic '31 Ford Woody	6251	assorted	1969	30	90
Classic '32 Ford Vicky	6250	assorted	1969	30	95
Classic '36 Ford Coupe	6253	blue	1969	20	60
Classic '36 Ford Coupe	6253	assorted	1969	35	100
Classic '57 T-Bird	6252	assorted	1969	30	100
Classic Caddy	2529	red/white/blue, Museum Exhibit car	1992	15	35
Classic Cobra		blue w/white hubs, Real Rider	1985	40	80
Classic Nomad	6404	assorted	1970	55	150
Cockney Cab	6466	assorted	1971	50	160
Cool One	9120	plum, blackwall	1977	20	40
Corvette Stingray	9506	chrome, blackwall set only	1977	55	n/a
Corvette Stingray	9241	red	1976	30	80
Corvette Stingray	9506	chrome	1976	20	50
Custom AMX	6267	assorted	1969	100	225
Custom Barracuda	6211	assorted	1968	80	400
Custom Camaro	6208	white enamel	1968	500	2500
Custom Camaro	6208	assorted	1968	100	450
Custom Charger	6268	assorted	1969	100	250
Custom Continental Mark III	6266	assorted	1969	20	60
Custom Corvette	6215	assorted	1968	90	300
Custom Cougar	6205	assorted	1968	80	275
Custom El Dorado	6218	assorted	1968	40	140
Custom Firebird	6212	assorted	1968	50	250
Custom Fleetside	6213	assorted	1968	60	250
Custom Mustang	6206	assorted	1968	80	425
Custom Mustang	6206	assorted w/open hood scoops or ribbed windows	1968	400	1200
Custom Police Cruiser	6269	assorted	1969	55	200
Custom T-Bird	6207	assorted	1968	50	165
Custom VW Bug	6220	assorted	1968	30	125
Datsun 200SX	3255	maroon, Canada	1982	75	175
Demon	6401	assorted	1970	25	50
Deora	6210	assorted	1968	60	375
Double Header	5880	assorted	1973	120	450
Double Vision	6975	assorted	1973	110	400

VEHICLES

HOT WHEELS VINTAGE

NAME	NO.	DESCRIPTION	YEAR	MNP	MIP
Dune Daddy	6967	assorted	1973	110	400
Dune Daddy	6967	light green	1975	25	75
Dune Daddy	6967	orange	1975	225	600
El Rey Special	8273	dark blue	1974	225	900
El Rey Special	8273	green	1974	40	75
El Rey Special	8273	light blue	1974	300	1200
El Rey Special	8273	light green	1974	75	175
Emergency Squad	7650	red	1975	15	65
Evil Weevil	6471	assorted	1971	75	150
Ferrari 312P	6973	red	1974	40	80
Ferrari 312P	6417	assorted	1970	30	60
Ferrari 312P	6973	assorted	1973	300	1100
Ferrari 512-S	6021	assorted	1972	75	250
Fire Chief Cruiser	6469	red	1970	15	45
Fire Engine	6454	red	1970	25	100
Flat Out 442	2506	orange	1979	8	10
Flat Out 442		green, Canada	1984	75	150
Ford J-Car	6214	assorted	1968	20	70
Ford MK IV	6257	assorted	1969	15	60
Formula 5000	9119	white	1976	20	50
Formula 5000	9511	chrome	1976	30	65
Fuel Tanker	6018	assorted	1971	75	200
Funny Money	7621	magenta	1974	60	150
Funny Money	7621	gray, blackwall	1977	20	65
Funny Money	7621	gray, redline	1977	60	150
Funny Money	6005	gray	1972	60	325
GMC Motorhome	9645	orange, redline	1977	400	1200
GMC Motorhome	9645	orange, blackwall	1977	10	25
Gold Passion		gold, Toy Fair promo	1992	40	100
Good Humor Truck		white	1986	55	125
Goodyear Blimp		chrome, Mattel promo	1992	65	n/a
Grass Hopper	6461	assorted	1971	45	100
Grass Hopper	7622	light green, no engine	1975	90	350
Grass Hopper	7621	light green	1974	40	100
Greased Gremlin		red, Mexican, Real Rider	1987	350	1000
Gremlin Grinder	9201	chrome, blackwall	1977	20	40
Gremlin Grinder	7652	green	1975	35	75
GT Racer	1789	blue	1989	50	100
Gun Bucket	9090	olive	1976	25	60
Gun Bucket	9090	olive, blackwall	1977	25	60
Gun Slinger	7664	olive, blackwall	1976	30	75
Gun Slinger	7664	olive	1975	25	50
Hairy Hauler	6458	assorted	1971	20	65
Hammer Down		red set only	1980	125	n/a
Heavy Chevy	7619	light green	1974	200	750
Heavy Chevy	6189	chrome, Club Kit	1970	75	300
Heavy Chevy	7619	yellow	1974	90	200
Heavy Chevy	9212	chrome, redline or blackwall	1977	40	120
Heavy Chevy	6408	assorted	1970	65	200
Hiway Robber	6979	assorted	1973	75	250
Hood	6175	assorted	1971	25	110
Hot Bird		blue	1980	60	125
Hot Bird		brown	1980	90	200
Hot Heap	6219	assorted	1968	20	65
Human Torch	2881	black	1979	20	40
Ice T	6980	light green	1974	25	75
Ice T	6980	yellow w/hood tampo	1974	200	525
Ice T	6980	assorted	1973	200	650
Ice T	6980	light green, blackwall	1977	20	35
Ice T	6184	yellow	1971	40	200
Incredible Hulk Van	2850	white, Scene Machine	1979	75	125
Indy Eagle	6263	gold	1969	75	240
Indy Eagle	6263	assorted	1969	15	40

HOT WHEELS VINTAGE

NAME	NO.	DESCRIPTION	YEAR	MNP	MIP
Inferno	9186	yellow	1976	30	60
Jack Rabbit Special	6421	white	1970	15	55
Jack-in-the-Box Promotion	6421	white, Jack Rabbit w/decals	1970	300	n/a
Jet Threat	6179	assorted	1971	45	160
Jet Threat II	8235	magenta	1976	35	80
Khaki Kooler	9183	olive	1976	15	30
King Kuda	6411	assorted	1970	25	100
King Kuda	6411	chrome, Club Kit	1970	75	300
Large Charge	8272	green	1975	25	60
Letter Getter	9643	white, redline	1977	175	550
Letter Getter	9643	white, blackwall	1977	8	15
Light My Firebird	6412	assorted	1970	35	75
Lola GT 70	6254	assorted	1969	20	60
Lotus Turbine	6262	assorted	1969	20	60
Lowdown	9185	gold plated, redline or blackwall	1977	15	30
Lowdown	9185	light blue	1976	30	75
Mantis	6423	assorted	1970	20	60
Masterati Mistral	6277	assorted	1969	50	125
Maxi Taxi	9184	yellow, blackwall	1977	20	60
Maxi Taxi	9184	yellow	1976	25	60
McClaren M6A	6255	assorted	1969	20	65
Mercedes 280SL	6962	assorted	1973	100	450
Mercedes 280SL	6275	assorted	1969	25	70
Mercedes C-111	6978	assorted	1973	300	1200
Mercedes C-111	6978	red	1974	40	90
Mercedes C-111	6169	assorted	1972	80	250
Mighty Maverick	6414	assorted	1970	45	130
Mighty Maverick	7653	blue	1975	50	100
Mighty Maverick	9209	light green	1975	300	750
Mighty Maverick	9209	chrome, blackwall	1977	25	50
Mod-Quad	6456	assorted	1970	20	60
Mongoose	6970	red/blue	1973	400	1400
Mongoose Funny Car	6410	red	1970	50	160
Mongoose II	5954	metallic blue	1971	75	350
Mongoose Rail Dragster	5952	blue, two pack	1971	75	n/a
Monte Carlo Stocker	7660	dark blue and green		55	70
Monte Carlo Stocker	7660	yellow	1975	45	90
Monte Carlo Stocker	7660	yellow, blackwall	1977	20	50
Motocross I	7668	red	1975	100	200
Motorcross Team Van	2853	red, Scene Machine	1979	50	125
Movin' On		white set only	1980	125	n/a
Moving Van	6455	assorted	1970	50	125
Mustang Stocker	9203	yellow w/red in tampo	1975	300	900
Mustang Stocker	7664	yellow w/magenta tampo	1975	90	300
Mustang Stocker	9203	chrome, redline or blackwall	1977	40	90
Mustang Stocker	7664	white	1975	400	1200
Mustang Stocker	9203	chrome	1976	40	90
Mutt Mobile	5185	assorted	1971	75	175
NASCAR Stocker	3927	white, NASCAR/Mountain Dew base	1983	90	165
Neet Streeter	9244	blue	1976	30	75
Neet Streeter	9510	chrome, blackwall set only	1977	40	n/a
Neet Streeter	9510	chrome	1976	20	40
Neet Streeter	9244	blue, blackwall	1977	15	30
Nitty Gritty Kitty	6405	assorted	1970	25	65
Noodle Head	6000	assorted	1971	40	150
Odd Job	6981	assorted	1973	100	600
Odd Rod	9642	yellow, redline	1977	30	50
Odd Rod	9642	yellow, blackwall	1977	20	40
Odd Rod	9642	plum, blackwall or redline	1977	200	400
Old Number 5	1695	red, no louvers	1982	10	20
Olds 442	6467	assorted	1971	400	800
Open Fire	5881		1972	100	400
Paddy Wagon	6966	blue	1973	30	120

VEHICLES

HOT WHEELS VINTAGE

NAME	NO.	DESCRIPTION	YEAR	MNP	MIP
Paddy Wagon	6966	blue, blackwall	1977	10	20
Paddy Wagon	6402	blue	1970	15	30
Paramedic	7661	yellow	1976	30	50
Paramedic	7661	yellow, blackwall or redline	1977	25	45
Paramedic	7661	white	1975	25	55
Peepin' Bomb	6419	assorted	1970	20	50
Pepsi Challenger	2023	yellow funny car	1982	20	25
Pit Crew Car	6183	white	1971	30	350
Poison Pinto	9240	green, blackwall	1977	15	30
Poison Pinto	9508	chrome, blackwall set only	1977	50	n/a
Poison Pinto	9240	light green	1976	25	65
Poison Pinto	9508	chrome	1976	20	40
Police Cruiser	6963	white	1973	200	550
Police Cruiser	6963	white, blackwall	1977	25	45
Police Cruiser	6963	white	1974	45	125
Police Cruiser	6963	white w/blue light	1977	30	65
Porsche 911	7648	black, six pack blackwall	1977	175	350
Porsche 911	9206	chrome, redline or blackwall	1977	20	40
Porsche 911	6972	orange	1975	25	65
Porsche 911	7648	yellow	1975	40	75
Porsche 917	6416	assorted	1970	25	65
Porsche 917	6972	red	1974	175	500
Porsche 917	6972	orange	1974	40	75
Porsche 917	6972	orange, blackwall	1977	15	25
Porsche 917	6972	assorted	1973	300	950
Power Pad	6459	assorted	1970	30	125
Prowler	9207	chrome, blackwall	1977	35	70
Prowler	6965	orange	1974	35	75
Prowler	6965	assorted	1973	200	1000
Prowler	6965	light green	1974	500	1000
Python	6216	assorted	1968	20	75
Race Ace	2620	white	1986	15	30
Racer Rig	6194	red/white	1971	100	375
Racing Team Van		yellow, Scene Machine	1981	60	125
Ramblin' Cruiser	7659	white without phone number	1977	15	25
Ramblin' Wrecker	7659	yellow	1975	15	20
Ramblin' Wrecker	7659	white, blackwall	1977	10	20
Ranger Rig	7666	green	1975	20	65
Rash I	7616	blue	1974	300	800
Rash I	7616	green	1974	50	75
Rear Engine Mongoose	5699	red	1972	200	600
Rear Engine Snake	5856	yellow	1972	200	600
Red Baron	6964	red, blackwall	1977	15	25
Red Baron	6964	red	1973	30	200
Red Baron	6400	red	1970	15	40
Red Passion		red	1994	10	20
Rescue Squad	3304	red, Scene Machine	1982	70	125
Road King Truck	7615	yellow set only	1974	600	1200
Rock Buster	9088	yellow	1976	20	35
Rock Buster	9507	chrome	1976	15	30
Rock Buster	9088	yellow, blackwall	1977	10	15
Rock Buster	9507	chrome, blackwall set only	1977	45	n/a
Rocket Bye Baby	6186	assorted	1971	60	200
Rodger Dodger	8259	magenta	1974	40	90
Rodger Dodger	8259	blue	1974	200	550
Rodger Dodger	8259	gold plated, blackwall or redline	1977	30	80
Rolls-Royce Silver Shadow	6276	assorted	1969	30	125
Ruby Red Passion		red	1992	25	45
S'Cool Bus	6468	yellow	1971	175	750
S.W.A.T. Van	2854	blue, Scene Machine	1979	70	125
Sand Crab	6403	assorted	1970	20	60
Sand Drifter	7651	green	1975	150	375

VEHICLES

NAME	NO.	DESCRIPTION	YEAR	MNP	MIP
Sand Drifter	7651	yellow	1975	35	75
Sand Witch	6974	assorted	1973	125	400
Scooper	6193	assorted	1971	100	325
Screamin'	9521	red w/light blue and yellow		10	15
Seasider	6413	assorted	1970	60	135
Second Wind	9644	white, blackwall or redline	1977	35	75
Shelby Turbine	6265	assorted	1969	20	55
Short Order	6176	assorted	1971	50	125
Show Hoss II	9646	yellow, redline	1977	300	600
Show Hoss II	9646	yellow, blackwall	1977	40	75
Show-Off	6982	assorted	1973	140	400
Sidekick	6022	assorted	1972	80	200
Silhouette	6209	assorted	1968	20	90
Simpsons Camper		blue, Scene Machine	1990	10	20
Simpsons Van		yellow, Scene Machine	1990	10	20
Sir Rodney Roadster	8261	yellow, blackwall	1977	40	70
Sir Sidney Roadster	8261	light green	1974	325	650
Sir Sidney Roadster	8261	orange/brown	1974	375	700
Sir Sidney Roadster	8261	yellow	1974	50	90
Six Shooter	6003	assorted	1971	75	225
Sky Show Fleetside (Aero Launcher)	6436	assorted	1970	400	850
Snake	6969	white/yellow	1973	600	1500
Snake Dragster	5951	white, two-pack	1971	75	n/a
Snake Funny Car	6409	assorted	1970	60	300
Snake II	5953	white	1971	60	275
Snorkel	6020	assorted	1971	90	200
Space Van	2855	gray, Scene Machine	1979	70	125
Special Delivery	6006	blue	1971	45	150
Spider-Man	2852	black	1979	15	35
Spider-Man Van	2852	white, Scene Machine	1979	50	125
Splittin' Image	6261	assorted	1969	15	50
Spoiler Sport	9641	light green, blackwall	1977	10	20
Spoiler Sport	9641	light green, redline	1977	25	50
Staff Car	9521	olive, blackwall	1977	500	750
Staff Car	9521	olive, six-pack only	1977	600	850
Steam Roller	8260	white w/seven stars	1974	100	300
Steam Roller	8260	white	1974	25	70
Steam Roller	9208	chrome w/seven stars	1977	100	300
Steam Roller	9208	chrome, redline or blackwall	1977	25	55
Street Eater	7669	black	1975	40	60
Street Rodder	9242	black, blackwall	1977	30	50
Street Rodder	9242	black	1976	40	85
Street Snorter	6971	assorted	1973	110	400
Strip Teaser	6188	assorted	1971	65	200
Sugar Caddy	6418	assorted	1971	45	120
Super Chromes	9505	chrome, blackwall, six-pack	1977	375	n/a
Super Van	7649	black, blackwall	1977	15	25
Super Van	7649	blue	1975	650	n/a
Super Van	7649	Toys-R-Us	1975	100	350
Super Van	7649	plum	1975	90	250
Super Van	9205	chrome	1976	20	40
Superfine Turbine	6004	assorted	1973	400	1100
Sweet 16	6007	assorted	1973	125	650
Swingin' Wing	6422	assorted	1970	25	75
T-4-2	6177	assorted	1971	50	175
T-Totaller	9648	brown, blackwall	1977	15	40
T-Totaller	9648	black, Red Line, six-pack only	1977	500	1000
T-Totaller	9648	black, blackwall	1977	15	40
Team Trailer	6019	white/red	1971	95	225
Thing, The	2882	dark blue	1979	20	50
Thor	2880	yellow	1979	15	30
Thrill Driver Torino	9793	red/white, blackwall, set of two	1977	275	n/a

HOT WHEELS VINTAGE

NAME	NO.	DESCRIPTION	YEAR	MNP	MIP
TNT-Bird	6407	assorted	1970	60	125
Top Eliminator	7630	blue	1974	50	165
Top Eliminator	7630	gold plated, redline or blackwall	1977	30	50
Torero	6260	assorted	1969	15	60
Torino Stocker	7647	gold plated, redline or blackwall	1977	30	70
Torino Stocker	7647	red	1975	35	70
Tough Customer	7655	olive	1975	25	55
Tow Truck	6450	assorted	1970	30	80
Tri-Baby	6424	assorted	1970	20	55
Turbo Mustang		blue	1984	35	65
Turbofire	6259	assorted	1969	15	50
Twinmill	6258	assorted	1969	15	50
Twinmill II	9502	chrome, blackwall set only	1977	45	n/a
Twinmill II	8240	orange, blackwall	1977	10	25
Twinmill II	9509	chrome	1976	20	45
Twinmill II	8240	orange	1976	10	35
Vega Bomb	7658	green	1975	250	800
Vega Bomb	7654	orange, blackwall	1977	40	75
Vega Bomb	7658	orange	1975	40	85
Volkswagen	7620	orange w/bug on roof	1974	30	60
Volkswagen	7620	orange w/stripes on roof	1974	100	400
Volkswagen Beach Bomb	6274	surf boards on side raised panels	1969	115	310
Volkswagen Beach Bomb	6274	surf boards in rear window	1969	7000	n/a
VW Bug		pink, Real Rider	1993	40	75
Warpath	7654	white	1975	50	110
Waste Wagon	6192	assorted	1971	90	325
What-4	6001	assorted	1971	50	150
Whip Creamer	6457	assorted	1970	25	60
White Passion		white, in box	1990	15	30
Winnipeg	7618	yellow	1974	90	300
Xploder	6977	assorted	1973	100	500
Z Whiz	9639	blue	1982	20	55
Z Whiz	9639	white, redline	1977	1500	n/a
Z Whiz	9639	gray, blackwall	1977	15	25
Z Whiz	9639	gray, redline	1977	35	70

Classic '36 Ford Coupe, 1969, Hot Wheels

HUBLEY

NAME	DESCRIPTION	GOOD	EX	MINT

Airplanes

NAME	DESCRIPTION	GOOD	EX	MINT
America Plane	trimotor, open cockpit, co-pilot, pilot, cast iron, 17" wingspan	2500	5000	7000
American Eagle Airplane	WWII Fighter, 11" wingspan	150	225	300
American Eagle Carrier Plane	cast metal, 11" wingspan, 1971	60	95	125
B-17 Bomber	15" wingspan	125	185	250
Bremen Junkers Monoplane	10" wingspan	1200	1750	2000
Corsair-Type Fighter Plane		30	45	65
Delta Wing Jet		60	95	125
DO-X Plane	six engines, 5-7/8" wingspan, 1935	165	200	285
Flying Circus	12" wingspan	45	70	90
Lindy Plane	cast iron, 10" wingspan	500	750	1000
Lindy Plane	cast iron, 13-1/4" long	1200	1750	2000
Navy WWII Fighter	folding wings and wheels	30	45	65
P-38 Fighter	camouflage paint, 12-1/2" wingspan	75	100	185
P-38 Plane	black rubber tires	70	95	165
Piper Cub Plane	pot metal	50	75	115
Sea Plane	orange/blue, two engines	35	55	75
Single Engine Fighter	3-1/2"	60	90	120
U.S. Air Force	12" wingspan	25	45	75
U.S. Army Monoplane	7-5/8" wingspan, 1941	50	75	100
U.S. Army Single Engine Fighter Plane	black rubber tires	20	35	50

Boats and Ships

NAME	DESCRIPTION	GOOD	EX	MINT
Penn Yan Motorboat	15" long	1700	2600	3500

Buses

NAME	DESCRIPTION	GOOD	EX	MINT
School Bus	metal, wooden wheels	60	85	125
Service Coach	cast iron, 5" long	675	900	1500

Cars

NAME	DESCRIPTION	GOOD	EX	MINT
Auto and Trailer	cast iron, sedan 7-1/4" long, trailer 7-1/8" long, 1936	185	245	315
Auto and Trailer	cast iron, 6-3/4" long, 1939	175	235	295
Buick Convertible	opening top, 6-1/2" long	50	65	90
Buick Convertible	top down, 6-1/2" long	45	60	80
Cadillac	black rubber tires, die cast w/tin bottom plate	25	40	70
Car Carrier With Four Cars	cast iron, 10" long	300	475	675
Chrysler Airflow	6" long	145	200	350
Chrysler Airflow	battery-operated lights, cast iron, 1934	1250	1900	2750
Chrysler Airflow	cast iron, 4-1/2" long	110	195	325
Coupe	cast iron, 9-1/2" long, 1928	900	1400	1800
Coupe	cast iron, 8-1/2" long, 1928	600	1100	1500
Coupe	cast iron, 7" long, 1928	400	650	800
Ford Convertible	cast iron, V/8, 1930s	65	100	185
Ford Coupe	cast iron, V-8, 1930s	65	100	185
Ford Model-T	movable parts	100	150	200
Ford Sedan	cast iron, V-8, 1930s	65	100	185
Ford Town Car	cast iron, V-8, 1930s	65	100	185
Limousine	cast iron, 7" long, 1918	250	325	400
Lincoln Zephyr	1937	250	350	450
Mr. Magoo Car	old timer car, battery-operated, 9" long, 1961	75	115	150
Open Touring Car	cast iron, 7-1/2" long, 1911	675	900	1250
Packard Roadster	9-1/2" long, 1930	90	145	250
Packard Straight 8	hood raises, detailed cast motor, cast iron, 11" long, 1927	7500	10000	15000
Race Car #22	cast iron, 7-1/2" long	40	55	85
Race Car #2241	7" long, 1930s	50	75	100
Racer	white rubber wheels, cast iron, 7" long	200	300	400
Racer	cast iron, 10-3/4" long, 1931	75	150	250
Racer	nickel-plated driver, cast iron, 4-3/4" long, 1960s	75	115	150

VEHICLES

HUBLEY

NAME	DESCRIPTION	GOOD	EX	MINT
Racer	red w/black wheels, silver grille and driver, 7-1/2" long	35	55	75
Racer #12	die cast, prewar	60	95	125
Racer #629	7" long, 1939	50	75	135
Roadster	cast iron, 7-1/2" long, 1920	75	150	225
Sedan	cast iron, 7" long, 1920s	175	265	350
Service Car	5" long, 1930s	75	115	150
Speedster	cast iron, 7" long, 1911	125	225	350
Station Wagon	die cast	50	75	100
Streamlined Racer	cast iron, 5" long	70	125	140
Studebaker	take-apart, 5" long	400	600	800
Tinytown Station Wagon and Boat Trailer		45	70	90
Touring Car	woman and dog seated in back, driver in front, 10" long, 1920	650	1000	1450
Yellow Cab	w/luggage rack, cast iron, 8" long, 1940	325	500	700

Emergency Vehicles

NAME	DESCRIPTION	GOOD	EX	MINT
Ahrens-Fox Fire Engine	cast iron, 11-1/2" long, 1932	5000	6500	8000
Auto Fire Engine	cast iron, 15" long, 1912	4200	5500	7000
Fire Engine	blue and green, large rear wheels w/smaller front wheels, cast iron, 10-3/4" long, 1920"s	4500	5750	7500
Fire Engine	cast iron, 14-1/2" long, 1932	1575	2250	3000
Fire Truck	5" long, 1930s	75	100	150
Fire Truck No. 468		60	95	125
Hook and Ladder Fire Truck	rubber wheels, die cast, 18" long	150	250	500
Hook and Ladder Truck	cast iron, 23" long, 1912	1850	3000	4500
Hook and Ladder Truck	cast iron, 16-1/2" long, 1926	850	1200	1700
Hook and Ladder Truck	cast iron, 8" long	100	125	200
Ladder Fire Truck	cast iron, 5-1/2" long	40	60	80
Ladder Truck	14" long, 1940s	150	275	500
Police Patrol	w/three policemen, cast iron, 11" long, 1919	900	1450	2500
Pumper Fire Truck	plastic, 1950s	25	45	65
Seven Man Fire Patrol	cast iron, 15" long, 1912	3575	5700	7500
Special Ladder Truck	cast iron, 13" long, 1938	465	575	975

Farm and Construction Equipment

NAME	DESCRIPTION	GOOD	EX	MINT
Avery	round radiator, cast iron, 4-1/2" long, 1920	175	300	450
Diesel Road Roller	plastic, 1950s	15	25	40
Elgin Street Sweeper	brush sweeps dirt into a bin in the body, uniformed driver, cast iron, 8-1/2" long, 1930	4000	8000	11500
Farm Trailer	w/gate, 8" long	30	45	60
Ford 4000	blue and gray, die cast, 1:12 scale	100	200	300
Ford 6000	blue and gray, die cast, 1:12 scale, 1963	125	250	400
Ford 961 Powermaster	red and gray, die cast, 1:12 scale, 1961	125	250	400
Ford 961 Powermaster	red and gray, row crop, die cast, 1:12 scale, 1961	100	200	300
Ford 961 Select-O-Speed	red and gray, die cast, 1:12 scale, 1962	125	250	400
Ford Commander 6000	blue and gray, die cast, 1:12 scale, 1963	125	225	300
Fordson	cast iron, 5-1/2" long	150	225	300
Fordson	w/loader, cast iron, 8-1/2" long, 1938	750	1250	1700
Fordson F	w/crank and driver, cast iron, 5-1/2" long	150	225	300
Huber Road Roller	large, w/standing driver, cast iron, 15" long, 1927	1675	2250	3750
Huber Steam Roller	cast iron, 1:25 scale, 1929	365	450	600
Huber Steam Roller	cast iron, 3-1/4" long, 1929	100	150	215
Junior Tractor		60	95	125
Oliver 70 Orchard	fenders over rear wheels, cast iron, 5" long, 1938	175	300	575
Road Scraper	plastic, 1950s	30	45	60
Steam Shovel	red, nickel-plated boom, cast iron, 4-3/4" long	75	115	150
Tractor	yellow, 5-1/4" long	35	55	75
Tractor and Farmer	plastic	25	35	55
Tractor Shovel	cast iron, 8-1/2" long, 1933	1250	1650	2000

Motorcycles

NAME	DESCRIPTION	GOOD	EX	MINT
Crash Car	motorcycle w/cart on back, cast iron, 9" long, 1930s	1000	1650	2000
Harley-Davidson Motorcycle	cast iron, 7-1/2" long, 1932	300	450	800

VEHICLES

NAME	DESCRIPTION	GOOD	EX	MINT
Harley-Davidson Parcel Post	cast iron, 10" long, 1928	1500	2500	4000
Harley-Davidson Sidecar Motorcycle	cast iron, 9" long, 1930	900	1625	1900
Hill Climber	cast iron, 6-3/4" long, 1935	375	500	900
Indian Air Mail	cast iron, 9-1/4" long, 1929	1575	2650	3500
Indian Armored Car	motorcycle police, cast iron, 8-1/2" long, 1928	1750	3500	6000
Indian Four-Cylinder Motocycle	cast iron, 9" long, 1929	1700	2425	3000
Indian Motorcycle	cast iron, 9" long	600	850	1500
Marathon Rider	bicycle, cast iron	200	300	400
Motorcycle	three wheels, cast iron	400	600	800
Motorcycle Cop With Sidecar	Harley-Davidson, cast iron	700	1000	1500
Motorcycle Crash Car	w/cart on back, cast iron, 5" long, 1930s	100	135	195
Motorized Sidecar Motorcycle	clockwork motor, cast iron, 8-1/2" long, 1932	4000	6250	10000
P.D. Motorcycle Cop	red plastic cycle	35	65	95
Patrol Motorcycle	green, 6-1/2" long	275	350	475
Popeye Patrol	cast iron, 9" long, 1938	425	600	950
Popeye Spinach Delivery	red motorcycle, cast iron, 6" long, 1938	375	500	750
Traffic Car	three-wheel transport vehicle, cast iron, 12" long, 1930	600	950	1500

Trucks

NAME	DESCRIPTION	GOOD	EX	MINT
Auto Dump Coal Wagon	cast iron, 16-1/4" long, 1920	800	1200	1500
Auto Express with Roof	cast iron, 9-1/2" long, 1910	500	875	1200
Auto Truck	spoke wheels, cast iron, 10" long, 1918	600	1200	1650
Auto Truck	five-ton truck, cast iron, 17-1/2" long, 1920	1000	1650	2250
Bell Telephone Truck	12" long, 1940	50	75	100
Bell Telephone Truck	spoke wheels, cast iron, 5-1/2" long, 1930	225	335	450
Bell Telephone Truck	white tires, winch works, cast iron, 10" long, 1930	500	1000	1500
Bell Telephone Truck	no driver, white tires, cast iron, 3-3/4" long, 1930	150	225	300
Bell Telephone Truck	white tires, cast iron, 7" long, 1930	300	400	500
Bell Telephone Truck	post-WWII, 24" long	85	150	200
Borden's Milk Truck	cast iron, 7-1/2" long, 1930	1650	2850	4250
Compressor Truck	1953 Ford	60	90	120
Delivery Van	cast iron, 4-1/2" long, 1932	365	475	675
Dump Truck	cast iron, 7-1/2" long	225	335	450
Dump Truck	white rubber tires, 4-1/2" long, 1930s	100	150	200
Dump Truck	plastic, 1950s	25	35	55
Gas Tanker	5-1/2" long	115	225	295
General Shovel Truck	dual rear wheels, cast iron, 10" long, 1931	500	750	1000
Ingersoll-Rand Compressor	cast iron, 8-1/4" long, 1933	3250	6500	10000
Lifesaver Truck	cast iron, 4-1/4" long	350	475	700
Long Bed Dump Truck	series 510, Ford, cast iron	110	175	300
Mack Dump Truck	cast iron, 11" long, 1928	600	800	1450
Merchants Delivery Truck	cast iron, 6-1/4" long, 1925	400	600	850
Milk Truck	cast iron, 3-3/4" long, 1930	115	200	295
Nucar Transport	w/four vehicles, cast iron, 16" long, 1932	675	1200	1500
Open Bed Auto Express	cast iron, 9-1/2" long, 1910	725	1200	1700
Panama Shovel Truck	Mack truck, cast iron, 13" long, 1934	750	1500	2000
Railway Express Truck	cast iron	135	225	275
Shovel Truck	metal, 10" long	250	375	500
Stake Bed Truck	cast iron, 3" long	75	115	150
Stake Truck	white rubber tires, 7" long, 1930s	85	130	175
Stake Truck	white cab, blue stake bed, 12" long	100	150	200
Stake Truck	die cast, 7" long, 1950s	75	115	150
Stockyard Truck #851	w/three pigs	60	95	165
Tanker	cast iron, 7" long, 1940s	85	130	175
Tow Truck	Ford, cast metal, 7" long, 1950s	50	65	165
Tow Truck	9" long	135	225	275
Truckmixer	Ford, mixer cylinder rotates when truck moves, cast iron, 8" long, 1932	50	85	185
Wrecker	whitewall tires, green/white, 11-1/2" long	25	50	75
Wrecker	cast iron, 5" long	60	95	125

VEHICLES

Bell Telephone Truck, Hubley

Nucar Transport, Hubley

Panama Shovel Truck, Hubley

HUBLEY

NAME	DESCRIPTION	GOOD	EX	MINT
Wrecker	6" long	70	125	145
Wrecker	red, die cast, 9-1/2" long, 1940"s	60	95	165

Wagons and Carts

NAME	DESCRIPTION	GOOD	EX	MINT
Alphonse in Goat-Pulled Wagon	13-3/4" long, 1900's	100	150	210
Alphonse in Mule-Pulled Wagon	6-1/2" long	225	335	450

JAPANESE

NAME	DESCRIPTION	GOOD	EX	MINT

Cars

NAME	DESCRIPTION	GOOD	EX	MINT
1935 Pontiac Four-Door Sedan	8", maroon, friction	30	65	90
1950s Cunningham Roadster	7-1/2", light blue, friction	40	90	125
1950s DeSoto	6", green, friction	20	45	65
1950s DeSoto	Asahi Toy, 8", green, friction	40	90	125
1950s Jaguar XKE Convertible	Tomiyama, 12", white, friction	195	455	650
1950s Jeep Station Wagon	Yonezawa, 7-1/2", two-tone brown, friction	100	210	300
1950s Kaiser Darren Convertible	6-1/2", red, friction	300	70	100
1950s Mercedes Convertible	Alps, 9", red, friction	105	245	350
1950s Studebaker Lark	5-1/2", blue, friction	20	45	65
1950s Volvo	5-1/2", red, friction	20	38	55
1950s Volvo PV-544	HoKu, 7-1/2", black, friction	165	385	550
1950s VW Convertible	9-1/2", dark blue, maroon, or light metallic blue, friction w/battery-operated engine light	85	195	275
1950s VW Sedan	7-1/2", gray, oval window, friction	45	105	150
1950s Zephyr Deluxe Convertible	11", maroon/yellow/blue, friction	120	280	400
1951 Cadillac Four-Door Sedan	Marusan, 12-1/2", gray, black, white, or red, friction	300	700	1000
1951 Cadillac Four-Door Sedan	Marusan, 12-1/2", gray, battery-operated, remote control, working headlights	480	1120	1600
1951 Ford Sedan	7", tan, battery-operated	30	70	100
1951 Futuristic Buick LeSabre	Yonezawa, 7-1/2", black, friction	240	560	800
1952 Ford Yellow Cab	Marusan, 10-1/2", yellow, friction, working money meter	165	385	550
1953 Chrysler Orion Convertible	6-1/2", blue/green, friction	25	60	85
1953 Studebaker Coupe	9", yellow, friction, working wipers	45	100	140
1954 Chevrolet Bel Air	Marusan and Linemar, 11", gray/black, friction	400	840	1200
1954 Chevrolet Bel Air	Marusan and Linemar, 11", rare orange/yellow, friction	660	1550	2200
1955 Buick Special	8-1/2", two-tone blue, battery-operated, working headlights	55	122	175
1955 Chevrolet Bel Air	Asahi Toy, 7" light green, friction	50	105	150
1955 Ford Convertible	Haji, 6-1/2", two-tone blue or red/white, friction	60	140	200
1955 Ford Thunderbird Convertible	8", orange, friction	45	100	140
1955 Mercedes 300 SL Coupe	9", metallic red, opening gull-wing doors, battery-operated	105	245	350
1956 Ford Two-Door HT	Ichiko, 10", two-tone blue or orange/white, friction	165	385	550
1956 Ford Two-Door Sedan	Marusan, 13", orange/white or blue/white	1050	2450	3500
1956 GM Gas Turbine Firebird II	8-1/2", red, friction	240	560	800
1956 Lincoln Premiere Two-Door HT	7-1/2", orange, friction	30	70	100
1956 Oldsmobile Super 88	Modern Toys, 14", orange, battery-operated, working headlights and signal lights	225	525	750
1956 Plymouth HT	Alps, 8-1/2", two-tone green, friction	165	385	550
1957 Chrysler New Yorker	6-1/2", red/black, friction	25	60	85

VEHICLES

NAME	DESCRIPTION	GOOD	EX	MINT
1957 Ford Convertible	HTC, 12", orange/pink, friction	115	265	375
1957 Ford Fairlane 500 HT	ToyMaster, 9-1/2", green/yellow, friction	45	100	140
1958 Dodge Four-Door HT	8-1/2", orange/white, friction	55	125	175
1958 Edsel Station Wagon	11", red/black, friction	225	525	750
1958 Ford HT Convertible	11", orange/white, battery-operated	60	140	200
1958 Ford HT Convertible	9-1/2", blue/white, battery-operated	85	195	275
1958 Oldsmobile	Asahi Toy, 12", gold/black, friction	540	1260	1800
1958 Oldsmobile Station Wagon	7-1/2", red/black, friction	30	70	100
1958 Pontiac Four-Door HT	Asahi Toy, 8", green/pink, friction	45	105	150
1959 Buick Convertible	11", orange/yellow, friction, dog and driver figures	115	245	350
1959 Buick HT Convertible	Linemar, 9-1/2" red/white, friction	50	105	150
1959 Buick Station Wagon	Yonezawa, 9", two-tone green, friction	50	105	150
1959 Chevrolet Highway Patrol Car	ASC, 10", black/white, friction	55	125	175
1959 Chevrolet HT	7", green, friction	30	70	100
1959 Dodge Two-Door HT	9", blue/white, friction	135	315	450
1959 Ford HT Convertible	11", blue/white, red/white, or green/white, battery-operated	70	160	225
1959 Ford Station Wagon	10-1/2", green/white, friction	40	90	125
1959 Oldsmobile Highway Patrol Car	Ichiko, 12-1/2", black/white, friction, working speed meter on trunk	75	175	250
1959 Oldsmobile Two-Door HT	Ichiko, 12-1/2", two-tone blue, two-tone green, or brown/white, friction	135	315	450
1959 Plymouth Convertible	Asahi Toy, 11", red/white, friction	330	770	1100
1960 Cadillac Four-Door Sedan	Yonezawa, 18" black or maroon, friction	300	630	900
1960 Chevrolet Impala HT	Alps, 9", red/white, friction	105	245	350
1960 Ford Gyron	Ichida, 11", red/white, battery-operated	135	315	450
1960 Ford Gyron	Ichida, 11", red/black, remote control, battery-operated	85	195	275
1960 Ford Gyron	Ichida, red/black, friction	45	100	140
1960s BMW Coupe	Yonezawa, 11" tan, battery-operated	50	105	150
1960s Ferrari Berlinetta 250 LeMans	Asahi Toy, 11", red, friction	115	265	375
1960s Ford Falcon	Marusan, 9", red/white, friction	25	55	75
1960s Jaguar XKE Coupe	10-1/2", red, friction	55	125	175
1960s Mercedes Convertible	HTC, 8", red, opening door w/swing-out driver, friction	45	105	150
1960s Porsche 911 Rally	11", red, friction	70	160	225
1960s Porsche 914 Rally	Daiya, 9", blue, battery-operated	25	55	75
1961 Buick Fire Department Car	16", red, friction, working wipers, revolving emergency light	50	105	150
1961 Mercedes 220-S	12", black, jack-up feature, friction	75	175	250
1961 Oldsmobile Rally Car	Asahi Toy, 15", red, friction	55	125	175
1962 Cadillac Polic Car	Ichiko, 6-1/2" black/white, friction w/siren	30	65	90
1962 Ford Thunderbird HT Convertible	Yonezawa, 11-1/2", red, battery-operated	105	245	350
1963 Corvette Coupe	12", metallic red or white, battery-operated, working headlights	180	420	600
1963 Ford Fire Chief Car	Taiyo, 12-1/2", red, battery-operated	23	55	75
1963 Ford Stock Car	Taiyo, 10-1/2", red/silver/blue, friction	25	60	85
1964 Ford Thunderbird HT Convertible	Ichiko, 15-1/2", red, working side windows, friction	120	280	400
1964 Lincoln	11", burgundy, battery-operated	165	385	550
1965 Ford Country Squire Wagon	9", white, friction	30	70	100
1965 Ford Mustang GT	15-1/2", red, friction	85	195	275
1966 Dodge Charger Sonic Car	16", red, battery-operated	145	335	475
1970s VW Rabbit Rally Team Car	Asahi Toy, 8", yellow, battery-operated	20	45	65
Ford Model-T	9", red, hard top, friction	25	55	75
Ford Model-T	9", black, open top, friction	25	55	75

VEHICLES

.Com cars (Internet program)

NAME	DESCRIPTION	MIP
Bikini.com	Mustang Trans-Am	5
CBS Sports	Monte Carlo	5
Ebay	Viper GTS-R	6
Millenium VW Bus		6
Playing Mantis Internet Car	Firebird	5
Yahoo!	IRL Car	5

America's Finest, Round 1

NAME	DESCRIPTION	MIP
'95 Caprice	Honolulu Police	6
'97 Camaro	Contra Costa County, CA	6
'97 Crown Victoria	North Carlolina State Police	6
'97 Crown Victoria	Indiana State Police, exclusive car	12
'97 Tahoe	Mesquite Texas Police	6

America's Finest, Round 2

NAME	DESCRIPTION	MIP
'95 Caprice	St. Louis Metropolitan Police, White Lightning	15
'97 Camaro	Texas Highway Patrol, White Lightning	20
'97 Crown Victoria	Niles Township Police, White Lightning	20
'97 Tahoe	Michigan State Police, White Lightning	20

American Blue, Round 1

NAME	DESCRIPTION	MIP
'95 Caprice	New Hampshire	5
'97 Camaro	South Carolina	5
'97 Crown Victoria	New Orleans	5
'97 Tahoe	Chevrolet	5
1977 Dodge Royal Monaco	Chicago	5
Dodge Royal Monaco	New York	5
Ford Galaxy 300	Cook County	5

American Blue, Round 2

NAME	DESCRIPTION	MIP
'66 Ford Galaxy 300	Kissimmee Police	5
'77 Dodge Royal Monaco	Mount Prospect	5
'95 Caprice	Key West Police	5
'97 Camaro	Nevada Hwy. Police	5
'97 Crown Victoria	New Orleans Harbor, bonus car	5
'98 Hummer	S.P.O.C.	5
Chevy Tahoe	Wisconsin State PD	5

American Blue, Round 3

NAME	DESCRIPTION	MIP
'66 Ford Galaxy 300	Missouri State Highway Patrol	5
'95 Caprice	California Hwy Patrol	5
'95 Corvette ZR-1	Baltimore Police, bonus car	5
'97 Camaro	Oregona State Police	5
'97 Chevy Tahoe	Spring Grove Police	5

American Blue, Round 3

NAME	DESCRIPTION	MIP
'97 Crown Victoria	Detroit Police	5
'97 Crown Victoria	Georgia State Police	5

American Chrome

NAME	DESCRIPTION	MIP
'53 Buick Super		5
'55 Chrysler C-300		5
'55 Ford Crown Victoria		5
'57 Lincoln Premier		5
'58 Chevy Impalla		5

Anniversary Cars, Round 1

NAME	DESCRIPTION	MIP
'70 Challenger R/T		5
'70 Cobra 429		5
'70 Superbird		5

Anniversary Cars, Round 2

NAME	DESCRIPTION	MIP
'70 AMC Rebel Machine		5
'70 Camaro RS		5
'70 Mustang Boss 302		5

Anniversary Cars, Round 3

NAME	DESCRIPTION	MIP
'70 Buick GSX		5
'70 Camaro Z28		5
'70 Olds 4-4-2		5

Anniversary Cars, Round 4

NAME	DESCRIPTION	MIP
'70 Chevelle		5
'70 Corvette		5
'70 Superbee		5

British Invasion, Round 1

NAME	DESCRIPTION	MIP
'58-'60 MGA Twin Cam		5
'58-'61 Austin-Healey Srite		5
'58-'61 Triumph TR3A		5
'62-'71 MGB		5

British Invasion, Round 2

NAME	DESCRIPTION	MIP
'58-'60 MGA Twin Cam		5
'58-'61 Austin-Healey Sprite		5
'58-'61 Triumph TR3A		5
'61 Jaguar Convertible		5
'62 Sunbeam		5
'62-'71 MGB		5

Camaros, First Shots

NAME	DESCRIPTION	MIP
'67 Camaro Z28		15
'68 Camaro		11

VEHICLES

JOHNNY LIGHTNING / PLAYING MANTIS

Camaros, First Shots

NAME	DESCRIPTION	MIP
'69 Camaro SS		11
'72 Camaro RS		12
'76 Camaro LT		10
'82 Camaro Z28		10

Camaros, Round 1

NAME	DESCRIPTION	MIP
'67 Camaro	bonus car	7
'67 Camaro RS/SS		6
'68 Camaro RS/SS		6
'69 Camaro RS		6
'70 Camaro RS/SS		5
'77 Camaro Z28		5
'82 Camaro Z28		4

Camaros, Round 2

NAME	DESCRIPTION	MIP
'67 Camaro RS/SS		6
'68 Camaro RS/SS		6
'69 Camaro RS		5
'70 Camaro RS/SS		4
'77 Camaro Z28		4
'82 Camaro Z28		4

Camaros, Round 3

NAME	DESCRIPTION	MIP
'67 Camaro RS/SS		5
'67 Coupe Camaro		5
'68 RS/SS Camaro		5
'69 COPO Camaro		5
'73 RS Camaro		4
'76 Coupe Camaro		4
'87 IROC-Z Camaro		4

Camaros, Round 4

NAME	DESCRIPTION	MIP
'67 Camaro RS/SS		5
'68 Camaro Z-28		6
'69 Camaro RS/SS 396		5
'72 Camaro RS		4
'76 Camaro LT		4
'89 Camaro IROC-Z		3

Cartoon Network Cars

NAME	DESCRIPTION	MIP
Flintstone's Sports Car		5
Speed Buggy		5
Wacky Racers Compact Pussy Cat		5
Wacky Racers Mean Machine		5

Classics Gold, Round 1

NAME	DESCRIPTION	MIP
'33 Willys		5
'56 Chevy		5
'63 Impala		5
'66 Mustang		5
'69 Camaro		5

Classics Gold, Round 1

NAME	DESCRIPTION	MIP
'69 Rambler		5
'70 Cougar		5
'70 Olds 442		5
'74 Olds		5
Grand National		5

Classics Gold, Round 2

NAME	DESCRIPTION	MIP
'69 AMX		5
'70 Buick GS		5
'78 Corvette		5
'84 Monte Carlo SS		5

Classics Gold, Round 3

NAME	DESCRIPTION	MIP
1941 Willy's Pro Street		5
1969 Mercury Cougar		5
1971 Challenger Convertible		5
1974 Ford Torino		5
1997 Chevy Tahoe		5
Midnight Express		5

Classics Gold, Round 4

NAME	DESCRIPTION	MIP
1941 Willy's Pro Street		5
1965 Mustang		5
1969 AMX Javelin	bonus car	5
1972 Olds Cutlass		5
1978 Mustang Cobra		5
1996 Dodge Viper GTS		5
1997 Chevy Tahoe		5

Classics Gold, Round 5

NAME	DESCRIPTION	MIP
1959 El Camino		5
1967 Pontiac GTO		5
1972 Boss Mustang		5
1996 Dodge Viper		5
1996 Impala SS		5
Yellow Cab		5

Classics Gold, Round 6

NAME	DESCRIPTION	MIP
1941 Willy		5
1969 AMX		5
1970 Olds 4-4-2		5
1978 King Cobra		5
1995 Impala SS		5
Boothill Express		5

Commemorative, Round 1

NAME	DESCRIPTION	MIP
Bug Bomb		5
Custom '32 Roadster		5
Custom El Camino		5
Custom GTO		6
Custom XKE		5
Movin' Van		5

VEHICLES

Camaros, 1968 Camaro
RS/SS 396, Playing Mantis

Classics Gold, Playing Mantis. Photo Courtesy Playing Mantis

VEHICLES

818

Commemorative, Round 1

NAME	DESCRIPTION	MIP
The Wasp		5
Vicious Vette		6

Commemorative, Round 2

NAME	DESCRIPTION	MIP
Custom Continental		4
Custom Mako Shark		6
Custom Mustang		4
Custom Spoiler		4
Custom T-Bird		4
Custom Toronado		4
Custom Turbine		4
Nucleon		4
T.N.T.		4
Triple Threat		4

Commemorative, Round 3

NAME	DESCRIPTION	MIP
Custom Camaro		4
Custom Charger		4

Commemorative, Round 4

NAME	DESCRIPTION	MIP
Custom Dragster		4
Custom Eldorado		4
Custom Stiletto		4
Flame Out		4
Mad Maverick		4
Sand Stormer		4

Commemorative, Round 5

NAME	DESCRIPTION	MIP
Custom El Camino		4
Custom GTO		4
Custom Mako Shark		6
Custom T-Bird		4
Custom Toronado		4

Commemorative, Round 6

NAME	DESCRIPTION	MIP
Beep Jeep		4
Commuter		4
Skinni Mini		4
Tow'd		4

Commemorative, White Lightnings

NAME	DESCRIPTION	MIP
Bug Bomb		10
Custom '32 Roadster		10
Custom Continental		12
Custom El Camino		12
Custom GTO		12
Custom Mako Shark		15
Custom Mustang		15
Custom Spoiler		10
Custom T-Bird		15
Custom Toronado		10
Custom Turbine		10
Custom XKE		10

Commemorative, White Lightnings

NAME	DESCRIPTION	MIP
Nucleon		10
T.N.T.		10
The Wasp		10
Triple Threat		10
Vicious Vette		15

Corvette Collection, First Shots

NAME	DESCRIPTION	MIP
'53 Corvette		10
'63 Corvette Sting Ray		10
'63 Grand Sport		10
'65 Corvette Sting Ray Coupe		10
'70 Corvette Sting Ray Coupe		10
'98 Corvette Convertible		10

Corvette Collection, Round 1

NAME	DESCRIPTION	MIP
'54 Corvette Nomad		8
'57 Corvette Roadster		4
'62 Corvette Convertible		4
'65 Mako Shark II		5
'67 Corvette 427 Sting Ray		4
'80 Aerovette		5
'82 Corvette		5
'95 Corvette ZR-1		5
Corvette Indy		4
Corvette Sting Ray III		4

Corvette Collection, Round 2

NAME	DESCRIPTION	MIP
'53 Corvette		4
'63 Corvette Sting Ray		4
'63 Grand Sport		4
'65 Corvette Sting Ray Coupe		4
'70 Corvette Sting Ray Coupe		4
'98 Corvette Convertible		4

Corvette Collection, White Lightnings

NAME	DESCRIPTION	MIP
'54 Corvette Nomad		120
'57 Corvette Roadster		65
'62 Corvette Convertible		65
'65 Mako Shark II		60
'67 Corvette 427 Sting Ray		65
'80 Aerovette		45
'82 Corvette		75
'95 Corvette ZR-1		95

VEHICLES

Cover Cars—Mustang Illustrated, Round 1

NAME	DESCRIPTION	MIP
'68 Mustang GT		5
'69 Mach 1		5
'73 Mach 1		5
'77 Cobra II		5
'94 Boss		5
Ford Mustang Convertible		5

Cover Cars—Mustang Illustrated, Round 2

NAME	DESCRIPTION	MIP
'65 Mustang Convertible		5
'67 GTA		5
'68 Shelby GT 350		5
'69 Mach 1		5
'72 Mustang		5
'88 GT		5

Cover Cars—Super Chevy, Round 3

NAME	DESCRIPTION	MIP
'54 Corvette		5
'57 Chevelle		5
'63 Nova SS		5
'66 Malibu		5
'68 Chevelle		5
'69 Z-28		5

Cover Cars—Super Chevy, Round 4

NAME	DESCRIPTION	MIP
'57 Chevy		5
'61 Convertible Corvette		5
'63 Corvette Grand Sport		5
'63 Impala Z-11		5
'68 Camaro SS		5
'72 Camaro RS		5

Cover Cars—Super Chevy, Round 5

NAME	DESCRIPTION	MIP
'57 Chevy		5
'61 Corvette		5
'63 Impala Z-11		5
'67 Camaro RS/SS		5
'69 Camaro RS/SS 396		5
'98 Corvette (Pace car)		5

Dragsters USA, Round 1

NAME	DESCRIPTION	MIP
Blue Max	'71 Mustang	4
Chi-Town Hustler	'72 Charger	4
Color Me Gone	'72 Challenger	4
Drag-On Lady	'69 AMX	4

Dragsters USA, Round 1

NAME	DESCRIPTION	MIP
Hawaiian	71 Charger	4
Motown Shaker	'71Vega	4
L.A.P.D.	'92 Camaro	4
Revellution	'71 Demon	4
Sox 'N Martin	'71 Cuda	4

Dragsters USA, Round 2

NAME	DESCRIPTION	MIP
Fast Orange—Whit Bazemore	'94 Daytona	3
Kendall GT-1—Chuck Etchells	'96 Avenger	3
King of the Burnouts—Spurlock	'95 Avenger	3
Mantis	'97 Firebird	3
Mooneyes—Kenji Okazaki	'95 Avenger	3
Otter Pops—Ed McCulloch	'91 Olds	3
Pioneer—Tom Hoover	'95 Daytona	3
Rug Doctor—Jim Epler	'94 Olds	3
Sentry Gauges—Bruce Larson	'90 Olds	3
Western Auto—Al Hofmann	'95 Firebird	3

Dragsters USA, Vintage cars, Round 3

NAME	DESCRIPTION	MIP
Barry Setzer	'71 Vega	5
Bob Banning	'72 Challenger	5
Don Garlits	'71 Charger	5
Gene Snow	'72 Charger	5
Jungle Jim	'71 Vega	5
Mantis	'71 Vega	5
Mr. Norm's	'72 Charger	5
Ramchargers	'71 Duster	5
Trojan Horse	'71 Mustang	5
Wildman	'72 Charger	5
Wonder Wagon	'71 Vega	5

Emergency Vehicles, Round 1

NAME	DESCRIPTION	MIP
2000 Chevy Silverado	extended cab w/ seats in back	4
2000 Chevy Silverado	pick up w/ oil dry bin	4
2000 Ford F-250 HD	extended cab w/ oil dry bin	4
2000 Ford F-350 Tow Truck		4

Emergency Vehicles, Round 2

NAME	DESCRIPTION	MIP
2000 Chevy Silverado	IRL	4
2000 Chevy Silverado	Indy 500	4
2000 Chevy Silverado Fire Equip.	IRL	4
2000 Chevy Silverado Fire Equip.	Indy 500	4

VEHICLES

Dragsters USA, Vintage cars, Playing Mantis

Evel Knievel, Playing Mantis. Photo Courtesy Playing Mantis

Emergency Vehicles, Round 2

NAME	DESCRIPTION	MIP
2000 Chevy Silverado Oil Dri	IRL	4
2000 Chevy Silverado Oil Dri	Indy 500	4

Emergency Vehicles, Round 3

NAME	DESCRIPTION	MIP
2000 Chevy Silverado	pick up w/ oil dry bin, Brickyard 400	4
2000 Chevy Silverado	extended cab w/ seats in back, Brickyard 400	4
2000 Chevy Silverado pick up	Brickyard 400	4
2000 Ford F-250 HD	extended cab, Nascar	4
2000 Ford F-350 Tow Truck	Nascar	4
Chevy Tahoe	Brickyard 400	4

Evel Knievel

NAME	DESCRIPTION	MIP
Harley Davidson 750 XR		5
Triumph T-120 Bonneville 650		5
X-2 Sky Cycle		5

Frightning Lightning, First Shots

NAME	DESCRIPTION	MIP
Drag-U-La		18
Heavenly Hearse		15
Meat Wagon		15
Munster's Coach		18
Surf Hearse		15
Undertaker		15

Frightning Lightning, Round 1

NAME	DESCRIPTION	MIP
Boothill Express		5
Christine		5
Elvira		5
Ghostbusters		5
Haulin' Hearse		5
Mysterion		5
Vampire Van		5

Frightning Lightning, Round 2

NAME	DESCRIPTION	MIP
Drag-U-La		5
Heavenly Hearse		5
Meat Wagon		5
Munster's Coach		5
Surf Hearse		5
Undertaker		5

Funny Car Legends, Round 1

NAME	DESCRIPTION	MIP
Al Vandewoude's Flying Dutchman	'68 Charger	5
Bruce Larson's USA-1	'70 Camaro	5
Don Schumacher's "Stardust"	'70 Cuda	5

Funny Car Legends, Round 1

NAME	DESCRIPTION	MIP
Jim Green's "Green Elephant"	'74 Vega	5
Jungle Jim	'75 Monza	5
Shirl Greer's "Chain Lightning"	'74 Mustang	5

Funny Car Legends, Round 2

NAME	DESCRIPTION	MIP
Dicky Harrell	'71 Vega	4
Gene Snow's Rambunctious	'70 Challenger	4
Jim Murphy's "Holy Smokes"	'73 Satellite	4
Lew Arrington's "Brutus"	'73 Mustang	4
Tom Hoover's "Showtime"	'78 Corvette	4
Tom Hoover's "White Bear Dodge"	'72 Charger	4

Funny Car Legends, Round 3

NAME	DESCRIPTION	MIP
Blue Max	'74 Mustang	4
Connie Kalitta	'73 Mustang	4
Dunn and Reath Satellite	'73 Satellite	4
Larry Arnold's "Kingfish"	'70 Cuda	4
Radice Wise	'74 Vega	4
Ramchargers	'70 Challenger	4

Funny Car Legends, Round 4

NAME	DESCRIPTION	MIP
Bunny Burkett	'94 Daytona	4
Cruz Pedregon "McDonald's"	'91 Olds	4
Gordon Mineo, Flash Gordon	'75 Monza	4
Kosty Ivanof	'78 Corvette	4
Malcom Durham	'70 Camaro	4
Mr. Norms Charger	'68 Charger	4

Future Pro Stocks

NAME	DESCRIPTION	MIP
Dynagear—Steve Schmidt	'96 Olds	5
Mama Rosa's Pizza— Osborne	'96 Olds	5
Six Flags—Tom Martino	'96 Firebird	5
Splitfire—Jim Yates	'96 Firebird	5
Summit—Mark Pawuk	'96 Firebird	5
Super Clean—Larry Morgan	'96 Olds	5

Hollywood on Wheels, Round 1

NAME	DESCRIPTION	MIP
Andy Griffith Police Cruiser		5
Back to the Future		6
Blues Brothers 2000		4
Blues Brothers		4

VEHICLES

Hollywood on Wheels, Round 1

NAME	DESCRIPTION	MIP
Dragnet		4
Monkee Mobile		5
Partridge Family		5
Starsky & Hutch		5

Hollywood on Wheels, Round 2

NAME	DESCRIPTION	MIP
'71 Hemi Cuda	Nash Bridges	4
Dodge Ram	Walker Texas Ranger	4
Jaguar XKE	Austin Powers	4

Hollywood on Wheels, Round 3

NAME	DESCRIPTION	MIP
Austin Powers (Felicity) '65 Corvette Convertible		4
Barrismobile		4
Black Beauty		5
Mod Squad Woody		5
Mystery Machine		6
Robocop	four-door hard top pickup	4
Supercar	Supercar	4

Hot Rods, Round 1

NAME	DESCRIPTION	MIP
'29 Crew Cab		5
'62 Bad Bird		5
'66 Pro Street		5
'69 Pro Street		5
'72 Goin Goat		5
'86 Beastmobile		5
Bumongous		5
Flathead Flyer		5
Frankenstude		5
Rumblur		5

Hot Rods, Round 2

NAME	DESCRIPTION	MIP
'23 T-Bucket		4
'27 T-Roadster		4
'32 Ford HiBoy		4
'33 Ford Delivery		4
'34 Ford Coupe		4
'37 Ford Coupe		4

Hummers, Round 1

NAME	DESCRIPTION	MIP
Atlantic Beach Rescue Hummer		5
Civilian Hummer	four-door wagon, black	5
M1025A2 Tow Missile Carrier		5
Rod Hall's Off-Road Racing Hummer		5

Hummers, Round 2

NAME	DESCRIPTION	MIP
ATR Rescue Hummer		4
Civilian - 2dr pickup		4

Hummers, Round 2

NAME	DESCRIPTION	MIP
Civilian Hummer	four-door wagon, silver, bonus car	4
St. Joe Sheriff Hummer		4
US Marines Humvee		4

Hummers, Round 3

NAME	DESCRIPTION	MIP
Army National Guard		43
Army Reserve Hummer		3
Civilian Hummer	four-door wagon (Red bonus car)	3
Gatorade Hummer		3
Tom Wamberg Race Hummer		3

Hurst Muscle

NAME	DESCRIPTION	MIP
'69 Hurst Olds		5
'69 SC/Rambler		5
'74 Hurst Olds		5
Hurst Hairy Olds		5
Hurst Hemi Under Glass		5

Indy Pace Cars, Round 1

NAME	DESCRIPTION	MIP
'69 Camaro		6
'70 Olds 442		4
'74 Hurst Olds		4
'75 Buick Century		4
'77 Olds Delta 88		4
'78 Corvette		4
'79 Mustang		4
'92 Allante		4

Indy Pace Cars, Round 2

NAME	DESCRIPTION	MIP
'68 Torino		6
'69 Camaro		6
'70 Olds 442		6
'71 Challenger		6
'72 Olds		6
'73 Cadillac Eldorado		6
'74 Hurst Olds		6
'77 Olds Delta 88		6
'78 Corvette		6
'79 Mustang		6
'98 Corvette Convertible		6

Indy Pace Cars, Round 3

NAME	DESCRIPTION	MIP
'64-1/2 Mustang		6
'67 Camaro		6
'68 Torino		6
'82 Camaro		6
'96 Viper GTS		6
'98 Corvette		6

VEHICLES

Frightning Lightning, Playing Mantis. Photo Courtesy Playing Mantis

Funny Car Legends, Playing Mantis. Photo Courtesy Playing Mantis

VEHICLES

Indy Race Cars, Round 1

NAME	DESCRIPTION	MIP
'69 Andretti		6
'70 A. Unser		6
'74 Rutherford		6
'75 B. Unser		6
'77 A.J. Foyt		6
'78 A. Unser		6
'79 Mears		6
'92 A. Unser Jr.		6

James Bond, Round 1

NAME	DESCRIPTION	MIP
'64 Aston Martin	Goldeneye	7
'64 Aston Martin	Thunderball	6
'87 Aston Martin	The Living Daylights	6
Ford Mustang Convertible	Goldfinger	7
Ford Mustang Mach 1	Diamonds are Forever	6
Lotus Espirit	For Your Eyes Only	5
Lotus Espirit	The Spy Who Loved Me	6
Mercury Cougar Convertible	On Her Majesty's	6
Sunbeam	Dr. No	10
Toyota 2000GT Convertible	You Only Live Twice	6

James Bond, Round 2

NAME	DESCRIPTION	MIP
'57 Chevy Convertible		6
'64 Aston Martin		6
'65 Ford Mustang Convertible		6
'95 Corvette		6
BMW Z-3	Goldeneye	7
BMW Z-8	The World Is Never Enough	5

Johnny Lightning Red Card Series, Round 1

NAME	DESCRIPTION	MIP
'41 Willy's Coupe		5
'57 Chevy		8
'72 GtO		5
'73 Trans Am		5
Bad Man		5
Bad News		5
Shelby 427 Cobra		5
Speedwagon		5

Johnny Lightning Red Card Series, Round 2

NAME	DESCRIPTION	MIP
'57 Vette Gasser		6
'69 SuperBee		5
Cheetah		5
Li'l Van		5

Jurassic Park

NAME	DESCRIPTION	MIP
Hum-Vee Hunter Vehicle		4

KISS Racing Dreams

NAME	DESCRIPTION	MIP
Ace Frehley	'97 Firebird	5
Gene Simmons	'94 Daytona	5
Paul Stanley	'91 Olds	5
Peter Criss	'96 Avenger	5

Lost In Space

NAME	DESCRIPTION	MIP
Jupiter II		5
Robot B-9		5
Space Chariot		5
Space Pod		5

Magmas, Round 1

NAME	DESCRIPTION	MIP
'70 A. Unser Indy	1:43-scale	7
Drag-u-la	1:43-scale	8
T'rantula	1:43-scale	7

Magmas, Round 2

NAME	DESCRIPTION	MIP
'68 Camaro	1:43-scale	7
'70 A. Unser Indy	1:43-scale	7
'70 Challenger Trans Am	1:43-scale	7
'71 Mustang Boss 351	1:43-scale	7
'71 Mustang Mach 1	1:43-scale	7
'71 Plymouth Roadrunner	1:43-scale	7
Drag-u-la	1:43-scale	7
T'rantula	1:43-scale	8

Magmas, Round 3

NAME	DESCRIPTION	MIP
Donkey Kong	Grand Prix, 1:43-scale	6
Smash Brothers	Taurus, 1:43-scale	6
Yoshi	Taurus, 1:43-scale	6
Zelda	Grand Prix, 1:43-scale	6

Military Vehicles

NAME	DESCRIPTION	MIP
'90's Humvee		4
'90's M1 Tank		4
WW II 6x6 Truck		4
WW II Half Track		4
WW II Jeep		4
WW II WC54 Ambulance		4

Modern Muscle

NAME	DESCRIPTION	MIP
Chevy Monte Carlo		4
Dodge Viper		4
Ford Mustang		4
Jaguar XK8		4
Miata		4
Pontiac Firebird Trans-Am		4

VEHICLES

Monopoly

NAME	DESCRIPTION	MIP
'33 Willys	Monopoly	5
'40 Ford	Reading Railroad	5
'57 Chevy	Illinois Ave.	5
'67 Mustang	Community Chest	5
'98 Corvette	Monopoly	5
Cameo	Water Works	5
Crown Victoria	Go To Jail	5
LA Dart	Chance	5
Tahoe	B&O Railroad	5
Tameless Tiger	Park Place	5
Utility Van	Electric Company	5
Viper	Luxury Tax	5

Mopar Box Set

NAME	DESCRIPTION	MIP
'70 Superbird, '71 440 Cuda, '59 Hemi Roadrunner, '70 Challenger, '68 Hemi	set of ten	12

Mopar Muscle

NAME	DESCRIPTION	MIP
'69 Charger		5
'69 Daytona		5
'70 Cuda		5
'70 Roadrunner GTX		5
'71 Duster		5
'71 Satellite/RR/GTX		5

Muscle Cars, Round 1

NAME	DESCRIPTION	MIP
'65 Pontiac GTO Convertible		7
'69 Mercury Cougar Eliminator		5
'69 Olds 442		4
'69 Pontiac GTO Judge		7
'70 Chevy Chevelle SS		5
'70 Dodge Super Bee		5
'70 Ford Boss 302 Mustang		7
'70 Plymouth Superbird		5
'71 Plymouth Hemi Cuda		5
'72 Chevy Nova SS		4

Muscle Cars, Round 2

NAME	DESCRIPTION	MIP
'66 Chevy Malibu		4
'68 Dodge Charger		4
'68 Ford Shelby GT-500		5
'69 Plymouth Roadrunner		4
'69 Pontiac Firebird		4
'70 Buick GSX		4
'70 Dodge Challenger		5
'72 AMC Javelin AMX		4

Muscle Cars, Round 3

NAME	DESCRIPTION	MIP
'65 Chevy II Nova		5
'67 GTO		6
'68 Chevelle		5
'70 AAR Cuda		5
'70 AMC Rebel Machine		5
'70 Challenger T/A		5
'70 Torino		5
'71 Demon		5
'71 GTO Judge		5
'73 Charger		5

Muscle Cars, Round 4

NAME	DESCRIPTION	MIP
'64 Pontiac GTO		4
'67 Cougar		4
'67 Cutlass		4
'67 Pontiac Firebird		4
'69 Chevy Nova		4
'70 Mercury Cyclone		4

Muscle Cars, White Lightnings

NAME	DESCRIPTION	MIP
'65 Chevy II Nova		25
'67 GTO		30
'68 Chevelle		25
'70 AAR Cuda		30
'70 AMC Rebel Machine		25
'70 Challenger T/A		25
'70 Torino		25
'71 Demon		25
'73 Charger		25

Pewter Cars, Round 1

NAME	DESCRIPTION	MIP
'57 Chevy	pewter	4
'68 Camaro	pewter	4
Corvette Lamans	pewter	4
Dodge Viper	pewter	4
Hummer	pewter	4
Jungle Jim	pewter	4
Mustang	pewter	4
Six Pack	pewter	4
Space Shuttle	pewter	4
Stealth	pewter	4
Topper El Camino	pewter	4

Racing Dreams, Round 1

NAME	DESCRIPTION	MIP
Army	'71 Charger	5
DQ-Dilly Bar	'71 Demon	6
Hawaiin Punch	'72 Challenger	6
Hershey's	'94 Olds	6
James Bond - Goldfinger	'71 Vega	6
Jurrassic Park the Ride	'94 Daytona	6
Mooneyes	'71 Mustang	5
Nintendo-Star Fox	'96 Avenger	6
Popsicle	'72 Charger	7

VEHICLES

Hollywood on Wheels, Playing Mantis. Photo Courtesy Playing Mantis

James Bond, Playing Mantis. Photo Courtesy Playing Mantis

Racing Dreams, Round 1

NAME	DESCRIPTION	MIP
Trix	'97 Firebird	6

Racing Dreams, Round 2

NAME	DESCRIPTION	MIP
Coast Guard	Monte Carlo	6
Lucky Charms	Grand Prix	7
Nintendo-Mario 64	Grand Prix	7
Pez	Monte Carlo	8
Planters-Mr. Peanut	Thunderbird	7
TGI Friday's	Thunderbird	6

Racing Dreams, Round 3

NAME	DESCRIPTION	MIP
Frosted Flakes		6
Fudgsicle		7
McDonald's Big Mac		6
Pennzoil		6
Reese's-Hershey		5

Racing Dreams, Round 4

NAME	DESCRIPTION	MIP
Blizzard		6
Cocoa Puffs		6
Grimace		6
Hawaiin Punch	orange	6
Monkees (Direct Mail car)		9
Mug Rootbeer		6
Nintendo-Zelda		6
Pez		9
Yohsi		6

Racing Machines, Round 1

NAME	DESCRIPTION	MIP
Current Camaro Trans Am	PLC Direct	4
Current Mustang Trans-Am	Preformed, Ruhlman	4
IRL Race Car	Powerteam	4
Viper GTS-R	Bobby Archer	4

Racing Machines, Round 2

NAME	DESCRIPTION	MIP
'94 Daytona	Bunny Car	4
'98 Avenger	Tom Hoover Pioneer	4
Current Camaro Trans Am	Glacier Tek	4
Current Mustang Trans-Am	Homelink	5
Viper GTS-R	Team Oreca	4

Racing Machines, Round 3

NAME	DESCRIPTION	MIP
'69 AMX	AMX Petes Patriot	5
'72 Charger	Gene Snow Funny Car	4
'98 Avenger	Red Line Oil Funny Car	4
94 Olds	McDonalds Funny Car	4
Firebird	Splitfire	4
Tameless Tiger	Tameless Tiger	4

Racing Machines, Round 4

NAME	DESCRIPTION	MIP
'69 Pontiac GTO Judge	The Judge, Arnie Beswick	5
'71 Vega	Wonder Wagon	4
'94 Daytona	Roland Leong's Hawaiian Punch	4
'96 Saleen Racer	Saleen Mustang	4
'97 Firebird	NAPA Dragster	4
'98 Avenger	PM Bug Car, Jim Dunn	4
'98 Avenger	JL Car, Jim Dunn, bonus car, No. 1	4

Racing Machines IRL Cars—1999

NAME	DESCRIPTION	MIP
IRL Race Car	Scott Goodyear	5
IRL Race Car	Kenny Brack	5
IRL Race Car	Greg Ray	5
IRL Race Car	Indy Event Car, 1999	5
IRL Race Car	Luyendyk '98 winner car, twin w/1990	7
IRL Race Car	Eliseo Salazar	5
IRL Race Car	Arie Luyendyk '99 car	5
IRL Race Car	Scott Sharp	5
IRL Race Car	Mark Dismore	5
IRL Race Car	Billy Boat	5

Racing Machines IRL Cars—2000

NAME	DESCRIPTION	MIP
IRL Race Car	Robby McGhee, Mall.com #5	5
IRL Race Car	Greg Ray, Menards #2 1999 and #3 2000 twin	5
IRL Race Car	Indy Event Car, 2000	5
IRL Race Car	Robby McGhee, Energizer #55	5
IRL Race Car	Robbie Buhl, Purex #24	5
IRL Race Car	Buddy Lazier, Tae Bo #91	5
IRL Race Car	Mark Dismore, Bryant #28	5
IRL Race Car	Scott Goodyear, Pennzoil #4	5
IRL Race Car	Greg Ray, Menards #3	5
IRL Race Car	Scott Sharp, Delphi #8	5

Rock N Rollers

NAME	DESCRIPTION	MIP
'64 Mustang		6
'67 GTO		6
Bad Bird		6
Cobra		6
Fink Speedwagon		6
Flathead Flyer		6

Show Rods—George Barris

NAME	DESCRIPTION	MIP
'41 "Tribute" Ford Phaeton		4
'51 Burgundy Mercury Converible		4
Emperer		4
Fireball 500		6
Kopper Kart		6

VEHICLES

Show Rods—George Barris

NAME	DESCRIPTION	MIP
Sam Barris—'49 Merc		4
Speed Coupe		4
Wildkat		4

Show Rods—George Barris, White Lightnings

NAME	DESCRIPTION	MIP
'41 "Tribute" Ford Phaeton		4
'51 Burgundy Mercury Converible		4
Emperer		4
Fireball 500		6
Kopper Kart		6
Sam Barris—'49 Merc		4
Speed Coupe		4
Wildkat		4
'41 "Tribute" Ford Phaeton		20
'51 Burgundy Mercury Converible		20
Emperer		20
Fireball 500		25
Kopper Kart		20
Sam Barris—'49 Merc		20
Speed Coupe		20
Wildkat		20

Show Rods—Tom Daniel Show Rods

NAME	DESCRIPTION	MIP
Baja Bandito		3
Desert Fox	Rommel's Rod	3
Dog Catcher		3
Fast Buck		3
LA Kid or Daddy's Deuce		3
Rat Vega or Poison Pinto		3
Smug Bug		3
TD's Ride	CA Street Vette	4
Triple T		3
Wild Bull Surfer		3

Showstoppers, Round 1

NAME	DESCRIPTION	MIP
Chuck Wagon		3
Dodge Rebellion		3
Hemi Xpress		3
Little Red Wagon		5

Showstoppers, Round 2

NAME	DESCRIPTION	MIP
Hemi Under Glass		3
Hurst Hairy Olds		3
LA Dart		3
Tameless Tiger		3

Showstoppers, Round 3

NAME	DESCRIPTION	MIP
Dodge Material		3
Frank Monaghan		3
Little Red Wagon		3
Thunder Wagon		3

Special Edition, Round 1

NAME	DESCRIPTION	MIP
'54 Chevy Panel		15
'56 Chevy		15
'60's VW Van		15
Dodge A-100		15

Special Edition, Round 2

NAME	DESCRIPTION	MIP
'33 Willys		15
'66 Mustang 350H		15
Bugaboo		15
Buick Grand National		15
NSX		15
Plymouth Prowler		15
The VW Thing		15
VW Concept One		15

Special Edition, Round 3

NAME	DESCRIPTION	MIP
'63 Chevy Impala		15
'69 AMC Hurst SC/Rambler		15
'70 Cougar Convertible		15

Speed Racer, Round 1

NAME	DESCRIPTION	MIP
Assassin		5
GRX: Fastest Car		5
Racer X Shooting Star		5
Speed Racer Mach 5		15

Speed Racer, Round 2

NAME	DESCRIPTION	MIP
Captain Terror		5
Mach 5		11
Shooting Star		5
Snake Oiler		5

Stock Car Legends, Round 1

NAME	DESCRIPTION	MIP
'67 Ford Fairlane	Mario Andretti	4
'69 Daytona	Bobby Isaac	4
'71 Mercury Cyclone	Donny Allison	4
'73 Dodge Charger	Marty Robbins	4
'81 Grand Prix	Rusty Wallace	4
'85 Ford Thunderbird	Buddy Baker	4

Stock Car Legends, Round 2

NAME	DESCRIPTION	MIP
'69 Torino Talladega	David Pearson	4
'70 Superbird	Pete Hamilton	4
'71 Plymouth Satellite	Pete Hamilton	4
'77 Olds Cutlass	Cale Yarborough	4
'79 Chevy Monte Carlo	Darrell Waltrip	4

VEHICLES

Muscle Cars, Playing Mantis. Photo Courtesy Playing Mantis

Racing Dreams, Playing Mantis. Photo Courtesy Playing Mantis

Stock Car Legends, Round 2

NAME	DESCRIPTION	MIP
'83 Chevy Monte Carlo	Cale Yarborough	4

Stock Car Legends, Round 3

NAME	DESCRIPTION	MIP
'67 Ford Fairlane	David Pearson	4
'69 Daytona	Buddy Baker	4
'69 Torino Talladega	LeeRoy Yarbrough	4
'71 Mercury Cyclone	Donny Allison, Purolator	4
'83 Chevy Monte Carlo	Darrell Waltrip	4
'85 Ford Thunderbird	Buddy Baker	4

Stock Car Legends, Round 4

NAME	DESCRIPTION	MIP
'70 Superbird	Richard Brooks	4
'71 Plymouth Satellite	Fred Lorenzen	4
'73 Dodge Charger	Neil Bonnett	4
'77 Olds Cutlass	AJ Foyt	4
'79 Chevy Monte Carlo	Benny Parsons	4
'81 Grand Prix	Geoff Bodine	4

Street Freaks, Round 1

NAME	DESCRIPTION	MIP
'67 Mustang		6
'67 Shelby		5
'69 Mach 1		4
'70 AMC Rebel Machine		4
'71 GTO Judge		6
'73 Mach 1		4

Street Freaks, Round 2

NAME	DESCRIPTION	MIP
1963 Mustang		5
1967 GTO		5
1968 Chevelle		5
1976 Cobra		4
1987 Mustang		4
1994 Mustang		4

Street Freaks, Round 3

NAME	DESCRIPTION	MIP
'65 Nova		4
'69 Camaro		5
'70 AAR		4
'70 Torino		4
'71 Demon		5
'73 Charger		7

Street Freaks, White Lightning 1

NAME	DESCRIPTION	MIP
'67 Mustang		20
'67 Shelby		20
'69 Mach 1		20
'70 AMC Rebel Machine		20
'71 GTO Judge		20
'73 Mach 1		20

Street Freaks, White Lightning 2

NAME	DESCRIPTION	MIP
1963 Mustang		20
1967 GTO		20
1968 Chevelle		20
1976 Cobra		15
1987 Mustang		15
1994 Mustang		15

Surf Rods, Round 1

NAME	DESCRIPTION	MIP
'29 Crew Cab	Laguna Longboards	4
'59 El Camino	Redondo Gonzos	4
'60's VW Van	Huntington Hunnies	4
Dan Fink Speedwagon	Woody	4
Rumblur	The Hang 10 Men	4
Surfbusters	Surf Daddies	4

Surf Rods, Round 2

NAME	DESCRIPTION	MIP
'29 Ford	Torrance Terrors	4
'50 Ford F-1	Hermosa Beach Bums 3	4
'54 Chevy Panel Truck	Waimea Mamas	4
Emperor	Malibu Babes	4
Haulin' Hearse	Santa Monica Maniacs	4
Meat Wagon	Cowabunga Boyz	3

Team Lightning, Round 1

NAME	DESCRIPTION	MIP
Black Beauty, Frankenstude		3
Crash Bandicoot Viper		3
Munsters '29 Crew Cab		3
Three Stooges Flathead Fly		3

Team Lightning, Round 2

NAME	DESCRIPTION	MIP
Bad Medicine	Bela Lugosi's Dracula	3
Bugaboo	Bozo the Clown	3
Count Chocula Pro Street		3
Dodge Ram	Blow Pops	3
Meatwagon	Alfred Hitchcock Vertigo	3
Willys	3 Stooges Moe	3

Top Fuel, Round 1

NAME	DESCRIPTION	MIP
'60's Front Engine Top Fuel	Ramchargers	3
'60's Front Engine Top Fuel	Tommy Ivo	3
'70's Rear Engine Car	Don Garlits "Swamp Rat 19"	3
'70's Rear Engine Car	Jeb Allen "Praying Mantis"	3
'70's Rear Engine Car	Warren Coburn and Miller "Rain For Rent"	5

VEHICLES

VEHICLES

Top Fuel, Round 2

NAME	DESCRIPTION	MIP
'60's Front Engine Top Fuel	Hawaiin	3
'60's Front Engine Top Fuel	Tony Nancy	5
'60's Front Engine Top Fuel	Soapy Sales	3
'70's Rear Engine Car	Tommy Ivo Rod Shop	3
'70's Rear Engine Car	Walton Cerny & Moody	3
'70's Rear Engine Car	Don Garlits	3

Top Fuel, Round 3

NAME	DESCRIPTION	MIP
'60's Front Engine Top Fuel	John Wiebe	3
'60's Front Engine Top Fuel	BB & Mulligan	3
'60's Front Engine Top Fuel	Steve Carbone '71 Dragster	3
'70's Rear Engine Car	Jungle Jim	3
'70's Rear Engine Car	Don Garlits Swamp Rat 24	3
'70's Rear Engine Car	Diamond Jim Annin	3

Top Fuel, Round 4

NAME	DESCRIPTION	MIP
'60's Front Engine Top Fuel	Creitz and Donovan	3
'60's Front Engine Top Fuel	Garlits Swamp Rat X	3
'60's Front Engine Top Fuel	Jerry Ruth Dragster	3
'70's Rear Engine Car	Benny Osborne	3
'70's Rear Engine Car	Jade Grenade	3
'70's Rear Engine Car	Keeling and Clayton California Charger	3

Truckin' America

NAME	DESCRIPTION	MIP
'29 Ford		6
'40 Ford		4
'50 Ford F-1		4
'55 Chevy Cameo		4
'59 El Camino		4
'60's Studebaker Champ		6
'71 El Camino		4
'78 Li'l Red Express		6
'91 GMC Syclone		7
'96 Dodge Ram		4

Truckin' America, White Lightnings

NAME	DESCRIPTION	MIP
'29 Ford		6
'40 Ford		4
'50 Ford F-1		4
'55 Chevy Cameo		4
'59 El Camino		4
'60's Studebaker Champ		6
'71 El Camino		4

Truckin' America, White Lightnings

NAME	DESCRIPTION	MIP
'78 Li'l Red Express		6
'91 GMC Syclone		7
'96 Dodge Ram		4
'29 Ford		20
'40 Ford		20
'50 Ford F-1		20
'55 Chevy Cameo		20
'59 El Camino		20
'60's Studebaker Champ		20
'71 El Camino		20
'78 Li'l Red Express		20
'91 GMC Syclone		20
'96 Dodge Ram		20

Trucks—KISS Album

NAME	DESCRIPTION	MIP
'29 Ford	KISS The Original Album	5
'40 Ford	KISS Destroyer	5
'59 El Camino	KISS Love Gun	5
'71 El Camino	KISS Unmasked	5
'78 Li'l Red Express	KISS Dressed to Kill	5
'91 GMC Syclone	KISS Dynasty	5

VIP

NAME	DESCRIPTION	MIP
Ford Mustang		4
Jaguar XK8		4
Miata		4

Volkswagens

NAME	DESCRIPTION	MIP
'60's VW Bug		5
2000 New Beetle		5
Karmann Ghia		5
Smug Bug		5

Wacky Winners

NAME	DESCRIPTION	MIP
Bad Medicine		4
Bad News		7
Badman		7
Cherry Bomb		5
Draggin' Dragon		4
Garbage Truck		4
Root Beer Wagon		4
T'rantula		5
Tijuana Taxi		4
Trouble Maker		4

Workhorses/True Grit, Round 1

NAME	DESCRIPTION	MIP
Basic Step Van	Tootsie Roll	3
Basic Step Van	Froot Loops	3
Utility Van	PEZ	3

NAME	DESCRIPTION	GOOD	EX	MINT
'32 Roadster		25	60	125
A.J. Foyt Indy Special	black wall tires	40	60	250
Al Unser Indy Special	black wall tires	100	200	500
Baja		45	125	200
Big Rig	came w/add on extras called Customs; prices reflect fully accessorized cars	65	150	275
Bubble	Jet Powered	45	75	150
Bug Bomb	black wall tires	40	90	225
Condor	black wall tires	150	200	1200
Custom Camaro	prototype, only one known to exist, value is for car in MNB condition	n/a	n/a	6000
Custom Charger	prototype, only one known to exist, value is for car in MNB condition	n/a	n/a	6000
Custom Continental	prototype, only six known to exist, value is for car in MNB condition	n/a	n/a	4000
Custom Dragster	without canopy	35	75	125
Custom Dragster	mirror finish	150	250	1000
Custom Dragster	w/plastic canopy	60	150	200
Custom El Camino	w/sealed doors	100	300	500
Custom El Camino	w/opening doors	150	275	475
Custom El Camino	mirror finish	200	350	1125
Custom Eldorado	w/sealed doors	150	300	1000
Custom Eldorado	w/opening doors	150	275	275
Custom Ferrari	w/opening doors, mirror finish	300	450	1000
Custom Ferrari	w/sealed doors	35	80	125
Custom Ferrari	w/opening doors	150	275	500
Custom GTO	mirror finish	200	475	1000
Custom GTO	w/sealed doors	200	350	1700
Custom GTO	w/opening doors	200	350	1500
Custom Mako Shark	w/sealed doors	40	75	225
Custom Mako Shark	w/opening doors, mirror finish	200	500	2000
Custom Mako Shark	w/opening doors	125	350	500
Custom Mustang	prototype, only one known to exist, value is for car in MNB condition	n/a	n/a	6000
Custom Spoiler	black wall tires	35	65	150
Custom T-Bird	w/opening doors	100	250	475
Custom T-Bird	mirror finish	200	400	5000
Custom T-Bird	w/sealed doors	150	300	700
Custom Toronado	w/opening doors	225	400	1000
Custom Toronado	mirror finish	450	600	2000
Custom Toronado	w/sealed doors	300	500	1500
Custom Turbine	red, black, white painted interior	50	150	200
Custom Turbine	w/unpainted interior	25	45	125
Custom Turbine	mirror finish	150	225	500
Custom XKE	w/opening doors, mirror finish	300	450	800
Custom XKE	w/sealed doors	35	80	100
Custom XKE	w/opening doors	150	275	400
Double Trouble	black wall tires	75	100	1500
Flame Out	black wall tires	60	125	350
Flying Needle	Jet Powered	45	100	225
Frantic Ferrari		35	45	90
Glasser	Jet Powered	40	75	150

VEHICLES

'32 Roadster, 1969, Topper Toys. Photo Courtesy Dennis Seleman

Custom Eldorado, 1969, Topper Toys. Photo Courtesy Dennis Seleman

Custom T-Bird, 1969, Topper Toys. Photo Courtesy Dennis Seleman

Leapin' Limo, 1970, Topper Toys

JOHNNY LIGHTNING / TOPPER

NAME	DESCRIPTION	GOOD	EX	MINT
Hairy Hauler	came w/add on extras called Customs; prices reflect fully accessorized cars	65	150	275
Jumpin' Jag	black wall tires	35	80	175
Leapin' Limo	black wall tires	50	125	400
Mad Maverick	black wall tires	75	150	450
Monster	jet powered	40	74	150
Movin' Van	black wall tires	35	65	90
Nucleon	black wall tires	35	80	225
Parnelli Jones Indy Special	black wall tires	40	60	250
Pipe Dream	came w/add on extras called Customs; prices reflect fully accessorized cars	65	150	275
Sand Stormer	black wall tires	20	35	90
Sand Stormer	black roof, black wall tires	50	100	200
Screamer	jet powered	45	75	200
Sling Shot	black wall tires	50	95	250
Smuggler	black wall tires	35	75	150
Stiletto	black wall tires	60	85	300
TNT	black wall tires	40	75	175
Triple Threat	black wall tires	40	90	200
Twin Blaster	came w/add on extras called Customs; prices reflect fully accessorized cars	65	150	275
Vicious Vette	black wall tires	35	80	225
Vulture w/wing	black wall tires	75	130	500
Wasp	black wall tires	80	100	400
Wedge	Jet Powered	45	75	200
Whistler	black wall tires	75	125	300
Wild Winner	came w/add on extras called Customs; prices reflect fully accessorized cars	60	125	250

Sand Stormer, 1970, Topper Toys

Smuggler, 1970, Topper Toys. Photo Courtesy Mark Rich

Amos 'N' Andy Fresh Air Taxi Cab, Marx

KEYSTONE

Airplanes

NAME	DESCRIPTION	GOOD	EX	MINT
Air Mail Plane	25", olive green, w/three propellors	1600	2400	2800
Air Mail Plane	25", olive green	1500	2200	3000
Rapid Fire Air Mail Plane	25", olive green	2000	3000	4200
Ride 'Em Air Mail Plane	25", seat and handles allowed child to ride	1200	1700	2400

Emergency Vehicles

NAME	DESCRIPTION	GOOD	EX	MINT
Aerial Ladder Truck	27-1/2"	800	1200	1500
Ambulance	27-1/2", w/canvas cover and stretcher	1000	1500	2000
Fire Truck	27-1/2", red w/hose reel	700	1000	1600
Water Pump Tower Truck	29", red cab, rubber tires	850	1200	1600

Miscellaneous Vehicles

NAME	DESCRIPTION	GOOD	EX	MINT
Coast to Coast Bus	31-1/4", blue	1200	1700	2500
Ride 'Em Locomotive	28"	300	500	650
Ride 'Em Pullman Car	25", silver or red passenger car	300	500	725
Steam Roller	20", black body, w/whistle and bell	200	300	600
Steam Shovel	20-3/4"	75	175	225
Truck Loader	tan w/black base, 20-1/4"	175	375	500

Trucks

NAME	DESCRIPTION	GOOD	EX	MINT
American Railway Express Truck	26-1/4", green body, screened back	600	1000	1600
Dump Truck	black w/red chassis; 26-1/4"; rubber tires	300	500	720
Koaster Truck	26", open cab w/flatbed, black cab, red body	700	1000	1900
Moving Van	26-1/4", black cab, red body, rubber tires	1000	1500	2000
Packard U.S. Mail Truck	26-1/4", black cab, tan body	400	1000	1700
Police Patrol Truck	27-1/2", Police Patrol decals	700	1200	1600
Ride 'Em Dump Truck	26-1/2", green cab, red body	250	450	700
Standard Dump Truck	Packard decal; black w/red chassis, 26-1/4"	350	500	800
Tank Truck	26-1/4", black cab, dark green body	1200	1800	2200
U.S. Army Truck	26-1/4", w/canvas cover	500	900	1300
World's Greatest Circus Truck	26-1/4", w/six removable animal cages, w/circus lithography	2500	5000	10000
Wrecker	27-1/2", red	800	1000	1500

VEHICLES

NAME	NO.	DESCRIPTION	MINT

100 Series

BRM Formula 1 Racer	101-A	unchromed or chromed	18
Citroen DS 21	113-A		23
Ferrari LeMans	109-A	unchromed or chromed	18
Fiat Multi Benne Skip Truck	114-A	orange w/red skip, 1:100-scale (later reissued as 222-A)	18
Hotchkiss Jeep with Cable Carrier	107-A		15
Peugeot 404 Saloon	116-A		23
Porsche Formula 1 Racer	102-A	uncromed or chromed	18

200 Series

'57 Chevy Hot Rod	223-D	Road Eaters assorted	5
'57 Chevy Hot Rod	223-D	Kool Kromes	5
'57 Chevy Hot Rod	223-D	assorted	4
1969 Plymouth Fury Police	216-B	metallic blue	8
20 Panel Truck	214-C		8
Airport Minibus	262-A	red w/Coca-Cola sun	7
Airport Minibus	262-A	red and yellow, 1:87-scale	5
Airport Minibus	262-A	various, 1:87-scale	4
Airport Minibus	262-A	white, marked "Air France" or "TWA," 1:87-scale	8
Alfa 75	271-A	red w/tan or white interior	5
Alfa 75	271-A	red w/black accents w/black interior, silver trim on grille	6
Alfa 75	271-A	red w/black accents w/black interior, no trim on grille	8
Alfa Romeo Giulietta	271-B	red w/black and silver accents	5
Alfa Romeo Giulietta	271-B	blue Polizia w/whit interior, 1:55-scale	6
Alpine A310 special Team Unit	264-A	various	10
Ambulance Truck	255-D	white w/orange accents, 1:60-scale	4
Aston-Martin DB7	229-D	blue	5
ATF	256-A		14
Audi 90	259-D	yellow, 1:60-scale	4
Audi 90	239-D	assorted, 1:60-scale	4
Audi Quattro	221-C	assorted	5
Autobianchi A112	269-B	assorted, 1:53-scale	8
Bank Security Armored Truck	204-C	assorted, 1:57-scale	4
Bernard Cattle Carrier	206-C	1:50-scale	15
Bernard Circus Truck	212-A		18
Bernard Dump truck	205-A		10
Bernard Fire Engine	204-A		18
Bernard Flat truck with Racks	206-A	1:50-scale	15
Bernard Flat Truck with Scraper	206-B	1:50-scale	15
Bernard Sanitation Truck	218-A		14
Bernard Sanitation Truck	218-A		12
Bernard Snow Plow	208-A	1:50-scale	15
Bernard Stake Truck	219-A		9
Bernard Truck with Chalet	236-B		14
Bertone Camargue	221-B		8
BMW 2800CS Coupe	235-A		9
BMW 3.0	235-C	yellow, 1:60-scale	6
BMW 3258i	257-C	various, 1:56-scale	4
BMW 325i	229-C	assorted	4
BMW 733	256-B	various, 1:60-scale	7
BMW Turbo	217-B		8
British Bus	259-E	red w/amber windows, w/"British Airways" label, 1:125-scale	8
British Bus	286-B	assorted, 1:125-scale	8

VEHICLES

NAME	NO.	DESCRIPTION	MINT
BRM Fi Racer	228-A		12
Bulldozer	255-A		6
Bulldozer	287-B	yellow w/black cab	5
BX4TC	225-B	white	7
Cadillac Allante	253-C	silver w/red roof	7
Cadillac Allante	253-C	various	4
Camping Trailer	259-B		8
Chevrolet Al Camino SS Pickup	296-A	assorted, 1:59-scale	4
Chevrolet Al Camino SS Pickup	296-A	Kool Kromes red w/pink flames, 1:59-scale	5
Chevrolet Al Camino SS Pickup	296-A	Road Eaters fluorescent lime green, 1:59-scale	5
Chevrolet Al Camino SS Pickup	296-A	Road Eaters dark blue, 1:59-scale	5
Chevrolet Blazer	236-E		4
Chevrolet Covered Truck	241-C	blue, marked "Cadbury Roses Chocolates"	8
Chevrolet Grand Prix Corvette	215-C	assorted, 1:57-scale	4
Chevrolet Grand Prix Corvette	215-C	metallic blue w/gold abd black accents	6
Chevrolet Impala Police Car	240-B	various	5
Chevrolet Impala Police Car	240-B	black w/white doors	4
Chevrolet Impala Taxi	213-F	yellow and black, 1:69-scale	4
Chevrolet Impala Taxi	213-F	yellow, 1:69-scale	5
Chevrolet Impala Taxi	219-D	assorted	5
Chevrolet Pickup	217-D		3
Chevy Blazer Pickup 4x4	291-A	assorted	4
Chevy Blazer Pickup 4x4	291-A	blue w/yellow interior or yellow w/red interior	5
Chevy Blazer Wrecker	228-B	assorted	4
Chevy Blazer Wrecker (Depanneuse)	228-B	red without markings, 1:62-scale	5
Chrysler 180	208-B	metallic green, 1:60-scale	13
Citroen Ambulance	206-E		10
Citroen CX	265-A	burgundy, silver or metallic brown, 1:60-scale	8
Citroen Ds19	213-A	blue w/red interior	14
Citroen DS21	213-B		12
Citroen DS21 with Boat	214-A		18
Citroen DS21 with Caravan	215-A		18
Citroen Dyane Raid	231-A		10
Citroen GS	201-B		8
Citroen Maserati SM	250-A		12
Citroen Visa Chrono Mille Pistes	201-C	yellow or white, 1:52-scale	4
Citroen XM	254-C	white	4
Citroen XM	254-C	metal flake silver	5
Container Truck	265-B	various, 1:100-scale	5
Container truck	265-B	white w/gold tampo, marked "Futura Motors Pty.Ltd.," Australian promotional issue, 1:100-scale	18
Container Truck	265-B	blue, marked "{Cadbury Roses Chocolate" or "Cadbury Dairy Milk," 1:100-scale	8
Container Truck	265-B	red, labelled "Coca-Cola," 1:100-scale	8
Container Truck	265-B	white, labelled "Total," 1:100-scale	6
Container Truck	265-B	Raod Eaters white, labelled "Diet Pepsi," 1:100-scale	6
Corvette Turbo Racer	268-B	assorted, 1:54-scale	5
Corvette Turbo Racer	268-B	black w/silver and gold accents, 1:54-scale	6
Corvette Turbo Racer	268-B	white, 1:54-scale	6
Crane Truck	283-A	assorted, 1:100-scale	4
Crazy Car	267-B	black w/white interior	5
Crazy Car 4x4	223-B		8

VEHICLES

NAME	NO.	DESCRIPTION	MINT
Custom Ford Transit Van Pickup	264-B	red w/white interior	6
DAF 2600 Bucket Truck	246-C	1:100-scale	17
DAF 2600 Covered Platform Truck	241-A	1:100-scale	9
DAF 2600 Crane Truck	247-A	1:100-scale	14
DAF 2600 Tanker	245-A	marked "Shell," 1:100-scale	8
DAF Covered Trailer	243-A		14
Datsun 260Z	229-B	yellow, 1:60-scale	5
Datsun 260Z	229-B	metallic turquoise or light green, 1:60-scale	7
Datsun 260Z	229-B	red, 1:60-scale	6
Desert Raider 4x4	223-C	black	5
Dodge Camper	209-A		15
Dodge Fire Rescue	204-B		8
Dodge Safari Truck	225-A	assorted	12
Dodge Snow Top truck with Plow	242-A		8
Dodge Wrecker Tow Truck	212-B	white wit blue light	8
Dune Buggy	232-C	hot pink, "Fun Buggy"	6
Dune Buggy	232-C	hot pink, "Ice Cream"	5
Dune Buggy	248-A	various colors, flowers and lightning decals on roof, 1:55-scale	8
Dune Buggy	258-A	various, w/awning and amber windshield, chrome spiral window wheel design	12
Dune Buggy	259-A		12
Dune Buggy Surfer JP4 with surfboards	252-A	various, 1:47-scale	6
Etalmobile Warehouse Vehicle	203-A	1:50-scale	18
Excalibur	267-A	metallic light blue w/white interior and black roof, 1:56-scale	7
Excalibur	267-A	yellow w/passenger, 1:56-scale	8
Excalibur	267-A	silver or metallic brown, 1:56-scale	6
Explorateur 4x4	260-B	various, 1:59-scale	7
Explorer	261-B		4
Extending Ladder Fire Truck	207-D	red w/gold lettering, wheat laurel or four-petal ensignia	4
Extending Ladder Fire Truck (Pompier)	207-D	red without lettering, 1:100-scale	6
F1 Racer	234-B		6
Farm Tractor	208-C	assorted	4
Farm Tractor	208-C	w/cultivator	4
Ferrari 456 GT	204-D		4
Ferrari F50 Coupe	204-E		4
Ferrari FA0	280-B	red w/or without red plastic window, 1:58-scale	4
Ferrari FA0	280-B	Kool Kromes red or yellow	5
Ferrari FI Racer	229-A	metallic purple	12
Ferrari GTO	211-E	assorted, 1:56-scale	4
Ferrari Testarosa	211-F		4
FI Ferrari	282-A	red and green marked "Benetton 8"	6
FI Ferrari	282-A	assorted	4
FI Ferrari	282-A	red and green marked "Benetton 23"	6
FI Racer	213-G		4
Fiat 127	203-B	blue, metallic blue or metallic yellow green, dog on back seat, 1:55-scale	10
Fiat 127	203-B	blue, metalillic blue or metallic yellow-green; doors open, dog on back seat looking out left rear window, 1:55-scale	8
Fiat Ritmo/Strada	239-C	assorted	6
Fiat Ritmo/Strada	239-C	red without markings	7
Fiat Skip Truck multi Benne	222-A	orange w/blue skip, 1:100-scale	10

VEHICLES

NAME	NO.	DESCRIPTION	MINT
Fiat Skip Truck Multi Benne	222-A	red w/yellow skip, 1:100-scale	8
Fiat Tipo	286-B	assorted, 1:54-scale	5
Ford 5000 Farm Tractor	253-A	blue w/white fenders, 1:55-scale	10
Ford Bronco 4x4	251-B	mutard yellow, 1:56-scale	6
Ford Bronco 4x4	251-B	black w/silver and gold accents, w/and without sunroof, 1:56-scale	4
Ford Capri	251-A	various	8
Ford Covered Truck	241-C	red w/white cargo cover w/Coca-Cola label, 1:100-scale	6
Ford Covered Truck	241-C	various, 1:100-scale	4
Ford Escort GT	275-B		4
Ford Escort XR3	212-C	assorted, 1:52-scale	4
Ford Model A Van	201-D	blue or metallic red, "Tea Shop," 1:60-scale	6
Ford Model A Van	201-D	blue, "Orange Company," 1:60-scale	4
Ford Model A Van	201-D	blue, 1:60-scale	8
Ford Model A Van	201-D	Road Eaters bright orange or red, 1:60-scale	5
Ford Mondeo	269-B		4
Ford Mustang GT Convertible	227-C	assorted, 1:59-scale	4
Ford Tanker	245-C	various	5
Ford Tempo/Sierra	272-A	assorted, 1:58-scale	4
Ford Thunderbird Turbo	217-C	blue w/red trim, 1:67-scale	5
Ford thunderbird Turbo	217-C	Smelly Speeders, white w/brown trim, 1:67-scale	5
Ford Thunderbird Turbo	217-C	assortes, 1:67-scale	4
Ford Transit Custom Tow Truck	230-D	assorted	4
Ford Transit Custom Tow Truck	295-A	red w/white bumpers, marked "Jack's Towing 24 Hr Service"	4
Ford Transit Custom Tow Truck	295-A	fluorescent orange, marked "Racing Service"	5
Ford Transit Van	243-C	various	4
Ford US Van	250-B	black, 1:65-scale	7
Formula 1 Brabham	232-B	assorted, 1:53-scale	4
Formula 1 Racer	238-B	green, red and white, "Benetton," 1:55-scale	8
Formula I Racer	238-B	assorted, 1:55-scale	4
Four Wheel Loader	211-B		10
Fourgon Commercial Van	234-C	blue, "Cadbury Dairy Milk Buttons"	8
Fourgon Commercial Van	234-C	red, "Coca-Cola"	6
Fourgon Commercial Van	234-C	assorted, 1:53-scale	4
Fourgon Ice Cream Van	259-C	yellow w/pink or blu windows, white awning	8
Fourgon Ice Cream Van	259-C	white w/red awning	6
Fourgon Ice Cream Van	259-C	various	7
Fourgon Motor Home	224-C	assorted, 1:67-scale	10
Fourgon Police Van	279-A	assorted, 1:65-scale	5
Front End Loader	263-A	orange, 1:87-scale	5
Front End Loader	263-A	yellow, 1:87-scale	4
GMC Jimmy	249-D		4
Honda Accord	219-C	assorted, 1:59-scale	5
Honda Accord NSX	220-C		4
Honda Prelude 4WD	252-B	red w/black and silver accents, 1:58-scale	5
Hotchkiss Jeep with Cattle Trailer	211-A		18
Jaguar E	207-B		10
Jaguar J6	293-B	assorted, 1:65-scale	4
Jaguar J6 Police	205-D		5
Jaguar XKE 2+2 Coupe	207-A		10
Jeep 4x4	244-B	various	5
Jeep 4x4 Rallye 4x4	289-A	assorted, 1:62-scale	4
Jeep Cherokee	236-D	yellow w/"Indian" on roof	4

VEHICLES

NAME	NO.	DESCRIPTION	MINT
Jeep Cherokee 4x4	236-D	red w/white and black, orange and bllue accents, w/dog, 1:65-scale	5
Jeep Cherokee 4x4	236-D	red w/white and black, orange and blue accents, no dog, 1:65-scale	4
Jeep Cherokee 4x4	236-D	yellow w/red and black accents, ribbed roof, w/dog, 1:64-scale	5
Jeep Cherokee 4x4	236-D	flourescent green, no dog, 1:64-scale	4
Jeep Cherokee 4x4	236-D	Road eaters, black, "Chee-tos Chester Cheetah," no dog, 1:64-scale	5
Jeep Cherokee 4x4	236-D	green	4
Jeep Cherokee 4x4	236-D	metallic brown, "Big Chief," w/dog, ribbed roof, 1:64-scale	7
Jeep Cherokee 4x4	236-D	flourescent orange, ribbed roof, 1:64-scale	4
Jeep Cherokee 4x4	236-D	Smelly Speeders, yellow, ribbed roof, 1:64-scale	4
Jeep Cherokee 4x4	236-D	white, "Coca-Cola" w/polar bear	12
Jeep Cherokee 4x4	236-D	light brown, "Big Chief," w/dog, ribbed roof, 1:64-scale	5
Jeep Cherokee 4x4	236-D	red, "Mad Bull," ribbed roof, 1:64-scale	6
Jeep Cherokee Ambulance	269-A	white w/red or blue accents, 1:64-scale	5
Jeep Cherokee Ambulance	269-A	white w/no markeings, 1:64-scale	6
Jeep Cherokee Limited	224-C	w/surfboards on roof, assorted, 1:60-scale	4
Jeep Cherokee Sheriff	285-B	assorted	4
Jeep CJ	268-A	assorted, w/conventional chassis, 1:54-scale	5
Jeep CJ	268-A	metallic brown, w/conventional chassis, 1:54-scale	6
Lamborghini Diablo	219-E	Road Eaters w/Pepsi logo, 1:58-scale	6
Lamborghini Diablo	219-E	assorted, 1:58-scale	5
Lancia Montecarlo	285-A	white w/red accents	5
Lancia Montecarlo	285-A	mustard yellow w/black interior	6
Land Rover 4x4	266-b	various, 1:60-scale	5
Land Rover 4x4	266-B	tan w/zebra stripes, 1:60-scale	4
Locomotive	234-A		17
Lotus FI Racer	227-A		10
Mack Dump Truck	297-A	assorted, 1:100-scale	4
Mack Tow Truck	256-C	red, 1:100-scale	4
Magirus Beton Cement Mixer	227-B	1:100-scale	10
Matra Simca 670	239-B	metallic blue	7
Matra Simca Bagheera	219-B	blue, 1:55-scale	7
Mazda Rx7 Daytona	257-B	various, 1:56-scale	4
Mazda RX7 Daytona	257-B	orange w/blue accents, narrow tires, 1:56-scale	6
Merceded-Benz 300TE Station Wagon	250-C	various, 1:63-scale	5
Mercedes Cattle Truck	254-B	yellow, w/one white and one black steer, 1:100-scale	8
Mercedes Public Works Truck (Trax Publics)	233-B	orange, 1:70-scale	7
Mercedes Public Works Truck (Trax Publics)	233-B	metallic light blue, 1:70-scale	6
Mercedes-Benz 190E 2.3-16	231-B	assorted, 1:59-scale	5
Mercedes-Benz 2.3-16	231-B	white, 1:59-scale	4
Mercedes-Benz 350SL Convertible	213-C	yellow, 1:60-scale	8
Mercedes-Benz 350SL Convertible	213-C	silver w/red-orange accents, 1:60-scale	6
Mercedes-Benz 450 SE	249-B	metallic silver, 1:60-scale	4
Mercedes-Benz 450 SE	249-B	metallic godl or light green, 1:60-scale	5
Mercedes-Benz 450SL	213-D		6
Mercedes-Benz 500 SL Roadster	260-C	Road Eaters nright red, marked "Willy Wonka NERDS," 1:58-sclae	5
Mercedes-Benz 500 SL Roadster	260-C	dark red witt maroon interior, 1:58-scale	5
Mercedes-Benz 500 SL Roadster	260-C	various, 1:58-scale	4

VEHICLES

NAME	NO.	DESCRIPTION	MINT
Mercedes-Benz Fire Engine	258-B	red, 1:70-scale	8
Mercedes-Benz Sanitation Truck	218-B	assorted, 1:100-scale	6
Mercedes-Benz Sanitation Truck	218-B	orange and gray	8
Mercedes-Benz Stake Truck	213-E	red w/yellow hay bales, 1:100-scale	8
Mercedes-Benz Stake Truck with Hay load	254-A	red and brown, 1:100-scale	8
Mobile Home Camping Car	278-B	assorted	6
Mobile Home Camping Car	278-B	red w/white camper	4
Mobile Office	223-A		10
Morgan	261-A	Kool Kromes blue w/white interior, 1:50-scale	5
Morgan	261-A	various, 1:50-scale	4
Motorboat and Trailer	235-B		15
Mustang SVO	220-B	metallic periwinkle, narrow or oversize tires, 1:59-scale	6
Mustang SVO	220-B	red w/narrow tires	4
Mustang SVO	220-B	metallic periwinkle w/red and white accents, oversize tires, 1:59-scale	4
Mustang SVO	220-B	white w/narrow tires, 1:59-scale	5
Mustang SVO	220-B	white w/oversized tires, 1:59-scale	4
Nissan 300ZX Turbo T-Roof	214-D	assorted	4
Oldsmobile Omega	253-B	various, 1:75-scale	8
Panther Bertone Course Racer	233-A	assorted, 1:65-scale	12
Peugeot 204 Roadster	230-A		12
Peugeot 205 CTI/GTI Cabriolet	210-C	assorted, 1:53-scale	4
Peugeot 205 GTI/CTI Hardtop	210-D	1:53-scale	4
Peugeot 205 GTI/CTI Hardtop Sedan	281-A	assorted, 1:53-scale	4
Peugeot 205 GTI/CTI Hardtop Sedan	281-A	white w/red and blue accents, marked "Police," 1:53-scale	5
Peugeot 404 Ambulance	206-D		15
Peugeot 404 Police	216-A		10
Peugeot 404 Saloon with Alpine	217-A		18
Peugeot 405 mi 16	218-C	assorted, 1:62-scale	4
Peugeot 405 T16	202-D	yellow or red	4
Peugeot 405 T16	202-D	Kool Kromes orange or blue	5
Peugeot 406	218-D		4
Peugeot 504	239-A		8
Peugeot 604	236-C		6
Peugeot 604	238-A	assorted	7
Police Motorcycle	203-C		23
Pontiac Fiero	206-F	assorted	4
Pontiac Firebird	212-D		4
Pontiac Firebird Trans Am	248-B	various, 1:55-scale	4
Pontiac Firebird Turbo	293-A		5
Pontiac Trans Sport SE	268-C	red or black w/white interior	4
Porsche 911 Turbo	209-B	yellow w/orange and blue accents, narrow tires, 1:57-scale	8
Porsche 911 Turbo	209-B	assorted, wide tires, 1:57-scale	5
Porsche 911 Turbo	209-B	assorted	4
Porsche 924	247-B	various, amber windows, 1:60-scale	8
Porsche 924	247-B	metallic blue w/orange accents, clear windows	6
Porsche LeMans Racer	232-A	metallic red, 1:65-scale	11
Power Shovel	242-B	yellow body w/black base and shovel, 1:100-scale	4
Power Shovel	242-B	red body w/yellow base and yellow shovel, 1:100-scale	5

VEHICLES

NAME	NO.	DESCRIPTION	MINT
Pro Stocker Firebird with Oversized Engine	258-C	various, 1:62-scale	4
Range Rover Rescue Unit	246-B	w/closed rear section, 1:60-scale	6
Range Rover Rescue Unit	246-C	w/closed rear section, red w/black or white interior, 1:60-scale	4
Refuse TrucK	247-C	green body w/gray container	7
Refuse Truck	247-C	lime green body w/orange container w/hippo on sides, 1:100-scale	5
Refuse Truck	247-C	vatious, 1:100-scale	4
Refuse Truck	247-C	green body, orange container, 1:100-scale	6
Renault 11 Encore	274-A	assorted, 1:54-scale	5
Renault 11 Encore	274-A	metallic green w/black, orange and silve accents, 1:54-scale	7
Renault 11 Encore	274-A	dark maroon w/yellow interior, 1:56-scale	6
Renault 17	260-A		8
Renault 18	266-A	yellow, no marking, w/passenger, 1:60-scale	8
Renault 18	266-A	various, 1:60-scale	6
Renault 18	266-A	metallic silver, 1:60-scale	8
Renault 19 Convertible	225-C		4
Renault 25 V6	222-B	assorted, 1:63-scale	4
Renault 4L Delivery Van	230-B	assorted, 1:55-scale	10
Renault 5 LeCar	280-A	metallic olive green, without rear-view mirrors or antenna, 1:51-scale	8
Renault 5 LeCar	257-A	various, w/antenna and rear view mirrors	10
Renault Acadiane Service Van	235-D	assorted, 1:53-scale	6
Renault Clio	270-B		5
Renault Espace	272-B	white ambulance	4
Renault Express Van	233-C	orange or white, "europcar rentacar"	7
Renault Express Van	233-C	blue, "Satellite Service"	5
Renault Express Van	233-C	red, "Avis"	6
Renault Maxi 5 Turbo	255-C	blue, 1:53-scale	5
Renault R16	221-A		12
Renault R5 Turbo	255-B	red w/yellow interior, 1:53-scale	6
Renault Safrane	221-E	assorted	4
Renault Super Cinq GT Turbo	205-C	blue, 1:51-scale	5
Renault Super Cinq GT Turbo	205-C	black, 1:51-scale	5
Renault Twingo Minivan	206-G		6
Renault X54	221-D		5
Repco FI Racer	226-A		12
Road Grader Shovel	211-D		6
Road Roller	226-C	assorted	4
Roadster	273-B	red, based on the Dodge Viper, 1:58-scale	4
Rock Motorcycle	207-C		15
Saab 900Turbo	284-A	assorted, 1:62-scale	5
Saab Scania Dump Truck	205-B	yellow or silver w/red dumper	8
Saviem Canvas Platform Truck	241-B	various	7
Saviem Container Truck	214-B	Adidas logo	7
Saviem Container Truck	214-B	Pepsi logo	8
Saviem Tanker	245-B	various, 1:100-scale	8
Saviem Tanker	245-B	red-orange w/white tank, marked "Ewig Oil Co.," 1:100-scale	22
Saviem Tanker	245-B	marked "Texaco," 1:100-scale	26
Service Broom Truck	251-C		4
Simca 1100	234-B		10
Simca 1308	240-A	dark silver or blue, 1:60-scale	8
Ski-Doo Nordic Snowmobile	249-A		16

VEHICLES

NAME	NO.	DESCRIPTION	MINT
Snowmobile	284-B	white w/silver skis	8
Snowmobile	284-B	white w/red skis	6
Sports Proto Racer	235-F		4
St. Tropez Travel Trailer	201-A	1:68-scale	12
Stock Car	279-A	assorted, 1:60-scale	4
Streckeman Lovely 400 Travel Trailer	236-A	1:65-scale	14
Super Dump Truck	274-A	yellow w/silver dumper, 1:100-scale	4
Toyota 4x4	276-A	metallic maroon	4
Toyota 4x4	276-A	red w/black interior	4
Toyota Celica 2.0 GT	249-C	various, 1:58-scale	4
Toyota Hi-Lux Pickup	287-A	assorted, conventional chassis, 1:56-scale	8
Toyota Hi-Lux Pickup	292-A	yellow w/black interior, modified 4x4 chassis	6
Toyota Hi-Lux Pickup	292-A	hot pink or metallic blue, modified 4x4 chassis	4
Toyota Hi-Lux Pickup	292-A	assorted, modified 4x4 chassis	5
Toyota Landcruiser	277-A	metallic green, conventional chassis, 1:53-scale	7
Toyota Landcruiser	277-A	black and white zebra stripes, conventional chassis, 1:53-scale	6
Toyota Landcruiser	277-A	red w/yellow interior, conventional chassis, 1:53-scale	5
Toyota Landcruiser	277-A	beige w/green accents and map of Africa on roof, conventional chassis, 1:53-scale	6
Toyota Landcruiser 4x4	277-B	bright green w/yellow interior or red w/black and gold accents, modified chassis, 1:53-scale	5
Toyota Landcruiser 4x4	277-B	red and black or white and black zebra stripes, modified chassis, 1:53-scale	6
Toyota Landcruiser 4x4	277-B	black w/gold accents and map of Africa on roof, modified chassis, 1:53-scale	6
Toyota Landcruiser 4x4	277-B	beige w/red interior and map of Africa on roof, modified chassis, 1:53-scale	5
Toyota Landcruiser 4x4	277-B	white w/red and gold accents, modified chassis, 1:53-scale	4
Toyota Lite Ace Van Wagon	216-C	yellow w/bluebird accents on side	6
Toyota Lite Ace Van Wagon	216-C	assorted, 1:52-scale	5
Toyota Tercel 4WD	273-A	assorted, 1:55-scale	6
Tractor with Plow	211-C		8
Triumph TR7	202-C	red or orange	4
Unimog Snow Plow	224-A		10
Unimog with Fork Lift	215-A	blue and white	8
Volkswagen 1302	203-D	blue or lime green, trunk does not open (Coccinelle)	5
Volkswagen 1302	203-D	light blue, trunk doesn't open (Coccinelle)	6
Volkswagen Ambulance	244-A	metallic blue w/white interior	10
Volkswagen Golf	210-B	assorted, 1:60-scale	6
Volkswagen Golf	264-C	red, silver or teal, 1:56-sclae	4
Volkswagen K70	210-A	assorted, 1:60-scale	10
Volkswagen Van	226-B		12
Volkwagen Ambulance	244-A	various	8
Volvo 245 DL Station Wagon	220-A	assorted, 1:60-scale	8
Volvo 760 GLE	230-C	assorted, 1:61-scale	5
VW 113	202-A		10
VW 1302 Beetle	202-B	red w/yellow lightening bolt on trunk, opening trunk, 1:60-scale	8
VW 1302 Beetle	202-B	red w/yellow flower on trunk, opening trunk, 1:60-scale	11
Western Train	278-A	metallic blue, 1:87-scale	12

VEHICLES

NAME	DESCRIPTION	GOOD	EX	MINT

Airplanes

NAME	DESCRIPTION	GOOD	EX	MINT
727 Riding Jet	jet engine sound	150	225	300
Air-Sea Power Bombing Set	12" wingspan, 1940s	325	450	650
Airmail Biplane	four engines, tin wind-up, 18" wingspan, 1936	225	325	450
Airmail Monoplane	two engines, tin wind-up, 1930	100	150	225
Airplane	mail biplane, tin wind-up, 9-3/4" wingspan, 1926	150	225	300
Airplane	monoplane, pressed steel, 9" wingspan, 1942	110	165	300
Airplane	no engines, tin wind-up, 9-1/2" wingspan	135	200	300
Airplane	two propellers, tin wind-up, 9 7/8" wingspan, 1927	200	300	400
Airplane	tin wind-up, 9-1/4" wingspan, 1926	150	225	300
Airplane	adjustable rudder, tin wind-up, 10" wingspan, 1926	150	225	300
Airplane	monoplane, adjustable rudder, tin wind-up, 9-1/4" wingspan	150	225	300
Airplane	medium fuselage, tin wind-up	125	150	250
Airplane	light fuselage, tin wind-up	125	175	250
Airplane	twin engine, tin wind-up, 9-1/2" wingspan	100	150	200
Airplane #90	tin wind-up, 5" wingspan, 1930	240	360	480
Airplane with Parachute	monoplane, tin wind-up, 13" wingspan, 1929	115	170	325
Airways Express Plane	tin wind-up, 13" wingspan, 1929	200	300	400
American Airlines Airplane	passenger plane, tin wind-up, 27" wingspan, 1940	130	190	400
American Airlines Flagship	pressed steel, wood wheels, 27" wingspan, 1940	200	300	500
Army Airplane	biplane, tin wind-up, 25-3/4" wingspan, 1930	225	340	450
Army Airplane	18" wingspan, 1951	150	225	300
Army Airplane	two engines, tin wind-up, 18" wingspan, 1938	125	190	250
Army Airplane	tin, mechanical fighter, 7" wingspan	125	170	230
Army Bomber	two engines, tin wind-up, 18" wingspan, 1940s	250	375	500
Army Bomber	monoplane, litho machine gun and pilot, 25-1/2" wingspan, 1935	300	450	600
Army Bomber	tri-motor, 25-1/2" wingspan, 1935	250	375	500
Army Bomber with Bombs	camouflage pattern, metal, wind-up, 12" wingspan, 1930s	100	150	250
Army Fighter Plane	tin wind-up, 5" wingspan, 1940s	100	150	250
Autogyro	tin wind-up, 27" wingspan, 1940s	150	225	375
Blue and Silver Bomber	two engines, tin wind-up, 18" wingspan, 1940	190	280	375
Bomber	four propellers, metal, wind-up, 14-1/2" wingspan	100	150	300
Bomber with Tricycle Landing Gear	four engine, tin wind-up, 18" wingspan, 1940	225	325	425
Camouflage Airplane	four engines, 18" wingspan, 1942	125	200	295
China Clipper	four engines, tin wind-up, 18-1/4" wingspan, 1938	100	150	250
City Airport	extra tower and planes, 1930s	125	190	250
Crash-Proof Airplane	monoplane, tin wind-up, 11-3/4" wingspan, 1933	100	150	200
Cross Country Flyer	19" tall, 1929	375	550	725
Dagwood's Solo Flight Airplane	wind-up, 9" wingspan, 1935	200	300	950
Daredevil Flyer	tin wind-up, 1929	115	170	325
Daredevil Flyer	Zeppelin-shaped, 1928	225	350	475
DC-3 Airplane	aluminum, wind-up, 9-1/2" wingspan, 1930s	125	190	300
Eagle Air Scout	monoplane, tin wind-up, 26-1/2" wingspan, 1929	200	300	400
Fighter Jet, USAF	battery-operated, 7" wingspan	90	135	250
Fighter Plane	battery-operated, remote controlled, 1950s	90	135	250
Fix All Helicopter		275	400	600
Flip-Over Airplane	tin wind-up	200	300	450
Floor Zeppelin	9-1/2" long, 1931	225	340	500
Floor Zeppelin	16-1/2" long, 1931	350	525	750
Flying Fortress 2095	sparking, four engines, 1940	150	245	400
Flying Zeppelin	wind-up, 9" long, 1930	225	340	475
Flying Zeppelin	wind-up, 17" long, 1930	350	525	750
Flying Zeppelin	wind-up, 10" long	275	400	600
Four-Motor Transport Plane	friction, tin litho	120	180	325
Golden Tricky Airplane		75	115	225
Hangar with One Plane	1940s	150	225	500
International Airline Express	monoplane, tin wind-up, 17-1/2" wingspan, 1931	200	300	425
Jet Plane	friction, 6" wingspan, 1950s	65	90	195
Little Lindy Airplane	friction, 2-1/4" wingspan, 1930	200	300	500

VEHICLES

NAME	DESCRIPTION	GOOD	EX	MINT
Looping Plane	silver version, tin wind-up, 7" wingspan, 1941	225	325	525
Lucky Stunt Flyer	tin wind-up, 6" long, 1928	150	225	350
Mammoth Zeppelin, 1st Mammoth	pull toy, 28" long, 1930	400	600	900
Mammoth Zeppelin, 2nd Mammoth	pull toy, 28" long, 1930	375	575	775
Municipal Airport Hangar	1929	100	150	425
Overseas Biplane	three propellers, tin wind-up, 9-7/8" wingspan, 1928	150	275	395
PAA Clipper Plane	pressed steel, 27" wingspan, 1952	125	175	525
PAA Passenger Plane	tin litho, 14" wingspan, 1950s	120	175	275
Pan American	pressed steel, four motors, 27" wingspan, 1940	90	150	525
Piggy Back Plane	tin wind-up, 9" wingspan, 1939	100	150	350
Pioneer Air Express Monoplane	tin litho, pull toy, 25-1/2" wingspan	125	190	300
Popeye Flyer	Popeye and Olive Oyl in plane, tin litho tower, wind-up, 1936	475	700	1250
Popeye Flyer	Wimpy and Swee'Pea litho on tower, 1936	600	900	1600
Pursuit Planes	one propeller, 8" wingspan, 1930s	125	200	300
Rollover Airplane	tin wind-up, forward and reverse, 6" wingspan, 1947	200	300	575
Rollover Airplane	tin wind-up, 1920s	200	300	575
Rookie Pilot	tin litho, wind-up, 7" long, 1930s	225	340	550
Seversky P-35	single-engine plane, 16" wingspan, 1940s	125	200	350
Sky Bird Flyer	two planes, 9-1/2" tower, 1947	275	400	550
Sky Cruiser Two-Motored Transport Plane	18" wingspan, 1940s	125	175	325
Sky Flyer	biplane and Zeppelin, 8-1/2" tall tower, 1927	225	340	450
Sky Flyer	9" tall tower, 1937	150	225	375
Spirit of America	monoplane, tin wind-up, 17-1/2" wingspan, 1930	325	500	650
Spirit of St. Louis	tin wind-up, 9-1/4" wingspan, 1929	150	225	595
Stunt Pilot	tin wind-up	175	250	425
Tower Flyers	1926	175	250	350
Trans-Atlantic Zeppelin	wind-up, 10" long, 1930	225	350	450
TWA Biplane	four-engine, 18" wingspan	225	350	450
U.S. Marines Plane	monoplane, tin wind-up, 17-7/8" wingspan, 1930	200	300	400
Zeppelin	all metal, pull toy, 28" long, 1929	400	600	800
Zeppelin	friction pull toy, steel, 6" long	100	200	250
Zeppelin	flies in circles, wind-up, 17" long, 1930	350	525	700

Boats and Ships

NAME	DESCRIPTION	GOOD	EX	MINT
Battleship USS Washington	friction, 14" long, 1950s	50	75	225
Caribbean Luxury Liner	sparkling, friction, 15" long	50	75	225
Luxury Liner Boat	tin, friction	100	150	250
Mosquito Fleet Putt Putt Boat		40	55	95
River Queen Paddle Wheel Station	plastic	50	75	150
Sparkling Warship	tin wind-up, 14" long	50	75	195
Tugboat	plastic, battery-operated, 6" long, 1966	50	75	195

Buses

NAME	DESCRIPTION	GOOD	EX	MINT
American Van Lines Bus	cream and red, tin wind-up, 13-1/2" long	65	100	130
Blue Line Tours Bus	tin litho, wind-up, 9-1/2" long, 1930s	150	225	425
Bus	red, 4" long, 1940	35	50	95
Coast to Coast Bus	tin litho, wind-up, 10" long, 1930s	125	200	325
Greyhound Bus	tin litho, wind-up, 6" long, 1930s	100	150	200
Liberty Bus	tin litho, wind-up, 5" long, 1931	75	125	200
Mystery Speedway Bus	tin litho, wind-up, 14" long, 1938	200	300	550
Royal Bus Lines Bus	tin litho, wind-up, 10-1/4" long, 1930s	135	200	450
Royal Van Co. Truck "We Haul Anywhere"	tin wind-up, 9" long, 1920s-30's	140	225	500
School Bus	steel body, wooden wheels, pull toy, 11-1/2" long	125	200	325

Cars

NAME	DESCRIPTION	GOOD	EX	MINT
Amos 'N' Andy Fresh Air Taxi Cab	tin litho, wind-up, 8" long, 1930	650	875	1600
Anti-Aircraft Gun on Car	5-1/4" long	50	75	225

VEHICLES

NAME	DESCRIPTION	GOOD	EX	MINT
Army Car	battery-operated	65	100	200
Army Staff Car	litho steel, tin wind-up, 1930s	125	200	425
Army Staff Car	w/flasher and siren, tin wind-up, 11" long, 1940s	75	125	400
Big Lizzie Car	tin wind-up, 7-1/4" long, 1930s	75	125	235
Blondie's Jalopy	tin litho, 16" long, 1941	325	500	850
Boat Tail Racer #3	tin wind-up, 5" long, 1930s	40	55	200
Bouncing Benny Car	pull toy, 7" long, 1939	325	500	750
Bumper Auto	large bumpers front and rear, tin wind-up, 1939	60	100	225
Cadillac Coupe	8-1/2" long, 1931	175	275	400
Cadillac Coupe	trunk w/tools on luggage carrier, tin wind-up, 11" long, 1931	200	300	525
Camera Car	heavy gauge steel car, 9-1/2" long, 1939	850	1300	1900
Careful Johnnie	plastic driver, 6-1/2" long, 1950s	100	150	350
Charlie McCarthy "Benzine Buggy" Car	w/white wheels, tin wind-up, 7" long, 1938	450	625	950
Charlie McCarthy "Benzine Buggy" Car	w/red wheels, tin wind-up, 7" long, 1938	600	900	1450
Charlie McCarthy and Mortimer Snerd Private Car	tin wind-up, 16" long, 1939	600	900	1500
Charlie McCarthy Private Car	wind-up, 1935	1450	2200	3500
College Boy Car	blue car w/yellow trim, tin wind-up, 8" long, 1930s	300	450	525
Convertible Roadster	nickel-plated tin, 11" long, 1930s	175	275	395
Coo Coo Car	8" long, tin wind-up, 1931	375	575	825
Crazy Dan Car	tin wind-up, 6" long, 1930s	140	225	395
Dagwood the Driver	8" long, tin wind-up, 1941	200	300	900
Dan Dipsy Car	nodder, tin wind-up, 5-3/4" long, 1950s	250	375	450
Dick Tracy Police Car	9" long	150	225	350
Dick Tracy Police Station Riot Car	friction, sparkling, 7-1/2" long, 1946	130	200	375
Dick Tracy Squad Car	yellow flashing light, tin litho, wind-up, 11" long, 1940s	250	375	525
Dick Tracy Squad Car	battery-operated, tin litho, 11-1/4" long, 1949	170	275	475
Dick Tracy Squad Car	friction, 20" long, 1948	125	170	300
Dippy Dumper	Brutus or Popeye, celluloid figure, tin wind-up, 9", 1930s	350	525	900
Disney Parade Roadster	tin litho, wind-up, 1950s	100	150	900
Donald Duck Disney Dipsy Car	plastic Donald, tin wind-up, 5-3/4" long, 1953	425	650	895
Donald Duck Go-Kart	plastic and metal, friction, rubber tires, 1960s	75	130	325
Donald the Driver	plastic Donald, tin car, wind-up, 6-1/2" long, 1950s	200	300	595
Dora Dipsy Car	nodder, tin wind-up, 5-3/4" long, 1953	400	600	725
Dottie the Driver	nodder, tin wind-up, 6-1/2" long, 1950s	150	225	450
Drive-Up Self Car	turns left, right or straight, 1940	100	150	225
Driver Training Car	tin wind-up, 1930s	80	120	225
Electric Convertible	tin and plastic, 20" long	65	100	295
Falcon	plastic bubble top, black rubber tires	50	75	175
Funny Fire Fighters	7" long, tin wind-up, 1941	800	1200	1600
Funny Flivver Car	tin litho, wind-up, 7" long, 1926	275	425	675
G-Man Pursuit Car	sparks, 14-1/2" long, 1935	190	285	750
Gang Buster Car	tin wind-up, 14-1/2" long, 1938	200	300	800
Giant King Racer	dark blue, tin wind-up, 12-1/4" long, 1928	250	375	725
Hot Rod #23	friction motor, tin, 8" long, 1967	45	75	90
Huckleberry Hound Car	friction	125	200	250
International Agent Car	friction, tin litho, 1966	60	100	195
International Agent Car	tin wind-up	30	55	125
Jaguar	battery-operated, 13" long	225	325	450
Jalopy	tin driver, friction, 1950s	125	200	250
Jalopy Car	tin driver, motor sparks, crank, wind-up	140	225	280
Jolly Joe Jeep	tin litho, 5-3/4" long, 1950s	150	225	375
Joy Riders Crazy Car	tin litho, wind-up, 8" long, 1928	340	500	675
Jumping Jeep	tin litho, 5-3/4" long, 1947	210	325	425
King Racer	yellow body, red trim, tin wind-up, 8-1/2" long, 1925	375	575	750
King Racer	yellow w/black outlines, 8-1/2" long, 1925	250	430	575
Komical Kop	black car, tin litho, wind-up, 7-1/2" long, 1930s	450	675	900
Leaping Lizzie Car	tin wind-up, 7" long, 1927	250	375	500

VEHICLES

Charlie McCarthy "Benzine Buggy" Car, Marx

Funny Flivver Car, Marx

NAME	DESCRIPTION	GOOD	EX	MINT
Learn To Drive Car	wind-up	110	165	225
Lonesome Pine Trailer and Convertible Sedan	22" long, 1936	375	600	795
Machine Gun on Car	hand crank activation on gun, 3" long	75	130	225
Magic George and Car	litho, 1940s	170	250	350
Mechanical Speed Racer	tin wind-up, 12" long, 1948	125	200	275
Mickey Mouse Disney Dipsy Car	plastic Mickey, tin wind-up, 5-3/4" long, 1953	425	655	875
Mickey the Driver	plastic Mickey, tin car, wind-up, 6-1/2" long, 1950s	170	250	450
Midget Racer "Midget Special" #2	miniature car, clockwork-powered, 5" long, 1930s	125	200	250
Midget Racer "Midget Special" #7	miniature car, tin wind-up, 5" long, 1930s	125	200	250
Milton Berle Crazy Car	tin litho, wind-up, 6" long, 1950s	250	375	595
Mortimer Snerd's Tricky Auto	tin litho, wind-up, 7-1/2" long, 1939	400	600	750
Mystery Car	press down activation, 9" long, 1936	125	200	275
Mystery Taxi	press down activation, steel, 9" long, 1938	160	250	375
Nutty Mad Car	red tin car, vinyl driver, friction, 4" long, 1960s	100	150	225
Nutty Mad Car	w/driver, battery-operated, 1960s	100	150	225
Nutty Mad Car	blue car w/goggled driver, friction, hard plastic, 1960s	75	130	200
Old Jalopy	tin wind-up, driver, "Old Jalopy" on hood, 7" long, 1950	225	325	425
Parade Roadster	w/Disney characters, tin litho, wind-up, 11" long, 1950	225	325	900
Peter Rabbit Eccentric Car	tin wind-up, 5-1/2" long, 1950s	250	375	500
Queen of the Campus	w/four college students' heads, 1950	250	400	525
Race 'N Road Speedway	HO scale racing set, 1950s	60	100	125
Racer #12	tin litho, wind-up, 16" long, 1942	225	325	625
Racer #3	miniature car, tin wind-up, 5" long	75	125	195
Racer #4	miniature car, tin wind-up, 5" long	75	125	195
Racer #5	miniature car, tin wind-up, 5" long, 1948	75	125	195
Racer #61	miniature car, tin wind-up, 4-3/4" long, 1930	75	125	195
Racer #7	miniature car, tin wind-up, 5" long, 1948	75	125	195
Racing Car	two man team, tin litho, wind-up, 12" long, 1940	125	200	425
Racing Car	plastic driver, tin wind-up, 27" long, 1950	100	175	450
Roadster	11-1/2" long, 1949	100	150	225
Roadster and Cannon Ball Keeper	wind-up, 9" long	175	250	350
Roadster Convertible with Trailer and Racer	mechanical, 1950	125	200	275
Rocket Racer	tin litho, 1935	275	425	550
Rolls-Royce	black plastic, friction, 6" long, 1955	40	60	80
Royal Coupe	tin litho, wind-up, 9" long, 1930	175	275	375
Secret Sam Agent 012 Car	tin litho, friction, 5" long, 1960s	40	65	165
Sedan	battery-operated, plastic, 9-1/2" long	175	275	350
Sheriff Sam and His Whoopee Car	plastic, tin wind-up, 5-3/4" long, 1949	200	300	475
Siren Police Car	15" long, 1930s	75	125	395
Smokey Sam the Wild Fireman Car	6-1/2" long, 1950	125	200	395
Smokey Stover Whoopee Car	1940s	175	275	525
Snoopy Gus Wild Fireman	7" long, 1926	500	750	1150
Speed Cop	two 4" all tin wind-up cars, track, 1930s	175	275	795
Speed King Racer	tin litho, wind-up, 16" long, 1929	325	500	650
Speed Racer	13" long, 1937	250	375	500
Speedway Coupe	tin wind-up, battery-operated headlights, 8" long, 1938	200	300	400
Speedway Set	two wind-up sedans, figure eight track, 1937	250	375	500
Sports Coupe	tin, 15" long, 1930s	125	200	250
Station Wagon	friction, 11" long, 1950	125	200	325
Station Wagon	green w/woodgrain pattern, wind-up, 7" long, 1950	50	75	250
Station Wagon	litho family of four w/dogs on back windows, 6-3/4" long	60	100	275
Station Wagon	light purple w/woodgrain pattern, wind-up, 7-1/2" long	60	100	275
Streamline Speedway	two tin wind-up racing cars, 1936	175	275	395
Stutz Roadster	driver, 15" long, wind-up, 1928	325	500	750
Super Hot Rod	"777" on rear door, 11" long, 1940s	200	300	400

VEHICLES

NAME	DESCRIPTION	GOOD	EX	MINT
Super Streamlined Racer	tin wind-up, 17" long, 1950s	125	200	400
The Marvel Car, Reversible Coupe	tin wind-up, 1938	125	200	400
Tricky Safety Car	6-1/2" long, 1950	100	150	200
Tricky Taxi	red, black, and white, tin wind-up, 4-1/2" long, 1940s	175	275	375
Tricky Taxi	black/white version, tin wind-up, 4-1/2" long, 1935	160	250	375
Uncle Wiggly, He Goes A Ridin' Car	rabbit driving, tin wind-up, 7-1/2" long, 1935	425	650	850
Walt Disney Television Car	friction, 7-1/2" long, 1950s	125	200	425
Western Auto Track	steel, 24" long	75	125	225
Whoopee Car	witty slogans, tin litho, wind-up, 7-1/2" long, 1930s	375	580	775
Whoopee Cowboy Car	bucking car, cowboy driver, tin wind-up, 7-1/2" long, 1930s	400	600	800
Woody Sedan	tin friction, 7-1/2" long	60	100	225
Yellow Taxi	wind-up, 7" long, 1927	275	425	575
Yogi Bear Car	friction, 1962	50	85	195

Emergency Vehicles

NAME	DESCRIPTION	GOOD	EX	MINT
Ambulance	13-1/2" long, 1937	225	350	650
Ambulance	tin litho, 11" long	125	175	375
Ambulance with Siren	tin wind-up	100	150	400
Army Ambulance	13-1/2" long, 1930s	250	375	750
Boat Tail Racer #2	litho, 13" long, 1948	125	200	425
Chief-Fire Department No. 1 Truck	friction, 1948	60	90	195
Chrome Racer	miniature racer, 5" long, 1937	85	125	250
City Hospital Mack Ambulance	tin litho, wind-up, 10" long, 1927	190	280	500
Electric Car	runs on electric power, license #A7132, 1933	225	325	500
Electric Car	wind-up, 1933	175	250	475
Fire Chief Car	working lights, 16" long	125	200	295
Fire Chief Car	wind-up, 6-1/2" long, 1949	75	125	275
Fire Chief Car	battery-operated headlights, wind-up, 11" long, 1950	100	150	325
Fire Chief Car	friction, loud fire siren, 8" long, 1936	150	250	425
Fire Chief Car with Bell	10-1/2" long, 1940	175	250	450
Fire Engine	sheet iron, 9" long, 1920s	100	175	335
Fire Truck	friction, all metal, 14" long, 1945	90	135	295
Fire Truck	battery-operated, two celluloid firemen, 12" long	50	75	300
Giant King Racer	pale yellow, tin wind-up, 12-1/2" long, 1928	225	325	575
Giant King Racer	red, 13" long, 1941	200	300	550
Giant Mechanical Racer	tin litho, 12-3/4" long, 1948	100	175	350
H.Q. - Staff Car	14-1/2" long, 1930s	325	500	750
Hook and Ladder Fire Truck	three tin litho firemen, 13-1/2" long	90	135	225
Hook and Ladder Fire Truck	plastic ladder on top, 24" long, 1950	90	135	225
Plastic Racer	6" long, 1948	50	75	150
Racer with Plastic Driver	tin litho car, 16" long, 1950	150	225	375
Rocket-Shaped Racer #12	1930s	275	425	600
Siren Fire Chief Car	red car w/siren, 1934	225	325	495
Siren Fire Chief Truck	battery-operated, 15" long, 1930s	100	175	325
Tricky Fire Chief Car	4-1/2" long, 1930s	250	375	625
V.F.D. Emergency Squad	w/ladder, metal, electrically powered, 14" long, 1940s	70	125	200
V.F.D. Fire Engine	w/hoses and siren, 14" long, 1940s	120	180	295
V.F.D. Hook and Ladder Fire Truck	33" long, 1950	140	225	325
War Department Ambulance	1930s	100	150	695

Farm and Construction Equipment

NAME	DESCRIPTION	GOOD	EX	MINT
Aluminum Bulldog Tractor Set	tin wind-up, 9-1/2" long tractor, 1940	250	375	500
American Tractor	w/accessories, tin wind-up, 8" long, 1926	150	225	300
Army Design Climbing Tractor	tin wind-up, 7-1/2" long, 1932	80	120	300
Automatic Steel Barn and Mechanical Plastic Tractor	tin wind-up, 7" long red tractor, 1950	85	125	475
Bulldozer Climbing Tractor	caterpillar type, tin wind-up, 10-1/2" long, 1950s	45	75	295

VEHICLES

NAME	DESCRIPTION	GOOD	EX	MINT
Bulldozer Climbing Tractor	bumper auto, large bumpers, tin wind-up, 1939	50	75	325
Caterpillar Climbing Tractor	yellow tractor, tin wind-up, 9-1/2" long, 1942	75	125	300
Caterpillar Climbing Tractor	orange tractor, tin wind-up, 9-1/2" long, 1942	100	175	325
Caterpillar Tractor and Hydraulic Lift	tin wind-up, 1948	50	75	295
Climbing Tractor	w/driver, tin wind-up, 1920s	50	100	275
Climbing Tractor	tin wind-up, 8-1/4" long, 1930	100	150	325
Climbing Tractor with Chain Pull	tin wind-up, 7-1/2" long, 1929	150	225	350
Co-Op Combine	tin friction, 6"	30	45	95
Construction Tractor	reversing, tin wind-up, 14" long, 1950s	100	150	465
Covered Wagon	friction, tin litho, 9" long	20	30	195
Crawler	w/or without blades and drivers, litho, 1/25 scale, 1950	75	125	150
Crawler with Stake Bed	litho, 1/25 scale, 1950	75	130	175
Farm Tractor and Implement Set	tin wind-up, tractor mower, hayrake, three-gang plow, 1948	200	300	400
Farm Tractor Set	40 pieces, tin wind-up, 1939	325	500	650
Farm Tractor Set and Power Plant	32 pieces, tin wind-up, 1938	200	300	400
Hill Climbing Dump Truck	tin wind-up, 13-1/2" long, 1932	140	210	375
Industrial Tractor Set	orange and red heavy gauge plate tractor, 7-1/2" long, 1930	145	225	395
International Harvester Tractor	diesel, driver and set of tools, 1/12 scale, 1954	75	125	150
Magic Barn and Tractor	plastic tractor, tin litho barn, 1950s	70	100	375
Mechanical Tractor	tin wind-up, 5-1/2" long, 1942	125	200	275
Midget Climbing Tractor	tin wind-up, 5-1/4" long, 1935	125	200	250
Midget Road Building Set	tin wind-up, 5-1/2" long tractor, 1939	200	300	400
Midget Tractor	red metal, tin wind-up, 5-1/4" long, 1940	30	45	125
Midget Tractor	copper color metal, tin wind-up, 5-1/4" long, 1940	40	60	125
Midget Tractor and Plow	tin wind-up, 1937	70	100	225
Midget Tractor with Driver	red metal, tin wind-up, 5-1/4" long, 1940	40	60	220
No. 2 Tractor	red w/black wheels, tin wind-up, 8-1/2" long, 1940	95	150	225
Plastic Sparkling Tractor Set	tin wind-up, 6-1/2" long tractor w/10-1/2" long wagon, 1950	40	60	195
Plastic Tractor with Scraper	tin wind-up, 8" long w/road scraper, 1949	50	75	195
Power Grader	black or white wheels, 17-1/2" long	50	100	125
Power Shovel		50	75	100
Reversible Six-Wheel Farm Tractor-Truck	tin wind-up, 13-3/4" steel tractor, 7-1/2" stake truck, 1950	80	125	425
Reversible Six-Wheel Tractor	red steel tractor, tin wind-up, 11-3/4" long, 1940	200	300	475
Self-Reversing Tractor	tin wind-up, 10" long, 1936	125	200	350
Sparkling Climbing Tractor	tin wind-up, 8-1/2" long, 1950s	100	150	300
Sparkling Climbing Tractor	tin wind-up, 10" long, 1940s	175	275	350
Sparkling Heavy Duty Bulldog Tractor	w/road scraper, tin wind-up, 11" long, 1950s	40	60	225
Sparkling Hi-Boy Climbing Tractor	10-1/2" long, 1950s	25	40	195
Sparkling Tractor	w/driver and trailer, tin wind-up, 16" long, 1950s	60	90	295
Sparkling Tractor	w/plow blade, tin wind-up, 1939	50	75	235
Sparkling Tractor and Trailer Set	"Marborook Farms," tin wind-up, 21" long, 1950s	55	75	255
Steel Farm Tractor and Implements	tin wind-up, 15" long steel bulldozer tractor, 1947	160	240	325
Super Power Reversing Tractor	tin wind-up, 12" long, 1931	100	150	325
Super Power Tractor and Trailer Set	tin wind-up, 8-1/2" tractor, 1937	125	200	375
Super-Power Bulldog Tractor with V-Shaped Plow	aluminum finish, tin wind-up, 1938	75	130	200
Super-Power Climbing Tractor and Nine-Piece Set	tin wind-up, 9-1/2" long tractor, 1942	160	240	395
Super-Power Giant Climbing Tractor	tin wind-up, 13" long, 1939	180	270	450
Tractor	tin wind-up, 8-1/2" long, 1941	100	175	315

VEHICLES

Joy Riders Crazy Car, Marx

Doughboy Tank, Marx

Coca-Cola Truck, Marx

NAME	DESCRIPTION	GOOD	EX	MINT
Tractor	red tractor, tin wind-up, 8-1/2" long, 1941	100	175	300
Tractor and Equipment Set	five pieces, tin wind-up, 16" long tractor, 1949	160	240	320
Tractor and Mower	tin wind-up, 5" long litho steel tractor, 1948	50	75	215
Tractor and Six Implement Set	tin wind-up, 8-1/2" long aluminum tractor, 1948	160	240	425
Tractor and Trailer	tin wind-up, 16-1/2" long, 1950s	40	60	115
Tractor Road Construction Set	36 pieces, tin wind-up, 8-1/2" long tractor, 1938	200	325	595
Tractor Set	five pieces, tin wind-up, 8-1/2" tractor, 1938	90	135	295
Tractor Set	40 pieces, tin wind-up, 8-1/2" long, 1942	300	450	800
Tractor Set	two-pieces, tin wind-up, 19" long steel tractor, 1950	65	100	215
Tractor Set	four pieces, tin wind-up, 8-1/2" long, 1936	100	150	325
Tractor Set	seven pieces, tin wind-up, 8-1/2" long tractor, 1932	125	200	400
Tractor Set	five pieces, tin wind-up, 8-1/2" long tractor, 1935	70	100	220
Tractor Set	32 pieces, tin wind-up, 1937	180	270	450
Tractor Trailer and Scraper	tin wind-up, 8-1/2" long tractor, 1946	80	120	200
Tractor Train with Tractor Shed	tin wind-up, 8-1/2" long, 1936	100	150	220
Tractor with Airplane	wind-up, 5-1/2" long tractor, 27" wingspan on airplane, 1941	250	375	675
Tractor with Driver	wind-up, 1940s	100	150	300
Tractor with Earth Grader	tin wind-up, mechanical, 21-1/2" long, 1950s	40	60	190
Tractor with Plow and Scraper	aluminum tractor, tin wind-up, 1938	70	125	295
Tractor with Plow and Wagon	tin wind-up, 1934	70	125	295
Tractor with Road Scraper	tin wind-up, 8-1/2" long climbing tractor, 1937	90	125	325
Tractor with Scraper	tin wind-up, 8-1/2" long, 1933	70	125	295
Tractor with Trailer and Plow	tin wind-up, 8-1/2" long, 1940	80	120	295
Tractor, Trailer, and V-Shaped Plow	tin wind-up, 8-1/2" steel tractor, 1939	85	125	325
Tractor-Trailer Set	tin wind-up, 8-1/2" long copper-colored tractor, 1939	70	125	295
Yellow and Green Tractor	tin wind-up, 8-1/2" long, 1930	90	135	335

Motorcycles

NAME	DESCRIPTION	GOOD	EX	MINT
Motorcycle Cop	tin litho, mechanical, siren, 8-1/4" long	75	125	235
Motorcycle Delivery Toy	"Speedy Boy Delivery Toy" on rear of cart, tin wind-up, 1932	175	275	500
Motorcycle Delivery Toy	"Speedy Boy Delivery Toy" on side of cart, tin wind-up, 1930s	175	280	525
Motorcycle Police	red uniform on cop, tin wind-up, 8" long, 1930s	125	200	275
Motorcycle Police #3	tin wind-up, 8-1/2" long	100	150	250
Motorcycle Policeman	orange/blue, tin wind-up, 8" long, 1920s	100	150	325
Motorcycle Trooper	tin litho, wind-up, 1935	80	120	275
Mystery Police Cycle	yellow, tin wind-up, 4-1/2" long, 1930s	75	125	225
Mystic Motorcycle	tin litho, wind-up, 4-1/4" long, 1936	75	130	235
P.D. Motorcyclist	tin wind-up, 4" long	40	60	195
Pinched Roadster Motorcycle Cop	in circular track, tin wind-up, 1927	125	200	365
Pluto Motorcycle with Siren	1930s	150	225	550
Police Motorcycle with Sidecar	tin wind-up, 3-1/2" long, 1930s	300	450	750
Police Motorcycle with Sidecar	tin litho, wind-up, 8" long, 1950	175	280	425
Police Motorcycle with Sidecar	tin litho, wind-up, 8" long, 1930s	425	650	950
Police Patrol Motorcycle with Sidecar	tin wind-up, 1935	110	165	400
Police Siren Motorcycle	tin litho, wind-up, 8" long, 1938	150	225	350
Police Squad Motorcycle Sidecar	tin litho, wind-up, 8" long, 1950	100	150	375
Police Tipover Motorcycle	tin litho, wind-up, 8" long, 1933	200	300	525
Rookie Cop	yellow w/driver, tin litho, wind-up, 8" long, 1940	175	275	425
Sparkling Soldier Motorcycle	tin litho, wind-up, 8" long, 1940	175	275	425
Speeding Car and Motorcycle Policeman	tin litho, wind-up, 1939	90	150	350
Tricky Motorcycle	tin wind-up, 4-1/2" long, 1930s	100	150	250

NAME	DESCRIPTION	GOOD	EX	MINT

Tanks

NAME	DESCRIPTION	GOOD	EX	MINT
Anti-Aircraft Tank Outfit	three cardboard tanks	150	225	350
Anti-Aircraft Tank Outfit	four flat metal soldiers, tank, anti-aircraft gun, 1941	90	135	300
Army Tank	sparking climbing tank, tin wind-up, 1940s	150	225	375
Climbing Fighting Tank	tin wind-up	90	135	250
Climbing Tank	tin wind-up, 9-1/2" long, 1930	125	200	325
Doughboy Tank	doughboy pops out, tin litho, wind-up, 9-1/2" long, 1930	150	225	425
Doughboy Tank	sparking tank, tin wind-up, 10" long, 1937	125	200	400
Doughboy Tank	tin wind-up, 10" long, 1942	150	225	450
E12 Tank	makes rat-a-tat-tat or rumbling noise, tin wind-up, 1942	100	150	375
E12 Tank	green tank, 9-1/2" long, tin wind-up, 1942	150	225	375
M48T Tank	battery-operated, 1960s	50	100	225
Midget Climbing Fighting Tank	5-1/2" long, 1937	100	175	375
Midget Climbing Fighting Tank	tin litho, wind-up, 5-1/4" long, 1931	90	135	235
Midget Climbing Fighting Tank	wide plastic wheels, supergrid tread, 5-1/4" long, 1951	100	150	300
Refrew Tank	tin wind-up	75	125	200
Rex Mars Planet Patrol Tank	tin wind-up, 10" long, 1950s	150	225	375
Sparkling Army Tank	tan or khaki hull, tin litho, wind-up, 1938	95	150	235
Sparkling Army Tank	yellow hull, E12 Tank, tin litho, wind-up, 1942,	100	150	300
Sparkling Army Tank	camouflage hull, two olive guns, tin wind-up, 5-1/2" long	100	150	275
Sparkling Army Tank	camouflage hull, two khaki guns, tin wind-up, 5-1/2" long	125	200	325
Sparkling Climbing Tank	tin wind-up, 10" long, 1939	110	165	310
Sparkling Space Tank	tin wind-up, 1950s	250	375	600
Sparkling Super Power Tank	tin wind-up, 9-1/2" long, 1950s	75	125	250
Sparkling Tank	tin wind-up, 4" long, 1948	75	130	195
Superman Turnover Tank	Superman lifts tank, 4" long, tin wind-up, 1940	250	375	600
Tank	pop-up army man shooting	150	225	400
Turnover Army Tank	camouflage, tan or khaki hull, tin wind-up, 1938	175	275	450
Turnover Army Tank	tin wind-up, 9" long, 1930	150	225	375
Turnover Tank	tin litho, wind-up, 4" long, 1942	100	150	275

Trucks

NAME	DESCRIPTION	GOOD	EX	MINT
A & P Supermarket Truck	pressed steel, rubber tires, litho, 19" long	50	100	275
Aero Oil Co. Mack Truck	tin litho, friction, 5-1/2" long, 1930	125	200	350
Air Force Truck	32" long	75	125	300
American Railroad Express Agency Inc. Truck	open cab, 7" long, 1930s	100	150	325
American Truck Co. Mack Truck	friction, 5" long	100	150	225
Armored Trucking Co. Mack Truck	black cab, yellow printing, wind-up, 9-3/4" long	200	300	400
Armored Trucking Co. Truck	tin litho, wind-up, 10" long, 1927	100	150	325
Army Truck	olive drab truck, 4-1/2" long, 1930s	125	200	350
Army Truck	tin, 12" long, 1950	60	90	150
Army Truck	20" long	50	75	125
Army Truck	canvas top, 20" long, 1940s	150	225	325
Army Truck with Rear Benches and Canopy	olive drab paint, 10" long	75	125	225
Artillery Set	three-piece set, 1930	100	150	225
Auto Carrier	two yellow plastic cars, two ramp tracks, 14" long, 1950	125	200	295
Auto Mack Truck	yellow/red, 12" long, 1950	50	75	175
Auto Transport Mack Truck and Trailer	dark blue cab, dark green trailer, wind-up, 11-1/2" long, 1932	150	225	375
Auto Transport Mack Truck and Trailer	medium blue cab, friction, 11-1/2" long, 1932	150	225	425
Auto Transport Mack Truck and Trailer	dark blue cab, wind-up, 11-1/2" long, 1932	150	225	400
Auto Transport Truck	w/three cars, 21" long, 1940	250	375	575

VEHICLES

VEHICLES

NAME	DESCRIPTION	GOOD	EX	MINT
Auto Transport Truck	w/three racing coupes, 22" long, 1933	250	375	525
Auto Transport Truck	w/two plastic sedans, wooden wheels, 13-3/4" long, 1950	75	130	225
Auto Transport Truck	21" long, 1947	175	250	400
Auto Transport Truck	pressed steel, w/two plastic cars, 14" long, 1940	75	125	225
Auto Transport Truck	w/dump truck, roadster and coupe, 30 1/2" long, 1938	275	425	575
Auto Transport Truck	w/three wind-up cars, 22-3/4" long, 1931	250	375	525
Auto Transport Truck	w/two tin litho cars, 34" long, 1950s	60	90	200
Auto Transport Truck	double decker transport truck, 24-1/2" long, 1935	275	425	575
Auto Transwalk Truck	w/three cars, 1930s	175	250	395
Bamberger Mack Truck	dark green, wind-up, 5" long, 1920s	200	300	525
Big Load Van Co. Hauler and Trailer	w/little cartons of products, 12-3/4" long, 1927	200	300	525
Big Load Van Co. Mack Truck	wind-up, 13" long, 1928	225	350	600
Big Shot Cannon Truck	battery-operated, 23" long, 1960s	150	250	325
Cannon Army Mack Truck	9" long, 1930s	175	250	325
Carpenter's Truck	stake bed truck, pressed steel, 14" long, 1940s	175	250	350
Carrier with Three Racers	tin litho, wind-up, 22-3/4" long, 1930	150	225	425
Cement Mixer Truck	red cab, tin finish mixing barrel, 6" long, 1930s	100	150	300
City Coal Co. Mack Dump Truck	14" long, 1934	225	350	525
City Delivery Van	yellow steel truck, 11" long	140	210	280
City Sanitation Dept. "Help Keep Your City Clean" Truck	12-3/4" long, 1940	60	90	250
Coal Truck	3rd version, Lumar Co. truck, 10" long, 1939	150	250	310
Coal Truck	battery-operated, automatic dump, forward and reverse, tin	75	125	175
Coal Truck	1st version, red cab, litho blue and yellow dumper, 12" long	140	225	280
Coal Truck	2nd version, light blue truck, 12" long	140	225	280
Coca-Cola Truck	stamped steel, 20" long, 1940s	175	250	350
Coca-Cola Truck	red steel, 11-1/2" long, 1940s	100	175	250
Coca-Cola Truck	tin, 17" long, 1940s	125	200	250
Coca-Cola Truck	yellow, 20" long, 1950	150	225	300
Contractors and Builders Truck	10" long	125	200	250
Curtiss Candy Truck	red plastic truck, 10" long, 1950	125	200	250
Dairy Farm Pickup Truck	22" long	60	100	150
Delivery Truck	blue truck, 4" long, 1940	100	175	225
Deluxe Delivery Truck	w/six delivery boxes, stamped steel, 13-1/4" long, 1948	100	150	200
Deluxe Trailer Truck	tin and plastic, 14" long, 1950s	70	100	145
Dodge Salerno Engineering Department Truck		600	900	1200
Dump Truck	4-1/2" long, 1930s	100	175	325
Dump Truck	yellow cab, blue bumper, red bed, 18" long, 1950	100	150	200
Dump Truck	red cab, green body, 6-1/4" long	50	75	100
Dump Truck	6" long, 1930s	100	150	250
Dump Truck	motor, tin friction, 12" long, 1950s	50	75	100
Dump Truck	red cab, gray bumper, yellow bed, 18" long, 1950	100	150	200
Emergency Service Truck	friction, tin	125	200	275
Emergency Service Truck	friction, tin, searchlight behind car and siren	150	225	300
Firestone Truck	metal, 14" long, 1950s	50	75	150
Ford Heavy Duty Express Truck	cab w/canopy, 1950s	60	100	175
Gas Truck	green truck, 4" long, 1940	60	90	165
Giant Reversing Tractor Truck	w/tools, tin wind-up, 14" long, 1950s	75	130	350
Gravel Truck	1st version, pressed steel cab, red tin dumper, 10" long, 1930	100	150	250
Gravel Truck	2nd version, metal, 8-1/2" long, 1940s	75	125	200
Gravel Truck	3rd version, metal w/"Gravel Mixer" drum, 10" long, 1930s	100	150	250

Hi Way Express Truck, Marx

Magnetic Crane and Truck, Marx

U.S. Mail Truck, Marx

MARX

NAME	DESCRIPTION	GOOD	EX	MINT
Grocery Truck	cardboard boxes, tinplate and plastic, 14-1/2" long	90	150	225
Guided Missile Truck	blue, red and yellow body, friction, 16" long, 1958	75	125	225
Hi Way Express Truck	metal, 15-1/2" long, 1940s	100	150	225
Hi Way Express Truck	pressed steel	95	150	185
Hi Way Express Truck	tin, tin tires, 16" long, 1940s	50	75	185
Hi Way Express Truck	"Nationwide Delivery," 1950s	100	150	225
Jalopy Pickup Truck	tin wind-up, 7" long	60	90	175
Jeep	11" long, 1946-50	75	130	200
Jeepster	mechanical, plastic	110	165	250
Lazy Day Dairy Farm Pickup Truck and Trailer	22" long	45	75	275
Lincoln Transfer and Storage Co. Mack Truck	wheels have cut-out spokes, tin litho, wind-up, 13" long, 1928	350	525	750
Lone Eagle Oil Co. Mack Truck	bright blue cab, green tank, wind-up, 12" long, 1930	225	350	550
Lumar Contractors Scoop/Dump Truck	17-1/2" long, 1940s	75	125	200
Lumar Lines and Gasoline Set	1948	250	375	725
Lumar Lines Truck	red cab, aluminum finished trailer, 14" long	125	200	300
Lumar Motor Transport Truck	litho, 13" long, 1942	75	130	250
Machinery Moving Truck		60	90	200
Mack Army Truck	friction, 5" long, 1930	125	200	350
Mack Army Truck	khaki brown body, wind-up, 10-1/2" long	125	225	400
Mack Army Truck	13-1/2" long, 1929	225	350	600
Mack Army Truck	pressed steel, wind-up, 7-1/2" long	70	100	250
Mack Dump Truck	dark red cab, medium blue bed, wind-up, 10" long, 1928	150	225	475
Mack Dump Truck	medium blue truck, wind-up, 13" long, 1934	200	300	525
Mack Dump Truck	silver cab, medium blue dump, wind-up, 12-3/4" long, 1936	225	355	525
Mack Dump Truck	no driver, 19" long, 1930	300	450	650
Mack Dump Truck	tin litho, wind-up, 13-1/2" long, 1926	225	350	575
Mack Railroad Express Truck #7	tin, 1930s	75	125	450
Mack Towing Truck	dark green cab, wind-up, 8" long, 1926	175	275	450
Mack U.S. Mail Truck	black body, wind-up, 9-1/2" long	250	375	500
Magnetic Crane and Truck	1950	175	275	350
Mammoth Truck Train	truck w/five trailers, 1930s	150	250	450
Meadowbrook Dairy Truck	14" long, 1940	150	275	375
Mechanical Sand Dump Truck	steel, 1940s	100	150	275
Medical Corps Ambulance Truck	olive drab paint, 1940s	100	150	275
Merchants Transfer Mack Truck	red open-stake truck, 10" long	225	350	450
Merchants Transfer Mack Truck	13-1/3" long, 1928	250	375	600
Military Cannon Truck	olive drab paint, cannon shoots marbles, 10" long, 1939	125	200	250
Milk Truck	white truck, 4" long, 1940	60	90	120
Miniature Mayflower Moving Van	operating lights	60	90	125
Motor Market Truck	10" long, 1939	100	175	225
Navy Jeep	wind-up	50	75	100
North American Van Lines Tractor Trailer	wind-up, 13" long, 1940s	100	175	225
Panel Wagon Truck		30	55	75
Pet Shop Truck	plastic, six compartments w/six vinyl dogs, 11" long	125	200	250
Pickup Truck	blue/yellow w/wood tires, 9" long, 1940s	50	75	150
Polar Ice Co. Ice Truck	13" long, 1940s	100	175	275
Police Patrol Mack Truck	wind-up, 10" long	200	300	475
Popeye Dippy Dumper Truck	Popeye is celluloid, tin wind-up	325	500	800
Pure Milk Dairy Truck	glass bottles, pressed steel, 1940	55	80	250

NAME	DESCRIPTION	GOOD	EX	MINT
Railway Express Agency Truck	green closed van truck, 1940s	90	135	300
Range Rider	tin wind-up, 1930s	250	375	500
RCA Television Service Truck	plastic Ford panel truck, 8-1/2" long, 1948-50	150	225	300
Reversing Road Roller	tin wind-up	60	100	125
Road Builder Tank	1950	125	200	250
Rocker Dump Truck	17-1/2" long	60	90	120
Roy Rogers and Trigger Cattle Truck	metal, 15" long, 1950s	60	100	225
Royal Oil Co. Mack Truck	dark red cab, medium green tank, wind-up, 8-1/4" long, 1927	200	300	500
Royal Van Co. Mack Truck	1927	250	375	600
Royal Van Co. Mack Truck	red cab, tin litho and paint, wind-up, 9" long, 1928	210	315	550
Run Right To Read's Truck	14" long, 1940	125	200	250
Sand and Gravel Truck	"Builder's Supply Co.," tin wind-up, 1920	150	225	400
Sand Truck	9" long, 1948	100	150	200
Sand Truck	tin litho, 12-1/2" long, 1940s	125	200	275
Sand-Gravel Dump Truck	tin litho, 12" long, 1950	150	225	300
Sand-Gravel Dump Truck	blue cab, yellow dump w/"Gravel" on side, tin, 1930s	140	225	285
Sanitation Truck	1940s	135	200	270
Searchlight Truck	pressed steel, 9-3/4" long, 1930s	160	250	325
Side Dump Truck	1940	90	130	275
Side Dump Truck	10" long, 1930s	140	225	280
Side Dump Truck and Trailer	15" long, 1935	150	225	300
Sinclair Tanker	tin, 14" long, 1940s	150	225	300
Stake Bed Truck	red cab, blue stake bed, 6" long, 1930s	75	125	150
Stake Bed Truck	red cab, yellow and red trailer, 14" long	100	150	200
Stake Bed Truck	medium blue cab, red stake bed, 10" long, 1940	75	130	185
Stake Bed Truck	red cab, green stake bed, 20" long, 1947	100	150	200
Stake Bed Truck	rubber stamped chicken on one side of truck, bunny on other	100	150	200
Stake Bed Truck	pressed steel, wooden wheels, 7" long, 1936	60	90	200
Stake Bed Truck and Trailer	red truck, silver stake bed	125	200	250
Streamline Mechanical Hauler, Van, and Tank Truck Combo	heavy gauge steel, 10 3/8" long, 1936	170	275	350
Sunshine Fruit Growers Truck	red cab, yellow/white trailer w/blue roof, 14" long	100	150	225
Tipper Dump Truck	wind-up, 9-3/4" long, 1950	75	130	175
Tow Truck	red cab, yellow towing unit, 6" long, 1930s	137	200	275
Tow Truck	10" long, 1935	125	200	250
Tow Truck	aluminum finish, wind-up, 6-1/4" long	95	150	190
Tow Truck	aluminum finsih, tin litho wind-up, 6-1/4" long	75	125	150
Toyland Dairy Truck	10" long	140	210	280
Toyland's Farm Products Mack Milk Truck	w/12 wooden milk bottles, 10-1/4" long, 1931	200	300	400
Toytown Express Truck	plastic cab	45	70	95
Tractor Trailer with Dumpster	blue/yellow hauler, tan dumpster	125	200	250
Truck Train	stake hauler and five trailers, 41" long, 1933	250	400	525
Truck Train	stake hauler and four trailers, 41" long, 1938	350	550	725
Truck with Electric Lights	battery-operated lights, 10" long, 1935	125	200	375
Truck with Electric Lights	15" long, 1930s	110	165	300
Truck with Searchlight	toolbox behind cab, 10" long, 1930s	150	225	400
U.S. Air Force Willy's Jeep	tin body, plastic figures	70	100	140
U.S. Army Jeep with Trailer		100	150	200
U.S. Mail Truck	metal, 14" long, 1950s	225	350	450
U.S. Trucking Co. Mack Truck	dark maroon cab, friction, 5-1/2" long, 1930	100	150	200
Van Truck	plastic, 10" long, 1950s	40	60	80
Western Auto Truck	steel, 25" long	60	90	125
Willy's Jeep	steel, 12" long, 1938	125	200	250
Willy's Jeep and Trailer	1940s	100	160	215
Wrecker Truck	1930s	145	225	290

VEHICLES

NO.	NAME	DESCRIPTION	GOOD	EX	MINT
	London E Class Tramcar	red, cream roof; News of the World decals,	25	60	90
	"B" Type London Bus	red w/black driver; black wheels; eight over four side windows; Dewar's labels,	45	60	85
1	Aveling Barford Road Roller	green body, canopy, tow hook, 2-5/8", 1962	7	10	15
1	Diesel Road Roller	dark green body, flat canopy, tow hook, driver, 1-7/8", 1953	15	25	35
1	Dodge Challenger	red body, white plastic top, silver interior, wide five spoke wheels, 2-15/16", 1976	3	5	8
1	Mercedes-Benz Lorry	metallic gold, removable orange or yellow canopy, 3", 1970	4	6	8
1	Mercedes-Benz Lorry	pale green body, removable orange plastic canopy, 3", 1967	5	7	15
1	Mod Rod	yellow body, tinted windows, red or black wheels, 2-7/8", 1971	10	15	20
1	Revin' Rebel	orange body, blue top, black interior, large five-spoke rear wheels, 1982	2	3	5
1	Road Roller	light green or dark green body, canopy, metal rollers, tow bar, driver, 2-3/8", 1958	20	25	35
1	Road Roller	pale green body, canopy, tow hook, dark tan or light tan driver, 2-1/4", 1953	25	45	65
2	Dumper	green body, red dumper, gold trim, thin driver, green painted wheels, 1-5/8", 1953	35	50	70
2	Dumper	green body, red dumper, no trim color, fat driver, 1-7/8", 1957	20	30	40
2	Hovercraft	metallic green top, tan base, silver engine, yellow windows, 3-1/8", 1976	4	8	12
2	Jeep Hot Rod	cream seats and tow hook, wide four-spoke wheels, 2-5/16", 1971	7	10	15
2	Mercedes-Benz Trailer	pale green body, removable orange canopy, tow hook, black plastic wheels, 3 1/2", 1968	5	7	15
2	Mercedes-Benz Trailer	metallic gold body, removable canopy, rotating tow bar, 3-1/4", 1970	3	5	15
2	Muirhill Dumper	red cab, green dumper, black plastic wheels, 2-1/6", 1961	10	20	25
3	Bedford Ton Tipper	gray cab, gray wheels, dual rear wheels, 2-1/2", 1961	10	15	20
3	Cement Mixer	blue body and rotating barrel, orange metal wheels, 1-5/8", 1953	25	35	45
3	Mercedes-Benz Ambulance	ivory interior, Red Cross label on side doors, 2-7/8", 1970	5	10	15
3	Monteverdi Hai	dark orange body, blue tinted windows, ivory interior, 2-7/8", 1973	3	6	8
3	Porsche Turbo	metallic brown body, black base, yellow interior, wide five-arch wheels, 3", 1978	4	7	10
4	1957 Chevy	metallic rose body, chrome interior, large five-arch rear wheels, 2-15/16", 1979	2	8	12
4	Gruesome Twosome	metallic gold body, wide five-spoke wheels, 2-7/8", 1971	5	7	10
4	Massey Harris Tractor	red body w/rear fenders, tan driver, four spoke metal front wheels, 1954	30	40	55
4	Massey Harris Tractor	red body, no fenders, tan driver, solid metal front wheels, hollow inside rear wheels, 1-5/8", 1957	25	40	50
4	Pontiac Firebird	metallic blue body, silver interior, slick tires, 2-7/8", 1975	2	7	12
4	Stake Truck	yellow cab, green tinted windows, 2-7/8", 1967	5	10	30
4	Stake Truck	cab colors vary, 2-7/8", 1970	5	7	15
4	Triumph Motorcycle and Sidecar	silver/blue body, wire wheels, 2-1/8", 1960	25	40	60
5	Jeep 4x4 Golden Eagle	brown body, wide four-spoke wheels, eagle decal on hood, 1982,	2	5	8
5	London Bus	red body, 2-1/4", 1957	20	45	65
5	London Bus	red body, white plastic seats, black plastic wheels, 2-3/4", 1965	5	10	30

NO.	NAME	DESCRIPTION	GOOD	EX	MINT
5	London Bus	red body, gold grille, metal wheels, 2", 1954	20	45	65
5	London Bus	red body, silver grille and headlights, 2-9/16", 1961	10	20	25
5	Lotus Europa	metallic blue body, clear windows, ivory interior and tow hook, 2-7/8", 1969	5	7	10
5	Seafire Boat	white deck, blue hull, silver engine, red pipes, 2-15/16", 1975	6	8	10
5	U.S. Mail Jeep	blue body, white base and bumpers, black plastic seat, white canopy, wide five-arch rear wheel, 2-3/8", 1978	5	10	15
6	Euclid Quarry Truck	yellow body, three round axles, two front black plastic wheels, two solid rear dual wheels, 2-5/8", 1964	15	25	30
6	Euclid Quarry Truck	yellow body, four ribs on dumper sides, plastic wheels, 2-1/2", 1957	10	20	25
6	Ford Pick-up	red body, white removable canopy, five spoke wheels, 2-3/4", 1970	5	7	15
6	Ford Pick-up	red body, white removable plastic canopy, four black plastic wheels, 2-3/4", 1968	10	15	20
6	Mercedes-Benz 350 SL	orange body, black plastic convertible top, light yellow interior, 3", 1973	5	10	20
6	Quarry Truck	orange cab, gray dumper w/six vertical ribs, metal wheels, 2-1/8", 1954	15	30	50
7	Ford Anglia	blue body, green tinted windows,, 2-5/8", 1961	10	15	30
7	Ford Refuse Truck	orange cab, gray plastic dumper, silver metal loader, 3", 1966	7	10	15
7	Ford Refuse Truck	gray plastic body, silver metal dumper, 3", 1970	6	8	15
7	Hairy Hustler	metallic bronze, silver interior, five-spoke front wheels, cloverleaf rear wheels, 2-7/8", 1971	5	7	10
7	Horse Drawn Milk Float	orange body, white driver and bottle load, brown horse w/white mane and hoofs, 2-1/4", 1954	25	55	90
7	Rompin' Rabbit	white body, red windows, yellow lettered "Rompin Rabbit" on side, 1982	2	3	5
7	Volkswagen Golf	green body, black base and grille, 2-7/8", 1976	4	8	12
8	Caterpillar Tractor	yellow body, no driver, plastic rollers, rubber treads, rounded axles, 2", 1964	10	15	20
8	Caterpillar Tractor	yellow body and driver, large smoke stack, metal rollers, rubber treads, crimped axles, 1-5/8", 1959	20	35	45
8	Caterpillar Tractor	driver has same color hat as body, metal rollers, rubber treads, crimped axles, 1-1/2", 1955	40	60	80
8	Ford Mustang	wide five spoke wheels, interior and tow hook are the same color, 2-7/8", 1970	10	25	50
8	Ford Mustang Fastback	white body, red interior, clear windows, 2-7/8", 1966	7	10	30
8	Pantera	white body, blue base, red/brown interior, five-spoke rear slicks, 3", 1975	35	45	60
9	Boat and Trailer	white hull, blue deck, clear windows, five-spoke wheels on trailer, 3-1/4", 1970	3	5	20
8	Caterpillar Tractor	yellow body and driver, large smoke stack, metal rollers, rubber treads, rounded axles, 1-7/8", 1961	10	15	25
9	Boat and Trailer	white hull, blue deck, clear windows, five-spoke wheels on trailer, 3-1/4", 1966	4	6	15
9	Dennis Fire Escape Engine	red body, metal wheels, no front bumper, 2-1/4", 1955	10	20	30
9	Fiat Abarth	white body, red interior, 1982,	2	3	5
9	Ford Escort RS2000	white body, black base and grille, tan interior, wide multispoke wheels, 3", 1978	3	5	7
9	Merryweather Marquis Fire Engine	1959	15	25	40
10	Mechanical Horse and Trailer	red cab w/three metal wheels, gray trailer w/two metal wheels, 2-3/8", 1955	15	25	35
10	Mechanical Horse and Trailer	red cab, ribbed bed in trailer, metal front wheels on cab, 2-15/16", 1958	25	35	45
10	Pipe Truck	red body, gray pipes, "Leyland" or "Ergomatic" on front base, eight black plastic wheels, 2-7/8", 1966	7	10	15
10	Pipe Truck	black pipe racks, eight thin five-spoke wheels, 2-7/8", 1970	4	6	15

VEHICLES

1 Ton Trojan Van, No. 47, Matchbox. Photo Courtesy Gary Linden

10 Ton Pressure Refueller, No. 73, 1959, Matchbox. Photo Courtesy Gary Linden

NO.	NAME	DESCRIPTION	GOOD	EX	MINT
10	Piston Popper	metallic blue body, white interior, 2-7/8", 1973	4	6	8
10	Plymouth Gran Fury Police Car	white body w/black detailing, "Police" on doors, white interior, 3", 1979	3	4	5
10	Sugar Container Truck	blue body, eight gray plastic wheels, "Tate & Lyle" decals on sides and rear, 2-5/8", 1961	30	55	75
11	Cobra Mustang	orange body, "The Boss" on doors, 1982	2	3	5
11	Flying Bug	metallic red, gray windows, small five-spoke front wheels, large five spoke rear wheels, 2-7/8", 1972	5	7	10
11	Jumbo Crane	yellow body, black plastic wheels, 3", 1965	5	10	15
11	Scaffolding Truck	silver body, green tinted windows, black plastic wheels, 2-1/2", 1969	4	7	25
11	Road Tanker	red body, gas tanks, "11" on baseplate, black plastic wheels, 2-1/2", 1958	20	55	80
11	Scaffolding Truck	silver/gray body, green tinted windows, yellow pipes, 2-7/8", 1969	5	10	25
11	Road Tanker	green body, flat base between cab and body, gold trim on front grille, gas tanks, metal wheels, no number cast, 2", 1955	60	265	360
12	Safari Land Rover	metallic gold, clear windows, tan luggage, thin five-spoke wheels, 2-13/16", 1970	10	20	30
12	Big Bull	orange body, green plow blade, base and sides, chrome seat and engine, orange rollers, 2-1/2", 1975	4	6	8
12	Setra Coach	clear windows, ivory interior, thin five-spoke thin wheels, 3", 1970	5	7	10
12	Safari Land Rover	clear windows, white plastic interior and tow hook, black plastic wheels, 2-1/3", 1965	7	10	20
12	Citroen CX	metallic body, silver base and lights, blue plastic hatch door, 3", 1979	4	8	12
12	Land Rover	olive green body, no driver, tow hook, 2-1/4", 1959	35	55	75
12	Land Rover	olive green body, tan driver, metal wheels, 1-3/4", 1955	20	25	35
13	Dodge Wreck Truck	green and yellow body, 1970,	10	15	25
13	Baja Dune Buggy	metallic green, orange interior, silver motor, 2-5/8", 1971	3	4	6
13	Snorkel Fire Engine	red body, yellow plastic snorkel and fireman, 3", 1977	3	5	7
13	Dodge Wreck Truck	yellow cab, rear body, red plastic hook, green windows, 3", 1970	10	15	40
13	Thames Wreck Truck	red body, bumper and parking lights, 2-1/2", 1961	15	25	30
13	Bedford Wreck Truck	tan body, red metal crane and hook, 2", 1955	30	40	55
13	Bedford Wreck Truck	tan body, red metal crane and hook, crane attached to rear axle, 2-1/8", 1958	30	45	60
13	Dodge Wreck Truck	green cab and crane, yellow body, green windows, 3", 1965	300	500	700
14	Iso Grifo	blue body, light blue interior and tow hook, clear windows, 3", 1968	5	7	15
14	Rallye Royal	metallic pearl gray body, black plastic interior, wide five-spoke wheels, 2-7/8", 1973	3	4	5
14	Daimler Ambulance	silver trim, "AMBULANCE" cast on sides, red cross on roof, 2-5/8", 1958	40	65	85
14	Bedford Ambulance	white body, silver trim, two opening rear doors, 2-5/8", 1962	15	60	80
14	Mini Haha	red body, pink driver, silver engine, large spoke rear slicks, 2-3/8", 1975	5	9	12
14	Daimler Ambulance	cream body, silver trim, no number cast on body, "AMBULANCE" cast on sides, 1-7/8", 1956	20	35	45
14	Iso Grifo	five-spoke wheels, clear windows, 3", 1969	5	10	15
15	Atlantic Tractor Super	orange body, tow hook, spare wheel behind cab on body, 2-5/8", 1959	15	30	40
15	Hi Ho Silver	metallic pearl gray body, 2-1/2", 1971	7	10	15
15	Refuse Truck	blue body, gray dumper w/opening door, 2-1/2", 1963	10	15	20
15	Volkswagen 1500 Saloon	off white body and interior, clear windows, "137" on doors, 2-7/8", 1968	10	20	30
15	Fork Lift Truck	red body, yellow hoist, 2-1/2", 1972	3	4	6

VEHICLES

NO.	NAME	DESCRIPTION	GOOD	EX	MINT
15	Volkswagen 1500 Saloon	clear windows, "137" on doors, red decal on front, 2-7/8", 1968	7	15	20
15	Prime Mover	silver trim on grille and tank, tow hook same color as body, 2-1/8", 1956	20	35	50
16	Atlantic Trailer	orange body, eight gray plastic wheels w/knobby treads, 3-1/4", 1957	15	50	80
16	Badger Exploration Truck	metallic red body, silver grille, 2-1/4", 1974	3	4	6
16	Scammel Mountaineer Dump Truck/Snow Plow	gray cab, orange dumper body, six plastic wheels, 3", 1964	10	20	25
16	Atlantic Trailer	tan body, six metal wheels, tan tow bar, 3-1/8", 1956	15	25	35
16	Case Tractor Bulldozer	red body, yellow base, motor and blade, black plastic rollers, 2-1/2", 1969	5	9	12
16	Pontiac Trans Am	white body, red interior, clear windows, blue eagle decal, 1982	2	3	4
17	Austin Taxi Cab	maroon body, 2-1/4", 1960	35	50	70
17	Hoveringham Tipper	red body, orange dumper, 2-7/8", 1963	7	10	25
17	Bedford Removals Van	maroon body, peaked roof, gold grille, 2-1/8", 1956	35	115	150
17	Horse Box, Ergomatic Cab	red cab, green plastic box, gray side door, 1969	10	15	20
17	Horse Box	blue tinted windows, thin five-spoke wheels, white plastic horses inside box, 2-3/4", 1970	5	10	15
17	Londoner Bus	red body, white interior, wide five-spoke wheels, 3", 1972	10	15	20
18	Hondarora Motorcycle	red frame and fenders chrome bars, fork, engine, black seat, 2-3/8", 1975	5	15	25
18	Caterpillar Bulldozer	yellow body w/driver, green rubber treads, 2-1/4", 1961	10	15	25
18	Field Car	yellow body, tan roof, red wheels, ivory interior and tow hook, 2-5/8", 1970	5	7	20
18	Field Car	yellow body, tan plastic roof, ivory interior and tow hook, green plastic tires, 2-5/8", 1969	50	145	200
18	Caterpillar D8 Bulldozer	yellow body and driver, red blade and side supports, 1-7/8", 1956	25	35	45
18	Caterpillar Bulldozer	yellow body and driver, yellow blade, No. 18 cast on back of blade, metal rollers, 2", 1958	30	45	65
18	Caterpillar Crawler Bulldozer	yellow body, no driver, green rubber treads, 2-3/8", 1964	30	45	60
19	Lotus Racing Car	white driver, large rear wheels, 2-3/4", 1966	10	15	20
19	Lotus Racing Car	metallic purple, white driver, wide five-spoke wide wheels w/cloverleaf design, 2-3/4", 1970	5	10	15
19	Aston Martin Racing Car	metallic green, metal steering wheel and wire wheels, black plastic tires, 2-1/2", 1961	10	30	45
19	MG Midget	silver or gold grilles, tan driver, 2-1/4", 1958	20	45	75
19	Road Dragster	ivory interior, silver plastic motor, 2-7/8", 1970	3	4	6
19	MG Midget	white body, tan driver, red seats, spare tire on trunk, 2", 1956	30	60	75
19	MGA Sports Car	white body variation, silver wheels, tan driver, silver or gold grilles, 2-1/4", 1958	50	95	125
19	Cement Truck	red body, yellow plastic barrel w/red stripes, large wide arch wheels, 3", 1976	4	5	7
19	Peterbilt Cement Truck	green body, orange barrel, "Big Pete" decal on hood, 1982	2	3	5
20	Chevrolet Impala Taxi Cab	orange/yellow or bright yellow body, ivory or red interior and driver, 3", 1965	10	15	20
20	Desert Dawg Jeep 4x4	white body, red top and stripes, white "Jeep" and yellow, red and green, "Desert Dawg" decal, 1982	2	3	5
20	ERF 686 Truck	dark blue body, silver radiator, eight plastic silver wheels, No. 20 cast on black base, 2-5/8", 1959	25	45	60
20	Lamborghini Marzel	amber windows, ivory interior, 2-3/4", 1969	15	20	35
20	Police Patrol	white body, "Police" on orange side stripe, orange interior, 2-7/8", 1975	6	8	12

VEHICLES

*Bedford Compressor Truck, No. 28, 1956, Matchbox. Photo
Courtesy Gary Linden*

Bedford Dunlop Truck, No. 25, 1956, Matchbox

NO.	NAME	DESCRIPTION	GOOD	EX	MINT
20	Stake Truck	gold trim on front grille and side gas tanks, ribbed bed, metal wheels, 2-3/8", 1956	50	75	100
21	Commer Milk Truck	pale green body, clear or green tinted windows, ivory or cream bottle load, 2-1/4", 1961	20	30	40
21	Foden Concrete Truck	orange/yellow body and rotating barrel, green tinted windows, eight plastic wheels, 3", 1968	3	5	15
21	Foden Concrete Truck	red body, orange barrel, green base and windows, five-spoke wheels, 2-7/8", 1970	2	10	20
21	Long Distance Coach	green body, black base, "No. 21" cast on baseplate, "London to Glasgow" orange decal on sides, 2-5/8", 1958	20	60	45
21	Long Distance Coach	light green body, black base, "London to Glasgow" orange decal on sides, 2-1/4", 1956	10	20	25
21	Renault 5TL	yellow body and removable rear hatch, tan interior, silver base and grille, 2-11/16", 1978	4	9	15
21	Road Roller	yellow body, red seat, black plastic rollers, 2-5/8", 1973	7	10	15
22	Blaze Buster	red body, silver interior, yellow label, five-spoke slicks, 3", 1975	4	6	8
22	Freeman Inter-City Commuter	clear windows, ivory interior, wide five-spoke wheels, 3", 1970	5	7	10
22	Pontiac Grand Prix Sports Coupe	light gray interior and tow hook, clear windows, four black plastic wheels, 3", 1964	6	9	12
22	Pontiac Grand Prix Sports Coupe	light gray interior, clear windows, thin five-spoke wheels, 3", 1970	2	4	6
22	Vauxhall Cresta	w/or without silver grille, tow hook, plastic wheels, 2-5/8", 1958	20	40	60
22	Vauxhall Sedan	dark red body, cream or off-white roof, tow hook, 2-1/2", 1956	15	30	45
23	Atlas Truck	metallic blue cab, silver interior, orange dumper, red and yellow labels on doors, 3", 1975	6	8	10
23	Audi Quattro	white body, red and black print sides, clear windows, "Audi Sport" on doors, 1982	2	3	5
23	Berkeley Cavalier Trailer	decal on lower right rear of trailer, metal wheels, flat tow hook, 2-1/2", 1956	10	30	40
23	Bluebird Dauphine Trailer	green w/gray plastic wheels, decal on lower right rear of trailer, opening door on left rear side, 2-1/2", 1960	45	135	200
23	GT 350	white body, blue stripes on hood, roof and rear deck, 2-7/8", 1970	3	4	5
23	Trailer Caravan	yellow or pink body w/white roof, blue removable interior, 2-7/8", 1965	4	7	15
23	Volkswagen Camper	orange top, clear windows, five-spoke wheels, 2-1/8", 1970	5	7	10
24	Datsun 280ZX	black body and base, clear windows, five-spoke wheels, 2-7/8", 1979	2	3	5
24	Rolls-Royce Silver Shadow	metallic red body, ivory interior, clear windows, silver hub caps or solid silver wheels, 3", 1967	10	15	20
24	Rolls-Royce Silver Shadow	ivory interior, clear windows, five-spoke wheels, 3", 1970	5	7	20
24	Shunter	metallic green body, red base, tan instruments, no window, 3", 1978	3	5	7
24	Team Matchbox	white driver, silver motor, wide cloverleaf wheels, 2-7/8", 1973	15	20	25
24	Weatherhill Hydraulic Excavator	metal wheels, "Weatherhill Hydraulic" decal on rear, 2-3/8", 1956	20	25	35
24	Weatherhill Hydraulic Excavator	yellow body, small and medium front wheels, large rear wheels, 2-5/8", 1959	10	15	20
25	Bedford Dunlop Truck	dark blue body, silver grille, 2-1/8", 1956	10	25	50
25	BP Petrol Tanker	yellow hinged cab, white tanker body, six black plastic wheels, 3" lon, 1964	8	15	20
25	Celica GT	blue body, black base, white racing stripes and "78" on roof and doors, 2-15/16", 1978	3	7	12

VEHICLES

NO.	NAME	DESCRIPTION	GOOD	EX	MINT
25	Celica GT	yellow body, blue interior, red "Yellow Fever" on hood, side racing stripes, clear windows, large rear wheels, 1982	2	4	6
25	Ford Cortina	clear windows, ivory interior and tow hook, thin five-spoke wheels, 2-3/4", 1970	3	6	10
25	Ford Cortina G.T.	light brown body in various shade, ivory interior and tow hook, 2-7/8", 1968	4	7	10
25	Mod Tractor	metallic purple, orange/yellow seat and tow hook, 2-1/8", 1972	10	15	20
25	Volkswagen 1200 Sedan	silver-blue body, clear or tinted windows, 2-1/2", 1960	20	40	55
26	Big Banger	red body, blue windows, small front wheels, large rear wheels, 3", 1972	4	6	8
26	Cosmic Blues	white body, blue "COSMIC BLUES" and stars on sides, 2-7/8", 1970	2	3	4
26	Foden Ready Mix Concrete Truck	orange body, gray plastic rotating barrel, w/or without silver grille, six gray wheels, 2-1/4", 1961	60	130	180
26	Foden Ready Mix Concrete Truck	orange body and rotating barrel, silver or gold grille, four silver plastic wheels, 1-3/4",, 1956	50	100	140
26	GMC Tipper Truck	red cab, silver/gray tipper body, wide four-spoke wheels, 2-1/2", 1970	10	15	20
26	GMC Tipper Truck	red tipping cab, silver tipper body w/swinging door, four wheels, 2-5/8", 1968	5	7	20
26	Site Dumper	yellow body and dumper, black base, 2-5/8", 1976	2	3	5
27	Bedford Low Loader	light blue cab, dark blue trailer, silver grille and side gas tanks, four metal wheels on cab, two metal wheels on trailer, 3-1/8", 1956	100	350	450
27	Bedford Low Loader	green cab, tan trailer, silver grille, four gray wheels on cab, two wheels on trailer, 3-3/4", 1959	20	55	75
27	Cadillac Sedan	w/or without silver grille, clear windows, white roof, silver wheels, 2-3/4", 1960	15	30	40
27	Lamborghini Countach	yellow body, silver interior and motor, five-spoke wheels, 2-7/8", 1973	5	7	10
27	Mercedes-Benz 230 SL	unpainted metal grille, red plastic interior and tow hook, black plastic wheels, 3", 1966	5	10	20
27	Mercedes-Benz 230 SL	metal grille, blue tinted windshield, five-spoke wheels, 2-7/8", 1970	5	10	20
27	Swing Wing Jet	red top and fins, white belly and retractable wings, 3", 1981	2	3	5
28	Bedford Compressor Truck	silver front and rear grilles, metal wheels, 1-3/4", 1956	15	35	45
28	Formula Racing Car	gold body, silver engine and pipes, white driver and "Champion," black "8" on front and sides, large cloverleaf rear wheels, 1982	2	3	5
28	Jaguar Mark 10	light brown body, off-white interior, working hood, gray motor and wheels, 2-3/4", 1964	35	65	90
28	Lincoln Continental MK-V	red body, tan interior, 3", 1979	10	15	20
28	Mack Dump Truck	pea green body, green windows, large balloon wheels w/cloverleaf design, 2-5/8", 1970	2	5	15
28	Mack Dump Truck	orange body, green windows, four large plastic wheels, 2-5/8", 1968	4	7	15
28	Stroat Armored Truck	metallic gold body, brown plastic observer coming out of turret, wide five-spoke wheels, 2-5/8", 1974	8	15	25
28	Thames Trader Compressor Truck	yellow body, black wheels, 2-3/4", 1959	20	25	35
29	Austin A55 Cambridge Sedan	two-tone green, light green roof and rear top half of body, dark metallic green hood and lower body, 2-3/4", 1961	10	20	25
29	Bedford Milk Delivery Van	tan body, white bottle load, 2-1/4", 1956	15	25	30
29	Fire Pumper Truck	red body, metal grille, white plastic hose and ladders, 3", 1966	3	7	20
29	Fire Pumper Truck	red body, metal grille, white plastic hose and ladders, 3", 1970	2	5	20

VEHICLES

BP Petrol Tanker, No. 25, 1964, Matchbox

Coca-Cola Lorry, No. 37, 1960, Matchbox

NO.	NAME	DESCRIPTION	GOOD	EX	MINT
29	Racing Mini	clear windows, wide five-spoke wheels, 2-1/4", 1970	5	7	10
29	Shovel Nose Tractor	yellow body and base, red plastic shovel, silver engine, 2-7/8", 1976	8	15	20
30	6-Wheel Crane Truck	silver body, orange crane, metal or plastic hook, gray wheels, 2-5/8", 1961	20	30	40
30	8-Wheel Crane Truck	green body, orange crane, red or yellow hook, eight black wheels on four axles, 3", 1965	15	20	25
30	8-Wheel Crane Truck	red body, yellow plastic hook, thin five-spoke wheels, 3", 1970	5	7	10
30	Articulated Truck	blue cab, white grille, silver/gray dumper, five-spoke accent wheels, 3", 1981	3	5	6
30	Beach Buggy	pink, yellow paint splatters, clear windows, 2-1/2", 1970	3	4	6
30	Ford Prefect	blue body, metal wheels, silver grille, black tow hook, 2-1/4", 1956	20	60	90
30	Peterbilt Quarry Truck	yellow body, gray dumper, silver tanks, "Dirty Dumper" on sides, six wheels, 1982	2	4	6
30	Swamp Rat	green deck, yellow plastic hull, tan soldier, black engine and prop, 3", 1976	2	4	6
31	Ford Customline Station Wagon	yellow body, no windows, w/or without red painted tail lights, 2-5/8", 1957	20	30	40
31	Ford Fairlane Station Wagon	green or clear windows, w/or without red painted tail lights, 2-3/4", 1960	10	30	35
31	Lincoln Continental	clear windows, ivory interior, five-spoke wheels, 2-3/4", 1970	5	10	30
31	Lincoln Continental	clear windows, ivory interior, black plastic wheels, 2-7/8", 1964	10	15	20
31	Mazda RX-7	gray body w/sunroof, black interior, 1982	15	25	35
31	Mazda RX-7	white body, black base, burgundy stripe, black "RX-7", 3", 1979	3	4	5
31	Volks Dragon	red body, purple tinted windows, 2-1/2", 1971	3	4	5
32	Atlas Extractor	red/orange body, gray platform, turret and treads, black wheels, 3", 1981	2	4	6
32	Jaguar XK 140 Coupe	w/or without silver grille, w/or without red painted taillights, 2-3/8", 1957	20	30	40
32	Jaguar XKE	metallic red body, ivory interior, clear or tinted windows, 2-5/8", 1962	15	20	35
32	Leyland Petrol Tanker	green cab, white tank body, blue tinted windows, eight plastic wheels, 3", 1968	25	40	50
32	Leyland Petrol Tanker	green cab, white tank body, blue tinted windows, thin five-spoke wheels, 3", 1970	10	20	50
32	Maserati Bora	metallic burgundy, clear windows, bright yellow interior, wide five-spoke wheels, 3", 1972	5	7	10
33	Datsun or 126X	yellow body, amber windows, silver interior, 3", 1973	5	8	10
33	Ford Zephyr 6MKIII	blue/green body shades, clear windows, ivory interior, 2-5/8", 1963	15	20	30
33	Ford Zodiac MKII Sedan	w/or without silver grille, w/or without red painted taillights, 2-5/8", 1957	20	30	45
33	Lamborghini Miura	clear windows, frosted rear window, five-spoke wheels, 2-3/4", 1970	25	40	50
33	Lamborghini Miura	metal grille, silver plastic wheels, red or white interior, clear or frosted back window, 2-3/4", 1969	10	15	20
33	Police Motorcyclist	white frame, seat and bags, silver engine and pipes, wire wheels, 2-1/2", 1977	5	7	10
34	Chevy Pro Stocker	white body, red interior, clear front and side windows, frosted rear window, 3", 1981	2	3	5
34	Formula 1 Racing Car	metallic pink, white driver, clear glass, wide four-spoke wheels, 2-7/8", 1971	7	10	15
34	Vantastic	orange body, white base and interior, silver engine, large rear slicks, 2-7/8", 1975	4	7	9
34	Volkswagen Camper Car	silver body, orange interior, black plastic wheels, raised roof, six windows, 2-5/8", 1967	15	20	30
34	Volkswagen Camper Car	silver body, orange interior, black plastic wheels, short raised sun roof, 2-5/8", 1968	10	20	25
34	Volkswagen Microvan	blue body, gray wheels, "Matchbox International Express" on sides, 2-1/4", 1957	30	40	50

NO.	NAME	DESCRIPTION	GOOD	EX	MINT
34	Volkswagen Microvan	light green body, dark green interior, flat roof, green tinted green window, 2-3/5", 1962	20	30	40
35	Fandango	white body, red interior, chrome rear engine, large five-spoke rear wheels, 3", 1975	3	5	8
35	Marshall Horse Box	red cab, brown horse box, silver grille, three rear windows in box, 2", 1957	20	25	35
35	Merryweather Fire Engine	metallic red body, blue windows, white removable ladder on roof, thin five-spoke wheels, 3", 1969	5	7	10
35	Pontiac Trans Am T Roof	black body, red interior, yellow "Turbo" on doors, yellow eagle on hood, 1982	2	3	5
35	Snowtrac Tractor	red body, silver painted grille, green windows, white rubber treads, 2-3/8", 1964	10	15	20
35	Zoo Truck	1981	4	7	10
36	Austin A50	silver grille, w/or without silver rear bumper, no windows, 2-3/8", 1957	15	20	30
36	Formula 5000	orange body, silver rear engine, large cloverleaf rear slicks, 3", 1975	5	7	10
36	Hot Rod Draguar	metallic red body, clear canopy, wide five-spoke wheels, 2-13/16", 1970	4	6	8
36	Lambretta TV 175 Motor Scooter and Sidecar	metallic green, three wheels, 2", 1961	25	35	45
36	Opel Diplomat	ivory interior and tow hook, clear windows, thin five-spoke wheels, 2-7/8", 1970	5	7	15
36	Opel Diplomat	metallic light gold body, white interior and tow hook, clear windows, black plastic wheels, 2-3/5", 1966	10	15	20
36	Refuse Truck	red metallic body, silver/gray base, orange plastic container, 3", 1980	2	3	4
37	Cattle Truck	gray plastic box, white plastic cattle inside, five spoke thin wheels, green tinted windows, 2-1/2", 1970	5	7	20
37	Cattle Truck	yellow body, gray plastic box w/fold down rear door, black plastic wheels, green tinted windows, 2-1/4", 1966	7	10	15
37	Coca-Cola Lorry	orange/yellow body, uneven case load, open base, metal rear fenders, 2-1/4", 1957	25	75	140
37	Coca-Cola Lorry	yellow body of various shades, even case load, silver wheels, black base, 2-1/4", 1960	25	55	125
37	Skip Truck	red body, yellow plastic bucket, light amber windows, silver interior, 2-11/16", 1976	3	5	7
37	Soopa Coopa	metallic blue, amber windows, yellow interior, 2-7/8", 1972	3	4	5
37	Sun Burner	black body, red and yellow flames on hood and sides, 3", 1972	2	3	4
38	Camper	red body, off white camper, unpainted base, 3", 1980	3	5	7
38	Honda Motorcycle and Trailer	metallic blue-green cycle w/wire wheels, black plastic tires, orange trailer, 2-7/8", 1967	10	15	20
38	Honda Motorcycle and Trailer	yellow trailer, thin five-spoke wheels, 2-7/8", 1970	5	7	20
38	Jeep	olive green body, black base and interior, wide five-spoke reverse-accent wheels, no hubs, 2-3/8", 1976	5	8	12
38	Karrier Refuse Collector	silver grille headlights and bumper, 2-3/8", 1957	15	25	30
38	Stingeroo Cycle	metallic purple body, ivory horse head at rear of seat, wide five-spoke rear wheels, 3", 1973	4	6	8
38	Vauxhall Victor Estate Car	yellow body, red or green interior, clear windows, 2-5/8", 1963	10	18	25
39	Clipper	metallic dark pink, amber windows, bright yellow interior, 3", 1973	3	4	5
39	Ford Tractor	blue body, black plastic steering wheel and tires, w/or without yellow hood, 2-1/8", 1967	5	10	20
39	Ford Zodiac Convertible	peach/pink body shades, tan driver, metal wheels, silver grille, 2-5/8", 1957	35	65	90
39	Pontiac Convertible	purple body, w/or without silver grille, cream or ivory interior, silver wheels, 2-3/4", 1962	30	50	75

VEHICLES

Jaguar XKE, No. 32, 1962, Matchbox

M3 Army Personnel Carrier, No. 49, 1958, Matchbox. Photo Courtesy Gary Linden

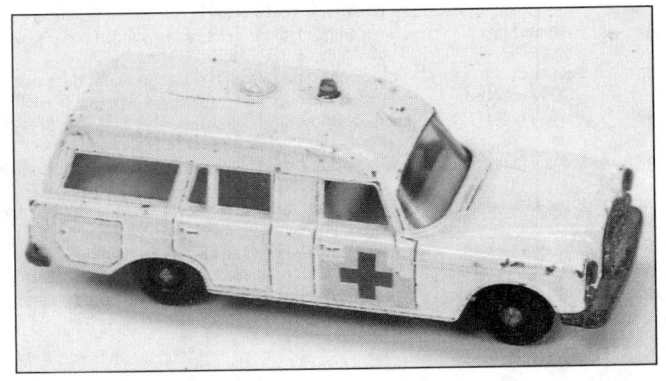

Mercedes-Benz Ambulance, No. 3, 1970, Matchbox

NO.	NAME	DESCRIPTION	GOOD	EX	MINT
39	Rolls-Royce Silver Shadow II	metallic silver gray body, red interior, clear windshield, 3-1/16", 1979	3	5	7
40	Bedford Tipper Truck	red cab, silver grille, two front wheels, four dual rear wheels, 2-1/8", 1957	25	40	50
40	Corvette T Roof	white body and interior, black "09" on door, red and black racing stripes, 1982	2	3	5
40	Hay Trailer	blue body w/tow bar, yellow plastic racks, yellow plastic wheels, 3-3/4", 1967	5	10	15
40	Horse Box	orange cab, off-white van w/tan plastic door, small wheels, 2-13/16", 1977	4	5	7
40	Leyland Royal Tiger Coach	silver-gray body, green tinted windows, four plastic wheels, 3", 1961	10	15	20
40	Vauxhall Guildsman	pink body, light green windows, light cream interior and tow hook, wide five-spoke wheels, 3", 1971	3	4	5
41	Chevrolet Ambulance	white body, blue windows and dome light, gray interior, 2-15/16", 1978	4	7	10
41	D-Type Jaguar	dark green body, tan driver, open air scoop, 2-13/16", 1957	15	30	55
41	D-Type Jaguar	dark green body, tan driver, silver wheels, open and closed air scoop, 2-7/16", 1960	50	100	150
41	Ford GT	white or yellow body, red interior, clear windows, yellow or red plastic wheels, 2-5/8", 1965	20	30	40
41	Ford GT	white body, red interior, clear windows, five spoke wheels, 2-5/8", 1970	5	7	20
41	Kenworth Conventional Aerodyne	red cab and chassis, silver tanks and pipes, black and white stripes on cab, 1982	2	3	5
41	Siva Spider	metallic red body, cream interior, clear windows, wide five-spoke wheels, 3", 1972	5	7	10
42	1957 Ford T-Bird	red convertible, white interior, silver grille and trunk mounted spare, 1982	3	5	6
42	Bedford Evening News Van	yellow/orange body, silver grille, 2-1/4", 1957	15	35	45
42	Iron Fairy Crane	four-spoke wheels, yellow plastic hook,, 3", 1970	25	35	50
42	Iron Fairy Crane	red body, yellow-orange crane, black plastic wheels, yellow plastic single-cable hook,, 3", 1969	7	10	30
42	Mercedes-Benz Container Truck	red body, black base and grille, removable ivory container w/red top and back door, six wheels, 3", 1977	4	5	7
42	Studebaker Lark Wagonaire	blue body, sliding rear roof panel, white plastic interior and tow hook, 3", 1965	10	15	20
42	Tyre Fryer	metallic red body, cream interior, clear windows, wide five-spoke wheels, 3", 1972	3	4	6
43	0-4-0 Steam Loco	red cab, bin and tanks, black boiler, coal, and base, 3", 1978	4	5	7
43	Aveling Barford Tractor Shovel	yellow body, yellow or red driver, four large plastic wheels, 2-5/8", 1962	10	15	25
43	Dragon Wheels Volkswagen	light green body, amber windows, silver interior, orange on black "Dragon Wheels" on sides, large rear wheels, 2-13/16", 1972	5	7	9
43	Hillman Minx	w/or without silver grille, w/or without red painted taillights, 2-5/8", 1958	15	20	30
43	Perterbilt Conventional	black cab and chassis, silver grille, fenders and tanks, red and white side stripes, six wheels, 3", 1982	2	3	5
43	Pony Trailer	yellow body, clear windows, gray plastic rear fold-down door, four plastic wheels, 2-5/8", 1968	7	10	15
43	Pony Trailer	yellow body, clear windows, gray rear door, thin five-spoke wheels, 2-5/8", 1970	3	5	15
44	Boss Mustang	yellow body, amber windows, silver interior, wide cloverleaf wheels, 2-7/8", 1972	3	4	6
44	Chevy 4x4 Van	green body and windows, white "Ridin High" w/horse and fence on sides, 1982	2	3	5
44	GMC Refrigerator Truck	red ribbed roof cab, turquoise box w/gray plastic rear door that opens, green windows, 1967	7	10	20

NO.	NAME	DESCRIPTION	GOOD	EX	MINT
44	GMC Refrigerator Truck	green windows, four-spoke wheels, gray plastic rear door, 2-13/16", 1970	5	7	15
44	Railway Passenger Car	cream plastic upper and roof, red metal lower, black base, 3-1/16", 1978	3	5	7
44	Rolls-Royce Phantom V	clear windows, ivory interior, black plastic wheels, 2-7/8", 1964	15	20	30
44	Rolls-Royce Silver Cloud	metallic blue body, no windows, w/or without silver grille, 2-5/8", 1958	15	20	25
45	BMW 3.0 CSL	orange body, yellow interior, 2-7/8", 1976	3	5	7
45	Ford Corsair with Boat	pale yellow body, red interior and tow hook, green roof rack w/green plastic boat, 2-3/8", 1965	10	15	20
45	Ford Group 6	metallic green body, ivory interior, clear windows, wide five-spoke wheels, 3", 1970	5	7	10
45	Kenworth Caboner Aerodyne	white body w/blue and brown side stripes, silver grille, tanks and pipes, 1982	2	3	5
45	Vauxhall Victor Saloon	yellow body, w/or without green tinted windows, w/or without silver grille, 2-3/8", 1958	10	15	25
46	Ford Tractor	blue body, black base, large black plastic rear wheels, 2-3/16", 1987	3	5	8
46	Hot Chocolate	metallic brown front lid and sides, black roof, 2-13/16", 1972	3	4	5
46	Mercedes-Benz 300 SE	clear windows, ivory interior, black plastic wheels, 2-7/8", 1968	5	10	20
46	Mercedes-Benz 300 SE	clear windows, ivory interior, thin five-spoke wheels, 2-7/8", 1970	5	10	20
46	Morris Minor 1000	dark green body, metal wheels, no windows, 2", 1958	20	30	45
46	Pickford Removal Van	green body, w/or without silver grilles, 2-5/8", 1960	15	30	50
46	Stretcha Fetcha	white body, blue windows, pale yellow interior, 2", 1972	6	8	12
47	1 Ton Trojan Van	red body, no windows, 2-1/4"	25	35	45
47	1 Ton Trojan Van	red body, no windows, 2-1/4", 1958	25	35	45
47	Beach Hopper	dark metallic blue body, hot pink splattered over body, bright orange interior, tan driver, 2-5/8", 1974	3	4	5
47	Commer Ice Cream Canteen	metallic blue body, cream or white plastic interior w/man holding ice cream cone, black plastic wheels, 1963	60	95	100
47	DAF Tipper Container Truck	silver cab, yellow tipper box, thin five-spoke wheels, 3", 1970	4	6	20
47	DAF Tipper Container Truck	aqua or silver cab, yellow tipper box w/light gray or dark gray plastic roof, 3", 1968	6	8	12
47	Pannier Tank Loco	green body, black base and insert, six large plastic wheels, 3", 1979	3	5	7
48	Dumper Truck	red body, green tinted windows, 3", 1966	10	20	25
48	Dumper Truck	bright blue cab, yellow body, green windows, 3", 1970	5	7	25
48	Meteor Sports Boat and Trailer	metal boat w/tan deck and blue hull, black metal trailer w/tow bar, 2-3/8", 1958	30	45	60
48	Pi-Eyed Piper	metallic blue body, amber windows, small front wheels, large rear wheels, 2-7/8", 1972	5	7	10
48	Red Rider	red body, white "Red Rider" and flames on sides, 2-7/8", 1972	2	3	4
48	Sambron Jacklift	yellow body, black base and insert, no window, orange and yellow fork and boom combinations, 3-1/16", 1977	4	7	10
48	Sports Boat and Trailer	plastic boat, red or white deck, hulls in red, white or cream, gold or silver motors, blue metal two-wheel trailer, boat 2-3/8", trailer 2-5/8", 1961	35	65	80
49	Chop Suey Motorcycle	metallic dark red body, yellow bull's head on front handle bars, 2-3/4", 1973	5	7	10
49	M3 Army Personnel Carrier	olive green body, gray rubber treads, 2-1/2", 1958	15	25	30
49	Mercedes-Benz Unimog	silver grille, four black plastic tires, 2-1/2", 1967	10	15	20
50	Articulated Truck	purple tinted windows, small wide wheels, wide five-spoke wheels, 2-3/4", 1973	6	8	12

VEHICLES

*Merryweather Marquis Fire Engine, No. 9, 1959, Matchbox.
Photo Courtesy Gary Linden*

*MG Midget, No. 19, 1958, Matchbox. Photo Courtesy Gary
Linden*

NO.	NAME	DESCRIPTION	GOOD	EX	MINT
50	Commer Pickup Truck	w/or without silver grille and bumpers, four wheels, 2-1/2", 1958	35	55	75
50	Harley-Davidson Motorcycle	silver and brown metallic frame and tank, chrome engine and pipes, brown rider, 2-11/16", 1980	2	3	7
50	John Deere Tractor	green body and tow hook, yellow plastic wheels, 2-1/8", 1964	10	20	30
50	Kennel Truck	metallic green body, clear or blue tinted canopy, four plastic dogs, 2-3/4", 1969	5	15	40
50	Kennel Truck	green windows, light blue tinted canopy, four plastic dogs, 2-3/4", 1970	5	15	45
51	8-Wheel Tipper	blue tinted windows, eight black plastic wheels, 3", 1969	7	10	15
51	8-Wheel Tipper	yellow cab, silver/gray tipper, blue windows, thin five-spoke wheels, 3", 1970	4	6	8
51	Albion Chieftan	yellow body, tan and light tan bags, small round decal on doors, 2-1/2", 1958	10	20	25
51	Citroen SM	clear windows, frosted rear windows, five-spoke wheels, 3", 1972	3	4	6
51	Combine Harvester	red body, black painted base, yellow plastic grain chute, 2-3/4", 1978	3	5	8
51	John Deere Trailer	green tipping body w/tow bar, two small yellow wheels, three plastic barrels, 2-5/8", 1964	20	35	50
51	Midnight Magic	black body, silver stripes on hood, five-spoke front wheels, cloverleaf rear windows, 1972	2	3	4
52	BRM Racing Car	blue or red body, white plastic driver, yellow wheels, 2-5/8", 1965	10	20	25
52	Dodge Charger	clear windows, black interior, five spoke wide wheels, 2-7/8", 1970	4	6	8
52	Maserati 4 Cl. T/1948	red or yellow body, cream or white driver w/or without circle on left shoulder, 2-3/8", 1958	10	17	25
52	Police Launch	white deck, blue hull and men, 3", 1976	2	4	6
53	Aston Martin DB2 Saloon	metallic light green, 2-1/2", 1958	20	30	40
53	BMW M1	silver gray metallic body w/plastic hood, red interior, black stripes and "52" on sides, 2-15/16", 1981	2	4	5
53	Flareside Pick-up	blue body, white interior, grille and pipes, clear windshield, lettered w/"326," "Baja Bouncer" and "B.F. Goodrich", 1982,	2	4	5
53	Ford Zodiac	clear windows, ivory interior, five-spoke wheels, 2-3/4", 1970	5	7	15
53	Ford Zodiac MK IV	metallic silver blue body, clear windows, ivory interior, four black plastic wheels, 2-3/4", 1968	7	10	15
53	Jeep CJ6	red body, unpainted base, bumper and winch, five-spoke rear-accent wheels, 2-15/16", 1977	2	3	5
53	Mercedes-Benz 220 SE	silver grille, clear windows, ivory interior, four wheels, 2-3/4", 1963	15	25	30
53	Tanzara	orange body, silver interior, small front wheels, larger rear wheels, 3", 1972	3	4	5
54	Cadillac Ambulance	white body, blue tinted windows, white interior, red cross labels on sides, 2-3/8", 1970	5	7	20
54	Ford Capri	ivory interior and tow hook, clear windows, wide five-spoke wheels, 3", 1971	3	4	6
54	NASA Tracking Vehicle	white body, silver radar screen, red windows, blue "Space Shuttle Command Center," red "NASA" on roof, 1982	2	3	5
54	Personnel Carrier	olive green body, green windows, black base and grille, tan men and benches, 3", 1976	4	5	7
54	S & S Cadillac Ambulance	white body, blue tinted windows, white interior, red cross decal on front doors, 2-7/8", 1965	10	15	30
54	Saracen Personnel Carrier	olive green body, six black plastic wheels, 2-1/4", 1958	10	17	25
55	Ford Cortina	metallic gold/green body, unpainted base and grille, wide multispoke wheels, 3-1/16", 1979	3	4	5
55	Ford Cortina	metallic tan body, yellow interior, blue racing stripes, 1982	2	4	6

NO.	NAME	DESCRIPTION	GOOD	EX	MINT
55	Ford Fairlane Police Car	silver grille, ivory interior, clear windows, four plastic wheels, 2-5/8", 1963	20	55	100
55	Ford Galaxie Police Car	white body, ivory interior, driver and tow hook, clear windows, 2-7/8", 1966	10	15	30
55	Hellraiser	white body, unpainted base and grille, silver rear engine, 3", 1975	3	5	7
55	Mercury Police Car	white body, ivory interior w/two figures, clear windows, four silver wheels w/black plastic tires, 3", 1968	10	15	40
55	Mercury Police Car	white body, ivory interior, two occupants, thin five-spoke wheels, 3", 1970	5	7	15
55	Mercury Police Station Wagon	white body, ivory interior, no occupants, wide five-spoke wheels, 3", 1971	5	7	10
56	BMC 1800 Pininfarina	clear windows, ivory interior, five-spoke wheels, 2-3/4", 1970	7	10	15
56	Fiat 1500	silver grille, red interior and tow hook, brown or tan luggage on roof, 2-1/2", 1965	10	15	20
56	Hi-Tailer	white body, silver engine and windshield, wide five-spoke front wheels, wide cloverleaf rear wheels, 3", 1974	4	6	8
56	London Trolley Bus	red body, two trolley poles on top of roof, six wheels, 2-5/8", 1958	45	70	90
56	Mercedes-Benz 450 SEL	metallic blue body, unpainted base and grille, 3", 1979	3	4	5
56	Mercedes-Benz Taxi	tan plastic interior, unpainted base, clear plastic windows, red "Taxi" sign on roof, 3", 1980	3	4	5
56	Peterbilt Tanker	blue cab, white tank w/red "Milk's the One", silver tanks, grille, and pipes, 1982	15	25	40
57	Chevrolet Impala	pale blue roof, metallic blue body, green tinted windows, 2-3/4", 1961	20	25	35
57	Eccles Trailer Caravan	orange roof, green plastic interior, thin five-spoke wheels, 3", 1970	5	7	10
57	Land Rover Fire Truck	red body, blue tinted windows, white plastic removable ladder, 2-1/2", 1970	5	7	20
57	Land Rover Fire Truck	red body, blue tinted windows, white plastic ladder on roof, 2-1/2", 1966	10	15	25
57	Wild Life Truck	yellow body, red windows, light blue tinted canopy, 2-3/4", 1973	3	4	6
57	Wolseley 1500	w/or without grilles, four wheels, 2-1/8" long, 1958,	20	30	35
58	BEA Coach	blue body, four wheels w/small knobby treads, 2-1/2", 1958	20	25	35
58	D.A.F. Girder Truck	green windows, thin five-spoke wheels, red plastic girders, 2-7/8", 1970	5	7	20
58	D.A.F. Girder Truck	cream body shades, green tinted windows, six black wheels, red plastic girders, 3", 1968	7	10	15
58	Drott Excavator	red or orange body, movable front shovel, green rubber treads, 2-5/8", 1962	35	50	70
58	Faun Dump Truck	yellow cab and dumper, black base, 2-7/8", 1976	5	10	15
58	Woosh-n-Push	yellow body, red interior, large rear wheels, 2-7/8", 1972	3	4	5
59	Ford Fairlane Fire Chief's Car	red body, ivory interior, clear windows, four plastic wheels, 2-5/8", 1963	35	75	125
59	Ford Galaxie Fire Chief's Car	red body, ivory interior, driver and tow hook, clear windows, four black plastic wheels, 2-7/8", 1966	5	10	40
59	Ford Galaxie Fire Chief's Car	red body, ivory interior and tow hook, clear windows, thin four-spoke wheels, 2-7/8", 1970	3	7	30
59	Ford Thames Van	silver grille, reads "Singer" on the side, four plastic knobby wheels, 2-1/8", 1958	35	75	110
59	Mercury Fire Chief's Car	red body, ivory interior, two occupants, clear windows, wide five-spoke wheels, 3", 1971	5	7	20
59	Planet Scout	metallic green top, green bottom and base, silver interior, grille and roof panels, large multispoke rear wheels, 2-3/4", 1975	4	5	7
59	Porsche 928	metallic brown body, black base, wide five-spoke wheels, 3", 1980	3	5	6

NO.	NAME	DESCRIPTION	GOOD	EX	MINT
60	Lotus Super Seven	butterscotch, clear windshield, black interior and trunk, wide four-spoke wheels, 2-7/8", 1971	5	7	10
60	Morris J2 Pickup	blue body, open windshield and side door windows, four plastic wheels, 2-1/4", 1958	15	25	30
60	Piston Popper	yellow body, red windows, silver engine, labels top and sides, large rear wheels, 1982	2	3	5
60	Site Hut Truck	blue body, blue windows, four black plastic wheels, 2-1/2", 1966	7	10	15
60	Site Hut Truck	blue cab, blue windows, thin five-spoke wheels, 2-1/2", 1970	5	7	15
61	Alvis Stalwart	white body, yellow plastic removable canopy, green windows, six plastic wheels, 2-5/8", 1966	20	30	50
61	Blue Shark	metallic dark blue, white driver, clear glass, wide four-spoke wheels, 3", 1971	3	4	6
61	Ferret Scout Car	olive green, tan driver faces front or back, four black plastic wheels, 2-1/4", 1959	10	20	25
61	Ford Wreck Truck	red body, black base and grille, frosted amber windows, 3", 1978	3	5	7
62	Corvette	metallic red body, unpainted base, gray interior, 1979	2	4	6
62	General Service Lorry	olive green body, six black wheels, 2-5/8", 1959	15	25	30
62	Mercury Cougar	red interior and tow hook, thin five-spoke wheels, 3", 1970	3	5	15
62	Mercury Cougar	metallic lime green body shades, red plastic interior and tow hook, silver wheels, 3", 1968	7	10	15
62	Mercury Cougar "Rat Rod"	red interior and tow hook, small five-spoke front wheels, larger five-spoke rear windows, 3", 1970	4	6	8
62	Renault 17TL	white interior, green tinted windows, green "9" in yellow and black circle, 3", 1974	5	7	10
62	Television Service Van	cream body, green tinted windows w/roof window, four plastic wheels, 2-1/2", 1963	25	40	50
63	Dodge Challenger	green body, black base, bumpers and grille, clear windows, 2-7/8", 1980	3	5	7
63	Dodge Crane Truck	yellow body, green windows, six black plastic wheels, rotating crane cab, 3"long, 1968	7	10	15
63	Dodge Crane Truck	yellow body, green windows, four spoke wide wheels, yellow plastic hook, 2-3/4", 1970	5	7	20
63	Foamite Fire Fighting Crash Tender	red body, six black plastic wheels, white plastic hose and ladder on roof, 2-1/4", 1964	10	15	40
63	Ford Service Ambulance	olive green body, four plastic wheels, round white circle on sides w/red cross, 2-1/2", 1959	15	20	45
63	Freeway Gas Truck	red cab, purple tinted windows, small wide wheels on front, cloverleaf design, 3", 1973	10	15	20
64	MG-1100	ivory interior and tow hook, one occupant and dog, clear windows, 2-5/8", 1970	7	10	15
64	MG-1100	green body, ivory interior, driver, dog and tow hook, clear windows, four black plastic wheels, 2-5/8", 1966	5	7	15
64	Scammel Breakdown Truck	olive green, double cable hook, six black plastic wheels, 2-1/2", 1959	15	25	30
64	Slingshot Dragster	pink body, white driver, five spoke thin front wheels, wide eight-spoke rear wheels, 3", 1971	7	10	15
65	Airport Coach	white top and roof, metallic blue bottom, amber windows, yellow interior, comes w/varying airline logo decals, 3", 1977	5	10	15
65	Claas Combine Harvester	red body, yellow plastic rotating blades and front wheels, black plastic front tires, solid rear wheels, 3", 1967	7	10	15
65	Jaguar 3.4 Litre Saloon	silver grille, silver or black bumpers, four gray plastic wheels, 2-1/2", 1959	7	10	15
65	Jaguar 3.8 Litre Sedan	red body shades, green tinted windows, four plastic wheels, 2-5/8", 1962	5	7	30
65	Saab Sonnet	metallic blue body, amber windows, light orange interior and hood, wide five-spoke wheels, 2-3/4", 1973	5	7	10

VEHICLES

Opel Diplomat, No. 36, 1966, Matchbox

Rolls-Royce Silver Cloud, No. 44, 1958, Matchbox

Saracen Personnel Carrier, No. 54, 1958, Matchbox

VEHICLES

NO.	NAME	DESCRIPTION	GOOD	EX	MINT
66	Citroen DS 19	light or dark yellow body, w/or without silver grille, four plastic wheels, 2-1/2", 1959	10	30	40
66	Ford Transit	orange body, unpainted base, yellow interior, green windows, 2-3/4", 1977	2	3	4
66	Greyhound Bus	silver body, white interior, amber windows, thin five-spoke wheels, 3", 1970	5	10	20
66	Greyhound Bus	silver body, white plastic interior, clear or dark amber windows, six black plastic wheels, 3", 1970	25	35	45
66	Harley-Davidson Motorcycle/Sidecar	metallic bronze body, three wire wheels, 2-5/8", 1962	20	45	75
66	Mazda RX 500	orange body, purple windows, silver rear engine, wide five-spoke wheels, 3", 1971	3	4	5
67	Datsun 260Z 2+2	metallic burgundy body, black base and grille, yellow interior, 3", 1978	3	4	6
67	Hot Rocker	metallic lime/green body, white interior and tow hook, wide five-spoke wheels, 3", 1973	3	5	7
67	Saladin Armoured Car	olive green body, rotating gun turret, six black plastic wheels, 2-1/2", 1959	15	20	25
67	Volkswagen 1600 TL	ivory interior, clear windows, five-spoke wheels, 2-5/8", 1970	5	10	20
67	Volkswagen 1600 TL	ivory interior, four black plastic tires, 2-3/4", 1967	10	15	20
68	Austin MK II Radio Truck	olive green body, four black plastic wheels, 2-3/8", 1959	20	25	30
68	Chevy Van	orange body, unpainted base and grille, large rear wheels, 3", 1979	3	5	7
68	Mercedes-Benz Coach	white plastic top half, white plastic interior, clear windows, four black plastic wheels, 2-7/8", 1965	30	40	55
68	Porsche 910	amber windows, ivory interior, five-spoke wheels, 2-7/8", 1970	7	10	15
69	Armored Truck	red body, white plastic roof, silver/gray base and grille, "Wells Fargo" on sides, 2-13/16", 1978	3	5	8
69	Commer 30 CWT Van	silver grille, sliding left side door, four plastic wheels, yellow "Nestle's" decal on upper rear panel, 2-1/4", 1959	10	30	40
69	Hatra Tractor Shovel	orange or yellow movable shovel arms, four plastic tires, 3", 1965	20	30	40
69	Rolls-Royce Silver Shadow Coupe	amber windshield, five-spoke wheels, 3", 1969	5	7	10
70	Dodge Dragster	pink body, clear windows, silver interior, wide five-spoke front wheels, 3", 1971	7	10	15
70	Ferrari 308 GTB	red body and base, black plastic interior, side stripe, 2-15/16", 1981	2	3	5
70	Ford Thames Estate Car	yellow upper, bluish-green lower, four plastic wheels, 2-1/8", 1959	10	15	30
70	Grit Spreader Truck	dark red cab, four black plastic wheels, 2-5/8", 1966	5	7	15
70	Grit Spreader Truck	red cab, yellow body, green windows, gray plastic rear pull, 2-5/8", 1970	6	8	15
71	Austin 200 Gallon Water Truck	olive green body, four black plastic wheels, 2-3/8", 1959	10	25	30
71	Cattle Truck	metallic brown body, yellow/orange cattle carrier, 3", 1976	4	6	7
71	Ford Heavy Wreck Truck	red cab, white body, green windows and dome light, wide four-spoke wheels, 3", 1970	15	25	30
71	Ford Heavy Wreck Truck	red cab, white bumper, amber or green windows, 3", 1968	25	75	100
71	Jeep Gladiator Pickup Truck	red body, clear windows, green or white interior, four black plastic wheels, fine treads, 2-5/8", 1964	18	25	30
71	Jumbo Jet Motorcycle	dark metallic blue body, red elephant head on handle bars, wide wheels, 2-3/4", 1973	4	6	8
72	Bomag Road Roller	yellow body, base and wheel hubs, black plastic roller, 2-15/16", 1979	2	4	6
72	Fordson Tractor	blue body w/tow hook, 2", 1959	10	20	25
72	Hovercraft	white body, black bottom and base, red props, 3", 1972	4	7	10
72	Jeep CJ5	red interior and tow hook, eight-spoke wheels, 2-3/8", 1970	5	7	10

VEHICLES

NO.	NAME	DESCRIPTION	GOOD	EX	MINT
72	Jeep CJ5	yellow body, red plastic interior and tow hook, four yellow wheels, black plastic tires, 2-3/8", 1966	10	15	20
72	Maxi Taxi	yellow body, black "MAXI TAXI" on roof, five-spoke wheels, 3", 1973	2	3	4
73	10 Ton Pressure Refueller	bluish gray body, six gray plastic wheels, 2-5/8", 1959	20	25	35
73	Ferrari F1 Racing Car	light and dark red body, plastic driver, white and yellow "73" decal on sides, 2-5/8", 1962	15	25	40
73	Mercury Station Wagon	red body, ribbed rear roof, ivory interior w/two dogs, 3", 1972	3	5	7
73	Mercury Station Wagon	red body, ribbed rear roof, ivory interior w/two dogs, 3", 1970	3	5	10
73	Mercury Station Wagon	metallic lime green body shades, ivory interior w/dogs in rear, 3-1/8", 1968	7	10	15
73	Model A Ford	off white body, black base, green fenders and running boards, 1979	2	3	5
73	Weasel	metallic green body, large five-spoke slicks, 2-7/8", 1974	3	4	6
74	Cougar Village	metallic green body, yellow interior, unpainted base, 3-1/16", 1978	3	4	6
74	Daimler Bus	double deck, white plastic interior, thin five-spoke wheels, 3", 1970	7	10	20
74	Daimler Bus	double deck, white plastic interior, four black plastic wheels, 3", 1966	10	15	20
74	Mobile Refreshment Canteen	cream, white, or silver body, upper side door opens w/interior utensils, "Refreshment" on front side, 2-5/8", 1959	15	40	65
74	Orange Peel	white body, wide orange and black stripe and black "Orange Peel" on each side, 3", 1971	3	4	5
74	Toe Joe	metallic lime green body, yellow interior, wide five-spoke wheels, 2-3/4", 1972	3	4	6
75	Alfa Carabo	pink body, ivory interior, black trunk, wide five-spoke wheels, 3", 1971	3	4	5
75	Ferrari Berlinetta	metallic green body of various shades, ivory interior and tow hook, wire or silver plastic wheels, 3", 1965	10	20	25
75	Ferrari Berlinetta	ivory interior, thin five-spoke wheels, 2-3/4", 1970	5	7	25
75	Ford Thunderbird	cream top half, pink bottom half, green tinted windows, 2-5/8", 1960	25	35	45
75	Seasprite Helicopter	white body, red base, black blades, 1977	3	5	7
Y-1	1936 Jaguar SS 100	1977	8	10	17
Y-2	1911 'B' Type London Bus	1955	25	50	90
Y-2	1911 Renault 2-Seater	1963	12	20	36
Y-2	Prince Henry Vauxhall	1970	8	10	21
Y-3	1907 London 'E' Class Tramcar	1955	30	75	120
Y-3	1910 Benz Limousine	1965	10	20	50
Y-3	1934 Riley MPH	1972	6	10	20
Y-4	Sentinel Steam Wagon	1955	30	75	120
Y-4	1909 Opel Coupe	1966	10	15	30
Y-4	1930 Duesenberg Model J	1976	5	8	10
Y-5	1907 Peugeot	1968	10	20	35
Y-5	1927 Talbot Van	1978	5	8	12
Y-5	1929 LeMans Bentley	1955	20	40	80
Y-5	1929 Supercharged 4-1/2 Litre Bentley	1960	8	15	30
Y-6	1916 A.E.C. "Y" type Lorry Truck	1955	25	50	75

VEHICLES

NO.	NAME	DESCRIPTION	GOOD	EX	MINT
Y-6	1913 Cadillac	1967	12	20	35
Y-6	1926 Type "35" Bugatti	1961	30	65	90
Y-6	Rolls-Royce Fire Engine	1978	6	10	15
Y-7	1913 Mercer Raceabout Sportcar	1961	4	8	15
Y-7	1912 Rolls-Royce	1967	10	25	50
Y-7	1914 4-Ton Leyland	1955	50	75	130
Y-8	1914 Sunbeam Motorcycle with Sidecar	1962	45	80	115
Y-8	1914 Stutz Roadster	1968	10	20	35
Y-8	1926 Morris Cowley "Bullnose"	1955	15	35	65
Y-8	1945 MGTC Sports Car	1978	5	10	15
Y-9	1924 Fowler "Big Lion" Showman Engine	1967	10	20	55
Y-9	1912 Simplex	1967	10	20	55
Y-10	1906 Rolls-Royce Silver Cloud	1968	8	10	20
Y-10	1908 Grand Prix Mercedes Racing Car	1957	8	15	30
Y-10	1928 Mercedes-Benz 36/220	1963	10	20	55
Y-11	1912 Packard Landaulet	1963	12	25	45
Y-11	1920 Aveling & Porter Steam Roller	1957	20	45	95
Y-11	1938 Lagonda Drophead Coupe	1972	5	10	20
Y-12	1899 Horse-Bus (London)	1957	30	60	100
Y-12	1909 Thomas Flyabout	1967	10	20	45
Y-12	1912 Model "T" Ford	1979	5	10	15
Y-13	1911 Daimler	1965	15	30	60
Y-13	1918 Crossley Truck	1972	5	10	25
Y-14	1911 Maxwell Roadster	1965	8	15	30
Y-14	1931 Stutz Bearcat	1972	4	8	15
Y-15	1907 Rolls-Royce "Silver Ghost"	1960	10	20	50
Y-15	1930 Packard Victoria	1969	5	10	20
Y-16	1904 Spyker Veteran Automobile	1961	10	25	50
Y-16	1928 Mercedes SS	1971	5	10	20
Y-17	1938 Hispano Suiza	1972	5	10	20
Y-18	1937 Cord 812	1979	5	10	20
Y-19	1935 Auburn 851	1980	5	10	20
Y-20	1938 Mercedes 540K	1981	5	10	20
Y-21	1929 Woody Wagon	1981	4	8	15
Y-22	Model A Van		4	6	10

VEHICLES

NYLINT

NAME	DESCRIPTION	GOOD	EX	MINT
Cars				
Howdy Doody Pump Mobile	8-1/2" long	250	450	650
Emergency Vehicles				
Ladder Truck	post war, 30" long	100	175	250
Farm and Construction Equipment				
Michigan Shovel	bright yellow, bucket tips automatically when raised to boom, boom raises and lowers, 10 wheels, steerable front wheels	150	225	275
Payloader	bright red, 3-3/4" rubber tires, 18" long, 1955	125	187	250
Road Grader	sturdy blade can be raised, lowered, or tilted; tandem-pivoted rear wheels, 3-3/4" steel wheels, 19-1/4" long, 1955	100	175	225
Speed Swing Pettibone	orange, raise or lower bucket and tip to dump, steerable wheels, 3-3/4" rubber tires, "Pettibone" decal on sides, 19" long	200	300	400
Street Sweep	wind-up, 8-1/4" long	175	275	350
Tournahopper	huge hopper, pull lever at rear opens wide clamshell jaws for bottom dumping, 3-3/4" rubber-tired steel wheels, 22-1/2" long,	100	150	200
Tournarocker	oversize hopper, crank action hoist, 3-3/4" rubber-tired steel wheels, 18" long, 1955	75	125	175
Tournatractor	yellow, big powerful adjustable blade on front, pivoted tow-bar on rear, 14-3/4" long, 1955	100	150	200
Traveloader	orange, synchronized feeders, buckets, and rubber conveyor belt, hand crank, steel wheels w/3-3/4" rubber tires, 30" long,	200	300	400
Trucks				
Guided Missile Launcher	1957	75	125	175
Tournahauler	dark green, tractor w/enclosed cab, platform trailer, slid-out ramps, 41-1/2" long w/ramp extended, 1955	125	150	250
U-Haul Ford Truck and Trailer	w/twin I-Beam suspension	125	187	250

SCHUCO

NAME	DESCRIPTION	GOOD	EX	MINT
Cars				
1902 Mercedes Simplex 32PS	wind-up, 8-1/2" long	125	187	250
1913 Mercer	wind-up, 7-1/2" long	87	130	175
Renault 6CV Model 1911	open two-seater, 7" long	125	187	250
Sedan	blue, tin litho, wind-up, 4-1/2" long, 1950s	200	300	400
Sets				
Highway Patrol Official Squad Car Road Set	1958	100	150	200
Tanks				
Military Miniature Tank	keywind	37	55	75
Trucks				
Van	battery-operated, 4" long	75	112	150

NAME	DESCRIPTION	GOOD	EX	MINT

Emergency Vehicles

"L" Mack Aerial Ladder	red w/gold lettering; polished aluminum surface, SMFD decals on hood and trailer sides, six-wheeler, 1950	375	475	795

Trucks

"B" Mack Associated Truck Lines	red cab, polished aluminum trailer, decals on trailer sides, six-wheel tractor, eight-wheel trailer, 1954	500	850	1200
"B" Mack Blue Diamond Dump	all white truck w/blue decals, hydraulic piston, 10-wheeler, 1954	600	950	1300
"B" Mack Lumber Truck	yellow cab and timber deck, three rollers, loading bar and two chains, six-wheeler, load of nine timbers, 1954	450	650	1000
"B" Mack Orange Dump Truck	construction orange all over, no decals, hydraulic piston, 10-wheeler, 1954	650	1150	1650
"B" Mack P.I.E.	red cab, polished trailer, six-wheel tractor, eight-wheel trailer, 1954	375	600	850
"B" Mack Searchlight	dark red paint schemes, fully rotating and elevating searchlight, battery-operated, 1954	500	775	1100
"B" Mack Silver Streak	yellow cab, unpainted, unpolished trailer sides, "Silver Streak" decal on both sides, six-wheel tractor, eight-wheel trailer, 1954	450	775	1050
"B" Mack Watson Bros.	yellow cab, polished aluminum trailer, decals on trailer sides and cab doors, 10-wheel tractor, eight-wheel trailer, 1954	650	1100	1500
"L" Mack Army Materials Truck	Army green, flatbed w/dark green canvas, 10-wheeler, load of three wood barrels, two boards, large and small crate, 1952	375	500	750
"L" Mack Army Personnel Carrier	all Army green, wood sides, Army seal on door panels, military star on roof, 10-wheeler, 1952	375	500	750
"L" Mack Bekins Van	white, covered w/"Bekins" decals, six-wheel tractor, four-wheel trailer, 1953	1000	1650	2000
"L" Mack Blue Diamond Dump	white cab, white dump bed, blue fenders and chassis, hydraulically operated, 10-wheeler, 1952	425	750	1050
"L" Mack International Paper Co.	white tractor cab, "International Paper Co." decals, six wheel tractor, four wheel trailer, 1952	375	650	900
"L" Mack Lyon Van	silver gray cab, dark blue fenders and frame, silver gray van box w/blue "Lyon" decal, six-wheeler, 1950	425	800	1100
"L" Mack Material Truck	light metallic green cab, dark green fenders and frame, wood flatbed, six-wheeler, load of two barrels and six timbers, 1950	400	600	875
"L" Mack Merchandise Van	red cab, black fenders and frame, "Smith-Miller" decals on both sides of van box, double rear doors, six-wheeler, 1951	425	695	1000
"L" Mack Mobil Tandem Tanker	all red cab, "Mobilgas" and "Mobiloil" decals on tank sides, six-wheel tractor, six-wheel trailer, 1952	450	725	1000
"L" Mack Orange Hydraulic Dump	orange cab, orange dump bed, hydraulic, 10-wheeler, may or may not have "Blue Diamond" decals, 1952	850	1500	1950
"L" Mack Orange Materials Truck	all orange, flatbed w/canvas, 10-wheeler, load of three barrels, two boards, large and small crate, 1952	400	650	900
"L" Mack P.I.E.	all red tractor, polished aluminum trailer, "P.I.E." decals on sides and front, six wheel tractor, eight-wheel trailer, 1950	395	550	850
"L" Mack Sibley Van	dark green cab, black fenders and frame, dark green van box w/"Sibley's" decal in yellow on both sides, six-wheeler, 1950	850	1375	1850
"L" Mack Tandem Timber	red/black cab, six-wheeler, load of six wood lumber rollers, two loading bars, four chains and 18 or 24 boards, 1950	400	550	725

VEHICLES

NAME	DESCRIPTION	GOOD	EX	MINT
"L" Mack Tandem Timber	two-tone green cab, six-wheeler, load of six wood lumber rollers, two loading bars, four chains, and 18 timbers, 1953	400	550	725
"L" Mack Telephone Truck	all dark or two-tone green truck, "Bell Telephone System" decals on truck sides, six-wheeler, 1952	475	750	975
"L" Mack West Coast Fast Freight	silver w/red/black or silver cab and chassis, "West Coast-Fast Freight" decals on sides of box, six-wheeler, 1952	475	775	1000
Chevrolet Arden Milk Truck	red cab, white wood body, four-wheeler, 1945	275	465	800
Chevrolet Bekins Van	blue die cast cab, all white trailer, 14-wheeler, 1945	275	350	750
Chevrolet Coca-Cola Truck	red cab, wood body painted red, four-wheeler, 1945	300	600	850
Chevrolet Flatbed Tractor-Trailer	unpainted wood trailer, unpainted polished cab, 14-wheeler, 1945	250	300	500
Chevrolet Heinz Grocery Truck	yellow cab, load of four waxed cases, 1946	225	325	475
Chevrolet Livestock Truck	polished, unpainted tractor cab and trailer, 1946	175	275	375
Chevrolet Lumber	green cab, load of 60 polished boards and two chains, 1946	150	195	275
Chevrolet Lyons Van	blue cab, silver trailer, 1946	165	325	500
Chevrolet Material Truck	green cab, no side rails, load of three barrels, two cases and 18 boards, 1946	135	185	225
Chevrolet Stake	yellow tractor cab	185	250	425
Chevrolet Transcontinental Vanliner	blue tractor cab, white trailer, "Bekins" logos and decals on trailer sides, 1946	200	350	495
Chevrolet Union Ice Truck	blue cab, white body, load of eight waxed blocks of ice, 1946	300	495	800
Ford Bekins Van	red sand-cast tractor, gray sheet metal trailer, 14-wheeler, 1944	275	500	750
Ford Coca-Cola Truck	red sandcast cab, wood body painted red, four-wheeler, 1944	400	650	900
GMC Arden Milk Truck	red cab, white painted wood body w/red stakes, four-wheeler, 1947	200	425	650
GMC Bank of America Truck	dark brownish green cab and box, 'Bank of America' decal on box sides, four-wheeler, 1949	115	165	275
GMC Be Mac Tractor-Trailer	red cab, plain aluminum frame, "Be Mac Transport Co." in white letters on door panels, 14-wheeler, 1949	250	350	700
GMC Bekins Vanliner	blue cab, metal trailer painted white, 14-wheeler, 1947	175	275	425
GMC Coca-Cola Truck	red cab, yellow wood body, four-wheeler, load of 16 Coca-Cola cases, 1947	400	675	895
GMC Coca-Cola Truck	all yellow truck, red Coca-Cola decals, five spoke hubs, four-wheeler, load of six cases each w/24 plastic bottles, 1954	275	450	750
GMC Drive-O	red cab, red dump body, runs forward and backward w/handturned control at end of 5-1/2 ft. cable, six-wheeler, 1949	175	300	450
GMC Dump Truck	all red truck, six-wheeler, 1950	150	200	285
GMC Emergency Tow Truck	white cab, red body and boom, 'Emergency Towing Service' on body side panels, four-wheeler, 1953	185	250	400
GMC Furniture Mart	blue cab, off-white body, "Furniture Mart, Complete Home Furnishings" markings on body sides, four-wheeler, 1953	135	275	295
GMC Heinz Grocery Truck	yellow cab, wood body, six-wheeler, 1947	250	325	450
GMC Highway Freighter Tractor-Trailer	red tractor cab, hardwood bed on trailer w/full length wood fences, "Fruehauf" decal on trailer, 14-wheeler, 1948	150	210	325
GMC Kraft Foods	yellow cab, yellow steel box, large "Kraft" decal on both sides, four-wheeler, 1948	200	300	450
GMC Lumber Tractor-Trailer	metallic blue cab and trailer, three rollers and two chains, 14-wheeler, 1949	185	250	350

VEHICLES

Scammel Breakdown Truck, No. 64, 1959, Matchbox. Photo Courtesy Gary Linden

Gasoline Truck, 1957, Tonka. Photo Courtesy Don and Barb DeSalle

NAME	DESCRIPTION	GOOD	EX	MINT
GMC Lumber Truck	green cab, six-wheeler, 1947	165	215	300
GMC Lyons Van Tractor-Trailer	blue tractor cab, "Lyons Van" decals on both sides, fold down rear door, 14-wheeler, 1948	165	250	400
GMC Machinery Hauler	construction orange, two loading ramps, 10-wheeler, 1953	200	295	425
GMC Machinery Hauler	construction orange cab and lowboy trailer, "Fruehauf" decal on gooseneck, 13-wheeler, 1949	150	225	335
GMC Machinery Hauler	construction orange cab and lowboy trailer, "Fruehauf" decal on gooseneck, 13-wheeler, 1949	150	225	335
GMC Marshall Field's & Company Tractor-Trailer	dark green cab and trailer, double rear doors, never had Smith-Miller decals, 10-wheeler, 1949	295	395	500
GMC Material Truck	green cab, wood body, six-wheeler, load of three barrels, three cases and 18 boards, 1947	115	150	250
GMC Material Truck	yellow cab, natural finish hardwood bed and sides, four-wheeler, load of four barrels and two timbers, 1949	125	175	265
GMC Mobilgas Tanker	red cab and tanker trailer, large "Mobilgas", "Mobiloil" emblems on sides and rear panel of tanker, 14-wheeler, 1949	135	225	400
GMC Oil Truck	orange cab, rear body unpainted, six-wheeler, load of three barrels, 1947	115	185	265
GMC P.I.E.	red cab, polished aluminum box trailer, double rear doors, "P.I.E." decals on sides and front panels, 14-wheeler, 1949	150	265	350
GMC People's First National Bank and Trust Company	dark brownish green cab and box, "People's First National Bank and Trust Co." decals on box sides, 1951	165	250	385
GMC Rack Truck	red or yellow cab, natural finish wood deck, red stake sides, six-wheeler, 1948	135	200	325
GMC Redwood Logger Tractor-Trailer	green or maroon cab, unpainted aluminum trailer w/four hardwood stakes, load of three cardboard logs, 1948	365	585	700
GMC Rexall Drug Truck	orange cab and closed steel box body, "Rexall" logo on both sides and on front panel of box, four-wheeler, 1948	500	750	1000
GMC Scoop Dump	rack and pinion dump w/a scoop, five spoke wheels, six-wheeler, 1954	275	350	575
GMC Searchlight Truck	four wheel truck pulling four wheel trailer, color schemes vary, "Hollywood Film Ad" on truck body side panels, 1953	300	415	695
GMC Silver Streak	unpainted polished cab and trailer, wrap around sides and shield, some had tail gate, 1950	140	200	300
GMC Sunkist Special Tractor-Trailer	cherry/maroon tractor cab, natural mahogany trailer bed, 14-wheeler, 1947	165	275	475
GMC Super Cargo Tractor-Trailer	silver gray tractor cab, hardwood bed on trailer w/red wraparound side rails, 14-wheeler, load of 10 barrels, 1948	150	225	395
GMC Timber Giant	green or maroon cab, unpainted aluminum trailer w/four hardwood stakes, load of three cardboard logs, 1948	175	285	495
GMC Tow Truck	white cab, red body and boom, five spoke cast hubs, "Emergency Towing Service" on body side panels, four-wheeler, 1954	95	135	200
GMC Transcontinental Tractor-Trailer	red tractor cab, hardwood bed on trailer w/full length wood fences, "Fruehauf" decal on trailer, 14-wheeler, 1948	150	210	325
GMC Triton Oil Truck	blue cab, mahogany body unpainted, six-wheeler, load of three Triton Oil drums (banks) and side chains, 1947	115	185	265
GMC U.S. Treasury Truck	gray cab and box, "U.S. Treasury" insignia and markings on box sides, four-wheeler, 1952	235	325	475

VEHICLES

STRUCTO

NAME	DESCRIPTION	GOOD	EX	MINT

Cars

NAME	DESCRIPTION	GOOD	EX	MINT
Auto Builder Auto	1918; red w/black fenders; 16"	550	1100	1500
Auto Builder Racing Auto	1919; 12-1/2"; red	600	900	1200
Bearcat Auto	1919; 16"	850	1400	2000
Roadster	1924; 10-1/2"; orange or red body	900	1500	2000

Miscellaneous

NAME	DESCRIPTION	GOOD	EX	MINT
Caterpillar Tractor	1921; 9"	325	500	850
Climbing Military Tank	1929; green tank; chain link treads	450	700	1100
Climbing Tractor	1929; 12-1/2"; chain link treads	450	600	1100
Excavator	1931; 29"	325	600	950
Fire Insurance Patrol	1928; 18"	250	500	700
High Wheel Tractor/Trailer	1919; 22", green w/red wheel guards	550	1000	1500
Hook and Ladder Truck	1930; 24"	300	450	690
Lift Crane	1924; 13"	100	150	225
Lone Eagle Airplane	1928; 19-1/2"; monoplane w/spring-driven motor; blue/green w/orange wing	600	800	1100
Moving Van	1928; 17"; orange w/green wheels and black tires	350	650	950
Pile Driver	1924; blue crane w/red roof; 10-3/4"	100	200	300
Police Patrol	1928; 16-1/2"; blue w/decals; red wheels w/white tires	350	650	950
Pumping Fire Engine	1928; 21"; red truck w/orange water tank	600	1000	1400
Road Grader	1922; four-wheel grader; green; 16"	150	350	650
Sky King Airplane	1929; 21-1/2"; blue w/gray wings	900	1000	1500
Whippet Military Tank	1920; 12"	425	650	1000
Yuba Tractor	1919; 20"	750	1000	1475

Trucks

NAME	DESCRIPTION	GOOD	EX	MINT
Ambulance Truck	1928; 17"; green w/Ambulance markings	550	800	1350
Contractor Truck	1924; 12-1/2"; orange dump truck w/black fenders	525	850	1000
Dump Truck	1924-1932; 14-1/2"; assorted colors and styles	200	300	450
Giant Truck Builder Dump Truck	1919; 18-1/2"	850	1300	1850
Motor Dispatch	1929; 24"; blue w/decals; orange wheels and black tires	850	1000	1400
Red Rider Truck	1932; 17-5/8"; red	250	450	750
Screen Side Truck	1928; 17"; white w/black wheels and white tires	350	650	1000
U.S. Mail Truck	1928; 17"; green w/red wheels and white tires	450	700	1100

NAME	DESCRIPTION	GOOD	EX	MINT
3-in-1 Hi-way Service Truck	1957, w/two snowblades, 13" long	275	400	700
Aerial Ladder Truck	1957	200	300	500
Allied Van Lines	1955	150	275	500
Big Mike Dual Hydraulic Dump Truck	1957, 14" long	325	595	1000
Dump	1955	100	150	350
Farm Stake Truck	1957	190	375	480
Freighter	1955	90	135	280
Gasoline Truck	1957, 15" long	350	525	1000
Green Giant Semi Reefer	1956	155	350	600
Hook and Ladder	1955	100	300	450
Jolly Green Giant Special	1960, white, green stake racks	375	450	850
Livestock Truck	1955	110	200	350
Loboy and Shovel	1955	150	300	450
No. 0001 Service Truck	1959, 12-3/4" long	100	150	350
No. 0001 Service Truck	1960	100	150	350
No. 0002 Pickup	1960	100	200	375
No. 0002 Pickup	1961	100	190	320
No. 0002 Pickup Truck	1958 Next Generation Cars	100	150	300
No. 0003 Utility Truck	1958 Next Generation Cars	100	150	300
No. 0004 Farm Stake	1961	85	175	370
No. 0004 Farm Stake Truck	1958 Next Generation Cars	100	150	300
No. 0004 Farm Stake Truck	1960	100	200	325
No. 0005 Sportsman	1959	100	175	350
No. 0005 Sportsman Pickup w/Topper	1958 Next Generation Cars, 12-3/4" long	150	225	450
No. 0006 Dump	1961	75	100	250
No. 0006 Dump Truck	1958 Next Generation Cars	100	150	300
No. 0006 Dump Truck	1960	75	125	290
No. 0008 Logger	1960	150	225	300
No. 0012 Road Grader	1958 Next Generation Cars	75	112	150
No. 0014 Dragline	1959, 20" long	100	175	375
No. 0014 Dragline	1961, yellow	100	150	250
No. 0016 Air Express	1959	350	425	700
No. 0018 Wrecker	1960, white sidewalls	100	150	375
No. 0018 Wrecker	1961	100	250	400
No. 0018 Wrecker Truck	1958 Next Generation Cars	100	250	450
No. 0020 Hydraulic Dump	1960	75	150	300
No. 0020 Hydraulic Dump	1961	75	110	250
No. 0020 Hydraulic Dump Truck	1958 Next Generation Cars	125	175	275
No. 0022 Deluxe Sportman	1961	100	200	450
No. 0022 Deluxe Sportsman	1959	150	325	500
No. 0022 Deluxe Sportsman	1960	100	250	400
No. 0028 Pickup & Trailer	1960	100	150	300
No. 0028 Pickup with Stake Trailer and Animal	1958 Next Generation Cars	125	175	350
No. 0029 Sportsman Truck w/Box Trailer	1958 Next Generation Cars	150	225	400
No. 0030 Tandem Platform Stake	1959, 28-1/4" long	240	450	800
No. 0032 Stock Rack Truck	1958 Next Generation Cars	175	300	500
No. 0033 Gasoline Truck	1958 Next Generation Cars, hinged back door, hose and nozzle	350	500	900
No. 0034 Deluxe Sportsman with Boat Trailer	1958 Next Generation Cars, 22-3/4" long	150	325	750
No. 0035 Farm Stake	1958 Next Generation Cars, w/two-horse trailer, 21-3/4" long	125	250	450
No. 0035 Farm Stake and Horse Trailer	1960	125	180	350
No. 0035 Farm Stake Truck and Horse Trailer	1961	100	180	350
No. 0036 Livestock Van	1958 Next Generation Cars	175	250	450
No. 0037 Thunderbird Express	1958 Next Generation Cars	150	300	600

No. 006 Dump, 1961, Tonka. Photo Courtesy Don and Barb DeSalle

No. 180 Dump Truck, 1956, Tonka. Photo Courtesy Don and Barb DeSalle

No. 200 Lift Truck and Trailer, 1948, Tonka. Photo Courtesy Don and Barb DeSalle

VEHICLES

NAME	DESCRIPTION	GOOD	EX	MINT
No. 0037 Thunderbird Express	1960	150	350	550
No. 0039 Allied Van	1961	120	250	450
No. 0039 Nationwide Moving Van	1958 Next Generation Cars, 24-1/4" long	250	475	800
No. 0040 Car Carrier	1960	100	225	450
No. 0040 Car Carrier	1961	100	250	450
No. 0041 Boat Transport	1960, 38" long	250	450	850
No. 0041 Boat Transport Truck	1961	150	300	650
No. 0041 Hi-Way Service Truck	1958 Next Generation Cars	100	200	400
No. 0043 Shovel & Carry-All Trailer	1958 Next Generation Cars	200	300	500
No. 0044 Dragline & Trailer	1959, 26-1/4" long	150	275	400
No. 0045 Big Mike Dual Hydraulic Dump Truck	1958 Next Generation Cars, w/snow plow	375	675	1000
No. 0046 Suburban Pumper	1958 Next Generation Cars	175	225	450
No. 0046 Suburban Pumper	1960	100	250	350
No. 0048 Aerial Ladder	1960	125	250	350
No. 0048 Aerial Ladder	1961	125	200	450
No. 0048 Hydraulic Aerial Ladder	1958 Next Generation Cars	100	250	450
No. 005 Sportsman	1960	100	275	400
No. 005 Sportsman	1961	100	150	375
No. 0050 Mini-Tonka Jeep pickup	1963, 9-1/4" long	35	52	70
No. 0056 Mini-Tonka Stake Truck	1963, 9-1/4" long	35	52	70
No. 0060 Mini-Tonka Dump	1963, 9-3/4" long	30	50	75
No. 0065 Trailer	1955, stake side	30	45	60
No. 0068 Mini-Tonka Wrecker	1963, 9-1/2" long	30	50	75
No. 0070 Mini-Tonka Camper	1963, 9-5/8" long	75	112	150
No. 0077 Mini-Tonka Mixer	1964, 9" long	30	50	75
No. 0086 Mini-Tonka Van	1964, 16" long	36	54	72
No. 0090 Mini-Tonka Livestock Van	1964, 16" long	50	75	100
No. 0096 Mini-Tonka Carrier	1964, 18-1/2" long, two cars	50	75	150
No. 0100 Bulldozer	1960, 8-7/8" long, plated roller wheels only in 1960	75	125	200
No. 0100 Steam Shovel	1947, 20-3/4" long	135	200	350
No. 0100 Stearn Shovel Deluxe	1949, 22" long	100	250	400
No. 0105 Rescue Squad	1960, 13-3/4" long	100	250	450
No. 0110 Fisherman Pick-up	1960, w/sportsman, cover, 14" long	100	175	375
No. 0115 Power Boom Loader	1960, 1960 only, 18-1/2" long	300	650	1000
No. 0116 Dump Truck with Sandloader	1961, 23-1/4" long	100	175	395
No. 0117 Boat Service Truck	1961, 1961 only	100	250	450
No. 0118 Giant Dozer	1961, 12-1/2" long	70	100	250
No. 012 Road Grader	1961, yellow	75	100	200
No. 0120 Cement Mixer	1960, 15-1/2" long	100	150	300
No. 0120 Cement Mixer	1961	100	150	300
No. 0120 Shovel and Carry-All (Loboy)	1956, 33" long total	188	280	475
No. 0120 Tractor and Carry-All Trailer	1949, w/No. 50 Steam Shovel.	155	280	475
No. 0125 Lowboy and Bulldozer	1960, 26-1/4" long	190	375	675
No. 0125 Tractor & Carry-All Trailer	1949, w/No. 100 Steam Shovel	150	250	550
No. 0130 Deluxe Fisherman	1960, also new boat and trailer	150	350	550
No. 0130 Deluxe Fisherman	1961	150	350	550
No. 0130 Tractor-Carry-All Trailer	1949, 30-1/2" long	100	150	350

VEHICLES

No. 425 Jeep Pumper, 1964, Tonka. Photo Courtesy Don and Barb DeSalle

No. 0530 Camper, 1963, Tonka. Photo Courtesy Don and Barb DeSalle

No. 0616 Dump Truck & Sand Loader, 1963. Tonka. Photo Courtesy Don and Barb DeSalle

NAME	DESCRIPTION	GOOD	EX	MINT
No. 0134 Grading Service Truck, Trailer and Bulldozer	1961, 25-1/2" long total	100	150	350
No. 0135 Mobile Dragline	1960	100	250	450
No. 0135 Mobile Dragline	1961	100	250	450
No. 0136 Houseboat Set	1961, 29" long total	200	400	800
No. 0140 Sanitary Truck	1960	350	550	900
No. 0140 Sanitary Truck	1961	400	700	1500
No. 0140 Tonka Toy Transport Van	1949, 22-1/4" long	150	300	500
No. 0142 Mobile Clam	1961, 27-1/4" long	100	250	450
No. 0145 Steel Carrier Semi	1950, 22" long	125	200	350
No. 0145 Steel Carrier Truck	1954	100	185	380
No. 0145 Tanker	1960, first Tonka w/major use of plastic, 28" long	100	250	450
No. 0145 Tanker	1961	100	250	350
No. 0150 Crane and Clam	1947, 24" long	135	200	350
No. 0170 Tractor & Carry-All Trailer	1949, w/No. 150 Crane and Clam	200	300	525
No. 0175 Utility Hauler	1950, 12" long	100	150	300
No. 0180 Dump Truck	1949, 12" long	100	175	375
No. 0180 Dump Truck	1956, 13" long	100	150	350
No. 0185 Express Truck	1950, 13-1/2" long	200	450	900
No. 0190 Loading Tractor	1949, 10-1/2" long	n/a	n/a	n/a
No. 0200 Jeep Dispatcher	1962, 9-3/4" long	50	75	100
No. 0200 Jeep Dispatcher	1963	30	50	75
No. 0200 Lift Truck and Trailer	1948	200	350	600
No. 0201 Servi-I-Cae	1963	55	82	110
No. 0201Serv-I-Car	1962, 9-1/8" long	75	125	200
No. 0249 Jeep Universal	1962	75	125	175
No. 0250 Military Tractor	1964, black seat	55	70	100
No. 0250 Tractor	1962, 8-5/8" long	50	75	100
No. 0250 Tractor	1963, yellow w/red seat	75	112	150
No. 0250 Wrecker Truck	1949, 12-1/2" long	125	250	375
No. 0251 Military Jeep Universal	1963, 10-1/2" long	25	38	50
No. 0251 Military Jeep Universal	1964	35	55	75
No. 0300 Bulldozer	1962	50	75	100
No. 0300 Bulldozer	1963	55	82	110
No. 0301 Utility Dump	1962, 12-1/2" long,	100	150	300
No. 0302 Pickup	1962	95	150	250
No. 0302 Pickup	1963	35	52	70
No. 0304 Jeep Commander	1964, canvas top, 10-1/2" long	30	50	75
No. 0308 Stake Pickup	1962, 12-5/8" long	50	100	200
No. 0308 Stake Pickup	1963	50	95	150
No. 0315 Dump Truck	1964, 13-1/2" long	40	60	90
No. 0350 Jeep Surrey	1963	50	75	100
No. 0350 Jeep Surrey, fringe top	1962, 10-1/2" long	75	125	200
No. 0352 Loader	1963	40	60	80
No. 0354 Style-Side Pickup	1963, 14" long	40	60	125
No. 0375 Jeep Wrecker	1964, 11" long	75	130	200
No. 0380 Troop Carrier	1964, 14" long	70	100	150
No. 0384 Military Jeep & Box Trailer	1964, 19-3/8" overall	50	75	150
No. 0400 Allied Van Lines Semi	1950, 23-1/2" long	175	260	400
No. 0402 Loader	1962, yellow and green	40	60	80
No. 0404 Farm Stake Truck	1962	50	95	150
No. 0404 Farm Stake Truck	1963	60	90	150
No. 0404 Stake Truck	1964, red	70	120	170
No. 0405 Sportsman	1962	75	100	200
No. 0406 Dump Truck	1962	75	150	275

VEHICLES

No. 640 Ramp Hoist, 1964, Tonka. Photo Courtesy Don and Barb DeSalle

No. 725 Minute Maid Orange Juice Van, 1955, Tonka

No. 880 Pick-up Truck, 1955, Tonka

NAME	DESCRIPTION	GOOD	EX	MINT
No. 0406 Dump Truck	1963	45	68	90
No. 0410 Jet Delivery Truck	1962, 14" long, 1962 only	200	350	850
No. 0420 Airlines Luggage Service	1962, 16-5/8 long	100	250	400
No. 0422 Back Hoe	1963, 17-1/8" long	100	175	350
No. 0425 Jeep Pumper	1963, 10-3/4" long	100	175	400
No. 0425 Jeep Pumper	1964, black steering wheel	100	150	275
No. 0500 Livestock Hauler Semi	1952, 22-1/4" long	100	150	350
No. 0504 Stake Pickup & Trailer	1964, 21-5/8" long	50	75	185
No. 0512 Road Grader	1962	45	68	90
No. 0512 Road Grader	1963, red clearance lights	80	120	160
No. 0514 Drag	1963	60	90	120
No. 0514 Dragline	1962	150	225	300
No. 0516 Jeep Runabout	1963, trailer and boat	75	150	300
No. 0516 Jeep Runabout, trailer, boat	1962, 25-5/8" long total	75	175	350
No. 0518 Wrecker	1962	75	175	325
No. 0518 Wrecker	1963	45	75	150
No. 0520 Hydraulic Dump	1962	75	100	220
No. 0520 Hydraulic Dump Truck	1963	45	68	90
No. 0522 Style-Side Pickup & Stake Trailer	1963, 22-3/4" long total	75	125	250
No. 0524 Dozer Packer	1962, 18-1/4" long total, Packer has eleven tires, sold only in 1962	100	250	400
No. 0524 Dozer Packer	1963, yellow	200	300	400
No. 0525 Jeep & Horse Trailer	1964, 19-1/4" long total, two horses	45	68	135
No. 0528 Pickup & Trailer	1962	50	75	150
No. 0530 Camper	1962, 14" long	75	150	250
No. 0530 Camper	1963	25	38	50
No. 0534 Trencher	1963, 18-1/4" long	40	75	150
No. 0536 Giant Dozer	1963	110	160	225
No. 0550 Grain Hauler Semi	1952, 22-1/4" long	125	180	350
No. 0575 Logger Semi	1953, wood flat bed	125	180	350
No. 0575 Logger Semi	1953, 22-1/4" long	125	180	350
No. 0600 Grader	1955	75	125	200
No. 0600 Road Grader	1953, 17" long	50	75	100
No. 0600 Road Grader	1956, 17" long	75	125	200
No. 0616 Dump Truck & Sand Loader	1963, yellow	100	150	235
No. 0616 Dump Truck & Sandloader	1964, orange and yellow	75	125	175
No. 0616 Dump Truck and Sand Loader	1962	75	125	240
No. 0618 Giant Dozer	1962	100	150	200
No. 0620 Cement Mixer	1962	85	150	300
No. 0620 Cement Mixer	1963	75	125	250
No. 0625 Stake Pickup & Horse Trailer	1963, 21-3/4" long overall	75	125	175
No. 0640 Ramp Hoist	1963, 19-1/4" long, red and white	175	350	550
No. 0640 Ramp Hoist	1964, park green and white, very rare	300	650	900
No. 0650 Green Giant Transport Semi	1953, 22-1/4" long	150	300	500
No. 0675 Trailer Fleet Set	1953, two tractors (five interchangeable trailers), per set	450	680	975
No. 0700 Aerial Ladder	1956, 32-1/2" long	150	300	450
No. 0700 Aerial Ladder Semi Fire Truck	1954, 32-1/2" long	175	260	450
No. 0720 Terminal Train	1963, 33-5/8" long, total, fifteen suitcases	105	175	300
No. 0725 Minute Maid Orange Juice Van	1955	275	650	950
No. 0725 Star Kist Van	1954, 14-1/2" long	250	575	950

No. 950 Pumper, 1956, Tonka. Photo Courtesy Don and Barb DeSalle

Thunderbird Express Semi, 1957, Tonka

Utility Truck, 1954, Tonka

TONKA

NAME	DESCRIPTION	GOOD	EX	MINT
No. 0735 Farm Stake and Horse Trailer	1962	75	125	225
No. 0739 Allied Van	1962	125	250	350
No. 0739 Allied Van	1963	118	175	235
No. 0739 Allied Van Lines	1964, black knob on door	75	125	175
No. 0750 Carnation Milk Delivery Van	1955	200	400	600
No. 0750 Carnation Milk Step Van	1954, 11-3/4" long	200	400	600
No. 0750 Parcel Delivery Van	1954, 11-3/4" long	200	300	500
No. 0775 Road Builder Set	1954, Road Grader, Semi T&T Crane and Dump Truck, five pieces	350	525	900
No. 0834 Grading Service Truck	1962	70	100	150
No. 0840 Car Carrier	1962	100	150	300
No. 0840 Car Carrier	1963	42	63	85
No. 0850 Lumber Truck	1955, six-wheel	175	260	400
No. 0860 Stake Truck	1955, six-wheel	175	360	500
No. 0880 Pick-up Truck	1955	125	280	450
No. 0880 Pickup Truck	1956, 13-3/4" long	150	350	650
No. 0900 Mighty Tonka Dump Truck	1964, one of the most popular Tonka vehicles ever made; there were 9,655,000 sold between 1964 and 1983	65	100	230
No. 0926 Pumper	1963	60	90	120
No. 0926 Pumper Truck	1962	100	150	300
No. 0942 Mobile Clam	1962	100	150	320
No. 0942 Mobile Clam	1963	75	112	150
No. 0942 Mobile Clam	1964, yellow	50	75	100
No. 0950 Pumper	1956, 17" long	150	275	450
No. 0960 Wrecker	1956	100	300	600
No. 0980 Hi-Way Dump Truck	1956, 13" long	130	280	395
No. 0991 Farm Stake Truck	1956, 13" long	150	250	460
No. 0992 Aerial Sand Loader Set	1955, Loader and Dump Truck	275	425	875
No. 0996 Wrecker	1956, white, 12" long, rare	390	525	800
No. 0998 Aerial Ladder	1964, two auxiliary ladders	50	75	100
No. 0998 Lumber Truck	1956, 18-3/4" long	130	225	360
No. 1001 Trencher & LoBoy	1963, 28-1/2" long total	75	112	150
No. 1348 Aerial Ladder	1962	100	150	350
No. 1348 Aerial Ladder Truck	1963	100	150	200
No. 2100 Airport Service Set	1963	150	225	300
Parcel Delivery Van	1957, 12" long	200	350	500
Pickup with Stake Trailer	1957, 20-1/2" long	150	250	400
Rescue Squad Van	1956, 11-3/4" long	225	400	850
Rescue Van	1955	200	450	800
Sanitary Truck	1959, square back	450	700	1000
Stake Trailer	1957	30	45	75
Standard Oil Company Wrecker Special	1960	400	600	1200
Stock Rack Truck with Animals	1957, 16-1/4" long	175	365	650
Tandem No. 36 Tandem Air Express	1959, w/trailer, 24" long	325	650	1000
Tandem No. 40 Car Carrier	1959	100	300	500
Tandem No. 41 Boat Transport	1959, 38" long	250	350	700
Tandem No. 42 Hydraulic Land Rover	1959, 15" long	550	825	1700
Thunderbird Express Semi	1957, 24" long	150	400	600
Utility Truck	1954	110	275	425
Wrecker	1953	125	200	350
Wrecker	1954	100	300	500
Wrecker	1957	100	300	500

VEHICLES

TOOTSIETOY

NAME	DESCRIPTION	GOOD	EX	MINT
Airplanes				
Aero-Dawn	1928	20	35	65
Atlantic Clipper	2" long	5	10	20
Autogyro	white, 1934	25	40	90
Beechcraft Bonanza	orange, front propellor	6	10	35
Bi-Wing Seaplane	1926, yellow	30	40	65
Bleriot Plane	1910	25	50	100
Crusader		25	50	75
Curtis P-40	light green	120	250	525
Dirigible U.S.N. Los Angeles	silver	40	60	90
Douglas D-C 2 TWA	1935	20	45	85
F-94 Starfire	green, four engines, 1970s	10	15	35
F9F-2 Panther Shooting Star		25	35	70
Fly-N-Gyro	1938	50	100	310
KOP-1 USN		20	30	60
Low Wing Plane	miniature Piper Cub	20	30	50
Navion	red, front propellor	10	15	35
Navy Jet	red, 1970s	5	10	30
Navy Jet Cutlass	red w/silver wings	10	15	30
P-38 Plane	9-3/4" wingspan	40	60	110
Piper Cub	blue, front propellor	10	15	30
S-58 Sikorsky Helicopter	1970s	15	30	50
Snow Skids Airplane	rotating prop, 4" wingspan	40	60	85
Stratocruiser		30	50	110
Supermainliner		20	30	50
Top Wing Plane	miniature	20	30	50
Transport Plane	1941, orange	40	75	110
Tri-Motor Plane	three propellors	50	85	150
TWA Electra	two engines, propellors	10	20	45
Twin Engine Airliner	10 windows, DC4	10	20	45
U.S. Army Plane	1936	15	25	50
UX214 Monoplane	4", 1930s	30	60	90
Waco Bomber	blue base/silver top or silver base	50	80	150
Boats and Ships				
Battleship	silver w/some red on top, 6" long, 1939	10	20	35
Carrier	silver	15	25	40
Cruiser	silver; some red on top, 6" long, 1939	10	15	25
Destroyer	4" long, 1939	10	20	40
Freighter	6" long, 1940	10	20	45
Submarine	4" long, 1939	10	15	30
Tanker	black, 6" long, 1940	10	20	25
Tender	4" long, 1940	10	15	25
Transport	6" long, 1939	15	20	30
Yacht	4" long, 1940	10	15	30
Buses				
Cross Country Bus		30	45	65
Fageol Bus	1927-33	20	40	65
GMC Greyhound Bus	blue/silver, 6", 1948	20	35	55
GMC Scenicruiser Bus	blue and silver, raised passenger roof w/windows, 6" long, 1957	20	35	55
Greyhound Bus	blue, 1937-41	25	60	80

VEHICLES

NAME	DESCRIPTION	GOOD	EX	MINT
Overland Bus	1929-33	45	65	125
Twin Coach Bus	red w/black tires, 3" long, 1950	20	35	55

Cannons and Tanks

NAME	DESCRIPTION	GOOD	EX	MINT
Army Tank	miniature	5	10	25
Army Tank	1931-41	35	50	100
Four Wheel Cannon	4" long, 1950s	10	20	45
Long Range Cannon		7	10	30
Six-Wheel Army Cannon	1950s	10	20	50

Cars

NAME	DESCRIPTION	GOOD	EX	MINT
Andy Gump Car	1932; Funnies series	75	300	500
Armored Car	"U.S. Army" on sides, camouflage, black tires, 1938-41	25	35	65
Auburn Roadster	red, white rubber wheels	15	35	50
Austin-Healy	light brown roadster; 6" long, 1956	20	30	60
Baggage Car		10	15	30
Bluebird Daytona Race Car		20	35	65
Boat Tail Roadster	red roadster, 6" long	20	35	55
Buick Brougham	tan/black	20	35	70
Buick Coupe	blue w/white wheels, 1924	30	42	65
Buick Coupe	4"	20	35	50
Buick Estate Wagon	yellow and maroon w/black wheels, 6" long, 1948	20	30	50
Buick Experimental Car	blue w/black wheels, detailed tin bottom, 6" long, 1954	25	50	85
Buick LaSabre	red open top, black wheels, 6" long, 1951	25	45	70
Buick Roadmaster	blue w/black wheels, four-door, 1949	25	40	65
Buick Roadster	yellow open top, black wheels, 4" long, 1938	25	45	65
Buick Sedan	6" long	25	35	55
Buick Special	4" long, 1947	15	25	50
Buick Station Wagon	green w/yellow top, black wheels, 6" long, 1954	20	30	45
Buick Tourer	red w/white wheels, 1925	25	45	70
Buick Touring Car		50	75	110
Cadillac	HO series, blue car/white top, 2" long, 1960	10	20	30
Cadillac 60	red-orange w/black wheels, four-door, 1948	20	35	60
Cadillac 62	red-orange w/white top, black wheels, four-door, 6" long, 1954	20	35	120
Cadillac Brougham		40	60	85
Cadillac Coupe	blue/tan, black wheels	40	60	85
Cadillac Sedan	white rubber wheels	40	60	85
Cadillac Touring Car	1926	50	90	120
Chevrolet Ambulance	4"	15	20	35
Chevrolet Bel Air	yellow w/black wheels, 3" long, 1955	15	30	50
Chevrolet Brougham		40	60	85
Chevrolet Coupe		20	35	90
Chevrolet Coupe	green w/black wheels, 3"	20	35	55
Chevrolet Fastback	blue w/black wheels, 3" long, 1950	15	20	35
Chevrolet Roadster		20	35	90
Chevrolet Sedan		20	35	75
Chevrolet Touring Car		60	150	200
Chrysler Convertible	blue-green w/black wheels, 4" long, 1960	15	25	35
Chrysler Experimental Roadster	orange open top, black wheels	25	40	60
Chrysler New Yorker	blue w/black wheels, four-door, 6" long, 1953	25	35	55
Chrysler Windsor Convertible	black wheels, 6" long, 1950	50	90	120

VEHICLES

NAME	DESCRIPTION	GOOD	EX	MINT
Chrysler Windsor Convertible	green w/black wheels, 4" long, 1941	20	30	45
Classic Series 1906 Cadillac or Studebaker	green and black, spoke wheels	10	15	25
Classic Series 1907 Stanley Steamer	yellow and black, spoke wheels, 1960-65	10	15	25
Classic Series 1912 Ford Model T	black w/red seats, spoke wheels	10	15	25
Classic Series 1919 Stutz Bearcat	black and red, solid wheels	10	15	25
Classic Series 1929 Ford Model A	blue and black, black tread wheels, 1960-65	10	15	25
Corvair	red, 4" long, 1960s	30	55	75
Corvette Roadster	blue open top, black wheels, 4" long, 1954-55	15	20	35
Coupe	miniature	20	25	40
DeSoto Airflow	green w/white wheels	20	35	60
Doodlebug	same as Buick Special	50	75	100
Ferrari Racer	red w/gold driver, black wheels, 6" long, 1956	30	40	65
Ford	red w/open top, black wheels, 6" long, 1940	15	25	40
Ford B Hotrod	1931	15	20	40
Ford Convertible Coupe	1934	30	50	70
Ford Convertible Sedan	red w/black wheels, 3" long, 1949	10	20	35
Ford Coupe	powder blue w/tan top, white wheels, 1934	30	50	75
Ford Coupe	blue or red w/white wheels, 1935	25	35	45
Ford Customline	blue w/black wheels, 1955	15	20	30
Ford Fairlane 500 Convertible	red w/black wheels, 3" long, 1957	10	15	30
Ford Falcon	red w/black wheels, 3" long, 1960	10	15	30
Ford LTD	blue w/black wheels, 4" long, 1969	15	20	35
Ford Mainliner	red w/black wheels, four-door, 3" long, 1952	10	20	30
Ford Model A Coupe	blue w/white wheels	25	35	50
Ford Model A Sedan	green w/black wheels	25	35	50
Ford Ranch Wagon	green w/yellow top, four-door, 4" long, 1954	15	25	35
Ford Ranch Wagon	red w/yellow top, four-door, 3" long, 1954	15	20	35
Ford Roadster	powder blue w/open top, white wheels	25	40	60
Ford Sedan	powder blue w/white solid wheels, 1935	25	35	50
Ford Sedan	lime green w/black wheels, four-door, 3" long, 1949	15	20	35
Ford Sedan	1934	35	50	70
Ford Station Wagon	blue w/black wheels, 3" long, 1960	10	15	25
Ford Station Wagon	red w/white top, black wheels, four-door, 6" long, 1962	25	40	55
Ford Station Wagon	powder blue w/white top, black wheels, 6" long, 1959	15	20	35
Ford Tourer	open top, red w/silver spoke wheels	20	30	45
Ford V-8 Hotrod	red w/open top, black wheels, open silver motor, 6" long, 1940	15	25	35
Ford w/Trailer	blue sedan, white rubber wheels	50	75	130
Graham Convertible Coupe	rear spare tire, rubber wheels, 1933-35	50	125	175
Graham Convertible Coupe	side spare tire, rubber wheels, 1933-35	50	125	175
Graham Convertible Sedan	rear spare tire, rubber wheels, 1933-35	50	125	175
Graham Convertible Sedan	side spare tire, rubber wheels, 1933-35	50	125	175
Graham Coupe	side spare tire, rubber wheels, 1933-35	50	115	150
Graham Coupe	rear spare tire, rubber wheels, 1933-35	50	115	150
Graham Roadster	side spare tire, rubber wheels, 1933-35	50	115	150
Graham Roadster	rear spare tire, rubber wheels, 1933-35	50	115	150
Graham Sedan	rear spare tire, rubber wheels, 1933-35	50	115	150
Graham Sedan	side spare tire, rubber wheels, 1933-35	50	115	150

VEHICLES

NAME	DESCRIPTION	GOOD	EX	MINT
Graham Towncar	rear spare tire, rubber wheels, 1933-35	50	115	150
Graham Towncar	side spare tire, 1933-35	50	115	140
Insurance Patrol	miniature	15	25	35
International Station Wagon	red/yellow, white wheels, 1939-41	15	25	50
International Station Wagon	red/yellow, 3" long	15	25	50
International Station Wagon	4" long, rubber wheels, 1940s	25	45	50
International Station Wagon	orange w/black wheels, postwar	15	20	30
Jaguar Type D	green w/black wheels, 3" long, 1957	10	15	25
Jaguar XK 120 Roadster	green open top, black wheels, 3" long	10	15	25
Jaguar XK 140 Coupe	blue w/black wheels, 6" long	20	30	50
Kaiser Sedan	blue w/black wheels, 6" long, 1947	25	45	55
KO Ice	1932; Funnies series	100	325	425
Lancia Racer	dark green w/black wheels, 6" long, 1956	30	50	75
Large Bluebird Racer	green w/yellow solid wheels	20	40	60
LaSalle Convertible	rubber wheels	80	200	300
LaSalle Convertible Sedan	rubber wheels	80	200	300
LaSalle Coupe	rubber wheels	100	200	300
LaSalle Sedan	rubber wheels	140	200	275
LaSalle Sedan	red w/black rubber wheels, 3" long	15	20	30
Limousine	blue w/silver spoke wheels; prewar	20	40	65
Lincoln	prewar; red w/white rubber wheels, four-door	110	400	500
Lincoln Capri	red w/yellow top, black wheels, two-door, 6" long	20	35	50
Mercedes 190 SL Coupe	powder blue w/black wheels, 6" long, 1956	15	25	40
Mercury	red w/black wheels, four-door, 4" long, 1952	15	20	40
Mercury Custom	blue w/black wheels, four-door, 4" long, 1949	15	30	40
Mercury Fire Chief Car	red w/black wheels, 4" long, 1949	25	35	50
MG TF Roadster	red open top, black wheels, 6" long, 1954	15	25	45
MG TF Roadster	blue open top, black wheels, 3" long, 1954	15	20	35
Model T Pick-up	3", black, spoked metal wheels	25	40	50
Moon Mullins Police Car	1932; Funnies series	130	200	425
Nash Metropolitan Convertible	red w/black tires, 1954	25	35	60
Observation Car		10	15	30
Offenhauser Racer	dark blue w/black wheels, 4" long, 1947	10	20	35
Oldsmobile 88 Convertible	yellow w/black wheels, 4" long, 1949	15	25	35
Oldsmobile 88 Convertible	bright green w/black wheels, 6" long, 1959	20	25	40
Oldsmobile 98	white body w/blue top, skirted fenders, black wheels, 4" long, 1955	20	25	40
Oldsmobile 98	red body w/yellow top, open fenders, black wheels, 4" long, 1955	20	25	45
Oldsmobile 98 Staff Car		20	25	45
Oldsmobile Brougham		25	35	50
Oldsmobile Coupe		25	35	50
Oldsmobile Roadster	orange/black, white wheels, 1924	25	45	75
Oldsmobile Sedan		25	35	50
Oldsmobile Touring		25	35	50
Open Touring	green convertible, white wheels, 3"	25	35	45
Packard	white body w/blue top, black wheels, four-door, 6" long, 1956	25	35	45
Plymouth	dark blue w/black wheels, two-door, 3" long, 1957	10	15	20
Plymouth Sedan	blue w/black wheels, four-door, 3" long, 1950	15	20	30
Pontiac Fire Chief	red w/black wheels, 4" long, 1950	20	35	50
Pontiac Sedan	green w/black wheels, two-door, 4" long, 1950	15	25	45
Pontiac Star Chief	red w/black wheels, four-door, 4" long, 1959	15	25	40

VEHICLES

Moon Mullins Police Car, No.5104X, 1932, Tootsietoy

Ford Wrecker, No. 0133, Tootsietoy

Federal Milk Van, No. 4634, 1924, Tootsietoy

NAME	DESCRIPTION	GOOD	EX	MINT
Porsche Roadster	red w/open top, black wheels, two-door, 6" long, 1956	20	25	40
Pullman Car		10	15	30
Racer	miniature	25	40	50
Racer	orange w/black wheels, 3" long, 1950s	10	15	30
Rambler Wagon	dark green w/yellow top, black wheels, yellow interior, 1960s	15	25	35
Rambler Wagon	blue w/black wheels, 4" long, 1960	15	25	35
Roadster		50	100	140
Roadster	miniature	15	25	40
Sedan	miniature	20	25	40
Sedan		50	100	135
Small Racer	blue w/driver, white wheels, 1927	50	110	175
Smitty	1932; Funnies series	170	250	500
Station Wagon	red w/tan upper, 3"	15	35	55
Studebaker Coupe	green w/black wheels, 3" long, 1947	25	35	50
Studebaker Lark Convertible	lime green w/black wheels, 3" long, 1960	10	15	25
Tank Car	miniature	20	25	40
Thunderbird Coupe	powder blue w/black wheels, 4" long, 1955	15	30	40
Thunderbird Coupe	blue w/black wheels, 3" long, 1955	15	20	30
Torpedo Coupe	gray; prewar	20	25	45
Torpedo Sedan	red	20	30	50
Triumph TR 3 Roadster	black wheels, 3" long, 1956	10	20	35
Uncle Walt	1932; Funnies series	150	300	450
Uncle Willie	1932; Funnies series	150	300	450
VW Bug	lime green w/black tread wheels, 3" long, 1960	10	20	35
VW Bug	metallic gold w/black tread wheels, 6" long, 1960	15	25	30
Yellow Cab Sedan	green w/white wheels, 1921	10	20	30

Emergency Vehicles

NAME	DESCRIPTION	GOOD	EX	MINT
American LaFrance Pumper	red, 3" long, 1954	15	20	35
Chevrolet Ambulance	army green, red cross on roof top, army star on top of hood, 4" long, 1950	15	25	50
Chevrolet Ambulance	yellow, red cross on top, 4" long, 1950	15	25	40
Fire Hook and Ladder	red/blue w/side ladders	25	40	50
Fire Water Tower Truck	blue/orange, red water tower	30	60	80
Ford Wrecker	3" long, 1935, brown, white rubber wheels	30	50	65
Graham Ambulance	white w/red cross on sides	40	95	125
Graham Wrecker	red/black; rubber wheels	50	110	150
Hook and Ladder	#1040	20	25	40
Hook and Ladder	w/driver; white rubber wheels, 1937-41	40	60	75
Hook and Ladder	red and silver; white rubber wheels	50	75	90
Hose Car	w/driver and figure standing by water gun; 1937-41	35	50	80
Hose Wagon	red, black rubber wheels, postwar	20	25	40
Hose Wagon	red w/silver hose, white rubber wheels, 3" long, prewar	25	30	45
Insurance Patrol	red, white wheels, prewar	25	30	45
Insurance Patrol	red, black rubber wheels, postwar	20	25	40
Insurance Patrol	w/driver	25	40	60
Jumbo Wrecker	6" long, 1941	25	40	60
Lincoln Wrecker	sedan w/wrecker hook	200	425	600
Mack L-Line Fire Pumper	red w/ladders on sides	35	65	75
Mack L-Line Hook and Ladder	red w/silver ladder	35	65	75

Farm and Construction Equipment

NAME	DESCRIPTION	GOOD	EX	MINT
Caterpillar Bulldozer	yellow, 6" long	25	45	55
Caterpillar Scraper	yellow w/black wheels, silver blade, 6" long, 1956	15	25	40

VEHICLES

NAME	DESCRIPTION	GOOD	EX	MINT
Caterpillar Tractor	1931	20	30	50
Caterpillar Tractor	miniature	15	25	35
D7 Crawler with Blade	1:50 scale, die cast, 1956	20	35	55
D8 Crawler with Blade	1:87 scale, die-cast	20	30	45
Farm Tractor	w/driver	60	100	145
Ford Tractor	red w/loader, die cast, 1/32 scale	30	40	65
Grader	1:50 scale, 1956, 6"	20	30	50
International Tractor		10	15	25
Steamroller	1931-34	75	150	200

Sets

NAME	DESCRIPTION	GOOD	EX	MINT
Box Trailer and Road Scraper Set	w/driver on road scraper	75	130	250
Contractor Set	pickup truck w/three wagons	50	100	130
Four-Car Transport Set	flatbed trailer carries cars	50	90	135
Freight Train	five-piece set	35	60	80
Grand Prix #1687 Set	seven vehicles, 1969	50	95	150
Midget Series	single engine plane, St. Louis, bomber, Atlantic Clipper, 1" long, 1936-41	10	15	25
Midget Series	assorted ships, 1" long, 1936-41	20	40	60
Midget Series	green cannon, blue tank, green armored car, green tow truck, green camelback van, 1" long, 1936-41	20	40	60
Midget Series	yellow stake truck, red limo, green doodlebug, yellow railcar, blue racer, red fire truck, 1" long, 1936-41	20	40	60
Milk Trailer Set	tractor w/three milk tankers	50	100	200
Passenger Train	five-piece set	40	60	100
Playtime Set	six cars, two trucks, two planes	200	500	850
Tractor with Scoop Shovel and Wagon	red w/silver scoop, flatbed trailer, 1946-52	125	185	250

Space Vehicles

NAME	DESCRIPTION	GOOD	EX	MINT
Buck Rogers Battlecruiser	1937	75	110	165
Buck Rogers Flash Blast Attack Cruiser	1937	50	90	165
Buck Rogers Venus Duo-Destroyer	1937	75	110	150

Trailers

NAME	DESCRIPTION	GOOD	EX	MINT
Boat Trailer	two-wheel	10	15	20
Horse Trailer	red w/white top, two-wheel, black tread wheels	10	15	20
House Trailer	powder blue w/black wheels, two-wheel, door opens	10	15	20
Restaurant Trailer	yellow w/black tread wheels, two-wheel, open sides	30	40	65
Small House Trailer	two-wheel, three side windows, 1935	30	45	65
U-Haul Trailer	red w/black tread wheels, two-wheel, U-Haul logo on sides	10	15	30

Trains

NAME	DESCRIPTION	GOOD	EX	MINT
Borden's Milk Tank Car	yellow; red base	15	20	35
Box Car	"Southern"	15	20	35
Caboose	red	10	15	25
Coal Car	red	10	15	25
Cracker Jack Railroad Car	embossed white metal, painted orange, black rubber tires, 3" long, 1930s	60	150	200
Fast Freight Set	five-piece set, 1940	35	60	80
Log Car	silver w/red wheels; logs chained on	10	15	25
Oil Tank Car	silver top, red base, "Sinclair"	15	20	35
Passenger Train Set	four-piece set, 1925	50	125	160

VEHICLES

NAME	DESCRIPTION	GOOD	EX	MINT
Pennsylvania Engine	red/silver	20	30	50
Refrigerator Car	yellow ochre, red base, black roof	10	15	30
Santa Fe Engine	black/silver	15	20	35
Stock Car	red	10	15	30
Tootsietoy Flyer	silver; three-piece set, 1937	35	60	90
Wrecking Crane	green crane on silver flatbed car w/red wheels	20	30	40
Zephyr Railcar	dark green, 4" long, 1935	35	60	90

Trucks

NAME	DESCRIPTION	GOOD	EX	MINT
Army Half Truck	1941	30	55	75
Army Jeep	windshield up, 6" long, 1950s	15	25	40
Army Jeep CJ3	extended back, windshield down, 4" long, 1950	10	15	35
Army Jeep CJ3	no windshield, 3" long, 1950	10	15	40
Army Supply Truck	w/driver	25	40	55
Box Truck	red w/white wheels, 3" long	15	20	30
Buick Delivery Van		25	35	50
Cadillac Delivery Van		25	35	50
Chevrolet Cameo Pickup	green w/black wheels, 4" long, 1956	15	25	40
Chevrolet Delivery Van		25	35	50
Chevrolet El Camino	red	20	25	40
Chevrolet El Camino Camper and Boat	blue body w/red camper, black/white boat on top of camper	25	35	45
Chevrolet Panel Truck	light green w/black wheels, 4" long, 1950	25	30	40
Chevrolet Panel Truck	green, 3" long, 1950	10	20	30
Chevrolet Panel Truck	green, front fenders opened, 3" long, 1950s	15	20	35
Civilian Jeep	burnt orange, open top, black wheels, 3" long, 1950	10	15	30
Civilian Jeep	red, open top, black wheels, 4" long, 1950	15	20	35
Civilian Jeep	blue w/black tread wheels, 6" long, 1960	15	20	35
CJ3 Army Jeep	open top, no steering wheel cast on dashboard, 3" long, 1950	10	15	30
CJ5 Jeep	red w/black tread wheels, windshield up, 6" long, 1960s	15	20	30
CJ5 Jeep	red w/black tread wheels, windshield up, 6" long, 1950s	15	25	35
Coast to Coast Van	9" long	40	75	100
Commercial Tire Van	"Commercial Tire and Supply Co."; white rubber wheels; prewar	70	150	200
Diamond T K5 Dump Truck	yellow cab and chassis, green dump body, 6" long	25	35	50
Diamond T K5 Semi	red tractor and light green closed trailer	25	45	55
Diamond T K5 Stake Truck	orange, open sides, 6" long, 1940	25	35	55
Diamond T K5 Stake Truck	orange, closed sides, 6" long, 1940	25	35	55
Diamond T Metro Van	powder blue, 6" long	35	75	100
Diamond T Tow Truck	red w/silver tow bar	25	35	55
Dodge D100 Panel	green and yellow, 6" long	25	40	55
Dodge Pickup	lime green, 4" long	20	30	40
Federal Bakery Van	black w/cream wheels, 1924	50	85	110
Federal Florist Van	black w/cream wheels, 1924	75	175	220
Federal Grocery Van	black w/cream wheels, 1924	45	70	100
Federal Laundry Van	black w/cream wheels, 1924	50	85	110
Federal Market Van	black w/cream wheels, 1924	55	85	110
Federal Milk Van	black w/cream wheels, 1924	55	85	110
Ford C600 Oil Tanker	red, 6" long, 1962	15	30	40
Ford C600 Oil Tanker	bright yellow, 3" long	10	15	20
Ford Econoline Pickup	red, 1962	15	25	35
Ford F1 Pickup	orange, open tailgate, 3" long, 1949	15	20	35
Ford F1 Pickup	orange, closed tailgate, 3" long, 1949	15	20	35

VEHICLES

NAME	DESCRIPTION	GOOD	EX	MINT
Ford F6 Oil	orange, 4" long, 1949	10	15	25
Ford F6 Oil Tanker	red w/Texaco, Sinclair, Shell or Standard on sides, 6" long, 1949	25	50	100
Ford F6 Pickup	red, 4" long, 1949	15	25	40
Ford F600 Army Anti-Aircraft Gun	tractor-trailer flatbed, guns on flatbed	20	30	45
Ford F600 Army Radar	tractor-trailer flatbed, yellow radar unit on flatbed, 6" long, 1955	20	30	45
Ford F600 Army Stake Truck	tractor-trailer box, army star on top of trailer box roof and "U.S. Army" on sides, 6" long, 1955	25	40	55
Ford F600 Stake Truck	light green, 6" long, 1955	15	25	35
Ford Pickup	3", beige; 1935; white rubber wheels	25	40	55
Ford Shell Oil Truck		45	60	85
Ford Styleside Pickup	orange, 3" long, 1957	10	15	30
Ford Texaco Oil Truck		45	60	85
Hudson Pickup	red, 4" long, 1947	25	40	55
International Bottle Truck	lime green	30	45	65
International Car Transport Truck	red tractor, orange double-deck trailer w/cars	35	50	70
International Gooseneck Trailer	orange tractor and flatbed trailer	30	40	55
International K1 Oil Truck	green, comes w/oil brands on sides, 6" long	20	30	45
International K1 Panel Truck	blue, 4" long	20	30	55
International RC180 Grain Semi	green tractor and red trailer	30	50	70
International Sinclair Oil Truck	6" long	35	75	100
International Standard Oil Truck	6" long	35	75	100
Jeepster	bright yellow w/open top, black wheels, 3" long, 1947	10	15	35
Jumbo Pickup	6" long, green w/black wheels, 1936-41	25	35	50
Mack Anti-Aircraft Gun		25	40	55
Mack B-Line Cement Truck	red truck w/yellow cement mixer, 1955	20	35	55
Mack B-Line Oil Tanker	red tractor and trailer, "Mobil"	20	35	55
Mack B-Line Stake Trailer	red tractor, orange closed trailer, 1955	20	35	55
Mack Coal Truck	"City Fuel Company," 10 wheels	60	120	175
Mack Coal Truck	orange cab w/blue bed, four wheels, 1925	90	100	250
Mack Coal Truck	red cab w/black bed, 1928	60	120	160
Mack Dairy Tanker	1930s; two-piece cab; Tootsietoy Dairies	75	100	225
Mack L-Line Dump Truck	yellow cab and chassis, light green dump body, 6" long, 1947	20	35	55
Mack L-Line Semi and Stake Trailer	red tractor and trailer	50	95	125
Mack L-Line Semi-Trailer	red tractor cab, silver semi-trailer, "Gerard Motor Express" on sides	60	115	145
Mack L-Line Stake Truck	red w/silver bed inside	25	35	55
Mack L-Line Tow Truck	red w/silver tow bar	25	35	55
Mack Log Hauler	red cab, trailer w/load of logs, 1940s	50	95	135
Mack Mail Truck	red cab w/light brown box, "U.S. Mail Airmail Service" on sides, 3" long, 1920s	40	70	100
Mack Milk Truck	"Tootsietoy Dairy," one-piece cab	50	110	175
Mack Oil Tanker	"DOMACO" on side of tanker	60	100	155
Mack Oil Truck	red cab w/orange tanker, 1925	25	40	55
Mack Railway Express	1930s; Wrigley's Gum	55	115	165
Mack Searchlight Truck	1931-41	25	40	55
Mack Stake Trailer-Truck	enclosed cab, open stake trailer, 'Express' on sides of trailer	50	90	120

VEHICLES

TOOTSIETOY

NAME	DESCRIPTION	GOOD	EX	MINT
Mack Stake Truck	orange cab w/red stake bed, 1925	25	40	60
Mack Trailer-Truck	open cab	50	85	110
Mack Transport	red, open cab w/flatbed trailer	60	150	200
Mack Transport	yellow, 1941, w/three cars at angle	150	500	700
Mack Van Trailer-Truck	enclosed cab and box trailer	50	100	140
Mack Wrigley's Spearmint Gum Truck	4", green w/white rubber wheels, red hubs	70	150	225
Model T Pickup	3" long, 1914	30	50	75
Oil Tanker	blue, three caps on top, 2" long, 1932	20	25	50
Oil Tanker	orange, four caps on top of tanker, 3" long, postwar	20	25	40
Oil Tanker	green w/white wheels; prewar	15	25	35
Oil Tanker	blue and silver, two caps on top of tanker, 3" long	20	30	40
Oldsmobile Delivery Van		25	35	50
Shell Oil Truck	yellow/silver, 6", white rubber wheels	50	85	120
Sinclair Oil Truck	6" long; green/silver	50	85	120
Special Delivery	1936	20	25	40
Stake Truck	miniature	25	40	55
Standard Oil Truck	red/silver; 6", white rubber wheels	80	100	150
Texaco Oil Truck	red/silver; 6", white rubber wheels	55	85	120
Tootsietoy Dairy	semi trailer truck	75	110	140
Tootsietoy Oil Tanker	red cab, silver tanker, "Tootsietoy Line" on side, 1950s	60	95	125
Wrigley's Box Van	w/or without decal, 1940s	45	60	75

WILLIAMS, A.C.

NAME	DESCRIPTION	GOOD	EX	MINT

Cars

NAME	DESCRIPTION	GOOD	EX	MINT
1930s Chrysler Convertible Coupe	6", operating rumble seat	300	400	500
1930s Chrysler Roadster	5"	100	200	300
1930s Coupe	5", rubber tires, turned metal wheels, twin sidemount spare tires	150	250	350
1930s Sedan	6-1/2", rubber tires, turned metal wheels, twin sidemount spare tires	250	350	450
1930s Sedan	5", rubber tires, turned metal wheels, twin sidemount spare tires	150	250	350
Dream Car	cast iron, 4-7/8" long, 1930	75	150	250
Ford Model A Fordor Sedan	6", nickel-plated cast spoke wheels	600	900	1200
Ford Roadster	1936	450	550	650
Lincoln Touring Cars	spoked wheels, cast iron, 8-3/4" long, 1924	400	600	800
Racer	yellow, cast iron, 8-1/2" long, 1932	300	450	600
Taxi	cast iron, 5-1/4" long, 1920	200	350	500
Touring Cars	solid wheels, cast iron, 11-3/4" long, 1917	500	750	1200
Touring Cars	disc wheels, cast iron, 9-1/8" long, 1922	400	600	800

Trucks

NAME	DESCRIPTION	GOOD	EX	MINT
Austin Transport Set	w/three vehicles, cast iron, 12-1/2" long, 1930	500	850	1250
Car Carrier w/Three Austin Cars	12"	800	1200	1600
Coast to Coast Cartage Semi Stake Trailer	6-1/2"	100	150	200
Coast to Coast Cartage Semi Stake Trailer	10", nickel plated stamped steel spoke wheels	400	600	800
Interchangeable Delivery Truck	cast iron, 7-1/4" long, 1932	175	250	350

VEHICLES

906

WILLIAMS, A.C.

NAME	DESCRIPTION	GOOD	EX	MINT
Mack Bulldog Gasoline Tank Truck	5", nickel plated stamped steel spoke wheels	125	175	225
Mack Bulldog Gasoline Tank Truck	7", nickel plated cast spoke wheels	300	450	600
Mack Bulldog Stake Truck	4-3/4", nickel plated stamped steel spoke wheels	100	150	200
Moving Van	cast iron, 4-3/4" long 1930	150	225	300
Pickup Truck	cast iron, 4-3/4" long, 1926	100	150	200

WINROSS

NAME	DESCRIPTION	GOOD	EX	MINT
AACA Hershey Region Fall Meet	long nose single axle (White 9000 cab), stk., wind screen doubles (incentive)	95	100	125
AACA Hershey Region Fall Meet	sleeper single axle (White 7000 cab) tanker, (incentive)	95	100	125
AACA Library and Research Center	FL/T stk. aerodynamic wind screen	60	65	75
ACME Printing	long nose tandem axle (White 9000)	30	45	50
Adirondack Beverage Co.	Ford cab (Ford C1 9000), long nose tandem axle, stacks, wind screen	20	25	35
Almond Joy	Ford cab (Ford C1 9000), long nose tandem axle, stacks, other side Mounds	45	50	60
Alpo	long nose tandem axle (White 9000 cab)	30	45	50
Amana	sleeper tandem axle (White 7000 cab)	35	45	50
American Red Cross	International 8300/T stacks Hanover top logo not Winross 1/600	55	65	75
Amoco Mileage Caravan	sleeper single axle (White 7000 cab) blue cab swing dolly	75	80	90
Anderson Windows	Internationl 8300/T stacks	50	60	65
Andes Candies	Mack cab (Mack Ultra-liner), sleeper tandem axle (White 7000 cab), wind screen, reefer	40	50	60
Antique Car Show (Hershey)	International 8300/T stacks	55	65	75
Antique Car Show (Hershey)	Ford cab (Ford C1 9000), long nose tandem axle stacks, drop bed	55	65	75
Avis Truck Rental	cab over single axle (White 5000 cab)	25	35	45
Bicentennial Trail Issue	long nose tandem axle (White 9000 cab)	40	50	60
Bon Ton Potato Chips	Ford cab (Ford C1 9000), long nose single axle, black tanks, old suspension	90	100	125
Bon Ton Potato Chips	Ford cab (Ford C1 9000), long nose single axle, chrome tanks	35	45	55
Borden	milk tanker, screw replaces the rivet in the ear of the floor trailer, w/ladder	80	90	110
Borden	Credit and Sales sleeper tandem axle (White 7000 cab), plastic dolly	35	40	50
Bowman Trans.	long nose tandem axle (White 9000 cab), stacks, wind screen	90	100	125
Bubble Yum	cab over single axle (White 5000 cab), red, plastic dolly	55	65	75
Bud Light (Fox Dist.)	Ford cab (Ford C1 9000), long nose tandem axle, stacks	90	100	125
Budd Movers	sleeper tandem axle (White 7000 cab), stacks, drop bed	135	175	200
Busch	Ford cab (Ford C1 9000), long nose tandem axle, stacks, wind screen (Hauck and Sons)	80	90	100
Butternut Coffee	sleeper tandem axle (White 7000 cab), stacks	25	35	45
California Raisins	Ford cab (Ford C1 9000), long nose tandem axle, stacks	60	70	80
Campbell's Soup	Mack cab (Mack Ultra-liner), sleeper tandem axle (White 7000 cab), aerodynamic wind screen, tanker Tomato Juice	70	80	90

NAME	DESCRIPTION	GOOD	EX	MINT
Cerro Cooper	sleeper tandem axle (White 7000 cab), stacks	30	40	50
Cherry Hill Orchard	Ford cab (Ford C1 9000), long nose tandem axle, stack, full fairing T-Bird reefer	45	55	65
Cherry Hill Orchard	Mack cab (Mack Ultra-liner), sleeper tandem axle (White 7000 cab), aerodynamic wind screen, full fairing T-Bird reefer	45	55	65
Cola-Cola	long nose single axle (White 9000 cab) unpainted doors	100	125	150
Cola-Cola	long nose single axle (White 9000 cab) red plain doors	100	125	150
Cola-Cola	Ford Aeromax 120 cab, aerodynamic conventional sleeper, tandem axle, stacks, Dearborn Convention	175	200	300
Coleman's Ice Cream	Ford cab (Ford C1 9000), long nose tandem axle, stack, aerodynamic wind screen tool box sleeper	40	50	60
Colorado Beef	long nose single axle and long nose tandem axle (White 9000 cab) and stacks	30	40	50
Coors	Ford cab (Ford C1 9000), long nose tandem axle, stack, full fairing drop bed "Bill Elliott"	185	200	250
Coors	Ford Aeromax 120 cab, an aerodynamic conventional sleeper, stack	55	65	75
Corning	sleeper tandem axle (white 7000 cab), "Lots for You" (both sides shown)	30	40	50
Cracker Jack	silk screen, plastic dolly	200	250	300
Dairymen	Ford cab (Ford C1 9000), stack, tanker	90	100	125
Dannon Yogurt	cab over single axle w/Beatrice logo	25	30	35
Diamond Crystal Salt	silk screen	50	55	60
Diefenbach's Potato Chips	Ford cab (Ford C1 9000), long nose tandem axle, stack, 25th Anniversary	40	50	60
Domino's	Kenworth T800, tandem axle, stack, T-Bird reefer	40	50	60
Downy's Honey Butter	Ford cab (Ford C1 9000), long nose tandem axle, stack, T-Bird reefer, chassis cylinder (fuel tank for a reefer)	40	50	60
Eastman Kodak	long nose tandem axle (White 9000 cab), metal dolly, Kodak logo	55	65	75
Eastman Kodak	Mack ultra-liner cab, sleeper tandem axle (White 7000 cab), stacks, drop bed, (racing team)	350	400	500
Eastwood Company	Kenworth T800, tandem axle, stack, turbo wind screen, parabolic shape, straight truck	55	65	75
Eastwood Company	Ford Aeromax 120 cab, an aerodynamic conventional sleeper, long nose tandem axle, stack, wind screen, doubles	40	50	60
Eastwood Company	Ford cab (Ford C1 9000), long nose tandem axle, stack, turbo wind screen (Motor Sports)	55	65	75
Emergency Fire	1500 cab light or dark red	100	125	150
Emergency Fire	3000 cab white	300	325	350
Evergreen Juice Co.	Mack cab (Mack Ultra-liner), sleeper tandem axle (White 7000 cab), stack	30	40	50
Firestone	International 8300, tandem axle	55	65	75
Florigold (Sealed Sweet)	sleeper tandem axle	55	65	75
Ford, Story of	Ford Aeromax 120 cab, tandem axle, stack, yellow cab (#1), 1905	150	175	200
Fourth of July	Ford cab (Ford C1 9000), long nose tandem axle, stack, aerodynamic wind screen	55	65	75
Foxx Paper (fictional company)	3000 cab, 32' flat bed w/side boards and simulated paper roll load	20	25	30
Georgia Pacific	Mack cab (Mack Ultra-liner), sleeper tandem axle (White 7000 cab), stack, wind screen, drop bed	250	300	350
Girl Scout Cookies	Ford cab (Ford C1 9000), long nose tandem axle, stack	55	65	75
Glade Spinfresh	long nose single axle (White 9000 cab)	25	30	35
Good & Plenty Candy	International 8300, tandem axle, stack	30	40	50

VEHICLES

NAME	DESCRIPTION	GOOD	EX	MINT
Good Poultry Services	Ford cab (Ford C1 9000), long nose tandem axle, stack, wind screen, tanker	30	40	50
Goodwill	Ford cab (Ford C1 9000), long nose single axle, stack	30	40	50
Goodwrench	International 8300, tandem axle, stack, drop bed #3 Dale Earnhart w/cars	100	125	150
Graebel	sleeper tandem axle (White 7000 cab), stack, wind screen, drop bed (Movers)	75	85	100
Graebel	sleeper tandem axle (White 7000 cab), stack, wind screen, drop bed (Van Line)	30	35	45
Great American Van Lines	single tandem axle (White 7000 cab), stack, drop bed	70	75	90
H & H Excavating	Ford cab (Ford C1 9000), long nose tandem axle, stack	30	40	50
H & R Block	Mack cab (Mack Ultra-liner), sleeper tandem axle (White 7000 cab), stack	30	40	50
Halls	long nose tandem axle, plastic dolly, smooth front trailer	90	100	125
Hanover Brands	silk screen, swing dolly (both sides)	125	150	200
Hanover Transfer Co.	International 8300, tandem axle, stack	70	85	100
Hardee's	Mack cab (Mack Ultra-liner), sleeper tandem axle (White 7000 cab), stack, reefer, under chassis cylinder (fuel tank for a reefer)	65	70	80
Hawaiian Punch	sleeper tandem axle (White 7000 cab), wind screen	100	125	150
Hershey's Chocolate	sleeper single axle (White 7000 cab), foil tanker	100	125	150
Hershey's Chocolate	Ford cab (Ford C1 9000), long nose tandem axle, stack, red cab foil tanker	100	125	150
Hershey's Chocolate	Kenworth T800, tandem axle, stack, Strawberry Syrup tanker	75	85	100
Hershey's Chocolate	Ford cab (Ford C1 9000), long nose tandem axle, stack, aerodynamic wind screen, milk tanker	75	85	100
Hertz	long nose single axle (White 9000 cab), 32' wheel, dolly cast doors	75	85	100
Hess Mills (Purina Chows)	Ford cab (Ford C1 9000), long nose tandem axle, stack. vert. brush tanker	40	50	60
Hostess Cake	Ford cab (Ford C1 9000), long nose tandem axle, stack, wind screen, other side Wonder	60	70	80
Iceland Seafood	sleeper single axle (White 7000 cab)	70	80	90
Iola Car Show	long nose single axle (White 9000 cab)	20	25	30
Iola Car Show	cab over single axle (White 5000 cab)	20	25	30
James River Corp.	Mack cab (Mack Ultra-liner), sleeper tandem axle (White 7000 cab), stack, wind screen	35	45	55
Jeno's Pizza	sleeper single axle (White 7000 cab), pin, plastic dolly	50	55	60
Johnson Wax	sleeper tandem axle (White 7000 cab), vert. brush tanker "Innobulk"	25	30	40
Juice Bowl	sleeper tandem axle (White 7000 cab), wind screen	45	55	65
Kraft	International 8300, tandem axle, stack, T-Bird reefer, "America Spells Cheese" top logo	60	70	80
Lancaster Farm Toy Show	Mack cab (Ultra-liner), sleeper tandem axle, brown cab, flatbed w/J.D. farm equipment	150	175	200
Lancaster Farm Toy Show	Ford cab (Ford C1 9000), long nose tandem axle, stack, met, maroon, flatbed w/J.D. farm equipment	150	175	200
Lancaster Farm Toy Show	Ford cab (Ford C1 9000), long nose tandem axle, stack, met, slate blue, flatbed w/J.D. farm equipment	150	175	200
Lancaster Farm Toy Show	Ford cab (Ford C1 9000), long nose tandem axle, stack, met, brown, flatbed w/J.D. farm equipment	150	175	200
Lancaster Farm Toy Show	Mack cab (Ultra-liner), sleeper tandem axle, red cab, flatbed w/Ford farm tractor	150	175	200
Lancaster Farm Toy Show	Mack cab (Ultra-liner), sleeper tandem axle, blue cab, flatbed w/International farm tractor	150	175	200
Lea & Perrins	sleeper tandem axle (White 7000 cab)	25	30	40
Leinenkugel Brewery	Ford cab (Ford C1 9000), long nose tandem axle, stack	35	45	55

VEHICLES

909

NAME	DESCRIPTION	GOOD	EX	MINT
Londonderry Fire Co.	Ford cab (Ford C1 9000), long nose tandem axle, stack, vert. brush tanker	40	50	60
Lysol	long nose single axle (White 9000 cab)	25	30	40
Mack Trucks "Story of Mack Trucks Set #1"	Mack cab (Mack Ultra-liner), sleeper tandem axle (White 7000 cab), stack 1893 new and old suspension	125	150	175
Mack Trucks "Story of Mack Trucks Set #1"	Mack cab (Mack Ultra-liner). sleeper tandem axle (White 7000 cab), stack 1905 new and old suspension	125	150	175
Mack Trucks "Story of Mack Trucks Set #1"	Mack cab (Mack Ultra-liner). sleeper tandem axle (White 7000 cab), stack 1909 new and old suspension	125	150	175
Martin's Potato Chips	Ford cab (Ford C1 9000), long nose single axle, stack, aerodynamic wind screen, white cab	35	45	55
Maxwell House (Sterling Martin)	Ford Aeromax 120 cab, an aerodynamic conventional sleeper	55	65	75
McDonald's	sleeper tandem axle (White 7000 cab), Martin Brower, T-Bird reefer	40	50	60
Michelob Fox District	Ford cab (Ford C1 9000), long nose tandem axle, stack, tanker	100	110	125
Monfort	sleeper tandem axle (White 7000 cab)	100	110	125
Morton Salt	sleeper single axle (White 7000 cab)	70	80	90
Mountain Dew	International 8300, tandem axle, stack	35	45	55
Mrs. Paul's	International 8300, tandem axle, stack, tanker	60	70	80
Mt. Joy Co-op	Ford cab (Ford C1 9000), long nost tandem axle, foil tanker w/graphics	70	85	100
Nabisco	sleeper single axle (White 7000 cab), Jr. Mints-Chuckles both sides shown	85	95	110
National Private Trucking Association	Ford cab (Ford C1 9000), long nose tandem axle, stack	20	25	30
National Toy Show	long nose single axle, Ford "F" Series, Ford cab w/pop-up hood, two tractors both sides and cabs	75	85	100
Nestle's Quik	sleeper tandem axle (White 7000 cab), vert. brush	70	80	90
Old Milwaukee	long nose single axle (White 9000 cab), metal dolly, black chassis	70	80	90
Old Style (Heileman Brewery)	sleeper tandem axle (White 7000 cab), plastic dolly, one shield	55	65	75
Old Toyland Shows	long nose single axle (White 9000 cab), stacks, white cab both sides shown	25	30	35
Owens Corning Fiberglass	sleeper single axle (White 7000 cab), vert. brush tanker	40	50	60
P.I.E. Nationwide	Ford cab, long nose single axle, wind screen, stacks, doubles, w/Olympic rings	300	350	400
P.I.E. Nationwide	long nose tandem axle (White 9000 cab), wind screen	55	65	75
Pennsylvania Pump Primers	Ford cab (Ford C1 9000), long nose tandem axle, stack, tool box #1	30	40	50
Pepsi	screw replaces the rivet in the rear of the floor of the trailer, plastic dolly	150	175	200
Pepsi	International 8300, tandem axle, stack, special edition	150	175	200
Pillsbury	sleeper tandem axle (White 7000 cab), Hungry Jack/Crescent Rolls	80	90	100
Prince Spaghetti	long nose single axle (White 9000 cab)	55	65	75
Quaker Oats	Mack cab (Mack Ultra-liner), sleeper tandem axle (White 7000 cab), stack, Kankakee Distribution Center	30	40	50
Quaker State	sleeper single axle (White 7000 cab), swing dolly	100	150	200
RCA	long nose tandem axle (White 9000 cab), stack, "Home Video"	80	85	100
Reading Railroad	long nose tandem axle (White 9000 cab), one stack	85	90	100
Reading Railroad	long nose tandem axle (White 9000 cab), no stack	65	70	80

VEHICLES

910

NAME	DESCRIPTION	GOOD	EX	MINT
Red Ball Movers	sleeper tandem axle (White 7000 cab), van red, metal dolly	80	90	100
Red Hawk Racing	Ford Aeromax 120 cab, an aerodynamic conventional sleeper, stack, tandem axle, double bed, Jeff McClure	90	100	120
Reese's	long nose tandem axle (White 9000 cab), cab logo, foil tanker, (peanut butter cups)	35	45	55
Rochester Smelting	long nose tandem axle (White 9000 cab), metal dolly, flat bed w/block load	150	175	200
Sakrete	screw replaces the rivet in the rear of the floor of the trailer	85	95	100
Schmidt's Beer	long nose tandem axle (White 9000 cab)	100	125	150
Seven Up	sleeper single axle (White 7000 cab), red wheels, red metal dolly	90	100	125
Shasta	sleeper single axle (White 7000 cab)	30	35	45
Silver Spring Fire Co.	Mack cab (Mack Ultra-liner), sleeper tandem axle (White 7000 cab), stack, tanker	40	50	60
Simon Candy	Mack cab (Mack Ultra-liner), sleeper tandem axle (White 7000 cab), stack, full fairing clear sided doubles; w/candy	55	65	75
Snyder's of Hanover	Mack cab (Mack Ultra-liner), sleeper single axle (White 7000 cab), stack	90	100	110
Sony	Mack cab (Mack Ultra-liner), sleeper tandem axle (White 7000 cab), stack, wind screen	60	65	75
Spickler's	Ford cab (Ford C1 9000), long nose tandem axle, stack, vert. brush, tanker	45	55	65
Stephens Boat Works (fictional company)	long nose single axle (White 9000 cab), blue 32'	150	175	200
Sunoco	Ford cab (Ford C1 9000), long nose tandem axle, stack, full fairing drop bed "Ultra Racing Team" (Marlin) plain	125	150	175
Sunoco	Ford Aeromax 120 cab, an aerodynamic conventional sleeper, tandem axle, stack, drop bed, Terry Labonte	200	250	300
SuperAmerica	long nose tandem axle (White 9000 cab), tanker	30	35	45
Superbubble	sleeper tandem axle (White 7000 cab)	25	30	35
Timberline	sleeper tandem axle (White 7000 cab), stack	35	45	55
TMI (Three Mile Island)	sleeper tandem axle (White 7000 cab), stack, wind screen, flat bed, nuc. waste load, each numbered	100	125	150
Toledo Toy Show	International 8300, tandem axle, stack	25	30	40
Totinos	sleeper tandem axle (White 7000 cab), stack, T-Bird reefer	35	40	50
Transport for Christ (Mobile Chapel)	Mack cab (Mack Ultra-liner), sleeper tandem axle (White 7000 cab), stack, wind screen	35	40	50
Transport Topics	long nose tandem axle (White 9000 cab), tanker, swing dolly	90	100	125
Tyson Foods	sleeper tandem axle (White 7000 cab), wind screen, reefer, "America's Choice"	80	90	110
U.S. Brands	sleeper tandem axle (White 7000 cab), wind screen	25	35	45
U.S. Gypsum	sleeper tandem axle (White 7000 cab), blue w/red letters	55	65	75
U.S. Mail	cab over single axle (White 5000 cab), "Zip" blue metal dolly	55	65	75
U.S. Steel	long nose tandem axle (White 9000 cab), long wheel base cab, green, 32' flat bed, silver I-beam	90	100	125
Union Carbide	sleeper tandem axle (White 7000 cab), vert. brush, tanker	55	65	75
Unique Garden Center	sleeper tandem axle (White 7000 cab), stack, reefer	25	30	40
United Auto Workers (UAW)	Ford cab (Ford C1 9000), long nose tandem axle, stack (America Works)	65	70	75

VEHICLES

NAME	DESCRIPTION	GOOD	EX	MINT
United Way	Ford cab (Ford C1 9000), long nose tandem axle, stack, tanker (Collector Model 1 of 500)	30	40	50
Warner-Lambert	Ford cab (Ford C1 9000), long nose tandem axle, aerodynamic wind screen, "Efferdent" on side	25	30	35
Watergate	cab over single axle (White 5000 cab)	20	25	30
Weaver Chicken	sleeper tandem axle (White 7000 cab), white metal dolly "Country Style"	80	90	110
Westmans 32' Transport Tanker	long nose single axle (White 9000 cab), white trailer, red letters, wheel dolly	150	175	200
Westmans 32' Transport Tanker	3000 cab w/wheels, blue w/red, logo on trailer, wheel dolly	175	200	250
White Oak Mills	sleeper tandem axle (White 7000 cab), stack, tanker w/catwalk	90	100	110
Wilbur Chocolate	Ford cab (Ford C1 9000), long nose tandem axle, stack, aerodynamic wind screen, T-Bird reefer, "Wilbur Buds"	60	65	75
Winross at Dyersville	Ford Aeromax 120 cab, an aerodynamic conventional sleeper, stack, Erie Canal	65	70	75
Winross at Hershey	Ford Aeromax 120 cab, an aerodynamic conventional sleeper, tandem axle, stack, quilts, different shade pink wind screen (Collectors Series)	40	45	50
Winross at Hershey	Kenworth T800, tandem axle, tent scene	30	40	50
Winross at Hershey	Mack cab (Mack Ultra-liner), tandem axle, chrome stacks, aerodynamic wind screen, car restoration	30	40	50
Winross at Hershey	Ford Aeromax 120 cab, an aerodynamic conventional sleeper, tandem axle	75	80	90
Winross at Hershey	Mack cab (Mack Ultra-liner), sleeper tandem axle (White 7000 cab), aerodynamic wind screen, farm scene	30	40	50
Winross at Hershey	International 8300, tandem axle, Hershey Commemorative	40	45	50
Winross at Hershey	Mack cab (Mack Ultra-liner), sleeper tandem axle (White 7000 cab), aerodynamic wind screen, green cab	30	40	50
Winross at Hershey	Ford cab (Ford C1 9000), long nose tandem axle, stack, aerodynamic wind screen, blue cab	30	40	50
Winross at Hershey	Mack cab (Mack Ultra-liner), tandem axle, gray stacks, aerodynamic wind screen, car restoration, Collector Series	30	40	50
Winross at Hershey	Ford Aeromax 120 cab, an aerodynamic conventional sleeper, stack, tandem axle, quilts	75	80	90
Winross at Rochester	Kenworth T800, tandem axle, stack, Erie Canal	30	40	50
Winross Hospitality Day	Mack cab (Mack Ultra-liner), tandem axle, stack, wind screen, blue cab, "You've Got a Friend in PA"	50	55	60
Winston Motor Sports	Ford Aeromax 120 cab, an aerodynamic conventional sleeper, stack, 20-year anniversary	45	50	55
Wonder Bread	Ford cab (C1 9000), long nose tandem axle, stack, wind screen, other side "Hostess"	70	75	80
Wyler's	sleeper single axle (White 7000 cab), pin, plastic dolly, "Realemon" on both sides	25	30	40
Y & S Candies	Mack cab (Mack Ultra-liner), sleeper tandem axle (White 7000 cab), stack, wind screen	55	65	75
Yellow Freight System	screw replaces the rivet in the rear of the floor of the trailer, rib trailer, plastic dolly	25	30	40
Yoplait Yogurt	sleeper tandem axle (White 7000 cab), stack, wind screen, reefer, trailer edged white	30	40	50
Zeager Bros. Inc.	Ford cab (C1 9000), long nose tandem axle, stack, flat bed w/two lumber stacks	100	125	150
Zembo Temple	Ford cab (C1 9000), long nose tandem axle, stack, wind screen, white wheels	85	95	100

VEHICLES

Soap Box Derby Racer, 1940s, Wyandotte

Circus Truck and Wagon, 1937, Wyandotte

Ice Truck, 1938, Wyandotte

WYANDOTTE

NAME	DESCRIPTION	GOOD	EX	MINT

Airplanes

NAME	DESCRIPTION	GOOD	EX	MINT
Army Bombing Plane	8-1/2" wingspan; rubber wheels	25	65	85
Autogyro Plane	9-1/4" long; rubber wheels	75	190	300
China Clipper Airplane	9-1/4" long; rubber wheels	90	200	300
Defense Bomber Airplane	9-1/4" long; "U.S. Army" marked on wing	70	150	225
Stratoship Mystery Plane	4-1/4" long	10	25	40

Boats

NAME	DESCRIPTION	GOOD	EX	MINT
Battleship	6" long, rubber wheels	35	55	70
S.S. America Boat	12-1/2" long, wood wheels	40	75	100

Cars

NAME	DESCRIPTION	GOOD	EX	MINT
Air Speed Coupe	5-7/8" long, rubber wheels	40	75	95
Coupe	6-1/2" long, wood or rubber wheels	40	75	90
Rocket Racer	6" long	50	75	100
Soap Box Derby Racer	6-1/4"	45	100	150
Station Wagon	woodgrain and passenger lithography; 21" long	200	300	450
Zephyr Racer	10" long	75	125	150
Zephyr Roadster	13-3/8" long; rubber wheels	400	600	750

Emergency Vehicles

NAME	DESCRIPTION	GOOD	EX	MINT
Ambulance	11-1/4" long; Red Cross and "Wyandotte Toys" on side	75	150	185
Ambulance	6", wood wheels	45	70	90

Miscellaneous

NAME	DESCRIPTION	GOOD	EX	MINT
Auto Hauler Set	trailer, sedan, dump truck, wooden wheels; 18-1/2" long	175	325	375
Coast to Coast Bus Lines	21" long; rubber wheels	200	300	450
Flash Strat-O-Wagon	6" long; rubber wheels	35	65	90
Gasoline and Service Station	Shell station; w/two vehicles	250	550	800
Land Cruiser Auto Set	sedan w/trailer; 11-3/4" long	50	100	150
Sand Hopper Set	7" high; w/shovel	20	35	50
Streamlined Wagon	5-1/4" long, rubber wheels	25	35	50

Trucks

NAME	DESCRIPTION	GOOD	EX	MINT
Circus Truck and Wagon	19" long; red/yellow; w/cardboard animals	650	950	1400
Contractors' Truck	11-1/4" long; metal wheels; w/miniature wheelbarrow	70	125	175
Engineer Corps Truck	17-1/2" long; wood wheels; marked "Army Engineer Corps"	75	130	190
Gasoline Truck	21" long; rubber wheels	100	200	300
Hook 'n Ladder Truck	10-1/4" long, detachable ladders, rubber wheels	90	130	160
Ice Truck	11-1/2" long, wood wheels	100	190	250
Medical Corps Truck	11-3/4" long; metal wheels; "U.S.A. Medical Corps" on side	90	175	250
Milk Truck	11-1/2" long, wood wheels	100	190	250
Semi-Trailer Dump Truck	17-3/8" long; rubber wheels	60	90	150
Stake Truck	6-3/4" long, rubber or wood wheels	35	65	80

VEHICLES

View-Master Reels

View-Master, the popular 3-D collectible, was first introduced at the 1939 New York World's Fair. Originally considered a "photographic" souvenir, it has since become a favorite toy of young and old alike.

During the 1940s and 1950s, the company mainly produced reels for various national parks and other scenic attractions. During World War II, View-Master produced millions of reels for the U.S. government to aid in airplane and ship identification and range estimation.

The company began producing reels for children with the development of their Fairy Tale series in the late 1940s. They went on to produce hundreds of other favorite cartoon characters. In 1951, View-Master purchased the competition, the Tru-Vue Company. Since Tru-Vue held the license to use Disney characters, this acquisition was a coup for View-Master.

Since 1939, the style and construction of the View-Master viewer has greatly changed. Originally made of black Bakelite, the first models were round. The Model "C," which debuted in 1946, was the first square viewer and became the model for all viewers produced since. This model is easily-found today and very affordable. Character viewers were added to the line in 1989 but have since been removed from the product line.

The new 3-D viewer — the Virtual Viewer — will be available in five colors, and was available in stores in the summer of 1999.

Tyco Toys purchased View-Master in 1989. In 1996, Mattel Toys acquired Tyco, bringing the View-Master name under its umbrella.

In pricing reels, the important thing to remember is condition. Three-reel packets consist of the reels, a book (if indicated on the packet reverse side), and the outer envelope with full-color picture. If any element is missing, the overall price drops dramatically. Also, if any part is torn or damaged in any way, the price should be adjusted accordingly.

Prices listed are for reels Mint in Package (MIP). Those in Excellent condition command about 85 percent of the MIP price.

Note: All packages listed have three reels unless otherwise noted.

Trends

Prices for View-Master reels have risen consistently over the past several years, but the market appears to have topped off. Scenic titles continue to be mod-

Toby Tyler

estly priced, but the demand for character reels, mostly by crossover character toy collectors, has resulted in a higher demand for these items. World's Fair titles are also very popular.

The Top 10 View-Master Reel Sets
(Mint in package; not including Movie Preview Reels)

1. It Came From Outer Space $250
2. House of Wax 250
3. Munsters 200
4. Charge at Feather River, The 150
5. Dangerous Mission 150
6. Devil's Canyon 150
7. Drums of Tahiti 150
8. Flight to Tangier 150
9. Fort Ti 150
10. French Line, The 150

Contributors to this section: Mary Ann and Wolfgang Sell, 3752 Broadview Dr., Cincinnati, OH 45208.

VIEW- MASTER

NO.	NAME	MNP	MIP
B506	$1,000,000 Duck	7	10
3014	101 Dalmatians	3	5
B532	101 Dalmatians	3	5
86	1939 New York World's Fair (single reel)	10	25
87	1939 New York World's Fair (single reel)	10	25
88	1939 New York World's Fair (single reel)	5	10
89	1939 New York World's Fair (single reel)	5	10
57	1940 Golden Gate International Expo (single reel)	12	25
56	1940 Golden Gate International Expo (single reel)	12	25
58	1940 Golden Gate International Expo (single reel)	5	10
59	1940 Golden Gate International Expo (single reel)	5	10
A272	1962 Seattle World's Fair (four reels)	20	30
A2726	1962 Seattle World's Fair (single reel)	7	15
A2725	1962 Space Needle U.S.A. (single reel)	7	15
B937	1970s America's Cup (ABC's WW/Sports)	45	50
B370	20,000 Leagues Under the Sea	7	15
4045	A-Team	6	12
BD199	Adam & the Ants	15	20
B593	Adam-12	10	12
B486	Addams Family	65	95
BD205	Adventures of Morph	7	8
3088	Aladdin	3	4
BD265	Alex	9	10
4082	Alf	5	10
4111	An American Tail II	5	6
N3	Annie	5	6
B470	Annie Oakley	12	25
B558	Apple's Way	14	16
B574	Archie	7	8
	Arena (Movie Preview Reel)	75	125
B365	Aristocats, The	5	6
B457	Astrix & Cleopatra	21	25
B948	Auto Racing, Phoenix 200 (ABC's WW/Sports)	35	50
B375	Babes in Toyland	21	25
H77	Bad News Bears in "Breaking Training"	7	8
B502	Banana Splits	10	20
BD239	Bananaman	9	10
4071	Barbie and the Rockers	7	10
35428	Barbie Prom Date	3	5
1998	Barbie Special Pink Viewer set; regular viewer in Barbie pink	7	10
1998	Barbie Special Pink Viewer set; Supershow viewer in Barbie pink; Target Exc	12	20
B500	Barbie's Around the World Trip	20	25
B576	Barbie's Great American Photo Race	20	35
1086	Batman	4	5
BB492	Batman (Adam West)	13	15
B492	Batman (Adam West)	9	10
3086	Batman - The Animated Series	2	4
4137	Batman Returns	7	8
4011	Batman, The Perfect Crime	7	8
L16	Battle Beyond the Stars	12	20
BD185	Battle of the Planets	13	15
3079	Beauty & the Beast	2	4
B366	Bedknobs & Broomsticks	5	10
1074	Beetlejuice	5	6
J51	Benji's Very Own Christmas	7	8
4018	Benji, Superstar	5	6
BD259	Bertha	7	8
B570	Beverly Hillbillies	12	25
B587	Big Blue Marble	10	12
D135	Black Beauty	9	10
K35	Black Hole	15	18
BK035	Black Hole	7	12
BD207	Bollie & Billie	7	8
BB487	Bonanza	10	20
B471	Bonanza	10	20
B487	Bonanza (w/o Pernell Roberts)	30	35
BD1484	Bozo	13	15
B568	Brady Bunch	17	20
B466	Brave Eagle	21	25
BD272	Bravestar	9	10
L15	Buck Rogers	7	8
4056	Buckaroo Banzai	10	12
965abc	Buffalo Bill, Jr.	21	25
B464	Buffalo Bill, Jr.	21	25
B531	Bugs Bunny	9	10
1077	Bugs Bunny & Tweety	2	3
800	Bugs Bunny and Elmer Fudd (one reel)	7	8
B549	Bugs Bunny, Big Top Bunny	5	6
M10	Bugs Bunny/Road Runner Show	3	4
B515	Bullwinkle	12	15
BD212	Button Moon	7	8
L1	Can't Stop the Music	17	20
H43	Captain America	4	5
755abc	Captain Kangaroo	14	16
B560	Captain Kangaroo	10	12
B565	Captain Kangaroo Show	10	12
BD264	Care Bears	5	6

VIEW- MASTER

VIEW- MASTER

NO.	NAME	MNP	MIP
B521	Cartoon Carnival with Supercar	50	75
BD171	Casimir Costureiro	7	8
B533	Casper The Friendly Ghost	5	6
BB533	Casper The Friendly Ghost	5	6
J22	Cat from Outer Space	7	8
1057	Centurions	3	4
	Charge at Feather River, The (Movie Preview Reel)	128	150
L2	Charlie Brown, Bon Voyage	4	6
B556	Charlie Brown, It's a Bird	4	5
1039	Charlie Brown, It's Your First Kiss	9	10
B321	Charlotte's Web	5	6
3075	Chip 'n Dale Rescue Rangers	4	5
L14	CHiPs	13	15
FT5	Cinderella (one reel)	1	2
960	Cisco Kid (one reel)	2	4
B496	City Beneath the Sea	15	30
J47	Close Encounters of the Third Kind	10	15
B461	Cowboy Stars	21	25
B564	Curiosity Shop	10	12
B498	Daktari	13	15
944abc	Dale Evans	26	30
B463	Dale Evans	23	27
BD214	Danger Mouse	15	18
	Dangerous Mission (Movie Preview Reel)	128	150
B479	Daniel Boone	15	20
4036	Dark Crystal	7	10
B503	Dark Shadows	30	60
935abc	Davy Crockett	64	75
BD244	Dempsey & Makepeace	7	8
1065	Dennis the Menace	2	3
B539	Dennis the Menace	3	4
B519	Deputy Dawg	30	50
	Devil's Canyon (Movie Preview Reel)	128	150
4105	Dick Tracy	7	8
BD188	Dick Turpin	9	10
4138	Dinosaurs (Disney TV show)	4	7
A177	Disneyland, Adventureland	6	20
A178	Disneyland, Fantasyland	6	20
A176	Disneyland, Frontierland	6	20
A175	Disneyland, Main Street U.S.A.	6	20
A180	Disneyland, New Orleans Square	6	20
A179	Disneyland, Tomorrowland	6	20
B525	Donald Duck	7	8
H2	Dr. Shrinker & Wonderbug	10	14
BD187	Dr. Who	35	75
BD216	Dr. Who	35	75
B324	Dracula	13	15
	Drums of Tahiti (Movie Preview Reel)	128	150
3055	Duck Tales	4	5
L17	Dukes of Hazzard	7	8
M19	Dukes of Hazzard #2	6	7
4000	Dukes of Hazzard 2	6	7
J60	Dumbo	7	8
BD1474	Dumbo	9	10
4058	Dune	7	12
4117	E.T. (reissued)	3	6
N7	E.T. The Extra-Terrestrial	15	18
4001	E.T., More Scenes from	15	18
K76	Eight is Enough	13	15
H3	Electra Woman & Dyna Girl	7	10
4125	Elmo Wants to Play	2	3
B597	Emergency	10	12
BD122	Emil	10	12
A071	Expo 67 Montreal	12	25
A073	Expo 67 Montreal	12	25
A074	Expo 67 Montreal	12	25
	Expo 70 Osaka	20	40
	Expo 74 Spokane	5	10
BD251	Fabeltjes Krant	10	12
B571	Family Affair	21	25
4118	Family Matters	4	8
K66	Fang Face	5	6
K36	Fantastic Four	9	10
B546	Fantastic Voyage	10	12
B554	Fat Albert & Cosby Kids	5	6
BD269	Ferdy	9	10
B390	Fiddler on the Roof	21	25
	Flash Gordon in the Planet Mongo	21	25
	Flight to Tangier (Movie Preview Reel)	128	150
1066	Flintstone Kids	2	4
L6	Flintstones	10	12
1080	Flintstones	2	3
BB480	Flipper	10	12
B485	Flipper	10	12
BD189	Flying Kiwi	10	12
B495	Flying Nun	21	25
BJ013	Fonz, The	7	8
H54	For the Love of Benji	7	8
	Fort Ti (Movie Preview Reel)	128	150
L29	Fox & Hound	7	8
3000	Fox & the Hound, The (Disney)	4	5
4053	Fraggle Rock	4	5
1067	Fraggle Rock	4	5
B323	Frankenstein	13	15
	French Line, The (Movie Preview Reel)	128	150
4119	Full House	3	6
B585	G.I. Joe	13	15
L28	Garfield	3	4

NO.	NAME	MNP	MIP
950	Gene Autry (one reel)	2	3
951	Gene Autry, "The Kidnapping" (one reel)	2	3
1062	Ghostbusters, The Real	4	6
BD225	Gil & Julie	7	8
	Glass Web (Movie Preview Reel)	128	150
J23	Godzilla	13	15
B945	Gold Cup Hydroplane Races (ABC's WW/ Sports)	34	40
FT6	Goldilocks and the Three Bears (one reel)	1	2
4064	Goonies	7	8
M7	Great Muppet Caper	4	5
B488	Green Hornet	30	60
4055	Gremlins	7	12
J10	Grizzly Adams	9	10
	Gun Fury (Movie Preview Reel)	128	150
B589	Gunsmoke	21	25
B552	Hair Bear Bunch	7	8
1081	Hammerman	3	6
	Hannah Lee (Movie Preview Reel)	128	150
BB586	Happy Days	7	8
J13	Happy Days	7	8
B586	Happy Days	9	10
B547	Hardy Boys	9	10
B590	Hawaii Five-O	17	20
B578	Herbie Rides Again	7	8
B588	Here's Lucy	43	50
956	Hopalong Cassidy (one reel)	2	3
955	Hopalong Cassidy (one reel)	2	3
	House of Wax (Movie Preview Reel)	213	250
4073	Howard the Duck	7	10
B343	Huckleberry Finn	5	8
B512	Huckleberry Hound & Yogi Bear	4	5
L32	I Go Pogo	7	15
	Inferno (Movie Preview Reel)	128	150
BD232	Inspector Gadget	7	8
B946	International Moto-Cross (ABC's WW/ Sports)	15	30
B936	International Swimming & Diving Meet (ABC's WW/Sports)	60	70
H44	Ironman	3	5
T100	Isis	10	12
B367	Island at Top of the World	21	25
	It Came From Outer Space (Movie Preview Reel)	213	250
FT3	Jack and the Beanstalk (one reel)	1	2
B393	James Bond, Live & Let Die	12	20

NO.	NAME	MNP	MIP
BB393	James Bond, Live & Let Die	17	20
K68	James Bond, Moonraker	13	15
4041	Jaws 3-D	4	6
1059	Jem	6	7
	Jesse James vs. The Daltons (Movie Preview Reel)	128	150
L27	Jetsons	5	6
K27	Jim Henson's Muppet Movie	4	5
BD261	Jimbo and the Jet Set	7	8
B456	Joe 90	70	95
BB454	Joe Forrester	9	10
937abc	Johnny Mocassin	21	25
B468	Johnny Mocassin	21	25
B572	Julia	15	25
4150	Jurassic Park	7	10
B392	King Kong	7	8
	Kiss Me Kate (Movie Preview Reel)	128	150
4054	Knight Rider	5	6
B557	Korg 70,000 B.C.	10	12
B598	Kung Fu	13	15
B504	Lancelot Link Secret Chimp	21	25
B494	Land of the Giants	25	50
B579	Land of the Lost	9	15
H1	Land of the Lost 2	9	15
BD190	Larry the Lamb	7	8
B472	Lassie & Timmy	13	15
B480	Lassie Look Homeward	9	10
B489	Lassie Rides the Log Flume	13	15
4057	Last Starfighter, The	5	6
B497	Laugh-In	13	15
J20	Laverne & Shirley	5	6
4092	Legend of Indiana Jones	5	6
L26	Legend of the Lone Ranger	7	8
4033	Legend of the Lone Ranger	6	8
BD203	Les Maitres Du Temps	7	8
B940	Little League World Series (ABC's WW/ Sports)	43	50
3078	Little Mermaid	2	3
3089	Little Mermaid - TV Show	2	3
B319	Little Red Hen/ Thumbelina/Pied Piper	7	8
B465	Lone Ranger	21	25
962abc	Lone Ranger, The	21	25
B482	Lost in Space	40	6
	Lost Treasures of the Amazon (Movie Preview Reel)	128	150
B501	Love Bug, The	9	10
B455	Lucky Luke vs. The Daltons	21	25

Buck Rogers, 1979

NO.	NAME	MNP	MIP	NO.	NAME	MNP	MIP
J11	M*A*S*H	9	10	B592	Partridge Family	21	25
BJ011	M*A*S*H	9	10	B569	Partridge Family	17	20
B441	Magic Roundabout, The	13	15	BB5924	Partridge Family	17	20
BD182	Maja the Bee	7	8	4074	Pee-Wee's Playhouse	9	10
B484	Man from U.N.C.L.E.	25	35	B943	Pendelton Round-Up (ABC's WW/Sports)	30	35
BB450	Mannix	21	25	BD184	Perishers, The	6	8
BB372	Mary Poppins	7	8	H38	Pete's Dragon	7	8
B376	Mary Poppins	7	8		Peter Pan, Disney's	5	6
1056	Mask	4	5	J12	Pink Panther	5	6
	Maze, The (Movie Preview Reel)	128	150	BJ012	Pink Panther	4	5
BD217	Metal Mickey	7	8	750	Pinky Lee's 7 Days (one reel)	21	25
K46	Meteor	9	10	D113	Pippi Longstocking	13	15
D122	Michael	26	30	B322	Pippi Longstocking	13	15
4047	Michael Jackson's Thriller	6	8	BB507	Planet of the Apes	30	35
B528	Mickey Mouse	5	10	B507	Planet of the Apes	30	35
B551	Mickey Mouse - Clock Cleaners	9	30	BB529	Pluto	4	5
865abc	Mickey Mouse Club	21	25	3013	Pluto	4	5
B524	Mickey Mouse Club Mouseketeers	21	25	B529	Pluto	9	10
J29	Mickey Mouse Jubilee	9	10	B442	Polly in Portugal	26	30
BB526	Mighty Mouse	4	5	D100	Polly in Venice	17	20
B526	Mighty Mouse	17	20	B516	Popeye	6	8
	Miss Sadie Thompson (Movie Preview Reel)	128	150		Popeye Talking View-Master Set	9	10
B505	Mission Impossible	15	18	B527	Popeye's Fun	7	8
B478	Mod Squad	16	20	BD226	Portland Bill	10	12
	Money From Home (Movie Preview Reel)	128	150	B391	Poseidon Adventure	21	25
B493	Monkees	12	25	BD218	Postman Pat	7	8
K67	Mork & Mindy	7	8	BD220	Pumcki	7	8
740	Movie Stars I (one reel)	13	15	4068	Punky Brewster	7	8
741	Movie Stars II (one reel)	13	15	4003	Puppets Audition Night	4	5
742	Movie Stars III (one reel)	13	15	L9	Puppets Audition Night, The	4	5
H56	Mr. Magoo	6	8	FT1	Red Riding Hood (one reel)	2	3
BD197	Munch Bunch	7	8	H26	Rescuers, The	5	6
B481	Munsters	105	200	BH026	Rescuers, The	5	6
4005	Muppet Movie, Scenes From The	4	5	J25	Return to Witch Mountain	5	6
L25	Muppets Go Hawaiian, The	4	5	930abc	Rin-Tin-Tin	13	15
K26	Muppets, Meet Jim Henson's	4	5	B467	Rin-Tin-Tin	13	15
BK026	Muppets, The	4	5		Robin Hood	21	25
B573	Nanny & The Professor	30	35	B373	Robin Hood Meets Friar Tuck	17	20
B935	NCAA Track & Field Championships (ABC's WW/Sports)	50	75	4115	Rocketeer, The	7	8
	Nebraskan, The (Movie Preview Reel)	128	150	BD240	Roland Rat Superstar	7	8
H9	New Mickey Mouse Club	5	6	K20	Romper Room	7	8
B566	New Zoo Revue	13	15	BB452	Rookies, The	13	15
B567	New Zoo Revue 2	13	15	948abc	Roy Rogers	21	25
B443	Old Surehand	43	50	B475	Roy Rogers	21	25
B377	One of Our Dinosaurs Is Missing	10	12	B462	Roy Rogers	21	25
A0250	Oregon Centennial Exposition (1959)	30	50	945	Roy Rogers (one reel)	2	3
BD266	Orm & Cheap	10	12	B594	Run Joe Run	13	15
				BD109	Rupert the Bear	12	15
				BB453	S.W.A.T.	10	12
					Sangaree (Movie Preview Reel)	128	150
				1079	Scooby Doo	2	3
				B553	Scooby Doo	4	5
				B591	Search	17	20
				D101	Sebastian	26	30

NO.	NAME	MNP	MIP
B452	Sebastian	26	30
	Second Chance (Movie Preview Reel)	128	150
B535	Secret Squirrel & Atom Ant	9	10
BD208	Secret Valley	10	12
4066	Sesame Street - Follow That Bird	4	5
4049	Sesame Street - People in Your Neighborhood	4	5
M12	Sesame Street - People in Your Neighborhood	4	5
4051	Sesame Street Alphabet	2	3
4072	Sesame Street Baby Animals	4	5
4097	Sesame Street Circus Fun	4	5
4050	Sesame Street Counting	4	5
4077	Sesame Street Goes on Vacation	4	5
4085	Sesame Street Goes Western	4	5
4083	Sesame Street Nursery Rhymes	4	5
4052	Sesame Street Shapes, Colors	4	5
4017	Sesame Street Visits the Zoo	4	5
b368	Shaggy D.A.	10	12
B550	Shazam	5	6
BD270	Shoe People, The	10	12
B595	Sigmund & the Sea Monsters (correct issue numbers)	15	18
B559	Sigmund & the Sea Monsters, (wrong issue number)	15	18
1058	Silverhawks	4	5
B556	Six Million Dollar Man	13	15
B308	Sleeping Beauty, Disney's	4	5
B490	Smith Family, The	10	30
BD194	Smuggler	7	8
BD246	Smurf, Baby	7	8
N1	Smurf, Flying	4	5
N2	Smurf, Traveling	4	5
BD172	Smurfs	5	6
B544	Snoopy and the Red Baron	7	8
BD250	Snorkes	8	10
K69	Snow White & the Seven Dwarfs	7	8
FT4	Snow White (one reel)	3	4
BD262	Snowman	7	8
	Son of Sinbad (Movie Preview Reel)	128	150
B509	Space Mouse	10	20
BD150	Space: 1999	21	25
BB451	Space: 1999	21	25
H11	Spider-Man	10	12
BH011	Spider-Man	7	8
K31	Spider-Man	9	10

NO.	NAME	MNP	MIP
B555	Star Trek (Cartoon Series)	9	10
B499	Star Trek (TV Series), "Omega Glory"	21	25
K57	Star Trek - The Motion Picture	10	12
4095	Star Trek - The Next Generation	7	8
M38	Star Trek - Wrath of Khan	10	12
B582	Steve Canyon	64	75
	Stranger Wore a Gun, The (Movie Preview Reel)	128	150
1064	Superman	4	5
BJ78	Superman	5	6
B584	Superman (cartoon)	4	5
J78	Superman - The Movie	10	20
L46	Superman II	17	25
4044	Superman III	7	15
J070	Superstar barbie	7	15
3081	Tailspin	4	5
B580	Tarzan	9	10
975	Tarzan (one reel)	4	5
976A	Tarzan Finds a Son (one reel)	3	4
976abc	Tarzan of the Apes	21	25
	Taza, Son of Cochise (Movie Preview Reel)	128	150
1073	Teenage Mutant Ninja Turtles	2	3
4114	Teenage Mutant Ninja Turtles - Movie II	3	4
4149	Teenage Mutant Ninja Turtles - Movie III	2	3
4109	Teenage Mutant Ninja Turtles - The Movie	3	5
BD243	Telecat	7	8
BD230	Terrahawks	10	20
	They Called Him Hondo (Movie Preview Reel)	128	150
BD238	Thomas the Tank Engine	6	10
H39	Thor	2	3
	Those Redheads from Seattle (Movie Preview Reel)	128	150
B453	Thunderbirds	43	50
B491	Time Tunnel	20	35
1076	Tiny Toon Adventures	2	3
BD205	Tiswas	7	8
B476	Toby Tyler	30	35
810	Tom & Jerry (one reel)	2	3
B511	Tom & Jerry, Two Musketeers	9	10
B581	Tom Corbett, Secret from Space	21	25
970abc	Tom Corbett, Space Cadet	21	25
B340	Tom Sawyer	7	8
D123	Tom Thumb	13	15
B513	Top Cat	13	15
BB513	Top Cat	13	15

NO.	NAME	MNP	MIP	NO.	NAME	MNP	MIP
B947	Tournament of Thrills (ABC's WW/Sports)	30	35	4084	Wind in the Willows	7	8
BD242	Tripods, The	10	12		Wings of the Hawk (Movie Preview Reel)	128	150
M37	Tron	8	10	B728	Winnetou	26	30
B477	TV Shows at Universal Studios	26	30	BB731	Winnetou	21	25
745	TV Stars I (one reel)	17	20	BB7284	Winnetou	21	25
746	TV Stars II (one reel)	17	20	B728	Winnetou & Halfblood Apache	26	30
747	TV Stars III (one reel)	17	20	K37	Winnie the Pooh & The Blustery Day	7	8
BD1161	Tweety & Sylvester	7	8	J14	Wiz, The	17	20
J28	Tweety & Sylvester	3	4	FT45abc	Wizard of Oz	13	15
4043	Twice Upon a Time	3	4	BD267	Wizard of Oz	7	8
B417	U.F.O.	38	45	D131	Wombles, The	13	15
BD198	Ulysses 31	7	8	BD131	Wombles, The	7	8
BD224	Victor & Maria	7	8	B522	Woody Woodpecker	13	15
B483	Voyage to the Bottom of the Sea	10	12	820	Woody Woodpecker Pony Express Ride (one reel)	3	4
BB596	Waltons, The	10	12	B949	World Bobsled Championships (ABC's WW/Sports)	60	80
B596	Waltons, The	10	12				
J19	Welcome Back Kotter	10	12				
4086	Who Framed Roger Rabbit	8	16	BD185	Worzel Gummidge	7	8
B473	Wild Bill Hickcock & Jingles	26	30	4067	Wrestling Superstars	8	10
BD215	Willo the Wisp	7	8	4140	Young Indiana Jones Chronicles	6	8
BD231	Wind in the Willows	7	8	B469	Zorro	34	40

VIEW- MASTER

Weebles

It's hard to separate the words "Weeble" and "wobble."

They go together as comfortably as a tiny Weeble fits inside a child's small hand.

Weebles, Hasbro's pint-sized egg-shaped plastic toys, brought the marketing phrase "Weebles wobble but they don't fall down" into the public consciousness.

Meant to infiltrate the market dominated by Fisher-Price's Play Family play sets, Weebles rolled onto the toy scene in 1972. Their weighted bottoms gave them the ability to wobble, yet amazingly they never tipped over. In the world of play people, they could be seen as the fat and friendly relatives of the more severely-shaped Play Family characters.

Jovial Weebles characters like Mom, Dad and kids found their way into dozens of play sets, including tree houses, boats, campers, playgrounds, cottages and airports. Each play set cleverly accommodated its wobbly inhabitants. Sets and even their boxes alone remain holy grail for collectors of Weebles and plastic play sets of that era. Early sets were marketed under the Romper Room name, capitalizing on the popular 1960s children's television program.

By the mid-1970s, Hasbro "weeblized" licensed characters like Winnie the Pooh, Raggedy Ann and Andy, Mickey Mouse, and the Flintstones. These licensed Weebles are among the most collectible today, fetching as much as $50-$100 for a single Weeble!

The earliest Weebles featured the wraparound character designs on a shrink-wrapped plastic covering. By the late 1970s, however, to prevent children from peeling the covering off, Hasbro redesigned the Weebles with a hard, clear plastic shell over the character design.

The heyday of the Weebles was around 1972-1982. But Weebles haven't entirely disappeared today. In the early 1990s, Playskool reintroduced larger, more chunky Weebles. Safety regulations forced toy companies to comply with size standards, and earlier Weebles apparently posed chocking hazards.

Trends

With a current rejuvenated interest in "everything '70s," the Weebles are returning to the forefront of pop culture and collecting. As Weebles brace for their 30th anniversary in 2002, yesterday's kids are searching for these vintage plastic playthings. They just may the new hot collectibles of the 21st century.

The Top 10 Weebles
(in Mint condition)

1. Weebles Winnie the Pooh Circus $200
2. Weebles Treasure Island 150
3. Weebles Family 140
4. Weebles Mickey Mouse Magic Kingdom 140
5. Weebles Haunted House 135
6. Weebles Dairy 130
7. Weebles Firebrigade 130
8. Weebles Super Hero 125
9. Weebles Playhouse At Pooh Corners 125
10. Weebles Winnie the Pooh Honey Tree 125

Contributor to this section: Sean Craig and Debbie Craig, toys96fp@aol.com.

VEHICLES

Weebles Airport. Photo Courtesy Sean and Debbie Craig

Weebles Circus. Photo Courtesy Sean and Debbie Craig

Weebles Marina. Photo Courtesy Sean and Debbie Craig

VEHICLES

NAME	DESCRIPTION	GOOD	EX	MINT
Flintstones	Fred, Wilma, and Pebbles on card	25	40	65
Flintstones Tumbler	Fred Flintstone w/Tumbler slide	15	30	55
Good Weebles Blimp	blimp w/turn able sign, and a tumble aviator Weeble	15	25	35
Holiday Weebles Set, Christmas	Santa and reindeer, Set 5	15	30	55
Holiday Weebles Set, Easter	Bunny and Chicken, Set 6	15	30	55
Raggedy Ann And Andy Weebles	Raggedy Ann ad Andy and wrinkle knees blue camel, carded	25	40	100
Raggedy Ann Tumbler	Raggedy Ann w/Tumbler Slide	25	40	100
Weebicycles	van-yellow van w/three seats and a man Weeble; sedan-pink sedan w/two seats and a woman Weeble; tow truck-orange tow truck w/two seats and a large boy Weeble. Values are for each set	15	25	35
Weebles Airport	hanger, large airplane "Weeair", small airplane, helicopter, windsock three-pieces of luggage, five Weebles-pilot, mom, girl, boy, and a baby	40	75	12
Weebles Boat	SS Little Putt, anchor, flagpole, fishing pole, four metal fish, four Weebles-dad, mom, boy, and a girl; peel type Weebles	30	50	70
Weebles Camp-About	car/camper, trail bike, picnic table, rowboat and trailer, two camper jacks, two Weebles-man and woman	25	50	70
Weebles Car And Camper	convertible car and camper, trail bike, table, four chairs, three pieces of luggage, luggage rack, rowboat, four Weebles including dad, mom, girl and boy	50	75	115
Weebles Circus	tent w/carrying handle, two trapezes, two-piece cannon, trampoline w/hoop, stilts, four flags, three Weebles-trapeze woman, clown, and a ringmaster	50	80	120
Weebles Cottage	house, pool, couch, chair, two beds, car, four Weebles-dad, mom, boy, and girl	50	70	90
Weebles Dairy	dairy milk truck and a Weebles dad	65	90	130
Weebles Family	six older style peelable weebles, carded	40	75	140
Weebles Firebrigade	fire truck w/cherry picker, two tools, and two Weebles firemen	65	90	130
Weebles Ghost Van	purple van, and glow in the dark ghost Weeble	25	40	75
Weebles Haunted House	house w/removable vestibule, couch, chair, bed, trunk, four Weebles-witch w/removable hat, scared boy and girl, and a glow in the dark ghost Weeble	60	85	135
Weebles Marina	SS Little Putt, motorboat, sailboat, three dock sections, two gas pumps boathouse, fishing pole, flagpole, anchor, four metal fish, four Weebles include boat captain, woman, boy, and girl	50	75	90
Weebles On Card	Set 1—boy and dog set; Set 2—pirate captain and red and white striped pirate; Set 3—baby and boat captain set; Set 4—cowboy and Indian. Values are for each set	5	13	25
Weebles Playground	swing set, merry go round, seesaw, slide, four Weebles include boy, girl, baby, and a dog	15	25	35
Weebles Playhouse	house, pool, picnic table, car, swing set, seesaw, slide, three Weebles include dad, mom, and a baby	50	75	90
Weebles Scotch Tape Mail-Away Promo	all black Weeble w/glow-in-the-dark hat, hands and feet	25	40	80
Weebles Super Hero	ice cream truck, office trailer, two Weebles include Mr. Trouble, and Walter Weeble (Super Weeble)	60	80	125
Weebles Tarzan Jungle Hut	jungle hut, three jungle leaf sections, hut, picnic table, winch and vine basket, swing vine, suction cup, two Weebles include Tarzan and Nkima	60	80	125
Weebles Train	three piece train blue and white color, three red train tops, two Weebles include boy and a girl	60	80	110

VEHICLES

Weebles Mickey Mouse Clubhouse. Photo Courtesy Sean and Debbie Craig

Weebles Playhouse. Photo Courtesy Sean and Debbie Craig

WEEBLES

NAME	DESCRIPTION	GOOD	EX	MINT
Weebles Treasure Island	pirate ship w/two removable sails and a wee old gang plank, two islands, three trees, look out w/telescope, hammock, longboat, hut, pick, shovel, map, treasure chest, four Weebles include pirate captain w/hat, red striped pirate w/feather hat and two other pirate Weebles	60	80	150
Weebles Tree House	tree house, three leaf sections, basket elevator, picnic table, rocking chair, trike, two Weebles include boy and a girl	40	60	80
Weebles Tub Sub	sub w/diving planes, periscope and a see through dome, one diver Weeble	15	25	35
Weebles Tumblin Funhouse	house w/elevator, car, four sections of track, two Tumble Weebles include boy and a girl	25	45	80
Weebles Tumblin Slide	banana-like slide w/one Tumble Weeble. This is a carded set; Set 1— clown, Set 2—Dog set, Set 3— football player, Set 4—Girl, Set 5—Boy, Set 6—Dog; Value is for each set	7	12	20
Weebles Weekender	Weemap of Weebleville, large plane "Weeair" car, sailboat, three pieces of luggage, four Weebles include dad, mom, boy and a girl	25	40	65
Weebles Wobble Race Set	turn-crank race board, hurdle, cardboard grandstand, four Weeblesinclude numbers 1-4	35	50	85

Disney Weebles Sets

NAME	DESCRIPTION	GOOD	EX	MINT
Carded Pooh Weebles	Pooh and Tigger on card	30	50	80
Disney Mickey Mouse Weebles On Card	Set 2: Mickey Mouse, Goofy, Donald Duck	15	30	55
Disney Mickey Mouse Weebles On Card	Set 1: Mickey Mouse, Goofy, Billy and Karen Mouseketeers	15	304	55
Disney Tumbler	Mickey Mouse Tumbler w/slide	15	30	55
Weebles Mickey Mouse Clubhouse	clubhouse, grandstand, swing, seesaw, rocking chair, TV camera, spotlight, playmat, mailbox, three letters, flagpole w/bumpy bucket ride, four Weebles include Pluto, Mickey and Billy and Karen Mouseketeer	35	50	80
Weebles Mickey Mouse Magic Kingdom	castle carrying case, monorail track, monorail station, monorail car, teacup ride and base, Dumbo ride, five flags, slide, playmat, three Weebles include Mickey, Donald Duck, and Goofy	60	85	140
Weebles Playhouse At Pooh Corners	playhouse, swing, slide, seesaw, picnic table, bed, rocking chair, pool, three Weebles include Pooh, Tigger, and Christopher Robin	60	85	125
Weebles Winnie the Pooh Circus	tent w/carrying handle, two trapezes, two-piece Tigger cannon, trampoline w/hoop, four flags, Tumbler slide, three Weebles inlcude Pooh Tumbler, Tigger and Christopher Robin	85	125	200
Weebles Winnie the Pooh Honey Tree	tree house, winch elevator, picnic table, car, Winnie the Pooh tree, sign, rocking chair, two Weebles include Pooh and Tigger	65	85	125

Other Weeble Items

NAME	DESCRIPTION	GOOD	EX	MINT
Weeble Puzzles	many different scenes-Circus, Tub Sub, Camper, Playground, Indian Camp, Fire Engine, Train, Tree house, Airport; values are for each puzzle	10	20	30
Weebles Bop Bag	ghost bop bag	15	25	40
Weebles Bop Bag	boy w/"Weeble" written on shirt	15	25	40
Weebles Pen & Ink Set	boxed set comes w/preprinted Weeble scenes and color pens	15	25	40

Sesame Street Weebles Sets

NAME	DESCRIPTION	GOOD	EX	MINT
Berts Convertible	convertible car and Bert Weeble	15	25	40
Big Bird and Grover Set	carded	15	25	40
Big Birds Plane	plane and Big Bird Weeble	15	25	40
Cookie Monster Sailboat	sailboat and Cookie Monster Weeble	15	25	40

Weebles Super Hero. Photo Courtesy Sean and Debbie Craig

Weebles Tarzan Jungle Hut. Photo Courtesy Sean and Debbie Craig

WEEBLES

NAME	DESCRIPTION	GOOD	EX	MINT
Ernies Helicopter	helicopter and Ernie Weeble	15	25	40
Sesame Street Submarine	Sub w/diving planes, periscope and a see through dome, w/Big Bird	15	25	40
Set 2-Cookie Monster and Oscar	carded	15	25	40
Set 3-Bert and Ernie	carded	15	25	40
Weebles Bert And Ernie's Play Ground	swing set, merry go round, seesaw, two Weebles-Bert and Ernie	25	35	50

Western Weebles

NAME	DESCRIPTION	GOOD	EX	MINT
Weebles Wagonmaster	covered wagon, brown horse, and a cowboy w/hat	15	25	40
Weebles West	ranch/bunk house, one covered wagon, one horse, one hitching post, one harvest table, two benches, one gate, six fence sections, one water trough, three tools-pitchfork, axe, shovel, four Weebles—a Native American, and a man, woman and a boy, all three have cowboy hats	35	50	80
Weebles Western Train	three-piece brown and cream train w/orange tops, four Weebles-a Native American, and a man, woman and a boy, all three have cowboy hats	50	70	110
Weebles Wigwam	white tepee, orange horse cart, white horse, and one Native American Weeble	15	25	40

VEHICLES

Western Toys

A quarter doesn't buy what it used to. In the 1940s and 1950s, American cowgirls and cowboys could plunk down their hard-earned silver for genuine articles endorsed (or at least bearing the names of) their Western heroes.

Heroes were aplenty — Gene Autry, Hopalong Cassidy, the Lone Ranger, and, of course, Roy Rogers and Dale Evans.

Today, grownup cowpokes drive hard bargains to get their hands on well-preserved toys to evoke well-preserved memories. That's because they don't make toys, or heroes, like they used to.

Remembering those days is only a toy away.

In the 1940s, straight shooters like Buck Jones, Red Ryder and Tom Mix were everywhere — not only were they peering down from the movie screen, but their images also graced cereal boxes, comic books and toy rifles.

By the time Hopalong Cassidy, Gene Autry and Roy Rogers became household words, merchandising of cowboy toys was everywhere. Soon every child could wear, eat, play with, read or decorate his room with cowboy memorabilia.

The heyday of cowboy fever blossomed in the 1940s and 1950s. Stores like Sears Roebuck had entire sections dedicated to cowboy merchandise.

Then, toys ranged from 25 cents to $5. There were six-guns of every size, both in sets and individually. Generic guns, hats and other pieces can still be widely found today at reasonable prices. Toys featuring the "Big Four" (Hoppy, Lone Ranger, Gene and Roy) command higher premiums. But other cowboy hereos enjoyed successful merchandising as well, including Rex Allen, Wild Bill Elliott, Tom Mix, The Cisco Kid and Tex Ritter.

Trends

Western toys, particularly those from the pre-World War II era, should only increase in collector interest and value. Paper ephemera, such as lobby cards, advertisements, food wrappers or club membership items, are especially valuable because they were often discarded and, ultimately, hard to find today.

Premium rings often bore the likenesses of cowboy heroes. These are among some of the most valuable items as well. Other premiums, offered by companies like Ovaltine, Kellogg's and Ralston, were available only by mail, adding to their frequent scarcity.

Beware of reproductions, however. In recent years, many unlicensed reproduction

Roy Rogers Nodder, Japanese

and fake items bearing the Lone Ranger, Roy Rogers or Hopalong Cassidy names have been encountered.

Roy Rogers' and Gene Autry's deaths may result in a renewed interest — and increased value — in related memorabilia.

Editor's Note: Most Western toy guns are listed in the Guns section of this book.

The Top 10 Western Toys
(in Mint condition)

1. Hopalong Cassidy Roller Skates, Rollfast $1,000
2. Hopalong Cassidy Radio, Arvin, 1950s 600
3. Hopalong Cassidy Cap Gun, Wyandotte, 1950s 600
4. Roy Rogers Toy Chest, 1950s 550
5. Buck Jones Rangers Cowboy Suit, Yankiboy, 1930s 500
6. Hopalong Cassidy Western Series, Timpo, 1950s 475
7. Lone Ranger Record Player, Dekka, 1940s 450
8. Roy Rogers Play Set, Amsco, 1950s 440
9. Roy Rogers Alarm Clock, Ingraham, 1950s 440
10. Tom Mix Big Little Book Picture Puzzles, 1930s 425

WESTERN TOYS

ANNIE OAKLEY

NAME	COMPANY	YEAR	DESCRIPTION	GOOD	EX	MIP
Annie Oakley Cut-Out Dolls	Watkins-Strathmore	1956	paper dolls	20	35	50
Annie Oakley Cut-Out Dolls	Whitman	1958	paper dolls	20	35	50
Annie Oakley Sewing Set	Pressman	1950s		20	35	50
Annie Oakley Sharpshooter Book	Golden	1956	Little Golden Books	3	5	10
Annie Oakley Sparkle Picture Craft	Gabriel	1950s		20	30	40
Annie Oakley with Tagg and Lofty Cut-Out Dolls	Whitman	1955	paper dolls	20	35	50
Holster Set	Daisy	1950s	leather holsters and cap pistols	30	100	200
Puzzle	Milton Bradley	1955	boxed jigsaw puzzle	5	10	25

BONANZA

NAME	COMPANY	YEAR	DESCRIPTION	GOOD	EX	MIP
Ben Cartwright and his Horse	American Character	1966	plastic figures	60	140	290
Bonanza Four-in-One Wagon	American Character	1960s		75	150	300
Foto Fantastiks Photo Coloring Set	Eberhard Faber	1960s		40	75	150
Hoss Cartwright and his Horse	American Character	1966	plastic figures	60	140	290
Hoss Range Pistol	Marx	1960s	carded plastic gun	35	65	125
Little Joe Cartwright Figure	American Character	1966		60	140	290
Mustang	American Character		the outlaw's horse	25	50	100
Outlaw Figure	American Character	1966		40	80	160
Palomino	American Character		Ben's horse	25	50	100
Pinto	American Character		Little Joe's horse	25	50	100
Puzzle	Saalfield	1960s	frame tray	20	40	75
Puzzle	Milton Bradley	1964		10	20	40
Stallion	American Character		Hoss's horse	25	50	100
Woodburning Set	ATF Toys	1960s		65	125	250

DANIEL BOONE

NAME	COMPANY	YEAR	DESCRIPTION	GOOD	EX	MIP
Daniel Boone Card Game	Ed-U-Cards	1965		7	10	15
Daniel Boone Figure	Remco	1964	5" tall, hard plastic body, vinyl head, cloth coonskin cap and long rifle	35	75	160
Daniel Boone Film Viewer	Acme	1964	w/two arms	7	10	20
Daniel Boone Inflatable Toy	Multiple Toymakers	1965		25	50	75

DAVY CROCKETT

NAME	COMPANY	YEAR	DESCRIPTION	GOOD	EX	MIP
3-D Moving Picture and Viewer	Armour-Cloverbloom Margarine	1950s	premium cardboard viewer w/ 3-D cards	40	80	150
Alamo Construction Set	Practi-Cole	1950s		40	75	150
Auto-Magic Picture Gun	Stephens	1950s	projection gun w/films	40	75	150
Baby Davy Crockett Doll	Spunky	1950s	8" tall vinyl squeeze toy	20	40	75

Hopalong Cassidy Chinese Checkers, 1950, Milton Bradley

Hopalong Cassidy Coloring Outfit, 1950s, Transogram

Hopalong Cassidy Frame Tray Puzzle, 1950s, Whitman

DAVY CROCKETT

NAME	COMPANY	YEAR	DESCRIPTION	GOOD	EX	MIP
Davy Crockett and His Horse Figures	Ideal	1950s	plastic	30	50	100
Davy Crockett Doll		1950s	8", hard plastic, sleepy eyes, leather clothes, two rifles, hat	60	130	250
Davy Crockett Doll	Exel	1973	Legends of the West series, 9-1/2"	30	55	95
Davy Crockett Frontier Target Game	American Toys		tin litho dartboard	35	75	130
Davy Crockett Guitar	Peter Puppet Playthings	1950s	24" long, wood	80	175	350
Davy Crockett Push Puppet	Kohner Bros.	1950s		30	65	100
Davy Crockett Ring		1950s	bronze-colored	40	50	60
Dispatch Case	Neptune Plastics	1950s	vinyl pouch, yellow graphics	15	30	50
Frontier Rifle	Marx	1950s	32" rifle	40	75	150
Frontierland Pencil Case	Hassenfeld Bros.	1950s	cardboard	45	75	100
Frontierland Pioneer Scout Outfit	Eddy	1950s	costume set	50	100	250
Iron-Ons	Vogart	1950s	three transfers on sheet	15	35	50
Magic Paint with Water Pictures	Artcraft	1950s	construction and art set set w/ Frontierland fort	75	150	275
Offical Davy Crockett Color TV Set	Lido		plastic viewer, four films	75	150	275
Official Davy Crockett Belt			on card	35	80	150
Official Davy Crockett Tool Kit	Liberty Steel Chest		w/tools	75	175	250
Pocket Knife	Disney	1950s	single blade, 2", yellow	20	40	75
Pony Express Bank	Randing	1950s	bown and white cloth pouch w/ lock and key	15	30	50
Puzzle	Whitman	1955	11-1/4" x 15"	15	40	75
Puzzle	Marx		Seige on the Fort	15	40	75
Ride-On Bouncing Horse	Rich Toys	1950s	37" x 31", white plastic w/black and yellow saddle	75	150	275
Sand Pail	Ohio Art	1950s	tin litho	20	30	50
Suspenders		1950s	tan w/Crockett graphics	25	50	90
Travel Bag	Neevel	1950s	6-1/2" x 12" x 10" heavy cardboard w/brass hinges and plastic handle	30	75	130
Wallet	Walt Disney	1950s	red vinyl w/faux fur	20	45	80

GENE AUTRY

NAME	COMPANY	YEAR	DESCRIPTION	GOOD	EX	MIP
Frame Tray Puzzle	Whitman	1950s	wood	15	21	38
Gene Autry Drum Set	Colmor	1940s		51	105	275
Gene Autry Guitar	Emenee	1950s	plastic	56	105	220
Gene Autry Jump-Up Book	Adprint Limited London	1955		30	52	82
Gene Autry Ranch Outfit	Henry	1940s	dress-up kit w/holster and gun	56	105	220
Gene Autry's Champion Slate	Lowe	1950s		15	26	49
Gene Autry's Stencil Book		1950s		15	31	55
Spurs	Leslie-Henry	1960s		25	57	176
Stringless Marionette	National Mask & Puppet	1950s	14-1/2" tall	45	78	165

Hopalong Cassidy Mechanical Shooting Gallery, 1950s, Automatic Toy

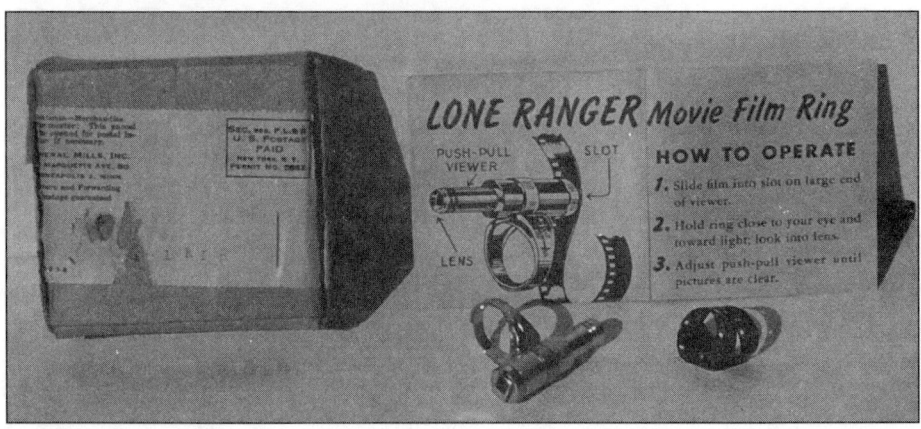

Lone Ranger Movie Film Ring, 1950s, General Mills

Lone Ranger Record Player, 1940s, Dekka

GUNSMOKE

NAME	COMPANY	YEAR	DESCRIPTION	GOOD	EX	MIP
Gunsmoke Puzzle	Whitman	1958	frame tray	19	34	60
Gunsmoke Puzzle	Whitman	1950s	boxed	18	33	55

HARTLAND FIGURES

NAME	COMPANY	YEAR	DESCRIPTION	GOOD	EX	MIP
Annie Oakley and Target	Hartland	1950s	9" plastic rider w/horse	70	140	250
Brave Eagle and White Cloud	Hartland	1950s	9" plastic rider w/horse	75	150	200
Bret Maverick	Hartland	1950s	9" plastic rider w/horse	20	40	80
Bret Maverick	Hartland	1960s	9" plastic rider w/horse	50	100	150
Buffalo Bill	Hartland	1950s	9" plastic rider w/horse	70	140	250
Cheyenne	Hartland	1960s	9" plastic rider w/horse	30	50	100
Cheyenne	Hartland	1950s	9" plastic rider w/horse	40	80	150
Cochise	Hartland	1950s	9" plastic rider w/horse	40	90	150
Dale Evans	Hartland	1950s	9" plastic rider w/horse	40	80	200
Davy Crockett	Hartland	1950s	9" plastic rider w/horse	45	90	150
Jim Bowie	Hartland	1950s	9" plastic rider w/horse	70	140	250
Lone Ranger	Hartland	1950s	9" plastic rider w/horse	45	90	150
Lone Ranger	Hartland	1960s	9" plastic rider w/horse	15	30	60
Marshal Matt Dillon	Hartland	1960s	9" plastic rider w/horse	50	100	175
Marshal Matt Dillon	Hartland	1950s	9" plastic rider w/horse	15	30	60
Paladin	Hartland	1950s	9" plastic rider w/horse	45	90	150
Paladin	Hartland	1960s	9" plastic rider w/horse	15	30	60
Roy Rogers and Trigger	Hartland	1950s	9" plastic rider w/horse	50	100	175
Roy Rogers and Trigger	Hartland	1960s	9" plastic rider w/horse	50	100	200
Tom Jeffords	Hartland	1950s	9" plastic rider w/horse	70	140	250
Tonto	Hartland	1950s	9" plastic rider w/horse	30	60	120
Tonto	Hartland	1960s	9" plastic rider w/horse	45	90	150
Wyatt Earp	Hartland	1950s	9" plastic rider w/horse	45	90	150
Wyatt Earp	Hartland	1960s	9" plastic rider w/horse	15	30	60

HAVE GUN, WILL TRAVEL

NAME	COMPANY	YEAR	DESCRIPTION	GOOD	EX	MIP
Have Gun, Will Travel Play Set	Prestige	1958		50	100	20
Have Gun, Will Travel Slate		1960s		10	25	50
Holster Set	Halco	1960s	holsters, belt, canteen	40	100	200
Paladin Checkers	Ideal	1960s	carded	25	50	75
Paladin Western Outfit	Ben Cooper	1959	mask, vest	n/a	65	150

HOPALONG CASSIDY

NAME	COMPANY	YEAR	DESCRIPTION	GOOD	EX	MIP
Automatic Television Set	Automatic Toy	1950s		60	100	200
Bar 20 Ranch Badge		1950s		25	50	75
Bar Twenty Shooting Game	Chad Valley	1950s		50	100	250
Bread Wrapper	Butternut	1950s	14" x 23"	50	70	95
Canvas School Bag		1950s		25	50	150
Cap Gun	Wyandotte	1950s	7", silver metal w/white handles, Hoppy pictured on sides	150	300	600
Coloring Outfit	Transogram	1950s		35	75	150
Compass Hat Ring		1950s	brass, features "HC" on one side and "20" on other; compass on top	195	250	300
Crayon and Stencil Set	Transogram	1950s		35	75	150
Frame Tray Puzzle	Whitman	1950s		10	20	35

Lone Ranger Sheriff Jail Keys, 1945, Esquire Novelty

HOPALONG CASSIDY

NAME	COMPANY	YEAR	DESCRIPTION	GOOD	EX	MIP
Hop-A-Long Cassidy Tin Toy	Marx	1950s	wind-up rocker toy	90	150	325
Hopalong Canasta	Pacific Playing Card	1950s		55	100	250
Hopalong Cassidy Chinese Checkers	Milton Bradley	1950		60	130	225
Hopalong Cassidy Figure	Ideal	1950s	plastic figure of Hoppy w/ Topper	40	65	150
Hopalong Cassidy Lasso Game	Transogram	1950s		35	75	150
Hopalong Cassidy Western Series	Timpo	1950s	British set of seven metal figures	100	250	475
Mechanical Shooting Gallery	Automatic Toy	1950s		75	150	350
Original Hopalong Pogo Stick		1950s		50	100	225
Picture Gun and Theatre	Stephens Products	1950s	projects film, Hoppy decals on sides, includes film, gun, cardboard stage	75	150	225
Pony Express Toss Game	Transogram	1950s		30	45	70
Puzzles	Milton Bradley	1950s	boxed set of three	30	50	100
Radio	Arvin	1950s	red metal case, embossed image of Hoppy and topper on front	200	450	600
Roller Skates	Rollfast			200	500	1000
Stationary	Whitman	1950s		20	50	100
Topper Rocking Horse	Rich Toys	1950s	plastic/wood	65	125	250
Wrist Cuffs		1950s		55	100	250

HOW THE WEST WAS WON

NAME	COMPANY	YEAR	DESCRIPTION	GOOD	EX	MIP
Dakota Figure	Mattel	1978		10	20	35
How the West Was Won Action Play Set	Timpo	1977		10	20	35
Lone Wolf Figure	Mattel	1978		10	20	35
Puzzle	HG Toys	1978	boxed jigsaw puzzle	5	7	15
Zeb Macahan Figure	Mattel	1978		10	20	35

LONE RANGER

NAME	COMPANY	YEAR	DESCRIPTION	GOOD	EX	MIP
Electric Drawing Set	Lakeside	1960s		5	10	20
Flashlight Ring		1948	premium	45	90	175
Hand Puppet		1940s	cloth body, blue and white polka-dot shirt w/bells in both hands	40	90	160
Lone Ranger and Tonto Target Set	Multiple Toymakers	1970s	3" figures w/horses, guns, darts	15	35	65
Lone Ranger Coloring Book	Whitman	1975	#1010	8	15	25
Lone Ranger Record Player	Dekka	1940s	12" x 10" x 6" wooden box w/ burned in illustrations, leather strap	100	225	450
Lone Ranger Sheriff Jail Keys	Esquire Novelty	1945	5", on ring, came on card w/ cut-out Sheriff card	30	63	125
Pencil Box	American Pencil	1940s		20	40	75
Tonto Indian Outfit	Esquire	1950s	costume set	50	100	350

WESTERN TOYS

Roy Rogers & Dale Evans Western Dinner Set, 1950s, Ideal

Roy Rogers Fix-It Chuck Wagon and Jeep, 1950s, Ideal

WESTERN TOYS

MISCELLANEOUS CHARACTERS

NAME	COMPANY	YEAR	DESCRIPTION	GOOD	EX	MIP
Bat Masterson Holster Set	Carnell	1950s	holster, belt, cane, yellow and black vest	75	200	300
Buck Jones Rangers Cowboy Suit	Yankiboy	1930s	costume set	60	200	500
Buffalo Bill Puzzle	Built-Rite	1956	frame tray	10	20	35
Cheyenne Book	Whitman	1958	Little Golden Book	6	13	24
Cheyenne Little Golden Record		1950s	45 rpm	7	15	25
Cheyenne Puzzle	Milton Bradley	1957	frame tray	12	25	45
Cisco Kid Puzzle Set	Saalfield	1950s	set of three puzzles	30	50	70
Johnny Moccasin View-Master Reels	Sawyers	1957	set of three reelse, booklet	20	45	60
Johnny Ringo Hand Puppet	Tops in Toys	1950s	15" full body puppet, vinyl head	65	100	200
Laramie Cowboy Holster Set	Clarke Bros.	1960s		65	100	225
Rin Tin Tin Magic Slate	Whitman	1950s		10	20	30
Rin Tin Tin Rusty Costume	Ben Cooper	1950s		25	40	65
Straight Arrow Target Game	Novel Novelties	1949	tin litho target w/crossbow	40	75	150
Wild Bill Hickok and Jingles Puzzle Set	Built-Rite	1950s	set of four	25	50	75
Wild Bill Hickok Treasure Map/Guide	Kellogg's	1950s	cereal premium	40	65	90

RED RYDER

NAME	COMPANY	YEAR	DESCRIPTION	GOOD	EX	MIP
Frame Tray Puzzle	Jaymar	1951	Red Ryder or Little Beaver	5	10	20
Little Beaver Archery Set		1951	cardboard target	10	20	30
Little Beaver Coloring Book	Whitman	1956		5	10	25
Red Ryder Corral Bagatelle Game	Gotham	1940s		25	45	75
Red Ryder Pop-Um Shooting Game	Daisy	1940s		30	50	100
Red Ryder Target Game	Whitman	1939		25	50	100
Red Ryder Whirli-Crow Game	Daisy	1940s		30	50	100

ROY ROGERS

NAME	COMPANY	YEAR	DESCRIPTION	GOOD	EX	MIP
Dale Evans Wristwatch	Ingraham	1951	dale inside upright horsehsoe, tan background, chrome case, black leather band	61	157	330
Give-A-Show Projector	Kenner	1960s	projector w/slides	25	52	82
Horsedrawn Wagon Pull Toy	Hill	1950s	18", wood w/paper litho	56	105	275
Ranch Lantern	Ohio Art	1950s	tin litho, battery-operated	56	105	275
Roy Rogers & Dale Evans Coloring Book	Whitman	1975		10	21	33
Roy Rogers & Dale Evans Paper Dolls	Whitman	1954		35	57	88
Roy Rogers & Dale Evans Western Dinner Set	Ideal	1950s	utensils in 14" x 24" box	35	68	104
Roy Rogers Alarm Clock	Ingraham	1950s	4", square ivory-color case, full-color graphics	153	315	440
Roy Rogers Crayon Set	Standard Toykraft	1950s		35	52	110
Roy Rogers Fix-It Chuck Wagon and Jeep	Ideal	1950s	set w/two horses, four figures, Nellybelle, accessories	71	157	330
Roy Rogers Horeshoe Set	Ohio Art		tin litho	40	105	275

WESTERN TOYS

ROY ROGERS

NAME	COMPANY	YEAR	DESCRIPTION	GOOD	EX	MIP
Roy Rogers Horseshoe Set		1950s	rubber horseshoes and pegs	30	52	143
Roy Rogers Nodder	Japanese		composition, blue shirt, white hat and pants and red bandana and boots	n/a	n/a	n/a
Roy Rogers Play Set	Amsco	1950s	cardboard w/magnetic figures	51	210	440
Roy Rogers Puzzle		1950s	frame tray	20	36	55
Roy Rogers Rodeo Board Game	Rogden	1949	four games in one	102	147	220
Roy Rogers Rodeo Sticker Fun Book	Whitman	1953		35	57	121
Roy Rogers Stagecoach	Ideal	1950s	14", plastic w/two harnessed horses, Roy, and accessories	10	68	99
Roy Rogers Toy Chest		1950s	17" x 17" x 12" w/Roy and Bullet graphics	178	315	550
Roy Rogers Toy Football		1950s	white vinyl w/logo	20	42	66
Roy Rogers Trigger Trotter		1950s	pogo stick	153	236	330
Roy Rogers Truck	Marx	1950s	14", tin litho, red, yellow and blue	102	157	275
Trigger Rocking Horse	Bell Toys	1950s	wood w/metal seat	51	105	220

TOM MIX

NAME	COMPANY	YEAR	DESCRIPTION	GOOD	EX	MIP
Big Little Book Picture Puzzles		1930s	boxed set of two	100	225	425
Bullet Flashlight		1930s	3" long	50	75	130
Riding Horse	Mengel	1930s	wood	75	150	365
Tom Mix Rodeorope	Mordt	1930s		75	250	425
Tom Mix Shooting Gallery	Parker Brothers	1935		75	150	320

ZORRO

NAME	COMPANY	YEAR	DESCRIPTION	GOOD	EX	MIP
Dart Rifle Target Set		1960s		40	70	175
Hand Puppet	Gund	1958	vinyl and fabric	25	50	75
Official Zorro Action Set	Marx	1950s	costume and weapons set	75	150	350
Paint by Number Set	Hasbro		canvas and paints	35	60	80
Pencil by Number Set		1960s		35	60	80
Puzzle	Jaymar	1960s	boxed jigsaw puzzle	7	20	35
Target Shoot		1950s	gun w/soldier targets	40	75	1510
Walt Disney's The Adventures of Zorro	Golden	1958	Big golden Book	10	20	30
Walt Disney's Zorro		1958	Little Golden Book	5	7	12
Walt Disney's Zorro	Golden	1958	Golden Book	5	10	20
Zorro Dominoes	Halsam	1950s		25	45	65
Zorro Fencing Set		1950s	swords, masks, face guards	45	75	150
Zorro Spring Action Target	Knickerbocker	1950s		45	75	150

WESTERN TOYS

Toy Manufacturers Directory

Have you ever wanted to reach a toy company but didn't know how? The following is a representative, but not all-inclusive, list of most of the current, notable toy manufacturers.

Remember: Most manufacturers are not able to answer questions about secondary market value of their toys. And many companies do not maintain comprehensive archives of past products, so they may not be able to answer questions about past toy lines. The addresses and phone numbers may be helpful, however, when trying to reach the company with a customer service question or product concerns.

Aladdin Industries (lunch kits)
703 Murfreesboro Rd.
Nashville, TN 37210
615-748-3000

Alexander Doll Company
615 W. 131st St.
New York, NY 10027-7982
212-283-5900

Applause (plush, plastic)
6101 Variel Ave.
Woodland Hills, CA 91365-4183
818-992-6000

Bachmann Industries (trains)
1400 E. Erie Ave.
Philadelphia, PA 19124
215-533-1600

Bandai America (action figures)
12851 E. 166th St.
Cerritos, CA 90701
310-926-0947

Binney & Smith (Crayola crayons)
1100 Church La., P.O. Box 431
Easton, PA 19042
610-253-6271

Cadaco (games)
4300 W. 47th St.
Chicago, IL 60632-4477
312-927-1500

Duncan Toys (yo-yos)
15981 Valplast Rd.
Middlefield, OH 44062
216-632-1631

Fisher-Price (preschool toys)
636 Girard Ave.
East Aurora, NY 14052
716-687-3449

Full Moon Toys (action figures)
1645 N. Vine St., 9th floor
Los Angeles, CA 90028
877-315-6666

First Gear (die-cast models)
P.O. Box 52
Peosta, IA 52068-0052
319-582-2071

Gund (plush)
1 Runyons Ln.
P.O. Box H
Edison, NJ 08818
908-248-1500

Hasbro (Milton Bradley, Galoob, Tonka, Kenner, Parker Brothers and Playskool)
1027 Newport Ave.
Pawtucket, RI 02862-1059
401-727-5582

Idea Factory (Meanies beanbag toys)
1350 Broadway Suite 2400
New York, NY 10018
212-564-7430

Kenner Products (Hasbro)
(G.I. Joe, Star Wars)
615 Elsinore Pl.
Cincinnati, OH 45202
513-579-4927

Larami Corp. (miscellaneous)
340 N. 12th St.
Philadelphia, PA 19107-1123
215-923-4900

LEGO Systems (construction toys)
555 Taylor Rd.
P.O. Box 1600
Enfield, CT 06083-1600
203-763-6731

Lionel Trains
50625 Richard W. Blvd.
Chesterfield, MI 48051
810-949-4100

Little Tykes (preschool toys)
2180 Barlow Rd.
Hudson, OH 44236
216-650-3000

Majorette (die-cast vehicles)
2898 NW 79th Ave.
Miami, FL 33122
305-593-6016

Mattel (Barbie, Hot Wheels, Matchbox, Tyco)
333 Continental Blvd.
El Segundo, CA 90245-5012
310-252-2000

Marx (modern reincarnation of original Marx company)
249 E. Georgia Ave.
Sebring, OH 44672
330-938-8697

McFarlane Toys (action figures)
15155 Fogg St.
Plymouth, MI 48170
313-414-3500

Meccano-Erector (Erector sets)
1675 Broadway, 31st Floor
New York, NY 10019
212-397-0711

Milton Bradley (games)
443 Shaker Rd. E.
Longmeadow, MA 01028-3149
413-525-6411

Nintendo (video games)
4820 150th Ave. NE
Redmond, WA 98052-5111
206-882-2040

Nylint (vehicle toys)
1800 Sixteenth Ave.
Rockford, IL 61104-5491
815-397-2880

Ohio Art (Etch-a-Sketch)
One Toy Street
Bryan, OH 43506
419-636-3141

Parker Brothers (games)
50 Dunham Rd.
Beverly, MA 01915
617-927-7600

PEZ Candy
35 Prindle Hill Rd.
Orange, CT 06477
203-795-0531

Playing Mantis (die-cast cars, model kits)
3600 McGill St., Suite 300
P.O. Box 3688
South Bend, IN 46619-3688
219-232-0300

Playmates (action figures)
611 Anton Blvd. #600
Costa Mesa, CA 92626
714-428-2000

Playmobil (figures)
11-E Nichols Ct.
Dayton, NJ 08810
908-274-0101

Racing Champions-Ertl
800 Roosevelt Rd., Bldg. C Suite 320
Glenn Ellyn, IL 60137
630-790-3507

Reeves International (distributor of Breyer)
14 Industrial Rd.
Pequannock, NJ 07440
201-694-5006

Revell-Monogram (model kits)
8601 Waukegan Rd.
Morton Grove, IL 60053
708-966-3500

Sega of America (video games)
255 Shoreline Dr.
Redwood City, CA 94065
415-508-2800

Sideshow Toy (action figures)
31238 Via Colinas, Suite E
Westlake Village, CA 91362
818-879-1996

Smith-Miller (vehicle toys)
P.O. Box 139
Canoga Park, CA 91305
818-703-8588

SpecCast (die-cast vehicles)
428 9th Ave. NW
Dyersville, IA 52040-1129
319-875-8706

Steiff USA (teddy bears)
200 Fifth Ave., Suite 1205
New York, NY 10010
212-675-2727

Thermos Co. (lunch kits)
Rt. 75 East
Freeport, IL 61032
815-232-2111

Thinkway Toys (Toy Story, etc.)
8885 Woodbine Ave.
Markham, Ontario
Canada L3R 5G9
905-470-8883

Today's Kids (miscellaneous)
13630 Neutron Rd.
Dallas, TX 75244
214-404-9335

Strombecker (Tootsietoy)
600 N. Pulaski Rd.
Chicago, IL 60624
312-638-1000

Toy Biz (action figures)
333 East 38th St.
New York, NY 10016
212-682-4700

Trendmasters (action figures)
611 North 10th St., Suite 555
St. Louis, MO 63101
314-231-2250

Ty, Inc. (Beanie Babies)
P.O. Box 5377
Oakbrook, IL 60522
630-920-1515

21st Century Toys (action figures)
2037 Clement Ave., Bldg. #33
Alameda, CA 94501

Winross (die-cast trucks)
Box 23860
Rochester, NY 14692
716-381-5638

Directory of Auction Houses

The following is a representative, but not all-inclusive, list of nationwide auction houses. Most hold general antiques and collectibles auction; some may specialize in toys. For information on upcoming auctions, contact the auction house directly.

Noel Barrett Antiques & Auctions
P.O. Box 300
6193 Carversville Rd.
Carversville, PA 18913
215-297-5109

Bill Bertoia Auctions
2413 Madison Ave.
Vineland, NJ 08360
609- 692-1881

Block's Box (marbles)
P.O. Box 51
Trumbull, CT 06611
206-926-8448

Brooks
81 Westside
London SWA 9AY
Great Britain

Butterfield & Butterfield
7601 Sunset Blvd.
Los Angeles, CA 90046
213-850-7500

Christie's
502 Park Ave.
New York, NY 10022
212-546-1000

Christie's East
219 East 67th St.
New York, NY 10021
212-606-0400

Continental Auctions
P.O. Box 193
Sheboygan, WI 53082
920-693-3371

William Doyle Galleries
175 E. 87th St.
New York, NY 10128-2205
212- 427-2730

Dumouchelle Art Galleries
409 East Jefferson Ave.
Detroit, MI 48226
313-963-6255 / 313-963-0248

Eldred's
P.O. Box 796
East Dennis, MA 02641-0796
508- 385-3116

Guernsey's
108 East 73rd St.
New York, NY 10021
212-794-2280

Hake's Americana & Collectibles
P.O. Box 1444
York, PA 17405-1444
717-848-1333

Henry/Pierce Auctioneers (banks)
1525 S. Arcadian Dr.
New Berlin, WI 53151
414-797-7933

Randy Inman Auctions
40 College Ave.
P.O. Box 726
Waterville, ME 04901
207-872-6900

Jackson's Auctioneers & Appraisers.
2229 Lincoln St.
Cedar Falls, IA 50613
319-277-2256

James D. Julia Auctioneers Inc.
Rte. 201, Skowhegan Rd.
P.O. Box 830
Fairfield, ME 04937
207-453-7125

Just Kids
310 New York Ave.
Huntington, NY 11743
516-423-8449

Manion's Auction House
PO Box 12214
Kansas City, KS 66112-0214
913-299-6692

Mapes Auctioneers & Appraisers
1600 Vestal Parkway West
Vestal, NY 13850
607-754-9193

Ted Maurer
1003 Brookwood Dr.
Pottstown, PA 19646
215-323-1573

McMasters Doll Auctions
P.O. Box 1755
Cambridge, OH 43725
614-432-4419

Mid-Hudson Auction Galleries
One Idlewild Ave.
Croton-On-Hudson, NY 12520

New England Auction Gallery
Box 2273-T
West Peabody, MA 01960
508-535-3140

Richard Opfer Auctioneering Inc.
1919 Greenspring Dr.
Lutherville Timonium, MD 21093-4113
410-252-5035

Phillips Fine Art & Auctioneers
406 East 79th St.
New York, NY 10022
212-570-4830

Lloyd W. Ralston
173 Post Rd.
Fairfield, CT 06430
203-255-1233

Skinner Inc.
357 Main St.
Bolton, MA 01740-1104
508-779-6241/ 617-350-5400

Smith House
P.O. Box 336
Eliot, ME 03903
207-439-4614

Sotheby's
1334 York Ave. at 72nd St.
New York, NY 10021
212- 606-7370 / 212- 606-7000

Theriault's (dolls)
P.O. Box 151
Annapolis, MD 21404
800-638-0422

'Tiques
545 Fifth Ave., Suite 902
New York, NY 10016
212-545-0800

Toy Scouts
137 Casterton Ave.
Akron, OH 44303
330-836-0668

Withington Inc.
RD2 Box 440
Hillsboro, NH 03244
603-464-3232

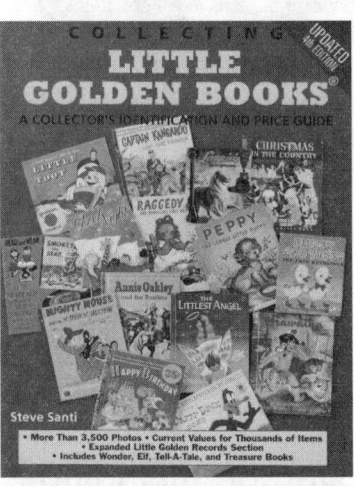

<u>NOTES</u>

NOTES

NOTES

NOTES